Selected Political and Economic Writings

Historical Materialism Book Series

The Historical Materialism Book Series is a major publishing initiative of the radical left. The capitalist crisis of the twenty-first century has been met by a resurgence of interest in critical Marxist theory. At the same time, the publishing institutions committed to Marxism have contracted markedly since the high point of the 1970s. The Historical Materialism Book Series is dedicated to addressing this situation by making available important works of Marxist theory. The aim of the series is to publish important theoretical contributions as the basis for vigorous intellectual debate and exchange on the left.

The peer-reviewed series publishes original monographs, translated texts, and reprints of classics across the bounds of academic disciplinary agendas and across the divisions of the left. The series is particularly concerned to encourage the internationalization of Marxist debate and aims to translate significant studies from beyond the English-speaking world.

For a full list of titles in the Historical Materialism Book Series available in paperback from Haymarket Books, visit:
https://www.haymarketbooks.org/series_collections/1-historical-materialism

Selected Political and Economic Writings

From the Hungarian Revolution to Orthodox Economic Theory in the USSR

Eugen Varga

Edited and translated by
André Mommen

Haymarket Books
Chicago, IL

First published in 2020 by Brill Academic Publishers, The Netherlands
© 2020 Koninklijke Brill NV, Leiden, The Netherlands

Published in paperback in 2021 by
Haymarket Books
P.O. Box 180165
Chicago, IL 60618
773-583-7884
www.haymarketbooks.org

ISBN: 978-1-64259-605-2

Distributed to the trade in the US through Consortium Book Sales and Distribution (www.cbsd.com) and internationally through Ingram Publisher Services International (www.ingramcontent.com).

This book was published with the generous support of Lannan Foundation and Wallace Action Fund.

Special discounts are available for bulk purchases by organizations and institutions. Please call 773-583-7884 or email info@haymarketbooks.org for more information.

Cover art and design by David Mabb. Cover art is a detail of *Long Live the New! no. 3*, Kazimir Malevich drawing on Morris & Co. design, paint and wallpaper on canvas (2016).

Printed in Canada.

10 9 8 7 6 5 4 3 2 1

Library of Congress Cataloging-in-Publication data is available.

Contents

Preface IX
Abbreviations XI
Tables XII
About Translations, Transliteration and References XXIV

Eugen Varga: An Introduction to His Life and Works 1
 André Mommen

PART 1
The Hungarian Councils' Republic (1919)

Introduction to Part 1 117

1 Political-Economic Problems of the Proletarian Dictatorship 118

PART 2
The Comintern Years (1920–38)

Introduction to Part 2 241

2 The International Situation: A Study of Capitalism in Collapse (Presented to the Moscow Congress, 1921) by Leon Trotsky and Prof. E. Varga 242

3 Economic Basis of Imperialism in the US of North America 262

4 The Economic Crisis of Germany 286

5 The Crisis of the Capitalist World Economy 343

6 The Situation of the World Economy and the Evolution of the World Economic Policy during the Last Three Years 393

7 The Process of Capitalist Decline (Report to the Fourth Congress of the Communist International) 414

8   The Decline of Capitalism   463

9   Introduction to: Materials on the Situation of the Peasant Movement in the Most Important Countries   544

10 The Decline of Capitalism: The Economics of a Period of the Decline of Capitalism after Stabilisation   548

11 Accumulation and Breakdown of Capitalism   661

12 The Great Crisis and Its Political Consequences: Economics and Politics 1928–34   700

PART 3
The General Crisis of Capitalism (1939–64)

13 The Imperialist Struggle for a New Redivision of the World   907

14 Changes in Capitalism during the War   922

15 Plans for Currency Stabilisation   933

16 World Currency Headache   936

17 Toward a New Crash?   939

18 The General Crisis of Capitalism (Features of the Home and Foreign Policy of the Capitalist Countries during the Epoch of the General Crisis of Capitalism)   946

19 Democracy of a New Type   959

20 Anglo-American Rivalry and Partnership: A Marxist View   971

21 The Increased Role of the State in the Economy of the Capitalist Countries   984

22 The Impoverishment Tendencies in the War Economy of the Capitalist Countries   1003

23 Concentration and Centralisation of Production and Capital during the War   1020

24 Economic Regulation and Absence of Planning in the Capitalist Countries during the War   1035

25 Towards an Economic Crisis in the USA   1050

26 Crisis Hits the USA   1057

27 Problems of the Postwar Industrial Cycle and the New Crisis of Overproduction   1061

28 The Problem of Inter-imperialist Contradictions and War   1088

29 Changes in the Reproduction Cycle Following the Second World War   1097

30 Problems of State-Monopoly Capitalism   1127

Bibliography   1147
Index   1175

Preface

This collection of Eugen Varga's writings contains texts he published after having joined the Hungarian Communist Party in 1919. Many of Varga's publications were also published in English translation. In several cases, however, the Comintern omitted translating them into English. The Comintern's language was German. The expanding Comintern bureaucracy in Moscow comprised mostly immigrants originating from Central Europe where German was the language of the educated layers of the population. This was certainly also the case in Varga's native Hungary.

Varga was a prolific writer, dictating his articles to secretaries. Personal assistants were also conducting additional research for his publications. This explains why his scientific and militant production could grow enormously. In 1964, when Varga died, his bibliography contained more than 1,300 articles and some 80 books and pamphlets. Making a selection of them was a hazardous task. Having worked as a newspaper journalist, Varga used to assemble and mix texts. As Varga never pretended to be an 'original' thinker, but only a Communist militant serving the cause of the revolutionary proletariat, he can hardly be called the Comintern's theoretician or ideologue. In the 1930s, when Stalin's hold on the Bolshevik Party had become absolute, Varga would become the dictator's propagandist and adviser. He authored policy papers largely based on actual economic reports, statistics and newspaper articles. Varga's 'industrial writing' was nonetheless framed within a strictly Marxist context in which Marx's *Capital* and *Theories of Surplus-Value* were many times quoted. Lenin and Stalin were also often quoted in order to stress the role of the victorious October Revolution and the revolutionary movements in the world.

This selection opens with Varga's report *Economic Problems of the Proletarian Dictatorship* written in 1919–20 during his detention in Austria after the fall of the Hungarian Councils' Republic. According to Lenin, this is probably the best account of the collapse of the dictatorship of the proletariat in Hungary. This report would also establish Varga's fame as an economic expert authoring all the economic reports to the Comintern congresses.

During the Second World War, Varga became Molotov's expert advising the latter on postwar issues, especially with regard to the problem of German reparation payments and the recently founded international institutions like the World Bank and the International Monetary Fund, or the Marshall Plan. Varga's academic and political disgrace in 1947 was the result of the so-called 'Varga controversy' breaking out and found its origins in the publication of his book

Changes in the Economy of Capitalism Resulting from the Second World War in which he reported on the changing role of the capitalist state.

This selection of Varga's writings is in some way a spin-off of my Varga biography entitled *Stalin's Economist: The Economic Contributions of Jenő Varga* (Routledge), published in 2011.

For this publication, some additional research was nonetheless required. For checking Varga's quotes and references, I spent much time in several archives and libraries. I only mention here the libraries of the University of Amsterdam, the University of Utrecht, the Library of the Erasmus University Rotterdam, the International Institute of Social History in Amsterdam or the Royal Library in The Hague. I could rely on the services of the RWTH Aachen Hochschulbibliothek, the Universitäts- und StadtBibliothek of the Universität zu Köln, the Universitätsbibliothek of the Freie Universität Berlin, the Niedersächsische Staats- und Universitätsbibliothek of the Georg-August-Universität Göttingen, the Österreichische Nationalbibliothek in Vienna, the Arbejdermuseet & Arbejderbevægelsens Bibliotek og Arkiv in Taastrup, the AMSAB Archives in Ghent and Antwerp, the Library and Archives of the Institut Émile Vandervelde (IEV) and the Documentation and Archives Centre of the Communist Movement (DACOB) in Brussels, the Library of Congress in Washington, the Widener Library at Harvard University, the Bodleian Library of the University of Oxford, the British Library in London and the Library of Harvard University. Dr. Ludger Syré of the Badische Landesbibliothek in Karlsruhe informed me about articles Isaac Deutscher published in *The Economist*. With the help of librarian Zsuzsa Nagy, I could often consult the rich collection of the Corvinus University Library in Budapest. In addition, I did some more research at the Hungarian State Archives (MOL), the archives of the Institute of Political History – Oral Archives, the Open Society Archives (OSA), the György Lukács Archives, and the archives and library of the Institute of Political History in Budapest.

My greatest pleasure at the completion of this project is to thank publicly those who have contributed directly and indirectly, in a major or minor part. Maurice Andreu read the introductory chapter and commented on the texts chosen for this collection. The Varga family remained interested in the progress of this project along the way, while Mira Bogdanović did the same when I was sometimes struggling with Varga's German-Austrian idiom. Without the help of the late Sergey S. Artobolevskiy this project would not have been completed.

André Mommen
Lanaken, July 2016

Abbreviations

AFL	American Federation of Labor
BHE	Bund der Heimatvertriebenen und Entrechteten
CENTO	Central Treaty Organization
CIO	Congress of Industrial Organization
CPSU	Communist Party of the Soviet Union
DNVP	Deutschnationale Volkspartei
ECCI	Executive Committee of the Communist International
ECSC	European Coal and Steel Community
FDR	Franklin Delano Roosevelt
GEC	General Electric Co.
GPD	Gross Domestic Product
ICI	Imperial Chemical Industries
IFTU	International Federation of Trade Unions
IRI	Instituto per le Renovazione Industriale
ITS	International Transportworkers Federation
KMP	Magyarországi Kommunisták Pártja
KPD	Kommunistische Partei Deutschlands
MICUM	Mission Interalliée de Contrôle des Usines et des Mines
MRBM	Medium Range Ballistic Missile
MSZDP	Magyarországi Szociáldemokrata Párt
NATO	North Atlantic Treaty Organization
NEP	New Economic Policy
PCF	Parti Communiste Français
PIL	Politikatörténeti Intézet Levéltára
POW	Prisoners of War
UAR	United Arab Republic
SFIO	Section Française de l'Internationale Ouvrière
SLI	Socialist and Labour International
SNCF	Société Nationale des Chemins de fer Français
SPD	Sozialdemokratische Partei Deutschlands
UN	United Nations
USA	United States of America
USPD	Unabhängige Sozialdemokratische Partei Deutschlands
USSR	Union of Socialist Soviet Republics
VKP-b	All-Union Communist Party – bolsheviks

Tables

0.1	Theories explaining business cycle in the 1920s	17
0.2	Varga's ten characteristics of decaying capitalism	44
3.1	Industrial statistics according to the data of American census (in millions)	265
3.2	The productivity of the United States amounted (in millions tons)	266
3.3	The number of officially registered automobiles in the United States	267
3.4	Development of the cotton industry (millions of pounds)	267
3.5	Export and import of manufactured goods	268
3.6	Cattle breeding (in millions)	268
3.7	The total cost of the farm produce in millions of dollars	269
3.8	Total sum of credit by US banks (in millions of dollars)	271
3.9	Data on the produce of farming according to the market statistics	271
3.10	American market prices	274
3.11	Exchange rates of the US dollar	280
4.1	Percentage rise of number of workers employed in industry and commerce	288
4.2	Total horsepower of steam engines used in industries in Prussia (its increase can easily be extrapolated for the whole Reich)	289
4.3	Amount and increase of agricultural machinery	289
4.4	Tonnage of sea ships (in net register tons)	290
4.5	Cattle stock in million heads of cattle	290
4.6	Agrarian production (average output per ha. in double hundredweight)	291
4.7	Industrial production	291
4.8	Cropland in million ha (without Alsace-Lorraine) (new territory)	293
4.9	Bread grains in million tons	295
4.10	Grain *import* – minus *export* – in 1920	295
4.11	Price increases in autumn 1920 compared to the pre-war period	297
4.12	Agrarian means of production and wages	297
4.13	Livestock on Germany's territory (in millions of heads)	297
4.14	In 1907, percentage of people having a chief occupation per sector	299
4.15	German industrial production (in million tons)	300
4.16	Steel and iron production (in million tons)	301
4.17	Textile industry: import minus export of raw materials in thousands of tons	301
4.18	Used textile machines exported in the period October 1919–September 1920	302

4.19	Production decline in some industrial branches (1913–20)	303
4.20	Industrial production	304
4.21	New buildings in cities with more than 50,000 inhabitants	305
4.22	German rolling stock	306
4.23	Employed workers and clerks	308
4.24	Grain harvest	310
4.25	Harvest in territorially reduced Germany	311
4.26	Meat production: cattle slaughtered after 'inspection' by the food administration	311
4.27	Consumption of some foodstuffs	312
4.28	Yearly tuberculosis mortality dead rate per 10,000 people in German cities having 15,000 or more inhabitants	312
4.29	Mortality rates per 1,000 inhabitants	313
4.30	Wholesale index	316
4.31	Index of needs of a working-class family (Berlin)	318
4.32	Foodstuff consumption per week	319
4.33	Index of rations	319
4.34	Wages (shift wages) of all workers. Costs of living 1913 = 100	320
4.35	Average of index for 1920	321
4.36	Four weekly wages in 1913 or in 1914 = 100, compared with wages of February 1920	321
4.37	Index of the cost of living in February 1920	321
4.38	Wage increases between 1914–20 according to the trade unions	322
4.39	Wage increases of commercial employees (1913 = 100)	322
4.40	Labour productivity in coal mining	325
4.41	Daily production per miner in kilogram	326
4.42	Coal production (without Alsace-Lorraine, Saar and Pfalz)	326
4.43	Productivity per shift per worker in the Ruhr Basin	327
4.44	Labour productivity	328
4.45	Argentinean tender for 10,000 rolling-stock wheels (per piece) (spring 1921)	329
4.46	Wages in US$	334
5.1	Germany: impoverishment and decline	346
5.2	French cattle stock (in millions of animals)	348
5.3	French industrial output	348
5.4	Production in millions of tons	349
5.5	Denmark's herd (in millions of animals)	350
5.6	Public debt increased during the war from 1913 to 1919	350
5.7	US industrial production (in million tons)	351
5.8	Livestock statistics (in millions of animals)	352

5.9	US bitumen and coal production	352
5.10	Export surplus of the United States in millions of dollars	353
5.11	Japan's industrial production	354
5.12	Total tonnage of ships arriving at British-Indian ports	355
5.13	Most important commodities exported from Great Britain to British India (in million £)	355
5.14	Industrial development in Australia	356
5.15	Index of wholesale prices	357
5.16	Currency rates at the end of the war	358
5.17	Declining exchange rates and inflation	359
5.18	Production in million tons	360
5.19	Yearly tax burden per inhabitant according to an assessment made by Entente experts	361
5.20	Yearly income tax rates	361
5.21	Evolution of the currency exchange rates	362
5.22	Production in millions	362
5.23	Highest wholesale prices in various countries in 1920	364
5.24	Evolution of wholesale prices in the United States and England	365
5.25	Total stock of sea ships (in 1,000 tons) according to *Lloyd's Register*	366
5.26	Indian-English freight prices	366
5.27	British shipping prices in 1920	367
5.28	Depreciation of the most important currencies *vis-à-vis* the US dollar in percentages at the end of 1920	368
5.29	Price index of goods	369
5.30	Prices of some goods having surpassed peacetime price levels	370
5.31	Some cases of fluctuating exchange rates on the London market during recent years	371
5.32	Average wages increased between 1914 and the end of 1920	374
5.33	Averages wages of Great Berlin	374
5.34	Data about wage increases of the coalminers (French Ministry of Labour)	376
5.35	Average wage increases paid by the English shipyards (for a working week of 53 or 54 hours in 1914, and 47 hours in 1920) between 4 August 1919 and 31 December 1920 according to the *Labour Gazette*	377
5.36	Wage increases in comparison with 1914 according to the *Manchester Guardian*	377
5.37	Wage increases of the miners compared to peace-time wages	378
5.38	Average wages of the workers of the state of New York	379
5.39	Average wages of all categories of workers	380
5.40	Performances of the *American mineworkers* in the bitumen and coal industry	381

5.41	Production per *English* miner in tons per day	382
5.42	Production per *German* miner in kg per day	382
5.43	Production per *French* miner in kg per day	382
5.44	Balance-of-trade deficit	384
5.45	Future state expenditures in percentages covered by tax revenues for the fiscal year of 1920	385
5.46	Paper money circulating from the end of 1918 until the end of 1920	385
5.47	US share of world production	391
5.48	US coal exports (in thousands of tons)	391
6.1	Average unemployment in 1921	395
6.2	The exchange rate of the British Pound in London	396
6.3	Foreign trade of England, Germany, France and the United States in 1913 and 1920 (gold value)	402
6.4	England's foreign trade with Europe decreased in percentages	408
7.1	Movement of foreign trade in the main countries in the last decade	422
7.2	General Index gives the following figures	424
7.3	Monthly average rates in percentages of the American dollar (at par)	425
7.4	World production of agrarian products in million double cwts (Russia not included)	426
7.5	World's life stock (including Russia) in million heads (according to the census taken immediately before 1911 and 1921)	427
7.6	European wheat and cattle production	428
7.7	The most important dates as to unemployment (in percentages of the organised or insured working people respectively)	429
7.8	Total sum of the net profits of all joint-stock-companies in million dollars	435
7.9	Total net profit, in million dollars	436
7.10	Average rates in July, in percentages of the dollar (at par) according to *Federal Reserve Bulletin* 1922, 8, 8, p. 1016	438
7.11	US surplus exports in the last decade in million dollars	440
7.12	For an English pound sterling the following rates were quoted in London	444
7.13	The following rates were quoted in London for £1	446
7.14	US industrial production index	449
7.15	British industrial production statistics	451
7.16	French industrial production statistics	453
7.17	Italian economics statistics	455
7.18	Average production per head in Germany according to official data	456
7.19	Exchange rate of the paper mark	456
7.20	German monetary statistics	457

8.1	The development of sugar production is characteristic in millions of double hundredweights	472
8.2	Production in heavy industries in millions of tons	473
8.3	Economic development in USA, England, France, Germany, Czechoslovakia, Poland	477
8.4	US foreign trade in millions of dollars	479
8.5	US employment in 1919 = index 100	481
8.6	Evolution of the number of unemployed (in thousands)	481
8.7	Capital flows from Europe to the US	483
8.8	Economic development of Australia and India	484
8.9	Exports in millions of monetary units	486
8.10	Division of the number of unemployed	486
8.11	Wheat prices, average 1913	490
8.12	Wheat prices and general prices	490
8.13	Cultivated grain areas, average (in 1,000 hectares)	493
8.14	The area under grain cultivation in Canada and Argentina, average (in 1,000 hectares)	494
8.15a	German agrarian prices	495
8.15b	German agrarian prices	495
8.16	German reparation payments	513
8.17	Figures for world production (without Russia)	524
8.18	Shift in mine production	526
8.19	Development of coal and iron production in the most important countries	527
8.20a	Economic statistics of the United States (1918 = 100). Monthly averages	528
8.20b	The most important data concerning English business. Monthly averages	529
8.20c	The most important data concerning French business	529
8.20d	The most important data concerning German business	531
8.21a	Emission of capital in the United States (million dollars)	532
8.21b	Emission of capital in England (in million £) (a)	533
8.22	Direction in which the Foreign Trade of the United States moves. (a)	533
8.23	Unemployment in %	535
8.24	Dollar-cents per unit of exchange	537
8.25	The foreign trade of important countries (a)	539
8.26	Price of wheat per quarter in gold francs (at the beginning of each month or the end of the preceding month)	540
8.27	The table shows the shift in the production of grain in the various parts of the world during the postwar period	542
10.1	Coal and pig iron production (a)	553

10.2	Unemployment among unionists in Germany (1923–7) 563
10.3	Development of the workforce and the volume of production 564
10.4	Development of labour forces and volume of production since 1919 565
10.5	Index figures for factory industry 565
10.6	Changes in American industry in 1923–7 566
10.7	The number of workers engaged in industry and transport amounted to, in thousands 567
10.8	Number of workers having found a livelihood in services 568
10.9	Reduction of types produced in industry 570
10.10	Rate of surplus value in American industry 574
10.11	Amounts of coal used by the Austrian Federal Railways 576
10.12	Production, million tons (5-yearly averages) 576
10.13	The number of horses in the United States 579
10.14	The total length of railways in the world amounted to … 584
10.15	Rate of surplus value in American industry in million dollars 589
10.16	Value of machines in industry (in million dollars) 589
10.17	Evolution of American wages and the number of workers 590
10.18	Wages and value added in million dollars 591
10.19	Capital of some British monopolies 597
10.20	State property in Germany 607
10.21	Percentages of US total production exported 614
10.22	The most important figures of production of world economy (in million units) 634
10.23	World population (in millions) (i) 636
10.24	European figures of production (in million units) 636
10.25	Europe-America 638
10.26	Index figures of the economy of the Soviet Union (taken from the Russian Control Figures for 1927–8) 638
10.27	Development of production in the USSR and the rest of Europe 639
10.28	Production in Germany (1) 640
10.29	Index figures of German production (1) (1924–6 = 100) 640
10.30	Production in France 641
10.31	Production in England (1) 641
10.32	Production in the United States (1) 642
10.33	Unemployment 643
10.34	Increase in output in Germany 644
10.35	Calculation of the rate of surplus value in American Industry (in million dollars) 646
10.36	Value added by manufacture amounted in American industry to the following (according to the article published in the *American Federationist*, October 1927–March 1928, and based on census returns): 1904 = 100 647

10.37	Average height of tariffs of the value of commodities for a few countries	648
10.38	Examples of differences between home and foreign prices	648
10.39	Capital issues and movement of capital	649
10.40	Comparative index figures of real wages (1)	650
10.41	Wage changes in Germany, 1913–27	651
10.42	Wage changes in England	652
10.43	Wages in the USA	653
10.44	Consumption per head of articles of general consumption in Germany (1)	654
10.45	British imports per head of the most important foodstuffs, etc. (3)	654
10.46	Industrialisation	655
10.47	Industrialisation	656
10.48	Industrialisation	657
10.49	Industrialisation	657
10.50	The great powers of the world (1)	658
10.51	The workers' share of profits in the USA	660
11.1	Otto Bauer's scheme	668
11.2	The Bauer-Grossmann scheme	670
11.3	Population growth in percentages	676
11.4	Growth of American capital (in milliards of dollars)	677
11.5	Organic composition of American capital (1925)	686
12.1	Changes in the industrial outlook of Germany according to cycles	725
12.2	United States of America: decline in production in %	726
12.3	Index of world industrial production (1928 = 100)	727
12.4	Index of world production without the Soviet Union	727
12.4	Index of world production without the Soviet Union (repeated)	728
12.6	Rolling stock orders	729
12.7	Number of installed spindles (in millions)	730
12.8	World sea-going tonnage – millions of gross tons	730
12.9	Loss of tonnage between the middle of 1929 and 1934 (millions of tons)	731
12.10	World production of artificial silk in thousands of metric tons	732
12.11	USA – duration of the decline in production (in months)	732
12.12	Index of wholesale prices (1913 = 100)	733
12.13	Price decline in percent from 1929 to 1933 (annual average)	734
12.14	Company balances of the most important industrial countries	736
12.15	Monopolies as against customers and producers	737
12.16	Losses made in the textile industry	737
12.17	Losses of heavy industry	738
12.18	Argentina's balance of payment during the crisis (millions of dollars)	742

12.19	Gold reserves of central banks and governments in millions of gold dollars	744
12.20	New issues of capital for foreign countries	745
12.21	Issue of capital – except for refunding (in millions)	746
12.22	World foreign trade in milliards of pre-inflation gold dollars	747
12.23	Agricultural sales income	748
12.24	Number of sheriff sales of peasant farms in Germany	748
12.25	The League of Nations index of world foodstuffs production (cereals, meat, wine, coffee, tea, cocoa, etc.) reveals the following picture (1925–9, taken as 100)	750
12.26	Proportion of fixed-charges increases with decreasing income following official data for the USA (in millions of dollars)	751
12.27	Wholesale prices in London	753
12.28	The movement of the English Sauerbeck Index during the agrarian crisis	754
12.29	Area under industrial crops	756
12.30	Prices of important industrial raw materials in gold francs (per hundred pounds)	755
12.31	World stocks of agricultural produce (in April of each year)	756
12.32	Data of prices of agrarian and industrial products	757
12.33	Decline in use of agricultural machinery	758
12.34	Sales of agricultural machinery in the USA (units)*	758
12.35	Sales of agricultural machinery	759
12.36	Prices of colonial products	760
12.37	Gold reserves of some of the colonial and semi-colonial countries (in millions of their respective currency units)	761
12.38	Foreign trade of India, year ending March 31 (millions of rupees)	761
12.39	Price indices (1913 = 100)	762
12.40	Index of imported manufactured goods in Shanghai, in silver (1926 = 100)	764
12.41	Import of manufactures in the colonies	765
12.42	Price index in Germany, Austria and Poland	768
12.43	Prices in gold francs, July 1932	771
12.44	German domestic production	771
12.45	Budgets of the most important countries during the crisis (in millions of the respective currency units)	774
12.46	Index of industrial output (1928 = 100)	775
12.47	Index of stocks of manufactures in the USA (1923–5 = 100)	776
12.48	World stocks of industrial raw materials	776
12.49	Utilisation of capacity of German industry (in percent)	780

12.50	Comparative wholesale and retail prices, annual average (1913 = 100)	781
12.51	The percentage of farmers in the USA working leased land exclusively according to census data	790
12.52	Percentage of unemployed industrial workers	794
12.53	Number of workers employed in industry and in craft trades in Germany (*in millions*) (In enterprises more than five workers)	795
12.54	US employment and production (1923–33) (1923–5 = 100)	797
12.55	Official statistics of American industry (1923–5 = 100)	798
12.56	Increase in output per worker in German industry	798
12.57	Output per pit-worker in German coal mines (1913 = 100)	799
12.58	Average output per shift in pounds	799
12.59	Increase in output in the Japanese textile industry	799
12.60	Number of Japanese workers per 100 looms	800
12.61	Shift in number of productive and non-productive workers employed in Great Britain (in thousands)	800
12.62	World unemployment	801
12.63	Unemployment in Germany	801
12.64	According to German official estimates, the number of persons reaching the working age was (in thousands)	802
12.65	Decline of average earnings in the building trades from August 1929 to August 1932 (in percent) (for all cities with more than 100,000 inhabitants)	803
12.66	Compared with this the official cost of living index (1913–14 = 100)	804
12.67	German average employment	804
12.68	Total income of German workers	805
12.69	Average weekly earnings of all industrial workers	806
12.70	Trend of the rate of surplus value in US industry	806
12.71	Index of wages paid in big American industries (Federal Reserve Board, 1923–5 = 100)	807
12.72	Savings bank deposits and depositors in the USA	807
12.73	Trend of real wages in Japan (1926 = 100)	808
12.74	Wages of agricultural workers	808
12.75	Registered unemployed in various categories (in percent)	809
12.76	Unemployment and overtime hours in Great Britain	810
12.77	Growth of industrial production (1929 = 100)	818
12.78	Ratio of industry and agriculture in the total production of the Soviet Union (at 1926–7 price level)	819
12.79	Ratio of divisions I and II in large-scale industrial production of the Soviet Union (at 1926–7 price level)	820
12.80	Development of collectivisation	823

12.81	Mechanical equipment in the Soviet farms and collective farms in 1933 823
12.82	Number of students 826
12.83	Approximate size of the Red Army 839
12.84	Open war expenditures in the budget of major countries (a) (percent of total budget) 853
12.85	Number of military airplanes 856
12.86	Index of real wages of the labour aristocracy (1900 = 100) 864
12.87	Weekly wages of skilled workers 865
12.88	Invalid insurance classification of German workers according to weekly wage (in percent) 865
12.89	The Fascist vote in Germany 877
12.90	Persons employed in agriculture 878
12.91	Rate of surplus value 902
12.92	Depreciation of machinery (millions of dollars) 902
13.1	Production of coal, iron, steel and cotton in Great Britain, the USA and Germany 911
13.2	Colonial possessions of the imperialist powers on the eve of the World War of 1914 912
13.3	Colonial possessions of the Great Powers (millions of km^2 and millions of inhabitants, 1932) 915
13.4	Great Britain's trade with her colonial empire (percentage of total trade) 917
13.5	France's trade with her colonial empire (percentage of total trade) 917
13.6	Output of coal. Brown coal, iron, steel aluminium and electricity in 1938 918
20.1	Industrial production of Britain and the United States 972
20.2	Production of coal, iron and steel in Britain and the United States 973
20.3	Britain's overseas trade by value 977
21.1	England's National Income (in percentages) 988
21.2	Relative share of US state expenditures (in milliards of dollars) 989
21.3	England's National Income and tax receipts (in millions of pounds sterling) 990
21.4	US tax receipts (in milliards of dollars) 991
21.5	Distribution of the labour force in the USA (in millions of people at the end of the year) 993
21.6	Workers working for the British 994
21.7	British public and war expenditures (in millions of pounds sterling) 994
21.8	Growing costs of living during the Second World War (in percentages) 995
21.9	Official price index in Germany (first semester of 1939 = 100) 996
22.1	New capital investments (in milliard dollars) 1007

22.2	Decrease of livestock in Germany	1011
22.3	Depletion of cattle stock by the end of 1942	1015
22.4	Changes in 'capital wealth' (in million pounds)	1016
22.5	Decrease in British national wealth between September 1939 and June 1945 (in million pounds sterling)	1016
22.6	US war expenditures in percentages of the National Product	1018
23.1	Capital centralisation in Germany	1021
23.2	State orders going to five US enterprises (in milliard US$)	1023
23.3	Large US trusts employing more than 100,000 workers	1025
23.4	US firms owning liabilities worth more than 1	1025
23.5	IG Farbenindustrie dominating different industrial sectors	1026
23.6	Return on invested capital in 1942	1028
23.7	Profits made by American corporations (in milliard US$)	1028
25.1	Index of physical volume of US industrial production (1934–5 = 100)	1052
25.2	Prices of typical monopoly commodities	1054
26.1	US military expenditure (calculated on the basis of expenditure in the first nine months)	1059
27.1	The course of the economic cycle in the US, UK and France	1065
27.2	US expenditures on armaments (US$ milliard)	1067
27.3	Prices of the most important kinds of industrial raw materials in the United States	1069
27.4	Amount of money in circulation (in milliards, at the end of the corresponding year)	1070
27.5	Bank deposits (in milliards, at the end of the corresponding year)	1070
27.6	General index of wholesale prices, annual averages (1953 = 100)	1071
27.7	Expenditures on new equipment in the United States (annual average in US$ milliards)	1072
27.8	Expenditures for fixed capital in Great Britain (in millions of £)	1072
27.9	Expenditures for fixed capital (in milliards marks)	1072
27.10	Index of physical volume of industrial production (1953 = 100)	1074
27.11	The fall of index (in %) of US production	1081
27.12	New orders received by industry in the United States (in US$ milliards)	1082
29.1	General index of the capitalist world's industrial output (1929 = 100)	1098
29.2	Index of the capitalist world's industrial production (1953=100)	1099
29.3	Industrial output in percentages in the world economy (1953 = 100)	1099
29.4	Index numbers of industrial production (1953 = 100)	1100
29.5	Military spending as a percentage of the National Income	1106
29.6	Idle capacities in the USA (%)	1107
29.7	Percentage expenditure on the main kind of war materials in the US	1108

29.8	Prices on industrial raw materials in the US	1109
29.9	Personal savings in the USA (thousand million US$)	1111
29.10	Money in circulation (thousand millions at the end of the year)	1111
29.11	Deposits (thousand millions at the end of the war)	1112
29.12	Average yearly general wholesale price index (1953 = 100)	1112
29.13	Expenditure on new equipment in the USA (thousand million US$, average per year)	1113
29.14	Gross fixed capital formation in Britain (million pounds sterling)	1113
29.15	West Germany capital investments in means of production and construction comprised (thousand million marks)	1114
29.16	Index of consumer prices (1958 = 100)	1117
29.17	Index of Industrial Production (1958 = 100)	1120
29.18	Distribution of capital investments in the USA (percent)	1123
29.19	Crisis of overproduction in the USA	1124
30.1	Data showing the development of the British coal industry	1140

About Translations, Transliteration and References

Varga used to write or dictate his papers in German, his intellectual language. Apart from Hungarian, his knowledge of other languages was rather basic. In Moscow he was allowed to listen to the BBC broadcasting in German. Most of his writings were published in the Comintern languages (Russian, German, French, English and Spanish). However, because of the weakness of the Communist parties of Great Britain and the United States, not all publications were translated into English. Hence, several Varga texts had to be translated from German into English. Apart from the German, 'original' Russian, French and sometimes Spanish translations were also used. The Comintern translators sometimes made their own interpretations of the texts they translated.

American and British editions of Varga's writings also circulated. These editions were used for this selection as well. The spelling and word use had to be actualised according to the *Concise Oxford Dictionary*. Hence, 'to-day' has become 'today'. American proper nouns and book titles have remained unchanged: American Federation of Labor or Department of Defense. Russian names and titles were transliterated according to the rules of the Library of Congress, but without adding soft and hard signs. For the same reason typical American words in Varga's American publications have been replaced by their British equivalents. But in quotations from American publications they were retained. Original Polish names kept their original spelling in cases where the person in question was a native Pole having also been active in Polish politics.

References in Varga's texts were checked as far as possible. Varga did not really care about the exactness of his references and quotations. He also used the most disparate sources and in addition he easily mixed them with official data. Sometimes Varga refers to newspaper articles which could not always be retraced in the issues indicated. In the latter case this is always mentioned in an editor's footnote.

Chapter references in Varga's texts are part of the original work and refer to chapters in the original work (which have been turned into sections in this collected volume). However, since these are archival texts we decided to preserve the original language.

Eugen Varga: An Introduction to His Life and Works

André Mommen

> Faites votre destin, âmes désordonnées,
> Et fuyez l'infini que vous portez en vous.
> CHARLES BAUDELAIRE

∴

Marxist Jenő (Eugen) Varga (1879–1964) belonged to the Marxist wing of the pre-1914 Hungarian Social-Democratic Workers Party (Magyarországi Szociáldemokrata Párt, MSZDP). He studied philosophy at the University of Budapest, but would soon also specialise in economic and sociological research. When breaking in 1903 with Judaism, he also, with his older brother Emil, changed his family name Weisz to Varga. In December 1905, Varga joined the MSZDP when the latter was campaigning for the franchise vote, but also announcing a new society without oppression and faith. Varga would become a Marxist, knowing the workings of history and explaining it by using a simple ontology. His Marxism was a mechanistic economic and social analysis accessible to all, written in a clear style and magnificently serviceable to party politics. Varga was thus a perfect propaganda officer when using his pen. One may also presume that his oratorical qualities must have been rather limited and that he preferred staying backstage instead of moving to the political front in the role of an agitator or organiser.

Varga belonged to a new generation of Hungarian intellectuals having emerged after 1900 in Budapest and who had founded at the turn of the century the Sociological Association, animated the Freethinkers Movement, Freemasonry and two associations specialising in adult education. These young social and cultural reformers had not only accepted urban life, but also constituted a 'reform generation' longing for a democratic society. They made of intellectual life in Budapest their stronghold, challenging the large landowners, the bureaucratic and military cast and the Catholic Church as well. In Budapest, these recently arrived students and intellectuals lost their former identity, but they gained a world of vastly enlarged experience in which the crowd played a basic role. French poet Charles Baudelaire once argued that the poetic city-dweller was also a cousin to the prostitute. Indeed, the modern big city had destroyed the validity of all inherited integrating creeds.[1]

Just before 1914 almost a quarter of the population of Budapest was constituted by Jews who were looking for a better life. Especially Jewish intellectuals were forming the hard core of the democratic reform movement, but many also mistook artifice and illusion for reality and substance. Their political influence remained marginal. Just before 1914 many of them would join forces within the tiny Radical. Others had already joined the MSDZP now mobilising the growing mass of industrial workers of the suburbs of Budapest. Both political parties nonetheless formed the backbone of an urban movement sweeping the streets of Budapest and challenging the ruling aristocracy, stressing 'Hungarianism' as an *antidote* to the democratic urban opposition.

From 1906 on, Varga started publishing in the socialist press and in journals founded by the 'reform generation'. He learned to combine political polemics with academic thoroughness. After a while he also served as a correspondent for Karl Kautsky's prestigious *Neue Zeit*. Meanwhile Varga had become a teacher of German language and history at a prestigious school for girls in Budapest. Chair of university professor remained, however, beyond his reach as long as the Budapest University was ruled by conservative professors opposing modernisation demanded by liberal and socialist intellectuals organised within the Sociological Society, the Freemasonry and freethinkers associations.[2] By joining these organisations and movements representing the Enlightenment, Varga had became a member of a 'reform generation' of radical liberals and socialist intellectuals rapidly acquiring an influential but nonetheless politically powerless position in pre-1914 Budapest.[3]

At that moment, Marxism had already penetrated into a Hungarian labour movement consisting of rather small trade unions of skilled workers. But Marxism had nonetheless acquired the favours of some labour leaders and left intellectuals. In 1906, the Hungarian edition of Karl Kautsky's introduction to Marx's historical materialism[4] sold 1,500 copies. However, this did not mean that Marxism had superseded anarchist and revolutionary-syndicalist currents within the trade unions constituting the MSZDP. The outbreak of the First World War in July–August 1914 would nonetheless lay the ground for a further radicalisation of the MSZDP. During the war, Varga still moved to the Hungarian pacifist left, but the party leadership nevertheless succeeded in preserving party

---

1 Schorske 1998, p. 50.
2 On Varga's early years, see Mommen 2011, pp. 13–22.
3 Lederer 1975.
4 Kautsky 1907.

unity. In October 1918, the Austrian-Hungarian Empire suddenly broke down. This would create a new situation in Budapest. The so-called Aster Revolution gave birth to a bourgeois republic whose government was led by Count Mihály Károlyi. This government could not prevent the breaking-away of the Slovak, Rumanian and Croatian territories, thus creating a 'small Hungary'. Meanwhile the MSZDP had joined the bourgeois parties in an effort to stabilise the economy and to conclude a peace treaty with the victor countries. Already on 21 March 1919, this loose coalition government of Social Democrats and Liberals was disbanded. Then the MSZDP leadership decided to merge with the tiny but dynamic Hungarian Communist Party. A Councils' Republic was installed and the dictatorship of the proletariat declared. Varga became People's Commissar of Finance, but after a few weeks he was charged with the direction of the government's economic policy. After only 133 days, the Councils' Republic collapsed. Soon a reactionary regime headed by Admiral Miklós Horthy was established.[5]

After the fall of the Councils' Republic, its leaders sought refuge in Austria, where many of them were interned. Meanwhile, Social Democrats and Communists re-established their former parties. Instead of joining the reconstituted MSZDP, Varga, together with other 'radicals', adhered to the reconstructed Hungarian Communist Party (Kommunisták Magyarországi Pártja, KMP). The fall of the Councils' Republic had meanwhile created a watershed in Varga's political and private life. In Vienna, he became very close to Communist leader Béla Kun and his faction. The small but deeply divided KMP would never find a mass following in Hungary. Beyond Budapest, the KMP would only gain some influence in two other Hungarian cities and in the mining districts.[6]

In Vienna, the Hungarian political migrants lived under the threat of extradition to Hungary, where the Horthy regime was savagely persecuting the former supporters of the Councils' Republic. From Vienna, Hungarian Communists tried also to emigrate to Argentina and some took temporary refuge in Italy.[7] In the summer of 1920, Varga emigrated together with several leading Communists – among them was Kun – to Moscow where many of them started working for the Comintern. In Moscow, Varga gained direct access to Lenin, Grigoriy Zinoviev, Lev Trotsky and Nikolay Bukharin. German-Soviet relations were constantly improving after the inking of the Treaty of Rapallo in April 1922.[8] Then,

---

5   On Varga and the Councils' Republic, see Mommen 2010.
6   Hevesi 1959.
7   In Bologna they formed a propaganda club with János Siebenhofer, András Havas, László and Béla Friedbauer, Alfréd Korak, László Leipnik and Wladimir Müller. Hevesi 1959, pp. 331–4.
8   Broué 2006, pp. 603–6.

Lenin sent Varga to Berlin. On 12 October 1924, a German-Russian trade treaty was signed. A Soviet trade delegation moved into the Victoria building at the Lindenstraße in Berlin-Kreuzberg.[9]

Economic Problems of the Dictatorship

During his stay as a refugee in Austria, Varga reported on his experiences as a People's Commissar during the Hungarian Councils' Republic in his book entitled *Economic Problems of the Proletarian Dictatorship*[10] (see Part 1, Chapter 1), which he wrote during his imprisonment at Karlstein Castle in Austria. This booklet was the first and only one of several pamphlets published by the revolutionary protagonists giving a comprehensive analysis of most economic problems the Councils' regime had to deal with. However, unlike Varga, most Hungarian Communists preferred focusing on the weaknesses of the ruling party having been formed after the merger of the Social Democrats and the Communists, rather than analysing the Councils' economic policy. Hence, it was always stressed that the Councils' Republic had been prematurely proclaimed at a moment the Communist Party was too weak to digest the merger with the Social-Democratic Party. Hence, Béla Kun could argue, in his pamphlet *From Revolution to Revolution*,[11] that the newly formed party had been too divided and eclectic to operate as a necessary vanguard of the revolution. The cardinal sin of the Communists had been that they had shared power with the reformists, the right-wing Socialists, meaning that their ideological purity had been diluted and class consciousness had been beclouded, all of which had ultimately served the enemies of the revolution. According to Kun, the dictatorship of the proletariat was not the result of a revolutionary take-over by the Communists, but of the cowardice of the reformists. The lesson to be learnt was now that an unrelenting and sharp struggle against the reformist traitors and the union bureaucracy should be carried out. But Kun also attacked the so-called left-wingers in the Hungarian Social-Democratic Party because of the harmful role they played during the Councils' Republic.

Lenin, who read Kun's pamphlet, was not very pleased by the latter's complete lack of facts. Lenin was also displeased by ultra-left tendencies dominating the Hungarian Communist Party. Hence, Lenin attacked György Lukács for his 'verbalism' and Kun for rejecting any collaboration with Hungarian centrists

---

9   Fischer 1979.
10 Varga 1921a.
11 Kun 1921.

like Zsigmond Kunfi or Vilmos Böhm having meanwhile reconstituted a new 'centrist' Hungarian Social-Democratic Party in exile. Hence, Lenin mounted a campaign in which he severely criticised Kun for having missed 'that which is most essential in Marxism, which is Marxism's living soul – the concrete analysis of a concrete situation'. Lenin's pamphlet *Left-Wing Communism: An Infantile Disorder of Communism*, written in preparation for the Comintern's Second Congress, was an open attack on the 'doctrinaires of the revolution', especially the Hungarian leftists publishing in the Vienna-based journal *Kommunismus*,[12] who defended a sectarian line.

Though belonging to Kun's faction, Varga was nonetheless at odds with his party leader because of the latter's violent character and his adventurous initiatives. Hence, Varga's analysis of the Hungarian revolution of 1919 was quite different from that of Kun who sought to establish a 'super-centralised' party directing the struggle directly from Moscow.[13] In his account, Varga pointed out that the objective political and economic circumstances had been very unfavourable, and as such had caused the breakdown of the dictatorship of the proletariat. In addition, the Hungarian workers had not been sufficiently prepared for their revolutionary tasks by the labour organisations still dominated by reformist trade union leaders and the 'egoistic psyche' persistently guiding the workers' attitude. Meanwhile the proletariat was more interested in increasing its individual consumption than in developing the productive forces able to fulfil society's needs. Hence, expropriation of capital could only be but one factor in this revolutionary process.

Varga and many others concluded that the Hungarian proletariat and its organisations had been unripe for the socialist revolution. On 28 April 1919, during a lecture at the Agitators' Training School, Karl Polányi stated that 'a real passion for purchasing' had broken out in Budapest. 'The duty of the proletariat today is to refrain from making purchases. You should only buy what you absolutely need, because if you can do without the object you have bought you have certainly deprived somebody who may need it more'.[14] Hence, Varga combined optimism with bitterness when commenting on the course of the Hungarian revolution. Completely in line with Kun, he argued that only a large and influential revolutionary party could overcome all these weaknesses affecting the proletariat. Hence, it was the task of the Communists to build such a party imitating the Russian Bolshevik Party. In line with Lenin, Varga pointed out that the international crisis of capitalism had broken out at the end of the war

---

12   Lenin 1965a, pp. 165–7.
13   Le Blanc 2013, pp. 52–3.
14   Quoted in Péteri 1984, p. 80.

and weakened the hegemonic capacities of the ruling classes in the major capitalist countries at a moment when the latter had mobilised the proletariat to save the Fatherland. Meanwhile the proletariat's self-determination had been fortified because of its struggle for a higher material and moral living standard that the bourgeoisie was reluctant to concede at a moment when the military and economic breakdown had increased misery in Central Europe.

Varga argued that the war had also revealed that a centrally planned economy was possible. However, capitalism was no longer able to accumulate and expand production and without accumulation there was no possibility to extract additional surplus, and thereby to increase the living standard of the masses. The proletarian revolution with the installation of a proletarian economy would thus be the logical outcome of the decay of the capitalist system as well. Varga's analysis of the postwar crisis of the capitalist system was thus also based on the assumption that capitalism was unable to accumulate in a normal way and that it would be the task of the proletariat to increase production after a successful takeover. According to Varga, four pillars determined labour's economic yield: labour rationality, labour productivity, labour intensity, and the relationship between productive and non-productive individuals in society. During the dictatorship of the proletariat it was a matter of increasing production by making use of all available possibilities to develop the productive forces as well. According to Varga, labour rationality and employability of the workers depended on the general educational level of the workforce, the industrial standards and technological development. Hence, the proletarian regime had to reform the educational system, decree an absolute prohibition of alcohol consumption, etc. In a capitalist system, labour productivity was lagging behind because of the repressive environment, the unwillingness of the workers to apply innovations, the existence of cartels and trusts keeping less productive factories in operation. Important gains could thus be obtained by rationalisations, concentration of production, suppression of idle production capacity, schooling of workers, application of industrial standards and norms and by sharing patents.

All the time Varga remained in favour of the principles of Taylorism, because important gains in productivity could be obtained by concentrating production in large factories where scientific methods of labour organisation could be easily applied. In capitalism, he added, Taylorism and piece-wage work were compelling workers to higher labour productivity. Hence, its introduction in a socialist economy could be extremely valuable. As long as workers' consciousness was insufficiently developed, piece-wages had to guarantee an increase of labour productivity. Taylorism and 'scientific management' were in this case very useful instruments for employing unskilled workers in new factories as well. Finally, Varga thought that average labour productivity would also increase after having eliminated all non-productive labourers, rentier capitalists, bourgeois women, and domestic servants.

Varga was thus a 'productivist' believing that all social evils and economic problems could be eradicated by increasing productivity, establishing labour discipline, introducing piece wages, and eliminating all non-productive workers and profiteers. All these ideas were in a certain sense common to sociologists having studied productivity and labour problems. In the first decades of the twentieth century, many factories came to reorganise production processes along the line set out by Fredrick W. Taylor and other reformers who had pointed out that production costs decrease by applying 'scientific' time and motion studies of the work involved.[15] Lenin defended already in 1918 the reintroduction of piece-work in Russian factories. The Union of Russian Metalworkers was then one of the first unions to carry out Lenin's instructions on raising labour productivity by introducing a system of piece-work and bonuses in order to stop the decrease of labour productivity. Lenin's arguments were similar to those used by Varga. Lenin: 'We must raise the question of piece-work and apply and test it in practice; we must raise the question of applying much of what is scientific and progressive in the Taylor system; we must make wages correspond to the total amount of goods turned out, or to the amount of work done by the railways, the water transport system, etc., etc.'.[16] Lenin's key discovery was thus precisely the fact that Russia had to assimilate the basic achievements of Western technology and cultural civilisation at the same time as attempting to create a new mixed economy.[17] Varga had been well aware of Lenin's preoccupations. In his book on the Hungarian dictatorship, he extensively quoted Lenin's pamphlet on the tasks of the Soviet Government which had been published in German translation by publisher A. Hoffmann in Berlin and by Verlag Neue Erde in Vienna in 1919.[18]

The introduction of piece-work and scientific methods of management met many resistances from the workers in the factories. That was the basic reason why the workers of the large factories in this period of the development of capitalism had joined the unions and occupied factories at the end of the First World War. The shop stewards movement in England or the *Vertrauensleute* in Germany were an emanation of a revolutionary syndicalist movement tran-

---

15   Chandler 1977, pp. 272–83.
16   Lenin 1972, pp. 235–77.
17   Krausz 2011.
18   There also exists a Swiss edition published in 1918 by Promachos-Verlag in Bern-Belp (Switzerland).

scending at the end of the First World War the cultural and occupational differences between skilled and unskilled workers while striving for workers' control on the shop floor.

Though their initial concern was the defence of skilled workers, technological change had meanwhile made arguments based on skill increasingly untenable. All workers now joined unions organised on an industrial base instead of on skills or trades. In Hungary, this transformation process was still going on when in 1919 the revolution occurred. Skilled workers still dominated the unions and occupied leading positions after having occupied the factories and the wharfs. Varga was disappointed by their prevailing mentality, which he thought was a sequel of bourgeois dominance. Proletarians now administering the nationalised factories were in his eyes only too prone to believe that these factories were their own property and not that of society. Hence, many workers were *sub titulo* of exercising controlling tasks occupying offices and multiplying the number of non-productive office workers. Because of a widespread reorganisation of the production process in the factories during the war, Taylorism had become a central theme in the debates among labour leaders. Obtaining productivity gains was in those days a goal backed by all European labour leaders, having visited factories in the United States. Indeed, 'American methods of production' had meant that the American workers were producing 'two or three times as much as the British worker', Henry de Man had observed during his journey to the United States.[19]

Varga discovered that in the beginning of the dictatorship of the proletariat, labour productivity had diminished and that, as a consequence, the standard of living of the urban workers had decreased. Varga also discovered that mobilising the proletariat for increasing productivity by re-establishing labour discipline was very difficult and even impossible. Expropriation of the bourgeoisie could not provide the proletariat with much more additional consumption goods unless the whole productive infrastructure could be reformed, the implementation of which would require a lengthy period of time. Expropriation of the landed aristocracy, however, led to an increased living standard of the peasantry, but in the meantime this also caused a reduction of foodstuffs the peasantry was willing to sell on the market. As a consequence, the living standard of the workers diminished.

In the meantime many incongruities had weakened the Councils' Republic authority. Necessary measures were not taken against the bourgeoisie. Public debt was not cancelled and foreign capital not expropriated. In order to

---

19   De Man 1919, p. 259.

hold the bourgeois experts in check, political commissars were appointed in the factories, while elected workers' councils had to establish labour discipline and to determine working conditions and wages, a task in which they failed to obtain significant results. In Varga's opinion, the complete and immediate socialisation of the whole economy had given better results than in Russia, where not all enterprises had been nationalised.[20] On the other hand, the creation of many sector ministries with local branches created a huge bureaucracy headed by a Supreme Economic Council allocating raw materials and machinery, organising commercial transactions and distribution, and deciding on quantity and quality of all produced goods. When running the centrally planned economy, Varga discovered many problems inherent to this type of organising production. Central decisions came into conflict with particular interests defended by local economic councils. Concentration of production into large factories was opposed by workers refusing to be lodged in other towns. Enterprise chauvinism, laziness, vicious behaviour of the workers, squandering of public goods, etc. had to be combated by financial controllers. They also organised distribution of raw materials in cooperation with the factory commissars and the commodity administrations. The factory directors and managers of state farms had meanwhile kept their bureaucratic style of management and they also tried to hoard raw materials, while the central administration did not receive adequate information about the factory's real shortages and the employed workforce. Therefore, Varga had pleaded for the introduction of a personal identification card in order to collect information about the available workforce and its employment.

Varga's analysis of the problems he had met when managing a centrally planned economy was rather original, because he gave a very fair description and evaluation of all its systemic flaws. About a quarter of Varga's book was also devoted to the rather disastrous agrarian policy of the Councils' Republic. The revolutionary workers' government had failed to win over the agrarian proletariat and the village poor and to neutralise the majority of the middle-peasants in order to continue producing foodstuffs for the hungry cities in combination with revolutionary changes in rural property relations. Varga could nonetheless agree with the principle of a complete socialisation of all landed property, but on the other hand he argued that the soil remained a natural means of existence. Hence, millions of land-hungry peasants were also able to keep in check the urban proletariat. In a country like Hungary, where big estates were

---

20   In a revised second printing of his booklet, Varga would also add some remarks on Russia's experience.

dominating agriculture and landless peasants and agricultural workers were numerous, the dictatorship of the proletariat should socialise all land. But in other countries where small property was dominating and evenly distributed among the peasantry, such a policy would meet many more difficulties. In Hungary, expropriation of the big estates had not been accompanied by a rigorous transformation of the big estates having become state property. In many cases the former managers or owners had remained in office, while the agricultural workers had been hardly touched by the revolutionary movement. In addition, because of high wage demands the living standard of the agricultural workers had been improved, while production had declined due to a relaxation of labour discipline. Meanwhile the urban population was starving. The dictatorship of the proletariat had thus failed to mobilise the agrarian masses by implementing reforms that had not met the real expectations of the rural poor. In order to explain this, Varga pointed here to the corrupt mind of the Hungarian peasants who refused to sell their produce to the cities and who even preferred returning to self-sufficiency instead of delivering their foodstuffs to the proletarian state. Therefore, this backward, egoistic and land-hungry peasantry had been responsible for the fall of the Councils' Republic. Meanwhile, Karl Kautsky had already argued in his *Dictatorship of the Proletariat*[21] that the poor peasantry would never give up the illusion of private property and that in all countries where feudalism had been overcome, the peasant had become the strongest defender of private property. The peasantry would thus never march with the proletariat. This idea was rejected by Varga.

Lenin was nonetheless very pleased when reading Varga's analysis. He quoted him when delivering a speech to the Second Congress of the Comintern on 30 July 1920 at a moment when Varga had yet to arrive in Moscow from Petrograd by train. Lenin said:

> Then there is the agrarian question. Here [Arthur] Crispien has got very worked up and tried to impute a petty-bourgeois spirit to us: to do anything for the small peasant at the expense of the big landowner is alleged to be petty-bourgeois action. He says the landed proprietors should be dispossessed and their land handed over to co-operative associations. This is a pedantic viewpoint. Even in highly developed countries, including Germany, there are a sufficient number of latifundia, landed estates that are cultivated by semi-feudal, not large-scale capitalist, methods. Part of such land may be cut off and turned over to the small peasants, without

---

21   Kautsky 1918.

injury to farming. Large-scale farming can be preserved, and yet the small peasants can be provided with something of considerable importance to them. No thought is given to this, unfortunately, but in practice that has to be done, for otherwise you will fall into error. This has been borne out, for example, in a book by Varga (former People's Commissar for the National Economy in the Hungarian Soviet Republic), who writes that the establishment of the proletarian dictatorship hardly changed anything in the Hungarian countryside, that the day-labourers saw no changes, and the small peasants got nothing. There are large latifundia in Hungary, and a semi-feudal economy is conducted in large areas. Sections of large estates can and must always be found, part of which can be turned over to the small peasants, perhaps not as their property, but on lease, so that even the smallest peasant may get some part of the confiscated estates. Otherwise, the small peasant will see no difference between the old order and the dictatorship of the Soviets. If the proletarian state authority does not act in this way, it will be unable to retain power.[22]

But Lenin only quoted Varga's analysis with regard to the agrarian question, especially the fate of the latifundia and the landless peasants, not his digressions on the functioning of the local councils or the behaviour of the workers or total management control.

In Moscow

After having arrived in Moscow, Lenin received Varga in order to discuss his book thoroughly. According to Varga, Lenin had 'made sharp notes of criticism in the margins of some pages'.[23] In particular, Lenin had underlined the sentence on the hostility of the prosperous peasants towards the proletarian state, once a serious step was taken to build up a socialist economy. But Varga refrained later on from giving more details about the other sharp notes of criticism in the margins. Many arguments contained in Varga's book must have irritated Lenin. Varga thought that after having expropriated big enterprises and estates, the proletarian state could take over the tasks of real accumulation and the development of the productive forces as such. Meanwhile he had reduced the phenomenon of a state-managed economy to some organisational

---

22 Lenin 1965a, pp. 249–50.
23 Varga 1947, p. 277.

questions and bookkeeping principles of a war economy. This organisational structure had been frustrated in its concrete functioning by sabotage of undisciplined workers, narrow-minded trade unionists and egoistic peasants who refused to carry out their chief task of producing goods under the strict conditions of a centrally planned economy. Varga's practical and theoretical conception differed from Lenin's in *State and Revolution*, although Lenin defended a reintroduction of piece wages and Taylorism in Soviet Russia. In Varga's view, all these *productivist* measures had to be interpreted as elements of an economic system which had all the characteristics of a war economy, not of a socialist society *in ovo* going beyond the stage of state capitalism. Varga's productivist ideas already announced his later preference for Stalin's industrialisation and collectivisation policy.

However, at that moment Varga was a jobless Hungarian Communist looking for a job in the recently founded Comintern bureaucracy. According to *Pravda* of 10 August 1920, Varga had been appointed a candidate member of ECCI.[24] When in September 1920 the Second All-Russian Conference of Hungarian POWs convened under the presidency of Béla Kun, Jenő Varga and József Pogány[25] read reports on the causes and fall of the Councils' Republic. Apparently, Varga belonged now to the top three party leaders of the Hungarian Communist Party in Moscow of which Kun had remained the party chief (albeit not without challenge). In Budapest, Pogány had been the man of the soldiers' soviet also belonging to the radical wing. Varga was reporting to the congress on the causes and consequences of the economic disaster of the Councils' Republic and Pogány on the White Terror in Hungary under the Horthy regime, while Kun was arguing that the Hungarian POWs residing in Soviet Russia should return home to organise an armed uprising there.[26] Meanwhile the Hungarian Communist Party was organising its structures and forming party workers by setting up in Moscow a party school where Varga and Pogány would teach some courses.[27]

At that time, the Comintern and the Soviet government established numerous cadre schools for functionaries of the different communist parties. A communist university for workers of the East started in April 1921 in order to school activists for the Middle East, the Caucasus and other regions as well. This university counted at the end of 1821 more than 600 students from 44 nations. At the end of November 1921, the Communist University for Minor-

---

24   Kahan 1976, p. 158.
25   Sakmyster 2012, pp. 17–33.
26   Borsányi 1993, p. 245.
27   Babitschenko 1993, pp. 42–3.

ities in the West was founded and many migrants from European countries were teaching here at their compatriots. There existed 11 national schools. The Communist J.M. Sverdlov University founded in 1919 stood as the model for this university. Varga was an experienced journalist having worked for the Hungarian social-democratic party press. Hence, in Moscow he started publishing articles on a wide range of economic and political subjects in most Soviet papers. *Narodonoe Khozyaystvo, Ekonomicheskaya Zhizn* and *Pravda* published his articles.[28] But he also sent articles to *Kassai Munkás* in Slovakia and *Előre* in New York. As a Comintern functionary Varga became involved in the Comintern organisation's press campaign. He gave many articles to *Internationale Pressekorrespondenz* in Berlin, *Kommunismus* in Vienna, *Russische Korrespondenz* in Leipzig, *Jahrbuch für Wirtschaft, Politik und Arbeiterbewegung* and *Die Kommunistische Internationale* in Hamburg. Though these articles were hastily written, they were nonetheless well researched and edited. Varga would collect numerous statistical and other data in the international press and bourgeois economic studies. These skills did not remain unnoticed for long. Already in November 1920 he was appointed the head of a newly founded office of economic statistics where he worked alongside Mikhail Pavlovich (Veltmann) and Avetis Sultan-Zade (Mikaelyan), also members of the ECCI.[29] From then on, Varga authored reports for the Comintern and its affiliated organisations, such as the Profintern and the Krestintern.

Together with Solomon A. Lozovskiy,[30] Varga wrote a report on the economic crisis in the west for the Profintern's first congress meeting in 1921.[31] These activities also enabled Varga to adapt to his new living conditions determined by his exile in Moscow. He arrived in Soviet in Russia at the end of July 1920 without reading or speaking Russian and without knowing the leadership of the Russian Bolshevik Party. In a letter written on 30 August 1920, he reported to his wife, who still lived in Vienna, that he felt cruelly alone in Moscow having nobody to talk to.[32] Varga blamed himself for his 'aristocratic behaviour' preventing him

---

28   His first article in *Pravda* appeared on 17 August 1920 and considered the peasantry and the agrarian question, a theme also discussed in his book on the Hungarian Councils' Republic.

29   Avetis Sultan-Zade (1889–1938) was an Armenian-born Persian, founder of the Persian Communist Party. He belonged to the party's radical wing. 'A. Sultan Zade', in Lazitch with Drachkovich (eds.) 1986, p. 454.

30   Also called Alexander Lozovskiy (1878–1952). He was General Secretary of the Profintern (1921–37). In May 1939 Lozovskiy was appointed (along with two others) a deputy people's commissar for foreign affairs handling the Far East and Scandinavia.

31   Varga and Lozovskiy 1921.

32   Party Archives, Budapest. Varga files, 783 f 11.

from looking for contacts. But in another letter to his wife written on 5 October 1920, he also mentioned that he was reading and writing, and at the end of the letter he begged to be sent 'warm gloves' and 'buttons'.[33]

In Moscow, Varga would experience the fate of an exiled revolutionary. Later, H.N. Brailsford would testify:

> Exile is a harsh discipline. It uproots a man from the landscape he loved: it severs him from kindred and comrades: his ears must grow familiar with strange sounds and his mind with uncongenial habits of thought: worst of all, in his new environment he is an alien who may not act on others, or use his will to influence society that harbours him. It is an experience from which few emerge without a corroding sense of frustration.[34]

Varga's participation in normal party life became possible with the arrival of more Hungarian Communists. Kun, who had been assigned to the southern front, attended with entire staff of the Comintern in the beginning of September 1920 the Congress of Eastern Nations held at Baku.[35] But Varga stayed in Moscow.[36] Only some years later would he become actively interested in the Eastern Question and the topic of the Asiatic mode of production. Meanwhile he would develop a life-long distaste for the masters of German Orthodox Marxism represented by Karl Kautsky and Rudolf Hilferding, but also by its Austrian counterpart in the form of Otto Bauer who had betrayed the revolution[37] and then the Republican institutions by advocating a 'policy of the lesser evil'[38] with regard to Fascism.

In Moscow and later in Berlin, where he settled down in 1922 as a member of the Soviet diplomatic service, Varga started working out the rudiments of his theory of the postwar economic production cycle he based on Lenin's imperialism theory. Lenin associated imperialism with monopoly capitalism having emerged at the beginning of the twentieth century as a result of the concentration of production and capital and the merging of bank capital with industrial capital. The export of capital acquired at the same moment an exceptional importance and international cartels organised in its wake, while the whole

---

33   Party Archives, Budapest. Varga files, 783 f 51.
34   Brailsford 1945, p. 7.
35   Tooze 1999, p. 527.
36   Party Archives, Budapest. Varga files, 783 f 45, 46, 48.
37   Varga 1921; Bauer 1919.
38   Varga 1935a, p. 148.

world was divided among the biggest capitalist countries. But Lenin did not specify very clearly all various elements of imperialism, nor the causal mechanisms lying behind its particular features. Lenin refers to the 'surplus capital' accumulated in the imperialist centres, but he does not explain why domestic investment opportunities were lacking. Both Hilferding and Bukharin had appealed to Marx's theory of the falling rate of profit, but Lenin neglected this factor. It was up to Varga to study these aspects thoroughly for his reports to the Comintern Congresses in which he reported on several cyclical aspects of monopoly capitalism he defined as 'declining capitalism'.

During his Berlin years, Varga must have been enticed by the works of the Berlin Institut für Konjunkturforschung established in 1925[39] by Dr. Ernst Wagemann.[40] The latter was wanted to provide the policy makers in the German government with up-to-date economic information and forecasts, a view he popularised in many of his writings.[41] According to historian Adam J. Tooze, Wagemann's dream was to establish in economics the kind of large-scale division of scientific labour that had been achieved by the natural sciences in the late nineteenth century.[42] At that moment the Weimar Republic sponsored efforts in empirical and policy-oriented economic and statistical research on an unprecedented scale. The consequences of the First World War meant that many European economists (especially statisticians) working for the different national economic research institutes believed that a structural change had taken place in the world economy,[43] and that business cycles had shifted 'as a consequence from the characteristic pattern of pre-War times to a pattern marked by persistent underemployment and intensified fluctuations'.[44] On the other hand, many American economists believed that business cycles were being 'ironed out'.[45] In the US, optimism reigned at the end of the 1920s. A good example of this optimism is reflected in an article of John R. Dunlap entitled 'Why panics now end quickly. How the Federal Reserve Banking System has abolished prolonged industrial depressions'.[46]

---

39 Varga would quote statistics published by the institute's *Vierteljahrshefte zur Konjunkturforschung* and the *Wochenberichte*.
40 Tooze 1999, pp. 523–43.
41 See Wagemann 1927.
42 Tooze 1999, p. 523.
43 Wagemann, Vogel and Bruere 1931.
44 Burns and Mitchell 1946, p. 382.
45 The influence of the American economist Wesley C. Mitchell (1927) on Varga's thinking is also mentioned in the doctoral research of Roh (2010) and Andreu (2000).
46 Dunlap 1927, pp. 5–8.

All this should have incited Varga to study the features of the 'business cycle' more closely[47] and to underpin his theory of 'declining capitalism'[48] for the first time more thoroughly than before. Hence, Varga needed to import 'bourgeois' theories related to the 'business cycle' (see *Table 0.1*), which Marxists had neglected in the past, but which had already been pioneered by Kondratiev when studying the 'long waves'.[49] Varga discovered the American economist Wesley E. Mitchell who had an 'endogenous perspective of the causes of the cycle'.[50] Mitchell argued that profits were the critical factor influencing investment decisions. In addition, Mitchell had also gathered and interpreted a huge amount of data about cyclical fluctuations.

In Moscow, Varga was even outpaced by Nikolay D. Kondratiev's Institute of Conjuncture, founded in 1920.[51] Kondratiev, a former Socialist Revolutionary and an agrarian expert as well, had developed the theory of the 'long cycles' which would make him not only famous, but also well acquainted with the expanding group of business-cycle researchers elsewhere.[52] At his institute he had attracted young researchers like the talented Eugen Slutskiy.[53] A host of researchers had already formed an international network with central figures like Wagemann in Berlin and Eugen Altschul of the Gesellschaft für Konjunkturforschung in Frankfurt.[54] In Germany, the trade-union movement became interested in the business cycle, especially with regard to the increasing unemployment level in monopolised industries[55] and governmental policies. The opinion prevailed here that 'underconsumption' was the main source of recurrent economic crises[56] and that the German Central Bank (Reichsbank) should therefore play a more active role.[57]

---

47   Varga 1927b.
48   Varga 1927c.
49   Barnett 1998 and 2004.
50   Roh 2010, p. 184.
51   Barnett 1998.
52   Kondratieff 1927 and 1944.
53   Barnett 2005.
54   This society published books of O. Anderson, H. Straehle, J. Sondek, K. Pribram, S. Kuznets, Fr. Neumark, M. Ezekiel, H. Schultz, H. von Schelling, Erich Preiser, E.J. Gumbel, A. Michaelis, E. Slutskiy, W. Lüttecke, S. Kohn, R. Frisch, F. Bauer.
55   Lederer 1927.
56   Woytinski 1927; Tarnow 1928; Neisser 1927.
57   Braunthal 1927.

TABLE 0.1   Theories explaining business cycle in the 1920s

Physical causes

William Stanley Jevons: Sunspots.
Henry L. Moore: Eight-year periods in the conjunction of Venus produce similar cycles in mundane weather, crop-yields, and business.
Ryamond H. Wheeler and Elsworth Huntington: Weather cycles affect health, which in turn affects business.

Psychological causes

Arthur C. Pigou: Optimistic error and pessimistic error, when discovered, give birth to one another in an endless chain.

Institutional causes

1. Processes of business management
Charles O. Hardy: Uncertainty gives rise to alternate over- and underproduction of goods.
Thorstein Veblen: Discrepancy between prospective profits and current capitalisation.

2. Processes of producing goods and of distributing and spending incomes.
Hudson B. Hastings, William T. Foster, and others: Incomes disbursed by business enterprises are alternately less and more than the full value of goods produced for sale.
Socialists: Overproduction resulting from exploitation of workers who receive in wages less than they produce.

3. Processes of consuming, saving, and investing capital in new construction.
Charles Henry Hull: Relatively slight changes in the demand for consumer goods and in costs of construction cause far more violent changes in the volume of construction work, which in turn react to heighten changes in demand for consumers' goods.
John A. Hobson: Large incomes, which grow rapidly in prosperity, lead to oversaving and overinvestment in new plants so that supply exceeds current demand.

TABLE 0.1   Theories explaining business cycle in the 1920s (*cont.*)

4. Processes of banking
Alvin A. Hansen: Banks increase purchasing power of businessmen when prospects are favourable by lending credit; later they are compelled to restrict advances. Following crisis and depression, idle funds accumulate in banks and enable them to start new expansion.
Irving Fisher: Discount rates lag behind when prices rise, giving borrowers increased profits and stimulating activity. Shortage of reserves forces a rapid advance of discount rates which pass prices. Crisis and depression are precipitated. Increasing reserves and dull business finally reduce discount rates faster than prices are falling and so prepare for a resumption of activity.

SOURCE: BASED ON TUGWELL 1927, PP. 92–3

A first attempt of Varga's study of the 'business cycle' is already apparent in his paper destined for the Third Congress of the Comintern in 1921. In his report[58] to the Third Congress (see Part 2, Chapter 4), Varga outlined that the capitalist world had fallen apart into two different economic areas: on the one hand a pauperised European part, and on the other the United States and Japan having developed their production capacity beyond the absorbing capacities of their home markets. The economic crisis was thus nothing more than a crisis of overproduction in the rich part of the world and a crisis of underconsumption in the pauperised areas. The only way out of the crisis for the capitalists was thus cutting wages, which could only aggravate the realisation problem. Varga interpreted the short slump of 1921 as a signal that capitalism was entering into a long phase of agony. Periods of economic upswing were growing shorter and shorter and the crisis was deepening. More and more countries were dragged into a process of general decay. Meanwhile the revolutionary movement of the proletariat was pushing capitalism into ever deeper crises, until eventually, after lengthy struggles, the social revolution would finally triumph.

In his report, in relation to the revolutionary perspectives and the military balance at that moment, Varga defended the thesis that the economic crisis of 1921 was by no means a normal overproduction crisis, but rather the result of several structural deformations caused by the war economy. Though not all countries had been evenly hit by the slump, all were nonetheless suffering from

58   Varga 1921b, pp. 3–4.

a world market having been broken up by growing protectionism, currency crisis and the rise of competing industries in the colonies. Now the masses had become sensitive to revolutionary changes as well, which would hasten the decay of the capitalist world system. However, for the time being, imperialism had succeeded in maintaining its hegemony, but revolutionary movements having appeared everywhere were announcing the end of capitalism.

Hence, Varga predicted the end of capitalism as a result of the postwar economic chaos and distortions in which imperialism tried to maintain its hegemony in the world. In this Varga was nearing Lenin's imperialism theory, because he accepted that capital exports were the key for analysing imperialist contradictions and wars. Apparently, Varga fell back on Rosa Luxemburg's *underconsumption* thesis that the disturbed world market was unable to absorb all produced goods, because an overproduction crisis had spread from the defeated European countries to other countries. In addition, Varga's analysis concentrated on Europe where the Russian Revolution and the defeat of the Central-European powers had engendered a 'business cycle of a special kind'. In Central Europe underproduction had created a situation of permanent crisis with only temporary and very short cyclical recoveries which could soon end up in a new world war for a new repartition of the world. Finally, Varga identified the United States as the most aggressive imperialist power now wanting to supersede the British Empire and acquire the latter's oil reserves in Mesopotamia.

Because chronic underproduction in Central Europe was met with chronic overproduction in other parts of the world, Varga rejected the probability of an economic recovery in the near future. In the past overproduction had caused falling prices on the world market, which had led to technological innovations stimulating higher productivity and lowering production costs. However, in the age of monopoly capitalism, big firms were regulating production and cutting wages in order to finance innovations. Here Varga used Hilferding's financial stabilisation thesis in order to avoid the traps of Rosa Luxemburg's imperialism theory and her underconsumption thesis that capitalism could not absorb all produced goods. Varga's theory neared Lenin's thesis that capitalism had stabilised. However, social-democratic parties and reformist union leaders had played a treacherous role in this process. Hence, the situation of the proletariat could be seen as completely hopeless. Only a proletarian upheaval and a revolution could give a valuable response to the fatal process of falling living standards, rising prices and growing mass unemployment.

Though Varga quoted Lenin in his report to the Third Congress of the Comintern, his text was rather heterodox. He referred to Alfred Weber's *Standort* (location) theory. Varga's *economism* was at that moment still patent. The imprint of Kautsky and Hilferding could not be denied. Varga's hope for a revolutionary upswing had certainly been inspired by Luxemburg's *spontaneism* and Béla Kun's ultra radicalism. His analysis of the capitalist cycle remained therefore articulated within purely geographical terms and was restricted to some immediate appearances of the political and economic situation. The content of Varga's report must have disappointed Lenin who was doubtful of the immediate prospects of a world revolution in a period of 'relative equilibrium' of world capitalism.

At the Third Congress of the Comintern, Trotsky and Varga presented a short report on the future prospects of the revolution. In this text they hopefully argued that, notwithstanding the defeat of the revolution in Europe, the bourgeoisie was unable to restore the social balance with the proletariat. Varga's imprint could easily be traced in this text. The Trotsky-Varga report stated that the industrial revival of 1919–20 was not in essence the beginning of a recovery, 'but a mere prolongation of the artificially stimulated state of industry and commerce, which was created by the war, and which undermined the economy of capitalism'.

Thus the crisis of 1920 was not a periodic crisis of a normal industrial cycle, 'but a profound reaction consequent upon the artificial stimulation that prevailed during the war and during the two years thereafter, and was based upon ruination and exhaustion'. Trotsky and Varga predicted rather mysteriously that the European economy was going to contract further and expand during a number of years to come, and that 'the expansions are going to be short-lived and of a speculative nature to a considerable extent, while the crises are going to be hard and lasting'. Thus the European crisis was one of underproduction, while capitalist Europe had completely lost its dominating position in the world due to the rise of Japan and the United States and the vigorous development of capitalism in China and India. The two authors of the report then concluded that all these unstable conditions also prevented the restoration of class equilibrium in its most essential domain, that of production. 'The instability of the conditions of life reflecting the general instability of the economic conditions nationally and internationally, is today the most revolutionary factor of social development'. Moreover, both authors connected this situation to the strategy of the Comintern: 'Revolution has always been and is today, nothing else than a struggle of living forces carried on within given historic conditions. The war has destroyed capitalist equilibrium all over the world, thus creating conditions favouring the proletariat, which is the fundamental force of the revolution'. Finally, no matter whether or not the revolution would break out rapidly, the Communists had to form the Party of action and to stand at the head of the struggling masses.

It is interesting that both authors of the report argued that the high tide of capitalism had already been reached during the two decades preceding the war and that the intervals of prosperity were superseded by periods of depression of comparatively shorter duration and intensity. The general trend was that of an upward curve, but while trusts, cartels, and combines were increasingly controlling the world market, 'the masters of world-capitalism well realised', Trotsky and Varga argued, that this growth of capitalism would finally strike a dead wall confining the limits of capacity of the market created by themselves. They therefore tried to get out of the difficulty by a surgical method. In place of a lengthy period of economic depression which was to follow and result in wholesale destruction of production resources, the bloody crisis of the world was ushered in to serve the same purpose. They also pointed to the fact that the imperialist war coincided with the industrial crisis having its origin in America (1913) 'and began to hover menacingly over Europe'.

> The normal development of the industrial cycle was checked by the war which had itself become the most powerful economic factor. It created an unlimited market for the basic branches of industry and secured them against competition. The war played the part of a solid customer ever in want of goods. The manufacture of productive commodities was supplanted by the fabrication of means of destruction. Millions of people not engaged in production, but in work of destruction, were continuously using up necessities of life at ever-increasing prices. This proved to be the cause of the present economic decline.[59]

At the Third Congress, Trotsky recognised that there were signs of stabilisation, but that the latter could only have a short-term character. At the end of the decade there would be new upheavals, because capitalism still lived by cycles of limited booms and subsequent crises. For the Soviet Union, the situation was not too dramatic because the capitalist countries were looking for investment opportunities in Russia's industry and railway system and would try to sign agreements with the Soviet regime. Trotsky addressed the question of whether capitalism was now achieving a new phase of equilibrium. Because capitalism was still alive, he argued, 'it will have to breathe, i.e. that fluctuations will occur'.[60] The war had, on the one hand, not only provoked an acute crisis, but also ruined the European economies. On the other hand, capitalism was still

---

59 Trotsky and Varga 1921f.
60 *Protokoll des III Kongresses* 1921, p. 73.

developing notwithstanding its complete social decay. Then Trotsky attacked German Social Democrats like Heinrich Cunow and Hilferding who had defended the possibility of an 'automatic equilibrium' providing a new social base for a reformist policy in a period when the accumulation of capital resumed. Instead, Trotsky predicted that this stabilisation policy would be followed by resurging class struggles. Because of the impoverishment of the European economy and China's and Latin America's resistance, the United States would be unable to find an outlet for their produce on the world market. 'Thus we are in a period of depression; this cannot be denied', Trotsky claimed.

During the debates, the radicals still forming an important faction were not convinced by the conclusion that an economic downturn would not be automatically followed by a revolutionary upheaval. Trotsky had only discovered a growing antagonism between French and British imperialism on the one hand, and between the United States and Great Britain on the other. But, for the time being, the revolutionary period was over. The Communists should therefore prepare for applying a defensive strategy to develop working-class support in the factories. In an intervention, Varga rejected any proposal in favour of a more radical strategy in a period when the bourgeoisie had gained the support of the majority of the peasantry against the proletariat.[61] The theses defended by Trotsky were, however, sent back to the preparatory commission in order to predict earlier upheavals. This compromise with the Left in the KPD especially opened the door to adventurism and an undermining of the United Front policy.

After the Third Congress of the Comintern, Varga thoroughly revised his preliminary report. A second and enlarged edition containing more statistics was published under the same title in 1922. In this second edition, Varga argued that he had worked on the concept of 'tendencies furthering the restoration of a new balance in the world economy', a concept explaining why postwar capitalism had recovered during the second half of 1921. This recovery, which he called 'volatile' and 'partial', was interwoven with revolutionary struggles and international conflicts and would be followed one day by a more serious economic crisis.[62] It was, however, strange that Varga published an enlarged edition of his report. Maybe it was a consequence of the discussions at the Third Congress of the Comintern where the KPD Left had succeeded in revising the theses presented by Trotsky. Although the KPD had agreed with the revised compromise text on paper, the KPD leadership was divided on the practical demands for action by the United Front tactics. Leading rightists were kept off the leadership, while

---

61   *Protokoll des III Kongresses* 1921, pp. 708–16.
62   Varga 1922a, pp. 122–31.

the moderate left around Koenen coalesced with ultraleftists like Fischer and Maslow. Every compromise in the Trotsky-Varga Report was now stressed and that which did not suit them was rejected.

Varga's analysis of the world economy had meanwhile been followed, because at the First Plenary Meeting of the ECCI in March 1922, theses were adopted reflecting Varga's theses concerning the international situation. He was asked to deliver a new report on it to the Fourth Congress of the Comintern convening from 5 November to 5 December 1922 in Moscow. This time he would refine his analysis by making a distinction between 'normal' pre-1914 liberal capitalism and declining postwar monopoly capitalism.

Meanwhile Varga had moved to Berlin where he was now working at the Soviet embassy as an expert in international trade, which enabled him to consult primary sources and publications on this subject. In Berlin, Varga acquired the stature of a well-respected economist publishing his quarterly reports on the international economic situation in *Internationale Presse-Korrespondenz* founded by his compatriot Irén Komját.[63]

Problems of Postwar Imperialism

Already in 1921 Varga had paid much attention to the development of postwar capitalism in the main capitalist countries. Inter-imperialist rivalries kept his attention as well. As such he refined Lenin's imperialism theory too. Especially the international position of Germany after the Versailles Treaty of 1919 remained an important topic in his research. The Communists were still hoping for a proletarian revolution bringing down the Weimar Republic and installing a Soviet regime. In addition, the appearance of the United States as a major economic world power was a phenomenon Varga liked to study because industrialisation was progressing there with rapidity. How to explain this economic success and what were the prospects for the future? Throughout his life Varga would study and discuss the rise of the United States as a super-imperialist power and the possibility of British-American inter-imperialist rivalries.

In an article Varga had probably written in March 1921 in Moscow, he analysed the economic basis of American imperialism (see Part 2, Chapter 2).[64]

---

63   Komját 1982. The weekly *Internationale Presse-Korrespondenz* was obviously modelled after the German weekly *Welwirtschaftliche Korrespondenz* founded by Emil Lederer in 1920 with the help of Hungarian refugee Adalbert (Béla) Halasi who was a member of the Radical Party and assisted Lederer at Heidelberg University.

64   Varga 1921e.

Parts of it were also used for his report on the international economic crisis for the Third Congress of the Comintern. This article contains some important features that Varga would highlight later in other publications about the economy of the United States. First of all, Varga argued that American imperialism was banking on military and financial supremacy. He noticed that the proportion of constant capital to total capital was very high in the United States. But he also pointed out that work was more rationally organised and mechanised in the United States than elsewhere. From a debtor country, exporting raw materials and agricultural products, the US was transformed into a capital exporting country. This process was even speeded up during the war, as Varga noticed, because of extremely favourable circumstances. Colossal profits were obtained thanks to competition among the warring countries. Meanwhile the United States could pay back all the money they owed Europe, but also more than half of the gold fund of the capitalist world. The combination of favourable natural conditions, a considerable accumulation of means of production and a more rational system of production had fostered excessively quick economic development which Varga illustrated with production statistics. But for the postwar period Varga predicted a further decrease of production and also falling prices due to overproduction capacity in sectors like the automobile industry, which had developed so greatly during the war, and to wage cuts.

In this study Varga also paid attention to the situation of the working class which was in a process of profound restructuring. The capitalists rationalising their production lines had decreed a war on the system of 'closed shop' which had compelled them to hire only organised workers in some branches and enterprises. Varga noticed that the class consciousness of the US proletariat was low, notwithstanding huge class antagonisms. Without citing Taylor and the already adopted theory and practice of scientific management, Varga pointed here to the existence of a labour aristocracy of skilled workers in unions enjoying a monopoly position in the closed shops despising the unskilled workers. Hence, Varga hailed the tendency of capitalists trying to destroy the hated system of 'closed shop'. 'We wish it success because this would mean a step forward on the road to the uniting of the proletariat. But the American proletariat will become revolutionary only when the United States are drawn into the European capitalist crisis: when American capital will not be able to ensure to the proletariat the customary high level of the material conditions of existence, when it will be impossible to overcome the present crisis painlessly'.

Finally, Varga analysed the relation between the United States and the European countries since the Great War. As a result of currency depreciations American goods could not compete on the European markets, which was at the origins of an acute crisis in the USA. Therefore American capital attempted to support the purchasing power of the European countries by investing in those countries. 'At the present moment the United States is the most imperialist power in the world!', Varga exclaimed. American imperialism did not differ in anything from German or British imperialism and was on its way to becoming the strongest military power in the world. Then Varga foresaw a clash between British and American imperialism for a new redivision of the world and the control of natural resources, such as the oil fields of Mesopotamia (Iraq). The fate of American-British rivalry would remain a recurrent topic in many publications and reports, which attested that Varga had made Lenin's imperialism theory his own.[65] However, Varga never made a thoroughgoing analysis of the rise and decline of the British Empire after the First World War.

Varga also mentioned in this article the question of war debts. The United States had lent money for carrying on the war to Great Britain and indirectly to France, Italy, Belgium. Under unfavourable exchange rates, these war debts were laying an extremely heavy burden on the countries of continental Europe. France's ruthless attitude to Germany was conditioned by this situation. Repayment of these debts had therefore become an issue revealing inter-imperialist contradictions after the Versailles Treaty was signed in 1919. Varga pointed here to John M. Keynes who, in his book *The Economic Consequences of the Peace*, had proposed an annulment of all war debts. But Varga concluded that 'the capitalist rulers of the United States are in no way inclined to sacrifice their milliards in order to restore European capitalism. This is to our advantage, but England was annoyed by this fiasco'. That Varga favourably referred to Keynes and his book *The Economic Consequences of the Peace* was caused by the fact that Lenin had largely based his foreign policy strategy on this book.

At the Second Congress of the Comintern (17 July–7 August 1920), Lenin had submitted two reports on the international situation and the fundamental tasks of the Comintern and the national and colonial questions raised by the Versailles Treaty. His analysis was that the Versailles Treaty had reduced Germany to the status of a semi-colony, thus to poverty, starvation, ruin, and loss of rights. Hence, Lenin argued that this treaty would bind the Germans for many generations, placing them in conditions that no civilised nation has ever lived in.[66] According to Lenin, the Treaty of Versailles would lead the whole world to bankruptcy. With Keynes he defended the proposal that all inter-war debts be

---

65 This applied not only to the independence of Ireland, but also to the special position that the Dominions with their white settler governments had acquired and the rise of the All-Indian Congress Party and the Muslim League in British India. Woodcock 1974; Ahmed 1986.
66 Lenin 1965b, pp. 213–63.

annulled and international trade normalised. By cancelling all debts as Keynes proposed, free commercial intercourse between Germany and Russia could be secured. In those days, Keynes was already a well-known economist and diplomat. His book had established his reputation in Moscow as well. Lenin had ordered a translation of *The Consequences of Peace* before the Second Congress of the Comintern met in July 1920.[67]

Keynes was in some ways an important source of inspiration for Lenin's tactics *vis-à-vis* the western powers. He drew attention to not only the interimperialist rivalries at Versailles, but also the political and economic situation of Germany. Hence Varga started studying the case of Germany from Lenin's point of view. In his report *The Economic Crisis of Germany*, published in 1921 under the pseudonym Eugen Pawlowski,[68] he analysed the reparation plan adopted at Versailles in the same sense as Keynes had done in his *Consequences of Peace* (see Part 2, Chapter 3). He reiterated that the USA would not annul Europe's war debts. Hence, the obligation of paying the reparation burden would seriously sharpen the crisis of capitalism. He underpinned Keynes's views with additional statistical materials and witnesses of contemporaries and attested that if Germany would be obliged to pay a yearly tribute of some 3.5 milliards of gold marks, then an average of some 800 paper marks per capita per year would be taken away from Germany's GDP as payments to the Entente bourgeoisie. Although intelligent English people like Keynes, Norman Angell et al. were raising their voice, the French bourgeoisie refused to listen to these warnings and was now pushing the German proletariat towards the revolution.

In these years of revolutionary turmoil it was not so unusual that one published a report under a pseudonym. Varga's report would only be published in German, and was considered unfit for export to Germany's victor countries.[69] The reason could be that Varga's report on the consequences of the Versailles Treaty was very technical and filled with numerous tables, which made for difficult reading. Varga's report was also rather one-sided because it lacked any thoroughgoing analysis of Germany's new economic position in the world economy.[70] Varga also stated that Germany was progressing day after day to a final breakdown. This decay was accompanied by the most vehement class struggles

---

67 Keins [Keynes] 1922.
68 Pawlovski [Varga] 1921.
69 A Russian translation (*Bankrotstkovo Germanii*) was only published in 1923 in Moscow under a pseudonym (V. Antropin).
70 Varga did not quote Emil Lederer's book *Deutschlands Wiederaufbau und weltwirtschaftliche Neueingleiderung durch Sozialisierung*, published in 1920 as a preliminary socialisation report to the German trade-union movement. See Lederer 1920.

between the proletariat and the property-owning classes. But Varga also argued that the ruling classes were deeply divided in their striving to acquire an ever increasing share of an ever shrinking GDP. Thus the Right and the Left were preparing for a final clash in a struggle of all against all. Varga did not make clear that this struggle of the German proletariat could also be victorious, only that the impoverishment of the great mass of the German population would provoke social, economic and political conflicts because of the reparation payments imposed by the Treaty of Versailles. But how could these conflicts give birth to a proletarian revolution? This problem of tactics would occupy the Comintern over the coming months.

In the meantime, German capitalists and petty-bourgeois nationalist groupings were mobilising all popular forces against the Versailles Treaty in a period when the German proletariat was politically divided and the German Social-Democratic Party (SPD) and the reformist trade unions still organised the hard core of the working class. The theory began to emerge in the Communist KPD that Germany was a colony of either France or the USA and that an alliance with other social classes, i.e. the petty bourgeoisie, would be necessary in order to reconquer national independence in a struggle for socialism. In a resolution carried by the KPD's Central Committee on 16–17 May 1923, the motivations and perspectives of the different strands of rightist nationalism were enumerated and the KPD's tactic proposed:

> ... [A]s long as the proletariat has not constituted itself as the nation, as long as it has not taken the future of the German people in its hands, the confused nationalist petit-bourgeoisie, in its rage over the national disgrace, will rise up because they do not understand that the German people are unable to attain their independence, and their national future, as long as bourgeois mastery has not been overcome. We must reach out to the proletarianised petit-bourgeoisie's misled and rebellious masses and tell them the whole truth, and say to them that they can only defend themselves and the future of Germany if they have allied themselves with the proletariat in struggle with the bourgeoisie.[71]

The Ruhr crisis of early January 1923 forced the KPD to organise a proletarian resistance movement to the occupation forces, but also to combat the Cuno government. The Fourth Congress of the Communist International held in November and December 1922 had previously already defined Central Europe,

---

71 Quoted in Mike Jones, s.d.

especially Germany, as a new colonial country exploited by France and its allies. Varga had subscribed to this theory and he would – conspicuously – further develop this thesis in his writings, but without embracing the KPD's leftist views. Therefore Varga updated and rewrote his pamphlet *The Economic Crisis of Germany* of 1921 just before the Franco-Belgian occupation of the Ruhr in January 1923 under the significant title *Germany a Colony?*[72] In a preface, Varga remarked that his first publication had been sold but not discussed in the media. Varga doubted whether Germany could become a French colony because France was impoverished by the war and was therefore economically unable to transform Germany into a colony![73] Of course, the United States was able to float the German economy and thus transform Germany into an industrial colony as well. Great Britain needed Germany as an export market, but feared the German export industry too. Hence, no clear-cut project of reducing Germany to a colony was available. 'We have to study the economic situation of Germany thoroughly again – as we already did in our previous publication – and found our insights on this', Varga advised his readers.[74] However, in his last chapter Varga remained unclear about the outcome of the conflict between Germany and the Entente. He only predicted a 'revolutionary class struggle' of the German proletariat together with the proletariat of other imperialist countries.[75] Thus Varga rejected an alliance of the German working classes with the German bourgeoisie against the Entente Powers and opted for a united front of the workers' parties and the trade unions, a tactic that was confirmed by E.A. [Eduard Alexander][76] who added a postface at the end of Varga's book in which this 'united front' idea was defended as well. That 'united front' with the reformists was visibly not wanted by the left in the KPD dreaming of a revolutionary clash with the occupation forces and the German coal and steel magnates. But an armed resistance in the now occupied Ruhr area, where the fascist right was concentrating its forces, could also lead to an alliance with the armed gangs financed by the Nationalist Right[77] against the French-Belgian intervention forces. This so-called 'Schlageter Line' was advised by Karl Radek in a famous speech at the plenum of the ECCI in June 1923[78] wherein he pleaded for the following tactics towards the nationalists:

---

72   Pawlowski 1923.
73   Pawlowski 1923, p. 7.
74   Pawlowski 1923, p. 8.
75   Pawlowski 1923, p. 90.
76   Eduard Alexander (1881–1945) was a barrister and journalist in charge of the KPD press. In 1929 he was excluded because of his reconciling attitude with regard to social democracy.
77   Dupeux 1979.
78   Broué 2006, pp. 727–31.

> If the patriotic circles of Germany do not make up their own minds to make the cause of the majority of the nation their own, and so create a front against both the Entente and German capital, then the path of Schlageter was the path into the void, and Germany, in the face of foreign invasion, and the perpetual menace of the victors, will be transformed into a field of bloody internal conflict, and it will be easy for the enemy to defeat her and destroy her.[79]

However, Radek's appeal to the Nationalist Right was mainly destined to the mass of people not belonging to the capitalist class, but following nationalist slogans:

> But we believe that the great majority of the nationalist-minded masses belong not to the camp of the capitalists but to the camp of the workers. We want to find, and we shall find, the path to these masses. We shall do all in our power to make men like Schlageter, who are prepared to go to their deaths for a common cause, not wanderers into the void, but wanderers into a better future for the whole of mankind; that they should not spill their hot, unselfish blood for the profit of the coal and iron barons, but in the cause of the great toiling German people, which is a member of the family of peoples fighting for their emancipation. This truth the Communist Party will declare to the great masses of the German people, for it is not a party fighting for a crust of bread on behalf of the industrial workers, but a party of the struggling proletariat fighting for its emancipation, an emancipation that is identical with the emancipation of the whole people, of all who toil and suffer in Germany. Schlageter himself cannot now hear this declaration, but we are convinced that there are hundreds of Schlageters who will hear it and understand it.[80]

Though Varga was confronted with growing nationalist sentiments and antidemocratic forces, he never paid much attention to what Hans Kohn would call the 'German mind'.[81] The recently created so-called Weimar Republic was threatened by social and economic forces rejecting parliamentarism. The universities were centres of nationalism and conservatism. The bureaucracy, the military and the judiciary were in their overwhelming majority enemies of the Republic and kept the forces of change easily in check. How could the German

---

79   Radek 1923.
80   Ibid.
81   Kohn 1960.

Communist gain power in a country tainted by authoritarianism? The absence of western statesmanship overcoming severe clashes by an effort at reciprocity and by the acknowledgement of binding laws would cause serious political tensions between the social classes. Hence, Carl Schmitt could proclaim that justice should be determined by the legislator enforcing the decision. He based his concept of politics on the inescapable antagonism between friend and enemy. Political conflicts were for him existential conflicts and enmity was existential negation of the existence of another.[82]

At the end of 1921 Varga wrote a report on the situation of the world economy during the past three years (see Part 2, Chapter 5).[83] On the situation in Germany he remarked that if Germany could be floated by new credits with a reduction of the reparation burden, it would regain its equilibrium and reappear as the most dangerous competitor of the other capitalist powers on the world market. He also predicted a sharpening of the world crisis which must lead to an underfed proletariat. He argued that the reparation problem could only be solved within a general framework restoring the economic equilibrium: 'each other specific attempt would lead to a *sharpening of the general crisis*'.[84] At the very end of his report Varga argued that capitalism had not consolidated economically and that in the defeated countries the situation was socially consolidated, but not for the long run! Again, he predicted periods of economic revival followed by crises. An acute economic crisis would thus appear after any short period of economic revival. In the defeated countries, the bourgeoisie had regained its strength and self-confidence and had reorganised herself and lined up White Guards. This ambivalence did not meet the expectations of the KPD Leftists still dreaming of a proletarian takeover in Germany and the establishment of a German Soviet Republic.

All these conflicts and problems confronting Varga can also be traced in his reports legitimating the Comintern's tactics in the period of general decline of capitalism.

At the First Plenary Meeting of the ECCI in March 1922, the adopted theses reflected Varga's way of analysing the international situation of that moment. For the Fourth Congress of the Comintern (5 November–5 December 1922)

---

82   Schmitt 1932.
83   Varga 1922b.
84   Varga 1922b, p. 14. [At the end of 1920, Varga already uses the concept of 'general crisis', but, according to Maurice Andreu, this concept refers in the first place to the 'crisis of overproduction' and not to the 'general crisis of capitalism'. The latter concept only appears in 1928 but not yet in Varga's report to the Sixth Congress of the Comintern. Letter of Maurice Andreu to the author, 2 February 2014].

Varga refined his analysis of the international economic situation in his report *The Process of Capitalist Decline*[85] (see Part 2, Chapter 6). Again he stressed that the falling apart of the world capitalist system had caused a *general decline* of capitalism and that the latter's uneven development, combined with a persisting agrarian crisis in Europe, had disturbed the *normal* economic cycle. In the meantime he prudently kept his distance from Rosa Luxemburg's accumulation theory as well: the origins of the imperialist wars were not to be found in the impossibility of peaceful inclusion of the non-capitalist world into capitalism, but in the profit-seeking activities of the capitalist class. Then he raised the following fundamental question: 'Is the present industrial crisis of the world a transitory and usual one within capitalism, which, after having run its course, will be followed by a period of prosperity and social consolidation of class domination, in order to give way, some time later, to a less severe and usual crisis. Or have we to do with a permanent crisis, which, while it may be broken by spells of prosperity, can no more be topped?'[86] Varga's answer to this question that so interested the Communist Left was rather elusive: without the 'self-sacrificing spirit of the proletariat', capitalism would not be defeated. Capital would strive to surmount its difficulties by pauperising the working class and driving down society to a pre-capitalist level rather than relinquish its class domination. But on the other hand, Varga also warned of fatalism by merely theorising the collapse of capitalism without calling for an offensive strategy. Again, Varga defined the crisis as a transitory phase 'within an upward development – the effects of the anarchy of the capitalist form of production', causing 'but superficial disturbances in the structure of capitalism'. The system as a whole, however, would lose nothing of its equilibrium.

Mixing Luxemburg, Hilferding and Lenin, Varga explained the difference between the pre-war crises of capitalism and the present one. Former crises of capitalism had occurred during its ascending line of evolution which had ended with the outbreak of the Great War. Capitalism had extended in that period its sphere of influence in the capitalist countries themselves and had expanded geographically in new countries. The falling rate of profit in the highly industrialised countries was compensated by capital export to the colonies and the less developed countries. Meanwhile the proletariat in the imperialist countries had obtained a small share of the extra profits the capitalists extracted through the exploitation of the colonies. The tendency of financial capital was now to amalgamate all possessing sections of the nation with one

---

85 Varga 1922c.
86 Varga 1922c, p. 5.

another. Varga then defined the postwar period as the stage of 'decaying' capitalism or 'the period of permanent crisis, or the crisis-period, for short', or a 'period of permanent crisis, or crisis-period, owing to its world dimensions must be of long duration'.[87] He distinguished three types of crises: acute crisis in the period of ascending capitalism; the crisis period, or the period of the decline of capitalism; acute crises within the crisis period of capitalism. After having made these distinctions Varga could warn his readers, especially those of the Ultra Left in Germany, that one was no longer in a phase of crisis, 'as we were at the time of the Third Congress', because 'we are in a phase of improving trade, but still within the crisis-period of capitalism'. He warned his readers that his conception would be opposed by all Social Democrats and also by certain adherents of the Left 'who deny that we have entered any phase of improving trade'. Against all he stressed that one had actually entered 'a period of permanent crisis; that the war which gave rise to this crisis-period was no "accident", but the necessary consequence of the imperialism which is the present evolutionary stage of capitalism; that an improvement of the economic situation is drawing near'.[88]

In this report Varga studied the essential features of his theory of declining capitalism by paying much attention to the disturbed accumulation cycles of capital and the lost equilibrium. Though in the time of Marx the capitalist mode of production had only touched a small part of the civilised world, Marx had integrated in his analytical model the capitalist world as a whole. Hence, Varga approached the equilibrium of economic life in capitalism from the point of view of the balance of exchange values. In the pre-war period, Europe received annually, without equivalent, from the whole world large masses of values and profits from investment abroad and from the colonies. The capitalist centre exported capital to the less developed countries. That a kind of equilibrium could establish itself was proved by the fact that the rates of the foreign bills fluctuated little. The Great War would destroy – at least temporarily – this equilibrium. The European belligerent powers consumed not only the profits of their early investments, but also their capitals. Accumulation of capital stopped and, partly, a disaccumulation took place destroying the exchange-value equilibrium of the capitalist world system. Currency chaos was its consequence. Regions formerly supplying raw materials and foodstuffs to the manufacturing centres were now establishing their own manufactures. Hence, goods made in the manufacturing centres could hardly find an outlet in the less developed

---

87 Varga 1922c, pp. 7–8.
88 Varga 1922c, p. 8.

countries. Instead of reproduction on an extending scale, there took place a reproduction on a shrinking scale giving birth to grave disturbances of the equilibrium of the capitalist system.[89]

In this report to the Fourth Congress of the Comintern, Varga's analytical framework had already reached a much higher degree of maturity compared to his report of 1921. Though he did not embrace Rosa Luxemburg's theory, he nonetheless accepted her idea that imperialism necessarily leads to war, but he differed as to its motivation. 'We do not believe that an accumulation or the continued existence of capital is impossible without an extension of the capitalist mode of production in hitherto non-capitalist strata'.[90] Varga now classified the various countries into categories to group them according to their position in the world economy. At the lowest level he situated the oppressed colonial regions in Africa inhabited by an uncivilised native population. Colonial countries having reached a higher level of civilisation constituted another subcategory. The subgroup of British settlement colonies still had recourse to protective duties moving along the direction of establishing a self-sufficient economic life.

The second group comprised fully developed and essentially intact capitalist countries like Japan, the USA, Great Britain and the neutral European countries. In some of these countries capitalist decay was not yet evident. In Great Britain as a fully developed country, the proletariat was on the way to a revolutionary conception of the situation notwithstanding the trade-union leaders co-operating with the capitalists. More hopeful for the revolutionary movement were those countries where decay of capitalism was evident because of the war. Their common feature was 'a large decrease of production as compared with the pre-war period'.[91]

France, Italy and Belgium formed another subgroup of victorious countries. France exercised a dangerous influence on several newly formed countries in Central Europe where economic decline was important because accumulation of capital had come to a standstill. Because their currencies had rapidly depreciated, the credit system had broken down, the rates of interest were reaching fantastic heights. Hence, the whole Central-European region was now sinking, economically and politically, to the level of *a colony* of the Allied Powers. Finally, the smaller countries and border states in Eastern Europe, among them Bulgaria and Hungary, were in a relatively better economic condition. Because the dominant classes were not united in their resistance, these countries were,

---

89   Varga 1922c, pp. 10–11.
90   Varga 1922c, p. 23.
91   Varga 1922c, p. 30.

nonetheless, nearer to a proletarian revolution than those of Central Europe. Finally, there was the 'group' of Soviet countries constituting a vanguard force against 'the capitalist class', which was 'still stronger than the proletariat', and this fact compelled isolated proletarian Russia to make 'serious concessions to capitalism' to accelerate the 'economic reconstruction of Russia'.[92] Thus, while the decline of capitalism was proceeding apace, 'the new governmental type, the Soviet power, so full of promise for the future', was 'growing in strength'.[93]

In this report, several features of Varga's later Stalinist concepts about world politics are already present. First of all, the decline of capitalism went hand in hand with the rise of the Soviet Union as a nucleus of a competing socialist world system. Secondly, Varga stressed the importance of existing inter-imperialist rivalries, but he situated the centre of the revolutionary movement in Germany and Central Europe. However, remnants of Kautsky's theory of super-imperialism were still present in Varga's analysis and new ideas about monetary problems remained absent in his analysis. Varga was still holding to the gold standard as a guarantee for currency stability. When making prospects for the immediate future, Varga preferred making overviews of possible developments, leaving room for different interpretations. He argued that capitalism had acquired 'a certain firmness' because of the system's 'inherent tendencies towards a restoration of the equilibrium'. Many capitalists preferred closing their factories, thus hampering economic recovery, because of overproduction in the region. Because of the depreciation of money, prices of the foreign goods in the 'underproduction regions' were increasing sharply, their consumption diminished and stimulated import-substitution production. Increased production at home eventually meant diminishing international exchanges. A tendency towards 'a restoration of the distributed equilibrium between the rich and the impoverished countries' was the result.[94] Varga also argued that the great powers were passing the bill of the economic crisis to the proletariat by transforming the whole world into a 'colonial region'. In this process millions of proletarians would perish from starvation.[95] Capitalism could overcome the crisis by opening up 'the still undeveloped regions to capitalist exploitation' and by reconverting 'former capitalist lands into non-capitalist in the meaning of Rosa Luxemburg'. Varga held on to his thesis of capitalist decline, which offered him the hope of a victorious proletarian revolution, but in the mean

---

92 Varga 1922c, p. 35.
93 Ibid.
94 Varga 1922c, p. 44.
95 Varga 1922c, p. 47.

time the 'proletarian control must be fought for' because the material development did not 'automatically result in the collapse of capitalism'.[96]

Already at the Fifth Congress of the Comintern in 1924, the leadership had to assume that the world revolution had suffered a major setback from its early hopes. Zinoviev admitted in his opening speech that he had misjudged the tempo of the world revolution.[97] His political report was immediately followed by Varga's economic report *The Decline of Capitalism*[98] in which Varga, who had made use of paragraphs of his report to the Fourth Congress in 1922, predicted the collapse of capitalism although the 'acute social crisis of capitalism' after the war had been 'by and large' overcome. Combining vagueness with revolutionary fervour Varga pointed to 'factors that are important for gauging developments' which could not be determined at that time. Although the American boom had already come to a standstill, it was impossible to qualify the sharp decline of the boom as the beginning of a steep crisis. The agrarian crisis was, however, still a key factor in the world economy. The outcome of the harvest was of great importance 'for shaping the course of the market during the ensuing business year' because a poor harvest would put an end to 'the sparse beginnings of a recovery of business in Middle Europe'.[99] Again Varga explained in a footnote of his rapport that he differed from Luxemburg with regard to the accumulation problem.

Varga nonetheless married Lenin's imperialism with Rosa Luxemburg's thesis that capital employs different means for combating the falling tendency in the rate of profit. Capital in a highly developed country is thus compelled, in order to retard the decrease in the rate of profit, to subjugate large colonial areas.

> The principal means, however, is the exportation of capital to countries where the time involved in labour is shorter and the rate of profit and for overtime is a higher one ... We therefore find ourselves in agreement with Rosa Luxemburg with reference to the fact that highly developed capitalism in the form of imperialism leads to warlike conflicts of world dimension. *The reason for this, however, is not the impossibility of accumulation without the existence of non-capitalistic elements, but the simple desire for higher rates of profit.*[100]

---

96   Varga 1922c, p. 48.
97   *Protokoll Fünfter Kongresses* 1924, p. 5.
98   Varga 1924, p. 3.
99   Ibid.
100 Varga 1924, p. 8 [my emphasis, A.M.].

The direct economic consequences of the past war were not only the separation of the world into spheres of relative overproduction and absolute underproduction, Varga argued in his report, but also the decline of capitalism. However, this did not mean that single sections of the world only recently encompassed within capitalism would not pass through an ascending stage of economic development, nor did this mean that there would be no economic booms in Europe in the future. This did mean that capitalism as a whole was proceeding along a downward curve and that, considered over a longer period of time, total production was decreasing, that crises were lasting longer and were more intensive, whilst booms were weaker and of a shorter duration. Unity of the capitalist world economy was not achieved, industrial cycles crossed one another's path, interlocking world-economic interests became less and less tight.

Varga's analysis of capitalist development differed thus from Hilferding's optimism with regard to 'organised' capitalism having emerged during and after the war. According to Varga, Hilferding and the SPD had concluded an accord with the bourgeoisie against the proletarian revolution by promising the workers an improvement in their living conditions within the capitalist system. Hence, Varga had to be less pessimistic about the economic situation and the chances of the world revolution as well, because nothing could alter the final downfall of capitalism, although many variations could occur in the form both of partial recovery and of incongruities between different countries now that capitalism no longer formed a uniform world system.[101] Though American capitalism was still healthier than European capitalism, that did not mean that an American upswing would last long. The capitalist world would thus remain in crisis and a further deterioration could be expected. Hence, stagnation and production decline in combination with declining living standards would create the objective possibility of a successful struggle for power. Although American finance capital was now more powerful than ever, it would get ever more deeply entangled in the contradictions and crises of European capitalism. Nothing could alter the final downfall of capitalism having already entered its last stage.

Much time was meanwhile spent in seemingly endless discussions and disputes. During these debates different positions nonetheless emerged illustrating accumulated tensions within the Comintern concerning the prospects of a revolution in Germany where the KPD had nonetheless failed to conquer power after having combated the Franco-Belgian intervention forces in the Ruhr area. Hence, Varga's report became the object of discussions about the 'elasticity' of

---

101 *Protokoll Fünfter Kongresses* 1924, pp. 109–21; Kozlov and Weitz 1989, p. 392.

his analysis of the world economy. The Right and the Left could easily clash during the debates at the Fifth Congress. French delegate Albert Treint supported Zinoviev against the Rightists. The Polish German delegate Gustaw Reicher declared that in October 1923 the KPD had been in a position to seize power. British delegate John T. Murphy pointed out that the united front was the essential basis of the tactics of the British party. Indian delegate Manabendra Nath Roy castigated the British proletariat as a class penetrated through and through by the unconscious and conscious spirit of imperialism. John Pepper (Pogány) scoffed at the idea that US real wages were moving downward and that the American working class was then undergoing a process of radicalisation.[102] Karl Radek attacked Zinoviev and turning on Varga, he read extracts from Varga's pamphlet of the previous month, contrasting them with the more bellicose passages of his report to the Congress. Predicting the imminence of an acute revolutionary crisis, Ruth Fischer rejected the united front slogan as 'obsolete'. Varga's theses on the economic situation, having been referred to an economic drafting commission, were adopted unanimously, though it was reported that, presumably as the result of pressure from the 'Left', they had been further modified in the commission in order to make them more favourable to the prospects of revolutionary action.[103]

Meanwhile the polemics against Luxemburg's accumulation theory had gained momentum in the Soviet Union because Yevgeniy A. Preobrazhenskiy's theory of 'primitive socialist accumulation' had endangered the theoretical foundations of NEP. Bukharin,[104] who had already 'ferociously' criticised Luxemburg's accumulation theory,[105] warned against Preobrashenskiy's concept that could engender a disruption of the peasants and workers alliance in the Soviet Union.[106] Moreover, at the Fifth Enlarged Plenum of the ECCI (21 March–6 April 1925), 'Luxemburgism' was categorically banned, together with Karl Radek, Heinrich Brandler and August Thalheimer, and from this moment on 'Leninism' would become the guiding theory of the Comintern.[107]

In 1924 Varga had sketched all recent economic improvements in a series of nations, such as the United States and France, as 'isolated' and not representative of the general trend of a 'decaying capitalist world economy'. In 1925 he had already revised his views now that European economies had expanded

---

102 Sakmyster 2012, pp. 129–31.
103 *Protokoll Fünfter Kongresses* 1924, pp. 415–16.
104 Andreu 2001.
105 Bucharin 1925a, 1925b.
106 Bucharin 1925c.
107 Hedeler s.d.

their productive potential as a result of technological changes and rationalisations. However, a gaping contradiction between the production and realisation possibilities of European industries still existed, because there did not exist enough demand for the increased output capacity. In 1921, Varga had nonetheless argued that low wages had been the result of economic chaos, but by 1925 he thought that they were causing the maintenance of an idle productive apparatus.[108] But these views were also in line with the guidelines Stalin[109] had developed at the Fourteenth Congress of the All-Union Communist Party (VKP-b) in December 1925 and the latter's claim at the Seventh Enlarged Plenum of the ECCI (22 November–16 December 1926)[110] that 'the starting point for the position of our Party is the recognition of the fact that present-day capitalism, imperialist capitalism, is moribund capitalism'.[111] Capitalism had not yet gone completely bankrupt, but it was nonetheless 'on its road to extinction'. Stalin added that the 'law of uneven development in the period of imperialism means the spasmodic development of some countries relative to others, the rapid ousting from the world market of some countries by others, periodic re-divisions of the already divided world through military conflicts and catastrophic wars, the increasing profundity and acuteness of the conflicts in the imperialist camp, the weakening of the capitalist world front, the possibility of this front being breached by the proletariat of individual countries, and the possibility of the victory of socialism in individual countries'.[112] Stalin had already used, in his polemic with Trotsky, Lenin's words that the uneven economic and political development was an absolute law of capitalism, and that the victory of socialism was possible in one country taken separately, but this time he also gave a brief outline of the basic elements of the law of uneven development under imperialism by completing them with Varga's analysis of international capitalism.

At the Enlarged Plenum of the ECCI meeting from 17 February to 15 March 1926 in Moscow, Varga was acting as a referee on the world's economic situation. Here he diagnosed a temporary and fragile economic stabilisation of capitalism at the expense of the European proletariat. But, because of a sinking living standard of the working class, a revolutionary tendency would develop at the end of this stabilisation period. In America, the economic boom would end up in a slow down initiating a worldwide economic crisis, putting an end to the

---

108 Kozlov and Weitz 1989, p. 392.
109 Stalin 1954, pp. 265–417.
110 *Protokoll* 1927.
111 Stalin 1975, p. 612.
112 Stalin 1975, p. 615.

period of economic recovery in Europe that had lost its predominant position, while revolutions were spreading across the Asian continent. This time Varga was talking about a 'structural change in world capitalism'.[113] At the end of his speech, which was nonetheless tainted by radicalism, he attacked ultra-leftist Werner Scholem (KPD) for criticising him as a 'rightist deviationist' who had adopted Hilferding's stabilisation theory. Varga forcefully repeated that there was no perspective on a period of further peaceful development of European capitalism. Conquering political power would require a long process of revolutionary upheavals the result of which would be highly uncertain. In order to reassure his audience, Varga added that the vanguard of the proletariat had prepared this bid for power. Though Varga was 'believing in and hoping for a fast final victory of the proletariat', he did not believe in an automatic collapse of capitalism. 'Without risking a revolutionary struggle against the bourgeoisie no revolution can succeed', he exclaimed. Thus it was up to the communist parties to launch revolutionary struggles.[114]

Meanwhile the Enlarged Executive of the ECCI was also treating the question of the relation between the communist parties and the individual peasant parties having emerged after the war in several countries. These peasant parties were dominated by big landowners and rich peasants. In 1923 the Bulgarian peasant leader Alexander Stamboliski had been defeated and murdered by the military when attempting to gain state power after having won the parliamentary elections. In other countries the peasants formed cooperative movements of a reformist nature, while the Communists failed to enrol them in revolutionary movements. Hence, the Comintern decided to organise a Peasants' International or Krestintern in order to study the possibilities of organising the toiling peasants in revolutionary organisations allying with the revolutionary workers. Varga, who already had spoken at the Fourth Congress of the Comintern in December 1922 on the agrarian question,[115] was now charged with the important task of collecting materials on the situation of the peasantry and their organisations in different countries. He prepared a report[116] on this question as well (see Part 2, Chapter 8), which indicates that his work for the Comintern had gained more and more importance now that the organisation had to reorient its strategy in order to find allies outside the working class to defeat the ruling landowners and military in Central Europe and the Balkans. But Varga also criticised the Social Democrats who had made a distinction between pro-

---

113   *Protokoll* 1926, p. 109.
114   *Protokoll* 1926, pp. 112–13.
115   *Toward the United Front* 2012, pp. 739–50.
116   *Materialien* 1925, pp. 5–11.

ducers and consumers and had identified the poor peasants as producers, while many of them had to buy foodstuffs.

In this period, the Comintern tried to broaden the peasants' revolutionary front by including the national bourgeoisie of the colonial countries by founding the League against Imperialism and for National Independence at an international congress held in Brussels in February 1927.[117] The Anti-Imperialist League intending to coordinate the struggle of the oppressed colonial peoples of Asia and Africa would be a failure in China. Already in the same year the nationalist Kuomintang broke up the alliance with the Communists. The latter were now forced to organise an armed struggle against the Nationalist government by trusting the revolutionary potential of the peasantry and immersing themselves in rural life.[118] Though Varga was interested in the national liberation movements in Asia, he would nonetheless not become involved in the Anti-Imperialist League set up on Willi Münzenberg's initiative in order to sustain the Comintern's united front tactics. It is noteworthy that George Lansbury was elected president of the League and Edo Fimmen vice-president, and that Münzenberg and Virendranath Chattopadhyaya were joint general secretaries. When in 1928 the Comintern accepted the leftist tactics of 'class against class', the organisation lost the support of the Labour Left in Great Britain, but also in India where Roy had opted for a more moderate course.

At its Ninth Plenum of February 1928, the ECCI would reverse its tactics on the question of British colonial policy. Varga presented there a thesis which held that British capitalism was trying to slow down India's industrial growth. In the next issue of *International Correspondence*, Varga devoted several columns in his quarterly review of world economic development to this question. Varga argued in this article that Great Britain had embarked on a policy of treating India as an agricultural colony and a source of raw materials, thus also an export market for British industrial products. At the Sixth Congress of the Comintern, Varga's thesis was contested by the British Communists, but Kuusinen attacked the view of Roy and certain British communists on the question of British economic policy with regard to India and the latter's gradual decolonisation, a view also held by the British Labour Party. A special commission drafted theses on the revolutionary movements in the colonies and semi-colonies, which stated that British imperialism had returned to its policy of hindering industrial development in India. However, the Comintern did not completely break with the national bourgeoisie in the colonies. It was

---

117   *Der Brüsseler Kongreß* [1927]; *Resolutions* [1928]; *The Colonies* 1931; *Report* 1931; *Der koloniale* 1931.
118   Harrison 1970, pp. 48–61.

admitted that the faction of the industrial bourgeoisie was backing nationalist movements. Having joined forces with the German opposition led by Heinrich Brandler, Roy was expelled from the Comintern. Having opposed the sectarian course of the Comintern, Roy pointed to the fact that the Indian petty bourgeoisie had adopted left-nationalist views against the big bourgeoisie and that the Comintern was missing a historical opportunity. In India the road to communism led through the national revolution.[119] Roy's exclusion weakened the communist movement in India in a period when the influence of the Congress Party increased.[120] The League was officially disbanded in 1937.

Finally, with some hindsight one can also see that Stalin was the one who could take advantage of Varga's theory of the decay of capitalism by using the latter against the United Left Opposition in Russia. In the meantime, Varga's thesis of the crisis of capitalism had become the Comintern's basic tenet, because his theoretical approach allowed the expanding bureaucratic organisation to develop a revolutionary discourse in a period when capitalism had stabilised and reached an international economic equilibrium. In addition, Varga was also able to use Lenin's law of uneven capitalist development with his underconsumptionist thesis for the prediction of economic crises and the appropriated moment of revolutionary struggles. The term 'Leninism' had spontaneously appeared in his writings as well.[121] Though capitalism had gained a more extended lease on life – also called a partial and temporary stabilisation – recovery of capitalism could be described as a mere postponement of the inevitable final breakdown. Meanwhile the Soviet Union had broken away from the capitalist orbit, cutting off capitalism from an important part of the world economy. The consequence was thus that capitalist production was proceeding on an ever-narrowing basis, meaning that the difficulties in the extraction and the realisation of surplus value were growing. Meanwhile, the higher organic composition of capital (fixed capital) and the decreasing proportion of wages (variable capital) had increased, forcing the monopolists to launch a fierce struggle for market shares. Aggravated conflicts among nations would therefore increase the danger of war. However, monopolistic surplus profits

---

119 Haithcox 1971, pp. 84–205.
120 Meanwhile the League's most important activity concerned the Meerut Trial in India. The trial of 32 leaders of the workers' movement in Meerut, India, lasted from 1929 to 1933. The trial involved prominent Communists, including S.A. Dange, Muzaffar Ahmad, and P.C. Joshi, and a number of other leftwing leaders of the labour movement. They were charged with conspiring to overthrow royal power in British India. Hutchinson 1935, Sharma 1963, pp. 91–4.
121 See Part 2, Chapter 8.

depressed the level of consumption, channelled investments into war industries, increased disproportionalities between *Department I* (capital goods) and *Department II* (consumer goods) and affected the reproduction capacities of the whole capitalist system.

Having studied during his Hungarian years the pitfalls of capitalist accumulation, Varga was well placed for debating this question. His analysis of the decline of capitalism or the chronic economic stagnation was largely based on a footnote Friedrich Engels had added to Volume III of Marx's *Capital* in which he had predicted long and indecisive depressions taking place in the various capitalist countries at different times as a consequence of protective tariffs and the growth of trusts regulating accumulation. Engels thought that capitalism was expanding overseas in order to escape from overproduction, falling prices and diminishing profits. The rise of international cartels and trusts inspired Karl Kautsky to propose the thesis that expanding foreign exchanges and investment would force the capitalists to dismantle tariff barriers as well. Hence, international cartels would prepare the ground for the stage of ultra-imperialism. According to Rosa Luxemburg in *Accumulation of Capital* (1913), Marx had ignored the fact that the workers could not buy the remaining portion of the surplus value intended for capital accumulation. Imperialism was thus the result of a search for additional outlets in non-capitalist countries where capital could find the possibility of realising surplus value for further accumulation.

Having rejected Luxemburg's accumulation thesis, Varga entirely subscribed to Hilferding's thesis in *Finance Capital* (1910), namely that due to changes in the organic composition of capital and the rise of the big corporation, the prolongation of the turnover period had lessened the adaptability of industrial firms to change their strategy, which had lengthened the time required for the transformation of money-capital through the stage of fixed capital back into money capital. This had made industrial firms dependent on credit provided by big banks which protected their interests by organising cartels and trusts or supporting imperialist projects. Thus, finance capital strove to raise profits by changing market forms and production, but meanwhile it fostered inter-industrial disproportionalities at the international level as well. However, cartels could also be broken up by redundant productive capacities, bankruptcies, relative overproduction and competition for market shares. Smaller outsiders could enter the market and destroy cartels. The class struggle and disproportionalities formed thus the objective limit to Hilferding's organised capitalism thesis. Varga now rejected Hilferding's assumption that capitalist reproduction could take place without hindrance. In this he followed Lenin in the view that contradictions between organised and unorganised capital would persist and that struggles for market shares and colonial territories would continue notwithstanding all forms of market organisation.

During the war, however, Nikolay Bukharin had referred to the rise of collective capitalism now that the state was regulating prices and output, thus also determining profits. The capitalist cycle had disappeared and capitalist anarchy had been suspended as well. Bukharin assigned here an important role to the state bank by transforming private accumulation of capital into public expenditures for financing the war economy. Hence, individual capitalists had now been transformed into stakeholders of the war economy. The spontaneous working of the law of value was thus banned in favour of a planned economy by the state deciding on investments and profits. However, during the 1920s Bukharin had changed his opinion by stressing the role played by technological innovations revolutionising the production processes. New industrial branches had developed and brought new products onto the market. Mass production of consumer goods had driven out small domestic producers and had created new markets. According to Bukharin, there existed thus some kind of dynamism in capitalism as well.

Varga's Law

Meanwhile, in his reports and articles Varga preferred focusing on several specific aspects of decaying capitalism (see *Table 0.2*), which one would soon call *Varga's Law*. Firstly, Varga highlighted labour-saving techniques and cost-cutting rationalisations. He pointed to increased competition for market shares as well. Varga thought that capitalism was suffering from a chronic problem of solvent markets now that the mass of productive workers was declining even during normal periods of cyclical upswings. Increased productivity was thus engendering growing industrial unemployment, while industrialisation of agriculture was eliminating the domestic non-capitalistic market. A transfer of income from the capitalists to the workers was, however, politically impossible. The capitalists would oppose wage increases. Varga's crisis theory was also based on Lenin's imperialism theory. Secondly, he argued that the contradictions between the capitalist world and the Soviet Union had also become characteristic for this new stage of history in which monopoly capitalism had triumphed over free capitalism. Thus capitalism's decay would also be the result of the Soviet Union's position and the coming revolutions in other countries, especially in China.

TABLE 0.2 Varga's ten characteristics of decaying capitalism

1. The geographic expansion of the capitalist form of production is slackening; in addition to capitalist countries there are countries in growing numbers where the proletariat is preparing for dictatorship.
2. Within various capitalist countries there is a growing tendency towards a reversion to pre-capitalist forms of industry.
3. The international division of labour is narrowing; foreign trade is shrinking, the economic life of the world, which used to arrange itself organically round the highly developed industrial nucleus of Western Europe, loses its centre of gravity and disintegrates into elements with very diverse economic structures.
4. The gold standard of the various countries, which, while it differed in the number of its gold units, was on the whole a uniform and stable currency, is being replaced by an unstable, violently fluctuating paper currency; and there is even a tendency to revert to barter.
5. The former accumulation of capital is being replaced by a progressive impoverishment – disaccumulation.
6. The volume of production is decreasing.
7. The whole credit system is crumbling.
8. The standard of life of the proletariat is getting lower, either through the normal wage not keeping pace with the rise of prices or through wage cuts or unemployment.
9. Among the various strata of the possessing class, a severe struggle is taking place for the division of the diminishing social product. This manifests itself, politically, in the disruption of the governing Coalition Parties, in the failure to form new political bodies, or to formulate new programmes, etc.
10. The faith in the unity and solidity of the capitalist order of society is being shaken. The governing class, losing its moral authority, has recourse to force and arms itself for the protection of its dominance.

SOURCE: BASED ON ANDREU 2003, PP. 175–8

The removal of Zinoviev from his post at the top of the Comintern in October 1926 did not alter Varga's position. In December 1927, he was officially called back from Berlin to Moscow where he was appointed director of the ailing Institute of World Economy and World Politics.[122] It seems that Stalin preferred hav-

---

[122] Roh 2010, p. 62.

ing Varga at his side at a time when he was still manoeuvring for taking over the party leadership. This new position would make Varga the uncontested leading economist of the Comintern developing his own theories of the crisis of capitalism.

During the power struggle between Trotsky and Stalin, Varga preferred to maintain a neutral stance, which may suggest that he could be classed as a repenting member of the Right current in the Comintern. Zinoviev's successor at the leadership of the Comintern was Nikolay Bukharin with whom Varga was still close. Both could be seen as experts in the international economy as well. But in the meantime Stalin was preparing for a radical change in the leadership of the Comintern after having eliminated Trotsky and his allies. In addition, when Varga reappeared in Moscow, the position of Bukharin and his right wingers had also been hollowed out. However, Bukharin was only formally expelled from the leadership of the ECCI at the Tenth Plenum in July 1929. All this occurred at the very moment Stalin had started edging his way towards forced collectivisation of agriculture and breakneck industrialisation. This would mark a clear turn to the left by adopting a policy of 'class against class' at the international level, which implied that the Comintern, having broken with the tactics of the 'united front', would define the reformist labour leaders as 'social fascists' constituting the last support of bourgeois hegemony.

Bukharin's disgrace was prepared before the Sixth Congress of the Comintern met in July–August 1928. As usual Varga published his preliminary economic report entitled *The Decline of Capitalism: The Economics of the Decline after Stabilization*, in which he argued that capitalism had become unstable.[123] Bukharin, who was still the Comintern's leader, argued in his drafted new Comintern programme[124] that state capitalism had further stabilised at a higher technological and organisational level.[125] Bukharin argued that new inventions and industrial processes – such as electrification, synthetic fuels, artificial silk, the use of light metals such as aluminium, the spread of automobiles in the US, and the assembly line – announced a period of ascending capitalist development. State capitalism was furthering this ongoing technological revolution, shaking individual countries. But as long as state capitalist systems would call for a policy of working-class unity, not for sectarian adventures, Western capitalism was not on the brink of a profound revolutionary crisis. Finally, Bukharin rejected the proposal of excluding an alliance with

---

123 Varga 1928a.
124 Bukharin 1928a, pp. 549–64.
125 Bukharin 1928b, pp. 727–40.

social-democratic workers beforehand. Thus Bukharin still stood for the tactic of the united front in this period of stabilisation of capitalism.

In his preliminary report on the world economy, Varga explained that 'the stabilisation of capitalism' did not mean the 'stability of the capitalist system' and that 'the internal contradictions of stabilised capitalism must necessarily lead to new revolutionary situations, that the period of decline of capitalism is not ended'.[126] After the war, capitalism had stabilised with the help of the reformist labour leaders, but concessions granted by the capitalists to the workers were soon wiped out by inflation. Postwar capitalism was leading to 'a peaceful super-imperialism, whose economic basis is international monopoly, economic co-operation between banks of issue and the balance of forces; whose form of organisation is the League of Nations'.[127] Hence, it would be 'blind stupidity to attempt to deny the fact of the economic and political stabilisation of capitalism as compared with the position in the years immediately following the war'.[128] Varga identified a new phenomenon having arisen from the industrial cycle: an important decrease had occurred in the number of workers employed in industry in the leading capitalist countries, while the increase in production per worker exceeded the extension of production. The displacement of workers by machinery was no longer compensated for by an extension of production, while the capacity of the distribution services to absorb workers was rather limited as rationalisation of all forms of office work tended to decrease employment in this sector as well.[129]

Capitalism was no longer a unified whole, Varga reiterated, because its world system was broken up into imperialist states struggling for hegemony. The overthrow of the capitalist system and the establishment of the dictatorship of the proletariat within the Soviet Union signified 'the beginning of the period of the decline of capitalism'.[130] Here, Varga gave his own interpretation of the character of the crisis which 'differed fundamentally from all previous crises of capitalism that could succeed in solving the contradictions ... within the framework of the capitalist system, while this crisis led to the break up of the system itself, to the overthrow of the bourgeoisie and the attainment of the prolet-

---

126 Varga 1928a, p. 1.
127 Varga 1928a, p. 6.
128 Varga 1928a, pp. 6–7.
129 At that moment, however, a debate already had developed in the German trade-union movement about the growth of the number of white-collar workers and the decline in the number of industrial workers. Especially professor Emil Lederer (Heidelberg) had pointed to this phenomenon. Thomas, Lederer and Suhr 1928.
130 Varga 1928a, p. 10.

arian dictatorship in one of the greatest States of the world'.[131] Varga rejected Hilferding's thesis that capitalism was approaching a new period of expansion and that today's capitalism differed from earlier forms of capitalism because it had become organised and planned. The state in the period of organised capitalism had thus not become of decisive importance to the fate of the working class; hence he therefore rejected the thesis that the transition from capitalism to socialism could be realised by a gradual attainment of economic democracy, not by the collapse of capitalism.

Like Bukharin, Varga noted that during the last two years a far-reaching technical progress had taken place, which in the US had already caused tremendous changes in the economic basis and in the structure of the working class. Increased productivity of labour due to technical changes in the production process and increased intensity of labour had led to a new kind of unemployment, which Varga qualified as being 'structural unemployment ... economically different from the industrial reserve army'. He saw a tendency towards the rise of a 'new type of privileged worker, a new type of labour aristocracy'. The conveyer system implied that any worker might learn in a few days the simple manipulations required by the function. Hence, a 'new class of workers' had arisen in the large factories, but in order to secure their employment, these new workers were systematically placing themselves at the 'service of the capitalists' against the working class 'as a whole'.[132] Structural unemployment was progressing since the crisis of 1921. 'Today we find that the expansion of the market no longer suffices to provide work again for those who have been previously thrown out of work in the imperialist countries'.[133] The peasants producing in the first place to satisfy their own needs had become farmers producing for the market and were purchasing industrial products. Varga denied that Rosa Luxemburg had inspired him,[134] but he subscribed to the thesis that increased mass unemployment would 'naturally' mean an increased discontent of the workers and a 'rise in the volume of revolutionary energy'. But, on the other

---

131   Ibid.
132   'Sixth World Congress' 1928, p. 819.
133   'Sixth World Congress' 1928, p. 818.
134   Varga said during the debates: 'I have tried to draw a very sharp distinction between my theory and that of Rosa Luxemburg. My point is not that it is impossible to realise surplus value within the capitalist system generally – there can be no question about that – but that the former expansion of the capitalist markets – which can only take place once in history – in these countries has now been completed. That is why we have a situation in which the workers who have been discharged from industry as a result of the improvement of technique and of rationalization, cannot find any other employment; their dismissal is final and complete'. 'Sixth World Congress' 1928, p. 1188.

hand, Varga noted that the living standard of the American proletariat had risen because the increased intensity of labour necessitated a 'well-fed worker'.[135]

During the debates, Varga's 'law' and the subsequent presumed effects did not impress Bukharin. The rationalisation crisis and the absolute growth of unemployment were for him a kind of Luxemburgism. 'I absolutely disagree with the argument advanced ... to the effect that the internal possibilities of American capitalism have been "exhausted" ... It is wrong both in theory and practice ... [I]t is a reiteration of Rosa Luxemburg's theory'.[136] Bukharin was not the only one commenting negatively on Varga's 'law'. In his attack, Stalinist Beso Lominadze saw in Varga's new law of development – under which the amount of variable capital, and consequently also the number of workers, would decline absolutely in the face of a simultaneous increase in constant capital – as contrary to Marx's *Capital*.

In her *Accumulation of Capital*, Rosa Luxemburg had argued that Marx's reproduction scheme in *Capital*, Volume II, was contradictory to the limits of consumption in *Capital*, Volume III. Varga's problem was that his crisis theory could be identified as a variant of Rosa Luxemburg's underconsumptionist thesis. In *Capital*, Volume III, Marx had stated that 'the ultimate reason for all real crises always remains the poverty and restricted consumption of the masses as opposed to the drive of capitalist production to develop the productive forces as though only the absolute consuming power of society constituted their limit'.[137] But in the same volume, Marx had remarked that 'things are produced only so long as they can be produced with a profit' and that the 'rate of profit is the motive power of capitalist production', which meant that 'new offshoots of capital' were seeking to find 'an independent place for themselves'.[138] Marx had observed that workers were hired only as they could be profitably employed and that the development of productivity of labour proceeded very disproportionately in degree but frequently also in opposite directions.[139]

Marx[140] had argued that the absolute volume of employment would tend to grow despite technological change, albeit at a slower rate than investment.

> The accumulation of capital, though originally appearing as its qualitative extension only, is effected, as we have seen under a progressive qualitative

---

135 'Sixth World Congress' 1928, p. 818.
136 'Sixth World Congress' 1928, p. 871.
137 Marx 1959, pp. 472–3.
138 Marx 1959, p. 254.
139 Ibid.
140 Marx 1954, pp. 612–712.

change in its compensation, under a constant increase of its constant, at the expense of its variable constituent ... The labouring population therefore produces, along with the accumulation of capital produced by it, the means by which itself is made relatively superfluous, is turned into a relative surplus population; and it does this to an always increasing extent. This is a law of population peculiar to the capitalist mode of production.[141]

'The greater the social wealth, the functioning capital, the extent and energy of its growth, and, therefore, also the absolute mass of the proletariat and the productiveness of its labour, the greater is the industrial reserve army. The same causes which develop the expansive power of capital, develop also the labour-power at its disposal'.[142]

Basing himself on *Capital*, Volume I, Varga argued that in 'pure capitalism' accumulation and technological progress automatically caused an absolute decline in the number of productive workers and, therewith, also engendered a chronic realisation problem. But Varga's interpretation of Marx was met by criticism on behalf of other Communist economists who did not appreciate Varga's proposal that crises occur because workers are not paid sufficient wages to consume the increasing output. They thought that Varga was here dangerously gravitating towards Rosa Luxemburg when arguing that crises occurred because workers were insufficiently paid and external markets were non-existent. Especially so in Varga's assertion that for the first time in history the number of productive workers had declined in the US in a period of industrial boom. In an article he had previously published in the journal of his institute, Varga had argued that during the postwar years US employment had fallen by 8 percent in mining, industry, rail transport and agriculture, which 'proved' that an absolute reduction in the number of workers was taking place in combination with an increasing output per worker.[143] Hence, the rate of labour displacement in some branches of production exceeded the absorption rate in others while new markets were available. At earlier stages the effects of technological changes had been offset by the use of machinery in agriculture and handicrafts, while labour power in these sectors could find employment in industry. But now that the American peasantry was mainly producing for the market and the working class was shrinking, absolute impoverishment would be their fate. Without renewed access to 'third-party' markets, the realisation

---

141   Marx 1954, pp. 631–2.
142   Marx 1954, p. 644.
143   Varga 1928b, pp. 3–12.

problem would become, despite the achievements of the monopolies in the regulation of production, so acute that further accumulation and realisation of surplus value would stagnate. Thus the only method to solve the problem was a transfer of income from the capitalists to the workers to sustain demand. In practice this would be impossible because of bourgeois resistance to any income redistribution. Varga referred to the American automobile industry where a realisation crisis had caused about 4 million jobless workers (about 10 percent of the working population or 18 percent of the wage earners). However, low interest rates were engendering a hitherto unknown stock-market speculation. This bubble would someday burst.[144] Varga's 'law' pointed to a chronic tendency towards a sharpening contradiction between the productive forces and the working classes' purchasing power. Hence, Varga's 'law' demonstrated the impossibility of continuously raising wages and subsequent workers' consumption.

Varga's 'law' met many oppositions and criticism from different Soviet economists. The latter did not share Varga's views on the impossibility of a normal 'business cycle' in the postwar period. Modeste I. Rubinshtein thought that American unemployment was exceptional. Bato Batuev argued that America was hit by an enormous underutilisation of its productive apparatus.[145] Spektator (Miron I. Nakhimson) stated that labour intensification was far more important than technological progress. Hence, high unemployment rates were due to insufficient investment rates sustaining or creating additional employment. He identified Varga's remarks on 'pure capitalism' as a return to Mikhail I. Tugan-Baranovskiy's thesis that capitalism might continue developing even in a period of growing unemployment.[146] In an address to the Communist Academy in April 1928, N. Osinskiy (Valerian Obolenskiy) rejected Varga's theory of the non-existence of expanded reproduction in the US. Hence, he predicted the take-off of a new reproduction cycle superseding the actual level of production in several branches.[147] But the Left also mobilised against Varga's 'law' in a period when the Stalinists campaigned against the presence of 'bourgeois specialists' in the institutes and the enterprises.[148] At the Sixth Congres of the Comintern, Beso Lominadze disqualified Varga's theory as being based on bourgeois statistics.[149] Left-winger Christoph Wurm (KPD) published in

---

144 'Sixth World Congress' 1928, p. 863.
145 Day 1981, p. 151.
146 Day 1981, pp. 152–3.
147 Day 1981, pp. 153–4.
148 McDermott 1995, p. 413.
149 'Sixth World Congress' 1928, pp. 933–4.

*Die Kommunistische Internationale*¹⁵⁰ a vile attack on Varga's 'unemployment law' as contrary to Marx's *Capital*. Wurm's thesis was that Marx had clearly stated that after a period of increased unemployment, a new investment cycle should create more employment. Though new machinery in the production process would destroy employment, workers would then find employment in the booming machinery industry. Lominadze, who had already developed the same reasoning during the Sixth Congress of the Comintern, had inspired Wurm's attack, in which he remarked that Varga's crisis theory came very near to Rosa Luxemburg's imperialism theory. Against Wurm's attacks, Varga defended himself by referring to statistics published by the Federal Reserve Board. He now argued that Marx had made a distinction between the concrete historical nature of unemployment and Marx's 'pure' theoretical analysis.

At the Sixth Congress of the Comintern, Varga also presented a report on the situation in the USSR and the problems confronting the CPSU in which he marked some differences from Bukharin's economic views concerning the peasantry and the possibility of 'transforming the country from an agrarian country into an agrarian-industrial country'.¹⁵¹ He warned his audience for the future because the alliance of workers and peasantry was 'beginning to decline in importance'.¹⁵² The fact that the Soviet Union obtained no foreign loans compelled the government to accumulate capital for the purpose of industrialisation in the form of the 'scissors'. Raising the price of manufactured goods in order to extract the largest possible share of income of the peasantry for the purpose of industrialisation would incite the peasants to 'weave his own cloths' and 'make his own syrup'.¹⁵³ They would also obtain from the handicraft workers their boots at a lower price than from the state factories. Class differentiation in the villages had led to the creation of a layer of a wealthy peasantry (kulaks), while the socialist sector was handicapped by its 'actual poverty'.¹⁵⁴ In a country 'where both a Socialist and a private economic sector exist', planning must 'keep stable the purchasing power of the currency in the home market'.¹⁵⁵

Varga also criticised the original draft programme of the Comintern on the question of war communism and the possibility of a war Communist policy. Varga did not hold the view that one 'must work for War Communism under

---

150 Wurm 1929.
151 'Sixth World Congress' 1928, p. 1118.
152 'Sixth World Congress' 1928, p. 1119.
153 Ibid.
154 'Sixth World Congress' 1928, p. 1120.
155 Ibid.

all circumstances or even to give it preference'. He rejected Bukharin's remarks that the opinion he had expressed here had 'historical connections with the mistakes we made in Hungary'. He also warned his audience that the capture of power in other countries will come about not in the way it did in Hungary or in Russia; it will come about in the form of a sanguinary civil war.[156] Moreover, during the first period of the dictatorship of the proletariat, all big enterprises, banks and 'perhaps also the big farms' had to be nationalised, but also labour discipline established. And what about distribution of land to the poor peasants? That would 'link up peasants and agricultural workers closely to the dictatorship'[157] without contradicting War Communism. 'When Comrade Bukharin reproached us for our wrong policy in Hungary he ought to know that since that time, during the past ten years, we have thought over these mistakes a thousand times and we are fully conscious of the great responsibility we bear for the failure of the dictatorship ... In my opinion, War Communism will be necessary in most countries as a means for retaining power'.[158] This minor incident between Bukharin and Varga clearly revealed that the latter was well aware of the difficulties Bukharin's industrialisation policy was meeting. Stalin, who had been 'especially heartily welcomed on his appearance'[159] and elected member of the congress presidium, must have noticed these differences between Bukharin's and Varga's tactical appreciations of the economic situation.

Already in the first paragraph of his report on the situation in the USSR, Varga had stated that 'the period of the proletarian dictatorship does not bring with it the cessation of the class struggle; it merely assumes another form. It would be a mistake to believe that there is no class war in the Soviet Union'.[160] Varga cited Lenin who had said that the kulaks could become dangerous when they could ally with the middle peasants and the urban bourgeoisie. Varga added: 'If this force turned against the proletarian dictatorship, it would naturally represent a dangerous force: it would mean civil war'.[161] However, this did not signify that Varga was breaking with NEP or wanted to return to a kind of War Communism. He only pleaded for supporting the poor peasants by getting them when 'the industry of the Soviet Union is able to turn out sufficient tractors, ploughs

---

156 'Sixth World Congress' 1928, p. 1188.
157 'Sixth World Congress' 1928, p. 1189.
158 Ibid.
159 'Sixth World Congress' 1928, p. 706.
160 'Sixth World Congress' 1928, p. 1098.
161 'Sixth World Congress' 1928, p. 1121.

and machinery to help these poor peasants, so that they can cultivate their land themselves, and if possible, to get them all organised on collectivist lines'.[162]

All this, however, did not mean that Varga's alleged 'Rightist' position would not be contested during the months to come. Especially Varga's 'law' that rationalisations had increased labour productivity and caused structural employment could easily be identified as a 'Luxemburgist deviation' the Comintern was combating. Varga's disgrace as the Comintern's official economist was meanwhile programmed and then consumed at the Tenth Plenum of the ECCI meeting on 3–19 July 1929. Otto Kuusinen, who had succeeded Bukharin at the head of the ECCI, gave a detailed analysis of the international situation and the revolutionary tasks of the Comintern. He also dealt with Varga's thesis of wage increases in a period of capitalist rationalisations and his 'unorthodox' appreciation of the recently signed Young Plan. He rejected Varga's 'law' as a superfluous ornament and linked it to Rosa Luxemburg 'who, in her desire to construct a simple, purely economic "law" of the collapse of capitalism, was diverted into the wrong channel'. Kuusinen discerned in Varga's law of the tendency of the decreasing number of workers 'the germ of a new theory of the gradual decay of capitalism'.[163]

But Kuusinen also attacked Varga for having defended the thesis that rationalisations and the conveyer system had contributed to a higher living standard of the American working classes. However, real wages could not possibly rise as intensification and rationalisation were creating mass unemployment. Increased labour intensity could only mean a declining general wage standard. Capitalist rationalisation should bring with it 'an absolute worsening of the position of the working class even when real wages are rising',[164] namely that, as Marx had said, 'in proportion as capital accumulates, the lot of the labourer, be his payment high or low, must grow worse'.[165] Monopoly capital not only enforces monopolist prices for goods, but also reduces the price of labour power well below its value. He attacked Varga on the latter's assertion that the real wages showed in America a tendency to rise without having investigated the extent of the rise, because such an investigation would have revealed that the standard of living of the workers was not rising. As a consequence of the worsening of the living conditions of the workers, proletarian consciousness would increase and shatter all reformist illusions. Finally, Kuusinen attacked Varga for the latter's treatment of the Young Plan. In the spring of 1929, Amer-

---

162 'Sixth World Congress' 1928, p. 1120.
163 'Tenth Plenum of the E.C.C.I.' 1929, pp. 839–46.
164 'Tenth Plenum of the E.C.C.I.' 1929, p. 839.
165 Marx 1954, p. 645.

ican diplomat Owen Young had renegotiated a reduction in the reparations annuity from 2.5 billion to 2 billion pre-war gold marks. Varga was now thinking that the Young Plan could prevent a sudden economic downturn and thus bridge over imperialist contradictions, but he had not solved the underlying reparations problem.

In his response, Varga opined that Kuusinen's report was 'too general, especially in regard to economics' and that the latter's theses did not pay 'sufficient attention to the concrete elements in the present situation'.[166] During the past period of 'uninterrupted economic revival', Varga argued, a revival of the labour movement had occurred leading to an increase in the volume of production on a world scale. This could, however, by no means be considered as the end of the general capitalist crisis. The American economy was not only suffering from overproduction in the agrarian sector, but also shaken by a huge overcapacity in the automobile industry. He signalled a new agrarian crisis in the United States, causing a sharp decline of wheat prices and the danger of an international credit crisis because of high interest rates. Varga also predicted the collapse of the stock market because of 'unprecedented speculation' in the United States and in other countries leading to a comprehensive rationalisation and dequalification process and announcing a general reallocation of the entire labour force.

During the Presidium discussions, Varga had also argued that the standard of living of the workers had been increased, not lowered. Unemployment was not the consequence of reduced production. 'It runs on the contrary, parallel with considerable increase of production' and does not 'disappear in a favourable economic situation'. The greatest unemployment could be found 'in the most highly developed capitalist countries' and 'partly disguised by the transference of wide sections of labour from the sphere of production to the sphere of consumption and distribution'.[167] Varga pointed now to the fact that average labour productivity had increased by 40 percent. The new unemployment was due to the rationalisation process in industry and the mechanisation drive in American agriculture. Varga criticised 'some comrades' having indulged in the joke of calling the definition a 'Varga law'. 'I cannot let that stand', he argued. 'I am a much too modest person to make a law ... I merely spoke of a tendency'.[168] A 'new type of privileged worker' had emerged: technical assistants, spies, members of company unions in the United States, but also the Stahlhelm in Germany. Varga pointed to the revolutionary potentials of the growing army

---

166   'Tenth Plenum of the E.C.C.I.' 1929, p. 863.
167   'Tenth Plenum of the E.C.C.I.' 1929, p. 866.
168   Ibid.

of unemployed workers. Features of those countries with high unemployment were related to the ongoing technological revolution in the developed capitalist countries. Unemployment was not the consequence of reduced production and it would not disappear in a favourable economic situation. The highest unemployment was registered in the most developed countries and the transfer of workers from industry to services was partially disguised unemployment. New unemployment was caused by the fact that there were 'not enough capitalist outlets to absorb again the young generation of the working class and the workers were thrown out of work!'[169]

Against this plethora of negative remarks, Varga stressed that he had 'never said that the living standard had risen, as was ascribed to me by some comrades here'.[170] He had only discerned a relative increase in the living standard of the working classes in some countries. In addition, a stock-market crash was imminent. Sure signs of a new economic crisis were visible. By 1930 there would be more fights between capital and labour. Finally, everything depended on the 'right interpretation' of the available statistics. 'To my mind, it is the greatest opportunism to keep silent because of fear to clash with the prevailing line of thought. This is the most dangerous kind of opportunism unworthy of a Communist'. Many times, Varga had been blamed for his alleged opportunism. Hence, he could refer to the Fourth Congress, where he had been 'described by Comrade Bukharin as an opportunist because I believed that the partial demands should be included in the Comintern Programme ... [A] few days afterwards Comrade Bukharin, on behalf of the Russian delegation, was bound to make a declaration in which the charge of opportunism was withdrawn'. At the Third Congress, Varga had been branded by a group of comrades as 'an opportunist'. However, these critics had now joined Social Democracy. Varga: 'The only one whom I still have the joy to see in our midst is my friend Bela Kun! (Béla Kun: "But at that time you were at one with Trotsky!") But also with Lenin on this question!'[171] Then Varga attacked Kolarov for having given 'the most opportunist speech ever made in the Comintern', for his 'liquidatorship of the purest brand' and for having used 'nothing else but the old vulgar theory of underconsumption', which was 'politically the theory of social-fascism' defended by Social Democrat[172] Fritz Tarnow in Germany.[173]

---

169   Ibid.
170   'Tenth Plenum of the E.C.C.I.' 1929, p. 1019.
171   Ibid.
172   Lange 1969.
173   'Tenth Plenum of the E.C.C.I.' 1929, p. 1020.

Notwithstanding his fierce defence, Varga's thesis was rejected by the Plenum. In his speech, Molotov connected Varga's Right opportunism to the faction of the German Reconcilers. He warned that Right-opportunist tendencies penetrate by other means too. 'An example of this is Comrade Varga'.[174] In his closing speech Kuusinen commented on the problem of Marxism's accuracy in the use of economic terms and the fact that the ECCI had differed from Varga's opinion about an absolute or only relative decline in the living standard of the working class. 'My whole argument was directed against Comrade Varga's assertion that there was only a relative, but no absolute decline in the living standard of the workers'.[175] In addition, Varga had overlooked the situation of the unemployed. He had not considered how much increase would be required in the wages to compensate merely for the increased intensity of labour. Kuusinen also criticised Varga for his 'deductions and generalizations' and for having drawn 'wrong conclusions from a whole series of absolute correct data'[176] on the question of reparations. Varga's so-called 'law' was thus a derivate of the American bourgeois economist Rexford G. Tugwell.[177] 'That is the baby, a bourgeois baby which Comrade Varga has wrapped in the napkin of "Marxian" phraseology'.[178] Although the number of workers in certain industries could diminish, this did not mean that one could speak 'about a general tendency'.[179]

It also appeared during the debates that Varga now counted many enemies among the delegates and that practically nobody wanted to defend him. For instance, Béla Kun blamed Varga for having been contaminated by 'bourgeois economics'.[180] John R. Campbell attacked Varga's analysis of the rationalisation process in British industry. British left-winger Harry Pollitt attacked Varga for having used bourgeois statistical evidences. According to Bulgarian Vasil Kolarov (Balkan Secretariat), the presumed rise in the living standard of the

---

174 'Tenth Plenum of the E.C.C.I.' 1929, p. 1045.
175 'Tenth Plenum of the E.C.C.I.' 1929, p. 1144.
176 Ibid.
177 Varga was certainly impressed by the writings of Rexford G. Tugwell who was then teaching at Columbia University (New York). Tugwell: 'Most economists now feel that the business cycle is to be understood not through any index of total business activity, but by movements among all the seemingly unrelated forces which function together in industrial life'. Tugwell 1927, p. 90. In 1932 Tugwell joined Franklin Roosevelt's Brains Trust. As Assistant Secretary of Agriculture he defended the idea of large-scale public works in order to absorb unemployment. Tugwell 1977.
178 'Tenth Plenum of the E.C.C.I.' 1929, p. 1145.
179 'Tenth Plenum of the E.C.C.I.' 1929, p. 1146.
180 'Tenth Plenum of the E.C.C.I.' 1929, p. 869.

working class remained a 'question of dispute between revolutionary Marxism and reformism'.[181] According to Varvara Moirova (ECCI Women's Department), Varga's thesis on the standard of living was wrong, Rafael M. Khitarov (Young Communist International) opined on the absolute lowering of the living standard, Thomas Bell congratulated Kuusinen for having taken him back to 'some fundamentals of Marxism, particularly on this question of the standard of living',[182] Ercoli (Palmiro Togliatti) defended the view that the workers in Italy had meanwhile lost a good part of their purchasing power, and German left-winger Hermann Remmele argued that Varga had given 'too much prominence' to the increase of production and reformist attempts by using bourgeois statistics. Only Ivan Teodorovich (secretary-general of the Krestintern), who had been closely associated with Varga and the latter's writings on the peasantry, was charmed by Varga's concrete analysis of the economic crisis.

Collapsing Capitalism?

At that time, Karl Korsch, who had already broken with the Comintern, blamed Varga for the latter's ability to provide the always changing strategy of the Comintern with economic 'foundations'.[183] Though Varga's position was nonetheless seriously weakened, he could keep his position at the head of the Institute of World Economy and World Politics, from where he started analysing the Wall Street crash of October 1929 wiping out US$ 25,000 million in fictitious value. This marked the end of the period of postwar stabilisation. Varga, who had stated at the Sixth World Congress of the Comintern that one was 'living the period of the decline of capitalism ... and that stabilization does not alter this fundamental fact'[184] would rapidly adjust his economic analysis now that investments were rapidly falling in the US and in Germany. Meanwhile he was also harassed by colleagues criticising him for his failure to analyse the very character of the crisis. Varga started debating with them in the press and during meetings organised by the scientific institutes as well, knowing that Stalin was now launching a merciless struggle against the Party's ideological enemies and that he was even putting the academic institutions under tighter control. This applied especially to the Institute of World Economy and World Politics headed by the 'deviator' named Varga.

---

181 'Tenth Plenum of the E.C.C.I.' 1929, p. 950.
182 'Tenth Plenum of the E.C.C.I.' 1929, p. 1040.
183 Korsch 1996, p. 151.
184 'Sixth World Congress' 1928, p. 1099.

The idea of an inevitable collapse of capitalism from within was shared by most Marxist thinkers. Although Eduard Bernstein and statisticians had raised some empirical objections to the prophecy of increasing proletarian impoverishment, many Communists defended the impoverishment thesis, because the proletarian revolution would be the result of an ever growing and impoverishing proletariat. The theory that capitalism could collapse from within was also inspiring other researchers like Rudolf Hilferding, Rosa Luxemburg, Heinrich Cunow, Otto Bauer and Tugan-Baranovskiy who had struggled with this issue from a more theoretical vantage point. Rosa Luxemburg and Fritz Sternberg developed the underconsumption theory of imperialism. Sternberg argued that imperialism was only a delaying factor in capitalism's demise and that the main task of capitalism was to find a profitable market for steadily growing mass commodities. 'The contradictions of the capitalist mode of production show themselves in the solution, or failure to find a solution, for this problem of markets. A favourable solution spells prosperity. The lack of one spells crisis'.[185]

In reality, the underconsumption theory of imperialism is based on some simple propositions, such as: 1) the output of consumable goods is steadily increased at a rate greater than that of population increase; 2) the purchasing power of the masses is always pressed down to a certain minimum standard of living by the capitalist system through mechanisation; 3) as a result, employment in the modern industrial sector increased more slowly than the speed of capital accumulation and output growth; 4) one day the accumulation process will slow down and the capitalist system will disintegrate; 5) this definite breakdown has hitherto been prevented only by selling out this surplus of commodities to noncapitalist countries.[186] This was also developed by the Polish researcher Henryk Grossmann in an article already published in 1922, but now more thoroughly in his book *Das Akkumulations- und Zusammenbruchsgesetz des kapitalistischen Systems (Zugleich eine Krisentheorie)*[187] (*The Law of Accumulation and Collapse*)[188] about a coming collapse of capitalism.

Grossmann explained that any enlargement of the apparatus of production could only take place, 'without disturbance, on condition that the coefficient m intended for accumulation be divided in strictly defined proportions: 1) Among different branches of joint production (the sphere producing instruments of

---

185   Sternberg 1947, pp. 10–11.
186   Neisser 1936, pp. 161–71.
187   Grossmann 1929.
188   Grossmann 1992.

production, the sphere producing goods for consumption, etc.); 2) Within each such branch among the component parts of capital $c:v$.[189]

In his book, Grossmann reconstructed Marx's account of economic crises deriving from the tendency for the rate of profit to fall. He also offered a theory of capitalist breakdown and the shaping of a revolutionary takeover as well. In the meantime it was also a critique of Luxemburg's voluntarism and Hilferding's belief in the virtues of organised capitalism. Grossmann rejected Luxemburg's imperialism theory for not being rooted in the immanent laws of the accumulation process of capital, but in the sphere of circulation. He thought that colonialism was driven by the need to exploit labour and create surplus value. Industrialisation of the colonial countries signified thus an increase in the possibilities for exports, which explains why booms and slumps had become internationally synchronised. This process of capitalist interdependent development of the productive forces of a country exercising a raw materials monopoly leads to monopolistic rises in prices and the pumping of supplementary surplus value from outside into the domestic economy. Grossmann also criticised Lenin, Bukharin, Hilferding and Bauer for having 'explained' capital export by way of higher profits that could be obtained abroad. But, according to Grossmann, Lenin offered no theoretical analysis of the facts that would demonstrate the necessity of capital export under high capitalism, because he limited himself to the explanation that the need to export capital arose from the fact that in a few capitalist countries capitalism was 'overripe' and that, owing to the backward state of agriculture and the poverty of the masses, capital could not find a profitable outlet. Grossmann certainly hit the nail on the head when remarking that 'what this over-ripeness consists of and how it is expressed, that Lenin has not demonstrated to us'.[190] Thus when further capital accumulation leads to a reduction of accumulation in the capitalists' own consumption instead of accumulating the surplus value, capitalists will earmark it for capital export or for speculation. Contrary to Varga, Bukharin, Hilferding and Bauer, Grossmann supposed that not higher colonial profits, but a shortage of domestic investment opportunities led to capital export.[191] In addition, capital export would also increase profits at home because domestic industries would be able to gain export opportunities and obtain higher prices. A rapid expansion of capital export in the form of loans was thus a consequence of a high level of capital accumulation. Though Grossmann adhered to Lenin's analysis that capital export was typical of imperialism, he nonetheless attacked

---

189   Grossmann 2000, pp. 171–80.
190   Grossmann 2000, pp. 182–3.
191   Grossmann 2000, pp. 191–2.

Lenin's and Hilferding's theory that finance capital was a historical tendency of capitalism. Preponderance of bank capital was only typical of a certain phase of capitalism when banks mobilised funds from outside in order to finance industrial expansion. Later industry could easily attract money from the market and dominate the banks. The historical tendency of capital was thus not to create a single bank dominating industries and federating them into cartels, but to accumulate capital leading to the final breakdown due to overaccumulation.[192]

The state was an instrument to overcome the tendency to the breakdown of capitalism by securing the flow of additional surplus values from the outside world. Grossmann, who had also studied Marx's *Capital*,[193] attempted to build on Bauer's mathematical models[194] derived from Marx's *Capital* a deductive system to prove Marx's crisis theory. According to Grossmann, the capitalists produce an unavoidable decline in the profit rate because of their tendency to overaccumulate. Countertendencies, such as the more efficient use of capital, might mitigate but will not forestall the terminal crisis of capitalism, because beyond a certain stage of accumulation the incentive for investment would decline and capitalists would look for more profitable alternatives elsewhere than in production, or they would export superfluous capital. Grossmann argued that the more free competition was replaced by monopoly capitalism on the domestic market, the more competition would sharpen on the world market and increase economic problems and instability.

Grossmann's book contained several passages which would provoke Varga's ire. Grossmann had argued that Varga belonged to those who thought that Lenin was the first to propose the law of uneven development and that Marx did not give a purely economic foundation to this law in *Capital*. In addition, Grossmann had classified Varga as somebody who had simply described the surface appearances and made no attempt to build these into Marx's overall system. He had even quoted Varga's *The Decline of Capitalism* (1928) about the importance of capital exports to monopolistic capitalism and claimed that Varga had argued that anything new could be added to Lenin's imperialism theory. Thus Varga had simply put aside any attempt to analyse the problem theoretically and simply produced facts about the volume and direction of international capital flows. Grossmann also quoted Varga who had ascertained that the rate of profit was regulating not only the influx of capital into indi-

---

192   Kuhn 2006, p. 7.
193   Kuhn 2013.
194   Bauer 1912–13. According to Rick Kuhn, Grossmann's choice of Bauer's model was, in part, a political one, designed to discredit Bauer's conclusions on the basis of his own assumptions. Kuhn 2004, pp. 181–221.

vidual branches of industry, but also its geographical migrations. Capital invested abroad whenever there were prospects of obtaining a higher rate of profit. Grossmann had then concluded that this was hardly original. Varga has thus failed to understand the dimensions of the question when arguing that capital was exported not because it is absolutely impossible for it to accumulate domestically without thrusts into non-capitalist markets, but because there was the prospect of higher profits elsewhere.[195] Hence, Varga had started from the false assumption that whatever its total amount, capital could always find an unlimited range of investment possibilities at home. Thus he had overlooked the simple fact that in denying the possibility of an overabundance of capital, he had denied the possibility of overproduction of commodities. In addition, Varga had imagined an argument that there were definite limits to the accumulation of capital, and that capital export necessarily followed, which was incompatible with Marx's concentration theory and thus could only be made by starting from Luxemburg's position.[196]

Varga reacted 'savagely'[197] to Grossmann's book in a very long review article published in *Unter dem Banner des Marxismus*[198] (see Part 2, Chapter 10). Against the above criticisms, Varga pointed to Grossmann's undialectical research method which was incapable of explaining the necessary breakdown of the capitalist system. Grossmann had furthermore omitted to study the Russian and Hungarian Revolutions as a part of the process of capitalist decay, and Varga discerned the influence of Luxemburg's imperialism theory on Grossmann's study of the overaccumulation phenomenon and the non-economic origins of the imperialist war. Without dialectics, there is no Marxist method, Varga claimed.[199] Varga also wrote a critical review article on Bauer's reproduction schemes which had influenced Grossmann's theory and his assertion that, finally, overaccumulation would lead to a breakdown. Bauer had demonstrated in his model that capitalism could go on forever without crises, so long as the output of exchange values from the industrial sectors was kept in the correct ratios. Grossmann had now discovered that this model could run without difficulties for 36 years before collapsing. Already after 20 years the incentive to invest would decline. Varga's preliminary remark was that both Bauer and Grossmann had formulated the problem in an 'undialectical way', turning violent clashes into abstractions. Hence, Grossmann's scheme was drawn from

---

195 Varga 1927a, pp. 363–9.
196 Grossmann 1992, p. 117 and pp. 180–1.
197 Kuhn 2007, p. 216.
198 Varga 1930a; Varga 1930b.
199 Varga 1930a, p. 65.

'pure capitalism' implicating an *automatic* collapse of capitalism, which was contrary to his and the Comintern's assumption that the decline of capitalism had already started and that only a revolutionary upswing could destroy the capitalist system.

Varga argued against Grossmann that the latter's crisis theory could be reduced to the problem of overaccumulation of capital in combination with an insufficient purchasing power of the whole population. He also claimed that Grossmann did not pay attention to the revolutionary struggles. This was quite unfair to Grossmann. The latter had only argued that a continuous deterioration of wages was only possible theoretically. Thus this was a purely abstract possibility. In reality, the constant devaluation of labour power accomplished by continual cuts in wages ran up against insuperable barriers. Every major cut in the living standard of the workers would inevitably drive them to rebellion and in this way, and through the very mechanism that was internal to it, the capitalist system moved incessantly towards its final end, dominated by the law of entropy of capitalist accumulation. Finally, Varga warned his readers that Grossmann's book, just like Luxemburg's accumulation theory, could convince people of the fact that capitalism was inevitably condemned and that the exact moment of it could be easily calculated.

Varga also called Grossmann an immodest 'scroundel' [Lumpe], a 'pseudo-Marxist', a 'forger', a user of 'Talmudism', a striver wanting to become a professor at the University of Frankfurt, a 'Seigneur' (Herr), etc. These ad hominem attacks were certainly influenced by the ongoing debates in Moscow on Varga's 'law' and crisis theory rejected by the new leadership of the Comintern after the demise of Bukharin. In addition, Grossmann was in close contact with some of Varga's opponents in the Soviet Academy of Sciences. Spektator (Nakhimson) of the International Agrarian Institute had rejected Varga's underconsumptionist views and he had preferred explaining crises in terms of disproportions between the spheres of production. Like Grossmann, he drew attention to the role of the turnover of fixed capital. In November 1930, before visiting Moscow, Grossmann was named a member of the Agrarian Institute, an institution belonging to the Comintern. Here Grossmann met director Sergey M. Dubrovskiy. The latter was the author of a book on Stolypin's land reforms.[200] Dubrovskiy told Grossmann that 'no one here takes Varga seriously'.[201]

---

200 Dubrovskiy 1963 [1925].
201 Letter from Grossmann to Mattick, 21 June 1931, Mattick papers, Stead, notes, box 6, folder 45. International Institute of Social History, Amsterdam. See Kuhn 2007, p. 140.

German communists having left the KPD were also interested in this polemic. In a letter to Paul Mattick[202] that Grossmann wrote in mid-1931, the latter argued that Varga had not gone into Grossmann's argumentations and objections. A discussion on Grossmannn's book emerged in which Alfred Braunthal,[203] Anton Pannekoek,[204] Ottó Benedikt,[205] Fritz Sternberg,[206] Arkadij Gurland,[207] Karl Muhs[208] and Hans Neisser[209] took a part. But Friedrich Pollock, who was Grossmann's colleague at the Institute for Social Research in Frankfurt, stayed out of the debate, although he had opined that the expanding services sector was extracting additional surplus value from the growing number of workers employed there. Most critics objected that Bauer's initial assumptions were unfit for analysing the actual process of accumulation and that the organic composition of capital was not given by technology, but depended upon the profitability of investment decisions. Grossmann's use of Bauer's example was therefore a mere play with numbers. In addition, Grossmann had ignored the Marxian concept of relative surplus value. Moreover, Grossmann treated 'the effects of technological change in cheapening the elements of both constant and variable capital as subsidiary factors which merely supply a correction to the underlying forces leading to economic breakdown. But these effects are an inherent part of the process of capital accumulation. They should have been integrated into Grossmannn's formal model, not simply tacked on at the end'.[210]

Varga's Shord Period of Disgrace (1929–33)

After having been defeated at the Tenth Plenum of the ECCI in 1929 and notwithstanding the attacks of the Stalinists, Varga would nonetheless survive his disgrace and re-emerge in 1934 as Stalin's preferred economist when the left course was abandoned by the Comintern and exchanged for the tactic of the Popular Front. Varga had to readjust his economic analysis of the postwar

---

202 Letter from Grossmann to Mattick, 21 June 1931. Kuhn 2007, p. 140.
203 Braunthal 1929, pp. 289–304.
204 [Pannekoek] 1934. An anonymous reaction to Anton Pannekoek's article would follow. See 'Zur Marxschen' 1934.
205 Benedikt 1919.
206 Sternberg 1929, pp. 26–7.
207 Gurland 1930.
208 Muhs 1931, pp. 16–18.
209 Neisser 1931.
210 Howard and King 1989, p. 330.

crisis having started in October 1929 in the USA and now spreading to Europe. World agricultural prices immediately plunged, as did raw materials. At a special meeting organised at the Institute of World Economy and World Politics on 17 December 1929, Varga's analysis of this sudden crisis was centred around the fact that the financial crisis was the result of the behaviour of the monopolists having insufficiently invested in new production facilities and that people had therefore been forced to speculate on the stock market.[211] But, as long as producers would not dump their produce at lower prices, the shock of the crisis could be absorbed. This analysis was very close to that of Hilferding. Indeed, well before the crisis, Hilferding had already argued that savers were preferring to invest in shares of monopolist firms because of their high return on investment. Thus Varga also believed that the monopolists were able to weather the crisis by cutting production and employment. Given the existing links between banks and big industry, a credit crisis would not happen because the American banking system was able to guarantee the industry's solvency,[212] but, on the other hand, many small businesses would collapse if taken over by larger competitors. Just like in the crisis years of 1920–1 he predicted that the monopolies would force the working classes and the better-off strata of the population to bear the burden of the crisis.

But soon Varga was forced during debates with prominent colleagues to readjust his analysis. This happened on 10 May 1930 in Leningrad during a debate before an audience of local economists.[213] In Leningrad, Varga argued that the characteristics of the *general crisis* were recognisable now that the expansion of the capitalist market had come to a halt, and that monopolistic pricing combined with his 'law' would lead to an inexorable industrial downturn and a prolonged crisis.[214] By defining the general crisis as being both 'unique' and 'classical', Varga tried to link the present crisis with the role played by finance capital and with the 'classical' capitalist contradiction between social production and consumption. Varga thought that a price fall would be inevitable, but, in the meantime, he did not exaggerate the moribund character of capitalism. He still believed that new investments had narrowed the market by making workers redundant and by destroying markets. However, Varga could not convince everybody at the Leningrad meeting. Opponents objected that his analysis was tainted by 'neo-Luxemburgism'. His Soviet colleagues

---

211   Varga 1929, pp. 142–51.
212   Varga 1930c, pp. 5–8.
213   All were members of the Leningrad Scientific Research Institute of Marxism.
214   Varga 1930d, pp. 89–110.

argued that the uneven development of fixed capital – due to differential variations in the rate of profit – constituted the 'material basis' of any crisis and that the share of the working class invariably rose at the beginning of an economic downturn. According to Sh.B. Livshits [ps. Lif], an increase in wages also implied a decline of profits.[215] Other Leningrad economists criticised Varga for his alleged Luxemburgism[216] and for omitting Marx's thesis that fixed capital is the material basis of the cyclical movement of capital. Varga argued that not Marx, but bourgeois authors like Werner Sombart and Cassel were their sources. Varga: 'When Marx speaks of the decline of the norm of profit, he relates it to the course of capitalist development in general – not of the separate phases of the industrial cycle. The thoughts developed by Comrade Livshits are characteristic of Hilferding and Cassel, not of Marx. This theory slurs over all the contradictions of capitalism; it is purely apologetic theory and in fact it is true'.[217] L. Karsharskiy summed up all criticisms and stated that Varga had directly attributed the cause of the crisis to the contradiction between production and consumption, thus to the 'narrowness of consumption resting on a capitalist basis. But amongst Marxists, it seems, there are few exceptions to the proper view that a crisis cannot be viewed as the direct result of this contradiction'. Thus, Varga's view did not include 'the conditions of the reproduction of capital'[218] which is the most crucial problem of all treated by Marx.

The debates at the Institute of Economy in Leningrad took place some weeks before the Sixteenth Congress of the CPSU met in June 1930 where Stalin would submit his report on the growing crisis of world capitalism and the external situation of the USSR.[219] Stalin saw a growing economic and agricultural crisis in nearly all the capitalist countries, while the Soviet Union was industrialising. According to Stalin, there was an overproduction crisis in the capitalist world. The industrial crisis also coincided with an agrarian crisis. Stalin regarded the present crisis as different from the old crises. Unlike in the old capitalism, monopoly capitalism was keeping up the high prices of goods, in spite of overproduction, which made the crisis ruinous for the masses. But the present economic crisis was also developing on the basis of 'the general crisis of capitalism' which had facilitated the advent of the economic crisis. Party Secretary

---

215   Day 1981, p. 188.
216   In 1934, a fifth edition of Rosa Luxemburg's *The Accumulation of Capital* was published in Russian translation with a long critical introduction by Wolf Motylev.
217   Varga 1930d, p. 109 (quoted in Day 1981, p. 189).
218   Quoted in Day 1981, p. 188.
219   Stalin 1955, Vol. 12, pp. 242–385.

Molotov in his speech to the Sixteenth Congress qualified the crisis as a crisis of overproduction as well.[220]

The Sixteenth Party Congress of June–July 1930 also marked the starting point of a merciless struggle against Stalin's enemies and a tighter control on the academic institutions. Troskyists and Right-wing deviators were unmasked, excluded and some executed. Economic literature was scrutinised, but it took some time to eradicate heterodoxy. In 1931, the Communist Academy was merged with the Institute of Red Professors. By 1934, all specific communist academic organisations were dissolved and integrated into the Soviet Academy of Sciences. The screening of academic manuscripts was imposed. Institutes were purged of their 'bourgeois' and Menshevik personnel as well. In this period, Varga's writings also became subject to criticism.

In December 1930, Varga published in *Bolshevik* an article on the prospects of the world economic crisis. The article featured an editorial footnote explaining that Varga's views were 'debatable and incorrect'.[221] A further comment on this issue was promised in a future issue. This would happen two months later, when geographer V.E. Motylev published an attack on Varga for having interpreted the 'general crisis' in a 'one-sided and wrong manner'.[222] Motylev rejected the idea of a 'normal' and 'classical' crisis in America. In addition, Varga had overestimated new capital expenditures and as a consequence he had explained the crisis of 1929 in *Luxemburgist* terms by stressing the exhaustion of third-countries demand. According to Motylev, Varga was a Luxemburgist deducing the inevitable crash of capitalism directly from the conditions in the market. Hence, he qualified Varga's 'law' of the absolute decline in the number of industrial workers as 'absurd'.[223] Thus Varga was thinking that the monopolists were unable to control prices and that accumulated losses would drive them to bankruptcy, thus leading to an inevitable credit crisis. Motylev, however, predicted a long-lasting crisis.[224] Varga's theory of a 'classical' and a 'normal' crisis was, in Motylev's words, nothing other than 'an opportunistic appraisal'[225] of future prospects for an upturn in America and later in Europe. For sure, Motylev's attacks formed an element in Stalin's campaign against heterodox views on the origins of imperialism. For instance, Motylev published a lengthy introduction to the Russian fifth edition of Rosa Luxemburg's *Accu-*

---

220 Molotov 1930, p. 7.
221 Varga 1930e.
222 Motylev 1931, pp. 56–70. See also Tikos 1965a.
223 Quoted in Day 1981, p. 193.
224 Ibid.
225 Ibid.

mulation of Capital in which enough Stalinist passages were stored in order to discredit Luxemburg's accumulation thesis. It was clear that with this introduction Luxemburg's accumulation theory had to be banned once and for all because this theory was now backed by renegades (Thalheimer), 'left' Social Democrats (Sternberg, Grossmann) and even Trotskyists.[226]

Lev A. Mendelson of the Moscow-based Institute of Red Professors blamed Varga in *Bolshevik* for having forgotten the revolutionary role of the proletariat and defected to the Hilferding camp. Underestimating both the economic crisis and the revolutionary role of the Soviet Union, Varga thus still believed that the crisis would become less severe. Hence, Varga's 'law' consisted of a denial of Lenin's imperialism theory and led, via Luxemburg, directly to Trotsky's stagnation theory. Mendelson could not understand why capitalism should be qualified as terminally ill when at the same moment American capitalism was undergoing a 'classical' crisis after a long period of expansion. Was the theory of the general crisis sometimes only applicable to Europe? For Mendelson, the classical cycle had now turned into a crisis in the US.[227]

These attacks by Mendelson and Motylev signified that Varga's future was compromised by his alleged Luxemburgist leanings. Hence, Varga was further disgraced at the Eleventh Plenum of the ECCI that met between 25 March and 13 April 1931. Here he was not allowed to deliver his usual report on the evolving world economy, but only invited to submit a report on the agrarian crisis.[228] Manuilskiy read a long report on the building up of socialism in the Soviet Union and on the deepening economic crisis in the capitalist world. Unfortunately, the 'subjective factor' was this time lagging behind the 'objective factor', thus it was a matter of launching revolutionary campaigns and actions. Finally, KPD Leftist Wilhelm Knorin was left with the task of attacking Varga for believing in an automatic collapse of capitalism.[229]

From now on, Varga would adopt a more critical stance in relation to Hilferding's theory of organised capital and the idea that monopoly capital could weather the crisis. In his adjusted views, he stated that the credit crunch spreading to several countries and causing monetary instability was a factor of the economic crisis.[230] According to Varga, the credit crunch of 1931 had been caused by a gulf of hoarding and speculation in the past, but he did not situate the origins of the financial crisis exclusively in the pre-1920 prosperity period,

---

226 Motylev 1931.
227 Mendelson 1931.
228 *XI Plenum IKKI* 1932, pp. 266–78.
229 *XI Plenum IKKI* 1932, pp. 398–425.
230 Varga 1931.

but also in recent developments of the general crisis of monopoly capitalism. Meanwhile he also operated a turn to the radical left when exclaiming that the 'period of the general crisis of capitalism is the period of the social revolution'.[231] However, these slightly readjusted views on the general crisis did not convince. On 24 December 1931, three young Stalinists – Boris S. Borilin, Nikolay A. Voznesenskiy, and Solomon P. Partigul – launched a frontal attack in *Pravda* on the Trotskyite Preobrazhenskiy, the Luxemburgist Varga and the Right-winger Stanislav G. Strumilin. Varga was also attacked for his theory drawn from Hilferding that monopoly capital could forestall bankruptcies. That theory was alien to Marxism.[232] In the case of Varga, this attack was more than perfectly timed, for the attackers must have known that he had meanwhile been compelled to organise on 29 December 1931 and 14 January 1932 two sessions of self-criticism at his institute.[233] At the sessions Varga reluctantly confessed his original sins, i.e. his theoretical mistakes and shortcomings. He confessed that he had not foreseen the recent credit crisis and the collapse of several big banks. He admitted having believed in Hilferding's theory that monopoly capital could weather the crisis by controlling output and prices. He recognised that the state was now refloating the banks and that the monopolised heavy industry was suffering from shrinking markets. Hence, Varga admitted that he had overestimated the powers of monopolistic capital and that he had not traced the current crisis to an earlier phase of cyclical expansion. Furthermore, he had also failed to predict the very moment of the banking crisis in combination with a possible revolutionary upheaval. All these confessions incited M. Engibaryan to ask for a meticulous study of the writings of Marx, Lenin and Stalin in order to elucidate the actual crisis. Pavel Łapiński even needed two hours for commenting on Stalin's speech to the Sixteenth Party Congress.[234]

Of course, the campaign against Varga did not stop immediately after this exercise. In *Bolshevik* of May 1932, Varga was ritually attacked by A. Amatuni for his belief that monopoly capital could forestall bankruptcies.[235] This article by Amatuni appeared in *Bolshevik* just before Varga's institute would organise a debate on monetary problems. Strange enough, but the participants at this debate paid some attention to Amatuni's diatribes. In his opening speech, I. Trakhtenberg could agree with Amatuni's analysis that the credit crunch originated with the stock-market collapse and that the credit crisis had exis-

---

231   Varga 1931, p. 2383.
232   Day 1981, p. 254.
233   Varga 1932a, pp. 198–210.
234   Day 1981, p. 253.
235   A. Amo [Amatuni] 1932.

ted for two years in a 'hidden form'. Not everybody was charmed by this hazardous analysis. During the debates Varga would nonetheless emerge as the leading analyst questioning the 'real meaning' of the presumed 'hidden credit crisis'.[236]

It is striking that Varga could save his position[237] in this period of witch-hunting and exclusion of Stalin's competitors. It was not clear how Varga could survive these conflicts in which he had become personally involved. It is likely that much had also to do with several institutional academic changes introduced in the scientific field under Stalin's guidance. Replacing Varga at the head of his institute would not have solved the problem of ideological changes dictated by the introduction of *partinost* (partisanship) in science. In addition, new personnel were attracted to Varga's Institute of World Economy and World Politics and doctoral students were recruited. A better knowledge of what was going on, especially in the Asian countries and the colonies, had become a priority of Stalin's Polit Buro. In the meantime, Varga and E. Khmelnitskaya (who had been working for him in Berlin) were made responsible for a military sub-section studying military-economic problems. A statistical department occupying some 50 researchers was now studying economic development in the capitalist countries as well. In 1932, Varga's institute became responsible for the Comintern's China Research Institute. All these changes may have saved Varga's position as an eminent director in a period when he was distancing himself explicitly from Hilferding and Luxemburg. But on the other hand, Varga's disgrace would keep him far from the leadership of the Comintern. At the Twelfth Plenum of the ECCI in 1932, Varga was this time absent as a speaker. He would only reappear at the Thirteenth Plenum of the ECCI in December 1933.

At the Seventeenth Congress of the CPSUb

Although the KPD leadership believed that the establishment of an open Fascist dictatorship in Germany would incite the workers to free themselves from

---

236   *Sovremennyi kreditnyi krizis* 1932.
237   It is striking that his wife and his daughter Mária Varga were allowed to stay in Berlin for his daughter's medical treatment during the spring of 1931. See the postcard (27 April 1941) sent by son Bandi Varga to his mother, address at [Adele] Elkan, Schwäbische Straße 27.IV, Berlin W30. Party Archives, Budapest, 783, f. 1, lap 261. Adele Elkan, born in Magdeburg, lived at that time at Berlin-Wilmersdorf. She was editor of *Mädchenpost*, a journal for girls. In 1943, she was murdered in Auschwitz.

the influence of the social-democratic leaders, Hitler's takeover in Germany nonetheless marked the failure of the ultra-left strategy of the Comintern. Hence, any discussions with the latter would be superfluous. Varga, who did not believe in the possibility of a real economic recovery, thought that the internal mechanisms working in accordance with the laws of capitalism to overcome every cyclical crisis were not strong enough owing to the pressure of the general crisis of capitalism. Hence, bourgeois optimism about an economic upswing was unfounded and inspired by a recent 'crisis rationalization'.[238] Profits were rising because of low wages, diminished earnings of the peasants, plundering of the state budget, subsidies, war production, etc.[239] Excess productive capacity still constituted an insurmountable obstacle to new investments that depended on higher consumption, thus on the volume of purchasing power.[240] Expansion of the market was impossible as in the colonies there were no additional groups of peasants to be exploited. Apparently, Varga had now returned to the imperialism theory of Rosa Luxemburg and Fritz Sternberg, but in the meantime he preferred quoting from Lenin's *The Development of Capitalism in Russia*, which contained an analogous explanation.

In this period Varga was also clinging to his 'law' when referring to the devastating effects of 'crisis realisation' on employment. Artificial state initiatives could not reverse this tendency. They only led to a sudden relapse, which was illustrated by the recent economic setback at the end of 1933 in the USA.[241] Varga fell back on his theory that the current crisis was not a 'normal depression', but one of a 'special kind'.[242] Meanwhile, Sergey Dalin and Esfir I. Gurvich[243] at Varga's Institute of World Economy and World Politics were analysing Roosevelt's *New Deal* and the development of American monopoly capitalism. They denied capitalism's capability of planning economic growth when pointing to financial capital domination. Varga maintained that the economic upswing of that period had to be attributed to 'internal forces' and that financial capital was unable to continue ruling in the old way. Varga denounced Roosevelt's *National Recovery Act* as a form of disguised Fascism and as a twin

---

238 Varga 1933, p. 1132.
239 Ibid.
240 Varga 1933, p. 1116.
241 Varga 1934, p. 665.
242 Varga 1935a, p. 73.
243 Sergey A. Dalin (1936) and Esfir I. Gurvich (1937) published two books on this subject. Gurvich's book published in 1937 reported, in a purely Stalinist style, on the economic policy of the Roosevelt Administration, while Dalin's paid more attention to the different capital factions competing for power. One should also note that Gurvich was Bukharin's former companion.

of Hitler's *Hereditary Farm Act* increasing agricultural prices.[244] His colleague V. Lan (Kaplan) saw in the close collaboration between capitalists and trade unions a form of Fascism.[245] Varga's Hungarian friend Lajos Magyar argued that the replacement of fixed capital had to occur at the end of the depression and that state subsidies financing capital were discouraging the normal recovery process. Hence, recent signs of economic recovery could have only been produced by a 'military-inflationary boom'.[246] M. Yuelson adhered to this analysis and proposed to use it as an analytical category. When the Thirteenth Plenum of the ECCI met on 28 November 1933, a new phase of revolutions was announced by the Comintern leadership.[247] In his opening speech, President O. Kuusinen argued that the slight revival of industry in 1933 was due to military-inflationary expenditures. Varga – now back on stage with a report on the international economic situation – did not believe in a real economic recovery at that moment. Backing the KPD Left, he also stressed the necessity of conquering the majority of the workers and mobilising the peasantry for a successful power struggle.[248]

When preparing the Seventeenth Congress of the CPSUb for 26 January–10 February 1934, Stalin invited Varga to the Kremlin in order to be informed on the global economic situation. Apparently, Stalin had not been satisfied by Kuusinen's analysis of the slump at the Thirteenth Plenum of the ECCI. During that interview with Varga, Stalin asked the latter to write a report on the characteristics of the actual slump. This report entitled *New Appearances in the World Economic Crisis*,[249] which contained many statistics and press clippings, defended the central thesis that the actual crisis was the first worldwide economic crisis since the war. Varga's report was divided into four chapters in which he analysed the general characteristics of the crisis, the features of the agrarian crisis, the development of the crisis per country, and finally the general conditions of the working class and the peasantry. In his report, he had assembled many statistics illustrating declining industrial output and showing that the monopolists had succeeded in upholding prices.[250] He also pointed to the fact that the industrial crisis had led to a catastrophic credit crisis in

---

244 German farming was facing many problems caused by the flight from the land to better-paid industrial jobs and investment in armoury instead of mechanisation of agriculture. Kershaw 2001, p. 162.
245 Day 1981, p. 260.
246 Day 1981, p. 261.
247 *XIII Plenum IKK* 1933.
248 See Varga's speech in *XIII Plenum IKK* 1933, pp. 417–23.
249 Varga 1934b; Varga 1979a, 2, pp. 307–92.
250 Varga 1979a, 2, p. 323.

Germany (1931) and the United States (1933).[251] Hence, Varga concluded that the role of the state had increased in order to 'artificially' overcome the crisis. The state appropriated and redistributed a growing share of the national economy. Meanwhile, the state had started regulating exchange rates and domestic prices, organised cartels and exercised a prominent influence on credit banks. Parliaments were losing their influence at the expense of bureaucratic organisations. Varga: 'Although finance capital is dominating the state and the state apparatus and, in general, determines economic policy making, ... state bureaucracies are growing because legal regulations are becoming increasingly complicated and are changing quickly'.[252]

All attempts to plan agricultural production had lamentably failed because of a declining purchasing power of the workers. Meanwhile, agricultural workers were unable to find employment in industry and, as a consequence, they returned to the villages. Because of increased protectionism, exports of agricultural products declined further. Therefore, Varga paid much attention to the economic policy practised by the Roosevelt Administration.[253] Obviously, Varga did not believe in a 'normal' solution to the crisis.[254] He saw the depression going over into a new boom characterised by an uneven evolution and an industrial output level well beneath the already low figures of 1932. 'It would be the biggest mistake to put on a par the end of stabilization with a "normal" depression'.[255] Though one certainly could speak of a 'cyclic overproduction crisis', he argued, this crisis was not a 'normal crisis, a simple "repetition" of former crises'.[256] Capitalism was obviously in its declining phase. 'The overcoming of the acute crisis phase, the evolution to a depression does certainly not mean a new stabilization of capitalism ... The industrial crisis had led to a further deepening of the general crisis of capitalism'. The agrarian crisis, chaos on the exchange markets, monopolisation of markets, etc. could induce 'at any moment' a new world war. 'This deepening of the general crisis of capitalism is furthering the ripening of the revolutionary crisis'.[257] Hence, Varga could qualify the capitalists' hope of a new upswing as being totally idle and lacking any foundation. Being confronted with the 'fast expanding revolutionary crisis', the bourgeoisie saw no other way out than breaking with parliamentari-

---

251   Varga 1979a, 2, p. 324.
252   Varga 1979a, 2, p. 335.
253   Varga 1979a, 2, p. 370.
254   Varga 1979a, 2, p. 392.
255   Varga 1979a, 2, p. 392.
256   Varga 1979a, 2, p. 309.
257   Varga 1979a, 2, p. 392.

anism and imposing an 'openly terroristic dictatorship of Fascism'. The present crisis brought also an end to the 'temporary stabilization of capitalism' and this signified a 'new stage in the shattering of the whole capitalist system'.[258] Varga concluded that since 1932, the crisis had gone over into a depression now determined by the general crisis of capitalism, which meant the end of capitalist stabilisation.

The Seventeenth Party Congress discussed in an 'atmosphere of appeasement'[259] Stalin's work report of the Central Committee, CPSUb.[260] On the reports of V.M. Molotov and V.V. Kuibyshev, the Congress adopted a resolution on *The Second Five-Year Plan of Development of the National Economy of the USSR (1933–37)* – a plan for the building of socialist society, thereby endorsing the grand programme for completing the technical reconstruction of the entire national economy, and for a still more rapid rise of the living and cultural standards of the workers and peasants.[261]

In some form or another, Stalin had used several paragraphs of Varga's report for his own report to the Seventeenth Congress. For instance, at the beginning of his report, Stalin asserted:

> in the economic sphere these years have been years of continuing world economic crisis. The crisis has affected not only industry, but also agricul-

---

258 Varga 1979a, 2, p. 310.
259 Broué 1977, p. 349.
260 The reports of the Central Auditing Commission, of the Central Control Commission and the Workers' and Peasants' Inspection, of the CPSUb delegation in the Executive Committee of the Comintern, and reports on the Second Five-Year Plan and on organisational questions (Party and Soviet affairs) were discussed as well.
261 The Seventeenth Party Congress emphasised that the basic political task during the Second Five-Year Plan period was the final elimination of capitalist elements and the overcoming of the survivals of capitalism in economic life and in the minds of the people. On the report of Lazar M. Kaganovich, the Seventeenth Party Congress adopted decisions on organisational questions (Party and Soviet affairs). The Congress pointed out that the principal tasks of the Second Five-Year Plan sharply raised the question of improving the quality of work in all spheres, and first and foremost the quality of organisational and practical leadership. The Congress adopted new Party Rules. It replaced the Central Control Commission and the Workers' and Peasants' Inspection by a Party Control Commission under the Central Committee, CPSUb, and a Soviet Control Commission under the Council of People's Commissars of the USSR. All speakers praised Stalin. In the election to the Central Committee some delegates refused nonetheless to vote for Stalin. Stalin had dropped the title of Secretary-General and was appointed as the first of four secretaries, including Lazar M. Kaganovich, Sergey M. Kirov and Andrey A. Zhdanov. For the Seventeenth Congress of the CPSU(b). *History of the C.P.S.U.(b)* 1954, pp. 496–503.

ture as a whole. The crisis has raged not only in the sphere of production and trade; it has also extended to the sphere of credit and money circulation, and has completely upset the established credit and currency relations among countries. While formerly people here and there still disputed whether there was a world economic crisis or not, now they no longer do so, for the existence of the crisis and its devastating effects are only too obvious. Now the controversy centres around another question: Is there a way out of the crisis or not; and if there is, then what is to be done?[262]

Stalin defined the actual economic crisis in the capitalist countries as different from all analogous crises. 'Formerly crises would come to an end in a year or two', he said, 'but the present crisis, however, is now in its fifth year, devastating the economy of the capitalist countries year after year and draining it of the fat accumulated in previous years'.[263]

Stalin explained the character of the actual economic crisis, first, by the fact that it had 'affected every capitalist country without exception, which has made it difficult for some countries to manoeuvre at the expense of others'. Secondly, there was the fact that the industrial crisis had become 'interwoven with the agrarian crisis' which had affected all the agrarian and semi-agrarian countries without exception. Thirdly, the agrarian crisis had grown more acute and had affected 'all branches of agriculture and it had brought about a retrogression of agriculture, a reversion from machines to hand labour ... a sharp reduction in the use of artificial fertilizers, and in some cases a complete abandonment of them – all of which has caused the industrial crisis to become still more protracted'. Fourthly, the monopolist cartels maintained high commodity prices, a circumstance which made the crisis 'particularly painful' and hindered the 'absorption of commodity stocks'. According to Stalin, the chief thing was that the industrial crisis had broken out in the conditions of 'the general crisis of capitalism', when capitalism no longer had, nor could have, either in the major countries or in the colonial and dependent countries, the strength and stability it had had before the war and the October Revolution. As a heritage from the imperialist war, the imperialist countries had received a chronic under-capacity operation of plants and armies of millions of unemployed.[264]

---

262   Stalin 1955, pp. 671–2.
263   Stalin 1955, p. 674.
264   Stalin 1955, p. 675.

These circumstances explained why the crisis was not confined to the sphere of production and trade, but had also affected the credit system and exchange rates. Hence, the traditionally established relations had broken down both between countries and between social groups in the various countries. The fall in commodity prices had played an important role. In spite of the monopolist cartels, the fall in prices had increased with elemental force, affecting primarily the commodities of the unorganised and small commodity producers and only gradually and to a smaller degree the producers united in cartels. The fall in prices made the position of debtors intolerable and 'placed creditors in an unprecedentedly privileged position'.[265] Mass bankruptcy of firms and of individual capitalists was the result. Bankruptcies were followed by currency depreciations, which slightly alleviated debtors' position, non-payment of international debts, a further decline in foreign trade. Stalin: 'Naturally, also, these destructive phenomena accompanying the industrial crisis, which took place outside the sphere of production, could not but in their turn influence the course of the industrial crisis, aggravating it and complicating the situation still further'.[266]

Stalin was thinking about a 'continuing *general* crisis of capitalism, in the circumstances of which the *economic* crisis is proceeding; the chronic undercapacity operation of the enterprises; chronic mass unemployment; the interweaving of the industrial crisis with an agricultural crisis; the absence of tendencies towards a more or less serious renewal of fixed capital, which usually heralds the approach of a boom, etc., etc.'. He even thought that one was witnessing 'a transition from the lowest point of decline of industry, from the lowest point of the industrial crisis, to a depression – not an ordinary depression, but a depression of a special kind, which does not lead to a new upswing and flourishing of industry, but which, on the other hand, does not force industry back to the lowest point of decline'.[267]

The prospects for the world revolution were good, but Stalin also warned that the victory of the revolution would not come automatically because '... only a strong proletarian revolutionary party can prepare for and win victory'. Thus everything depended on the existence of a revolutionary party of the proletariat 'with sufficient strength and prestige to lead the masses and to take power'.[268] Stalin remarked that the ruling classes in the capitalist countries were destroying the last vestiges of parliamentarianism and bourgeois

---

265   Stalin 1955, p. 676.
266   Ibid.
267   Stalin 1955, p. 680.
268   Stalin 1955, p. 687.

democracy 'which might be used by the working class in its struggle against the oppressors'. Meanwhile, they were 'driving the Communist Parties underground and resorting to openly terrorist methods of maintaining their dictatorship'.[269]

In his speech, Stalin paid much more attention to his peace offensive in Europe than to the prospects of the proletarian world revolution. According to Stalin, the USSR could rely on its growing economic and political might, on the moral support of the vast masses of the working class of all countries, who were vitally interested in the preservation of peace, on the prudence of those countries which for one motive or another were not interested in disturbing the peace, and which wanted to develop trade relations with such a punctual client as the USSR, and, finally, on the Red Army to defend the country against assaults from without. But Stalin did not attack Nazi Germany, although there had been 'some changes in the policy of Germany which reflect the growth of revanchist and imperialist sentiments in Germany'. He argued that although he was 'far from being enthusiastic about the fascist regime in Germany, it is not a question of fascism here, if only for the reason that fascism in Italy, for example, has not prevented the USSR from establishing the best relations with that country. Nor is it a question of any alleged change in our attitude towards the Versailles Treaty. It is not for us, who have experienced the shame of the Brest Peace, to sing the praises of the Versailles Treaty'. Having 'smashed the enemies of the Party, the opportunists of all shades, the nationalist deviators of all kinds', Stalin warned that 'remnants' of his enemies' ideology were still living in the minds of individual Party members, and not infrequently were finding their expression in the Party.

Popular Front Tactics

Though Stalin believed that parliamentarianism could no longer be an instrument in the hand of the working classes now that the bourgeoisie had opted for Fascism, he would become more and more suspicious of recent developments in France where fascists *ligues* were threatening the Republican institutions. When Georgi Dimitrov arrived at the end of February 1934 in Moscow after being acquitted for lack of evidence after the burning of the Reichstag in Berlin, he was received by Stalin and his Politburo. Dimitrov pleaded for a closer collaboration with the Social Democrats against the Fascists. In a let-

---

269 Stalin 1955, p. 681.

ter to Stalin dated 1 May 1934, Dimitrov pleaded for dropping the ultra-left course and for discarding the slogan on social fascism. Though Stalin still hesitated, he nonetheless could agree with Dimitrov on many points. Stalin invited Maurice Thorez to Moscow to discuss with Dimitrov about united front tactics. Dimitrov pressed Stalin in a letter of 1 July 1934 to drop the disqualification of Social Democracy as the bourgeoisie's main pillar. But Stalin still categorised the Social-Democratic leadership as 'social fascist'. However, Dimitrov could now find a majority in the Comintern leadership for an alliance with the Social Democrats. But a minority with Solomon Lozovskiy, Osip Pyanitskiy, Wilhelm Knorin, Béla Kun and Varga was still holding to the old slogan on social fascism.[270] That Varga stood side by side with V.G. Knorin and Kun during the debates on the united front tactics is not surprising. With Béla Kun and Serafina Gopner (Hopner) of the Agitprop department of the Comintern, Varga had published a book called *Social Fascism – Organizer of Intervention*,[271] in which he argued that Social Democracy was stimulating an armed intervention against the Soviet Union. But on 1 September 1934, Dmitry Z. Manuilskiy called the united front a promising experiment. Varga, who was writing a final draft of his report to the Seventh Congress of the Comintern, was now asked to rewrite his report in light of the new tactics. In the meantime, the PCF was now tempted by an electoral alliance with the Socialists, but also with the Radical Party for the district elections of October 1934. Maurice Thorez would call this alliance a 'front commun de la liberté et de la paix', but also a 'large front populaire antifasciste'.[272]

Much had changed in Varga's attitude now that he was invited to support the Popular Front tactics of the Comintern. He had not only to overcome his visceral repugnance for Social Democracy, but also to reformulate the text of his report in a much less radical way. Hence he argued that the third period of postwar capitalism was a period of the most intense development of the contradictions of world capitalism which was determined 'by the entire course of the general crisis of capitalism: shrinking markets, the existence of the Soviet Union, colonial liberation movements, and growth of the internal contradictions of imperialism. In this third period of sharpening contradictions between the growth of the productive forces and the shrinking markets, imperialist clashes or wars against the Soviet Union would be inevitable'.[273] But in the

---

270 Hochman 1984, pp. 84–5; Borsányi 1993, p. 397. Lejbzon and Sirinja 1975.
271 Varga 1932b, pp. 6–14.
272 Before the district elections, Klement Gottwald and Palmiro Togliatti had arrived in Paris in order to control the situation. Robrieux 1975, p. 193; Kriegel and Courtois 1997, p. 236.
273 Varga 1935a, p. 7.

meantime he also defended his previous conception of the utter emptiness of the Social Democrats' apologetics. He indicated that the cyclic crisis of 1929–33 still played a 'special role' in capitalism's history, because each upward swing ended with a violent explosion of all the contradictions of the capitalist system in the cyclic crisis of overproduction. He liberally referred to the Sixteenth Congress of the CPSUb when Stalin had defined the postwar crisis as a crisis of overproduction, and by no means a 'normal' crisis.

According to Varga, the course of the crisis was greatly influenced by the general crisis of capitalism, by the increasingly monopolistic character of postwar capitalism, by its intertwining with the agrarian crisis, and by the extraordinarily sharp fall in prices. He repeated that artificial measures taken by the monopolists had caused a considerable delay in the outbreak of the credit crisis of 1931 and to the deepening and prolongation of the crisis as a whole. Hence, the first world crisis in the era of the general crisis of capitalism had proven to be much deeper and longer than any other cyclic crises. Varga noted that qualitatively *new* aspects 'not present in any of the previous crises'[274] were developing with currency depreciation, non-payment of foreign debts, and practically complete cessation of capital export. His conclusion was that at the time the crisis had caused a general economic war of all countries, and that the cyclic crisis was hastening 'the end of capitalism's temporary stabilization' and resulting in 'the maturing of the objective prerequisites for the revolutionary crisis'.[275]

Varga based this revolutionary assumption on the realisation problem of capital. 'No basis for a further prosperity phase' could be expected during this period of a 'depression of a special kind'.[276] Hence, the correctness of Marx's theory of revolutionary collapse could be verified during the current crisis. This crisis of overproduction was thus due to the contradiction between the limited consuming power of society, and the boundless expansion drive of capital, due chiefly to the proletarian condition of the masses. The relative diminution of consuming power compared to the development of the productive forces must thus necessarily lead to a chronic accentuation of the contradiction between the productive power and the consuming power of capitalist society. An absolute impoverishment of the working classes hampered the accumula-

---

274 Varga 1935a, p. 13.
275 Varga also warned his readers for regarding 'the cyclic crisis as the cause of the end of stabilization', because theoretically the Comintern never had considered stabilisation 'anything but a transient phenomenon within the enduring general crisis of capitalism, as a trough in the waves of the revolutionary movement'. Varga 1935a, p. 13.
276 Varga 1935a, p. 15.

tion process and limited the production of capital goods. Prosperity could only continue 'as long as the process of real accumulation' was in full swing, 'as long as new factories, harbours, railways are built, and old machines are replaced by new ones'. But the contradiction between the development of productive power and consuming power would necessarily grow 'more acute' and determine to 'an ever increasing extent the course of the industrial cycle', which would lay down 'the economic basis for the accelerated maturing of the revolutionary crisis'.[277] The growth of monopoly capital had distorted the functioning of the market and the accumulation process. The great crisis of 1929–33 had chronically developed because of a narrowing of the market, a sharp competition for sales opportunities and growing imperialist antagonisms. Capital's manoeuvring possibilities were 'considerably restricted' in these circumstances. The chronic agrarian crisis, the chronic surplus of capital, and chronic mass unemployment should be added to the major characteristics of the actual general crisis of capitalism with its 'exceptional depth, intensity and duration'.[278]

In his report, Varga referred several times to Stalin's report at the Seventeenth Party Congress. Like Stalin, he enumerated some aspects of the crisis. For instance, only branches directly involved in war production had been exempted, price declines had engendered falling profits and then caused a credit crunch. A far-reaching fusion of bank capital and industrial capital into finance capital had delayed the outbreak of a credit crunch in all countries, but the longer this outbreak had been delayed, the more catastrophic were the forms assumed by the credit crisis. The depreciation of currencies was a qualitatively new factor not found in any previous crisis. There were still countries holding on to the gold standard, others were with a formal gold standard. All other countries had an openly depreciated currency tied to sterling or the dollar. Together with the currency crises, inflation, and the debt burden, the credit system had disintegrated. Payment of international debts became impossible owing to a lack of gold reserves and export surpluses or due to war reparations. The consequence was an almost complete standstill of capital export, which was 'an important factor in the exceptional nature of the present depression'.[279] As every crisis entailed a drop in the volume of foreign trade, the ideology of 'autarchy' could gain many adherents. Meanwhile, the bourgeoisie had been all this time unsuccessful in its endeavour to overcome the crisis artificially. Hence, the general crisis of capitalism was a historically transient form of society that was passing through a period of revolutionary collapse.

277 Varga 1935a, pp. 24–5.
278 Varga 1935a, p. 29.
279 Varga 1935a, p. 45.

In his account of the crisis of 1929–33, Varga paid much attention to the world agrarian crisis he defined as being interwoven with the industrial crisis. Nonetheless he pointed out that peasant agriculture still outweighed capitalist agriculture. The bulk of the agricultural produce was produced not by capitalist farmers, but by peasants. Agriculture's low organic composition of capital still reflected its backwardness. Due to slight development of capitalism in agriculture, the crisis did not take on the form of a sudden decline in production. Other factors, such as the ground rent in the form of leasehold and mortgages, also played a role. The peasant would continue production even when he could not make a minimum living. Varga connected the industrial crisis to the situation in agriculture: every industrial crisis made the situation in agriculture worse, and vice versa.

Varga was, however, fascinated by Roosevelt's 'New Deal' as 'the most grandiose effort to overcome the crisis by governmental measures'.[280] Roosevelt's policy aimed at: saving the credit system by (1) a government guarantee of deposits; (2) a reduction of the debt burden through depreciation of the US dollar; (3) an artificial increasing of agricultural prices; (4) the establishment of compulsory cartels; (5) combating unemployment by means of public works; (6) minimum wages. These measures had resulted in a zigzagging sharp rise in industrial output. Varga also prudently noted that the increase of production remained 'within the bounds' of what the 'inner forces of capitalism would have reached'. Varga's view was that 'in the long run' all efforts to overcome the crisis would fail. According to Varga, the fact that the acute phase of the crisis had passed into the 'depression of a special kind', was due not to the bourgeoisie, but rather to the inner forces of capitalism tending to overcome the cyclic crisis by preparing for war. About the role of price policies pursued by European governments, Varga noticed that through several measures domestic agrarian prices had risen two to three times higher than world market prices. On the other hand, the exporting countries tried to raise world market prices by retaining grain from the world market, but all these efforts had ended in failure. Only production restriction could stabilise prices at a higher level. But these measures had also failed because of fixed costs and defective control. The only recourse left was a systematic, wholesale destruction of agricultural produce of every kind. Hence, the decay of capitalism was 'tangibly obvious to every peasant and worker'.

According to Varga, the bourgeoisie was in a process of strengthening state-capitalism tendencies: (1) an increased role of the government budget; (2) for-

---

280   Varga 1935, p. 66.

eign trade concentrated in the hands of the state; (3) credit becoming state credit with banks depending on the state; (4) increasing state control over the distribution of labour power; (5) commodity prices determined by the state.[281]

Repeating Stalin's definition given in the latter's report to the Seventeenth Party Congress of January–February 1934, Varga asserted that the crisis had passed into a depression of a special kind. Considered mechanically, the present depression was hardly to be distinguished from all preceding phases of depression, as characterised by Marx. Considered dynamically, there was a fundamental difference. The present depression (in contrast to 'normal depressions') did not furnish a sufficient basis for an ensuing boom. The special nature of the depression consisted in the deformation of the industrial cycle under the influence of the general crisis of capitalism.[282] The ascending line of the economy had snapped in the summer of 1934. Hence, he predicted that the condition of the world economy 'as a whole' would be worse than in the previous years and that the 'contradiction between the productive forces and the production relationships' was so acute that 'increased production prematurely' would hit a snag 'in the market's limited absorption capacity'[283] before the boom phase could be reached. The 'inner mechanism of capitalism' was effective enough to overcome the lowest point of the crisis and to bring about the transition to a depression, but no real boom or prosperity phase. Varga explained why the rise in production had been prematurely blocked. Varga identified seven 'decisive factors': (1) a chronic failure in the process of real accumulation with a chronic surplus of industrial capital; (2) the formation of monopolies putting a brake on technical progress and on investment in fixed capital; (3) the rise in turnover taxes and the formation of monopolies lessened the fall in prices of monopoly goods; (4) the chronic agrarian crisis was one of the main obstacles in the path of a new boom; (5) in the former cycles the capitalist market was enlarged by drawing new regions into the capitalist mode of production, but in the actual world no more regions were left to conquer, while in the colonies new industries were developing; (6) the export of capital had almost completely ceased; (7) the income of the working class had declined as a result of mass unemployment.[284]

Varga preferred returning to his famous 'law' when arguing that during the transition period to the depression, the number of exploited workers had augmented, but the total purchasing power of wages had scarcely risen. Reduced

---

281 Varga 1935, pp. 69–70.
282 Varga 1935a, pp. 73–4.
283 Varga 1935a, p. 74.
284 Varga 1935a, pp. 75–8.

output in thoroughly rationalised and mechanised plants had increased production costs per unit product more than in less modern factories. In the period of the general crisis of capitalism, there were thus 'very narrow limits to the expansion of the capitalist market'.[285] Varga also focused on plants running at far below capacity and forms of rationalisation enabling monopoly capital to increase the workers' productivity and to make the proletariat bear the burden of the crisis. Meanwhile, 'the economic prerequisites for the revolutionary collapse of capitalism' were developing 'by leaps and bounds' so long as the bourgeoisie was 'incapable of utilizing the productive forces'.[286] The financial oligarchy tried to improve its position at the cost of everybody and to plunder the population with the help of the state apparatus. By restricting the consuming power of society, the monopolists were intensifying the general crisis of capitalism. The end of temporarily stabilisation would be followed by a 'new, deeper and more devastating economic crisis'.[287] Therefore, the bourgeoisie was looking forward to a new war to improve the return on capital in the present 'depression of a special kind'.[288]

Varga gave an extensive description of the social consequences of the economic crisis, including the impairment of the condition of the urban petty bourgeoisie, the so-called 'new middle classes', the various sections of the peasantry, and the impoverishment of the proletariat. Mass unemployment, increased labour output, a reduction of real wages, longer working hours combined with periodical reductions of working hours, increased intensity of labour, and forced labour in the colonies reflected the worsening social conditions of the proletariat during the economic crisis. Varga did not connect these deteriorating living conditions of the toiling masses and the working classes to a rather hypothetical rising tide of class struggle and revolutionary movements.[289] Instead, he preferred telling the 'truth' about the Soviet Union now that 'bourgeois individuals and Social Democrats of all kinds' were changing their minds. Since the Sixth Congress of the Comintern, the Soviet Union had realised a big economic leap forward. Varga noticed that people like Kautsky, the Archbishop of Canterbury, Trotsky, Dan, Bauer, etc. were denying the gigantic advances of the Soviet Union and that the 'bourgeoisie, the fascists, and the social-fascists [!] combat the revolutionising influence of the Soviet

---

285   Varga 1935a, p. 78.
286   Varga 1935a, pp. 79–80.
287   Varga 1935a, p. 80.
288   Ibid.
289   Varga 1935a, pp. 111–12.

Union with all sorts of lies, libels and slanders'.[290] The birth of the Soviet Union had been the first breach in the capitalist world system. Soviet China was its second breach. An attack on the Soviet Union was improbable, because of (1) the increased military strength of the Soviet Union; (2) the Soviet Union's entrance into the League of Nations; (3) imperialist antagonisms; (4) accentuated internal class antagonisms.[291]

With the unsettling of temporary stabilisation, the world had come close to a new round of wars and revolutions. The collapse of the Versailles system was near, because of the three pillars – reparations, disarmament, and territorial provisions – the latter one was still in force. Varga did not forget interimperialist rivalries outside Europe: a war between Britain and the USA was 'unavoidable if the proletarian revolution does not forestall it'.[292] Varga also noted a shift of the centre of gravity from Europe to the pacific where the four big powers are competing for 'their share in the exploitation of China'.[293]

Varga paid some attention to the position of Japan in the imperialist struggle for a redivision of the world market. Japan had not first resorted to arms because of its strength, but because of its economic weakness. Japan is a poor country, Varga argued, with a per capita income of the population equal to that of the poorest European countries. Japan's limited consumption power had forced Japanese industry 'to seek foreign markets for a large part of its production'.[294] The army of the next world war would be a mass army arming 'the entire male population'. Varga's strategic position was clear. The proletariat was placed by history before the alternative either to be sacrificed once again or 'to turn its weapons against its own bourgeoisie under the leadership of the Communist Party, turning the imperialist war into a civil war for the overthrow of the rule of the bourgeoisie!'[295]

Varga limited his analysis of this coming revolutionary crisis to the changes in the method of the dictatorship of the bourgeoisie and the subsequent fight for a 'united front'. Varga argued that the 'democratic-parliamentary disguise of the bourgeoisie's dictatorship' had fulfilled 'its historical mission of developing the forces of production' and in the period of the general crisis of capitalism 'bourgeois democracy had to be undermined and abolished since the capitalist mode of production has become an obstacle to the further development of

---

290   Ibid.
291   Varga 1935a, pp. 124–6.
292   Varga 1935a, p. 128.
293   Varga 1935a, p. 129.
294   Ibid.
295   Ibid.

social productive forces'.[296] Varga noticed that the struggle among the various factions of the bourgeoisie for a share in the decreasing social profit was growing acute. The splits in the bourgeois parties and the rapid succession of cabinets undermined the prestige of the ruling classes. Governments were becoming more and more independent from parliament and governing by decree. Varga recalled that in Germany and 'in several smaller countries', the bourgeoisie had established 'the fascist form of its dictatorship' against the 'revolutionary proletariat'.[297] He also called, according to the *Theses and Decisions of the Thirteen Plenum of the ECCI*, an 'open terrorist dictatorship' of capital.

In his chapter treating the changes in method of the dictatorship of the bourgeoisie, Varga argued that the bourgeoisie after having used Social Democracy as its main political support had turned its attention to Fascism in order to save its supremacy. In particular, the crisis of Social Democracy as a precondition for the rise of Fascism was sketched.

Apparently, Varga's main problem was not defining Social Democracy's fundamental character, but its reformist role and the decay of the labour aristocracy as a guiding force. Varga conceded, however, that the impairment of the labour aristocracy's condition concretely, in figures, met 'with the difficulty of determining what categories and groups of the working class' were to be considered 'as belonging to the labour aristocracy'.[298] Varga solved this 'Leninist problem' by differentiating Social Democracy according to groups of countries where Social Democracy usually participated in the government (Sweden, Denmark, England, Czechoslovakia); countries where they constituted legal opposition parties (Spain, France, USA, etc.); countries where they legally or semi-illegally existed under a Fascist regime (Hungary, Poland); countries where they were persecuted as a party (Germany and Austria). Varga focused on the fact that the illusions of the working class regarding bourgeois democracy and the possibility of improving its conditions under capitalism had grown immediately after the war. In the defeated countries all 'the traditional demands of the Social-Democratic workers were met'.[299] Participation in the Government enabled German and Austrian Social Democrats to expand their electoral base within the state bureaucracy. The great crisis undermined, however, 'the privileged position of the labour aristocracy by reducing its numbers and its privileged positions'.[300]

---

296 Varga 1935a, p. 139.
297 Varga 1935a, p. 140.
298 Varga 1935a, p. 143.
299 Varga 1935a, p. 142.
300 Varga 1935a, pp. 142–3.

The levelling out tendency of the condition of the working class during the crisis was, according to Varga, at the disadvantage of the labour aristocracy. Meanwhile, the possibility of advance within the framework of capitalism had 'evaporated' during the crisis. Varga argued that the social-democratic parties had been transformed 'into the main social support of the bourgeoisie'. He concluded that the political essence of the crisis of Social Democracy was 'the conflict between its function as the main social support of the bourgeoisie and its proletarian (and petty-bourgeois) mass base'.[301]

Hence, Varga concluded that the bourgeoisie demanded that the reformist leaders got the working class to accept the impairment of their working conditions, but that the workers demand that they organise resistance or to take advantage of their governmental power against the bourgeoisie. Varga therefore concluded that the 'Social-Democratic workers' were looking for an alliance 'with the Communists against the bourgeoisie'. Moreover: 'They demand the united front, negotiations and reconciliation with the Communist International' now that they understand that the Soviet Union is realising the ultimate socialist goal for which the labour movement 'has been fighting since its beginning; not only do they reject any war against the Soviet Union, but they demand that the latter be defended, in struggle against their own bourgeoisie if necessary'.[302]

Varga remarked that a united struggle or front against the bourgeoisie had little chance to come into existence as long as the Social-Democratic parties were particularly dominant on the Left and where the conditions of the workers had grown worse to a lesser extent. Varga also noted that the Social-Democratic workers wanted to struggle together with the Communist workers in a united front against the bourgeoisie, but he also admitted that the political crisis of Social Democracy was less acute in those countries where the influence of the Communist Parties was weaker and where Social Democrats still participated in their governments. Apparently, nowhere could identical conditions be met. This complicated Varga's analysis of the Social-Democratic parties. Varga eagerly turned his attention to the German Social Democracy that had gone as far as complete disintegration. He noticed that the Social Democrats had reduced the wages, prevented strikes, expelled the Communists from the trade unions, and allowed policemen to shoot down demonstrating workers.[303] This 'anti-working class policy' had led, according to Varga, to the undermining

---

301 Varga 1935a, p. 144.
302 Varga 1935a, p. 145.
303 Varga 1935a, pp. 146–7.

of the SPD's influence among the workers and the rapidly growing influence of the KPD. But the SPD refused the KPD's offer for common struggle.

Varga concluded that the ideological crisis of Social Democracy was interlinked with its political crisis and its theory of the state: the state is above classes; parliamentary democracy is the only road to socialism. Varga remembered that Hilferding, Kautsky, and Fritz Tarnow had announced 'that there was no general crisis of capitalism', or that 'the October Revolution had been a bourgeois revolution', or that capitalism was developing 'into a planned state capitalism, free of crisis; and that the transition to socialism had already begun'.[304] He argued that the ideological crisis had grown 'ever greater after the victory of fascism in Germany and Austria', because the 'ideology of peaceful parliamentary democracy had to be sacrificed for the time being'.[305] But, even locked up in concentration camps, Social Democracy was still serving the bourgeoisie by 'employing the vestiges of its remaining influence among the working masses against the united front of the proletariat, against the proletarian revolution, and for the re-establishment of a legal dictatorship of the bourgeoisie'.[306] Programmatically, the problem of Social Democracy was not easy to solve, because on the one hand this programme had to satisfy the workers' demands, and on the other hand it had to keep the bourgeoisie from driving out the reformists and making the Fascists their main social support. The most successful attempt had been made by Henry de Man with his Labour Program that had married 'a "Left" phraseology with a semi-fascist content'.[307] Finally, Varga remarked that more and more Social-Democratic workers were on the road to a 'united front in the struggle against fascism and the bourgeoisie'.[308] However, Varga omitted analysing the profound ideological and theoretical changes and conflicts shaking western Social Democracy after the fall of the Weimar Republic.[309]

Summing up, one can conclude that no real new insights were presented in Varga's report to the Seventh Congress of the Comintern. Combating Fascism was not listed as the most urgent task of the Comintern. Most themes and subjects Varga had already developed elsewhere. Growing Fascist agitation against the 'inferior' races was not listed in Varga's report. In the last chapter of his report, Varga nonetheless criticises the sectarian use that the KPD leadership

---

304   Varga 1935a, p. 149.
305   Varga 1935a, p. 150.
306   Varga 1935a, p. 151.
307   Ibid. See also Varga 1934c.
308   Varga 1935a, p. 153.
309   Horn 1996; White 1992.

had made of the concept of 'Social Fascism', but, as we saw, he had forgotten to suppress it in the English edition of his own report.[310] He even attacked in a footnote his former rival Nikolay. D. Kondratiev by associating him with Trotsky![311]

Notwithstanding some flaws in Varga's final draft of his report, the latter would acquire the status of a guiding document for the debates at the Seventh Congress of the Comintern and later, when the Popular Front in France and Spain got some momentum, it would achieve some notoriety as well. Many things can nonetheless be said about Varga's contribution to the Popular Front tactics. Varga remained a loyal executioner of Stalin's directives and the Comintern now following Dimitrov and his associates in their tactical move to include not only the Social Democrats, but also the bourgeois democrats in an alliance defending the democratic state system. On the other hand, Varga must have still felt some sympathy for the radical Leftists dominating the leadership of the Hungarian and German parties. Varga's Institute of World Economy and World Politics did not research the phenomenon of Fascism thoroughly. Varga's biographer Gerhard Duda even called Varga a 'longstanding protagonist of the Social-Fascism thesis in the Comintern'.[312] However, he was not the only one. The ECCI had many times in the recent past estimated that both Facism and Social Fascism stood for the maintenance and the strengthening of capitalism and bourgeois rule. Social Fascists restrained the workers 'from revolutionary action against the capitalist offensive and growing Fascism'.[313] At any rate, in January 1935 Varga's leftism had not disappeared, because he then still believed that the German working class had remained immune to Nazi propaganda, that the oppositional movements within the German army and bourgeoisie were gaining ground, and that the Nazi regime was unable to offer advantages to the petty bourgeoisie and the toiling peasants without affecting the interests of the capitalists and the big landowners. The Nazi economy would thus collapse because of its internal contradictions and a return to normal bourgeois rule would then happen with the help of the Social Democrats.[314]

---

310   It was suppressed in the French edition.
311   Varga: 'Kondratiev's wrong theory of "long cycles", which was largely accepted also by Trotsky, is based on the effect of the great nineteenth century agrarian crisis upon industry'. Kondratiev was arrested in 1931 and at the moment Varga attacked him he was in prison at Suzdal. Kondratiev was at that moment the most prominent Soviet economist for having travelled in Western Europe and America where he had met several famous economists, like John M. Keynes.
312   Duda 1994, p. 112.
313   *Theses and Resolutions* [1932], p. 11.
314   This point of view was also published in the Soviet media. Varga 1935b, pp. 57–75; Varga 1935c, pp. 63–84.

Historian E.H. Carr[315] remarked that the advance of the Popular Front was so slow because of persisting reservations about cooperation with the Social Democrats. Indeed, in the preparatory commission to the Seventh Congress of the Comintern, controversies appeared between those functionaries who connected the struggle against Fascism directly with the overthrowing of bourgeois power, and those who held the general democratic struggle as a normal phase on the road to socialism. These internal divisions had obliged the Presidium of the ECCI to postpone the Seventh Congress to July 1935. Meanwhile the Comintern remained divided. On 1 May 1935, the ECCI called for a united proletarian front, not for a Popular Front. In the Comintern leadership, Knorin and Pyatnitskiy were still backing the German sectarians against Wilhelm Pieck and Walter Ulbricht, while Béla Kun remained an opponent of the Popular Front. Kun still argued that only a proletarian revolution could smash the Horthy regime in Hungary, a broad anti-Fascist front for democratic reforms would thus be superfluous. Hence, the Comintern leadership went disunited to the Seventh Congress opening on the evening of 25 July 1935.[316]

Stalin had many reasons for not being present at the Seventh Congress of the Comintern. First of all he did not want to hinder his foreign policy by being associated with the Comintern. Secondly, the Comintern's Popular Front tactic consecrating the struggle for the unity of the working class and the democratic liberal bourgeoisie against Fascism had to be the outcome of Dimitrov's new leadership. Dimitrov's report[317] was therefore presented as the major event of the Seventh Congress. Hence, Dimitrov gave a long analysis of Fascism which he defined as neither a dictatorship of the bourgeoisie nor one of the petty bourgeoisie. He criticised the sectarians and their errors for having not understood the difference between a Fascist and a bourgeois dictatorship. Dimitrov also announced that the Comintern was preparing for the restoration of unity between the two internationals against the capitalist offensive, against Fascism, and against the danger of war.

Parts of Dimitrov's report had in reality been written, or at least edited, by Varga and others. For instance, parts of Dimitrov's report, such as his criticism of Henry de Man's Belgian Labour Plan, can be found in Varga's polemical writings against the Belgian Socialist. The difference was that Dimitrov appealed to Émile Vandervelde for constituting a common front for the defence

---

315 Carr 1982, pp. 149–50.
316 The speeches of Wilhelm Pieck, Dimitrov, Palmiro Togliatti, and Manuilskiy were later edited and published by Elfriede Lewerenz (1975) of the Institute for Marxism-Leninism in the GDR.
317 Dimitrov 1951.

of working-class interests against capital. However, Dimitrov's forceful synthetic constituted a hallmark in the Comintern's strategy against the rise of fascism. Dimitrov explained why the ruling bourgeoisie was seeking salvation in fascism: because the ruling circles were 'trying to shift the whole burden of the crisis onto the shoulders of the working people'.[318] Although Dimitrov adhered to the analysis of fascism described by the Thirteenth Plenum of the ECCI 'as the open terrorist dictatorship of the most reactionary, most chauvinistic and most imperialist elements of finance capital',[319] he conceded that the 'accession to power of fascism' was not 'an ordinary succession of one bourgeois government by another, but a substitution of one state form of class domination of the bourgeoisie – bourgeois democracy – by another form – open terrorist dictatorship'.[320] Success of fascism had to be explained by its ability to attract the masses by appealing 'to their most urgent needs and demands'.[321]

According to Dimitrov, the German working class could have prevented the Nazi victory, provided there would have been a 'united anti-fascist proletarian front'.[322] Dimitrov argued that 'fascism also attained power for the reason that the proletariat found itself isolated from its natural allies'.[323] Fascism could attain power because it was able to win over large masses of the peasantry and the youth. Dimitrov admitted the mistakes of the Communists having underestimated 'the fascist danger'.[324] Moreover, Dimitrov loudly criticised the German comrades for having regarded the Brüning Government as already fascist. 'Our comrades in Germany for a long time failed to fully reckon with the wounded national sentiments and the indignation of the masses against the Versailles Treaty'.[325] Dimitrov's changing attitude to Social Democracy was explicitly influenced by the 'lessons learned from the defeat of the workers in Germany, Austria and Spain, a defeat which was largely the result of the Social-Democratic policy of class collaboration with the bourgeoisie, and, on the other hand, under the influence of the victory of socialism in the Soviet Union'.[326] His answer to Fascism was the united front of Communist, Socialist and bourgeois parties.[327] He corrected Varga's previously formulated criticism

---

318 Dimitrov 1951, p. 39.
319 Dimitrov 1951, p. 40.
320 Dimitrov 1951, p. 42.
321 Dimitrov 1951, p. 43.
322 Dimitrov 1951, p. 49.
323 Dimitrov 1951, p. 51.
324 Dimitrov 1951, p. 52.
325 Dimitrov 1951, pp. 52–3.
326 Dimitrov 1951, p. 124.
327 Dimitrov 1951, pp. 63–5.

of Henry de Man's Labour Plan and stressed that the Belgian Workers Party had entered a coalition government without repealing all reactionary emergency decrees of the preceding governments.[328] However, the Labour Plan also promised 'a number of good things', such as the shortening of the working day, standardisation of wages, a minimum wage, a comprehensive system of social insurance, etc. Hence, Communist attitudes to bourgeois democracy could not be the same under all conditions in all countries. Now that in the capitalist countries the fascists were 'attacking bourgeois democracy in an effort to establish the most barbaric regime of exploitation and suppression of the working masses', the choice was 'not between proletarian and bourgeoisie democracy, but between bourgeois democracy and fascism'.[329] In addition, the question of whether Communists would take part in a coalition government was 'determined entirely by the actual situation prevailing at the time'.[330] Near the end of the Seventh Congress, Dimitrov declared that a united front could be formed, even a non-Communist one, and if it would be anti-fascist and not anti-Communist, Communists should join and support it. Hence, sectarianism was condemned not simply as an infantile disorder, but as an ingrained vice. Even the Chinese Communists were now willing, on certain conditions, to enter into an agreement with the Kuomintang. Mao Tse-tung was elected to the ECCI, which ended his period of disgrace by making him the ranking member of the Comintern active in China.[331] The Chinese Communists demanded immediate war against Japan and immediate cessation of the civil war against them. But only in February 1937 could discussions about a United Front commence with the Nationalists.[332]

With the rising tide of the Popular Front and Hitler's aggressive foreign policy, Varga's role would change. As Stalin's faithful propagandist he praised the merits of the Soviet regime and denounced capitalism's inability to cope with the economic slump. However, President Roosevelt's New Deal and Hitler's economic planning nonetheless had a profound impact on Varga's analysis of capitalism, even if he still believed that no real recovery was possible and that economic stagnation at a low level of production with small recoveries would be the irremediable fate of the capitalist system. As Stalin's propagandist, Varga now published commissioned books and articles under supervision

---

328 Dimitrov 1951, p. 82.
329 Dimitrov 1951, p. 129.
330 Dimitrov 1951, p. 128.
331 Van Slyke 1967, pp. 52–5; Rue 1966, pp. 266–91.
332 Kuo 1975, pp. 225–8.

of the Central Committee's propaganda department. His book *Two Systems*,[333] originally published in 1938[334] but also later destined for an international public, was an entirely rewritten version of his report to the Seventh Congress of the Comintern. Varga also contributed, together with Stalin's private secretary Lev Mekhlis and V. Karpinskiy, to the propagandistic book *The USSR and the Capitalist Countries*.[335] Again, Varga used previously published materials for this book.

One can imagine that Varga had now become an important advisor to the Prince in the Kremlin, directing the Soviet Union's external propaganda in a period when Hitler had started his annexation politics and the Western bourgeoisie and reformist labour leaders had become more an more inclined to neutralism or pacifism. Hitler was allowed to annex Austria in March 1938. In September 1938, Stalin discovered that 'the unwritten maxim of Munich was to keep Russia out of Europe'.[336] He was not invited by the British and French governments to discuss with Hitler and Mussolini the fate of his Czechoslovak ally. On 15 March 1939, during the Eighteenth Congress of the CPSUb, Hitler's Wehrmacht marched into Czechoslovakia. Stalin told his audience at the Eighteenth Party Congress that a new imperialist war was already in its second year, a war waged over a huge territory stretching from Shanghai to Gibraltar, and involving over 500 million people.[337]

Stalin's report also contained a chapter on the international economic crisis which was largely inspired or at least written by Varga. In this chapter, Stalin argued that the economic crisis had passed into a depression and that a certain revival, a certain upward trend of industry, had occurred in 1933 without developing into a boom. In 1937, a new economic crisis had begun in the United States and then in Britain, in France and in other countries. The present crisis was thus hitting those countries that had not been put on a war economy basis. It was thus clear that a new economic crisis was developing in the aftermath of a certain revival now that capitalism possessed fewer reserves to combat the effects of the crisis. The Fascist states had only delayed the outbreak of a crisis in their countries by putting their economies on a war footing. Hence, this new economic crisis was bound to lead to a further sharpening of the imperialist struggle. Stalin attributed the weakness of the non-aggressive states to the fear that a revolution might break out if the non-aggressive states were taken to war

---

333 Varga 1939a.
334 Varga 1938.
335 Mekhlis, Varga and Karpinsky 1938.
336 Deutscher 1949, p. 427.
337 Stalin 1947, p. 596.

and the war were to assume worldwide proportions.[338] It was clear that Stalin was now convinced of the fact that the British bourgeoisie wanted to divert Germany's expansion eastward. Hence, in case of a conflict with Hitler, the Soviet Union would have to bear all the weight of an eventual war. The German Soviet Non-Aggression Pact, signed on 23 August 1939, would be the logical outcome of Stalin's dilemma, allowing Hitler to start the war with Poland. Meanwhile Varga would pay much attention to the political, economic and military situation in Europe and would study recent British publications on the war and its economy.[339]

Problems of Postwar Capitalism

In the summer of 1943, Varga even became a regular adviser to Molotov's Ministry of Foreign Affairs concerning the problem of German reparation payments, a subject already well studied with regard to the Versailles Treaty two decades earlier. Meanwhile he studied the development of the war economies and the ability of the capitalist state to plan investment. Varga had to admit this time that capitalist governments were able to manage a war economy very successfully. In this period Varga also studied the possibilities of a further economic cooperation between the Allied Powers after the defeat of the Axis Powers. However, this would also cause the end of Varga's eminent scientific position in the Soviet Academy of Sciences after his Institute of World Economy and World Politics was closed down in autumn 1947.

Of course, Varga had applauded the signing of the Molotov-Ribbentrop Agreement or the so-called Hitler-Stalin Pact of 23 August 1939. With the German invasion of Poland on 1 September 1940 and the subsequent declaration of war by France and Britain on 3 September 1940, the Second World War was officially a fact. Basing himself this time on Lenin's imperialism theory, Varga argued in an article in *Bolshevik* and later in translation in *The Labour Monthly* that the war between Germany on the one hand and France and Britain on the other was a clash between two imperialist blocs for a new redivision of the world (see Part 3, Chapter 1). Varga also pointed to growing contradictions between American and British imperialism and the struggle of monopoly

---

338 Stalin 1947, pp. 598–602.
339 Varga reviewed Winston Churchill's book *Step by Step* (1939) and John M. Keynes's book *How to Pay for the War* (1940) in *Mirovoye khozyaystvo i mirovaya politika*. At that time (1939), British newspapers were demanding Churchill's inclusion in the Neville Chamberlain government. Gilbert 2006, p. 173; Manchester 1989, pp. 242–8.

capital to bring foreign countries under its political sway. This new war was weakening the imperialist powers and the entire capitalist system and thus the conditions for a successful proletarian revolution and colonial upheavals were ripening in several countries.

In the meantime Germany also signed with the Soviet Union on 11 February 1940 a new economic treaty for deliveries of petroleum and other natural resources in exchange for investment goods. According to *Die Deutsche Volkswirt* of 23 February 1940, this accord was of an 'extraordinarily significance', because Germany now had access to the natural resources of the Soviet Union.[340]

Disarray and confusion would soon increase with Hitler's easy victory over France in May and June 1940. Though Britain kept on fighting, Stalin was now confronted with a victorious German army on continental Europe and a Hitler he could not trust. It was clear that this war could drag on for a lengthy period of time. On 22 June 1941, the German attack on the Soviet Union would create a new momentum in world history which forced Stalin to adopt a new approach to the ongoing armed conflict and to ally with British imperialism against the common enemy. Meanwhile Varga had already designed the way in which the monopoly bourgeoisie in the belligerent countries was managing the war economy by putting its personnel at the top of state capitalist organisations. This happened against the revolutionary working class and the toiling masses. However, the monopoly bourgeois was unable to eliminate the contradiction between the tendency of capital to expand and the limited consuming capacity of society. He also remarked that the economic difference between peacetime capitalism and wartime capitalism was disappearing (see Part 3, Chapter 2). Varga's analysis of wartime state capitalism also contained the impoverishment thesis. The longer the war lasted, the more the belligerent countries would become poorer. In order to continue the war, the belligerent countries would be compelled to control their economies more strictly as well.

Varga, who still commented on the inter-imperialist conflict before the Soviet Union entered into the war, readjusted his analysis in the light of the Soviet Union's armed struggle against Hitler. Varga studied the impoverishment tendencies of the German war economy and he even predicted its near economic collapse. This wrong interpretation of the impoverishment of Germany would cause him some troubles for having endangered the Soviet Union's war effort. In August 1943, Varga started working for the Ministry of Foreign Affairs

---

340   'Das Wirtschaftsabkommen mit der Sowjet-Union' 1940, pp. 658–9.

as a specialist of postwar German reparation payments.[341] One may presume that Varga had been called in by Molotov with regard to the conference to be held at Tehran. On 31 August 1943, Varga lectured for the first time on the reparation problem. The text of this lecture was widely disseminated and captured the attention of the western media as well. It was even rumoured that Stalin, following Varga's advice, was planning a complete destruction of Germany's industrial capacities. Varga's proposal for deporting four to five million German workers to the Soviet Union was confirmed by French politician Pierre Cot.[342] Meanwhile, the reparations and reconstruction problem had become a hot policy issue. In the US, Hans Neisser drafted a policy paper treating postwar reconstruction.[343] In Britain, 'Keynesian' economists, like Hungarian-born Nicholas [Miklós] Káldor,[344] were working out reconstruction scenarios.[345]

Germany's economic demise was, however, not Winston S. Churchill's preferred war aim, while Roosevelt and Stalin were thinking of a Carthaginian future.[346] But at Tehran, no mention was made of dividing Germany into demilitarised duchies or reparations to be paid. Meanwhile Varga's policy proposals had already met unfavourable comments. Lord Keynes criticised Varga's ideas for being very 'dangerous'.[347] Rumours about Varga's proposals spread to Germany where Nazi propaganda tried to intimidate the population with the consequences of a military defeat and Varga's plan to enslave millions of German workers.[348] Meanwhile, Varga reformulated his impoverishment and breakdown theory by pointing to the fact that Germany was plundering the occupied countries. This explained why the German war economy had not yet collapsed. But he still believed in the revolutionary potential of the German working class. Varga likely had in mind a replay of the breakdown of the German Empire in 1918. The reparation question was still hanging when a Council of Foreign Ministers was set up by the Potsdam Agreement of 1945.[349]

Stalin was nonetheless impressed by America's role in the rehabilitation of postwar capitalism and geopolitical stabilisation and recovery initiatives. Hence, Stalin's representatives dutifully attended the July 1945 conference at

---

341   Maiski 1967, pp. 823–6.
342   Cot 1974, p. 260.
343   Neisser 1944.
344   Miklós Káldor also contributed much to the famous Beveridge Report outlining the basis for the postwar welfare state.
345   Kaldor and Joseph 1943.
346   Manchester and Reid 2013, pp. 747–74.
347   Keynes to Ronald, 2 December 1943. Foreign Office Records, FO 371–35309.
348   Goitsch 1944.
349   Dobbs 2013, p. 345.

Bretton Woods which established the Reconstruction Bank (World Bank) and the International Monetary Fund and which set the principles of price stability through fixed exchange rates, reductions of trade barriers and market integration. Until December 1945, Soviet trade and foreign ministers were recommending ratification on the grounds that this might yield reconstruction credits that the Soviet Union so badly needed.[350]

Varga was well aware of the importance of several postwar reconstruction plans debated between the allied powers. In the beginning of 1944, he commented on them in *Commercial and Financial Chronicle* (see Part 3, Chapters 3 and 4) published in New York in which he reported being impressed by the plans of establishing an international reconstruction bank and a stabilisation fund. However, Varga preferred a return to the gold standard proposed by American civil servant Harry Dexter White to Lord Keynes's plan for an international clearing union. It would be to the Soviet Union's interest to base international trade on a basis of gold currency with unchanging value. Moreover, the Soviet Union was also interested in restoring its own economy. In a commentary in *The Economist* of 11 December 1943, it was already argued that the rouble had 'at no time maintained a close relation to its internal purchasing power. The problem of maintaining equilibrium with international cost and price structures hardly arises in a wholly planned a socialised economy, where the State undertakes the whole of foreign trade'. In that commentary, *The Economist* pointed out that the Keynes plan would be viewed suspiciously by Moscow because it envisaged the possibility of changing the unit price of gold, and thus endangering the world-price on which Russia depends for its output of the metal. Varga's commentary was visibly inspired by past Soviet attitudes to the role of the gold standard. Soviet gold mines were built up to maintain a gold stock in order to meet temporary disequilibria in the balance of external payments. Diplomat Harry Dexter White, who wanted to make Bretton Woods work in a truly global sense, had proposed in early 1944 a large credit to the Soviet Union in exchange for needed strategic materials as a sound basis for continued collaboration in the postwar years. But from the perspective of the Soviet Union, the continuation of the Lend-Lease was nonetheless more important than these projects concocted in the conference rooms. Hence, at the end of 1945, Stalin had already lost any interest in joining the IMF.[351]

Meanwhile Varga remained preoccupied with the problems of war capitalism. In an article published in his institute's journal *Mirovoe khozyaystvo*

---

350 Gaddis 1997, pp. 187–220.
351 James 1996, pp. 68–70.

i mirovaya politika in May 1945 (see Part 3, Chapter 5), Varga discussed the postwar prospects. He predicted a new crash similar to that having occurred just after the First World War. Again, all countries had been exhausted by war expenditures, large-scale destructions and human losses. Again, accumulated consumers' demands were awaiting the end of the war. He also reflected on the situation just after the First World War when a rise in production lasted only about fifteen months. He argued 'with full assurance' that at the end of the war 'the distortion in the capitalist world will be much greater than in 1918'. On the other hand, the United States, Canada, South Africa, etc., would come out of the war with their productive apparatus much increased and improved, while continental Europe was ravaged by the war. In the countries of Eastern Europe allied with the Soviet Union, the crisis of underproduction would not be so sharp 'thanks to their closer economic relations with the Soviet Union'. Varga foresaw many problems in the United States where enterprises had to changeover from their war production to peace production. He closed his article with the claim that the Soviet Union would play a 'stabilising factor for the economy of the countries of Eastern Europe', while the cyclical crisis of overproduction would hit the United States and Britain and then affect all other countries in the capitalist world, while the absence of crisis in the USSR would be a beneficent influence on countries which are linked.

In the latter article published in May 1945, Varga did not comment on the future of the Soviet Union's alliance with Britain and the United States or the critical state of the British balance of payments. Even his favourite theme of inter-imperialist rivalries is absent. Later, when relations with the Anglo-Saxon powers had already deteriorated, he would return to this item in several publications. In his article of May 1945, however, Varga also mentioned that the countries of Central Europe would have their economy linked to the Soviet Union, but without commenting on their political future. In his native Hungary, but also in the other countries liberated by the Red Army, the Communists had formed coalition governments with other anti-fascist parties. Varga would call these democratic regimes having emerged with Soviet help 'democracies of a new type' (see Part 3, Chapter 7). Those democracies of a new type had broken with the feudal remnants, such as large-scale landownership, and they nationalised large enterprises and banks.

> It is neither a bourgeois dictatorship nor a proletarian dictatorship. The old State apparatus has not been smashed, as in the Soviet Union, but reorganised by means of a continuous inclusion in it of the supporters of the new regime. They are not capitalist States in the ordinary sense of the word. Neither, however, are they Socialist states. The basis for their

transition to Socialism is given by the nationalisation of the most important means of production and by the essential character of the State. They may, with the maintenance of the present State apparatus, gradually pass over to Socialism, developing to an ever increasing extent the socialist sector which already exists side by side with the simple commodity sector (peasant and artisan) and the capitalist sector, which has lost its dominant position.

Of course, Varga admitted that the Soviet Union was interested in having friendly relations with these states, not just because they had been liberated by the Soviet Union and were all Slave states, but primarily because the new social order had brought them nearer to the Soviet Union. Curiously enough, Varga mentioned only Yugoslavia, Bulgaria, Poland, Czechoslovakia and also Albania where the new democracies had emerged, not his own Hungary or Rumania. According to Varga, these two did not belong to the countries of democracy of a new type, but they were clearly developing in that way.

Political development in Central Europe and the Balkans, however, was not as simple as outlined by Varga. One has to keep in mind that although the Communists had led the most active forces of resistance and gained popular support in Yugoslavia, Albania, Greece, as well as in Bulgaria and Slovakia, elsewhere the social and political forces of the Right remained strong and had formed rival resistance movements. This was especially the case in Poland. The Communist resistance movement *Armija Ludowa* was small, while the well-organised Home Army had taken a leading role in the struggle against the German occupier. Meanwhile, Russophobia had revived and the Polish Communists enjoyed little popularity. In Poland and Rumania, the Soviet Union had put coalition governments in power by direct intervention. In Bulgaria, a broad coalition was formed. In Czechoslovakia and Hungary, provisional governments had been formed before the country was completely liberated. In an article written by a 'special correspondent', it was argued that there existed three types of regime in Eastern Europe. In Yugoslavia and Albania, the Communists had gained power. In Poland, Rumania and Bulgaria, coalition governments of Communists and Socialists together with the Peasants had been installed. Hungary could be added to this trio. The third type was Czechoslovakia where the Communists were the dominant party.[352] Meanwhile 'popular democracy' had been established in these countries.[353] According to the 'spe-

---

352 X 1947, pp. 893–4; pp. 942–3.
353 X 1947, p. 942.

cial correspondent', this regime was not intended to be a 'dictatorship of the proletariat', because specific guarantees of private property were included.

Varga's article on the new democracies was published in English translation in *The Labour Monthly*[354] and in German translation by the Berliner publisher *Tägliche Rundschau*[355] in 1947. A complete version of the article would be published (in 1946) in a Russian book on changes in the politics of capitalism during the Second World War. In the same period, Varga published an article in his institute's journal[356] about the general crisis of capitalism (see Part 3, Chapter 6) in which he explained that in the postwar period a swing to the left in the United States and Britain had occurred, but that the Communist parties were not yet 'an important factor' in the domestic policy of these countries. 'The capitalist system in these countries has not been shaken in consequence of the war'. However, the situation was different in continental Europe where the Communists had won great popularity. In Czechoslovakia, the Communists had become the strongest party mobilising 2.7 million voters. In Germany, a united party of the working class had emerged. The movement against colonialism had become stronger. On the other hand, Varga discerned in the plans for a Western European Union uniting Britain, France, Belgium, Holland, Portugal and perhaps the Scandinavian countries an attempt to defend the colonies against the USA wanting to smash the old colonial regime and assimilate them economically.

Meanwhile, Varga had become a well-known Soviet scholar having lost his former Comintern profile of a revolutionary Bolshevik, but now having gained the aura of an academician and advisor to the Soviet government at a moment when 'Russian Studies' became popular in the United States. With the support of the Rockefeller Foundation, the Russian Institute was developed at Columbia University in New York, where the idea was endorsed that leading Soviet scientists should be invited for a lecture. Historians like I.I. Mints, A.M. Pankratova and E.V. Tarle joined the names of economists like P.I. Liaishchenko and E.S. Varga. However, this initiative was not met with great enthusiasm by the Soviet and American governments.[357] However, Varga's reputation exceeded that of many of his colleagues who were playing no political role at all. *Foreign Affairs*, a journal published by the Council on Foreign Relations in New York, published an article by Varga on British-American rivalries[358] that

---

354 Varga 1947a.
355 Varga s.d. [1947].
356 Varga 1947b.
357 Engerman 2009, p. 31.
358 Varga 1947c.

was published (see Part 3, Chapter 8) in the same March issue as the famous article 'The Sources of Soviet Conduct' by X (George Kennan) in which the latter argued that the Soviet Union was pursuing a policy of economic autarchy.[359] Varga used in his article a 'scientific' approach by dealing with presumed growing tensions between American and British imperialism.[360]

Hence, a rather 'moderate' Varga – Stalin was not quoted – explained the thesis that high American tariffs were impeding the import of British manufactures, and that the British imperial preferences established at the Ottawa Conference in 1931 were also hampering free trade. Varga pointed out that the European countries could only buy American goods on credit and that the US wanted to break up the institutions of the British Empire. Though the British government was opposing American ambitions during the framing of the Atlantic Charter, Varga insisted on the fact that the US was now assuming the leading position in the world economy. The US was thus pursuing 'a world policy of imperialism in the fullest sense of the term' as 'the land in which militarism is most in vogue. Big business is bent on using the country's military power for the economic subjugation of the world'.

In order to mark the difference between the Roosevelt and the Truman Administrations, Varga called Roosevelt 'a great statesman' who had understood that it was 'in the interests of the American bourgeoisie itself to blunt the edge of the class struggle between the bourgeoisie and the proletariat by timely concessions which did not imperil the existing system'. But after Roosevelt's death, 'the forces of social reaction' had, however, gained the upper hand. The danger of Fascism was even growing now that the Republicans had won the last Congress elections and Truman had ordered the removal of 'all persons suspected of Communist sympathies' from the civil services. Fortunately, the British Labour Government was moving into the opposite direction with its programme of nationalisations and 'peaceful transition to Socialism', while the British bourgeoisie was displaying 'flexibility in avoiding a showdown fight with the working class'.

The US and Britain were, however, forming a bloc. Varga explained this paradox by referring to their common interest in maintaining 'the system of society

---

359   Kennan 1947, pp. 566–82; 1967, pp. 271–97 and pp. 354–67.
360   Varga's article was probably written before Truman's Cold War speech in Congress on 12 March 1947 in which it was said that the US would support 'free people who are resisting attempted subjugation by armed minorities or by outside pressure', but well before the George Marshall speech of 5 June 1947 announcing an international recovery plan. Varga's article had probably been solicited by the editorial board of *Foreign Affairs* in connivance with both Kennan in Moscow and the State Department.

existing outside the USSR' and in countering 'the influence of the Soviet Union in world affairs'. The Truman doctrine was 'a turning point in American foreign policy' and thus 'a clear departure from Roosevelt's policies'. Although Bevin continued Churchill's foreign policy, Varga looked nonetheless hopefully to the Labour Party rebels contesting Bevin's foreign policy. For the same reason he acclaimed Henry Wallace who was opposing Truman's foreign policy. But Varga's digressions on the situation of the European countries were certainly not all endorsed by Zhdanov, now tightening control on the academic world and having the confidence of Stalin in ideological matters.

The Varga Controversy

Between 1945 and 1948 Varga regularly travelled to Budapest where he met party leader Mátyás Rákosi, who he advised on economic and monetary policies.[361] In the beginning, all this remained beyond direct supervision of Andrey Zhdanov who was already tightening control over Varga's activities abroad.[362] Varga's many articles – especially in the weekly *New Times*[363] – on international politics must have displeased Zhdanov because they reflected Molotov's views on dealing with Washington. When in June 1947 Washington launched the Marshall Plan urging the European allies to align their economies, Molotov travelled with a delegation of advisers – among them was also Varga – to Paris in order to discuss the American proposals with the French and the British governments. After consulting Stalin, Molotov refused to accept the terms of the Marshall Plan. On 27 August 1947, Varga gave a lecture in which he argued that the American plan aimed at the creation of a Western bloc, 'this time under the aegis not of Great Britain but under the United States. The backbone of this bloc is to be Western Germany'.[364]

The implementation of the Marshall Plan placed doubts over Varga's analysis of growing Anglo-American rivalries. It was clear that the US had taken the lead in the postwar reconstruction policy[365] and was subjecting the European capitalist nations to its economic plan. Meanwhile Varga had already changed

---

361 Göncöl 1969, pp. 92–3.
362 In August 1946, Varga published five articles on monetary stabilisation in Hungary in *Szabad. Nép*. A copy of Varga's report to Zhdanov, with a copy to G.F. Aleksandrov, is kept in the Rákosi files at the Party Archives in Budapest, 274 fond, 10/122, lap 61–64.
363 *New Times* was published in several foreign languages and was Molotov's mouthpiece.
364 Varga 1947d, p. 5.
365 Trachtenberg 2005, pp. 135–40.

his opinion about future revolutionary developments in Europe. In a speech on 13 January 1948, he predicted a temporary ebb tide of the revolutionary movement in Europe, while the situation in Germany was still undecided.[366] These opinions, however, contradicted Zhdanov's plans with the Cominform created in 1947 and Communist-inspired strikes organised in Italy and France, but were in line with Molotov's plans to reach an agreement on a united but neutralised Germany paying US$10 billion in reparations out of current industrial production. Hence, Molotov demanded four-power control over the Ruhr.[367]

The political forces organised around Zhdanov were now preparing for Varga's fall by launching an attack on his recently published book *Changes in the Economy of Capitalism Resulting from the Second World War*.[368] When Varga's book appeared in the shops at the end of 1946, its content was certainly not controversial. Some chapters had already been published in the journal of Varga's institute as well (see Part 3, Chapters 7, 9, 10 and 11). The so-called 'Varga controversy'[369] was already initiated by an unsigned article in *Kultura i zizhn* criticising Varga's institute for having neglected the study of 'actual' imperialism and 'actual' tendencies in the development of state-monopoly capitalism. In his New Year's speech at his institute in December 1946, Varga promised to exercise a stricter 'quality control' on research and publication.[370] In January 1947, K.V. Ostrovityanov of the Institute of Economics, however, asked for a public debate on Varga's *Changes in the Economy of Capitalism Resulting from the Second World War* and the functioning of Varga's institute. Varga's journal *Mirovoe khozyaystvo i mirovaya politika* did not treat current problems in an adequate way, Ostrovityanov argued. Some authors had even praised American industrial superiority while the Soviet Union was making a formidable leap forward. A commission was charged with writing a report in which Varga's book was mentioned for its ideological and scientific shortcomings. Hence, a public discussion of these shortcomings was scheduled for 7, 14 and 21 May 1947.

During the debates a number of Varga's outspoken enemies, among them A.N. Shneyerson who had authored the report, argued that Varga's book contained many ideological and scientific shortcomings. Varga had overvalued the role of the capitalist state in conducting the war economy and neglected the dominating influence of monopoly capital. He had misinterpreted the dependency of the colonies (in this case India) on British capital. Thus the colonies

---

366 Akademiya Obshshestvennych Nauk (AON), Moscow, Varga file, 1513.1.54.
367 Smyser 1999, pp. 59–61; Adibekov 2002.
368 Varga 1946.
369 Roh 2010, pp. 254–303.
370 Tikos 1965b.

could not liberate themselves by a purely economic process, only by revolution. Varga had also incorrectly evaluated the role of the new democracies and disqualified them by calling them 'neither capitalist, nor state capitalist'. Varga's book was also theoretically inconsistent and political problems had been omitted. He had made prognoses in an incorrect way by making analogies with postwar developments after the First and the Second World War. The most important defect of Varga's book, however, was its treatment of the class role and the character of the state in the war economy, the impoverishment process, the excess of demand over supply, the disappearance of the realisation problem, state regulation, in which the state was in constant conflict with the private interests, and the dominance of the monopolies in the planning offices of the government. In his closing speech, Ostrovityanov summarised that Varga had not tried to approach the analysis of the phenomenon of contemporary capitalism from the point of view of the problem of the general crisis of capitalism, and that he had abstracted himself from politics when analysing economic phenomena. Thus Varga had omitted to touch upon political questions in his book and his analysis of the role of the bourgeois state had met unanimous criticism. In his reply Varga rejected most criticisms, as well as the incrimination that his book did not speak of the general crisis of capitalism. Concerning the problem of impoverishment, he referred to Marx and Stalin: a war meant eating up all the resources of a country. In short, Varga refused to admit all his reformist sins: 'It would be dishonest if I were to admit this or that accusation while inwardly not admitting it'.[371]

The result was that the Central Committee of the CPSUb decided on 18 September 1947, following a decision prepared by Aleksandrov and made by the Politburo, to close Varga's institute. It was merged with the Institute of Economics directed by Ostrovityanov.[372] Varga addressed a letter to Stalin in which he protested against this decision,[373] but without any result. Attacks on Varga would nonetheless continue in the press in what was now called the 'Varga controversy'. All 'moderates' in the academic institutes were screened, accused of scholasticism, lack of self-criticism, nepotism and mutual flattery. Their estrangement from Soviet reality was interpreted as the result of a lack of understanding of Marxist-Leninist theory. Meanwhile the campaign against the 'bourgeois objectivists' and 'cosmopolitans' at the Institute of Economics intensified. As long as Varga did not confess his errors, he would remain under fire from his enemies at the Institute of Economics who only repeated their

---

371   *Soviet Views Soviet* 1948, p. 125.
372   *Pravda*, 7 October 1947.
373   Undated draft of a letter to Stalin, AON, Moscow, Varga file f, 1513/1/198.

former arguments against Varga's overvaluation of the role of the bourgeois state in capitalism, the role of British capital in India after independence, etc. Finally, Varga repented publicly on 15 March 1949 in a letter to the editor of *Pravda*. He did that in style by referring to the Western press having slanders about him over his alleged Western orientation. A close reading of this letter, however, reveals that Varga was only making general concessions to his critics. This letter in *Pravda* was mainly destined for the Western press, in casu *The Times* of London, in which his 'Western orientation' had been highlighted in an article on 16 February 1949.[374]

On the other hand, Varga also admitted his errors in a more reasoned article published in *Voprosy ekonomiki*.[375] Varga argued now that his incriminated book and also other works of his former institute contained errors of a reformist tendency, signifying a departure from a Leninist-Stalinist evaluation of modern imperialism. The fundamental reason why such a mistake could have slipped into his book was due to a methodologically erroneous separation of economics from politics. This had unintentionally led to mistakes of a reformist tendency. He had thus wrongly asserted that the state played a 'decisive role' in the war economy and that the ruling oligarchy did not play the decisive role in the bourgeois state. On the basis of such a superficial, 'purely economic', investigation, replacing a Marxist-Leninist class analysis, the erroneous conclusion was drawn that in the interests of conducting war, the state comes out against the interests of individual monopolies. When the Communists participated in the governments of bourgeois states, they had always attempted to defend the proletariat's interests. In the countries of the people's democracy, however, the representatives of the propertied classes could be excluded from the government 'with the help of the Soviet Union'. It had been groundless and wrong to call these states 'capitalist' now that they were rapidly moving to socialism. The 'people's democracies' were thus 'states of the working people' fulfilling the functions of the dictatorship of the proletariat in the interests of all working people. Varga admitted that his inconsistent application of the Marxist-Leninist theory of the state had led to an incorrect analysis of the changing relations between India and England. India had turned thus from a colony into a semi-colony. 'At the time, an undialectical, purely "economic" approach

---

374 Varga tried to get Molotov's help in this case. On 29 April 1949 he wrote a letter to Molotov pledging his help for having inserted a letter in *The Times*. But on 4 March 1949, Molotov had already lost his position as Minister of Foreign Affairs. He remained nonetheless in charge of the Foreign Policy Commission of Stalin's Politburo that seldom gathered. Cherkasov 2005, p. 105; Watson 2005, pp. 238–40.

375 Varga 1949, pp. 78–88.

to the study, a neglect of Comrade Stalin's instructions on the need to orientate oneself toward what is new and developing, blocked my path toward correct evaluation of the character and significance of the countries of people's democracy', Varga confessed.

The overall effect, however, was that Varga's reputation had been destroyed. In the new edition of the *Great Soviet Encyclopedia*,[376] he was described as a 'bourgeois reformist'. Although he could keep his position of deputy director of the Institute of Economics, his academic prestige was undermined. His research project was limited to preparing a new book on postwar economic and political development of capitalism in which he would correct his old errors. Notwithstanding all these difficulties, he did not return to Hungary where his close associate Mátyás Rákosi had gained absolute power and sometimes invited him for economic advice.[377] In Budapest, Varga would acquire the status of an éminence grise in close contacts with the Kremlin. Honorofic distinction followed. In March 1949, he received the Medal of Merit with Golden Palms out of the hands of the Hungarian President Árpád Szakasits.[378] In 1954, he also became a member of the Hungarian Academy of Sciences. But, strangely enough, no publication of his hand appeared on the economic and political situation in his former homeland. The reason could have been that he had been absorbed by his work in Moscow, centre of power of the Communist world, while Budapest was the capital of a relatively small Socialist country heavily dependent on Soviet support. After the fall of Rákosi and the Hungarian upheaval in 1956, Varga would nonetheless be invited to Budapest for advice by the new party leadership,[379] but without any political or economic consequences. At the end of his long life, Varga was still defending a system of rigid state planning based on heavy industry and collectivised agriculture.

Problems of Monopoly Capitalism

After 1949, when the controversy about his scientific and political views had been definitively settled, Varga worked on a new book in which he had to

---

376 *Bolshaya Sovetskaya Enziklopediya*, Volume 6, Moscow 1951, p. 626.
377 Varga remained Rákosi's confidant in economic matters. In December 1951, the Hungarian government decided on the introduction of large-scale price reforms during a conference in which Varga participated. 'Eugen Varga greift ein', *Der Spiegel*, 30 January 1952, pp. 20–1.
378 *Szabad Nép*, 27 March 1949.
379 Letter Károlyi Kiss of 12 Fabruary 1957 and letters of Desző Szilagyi of 21 March 1957 and 7 April 1957 to Varga. Party Archives, Budapest, 783, f. 9, lap 24, 25, 26.

correct his past errors. This book, *Osnovnye voprosy ekonomiki i politiki imperializma posle vtoroy mirovoy voyny* (*Basic Economic Problems and Political Problems of Imperialism*), was published after Stalin's death by Gosudarstvoe Izdatelstvo Politicheskoy Literatury. This publication contained many Stalin quotes, but contained no new insights or facts. Again, the general crisis of capitalism had developed further and announced the end of the capitalist system as well. The masses were mobilising against capitalism and colonialism. However, Varga's much anticipated postwar slump had been postponed by America's military expenditures and the overproduction crisis had been absorbed by the Korean War boom (1950–3).

Varga argued that the working conditions of the labouring classes deteriorated while the American monopolists were solving their own overproduction crisis at the cost of the American and foreign people. The capitalist state operated now as a pump station siphoning taxes and transmitting them to the monopolies. Hence, the capitalist state was nothing more than a 'mighty instrument for the enrichment of the financial oligarchy on the costs of other classes'.[380] Varga, however, believed that increased international trade could nonetheless serve the economic interests of all nations. Decolonisation also played an important role. France and Britain were losing important chunks of their empires. Hence, both imperialist states were now lowering wages in order to compensate for the colonial markets they had lost, and together with the USA they were forming an alliance against the Soviet Union.[381] In full accord with Stalin, he believed that new inter-imperialist wars could not be excluded in the near future.[382] The formation of a strong socialist bloc had narrowed the capitalist world market, thus causing additional realisation problems to capitalism. In the meantime, the US tried to prohibit trade with the socialist countries, which deepened the ongoing general crisis of capitalism.

Meanwhile Varga commented on decaying capitalism sometimes in *Pravda*.[383] In these articles he could prove that he was following the correct party line. The problem, however, was that his much discussed downturn had not occurred. It was clear to him that the postwar economic crisis had been postponed by military expenditures which had caused a commodity boom. The end of the Korean War in 1953 would thus mark the beginning of a general slump spreading from the United States to Europe and the semi-colonies.

---

380   Varga 1955, p. 83.
381   Varga 1955, p. 240.
382   Varga 1955, pp. 335–6.
383   *Pravda*, 19 March, 10 May and 22 October 1950; 22 October 1951 and 25 November 1952; 18 October 1953.

In an article he published on 28 January 1954 in *Pravda* (see Part 3, Chapter 13), Varga argued that the crisis was already a fact because American monopolists had to diminish their prices and contract their production. Meanwhile poverty had increased and workers had been dismissed. This analysis focussed on production of basic materials (such as steel, copper, aluminium, oil, etc.) and made abstraction of the international economic situation. Conflicts of interests between firms producing for export markets and those producing for domestic markets were not analysed. The relation between the state and monopoly capital was not even mentioned.

American media and also the CIA paid some attention to Varga's *Pravda* article. *The New York Times* of 9 February 1954 referred to it and then Will Lissner published, on 11 April 1954, a full comment in which he recalled that Varga's authorship was disclosed 'by a statistical confusion, by a peculiar combination of outdated statistics, and by a remarkable succession of parallel statements in his analyses of United States economic conditions and in the analysis set forth by the party program'.

Not all Communist economists were impressed by Varga's crisis theory. The central feature of the crisis of capitalism in the interwar years was undercapacity working. Maurice Dobb (1957) pointed to not only the anti-cyclical influence of US state expenditures Varga had highlighted, but also consumers' expenditures and the investment boom affecting also the housing sector. Dobb: 'Maybe the crisis when it comes will be another 1929: this I do not profess to know ... It may well be that we are in a phase where crises of inflationary pressures ... are more likely to be on the agenda of the next year or two'.[384] In addition, for several reasons (industrial overcapacity, military expenditures, unemployment) Varga believed that the slump would nonetheless break out in the United States. Just like after the First World War, economic stabilisation would come to an end after a decade of prosperity. In 1958 Varga nonetheless thought that a cyclical crisis of overproduction had started in the USA.

In an interview given to a correspondent of *Neues Deutschland* (see Part 3, Chapter 14), Varga argued that after December 1956 industrial production had declined. This was partly due to an acute dollar shortage caused by American export surpluses, while rising unemployment because of falling export activities had caused overproduction in the sector of durable consumer goods. American capitalists were relying on increasing military expenditures to help them, but these hopes had no real foundation. Hence, Varga concluded that 'the crisis in the USA will involve all other capitalist countries in a world economic crisis.

---

384 Dobb 1957, p. 7.

The United States is responsible for half the total industrial production in the capitalist world. A crisis of over-production in the USA must extend itself to all other capitalist countries through its repercussions on foreign trade, the Stock Exchanges, international credit, and the undermining of confidence, especially when in each of these countries conditions for a crisis have been maturing'.

These politically sensitive digressions on the coming slump raised some protests from other Soviet economists. In addition, Varga's more theoretical underpinning of his analysis in a long article published in *Kommunist* (see Part 3, Chapter 15) in early 1958 and translated into many foreign languages, did not have the intended impact on his colleagues who had become very critical of Varga's prediction based on the thesis that the world war had interrupted the normal industrial cycle. His opponents, however, had argued that the cyclical character of reproduction was a result of the action of the general laws of capitalism and that capitalism remained capitalism even during the war. Varga called this approach a dogmatic one! He also rejected the opinion that industries producing war procurements create the premises for a crisis of overproduction, i.e. 'war creates great disproportions within the capitalist economy'. Varga called this a bourgeois or revisionist theory.

But all this did not convince Varga's colleagues. Young scholars rebelled against scientific sclerosis in the Soviet Academy of Sciences. They founded a new journal in 1956, with the backing of leading economist N.N. Lyubimov,[385] entitled *International Affairs*, which would publish new and original research in the field. Varga was apparently excluded from all changes that occurred with the rise of Nikita Khrushchev to power. When on 15 April 1958 the journals *Mezhdunarodnaya zhizn* and *International Affairs* organised a conference on the situation in the capitalist countries, Varga was not among the speakers. When on 4 October 1958, an international conference on the international economic crisis convened at the Humboldt University in Berlin (GDR), Varga's name was not listed. On 11 and 12 May 1959, the editorial board of *International Affairs* and the Chair of Political Economy of the Soviet Academy of Social Sciences dedicated a joint session to the contemporary conditions of the working classes in the capitalist countries, but Varga was not among the speakers or discussants. One may presume that Varga was kept out of these conferences, but afterwards he would publish his criticism, especially against his Stalinist enemies I.I. Kuzminov and also Adolf I. Katz, in the volume *Politico-Economic Problems of Capitalism* published in 1964.[386] On the problem of absolute impov-

---

[385] N.N. Lyubimov was Varga's former colleague at the Institute of World Economy and World Politics and the translater of Keynes's *General Theory* into Russian (1948).
[386] Varga 1968.

erishment, Varga's opinion differed from those of 'dogmatists' like Kuzminov of the Institute of Economics, who defended the point of view that the position of the working class was worsening all the time.[387] Varga now admitted that technological progress could have a positive effect on a worker's family consumption and that American workers could buy cars and other durable consumer goods and spent money on ready-to-cook foods. They ate more chicken and fewer potatoes.[388] But meanwhile a redistribution of the aggregate profit in favour of the monopolies was effected through price mechanisms and rich capitalist countries were earning super profits through the mechanism of unequal exchange. In his analysis Varga returned to the debate he once had with Henryk Grossmann in the late 1920s (see Part 2, Chapter 10) about the fact that under monopoly capitalism and under non-monopoly capitalism, the rates of different branches tend to equalise and form an *average profit*. Varga argued that the monopolies were making additional profits which did not tend to equalise, and hence there was no such thing as an average rate of monopoly profit.[389]

Varga's views on the development of capitalism did not change fundamentally after the Second World War. He repeatedly argued that the alliance of the monopolies and the state was effected primarily in the form of a merger between the monopolies and the state machinery. The alliance also takes the form of joint decisions on important economic issues. In various ways the state helps the monopolies fix high monopoly prices on the home market. State-monopoly capitalism is extremely reactionary, he asserted, because it defends a social system doomed to collapse (see Part 3, Chapter 18). With regard to the economic cycle, he thought that the period just after the Second World War should be excluded from the cycle, that the postwar cycle only started in 1947 and that the first postwar cycle then continued until 1957–8 when the first serious crisis broke out.

In conformity with Marxist-Leninist theory, Varga regarded monopoly capital as a 'single force' and the whole monopoly bourgeoisie as a class or as the layer of the capitalist class 'with common class interest'. Thus, the coalescence of these two forces, the monopolies and the state, form the basis of state-monopoly capitalism. Varga nonetheless stressed the fact that monopoly capital and the state were forming 'independent forces'.[390] He singled out that there were constant contradictions among the different factions of the various monopolies in a single branch. However, the monopoly bourgeoisie as

---

387 Varga 1968, p. 114.
388 Varga 1968, p. 120.
389 Varga 1968, p. 161.
390 Varga 1968, pp. 51–2.

a whole had several interests in common such as safeguarding the capitalist system or keeping wages at a low level. These conflicts explained why under state-monopoly capitalism the state represents the common interests of monopoly capital, sometimes contradicting the particular interests of the monopoly bourgeoisie. Hence, there was 'no "one-sided subordination" but a joining of forces, which, in spite of this merger, still maintain a certain autonomy'.[391]

In an article on the problems of inter-imperialist contradictions and war (see Part 3, Chapter 16), Varga argued that Stalin had completely forgotten Lenin's law of uneven development under imperialism. Hence the USA could no longer dictate the economic field as they did just after the Second World War. The other imperialist powers did not need a war with the USA to advance their economic development. But on the other hand, they were also unable to wage a war because of US supremacy in the imperialist camp. 'There is no political stabilisation of capitalism', Varga exclaimed, but on the other hand that did not mean that inter-imperialist wars were inevitable. The imperialist powers had learned a lesson from history as well, because a third world war would have devastating consequences for the capitalist system as a whole. Thus Stalin's theory on inter-imperialist war was incorrect.

Apart from the problems of state-monopoly capitalism (see Part 3, Chapter 17), Varga remained fundamentally interested in the capitalist cycle, which was now showing a tendency to become shorter because of investment in rapid technological changes. However, the general crisis of capitalism had not yet emerged. Was all this due to the competition between the two systems and the changing power balance in favour of socialism? Varga thought, however, that the fate of capitalism was already decided because of a superior socialist system.

Though Varga saw in Keynes a 'false prophet', he would later recognise that the 'reformist leaders value Keynes' because the latter had not attempted 'to refute Marx or argue with him'.[392] Varga would never link the Marshall Plan to Keynesianism or any other form of macroeconomic management, but he nonetheless would recognise that the Marshall aid had enabled countries to rebuild their industries and to boost production. He also saw Keynes as a 'typical eclectic' only dealing 'with the superficial phenomena of capitalist economy' and his theory was a 'confused rag-tag' for not having created an economic theory of his own or having refuted the teachings of the 'founders of bourgeois political economy'.[393] Varga's main charge against Keynes's 'muddled think-

---

391 Varga 1968, p. 55.
392 Varga 1968, p. 319.
393 Varga 1968, pp. 305–6.

ing'[394] was that any class analysis or historical approach was absent from it. He had forgotten in his 'pseudo-psychology' that competition forced 'the individual capitalist to make a profit or perish'. Keynes's abstract economic man and psychological laws had no validity in the 'real capitalist world' in which there were at least 'a thousand million people whose incomes are so low that they are forced to live in perpetual hunger' or people whose incomes 'are so large that it would be simply impossible to spend them on consumer goods'. Hence, Keynes's policy of overcoming the narrowness of the market by increasing unproductive consumption among the non-working classes was 'not as absurd as it would seem at first glance'.[395] Deficit spending was also intended to justify the expenditure on arms. According to Keynes, unemployment emerged because the more workers an employer hires, the less profit he could expect as a consequence of the working of the law of diminishing returns. Secondly, not all people wanted to spend their whole income on consumption or on investment. Varga remarked that the principal cause of unemployment was the capitalist system itself.

Varga's criticism of Keynes's *General Theory* was intimately related to the fact that in the 1960s neo-Keynesian thinking on economic growth had acquired some influence in Soviet economic thought. Keynes's growing popularity was mainly due to his recommendation that state intervention in the economy could avoid crises of overproduction and mass unemployment. However, that was, Varga wrote, in 'complete harmony with the interests of the monopolies'.[396] The union between reformism and Keynesian theories thus suited the requirements of the reformist leaders as well.

However, this benevolent criticism of Keynes was not without some afterthoughts, because of an incident at the Institute of Economics on 1 July 1949 in which Varga had been implicated. On that day, a dissertation written by Viktor S. Volodin had been accepted by the Academy of Sciences.[397] Volodin was a young Stalinist extremist who had already written a review of a Russian translation of *The General Theory* published in 1948 in Moscow. The translator was N.N. Lyubimov. I.G. Blyumin had written a lengthy introduction to the book. In that review article entitled 'The False Theory of Keynes',[398] Volodin argued that Blyumin and translator Lyubimov had done poor work and that this book consisted of false and deliberately confused reasoning. Blyumin, suffering from

---

394   Varga 1968, p. 320.
395   Varga 1968, pp. 307–9.
396   Varga 1968, p. 316.
397   Turner 1969, pp. 53–112.
398   Volodin 1950, pp. 108–14.

elements of pseudo-academism and objectivism, had failed to unmask Keynes as an apologist reflecting the ideology of monopolistic capital. Viktor S. Volodin worked at the Institute of Economics and must have obviously received Stalinist protection for this attack on respected economists like Lyubimov and Blyumin. Moreover, Volodin was allowed to write a doctoral dissertation in which he made a critical analysis of Keynes's *The General Theory* without doing any extensive research concerning the concrete situation in Britain during the Great Slump. During the discussion in the commission, I.N. Dvorkin hailed Volodin's work for its criticism of Keynes who was the worst enemy of the working class. The other members of the commission did not oppose this view. Finally, only Varga had some doubts as to whether Volodin's work had met the official standards of a dissertation. However, Volodin received his doctor's degree. His dissertation was published in 1953, the year of Stalin's death and Beria's execution.[399]

Conclusion

Because of his longevity and long-standing academic career, it is not easy to classify Varga's writing. Varga was a militant and most of the time working and writing for the cause of the world revolution and Soviet power. Having started as an adept of Karl Kautsky and Rudolf Hilferding before the First World War, Varga developed from a Marxist orthodox to a Bolshevik after the Bolsheviks had come to power. One may also argue that Varga never would become a *Russian* Bolshevik, but would remain at least a Hungarian Marxist well versed in Central-European thought and its positivistic methods. He would refuse to join one of the various Bolshevik factions competing for political power in the 1920s. Later he would support Stalin's rule and he would become acquainted with the master in the Kremlin as well, but a 'true' Stalinist he would never become. His scientific enemies sided with the faction of second-generation Bolsheviks represented by Andrey Vishinskiy and Andrey Zhdanov. Varga's fall in 1947 had been their work.

During the 1920s and 1930s, Varga was known as the author of all Comintern reports. His reputation was at its zenith in 1935 when his report to the Seventh Congress of the Comintern marked the end of the leftist period and the adoption of the popular front tactics. However, many were not really convinced of Varga's genius and his ability to predict the moment of the next economic

---

399   Volodin 1953.

crisis. Scholars of the history of Marxist thought usually neglected Varga's contribution to economic analysis. M.C. Howard and J.E. Even would even argue in their *History of Marxian Economics* that Varga was 'an original if unpenetrating thinker whose dominance was achieved largely by default'.[400] And also that he had made much of the temporary stabilisation of capitalism in 1920s, 'which in practice amounted to little more than a recognition that the world economy had recovered from the deep slump of 1920–1 and that the Dawes Plan was limiting the damage done by the reparation crisis'.[401] Indeed, Varga argued then that the recovery would be short-lived, that industrial rationalisation and increasing organic composition of capital would reduce employment and workers' consumption as well, thus leading to mass unemployment and a slump. 'In the light of what happened after 1929 this must be regarded as remarkably prescient, but it was very loosely argued and open to all the traditional Marxian objections to underconsumptionism'.[402]

One has to keep in mind that Varga had been an economic journalist reporting on actual problems for which he used various sources of unequal quality. Varga's 'economism' should also be highlighted. Like Kautsky, he saw Marxism as the science of history and his economic analysis rested firmly on this foundation. Capitalism would lead to the dispossession of the small producers by big enterprises (monopolies) and the disappearance of the toiling peasants and small masters. Like Lenin, however, he believed that capitalism in its highest stage was an unviable economic system leading to economic crises and interimperialist rivalries. Though he admitted that the capitalist economy after the Second World War could be managed for several years by government, capitalism was nonetheless moribund. In the meantime, class antagonisms would become increasingly intense and would be exacerbated by economic crises, increasing the proletariat's misery and insecurity. Varga did not believe in the American miracle of a crisis-free capitalism, but he was nonetheless aware of the country's fast economic growth laying the ground for mass consumption and, in the case of Europe, for extended welfare provisions. With regard to the postwar economic slump, he predicted that it could be easily absorbed by new cycles of investment and increased purchasing power of the masses. The communist parties in the developed capitalist countries would soon adjust their strategies to this reality and see in state-monopoly capitalism a further stage of capitalist development offering the proletariat the possibility of struggling

---

400 Howard and Even 1989, p. 298.
401 Ibid.
402 Ibid.

for a democratic revolution,[403] while in the post-colonial world revolutionary perspectives had remained intact. In general, these strategic assumptions were also largely characterised by a return to the basic tenets of the Orthodox Marxism of the Second International. It was mainly from this that Varga would resist many attacks of his Stalinist enemies in the Soviet Academy of Sciences and in the Central Committee of the CPSU.

After Varga's death in October 1964, nobody was seriously thinking of publishing his complete works, amounting to some 1,300 items. In 1969, Varga's selected writings in three volumes were published in the GDR.[404] Later on, other selections of Varga's works were published in Moscow and Budapest as well.[405] Elmar Altvater published in 1969 a selection of Varga's economic writings about the economic crisis in capitalism.[406] Though they were helpful to those studying the origins of the economic theory of state-monopoly capitalism, they failed to popularise Varga's contribution to the latter theory. Only a few students of Soviet Communism would use these selections. Hence, the person and works of Varga remained largely neglected by historians of economic and political theory. Only a few researchers have devoted their time and energy to studying Varga's works. Some have also pointed to his eminent role as the Comintern's and Stalin's famous and eminent economist.[407] But, in general, Varga's works are still largely unknown by most students of Communism, who pay more attention to the economic writings of Bukharin.

---

403 Boccara 1966.
404 Varga 1979b.
405 Varga 1974; Varga 1976, 1978, 1981.
406 Altvater 1969.
407 Wahl 1953; Gansauge 1889; Duda 1994; Andreu 2000, 2003; Day 1981, 1995; Mommen 2002, 2011; Roh 2010.

PART 1

The Hungarian Councils' Republic (1919)

Introduction to Part 1

Part One contains a long analysis of the Councils' Republic which Varga wrote during his detention at the Karlstein Castle in Austria after having fled from Budapest on 1 August 1919. The text was originally published in 1920 by publishing house Neue Erde in Vienna, and it met with considerable success. In 1921 the text was reprinted by Verlag der Arbeiter-Buchhandlung in Vienna and by Carl Hoym Nachf. in Hamburg. The book was also translated into Italian (1921), Dutch (1921, abridged version), French (1922), and Russian (1925), but there was no English translation.

CHAPTER 1

Political-Economic Problems of the Proletarian Dictatorship

To the memory of the loyal, bold, noble-minded champions of the proletariat, who have fallen victim to White Terror after the breakdown of the Hungarian Councils' Republic.

∴

Preface[1]

Bourgeois revolutions, like those of the eighteenth century, storm more swiftly from success to success, their dramatic effects outdo each other, men and things seem set in sparkling brilliants, ecstasy is the everyday spirit, but they are short-lived, soon they have attained their zenith, and a long crapulent depression seizes society before it learns soberly to assimilate the results of its storm-and-stress period. On the other hand, proletarian revolutions, like those of the nineteenth century, criticise themselves constantly, interrupt themselves continually in their own course, come back to the apparently accomplished in order to begin it afresh, deride with unmerciful thoroughness the inadequacies, weaknesses and paltriness of their first attempts, seem to throw down their adversary only in order that he may draw new strength from the earth and rise again from the indefinite prodigiousness of their own aims, until a situation has been created which makes all turning back impossible ...[2]

Undermined by the labour leaders 'shrinking back before indeterminate immensity of their own goals', deserted by the proletarians of the neighbour-

---

1 [Translation based on *Die wirtschaftspolitischen Probleme der proletarischen Diktatur*, von Dr. Eugen Varga, Univ.-Prof., gewesenem Volkskommissar und Präsidenten des Obersten Wirtschaftsrates der Ungarischen Räterepublik, Vienna 1920 [1921], II. Unveränderte Auflage 4.–8. Tausend, Verlag der Arbeiter-Buchhandlung, Wien VIII].
2 [Marx 1979, pp. 106–7].

ing states, the Hungarian Councils' Republic, this most advanced Western offshoot of Russia's revolutionary sea of flames, collapsed in the fight against a Rumanian-Czech soldiery supported by all imperialist powers. The most exposed leaders, foreseeing the historically unavoidability of the White Terror, fled the country and found a poverty-ridden asylum in Austria. Interned at Karlstein Castle and isolated from contacts with the outside world, I had the opportunity and enough time to make up my mind about the 'inadequate, weak and wretched aspects of the first attempt'. The result of this meditation is this writing. It bears the marks of its origins. Books were only in a very limited number at my disposal; no statistical materials at all. Writing and even quoting were a matter of memory. Hence, a lot of inaccuracies ...

Persecuted by the hangmen of the Hungarian White Terror; accused of murder, robbery and false coining; slandered by the capitalist press of the whole world; abandoned by many a good old comrade appalled by the harsh reality of the proletarian class struggle taking refuge in the idyll of bourgeois democracy, I confess, notwithstanding the defeat: there is no other way to the construction of a socialist society than the dictatorship of the proletariat. There will probably be countries, where even parliamentarism will be maintained in the period of the dictatorship. And there will be – we hope – countries where the dictatorship will be realised without any terror. It would be foolish to predict the forms of a social order in the making. So much is certain: without the dictatorship of the proletariat, i.e. without a period of transition, in which the proletariat constitutes the ruling class, and with the exclusion of all other classes of capitalist society determining the country's politics,[3] the transition from capitalism to socialism will be impossible.

This conviction, which was already formulated by Marx a half a century ago, gains uncommonly many adherents notwithstanding the fast collapse of the Finnish, Bavarian and Hungarian dictatorships. The German Independent Social-Democratic Party adhered unanimously to this platform at its last

---

3 This is the right sense of the concept: Dictatorship of the proletariat is thus not how Kautsky is putting it '... policy of oppression ... to liberate itself from the shackles of laws which itself has formed, and to have recourse to lawless oppression ... represents arbitrary force, which by its very nature can be put into practice by one person alone, or only by a very small circle of persons' [Varga quotes Kautsky 1919, p. 32]. This is the definition of tyranny, of dictatorship in general, but not of the proletarian dictatorship, which means the transitory state form of the exclusive political hegemony [Herrschaft] of the proletariat as a class, just like bourgeois democracy is the state form of the exclusive political hegemony of the bourgeoisie. The dictatorship of the proletariat does not mean 'to liberate itself from the shackles of laws'. On the contrary: the stricter all laws are observed, the most severe the dictatorship is exercised, the shorter the period of its historical necessity will be.

party congress. The Italian Socialist Party gained with this programme an overwhelming electoral victory. The labour movement in England and in America is coming very near to the idea and methods of the dictatorship. The unprecedented military successes of the Russian Councils' Republic in the year 1919, the decomposition of all counter-revolutionary armies in Russia prove that the hegemony of the proletariat in Russia has gained a foothold in the souls of the majority of the politically active part of the population and has become invincible. It is impossible that in the long-run the proletariat of Germany, England and America, although they constitute an absolute majority of their population, will stay passively under the yoke of capitalism, and that in Russia the proletarian regime will not only survive, but will also grow militarily, economically and culturally stronger, as recent events have already proven. Proletarian Russia must either be ruined or the proletariat of the other capitalist countries must also conquer political leadership.

I believe in the progress of the revolution, because capitalism is incapable – as I explain in the *First Chapter* of this publication – to secure for the proletariat a real increase in its living standard, being the only method to curb the revolutionary pressure of the proletariat. This belief in a continuing advance of the proletarian revolution urged me to publish this book, as incomplete and defective it may be. May it only slightly contribute to a 'shortening of the birth woes of the new society'.

My work is nothing but an agitational or justificational writing. I am revealing without any shame all mistakes we committed during the period of the Hungarian Councils' dictatorship; I notice at any rate when a decree was really implemented or had, on the contrary, remained on paper. I am refraining from giving prescriptions for the activities of proletarians in other countries. This would be an unhistorical naivety. My aims are: to discuss the general political-economic problems of this proletarian dictatorship, to look at the theoretically possible solutions and, finally, to delineate the experiences we really had when working out our solutions. Knowing more about these facts should be useful to the proletariat of all countries. It will be up to you to discover what may be useful in the Hungarian experiences ...

Something more about the method used. The latter is a Marxist one. Just like Marx, I started methodologically from the presupposition that the capitalist method of production is predominant and paid little attention to the remnants of the feudal economic system; the stress is here put on the development of new forms of the economy: forms having already developed in capitalism were further developed and stripped from their antagonistic character during the dictatorship. In this period of the dictatorship, economic life was split into two parts. Apart from the proletarian collective economy, remnants of a private economic system still subsisted. The latter were slowly dissolved and integrated into the collective system. If this process is completed, the dictatorship of the proletariat will have come to an end. There will be no proletarians and bourgeois anymore: there will be only a community of freely working civilised people ...

It is assumed that with the disappearance of private property the greedy-egoistic ideology corresponding with these property relations will also disappear. The necessity of the dictatorship of the proletariat does not end with the disappearance with private property of the means of production, but only with the disappearance of the capitalistic, greedy-egoistic ideology. The dictatorship of the proletariat can only be succeeded by Socialism if an ideological change has been completed and the greedy-egoistic psyche, which is so characteristic of capitalism, has also disappeared. This will take rather a generation.

The role of ideology, here by its unimpeding intellectual penetration during the Hungarian Councils' dictatorship, becomes more significant in a revolutionary situation than most Marxists will believe. The proletarian regime is much less endangered by the well-conceived class interests of the dispossessed ruling classes, than by the passive resistance of broader layers of the proletariat having not freed themselves from the ideology forced upon them by the culturally oppressive system of the capitalist state. The important role played by ideology, and by political practices based on it, meant that we included politics and ideology as determining factors in our analysis when discussing economic problems. A stricter concentration on purely economic aspects would have resulted in a better-delineated account, but one that was also further from reality ...

During my research I received the support of my comrades in jail: I thank Béla Kun and Julius [Gyula] Lengyel for having given me many valuable hints; I want to express my heartfelt gratitude to each of them.

    Karlstein, 10 January 1920
      The Author

1   The Crisis of Capitalism

The world war unleashed the crisis of capitalism. The proletariat of the whole world is now in a revolutionary ferment. Setting out from the victorious Russian fireplace, the revolutionary wave is irresistibly spreading to the West. Absolute relaxation of labour discipline; profound labour unrest under capitalist conditions; gigantic strikes shaking by their expansion the foundations of the capitalist economic system; inflation and misery; plundering in the cities; mutiny in the army: these experiences are showing that they are the signs of a coming armed upheaval of the proletariat.

The hirelings of the bourgeoisie maintain, of course, that this is actually only a temporary crisis of capitalism and not the beginning of the end. 'Bolshevism is the disease of the defeated countries' – that is their slogan. We will try to establish whether the actual crisis should be considered as a temporary or as a final one.

The capitalist social order is an antagonistic one. As a class-based hegemony it could only remain stable for such a long period of time as long as the interests of the bourgeoisie were suited to those of the large majority of the population. This situation only lasted for a short period of time. The immanent development tendencies of the capitalist mode of production brought the antagonistic character of this social order even sharper to the fore. Not the will of the majority of the stakeholders, but the repressive organisation of the ruling class kept the system upright during the decades of latent crisis. The proletarian masses organised themselves to fight capital. But this only led to isolated outbursts. Capitalism had not yet developed all its strength and utilised all its possibilities: it still expanded some more, occupied new countries and new continents which procured the capitalist huge profits and the possibility of providing the advance guards of the proletariat with the crumbs of them and offering them a slowly rising standard of living, which was dampening their revolutionary energy.[4] Concentration of enterprises and centralisation of capital was still less developed and those interested in private property of the means of production were very numerous. Conservative ideology, belief in the perenniality of the capitalist world order was still firmly rooted in the proletarian masses. The 'evolutionist' teachings of Social Democracy postponed the revolutionary change of society until an indefinite future; the trade-union praxis entirely dedicated to an improvement of the conditions of the working class within the capitalist social order was not appropriate to transform latent contradictions into active revolutionary energies. Finally, the repressive organisation of the ruling classes was intact and strong enough to put down any attempt at an armed uprising of the proletariat and, owing to this, reinforced in the proletariat the dogma preached by the advocates of the ruling class and transmitted to the proletariat the belief in the perenniality and eternity of the capitalist social order.

---

4 This lasted until the turn of the century; an upsurge of inflation led to increased money wages but also diminishing real wages. Kautsky 1910, p. 85.

The world war engendered thoroughgoing changes into the structure of capitalist society. First of all, we want to study the changes of the economic fundamentals during the war.

A part of these changes took place according to the general tendencies of the capitalist mode of production, but faster than if there had been no world war. Concentration progressed unusually fast. Hundreds of thousands of small craftsmen and peddlers were mobilised and their businesses were ruined. On the other hand, the big enterprises could enrich themselves with lucrative war supplies. The gap in society between wealthy capitalists and proletarians having nothing but their labour power to sell, became sharper than before the outbreak of the world war.

The tendency of the imperialist stage of capitalism to overcome anarchy by creating state-controlled compulsory economic organisations that permitted a better control by capital of the market, received an enormous impetus during the war. One was now speaking of war socialism, but a better definition could have been state-led organised capitalism.

We can define a series of other changes as war-economic deformations of economic life. The most important phenomena of these deformations are as follows:[5]

Instead of real accumulation, real impoverishment, accompanied by an unprecedented accumulation of fictive capital, occurred. The belligerent state is absorbing – together with consumption of the civil population – a much more important mass of goods than ever can be produced. Instead of normal capital accumulation, a disaccumulation, i.e. a decrease of real wealth, happens. The capitalist state lays claim to goods. Meanwhile property rights are recognised because the state pays the full price. This cash money is furnished by emissions of war loans. Unproductively used goods are replaced by fictive capital, by promissory loans financing future production, and by taxing realised surplus value. The amount of fictive capital is rapidly swelling because of rising prices because of growing shortages.

'These promissory loans, which are issued for the originally loaned capital long since spent, these paper duplicates of consumed capital, serve for their owners as capital to the extent that they are saleable commodities and may, therefore, be converted into capital'.[6]

In a war economy, this conversion can only happen to the individual owner of war loans; as real elements of productive capital are not available on the market of goods, conversion is in general socially impossible.

---

5 Varga 1916.
6 Marx 1957, p. 466.

During the war, real impoverishment of the population was not spreading evenly. Simultaneously, far-reaching changes occurred in the distribution of continuously shrinking real wealth. Suppliers of war-equipment, foodstuffs producers, thus all economic groups involved in the war economy, were getting rich. Small businesses, whose capital was not sufficient to continue production because of price increases of raw materials, were ruined. All social layers with fixed capital revenues were impoverished because of devaluation of their money.

The disappearance of real goods and the selling of fictive capital reflect an analogous evolution with regard to income distribution. The nominal amount of national income increases very much, but the counterpart of real goods for realising this income is missing. Prices are rising very fast, money is losing its character as a general medium of exchange. A primitive barter between city and countryside begins.

'The bourgeoisie has subjected the country to the rule of the towns'[7] – as is written in the *Communist Manifesto*. In the war economy, the countryside has subjected the city.

During the period of general shortages, peasants were hoarding the most indispensable goods: foodstuffs; they produced, acquired economic predominance, robbed the urban population, and forced the proletarians to swap their poor things for food at the farms.

In general, the living standard of the belligerent nations diminished rapidly and this decrease was not equally spread over all social classes. Landowners and wealthy bourgeois could keep their former living standard; peasants could even increase their living standard, while the living standard of the white-collar workers and industrial workers diminished by leaps. A real impoverishment of the toiling masses occurred because wage increases were not keeping pace with inflation. On the other hand, soldiers' lives improved because the traditional living standard of conscripts originating from the category of agricultural workers and unskilled workers from East and Central Europe rose considerably: people normally eating meat only once a fortnight now received a daily portion of meat in the army; proletarians walking barefoot during a good part of the year and having scarcely a shirt to their back were now dressed by the army, etc.

All these changes in the basic structures of the economy brought about thoroughgoing changes in the social superstructure. A significant change occurred in particular in the ideology of the proletariat: an activation of its latent revolutionary energy.

---

7 [Marx and Engels 1976, p. 488].

These moments coinciding with the general tendencies of capitalist development in the war economy, and accelerating the concentration and extension of compulsory economic syndicates, were only strengthening the latent resistance of the proletariat. The worsening of the living conditions of the working class is preparing a new revolutionary event. We have to stress that, notwithstanding all exploitation and misery the working class is suffering from in a capitalist society, its living standard has nonetheless – except for temporary setbacks in periods of crisis – increased in general during the epoch of the nineteenth century under modern capitalism. This is clearly revealed by data of food production and consumption. The decline of the proletariat's living standard in Central and Eastern Europe is an unprecedented experience in the history of the modern working class. *However, it is a basic psychological fact that losing one's formerly acquired living standard will cause a stronger revolutionary impulse than the drive for an improvement of the normal living conditions.* During the war the proletariat grew numerically because of the destitution of the petit-bourgeois and the sinking of the living standard of the white-collar workers to that of the proletariat. These declassed but undisciplined elements brought nonetheless a strong revolutionary impetus into the ranks of the proletariat.

Material impoverishment was affecting the proletariat in such a particular way that a further reinforcement of its social consciousness was highly favoured. During the war the ruling classes of all countries had appealed to the patriotism of the proletariat: in the fields, in the factories, in the countryside. One was always calling: the proletarians must save the fatherland, because their readiness for fighting on the battlefields and their labour productivity in the factories will both determine the 'fate of the fatherland'. The proletariat experienced in this manner its overwhelming importance in modern society from the spokesmen of capitalism. In the officially scientific ideology, the workers had hitherto only heard talk of their own inferiority in relation to the members of the ruling class. The opposite was now being said. In addition, the worker had experienced that he could manipulate weapons as well as the members of the ruling class and their followers – the latter had always served in the past as guardians of class hegemony and they had always been used *against* the workers. This experience had made a profound impression on the proletarians. As a matter of fact, we want to establish *that the proletariat of all countries came out of the war with a diminished standard of living, but also with a strengthened social conscience.* Due to this strengthened conscience, the proletariat now demands a higher material and moral standard of living, an increase over not only its actual but also its pre-war standard of living. We will prove that capital cannot possibly meet these demands. *This is the root of the actual crisis of capitalism.*

Quantitatively this development occurred unevenly. The deformation of economic life was more profound in the defeated countries than in the victorious ones. The result was a worsening of the living standard of the workers and their growing discontent, hence also an increase of their revolutionary drive. Because this strengthened revolutionary mood in the defeated countries coincides with the *decay of the repressive organisations of the state* because of the military defeat, the political revolution could break out in all these defeated countries. In Russia, where the past of the proletariat was strongest and where the ruling classes were weakly organised, a really proletarian revolution could be victorious, but a similar attempt would be later crushed in Finland, Bavaria and Hungary.

In the victorious countries, where the repressive organisations of the state had remained intact, the revolution did yet not occur. But the existence of the crisis cannot be denied. *The working class is loudly calling for a higher living standard. The capitalists are eagerly willing to give in to the bargain of a higher moral standard of the workers within bourgeois democracy.* Universal suffrage for the workers, participation of labour leaders in the government. Workers' communities, workers' councils with limited competences, yes, even socialisation with full compensation for the owners: the proletariat could 'easily' obtain this within the limits of bourgeois democracy.

But the working classes of the Entente countries are making sure that these kinds of political concessions do not suppress economic bondage. The proletariat of all countries cries out for a higher living standard: a shortening of the working day to seven hours, yes, to six hours in America, and it is trying – often unconsciously – to gain these measures by socialist-revolutionary methods. The experiences of the war economy have changed the organisation of a proletarian common economy [Gemeinwirtschaft] from a misty and distant social utopia into an accessible project for the near future. Although the compulsory organisation of the war economy is giving a distorted image of the communist economy, it proved to the masses that a centrally organised economic leadership is no utopia anymore, but arising from necessary relations, hence its tasks can be fulfilled by using the actual social expedients. That is why the British trade unions, which are always depicted as conservative, are now demanding the nationalisation of the mines, railways, banks and the most important commercial sectors; if accepted, these demands will mean the end of capitalism. The German workers demand the right of approval and co-partnership in the workers' councils of the capitalist enterprises, etc.

The struggle for increasing the living standard is predominantly fought with economic means, but also with a revolutionary energy. Gigantic strikes mobilising hundreds of thousands of railway workers, miners, metalworkers are stirring up economic life in Europe and America. Then, though economic demands are only clearly at stake in the conscience of the workers, an unprecedented expansion of this movement is transforming itself into a revolutionary class struggle. But because the bourgeoisie is unable to meet these demands, a general unrest is spreading among the workers in the capitalist world, together with a progressive fading away of capitalist labour discipline and a continually diminishing production.[8]

The capitalist class is, however, unable to meet the demands of the working class for an increase of the living standard to a pre-war level. This would mean the end of capitalism, because it also means the end of appropriation of surplus value. The capitalist class should completely renounce profits in the mere interests of the worker and continue the hope for a better future. One could now image that the leading bureaucracy of anonymous capital, the directors of limited liability companies, would continue production notwithstanding the prospects of some years without dividend. For the capitalist class in its totality, however, this is an unrealistic perspective.

---

8   The following data, which can be multiplied at will, illustrate the decline of production in Germany: 'Net losses of the Vereinigte König- und Laurahütte were 10.8 millions of marks in the year 1918–19. Cause of these losses were ... endless demands of workers and clerks, terrible increases of all costs, in particular *a steep decline of labour productivity*' (*Berliner Tagblatt*, 9 October 1919). [The Vereinigte König- und Laurhütte were located in Upper Silesia].

The Harpener Bergbau A.-G. [near Bochum] published the following report:

	Average productivity per worker (in deciles)	Worker's wage in marks
1913–14	9.49	6.63
1915–16	9.38	7.73
1916–17	8.54	9.86
1917–18	8.55	12.06
1918–19	7.65	16.71
July 1919	6.90	23.33
August 1919	6.02	26.87

Average productivity decreased since the end of the war from 8.55 deciles to 6.02 deciles (Berliner Tagblatt, 23 October 1919). General director Hilgner reported to the general assembly of Laurahütte that production was only half of peace production. The main cause of this decrease was *failing achievement of the workers (Berliner Tagblatt*, October 1919.) At the turn of the year 1919, labour productivity seems to have recovered. This will only be a passing by phenomenon.

But the contradiction between the demands of the workers and the possible results of capitalist production are so important that even – in practice completely unimaginable – the renouncement of the capitalist class on that profit would not solve that contradiction. The war has strongly diminished the possibility of production in all countries; composition and age of population have changed, the part of the employable layers of the population has diminished; the means of production are worn out, destroyed, stocks of goods, raw materials and means of production are consumed. With the help of these means of production it will be impossible to produce under capitalist production relations the necessary goods to meet the demands of the working class. *In its entire organisation, capitalist production is adapted to the former income distribution.* The capitalist class will never deny itself the temporary appropriation of surplus value. This would probably allow the working population to increase the value of its income in money, but not in goods necessary for raising the required real standard of living. But the means of production used for the production of luxury goods are not entirely suited to the production of those goods the working class is consuming.[9] The demands of the working class for a real increase in the living standard can only be realised by a production growth by leaps of all goods destined to workers' consumption.

Extension of production is, however, characteristic of capitalism: *increase of productivity* means growth by means of production set in motion by workers or – as Marx says – *by the increase of the organic composition of capital.* All other means – this will be discussed in the following chapter – are beyond the direct course of capitalist development. Production growth presupposes an increase of the means of production, thus real accumulation. This accumulation is only a function of the capitalist class, which means that a part of the appropriated surplus value is not consumed as income, but is used for a further increase of the means of production. But how can the capitalist class accumulate if it has to renounce its profits to meet the violent demands of the workers for an increase in their standard of living in order to curb their revolutionary upheavals? *Without profits, no accumulation; without accumulation, no possibility of increased production;*[10] without increased production, no

---

9   This is a problem also known under the dictatorship of the proletariat. We will discuss this in chapter 3. The question is thoroughly discussed by Marx in *Capital*, Volume II.

10 The increase of the production of goods is also hampered by the chaotic situation of the world market. Russia and Siberia have stopped delivering raw materials: the Balkans, Hungary, Poland are economically uncompetitive. Long-lasting instability of the exchange rates, the absence of the formerly absolute stability of the English world currency dominating the world market is seriously hampering international trade and production growth.

possibility to increase the living standard of the workers. But if capital tries it the other way – by refusing workers' demands to use the means of production for rapid accumulation, and thus for increasing surplus production necessary for the rise of the demanded real living standard – it would meet the most violent resistance of the proletariat. Strike after strike will follow, disappearance of discipline, refusal of the workers to work anymore under such conditions,[11] a wilful or unwilful decrease in productivity. Production will decline, contradictions between the demands of the workers and the available stocks of goods able to meet these demands will grow: the crisis of capitalism will automatically sharpen.

For capitalism there was only one way out of this dilemma: by inspiring the proletariat, who is already working at full capacity, to postpone at least their demands, thus giving the capitalist class the possibility of limiting in this way their personal expenditures in exchange for faster accumulation, for replacing the destroyed and worn-out means of production producing consumer goods, thus enabling later on a higher living standard of the proletariat. The *knights of social peace* are preaching the necessity of this solution to the working class. They ask the working class to suspend the class struggle, to work hard, to even work overtime, to demand no '*exaggerated*' wage increases – i.e. which are threatening profits and capitalist accumulation – and, above all, no shorter working time. The Scheidemanns[12] in Germany and Gompers[13] and Co. in America are operating in this way. But with little success! The grumbling proletariat is not hoping for a highly uncertain improvement of its living condition under a capitalist regime in the future, hence, the proletariat is not renouncing its attacks on capitalism by demanding an immediate improvement in its living conditions.

There is also a violent way. During the war the proletariat's consciousness was fortified and the proletarians acquired skills in handling weapons; hence, risking one's life had increased. Because of the decomposition of all repressive organisations of the ruling class, using violence had become either completely impossible or invited the professional soldiery, as we already saw in Hungary, to exercise the *most brutal repression. This form of violence can be used for*

---

11   The constant complaint of the capitalists about not finding workers for heavy, unskilled work, although huge unemployment exists, is revealing the revolutionary spirit of the workers. The workers are in such a mood that they prefer starving jobless to accepting the proposed working conditions.
12   [Philipp Scheidemann (1865–1939), German Social-Democratic politician].
13   [Samuel Gompers (1850–1924), president of the American Federation of Labor].

everything, except for securing the profitability of capitalist production. Choosing this way of destroying modern culture will lead back to the medieval production relations of a closed domestic barter economy, but not to normal capitalist production relations.

The dilemma of capitalism cannot be solved. The revolutionary turmoil is gaining ever broader social layers. Russia's violent example of a big country with a hundred million inhabitants ruled for more than two years by a victorious proletariat, whose military forces have crushed all adversaries, whose economic power is now visibly growing, notwithstanding a boycott by the imperialist Western powers and six years of war, is urging the class-conscious workers of all countries to the overthrowing of the capitalist system. The defeated attempts in Finland, Hungary and Bavaria do not change the fact that the revolutionary turmoil is gaining ever broader social layers and that nothing can save the cause of capitalism. The crisis will probably last for many years, the revolutionary transformation will last for decades and cost tens of thousands of lives: a return to a peaceful capitalism seems to be excluded.

The insight that all attempts to restore capitalist production must fail because of the insoluble contradiction that the class struggle will end 'with the common downfall of the struggling classes' themselves, if 'the revolutionary transformation of the whole society does not succeed', has brought many economically schooled Marxists – I was one of them – to the army of the Bolsheviks. Although in the beginning the dictatorship of the proletariat also strongly contributes to the economic decay, the basis of a definite solution is nonetheless laid here for the construction of a socialist society.

2   The Problem of the Productivity of Labour

Increasing productivity! That is the slogan currently returning in the collected speeches of bourgeois statesmen of all countries. We have closed our previous paragraph with the declaration that the real increase of the living standard demanded by the proletariat can only be met by a thoroughgoing increase of production. We have pointed out that this increase of production is impossible in countries crippled by the war. But in capitalism it is quite impossible to maximise wealth. In order to prove this, we only want to inquire into the general conditions of producing wealth. This means: inquiring into the factors of labour's wealth creation, i.e. of use value creation, which has to be sharply distinguished from profitability of capital invested in the production process. Profitability in a capitalist sense means putting a brake on production increases, a brake on maximising the creation of use values.

In the first place, wealth creation by people's labour is depending on physical conditions, on 'secular basic conditions'.[14] Because these conditions are only slowly changing, we may consider them as being of a constant character and thus we can make abstraction of them with regard to our problem.[15]

The variable factors are the following:
1. *rationalisation of labour;*
2. *productivity of labour;*
3. *intensity of labour;*
4. *the relation between productive and unproductive individuals of a community.*

1. *By rationalisation of labour I mean differences based on intellectual qualities in productivity of workers, both conductors and operators.* All other factors being equal, labour productivity is depending on psychological factors such as general culture, labour skills, rational organisation of labour of all people participating in the labour process. We only want to give here two examples. In China, weaving-mills installed by English manufacturers were using the same mechanical weaving looms as in Lancashire. However, it appeared that these weaving-mills, notwithstanding long working days and unusually low wages, were not only unproductive in our sense, but even not profitable in a capitalist sense. While the English wool weaver can operate four, exceptionally six, power looms at high speed, two Chinese workers have to be put at one power loom running at a lower speed; in China, power looms are nonetheless stopped for a longer period of time – or they are running empty – than in England.

Similar experiences were made in Japan.[16] Even more revealing is that I once carried out research on the causes of productivity differences in grain yields among European countries by using the *Annuaire de la statistique agricole internationale* of 1915. I wanted to obtain the aggregate average yield per ha between 1905 and 1914 of the four most important grains, i.e. wheat, corn, barley and oats, of which I listed the countries by virtue of their productivity. It appeared that this list did not correlate with the average farm size, with tariffs on grains or with grain prices, nor even with climate differences. On the other hand, this

---

14 The concept was coined by Karl Renner (Renner 1906).
15 Marx, whose research does not focus on wealth creation by labour in production of use value, but on value and surplus value problems, formulated the concept of productivity which partly covers our concept of use value based on the concept of labour productivity [Ergiebigkeit]: 'This productiveness is determined by various circumstances, amongst others, by the average amount of skill of the workmen, the state of science, and the degree of its practical application, the social organization of production, the extent and capabilities of the means of production, and by physical conditions'. Marx 1954, p. 40.
16 Koch 1910; Vialatte 1907; and also other authors.

list correlated unmistakably with a country's general culture and with its level of literacy. The lower its number of illiterates, the higher its agricultural productivity. That is why culture of the workers is of crucial importance to labour's productivity.[17]

2. *By productivity of labour I mean differences between labour productivity due to the different production methods used.* The nature of the means of production used also determines a low or a high degree of cooperation. These facts are all well known, particular evidences are thus not necessary. Workers in a modern weaving-mill or in a shoe factory produce a multiple amount, in many cases a thousand fold, as if that amount would have been produced by handicraft. *The larger the volume of constant capital of a country's means of production is in relation to its inhabitants, the larger production and productivity of labour [Ergiebigkeit] will be.*

3. *By labour intensity I mean the differences in labour productivity due to a range of different productive movements a worker is making during a longer average period of time.*[18] All other circumstances being equal, productivity of labour

---

17 'According to Hodgskin, circulating capital is nothing but the *juxtaposition* of the different kinds of social labour (coexisting labour) and accumulation is nothing but the amassing of the productive powers of social labour, so that the accumulation of the skill and knowledge (scientific power) of the workers themselves is the chief form of accumulation, and infinitely more important than the accumulation – which goes hand in hand with it and merely represents it – of the *existing objective* conditions of this accumulated activity. These objective conditions are only nominally accumulated and must be constantly produced anew and consumed anew ... [P]roductive capital and skilled labour are ... one ... Capital and a labouring population are precisely synonymous. Hodgskin [*Labour Defended against the Claims of Capital*, London, 1825] p. 33. These are simply further elaborations of Galiani's thesis: ... The real wealth ... is man (*Della Moneta, Custodi. Parte Moderna* Volume 3, p. 229). The whole objective world, the "world of commodities", vanishes here as a mere aspect, as the merely passing activity, constantly performed anew, of socially producing men'. Marx 1972, pp. 238–325.

18 This concept of the length of the working day is conceived as a special factor of labour intensity explaining also the problem of the effects of a shortening of the working day. 'Otherwise, however, so soon as the compulsory shortening of the hours of labour takes place. The immense impetus it gives the development of productive power, and to economy in the means of production, imposes on the workman increased expenditure of labour in a given time, heightened tension of labour-power, and closer filling up of the pores of the working-day, or condensation of labour to a degree that is attainable only within the limits of the shortened working-day. This condensation of a greater mass of labour into a given period thenceforward counts for what it really is, a greater quantity of labour. In addition to a measure of its extension, i.e. duration, labour now acquires a measure of its intensity or of the degree of its condensation or density. The denser hour of the ten hours' working day contains more labour, i.e. expended labour-power, than the more porous hour of the twelve hours' working-day'. Marx 1954, p. 410. As we have taken a longer average working time for measuring labour intensity, we eliminated this.

depends on how the workers are using their tools. '... [T]he normal intensity of labour, its intensive magnitude, whereby a given quantity of labour is expended in a given time ...'.[19] Labour intensity also has a qualitative aspect, such as not wasting raw materials or not breaking tools during the production process and, finally, meeting the required quality standards. As far as it depends on the worker, we will classify all this under the category of labour intensity. Hence, intensity partly depends on the will of the workers, but also partly independent of their own will, on their nourishment, their housing conditions, their individual aptitudes to accomplish the actual tasks of their work and other psychological aspects. The mechanist point of view also predominating in Marx's writings is that labour productivity exclusively depends on the way the means of production are employed and how the 'machine is using the worker'. Hence, the worker is fatally compelled to adapt his labour intensity to the running of the machine. This point of view ought to be discussed at the hand of newer and more thoroughgoing observations.

4. *Total output of a people considered as a producing whole will depend* – at a given degree of labour rationalisation, productivity and intensity – *on the relations between the productive workers with the consumers.*

∴

It can now easily be understood that the highest level of labour productivity cannot be reached in a capitalist society. We will now study one by one all individual factors contributing to labour productivity. Nonetheless we firstly want to point to *a major obstacle to the maximisation of productivity, i.e. the capitalist profit logic*. As long as all means of production, as well as the not-producing land units, are in private ownership, they will only be exploited if profitable. The consequence will be as follows:

Highest labour productivity (production of the possibly largest amount of use values) will never coincide with entrepreneurial profitability – never in a capitalist agriculture, accidentally in industry. In a capitalist mode of production, profitability is the only dominant factor. Hence, the consequence is that workers are jobless because means of production are standing idle, while workers are nonetheless available. In European countries with a high performing agriculture, large areas are encompassing fallow lands that could easily be fertilised by applying appropriate methods, by using waterpower and other unexploited natural resources. The profit logic, however, prevents their exploit-

---

19   Marx 1954, p. 519.

ation. In capitalist agriculture, productivity remains below its highest level, because of a diminishing return on additional capital invested in land exploitation; hence, production increases stop if newly invested capital is not reaching the average rate of profit. These basic facts of the capitalist mode of production cannot be altered by taking political-economic measures within a capitalist mode of production.

Within capitalism, labour rationalisation is necessarily very low. Millions of workers have still not acquired the lowest level of cultural development, i.e. literacy. An artificially fostered conservative mood among the toiling masses necessary for preserving class hegemony is hampering the development of labour rationalisation. Some 60 to 80 percent of arable land is owned by an uneducated, conservative peasantry refusing any kind of rational innovation by tenaciously defending their inherited conservatism. In contrast to the capitalist class, profitability is not even of decisive importance to these millions of landowning peasants. They only produce as much as necessary in order to cover the traditional needs of their slowly rising living standard. And nourishment of the population depends on such economic leaders!

Conservatism and the lack of rationalisation are also strongly influencing industrial production. Industrial standards were kept for many decades, even when they were already outdated because of changing technology. As far as he could obtain a substantial profit, the capitalist kept on producing in his traditional, irrational way.[20]

In a capitalist mode of production, labour productivity remains far beneath its theoretically attainable maximum level. First of all, the profit logic is, however, exerting its influence here. Improved means of production, the growth of the share of constant capital, and within that context the share of fixed capital, constitute an immanent tendency of a capitalism still based on free competition. But the volume of productive new investments also depends on the total amount of privately accumulated capital. From the point of view of profitability, however, not the possibility of increasing production but that of saving human labour constitutes the only determining factor for having any new technical discovery practically applied. *The more the working class of a particular country is enslaved, the less the capitalist class needs incentives to increase productivity.*

Productivity is low because millions of workers are working in small shops using primitive tools. The personal effort of the owner, who is exploiting himself, his family and one or two workers receiving a low salary according to the

---

20   Very interesting examples can be found in Friedrich Otto Herz [1918].

value of their labour power, ensures that these kinds of backward enterprises vegetate to the disadvantage of total labour productivity.

At the present stage of 'organised capitalism', free competition has disappeared in most sectors of big industry. Cartels and trusts replaced them. While the American trusts increased their labour productivity and profitability by crowding out badly organised and unfavourably located enterprises, loosely organised cartels were pursuing an opposite policy. All existing enterprises were kept producing and selling-prices were kept high in markets protected by tariffs, so that even enterprises producing at the highest costs were making a profit. *Backward enterprises, that would otherwise have gone bankrupt because of free competition, were from that moment on kept artificially afloat.* Many cartels even prevented the constitution of modern enterprises. In a cartel agreement concluded between Austrian and Hungarian iron works and iron manufacturing industries, a stipulation forbade selling any raw materials to newly established iron manufacturing enterprises not belonging to the cartel. Establishing new, more modern enterprises was now becoming impossible.

Finally, labour productivity is kept low by a multiple anarchy of production. Anarchy ensures that the most diverse goods are produced for the same purpose, serving either the buyer's caprice or producer's arbitrariness. Organised capitalism even tries to limit anarchy of production by introducing standardised models, by normalisation of components (for instance in the machine-building industry), by far-reaching specialisation of individual works, but all this fails because of the contradictory interests of the individual enterprises.

Anarchy in the total process of capital appears *in periodically returning commercial crises*. In capitalism, no regulatory forum is deciding on production in relation to priority needs. A capitalist is producing those goods he expects to sell at the highest profit. The market price is the production regulator. However, output of many goods periodically exceeds consumers' purchasing power, large quantities of goods remain unsold and are wasted,[21] or they have to be sold for a price lower than their value, the production process is halted, the workers are

---

[21] To what kind of squandering anarchy this can lead if compared to a better organised production, is proved by a statement of Mr. C.A. McCurdy, K.C., M.P., Parliamentary Secretary to the Food Controller, speaking at Histon, during a political meeting. 'Take the question of coal. Coal is the principal source of England's wealth. Every year we use in this country 80,000,000 tons of coal for motive power. Man for man, we use in industry half as much coal again as they do in America, but we do it so wastefully, so badly, that one ton of coal used to assist the worker in the United States gives him 50 per cent. more help, more motive power, than one-and-a-half tons used to assist the British worker'. *The Times*, 10 October 1919, p. 7. One can imagine that one is spilling coal in the backward enterprises of the European continent.

laid off. Means of production and workers remain idle. Labour productivity is falling to a lower level. Increased organisation of capital is altering the character of the crisis and putting the latter's burden entirely on the shoulders of the working classes. In the era of 'free capitalism', the market could easily get rid of unsaleable, superfluous goods by lowering their price to a level reflecting their value, but on the sole condition that only a 'socially necessary quantity' would be produced. Important price falls, huge losses, crashes and fraudulent bankruptcies occurred. An equilibrium was mostly attained at the detriment to the capitalists. Unemployment lasted only for a short period of time.

In the epoch of finance capital, cartels and trusts, overproduction cannot increase to the same extent as in free capitalism, because there exists a better knowledge of the situation on the world market. If there is overproduction, surplus goods are not liquidated by lowering prices. Cartels keeping prices high reduce production or adapt output to demand. A crash will be prevented and fraudulent bankruptcies will become exceptional and insignificant. *Capitalists will only lose their possible profits. On the other hand, an expanding, long-lasting unemployment combined with an unchanged high price level will put the burden on the working class.* This is a new, 'creeping' form of crisis that is affecting labour productivity much more seriously than the short-lived, acute crises of free capitalism.

Much more underestimated for labour productivity are the harmful consequences due to anarchy reigning within the field of career choices. In capitalism, parents' class position determines the careers and professions that are chosen. Sons of the ruling class have to study; at any price, they must go to a secondary school. A child of poor parents, even if a genius like Newton or Leibniz, will never accede to the higher classes of the secondary school, and, of course, he will not enter university. He will become an apprentice, or he will work in the fields or in the factory. The top of the cultural elite, the technicians, the inventors and organisers do not form more than ten percent of the young generation. The talents of the other 90 percent are wasted; during their lifetime they are exercising a job whose productivity only represents a small part of their potential capacities.

Within the actual circumstances, no planned vocational training is available to the toiling population. Whether the son of a proletarian becomes an agricultural labourer, a cabinet-maker, an ironworker or somebody else is only decided by chance. His physical and psychological capacities are not considered. Hence, many people, who otherwise would have achieved very well in some trade, will be ruined by their wrong vocational choice. But also in the same trade some workers may well and easily fulfil other tasks which other workers with the same skills cannot fulfil. It is the merit of Taylor's School of 'Scientific Management' for having done research on this topic. There are workers who are unfit for exercising continually monotonous tasks, while, on the other hand, they may excellently perform a job requiring skill for adapting to often changing situations. There are jobs demanding the exercise of a continual, evenly physical effort, and jobs alternating periods of utmost physical efforts with dull moments. Enumerating all these different types of work fitting the best with the psychological and physical types of workers would lead us much too far. We only want to assert here that anarchy in vocational choice and the division of labour is to the detriment of labour productivity.

Notwithstanding management control in the mechanised big enterprises exists, in capitalism labour intensity remains far beneath its theoretical level. Workers are especially missing a real interest in the production process itself:

> When this example [i.e. of the Irish] is considered in connexion with the unremitted labour of the whole population engaged in the various branches of the cotton manufacture, our wonder will be less excited by their fatal demoralization. Prolonged and exhausting labour, continued from day to day, and from year to year, is not calculated to develop the intellectual or moral faculties of man. The dull routine of a ceaseless drudgery, in which the same mechanical process is incessantly repeated, resembles the torment of Sisyphus – the toil, like the rock, recoils perpetually on the wearied operative. The mind gathers neither stores nor strength from the constant extension and retraction of the same muscles. The intellect slumbers in supine inertness; but the grosser parts of our nature attain a rank development. To condemn man to such severity of toil is, in some measure, to cultivate in him the habits of an animal. He becomes reckless. He disregards the distinguishing appetites and habits of his species. He neglects the comforts and delicacies of life. He lives in squalid wretchedness, on meagre food, and expounds his superfluous gains in debauchery.

This is how Engels[22] characterised modern industrial labour in *The Conditions of the Working Class in England.*[23] Because of the division of labour, a worker's interest in his job, his joy at work are disappearing. Being used to fulfil partial tasks, he does not even know the purpose of his work's product. Paid on an hourly base, he has the slightest interest in productivity. His labour intensity

---

22 [However, it was not Engels, but Dr. James Phillips Kay-Shuttleworth (1804–77) who was the author of this quote taken from *The Conditions of the Working Class*].
23 Engels 1977, pp. 295–6.

would only increase the profit of the capitalists. In the same way, he has no interest in saving raw materials and natural resources or in carefully handling his tools. The working-class man is groaning under the eternal strain of his overseers. Only his fear of being laid off in the case of a below-average productivity will guarantee a certain labour productivity. Contract-wages or piece-wages are not altering the heart of the matter. The capitalists will diminish basic wages as soon as weekly earnings of the workers of a particular capitalist exceed a certain rate of labour productivity. The workers know this and anticipate reductions in their contract-wages: they decide themselves that no worker should produce more units than convened with the capitalist for their weekly pay. Notwithstanding contract-wages there exists a systematic limitation of labour intensity and, subsequently, of labour productivity! Only Taylor's system, i.e. the last response of highly developed American capitalism, has tried to realise the highest profit rate and to obtain a very high rate of productivity by imposing its system of labour intensity, but at the price of pumping out all human energy, a situation a man's health cannot sustain for a longer period of time. At this moment the application of scientific management is so insignificant that we do not have to change our judgement with regard to labour's low degree of intensity and productivity. In the words of Marx: 'The labour time socially necessary is that required to produce an article under the normal conditions of production, and with the average degree of skill and intensity prevalent at the time'.[24]

In capitalism, the rate of productive and unproductive members of society is necessarily unfavourable. Child mortality is enormous due to extreme poverty and ignorance of the populace. As the children of poor people undertake hard labour at an early age, the workers die at a young age or they become early disabled workers. In capitalism the population as a whole disposes of fewer working-age people fit to work than there would be under a rationalised regime of human resources management. Many working-age people fit to work are not in the labour force, *because they are also enabled to make their living without working*. Real estate owners, house owners, rentiers of all sorts are consuming surplus value without doing any kind of work. All women of the wealthy classes, who are not allowed to have a productive occupation, belong to this category. Whilst in Europe 60 percent of the total male population is employed, this percentage is only 25 percent for women.[25] But in capitalism millions of the 'employed' people also do work which appears to be useless, unproductive, i.e.

---

24 Marx 1954, p. 39.
25 Philippovich 1980, 1, p. 83.

all those people whose income is representing the *faux frais* of capitalism, such as: all people employed in bodies 'guarding property rights' (guards, policemen, judges, lawyers, civil servants, etc.), the whole military and all those workers producing all sorts of military goods, all those superfluous agents of the circulation sphere of capital (salesmen, commercial agents, bank employees, etc.), and furthermore all servants and domestic personnel, insofar as they are not productively occupied in a secondary job. From detailed occupational statistics, one can approximately establish that a large amount of the employed are contributing nothing to the enhancement of labour productivity.

Hence, we see that capitalism is working by squandering an incredible part of human labour power. The nonworking rich, women of the better-off, a fair part of the unproductively employed, all people having become chronically sick at an early age because of under-nourishment and the victims of innumerable work accidents shortening life expectancy of the working class, and, finally, all victims of imperialist wars: *hence, the outcome is that capitalism is only employing about a half of all workers fit to work really productively who would otherwise have been employable in a rationally organised society.*

∴

We shall now study all distinct factors of labour productivity considered from a political point of view when the means of production are not in private hands, but instead belong to the community that is planning production and distributing its output to the workers according to fixed regulations excluding any kind of workless income. We are thus not talking about a situation of full communism in which everybody is working according to his needs. An economy based on such a system can only exist on condition that the selfish-greedy state of mind, formed by a system of private property during thousands of years, has disappeared. About this we cannot forecast. History is showing us how tenacious are the ideological remains; they are lasting in the minds for a long time after the revolution has shaken the material infrastructures. 'The tradition of all the dead generations weighs like a nightmare on the brain of the living', said Marx.[26] *We are therefore researching labour productivity during the transition period from capitalism to communism. This period will be politically characterised by the dictatorship of the proletariat, but economically by the actual situation that the means of production are already for the main part socialised, but utilised by a generation of workers still living in a selfish-greedy state of mind determined*

---

26 Marx 1979, p. 103.

by capitalism. In this chapter, our research will be *purely theoretical*. In the next chapter, we shall reveal *sine ira et studio*[27] all difficulties the praxis of the Russian and Hungarian experiences has taught us.

∴

Rationalisation of labour is rapidly increasing together with the upgrading of the intellectual level of the toiling masses. A proletarian dictatorship will start with an absolute *prohibition of alcohol*: it immediately expands the schooling system with its primary education as well as its education system for children, juveniles and adults; it transforms its purely theoretical education system into an active education system dispensing at the same time physical training and the basic knowledge of sciences; it replaces the conservative ideology based on an authoritarian belief system by a free, rational view on the world. Even authors absolutely hostile to Bolshevism recognised the great accomplishments of its cultural policy. The cultural level of the working population was very rapidly enhanced and the base for an increased rationalisation of production and labour productivity was laid, although in the beginning management rationalisation was negatively influenced by aloofness or sabotage committed by the best bourgeois technicians. At any rate, a rapid dissemination of technical and technological know-how among the workers curtailed the former technicians' monopoly in a very short space of time.

Productivity of labour can better be enhanced after the disappearance of the profit logic of capitalism. The introduction of technical innovations and the establishment of new factories are at least no longer connected to the average profit rate. Increasing labour productivity and diminishing labour costs will suffice.

> The use of machinery for the exclusive purpose of cheapening the product, is limited in this way, that less labour must be expended in producing the machinery than is displaced by the employment of that machinery, For the capitalist, however, this use is still more limited. Instead of paying for the labour, he only pays the value of the labour-power employed; ... Hence the invention now-a-days of machines in England that are employed only in North America; just as in the sixteenth and seventeenth centuries, machines were invented in Germany to be used only in Holland ...[28]

---

27   ['Without hate and zealousness'].
28   [Marx 1954, pp. 392–3].

Although in the beginning technical innovation had to face important problems, a reconstruction of the economy can nonetheless immediately be planned, in particular by concentrating industrial production into the biggest and best equipped and located enterprises.

Kautsky pretends that:[29] In 1907 about a million workers were occupied in Germany's textile industry and that 368,000 of them were working in enterprises employing more than 200 workers. Concentrating all workers into these big enterprises and running all machines there would mean that all workers should work in three shifts. In order to avoid night work, Kautsky proposes five-hourly shifts! Notwithstanding a five-hour working-day, total output of that number of workers would – according to Kautsky – double if compared to the output of the former small enterprises with their ten-hour working day. It can be left out of consideration whether Kautsky's assumption, or the very interesting calculations made by Ballod in his book *Zukunftstaat*,[30] were right or wrong. We also know from experience that concentration of the whole production into big enterprises will meet important difficulties. But we surely know that a planned economy and a thoroughgoing concentration of production can only be organised under the dictatorship of the proletariat.

In the meantime, *one can begin by abolishing anarchy in production.* Instead of producing a great variety of goods, one will only manufacture normalised and standardised products. No private interests are now hindering the most far-reaching production specialisation of the enterprises. Patents and production secrecies are no longer at the service of profit-seeking activities hampering productivity increases. Crises will gradually soften now that one is no longer disorderly producing for the market, but is adapting production to the needs of the population. During the dictatorship of the proletariat it would hardly be possible that goods would not be sold now that only solvent buyers will be left due to the newly established income distribution! There will be no overproduction anymore; only underproduction is possible!

Anarchy in vocational training and labour exchange will progressively be suppressed. Managers and cultural elites will be selected among all children, not only among that small minority of bourgeois children. Vocational selection should not be a matter of chance: specialists deciding on scientific criteria will decide which profession and which kind of work will be best suited to somebody. All these measures will foster an increase of labour productivity.

---

29   Kautsky 1907, p. 87.
30   Ballod 1919.

Intensity of labour will decrease during the beginning of the dictatorship of the proletariat, but the capitalist countries will later largely be surpassed. However, in the interest of productivity growth the most extreme forms of specialisation and division of labour, i.e. monotonous form of work should be maintained. On the other hand, labour intensity will increase by a shortening of the working day, by a hygienic-aesthetic rearrangement of the workplace, by the awareness that one is working for the commonwealth, thus also for oneself, thus not for an exploiting capitalist. Workers' self-management in the factory supervising the whole production process, the possibility of getting a different job due to a wide variety of vocational programmes, will soften the soul-killing monotony of the division of labour in the production processes of the big industrial enterprises. However, we do not deny that all these measures will only enact their full effect after a certain period of time. During an early period of transition, maintaining the contract-wage system and the Taylor system adapted to these circumstances will be absolutely necessary as long as the selfish-greedy ideology will be dominant.

An increase in the rate of productive workers will be of extraordinary importance. Expropriation of the sources of non-labour income will incite [the rich] to dismiss their personal servants immediately: force the rentiers to get a job! Systematically forced labour will do the rest. Organisation of the economy will diminish the number of unproductive workers and capitalism's *faux frais* will disappear. After having won the revolutionary liberation war, the mass of people active in the military sector will be freed for doing productive work. The transformation of commerce into a state-owned distribution system and the centralisation of the banking system will also lead to the freeing of a large mass of workers. We must admit that *they will only constitute a potential labour force: the principle of organising forced labour and transforming everybody fit to work into a productive worker will be one of the most difficult tasks of the dictatorship.*

Theoretically there is no doubt that the communist mode of production is largely superior. Later we will discuss all practical difficulties arising during the transition period. We are repeating it: *all these difficulties are due to the basic fact that all means of production had not been expropriated at once and that a generation of workers having been corrupted by a capitalist ideology and educated in a selfish-greedy ideology, had become the owners of the means of production.* The ideological superstructure can only follow with some delay the revolution occurring in the material infrastructure.

3   The Falling Living Standard of the Industrial Proletariat during the Beginning of the Dictatorship

We discovered that the central problem of the actual world crisis of capitalism is the contradiction between, on the one hand, the demands of the workers for a real increase of their living standard, and, on the other, the economic impossibility to meet these demands within a capitalist system. We have already indicated that – purely theoretically – communist production is much more productive than the capitalist one and that this can guarantee a higher living standard.[31] However, we must add, especially with regard to the industrial proletariat, i.e. the vanguard of the revolution, that in the beginning of the dictatorship – however, this may also happen later – a decrease in the living standard of the urban proletariat will be inevitable.

This assertion seems to be in contradiction with the fact that the dictatorship begins with the expropriation of the privately owned means of production, with the confiscation of milliards of idle income. Hence, one could assume that by then a significant increase in the living standard of the proletariat would be possible.

This will be, however, not the case. Again, we must refer to the fact that Quesnay and then Marx have thoroughly treated this subject,[32] i.e. that consumption of the capitalist class in its natural form consists of such a kind of goods which do not belong to the consumption pattern of the workers and we argue that [these goods] are also not fit for consumption during the dictatorship for they are not contributing to a rising living standard of the working masses. Under harsh coercion the proletarians can be billeted in the palaces of the rich. But this will only be a drop in the ocean. However, other goods, such as luxury cloths, jewels and servants, horses and hounds, automobiles and yachts, etc. etc., on which the ruling classes are spending milliards of their yearly income, are useless in their natural form for mass consumption by the proletariat. *In order to increase its living standard the proletariat needs first of all foodstuffs*,[33] then some *industrial goods of mass consumption*, i.e. furniture, clothes, bedding goods, fuel. The stock of the *latter* goods destined to

---

31   Marx 1957, pp. 351–523.
32   Marx summarises this in his *Theories of Surplus-Value*. Marx 1969.
33   It is a matter of evidence that an increase of the lower income categories will lead to a sharp increase in food consumption, while at the same moment the percentage of income spent on nourishment decreases. Here is one of these many examples. The German survey of the year 1907, *Erhebungen von Wirtschaftsrechnungen minderbemittelter Familien im Deutschen Reich*, gives these figures:

the working class will not grow by expropriating the means of production, by confiscating labourless incomes. Even if one radically expropriates the means of production of the bourgeoisie, the latter will still dispose of cash money, jewels, clothes, bedding goods, furniture. That will be enough for years of living in luxury. Restriction of consuming luxury goods by the ruling class does not lead to an increase of consumption goods for the proletariat.

However, during the first period of the dictatorship there is no possibility of increasing the production of these goods as well. We already argued in Chapter 1 that in capitalism production is adapted to the patterns of its income distribution. 'Demand' decides the kind of goods that will be produced for which kind of profits. And one will not only produce for market demands of wealthy people – from glittering clothes for demimondaine women or embroidery for holy altars – *the whole production apparatus will be organised in function of all 'marketable' goods*. This does not mean that expropriation of the expropriators would not lead to a momentary surplus of consumption goods for the proletarians: the existing means of production cannot be used without some adjustment for the production of these consumption goods specifically destined to the working classes in order to increase their living standard. *This will require a reconversion of the production apparatus and a retraining of the workers of the luxury industry for the production of goods of mass consumption before a productivity increase in the sector of these consumption goods can be realised.* Meanwhile, under the dictatorship of the proletariat, thoroughgoing changes in the distribution of the available and currently produced foodstuffs were occurring, which led to an unavertable worsening of the living standard of the urban proletariat. For a better understanding of this we have to dwell extensively on these questions.

In peacetime the cities of all European countries, also those in the so-called poor agrarian countries of East and Central Europe, had always been well

Income in marks	Average income in marks	Food expenditures in marks	Percentages
Minus 1,200	1,074	582.10	54.2
1,200–1,600	1,437	784.60	54.6
1,600–2,000	1,802	919.20	51.0
2,000–2,500	2,213	1,062.24	48.1
2,500–3,000	2,714	1,151.68	42.7
3,000–4,000	3,386	1,280.06	38.1
4,000–5,000	4,333	1,421.22	32.8

provided with foodstuffs. It would have been unimaginable that somebody could not buy food with his money. However, that does not mean that everybody could sufficiently eat; in those days people without income had to starve. But any money income could then have been exchanged for foodstuffs.

How did the city get the foodstuffs from the countryside? Of course, *formally* by paying with money, the general equivalent. *Materially* by using diverse sources and even partly by exchanging urban goods, industrial products the city delivered to the countryside, partly by *embodiment of labourless income: ground rent of the big landowners, taxes and interests of the farmers*. The big landowners were spending their ground rent in the cities, they sold their foodstuffs embodying their ground rent at the markets of the cities! Peasants also brought foodstuffs to the urban markets without receiving a material compensation, because they paid taxes of all kind from their yield. Yes, these countries could not only feed their cities, *but they had a large quantity of foodstuffs in stock for export to the western countries too.*

Feeding the cities and foodstuff export were only possible because the consumption of agricultural servants, of millions of unskilled workers, *was exceptionally low*. Average consumption of bread, meat, sugar by the Hungarian people remained notably below the average level of the German, French or English population. What could have been the consumption of the Hungarian agricultural worker considering the fact that – according to official statistics – his yearly salary for the year 1913 was less than 400 korunas? But also the nourishment of the independent small peasants was rather poor: although there was no shortage of bread, they usually had only meat on Sundays. Exports of foodstuffs and a sufficient feeding of the cities were only possible by undernourishing the toiling agricultural population. This happened not only in Hungary, but also in Russia and Rumania.

The balance between income distribution and nourishment was disturbed by the war. Inflation had disequilibrated the income balance at the advantage of the producers and to the detriment of the wage earners. The urban population could now afford fewer foodstuffs because wage increases did not keep up with inflation. On the other hand, the nominal value of taxes, interests and rents the agrarian producers were paying remained the same. For former Hungary [before 1919] we estimate these three items at about a half a milliard korunas a year, here calculated on a pre-war price basis of 25 korunas per hundredweight for 20 millions of hundredweights of wheat. (Food mainly consists of wheat). At a war-time wheat price of 60 to 80 korunas, farmers could meet the obligations the village had contracted with the city by selling only six to nine millions of hundredweights of wheat. An individual peasant had to contribute a smaller part of his harvest for paying his taxes, interests and eventually rents to the city. Income distribution changed to the advantage of the villages, i.e. agriculture. The peasant could easily pay off his debts while the city could not acquire foodstuffs in exchange for its ground rent.

The peasantry's standard of living has increased. This increase appeared first as an improvement of the nourishment situation of the rural population. A Hungarian peasant once described it in a very colourful way: 'In those days I took the geese to the market and I ate potatoes; nowadays I sell the potatoes and I eat the geese'. Again and again the city got fewer and fewer foodstuffs of ever decreasing quality from the peasants. But the city was also unable to deliver real goods in exchange. The function of money – having played until then only a mediating role between city and countryside – was now changing. Traditionally, the city used money as a *legally established means of payment* in the villages. But the cash money now circulating could not be used for acquiring real goods. The peasant accepted this situation for a while: he wanted to keep this money as *treasure* in an old sock. Finally he got fed up with collecting golden and silver coins and blue-coloured banknotes. His rising living standard took a dangerous form: *the farmer was working less, producing less and exchanging his food stocks only for real goods*. Money, that hot-desired general embodiment of social wealth, ceased to be a general means of payment in Hungary, as well as in Germany, Austria and Russia.

Hence, the peasantry was delivering smaller and smaller quantities of foodstuffs. Foodstuff surpluses arriving in peacetime in the cities as an embodiment of the big landowners' ground rent disappeared during the Károlyi Revolution[34] and even more radically during the dictatorship of the proletariat. Wages of agricultural servants and labourers (reapers, seasonal workers) were increasing very fast. And these increases were real, because wages were paid not in devalued cash money, but in physical goods. Payments in kind, i.e. in grain, bacon, milk, doubled. Reapers, earning a one-tenth share of the harvest before the war, were now earning a one-seventh share during the dictatorship of the proletariat. *The winners of the Károlyi Revolution and the dictatorship of the proletariat were the agricultural labourers and the village poor whose standard of living, i.e. mainly their nourishment, improved considerably.* A part of the agricultural labourers had very well grasped the essence of the dictatorship: the rural regiments of the Red Army courageously resisted until the bitter end. Unfortunately educational work carried out during the four-and-a-half months of the

---

34 [Károlyi Revolution: the bourgeois revolution or 'Aster Revolution' of October 1918. Count Mihály Károlyi became Prime Minister of a coalition government uniting the progressive wing of the Independence Party, the Radical Citizens Party and the Hungarian Social-Democratic Workers' Party].

dictatorship was insufficient to awake hundreds of thousands of agricultural labourers from their millennial lethargy in order to activate them politically.

A generous increase in the living standard of the agricultural labourers – to be realised during any proletarian dictatorship – means in reality the suppression of ground rent for the socialised large estates. Compared with the period when the agricultural proletariat was starving, a much smaller part of all foodstuffs produced on the large estates was now arriving in the cities and could thus be used for the nourishment of the urban proletariat. This happened because in the past the landowner did not consume his ground rent himself, but sold it in kind in the city where he exchanged it for industrial products, i.e. luxury goods.

Notwithstanding the appropriation of the idle incomes of the ruling classes, the dictatorship of the proletariat cannot increase the real living standard of the industrial proletariat, because a necessary foodstuff surplus is lacking. Apart from the already mentioned economic factors, the political preconditions are also absent. Hence, the peasants refused to deliver foodstuffs to the workers.

Having established the dictatorship – at least in the eastern countries of Europe where payment in kind of the agricultural proletariat is usual – the proletariat could possibly improve its nourishment during the first years of the dictatorship, but soon a worsening of that situation had become inevitable, because the rising living standard of the agricultural proletariat had laid a claim on a significant part of the foodstuffs once delivered to the cities. Yes, even in countries like England, where wages in cash are usual, it is probable that the agricultural proletariat living and working on the farm gets its increased income paid in the form of a foodstuff surplus, so that there is less left to the industrial proletariat. For those countries constantly relying on food imports, the problem is even harsher. We shall discuss this more in a chapter on international trade.

Without a thoroughgoing reform of the production system, the other demands of *the industrial proletariat cannot be met*. Housing shortages can only partly be solved by occupying bourgeois houses and by using superfluous commercial buildings; this is a fact proven by similar actions by the housing agencies in Budapest and in the provincial towns. We had the same experiences with the distribution of furniture. There was an enormous demand of mass-manufactured furniture due to rising incomes. But the existing production capacity, previously adjusted to a capitalist mode of income distribution, was temporarily unable to respond to these new demands.

We now arrive at the item *that the dictatorship of the proletariat can only provide for the time being a moral and cultural (theatre, music, libraries, bath houses, etc.) improvement of the living standard to the standard bearers of the new society, i.e. the industrial proletariat. With regard to material goods, a further fall of the living standard will nonetheless be inevitable.* One must say that openly and frankly to the elite of the industrial working class. This will absolutely not hinder a further strengthening of the proletarian rule. This is proven by the example of Russia where, notwithstanding the most gruesome hardships, a class-conscious industrial proletariat is clinging to the dictatorship. On the other hand, one should stress that the industrial population of Hungary was absolutely and relatively better nourished during the dictatorship of the proletariat than today under the dictatorship of the bourgeoisie. *The proletariat is now starving, while the bourgeoisie is freely guzzling and carousing.* During the dictatorship of the proletariat, the state's food provision aimed mainly at enhancing the proletariat's wellness; the guiding principle was that the toiling proletarians were allowed 'class rations' providing them with additional foodstuffs.

The contradictions between the political domination of the proletariat and the inevitable decline of production due to a new income distribution should be solved by *abolishing any luxury production and by increasing the large-scale production of goods for mass consumption, mainly financed by the agricultural surplus*. Expropriation of the means of production and elimination of profiteering constituted the sole investment guidelines underpinning this project theoretically.

A larger section of the workers employed in the production of articles of consumption which enter into revenue in general, will produce articles of consumption that are consumed by – are exchanged against the revenue of – capitalists, landlords and their retainers (state, church etc.), [and a smaller] section [will produce] articles destined for the revenue of the workers. But this again is effect, not cause. A change in the social relation of workers and capitalists, a revolution in the conditions governing capitalist production, would change this at once. The revenue would be 'realised in different commodities', to use an expression of Ricardo's. There is nothing in the, so-to-speak, physical conditions of production which forces the above to take place. The workmen, if they were dominant, if they were allowed to produce for themselves, would very soon, and without great exertion, bring the capital (to use a phrase of the vulgar economists) up to the standard of their needs. The very great difference is whether the available means of production confront the workers as capital and can therefore be employed by them *only* in so far as it is necessary for the increased production of surplus value and surplus produce for their employers, in other words whether the means of production employ *the workers*, or whether the workers, as subjects, employ the means of production – in the accusative case – in order to produce wealth for themselves. It is of course assumed here that capitalist production has already developed the productive forces of labour in general to a sufficiently high level for this revolution to take place.[35]

Here Marx clearly confronts the economic policy of capital with the policy of a proletarian government. By expropriating the means of production, the proletarian government can really increase the living standard of the toiling masses. However, this aim cannot be achieved 'immediately'. Even not – and this is quite understandable – if the proletariat has acquired from the bourgeoisie a completely intact production system together with its usual stocks of goods. The basic condition for increasing the living standard is an increase of agricultural production; but such an increase is also preconditioned by yearly growth periods and by the fact that many crops require growth periods lasting for several years. In order to meet the growing quantities of consumption goods demanded by the proletariat, new big production units and plants have to be built. Reconversion can 'immediately' be carried out, *but in most cases their results will only be seen after a period of several years*.

The Russian and Hungarian proletariat did not, however, acquire an intact production apparatus, but a crumbling one having been exhausted during the war. Marx himself stated in the pages already cited: 'It is of course assumed here that capitalist production has already developed the productive forces of labour in general to a sufficiently high level for this revolution to take place'.[36]

The production apparatus inherited by the Russian and Hungarian proletariat had nonetheless reached a sufficiently high degree of development that the proletarian revolution could be possibly successful. Although there already existed many small firms, big enterprises and concentration of production facilities were available; Kautsky was already right when arguing that the ripening of the social revolution cannot be measured by the size of the remnants of the old mode of production, but by the presence of big enterprises, those bearers of the coming mode of production. It is a matter of fact that advantageous preconditions were already present: masses of workers, technicians, managers.

---

35 [Here Varga quotes Karl Marx, *Theorien über den Mehrwert. Aus dem nachgelassenen Manuskript 'Zur Kritik der politischen Ökonomie' von Karl Marx*, edited by Karl Kautsky, Zweiter Band, *David Ricardo*, Zweiter Teil, Stuttgart: Verlag von J.H.W. Dietz Nachf., 1910, p. 376. Marx's texts edited by Kautsky differ from the texts published in the *Marx-Engels Werke*, Volume 26, Part 2, Berlin: Dietz Verlag, 1974, p. 583].

36 Ibid.

On the other hand, reconversion and development of production necessary for increasing the living standard were seriously hampered by the circumstances that neither the Russian nor the Hungarian proletariat had taken over an intact, but a ruined, worn-out, half-destroyed production apparatus which had to be restored before production could be continued on its old footing.

The dictatorship of the proletariat did not occur where and when the material preconditions for a new society had already developed within the womb of the old society. The repressive organisations of the ruling classes had largely been weakened as a result of a military defeat. That defeat on the battlefields was, however, previously engendered by decaying material and human resources and their inadequacy to continue the war. Finally, neither the Russian nor the Hungarian proletariat spent all their efforts to have the production system restructured because they were defending in the first place their political regime against the imperialists invading their country from outside and against the domestic counterrevolutionaries supported with foreign money and weapons.

Summarising one may conclude that the proletariat conquers political power in order to increase its living standard. This can be immediately realised for the agricultural proletariat; but, on the other hand, this will be impossible for the elite of the revolution, i.e. the industrial proletariat. The living standard of the proletariat can temporarily rise by plundering the economy, by slaughtering cattle, but this increase has no permanent effects. The inner contradiction is that the proletariat can only take power when the repressive power of the ruling class is unsettled. However, this is usually preceded by such a serious disorganisation of the means of production that a real increase in the living standard of the industrial proletariat will be impossible. One should repeatedly and with emphasis say this to the proletarians so that they cannot later blame, as occurred in Hungary, the dictatorship for not keeping its initial promise of a better provision with consumption goods.

Finally, we also want to mention that wages increases paid to the proletariat in paper money without gold coverage will be unfit to deal with the provision problem. During the war, currencies of all the countries have become paper moneys without gold coverage. Adjustment of the total nominal value of the circulating money to the value of the circulating goods did not occur anymore.[37] Real money – gold or banknotes with or without gold coverage, that is all the like, destined to private persons for paying for real goods transactions

---

37 Quantity of circulating money = Sum of prices of goods: sum of coins in circulation. See Marx 1954.

only – will flow back to the emission bank after the transaction has been concluded or, if the money is no longer needed, it will be hoarded by individual businessmen in the form of a real treasure. We say *real* because money may always be used for purchasing goods; hence, this money can be transformed into real capital.

The mass of circulating paper money formally covering state expenditures cannot be adapted to the changes having occurred in the total value of the goods' circulation. On the contrary, the prices of goods increase proportionally – in case of free competition – with the growth of the total face value of the paper money in circulation.[38] Unlimited competition will disappear under the dictatorship of the proletariat. Consumption of the most important consumer goods is then regulated. Notwithstanding their high wages, the industrial working class cannot really increase its standard of living; the only consequence of high nominal wages is that this money will be accumulated at the workers' home as a worthless treasure, i.e. a treasure which is not convertible into goods, or that it will lead to incredible price increases of the not rationed goods and consumer goods traded by intermediaries. High nominal wages are thus only important to the proletariat so long as the latter can buy foodstuffs in competition with the bourgeoisie on the black market during an initial period of persisting anarchy. The living standard of the proletariat can thus only be increased after having previously developed the new proletarian production process. The consequence of all this is: *each conscious proletarian must not only struggle for the realisation of socialism, but also endure a period of hardship.*

Because of a lack of revolutionary schooling and the inexistence of an organised communist party, the Hungarian workers were not willing to endure any hardship for their regime and for their socialist future. They wanted an immediate rise in their living standard and as this could not possibly be realised, they turned their backs on the ideal of proletarian hegemony. Counterrevolutionaries of all sorts could exploit the proletariat's discontent and that was one of the main reasons why the Rumanian attack[39] could be successful.

---

38   Hilferding 1910, p. 50.
39   [The Rumanian troops attacked at the end of July 1919 and marched on Budapest. On 3 August 1919 they entered Budapest].

4 Expropriating the Expropriators

The armed political force makes the expropriation of the expropriators possible. The biggest problem, i.e. resistance by the class state with its armed class power, is then liquidated. Meanwhile, serious problems would arise with regard to its practical realisation.

Firstly, one had to decide *what* is to be expropriated: the whole business group or individual factories or the means of production in their natural form? If the whole *business group* has to be expropriated, all plants with their claims and debts will be taken over as a going concern. If individual plants are to be expropriated, the previously existing unity will be broken up, claims and debts will or can nonetheless be taken over. If the means of production are expropriated in their natural form, i.e. machinery, buildings, raw materials and stocks of finished goods, claims and debts will also disappear. The latter solution is, however, the most radical measure reflecting the essence of the proletarian dictatorship. In Hungary – we think also in Russia – the first solution was chosen. In Hungary, two moments were decisive: firstly, the problem of foreign capital (we will later return to this topic); secondly, the problem of small trades remaining in private hands. Simply annulling the debts of peasants, small tradesmen and artisans by *expropriating them as such* appeared to be impossible. Maybe that by this measure the debts of these expropriated enterprises could have been cancelled, but, because the sum to be used for private consumption was limited to 200 korunas a month, the *provisionally* recognised debts were in general not compensated by maintaining the claims on the not expropriated owners.

Then the question was raised of how to carry out the expropriation technically.

First of all, the enterprises should be owned by *all workers*. Hence, one should *prevent the working classes from considering the means of production their own private property*, or from stealing them as often occurred with cattle and agricultural implements at the large agricultural estates in Russia. Secondly, one should guarantee that continuity of production will not be interrupted when the former bourgeois managers and the owners had lost command of their means of production. In Hungary one succeeded in both projects. Property of enterprises was not stolen on a large scale.[40] And continuity of production was hardly interrupted after the proclamation of the dictatorship of

---

40 Occasionally it happened that tailors made clothes for themselves by using textiles in stock at a low price, but cases of direct stealing were reported hardly anywhere.

the proletariat. The Hungarian Councils' government, showing the world that the dictatorship did not mean the ruin of the economy, tried to prevent any interruption of the production process, often by damaging its political goals ...

In order to bring the enterprises from capitalist to proletarian management, new proletarian organisations had to be set up: the *enterprise councils* and *production commissars*. Before discussing this topic, we must answer often raised question about the capacity of the proletariat to manage the production process.

The Communists disagree with the Social Democrats on the tasks of the proletariat in our present lifetime. The Communists think that the proletariat is mature enough to manage the production process without the help of capitalist managers, because they think that the proletariat, by taking over political and economic power, can often acquire the required qualifications for managing the production process. On the other hand, the Social Democrats think that the proletariat does not yet possess the necessary maturity to lead the production process. They think that the proletariat should develop itself intellectually and morally before taking over political and economic power; in order to avoid economic chaos during the introduction of socialism, expropriation should only be implemented progressively by keeping pace with the growing maturity of the proletariat.

Those who deny the proletariat's necessary maturity to manage the economy refer to the extensive knowledge, specialised qualifications and organisational talents required for directing a modern enterprise. Hence, we want to examine in the first place the management functions in capitalism. We think that these functions can be divided into three categories:

1. *Commercial management*: this function contains investment and financial tasks, acquisition of raw materials and auxiliary goods, price calculation, marketing, etc. They are mainly routine tasks requiring qualifications such as knowledge of markets and people, organisational talents and unscrupulousness.
2. *Technical management*: this function is only important in industrial enterprises producing material goods and consists of choosing the best management methods and machines and managing the enterprise technically. Calculation is the link between this function and that of commercial management.
3. *Disciplinary management*: this function consists of controlling the workers and their productivity in order to guarantee the production of a surplus in the enterprise.

The three functions have the common task of guaranteeing the highest possible profitability of the enterprise.

Formulating in this way the question of the maturity of the proletariat whether the qualifications of workers and clerks are *today* sufficiently or not motivated to assume *this kind of* management tasks, means that every unprejudiced observer should answer this question by saying '*no*'!

But the question is wrongly formulated!

Expropriation of a large enterprise under proletarian rule does not only signify a personal change in the composition of the enterprise's management, but also means that surplus value, i.e. surplus product, will not be appropriated by capitalists, but by the collectivity permitting a restructuring of the whole economic system itself, thus rendering the most important functions of the capitalist management system superfluous.

In a socialist economy, the manager of a particular enterprise does not need to know marketing, he cannot swindle, he does not need to speculate or to cheat. He gets his raw materials and auxiliary goods at a fixed price from other enterprises owned by the community. *Hence, with the end of economic anarchy, commercial management will be reduced to a simple bureaucratic function.*

Under the dictatorship of the proletariat, the exclusive political hegemony by the toiling classes and their control of the enterprises will become very important. A new kind of labour discipline can only be realised under proletarian leadership. In capitalism discipline is used for swindling. Capitalism is authoritatively bringing labour discipline under class hegemony. Unemployment and starvation are the whips used by the capitalist drivers, foremen, etc., particularly hated by the workers. After the fall of capitalism and its labour relations, the old authoritarian managers of the capitalists will be unable to keep discipline in the enterprises; thus they will have to be replaced by a new proletarian organisation.

Secondly, the question is wrongly formulated, because after the fall of capitalism the intellectual talents of the proletarians will increase quickly by schooling and training. We want to stress the following. Many Social Democrats argue: we should wait for a long period of time until the proletariat is intellectually and morally completely mature before taking over political and economic power. This is absolutely impossible. In a firmly established capitalist system, the worker has no chance of acquiring that necessary knowledge, just as one cannot learn to swim without jumping into the water.[41] The simple fact of get-

---

41   'There is another sort of artificial superiority which also returns an artificial rent: the superiority of pure status. What are called "superiors" are just as necessary in social organization as a keystone is in an arch; but the keystone is made of no better material than many other parts of a bridge: its importance is conferred on it by its position, not its position by its importance. If half-a-dozen men are cast adrift in a sailing boat, they will need

ting a job requiring a large and personal responsibility will bolster valuable qualifications many proletarians would have otherwise not acquired as long as they would exercise only manual tasks. – We do not deny that a transition from a capitalist to a proletarian management system will be accompanied by serious problems, which will negatively influence labour productivity. However, this will be inevitable. The best, yes, the only remedy will be the functioning of the already existing workers' and enterprise councils in Germany, Austria and England.

But let us now return to the new management organisation of the expropriated enterprises.

The new organisational structures should deal with the following tasks:
1. They should be rooted in the workers' community of the enterprises in order to guarantee discipline.
2. They should allow the integration of the enterprises into the economic organisational structures.
3. They should not acquire a bureaucratic rigidity.

In Hungary, one tried to find a solution to all these problems in the following way (Decree 9 of 26 March 1919):

In each expropriated enterprise the workers choose the members of the enterprise council; according to the size of the enterprise they comprised three to seven delegates (workers or clerks). The tasks of the enterprise councils consisted of deciding, together with the *production commissar*, on maintaining labour discipline, protection of the patrimony of the enterprise, enlisting and dismissing workers, deciding on work classification and pay-role scales, etc.

A *production commissar* was appointed within each expropriated enterprise, eventually for several small enterprises. The latter represents the interests of the national community against the workers of the enterprise represented by the enterprise council. He occupies the function of the former 'general director'. He purchases and sells. Together with the president of the enterprise council, he disposes of the funds and the bank accounts. If there is a conflict with the enterprise council or the workers' council of the enterprise, his directives should be obeyed until a higher authority decides. He operates as a permanent

---

a captain. It seems simple enough for them to choose the ablest man; but there may easily be no ablest man ... In that case, the captain must be elected by lot; but the moment he assumes his authority, that authority makes him at once literally the ablest man in the boat. He has the powers which the other five have given him for their own good ... As "the defenders of the system of conservatism" well know, we have for centuries made able men out of ordinary ones by allowing them to inherit exceptional power and status'. Shaw 1919, pp. 18–19.

link between enterprise and higher authorities. At any moment, the workers can replace the members of the enterprise council by other members.

This system is entirely in accord with the already mentioned four conditions – provided that the production commissar is the right person! The enterprise council emanates from the workers of the enterprise, while the production commissar represents the interests of the national community. The system is not bureaucratic because the enterprise council and the production commissars can be recalled at any moment.

The imperfections of this organisation are the following:

The members of the enterprise councils will try to get rid of their production work. They will prefer sitting in the offices by using the excuse they are controlling tasks. Hence, the number of unproductive workers will increase. In order to keep the agreeable functions, they will try to curry favour with the workers by compromising on discipline, labour productivity, wages, at the disadvantage of the general interest. In Russia, some members of the enterprise council were therefore attracted from outside. In Hungary we tried to give the trade unions some say over the elections of the enterprise councils. Whether this measure was successful could not be verified.

Selecting the already mentioned enterprise commissars was the biggest problem. One was confronted with a hardly solvable contradiction. The nomination of a commercially and technically qualified person was preferable for guaranteeing a good continuation of the production process. But those persons are politically unreliable under a workers' government.[42] In case a manual worker is selected, the latter should be recruited from the working-class movement. There is, however, no guarantee that a good agitator and organiser against capitalism will also possess the required qualifications for managing an enterprise. The conflict between professional skills and political reliability really exist. Industrial engineers having already joined the working-class movement and otherwise excellent workers were appointed commissar, but this did not change for the time being the existing technical and commercial-bureaucratic structures. Due to a lack of valuable candidates, the workers of the enterprises proposed their own candidates. This worked to the detriment of the commissar's authority. Local interests could also come to the surface. It was typical of the low-developed class consciousness of the Hungarian working class that the workers of many enterprises appointed former owners or general directors to

---

42   After the fall of the Hungarian Council's Government, many production commissars recruited from the '*technicians*' would boast that they had prevented or hampered the production process by organising sabotage.

the function of production commissars. Much energy was often spent dissuading the workers from doing this. In case their very specialised technical skills were required, these former managers were exceptionally maintained in the function of commissar. One often created a double structure: a political controller was then sitting next to a bourgeois technician, or a worker-commissar was sitting next to a technician.

In the beginning, the People's Commissariat functioned as a higher authority for social production and grouped all industries into sectoral branches. All technical, commercial and organisational tasks were here treated in the best possible way.

∴

What kind of enterprise should be expropriated?

An abundant literature already provided an answer to this socialisation question.[43] Big enterprises in the extractive industry and the transport sector, blast furnaces, the machine-building industry, etc. – all these studies are showing the same hiatus, i.e. they identify socialisation with a simple change of property relations within a capitalist economic system. *The state simply buys all enterprises.* However, [Otto] Bauer wants to realise this by transferring property rights and making the state the owner of all enterprises. According to Kautsky, interests paid by the state to the former owners should soon fade away by levying high income taxes and succession rights.[44] Meanwhile, the country's capitalist structure will nonetheless remain unchanged. A complete socialisation of a communist character, i.e. an immediate expropriation without compensation, is an economic and revolutionary action. A fast decision should make a bourgeois counterrevolution materially impossible. A slow and planned expropriation accompanied by compensations will make the proletarian dictatorship politically impossible. We can agree that losing all property rights is 'unfair' when other people owning only smaller estates may keep theirs. Hence, expropriation is an act of class struggle and during this struggle the ruling class does not respect fairness.

Hence, only effectiveness can motivate expropriation. One should expropriate as quick as possible and as much as necessary in order to break the economic power of the ruling class. The availability of human resources is important for the realisation of this project.

---

43 See Bauer 1919.
44 Kautsky 1907.

In Russia, only enterprises with more than 50 workers or with a capital exceeding half a million or a million roubles were expropriated[45] at a rather slow pace. Expropriation was in many cases only finished a year after the revolution.[46] By Decree of 2 July 1918, the expropriated enterprises were given in long-term lease to the former owners who were freed from paying rent. The state authority and the former owners are financing them in the same way as before. In March [1919], however, all Hungarian enterprises with more than 20 workers were expropriated at once. In many cases this limit was not really respected, because class-conscious workers of enterprises with 10 to 19 workers no longer accepted the authority of the entrepreneur and they expropriated their enterprises as well.

These two different methods of expropriation were caused by the following factors. In Russia, industry was developed very lately and mostly by foreign capital investment. In Russia, capitalism could thus immediately acquire its most outspoken industrial pattern, i.e. the large enterprise, while middle-sized manufacturing enterprises were completely absent. Hence, the expropriation of enterprises employing more than 50 workers was politically and economically correct. On the contrary, Hungary had comparatively very few large enterprises and many enterprises employing 20 to 50 workers. Hence, one had to draw the line lower. Huge shortages of goods called out for a regulated material economy drawing such a low bottom line for the size of the enterprises to be expropriated. (Later we will discuss the expropriation of banks, enterprises and big estates).

In Russia, the civil war, the enormous size of the country and sabotage by a bureaucracy hostile to the Bolsheviks slowed down the process of expropriation. In Hungary, where the dictatorship was established without civil war, the whole state apparatus and the technical bureaucracy initially accommodated without resisting; because of the country's smallness, carrying out expropriation went very fast. The Hungarian system of expropriation has been, without any doubt, politically and economically much better carried out. The faster and the more radically the expropriation is carried out, the faster the members of the bourgeoisie will tend to drop their bourgeois mentality, and the faster and smoother the transition will be achieved. In the western countries, where the working class is better educated and thus better able to manage an enterprise, expropriation can be faster and more radically carried out after political power is taken.

---

45   Berliner 1919, p. 30.
46   Hirschberg 1919. This is the relatively most objective account of the proletarian councils' dictatorship.

Expropriating the expropriators is only the first step to the creation of a new economy. Replacing capitalists with proletarian leaders assured continuity of production. Labour productivity, however, decreased due to declining labour intensity (we will later discuss this phenomenon thoroughly), *but economic chaos was anyway avoided*. Hence, we only want to describe the attempts made to organise a proletarian economy and the problems that created. The removal of the capitalists from the enterprises, the management takeover in the enterprises by trusted agents of the working class can only create the preconditions of a [socialist] reconstruction. These expropriated enterprises had to be merged with others and then organisationally transformed into a going concern. This is the essential task of the dictatorship of the proletariat: *realising the transition of the proletarian dictatorship from a capitalist to a communist economy*.

5 The Organisational Problems of the Proletarian Economy

> In bourgeois revolutions, the principal task of the mass of working people was to fulfil the negative or destructive work of abolishing feudalism, monarchy and medievalism. The positive or constructive work of organising the new society was carried out by the property-owning bourgeois minority of the population.
>
> In every socialist revolution, however – and consequently in the socialist revolution in Russia which we began on October 25, 1917 – the principal task of the proletariat, and of the poor peasants which it leads, is the positive or constructive work of setting up an extremely intricate and delicate system of new organizational relationships extending to the planned production and distribution of the goods required for the existence of tens of millions of people. Such a revolution can be successfully carried out only if the majority of the population, and primarily the majority of the working people, engage in independent creative work as makers of history.

That is how Lenin characterised the basic differences between bourgeois and proletarian revolutions.[47]

---

47 V.I. Lenin, *Die nächsten Aufgaben der Sowjetmacht*, Berlin-Wilmersdorf: Verlag der 'Kommunistischen Bibliothek' 3, 1919. [See Lenin 1964a, pp. 235–77]. In this characterisation of the tasks of the proletarian revolution, Lenin completely agrees with the views of Karl Renner, somebody who has to be situated at the extreme right wing of the Marxists: Renner also situates the basic problem of socialist transformation in its organisation. He

Organisational work can only begin when the means of production are in the hands of the proletariat. The fact of expropriation does not mean so much. The whole economy has to be reorganised, because the most urgent problem, i.e. increasing labour productivity, can only be solved in this way. The organisation of a proletarian economy is not an completely new task. All organisational forms of social economy are already represented in modern financial capitalism: *they only have to be rebuilt and extended according to the changed social relations and transformed from organisations of capitalism into organisations of a collective economy.*

The most difficult problem is making a good selection of that which should be *centrally organised* and that which should be *delegated to local initiatives*. With regard to the material relations, the following domains can be distinguished:

1. *The organisational-technical reconstruction of the economy.*
2. *The material economy.*
3. *The human economy.*

In Hungary, all these functions were initially indistinctly concentrated at the Directorate of Social Production. In lieu of a special institution, all decision making was concentrated here. A differentiation would gradually be implemented and the contours of a new organisation would appear after four months.

One has to make a distinction between enterprises falling under a central organisational body and those having to be locally administered during the technical reorganisation of the collective economy. This was in the first place determined by *location criteria*. Enterprises located in the neighbourhood of their consumers' markets and producing goods which cannot stand long-distance transport, should be locally administered. Those enterprises are: waterworks, gasworks, local electric power plants, city transport, brick-yards and sandpits, cloth and shoe repairing, bakeries, kitchen-gardens, etc. These kinds of enterprises should therefore not be taken over by the central state, but administered by the local state. On the other hand, enterprises distributing their output as consumption goods to consumers all over the country need a uniform, technical management organisation. This management organisation should best be organised like a capitalist trust. The ideal example of such an organisational structure is given by the central enterprise agencies in Hungary:

---

thinks that the basic forms of socialist collective property are already prefigured in capitalist society like germs which have to be further developed, while the Communists estimate that a basic change in the construction of state power is absolutely necessary for the establishment of a socialist organisation. Renner 1919.

All enterprises of an industrial branch were organisationally merged into one concern. Individual enterprises become simple departments of a central enterprise. Bookkeeping of individual enterprises will be limited to registration of materials and costs; the central office draws up the balance sheet. Raw materials and auxiliary goods for all enterprises will be delivered by the central enterprise. Payments will be executed by a central agency administering all assets of the merged enterprises. In agreement with the Supreme Economic Council, the central enterprise organisation will decide on the kind and quantity of goods to be produced in the individual enterprises. The old names remembering the former capitalist property relations were abolished and replaced by more striking names like, for instance, Budapest Steam Mill of the Councils' Republic No. 1, 2, 3, etc.

Centralisation of management should of course not degenerate into a bureaucratic excess. Management of individual enterprises located at different places should have enough autonomy: hiring and firing of workers, local distribution, a certain freedom of organising production, etc. Centralisation should not be so extremely organised that for a minor reparation of the machinery a written agreement of the central organisation would be requested. It is obvious that a balanced repartition of responsibilities between central and local management can only be reached by practice.

In Russia, the entrepreneurial central organisations seem to be organised in the same manner. According to an article published by [Yuri] Larin,[48] entrepreneurial central organisations existed in Russia for these industrial branches: textiles, metals, paper, rubber, copper, cement, coal, timber, peat, salt, safety matches, tobacco, starch, alcohol, sugar; and also for leather, electric power plants, shoe factories, bakeries, etc. In Hungary, the merger of individual enterprises into entrepreneurial central organisations was delayed due to unsolved problems of foreign relations. Surrounded by hostile capitalist countries, the Hungarian Councils' Government declared not wanting to expropriate properties of foreign capitalists, or, otherwise, wanting to compensate fully for expropriations. Proletarian management was introduced in all enterprises without paying attention to the nationality of their owners. But respect for foreign ownership postponed the suppression of the autonomy of many enterprises in which foreign capital had massively invested. At any rate, the government tried to gain time in order to postpone for as long as possible an armed intervention of the capitalist countries until the revolution in the neighbouring countries

---

48   [Yuri A. Larin (1882–1932), Soviet economist and former Menshevik. He became N. Bukharin's father-in-law].

would have further developed, or until a military connection could have been established with Russia. Hence concessions had to be made so that the expropriated foreign enterprises could further exist as separate entities. Under these circumstances a complete merger of the enterprises was hampered. To this a silent but tenacious sabotage by the clerks should be added, because they saw their function endangered by an energetically imposed centralisation; this phenomenon may reappear in any other dictatorship.

The special interests of individual branches remained a persistent difficulty for the central production management. Because of general shortages, confiscation of goods produced on their territory by local political authorities became a normal procedure. The central organisations were continually combating these local interferences. They had to trust on the authority of the People's Commissariat of Home Affairs against the interferences of these local political authorities. And they were certainly not always successful. The necessity of establishing local branches of the central economic agencies in the territorial centres was felt. These economic offices were staffed by civil servants appointed by the central state and they were to be assisted by local economic councils – later on we shall report on these organisational bodies. The economic administration imposed the decrees of the central economic administration, drafted reports on all kinds of economic matters and participated in the management of local municipal enterprises.

Apart from these centralised management structures, production concentration was also broached in Hungary. One was facing enormous difficulties. Although localisation factors remained a very strong factor in case of concentrating similar enterprises in one production centre, concentration of production was nonetheless carried out relatively easily. But even in these cases the workers were causing problems; partly because of their laziness – they were refusing longer commutes to their workplace; partly because they were anxious to not lose their job, as if the dictatorship would not care about workers having become redundant due to increasing labour productivity. Factory chauvinism was also playing a typical role in this. When in Budapest construction of tugboats was stopped in a shipyard and then concentrated in another shipyard, protesting workers appealed first of all to the good reputation of 'their' shipyard. However, this resistance can easily be overcome by informing and persuading the workers. On the other hand, concentration of production failed in some cases because of housing shortages. Concentrating production successfully in one single enterprise requires the creation of housing facilities for the workers, thus new houses had to be built for them. In the beginning of the dictatorship, a longer period of time will be necessary to build them because of shortages of building materials.

Management control of enterprises and state assets is a problem that created in Russia enormous difficulties. Lenin sees in systematic control one of the most important reconstruction tasks. In his article 'The Immediate Tasks of the Soviet Government' [published on 28 April[49] 1918 in *Pravda*], Lenin tackles the problem as follows:

> The principal difficulty lies in the economic sphere, namely, the introduction of the strictest and universal accounting and control of the production and distribution of goods, raising the productivity of labour and *socialising* production *in practice* ... Keep regular and honest accounts of money, manage economically, do not be lazy, do not steal, observe the strictest labour discipline – it is these slogans, justly scorned by the revolutionary proletariat when the bourgeoisie used them to conceal its rule as an exploiting class, that are now, since the overthrow of the bourgeoisie, becoming the immediate and the principal slogans of the moment ... The decisive thing is the organization of the strictest and country-wide accounting and control of production and distribution of goods. And yet, we have *not yet* introduced accounting and control in those enterprises and in those branches and fields of economy which we have taken away from the bourgeoisie; ... [O]ur work of organising proletarian accounting and control has obviously – obviously to every thinking person – *fallen behind* the work of *directly* 'expropriating the expropriators'. If we now concentrate all our efforts on the organization of accounting and control, we shall be able to solve this problem, we shall be able to make up for lost time, we shall *completely* win our 'campaign' against capital.[50]

Dealing carelessly with public goods and expropriated goods of the bourgeoisie arises from the capitalistic-egoistic mentality present in the whole society and from the long war having undermined morals. Some ambiguity about the new property rules also plays a role. Proletarians administering the expropriated enterprises too easily believe that the enterprise is theirs, thus that it does not belong to the entire community [Gemeinschaft]. That is why a well-functioning controlling system is of particular importance: it is meanwhile also an excellent educational instrument.

In Hungary, the problem of control had been very well solved. Accountants formerly serving the capitalists had been re-educated for this job by lawyers

---

49 [Varga gives the wrong date of 29 April 1918].
50 [Lenin 1964a].

and teachers of grammar schools and they were appointed civil servants at a special section of the Economic Council. This section counted branch agencies; hence, the same accountants were continually supervising the same industrial branches. Not only money and material transactions were controlled, but also a correct employment of the labour force and inquiries were made in case of disappointingly poor labour productivity or low output in general. At intervals, competent accountants regularly controlled the enterprises and their bookkeeping and they reported, not only detected, cases of fraud and mistakes, but also made suggestions for reforms. The accountants did not even possess a right of say in the enterprises. They were just controlling; they only reported and gave their opinion to the administration in charge of the organisation. In the meantime, a form of cooperation between the bookkeeper, the production commissar and the enterprise council could be established. The accountant's advice was often spontaneously observed. A journal entitled *The Review of Accounts* was founded. Its copies were sent to the expropriated enterprises. This had to contribute to making workers sensible for organisational questions. Systematic control was not only exercised on the enterprises, but also on the activities of the People's Commissariat.

During and after the Councils' Dictatorship, there was very much ado about *corruption* in the new Soviet bureaucracy. We repeatedly reacted against corruption in our writings and discourses. It could be asserted that the administration of public assets was by no means worse during the dictatorship than under the former bourgeois regime. The perception of extensive corruption could be created because in bourgeois society only a small part, here the members of the ruling classes, have an opportunity of practising corruption and in most cases they can easily hide their corruptive activities because they have acquired in this matter an impressive routine with the help of the machinery of the bourgeois state. During the dictatorship of the proletariat a larger part of the population could participate in public affairs. Hence, the number of corruption cases could increase. These proletarian thieves were clumsily and awkwardly stealing small sums of money when keeping the books of the enterprises. *While important robberies by bourgeois criminals were hidden by the bureaucratic system, many unimportant thefts committed by Soviet bureaucrats were discovered in much larger quantities because of systematic control and democratic institutions.* Organising a good controlling system is therefore also an important instrument against corruption always appearing in the early period of the proletarian dictatorship. From that moment on, the accountants will become personally honest and competent, thus not merely convinced supporters of the proletarian system, controlling tasks will be carried out more easily.

The *material economy* constitutes a serious problem to be addressed by the dictatorship. In this case we define 'material' not only as related to all raw materials and auxiliary goods, but also to all actual means of production and *all finished goods except those destined to unproductive consumption*. The central problem was that economic recovery was hampered by exhaustion of all stocks during the war, that production difficulties were caused by economic isolation, and that the proletarian classes demanded an increase in the real living standard; all this made sure that *there would be material shortages for many years*. Available and newly produced materials should therefore not be distributed in an anarchical way, but according to the principle of highest labour productivity and priorities defined by needs.

The material agencies were established to meet the material demands of the economy; some were already formerly existing central agencies of the war economy. The tasks of these agencies consisted of nominating an *executive staff* of civil servants and a *managing council was formed by delegates of the trade unions in factories utilising these raw materials*. Material agencies existed for coal, timber, iron and metal products, building materials, chemicals, petroleum and petrol, glass, leather, textiles, bags, and also for some consumption goods like corn, fodder, sugar, spirits, furniture, etc. *These material agencies administered and also collected information about stocks and their distribution*. In practice, distribution was regulated by urgency schemes based on the most urgent consumer demands. The waterworks, the electric light and power stations, the railways, the war industry and also the important food industry, such as the flour mills, slaughterhouses, yeast factories, etc., received special treatment for coal deliveries. For them delivery quotas were fixed for a longer period of time. From time to time one had also to decide on the utilisation of the remaining stocks of coal. Participation of workers' representatives in the managing councils was necessary not only to initiate them in questions of economic management, but also to inform them objectively about those industrial branches or industries having become idle because of a lack of coal or raw materials: these withdrawals of coal deliveries were not due to malicious complots, but were in the interest of the total economy.

Management by the material agencies was finally responsible to the Supreme Economic Council which defined the regulations of material management together with the production managers. At any rate, the foundation of that supreme authority was necessary, because some enterprises would get the indispensable materials for production, while others would not, something that often had been the case during the war. A highly organised and energetically directed material economy is the best leverage for proletarian economic policy making. The not expropriated and centrally or locally managed *small enterprises would obtain their orders from the material economy*, or, in case of emergency, they would be ordered to stop their production. Concentration of production in the best-performing enterprises can be obtained by using an adequate system of coal distribution or other essential materials, even against the will of the workers and the civil servants. *A well-organised material economy cares about the newly established common economy acquiring an absolute hegemony over the remaining sections of the private economic system.*

Meanwhile the material economy was already well established in Hungary and the functioning of the material agencies was only disturbed by the already mentioned interferences and the abuses by the local authorities and some enterprises taking away materials allocated by the agencies and then selling them illicitly. Mineworkers of a coal mine sometimes also organised Sunday shifts and they exchanged this coal for food. But this occurred very exceptionally. The material economy of the Hungarian Councils' Government did certainly not obtain a smaller portion of total output of the monopolised sector than during the period of the capitalist war agencies.

During the Hungarian Councils' Government, many complaints were heard about bureaucratic practices of the different material agencies hampering production. Chronic shortages of materials incited to a rigorous examination of any demand because the proletarian managers boosting production of 'their' enterprise demanded larger quantities of materials than required. Hence, any not ever-recurring demand had to be checked by the responsible section of social production and tested on its correctness. Such a bureaucratic chicanery can be at once lifted if supply of materials is guaranteed. A rapid and smooth functioning of the material agencies was, however, permanently hampered by secret sabotage committed by some counterrevolutionary-minded clerks or technicians in the enterprises, by an insufficient number of outlets in the provinces and by the fact that the stocks of the material agencies were partly administered by merchants in whose interests it was to neglect the directives of the material agencies while illicitly selling as many goods possible at a high price on the black market.

The attentive reader will already have noticed that the activities of the material agencies are coinciding and overlapping with those of the central enterprise agencies being in those days still under construction. This is absolutely true. The material agencies were then not only distributing raw materials, but also managing production. The timber agency, for instance, was not only in charge of distribution of construction timber and firewood, but also active in all sectors of the timber and wood industry. The situation of the textile agency was quite the same. As far as I know, it seems to me that this was also the case in the Russian controlling agencies. *Hence, the principal question has to be raised as to whether it would be necessary and profitable to establish material agencies and enterprise central agencies and whether the functions of enterprise management and distribution of goods could not be better united like in a capitalist trust?*

This question cannot be directly answered by referring to the Hungarian experiences. Due to the reasons already mentioned, the enterprise central agencies were only seriously in operation during the last weeks of the Councils' Republic. We think that both organisations are indispensable, but only when operating within their strictly defined competences. Enterprise central agencies have to manage the production process of their enterprises. Material agencies have no say on individual enterprises. On the other hand, they are in charge of managing all stocks, they decide on what should be produced in the country, and on what should eventually imported from abroad. The enterprise central agencies, once liberated from their distribution tasks, can later entirely concentrate on increasing output, while the material agencies can focus on the important task of a correct distribution. Management of the enterprise central agencies requires in the first place technically trained functionaries. Management of the material agencies is predominantly of a statistical, economic and political nature. *Technical reasons also call for a separation of functions.* Sometimes production and distribution are hardly qualitatively completing each other. For instance, Thomas slag is produced by blast furnaces and is distributed by the iron central agency. That was certainly not a good combination. Slag belongs to the chemical industry agency or eventually to a special agency of artificial fertilisers. Merging enterprise central agencies with distribution agencies creates giant organisations with an oversized bureaucracy. Such was the case of the coal and timber agencies. These considerations may lead to the conclusion that two organisational structures responsible for two strictly separated domains could work efficiently. Later, these material agencies can then be abolished in case material shortages and stagnation have disappeared. Distribution can than be taken over by enterprise agencies receiving instructions from the institute of statistics.

∴

The exceptionally important *problem of human resources management* [Menschenwirtschaft] was only worked out in a general form during the last month of the Councils' Government. In any proletarian dictatorship, the general obligation to work remains a basic principle of human resources management. In principle, this obligation was decreed for any healthy person. During the last month of the Councils' Republic, a special section of the Supreme Economic Council was created to apply this principle. The section's task was:

1. *A permanently actualised registration of all workers in the country.* Therefore any person considered fit to work had to carry an identity card. This identity card mentioned not only the owner's coordinates, but also information about his job or his unemployment allowances. *When registering a general medical report, a note on his suitability for work would be added.* The sick funds also paying unemployment benefits would keep these data up-to-date. *Hence, one could prevent the same person from obtaining an unemployment and a sick benefit at the same time.* This labour identity card could also be used as an identity card and a sick and unemployment card.

2. *Labour exchange.* Labour exchange is not conceived in a mechanical way, as in capitalism, and the unemployed are not only sent to a vacancy, if there is one, for *creating productive labour*. Completely different laws are in force in a proletarian economy. A profit-seeking capitalist will only hire workers if there is any outlook on producing surplus value. In a proletarian state, *the principle reigns that all citizens fit to work should possibly work, even if the produce of their labour does not equal the value of their pay.* According to capitalist standards, that labour will not be profitable. But in a proletarian state, all labour can be usefully employed. Hence, employing all workers, even those whose labour productivity is low, is desirable. Creating employment is certainly not easy in a situation of general shortages of raw materials and auxiliary goods. Of course, in agriculture and in similar activities like water regulation, soil improvement, and also construction of roads, canals, waterworks, etc., huge masses of workers can be productively employed on the condition that the already mentioned housing problems are solved. The most important, but also the most difficult, role is assigned to the section of the Supreme Economic Council for the construction of the proletarian economy. The dictatorship of the proletariat should be strictly applied on this point. In the near future, the living standard of the proletariat should be increased as well. We already pointed to the fact that this can only be realised after a full restructuring of the nation's social structure originating from capitalism and that this social structure is based on a capitalist mode of income distribution. Workers employed in the luxury industry have to be transferred to industries producing goods for mass consumption; civil servants formerly guarding and administering private goods in the broadest sense should be, just like the members of the bourgeoisie, employed productively. For the members of the bourgeoisie, coercion is also important in order to

prevent them from organising fraud and illicit trade which would hamper the proletarian up-building of the distribution system. It is evident that in these circumstances the workers should be enlisted in all kinds of tasks for which they are physically apt without regard to their formal education. *In such a case any kind of trade-union narrow-mindedness should be mercilessly sacrificed!* Retraining of generations of workers for new jobs is a painful process, but it is necessary for raising the living standard. In Hungary, a further retraining was temporarily decreed for only those branches having become partly or entirely superfluous in a future society. Hence, a retraining of lawyers and clerks was decided, a further recruitment of apprentices in luxury industry and in coffeehouses was forbidden and apprentices and young workers in these branches could break their contracts even without obtaining their masters' consent.[51] Reconversion of specific trades caused very serious problems. Of course, a worker becoming unemployed in a trade should be entitled to an unemployment benefit. But high benefits will damage the national economy. A narrow difference between wages and unemployment benefits will not incite the workers to accept the heavy burden of a job. When the situation is rather unclear, they can also easily earn an additional income by getting occasional jobs and by smuggling or peddling. The same applies to high sick benefits. *But if the unemployment benefits are low, the workers will protest very loudly against any attempt to close down unproductive enterprises, against any concentration of production*, because they will become jobless through no fault of their own. It is even more difficult to solve this problem when civil servants and clerks are laid off. We will treat the problem of civil servants in a separate paragraph as well. There is no other solution to the problem than a system of not very high unemployment benefits combined with very strict and systematic controls by the local councils. This problem was not entirely satisfactorily solved in Hungary. Its enforcement was particularly lax. Civil servants and workers becoming unemployed could provisionally keep their full salary paid by their enterprises; this had a very demoralising effect. Opportunism, especially of the trade-union leaders of the big unions of white-collar workers, obstructed measures taken against these practices. Organisational preparations were also not completed. Finally, concentration of economically product-

---

51   This prohibition was in force in the following trades: goldsmith, confectioner, coffeehouse and hotel employee, gilder and carpet weaver, poster artist, hatter, bookbinder, barber, commercial assistant, private secretary, bank employee. Retraining of lawyers and army officers was suspended.

ive enterprises implied a transfer of workers from the cities to the countryside. There they could only become productive by using very few raw materials. But this transfer was hindered because of a shortage of housing facilities. Hence we see: it is a long way from declaring a general obligation to work to its realisation.
3. *Fixing wages.*
4. *Defining and maintaining labour discipline.* Because both problems are intimately linked to the question of labour intensity, we will treat them in the following chapter.
5. This belongs to the human economy in its broadest sense: formal education, vocational training and choice of a career, protection of the worker by advanced hygiene and safety of production processes in the workshop, etc. All these problems can only be solved by development processes in the future.

∴

We only want to briefly describe the organisation of the Supreme Economic Council and its task of constructing and managing the economy of the proletarian state.

People's Commissars had replaced the former Ministers; the former economic departments of Agriculture, Finance, Commerce and Food Supply led by People's Commissars were for the time being functioning with the old officialdom. Reputedly conservative higher civil servants were placed on half-pay or dismissed; the civil service was rejuvenated by recruiting intelligent proletarians and intellectuals devoted to the proletarian state. The number of People's Commissars was meanwhile increased with a *Commissariat of Social Production* and soon a *Commissariat of Economic Organisation and Control*. Just like before the individual commissariats were functioning autonomously and separately. All decrees were debated in the Government Council. This way of functioning caused insufficient coordination between the individual economic commissariats while too much time was wasted by discussing trivialities.

Hence, a Supreme Economic Council was created by the Soviet Congress. Independence of the individual economic commissariats was abolished; they would only function as sections of the Supreme Economic Council; they were no more led by people's commissars; they could no longer promulgate decrees autonomously; that had become the competence of the Council of People's Commissars; all other competences were now delegated to the production level of the enterprises.

The Supreme Economic Council was organised as follows:

1. The *Presidency* was formed by four People's Commissars managing as higher civil servants as well as their own department of the Supreme Economic Council. The leaders of the other departments were also invited to the meetings of the Presidency. *The mission of the Presidency consisted of directing the People's Commissariats, preparing all decrees and proclaiming them after a debate, and managing the planned economy still under construction.*
2. The *Council* of the Supreme Economic Council, i.e. the enlarged economic council, comprised among its members delegates from the local economic councils (we will report on them later), the delegates of the consumers' associations, the central agency of the agrarian production cooperatives and the material agencies. This body counted about 80 members. The leaders of the departments of the Supreme Economic Council were also members of the Council. The directors of the accountants were also admitted, but without voting rights. *These important decrees, especially those concerning the organisation of labour discipline, wages and food provision were debated in the Council.* This body functioned excellently; deliberations were seriously and efficiently conducted. Subcommittees were regularly formed for debating special questions and, if necessary, specialists were invited to submit a written report. The trade unions were represented by their best leaders, and it was striking how the trade unions were meanwhile transforming themselves from a movement struggling against capital into a constructive organisation. 2a. *The Agricultural Council.* Agriculture is of great importance in Hungary. Hence, a special central controlling body for agrarian affairs was formed. This Council consisted of 40 members representing the agricultural workers and industrial unions closely associated with agriculture, i.e. the representatives of agricultural production cooperatives, consumers associations and agrarian professionals. As this Council was only established at the end of the Councils' Republic, no reports on its functioning are available. 2b. *The Supreme Technical Council.* The best technicians of the country were recruited for solving purely technical problems. As there were not many politically reliable people, a collegial system was installed. In Hungary, a Technical Council was formed with 60 members grouping the best engineers, professors of the technical universities and some representatives of the trade unions. This council was divided into sections representing the different industrial branches. *The tasks of this council consisted of advisory work on actual technical problems of production, on the introduction of technical innovations, on normalisation and specialisation of production, on the technical base of the material base of the material economy and on*

state investment. Unlike the members of the other councils, those of the Technical Council were paid a monthly fee of 100 korunas. Extra fees were paid for special tasks. This exceptional treatment of the members of the Technical Council was inspired by the bourgeois background of the recruited technical specialists. The Technical Council was only installed at the end of the Councils' Republic. Little can be said about its functioning. Without any doubt, this institution could have been of great value in improving labour productivity, but on the condition that no systematic sabotage would be committed. However, one can prevent this by paying its members high wages.

3. *The local economic councils.* In the provincial towns local economic councils comprising delegates from the local political councils, the trade unions, representatives of big enterprises and consumers organisations were appointed. The local economic councils functioned separately from the already mentioned economic agencies and they sent delegates to the Supreme Economic Council; they managed the local collective economy and made proposals to the Supreme Economic Council concerning any problem.

∴

The main shortcoming of the central agencies was their lack of qualified civil servants combining a specialised knowledge with a devotion to the new social order. The best technicians and managers belonged of course to the bourgeoisie and only a few of them would honestly support the new regime. The functionaries of the trade unions, i.e. at least those knowing the basic characteristics of the production branches, the size of the enterprises, their technical equipment, etc., had in general an aversion to the dictatorship and they preferred staying trade-union functionaries instead of supporting actively the construction of the proletarian economy. Administrators and leading civil servants of the central economic agencies were, however, either technicians with bourgeois leanings or workers with a very low technical knowledge, and they were in many cases enthusiastic young intellectuals missing technical experience; but, after the unexpected revolution and during that early period of reorganisation, one had to hire these young men having developed a special sense and ambition for these functions. It would have required a long selection process for having the right men on the right place.

When comparing the Hungarian organisation with the construction of the proletarian economy in Russia, we discover that *in Hungary the transitional and organisational reconstruction progressed faster and that it was more energetic-*

ally carried out than in Russia. All enterprises of the designated size were expropriated, while in Russia today expropriation is not yet completely carried out. The Hungarian organisation was *centralistic, bureaucratic* and gave the workers a smaller role than in Russia in the construction of the economy. These differences are due to distinct social relations. Hungary is, if compared to Russia, an insignificant little country; its population is only a one-tenth and its territory is only a one-hundredth of Russia's. Hence, many things could be centrally organised, which was completely impossible in Russia because of the latter's large territory. Due to the smallness of the country's territory and because the dictatorship was established without revolution and civil war, a transition could immediately be possible. The civil servants and the technicians did not openly commit sabotage; at the first onset they remained willingly at their post and many of them were convinced adherents of communism. Because there existed no well-organised Communist Party able to wake up and lead the proletarian masses through the transformation process of the economy, the whole economic organisation had become more bureaucratic than in Russia. One cannot simply copy the organisational structures of another state.

6   The Problem of Labour Discipline and Labour Intensity

Any kind of class rule is based on the ideas of the ruled classes that changing the existing situation is impossible. But when that opinion is challenged, revolutionary upheavals will necessarily follow. Because workers' discipline in the factories is exercised by means of class domination, any revolution will cause a serious weakening of labour discipline. A petit-bourgeois revolution bringing by violent means a new layer of the ruling class to power by replacing the old one with a new one, will also shake the belief of the masses in the authorities and thus undermine labour discipline. We could observe this in all countries after the October Revolution. The revolution in Hungary led, just like under Kerenski[52] in Russia, to a complete disappearance of capitalist labour discipline. Workers' councils were formed in the factories arbitrarily deciding wages, arbitrarily firing unpopular factory directors, 'socialising' individual enterprises, i.e. declaring the enterprise workers' property. Because there was longer an army exercising class domination and class discipline, capitalism was now completely disturbed. Day after day labour productivity diminished;

---

52   [Alexander Kerenski (1881–1970) headed the provisional Russian government from July to October 1917. He represented the Socialist Revolutionary Party].

the whole production process was ruined. This situation convinced the Social Democrats – the author of these paragraphs belonged to them – that only the dictatorship of the proletariat could restore production. Obviously, only a proletarian or a bourgeois dictatorship could restore the production process. Reintroduction of labour discipline on a capitalist base could only be possible by imposing brutal force as was tried in Germany. Under these circumstances, making a choice was therefore not that difficult, because unmistakable symptoms of decay had also become obvious in the victorious capitalist countries while Russia gave the example of a really proletarian government and production renewal on a socialist foundation.

In the first place, the proletarian revolution caused a disorganisation of labour discipline and a further decline of labour productivity in Russia as well as in Hungary. These workers having broken the chains of class rule refused now to conform themselves to labour discipline. All this is psychologically easily understandable. The former expedients of violently disciplining the working masses by punishments such as lock outs and threatening them with starving to death and with using machine guns in case of a proletarian upheaval, had lost any sense now that the workers were running the enterprises and the government, and now that the armed forces had come under their command. *The heavy task of implementing a new kind of voluntary labour*[53] *discipline adapted to these new social relations* had to be fulfilled, because without this – we already mentioned this in Chapter Two – an increase in labour intensity and labour productivity would be theoretically impossible.

First of all, one had to pass through a deep crisis. The piece-wage system, which was one of the strongest pillars of maintaining labour intensity in capitalism, but which nonetheless guaranteed at least a minimal productivity, had to be abandoned. The abolishment of the system of accord wages and the introduction of hourly wages was an old, but already ideologically stunted demand of the working class from the early period of the capitalist system. *The latter's ideological influence meant that this demand had been explicitly maintained although it was contrary to the interests of the toiling masses supporting the proletarian state.* Therefore this demand was only temporarily met. Thus, one of the first decrees of the Hungarian Councils' Government concerned the abolishment of accord wages and the introduction of a uniform system of hourly wages and the classification of the industrial proletariat into three categories of workers: unskilled, semi-skilled and skilled workers. In accord with the principle of income levelling, the wages of unskilled workers were significantly

---

53 [Varga writes 'freie Arbeit', i.e. 'free labour'].

increased, while those of the skilled workers were kept practically unchanged. Accord wages were only maintained for the mineworkers, civil servants and clerks could keep their monthly pay.

The other demand of the workers, i.e. the eight-hour day, was immediately conceded; the working day of a young worker was fixed at six hours a day.

The generalisation of the system of hourly wages, combined with a degradation of labour discipline, led to a further important decrease in labour productivity and output. Workers now freed from class discipline showed a far-reaching lack of labour discipline. Working hours were not correctly registered, instructions of foremen were neglected. Labour productivity declined sharply. This was of course a consequence of the greedy-egoistic mentality of the predominant majority of the working class. Having got rid of their capitalist mentality, workers could not understand why a weaker and slower worker should be paid the same wage as a better worker obtaining a higher output. Due to this generalisation of the system of hourly wages, *labour intensity diminished, while labour productivity tended to decline to the productivity level of the most unproductive workers*. All this happened openly. The foundries of three engineering works producing agricultural machines in Budapest merged into one enterprise. Then it appeared that a productivity difference of about 50 percent existed between the two factories. The more productive workers now argued about what should be done: the other factory should reach their productivity level, or their productivity should be lowered to the level of the other factory. This characterises the general workers' mentality very well. In the beginning of the dictatorship of the proletariat, labour productivity declined sharply, sometimes often up to 50 percent of its former level. As a referee and People's Commissar for Soviet Production at the Soviet Congress, I openly revealed, perhaps with a little bit of exaggeration but without using them as an excuse, all shortcomings of this new labour organisation.

Drawing attention of the workers to declining output and inciting them to accept reforms became in those days a relatively normal procedure. But one should also remark that in the period of sharp decline some joyful moments could already be noticed. First of all, declining labour productivity was not a general phenomenon. For instance, in the big ammunition factories of Csepel,[54] the iron-works in Diósgyőr,[55] etc., labour productivity did not decline. *And in all factories there were at least some departments where labour productivity did not decline due to the ascendancy of very class-conscious workers. Not-*

---

54 [Csepel is an industrial area south to Budapest].
55 [Diósgyőr is a historical city in the north of Hungary].

withstanding a transition from a system of accord wages to a system of hourly wages, productivity even increased in some cases. Declining labour productivity should also be explained by the fact that on 2 May [1919] the Rumanians threatened for the first time the Councils' Republic; all workers having been soldiers were mobilised. Hence, only less-valid workers and incomplete gangs of workers remained in the factories. Increasing shortages of fuel, raw materials, machines and tools caused by the persisting blockade continually hampered normal production. We should not commit the mistake, like bourgeois slanders are doing, of blaming the decline in production and the decrease in labour productivity during the Councils' Republic exclusively on the type of government. It is generally known that in 1919 labour productivity declined in all countries, but especially in those countries which lost the war, and this is so irrespective of their governmental system.

As soon as the most elementary organisational work was done, the struggle for restoring labour discipline and raising labour productivity was immediately launched. In countless articles and speeches the workers were informed of the fact that in the long-run the proletarian state could no longer distribute more goods than it produced and that under any political regime a raising of the living standard could only be obtained by increasing production. This intensive agitation was also bearing fruit: the working classes spontaneously began discussing means and ends of increasing productivity. The working class already reacted positively: workers did not openly oppose productivity increases; its way of realisation was debated in all factory meetings. *Finally, in many factories metalworkers spontaneously returned to the accord-wage system. The elite of the working class was thus inciting the less class-conscious masses to increase their labour productivity.*

As we already explained in Chapter Three, we stress that increases in accord-wages do not have the same meaning under the dictatorship of the proletariat as under a pure form of market capitalism in which any money income can be transformed into goods. Already during the capitalist war economy, the workers often demanded, when struggling for higher wages, that wage increases in money were not to their advantage now that the most important foodstuffs were rationed and thus not obtainable for money. Due to persisting ideological beliefs, the wages of the workers, especially those of the lowest paid mass of unskilled workers, had to be increased considerably. This rise of money income, however, did not correlate to output growth because output had seriously declined in the first period of the dictatorship of the proletariat. The difference between income in money and income in goods in terms of a potential purchasing power in relation to the available stock of goods was thus too important. The better distribution by the state is carried out, the more successfully illicit trade and speculation can be repressed, thus the more difficult it will become to realise a higher than average profit on goods transactions, and the less wage increases will benefit the workers. *One should nonetheless notice that there will be a persistent shortage of goods, that rising money wages can only have a minimal effect on the growth of labour intensity and labour productivity.* Increasing output by enforcing labour intensity and material incentives should thus be better realised by paying wages in kind. In Hungary, a plan was drafted for boosting individual and collective productivity growth by distributing sometimes clothes and luxury goods in the enterprises. But this plan could not be realised.

Labour discipline and increased labour intensity can better be realised by ideological incentives, by appealing to workers' judgement, by continuous agitation. All these measures reflect the quintessence of the dictatorship. The ideological remains, inciting the workers to oppose state or community like they previously resisted capitalists, can only be superseded by organising harsh and intensive propagandistic work. *The ideology of the workers has to be changed in accord with the changing economic base.* This is an exceptionally difficult task, because the remains of the old ideology – we already mentioned it – are, apart from the expropriated enterprises, also influenced by the presence of hundreds of thousands small, privately owned enterprises employing workers. One can generally argue that during the first year of the dictatorship, about half of the employed workforce was employed by privately owned enterprises. It is obvious that exploitation was reduced to a minimum in the privately owned enterprises after the establishment of the proletarian government. Higher wages, shorter working days and lower labour productivity were absorbing the largest share of the employer's profits. *But the social relations between exploiters and workers had remained unchanged, making the old fighting mentality of the workers still socially acceptable.* Because the trade unions were still organising all workers employed in the same trade, either in expropriated or in privately owned enterprises, being transferred from a private to an expropriated enterprise, and vice versa, was still possible. Because the trade-union officials had a strong interest in maintaining the unions as fighting organisations, it was very difficult to change the social structure of the working population. This was an additional argument in favour of carrying out as soon as possible a more thoroughgoing and integral expropriation.

Opaque relations between workers and clerks remained a disturbing factor in the enterprises. The function of clerk was already sowing discord in the capitalist factory. Apart from the technical staff, clerks represented the interests of capital against those of the workers: they were fixing wage scales, controlling labour productivity, maintaining discipline, etc. Although most clerks are wage workers and belong to the proletariat because of their income and social position, they were strongly distrusted because of their controlling functions and this often degenerated into senseless fanaticism. We shall discuss this problem of the white-collar workers in a following chapter. We only want to argue here that restoring labour discipline under new social conditions will be impossible by using clerks who have previously been at the service of capital. Only the newly established proletarian organisations, i.e. the enterprise councils and the production commissars, can fulfil this task. *Defining the competences of these organisations with regard to restoring workers' discipline is necessary*. The most essential points were the following:

The following disposals are in force when a worker commits a disciplinary offence such as arriving late, interrupting his work wilfully, neglecting the directives of his superiors, etc.:

1. *A rebuke by the enterprise council.*
2. *An announcement at the black board of the factory mentioning his name and the reason why.*
3. *A transfer to another workshop of the factory.*
4. *A wage cut proportional to his lower labour productivity.*
5. *A dismissal from the enterprise; eventually an exclusion, with or without unemployment benefits, from all public enterprises.*
6. *An exclusion from the trade-union organisation, implicating a change of trade.*

Only the enterprise council can inflict the last two severe punishments with the commitment of the implicated trade union. Any punishment should be communicated as a warning to all workers of the enterprise.

In order to increase labour productivity one should register the lowest output achievements in each enterprise; a worker not meeting the productivity standards should be punished (see above). Public congratulations and material compensations were exceptionally awarded in cases of exceptional achievement. *Emphasis put on disciplining individual workers in the factories was topical*. The functioning of this system was thus dependent on the worker's morality. Enterprise councils and production commissars were only allowed to enforce strict rules if they also enjoyed the moral support of the majority of the workforce in the enterprises and their backing when pushing for increased labour productivity. Otherwise the enterprise council would remain powerless and, if taking tough measures, it would be dismissed and then replaced by more docile delegates after holding new elections. Although they were not removable, the production commissars could also be lamed by an overwhelming majority of demoralised workers. In that case they should call for support from outside. Then, the Commissariat of Labour had to intervene. In order to restore the confidence of the workers, agitators should then visit the enterprise and explain at a meeting held at the end of the working day the necessity of maintaining labour discipline and labour intensity. Class-conscious workers could be transferred to badly functioning enterprises and set an example there. Hence, without using means of coercion, labour productivity can be increased to a normal level.

But it also may happen that the application of this necessarily very slow working method is not in the interest of the whole proletariat. *The general psychological situation of workers in individual enterprises or in whole branches can be poisoned in such a way that coercive measures must be taken.* In case of a run down, the better workers of the concerned enterprise should be transferred to other enterprises. Hence, the less able workers will become temporarily unemployed. In case of a run down of an entire industrial sector, *dictatorial measures* [*Personaldiktatur*], as taken by the railways in Russia, should be taken against the will of the workers. On the principle of appointing dictatorial leaders, Lenin says: '... on the other hand, they [the workers] demand of us a higher [degree of] democracy than bourgeois democracy and say: personal dictatorship is absolutely incompatible with your, Bolshevik (i.e. not bourgeois, but *socialist*), Soviet democracy'.

Lenin answers this question in *The Immediate Tasks of the Soviet Government*. He says:

> These are exceedingly poor arguments. If we are not anarchists, we must admit that the state, *that is*, *coercion*, is necessary for the transition from capitalism to socialism. The form of coercion is determined by the degree of development of the given revolutionary class, and also by special circumstances, such as, for example, the legacy of a long and reactionary war and the forms of resistance put up by the bourgeoisie and the petty bourgeoisie. There is, therefore, absolutely *no* contradiction in principle between Soviet (*that is*, socialist) democracy and the exercise of dictatorial powers by individuals ... In regard to the second question, concerning the significance of individual dictatorial powers from the point of view of the specific tasks of the present moment, it must be said that large-scale machine industry – which is precisely the material source, the productive source, the foundation of socialism – calls for absolute and strict unity of will, which directs the joint labours of hundreds, thousands and tens of thousands of people. The technical, economic and historical necessity of this is obvious, and all those who have thought about socialism have always regarded it as one of the conditions of socialism. But how can one ensure a strictly defined unity of will? By thousands sub-

ordinating their will to the will of one. Given ideal class-consciousness and discipline on the part of those participating in the common work, this subordination would be something like the mild leadership of a conductor of an orchestra. It may assume the sharp forms of a dictatorship if ideal discipline and class-consciousness are lacking. But be that as it may, *unquestioning subordination* to a single will is absolutely necessary for the success of processes organised on the pattern of large-scale machine industry.[56]

Of course, appointment of managers with dictatorial powers should not be considered as a final solution to this problem. The final solution can only be achieved by adapting the workers' mentality to the newly created social situation. Although urgently requested, such a homogenised attitude of the workers can only be arduously obtained. This process was already in progress in Hungary and one may ascertain that the lowest degree of undisciplined behaviour and labour productivity was already superseded during the dictatorship of the proletariat. Unfortunately, no figures underpinning this assertion are available; data we often obtained from individual enterprises in Russia do not give clear and convincing evidence. We are nonetheless convinced that labour discipline and a corresponding labour productivity can be obtained by a systematically enforced moral coercion. The better a proletariat of a country is educated, the more a country's public opinion will grow influential, and the more communist persuasion will imbue the masses because of good education, the easier a new voluntary discipline can grow and function. The English people with their self-organising sense and voluntary discipline will adopt this new discipline more easily than any other people having been submitted for a long period to an authoritarian regime.

7   The Problem of the Non-manual Workers[57]

The problem of the non-manual workers is closely related to the question of the maturity of the proletariat and also to productivity and output growth. In capitalism, office workers and the like are constituting a social layer of privileged wage earners – the state or military bureaucracy is forming a real ruling cast.

---

56   Lenin 1964b.
57   [Varga indistinctively uses the German word 'Beamtenschaft' for all categories of non-manual workers, i.e. office workers, commercial agents, clerks, civil servants, technicians, teachers, people working in public enterprises and services, military, judges, etc.].

Though the modern bourgeoisie is the real ruling class, she has no time to rule by herself. Ruling is in general an activity of a hierarchically organised class opposing the proletariat's rising hegemony. This social layer of non-manual workers is constituted by individuals possessing the qualifications acquired by vocational training and professional routine required for managing the production process, the workers are lacking and cannot obtain overnight. *The problem is thus how one can eliminate and break the power of these non-manual workers organised as an independent class and how one can win the support of these hardly replaceable technicians for the proletarian economy.* Losing their support would immensely harm the organisational and controlling system, thus also production. We intentionally used the expression 'to win support for the proletarian economy'. *Accomplishments obtained under extreme coercion are most of the time worthless when higher intellectual functions are involved.* We do not believe that the Russian system of workers' control, which is essentially based on coercion, will constitute a final solution to the problem. Sufficiently experienced workers able to judge the accuracy of instructions given by technicians. This would in reality make these non-manual workers redundant. Workers' control would become an empty formality in case the workers are missing any technical skills. Because this is in general the case during the beginning of the dictatorship, the technicians can pull the supervising workers' leg. Finally, the utility of workers' control will contribute to get the workers progressively acquainted with the matter. Hence, winning over all intellectual workers would make more sense.

Because the Russian and the Hungarian Councils' Government agreed that no differences between manual and intellectual workers existed, thus that their labour relations, i.e. their wages, working hours, healthcare insurance, etc., were the same, the latter process was disturbed. In Russia, the 'specialists' were nonetheless treated differently, which was a prelude to the second stage of the dictatorship of the proletariat, when manual as well as intellectual skills were taught in the newly established labour schools [Arbeitsschule]. But during the first period of the dictatorship of the proletariat, this problem could not be solved as such. Therefore we will discuss this question later.

Office workers form a part of the working class because these two social layers sell their labour force for a wage. This happens, however, in a different setting creating clear-cut differences with regard to lifestyle and ideology. A worker, however, sells his labour force daily; he is paid per hour; his employer may dismiss him at any moment and without reason; it will take him only a few days, or not more than two weeks, to fire him. Clerks are paid a monthly or annual salary; their term of notice is up to a year; civil servants of the central and local state, and also some private secretaries, can only be dismissed on disciplinary grounds. *Job security creates extreme differences between the social conditions of workers and clerks and makes office workers ideologically conservative.*

Workers are paid per hour. Thus they have no holidays. Any half hourly leave will be deducted from their pay. An office worker gets a monthly salary; his holidays are paid; absenteeism is overlooked. A worker will not be paid during his sick leave: he gets sick-pay. When ill, an office worker will keep his full pay. An old, incapacitated worker will be sacked, while an office worker will receive a pension. A worker never goes on holiday; an office worker gets a yearly paid holiday.

This different treatment of worker and clerk is not clearly related to differences between intellectual and manual work – sometimes manual work requires more intellectual capacity than routine office work – but *rather related to the different social functions of both social groupings*. The ruling classes use the office workers in order to keep down the manual workers; the rulers erect a wall between themselves and the working class; they artificially extend the narrow social base of the ruling class. *The hard core of the bureaucracy inclines to the opinion that they are forming a part of the ruling class.* The summits of the state are recruited from the ruling class; they share the same lifestyle and maintain mutual family ties, which creates the sense of belonging to the ruling class within the whole class of intellectual workers. This ideology is reinforced by common habits, education, clothing, etc., differentiating office workers from manual workers. During the past decades this ideology of belonging to the ruling class was shaken by a rapid fall in their living standard due to an unprecedented inflation.

In general there does not exist a class of office workers. This class is formed by different social layers and groupings. We will now study them more closely. They are composed of the following categories:

1. *Office workers directly involved in the repressive apparatus of the ruling class*: army officers and non-commissioned officers of the armed forces, government officials and judges. This social layer is closely related to the ruling class, possesses a highly developed class consciousness, and inclines to pursue its own political aims which may be different from those of the economic ruling class. We do not have to deal with them because they do not belong to our problem field.
2. *Teaching personnel of all degrees*: they form the worst paid and most despised grouping of all civil servants in capitalism and they are closely related to the proletariat.
3. *Commercial office workers*: they are employed in the spheres of production and circulation. A part of them exercises indispensable productive tasks:

engineers, chemists, technicians, economists, organisers, workshop conductors; another category is only involved in marketing activities and they belong as such thus to the faux frais of the capitalist economic system. Of course, intermediary groupings exist as well: railway and post-office workers who partly belong to the repressive organisations, and partly fulfil productive functions. Though all railway workers, service workers, etc. are all appointed officials, they are nonetheless workers.

The first and the second groupings of officials do not cause difficulties for the dictatorship of the proletariat. The first grouping of civil servants belonging to the repressive organisations of the old regime must be disbanded and their organisational structures destroyed. Only after having completely destroyed the old repressive organisation can individual officials be reintegrated into the civil service of the proletarian state.[58] The situation of the teachers was completely different: in general they could all be reintegrated into the proletarian state; only their summits had to be purged and their whole mentality had to be reformed in accord with the newly installed social order, which did not cause serious problems with this social layer.

The real problem should be situated within the sphere of production and repartition, where the productive office workers are in a direct contact with the working class. In capitalism, this social grouping occupies an equivocal position. As factory managers, controllers, wage calculators, foremen, all these office workers represented the invisible hand of capital against the manual workers. Because of that function the manual workers hated the office workers. In addition, they were also exercising important tasks in production as managers, engineers, technicians, i.e. all those functions the proletariat could hardly take over. A mutual understanding between workers and technical staff was therefore urgently necessary in order to obtain a significant increase in labour productivity in the enterprises. But some peculiarities of the dictatorship meanwhile hindered such an accord. *Workers occupying management*

---

58 That is what happened in Russia. In Hungary, the dictatorship was the result of a peaceful class revolution. The whole repressive bureaucracy collaborated 'voluntarily' with the proletarian state. General secretaries and state secretaries were zealously collaborating. The interest organisations of civil servants immediately adhered to the principles of the dictatorship. It is not a little wonder that in such circumstances the destruction of the old repressive apparatus was superficially accomplished. Most civil servants were mostly confirmed in their former functions and an important part of them committed, more or less prudently but nonetheless intensively, sabotage. Because of having not destroyed the former civil service, the reactionary regime was able to restore its rule within a relatively short span of time.

functions in the enterprises during the dictatorship of the proletariat now asked that the already recognised principle of equal pay and identical labour conditions be immediately applied to all categories of clerks and workers. That implied abolishing all privileges of the office workers or extending them to all categories of workers. However, during the Hungarian Councils' Regime, a continually growing discord between clerks and workers was frustrating the production process in the factories.

Though there were many enthusiastic followers and even militants among the office workers before the dictatorship, many, but for a small but convinced minority, lost their joy at work because they did not secure a leading position in the production process and in politics while they saw their former privileges threatened. The trade unions of office workers formed a united front for the maintaining the status quo. Individual conflicts were simply settled by mixed commissions of the involved trade unions. However, when the productive office workers threatened a general boycott, a reaction was imperatively necessary. Then, the Supreme Economic Council appointed a study commission that was not able to accomplish its mission.

After conquering political power, the Russian proletariat excluded the office workers. They went over to the camp of the enemy and openly resisted. Hence, they had to be crushed. The contradiction between technical knowledge and social reliability was then decided without any hesitation in favour of the latter.

In his speech of 28 May 1918 [at the City Conference of the Russian Communist Party in Moscow], Trotsky stated:[59]

> The military opposition of the bourgeoisie was broken in a very short time. So the bourgeoisie selected another mechanism of opposition in the form of sabotage by officials and technicians, all the specialized and semi-specialized intellectual elements who serve in bourgeois society as the natural mechanism of technical administration and incidentally of class rule and class government.
>
> All these elements revolted after the conquest of power by the working class ... Hence the sabotage, the desertion, the disorganizing of all government and of many public and private institutions by the directing technical and administrative personnel. This sabotage, in as far as it was not simply a product of the panic of the intellectual elements before the heavy hand of the working class which had taken the political power into their hands, and in so far as it pursued a political aim worked toward

---

59   Trotzky 1919, p. 10.

the future Constituent Assembly as its natural object, as a new bridge to those possessing the power.

But this victory was obtained at the price of a 'reinforcement of the decaying process'. And the working class was unable to stop that!

> The misfortune of the working class lies in the fact, that it has always been in the position of an oppressed class. This fact has reflected itself everywhere – not only in its educational level but also in the fact that it has not the experience and usage in administration that the ruling class possesses and transmits through its schools, universities, and the like. Nothing of all this does the working class possess, all this it must attain. Once it has come into power, it must look upon the old apparatus of state as an apparatus of class oppression. But at the same time it must draw out of this apparatus all the valuable specialized elements which it needs for technical work, put them into the proper places, and use these elements to heighten its proletarian class-power ... Now that the power of the Soviets is assured, *the fight against sabotage must express itself in the conversion of the late saboteurs into servants, into executives and technical directors, wherever the new regime requires it.* If we cannot manage it, if we do not avail ourselves of all the forces we need and place them in the service of the Soviets, then our late struggle against sabotage, the military-revolutionary struggle, would be condemned as entirely useless and fruitless.

For Trotsky, the solution consisted in workers' control and self-restrain:

> The next step must consist in the self-restriction of comradely initiative, in the healthy and redeeming self-restraint of the working class which knows when the elected representative of the workers can speak with decision and when it is necessary to give place to the technician, the specialist, who is equipped with definite knowledge, who must be given greater responsibility, and who must be kept under watchful political control.

The problem is here exposed in all its importance, but no practical solution is really given. The problems of describing the authority of technicians and workers' councils – we already mentioned this problem in the chapter on organisation – can easily be solved *by mutual consent*. Would it therefore be possible to convince these technicians struck by a greedy-egoistic ideology to work with heart and soul for a worker's wage? Would it otherwise be possible that the ruling manual workers obey the directives of the technicians in the production process and renounce the equality principle in labour conditions by guaranteeing them higher wages and better working conditions. An answer to this question requires making a further distinction between all categories of office workers in the production and circulation process: banking personnel, industrial clerks, office workers in transport and commercial firms, who are also called private-sector office workers in order to distinguish them from the civil servants. They formed a homogeneous grouping represented by an overall trade-union organisation. Two very different groupings can be discerned with regard to their role played in the production process. About 90 percent had a routine job that anyone with a normal intelligence can learn within a very short space of time: the army of typists, bookkeepers, correspondents, warehouse clerks, salesmen, etc. In no way do their intellectual capacities exceed those of most skilled workers. Standardisation of work tasks has made an enormous progress during the last decades. [Richard] Woldt[60] writes somewhere that correspondents in big enterprises do not even have the liberty of deciding for themselves to end a letter with 'Yours truly' or 'Yours sincerely', or another formula of courtesy. These formulas are numbered with 1, 2, or 3 and the correspondents receive an instruction as to which is to be used. The Taylor system was introduced, and not without success, in order to mechanise office work. Hence, there is no reason to grant these categories of office workers better working conditions than those of skilled workers,[61] as with the end of anarchy

---

60   [Varga refers to Richard Woldt 1911, whose book he reviewed in *Huszadik század* 1911, 23, pp. 748–50].

61   A half a century ago, Marx already argued: 'The commercial worker produces no surplus value directly. But the price of his labour is determined by the value of his labour-power, hence by its costs of production, while the application of this labour-power, its exertion, expenditure of energy, and wear and tear, is as in the ease of every other wage-labourer by no means limited by its value. His wage, therefore, is not necessarily proportionate to the mass of profit which he helps the capitalist to realise. What he costs the capitalist and what he brings in for him, are two different things. He creates no direct surplus value, but adds to the capitalist's income by helping him to reduce the cost of realising surplus value, inasmuch as he performs partly unpaid labour. The commercial worker, in the strict sense of the term, belongs to the better-paid class of wage-workers – to those whose labour is classed as skilled and stands above average labour. Yet the wage tends to fall, even in relation to average labour, with the advance of the capitalist mode of production. This is due partly to the division of labour in the office, implying a one-sided development of the labour capacity, the cost of which does not fall entirely on the capitalist, since the labourer's skill develops by itself through the exercise of his function, and all the more

in production and the organisation of a centrally directed economy most office work will be simplified and standardised. *There is thus no ground for creating a special status for a gigantic army of office workers and for preserving their rights based on their services rendered to the ruling class.* Their labour conditions can therefore easily be put on a par with those of manual workers. Labour conditions of manual workers should be improved. A paid holiday for all workers should be decreed. Examples from the capitalist praxis show that labour time lost by manual workers during holidays can easily be compensated by increasing labour productivity. There is no reason for fearing alienation and sabotage by these groupings of office workers because they can be easily watched and, if necessary, replaced by manual workers.

The situation of the remaining 10 percent or less of the numerous grouping of technical specialists, i.e. technical managers, organisers, chemists, etc., is completely different. They cannot be replaced and it is, as we already said, very difficult to put them under workers' control. One should therefore win over these people.

> Without the guidance of experts in the various fields of knowledge, technology and experience, the transition to socialism will be impossible, because socialism calls for a conscious mass advance to greater productivity of labour compared with capitalism, and on the basis achieved by capitalism. Socialism must achieve this advance *in its own way*, by its own methods – or, to put it more concretely, by Soviet methods. And the specialists, because of the whole social environment which made them specialists, are, in the main, inevitably bourgeois ... The mass of saboteurs are 'going to work', but the best organisers and the top experts can be utilised by the state either in the old way, in the bourgeois way (i.e. for high salaries), or in the new way, in the proletarian way (i.e. creating the conditions

---

rapidly as division of labour makes it more one-sided. Secondly, because the necessary training, knowledge of commercial practices, languages, etc., is more and more rapidly, easily, universally and cheaply reproduced with the progress of science and public education the more the capitalist mode of production directs teaching methods, etc., towards practical purposes. The universality of public education enables capitalists to recruit such labourers from classes that formerly had no access to such trades and were accustomed to a lower standard of living ... With few exceptions, the labour-power of these people is therefore devaluated with the progress of capitalist production. Their wage falls, while their labour capacity increases. The capitalist increases the number of these labourers whenever he has more value and profits to realise. The increase of this labour is always a result, never a cause of more surplus value'. Marx 1959, pp. 295–6.

of national accounting and control from below, which would inevitably and of itself subordinate the experts and enlist them for our work).[62]

We do not believe that these specialists can be forced to a higher labour productivity by introducing a good management organisation. In Russia this organisation was not even available. Hence, Lenin argued:

> Now we have to resort to the old bourgeois method and to agree to pay a very high price for the 'services' of the top bourgeois experts. All those who are familiar with the subject appreciate this, but not all ponder over the significance of this measure being adopted by the proletarian state. Clearly, this measure is a compromise, a departure from the principles of the Paris Commune and of every proletarian power, which call for the reduction of all salaries to the level of the wages of the average worker, which urge that careerism be fought not merely in words, but in deeds ... it is also *a step backward* on the part of our socialist Soviet state power, which from the very outset proclaimed and pursued the policy of reducing high salaries to the level of the wages of the average worker.[63]

In opposition to Lenin, higher wages and higher payments of specialists did *not cause a break with Soviet power, did not mean making a fundamental concession to the inherited greedy-egoistic capitalist mentality of the actual generation.* If a strong and capable worker is earning under a regime of accord wages twice as much as a puny and sick worker, it would then be understandable that an excellent technician or manager, whose work is maybe hundred times more productive than that of an average worker, gets a much higher salary. The principles would have been broken in both cases.

In Russia, this question was nonetheless explicitly discussed, but in Hungary the problem of wage differences and higher salaries paid to specialists remained all the time an unsolved question. One should in the first place reach an agreement with the trade unions on the question of the specialists and the ordinary office workers, and, if necessary, the white-collar unions should be abolished. Otherwise, all certified workers, even those workers doing typical office work, would demand, just like in Hungary, a specialist's salary. One should, however, be aware of the fact that specialists can buy real goods with their higher salaries; these higher wages will, however, create a money illusion if these goods are not available.

---

62 Lenin 1964a, p. 248.
63 Lenin 1964a, pp. 248–9.

As in most matters of economic policy making, success is intimately dependent on political achievements. If one can convince that a return to the capitalist system is highly improbable, the office workers, and notably the specialists, will unite all their forces. It will then become obvious to them that reviving the economic forces of the nation would be to their own advantage. Creativity also plays an important role in the life of a generous technician and manager. On the one hand, office work will rapidly diminish in importance due to the increasing educational level of the population. On the other hand, a new generation educated in the spirit of true fraternity and freed from greed and bourgeois prejudices is now growing up and intellectual and manual jobs are for them interchangeable. The problem of the office workers can only disappear together with this new generation.

But already in the beginning of the dictatorship, a number of brilliant intellectuals were at the service of the proletariat. The prophecy of the *Communist Manifesto* had come true:

> Finally, in times when the class struggle nears the decisive hour, the progress of dissolution going on within the ruling class, in fact within the whole range of old society, assumes such a violent, glaring character, that a small section of the ruling class cuts itself adrift, and joins the revolutionary class, the class that holds the future in its hands. Just as, therefore, at an earlier period, a section of the nobility went over to the bourgeoisie, so now a portion of the bourgeoisie goes over to the proletariat, and in particular, a portion of the bourgeois ideologists, who have raised themselves to the level of comprehending theoretically the historical movement as a whole.[64]

We can here proudly announce that the cream of the younger generation of the Hungarian intelligentsia was supporting the Councils' Republic and passionately backing the cause of the proletariat.

The problem of the office workers has also a quantitative aspect. By organising the social economy the number of office workers employed by the social economy increased impressively. On the other hand, the number of former private-sector office workers employed in the expropriated enterprises declined even faster, especially when counting the number of jobless agents employed in the circulation process of capital. Hence, the proletarian state had to face the very difficult social-economic problem of transforming *unproduct-*

---

64   Marx and Engels 1976, p. 494.

ive consumers into productive workers. In Hungary, we were soon aware of this problem of the human economy. Something positive was not achieved because of the organisation of the social economy that was still in its first period of development; the unions of office workers were strongly opposed and the right wing of the government, i.e. the Social Democrats, argued that no civil servant should be dismissed before having already got a new job. This created an untenable moral situation. Tens of thousands of office workers in enterprises having been closed down, clerks in offices not functioning anymore and in banks with minimal activities kept their full payment although they were doing nothing; and sometimes they even got a higher wage when coming and hanging around at their office; they refused taking another job with the excuse they were having a 'post'; civil servants of the Councils' Republic lost their joy at work because they were working hard while others were hanging around with the same pay. The important conclusion to be drawn from the Hungarian experience is that unemployed clerks should not, even for a while, be kept in office.

There are enough possibilities for employing these redundant office workers productively somewhere. The younger and able generation can be transferred without any problem to the agrarian sector where unlimited possibilities exist to intensify the labour process and increase labour productivity by employing an intelligent workforce. Productive work can be found in several industrial sectors. After having been retrained, others may become teachers. There is a great demand for teachers in order to increase the general cultural level of the population. The largest group is employed in the distributing and supervising agencies of the central and local state. The precondition of retraining these redundant office workers is their direct dismissal. If not they will only exceptionally leave their unproductive job for a productive one.[65] Trade-union resistance should be broken by intensive agitation and, in the worst case, by their dissolution.

8   The Agrarian Policy of the Proletarian State

The agrarian question is economically and politically the most difficult problem challenging the dictatorship of the proletariat. Economically, because providing the urban proletariat with indispensable foodstuffs is the real solu-

---

65   During the Hungarian Councils' Republic, the officials of a Finance Institute already in liquidation decided that the offices should be for other purposes: *they considered their own writing-table as their patch of ground for their own survival*. Those were the days when they had hardly anything else to do than sitting at their desk and cleaning their fingernails!

tion to the agrarian question; politically, because the agrarian countries of East and Central Europe cannot be governed in the long-run by the urban proletariat against the will of the agrarian population. *Hence, only an economic policy not hampering production, but possibly stimulating production and thus assuring food provision of the cities, can create a base for the proletarian regime in the villages.* A policy favouring the support of the agrarian proletariat and the village poor (subsistence peasants not employing wage workers and being sometimes wage workers) to the dictatorship of the proletariat should be pursued. That would, at least, neutralise the middle peasants politically. Nourishing the army and the cities will be the most urgent and the most difficult task during the first stage of the dictatorship.

We already explained in our third chapter its reason. In the beginning of the dictatorship, continuity of production must be a primary task. Interruption of industrial production may cause important damages, but in agriculture this may have a fatal consequence. Because of its productive-technical nature, agricultural production has a seasonal character: a temporary neglect cannot possibly be repaired later that year. As agriculture produces the most indispensable goods, i.e. foodstuffs, continuity of production should nonetheless be assured.

The necessity of assuring continuity of production will also influence the modalities of expropriation. *Though below a certain dimension landed property cannot be put to use as a means of exploitation, but only as a means of survival; landed property, as well as all other means of production, should nevertheless be completely expropriated.* Apart from this principal point of view, it is nonetheless obvious that there will be, from a practical point of view – just like in industry – no expropriations should be carried out below a certain size. *From a political point of view*: millions of small peasants fanatically clinging to property rights should not be transformed into political enemies becoming active in the counterrevolutionary camp. *From an economic-organisational point of view*: the proletariat does not dispose of a sufficiently large number of class-conscious followers ready to replace at least one million farmers, the more so as that any bad harvest can threaten the provision of the cities.

Just like in industry, farm size cannot be defined in advance. All depends on class differences engendered by the overall repartition of landed property at the countryside. The larger the proportion of big landownership and the larger the numbers of agricultural workers, the firmer the dictatorship will be established at the countryside, thus the more thoroughly the expropriation of the landed property must be carried out. The more landed property is equally divided up, the smaller the number of really landless proletarians will be. The less class differences are developed, the more the conditions for a proletarian dictatorship will be unfavourable and the more one should proceed cautiously. In addition: the agrarian question is creating a fundamental division between social-democratic revisionism and revolutionary bolshevism. Large estates are to be linked to the existence of a feudal reaction, agrarian economic policies and expensive foodstuffs in a bourgeois-democratic environment. Hence, extreme forms of class antagonism are forming an excellent precondition for a proletarian revolution. Domination of small property owners means democracy, hence fewer class antagonisms in the countryside, thus an unfavourable situation for waging a proletarian revolution. That is why the revisionists are in favour of breaking up the large estates, while the Communists intend to keep them intact.[66]

It is well known that landed property is very unequally distributed in Hungary. In 1916, enterprises larger than 100 joch (57 ha) owned 35 percent of all arable land. A larger part of all land is owned by large estates. This proportion was even more unfavourable in those areas of Hungary not occupied by the enemy during the period of the Councils' Republic. As a consequence, a class of millions of absolutely landless agrarian workers existed in Hungary. Apart from Rumania and Ireland, there existed nowhere else than in those parts of former Hungary, where the Magyars were dwelling, such a gigantic mass of landless agricultural workers owning not even the smallest patch of land, labouring not even a rented plot for their own account, and surviving as homeless [heimatlos] industrial workers.

Under these circumstances, expropriation of landed property could energetically be carried out. *All big and middle-sized estates with their complete inventory, claims and bank deposits were expropriated without paying compensations by Decree of 3 April [1919]*. However, this decree on landed property did not define the minimum size of the farms to be expropriated. Finally, this minimum was fixed at 100 yokes (59 ha).[67] As a result, many millions of ha of land, about 50 percent of the total territory; thus 30 to 40 percent of all arable land was given in a *juridical* sense to the toiling classes.

---

66 That the Bolsheviks allowed a partitioning of the large estates in Russia does not invalidate this principle. The Russian Bolsheviks were entangled in a political dilemma; in this manner they could strengthen the revolution in the countryside with its large agrarian population. Nowadays they are actively organising the remaining large estates into Soviet farms and reconstituting the big farms on a cooperative base.

67 It is obvious that an assessment taking the surface of a property as a base for expropriation may produce a very unequal outcome. 100 yokes of very fertile arable land have a higher intrinsic value than 500 yokes of barren land. No better method could be developed to determine the minimal size of a farm that should be not to be expropriated. Committed injustices should later on be systematically repaired.

Hungary's way of carrying out expropriations was economically superior to Russia's. In Russia, landed property was not at all expropriated, but lawlessly portioned by the peasants, while the inventory was stolen and taken away. It was not an expropriation, but a revolutionary repartition. Its damaging effects were strikingly described in Lenin's *The Struggle for Bread*.[68] *But in Hungary, expropriation of the great estates was not accompanied by a partitioning; this did not affect the production capacity of the enterprises.* This was in no way an achievement of the Hungarian functionaries of the Councils' Government, but the outcome of a totally different historical situation. In Russia, peasants – even the wealthier among them – actively participated in the revolution. They could thus solve the agrarian problem in their own way. The peasants portioned the land and took away the means of production. Not the poorest, but the wealthiest among them acquired the largest share. Strictly speaking, no proletarian revolution has occurred in Hungary. So to say, a legal transfer of political power to the proletarians occurred overnight. On the Great Plain,[69] the revolutionary movement was rather insignificant, but armed resistance was also non-existent. Legal expropriation could thus be realised without meeting obstacles. Legal expropriations could easily be carried out and big estates were maintained intact. In Russia, however, one is nowadays reconstituting state-owned large agricultural exploitations. Since the autumn of 1918, the Soviet Government became more and more concerned with keeping the large estates in the legal form of Soviet properties, cooperative farms and agrarian communes. Notwithstanding peasants' resistance, these new legal forms of agrarian exploitation were rapidly developing. In the beginning of February 1919, there already existed 1,510 cooperative farms and agrarian communes. At the end of July more than 5,000 units of them existed. They owned more than 2 million desyatins [100 acres = 37 desyatins].[70]

We are stressing here the word *judicial* to make clear that in most cases expropriation was only executed in a judicial sense while little had changed socially, and that the rural population had any clear-cut idea about the real sense of the expropriation carried out.

How was this expropriation process now carried out?

The former agrarian managers often remained in office, because one feared endangering the harvest. They were managing the enterprise in the same way as before, but now for the state. In many cases, the former proprietor was also the

---

68   Lenin 1964c.
69   [The Great Plain (Alföld) around the River Tisza in the eastern part of Hungary].
70   See *Russische Korrespondenz* 1920, 1, 2 (January), p. 14.

manager having remained in function as chief executive officer managing his expropriated enterprise. In general, this procedure was also followed in Russia where the big industrial enterprises were expropriated. But in Russia workers' councils in the expropriated enterprises had become immediately active and they exercised in practice workers' control, while the workers' councils of the Hungarian expropriated large estates only existed on paper. In case the former proprietor was staying as a state manager at the expropriated farm, any social change was hardly possible. The [former] proprietor was still living in his big mansion, he was still driven in his four-in-hand and the workers addressed him as 'My Lord!'. The only change was that he could not freely dispose of his goods, because he had to execute the directives of the central agency. The agrarian worker could only slightly discern the difference. The only importance of the social revolution was that his salary was now much higher than before. All thoroughgoing social changes were now postponed until the next autumn when the risk of disturbing continuity of production would be much lower.

Though this policy could be defended from an economic point of view, it hampered and postponed the social and political moment when the agrarian population would join the revolution. *Hence, only a small part of the agrarian proletariat could be aware of the meaning of the revolution and only a tiny minority of them would risk their lives as soldiers fighting in the Red Army on the battlefields.* It is true that an eventual political uprising of the toiling masses could have been very dangerous. It is also true that the industrial workers of Hungary were not yet 'mature' enough to manage their industrial enterprises, but the agricultural workers were certainly not. They lacked any degree of economic and social education; one out of two agricultural workers was illiterate and all were predominantly interested in becoming owners of their plot of land; they had no sympathy for the Communists, not even for the Social Democrats, because all agitation among the agricultural workers had already failed before the revolution due to repressive measures taken by a government dominated by landlords. Hence, one had to proceed cautiously with regard to those masses of uncultivated, unprepared human beings and not endanger the already obtained achievements in agriculture that year.

The structure of the expropriated large estates was as follows:

Individual estates formed production cooperatives. Cooperatives of a region were united into an overall organisation. All production cooperatives were covered by the Central Agency for Agricultural Production Cooperatives directly falling under the authority of the Direction of the Section Arable Land of the Supreme Economic Council. The legal form of a productive cooperative was chosen because of the agricultural workers' social backwardness. If we had simply nationalised the large estates, wage demands of the workers would have become unmanageable and labour intensity would have become minimal. Hence, when agitating for stricter labour discipline and higher labour intensity, we argued that net output of the estates would belong to the workers. Hence, demands of agricultural workers longing for property rights could anyhow be satisfied. Impairing the influence of the counterrevolutionary propaganda that the agricultural workers only had replaced their old masters, i.e. the 'Honourable Count', by 'officials of the urban proletariat', had become politically advisable. Because bookkeeping of all enterprises had been centralised, this concession to the agricultural workers was not really important. Transforming all agricultural workers into state officials, as had been the case with the industrial workers, was our ambition. Transforming the expropriated big estates into state farms and agricultural workers into state officials would only be carried out after having sufficiently informed them about that project.[71]

Management of the production process of individual farms was organised like in industrial enterprises. From now on the acting manager, i.e. the production commissar, was a civil servant appointed by the state. *All regular workers, i.e. workers with a yearly contract and casual workers having signed a contract for a period of at least 120 working days, became members of the production cooperative.* They chose an enterprise council functioning like that of the big industrial enterprises. Because of the agricultural workers' low educational level and their conservative ideology, managerial authority was high and, in general, the acting manager strongly dominated the enterprise council having not always been elected. Most agricultural councils were only formally functioning. Organisational changes were only planned for the end of the autumn [of 1919]. One was afraid to disturb the summer harvest being very important for provisioning the cities with foodstuffs. As in the factories, the same kind of conflicts emerged between workers and managers, causing problems hard to settle. Because entirely trusting on deliveries by the peasantry was too dangerous, one was very preoccupied with providing the urban proletariat with foodstuffs from the expropriated big estates. *Hence, we tried to increase production of the expropriated big estates by using all means.* First of all, already depleted stocks

---

71   The question is pending as to how one can transform agricultural workers into state officials and socialise the big estates without partitioning them. There are many signs confirming that the Hungarian agricultural worker would have freely accepted, after a thoroughgoing information campaign, giving up his not at all brilliant existence of isolated small peasants. After all, the distribution of small plots not larger than 1 ha to the village poor would have been more advantageous. This can also be accomplished by a *land-lease* contract.

of raw materials, coal, petrol, fertilisers and means of production (machinery, ploughs, tools) were distributed to the expropriated estates. A plan was drafted for developing large market-garden belts in the periphery of the big cities. Already during the first month of the dictatorship a very large market garden was developed on the territory of a former racecourse in the environment of Budapest. Other market gardens would be installed in the autumn of 1919. On many big estates narrow-gauge railways were built or the old rolling stock of the army was used. Milk-cows from farms situated far from the railways were concentrated in dairy farms near railway stations for the provisioning of the capital and other cities with milk. Workers and clerks having become redundant in the luxury industry and other sectors of the economy could be employed at the expropriated estates where they can do productive, healthy work and also enhance the intellectual level of the agricultural workforce and increase the latter's labour productivity. Hundreds of happy and highly motivated former clerks and other members of the former leading classes were already employed there. In brief, a plan for increasing the output of about 40 to 50 percent of the expropriated farms within a very short period of time was drafted in order to meet the most urgent demands of the urban population and to break the foodstuff monopoly of the peasantry. *The myopic leaders of the trade union of the agricultural workers, who were hostile to the dictatorship and benumbed by their inherited prejudices, formed a formidable obstacle to the realisation of this plan.* They urged the agricultural workers to formulate such unrealistic wage demands that, if accepted, the complete agrarian gross product would have become theirs and the urban population would have received nothing. Maybe a forceful agitation could have solved this problem.

Without exception, all expropriated big estates were now provisionally brought under control of a central state agency. In order to enhance efficiency and increase production with the help of local authorities and their control, one was thinking of communalising individual big estates. Industrial workers of big enterprises proposed to exploit the agricultural enterprises themselves; after their regular working day they wanted to participate directly in the exploitation of 'their' farm. Although this proposal was a very tentative one, we nonetheless had to decline it on principled grounds. Apart from a general tendency towards particularism, which is always so characteristic of a revolutionary period, such a decision could have thwarted the centrally organised system of food supply. In Russia, with its enormous distances, it seems that the advantages to be obtained from local interest groups increasing production outweigh the disadvantages of disturbing a centrally organised distribution system. In an article published by Larin in *Die Rote Fahne* at the end of December, it is said:

In order to develop and make agriculture subservient to the interests of the proletariat, the Soviet Government transferred large landed estates to factories, enterprises, agricultural associations and to municipalities as well. The Decree of 15 February 1919 of the Council of People's Commissars even encouraged that. Apart from rural associations of small peasants, private enterprises or enterprises of small producers, a socialist type of agriculture was created on the former big estates of the landlords after having been portioned by the peasants. Rural centres were created in the presence of the peasants which had to convince them of the advantages of joining a rural cooperative and imitate a rational organization of agriculture.

We think nonetheless that Larin's optimism about peasants spontaneously giving up their privately owned farm, when confronted with the model of a state farm, is as utopian as Kautsky's optimism concerning the agrarian question. This possibility may exist in Russia, which, because of common ownership of land, i.e. the basic mentality inspired by the mir, is still close to communism. But in those countries where private ownership of land and soil already existed for a long period of time and where the greedy-egoistic ideology had already fully developed, a free abandonment of privately owned farms would be unthinkable. It is our opinion that any political regime should be aware of these facts.

What should happen to the peasantry?

The peasantry problem is intimately related to the foodstuff problem. In Hungary, half of the arable land owned by big landowners was expropriated. Because the problem of feeding the industrial proletariat seemed to be at least solved, further decisions with regard to the agrarian question could be postponed. Our task consisted of improving farmers' productive practices by developing the educational system, by increasing their consumptive demands and *by preventing a return to a system of subsistence agriculture*. Acquisition of the peasants' surpluses should be tried by using peaceful methods by purchasing or exchanging them for industrial products. Force should only be employed if necessary when the rich peasants systematically refuse to sell or deliver their food surpluses because of political opposition. In such a case expropriation of land and soil should be decided. But requisition cannot be an appropriate method because it will lead to a decrease in output. As the expropriated estates can only be locally managed and as they are also parcelled out, normal management methods for large estates cannot be applied. Hence, the proletariat had to develop local economic agencies to meet the new demands. In Russia the so-called village communes – i.e. associations of landless and poor village dwellers[72] – were created in order to control food deliveries of the rich peasants. As we already said, this was hardly successful. Similar agencies, but this time *formed by village proletarians and supervised by local councils representing small communities, farmed the expropriated estates collectively and they paid their rent in kind.* We are talking here about small communities, because, for the time being, labouring small fields requires, at least, tools for these small plots.

Making that possible required many efforts: the proletarians in the villages had to break with the rich peasants, the idea of the class struggle had to be introduced into the villages and solidarity among the agricultural workers with the urban proletariat had to be awakened. This is an unusually heavy task. This task was probably easier to achieve in Hungary, where a deep divide existed between the wealthy property-owning farmers and the poor crofters. But in countries where land is equally distributed, it is impossible to make such a sharp distinction between rich and poor villagers; therefore other solutions should be found.[73] In this case, *one can only solve the problem by changing the whole peasant ideology.* Hence, gaining the confidence of the teachers will be indispensable. It is also possible to send communist industrial workers as agitators, leaders of the village council, etc., back to their native villages and where they have grown up. So the proletarian regime will get reliable and confidential militants constantly watching all counterrevolutionary peasant movements, which should be combated ideologically by means of newspapers, leaflets, speeches, education, etc. Because of the inevitable food shortages in the cities, sufficient numbers of industrial workers can everywhere be found for accomplishing these tasks. However, this difficult and lasting task has to be accomplished in order to stabilise the civil war between countryside and city!

---

72 [Varga is here referring to the Decree of 11 June 1918 leading to the creation of 'committees of poor peasants' in the villages falling under the general direction of the People's Commissariat (Narkomprod)].

73 We are thinking here of Marx's famous description in his *The 18th Brumaire of Louis-Bonaparte*:

'Each individual peasant family is almost self-sufficient; it itself directly produces the major part of its consumption and thus acquires its means of life more through exchange with nature than in intercourse with society. A smallholding, a peasant and his family; alongside them another smallholding, another peasant and another family. A few score of these make up a village, and a few score of villages make up a department. In this way, the great mass of the French nation is formed by simple addition of homologous magnitudes, much as potatoes in a sack form a sack of potatoes'. Marx 1979, p. 187. Seven decades after Marx's comment certain differences have already appeared in the peasantry depicted here. But today this basic assumption is still relevant in many a country.

9 Food Provisioning

Food provisioning of the proletariat will be a problem during the first years of the dictatorship. We already mentioned this in Chapter Three. The dictatorship will bring about important wage increases, partly in kind, for the agricultural proletariat; but at the countryside these higher wages in cash money cannot be converted into foodstuffs. All things being equal, the foodstuff provisioning of the cities will substantially diminish now that the cities will receive a smaller part of the same harvest. Surpluses delivered by expropriated farms managed by state and municipal authorities will be put at the disposal of the central agency of food supply, though certain particularistic resistances by local councils wanting to provide their own territory before all others first with foodstuffs may always arise.

In Hungary, where expropriation of big estates had brought 40 to 50 percent of arable land – and even a higher proportion of the most fertile land – under direct control of the central state, the problem of food provisioning could be fairly solved. One could patiently wait and see how the peasantry would adapt to the system of foodstuff deliveries.

In Russia, after two years of disastrously pursued experiences with the peasantry, the state also tried to charge the recently created big cooperative farms with the task of feeding the cities. In *Russische Korrespondenz* of January 1920, we read:

> Even if the farms of the communities and the cooperatives, especially those on Soviet land, are in many cases operating inefficiently because of shortages of skilled workers, agricultural machines and breeding cattle, this nonetheless means an important turning point in the agrarian question ... because the creation of big farms is ... certainly a matter of progress; without any doubt these new economic entities will become, after some initial problems, a sound base for feeding Russia. In mid-1919, one was thinking in Soviet circles that these farms could produce about 50[74] millions of pouds of cereals; this corresponds somehow with the amount the People's Commissariat of Supply [Narkomprod] was able to deliver in 1918.[75]

Hence, *by shifting the centre of gravity of agricultural production to the big estates, production will partly increase and that will break the peasantry's mono-*

---

74 [Varga wrongly mentions 100 millions of pouds].
75 *Russische Korrespondenz*, 1920, 1, 2(January), p. 14.

poly of food supply and, subsequently, the peasantry's semi-passively autonomous position; however, this solution cannot be applied everywhere. In most countries, 80 to 90 percent of total surface of arable land is cut up into small farms not larger than 50 ha. Feeding the cities is only possible by producing agrarian surpluses. Therefore one should find out how to incite the peasant to deliver his produce. (In general, one does not have to push the peasants; it is rare when they do not work on their land). Cereal monopoly or other monopolies already established during the war can show us the way. However, in Russia and in Central European countries, experiences prove that a legally established cereal monopoly combined with forced delivery does not always work perfectly. *All depends on the prestige and power of the authorities whether the peasant will deliver his produce to the monopoly agency*. The peasant will always find a way to refrain from delivering: he can use his corn as fodder; he can burry it; he can sell it illicitly, etc. It is predictable that the peasants are the enemies of the proletarian state[76] in most countries and that they do not want to execute their delivery obligations. We must therefore find out how the dictatorship can break the peasantry's resistance and secure food provision of the cities. With regard to economic, political and agitprop we stress that when applied they also should mutually interact. Hence, we distinguish:

1.   *Economic means:*
     a.   *Payment in cash;*
     b.   *Payment in kind with industrial products.*
2.   *Political means:*
     a.   *Taxes;*
     b.   *Confiscations;*
     c.   *Expropriation of rich peasants.*
3.   *Agitation* for re-establishing solidarity between urban rural proletariat.

1.   *Economic means*
a. In countries where the peasants had not enriched themselves extraordinarily during the war, where they had not accumulated so much cash, thus where the instinct of hoarding still exists, it would be, at least during the first years of the dictatorship, the best accepted and cheapest way for the proletariat to buy foodstuffs from the peasants by paying them with paper money. If pos-

---

76   The hostility of the prosperous peasants farmers and all strata of the ruling classes towards the proletarian state does not depend on the form the latter takes: whether this system is Soviet, a government of trade unions or a parliament with a Labour majority – this is all the same to the ruling classes. They will offer equally strong resistance to whatever form is assumed, once serious steps are taken to build a socialist economy.

sible, the demands of the peasants can also be met by fixing prices. One should also increase significantly the wages of industrial workers and the prices of agricultural products delivered by the peasants to the state agencies. For the proletarian state this will be only a matter of bookkeeping.

Unfortunately, *the Hungarian Councils' Republic could not apply this operation*. Firstly, the peasants had already accumulated so much cash during the war that their hoarding instinct had already disappeared. Secondly, we were so unhappy – we can hardly say it otherwise – to lack an office printing the so-called *blue* banknotes that were the peasantry's only accepted means of payment. We discuss this money problem of the proletarian state later. We only want to stress that the peasants refused to sell their foodstuffs for the money we offered. It seems that in Russia the peasants still are hoarding the old paper rouble and that this paper rouble was still accepted even when its exchange value had already sharply declined.

b. Apart from the peasants' conservative mind and their distrust of everything that is new, circumstances were also playing an important role in their refusal of banknotes; *according to them, all banknotes, new ones as well as old ones, were no longer currency in the economic sense of the word, because the peasants could not exchange their banknotes for industrial products*. Hence, cash money can only be a means of payment for buying goods of the proletarian state if all potential purchasing value of the capitalist era has disappeared.

In order to eliminate all potential purchasing power accumulated by the peasants in the form of cash, *a primitive exchange system in kind was set up in Hungary* for obtaining foodstuffs in exchange for industrial products of an equal or a higher value. Wagon-loads of industrial products that the peasants highly needed – such as salt, petroleum, spades, textiles, pictures – were sent to the larger peasant villages, where they were directly exchanged for agricultural products – lard, bacon, eggs, etc. Storehouses administered by the already mentioned local economic agencies were to replace these mobile wagons for the exchange of foodstuffs for industrial goods.[77]

---

77 Something similar had been tried out in Russia. In several places agreements were concluded between the urban consumers' cooperatives and the peasant communes. After an evaluation of the last harvest, a certain amount of foodstuffs had to be delivered. On the other hand, the supply agency of the state had to guarantee the delivery of a certain amount of industrial products to the peasant communities according to the terms defined in the agreement. The peasants experienced here indirectly that obtaining industrial products was related to the quantities of surplus grains delivered to the city. In last spring, this was tried out in the province of Tula, where within six weeks some 1,600,000 pouds of corn could be collected in one district. (From an article of Lenin) [Varga gives no further references].

However, the results obtained by these first experiences were ambiguous. The agricultural workers and the poor peasants, on whom the councils' system trusted in the countryside, became increasingly hostile to this exchange system; although possessing enough cash, they lacked sufficient food surpluses to be exchanged for the offered industrial goods. Only the rich peasants could acquire these industrial goods. Hence, workers and poor peasants wondered about real changes having occurred now that the dictatorship was favouring the rich peasantry. One could have settled this conflict by selling these industrial goods to the poor peasantry for cash money. But – and this is the major problem – the state did not have sufficient quantities of industrial goods at its disposal to meet all demands, and meanwhile exchanging grain surpluses for industrial products had also become impossible. *One was thinking about paying the peasants with a special kind of banknotes giving them the opportunity to buy goods offered by the state monopoly*. Hence, the purchasing power of the old paper money accumulated by the peasants would have been liquidated. This plan could not be executed, because of the collapse of the dictatorship.

A second interesting point is that the rich peasants refused to buy the offered goods because they found them too expensive. One can only understand this through knowledge of Hungary's particular situation. Hungary is a small country surrounded by countries having the same paper money as legal tender. Thus the peasants can also buy smuggled goods from abroad by paying them cash. Hence, they refuse paying a higher price for domestic goods than those offered on the world market.

These failures are certainly partly due to very special circumstances particular to Hungary. In large countries, where smuggling is comparatively not widespread and where the exchange rate of the own currency rapidly collapses after the establishment of the dictatorship, thus making imported goods expensive, there it would be possible to exercise economic pressure on the peasants in order to deliver sufficient quantities of foodstuffs for feeding the urban population and to impose a strong state monopoly and high monopoly prices to provide the peasants with industrial goods – salt, petroleum, iron, agricultural machines and tools, textiles. One should also keep in mind that this can only happen after the state has already started up production, i.e. the existence of a sufficiently large stock of industrial products to be exchanged for foodstuffs, which will not be the case in the very beginning of the dictatorship. The exchange conditions should not be too unfavourable to the peasants as well! We stress: *There is no such social category as a peasantry that can refuse consuming imported goods made in foreign factories*. If the peasant thinks that petroleum is too expensive, then he will use oil or fat for his lamp; if textiles become too expensive, then he will start spinning and weaving his own clothes; if the agricultural machines become too expensive, then he will start sowing his land by hand, beating his grain with a flail and digging his soil with a spade. Because he is the owner of the land, i.e. the most important of all means of production, exercising economic coercion on him will be in a certain sense inadequate. Then he will even return to a more primitive form of agriculture instead of buying urban products.

2. *The role of state coercion*

Our guiding premise was that economic motives are inspiring the peasants' behaviour with regard to the proletarian economic policy. This assumption is, however, wrong: *The class-conscious social layer of the rich peasantry refused to provide the proletarian cities with foodstuffs because of political reasons*. As long as the idea of the class struggle has not yet penetrated the villages, the rich peasantry can mobilise the middle peasantry and even elements of the village proletariat for their boycott actions. As we already argued, one should therefore *mobilise ideologically and politically the proletarians and the poor peasants against the rich peasants* by agitation, education and by organising appropriate agencies supporting in each village the dictatorship of the proletariat and by collecting foodstuffs. At any rate, carrying out this plan will require some time. Time that the starving urban proletariat living in the peasant countries does not have. Hence, the peasants should be compelled to deliver foodstuffs by employing political means of coercion. The question is now how this should be organised.

a. *Taxation* is the most appropriate psychological method to be used against the peasants because it is a traditional way of public intervention into income distribution. *But in Hungary we made the mistake of maintaining the already existing low land-tax scheme.* However, this was not a financial faux pas. The sum of 20 to 30 million in land-taxes that the peasants had to pay under the old land-tax schemes were not at all that important when compared to the huge budget of the Councils' Government. We rather committed a *political* mistake. This decision was wrong, because it did not contribute to gaining the sympathy of the peasants, but only strengthened them in their opposition. Tax remissions were interpreted as a sign of weakness of the proletarian regime inciting them to transgress other rules. Adverse measures should be taken immediately: turning on the tax screws, introducing a higher and fairer land-value tax to be paid in kind.[78] Only if the proletarian state is sufficiently powerful and

---

78 Many communists think that the land owned by the peasantry will soon be expropriated

prestigious can plenty of foodstuffs be extracted from the peasantry without compensation.

b. *Confiscation of foodstuffs*, also occurring under a capitalist regime, is a second thoroughgoing measure of exercising state power. *Confiscation combined with cash payment* or *banknotes* giving priority rights for purchasing industrial goods, and in Bolshevik Russia sometimes even without any payment at all, should also be tried out. The last measure was the cheapest solution for the proletarian state, but many communists also thought it the best method. From a purely economic point of view, we think, however, that it should not be applied. Confiscation without compensation is, strictly speaking, only possible for one year's harvest. Any peasant treated in such a way would immediately diminish his production for the next year and replace easily grabbed corn by other plants ripening at different times of the year. Later he would hide his harvest, bury it, use it as fodder for the animals, etc. Sending out armed groups of industrial workers from the cities using violent methods in the villages when confiscating foodstuffs can only have a temporary result. Normally feeding the cities will thus become impossible. In Russia, as we already mentioned, one tried to launch the class struggle into the villages by forming committees of proletarians and poor peasants which were permanently controlling harvests and deliveries by the peasants. How these institutions were concretely working we do not yet know.[79] In Hungary, the local political councils were supervising the harvesting peasants and exercising the monopoly tasks of the state agency. This system could not help overcoming the enormous problems. Because the rich peasants of many village councils could exercise leadership, the provincial [komitat]

---

or become state property when the peasants will voluntarily join the big state farms, but systematic taxation of the peasantry is for them a superfluous measure. However, our opinion is that this will not happen very soon. Not only because of political and ideological reasons but also because of economical-technical circumstances. *Millions of small peasant farms cannot collectively produce*. Merging them all into one large enterprise will create disadvantages of scale because the available agricultural machines and tools are not appropriated to labour on big estates as long as industry cannot produce these agricultural means of production quickly. Hence, we argue that an appropriate system of taxation will be undoubtedly necessary during a rather longer transitional period.

79 [Obviously Varga did not know that the committees of poor peasants having established by decree of 11 June 1918, had already been abolished in December 1918, and that the Soviet authorities had switched their appeal to the so-called 'middle-peasants', who rose above the indigent level of the 'poor peasants', but did not qualify for the label of 'rich peasants' or 'kulaks'].

councils showed a strong tendency toward particularism; they preferred feeding the inhabitants of their own province before all others.

c. *If the class of the rich peasants organises harsh political resistance against the delivering of foodstuffs, then it would be better* – because of the already mentioned reasons – *not to opt for violent measures when confiscating the harvest*. This could only happen once with a fair chance of success, *but only when expropriating the estates of the rich peasants*. If after being defeated, soil and land would remain the property of the rich peasants, the latter will wreck production; afterwards nothing will be left to confiscate. Hence, production should be put under control of other people. The question is: under the control of whom?

As we did not reach this stage of development in Hungary, we are missing any practical experience in this matter. It seems that in Russia the next stage of development can be observed: committees of the village poor acquired expropriated estates in the form of cooperative farming land.[80] The mir, i.e. the old agrarian system of collective property, will thus subsist, but on a new proletarian-political base. The problem of property transfer from the rich peasants to one or more cooperative farms will nonetheless guarantee at least an agrarian surplus to nourish the urban proletariat. It is possible that the cooperative organisations of the village poor will stimulate an *opposition movement of rich peasants* having not received real economic compensations.

3. We now arrive at a third set of problems: creating a common class consciousness and solidarity between the urban and rural proletariat.

In general, it is not sufficient to introduce the class struggle in the village communities by mobilising the village poor against the well-to-do peasants and by supporting them against the latter with the help of state power when the rich peasantry are expropriated. A clear-cut consciousness should be awoken about the necessity of breaking the big landowners' and rich peasants' yoke, which can only be realised with the help of the urban proletariat, i.e. the vanguard of the revolution. A consolidation of the revolution's realisations can only be secured by providing the cities with the most necessary goods. *The conscience*

---

80 [A number of agricultural communes of 'collective farms' (kolkhozy) were established by communist idealists on a working and living together base. Soviet farms (sovkhozy) were set up by the Soviet Government, by provincial or local soviets, or sometimes by industrial enterprises under the control of Vesenkha, for the specific purpose of providing food to urban and factory workers; they employed wage-labour and sometimes they were called 'socialist grain factories'].

of class solidarity has to be developed so that the village poor will voluntarily back the privatisation measures in order to provide the urban proletariat with the most necessary goods. This task will be as immense as the awakening of the industrial proletariat's class consciousness in the past. But this should now be realised within as short a time span as possible, otherwise the dictatorship of the proletariat collapses. In a few years one should now realise what previously had required several decades.

Completely different means of education and agitation are available to the industrial proletariat having become the ruling class than when she was struggling against a state dominated by the class of big landlords and rich peasants. The press monopoly, the printed and oral means of agitation, as well as the possibility of sending at least one class-conscious industrial worker to each village for leading, educating and organising are available for inciting the village poor to class solidarity. Schools are at the service of the proletarian dictatorship as well! *All these means should realise a possibly rapid transformation of the ideology of the village people, and thus also secure the provision of the urban proletariat with foodstuffs, but on the condition that the industrial proletariat can mobilise enough resources to fulfil this heavy task.* Of course, there will be very interesting 'national variations' on this theme. There are relatively few industrial workers living in the eastern countries of Europe and the agricultural proletariat's class conscious is low. This also applies to the rich peasants. In the western countries, the industrial proletariat dominates: the agricultural workers are already acquainted with the phenomenon of the class struggle and class solidarity because of their daily contacts with the industrial proletariat in the industrial centres and individual enterprises having been established in the countryside. On the other hand, the land-owning peasantry is here much more class-conscious, more pugnacious and also better mobilised. History will teach what will be most advantageous to the proletariat.

In order to avoid any misunderstanding, we conclude that the economic, political and ideological measures proposed remain rather abstract. They are practically all intertwined and they also mutually reinforce each other. If the proletarian state can increase its industrial output and will be able to deliver industrial products to the peasantry, then the state will increase its prestige in the eyes of the peasants. The greater the political prestige of the proletarian state, the easier economic problems can be solved. The deeper agitation reaches into the villages and the more convinced followers of Communism are recruited, the stronger the proletarian state will become. In other words: agitation will become more successful when state power grows stronger. Between these individual moments there are not only simple causal relations, but also interactions.

In capitalist countries with a high population density, the problem of domestic food production is also related to the question of food imports. That may create a serious problem as well. In the beginning of the revolutionary turmoil and as long as the capitalist countries are victorious, the emerging proletarian countries will be boycotted and excluded from world trade. Hence, food shortages will become a very serious problem if trade relations with other proletarian countries are impossible. This may explain why in food self-sufficient countries like Russia, Hungary and Bavaria the dictatorship of the proletariat got a foothold and why Bolshevism could easier take hold than in countries that were dependent on food imports to feed their population. However, the more the revolution spreads and the more countries that come under proletarian rule, the stronger the revolution and the new political system will become rooted in the countries spearheading the revolutionary struggle, thus the easier the problem of food shortages can be solved under the dictatorship of the proletariat.

10   The Distribution Problem of Goods

Limiting trade became a strong tendency under finance capitalism. This tendency has a triple character:
1. Monopoly cartels – among them one also counts the monopolies of the capitalist state – are eliminating intermediaries by selling their produce directly to the consumers: the retailer only receives a fixed provision. This is the case with the petroleum cartel, the beer cartel, etc. Functions and profits of commercial capital are transferred to productive capital by which the latter's circulation will proportionally grow.
2. Consumers unite into cooperatives directly buying goods on a large scale.
3. Small producers will join so-called producers' cooperatives, but in reality they are only selling agencies bypassing intermediaries.

Finally these voluntary agencies will join the compulsory agencies of the war economy, i.e. the different agencies distributing rationed foodstuffs. Hence, capitalism contains many valuable elements contributing to socialism. It will thus be only a matter of transforming these capitalist agencies – except for the consumers' associations – into proletarian organisations. *Distribution of goods, which is certainly a necessary function* in any social system not based on a 'closed household' economy, should be *distinguished from a system of independent commerce selling goods to make profit*. During the dictatorship of the proletariat in a period of shortages, such commerce will surely transform itself into speculation and usury. *Independent farms not belonging to the state eco-*

nomy are not disorganising the latter though independent trade is a disturbing factor in a system of officially regulated commodity production. Commerce is essentially an anarchistic and counterrevolutionary element masking people's needs, disturbing adjustment of production to demand and hampering the state's productive capacity. Therefore, trade should be eliminated at once.

From a theoretical point of view, everything should be clear. Expropriation of big enterprises will put an end to wholesale trade. Central entrepreneurial agencies will distribute raw materials and other means of production to all associated enterprises. Distribution of finished products will be organised either by the central or by material agencies. The expropriated enterprises having become state or municipal property, as well as the big agrarian enterprises, can no longer make profits, neither by selling nor by buying goods. Hence, we are now talking about Hilferding's 'general cartel', i.e. the well-known capitalist trust encompassing a country's whole output.

Cartelisation is accompanied by elimination or nationalisation of all international trade, which is normally also a matter of wholesale trade. Informed by the central entrepreneurial and material agencies about the most urgently demanded goods, the Foreign Trade Office, of course, receives utmost power to decide on commodity import and export. This extensive controlling system of international trade was developed by the state during the war.

Distribution of consumer goods can, strictly speaking, *easily be organised by making everyone a member of a local consumers' organisation*. Each inhabitant with a household will obtain his rationed foodstuffs and other consumption goods from distribution centres located in his own neighbourhood. People will not be allowed to purchase goods elsewhere (area distribution system). Restaurants will be opened for people without a household or those unable to join a family. Only the distribution centres in the villages will be provided with industrial goods. Local councils will supervise local distribution. We shall discuss later why class criteria should be used for distributing scarce goods.

As far as this trade is not a mater of state monopoly, an agency collecting the output of not yet expropriated enterprises should eliminate speculation. Handicrafts can easily be regulated if the proletarian state provides them with raw materials and governmental or municipal organisations distribute their produce; these handicrafts can, if necessary, be merged into larger enterprises or disbanded after a certain period of time. Threatening them with a withdrawal of fuel, iron, leather, etc. deliveries will incite them to join a distribution agency set up by the state or the municipalities, thus giving up speculation and illicit commerce, because all materials necessary for production will otherwise be withdrawn. The peasantry forms a more difficult case. Monopolistic organisations should be established for collecting corn, butter, milk, meat, etc.;

railways and ships should only transport goods provided by chartered organisations. Private trade should be confined to a well-defined sector. These chartered organisations should nonetheless acquire some local autonomy and not be completely bureaucratised. Workers' families should be set free to buy foodstuffs in their villages from local peasants.

We also want to discuss here some practical difficulties we experienced in Hungary.

One of the first measures to be discussed by the Councils' Government was the closing down of all wholesale shops and other large outlets in the cities, but not the groceries, book- and paper-shops, etc. This was one of the measures that has been loudly criticised by the Mensheviks: because of insufficient distribution centres, people do not easily find some consumption goods. *Such measures are, however, necessary and inevitable.* Firstly, large stocks of goods were stored in the enterprises and warehouses owned by merchants and the organisation of material distribution would have been hindered if these stocks had not been seized. Secondly, if this measured had not been taken, the bourgeoisie and peasantry would have used their accumulated savings, as occurred in Russia, in order to buy scarce stocks of shoes and textiles, etc. Hence, they would have not only replenished their abundant stocks for a longer period of time, *but also deprived the proletarians of the possibility of covering their most urgent needs of industrial products*, thus having prevented them from realising their wages by buying goods. Free trade of all available goods would have possibly allowed the bourgeoisie to destabilise the proletarian regime. Stocks of wholesalers were expropriated without compensation and assigned to the material agencies; small traders received a compensation, but this was limited to a monthly payment of no more than 2,000 K [korunas]. Although the shops had been closed down, many goods were nevertheless illicitly traded. Shop assistants inspecting the goods in the function of confidential agents of the proletariat were now making common cause with the merchants. They took away goods and sold them illicitly. This occurred practically everywhere because of the egoistic-selfish mentality of the actual generation.

The mistake we made was not the closing down of the shops, but the fact that proletarian measures were not applied energetically enough and that the functioning of the distribution organisations replacing the private trade system had been neglected. Hence, goods stored in private shops and storehouses must be, as soon as possible, transferred to the material agencies, the empty shops must be transformed into apartment houses, consumers must be organised into consumers' organisations and a sufficient number of state and cooperative distribution centres must be set up. But the energetic realisation of this programme was delayed because of sabotage by shop-assistants and civil servants afraid of losing their jobs, by the action of the Social Democrats wanting to 'protect the little man', and, finally, by pressure exercised by many foreign-owned businesses protected by the governments of the capitalist countries.

Trade in products made by the expropriated enterprises was indeed completely suppressed. The big state farms delivered their total agricultural produce, corn, cattle, wool, etc., directly to the assigned central agencies, as did the factories when delivering their output to the assigned entrepreneurial central agencies or the material agencies. Only a very small portion of the output of the expropriated enterprises disappeared abusively to the illicit market.

Foreign trade developed in a very particularly way. In the beginning, the country was not yet hit by a complete blockade by the Entente. But international trade was nonetheless subjected to important constraints, because foreign capitalists did not recognise the Foreign Trade Office, i.e. the trade agency of the proletarian state, as a trustworthy business partner. This would seriously hamper foreign trade. Hence, we had to trade under the name of a well-known capitalist trading firm. Many expropriated enterprises were in reality foreign-owned subsidiaries obtaining goods provided by their mother enterprises, which the proletarian state was unable to acquire. Foreign capital even considered the dictatorship as a temporary phenomenon. Later, when the Entente installed a strict blockade, smuggling became generalised and this was accompanied by all kinds of demoralising abuses like swindle and theft, phenomena which are of course accompanying all forms of illicit business.[81] Unfortunately, we were then cut off from the only (in those days) existing proletarian country, i.e. Russia. Mentioning that free flows of goods between all countries will fortify the proletarian economy would be therefore superfluous.

During the Hungarian Councils' Republic, a distribution system at the service of the final consumers was seriously organised. Consumers' associations were very well developed in Hungary; a big working-class consumers' association with some 200 outlets existed in the Hungarian capital. The consumers' association now forming the hard core of the new distribution system was put under supervision of the state. This decision was strongly opposed by the leaders of the consumers' associations themselves, because they were anxious for the survival of their institution after the collapse of the dictatorship. The introduction of a centralised, compulsory and territorial system was hampered by the so-called *'purchasing groupings'* [Anschaffungsgruppen] having been

---

[81] A typical example of the capitalist morality is the way the Czech capitalists were doing business with the Hungarian State firms when bartering tanning skins in a period the Hungarian troops were clashing with the Czech army.

established during the war period. All workers and clerks belonging to a particular factory or ministry, all railway workers, all employees of the postal service, etc., had already formed groupings purchasing their consumer goods collectively. The state agencies, however, had to pay the maximum price for buying foodstuffs, while these groupings, which were not subjected to any price control, could deliver foodstuffs at better conditions to their members than the state agencies or any individual ever could. In families with more than one person economically active in more than one single enterprise, all economically active family members could become family heads; hence they all could obtain more than one family-head ration per family. Because of these advantages they had to face harsh opposition from the others. Clerks and the industrial workers in the big enterprises were against an area distribution system for consumer goods and, hence, also against a dissolution of the purchasing associations. In Russia, a similar distribution system of consumer goods was set up, but with the difference that an important network of consumers' organisations had already been set up during the first year of the dictatorship. In *Russische Korrespondenz* of January 1920, we read that by Decree of 20 March

> the state took over the cooperation associations (that was the name of the consumers' associations in Russia) having already proved their efficiency because of their deep rooting in society, and one had them adjusted to the demands of a socialist distribution system. Distribution should also pass into the hands of the population itself. The distribution system providing the population with all necessary goods should be based on the autonomy principle. Hence, all people can participate into purchasing and the distribution associations. The whole population of the Soviet Russia is nowadays adhering, in some way or another, to the cooperative movement. The Decree of 20 March [1919] made membership of the cooperative movement even compulsory. One should of course take care of a well-organised distribution system organised by the state. For that purpose the state merged the previously independently operating cooperative associations into centralized organisations with a central pay-desk, a centralized management and a membership administration covering the whole population.

After having established this centralized distribution system, the Russian state is now thinking of abolishing its direct participation in the distribution system and only assuming general supervising tasks. That Decree was promulgated on 20 March 1919. Preparing its implementation lasted for five months. After having accomplished this preparatory work consisting of organising many congresses and meetings, drafting many instructions, etc., the cooperative associations could be merged. Since 31 July a centralized consumers' association exists in Moscow where a central office is registering all inhabitants of the city. That merger was carried out in a very disciplined way without causing problems. In the province, however, such a centralized distribution system will not as be organised easy as in the big cities, where the existing registry offices can simply carry all this out. Preparatory work for the implementation of this Decree has practically been accomplished everywhere.[82]

(This report was published in the autumn of 1919).

Provision and distribution of goods will be entirely delegated to the consumers and to the central consumers' organisations themselves. The state will only provide requisitioned products (corn), but distribution will remain in the hands of the cooperative organisations. Unfortunately, we do not have reliable information about these newly created Russian organisations and about the way they are functioning.

We will now treat the difficult problem of how the state collects food surpluses from the peasantry, i.e. a question we have already explored. In Russia, *rucksack travelling* [*Rucksackverkehr*] is also causing many troubles to the provisioning of the cities. We have already argued that during the war the peasants did not want to sell their foodstuffs for cash at a fixed maximum price. They preferred bartering them. The capitalist state could not accept this preference and decided to requisition them. The peasants, refusing to carry their foodstuffs to the market, preferred hiding them until the moment an illicit trader or a consumer showed up and would pay any price for them. Hence, the food situation was continuously worsening. Foodstuff provision became even more and more anarchistic. Thousands of people travelled by train from the cities to the countryside, to their relatives, friends, acquaintances in order to acquire foodstuffs; bed-clothes, shoes, jewels, all these things were now carried to the farms in the form of barter goods. An insatiable demand for consumer goods forced up prices while peasants' greed was at first sight growing to unlimited highs.

The proclamation of the proletarian dictatorship did not change this situation fundamentally. *Political resistance reinforced this economically inspired refusal of the peasantry to feed the cities*. Meanwhile the dictatorship was confronted with a serious dilemma. Hence, without repressing rucksack travelling collecting food surpluses efficiently and feeding of the urban population regularly could not be realised. Bread and flour demand could still be covered by

---

82 ['Der einheitliche Konsumverein in Sowjetland' 1920, p. 7].

the harvest of the previous year. The municipalities met their meat demand by claiming a certain percentage of the existing livestock. Milk provision could be secured by providing the peasantry with bran, sugar, etc. Serious shortages of agrarian products nonetheless existed: eggs, fat, fowls, all sorts of vegetables, etc. These shortages were of course also caused by important wage rises that the dictatorship had conceded to the broad masses of the urban proletariat. *Attempts to set up a rationally organised system of collecting foodstuffs were nonetheless hampered by a considerable growth in rucksack travelling.* On the other hand, a prohibition of this rucksack travelling would only be possible if governmental measures could guarantee foodstuff provision of the cities. As in Russia, the Hungarian Councils' Government was hesitating. Though rucksack travelling was forbidden, this prohibition could not strictly be applied because pettybourgeois women and workers of small enterprises, whose foodstuff provision was poorer than for people working in big enterprises, protested against this measure. An off-hand decree of commander-in-chief [Vilmos] Böhm[83] deciding that soldiers returning home from the front would be allowed to take some 25 kilos of foodstuffs with them, meant that the prohibition of rucksack travelling was cancelled. From now on, all food hoarders would travel in a soldier's uniform.

One was now increasingly reliant on democratic means of information when organising agitation campaigns. The workers were informed during meetings of the councils and during mass meetings that unorganised rucksack travelling would cause the decay of the proletarian provision system and would first of all permit the bourgeoisie to live a good but idle life. That kind of agitation was working. In the big factories workers now approved of resolutions which absolutely forbade smuggling of foodstuffs. But at that moment the Councils' Republic had already collapsed.

Effective means of coercion making illicit rucksack travelling impossible nonetheless existed. *Though we accepted the guiding principle that the dictatorship could not permit chaos or cultural decay, we nevertheless hesitated to prohibit all passengers' traffic by train or ship*, a measure that had nonetheless promulgated in the autumn of 1919 by capitalist countries like Germany and Austria in order to save coal. If only officials would have been permitted to travel by train, rucksack travelling and illicit trade would have become impossible and organising the counterrevolution would then have been seriously hampered. In the meantime, a large quantity of coal would also have been saved. Dur-

---

83 [Trade-union official and Social-Democratic politician Vilmos Böhm (1880–1949) was People's Commissar of War].

ing the dictatorship no business trips should be made. Making excursions can easily be denied for a short period of time. Parcel post delivering foodstuffs should meanwhile also be completely prohibited. Wagon-loads of illicitly traded goods sent by rail or ship can be halted in case these goods are not exclusively addressed to state agencies such as central entrepreneur agencies, raw materials agencies or local economic agencies. Without taking such tough measures, no efficiently organised provision of foodstuffs will be immediately possible. When the peasant sees that the buyer is not showing up or that he has no barter goods to offer, he will prefer to sell his food surpluses to the state agencies. Though survival will remain certainly difficult in the city, no other solution can be found.[84]

∴

At present we now want to look at the distribution problems from the point of view of the class struggle. We already argued that the industrial proletariat was first of all expecting an increase in its living standard, notwithstanding that this could not be realised before completely adapting capitalist income distribution to a reorganised production system and increasing productivity. Yes! A real rise in the living standard of the agricultural proletariat can be obtained, but at the detriment to the cities. No political-economic measure can solve this problem. If the working classes, especially the less-determined communist elements, refuse to be, as happened in Hungary, victims of counterrevolutionary agitation, they should adopt *a system of class-defined rationing and pricing system!*

The capitalist war economy had already led to a system of class-related food rationing for the hard-working and the very hard-working manual workers who could obtain larger bread and flour rations. A system of class-related food rations, as exists in Russia, means a further development of the idea that physically hard-working people should receive larger rations than clerks or bourgeois people doing lighter work. First, this should be a political and not an economic decision. Rations were kept so low during the beginning of the dictatorship because of problems with the food-distribution system. Diminishing food rations of the not so numerous class of non-proletarian workers would

---

84 A traffic interruption by the Austrian railway during the past Christmas holidays of 1919 splendidly confirmed our views. Normally, Vienna's daily milk provision amounted to 60,000 litres [a day]. But during the Christmas holidays one was forecasting a normal daily decrease of about 10,000 litres [a day]. Because rucksack travelling had now been made impossible, milk provision increased to 87,000 litres daily.

have only slightly improved the proletariat's nourishment. As we already saw, workers can better support privations when seeing that rich people get smaller quantities of foodstuffs from the state agencies than the hard-working manual workers. But the situation is completely different under a capitalist regime, when the rich – even in hard times – can secure the most delicate titbits.[85] Class-related rations are in the first place also a matter of increasing the class consciousness of the proletarian masses who should now consider themselves as the ruling class during the dictatorship of the proletariat. That was why in Hungary the finest foodstuffs, i.e. fowls, fish, etc., as far as the state distribution agencies could acquire them, were directly assigned to the factory proletarians. The system of class-defined rations had an excellent effect too. The smaller the bourgeois rations and the more illicit trade is successfully combated, the higher the prices of illicitly traded foodstuffs will rise for the bourgeoisie, thus the faster their savings will disappear and the earlier their productive labour will contribute to the construction of the proletarian state.

The system of class-defined rations was criticised by the Social Democrats because of its inhuman character, especially with regard to the children. During the first period of the dictatorship, the bourgeoisie will normally, notwithstanding the smaller rations they get, be better supplied than the workers because of their remaining funds. We could also have argued that the ruling bourgeoisie had never been preoccupied by the idea that the children of the proletarians were not decently nourished. One should nonetheless stress *that the whole system of class-defined rations will only be applied during the first period of the dictatorship. In Russia, all children of the bourgeoisie now get food rations which are as big as those of other children.*

Class-specific prices are of a similar significance. The selling-price of goods produced by the state, i.e. flour, meat, etc., is standard. But proletarian buyers

---

85   Unfortunately, the Hungarian proletariat experienced at its own cost that there is a big difference between a proletarian and a capitalist food economy. During the dictatorship, when the industrial workers were in general well provided with foodstuffs, complaints disappeared about the fact that the cities were insufficiently provided with foodstuffs, because the workers could not spend all their money on foodstuffs. Nowadays, there is plenty of food in Budapest. The shop-windows are overloaded with all sorts of delicacies. All things people were longing for can now be purchased. Of course, this only applies to the rich. The worker cannot afford all the foodstuffs now brought to the market. His wage is merely sufficient for purchasing bread and vegetables. Rationed bread does not exist anymore. But at every street corner, one can buy expensive white bread at a high price from illicit merchants. Sugar disappeared [from the shops], but confectionaries still sell plenty of expensive pastries. It is a horrible situation, but in the meantime it is also a historically necessary lesson to the Hungarian proletariat for having refused to wait until the real conditions would be fulfilled during the dictatorship for raising the living standard.

could buy them at a reduced rate. Because of shortages under the dictatorship, the money wages of workers were in general higher than the population's average living standard. Hence, the workers were able to buy all rationed foodstuffs without asking for price reductions. Price reductions, however, confirmed the workers in their opinion that '*their state*' was allowing these advantages to the rich because of all their past sufferings and efforts. If the rule of the toiling masses is definitely established, expropriation of the means of production is completely executed, public management and distribution are functioning and the bourgeoisie as a class has disappeared, then all people will have to work for their income, hence differences between former workers and bourgeois will then have disappeared and the reason for fixing class-specific rations and prices will then also have become superfluous. Both measures have thus a transitory character. The faster they become redundant, the better it will be for the country's suffering population.

11   Monetary Problems during the Dictatorship

Money has different economic functions in a capitalist economic system. It is a general equivalent of all goods, it is an ideal means of payment, it is a measure of all prices. It is used as a means of circulation and payment on the domestic and international market. It will be used for storing wealth, accumulated as a potential purchasing power. In modern capitalism it accomplishes all these functions without referring to its metal or paper form on the condition that the total nominal value of the banknotes put into circulation does not exceed the 'social circulation value', i.e. that there are not more banknotes circulating than necessary for the circulation process of goods.[86]

The war economy of *all countries* was characterised by the fact that the real amount of goods decreases, *that more is consumed than produced*, which means that *the real total value of the circulating goods finding expression in socially necessary labour time is diminishing*. This does not mean, however, that the quantity of money in circulation diminishes. On the contrary. This quantity will continually increase. The state is the most important consumer of the war economy. The state buys real goods from private owners for cash money. The state receives that cash money either directly from the emission bank in the form of the so-called floating debt, or from emitting war loans. If the state directs the emission bank itself, banknotes will simply replace consumed stocks of

---

86   Hilferding 1910.

goods. This paper money is only money in its superficial appearance. *In essence, it is only paper money that was not put into circulation for meeting the circulation demands of the economy, but for covering the war expenses of the state.*[87] Because real consumption now considerably exceeds production, this paper money can no longer be exchanged for goods. But that cannot be in harmony with an anarcho-capitalist economy. Hence, all prices will increase to the point where everybody will exchange his money for real goods representing an equivalent share of the national income. Prices will then rise proportionally to the amount of superfluous money put into circulation. One can now buy only a smaller quantity of goods than in the past for the same amount of money.

A quantity of paper money is then hoarded in the form of a treasure, deposited at monetary institutions or hidden in the trunks of the peasants. Because shortages make it impossible to buy capital goods on the market, there is no possibility of converting this money capital into productive capital. There is still the possibility of converting cash money into fictive capital. But only a small part of it can be transformed into interest-bearing capital because the monetary institutions are rolling in liquid assets. For instance, provincial banks in Hungary refused to accept interest-bearing deposits during the last year of the war. Hence, the only escape is to convert that fictive capital into an eminent but very typical monetary form: war loans. The state borrows from the propertied classes their accumulated paper money and transforms it continuously into interest-bearing loans: this means that a part of the later produced wealth of the next generations will be taxed away. Meanwhile the fictive national income of the country grows as a result of these war loans, which will lead to a further devaluation of the currency. Of course, it is not the quantity of banknotes put into circulation, as the vulgar money quantity theory pretends, that is causing inflation, *but the dominance of money income on the production of real goods*. Because of inflation the role of money declined as a means of payment in the war economies of the Central Powers. Hence, selling for cash money was gradually replaced by a primitive system of barter.[88] That was the situation of the Hungarian monetary system when the proletariat took over political power.

There exists no monetary problems in a fully developed communist economy, because money does not function here as it does in capitalism. A communist economy is a goods-producing economy *in which some kind of token money* [*ein geldähnliches Zeichen*] *is circulating, but that money is not as fatally*

---

87   The next European countries are today indebted to their circulation bank: Italy: 12 milliards of lires; France: 26 milliards of francs; Austria-Hungary: 22 milliards of kronen; German Austria: 5 milliards of kronen; Hungary: 7 milliards of kronen.
88   Varga 1916.

functioning as a social process for the people. It is not the realised sum of money that informs the producer as to whether or not the produced goods meet the social needs or whether labour time contained in them is also social labour time. Hence, the mysterious concept of the 'commodity market' and the 'fetish character' of goods in the form of commodities will disappear together with the money problem and the anarchistic way of producing for an impersonal market.

Hence, the money problem is the most difficult problem to be solved in the beginning of the dictatorship of the proletariat, i.e. during the transition period of a commodity to a goods producing economy. The problem is now how to transform the role of money in such a manner that some functions of it are maintained while others are suppressed. In the beginning, the proletarian state cannot use money as a price measure and a means of circulation as long as a egalitarian natural distribution of wealth is not yet fully realised and, except for the socialised enterprises, production of the private economic system is still important. Economic chaos would be the result of an immediate abolition of money.

A proletarian economy formally needs money to cover its spending deficit. In the beginning, the proletarian economy is confronted with a huge spending deficit, something the capitalist countries are also experiencing nowadays.[89] The capitalist governments can partly cover their spending deficits by contracting new loans. Because the proletarian state had cancelled the old state debt, no new loans could be contracted, thus no new sources of idle income could be created. Hence, no other solution for covering the deficit existed than printing more paper money.

The following money functions should be abolished:

The function of *money capital* is contrary to the essence of the proletarian economy. It is a means of acquiring surplus value in the form of *loan capital* and *commercial capital* or by its transformation into productive capital.

The *treasure* function of money inherited from capitalism constitutes a source of accumulated purchasing power for its owner and thus creates the possibility of making a living without taking a job until all saved money has been spent.

At the proclamation of the dictatorship, the function of *international currency* will be limited to gold and silver. Because the capitalist countries will not

---

89 For 1919–20, the deficit of the Union is about 2 milliards of dollars = 100 milliards, England 600 milliards of pounds sterling = 174 milliards of marks, France 20 milliards of francs = 100 milliards of marks, Germany about 20 milliards of mark, Italy 20 milliards of lire = 70 milliards of marks.

accept banknotes issued by the proletarian state, the latter cannot intervene in that matter. Hence the proletarian state will be unable to pay with banknotes imports of investment and consumer goods. These banknotes will thus play no role in economic exchanges between proletarian and capitalist countries.

We now discuss the money problem of the Hungarian Councils' Republic from the latter point of view. The first measure with regard to the currency system consisted in *putting the monetary institutions, i.e. the centres of the capitalist economic system, under state control*. Hence, the managing directors of the capitalists were removed from their leading positions and replaced by socialist-minded bank employees getting the same competences as those possessed by the commissars in the factories. From now on the Councils' Government could control the whole financial and banking system. Formal expropriations and nationalisations were, however, circumvented because of existing foreign-owned financial institutions and the far-reaching interests of foreign capital in the Hungarian credit institutions. All credit institutions were nonetheless brought under public control without meeting the slightest resistance. Transformation of the currency function could thus be undertaken at once.

In the beginning of the dictatorship, a shortage of circulation means [Zirkulationsmittel] could nonetheless cause a catastrophe: production could collapse because of liquidity shortages if workers' wages could not be paid immediately. Hence, the financial institutions received the instruction to pay the wages of the workers by ordering the banks to take over the payrolls of the factories and enterprises that the production commissars had already transmitted to them for that task. The financial institutions also paid the commodities that the expropriated enterprises had bought from private companies. A system of bank transfers was immediately started up for carrying out exchanges between the expropriated enterprises. Enterprises short in cash for paying wages were given a state guarantee. *But this was only a provisional measure.* After having organised the enterprise central agencies, the latter had to manage the bank accounts of all enterprises of the same branch. According to this regulation money was, however, only provisionally kept as a means of circulation. This made it possible to cover the state deficit by printing more banknotes.

The function of money capital was thus abolished. Hence, all money institutions stopped paying interest at once.[90]

---

90 Later, a general shortage of cash money was threatening the circulation system because there was no paper and no printing office for printing new banknotes; then we tried to solve this crisis by reintroducing the already abolished system of interest-bearing bank deposits. Anybody having deposited cash money at any money institution controlled by the state after the establishing of the Councils' Government, would obtain an interest of 4

A transformation of monetary capital into productive capital was impeded not only by the menace of expropriation, but also by the impossibility of buying productive capital goods. Big estates and also tenement houses in the bigger cities were expropriated. Small estates, i.e. farmers' land, were not sold by their proprietors. *Hence, transforming money capital into capital was impossible* with the exception of illicit trading, smuggling and other illegal transactions that have nonetheless become more and more of a secondary influence because of the expanding public sector.

The elimination of the treasure function of money is of much more importance. It prevents the mass of money accumulated under capitalism from becoming real purchasing power, meaning the money owners can buy goods and continue their idle existence until the moment they have run out of all their savings. The problem with money having already been transformed into interest-bearing capital and deposited at monetary institutions could easily be solved. The monetary institutions received the instruction that not more than 10 percent of a deposit could be withdrawn at a monthly maximum of 2,000 korunas. Deposits belonging to several members of the same family were put into a single bank account in order to prevent multiple monthly withdrawals of cash. *Seizing all bank accounts and claims would have been too radical a decision.* We did not take this decision because of the foreign account owners and also because we otherwise would have had to take care of all disabled persons as well. We did not want all disabled persons, i.e. the old and the sick, to immediately fall into misery. A seizure of all accounts should only follow after having organised a comprehensive welfare system for all disabled workers.

The purchasing power of all accumulated wealth in the form of treasure money – here we are thinking of millions of peasants and bourgeois storing huge sums of cash at home because of the confused political situation – can theoretically be eliminated in three ways:

1. *Nullification of all bank accounts and claims and the creation of new means of circulation is the most radical solution.* Such a decision destroys at once the purchasing power of all accumulated moneys; but such a decision would also suppose the existence of a very powerful proletarian state: the power of imposing the new currency on the peasantry. In the beginning, the proletarian state is, however, the peasantry's weaker trading part-

---

percent for his so-called 'free deposits'; the account owner could withdraw at any moment the whole sum from his account. This experiment failed too. Only small sums were deposited at the branch offices of the central cooperative peasants' bank by backward peasants without any clear idea about recent social changes. Later on, it appeared that the rule of not paying interest had not been suppressed.

ner, because the proletarian state has to get from the peasants quantities of goods of a higher total amount of value than can be provided. Thus the state has to balance its deficit by means of only formal payments.[91] Because the goods that the state offers to the peasants are for them less indispensable than their foodstuffs for the urban proletariat, applying the most radical measures would be hardly possible during the first period of the dictatorship; it would create enormous difficulties to the system of food deliveries.

2. *Reducing the accumulated money's purchasing power to a minimum by organising a radical currency devaluation* can be a second solution. The proletarian state can be forced into a currency devaluation when the budget deficit can only be covered by issuing more banknotes. But one can also opt for a devaluation. Or one can try to stop inflation and avoid a devaluation by means of an alternative payment system making cash payments redundant and by setting prices related to their production costs of goods produced by state enterprises. Repeated and fast devaluations are harmful because they impede wage stabilisation, thus they lead to wage fluctuations and cause conflicts between the workers and the proletarian state, they engender incessant wage increases, they hamper making calculations and disturb the drafting of a formal economic plan and they make the latter's implementation impossible. All depends thus on the quantity of money the wealthy classes have accumulated when planning a currency devaluation.

3. *The third and definitive way consists of letting money slowly disappear.* The proletarian economy is essentially a goods-producing economy, i.e. a natural economy [Naturalwirtschaft]. With the growth of the state sector money will disappear in exchange processes between state and enterprises. Coal mines will provide their coal to the railways and the iron works without making cross payments. The blast furnaces will deliver their iron to the engineering works without a making payment. The workers will receive an ever-growing part of their wages in kind: housing, heating, bread, meat, etc. Hence, the tighter the network of the state production and the growth of the distribution system, the more the peasants will have to participate in the commodity producing system, the less they will have a chance of transforming the money amassed under capitalism into a potential purchasing power. They will be forced to exchange their own goods for goods produced by the state and to pay their taxes in

---

91 See our previous chapter on the possibility of balancing this gap by means of taxation.

kind. Hence, money will disappear as a means of circulation well before the process of expropriation of the peasants is finished or before they have voluntarily abandoned their private means of productions. By then the treasure problem will be solved as well. A far-reaching organisational and political consolidation of the proletarian state will not be its only precondition; it will also require a balanced budget, having coped with inflationary deficit spending.

Invalidation, devaluation and a gradual disappearing of money are the three possible forms for liquidating the purchasing power of accumulated paper money. These three forms are not mutually exclusive. Any proletarian government will pursue a policy of economic expansion and will try as soon as possible to abolish the capitalist role of money. Any proletarian government will be forced to put paper money into circulation to cover the spending deficit and will devalue large quantities of cash money having been accumulated during the capitalist period. Finally, one should find a good occasion to give the circulating old money a severe blow by invalidating its value. It will depend on the historical and political circumstances which solution should be chosen.

Because of several coinciding circumstances, the Hungarian Councils' Republic struggled with very serious difficulties when dealing with the currency problem. In the capitalist period, Hungary did not have its own currency. Thus after the collapse of the Austrian-Hungarian Monarchy, banknotes of the Austrian-Hungarian [National] Bank were still circulating in all successor states. In some of these countries the old banknotes had been rubberstamped. Apart from this, these banknotes could also be easily counterfeited. The printing office of the emission bank was located in Vienna: in the successor states, demand of banknotes was met by deliveries of the emission bank, an operation covered by a blank credit. However, the emission bank [in Vienna] refused to open a blank credit to proletarian Hungary. Meanwhile, notes were needed to finance normal public expenditures, especially to cover war costs. Only the 200 and 25 koruna bills could be printed by the emission bank in Budapest. When these bills were running out of stock, they were reprinted.[92] Having been put into circulation only a few weeks before the war's end, these bills mentioned that they would be retreated from circulation well before the end of June 1919.

---

92 It was not only a matter of 'counterfeiting', as often was said. Banknotes reprinted by the Council's Government had received series numbers differing from those of the old regime. This fact was widely used by the counterrevolutionary agitation in order to discredit Soviet [sic!] money. The bills were reprinted after having previously informed the direction of the Austrian-Hungarian Bank. In reality, it was a loan enforced by the government on the country's national bank.

POLITICAL-ECONOMIC PROBLEMS OF THE PROLETARIAN DICTATORSHIP 223

Hence, they could never become popular among the peasants. Because only one side of the banknotes had received a print, they became unpopular and were therefore called 'white money'. In all successor states, the old 'bleu money' was circulating together with the new 'white' banknotes before the dictatorship [of the proletariat] was established. That the peasantry refused to be paid with white banknotes was then not at all very important. The peasants were now paid with blue banknotes, while the white ones were only put into circulation in the cities.

During the third month in power, the Councils' Government printed more white banknotes.[93] Because the Austrian-Hungarian Bank had invalidated these reprinted banknotes and had taken out of circulation all 200 and 25 koruna bills, these white banknotes were no longer legal tender in the adjacent successor countries. The peasants refused to accept these new white banknotes just as they had earlier refused to accept the white original ones. A well-known phenomenon reappeared: *bad money was driving out good money from circulation*. The blue bills were hoarded; everybody tried to get rid of the white banknotes. Because the peasants only wanted to sell their produce for blue banknotes, major difficulties arose when buying foodstuffs or other farm products. Railway workers, officials and workers living in the rural areas got into trouble, because they could not buy from the peasants. The Department of Finance of the Councils' Government was daily assailed by deputations demanding payment in blue banknotes. *The nearer one lived to the state border, the worse the situation became*, because the blue banknotes were still legal tender on the other side of the border where the white bills were not accepted. A *disagio* was growing between both currencies not only because prices were lower in the adjacent successor states, but also because of the conservative and even counterrevolutionary attitude of a peasantry not willing to accept the white banknotes.

Under these particular circumstances, the Councils' Government could only put a new currency into circulation. Meanwhile, the banknotes of the Austrian-Hungarian Bank, *the blue notes as well as the white notes, lost their status as legal tender*: the blue banknotes having a high face value ceased immediately to be legal tender and the white notes only after a certain period of time. The blue notes were considered a foreign currency. At the same moment the postal sav-

---

93 [Gresham's law says: When a government compulsorily overvalues one type of money and undervalues another, the undervalued money will leave the country or disappear from circulation into hoards, while the overvalued money will flood into circulation. It is also stated as: 'Bad money drives out good'].

ings bank, which was the most popular financial institution in Hungary, issued new legal-tender banknotes of 5, 10 and 20 korunas; refusing them would be severely punished. All old banknotes, blue and white ones, were exchanged at face value. The public, however, preferred these new banknotes to the white ones, not only because there was a shortage of low-value banknotes, but also because of their beautiful design.

Though normalisation was more or less realised, the currency problem was not yet definitely solved. The new currency was easily accepted in the collectivised sector for transactions between the expropriated enterprises and also in practically all urban trades. But the peasants resisted: they refused to accept the new banknotes and they did not exchange their blue banknotes in time; *the state lacked adequate power to enforce that exchange*. As we already argued, *not economically*, because the private economy of the peasantry was still more powerful than the collectively organised economy; *not politically*, because the proletarian state could not mobilise adherents in the rural areas really willing to combat the well-to-do peasants.

Hence, a very particular monetary situation was created. *Two different economic systems with two different currencies had now emerged in one country*. The various institutions of the collective sector adopted the new currency as a means of circulation. The state paid clerks and workers with the new banknotes with which they could buy all products provided by the state sector. The peasantry and all other private businesses formed a second economic sector. Their members were using the old bleu banknotes as a means of circulation. Private businessmen used the new banknotes they already had received for their transactions with the state sector. Apart from exceptional circumstances, enterprises and people belonging to the state sector would pay the peasants with blue banknotes. For instance, a civil servant receiving his salary in white banknotes could only use these notes to pay for his rent and goods produced by the state sector, but not to buy himself an egg. Because the state bought more goods from the peasants than the peasants bought from the state, *the private sector accumulated a surplus on its balance of payments with the state sector. All blue banknotes were then hoarded by the private economic sector; hence the blue notes could realise a premium*. A profitable but nonetheless forbidden exchange rate developed between the two currencies: at the end of the dictatorship the disagio of the new banknotes was already 50 percent of their face value. The state sector had been largely left behind by the private economic sector because its means of circulation were also legal tender in the adjacent successor states where they were easily rubberstamped and considered a hard currency. Because the new banknotes issued by the Councils' Government were refused by all capitalist countries, the government was forced to use the blue notes for trading with the capitalist world; no trade relations existed at that time with the non-capitalist countries.

The Hungarian Councils' Government now ran into trouble. As reprinting of the old banknotes was impossible on technical grounds, the risk of a premature invalidation of the old banknotes was now taken and a new currency was introduced. Prematurely, because the collectivised sector was not yet sufficiently built up to withstand the predominant private sector. Thus the new currency could not be imposed by state violence. The fall of the Council's Republic would cut this Gordian knot.

12   The Economic Policy of the Proletarian State

In the capitalist countries the state works as a coercive organisation of the ruling class by oppressing the population. All activities organised by the state, even those at the ideological level, are adapted to fulfilling that mission. Education of the working-class youth will only be carried out as far as this is necessary for transforming them into qualified workers. The aim of the whole educational system is the transmission of a chauvinist, conservative ideology that also eliminates class conscious. The economic policy of the state changes within the function of capitalist development: a simple guard of private property in the age of free-trade capitalism; a regulator of market prices in the age of tariff walls; a conqueror of new markets and new territories to be exploited in the period of modern capitalism; an organiser of the whole economy during the world war.

The dictatorship of the proletariat adopt these policy aims. State power continuously grows when expropriating and nationalising the means of production and will finally determine the whole production process. Hence, the economic policy of the state will have been completely transformed. Though the capitalist state had already managed productive enterprises – railways, mines, etc. – this was not of great importance. Furthermore, the state had to trust on tax revenues paid by the citizens for financing the predominantly unproductive costs of the repressive organisations of the state. One can argue that the revenues of the capitalist state are generally drawn from the following sources:

1. *Property taxes*: death-duties; property taxes and deliveries in kind.
2. *Ground-rent taxes*: ground tax; land value taxes.
3. *Taxes on surplus value*: all sorts of income taxes.
4. *Wage taxes*: practically all sorts of consumer taxes and revenues from monopolies, as well as the so-called direct taxes usually passed on to wages.

The dictatorship of the proletariat divides economic activities into two well-defined sectors: the new common economy and the remainders of the private economy now doomed to disappear. The proletarian state therefore wants to reform the tax system in function of the still remaining private ownership, but on condition of applying the already mentioned three tax policies ruthlessly. High death duties, if possible a land-value tax absorbing the entire net ground rent, and an income tax so high that the real living standard of the independent small businessmen or small peasants will not be higher than the living standard of a wage worker employed by an expropriated big enterprise.

The proletarian state is freer than the capitalist state to increase taxes levied on private property. In capitalism, social accumulation, i.e. the development of the means of production, is a task of the capitalist classes: social accumulation is the result of private accumulation of individual capitalists. *If the capitalist state taxes away too large a part of the surplus value for its unproductive expenditures – and the capitalist state is in general only in charge of that kind of expenditure – so that individual capitalist will lose their means of accumulation, then social accumulation will stop shortly, making any progress impossible.* By expropriating big enterprises the proletarian state will be in charge of real accumulation, and thus the development of the productive forces. Accumulation of wealth by private persons has become not only superfluous, but also harmful to the interests of the workers in a proletarian state. No economic limitations exist in the proletarian state for taxing any kind of wealth and surplus income. But this tax income will nonetheless remain unimportant, because the expropriated big enterprises, which were in general also the big tax payers, have now disappeared, while the added surplus value of the not yet expropriated privately owned enterprises is very small because of the low degree of exploitation of the working class in this sector.

The problem raised here is: if the proletarian state is powerful enough to impose high taxes and to collect them, then the state should also be strong enough to expropriate all means of production of the property-owning classes. This is maybe partly right, but a full expropriation of the land of millions of peasants would certainly engender a much more forceful counterrevolutionary opposition movement than imposing a high but fair land-value tax or a very high death duty only affecting some individuals, but not the whole population at once. But apart from all political aspects, *the expropriation of millions of enterprises will not be in the first place a matter of power politics, but rather a problem of organisation*. Expropriation is not to the advantage of the proletariat: the expropriated enterprises should be organically integrated into a collective economy. There will be a shortage of competent workers during the first years of the dictatorship before a new generation of workers would be educated.⁹⁴ Hence, it would be better to impose taxes on the net profits of the private businesses at the advantage of the proletarian state than having all small private enterprises nationalised.

On the other hand, consumption taxes and tariffs will be generally of little benefit to the proletarian state: most goods taxed by the capitalist state are bulk goods, such as sugar, spirits, petroleum, etc., produced by big enterprises and this trade will now be monopolised by the proletarian state. Hence, it would be completely senseless to have the state fixing prices and imposing consumption taxes afterwards. Once foreign trade is monopolised, tariffs will become superfluous. All former revenues from consumption taxes will be unified by the enterprise centrals of the state. Hence, all tariffs and consumption taxes will disappear. But an entirely new problem arises: the problem of *pricing*. We will discuss this problem later.

One should raise here the question of *how taxes levied in cash can possibly be integrated into an economic system of the proletarian state heading in principle for a plain goods-producing economy*. If the petit-bourgeois and peasant are so heavily taxed that their income equals that of a worker's wage, that would mean that the former cannot buy and consume more goods than a worker in a goods-producing economy. The problem is totally different if the rich and middle peasants have previously accumulated milliards [of korunas] of paper money. In a goods-producing economy, taxes paid in cash by the peasants will have a completely neutral effect as far as these taxes are paid with hoarded banknotes. Hence, the printing costs of new banknotes will at any rate be saved. Because putting a new currency into circulation and devaluing at the same moment the money hoarded by the peasants is impossible, imposing taxes in kind and levying a land-value tax based on corn deliveries should therefore be introduced as soon as possible. From the moment when the devaluation of the old paper money has succeeded and more and more new money is put into circulation, a high tax payable in cash imposed on the peasants will force the latter to sell their crops for cash because they now will need that money to pay taxes.⁹⁵

The really unproductive *expenditures* by the proletarian state – thus after deduction of the productive expenditures of the enterprises – are much higher in the beginning of the dictatorship than those of the capitalist countries. The isolated proletarian state is pushed to war by the neighbouring countries. It

---

94 That is at least the situation in Russia, Hungary and finally also everywhere in Eastern Europe. Western Europe, where the general level of education of the proletariat is much higher, where each industrial worker is at least able to read, write and count, the organisation problem can be easily solved.

95 See Chapter 11 on the monetary problems.

had to mobilise a large army staying under arms. The department of education budget grew by leaps and bounds, as did social-political payments: healthcare costs, unemployment benefits, etc. The adjournment of the state debt service only meant a real saving.

Without providing any statistical evidences for this assertion, it is nonetheless obvious that even a heavy taxation of the not yet expropriated private economic sector – on the condition that the collection of these taxes will not be disturbed by any political struggles, which is, by the way, an unrealistic assumption – will be by no means sufficient to cover all expenditures of the state. From the point of view of a goods-producing economy, the amount of goods taxed away from private producers will be insufficient to keep alive the unproductive social groupings of the population: soldiers, civil servants, teachers, unemployed people, sick and disabled persons. Hence, the state-owned enterprises will have to contribute to the coverage of public expenditures. This means: *People productively employed in the state-owned enterprises will normally not receive the full produce of their work*. A huge part of the produced goods will be transferred to the not directly productive people, who are nevertheless indispensable for keeping the proletarian state afloat and all kind of disabled persons alive. Because temporary money wages and prices exist, we are now touching on the already mentioned item of price fixing by the state.

How high will be the price level fixed by the state producers?

If these goods produced by the state are sold at their cost price, there would be no revenues to support the already mentioned unproductive social layers of the population. Hence a genuine accumulation of the means of production would also be impossible. In a proletarian state, however, accumulation is even much more necessary than in capitalism in order to increase the living standard of the population. All goods produced by state enterprises should be in principal sold at their 'social cost price'.[96] Social cost price is here *a price increased by a fee for supporting the non-working population and by an additional charge for financing the real accumulation process*. In other words: the selling price has to be fixed in such a manner that the state is not generating a deficit, but a surplus to be invested in new productive capacity.

That should be in principle the solution. In practice any dictatorship will nevertheless be confronted in the beginning period with a huge spending deficit and will have to cover that by issuing banknotes. We only want to stress that, viewed from a goods-producing economy, there exist practically no differ-

---

96 This concept was coined by People's Commissar Lengyel during the dictatorship. [Gyula Lengyel was a Commissar of Finance].

ences whether an economic equilibrium is reached by selling goods produced by the state at a social cost price, or by covering the fiscal deficit by increased monetary financing. The amount of goods produced and distributed will not be affected by this. It does not matter whether or not the state is running a deficit, because the unproductive not-working people will anyway get the amount of available goods necessary for survival. *The monetary deficit of the proletarian state is by no means economically identical to the production deficit, thus not identical to the decrease in the stock of real goods produced by the state.* An overarching real accumulation process, thus a development of the means of production, can be simply financed in a proletarian economic system by creating a gigantic spending deficit. The unpleasant consequence of such an economic deficit with its monetary financing is a widening of the gap between money income and real income and that in the perception of the would-be-buyers the shortages of goods will even grow harder than when all goods produced by the state would be sold at social cost prices and the proletarian economic system would run a deficit. Hence, it will depend on the monetary policy of the proletarian state to balance the budget. Once the paper money amassed during capitalism is devalued by putting into circulation a new currency, any devaluation of the new currency should then be avoided by refraining from financing the budget deficit monetarily. If one does not succeed in balancing state expenditures, a further monetarily financed deficit will cause a radical devaluation of the amassed stock of banknotes and speed up the transition to a goods economy. *However, the problem of shortages of real goods cannot be settled by taking financial measures.* That will possibly mean consuming all stocks (foodstuffs, cattle, wearing out machines without replacing them) or a necessary curtailing of consumption in order to balance consumption and production. The economic deficit problem will, however, disappear in a full-fledged communist economy of goods and will totally dissipate into a full-fledged collective people's economy.

Under the proletarian dictatorship, the remnants of the private economy of the peasants and the petty-bourgeoisie will still exist together with the social economic system. In order to eradicate the impact of these remnants of the private ownership of the means of production on the real income distribution – as long as a complete abolishment is politically and organisationally impossible – we had a far-reaching tax scheme in mind in order to lower the income level of the peasants and the petty-bourgeois to the wage level of the workers. But imposing such a kind of well-targeted direct taxation on these social layers would be very difficult during the first period of the dictatorship. It would therefore be a matter of attaining that target, as also was the case with balancing the budget, by applying a new form of indirect taxing of these social layers by applying a class pricing policy by the state which we already discussed in the policy of income distribution. Selling the monopolised consumption goods cheaper to the proletariat while selling them at a social cost price to the petty-bourgeoisie is possible.

It is quite impossible to impose a pricing policy discriminating the peasantry with regard to the most important monopolised goods by the state and foodstuffs, because the peasants themselves are producing these goods and are partly selling them. These goods, i.e. salt, petroleum, iron, tools, machinery, which they are not producing themselves and which they can hardly miss, should therefore be indirectly taxed. They can be sold to the peasants at a high price, but, as we already remarked, one should not transgress a certain price limit, because the peasants would otherwise return to a subsistence economy by which agrarian production declines.[97]

A very fast expansion of the common economy and also a very fast transition from a capitalist economic system to a full-fledged goods economy directed by the communist state will be the best and final solution to this problem.

13   The International Economic Problems of the Dictatorship

During our research we have already very often spoken about international problems. We nonetheless feel the need to summarise and discuss these data.

The isolated proletarian state will be boycotted by the surrounding capitalist countries. The proletarian is thus excluded from the advantages of the international division of labour. All goods have to be produced, as far as possible, on the proletariat's own territory; this is a very serious handicap for labour productivity, because many goods will have to be produced at unfavourably situated locations. *Production will thus require more labour time than would be necessary in the world economy.* Many important raw materials – rubber, cotton, copper, petroleum, etc. – can only be find in some remote areas of the globe, and the proletarian state can be totally cut off from them. Apart from this division of labour based on the spread of natural resources, modern capitalism has also created a thoroughgoing economic specialisation of industrial production. Some kind of machine tools are only produced in America, some kind of wood-working machinery only in Sweden, some chemical and optimal apparels only in Germany, etc. Patents, trade secrets and a lack of institutions

---

97   During the dictatorship, the development of the schooling system and general education enhanced the needs of the peasantry and constituted a counterweight to the tendency towards a culturally backward subsistence economy.

necessary for production have, during many years, hampered production of these goods, even when all raw materials were available.

However, even in case of a full blockade, smuggling can never be excluded. Hungarian experiences show that smuggling cannot by far replace legal trade. Because of its related practices such as fraud, bribery, etc., smuggling will also contribute to a profound demoralisation within the economic structure of the proletarian state. Smuggling practised by the state stimulates private smuggling and illicit trade. Hence, it is doubtful that the advantages obtained by smuggling outweigh its disadvantages. According to the Hungarian experiences, it would be more efficient to forbid smuggling of all consumer goods and to confine smuggling to some specific goods, such as apparels, machine parts, etc.

One can imagine that individual capitalist countries, respectively individual capitalist groups in these countries, will trade with the proletarian state, as happened in Hungary. The same will happen *if the proletarian state can provide its capitalist adjacent countries with important and hard to replace products*. As in Hungary, trade could develop through individual enterprises importing and exporting goods under their old company name from abroad. However, this is only possible in the first period of the proletarian dictatorship as long as the foreign capitalists see the dictatorship as a temporary political phenomenon. The form of international trade will also change when the proletarian dictatorship is well established. *Because property relations and legal rules of the proletarian state are not an appropriate ground for credit operations of the foreign capitalists, international credit provisions should be organised*. Money no longer exercises its international function. As the capitalists are not sure that they may exchange it for real goods or sources of income, they do not accept the money issued by the proletarian state. Hence, the proletarian state can also only use foreign currencies in a limited quantity because the possibility of importing goods will remain uncertain due to the continual threat of a blockade. In a capitalist economy, gold, i.e. capitalism's true world currency, is playing a totally different role than in a proletarian country. In capitalism, gold is used as a '*general equivalent of human labour*', as an 'embodiment of materialised form of value'.[98] Whatever may be its origins, gold is an absolute medium of payment. The proletarian state can buy everything with gold – if trade is possible – from

---

98 [Varga writes about 'allgemeiner Materiatur der menschelichen Arbeitskraft' and 'allgemein gültige verdinglichte Form des Wertes' (p. 130) without explicitly referring to *Capital*, Volume I. But in reality Marx writes: 'An adequate form of manifestation of value, a fit embodiment of abstract, undifferentiated, and therefore equal human labour, that material alone can be whose every sample exhibits the same uniform qualities'. Marx 1954, p. 89].

capitalists in capitalist countries. Because of its transition to a goods-producing economy, gold is, however, of low utility in a proletarian state and in the capitalist world its worth is that of means of payment. The proletarian state will therefore use without any hesitation its gold stock for buying goods abroad. The proletarian state will only export goods for gold payments if there is hardly a possibility to exchange them on the world market for real goods. Imagine now that there is a peaceful coexistence between a proletarian and a capitalist state; in that case foreign trade can only occur in the form of a barter system, just like already occurred during the war with the so-called '*compensation agreements*' of the state. The basic differences between the proletarian and capitalist economic system can easily be discerned in these barter programmes. In a proletarian state progressing towards a natural economy, only their use value is of decisive importance to the exchange of goods. This would be completely senseless for a capitalist. Capitalists only want to exchange goods if they can make profit in a hard currency. Hence, payments will occur in the currencies of the capitalist states.[99] The capitalists will unilaterally determine the quantitative terms of trade which reflect the capitalist world market price. The proletarian state, however, receives the new mission of quantifying the relative utility of goods: The state will decide how to compensate utilities lost by selling a particular good by utilities acquired by bartered goods. This valuation can be done by calculating costs of locally produced goods of the same kind. In the capitalist economic system, utility valuation standards of goods are a private affair of individual buyers and manifest anarchically as a reification by taking the form of market prices. But in the proletarian state, this function will, however, be taken over by the economic decision makers.

Trade between the proletarian and the capitalist countries will smoothly develop as long as the proletarian state still holds goods in stock, or, by selling gold and silver objects, jewels, luxury furniture and carpets, some textiles, etc., in case a fast reconversion of the means of production is impossible and a further production of goods for bourgeois consumption is, for the time being, unfeasible because these goods do not meet the needs of the worker whose living standard is still too low. One should also mention the auctioning of all sorts of foreign securities. These securities are of little value to the proletarian state, but they have a high market value for capitalists in the capitalist countries. Hence, they can easily be bartered. Efficiently trading goods is a very difficult matter when raw materials and consumer goods of the proletariat are

---

99 International trade payments are often settled in a foreign currency, in most cases here in British pounds or, more recently, also in American dollars.

concerned because of general shortages occurring in the proletarian state as a result of rising monetary incomes without a corresponding growth of domestic output.

Trade between proletarian states is, of course, easier to organise, but here will arise very particular problems as well. *In the beginning the former state borders will subsist as economic borders, partly because of organisational-technical reasons* – managing a centrally planned economy is a very difficult task – *partly because in the beginning the better-off proletarian countries may refuse to form a common economic and distribution area with the poorer countries.* It is also possible that a further geographical restructuring will proceed by leaps, that the newly emerging proletarian states may be temporarily – completely or partly – surrounded by capitalist states – as just happened to Hungary and Russia – and that establishing a single economic area will be geographically impossible. *Qualitative exchange ratios based on utility criteria would possibly not be established* when goods were organised between proletarian states, *because both countries can always come up with very different outcomes notwithstanding the fact that they start from the same criteria.* In case two countries exchange goods on a mutually beneficial basis, both should then obtain a surplus of utility. But an objective basis is nonetheless absent for a principled distribution of utilities between both trading partners. Calculating the quantity of labour time of the goods for export and making labour time the standard for establishing the exchange ratio would, however, conform well to the guidelines of a proletarian economy too. Hence, two questions of 'national particularities' with regard to the labour force can be raised here. An English worker produces on average during his working day more than a Russian or Hungarian worker, because he is operating under better natural conditions and using better tools, because he has received better professional training, because he is smarter, because he is better nourished, etc. The question is thus: should the working day of an English worker be considered as an equivalent for the working day of a Russian or Hungarian worker for exchanging goods? According to the basic principles of Communism they should be considered as equivalents. But a persisting greedy-egoistic ideology also forces one to make compromises. Like under the dictatorship, productivity of the individual worker, thus not his needs, should account for calculating his wage; in international trade one should take into account the existence of a difference in national labour productivity between the proletarian countries as well. In practice, one should probably establish permanent or ad hoc governmental committees fixing the exchange ratios.

One should also notice that the relations between proletarian countries are economically totally different from those between capitalist countries. Any proletarian regime has an urgent interest in strengthening other proletarian countries economically, because this will underpin its own consolidation, strengthen proletarian regimes in other countries, and guarantee a further existence in its own country. *During the first revolutionary period, a very serious momentum will occur with regard to the exchange of goods between the proletarian countries.* At any rate, countries having been the first to realise a proletarian revolution and having already consolidated their economy will aspire – for political reasons – to facilitate the the latecomers' transition from a capitalist to a proletarian economy. This can be best organised by opening a state-guaranteed credit line.

This situation will change as soon as the dictatorship of the proletariat is firmly established in all civilised countries. The isolated proletarian state will be possibly forced to produce all goods domestically. Apart from all other circumstances, labour productivity will thus be lower than in capitalist countries profiting from the international division of labour. However, if a proletarian country enters into contact with another, then Ricardo's principle of a country producing a particular good at a lower marginal and opportunity cost will fully come into operation. Hence, the location theory[100] will also be consciously applied within the context of the proletarian international economy. Each country will produce only those goods for which it owes the best location. All those greenhouse-like industrial activities capitalism developed behind high tariff walls in individual countries at the cost of labour's total productivity will be dismantled. *Hence, establishing a supranational economic organisation, a World Statistical Office and a Supreme World Economic Council for solving all interstate problems, will become necessary* as long as the individual countries remain independent economic entities. Because of this restructuring process, national differences in labour productivity will therefore successively disappear. Under the dictatorship of the proletariat, the toiling masses of the hitherto backward countries will make a fast cultural progress which will automatically lead to a higher labour productivity. An internationally planned dissemination of production facilities according to the location principle will reinforce this tendency. After a lifetime labour time will be indifferently applied as a world standard for calculating costs of all internationally exchanged goods. But we are at present digressing from the main point into utopian thoughts ...

The question of foreign direct investment and the colonial problem embody a cunning reality. The West-European countries, England, France, Holland, Belgium, Switzerland have invested gigantic amounts of capital abroad and their balance of trade already showed a deficit before the war. They import large

---

100 [Meant is Alfred Weber's cost theory of industrial location].

quantities of goods from abroad paid out of the profits made on productive capital investments and the interests on loans. All this will be finished with the dictatorship of the proletariat. The people on whose territory the means of production and other real assets are located will expropriate them without paying any compensations. The inflow of profits and interest earnings will stop shortly. For the creditor nations this will mean a huge loss, not only of money income, but also of supplied goods.

All income from the political exploitation of the colonies will meanwhile disappear. Continuing colonial politics in the old-fashioned way by oppressing and exploiting weaker people by force would be absolutely contrary to the disposition of the proletarian dictatorship. The proclamation of proletarian rule means the liberation of all colonial people. For the hitherto ruling people [Herrenvölker] this will directly signify a huge loss of real assets.

What we already clarified in Chapter Three about the position of the isolated proletarian state at the national level will here be rehearsed at the international level. Just as the vanguard of the proletarian struggle, i.e. the skilled industrial workers, were worse off at the beginning of the dictatorship of the proletariat than during capitalism when foodstuffs were withheld from the cities because of the fast-rising wages of agricultural workers. *At the international level, the dictatorship will also withhold all goods that the creditor and colonial powers had hitherto obtained from their debtor countries and colonies*: this circumstance strongly influences the proletariat's opinion in these countries into a conservative sense.

Transition from capitalism is accompanied by very intense struggles and privations of all kinds. *The European-American capitalist culture is founded not only on the exploitation of its own proletariat, but also on that of the entire colonial world.* This culture of the privileged social layers to which also belongs a part of the skilled workers, i.e. the labour aristocracy, and the fact that some countries are the workshop of the whole world, should disappear and be replaced by a general popular world culture. This transition will be a serious ordeal for the populations of these countries; but, on the other hand, the hitherto oppressed people, now freed from their colonial and national chains, will quickly develop their productive forces to a higher level. The production of wealth in the whole world will increase by leaps as a result of a fast extension of education, a general increase of popular culture [Volkskultur], a systematic exploitation of all natural resources and an international distribution of goods produced at the most advantageous locations in the world, thus, in one word, as the outcome of a planned world economy. Within a short period of time, production will grow to such a high level that all people, all proletarian layers, will acquire a standard of living which the labour aristocracy enjoyed in capitalism just before the outbreak of the war. At the international level, a levelling of income will happen. On this basis, a new and general world culture open to everybody will develop: a free empire [Reich] of a humanity freed from any material needs.

Epilogue

Many readers will disappointedly put this publication aside. Many will be deterred by the 'monstrosity' of the targets of the proletarian revolution and by the harsh privations the vanguards are enduring. But the creation of an ephemeral enthusiasm cowardly disappearing at the first setback is not our aim. The proletarian revolution needs nonetheless vanguards tough enough to endure privations and surmount all difficulties ...

The evolutionary interpretation of Marx's teachings created a passive, fatalistic ideology among broader layers of the proletariat. Marx's teachings of a necessary decay of the capitalist mode of production, his scientific foundation of the principles of socialism were thus wrongly explained as the coming of an automatic downfall of capitalism without any revolutionary struggle of the proletariat. This is a fatalistic misinterpretation of Marx: the revolutionary action of the proletariat will be one of the main causes of the downfall of capitalism. If the proletariat accepts the fait accompli of capitalism, the latter will always survive and overcome all contradictions at the cost of the proletariat. Neither anarchy of production and crises, nor a declining rate of profit or an impoverishment of the masses will then lead to the downfall of the capitalist social order. Hence, only a consciously revolutionary struggle by the working classes can lead to the downfall of capitalism.

We should not underestimate the enormous problems faced by a proletarian regime. We already had that experience in Hungary. The most difficult problem to solve is that of international isolation. We already referred to economic abuses caused by isolation. However, it is not economic abuses, but psychological demoralisation resulting from the isolation of the newly founded proletarian state that is the determining influence here.

The non-revolutionary layers of the population, yes, even those of the working classes, viewed the isolated proletarian regime as a temporary political phenomenon. The actively counterrevolutionary elements took refuge in the surrounding capitalist countries and there they set up an armed counterrevolution. The bourgeoisie also organised a financial and economic boycott of the new government. *At the same time psychological demoralisation was stimulated.* Messages, letters and oral accounts of the coming armed intervention by the capitalist neighbouring powers were uninterruptedly published in the newspapers. A general sentiment of vague anxiety, uncertainty and international abandonment then grew within the not absolutely convinced adherents of the regime. This would hamper the organisational setting up of the new state. The best intellectual elements kept their distance from organisational work; those participating in it secretly practised sabotage. The same was done – consciously or unconsciously – by a majority of the Soviet (sic!) functionaries of working-class origin. They tried to make friends with bourgeois people by rendering them a personal service, they were collecting evidences to prove their innocence, they were looking for an escape in order to save themselves. The dictatorship became 'pulpy', its regulations were no longer strictly observed, hardship was not courageously endured. *Instead of a revolutionary élan, petit-bourgeois lamentations became dominant, ensuring that all upright members of the working class wavered, trying to save their lives by demolishing the dictatorship, contacting the bourgeoisie to make compromises and by doing so they became traitors ...*

An isolated dictatorship of the proletariat can only survive in a big country like Russia, where the proletariat is well-experienced, that has a revolutionary character as hard as steel, that has a communist party, that party of socialism, that has brought down a decaying capitalism, that had declared the proletariat capable of organising a socialist society, and that has a strong and convinced following. In Hungary, where before the dictatorship practically no organised communist party existed, the dictatorship broke down because no revolutionary movement was strengthening it in the adjacent countries. The sad story of the Hungarian Councils' Republic proves the necessity, yes, even the urgency, of organising – not only in words but also in deeds – an international revolutionary solidarity movement contributing to the success of the proletarian revolution. However, not withstanding its many mistakes, the Hungarian Councils' Republic will not leave an inglorious headline in the history of the international revolution!

PART 2

The Comintern Years (1920–38)

Introduction to Part 2

Part Two brings together the reports Varga submitted to the Comintern Congresses of 1921, 1922, 1924, 1928 and 1935, along with some minor writings illustrating the diversity of his research. Varga also concentrated his research on the growing political and economic power of the United States and the political-economic situation in Germany.

CHAPTER 2

The International Situation: A Study of Capitalism in Collapse (Presented to the Moscow Congress, 1921) by Leon Trotsky and Prof. E. Varga

1   The Root of the Problem[1]

1. The revolutionary movement at the close of the imperialist war, and during the succeeding period, has been marked by unprecedented intensity. The month of March 1917 witnessed the overthrow of Tsarism. In May 1917, a vehement strike movement broke out in England. In November 1917, the Russian proletariat seized the power of Government. The month of November 1918 marked the downfall of the German and Austro-Hungarian monarchies. In the course of the succeeding year, a number of European countries were being swept by a powerful strike movement constantly gaining in scope and intensity. In March 1919, a Soviet Republic was inaugurated in Hungary. At the close of that year the United States was convulsed by turbulent strikes involving the metalworkers, miners and railwaymen. Following the January and March battles of 1919, the revolutionary movement in Germany reached its culminating point shortly after the Kapp uprising in March 1920. The internal situation in France became most tense in the month of May 1920. In Italy we witnessed the constant growth of unrest among the industrial and agrarian proletariat leading in September 1920, to the seizure of the factories, mills and estates by the workers. In December 1920, the Czech proletariat resorted to the weapon of the proletarian mass strike. March 1921 marked the uprising of workers in Central Germany and the coal miners' strike in England.

Having reached its highest point in those countries which had been involved in the war, particularly in the defeated countries, the revolutionary movement spread to the neutral countries as well. In Asia and in Africa, the movement aroused and intensified the revolutionary spirit of the great masses of the colonial countries. But this powerful revolutionary wave did not succeed in sweeping away international capitalism; nor even the capitalist order of Europe itself.

---

1   [Originally published by the Communist Party of Great Britain, 16 King Street, Covent Garden, London, WC2].

2. A number of uprisings and revolutionary battles have taken place during the year that elapsed between the Second and Third Congresses of the Communist International, which resulted in sectional defeats. (The Red Army offensive near Warsaw in August 1920, the movement of the Italian proletariat in September 1920, and the uprising of the German workers in March 1921).

Following the close of the war which has been characterised by the elemental nature of the revolutionary onslaught, by the considerable formlessness of its methods and aims, and the extreme panic of the ruling classes, the first period of the revolutionary movement may now be regarded as having reached its termination. The self-confidence of the bourgeoisie as a class, and the apparent stability of its governmental apparatus, has undoubtedly become strengthened. The fear of Communism haunting the bourgeoisie, without having disappeared, has nevertheless somewhat relaxed. The leading spirits of the bourgeoisie are now even boasting of the might of their governmental apparatus, and have assumed the offensive against the labouring masses everywhere, on both the economic and political fields.

3. This situation presents the following questions to the Communist International and to the entire working class:

To what extent does this transformation in the relations between the bourgeoisie and the proletariat correspond to the actual balance of the contending forces? Is it true that the bourgeoisie is about to restore the social balance which had been upset by the war? Is there any ground to suppose that the period of political upheaval and of class war is going to be superseded by a new epoch of restoration and capitalist development? Does not this necessitate a revision of the programme and tactics of the Communist International?

2 The War, Artificial Business Stimulation, the Crisis, and the Countries of Europe

4. The high tide of capitalism was reached in the two decades preceding the war. The intervals of prosperity were superseded by periods of *depression* of comparatively shorter duration and intensity. The general trend was that of an upward curve; the capitalist countries growing rich.

Having scoured the world market through their trusts, cartels, and combines, the masters of world capitalism realised that this mad growth of capitalism would finally strike a dead wall confining the limits of the capacity of the market created by themselves. They therefore tried to get out of the difficulty by a surgical method. In place of a lengthy period of economic depression which was to follow and result in wholesale destruction of productive resources, the bloody crisis of the world war was ushered in to serve the same purpose.

But the war proved to be not only extremely destructive in its methods, but also of an unexpectedly lengthy duration. So besides the economic destruction of the 'surplus' productive resources, it also weakened, shattered, and undermined the fundamental apparatus of European production. At the same time it gave a powerful impetus to the capitalist development of the United States and quickened the aggrandisement of Japan. Thus the centre of gravity of world industry was shifted from Europe to America.

5. The period following the termination of the four years' slaughter, the demobilisation of the armies, the transition to a peaceful state of affairs, and the inevitable economic crisis coming as a result of the exhaustion and chaos caused by the war – all this was regarded by the bourgeoisie with the greatest anxiety as the approach of a most critical moment. As a matter of fact, during the two years following the war, the countries involved became the arena of a mighty movement of the proletariat.

One of the chief causes which enabled the bourgeoisie to preserve its dominant position was furnished by the fact that the first months after the war, instead of bringing about the seemingly unavoidable crisis, were marked by economic prosperity. This lasted approximately for one year and a half. Nearly all the demobilised workers were absorbed in industry. As a general rule wages did not catch up with the cost of living, but they nevertheless kept rising, and that created the illusion of economic gains.

It was just this *commercial and industrial revival of 1919 and 1920*, which to some extent relieved the tension of the postwar period, that caused the bourgeoisie to assume an extremely self-confident air, and *to proclaim the advent of a new era of organic capitalist development*. But as a matter of fact, the industrial revival of 1919–20 was not in essence the beginning of the regeneration of capitalist industry, but a mere prolongation of the artificially stimulated state of industry and commerce, which was created by the war, and which undermined the economy of capitalism.

6. The outbreak of the imperialist war coincided with the industrial crisis which had its origin in America (1913) and began to hover menacingly over Europe. The normal development of the industrial cycle was checked by the war which had itself become the most powerful economic factor. It created an unlimited market for the basic branches of industry and secured them against competition. The war played the part of a solid customer ever in want of goods. The manufacture of productive commodities was supplanted by the fabrication of means of destruction. Millions of people not engaged in production, but in work of destruction, were continuously using up necessities of life at ever-

increasing prices. This process is the cause of the present economic decline. By the contradictions of capitalist society the masters lent the cloak of prosperity to this ruinous prospect. The State kept issuing loan after loan, one issue of paper money following upon another, till State accounting began to be carried on in billions instead of millions. The wear and tear of machinery and of equipment was not repaired. The cultivation of land was in a bad state. Public constructions in the cities and on the highways were discontinued. At the same time the number of government bonds, credit and treasury bills and notes kept growing incessantly. Fictitious capital increased in proportion as productive capital kept diminishing. The credit system, instead of serving as a medium for the circulation of goods, became the means whereby national property, including that which is to be created by the growing generations, was being mobilised for military purposes.

The capitalist State, dreading the impending crisis, continued after the war to follow the same policy as it did during the war, namely: new issues of paper money, new loans, regulation of prices of prime necessities, guaranteeing of profits, government subsidies, and other additions of salaries and wages, plus military censorship and military dictatorship.

7. At the same time the termination of hostilities, and the renewal of international relations, limited though it was, brought out a demand for various commodities from all parts of the globe. Large stocks of products were left without use during the war, and the enormous sums of money centred in the hands of dealers and speculators were mobilised by them to where they could produce the largest profits. Hence the feverish boom accompanied by an unusual rise of prices and fantastic dividends, while in reality none of the basic branches of industry, anywhere in Europe, approached the pre-war level.

8. By means of a continuous derangement of the economic system, accumulation of inflated capital, depreciation of currency (speculation instead of economic restoration), the bourgeois governments in league with the banking combines and industrial trusts succeeded in putting off the beginning of the economic crisis until the moment when the political crisis, consequent upon the demobilisation and the first squaring of accounts, was somewhat allayed.

Thus, having gained a considerable breathing space, the bourgeoisie imagined that the dreaded crisis had been removed for an indefinite time. Optimism reigned supreme. It appeared as if the needs of reconstruction had opened up a new era of lasting expansion of industry, commerce, and particularly of speculation. But the year 1920 proved to be a period of shattered hopes.

The crises – financial, commercial, and industrial – began in March 1920. Japan saw the beginning of it in the month of April. In the United States it opened by a slight fall of prices in January. Then it passed on to England, France, and Italy (in April). It reached the neutral countries of Europe, then Germany, and extended to all the countries involved in the capitalist sphere of influence during the second half of 1920.

9. Thus *the crisis of 1920 was not a periodic stage of a 'normal' industrial cycle, but a profound reaction consequent upon the artificial stimulation that prevailed during the war and during the two years thereafter, and was based upon ruination and exhaustion.*

The upward curve of industrial development was marked by turns of good times followed by crises. During the last seven years, however, there was no rise in the productive forces of Europe, but, on the contrary, they kept at a downward sweep.

The crumbling of the very foundation of industry is only beginning and is going to proceed along the whole line.

European economy is going to contract and expand during a number of years to come. The curve marking the productive forces is going to decline from the present fictitious level. The expansions are going to be short-lived and of a speculative nature to a considerable extent, while the crises are going to be hard and lasting. *The present European crisis is one of under-production.* It is the form in which destitution reacts against the struggle to produce trade, and resumes life on the usual capitalist level.

10. Of all the countries of Europe, *England* is economically the strongest and has been the least damaged by the war, but even with regard to this country, one cannot say that it has, in any way, gained its capitalist equilibrium after the war. Owing to its international organisation and to the fact that it came out victorious from the war, England did indeed achieve some *commercial* and *financial* success. It improved its commercial balance, it raised the rate of the pound and reached an accounting surplus in its budget. But, in the industrial sphere, England, after the war, not only did not progress, but made big strides backward. The productivity of labour in England today, and her national income, are much below that of the pre-war period. The coal industry, which is the fundamental branch of her national economy, is getting ever worse, pulling down all the other branches of industry. The incessant disturbances caused by the strikes are not the cause but the consequence of the derangement of English economy.

11. The ruin of *Belgium, Italy* and *France* brought about by the war is no less than that inflicted on Germany. The *post bellum* 'reconstruction' of France is being parasitically carried on by means of the progressive ruination of Germany, robbing the latter of her coal, machinery, cattle and gold. The French bourgeoisie is striking heavy blows at the entire capitalist order. France is gaining much less than what Germany is losing. The so-called reconstruction of

France is nothing more than piracy accompanied by diplomatic blackmail. The economic decline of that country is imminent. When the last period of expansion came to its end (in March 1920) the depreciation of French paper money reached 60 percent, while that of Italy came down to 75 percent of its face value.

12. A striking illustration of the illusory nature of this kind of business expansion is presented by Germany, where a seven-fold increase in prices coincided with a sharp decline in production. Germany won her apparent success in international trade relations at the cost of both the deterioration of the nation's basic capital (the destruction of industry, transportation and credit systems) and the progressive lowering of the standard of living of her working class. From the social and economic standpoint, the profits gained by German exporters represent pure loss. For this export in reality amounts to selling out the country's resources at a low price, while the capitalist masters of Germany are securing for themselves a constantly increasing share of the ever decreasing national wealth, the workers of the country are becoming the coolies of Europe.

13. As to the *smaller neutral countries*, they preserve their deceptive political independence thanks to the antagonistic contentions of the great powers. They maintain their economic existence on the fringes of the world market, whose essential nature used to be determined in the *antebellum* period by England, Germany, America and France.

During the war, the bourgeoisie of these countries were making enormous profits, but the devastation of those countries that had been involved in the war led to the economic disorganisation of the neutral countries as well. Their debts have increased, their currency exchange has dropped. The crisis spares them no blows.

3   The United States, Japan, Colonial Countries and Soviet Russia

14. The development of the United States during the war proceeded in an opposite direction, in a certain sense, to that of Europe. The part played by the United States in the war was chiefly that of a salesman. The destructive consequences of the war had no direct effect upon that country, and the damage caused to its transport, agriculture, etc., was only of an indirect nature and of a far smaller degree than that caused to England, not to speak of either France or Germany. At the same time, the United States, taking full advantage of the fact that European competition had either been removed entirely or had become extremely weak, succeeded in raising some of its most important industries

(such as petroleum production, ship-building, automobile and coal industry) to such a height as it had never anticipated. Today most of the countries of Europe are dependent on America not only for its petroleum and corn, but also for its coal.

While America's export prior to the war consisted chiefly of agricultural products and raw materials (making up more than two-thirds of the entire export), her main export at the present time is made up of manufactured articles (60 percent of her entire export). Having been in debt prior to the war, the United States is now the world's creditor, concentrating within its coffers about one-half of the world's gold reserve and continually augmenting its treasury. The dominant role played by the pound sterling in the world's financial market has now been taken over by the American dollar.

15. This extraordinary expansion of American industry was caused by the special combination of circumstances, namely, the withdrawal of European competition and, above all, the demands of the European war market. But American capitalism today has also lost its balance. Devastated Europe as a competitor of America is not in a position to regain its pre-war role on the world market. And the American market can only preserve an insignificant part of its former position with Europe as a customer. At the same time, America today is producing goods for export purposes to a much greater extent than prior to the war. The over-expansion of American industry, during the war, cannot find any outlet owing to the scarcity of world markets. As a consequence, many industries have become part-time, or seasonal, affording employment to the workers only part of the year. The crisis in the United States resulting from the decline of Europe signifies the beginning of a profound and lasting economic disorganisation. This is the result of the fundamental disturbance of the worldwide subdivision of Labour.

16. *Japan* also took advantage of the war in order to extend its influence on the world market. Her development has been of a much more limited scope than that of the United States and some branches of Japanese industry have acquired the character of what might be termed 'hothouse' production. Her productive forces were sufficiently strong to enable her to take hold of the market while there were no competitors. But they are utterly insufficient to retain that market in a competitive struggle with the more powerful capitalist countries. Hence the acute crisis which had its starting point particularly in Japan.

17. The *Trans-Atlantic* countries and the colonies (such as South America, Canada, Australia, China, Egypt and others), which used to export raw materials, in their turn took advantage of the rupture in international relations for the development of their home industries. But the world crisis has now involved

these countries as well, and their internal industrial development is going to be checked, thereby serving as an additional cause for the trade handicap of England and of the whole of Europe.

18. Thus, there is no ground whatsoever to speak of regarding any restoration of lasting balance, today, either in the sphere of production, commerce or credit with reference to Europe or even with reference to the world as a whole. The economic decline of Europe is still going on, and the decay of the foundation of European industry will manifest itself in the near future.

The world market is in a state of disorganisation. Europe wants American products, for which, however, it can give nothing in return. While the body of Europe is suffering from anaemia, that of America is affected with plethora. The gold standard has been destroyed, and the world market has been deprived of its general exchange medium.

The only way by which the restoration of the gold standard in Europe could be achieved would be by getting the export to exceed the import. But this is just what devastated Europe is not in a position to do. America, on the other hand, is trying to check the influx of European goods by raising her tariff.

Thus, Europe has become a bedlam. England has introduced prohibitive customs duties. The export as well as the entire economic life of Germany is at the mercy of the Parisian speculators. The former Austria-Hungary is now broken up into a number of provinces divided by custom borders. The net in which the Versailles Treaty has entangled the world is becoming more and more tightened.

19. The reappearance of Russia on the world market is not going to produce any appreciable changes in it. Russia's means of production have always been completely dependent upon the industrial conditions of the rest of the world, and this dependence, particularly with regard to the allied countries, became intensified during the war, when her home industry was almost completely mobilised for war purposes. But the blockade cut off these vital connections between Russia and the other countries. There could be no question of setting up any new branches of industry which were needed to prevent the general decay caused by the wear and tear of machinery and equipment in a country completely exhausted during three years of incessant civil war. In addition to this, hundreds and thousands of our best proletarian elements, comprising a great number of skilled workers, had to be recruited for the Red Army. Under these conditions, surrounded by the iron ring of the blockade, carrying on incessant wars and suffering from the heritage of an industrial collapse, no other could have maintained the economic life of the country and create such conditions as would permit of its centralised administration. There is no denying, however, that the struggle against world imperialism was carried on at

the price of the progressive diminution of the productive resources of industry in various branches. Now, since the blockade has relaxed, and the relations between town and country are becoming more regular, the Soviet power has, in a centralised manner, been enabled for the first time gradually and steadily to direct the country upon the road to economic prosperity.

4 Social Conditions Intensified

20. The unprecedented destruction of industrial resources brought about by the war did not check the process of social differentiation. Quite the contrary, the proletarianisation of the intermediary classes, including the new middle-groupings of employees, officials, etc., and the concentration of wealth in the hands of the small clique of trusts, combines, and so on, have for the last ten years made enormous strides in the more backward countries. The Stinnes combine is now the most important factor of the economic life of Germany.

The soaring of prices of all commodities coincident with the catastrophic depreciation of currency in all countries involved in the war meant a redistribution of the national incomes to the disadvantage of the working class, officials, employees, and small owners and all other persons with a more or less fixed income.

Thus we see that though Europe has been thrown back for a number of decades with reference to its material resources, the intensification of the social contradictions, so far from having retrograded or been suspended, has, on the contrary, assumed a particular acuteness.

This cardinal fact is, of itself, sufficient to dispel any illusions of the possibility of a lasting and peaceful development under a democratic form of Government. *The social differentiation proceeding along the line of economic decline predetermines the most intense, convulsive, and cruel nature of the class struggle.*

The present crisis is only a continuation of the destructive work done by the war and the *post-bellum* speculative boom.

21. Owing to the fact that agricultural products have risen in price, the country places have accumulated a large amount of cheap money. This produced the illusion that the villages were prosperous. The farmers did, indeed, succeed in paying off in paper money the debts they had contracted in currency at its face value. But the well-being of the farmer is not to be brought about merely by settling mortgages. The lack of labour power, the diminution of cattle, the scarcity of fertilisers, and the high cost of manufactured products brought European agriculture into a state of complete decline.

On the other hand, the universal impoverishment of Europe, rendering it incapable of purchasing the necessary amount of American or Canadian corn, resulted in getting the farming industry of the transatlantic countries into a critical situation. The ruin of the peasants and small farmers is going on not only in Europe, but also in the United States, Canada, Argentine, Australia, and South Africa. The capital newly acquired during the war is being used to buy up country estates. The village is being disintegrated, proletarianised, and pauperised, and is becoming a hotbed of discontent.

22. Owing to the fall of the purchasing power of money, the position of *State and private salaried employees* has, as a rule, become even worse than that of the proletarians. This condition is tending to go on in the same manner. Having lost their usual stability, the middle and lower officials are becoming the factors of political unrest and undermine the government apparatus which they are called upon to serve. This 'new middle state', which has been regarded by the reformists as the bulwark of conservatism, is in the present transitional period becoming a factor of revolution.

23. Capitalist Europe has completely lost its dominant position in the world economy. But it was just this domination that had lent some relative equilibrium between its social classes. All the efforts of the European countries (England and partly France) to restore former conditions only tend to intensify their instability and disorganisation.

24. While the concentration of wealth, going on in Europe, has its foundations in the ruinous conditions of that Continent, in the United States the concentration of property and the extreme intensification of class distinctions are proceeding on the basis of the feverish growth of capitalist accumulation. The class struggle going on in America has assumed an extremely tense revolutionary character owing to the sharp vacillations produced by the general instability of the world market. The period of an unprecedented rise of capitalism is bound to be followed by an extraordinary rise of revolutionary struggle.

25. The emigration of workers and peasants across the ocean has always served as a safety valve to the capitalist regime in Europe. It grew during prolonged periods of depression and upon unsuccessful revolutionary outbreaks. At present, however, America and Australia are putting ever-growing obstacles in the way of emigration. Thus this safety valve, so necessary to the capitalist regime, has ceased to exist.

26. The vigorous development of capitalism in the East, particularly in India and in China, has created new social foundations for the revolutionary struggle. The bourgeoisie of the Eastern countries has bound up its fate even more closely with foreign capital, and has thus become a very important weapon of capitalist domination. The contest between this bourgeois and foreign imper-

ialism is the contest of a weaker competitor against a stronger rival, and is by its very nature only half-hearted and unreal. The development of the native proletariat paralyses the nationalistic-revolutionary tendencies of the capitalist bourgeoisie: At the same time the great masses of the peasants of the Oriental countries look upon the Communist vanguard as their real revolutionary leader. This is particularly true of the more progressive elements of these masses.

The combination of the military nationalistic oppression of foreign imperialism, of the capitalist exploitation by foreign and native bourgeoisie, and the survivals of the feudal disabilities is creating the conditions in which the immature proletariat of the colonial countries must develop rapidly and take the lead in the revolutionary movement of the peasant masses.

The revolutionary national movement in India and in other colonies is today an essential component part of the world revolution to the same extent as the uprising of the proletariat in the capitalist countries of the old and the new world.

5 International Relations

27. The economic condition of the world in general, and the decline of Europe in particular, presages a long period of hard times, disturbances, crises of a general and partial character, and so forth. The international relations inaugurated by the war and the Versailles Treaty are rendering the situation more and more hopeless. The trend of the economic forces tending to sweep away national boundaries and convert Europe and the rest of the world into one economic territory gave birth to imperialism, but, on the other hand, the scuffle between the contending forces of this imperialism led to the creation of a multiplicity of new national boundaries, new custom barriers and new armies. With regard to State administration and economy, Europe has been thrown back to the medieval state.

The soil which has been exhausted and laid bare is now being called upon to feed an army exceeding in numbers that of 1914, the heyday of the 'world in arms'.

28. The policy of France, which is playing a dominant part in Europe today, is based upon the following two principles:

The blind rage of the usurer, ready to pounce upon and strangle an insolvent debtor and the greed of the predatory heavy industry striving to create favourable conditions for industrial imperialism to supplant financial imperialism with the aid of the Saar, Ruhr, and Upper Silesian Coal Basins.

But this striving runs counter to the interests of England, whose aim it is to keep the German coal away from the French ore, which, if brought together, would create the conditions necessary for the reconstruction of Europe.

29. Great Britain today has reached the high-water mark of her power. Having retained all her dominions, she also acquired new ones; nevertheless, it is just at this moment that it is becoming most evident that the dominating international position of England stands in contradiction to its actual economic decline. German capitalism, which from the standpoint of technique and organisation, is much more progressive than that of England, has been crushed by force of arms. The United States, having taken possession of both Americas, has now come out as a triumphant rival even more menacing than Germany was. The productivity of labour and of industry in the United States, owing to its superior organisation and technique, is now above that of England. Within the territory of the United States, from 65 to 70 percent of the world's petroleum is being produced upon which depends the automobile industry, tractor production, the fleet and aviation. England's dominant position in the coal market, which used to be almost a monopoly, has been shaken. America has now assumed first place and her European export is ominously increasing. America's commercial marine has nearly come up to that of England, nor is the United States content to any longer put up with England's monopoly over the Atlantic cables. Great Britain has taken up a defensive position with regard to her industry and is now resorting to protective legislation against the United States under the guise of combating the 'unwholesome' German competition. Finally, while the English fleet, comprising a large number of battleships of the old-type, has been checked in its latest development, the Harding administration[2] has taken up the Wilsonian programme of naval construction intended to secure the superiority of the American flag on the sea within the next couple of years.

The situation has become such that either England will be automatically pushed back, and, in spite of her victory over Germany, will become a second-rate power, or she will be constrained in the very near future to gather up all the power she had inherited from former times and engage in a mortal struggle with the United States.

This is just the reason why England is maintaining her alliance with Japan and making concessions to France in order to secure the latter's assistance or neutrality at any rate. The growth of the international role of the latter country within the European continent during the last year has been caused not by a strengthening of France, but by the international weakening of England.

---

2 [Warren Gamaliel Harding (1865–1923) was President of the United States (1921–3)].

Germany's capitulation last May on the indemnity question signifies, however, a temporary victory for England, including as it does a supplementary guarantee of further economic decay of Central Europe, without in any way excluding seizure by France of the Ruhr district and Upper Silesian basin in the near future.

30. The antagonism between Japan and the United States which was temporarily veiled by the former's participation in the war against Germany is now tending to come out into the open. In consequence of the war, Japan has approached the American coast having secured for itself a number of islands on the Pacific which are of great, strategic importance.

The crisis of Japanese industry, following upon its rapid expansion, has again put to the front the problem of emigration. Being very thickly populated and poor in natural resources, Japan must export either her goods or her men, but, whether she does the one or the other, she gets into collision with the United States: in California, in China, and in the Yap Islands.

Japan is spending one half of its budget on the maintenance of its army and fleet. In the impending struggle between England and the United States, Japan is going to play on the sea the same part as that played by France on land during the war with Germany. Japan today is making use of the antagonism between Great Britain and America but, when the final struggle between these two giants for world hegemony breaks out, Japan is going to be the battleground of that fight.

31. Both the original causes that called forth the recent great slaughter and the chief combatants that took part in it marked it as a European war, the crucial point of which was the antagonism between England and Germany. The intervention of the United States only widened the scope of the struggle, but it did not divert it from its original direction. The European conflict was being settled by worldwide means. The war settled the English-German and German-American quarrel in its own way, but it did not solve the problem of the relations between the United States and England. Now, however, this problem has been put forward prominently as one of the first order and the question of the American-Japanese as one of the second order. Thus the last war was in reality only a prelude to a genuine world war which is to solve the problem of *imperialist autocracy*.

32. This, however, forms only one focus of international policy which has yet another focus located in the Russian Soviet Federation and the Third International, brought about by the war. All the forces of the world revolution are arraying themselves against all the imperialist combinations.

Whether the alliance between England and France is going to be maintained or broken up, whether the Anglo-Japanese treaty is going to be renewed or not, whether the United States is going to join the League of Nations or not – all this is of little value so far as the interests of the proletariat or the securing of peace is concerned. The proletariat can see no guarantee for peace in the vacillating, predatory, and treacherous combinations of capitalist powers, whose policy turns to an ever increasing extent around the antagonism between England and America, fostering that antagonism and preparing for a new bloody outbreak.

The fact that some of the capitalist governments have concluded peace and commercial treaties with Soviet Russia does not mean that the bourgeoisie of the world has given up the idea of destroying the Soviet Republic. What we are witnessing now is nothing but a change, a temporary change perhaps, of the forms and methods of struggle. The uprising caused by the Japanese troops in the Far East may serve as an introduction into a new stage of armed intervention.

It is altogether obvious that the longer the revolutionary movement of the world proletariat will go on, the more inevitably will the bourgeoisie be impelled by the contradiction of the international economic and political situation to make another bloody denouement on a worldwide scale.

If this should come to pass, the 'restoration of capitalist equilibrium' consequent upon a new war would have to proceed under conditions of economic exhaustion and barbarity in comparison with which the present state of Europe might be regarded as the height of well-being.

33. In spite of the fact that the late war has furnished terrible evidence of the fact that 'wars are unprofitable' – a truth lying at the bottom of bourgeois and socialist pacifism – the process of political, economic, ideological and technical preparation for a new war continues apace all through the capitalist world. Humanitarian anti-revolutionary pacifism has become an auxiliary force to militarism.

The social democrats of every variety and the Amsterdam trade unionists[3] who are trying to make the workers of the world believe that they ought to adapt themselves to the economic and political conditions resulting from the war, are rendering the imperialist bourgeoisie most valuable services in the matter of preparing a new slaughter which threatens to completely annihilate civilisation.

---

3 [The International Federation of Trade Unions (IFTU) (also known as the Amsterdam International) was an international organisation of trade unions existing between 1919 and 1945. The IFTU was opposed by the Communist-controlled trade unions. After the American AFL dropped out in 1925, the IFTU became a mainly European body with social-democratic orientation. There were various International Trade Secretariats (ITS). The major ITS was the International Transportworkers Federation].

6   The Working Class and the Post-bellum Period

34. The problem of capitalist reconstruction along the lines outlined above, essentially puts forward the question as to whether the working class is willing to bear any more heavy sacrifices in order to perpetuate its own slavery, which is going to be ever more heavy and more cruel than it has been prior to the war.

The industrial and economic reconstruction of Europe requires the setting up of new machinery to replace that destroyed during the war and the creation of new capital. This would be possible only if the proletariat were willing to work more and to accept a lower standard of living. The capitalists are insisting on this, and the treacherous leaders of the Yellow International[4] urge the proletariat to assist in the reconstruction of capitalism in the first place, and then to proceed fighting for the betterment of their own conditions. But the European proletariat refuses the sacrifice. It demands a higher standard of living, which is utterly incompatible with the present state of the capitalist system. Hence the everlasting strikes and uprisings; hence the impossibility of the economic reconstruction of Europe.

To restore the value of paper money means for a number of European countries (Germany, France, Italy, Austria, Hungary, Poland, the Balkans, etc.) first of all to throw off the burden of too heavy obligations, i.e. to declare themselves bankrupt; but this would mean a strong impulse to the struggle of all classes for a new distribution of the national income. To restore the value of paper money means further reduction of state expenditures to the detriment of the masses (to forego the regulation of wages and of articles of prime necessity); to prevent the import of cheaper foreign manufactures and increase the amount of exported articles by lowering the cost of production which can be achieved, above all by increasing the exploitation of Labour.

Every radical measure tending to restore capitalist equilibrium must by the very nature of the case tend to disturb class equilibrium to a still greater extent than heretofore, lending additional impetus to the class war. Thus the attempt at a revival of capitalism involves a contest of vital forces, of classes and parties. If one of the two contending classes, namely, the proletariat, should decide to refrain from the revolutionary struggle, the bourgeoisie would undoubtedly establish some sort of a new capitalist equilibrium, an equilibrium based upon material and spiritual deterioration, leading to new wars, to the progressive

---

4   [The International Federation of Trade Unions (IFTU) was dubbed the 'Yellow International' by the Profintern, the Communist 'Red International'].

impoverishment of entire countries, and to the continuous dying out of these millions of toiling masses.

But the frame of mind of the world proletariat today furnishes no ground whatever for any such supposition.

35. The elements of stability, of conservatism, and of tradition have, to a considerable extent, lost their power over the minds of the labouring masses. It is true that social democracy and the trade unions still exercise an influence over a considerable part of the proletariat, thanks to the apparatus of organisation that has come down to them from former times. But the nature of this influence as well as that of the proletariat itself has undergone considerable changes in no way consistent with the 'step by step' methods of the pre-war period.

The upper crust of the proletariat, the labour bureaucracy, being closely knit together, and resorting to certain methods of domination that have become habitual, still preserves its usual position and is bound up by numerous ties with the institutions and organisations of the capitalist state. Then come those of the skilled rank and file whose position is more favourable than that of the rest of the workers, who occupy or look forward to occupying some administrative post in the industry itself, and on whom the labour bureaucracy mainly relies for its support.

The older generation of social democrats and trade unionists, consisting in the main of skilled workers, have become attached to their organisations through decades of struggle, and cannot make up their minds to sever connections with them, disregarding the treacherous nature of their activity. But in many industries unskilled workers and female workers are entering the ranks in considerable numbers.

Millions of workers having gone through the experiences of the war, and having acquired the ability to use the rifle, are now prepared, in some countries, to turn these weapons against their class enemies, provided they are given the strong leadership and serious training which are essential for victory.

Millions of working men and particularly women have been newly recruited for industrial pursuits during the war. These new workers brought with them their petty-bourgeois prejudices. But they also brought along their impatient claims for better conditions of life.

There are also millions of young working men and women who have grown up in the storm and stress of war and revolution, who are more susceptible to the communist ideas and are anxious to act.

The ebb and flow of the gigantic army of unemployed, some of whom are unattached to any class, while others possess only partial class attachments, form a striking illustration of the disintegration of capitalist production, and represent a constant menace to the bourgeois order. All these proletarian elements, varying so much in origin and character, have been enlisting in the *post-bellum* revolutionary movement at various times and in varying degrees. This explains the vacillations, the ebbs and flows, the attacks and retreats, characterising the revolutionary war. But the shattering of old illusions, the terrible uncertainty of existence, the arbitrary domination of the trusts and the practical methods of the militarised state – all this is rapidly welding the overwhelming majority of the proletarian masses together. The great masses are searching for a determined and definite leadership and for the closely welded and centralising Communist Party to take the lead.

36. During the war, the condition of the working class became perceptibly worse. It is true that some groups of workers improved their condition, and in those cases where several members of a working man's family were in a position to hold their place near the loom, the workers succeeded in maintaining and even in raising their standard of life. But as a general rule wages did not keep up with the rise in prices.

The proletariat of Central Europe has been doomed to ever greater privations since the war began. The lowering of the standard of life was not so noticeable in the allied countries until recently. In England the proletariat succeeded in stopping the process of lowering the standard of life by means of an energetic struggle carried on during the last period of the war. In the United States some of the workers succeeded in improving their conditions, others only retained their previous standard of living, while still others have had their standard of living lowered.

The economic crisis has come down upon the proletariat at a terrific rate. The falling of wages began to exceed the fall in prices. The number of unemployed and semi-employed has reached such dimensions as have never been equalled in capitalist history.

The ups and downs in the condition of existence not only have an unfavourable effect on productivity, but also prevent the restoration of class equilibrium in its most essential domain, that of production. The instability of the conditions of life, reflecting the general instability of the economic conditions nationally and internationally, is today the most revolutionary factor of social development.

7   The Perspective and Problems Involved

37. The war did not have, as its immediate consequence, a proletarian revolution, and the bourgeoisie has some ground to register this fact, as a great victory for itself.

Only dullards can find consolation in the fact that because the European proletariat did not succeed in overthrowing the bourgeoisie during the war or immediately after it, this is an indication that the programme of the Communist International failed. The Communist International is basing its policy on the proletarian revolution, but this by no means implies either dogmatically fixing any definite date for the revolution, or any pledge to bring it about mechanically at a set time. Revolution has always been, and is today, nothing other than a struggle of living forces carried on within given historic conditions. The war has destroyed capitalist equilibrium all over the world, thus creating conditions favouring the proletariat, which is the fundamental force of the revolution. The Communist International has been exerting all its efforts to take full advantage of these conditions.

The distinction between the Communist International and the Social Democrats of all colours does not consist in the fact that we are trying to force the revolution and set a definite date for it, while they are opposed to any utopian and immature uprisings. No, the distinction lies in the fact that Social Democrats hinder the actual development of the revolution by rendering all possible assistance in the way of restoring the equilibrium of the bourgeois State, while the Communists, on the other hand, are trying to take advantage of all means and methods for the purpose of overthrowing and destroying the capitalist government and establishing the dictatorship of the proletariat.

During the two and a half years following the war, the proletarians of certain countries exhibited such self-sacrifice, energy and readiness for the struggle as would have sufficed to have made the revolution triumphant, provided there had been a strong centralised international Communist Party on the scene ready for action. But, during the war, and immediately thereafter, by force of historic circumstances, there was at the head of the European proletariat the organisation of the Second International which has been and remains the invaluable political weapon in the hands of the bourgeoisie.

38. By the end of 1918 and the beginning of 1919, the power of the government in Germany was practically in the hands of the working class, but the social democracy and the professional unions used all their traditional influence and all their apparatus for the purpose of returning the power into the hands of the bourgeoisie.

In Italy, the revolutionary movement of the proletariat during one and a half years has been marked by abundant force, and it was the petty-bourgeois impotence of the socialist party, the treacherous policy of the parliamentary fractions, and the cowardly opportunism of the trade-union organisations that enabled the bourgeoisie to get into a position to reconstruct its apparatus, to mobilise its white guards, and to assume the offensive against the proletariat which has thus been temporarily discouraged by the bankruptcy of its leading organs.

The mighty strike movement in England has been frustrated once again during the last year, not so much by the government police forces as by the conservative trade unions whose apparatus has been most shamefully used to serve counter-revolutionary ends. Should the machinery of the English trade unions develop half the amount of energy in the interests of socialism which it has used in the interests of capitalism, the English proletariat would conquer power and would start the reconstruction of the economic organisation of the country with only an insignificant amount of sacrifice.

The same refers to a greater or less extent to all other capitalist countries.

39. It is absolutely beyond dispute that the open revolutionary struggle of the proletariat for power has been temporarily halted and its tempo delayed. But, in the very nature of the case, it was impossible to expect that the revolutionary offensive after the war, not having resulted in an immediate victory, should go on developing incessantly along an upward curve. The political evolution proceeds in cycles and has its ups and downs. The enemy does not remain passive but fights for his existence. If the offensive of the proletariat does not lead to direct victory, the bourgeoisie embraces the first opportunity for a counter-offensive. The proletariat in losing several of its positions, which were too easily won, usually experiences some confusion in its ranks. But it is undoubted a mark of our time that the curve of the capitalist evolution proceeds through temporary rises constantly *downwards*, while the curve of revolution proceeds through some vacillations constantly *upwards*.

40. Should the rate of development prove to be more protracted and should the present industrial crisis be superseded in a number of countries by a period of prosperity, this would not in the long-run signify the advent of the 'organic' epoch. So long as capitalism exists, periodic vacillations are inevitable. These vacillations are going to accompany capitalism in its agony, as was the case during its youth and maturity. The proletariat, having been somewhat repulsed during the present crisis, by the onslaught of capitalism, is going to assume the offensive as soon as the situation begins to improve. The offensive character of the economic struggle of the proletariat which would inevitably be carried on under the slogan of revenge for all the deceptions of the war period, and for all the plunder and abuses of the crisis, will tend to turn into an open civil war just as the present defensive stage of the struggle does.

41. No matter whether the revolutionary movement in the near future is going to proceed at a rapid or protracted rate, the Communist Party must, in either case, be the *Party of action*. The party stands at the head of the struggling masses, it must firmly and definitely proclaim their war cries and must expose

and sweep aside all equivocal slogans of the Social Democrats which always tend towards compromise. Whatever the turns in the course of the struggle, the Communist Party always strives to fortify the contested positions, to get the masses used to active manoeuvring, to equip them with new methods calculated to lead to an open conflict with the enemy forces. Taking advantage of every breathing space offered in order to appreciate the experience of the preceding phase of the struggle, the Communist Party strives to deepen and widen the class conflicts, to combine them nationally and internationally by unity of goal, and of practical activity, in such a way as to remove the hindrances in the way of the proletariat and lead it on to the socialist revolution.

CHAPTER 3

Economic Basis of Imperialism in the US of North America

Of all the capitalist Powers in the world, the United States of America is at the present moment distinguished by the most vividly expressed Imperialist character.[1] Whereas in England there is to be observed an almost general tendency in favour of a limitation of the military expenses and the liquidation of the Mesopotamian and Persian adventures, the United States is gradually developing into the largest military Power in the world – both on land and at sea. Their programme of shipbuilding is so great that its execution must lead by 1924 to a decisive supremacy of the American fleet over the naval powers of both England and Japan. As regards the land forces, it is proposed to form cadres, which will render possible a mobilisation of seven million soldiers.[2]

The *Neue Züricher Zeitung* gave notice in December [1920] of the agreement entered into by Portugal and the United States, in virtue of which the latter guaranteed the inviolability of the Portuguese colonial possessions, while Portugal on the other part entitles the United States to organise in case of war a base for the American fleet on the Azores in the Atlantic. The United States is protesting against the privileges granted to England in Mesopotamia, demanding the right to participate in the exploitation of the oil fields of that country. The United States is disputing with Japan the right of ownership in respect to the telegraphic cables which formerly had belonged to Germany, etc. Everywhere the United States is profiting by its military (and financial) supremacy to obtain the extension of its military and economic power throughout the whole world. This evolution in the American policy has taken place only quite recently. True, already the war with Spain, which ended in the conquest of the Spanish possessions in the West Indies and the Philippine Islands, showed that American capital is striving to direct the policy of the Entente along the course of Imperialism. But only the last two or three years have revealed the full development of this tendency. Our task therefore consists in determining the changes in the economic policy of America which have called forth the above-mentioned political evolution.

---

1 [Originally published in *The Communist International*, 1921, 2, 16–17: 58–67].
2 *Die Rote Fahne* (Berlin), 1 September 1920.

Basis of the Economic System of the United States

The distinguishing feature of American economic management for a long time has been the enormous productivity of labour. Unfortunately we are not in a position to cite any statistical data which would confirm the fact, but it is well known and widely accepted.[3] Another equally well-known fact is that the American workers of the white race enjoy a higher degree of material prosperity than any others in the world.

The great productivity of labour in America is called forth by the following three chief factors:
– The favourable natural conditions of the country;
– The considerable accumulation of means of production;
– A most rational system of production.

The favourable natural conditions may be summarised thus: a large area of fertile land in comparison with the population; in view of the favourable climatic conditions all the European as well as the most important tropical plants may be cultivated, and first of all – cotton. Colossal underground riches, such as coal, oil, iron, copper, lighting gas, etc. Large navigable rivers and a country which is most convenient for the construction of railways and which is able to find within the limits of its territory all the most important kinds of raw materials which a cultured people needs.

The proportion of constant capital to the total capital is very high in the United States. In other words the worker in America sets in motion a much greater mass of machinery than his fellow in Europe: This fact may be observed most in the agricultural industry, in which all the work is done by machinery (the agricultural machines employed in Russia are mostly of American invention); in the mining industry where the use of machines is much more considerable than in Europe: finally, in the process of industrial production itself, as well as in transport (the number of automobiles constructed in the United States is increasing with a furious rapidity. *The Times* of 20 October 1920 says that by 1922 this number will amount to 12 millions).[4] To the above must be added that as a general rule the machines in the United States are not subject to 'moral wearing out', as Marx says; while in Europe people are very careful with their machines. Constantly repairing them, endeavouring as far as possible to prolong the time of their functioning, in America it is the custom to give up a worn-out machine to be demobilised, replacing it with a

---

3 We refer the reader to the interesting book of A. Shadwell 1920, in which he examines and compares the productivity of labour in America, England and Germany.
4 *The Times*, 20 October 1920. [This reference could not be found in *The Times*].

more modern one. Therefore in the United States industry is using the latest and best technical methods.

Work is more rational in the United States than in Europe, and this circumstance is closely connected with the social development of America. The latter's population, not counting the coloured races, consists of the best elements from the population of Europe. Only people who are least conservative resolve to emigrate, who have known how to break with tradition, family ties, the mother country. In a word, the most advanced people of a given period. Owing to this circumstance, the whole intellectual life of America is much less conservative than that of Europe. America has never known feudalism, or nobility, titles, honorary posts or functions. The chasm dividing intellectual and physical labour is far less deep in America than in Europe. In America there is no backward illiterate peasantry like that of Eastern Europe – a peasantry which stubbornly repudiates all reasonable improvements in agriculture. Nor is there any of the guild standoffishness of the intellectual classes. Factory workers become intellectual workers while the students of the higher educational institutions work when necessary in factories, like ordinary factory hands. The result of such conditions is the rule of rationalism in production, unrestrained by conservatism, which greatly increases productivity of labour.

In examining the results of this productivity in pre-war times, we find that up to the end of the last century the influence of the first of the three factors mentioned by us, namely, that of the favourable natural conditions, was particularly felt. The United States was a country exporting an enormous quantity of raw materials, chiefly grain, wool and kerosene, and importing factory products. The centre of gravity of the public economy was agriculture. The cultivated area of land increased from 536 million acres in 1880 to 839 millions in 1900 (and 878 million acres in 1910), while the value of the agricultural products increased from 22 million dollars to 47 million dollars in 1900 and to 86 millions in 1910.[5] A colossal quantity of grain was thrown on the European market: Europe was then passing through an 'agrarian crisis'. In 1905, with a general export to the amount of 1,718 million dollars, the value of manufactured articles exported was only 160 million dollars: half-products 226 millions, foodstuffs and raw materials over 1,000 million dollars,[6] out of which were 401 million dollars of cotton, 4,186 dollars crops, 211 million dollars foodstuffs (bread, meat, etc.). We see that in spite of the rapid industrialisation (to which we shall again refer) we have a characteristic picture of a colonial country. It must be added

---

5 *The Statesman's Yearbook*, 1907 and 1920.
6 Ibid.

that a considerable share of European capital has been invested in American industry: that the steamship traffic was wholly in the hands of England and Germany, that the United States had no colonies and was not engaged in world politics: the basis for the foreign policy being the American continental doctrine of Monroe.

Meanwhile, however, the process of industrialisation of America had progressed with great rapidity, as the following figures will show:

TABLE 3.1 Industrial statistics according to the data of American census (in millions)

Year	Capital	Workers and employees	Cost of product	Cost of material
1870	2,128.2	2.05	4,232.3	2,488.4
1880	2,790.3	2.73	5,369.7	3,396.8
1890	6,525.2	4.71	9,372.4	5,162.0
1900	9,817.4	5.71	13,004.0	7,345.4
1905	13,872.0	6.72	16,866.7	9,497.6
1910	18,490.7	7.43	20,767.5	12,195.0
1915	22,790.9	8.00	24,246.4	14,368.1

An extraordinarily rapid rate of development of the mining and other industries may be observed. It is clear that the time is not far off when the United States will become transformed from a debtor country, exporting raw materials, into an Imperialist capitalist Power. Even though these figures are of a too general character, they nevertheless show that while in 1880 the share of each worker was 1,000 dollars of capital and 2,000 dollars of worked product per annum, in 1915 the capital expended was already 3,000 dollars, and the cost of the manufactured products also 3,000 dollars. While in 1880 the value of the products manufactured per annum constituted a figure which was double the amount of capital, both figures are almost equal in 1915. The turnover capacity of capital is slowing down as its organic accumulation is rapidly increasing, serving as a typical illustration of Marx's doctrine.

Economic Development of the United States during the War

At a time when in all the other warring countries the public economy was subjected to deep changes in consequence of the war, showing itself chiefly in the decline of material well-being, paper currency, high cost of living, stoppage in the growth of the population, and even reduction of the latter – not only had America not suffered from the war, but moreover she had gained by it. True, the prices had also risen greatly during the war, but this was not owing to a decrease in the productivity and the shortage in commodities ensuing therefrom, as in the other warring countries but was called forth by the favourable business conditions which had been created for America as the purveyor of the Entente.

Here are a few figures illustrating this fact:

TABLE 3.2   The productivity of the United States amounted (in millions tons)[7]

Year	Coal in tons	Iron Ore in tons	Copper in double cwts	Tin in ons	Kerosene	Cotton in bales	Wheat in quarters
1913–14	157	31.5	5.49	4.90	32.3	14.89	–
1914–15	466	23.7	5.26	5.68	42.3	15.07	111.4
1915–16	482	30.4	6.46	5.82	44.7	12.95	124
1916–17	552	40.1	8.81	6.06	40.1	12.97	86
1917–18	570	39.3	8.56	–	–	11.91	82
1918–19	586	39.5	–	–	49.1	–	116
1919–20	–	–	–	–	–	12.12	–

Some facts concerning the manufacturing industry are also well known: thus the colossal development of shipbuilding in America and the abnormal growth of the construction of passenger motor cars.[8]

---

7 These data are taken from *Statistisches Jahrbuch für das Deutsche Reich 1919* and from *Statesman's Yearbook*, 1920. For the products of the mining industry the calendar year is used, and for agriculture the year of operation.

8 In a most interesting article published in *The Contemporary Review*, November 1920, J. Ellis Barker writes on the question of kerosene which is now the most vital one in the Anglo-Saxon press. Barker 1920, pp. 671–80.

TABLE 3.3 The number of officially registered automobiles in the United States[9]

Year	Quantity
1915	2,445,664
1917	4,983,340
1919	7,558,848
1920	9,000,000
1922 (estimated)	12,000,000

Out of this number of motor cars only four percent are trucks, the rest are passenger cars, mostly private ones. Out of 50 million tons of kerosene produced in the United States, half is consumed by automobiles.

Finally we must mention the gigantic development the cotton industry, namely, in millions of pounds.

TABLE 3.4 Development of the cotton industry (millions of pounds)

Year	Consumed within the country	Exported
1910	2,250	3,106
1915	3,588	4,404
1918	3,863	2,320

The period of war was an extremely favourable combination of circumstances for the United States. All the productive forces of the country were drained to the utmost. 'All the workers found employment, all the machines were in operation. The factory owners sent agents to the rural districts in order to obtain workers from the farming industry. From 30 to 50 percent of workers (on an average) changed their place of work every month finding a better one in regard to the conditions of labour', as George E. Roberts, vice-president of the National City Bank of New York, writes in an article entitled 'The present price and credit situation as preliminary to a return to normal times'.[10]

---

9   This number of automobiles is cited in the *Scientific American*, January 1920, 89, 2292.
10 This quote is a free interpretation of what is printed: 'But when every man is at work and

The rapidly developing industrialisation is showing itself in the modification of the forms of foreign trade. It is a well-known fact that the excess of the American exports over the imports constituted in 1919 over three milliard dollars, i.e. almost half of the total exports. The export of the manufactured goods had already then exceeded that of agricultural products. Here are the corresponding figures in millions of dollars:

TABLE 3.5   Export and import of manufactured goods

	Imports	Exports	Export surplus
Foodstuffs, raw	545.3	678.5	123.2
Foodstuffs, in prepared form	555.7	1,963.7	1,408.0
Raw materials	1,674.3	1,610.1	–
Half-products	610.3	922.4	312.1
Manufactured goods	492.3	2,564.6	2,072.0

After the end of the war, the United States appears as an industrial country, exporting chiefly manufactured goods.[11]

Agriculture has not suffered either from the surplus consumption called forth by the war, as had been the case in the warring countries of Europe. The best proof thereof is the development of cattle breeding. This department of rural economy shows the following picture in *Table 3.6*:[12]

TABLE 3.6   Cattle breeding (in millions)

Horses	19.8	21.6
Horned cattle	61.8	68.1
Sheep	52.0	48.8
Pigs	58.2	72.9

every machine running, that is about all you can do. You reach the point where the only way any one employer can increase his output is by stealing labour away from some other employer. And that is what we did. We had a procession of wage-earners moving from one shop to another, and getting their wages raised at every move. There was labour "turnover" in some of the shipyards of something like 30 to 50 percent a month'. Roberts 1920, p. 761.

11   The change in the nature of the export is reflected in the movement of the population: the census of 1920 shows for the first time the preponderance of the town population over the rural one.

12   *Statesman's Yearbook*, 1920.

TABLE 3.7 The total cost of the farm produce in millions of dollars

1910	8.56
1917	19.33
1918	22.48
1919	24.98

In ten years the cost had increased by three times, and as the rise in the prices had not nearly reached these proportions it is clear that a considerable increase of production has taken place. Therefore the rise in the prices in America must be examined from a different plane than that of Europe. In the latter the high cost of living must be ascribed to a shortage of commodities called forth by the abrupt fall of the productivity, whereas the State standardising of the prices was unable to suppress their rise. In America the rise in the prices and the colossal profits of the capitalists were the result of the competition among the warring countries in regard to the products of American industry, notwithstanding that the latter had been working under increased productivity.[13]

The profits were received by the capitalists of the United States in two forms. First, the American investments (interest-bearing papers), which had been in the hands of the citizens of the countries of the Entente before the war, were claimed by the American Government and returned to the United States. Second, enormous masses of gold began to stream into the United States. The result of this was that out of the total quantity of the actual gold fund belonging to the State and emission hanks of the whole capitalist world, and amounting by the end of 1920 to 1,501.3 million pounds sterling, not less than 853.4 million pounds sterling, consequently over one half, belong to the United States.[14]

But the United States have not only paid all the money which they owed Europe, they have not only taken to themselves more than half of the gold fund of the capitalist world, they have besides this acquired claims of the value of many milliards on the European countries and especially England. From a

---

13 Notwithstanding that there is but a slender connection between the rate of discount and the share of capitalist profit, we must still note as an index of the height of the capitalist profit that the rate of discount in the US, by 1 May 1920, was equal to 6 percent, and since that day it has been invariably 7 percent.

14 Based on a table in *The Economist*, 19 February 1921, p. 348.

debtor-country the United States has become a creditor-country – the world creditor. The paper currency of the United States is on par with the gold.

The causes which in other countries had called forth a deep change in the structure of the public economy had exercised but an insignificant influence in America. The United States entered the war rather late and with such comparatively small forces that the hindrance to production in the presence of such rich resources as the United States has at its disposal was of no significance.[15] The direct development of the United States from a colonial agricultural, indebted State into an Imperialist industrial Power was not only not delayed by the war, but it was undoubtedly accelerated by it.

Period of Time Since the End of the War to Spring 1920

The above favourable business conditions continued after the war approximately up to the spring of 1920. The States of Central Europe, which had up to then been under boycott, began to take part, directly or indirectly, in the purchase of American goods. But it was soon evident that Europe, including the countries of the Entente, had become economically weakened and deprived of purchasing power. Even England was not in possession of a sufficient reserve fund in gold or American investments to be able to properly finance the purchasing operations in the United States; the rate of exchange of sterling had fallen in comparison with the dollar by 20 percent, and the currency of the other European countries had fallen to one-tenth and even to one-hundredth of the nominal value in gold. This inevitably led to the decrease in the purchasing capacities of these countries in relation to the United States and called forth an over-production crisis which had to take place in the United States for the very reason that the public economy had not been disorganised by the war.[16]

It is interesting to note how the crisis panned out. The capitalist circles, as usual, would not believe that the favourable trade conditions had passed away. According to the report of the 'Comptroller of the Currency', the total sum of credit opened by all the banks of the US amounted to:

---

15   The war expenses of the US were nevertheless considerable; the State expenses rose from 7.4 dollars in 1913 to 70 dollars per head in 1920.
16   See the above-mentioned article of G.E. Roberts.

TABLE 3.8   Total sum of credit by US banks (in millions of dollars)

On 30 June 1919	25,086
On 30 June 1920	30,892

The credit increased by 20 percent in one year and during an evident fall of production. These are the data given by Professor [Emil] Lederer;[17] the average production for the period of time from 1911 to 1913 estimated at 100 percent.

TABLE 3.9   Data on the produce of farming according to the market statistics

	October 1919	Spring 1920 (max. figure)	October 1920
Cattle (total)	151	139	116
Bread and flour	127	102	122
Wool	124	132	89
Sugar	127	184	59
Coal	152	131	137
Iron	102	159	146

The same process is to be observed with regard to many other commodities and also in the transport enterprises. Furthermore, in spite of the decrease in production, the reserves in the warehouses have only decreased insignificantly, constituting, for instance, (in February 1920) 534 percent, and (in October 1920) 504 percent of the turnover for the last month at the same time as, on the contrary, the unexecuted orders have decreased from 32 percent in February 1920 to approximately 10 percent of the turnover in October 1920. One may say that with the exception of separate cases, the quantity of manufactured products has in general considerably diminished from the autumn of 1919 to the spring of 1920.

There are certain signs indicating that the advent of the crisis had been artificially accelerated by the large American capital. The concentration of property

---

17   Lederer 1921, p. 1.

in trusts and the centralisation of the practical management of the enterprises has gone nowhere so far as in the United States. Therefore nowhere else can the market be so much under the direction of ruling capitalism as in the United States. Consequently there may be conditions which allow for the acceleration of the crisis. Unfortunately we have not got the corresponding American data on the basis of which we might judge how far our presumptions had been practically carried out. In the above-mentioned article, Professor [Emil] Lederer says:

> When in spring, 1919, together with the fall of American prices the rate of exchange of the European drafts and consequently also the purchasing capacity of the European countries decreased, the larger organisations of American capitalism, the banks, decided to limit the credits in future and to demand the return of loans advanced; this was soon carried out on a large scale. The limiting and the refusal of credit placed the industrial and commercial enterprises in a difficult position, compelling them to sell their goods promptly for the settlement of their liabilities. They could not keep their goods but were compelled to get rid of them even at a loss. True, they had received large profits under the favourable war conditions but nevertheless they looked upon their losses as a threat against their very existence, because they had to – and this was a second consequence of their situation so obviously pointed out by the above figures – reduce production, and consequently dismiss the workers, annul the orders for half-products, raw materials, etc. Thus, the crisis spread throughout the whole department of public economy. And in this way at the time when the whole world was still experiencing the greatest and most urgent need of American commodities, their production was forcibly reduced in order to avoid a worse evil, namely, the accumulation of stale goods, hopeless in the sense of finding a good sale. From the capitalist point of view such a limitation of credit was naturally most efficient, in that it averted a catastrophic over-production.

It is significant that the rate of discount was raised on 1 May to 7 percent, and has remained at that rate ever since.

The Present Economic Crisis ... Decrease in Production and Fall in Prices

In describing the course of the crisis we must base our statements almost exclusively on English sources of information, owing to the absence of American statistical material. Judging by the information given by *The Economist*, the crisis developed very slowly: capitalism tried to send the surplus of its goods to the world market: that is why the exports of the United States continued to increase up to October 1920 and the possibility of a greater economic catastrophe was averted by the organised action of the larger capital. Nevertheless the fall in the prices and unemployment attained really gigantic proportions.

We have already given figures in relation to the dimensions of the reduction in production for the period from spring to autumn of 1920. In September, *The Economist* says: 'Trade and industry are most irregular'. In October, 'the number of annulled orders is increasing rapidly, the reserves in the stores, instead of diminishing, are increasing. The public refuses to buy'. In November [1920], the consumption of cotton fell lower than it had ever been since August 1914 (see the different numbers of *The Economist*). The crisis is greatly influencing the cotton industry. The textile factories are closing one after another.[18]

The crisis also affected the manufacture of automobiles, which had developed so greatly during the war.

The Ford enterprises of worldwide renown were closed at the beginning of the year because the storehouses contained ready but unsold automobiles to the value of 25 million dollars.

L'Information[19] thus depicts the general state of affairs just before the advent of the New Year:

> The Europeans are now experiencing a feeling of satisfaction at the thought that the United States, a country abounding in gold and products, the creditor of the whole world, the only country in which gold is in circulation – begins to suffer like all the other nations: but oh! the irony of fate! To suffer not from penury, but from its wealth. The United States are suffering at present from the acute decline of their commerce, which in connection with the approaching winter is revealing all the symptoms of growing intensity. The number of bankruptcies is increasing day by day. The Stock Exchange is demoralized. The export trade, so flourish-

---

18   'Cabinet and local relief', *The Times*, 23 December 1920, p. 12.
19   *L'Information*, 20 December 1920.

ing during the war is rapidly falling – true, with the exception of foodstuffs and raw materials; a catastrophic fall of the prices in all branches of public economy is causing the despair not only of the factory owner, but of the farmer as well. The crisis has especially exercised its influence over industry; the latter is, in its turn, weekly dismissing the workers and reducing production: in view of the diminution of orders not only in the country itself, but abroad also. Fabulous sums invested in interest-bearing papers at the rate of exchange of six months ago are not redeemable, as these papers do not find purchasers even at considerably reduced prices.

The fall in the prices on the American market acquired great proportions in 1920. The general figures give the following picture:

TABLE 3.10 American market prices

Year	Month	*The Statist* Index	Broad Street	Bureau of Labour
1913	–	100	100	100
1920	January	225	227.2	248
1920	May	215	216.4	272
1920	August	200	195.7	262
1920	September	183	184	250
1920	October	170	170	242
1920	December	–	141	–

We have no more symptomatic figures; but by the notices in *The Times* we are able to follow the course of the extremely rapid fall of the prices of separate goods:

> 4 November 1920 – wheat 202; maize, 93.5; flour, 8.70; suet. 20.40; coffee, 7.23; sugar, 3.12; cotton, 15.85; copper, 15; iron, 44.50.
>
> 19 March 1921 – wheat 179.5; maize, 84; flour, 7.00; suet. 12.55; coffee, 5.34; sugar, 5.13; cotton, 11.45; copper, 12; iron, 29.

These goods are noted down not according to a certain system but only in the order they are set down in the weekly reports from *The Times*. The figures show the stupendous fall in prices, especially in copper, iron and cotton.

The manufactured articles do not permit of such comparative statistics. But here also the fall in prices was at least the same, especially in the prices for clothes, shoes, furniture, etc., where the strike of the purchasers showed itself more acutely.

It is interesting that in face of such a colossal fall in prices, American capitalism displayed an extraordinarily stubborn power of resistance. It is true, the number of bankruptcies was doubled but there were no crashes of banks or large capital enterprises. Some of the banks, it is true, were compelled to stop payment because the farmers refused to bring their produce to the markets at the diminished prices. The number of bankruptcies and the dimensions of the bankrupt concerns were approximately three times greater in the autumn of 1920 than in 1919 but we do not find here the gigantic crash which formerly generally accompanied such a fall in prices. The colossal organisation of American capital, the close contact between the banking and the industrial capital did not admit of any greater upheavals. As regards the petty trade and industry it must be specially marked that the prices fell much more slowly there than in the large trade.

According to the *Federal Reserve Board Bulletin* for January, the prices for instance of foodstuffs fell in the United States in November 1920: in the wholesale trade by 8.5 percent, in the retail trade only by 2.5 percent. This enabled the petty shopkeepers to get rid of their supplies without too great losses. But the whole burden of the crisis fell on the working class.

The Crisis and the Working Class

During the war the American working class passed through a period of favourable trade conditions. Everything tends to show that the material conditions of life of the American working class had improved during that time. I have no precise data on the subject at my disposal. The immigration of unskilled workers that is to say or cheap labour force had practically ceased; the new crisis fell more heavily on the American working class.

This crisis is revealing itself chiefly in colossal unemployment. The number of unemployed was estimated to be four million by the end of the year. In view of the absence of a workers' insurance in the US, we cannot obtain the precise information on this subject, as in England and Germany. At any rate, unemployment in the US is colossal. At the same time there is also a considerable number of proletarians working only half-time.

In connection with unemployment, American capitalism has greatly reduced wages.

All the American and English papers are full of news items concerning reductions in wages of between 10 and 40 percent. On a par with this, piece-work is being introduced in branches where labour has been hitherto remunerated on the principle of working hours, for instance in the tailoring industry. Furthermore, the capitalists are carrying on an attack against the system of 'closed shop', which compels them to receive only industrially organised workers in some of the enterprises. Finally, there is the law against the freedom of strikes. We have not got the full text of the law, which came into operation in the beginning of April. It was passed by the Senate in December of last year under the name of the 'Poindexter anti-Strike Law'.[20]

According to data of the International Bureau of Labour, it was the armaments industry that had created and defended this law. It purported to create special legal 'protection' for the workers who wish to work and chiefly to ensure the normal functioning of transport. The law prescribes Draconian penalties up to ten years' imprisonment.

The regulations of the law (which we do not cite here for lack of space) are such that their direct application permits the instigation of law proceedings against every leader of a strike and every striker. In other words, the American capitalists have started a war on all the fronts against the working class. And they are meeting with success.

But what is the position of the working class in this struggle?

It is necessary to remark that among the American workers one does not observe the unanimous organised resistance which the working class of England is displaying now. We are meeting daily in the American capitalist press notices regarding the consent of the workers to the reductions in wages, and even in some cases the workers are proposing the same on their own initiative. The capitalist press is naturally searching first of all for facts which might be useful to capitalism, but in the American papers[21] available to us, although we do find communications regarding separate instances of acute struggle, we see no indications of an organised struggle such as has engaged the whole working class of England. Notwithstanding the greatest development of capitalism, the class consciousness of the proletariat of the United States has attained a very low level; otherwise how could it have happened for instance that millions of workers should have given their votes at the last Presidential elections

---

20 [Miles Poindexter (1868–1946) was a member of Congress from Washington State, Progressive Republican politician, anti-Bolshevik and anti-anarchist campaigner. He ran for the Republican presidential nomination in 1920 against Warren G. Harding, but lost].

21 We have read *The Communist*, *The Toiler*, *Industrial Worker*, *The World*, *Advance*, and the radical bourgeois *The Nation*.

to such a glaringly expressed type of a reactionary as [Warren] Harding?[22] How could it have happened that the leader of the organised workers was [Samuel] Gompers,[23] a man whose anti-proletarian sentences are published in italics even by the capitalist press; the same Gompers who left the Yellow International[24] because the latter was 'too revolutionary' for him; the same Gompers who publicly censured the appeal of the transport workers protesting against the sending of war materials to Poland?

'It is quite possible', says Gompers, that 'the Polish invasion was undertaken as the only means of averting the offensive organised by the Soviet Government. Moreover, the present Polish Government is perhaps the most democratic in Europe'.[25]

How could it have happened that the hero of American social democracy, the imprisoned Eugene Debs, whom the 'humane philosopher', [Woodrow] Wilson, would not allow to leave the prison even as a candidate for the Presidency; how could Debs have asserted publicly: 'if you had brought the American Socialist Party to Lenin's programme, you would have killed the party'? How could he have been against any attempt at an armed class struggle? How could it have come to pass that in a country of the most ruthless class inconsistencies, in a country where [Daniel] De Leon[26] had anticipated the most important elements of the Bolshevist doctrine – there are three Communist sects, but no Communist mass party?

What is the cause of this inconsistency between the fact of a colossal class antagonism on the one hand, and such a weak class consciousness of the American proletariat on the other?

It is no easy matter to give an answer to this question which is so important to the whole course of the world revolution. We think that the answer will be given by the internal discord among the proletariat, the sharp differences between the condition of life and the ideology of the separate workers' grades.

We shall endeavour to explain this briefly.

---

22 [Warren G. Harding (1865–1923) was a Republican politician from Ohio, and President of the United States from 1921–3].
23 [Samuel Gompers (1850–1924) was a trade-union leader, President of the American Federation of Labor].
24 [Yellow International: the reformist International Federation of Trade Unions created in July 1919].
25 *New Republic*, 15 November 1920.
26 [Daniel De Leon (1852–1914) was an American socialist militant and labour leader, one of the founders of the Socialist Labor Party (SLP) and the Industrial Workers of the World (IWW)].

The American proletariat possesses a labour aristocracy. The latter consists of skilled workers organised in unions: they enjoy a monopolist position in the closed shops: by means of high initiation fees they make it difficult for new members to join their union; they despise the 'unorganised lumpenproletariat'. They consider themselves the aristocrats of the working class, leading the lives of petit bourgeoisie, fencing themselves off from the general mass of workers. The second stratum, which has become separated from the general mass of the proletariat, is the group of immigrant foreigners, who have no intention of ending their lives as American wage workers but who are striving at whatever cost to save as soon as possible enough money to buy a piece of land in the home country and to farm it as small landed proprietors. The third stratum includes the most militant elements – it is composed of acclimatised immigrants, unskilled or partly skilled workers. The coloured races occupy a special position; up to quite recent times they were not allowed to join the union on principle. The conditions of pay and of the mode of life of the above-described grades of the proletariat are so different that it is very difficult to weld these groups together on the basis of a homogeneous class policy.

The growth of class consciousness is impeded by the circumstance that it is not so difficult for the ablest representatives of the American working class to join the class of petty-bourgeoisie or to enter the circle of persons exercising the 'free professions' – it is much easier than in Europe. The absence of the need of a qualification for the occupying of any official position, the great number of educational institutions, which give the necessary instruction and training for becoming an engineer, lawyer, doctor, and the possibility of rising above the level of the working class by means of skilful speculation or some invention – all this induces the best minds of the American proletariat to seek their well-being, not in the conditions of a class struggle in the ranks of the proletariat, but in the endeavour to pass on to a higher rung in the social ladder along the individualistic road.

In conclusion it must be noted that the high level of material prosperity of the American skilled workers which has been rising ever higher during whole decades (with the exception of the first decade of the nineteenth century) has probably contributed most of all to the fact that in the United States revolutionary class consciousness has not attained the requisite development. True, there have been instances of frequent cruel and sharp collisions, but there was no revolutionary proletariat as a whole class. At the present moment a fierce struggle is going on chiefly around the question of the 'closed shop'. As all indication of obduracy with which the bourgeoisie is conducting the struggle, the fact may be observed that the Bethlehem Steel Co. is refusing to sign agreements with their contractors in New York and Philadelphia who do not agree to the principle of 'open shops'.[27] Capitalism is trying to destroy the hated system of 'closed shop'. We wish it success because this would mean a step forward on the road to the uniting of the proletariat. But the American proletariat will become revolutionary only when the United States is drawn into the European capitalist crisis: when American capital will not be able to ensure for the proletariat the customary high level of the material conditions of existence, when it will be impossible to overcome the present crisis painlessly.

The Imperialist Attempt to Overcome the Crisis

The causes of the actual economic crisis are of two kinds: on the one hand, they evolve out of the 'normal' course of capitalist production. A crisis usually follows a period of favourable trade conditions. On the other hand, the crisis is rendered more acute by the economic breakdown of continental Europe – a breakdown which we have described in No. 14 of our journal. The situation of the United States in comparison to Europe is analogous to that of England in comparison to continental Europe. The United States cannot sell their goods on the European markets because the countries ruined by the war are not in a position to purchase them. Hence the depreciation of the currency of the whole world; a colossal agio on the American currency, which leads to the result that American goods cannot compete in the world market, and even more than that, the goods of the countries with a low rate of exchange are competing with American goods within the limits of the United States. This agio on American currency has greatly increased since the war, and it is continuing even now, notwithstanding the acute crisis through which the United States are passing.

The rate of exchange of the dollar in comparison with the currency of the other principal countries amounted on 21 March 1921 to:[28]

---

27 *The Nation*, 19 January 1921.
28 *The Times*, 21 March 1921, p. 20.

TABLE 3.11 Exchange rates of the US dollar

Money exchange	Taxed unit	Parity	Previous day rate of exchange
London, stp. term	£1	4.86	3.92
Amsterdam, short sight	–	40.20	34.70
Russian roubles	100 r	61.46	0.50
Paris, short term	100 fr.	19.30	6.95
Berlin (telegraph)	100 mks	23.80	1.60
Christiania	100 kl.	26.80	16.05
Stockholm	100 kr.	26.80	22.90
Copenhagen	100 kr.	26.80	17.30
Rome	100 lira	19.30	4.05
Montreal on London (Telegr. draft)	£1	4.86	4.48

We see that the currency of all the European countries, even that of the rich neutral Holland, has greatly fallen in comparison with the dollar; in respect to pounds sterling the decrease amounts to over 20 percent.; the Italian lira is quoted at 18 percent of its value; the mark about 7 percent; the rate of exchange of the East European countries, for instance, Austria, Hungary, Poland, has sunk to 1 percent of the nominal value.

It is quite comprehensible that under these conditions the normal sale of American goods in the above-mentioned countries is almost impossible. Of all the countries of the world only Japan and Switzerland have a full-value currency in comparison with the United States; the currency of Canada is almost on a par, as well as that of some of the South American States. But the population and the purchasing capacity of these countries are too insignificant for the United States export.

American capital has made an attempt, in the same way as English capital, to support the purchasing power of the foreign countries by investing American capital in foreign enterprises. The United States has become the world banker. During the war American capital was mostly invested in the State loans of the allied countries: the debts of the countries of the Entente amount to approximately 15 milliard dollars. After the war almost all the countries and loans, as well as the larger joint-stock enterprises, knocked at the doors of the American money market and begged for a loan. If we look through the communications in *The Economist* for the last six months, we shall find the names of almost all the countries of the world as debtors of America: the states of South America, the Belgian railways, Danish towns, English banks, 'completely trustworthy enterprises paying 8 percent interest'. The direct investment of American capital is also widely practised. Formerly the European capitalists owned American shares and bonds; at present the American capitalists are buying up shares and enterprises throughout the whole of Europe, and paying fabulously low prices. One million dollars is equal in Central Europe to 25 million lire, or 60 million marks, or 600 million Austrian kroner, etc.

In this way, in spite of the bad trade conditions and unfavourable exchange, American capital succeeded in maintaining its export trade during the first period of the crisis. In October 1920, the export trade of the United States was higher than ever. Only in November an abrupt fall began; the export trade was 67 million dollars less than in 1919. Since that time affairs are going on in the same way from month to month.

The investing of capital in foreign enterprises, the danger of the loss of the European market in consequence of the disorganisation of the European public economy – all this compels the United States to carry on a world policy in spite of the resistance of some of the conservative circles! All the attempts to return to the old American continental policy, all attempts to 'fence oneself off' from Europe, suffer a defeat before the exactions of economic necessity. At the present moment the United States is the most imperialist power in the world!

In order to complete the picture we must stop to consider closely the facts, which characterise this American Imperialism and the tendencies of the latter. In substance it does not differ in anything from British and German Imperialism, except perhaps by its still retaining false pacific phraseology. During the last five years, ever since the Americans occupied Haiti, American soldiers and sailors have killed 3,250 men, according to the official data of the Ministry of Marine. Under the sound of Wilson's pathetic speeches on the 'rights of peoples', the United States has occupied Nicaragua and Costa Rica, and introduced a military dictatorship in these states.[29] Militarism is revealing itself ever more acutely, both on land and sea. The United States withdrew from the League of Nations because they would not submit to the hegemony of England. At present the United States are on the surest way to become the strongest military power in the world. They are entering into a conflict which is acquiring an ever more acute form with the two other world powers, England and Japan (we cannot consider France a world power in spite of her high sounding policy). Affairs have reached a point when America is seriously looking forward to the possibility of an Anglo-American war.

---

29 *Labour Leader*, 21 October 1920.

What is the cause of Anglo-American antagonism?

First of all is the question of the war debts. The cautious United States lent money for carrying on the war to England directly – chiefly to England, and the latter supplied France, Italy, Belgium, etc. under the present unfavourable rate of exchange these debts are now laying an extremely heavy burden on the countries of continental Europe. The demands of England on these countries are creating a considerable risk. France's ruthless altitude towards Germany is partly due to the fact that she is oppressed by her debts to England. Therefore the English politician, Keynes, in his book on the peace of Versailles,[30] proposed as the only way of solving the question that America should annul her demands to all the allies and debtors, that England should do the same in respect to the continental countries of Europe, while France should reduce her demands for the reparation of her war losses to the proportions which would be acceptable to Germany. However, the semi-official attempt of England to obtain the consent of the United States for the carrying out of this financial plan met with a decisive refusal. The capitalist rulers of the United States are in no way inclined to sacrifice their milliards in order to restore European capitalism. This is to our advantage, but England was annoyed by this fiasco.

On the other hand, the United States is displeased with Europe: 'Europe has fallen in the eyes of all respectable Americans, in view of her constant wars and revolutions and her non-desire to implant a peaceful industry', and so on.[31]

The activities of the League of Nations are arousing to a still greater degree the displeasure of the United States, especially when the mandate for Mesopotamia was given to England and the mandate given to Japan for the possession of the former German cable station on the Isle of Yap, and also for the possession of the German cables. The United States is interested in Mesopotamia chiefly on account of the latter's oil fields. On 26 November of last year, the United States protested sharply against the Mesopotamian mandate for England. At first sight it is difficult to understand why the United States, the largest producer of oil in the world, should protest so strongly on the subject of Mesopotamia. But at present oil is the only commodity which in spite of the crisis is in great demand on the market: therefore its price is continuing to increase in spite of the general fall in the prices in the world market. The American production of oil (kerosene) is utterly unable to keep pace with the rapid increase in the number of automobiles. Matters have become still more complicated by the fact that British capital has secretly bought up or taken possession of the oil

---

30 [Keynes 1920].
31 *The Nation*, 6 November 1920.

areas lying beyond the limits of the United States territory, including the Mexican oil fields. The situation was described by Senator [Kenneth] McKellar[32] in the Senate on 1 January 1921: 'Great Britain receives from the United States about 8 percent of the oil for her commercial and military fleet at a price varying from 10 shillings to 13 shillings and 4 pence per barrel, while she herself is supplying American ships in the Near East at the price of £2 to £3 0s. 6d. per barrel'.

America possesses only one-sixth of the world reserves of oil, but she consumes approximately three-quarters of the world output. McKellar gave a list of the British oil possessions: 'large areas in Persia, Mesopotamia, Egypt, India and smaller fields in Canada, the East Indies, producing almost one-fourth of the world output'. He adds: 'Great Britain or her citizens are greatly interested in the oil fields of Mexico, the United States, Russia, China, the East Indies and other countries. This circumstance permits her to control almost half of the world output of oil'. The orator remarks that under the actual consumption the American reserves will be exhausted within approximately 15 to 30 years because England is grasping the diminishing American reserves while keeping her own untouched. The United States has sufficient power to 'press England to the wall' by refusing to permit her to purchase American oil. England asserts that she cannot pay her debts to America, while at the same time she is buying up the oil fields of the whole world.

But McKellar was surpassed by Mr. Phelan,[33] a Democrat from California, who said that the Englishmen 'are imitating the Huns'. When they appealed to America to help during the war, saying they were 'in a fix', they simultaneously began to purchase oil fields in foreign countries: they obtained from America four milliard dollars (one milliard pounds sterling), and used their own money in order to monopolise the world output of oil.

Mr. Phelan then passed over to the Japanese question. In California the Japanese are buying kerosene from the British Company at the price of 10 shillings per barrel while the Californians have to pay 13 shillings and 4 pence. A limit will be laid to the acquisition of the Californian oil field by the English by the passing of a general bill 'against foreigners'. The orator mysteriously mentioned 'underground sources' through which he had obtained information regarding a recent meeting of English and Japanese representatives at which the Japanese were being encouraged to oppose this bill as being 'cause for war'.

---

32   [Kenneth Douglas McKellar (1869–1957) was a Democratic Senator for Tennessee].
33   [James D. Phelan (1861–1930) was a Democratic Senator for California].

In view of such an acute state of affairs, it is not surprising that one of the most aristocratic of American papers, *The Nation*, speaks openly of the possibility of an Anglo-American war.[34]

The English are trying by all means to mollify the displeasure of the United States in regard to the oil question – but evidently without success (see Barker's article on 'The world's oil resources and the United States' in the November 1920 issue of the *Contemporary Review*[35] and other English papers). This displeasure has increased under the influence of the Anglo-Japanese alliance. The results are obvious; an ever-increasing armament on the land and on the sea. We have already mentioned the gigantic shipbuilding programme of America; it is being carried out without respite, especially after the proposition on the part of America (made probably only for form's sake) regarding the cessation of all military construction for a whole year had been rejected by Japan, At the end of 1920, the Senate passed a resolution to reinforce the Panama Canal by constructions supplied with the strongest artillery in the world.[36] The work for the preparation of military technical means is continuing, liquids as well as gases producing an absolutely deadly effect are being manufactured. The United States are striving to create bases on all the seas, and they are carrying on an Imperialist world policy in the spirit of old times, They are protesting against the cession of the isle of Yap to Japan, and entering into an agreement with Portugal for the right to create an American marine base on the Azores, etc.

But they have directed their chief attention to the countries which are as yet on the threshold of capitalist development, without being at the same time colonies of some European State, such as South America and China. America wishes to guarantee for herself the possession of these States as colonies, and then not only to separate herself from 'sick' Europe by a wall of high custom duties or if necessary by prohibiting all imports – but to fence herself off from all imports on the part of countries with a low rate of exchange. Such is the economic significance of the victory of the Republican Party at the election, such is the inner meaning of Harding's policy, i.e. of the policy of big American capitalism, which, like England and Germany of pre-war times, has but one issue at present, the policy of Imperialism.

---

34   [Varga refers here to *The Times* of 5 February 1921 where nothing is said about this conflict. However, the *New York Herald* was cited as a source with regard to Californian oil interests and Phellan's polemics in *The Times*, 8 January 1921, p. 8].
35   Barker 1920, pp. 671–80.
36   *Frankfurter Zeitung*, 31 December 1920.

What is the prognosis of the economic future of the United States? We presume that the highest point of the crisis has been attained already, symptoms of improvement of the economic conditions are to be observed. One may say with assurance that, owing to the colossal wealth of the country, imperialist capitalism will be able to cope with the crisis. But, notwithstanding all this wealth, in spite of the efficacy of the policy that seeks in South America and China compensation for the loss of the European markets – the restoration of American public economy is impossible if the breakdown of European capitalism should continue at the former rate. The future must lead inevitably to a collision between three world Powers – the United States, England and Japan – a collision which is called forth by the efforts of each of these countries to acquire possession of the, as yet healthy, elements of the world public economy. This second world war will call forth then a crisis of the capitalist countries similar to the one which has at present taken hold of continental Europe.

CHAPTER 4

The Economic Crisis of Germany

Preface[1]

This brochure defends the thesis that Germany is on its way to an economic and financial breakdown. The exactness of this opinion is proven by the unprecedented worsening of the economic situation which already set in when writing these pages. The huge inflationary wave reaching its highest levels after January 1921 and then the closing of any discussion about price formation led to wage cuts during the first half of the year; the fast devaluation of the mark losing a third of its value within a half a year; a tax reform imposing on the proletariat a tax burden of nine milliard mark without solving so far the financial crisis: all this shows that Germany is progressing day after day to a final breakdown.

This decay is accompanied by the most vehement class struggles. Not only is the proletariat struggling against the totality of the property-owning classes, but also the ruling classes are at loggerheads in their attempts to acquire an ever increasing share of an ever shrinking real domestic product, but they want to choke off the costs of financing the state, having become a more or less undesirable burden to other classes. The class struggle of the proletariat against the property owners is connected with the struggle of all property-owning classes among themselves. Vehement struggles were until now mitigated by the centre parties, especially by the Social Democrats, at the proletariat's cost. But this mitigation cannot last for a too long a period of time. The Right and the Left are preparing for a clash. The objective situation will soon incite a wave of class struggles in Germany. It will be a struggle of all against all, a life-and-death struggle. It will be the great task of the Communist Party of Germany to give a direction to these chaotic struggles, to unite the proletarian masses and to lead them to victory.

 Moscow, 23 September 1921
 The Author

---

1 [Originally published in Dr. Eugen Pawlowski, *Der Bankrott Deutschlands*, Hamburg: Verlag der Kommunistischen Internationale, Auslieferungsstelle für Deutschland: Carl Hoym Nachf. Louis Cahnbley, 1921, Druck von Konrad Hanf, Hamburg 8, pp. 1–77].

Introduction

The tax problem appears *as a financial problem*: how could one balance state receipts and expenditures? It is, however, primary an *economic problem*: would it be possible to take away enough goods from a decreased production of commodities in an impoverished Germany and have them transferred to unproductive consumption for maintaining unproductive civil servants and to rentiers living off public debt interests, and to the requested reparation payments? Secondly, it is a *social and political problem* as well: whose income of which social class should be curtailed in real terms to provide the state with enough financial means?

It must be clear that the first problem cannot be solved in the long-run. A capitalist country like Germany is not capable of extorting sufficient resources from the productive classes in order to restore its economic equilibrium. Hence, an attempt to withdraw the necessary goods from the working class must either lead to an absolute impoverishment of the working class, thus to a relapse into barbarism, or to a social revolution!

The problem can only be solved at the international level. If Germany had not been internationally indebted and if it had not to carry the gigantic burden of the reparation payments, it would have solved the financial problem by overthrowing the power balance between the social classes inside Germany. But Germany should now pay – regardless of the internal repartition of its domestic product – goods valued at 4–5 milliards, later maybe 8–10 milliards of gold marks, to foreign capitalists, a tribute to be paid that can only be ended by revolutionary means; the idea of a possibly victorious war of revenge can only appear in the brains of the incorrigible German military.

The tasks of the Communist Party cannot be limited to denouncing the insolubility of this problem within capitalism and to rejecting as ill-fated any solution founded by the Social Democrats and the Independent Social Democrats[2] on a capitalistic base. The Communists cannot limit themselves to a negative stance. The party should propose positive solutions to the working masses. These solutions should be different from those of the capitalists and the Social Democrats of both filiations still believing in capitalism's eternal duration; they have to surpass capitalism because they are not constituting pillars of decaying capitalism, but foundations of the transition to a proletarian social order ...

---

2 [Unabhängige Sozialdemokratische Partei Deutschlands (USPD), Independent Social-Democratic Party of Germany].

The Base of the Capitalist Development of Germany

The latent bankruptcy of the state is an independent feature; it is only a reflection of the crisis of the capitalist social order of Germany. First of all we want to reveal the essence of the matter. We must therefore give a short overview of the basic structure and the development of capitalism in Germany.

In the period of 1871–1914, capitalism exhibited a stormy development. Natural advantages of location and cultural factors formed its core element. These natural basic elements were: a climate favourable to agriculture; a not very rich soil, but nonetheless suitable for quality improvement. An enormous mineral wealth: coal, iron ore, salt. Advantageous internal transportation facilities: navigable rivers, railway constructed at a low price. Centrally located in Europe. Practical all important countries, i.e. Russia, England, Scandinavia, Belgium, Holland, France, Austria, Bohemia, are accessible either directly or by sea. Cultural infrastructures: an educated population, almost no illiterates, organisational capabilities, a high average labour productivity, persevering and resolutely industrious workers.

The result of these factors was *an astonishing production growth, a colossal development of the means of production, an accumulation of real wealth*. Germany had become one of the *industrial workhouses* of the world.

TABLE 4.1 Percentage rise of number of workers employed in industry and commerce[3]

1882	41.96
1895	46.37
1907	49.99
1913	51.20

Even agriculture was industrialised,[4] it imported huge quantities of fodder, developed subsequently an 'industrial' form of cattle breeding and fattening; imported fertilisers and dumped huge quantities of manure in the soil. Ger-

---

3 Figures are from Zahn 1909, p. 801. Further data are taken from the industrial and occupational survey of 1907; the number for 1913 is only an estimation based on earlier development.
4 See Dade 1921, p. 42.

THE ECONOMIC CRISIS OF GERMANY

many imported cotton and exported textiles; imported ore and exported metal products; German ships sailed all over the world. German capital was invested in all countries. We shall underpin this well-known development with some data.

TABLE 4.2 Total horsepower of steam engines used in industries in Prussia (its increase can easily be extrapolated for the whole Reich)

	Horsepower	Increase since 1882 in %
1882	1,222,000	
1895	2,385,000	95
1907	5,190,000	325

The increase of machinery driven by gas, oil, petrol or hydropower could have been as important as that of horsepower.

TABLE 4.3 Amount and increase of agricultural machinery

	1882	1907	Increase in %
Threshing machines	268,367	947,003	353
Steam threshing machines	75,690	488,867	644
Sowing machines	63,842	290,039	283
Mowing machines	19,634	301,325	1,500
Steam ploughs	836	2,995	357

Between 1885 until 1911, total length of the railway network increased by 118 percent.

TABLE 4.4   Tonnage of sea ships (in net register tons)[5]

Year	Steam ships
1871	81,994
1914	2,832,312

TABLE 4.5   Cattle stock in million heads of cattle[6]

	1873	1883	1892	1904	1913
Horses	3.4	3.5	3.8	4.3	4.5
Horned cattle	15.8	15.8	17.6	19.3	21.0
Pigs	7.2	9.2	12.2	18.9	25.7
Sheep and goats	27.3	21.8	16.7	11.2	9.0

Notice: these figures do not give a sufficient insight into progress accomplished. In the meantime, an important improvement of the cattle stock occurred: taller and better animals were bred, carcass weight[7] increased a lot. 'Since the middle of the past century, meat consumption has doubled in Germany, i.e. 52 kg a year, of which three-fifths pork'.[8]

The increase of the means of production resulted in a growth of production.

---

5 *Statistisches Jahrbuch für das Deutsche Reich* 1919, p. 160.
6 Ritter 1921, p. 93.
7 [Carcass weight is the weight of the slaughtered animal's cold body after having been bled, skinned and eviscerated, and after removal of the head, the feet, the tail and the genitals].
8 Ritter 1921, p. 100.

TABLE 4.6   Agrarian production[9] (average output per ha. in double hundredweight)

	1883–7	1908–12	Increase in %
Wheat	13.4	20.7	55
Rye	10.0	17.8	78
Barley	12.8	20.1	57
Oats	11.3	19.0	75
Potatoes	28.5	133.4	368.4

TABLE 4.7   Industrial production

		Increase in %
Coal	1887–1911	208
Cast iron	1887–1911	287
Steel	1887–1911	1,335
Sugar	1887–1911	600

We do not want to discuss all different estimations of 'national' wealth and income growth during this period: they are of very dubious worth. We only want to argue that in Germany capitalists have actually invested capital estimated at about 30–40 milliard mark in foreign countries.[10]

∴

What was the working class's share of this rapid increase of Germany's 'national' wealth?

At any rate a very small one! The living standard of the German workers was always, though very slowly, growing. Growing output of products for mass-consumption reveals this. Totalling a multiple of 100,000 people during the

---

9   Real increases are maybe smaller because output has been better checked since the beginning of the 1890s.

10   Sartorius von Waltershausen (1907) estimates the stock of German capital abroad at 26 milliard of marks in 1906.

third quarter of the nineteenth century, migration out of Germany declined and then stopped shortly and turned over into migration of eastern workers into Germany.

In this period the labour movement is showing a gradual improvement in the proletariat's living conditions. The trade-union movement, which is very proud of its realisations, is basically defending the same positions as Kautsky's opportunism, albeit occulted by revolutionary phraseology and clearly by Bernstein's revisionism: a continuously economic and political strengthening of the proletariat will occur within democratic capitalism or capitalist democracy until a peaceful conquering of power is obtained by the proletariat. However, Kautsky was striking another tone in his *Road to Power*.[11] But in practice, they were both waiting for the fatal collapse of capitalism and both were welcoming the growing number of votes in the elections and small successes obtained by the trade unions.

The Impoverishment of Germany as a Consequence of the War

The proud development of German capitalism was suddenly interrupted by the war. Production shrank because everything had to serve the war effort. Instead of increasing the means of production, instead of accumulating capital, a fast impoverishment began. This real impoverishment was, however, occulted by a growing amount of fictive capital, by a false appearance of unprecedented enrichment. The state purchased with cash money at a high price all goods which were indispensable for warfare. Money was obtained by selling high-rented state bonds to its citizens. The amount of real wealth destroyed by the war was substantial, because it was converted into interest-bearing war loans.

> These promissory loans, which are issued for the originally loaned capital long since spent, these paper duplicates of consumed capital, serve for their owners as capital to the extent that they are saleable commodities and may, therefore, be converted into capital.[12]

The war made conversion of loan capital into productive capital impossible, because the real elements of conversion, the natural form – buildings, machinery, raw materials – as well as the necessary labour force were missing during

---

11   [Kautsky 1909].
12   Marx 1959, p. 466.

the war, and also partly today. The apparent wealth created by the disastrous method of financing the war – we shall dwell at length on this item later on – occults a profound real impoverishment; we shall illustrate this with some figures.

a)   *The decay of agriculture*
We already mentioned the fact that pre-war Germany's agriculture was very intensive, strongly interwoven with the world economy[13] and in a certain sense 'industrialised': it imports fodder from foreign countries and produces with it high-quality animal products intended for human consumption: milk, lard, meat, breeding-stock. 'It is hardly noticed that before the war the yearly average excess import of bread, grains and flour did not exceed hardly 200 million mark, but of fodder, means of production and fertilizers one and a half milliard mark'.[14]

Import of fodder creates the possibility of large-scale cattle breeding, which facilitates the creation of an abundant livestock manure and high yielding crops. This system collapsed during the war. Neither fodders nor fertilisers could be imported from abroad. German production of phosphates declined sharply. The fertile soil was rapidly exhausted, livestock diminished. H. Dade writes: 'The actual situation of German agriculture can be summarized as follows: a decimated livestock and a soil which fertility has declined with about one-third'.[15]

We illustrate this development with the help of some figures:

TABLE 4.8   Cropland in million ha (without Alsace-Lorraine) (new territory)

	Wheat	Rye	Oats	Barley	Potatoes	Sugar beet
1913	1.84	6.36	4.33	1.60	3.32	0.57[16]
1918	1.44	5.75	3.27	1.37	2.73	0.40
1919	1.30	4.40	2.99	1.13	2.18	0.30[17]
1920	1.38	4.33	3.24	1.20	2.46	0.33

13   Ritter 1921.
14   Dade 1921, p. 42.
15   Ibid.
16   Ritter 1921, p. 102.
17   *Reichsanzeiger*, 31 December 1920.

Total crop in millions of tons[18]

	Wheat	Rye	Oats	Barley	Potatoes	Sugar beet
1913	4.06	10.22	8.72	3.05	44.77	13.70
1919	2.17	6.10	4.49	1.67	21.48	5.82
1920	2.26	4.97	4.87	1.80	28.25	7.96

The average output per ha in tons: averages[19]

	1909–13 average	1919	1920	Decrease from 1903–13 until 1920 in %
Wheat	2.15	1.67	1.63	24.2
Rye	1.82	1.39	1.15	36.8
Oats	2.08	1.48	1.50	27.9
Barley	1.98	1.50	1.50	24.2
Potatoes	13.71	9.85	11.48	16.2

These figures show a catastrophic picture: agricultural areas have decreased by some 20–25 percent, total crops are by 24–37 percent lower, total harvest is about a half lower! One could at least presume that the output of cash crops had been in reality much larger than the official figures were showing: the agrarians had all interest in keeping their official output figures as low as possible in order to sell a lower share of their crops at convened prices. But a sharp decline in total output is nonetheless a fact.

Let us roughly calculate consumptive needs. In the period of 1909–13, total output of wheat and rye was 14.28 million ton in the actual cropland. Consumptive needs were, however, higher because: 1) 8 percent of the net consumptive need of bread grains was imported; 2) the ceded territories encompassed only 6 percent of the industrial population, but 12 percent of the agrarian population, thus 16 percent of total cropland of bread grains, 18 percent of that of potatoes, 20 percent of that of sugar beets were lost. Germany's internal bread provision worsened because of these lost territories. If we forget

---

18   'Der Rückgang der Ernteerträge in Deutschland', *Wirtschaft und Statistik* 1921, 1, 3, p. 107.
19   'Der Rückgang der Ernteerträge in Deutschland', *Wirtschaft und Statistik* 1921, 1, 3, p. 108.

about the latter and see the 8 percent imports and the output of the lost territories as a compensation for the peasantry's inadequate tax declaration, we finally obtain the following results:

TABLE 4.9   Bread grains in million tons

	Output	Shortages to be covered by imports (in million tons)
1909–13	14.28	–
1919	8.27	6.01
1920	7.23	7.05

We see: if popular demands are met in the same proportion and each proletarian wants to consume as much bread as before the war, then one should import as much bread grains in Germany as the latter's domestic production. Yes, even more! The consumption of domestic grain production is not evenly spread over the whole population! The ruling classes and the peasantry, that is the food producer, are both consuming today as much bread as before the war. *Thus the bread consumption by the German proletariat decreased with six to seven millions of tons!*

TABLE 4.10   Grain *import* – minus *export* – in 1920[20]

	Tons
Wheat and rye	992.22
Rye and wheat flour	49.81
Total	1,042.03

Instead of the required 6 to 7 millions of tons, only 1.04 million of tons were imported. *Compared with 1913, consumption of bread by the German proletariat had decreased by 4–6 millions tons in 1920!*

---

20   *Wirtschaft und Statistik* 1921, 1, 7, p. 307.

Apart from exhaustion of the soil due to a lack of cattle and fertilisers, the decrease in arable land and agrarian output was also caused by the peasants' pursuit of profit. Tables found in the journal *Wirtschaft und Statistik* nos. 3 and 4 [1921] reveal *that the decrease in rye output was sharpest in those areas where big landownership was heavily dominant*. Big landownership is returning to extensive forms of farming for two reasons: 1) because of fixed grain prices, arable land was transformed into meadows because cattle breeding was more profitable;[21] and 2) because a shortage of cheap Polish agricultural workers had made intensive farming less profitable! Here, territorial size is influencing the art of farming. The small peasant using his own labour force, and who produces no more – or less – than his needs, will try to extort as much as possible crops from his soil, and even much more foodstuffs, irrespective of agricultural prices. The big farmers and the landowners are not interested in gross product, but only in making high profits and in their return on investment. Hence, they will farm in such a way that their invested capital yields the highest net return on investment. In industry – where production increase also means cheaper output – the pursuit of higher profits is in general and in the meantime leading to increased production (with the exception of an artificial production restriction due to cartels and trusts), but this is not the case in agriculture. Operating independently of all other producers, the *individual* farmer has no interest in diminishing his output to obtain higher prices. This is in particular the case when prices are not administratively linked to production costs, or when they are partly fixed administratively and partly fixed freely, which is the case today. The agricultural capitalist will grow those crops generating highest profits but without paying attention to the produced quantity of foodstuffs.[22] The Prussian farmers have halved unscrupulously their grain production; instead of growing grains, they have transformed their arable land into permanent meadows

---

21 Output of artificial and natural prairies was more important in the year 1920 than in the years 1909–13. *Wirtschaft und Statistik* 1921, 1, 4, p. 160.

22 Kuczynski (1921) says: The peasant has the choice between selling or using his grain as fodder for his animals. Are grain prices in his eyes too low in comparison with cattle prices, then he will be tempted to use his grain as fodder. The desired price relation between grain and cattle prices can now be calculated with enough precision. In order to grow 100 kg of pork meat one needs 315 kg power-fodder and 30 kg edible proteins. This volume of power-fodder and also some remnants of proteins are contained in 440 kg of rye. At a price of 1,400 mark for one ton of rye, then 440 kg cost 616 mark. If one adds ¼ to the costs of fodder for losses, waiting and other costs, then producing 100 kg of live pork with 100 kg rye, at a price of 1,400 mark per ton, will cost 770 mark to the pig breeder. In fact, the pig breeder will, however, obtain for 100 kg live pork not 770 mark, but two to three times as much.

without paying any attention to the hungry proletarians in the cities! Hence, the impoverishment of German agriculture can thus not only be imputed to technological circumstances, but also to social abuse caused by the fact that the arable land is in the hands of agrarian capitalists who are not interested in food production, but in rising profits![23]

In this cattle-breeding is given an even gloomier picture.

TABLE 4.13 Livestock on Germany's territory (in millions of heads)

	Horses	Horned cattle	Pigs	Sheep and goats
1 December 1913	3.82	18.65	22.78	8.25
1 December 1919	3.47	16.32	11.52	9.48
1 December 1920	3.58	16.79	14.15	10.52

---

[23] The agrarian press is not tired of yammering about wage increases of the agrarian workers. The following tables, taken from Kurt Ritter's book – page 117 – (which is published by Agrarverlag Parey!), prove that the agrarians have found out that agrarian prices increased much faster than wages:

TABLE 4.11 Price increases in autumn 1920 compared to the pre-war period

Agrarian products	%	Agrarian products	%
Sugar	2,000	Hay and straw	1,400
Pulses	1,700	Fodder-beets	800
Rye	830	Wool	2,500
Wheat	770	Pork lard	2,500
Barley	800	Butter	1,350
Oats	850	Beef	1,800
Potatoes	1,600		

TABLE 4.12 Agrarian means of production and wages

Phosphates	2,300	Chaff-cutters	1,600
Potash	600	Sowing-machines	1,300
Nitrogenous fertilisers	900	Wages	700
Ploughs, rollers, barrows	1,700		

Cattle-stock was reduced by 10 percent and pigs by 38 percent. Only the flocks of sheep and especially those of goats have grown: a typical evidence of the overall transformation of agriculture and the impoverishment of the country. Counting heads of cattle is not enough: absolutely pertinent are the following comments of the statistical state office:[24]

> Hence, one should especially keep in mind that *only counting heads of cattle cannot give a clear picture of the evolution of livestock*, especially in case of horned cattle and pigs, but also concerning other animals showing a propitious development and multiplying better. However, the actual livestock remains far behind its high-level standard which having been already attained before the war thanks to planned breading and feeding. Today's average output of meat is lagging behind, dairy cows are giving less milk in particular due to fodder problems. That a comparison based on statistics of *heads of cattle* is not reflecting real development of the livestock population is revealed by the *average carcass weight* of cows being 155 kg in the period October 1919–September 1920. But before the war, the average carcass weight attained 250 kg; for the calves it was 31 kg in the period October 1919–September 1920, but 40 kg before the war; for sheep it was 17 kg in the period October 1919–September 1920, but 22 kg before the war; for pigs it was 75 in the period October 1919–September 1920, but 85 kg before the war. The decline is thus significant.

Apart from this 10 percent decrease of the livestock of horned cattle, carcass weight had declined by 24–38 percent; the number of pigs decreased with 38 percent and their carcass weight with 13 percent. The yearly increase in meat production is today about 50 percent less than before the war.

In sum, we can say that *the German agrarian economy is now producing about half of its pre-war output of bread and meat on the same territory. Agrarian development has thus economically fallen back to the level attained in the 1880s.*

b) *The crisis of industry*

Germany's industrial decay was not lower than its agricultural decline. Because of the blockade, imports of all raw materials from overseas had come to a standstill. A large part of the skilled working class was mobilised for the war. Enterprises producing for the war were exhausting human and material means

---

24 'Der deutsche Viehstand am 1. Dezember 1920', *Wirtschaft und Statistik* 1921, 1, 4, p. 158.

of production. Buildings were not repaired, machinery was not renewed, etc. One should mention the fact that in a territorially reduced Germany, industrial population has grown in percentages, but the country's industrial base, i.e. coal and iron ore production, has declined much more in percentages when compared to 1913.

TABLE 4.14 In 1907, percentage of people having a chief occupation per sector

	Former Germany	New Germany[25]
Agriculture and forestry	32.7	31.4
Industry and mining	37.2	38.3
Commerce and transport	11.5	11.8

Because of the secession of Alsace-Lorraine and the leave of Luxembourg, Germany lost about 75 percent of the quantity and about 69 percent of the quality of iron ore, and until a definitive decision is taken about the Silesian question, an important portion of its coal production will be lost as well. *Thus, proportionately more industrial workers will have to be supplied with fewer natural resources and they will have to produce with worn-out means of production. This is one of the causes of the crisis.*[26]

Because no postwar industrial and social census exists, we cannot easily calculate the decay of German industry and provide statistics similar to those for the agricultural sector. We only can refer to a yearly falling output caused by decreasing productivity.

---

25 The figures for new Germany are taken from data of the economic and social census of 1907; they do not give any information about changes having occurred in the professional occupations during the past years. 'Die berufliche Gliederung der Bevölkerung des neuen Deutschland', *Wirtschaft und Statistik* 1921, 1, 1, pp. 44–9.

26 According to Franz Eulenburg, quoted in Angell 1919, p. 91.

TABLE 4.15 German industrial production (in million tons)

	Coal[27]	Brown coal[28]	Nitrogenous fertilisers[29]
1913	190.1	87.2	11.6
1917	167.7	95.5	8.9
1918	158.3	100.6	9.4
1919	116.7	93.8	7.8
1920	140.8	111.6	11.4

If one converts brown coal into coal, it appears that production has decreased by 21.7 percent, but also that its caloric value has declined even more, while its quality has worsened.[30]

One should notice that the Saar is now producing for France, thus *in 1920 Germany had only 131.3 million tons of coal at its disposal for the same territory, against 173 million tons in 1913*. Reparation coal must be deducted from this total amount of coal. Hence, Germany has only about 60 percent of the prewar quantity of coal at its disposal; this shortage is only very partly covered by increased production of inferior brown coal. Coal shortages already lamed German industry during the period of postwar economic upswing when German products were sold on the world market; coal shortage is one of the most important causes of today's underproduction crisis.

---

27   'Deutschlands Kohlenversorgung', *Wirtschaft und Statistik* 1921, 1, 2, p. 55.
28   Ibid.
29   'Deutsche Kalisalz-Gewinnung', *Wirtschaft und Statistik* 1921, 1, 6, pp. 253–4. One should notice that sales of nitrogenous fertilisers were much lower in 1920 than production: that would have a profound impact in 1921.
30   See draft project of the German Government in Brussels: *Akten der Brüsseler Sachverständigenkonferenz* 1921, p. 219.

TABLE 4.16 Steel and iron production (in million tons)

		Steel production[31]	Iron production[32]
1913	Old Germany	18.9	19.3
	New Germany	–	11.5
1919	New Germany	7.0	7.0
1920	New Germany	7.0	5.0
	Decrease	67.0%	75.0%
		i.e.	57.0%

TABLE 4.17 Textile industry: import minus export of raw materials in thousands of tons[33]

	1913	1920
Cotton	4,850.8	1,633.1
Cotton fabrics	165.8	73.0
Wool and fabrics	3,994.1	613.8
Hemp, flax, jute and fabrics	3,052.1	841.0
Silk, rayon and fabrics	67.4	17.4
	12,130.2	3,178.3
	Decrease in production	73.5%

Capital export in its natural form of machinery is another cause of decreasing production. We read in the *Volkszeitung für das Vogtland* of 10 December 1920 about the number of used textile machines that were exported in the first half of 1920 (see *Table 4.18*).

---

31   *Hamburger Volkszeitung*, 14 May 1921. After 1919 no official data were published!
32   Ibid.
33   *Wirtschaft und Statistik* 1921, 1, 7, p. 310.

TABLE 4.18 Used textile machines exported in the period October 1919–September 1920

Weaving looms	1,949
Tulle making machinery	10
Spinning mules	68
Other spinning machinery	208
Fulling machines	29
Tricot (ribbed woollen) machinery	180
Ribbon weaving looms	10
Curtain weaving looms	10
Card machinery	139
Spools	25
Knitting machinery	20
Cord	580
Other machinery	159
Total machinery	3,387

In many cases the real number of machines is not indicated, and there is only mentioned 'old weaving looms or so-called out-of-use machinery', hence it is plausible that at least 4,000 to 5,000 of these exported textile machines had been previously dismantled.

Many machines are exported secretly. We mention a very particular case. The cotton spinning-mill of Uerdingen near Krefeld had become idle. The factory possessed 35,000 spools in a wire-winding factory which also held 1,200 bales of cotton in stock. The Krefelder Baumwollspinnerei wanted to buy this factory in order to restart it. This acquisition was not to the advantage of the Hammersen firm. Thereupon Hammersen dismantled the machinery park and carried it away. The machinery was then sold by Hammersen to the N.V. Tilburgsche Katoenspinnerij, a Dutch firm that had been founded by Hammersen in Amsterdam in the beginning of June [1921].[34] One can hence conclude that these machines were sold abroad. In September and October [1921], an export request for 1,885 machines was submitted. – In the knitting area of Plauen, 5,000 knitting machines were dismantled and sold abroad in the form of components.

---

34 [The N.V. Tilburgsche Katoenspinnerij was founded in January 1921].

A huge number of such incidents can certainly be found. Capitalists feel no patriotic scruples when profits are at stake. Fictive capital transactions and transformations of limited liability companies into foreign companies are primarily used as tax-avoiding manoeuvres.

In short, we want to give some approximate data on production decline in some important industrial branches between 1913 and the beginning of 1920.[35]

TABLE 4.19 Production decline in some industrial branches (1913–20)

Production		Before the war	1920–1	Decline in %
Concrete	Per month	6–700,000 t		65
Chalk	Per month	600,000 t		50
Tiles/Bricks	Per year	23–27 milliard bricks	3.5 milliard bricks (1919)	85
Glass				50
Porcelain				60
Paper				60
Milling				50
Soap				80
Beer				88
Spirits				84
Phosphates				80

(in million tons)

	1913[36]	1920	1918	Decrease in %
Raw copper	0.05	0.02		60

---

35 According to the *Frankfurter Zeitung* of 15–28 June 1921, based on *Denkschrift des Reichswirtschaftsministeriums*.

36 These data are taken from *Indexzahlen*, 5. Auflage, p. 53.

(in thousand tons)

Raw zinc	281.1	97.5	60
Raw lead	188,–	54,–	70
Raw tin	11.4	2,–	
Raw nickel	5.2	1.2	

The following figures give a good picture of declining industrial production (they are, however, only published until 1916 by the Statistical Office):[37]

TABLE 4.20 Industrial production

	Coal	Brown coal	Iron ore	Cast iron	Zinc	Lead	Copper
1913	2,470	1,401	690	277	3.4	3.4	4.0
1916	2,079	1,463	486	192	2.6	1.4	1.2

c) *The building industry*

A country's enrichment or impoverishment process can best be illustrated by way of current building activities. All building activities contribute to real accumulation because of their technical background. Housing demands cannot be met immediately; a house built today will serve three or four generations for their whole life. Building today means saving actual labour for the coming years.

Germany's impoverishment can best be illustrated by declining building activities and terrible housing shortages. We already gave data about the enormous production decline in building materials. These data are given in *Table 4.21*.

---

37 *Statistisches Jahrbuch* 1920, p. 149.

TABLE 4.21 New buildings in cities with more than 50,000 inhabitants[38]

	Buildings	Houses
1912	17,520	
1913	15,267	59,903
1914	13,887	
1915	6,363	
1916	3,993	
1917	2,457	
1918	1,964	
1919	4,078	8,212
1920	5,124[39]	18,791[40]

Since the beginning of the war, the number of houses built yearly decreased by about 70,000–80,000 units, thus in total to some half a million houses. The *Frankfurter Zeitung* writes: 'As is widely known, building costs have recently prevented large-scale building activities. Since the pre-war period, construction costs have risen fifteen-fold, which is in general caused by insane price rises for building materials. In 1913 wage costs constituted about 40–50 percent of total construction costs, but nowadays, notwithstanding a rise of the hourly paid wages by seven to nine-fold, they only represent about 30 percent of total building costs'. We also see here how the pursuit of profits by the capitalist class is hindering production increases.

The decrease in building and industrial production in Germany can thus be estimated at some 50 percent related to a total loss of population of about 9 percent. Industrial decline is here nearing Russia's decay, i.e. a country encircled by enemies. And this already half-impoverished country should pay a yearly counterpart of goods valued at 3½ milliards of gold marks equivalent to the Entente countries, or a third of the 1913 export value of a prospering Germany!

---

38 *Frankfurter Zeitung*, 28 June 1921; for housing: *Wirtschaft und Statistik* 1921, 1, 3, p. 147.
39 The low number of buildings compared to the amount of new houses built can be explained by the fact that mainly '*community houses*', i.e. small houses, were built.
40 Only dwellings!

d) *The decay of the transport system*

The German transport system reflects the situation of the country's fast impoverishing and decaying means of production. Worn out railway tracks and infrastructures are not represented in these statistics. We possess nonetheless detailed[41] information about rolling stock thanks to the *Akten der Brüsseler Sachverständigenkonferenz vom 16. bis 22 Dezember 1920* (see Table 4.22).[42]

TABLE 4.22 German rolling stock

	1 April 1913	1 April 1919	1 October 1920
A. Wagons			
Locomotives	29,996	36,500	30,000
Passenger and luggage wagons	85,000	81,000	60,000[43]
Freight wagons	660,951	739,000	546,800
B. Wagons needing reparation			
Locomotives	5,125	10,500	11,315
Passenger and luggage wagons	5,000	10,800	9,000
Freight wagons	22,500	60,500	75,000
C. Wagons in working order			
Locomotives	24,771	25,000	18,685
Passenger and luggage wagons	80,000	70,200	51,000
Freight wagons	638,451	679,100	471,800

From these tables we can draw the following conclusion that:
1. the units of rolling-stock listed on 1 April 1919 also include vehicles to be ceded to France in 1919, or otherwise lost during the war;
2. the units listed on 1 October 1920 do not include the rolling-stock still to be ceded to the lost territories (Poland, Free State Danzig, Memel Province, Czechoslovakia, Denmark, Belgium), except for the rolling-stock having already been ceded.

---

41   Detailed information on the Brussels Conference can be found in *Sammlung von Aktenstücken* 1921, R 43-, 456-, pp. 63–168.
42   *Akten der Brüsseler Sachverständigenkonferenz* 1921, p. 184.
43   This estimation is probably too high.

Rolling-stock in working order has decreased by some 25 to 30 percent because of huge transfers to the Entente. For these transfers, the Entente made a choice among the best rolling material available. The consequences of these transport demands are:
a) 'rolling-stock shortages *vis-à-vis* transport demands;
b) cancelled trains: congestion when receiving goods;
c) an uneconomic use of passengers locomotives for pulling freight wagons;
d) shortages of reserve locomotives in case of obstructions: hence, many operating problems'.[44]

The German commercial fleet is even more heavily affected by Entente measures.

In 1914, Germany owned 2,170 steamships with a gross register tonnage of 4,694,190.

According to Lloyd's Register, all steamships registered in Germany on 30 January 1920 totalled 673,000 gross register tons.

Up to 17 percent of Germany's fleet was stolen by Entente capital; it was not German shipping capital that took the losses, but the German proletariat; the capitalist state supported by Social Democracy compensated the losses suffered by shipping capital by charging the population.

We see thus that production was almost halved in Germany. During the first half of 1921 an apparent improvement occurred; but a bad harvest and the first reparation payments have practically annihilated any propsect of economic recovery. *We can entirely agree with Rathenau's opinion that Germany is still consuming more than it is actually producing.* Rathenau[45] writes:

> In our case there are evidences that because of losses of surpluses, ores, coal, ships, foreign assets, foreign investments, combined with a decrease in arable land and a decay of the transport system, the means of production and the working force, German total production will be insufficient to feed the country and to pay for imports of necessary foodstuffs and raw materials to sustain production. One can also state that *we are consuming more than we are producing* since the end of the war by living on our accumulated wealth and credit. This realist analysis of the material balance is conclusive.[46]

---

44 *Akten der Brüsseler Sachverständigenkonferenz 1921*, p. 185.
45 [Walther Rathenau (1867–1922) was a German industrialist, liberal politician and ideologue].
46 [Varga gives no references for this quote].

And this is a reality: Germany's economic and financial situation is desperately bad!

Where Are the German Workers?

The attentive reader will already have questioned about the agricultural, mining and industrial production and also about the building industry having suffered a decline of its activity by 40 to 84 percent: where are the proletarians? How is it possible that the number of unemployed workers is not amounting to millions, but – according to official statistics – only to hundreds of thousands?

We will give a provisional answer to this question. There are, as far as I know, no data available to give an answer to the question of how many workers and clerks are employed in Germany. We can nonetheless give some estimations in Table 4.23.

TABLE 4.23 Employed workers and clerks

	In millions
Total population 1905[47]	60.64
Total population 1910[48]	64.93
Total population 1917 (interpolation)	62.36
Agricultural and industrial workers and clerks 1907	17.8
Percentage of workers on total population	± 28

Germany's population, which amounted to 64.9 million people according to the census of 1910, had attained 68 million people at the outbreak of the war. Population should have, however, increased to 72.5 million people if natural growth rates are taken into account. Because of a 3.7 million *natality* decrease, increased *mortality* with 0.8 million among the civil population, some 1.7 million war casualties – hence in total 6.2 million people – and, in addition, Germany lost about 6 million inhabitants because of territorial losses and the secession of the Saar; hence, some 60.3 million inhabitants remain. Now due to

---

47   Results of the population census; *Statistisches Jahrbuch für das Deutsche Reich* 1919, p. 1.
48   Social census 1907 in *Statistisches Jahrbuch für das Deutsche Reich* 1919, p. 29.

prisoners of war coming home and the remigration of people predominantly coming from the lost territories, this total might increase to 61 million inhabitants.

If calculated on the basis of a 28 percent workers ratio in 1907 there should be 16.88 million workers among these 61 million people.[49] Agricultural and industrial production has decreased by 30 to 85 percent. Because of all lost territories we have to deduce a subsequent production decrease of 40 percent. Thus there must be about 6 million unemployed workers available.

There are several hundreds of thousands of entitled unemployed workers in Germany. There may be as many not-entitled full-time unemployed workers. Let us therefore assume that there are one million full-time unemployed people. The question is then: where have those remaining five million workers gone? These workers have disappeared as unproductive workers in the economy. Some of them are disabled persons. Others have become market-vendors or speculators. The number of these workers also increased after the dissolution of the standing army and the marine.

We can in no way deny that, *although production has declined in comparison with the pre-war period, some more millions of workers have found employment somewhere in the economy!* Where have they gone? They have disappeared in the enterprises. They are working – partly part-time – in the production process, even if production has slowed down. *Germany's labour productivity has sharply fallen!* In a separate section we will give some specific data underpinning this assertion.

The latter phenomenon is caused by:

1. *An impoverishment of the German working class* as a result of war-time hardship and postwar under-nourishment and diseases;
2. *A revolutionising of the working class* because of continual economic and political struggles; the German proletariat does not want to foster capitalist recovery by hard working;
3. *A decay of all means of production* in Germany;
4. An impoverishment of the working class in Germany.

a) *The collapse of food supply*

We already pointed to the fact that Germany's food condition worsened year after year due to a decrease in the arable surface and declining productivity.

---

49 Dr. [Friedrich] Syrup, President of the *Reichsamtes für Arbeitsvermittelung*, calculated for 1920: '19 million employed workers in the broadest sense', thus commercial clerks and civil servants are not included.

Bread. An exact calculation of bread consumption can only be obtained after making complex calculations for which the basic data are missing. We should make the following sum: the remnants of the former harvest, plus the harvest of the current business year, minus seeds, plus net grain and flour imports in the corresponding business year – from August until August. Meanwhile consumption has decreased in such huge quantities that making precise calculations would nonetheless be superfluous. Pre-war imports can be estimated at some 8 to 10 percent of total consumption, i.e. an equivalent of the harvested grains the farmers did not declare; we may deduce about 10 percent of it because these were used as sowing-seed; for the year 1920 we may forget about imported grains. Hence, we can give in *Table 4.24* the following data for the actual grain situation in new Germany.

TABLE 4.24 Grain harvest

	Harvest of domestic wheat and rye in million tons	After a deduction of 10 percent for sowing-seeds	Imports[50] in million tons	Together	Domestic harvest plus imports in kg per head[51]
1909	14.28	12.85		12.85	2.14
1920	7.23	6.51	1.03	7.54	1.26
Decrease				5.31	0.88

Bread consumption decreased thus by about 41 percent.

Official data provided for the London Conference give a decrease of 125 kg to 83 kg in flour consumption; according to this calculation, decrease in percentages is here even more important: 44 percent.

Potatoes. A calculation is here even more difficult to make, because potatoes are not only destined for human consumption, but also used as cattle fodder and basic materials in industry. Hence, we only want to give figures of consumption per head of the population (see *Table 4.25*).

---

50 'Der Außenhandel Deutschlands im Jahre 1920', *Wirtschaft und Statistik*, 1921, 1, 7, p. 307: rye and wheat: 0.992 million tons; rye and wheat flour: 0.022 million tons; increase of 20 percent: 0.006 million tons; total: 1.020 million tons.
51 About 60 million souls.

TABLE 4.25 Harvest in territorially reduced Germany[52]

	In million tons	Per head of population in kg
1913	44.77	746
1919	21.48	358
1920	28.25	471

Imports can be neglected, because they only consisted of 0.75 tons in 1920. *Decrease in consumption amounted to some 36 percent.*

TABLE 4.26 Meat production: cattle slaughtered after 'inspection' by the food administration[53]

	Cows (I)	Calves (II)	Pigs (III)	Meat (tons) I + II + III = (a)	Import (tons) (b)	Totals (a + b)	Per capita consumption
1913	3,629,958 at 250 kg per head	4,538,875 at 40 kg per head	13,293,319 at 85 kg per head	2,218.9	63.7	2,282.6	35.7
1920	2,089,483 at 155 kg per head	1,223,735 at 31 kg per head	3,011,567 at 75 kg per head	569.50	222.50	792	13.2

Decrease in consumption is 63 percent per head of the population.

In the official data provided by the London Conference one mentions 52 kg per head in 1913 and 20 kg per head in 1920. Obviously, slaughtered cattle that was not inspected by the food administration had also been included. Hence, decrease in percentages was 63 percent.[54] Of course, most cattle having been slaughtered without official inspection by the food administration disappears to the 'black market'! Its amount cannot be retraced in the official statistics. Decreased consumption is nonetheless conforming to reality,

---

52   *Wirtschaft und Statistik* 1921, 1, 1, p. 9.
53   'Rückgang der Ernteträge in Deutschland', *Wirtschaft und Statistik* 1921, 1, 3, pp. 110, 114.
54   Average carcass weight of cattle, see *Wirtschaft und Statistik* 1921, 4, p. 58. In the first quarter of 1921, the number of cattle slaughtered increased strongly. However, because the herds did significantly grow, we cannot compare them with those of the previous years.

which is confirmed by the results of the cattle census and by the fact that meat quality is declining.

The proceedings of the Brussels Conference give data on some important foodstuffs (see *Table 4.27*).[55]

TABLE 4.27 Consumption of some foodstuffs

	1913	1920	1913	1920	Decrease in %
			kg per capita		
Sugar (1,000 t)	1,283	860	19.2	14.1	26
Coffee (1,000 t)	64	45	2.5	0.7	72
Tea (1,000 t)	4.3	2	0.065	0.033	50
Beer (million hl)	68.8	25	103.3	41.0	60
Wine (million hl)	3	2	4.5	3.3	35

These figures illustrate that Germany's food situation had collapsed during the war. The consequences of under-nourishment are easily traceable in the country's general health condition of the population.

TABLE 4.28 Yearly tuberculosis mortality dead rate per 10,000 people in German cities having 15,000 or more inhabitants

1913	15.7	1917	25.2
1914	16.0	1918	28.7
1915	16.8	1919	27.1
1916	18.0	1920	18.4

An amelioration could be discerned in 1920; however, as a consequence of recently levied new taxes a further decline of the living standard of the masses should be attended.

---

55 *Akten der Brüsseler Sachverständigenkonferenz* 1921, pp. 165–6.

TABLE 4.29   Mortality rates per 1,000 inhabitants[56]

1913	15.8	1917	20.8
1914	19.9	1918	25.1
1915	22.0	1919	16.1
1916	19.7	1920	16.3

Professor E.H. Starling,[57] a professional expert from England, reports on the collapse of nourishment:

> The effects of these conditions, deficient production and defective distribution, have been felt by the consuming classes forming two-thirds of the population, and this chronic starvation has caused a great loss of body-weight and diminished resistance to disease. The death-rate has increased, and the birth-rate has diminished, so that the number of deaths now considerably exceeds the number of births, and the population is diminishing in numbers. Under-feeding has caused not only inefficiency in work and a diminution of national output, but has also had a marked effect on the mentality of the people, who are listless, apathetic and hopeless and have lost their respect for the laws, and the feeling of nationalism which has been so marked a feature in Germany during the last 20 years. There is a widespread increase of tuberculosis, the deaths from this disease having increased, according to the locality, from 2½ to 6 times. The Lack of milk has seriously affected the health of the children. In all classes rickets and associated diseases are of common and increasing occurrence.[58]

One goes on reading such reports.[59] 'Turnips, the staple food, even in the hospitals. The hospitals can no longer be heated properly, blankets were used up

---

56   Kuczynski 1921, p. 35.
57   [Professor Ernest Henry Starling (1866–1927) was a famous British physiologist, professor at University College London].
58   Quoted in Angell 1919, pp. 5–6; on food conditions in Germany, see Angell 1919, pp. 14–17; on nourishment situation, see Angell 1919, pp. 12–13. Here is quoted from Starling 1919.
59   See especially the HMSO command papers Cmd. 280, Cmd. 52, Cmd. 54, Cmd. 208.

... mothers naturally suffered in a special degree. Children could not be kept clean ... no soap ... no clothes. Many children living on half a litre of vegetable soup a day, cooked without fat or meat ... Children too destitute of clothes to appear in the street at all and perished slowly at home ... No wood for coffins ... Boxes for the children, but adults buried in mass graves, 10 bodies, one over the other with a layer of earth and lime between ... No swaddling clothes ... The dead wrapped in paper ...'.

Statistician [René] Kuczynski[60] writes that about 1,000 Berlin families of a total of one million are living in luxury, that about 10,000 families are having a 'good life', i.e. just like during the pre-war period, with having some 10,000 mark a year to spend, but that about 100,000 families are living at a subsistence level:

> *All others, the large majority of the population, earn less than the subsistence minimum.* Most working-class families are unable to protect their children from distress. The former middle classes, however, are often facing even worse conditions than the proletariat.
>
> Misery in Germany is not confined to Berlin. There are many cities where misery is even deeper. *In Berlin, the minimum subsistence level has grown elevenfold if compared with the pre-war period. Elsewhere poverty growth was sometimes steeper. Average income only grew fourfold. It declined from 600 to 170 if converted into gold marks*, a fact gaining some importance if one considers that not very few landowners, farmers, industrialists and merchants are earning about the same income as before the war if converted into gold marks.
>
> Unfortunately, it is not clear to everybody that Germany is the only country where *misery is really complete.* For sure, the *Viennese* are living in an even worse condition than the Berlinians. But Vienna is the only big city in German Austria, and, because the situation is supportable in the rural areas, the number of really needy people in German Austria is estimated at less than two million persons. For sure, the *Petersburgers* and the *Moscovites* are suffering more than the Berlinians. But the large masses of Russia's population are living in rural areas and today's living conditions are there not worse than before the war. Also only a few million people are worse off than before. About the same level of distress as found in Berlin can also be found more or less and in the same measure in the 50 other big cities, in countless average cities, and in a lot of small cities. For sure,

---

60   Kuczynski 1921, p. 35 (written on 1 April 1921).

assuming that *in Germany at least 15 million people are irrevocably lost if they are not immediately and generously relieved*, is not an exaggeration at all.

But such general data and descriptions do not inform us about what we are mainly interested in, i.e. the condition of the German *working class*. Data informing about the general decline in average consumption do not inform us about what the workers are really getting. For sure, they do not receive that average. The ruling classes, i.e. the bourgeoisie, the big landowners, the rich farmers, yes, even the majority of the middle peasants, are not in need of bread, meat, milk and lard. They are not consuming less than before the war. They are eating more than the population at average. Thus the worker is getting less. He gets his income in cash. If we want to know the living conditions of the German worker, then we must compare wages with prices. Hence, statistics will show us the average quantity of bread, meat and milk assigned to each person and reveal to us that a worker's pay does not suffice to acquire these victuals.

b) *Inflation and wage increases*

How high is inflation? In Germany, all proletarians are suffering from a terrible inflation; but one can hardly say that life is today more expensive than during the war. Even the scientists do not know it. Or they do not want to know it!

For measuring inflation a so-called *consumer price index* is used, i.e. scheduled data updates on changes in the prices paid by consumers for a representative basket of goods. Normally, prices are set to 100 for a particular year and price changes are then given in percentages. Prices of wholesale goods have a *wholesale price index* and retail prices have a *retail price index*. They are used for establishing an *index of the costs of living*. A given quantum of foodstuffs, clothes, housing, heating, etc. necessary for sustaining a family, is calculated and the price of the total quantum is fixed. This is the index of the costs of living!

Two wholesale indexes exist in Germany. The first one provided by the *Frankfurter Zeitung* encompasses the monthly prices of 77 goods, and the second one, here provided by the *Statistisches Reichsamt*, encompasses only monthly prices of 38 goods. This gives the following results in *Table 4.30*.

TABLE 4.30 Wholesale index

		Frankfurter Zeitung	*Statistisches Reichsamt* (official index of 38 goods)
1913			100
1914	July	100	
1920	January	1,099–100	1,243
	March	–	1,694
	May	1,714	1,502
	July	1,495	1,363
	August	1,550	1,446
	September	1,582	1,495
	October	1,604	1,462
	November	1,670–148	1,506
	December	1,681–153	1,437
1921	January	1,626–148	1,436
	February	1,494	1,372
	March	1,440	1,334
	April	1,429–130.1	1,323
	May	1,448–131.1	1,306
	June	1,392–128.0	1,365
	July	1,488–135.4	1,425
	August	1,714–156.0	

According to the *Frankfurter Zeitung*, wholesale prices have increased elevenfold; until January 1920 they had increased seventeenfold; they had increased between fourteen- and sixteenfold and, again, in August [1920] they had increased seventeenfold. They reached thus the highest level of price increase since May 1920. All talk of falling prices has become superfluous. Wage cuts have furthermore caused a decrease in the standard of living of the workers. The index of the *Statistisches Reichsamt* contains a too low an inflation percentage. The *detail price index* is fluctuating like the wholesale price index, but with the exception that retailers increase their prices immediately when wholesale prices rise; but they keep their prices high for some months when prices are declining.

Our aim is to determine the living conditions of the working class; calculating the costs of living is therefore important. For Germany three indexes exist, i.e. that of the

1. *Statistisches Reichsamt;*
2. *Calwer's index;*
3. *Kuczynski's index.*

The results of these calculations differ because of their different basics. *Calwer* gives us only foodstuff prices based on a triple ration of a German marine in peacetime.[61] The index of the *Statistisches Reichsamt* includes, apart from foodstuffs, also heating, housing and lighting costs; this means that the costs of living are presumably *lower* because rents are rising slower, while faster rising prices of clothes are not included! That is to the advantage of the employers who are now protected from '*exaggerated*' wage demands by the workers, as A. Heinchen openly argues in the very capitalist *Berliner Tageblatt* of 13 August [1921]. He writes:

> That the price index of the Statistisches Reichsamt is misleading is not that astonishing; this can be explained by the fact that *its construction was aiming to give a misleading picture of prices increases*. Political reasons have also mainly contributed to its conception! Thanks to this index, these falsified prices were able to prevent wage demands the impoverished German economy cannot afford; this can be welcomed from an economic point of view. This price index is thus playing the role of a dam to growing inflation. This does not alter the fact that at home and abroad, an objectively false idea was created in the public mind by a politically profiled ad hoc idea about inflation in Germany. As already is argued and that can make us glad from more than one point of view, not at least with regard to the entrepreneurial interests, its consequences are now fatally disadvantageous to Germany's general interests. When wage statistics show that actual wages increased six, seven, eight or nine times compared to peacetime wages and that, on the other hand, inflation only increased eight or nine times, then the conclusion can easily be drawn from a foreign point of view, i.e. especially from the particular point of view of the reparation creditors, that Germany's impoverishment is not at all that serious and that the country is more solvent than admitted from the German side. Reparation creditors will argue that the Germans now in tears should be confronted with the figures of their own official statistics for the sake of clarity! Nothing would be easier than confronting the German negotiators with the gap between their wage index and their living costs.

Finally, Kuczynski gives an index of *all* needs of a working-class family, but only for Berlin. We shall juxtapose all these figures in *Table 4.31*.

---

61 On the *little* Calwer index later.

TABLE 4.31 Index of needs of a working-class family (Berlin)

	Statistisches Reichsamt[62]	Calwer[63] (big)	Calwer (little)	Kuczynski: couple with 2 children in Great Berlin[64]
	Only foodstuffs	Foodstuffs, heating, lighting, housing			
	1913/14 = 100	1913/14 = 100	January 1914 = 25.57	January 1914 = 6.48	August 1913– July 1914 = 28.95
January 1918	–	–	56.50	–	–
January 1919	–	–	63.75	–	–
January 1920	–	–	130.65	–	220
February	854	623	147.65	–	254
March	1103	741	167.60	–	322
April	1123	836	189.78	–	375
May	1178	876	224.63	–	365
June	1133	842	232.15	–	304
July	1156	842	252.38	–	324
August	1049	795	261.38	–	308
September	1032	777	273.95	–	299
October	1129	827	332.20	–	318
November	1184	872	357.05	–	316
December	1272	916	369.76	–	327
Yearly average	1110	804	245.00	–	311
January 1921	1265	924	381.70	120.22	320
February	1191	901	359.56	–	313
March	1188	901	356.19	–	298
April	1171	894	351.27	106.73	281
May	1152	880	353.14	109.75	285
June	1175	896	351.55	107.06	311
July	–	963	359.04	121.97	324
August	–	1045	–	–	339

62 *Wirtschaft und Statistik*, 1921, 1, 7, p. 320.
63 Monthly overviews of foodstuff prices from Calwer.
64 Kuczynski 1921, p. 72; *Finanzpolitische Korrespondenz*, August 1921.

The 'little' Calwer index was set up in order to refute employers' criticism that the 'big' Calwer index is exaggerating inflation because it contains meat rations of 14 pounds a week.

'This criticism – Calwer writes – is now often heard. However, I want to demonstrate that even with a possibly smaller food portion, the evolution of a rising curve is in general not different from another one containing a large portion of food. I started from the poor *nourishment situation of the North-German worker* which was recorded during the previous decades, but I nonetheless added a weekly ration of one pound of lard. A four-person family, equalling three adults, consumes the following quantity of foodstuffs a week:

TABLE 4.32 Foodstuff consumption per week

2,500 g. potatoes
300 g. flour
7,500 g. bread
1,000 g. pork meat
500 g. lard
300 g. rice

In this, meat is of little importance, nourishment is qualitatively poor'.[65]

The composition of this index obviously *reflects much better the real nourishment situation of the German proletariat than the one with 'large' rations; hence it must be clear that between the pre-war period and July 1921 the costs of living increased with 1,850 percent.* Other indexes are giving the following results (see Table 4.33):

TABLE 4.33 Index of rations

Big Calwer Index	1,404%
Statistisches Reichsamt (foodstuffs)	1,175%
Statistisches Reichsamt (June, also housing, heating, lighting)	896%
Kuczynski	1,110%

---

65 [Varga gives no reference for this quote].

Thus *the poorer a worker is and the more numerous is the family he has to nourish, the higher the price of the food he consumes*. The standard of living of the 'better-off' social layers who are consuming about the same amount of foodstuffs as the marines did in peacetime, is only a fourteenfold of the price paid during the pre-war period. The poor worker with a large family, who is vegetating on bread and potatoes, pays an eighteen-and-half-fold increase.

Let us ask here the following question: how much more does a worker now pay for his maintenance compared with the pre-war period? Statistics are here giving a very different data. If one also includes the sharp price increases of August and September [1921], prices of living costs would have risen sixteen times. This would be an underestimation rather than an overestimation. What does this now mean?

Thus if the German workers want to keep their pre-war living standard – and in those days they were not squandering – then they must earn sixteen times their actual wages! Because we are missing the necessary data, we do not want to calculate and compare them with the actual peacetime wages. The available data are furthermore not reliable. That inquiry would necessitate a book publication. We will therefore only give some selected data: It is generally very well-known that the miner was the most wanted of all workers because of coal shortages; one may therefore assume that the miners were also the best paid of all workers during the pursuit between rising prices and wages. Official statistics[66] provide the following figures (see *Tables 4.34* and 4.35).

TABLE 4.34 Wages (shift wages) of all workers. Costs of living 1913 = 100

	1913	1919	1920
Upper-Silesia	100	367	996
Ruhr basin	100	307	810

66 *Wirtschaft und Statistik*, 1921, 1, 4, p. 187.

TABLE 4.35 Average of index for 1920

Reichsamt foodstuffs	Reichsamt complete index	Calwer (big)	Kuczynski
1,110	810	907	1,110

The wages of the overwhelming majority of the mineworkers in the Ruhr basin are thus lagging behind inflation!

For the other crafts we only have the data of the 'wage census' of February 1920. They only cover about one-tenth of the whole workers' population. Figures for 1920 are provided by the enterprises, but they were afterwards confirmed by the workers themselves. Reliability and correctness of this wage census are, according to the workers' organisations, open to serious doubts. We only give these figures with many reserves.[67]

TABLE 4.36 Four weekly wages in 1913 or in 1914 = 100, compared with wages of February 1920

Metal industry		Textile industry		Building industry	
Locksmith	559	Spinner	730	Bricklayer	554
Machine worker	633	Weaver	790	Carpenter	541
Relief man	800	Female weaver	932	Unqualified building worker	613

TABLE 4.37 Index of the cost of living in February 1920

Statistische Reichsamt foodstuffs	1,181
Statistische Reichsamt foodstuffs, housing, heating	901
Calwer (big index)	1,460
Kuczynski	1,080
Wholesale price index of the Reichsamt	1,694

One can at any rate conclude from these figures that when compared with the pre-war period, the workers have lost half of their purchasing power.

---

67 'Lohnsteigerung bis 1913 bis 1920', *Wirtschaft und Statistik* 1921, 1, 2, p. 83.

The General Commission of the German trade unions, in its report *Die wirtschaftliche Lage der deuschen Arbeiter und die Beschlüsse der Pariser Konferenz*, drew the same conclusion with regard to the wage level of *end 1920*.

TABLE 4.38 Wage increases between 1914–20 according to the trade unions

	Costs of living	
For wages	Calculations of the trade unions	Calwer index
For 1,444,851 workers × 9		
For 817,706 workers × 6.5	15.5 fold	14.7 fold
For 37,496 workers × 4.2		

'Wages of German workers should have roughly doubled in order keep up the pre-war living standard', is the conclusion of the trade unions.

We also give the wages of commercial employees who receive, just like civil servants, a monthly salary.

TABLE 4.39 Wage increases of commercial employees (1913 = 100)[68]

	1913	February 1920	January 1921
Male employees	100	432	662
Female employees	100	473	989
Statistisches Reichsamt, foodstuffs	100	1,191	1,265
Calwer (big)	100	1,460	1,480
Kuczynski	100	1,080	1,130

The living conditions of the employees ameliorated in 1920, but the purchasing power of the wages of male employees declined to about half of the pre-war level; the living standard of female employees had slightly improved, otherwise they would have starved because of decreasing real wages.[69]

⁂

---

68   *Wirtschaft und Statistik* 1921, 1, 4, p. 185.
69   About the misery of the employees, Dr. [Walter] Grützer, i.e. the President of the Düs-

These figures without doubt give an appalling picture of a monstrous worsening of the living conditions of the working classes. If the data about a declining agricultural and industrial production are right – there are only official data available – *then Germany's production has declined by about a half – or even maybe 60 percent – of the peacetime production level; hence, inevitably, a comparable real decline of the living standard must at least have occurred.* Producing less also means consuming less. And because the ruling classes are nowadays not consuming less than before the war, it must be the working class which is consuming less. This economic evidence can be grasped without producing statistics.

⁂

Without wages guaranteeing a subsistence minimum, the German working class is really being impoverished. Kuczynski has many times pointed to this fact. We do not want to repeat that. This impoverishment is a slow but changing process. The fate of the German workers varies with the exchange rate of the mark. If the exchange rate rises, imported goods will become cheaper and that will lower the costs of living, thus making it easier for the workers to make ends meet. Because of a rising exchange rate of the mark, exports are also declining. Hence, German goods are no longer competing in the world market. Economic activities will also slow down. Hence, unemployment and short-time work will rapidly grow. Thus industrialists will now plead for wage cuts and increase productivity in the name of a threatened German industry. Wages will diminish. Wages of workers will fall beneath the existence level. In addition, Germany will be obliged to pay a yearly tribute of some 3½ milliards of gold marks, i.e. some 50 milliards of paper marks. On average, some 800 mark per capita per year will be taken away from Germany's gross domestic product as payments to the Entente bourgeoisie. Hence, intelligent English people like Keynes, Norman Angell et al. are raising their voices. But the French bourgeoisie turns a deaf ear and is pushing the German proletariat towards the revolution, although the leaders of the Social Democrats and the Independent Social Democrats together with the trade-union leaders are opposing that tendency.

seldorf Government, declared: 'For months children of my civil servants are going to school without wearing a shirt'. *Frankfurter Zeitung*, 29 December 1920. [Dr. Walter Emil Grützer (1881–1951) was since 1909 member of the city council of Düsseldorf; in 1920 he was appointed President of the Düsseldorf Government. In 1923, the French occupation authorities dismissed him].

Declining Labour Productivity

That Germany's gross domestic product has fallen back to some 50–60 percent of the pre-war level can be interpreted from the vantage point of the production process as a result of declining labour productivity. This is obviously the case, but the controversy about its causes remains.

Labour productivity is the ratio of the amount of goods produced within a certain span of time. Hence, labour productivity depends on:
1. the quality of the used means of production: machinery, tools, raw materials, transport systems, etc.
2. the labour power daily employed by the workers; this is once more related to their nourishment;
3. the workers' willingness to sell their labour power to the capitalists employing it in the most rational and productive way.

That the means of production the German working class is actually using are in general of a much lower quality than before the war is obvious. The soil has been exhausted, livestock has diminished, factories are worn out, the transportation system has broken down. This can partly explain the economic decline. There is furthermore no doubt that the actual nourishment situation of the German working class is worse than before the war: in most cases it is so inferior that the quantity of incorporated nutritious substances is insufficiently replacing energy spent during a labour day. Notwithstanding decreasing output, the German working class is slowly decomposing and being impoverished in the psychological sense of the word. German capitalists communicating with foreign countries can openly agree on this fact. 'The general average wage level in Germany has in reality not been adjusted to the low exchange rate of the German currency; *this applies in particular to those wages attaining only the level of seven- to thirteenfold of the peacetime wages*'.[70]

> Because of being insufficiently nourished during the war and later on ... the qualitative and quantitative labour performances of the German workers have considerably diminished and ... remain substantially beneath the labour-productivity level of the workers in the neutral and Entente countries ... About the same applies to the means of production, machinery etc., of which the employability has eroded during the war because of surrogates used and the introduction of a reckless spoiling system; because of enormously increased costs and replacement of good materials by surrogates no improvement could until now be obtained.[71]

---

70   *Akten der Brüsseler Sachverständigenkonferenz* 1921, p. 81.
71   *Akten der Brüsseler Sachverständigenkonferenz* 1921, p. 83.

THE ECONOMIC CRISIS OF GERMANY

The local capitalists do not want to avow this. They only see decreasing labour productivity, strikes, political uproar, absent working motivation of the working class. It is nonetheless obvious that the German working class refuses to carry the burden of capitalism, that the workers are rebelling, that they have lost their faith in the eternity and the firmness of the capitalist social order. This is at the social origins of the subjective factor causing a declining labour productivity and one of the most fundamental causes of the crisis of the capitalist social order in Germany.

How important is the decline in labour productivity?

This question is not precise enough in its formulation. Let us have a look at Germany's total working class, i.e. with the self-employed workers included. Declining productivity equals here declining production. When thinking of declining labour productivity, one is not necessarily immediately talking about the performance of the 'total worker' (*Gesamtarbeiter*), but about the performance of the *individually employed real worker* in the production process for a certain period of time. Except for continuous complaints and not very reliable reports provided by the capitalists, some partly reliable data about declining labour productivity are nonetheless available.

German public opinion is concerned with declining labour productivity in the coal-mining industry. However, available data are often contradictory (see *Table 4.40* and *Table 4.41*).

TABLE 4.40 Labour productivity in coal mining

		Total manpower			Daily production in 1,000 tons	
		Ruhr Basin	Upper-Silesia		Ruhr Basin	Upper-Silesia
End	1913	390,647	123,349	1913	380	145
End December	1918	405,465	143,452	1918	284	139
End June	1919	413,930	151,719			
End December	1919	471,359	161,718	1919	230	86
End June	1920	484,500	173,900			
End December	1920	532,798	182,255	1920	289	106

TABLE 4.41 Daily production per miner in kilogram[72]

	Ruhr Basin	Upper-Silesia
1913	972	1,127
1919	555	566
1920	596	609

Compared with 1919, daily production per worker increased in 1920. It is noteworthy that increased productivity was obtained by introducing *extra shifts* accompanied by patriotic slogans of the trade-union leaders, by paying important extra benefits and distributing additional foodstuffs (the so-called pork and butter shifts). The extra shifts were cancelled in 1921. Total production is, however, higher than in 1920,[73] but the number of workers also increased.

In *Table 4.43*, Calwer (*Das Wirtschaftsleben*, July 1921) gives the following data of the Ruhr Basin for the year 1921.

---

[72] The calculation is not totally correct, because man-power data for June are only giving a half in stead of an exact yearly average.

[73] TABLE 4.42 Coal production (without Alsace-Lorraine, Saar and Pfalz)

1921	Coal	Brown coal in million tons	Cokes
January	12.00	10.07	2.47
February	12.00	10.04	2.27
March	11.46	9.88	2.44
April	9.00	10.40	2.15
May	7.80	9.34	2.15
June	8.69	10.06	2.09
July	10.73	10.06	2.21
Total 7 months	71.68	69.85	15.78
Total Springtime	73.40	61.44	13.86

TABLE 4.43 Productivity per shift per worker in the Ruhr Basin

1920 June	0.63 tons
1921 February	0.59 tons
1921 June	0.56 tons

In all basins labour productivity declined in this period!

With regard to the other industrial branches, only non-official data of individual industrial enterprises are available and they contain laments about low labour productivity of the German worker. We do want to discuss this again.[74]

The German Government has submitted to the Brussels Conference conspicuous data about productivity of the railway workers:[75]

In 1913, the German railways employed 440,205 workers; after the war this number increased to about 1.1 million workers in 1919 because former railway men and other jobless workers had come back home, in particular from the territories ceded to foreign powers and also because of the impossibility of firing temporary workers hired during the war. The 1920 annual report mentions 1,053,620 people. Meanwhile, labour productivity has considerably decreased, which is shown in *Table 4.44*:

---

[74] Reports of industrial enterprises or the economic reports of the former Socialist Calwer provide enough information for interested people. [Richard Calwer (1868–1927) studied theology and economy. He left the SPD before the First World War, but remained close to the trade unions].

[75] *Akten der Brüsseler Sachverständigenkonferenz* 1921, p. 47.

TABLE 4.44 Labour productivity

Personnel employed per 1 km railway
1913   13.10 employees
1919   20.66 Ibid.
1920   19.63 Ibid.

Personnel per 1,000 km/locomotive
1913   0.61 Ibid.
1919   1.40 Ibid.
1920   1.19 Ibid.

Personnel per 1,000 km/wagon axle
1913   0.04 Ibid.
1919   0.06 Ibid.
1920   0.04 Ibid.

Worker's productivity per km/wagon axle per year
1913   5,000 wagon km
1919   1,667 Ibid.
1920   2,500 Ibid.

Apart from the effects caused by the eight-hour day, low labour productivity is not only characteristic for the railways. A similar productivity decline is observed in other economic sectors because of harsh war efforts, inadequate nourishment and a general physical and psychological decay.

The Post Office provides comparable data:[76]

In 1913, the Reichspost- & Telegraphenverwaltung employed 256,200 people and actually 385,170 people. This increase was in particular caused by the eight-hour working day; compared with 1913 an estimated personnel increase of some 25 percent was caused by this measure. Acceptance of working overtime in case of a temporarily higher workload was in former days a typical attitude of a well-tried and willing officialdom, but today such a request would easily necessitate hiring additional workers in order to guarantee a further functioning of the enterprise. Labour force and joy at work was affected by war sequels especially engendered by the war's very unfortunate end. Because of under-nourishment

---

76   *Akten der Brüsseler Sachverständigenkonferenz* 1921, p. 51.

diseases spread widely; in 1913 a civil servant was reported ill during 18 days a year, but in 1919 already during 27.6 days a year. More holidays, membership of workers' councils and office councils, war invalids, employment of unskilled workers increased the number of people employed.

Declining labour productivity is a reality. But yammer of the capitalists is not justified. The German worker, though he is harder working than the Western-European one, gets less for his wage. Notwithstanding an important decline in its labour productivity, Germany's industrial strength in the world market is nonetheless based on this!

Misery of the German Working Class; German Industry Makes German Industry Competitive in the World Market

Two facts come here to the fore: 1) a declining labour productivity in Germany; 2) a growing competitiveness of German industry in the world market! We dealt with the first item in the previous paragraph. According to the second item, consulting any French, English or American economic journal would suffice to get data and complaints about German unfair trade and dumping practices. Tariff increases with 300 percent in France, a bill protecting key industries in England, a new American tariff law based this time not on cost prices in Germany, but on production costs in the United States; all this reveals that German industry has kept its full competitiveness in the world market. We will, however, add some concrete data to these allegations (see also *Table 4.45*):

TABLE 4.45   Argentinean tender for 10,000 rolling-stock wheels (per piece) (spring 1921)

	Gold Pesetas	
Bochumer Verein	35.65	at Buenos Aires
Krupp	49.60	at Santa Fé
Orenstein & Koppel	55.00	at Santa Fé
Gutehoffnungshütte	56.30	at Santa Fé
Bromberg & Co	58.50	at Corsario
Thyssen	74.80	at Santa Fé

Bids of North-Americans firms were ranging between 57.58 and 67 gold pesetas; those of English firms were, however, ranging between 118.80 and 240.45 gold pesetas. One heard grumbles not just on foreign continents, but also in England over the always underbidding German industry.

'Since last week Scottish bar iron has been reduced by £16 per ton. Thirteen months ago the quotation was as high as £30 a ton. As against £30 a ton. As against £16 per ton for home make at present, it is instructive to note that continental steel bars are selling at about £10 ton, delivered Forth ports'.[77]

'For no. 1 £8 15s f.o.t. at the works is named and £8 10s for no. 3 ... large quantities of basic steel are being offered from Belgium and Germany round about (and under) £6 a ton. This iron is going, it seems, into ship plates, and is being mixed with Scotch for special qualities and purposes'.[78]

'There is an entire absence of business in pig-iron for consumption either at home or abroad. The costs of manufacture are still too high to enable British ironmasters to compete with foreign pig-iron'.[79]

'The wool trade ... but Germany is still a serious competitor in this section of industry. In this connection it is worthy of note that while a considerable proportion of the Bradford combing plants is idle, most German combing establishments are fully booked up for at least six months ahead'.[80]

> ... [B]ut the prospect is certainly not a pleasing one of German mills working full time, selling freely, and buying twice as much wool in London as anybody else, while our own are only running on average 70 per cent. of their capacity. Of course, the German conversion costs are so very much lower than ours that of themselves they account for the difference between employment in the two trades, and although coal prices are expected to fall considerably before Christmas (offers being made now at 5s per ton less than a fortnight ago), it is certain that wages will have to come down still further. German combing rates today are only about half those ruling in this country in spite of our recent reduction, and how much this is due to wages may be gauged from the fact that they pay their workpeople on average about 24s per week of 60 hours, compared with our payment of an average of about £3 for a week of 48 hours.[81]

---

77   *The Economist*, 2 July 1921, p. 37.
78   *The Economist*, 9 July 1921, p. 79.
79   *The Economist*, 23 July 1921, p. 117.
80   *The Economist*, 23 July 1921, p. 167.
81   *The Economist*, 6 August 1921, p. 246.

The blast-furnaces[82] of *Kladno*[83] and *Königshof*,[84] producing some 4 million quintals cast iron during the last war year, have been put out, and one may be sure that they will not be soon put in operation, just like the iron mines of *Nuschitzer Erzberg*,[85] which are known for their iron ore wealth and having already produced ten million quintals of iron ore, and the neighbouring narrow-gauge railway, while the workers have already be laid off ... *German competition and the falling-apart of the former economic area* ... are at the origins of the serious crisis. With regard to German competition one can remark that the Czech factories, notwithstanding prices of German fabricates are 30, frequently 40 mark per quintal more expensive, had to diminish their prices substantially and that they are nonetheless operating at higher costs than the German factories, a fact that can be deduced from the following examples: *Bohemian ingots cost 315 Czech Kronen per quintal – German ingots, however, only 210 marks; Czech white iron 395 Czech Kronen – German tinplate 182 marks*. These prices were in force at the beginning of August, in a period the exchange rate of Czech kronen and the mark was about equal, maybe that the Czech Kronen had slightly appreciated.[86]

France tried to protect itself against German competition behind high tariff walls. But German competition is also felt in *Belgium*.

Higher general tariffs are in many cases considered as insufficient measures. Differences between production costs of iron in both countries are too considerable and, notwithstanding high tariff walls, German industry is very easily resisting competition coming from French industry in the French domestic markets. Because of the annexation of Alsace-Lorraine French industry is forced to export a fair part of its output. France has to sell its output on the international market, i.e. at the price level of its production costs, thus by competing with German exporters in the worst imaginable conditions. German prices – which are indicative in all world markets – are boosting imports coming from countries French tariff walls can hardly stop. For example, a French product protected by a *maximum tariff of 150 Fr. and a minimum tariff of 50 Fr., is costing in Germany 300 Fr.*

---

82 [Prager-Eisen-Industriegesellschaft].
83 [Kladno is a city in Central Bohemia near to Prague].
84 [Králův Dvůr (German: Königshof) is a small town in the Central Bohemian Region].
85 [Nuschitz and the Ore Mountains].
86 *Industrie- und Handelszeitung*, 29 August 1921.

per ton. Because the minimum tariff is applicable, Belgian and Luxembourg steel makers are now trying to sell their produce *at a price of 305 or 310 Fr. per ton in France*, thus at 355 or 360 Fr. per ton. Germany is even dictating Belgium's and Luxembourg's selling prices and, notwithstanding the 150 Fr. French maximum tariff, Germany can indirectly compete with France as if there would have exist a minimum tariff between both countries.[87]

In the *Vossische Zeitung* of 21 August 1921,[88] we read this about competition by German industry in Denmark:

> The Danish Industrial Council has transmitted us information on the situation of the Danish industrial sectors of which we are giving the following overview:
>
> *The textile industry*. Nowadays only 30–50 percent of the textile workers are employed. Some enterprises sell their output at loss. The Danish textile enterprises are indirectly much suffering from the consequences of the low exchange rate of the German mark, because large quantities of ready-made clothing are imported from Germany. Only 6,000 of the 12,000 textile workers are employed, and most of them only during four days a week.
>
> *The cigar industry*. In June 1950, 5 million cigars and cigarillos were imported, for the most part from Germany. If the Danish industry had produced this number of cigars, 1,300 jobless workers of the cigar industry would have been employed.
>
> *The tinplate industry*. The import of cheap tin-plated ware from Germany is continuously increasing. Compared to the year 1913, a 25-fold of an important specific product was imported during the first quarter of 1921. Import of other tin-plated wares increased with 50–400 percent.
>
> The *wood-packaging factories* are suffering heavily from German competition because making crates for the export of eggs had been hitherto an exclusively Danish activity, but they are nowadays practically all imported from Germany. Wood-wool is also mainly imported from Germany.
>
> *The bicycle industry*. In 1913, 3,500 bicycles were imported; in the first quarter of 1921, 24,000 coming mainly from Germany.

---

87   From an article by Albert Despaux in *Information* [Paris]. [Varga does not give more references].
88   [The left-liberal *Vossische Zeitung* was published in Berlin].

The Industry Council ends its message with the appeal at the Ministry of Commerce for taking radical measures in order to meet abnormal foreign competition having a catastrophic influence on Danish industry.

Because of low prices, German industry is everywhere emerging as a dangerous competitor.

The *Chicago Economist* significantly concluded from the narrow-minded vantage point of bourgeois economics that the German economy is recovering!

'Germany seems to recover faster than any one other European country. This proves the strength and the good entrepreneurship of the German people'.[89]

∴

We are facing the following problem: because the German worker is working with degraded means of production, his labour productivity is sharply declining and is today significantly lower than that of the English or American workers. The same goods produced in Germany contain more real working hours than those produced in England or in America. German working hours are no longer '*social*' working hours within the framework of a world economy. *If these German goods would be sold according to their incorporated value on the world market, they could not compete with American or English goods.* Bourgeois economists are blaming it on unfavourable exchange rates making German goods competitive. However, this means staying on the surface. It should be explained by referring to the real production and repartition relations. Marx says about the wages of the workers: 'In contradiction therefore to the case of other commodities, there enters ... necessary wants, as also the modes of satisfying them, are themselves the product of historical development, and depend therefore to a great extent on the degree of civilization of a country'.[90]

The 'historical and moral elements' as a consequence of the war caused a lowering of the living standard of the German working class back to the level of some 50 years ago. But the latter working class is nonetheless producing with the technical means of the twentieth century. It is obvious that a larger quantum of labour time is incorporated into German goods than in similar products made in England or in the neutral countries: *undervalued German labour productivity is compensated by the exceptionally low wages German work-*

---

89 *Chicago Economist*, 30 July 1921, p. 233.
90 Marx 1954, p. 171.

ers *obtain from surplus value created by their labour and the rate of surplus value is so exceptionally high that, notwithstanding high tariff walls*, German capitalists can nonetheless sell their goods wherever they want! Putting it differently: productivity of the German worker is clearly lower than that of a well-fed French, English or American worker and his real wage is even uncomparatively lower.

Kuczynski writes about this:[91]

> If comparing *real wages*, then our wages are possibly some two-fifths lower than in Northern Europe and in England, and possibly a quarter higher than in the United Sates. If comparing actual wages with labour productivity, i.e. with a worker being paid 1 mark = 3½ d. = 6 cents, then our wages are significantly lower than in Northern Europe and England and they are even only one-third of those in the United States.

To be clear: the exchange rate of one mark is today about 6 cents. But for one mark a German employer buys a threefold of that amount of labour power, three times more 'human muscles, nerves and brains' from a German worker than an American employer gets for 6 cents. This explains why German goods, although they contain less than the socially necessary average labour time, are competitive in the world market. Impoverishment of the German working class made German capital the dominating force of the world market.

According to the *Industrie- und Handelszeitung*, a US Congress Committee published an overview of the wages paid in the branches of the textile industry in the most important producing countries.

TABLE 4.46 Wages in US$

	Cotton weaving-mills	Wool spinning-mills	Wool weaving-mills
North America	20.80	39.33	38.98
England	12.39	15.58	17.70
Belgium	12.29	9.54	9.63
France	9.12	12.9	–
Italy	5.14	–	–
Japan	4.56	–	6.0
Germany	4.35	4.74	4.35

91   Kuczynski 1920, p. 64.

Wages of the German industrial workers are even *lower than those of the Japanese workers*.

Unfortunately, original American documentation is not available.

The British Secretary of State McKenna[92] gave on 15 June [1921] an interesting speech on this subject to a meeting of financiers. According to Wolff's Telegraphisches Bureau, he said:

> German foreign trade could not grow in such a way and not realise such an important trade surplus *without keeping wages very low* in comparison to those paid in the competing countries. A lowering of the living standard of the working class must be imposed in order to pay for the reparation debt. *Will the German working class agree on this?* As far as one can guess the answer should be *positive. Nowadays, wages paid in Germany are not higher than half of those paid in England*. The consent of the German worker can easily be explained by the fact that his actual situation has improved after the war during which all social classes were suffering in Germany – more than in any other country – from very harsh privations caused by the blockade. Answering to the question why the German worker did not improve his living standard when the industrial enterprises saw their exports and wealth growing, McKenna argued that this would have certainly occurred under normal conditions, because a nation cannot keep the advantages of low production costs based on comparatively low wages for a very long period of time. Hence, the German government, the press and the entrepreneurs make it clear to the German workers, who are dissatisfied with their low wages, that the huge German debt cannot be paid otherwise and that it would lead to a foreign invasion. These assertions of the German press are reinforced by statements of politicians in the Supreme Council threatening the German workers with a new occupation if Germany does not meet its obligations. *An active resistance by the German worker can thus hardly be probable, but only on the condition that the German worker gets enough means of subsistence to restore his labour force*. It is nonetheless possible that he will obey until the moment the whole debt has been paid.

In a characteristically British way, the enslavement of the German working class is here described in all its brutal openness.

---

92   [Reginald McKenna (1863–1943) was a British banker and Liberal politician. He notably served as Home Secretary and Chancellor of the Exchequer during the premiership of H.H. Asquith].

The Crisis of Capitalist Society in Germany

In Germany, the capitalist social order remains in a prolonged crisis which will lead to either a social revolution, or barbarianism, i.e. *'the total decay of the struggling classes'*, Marx once said.

This crisis is caused by the contradiction between a living standard of the working class having been reduced to its pre-war living standard and labour productivity demanded by modern technical conditions.

This problem cannot be solved:

The German working class demands an increase in its living standard at least as high as the pre-war level. Resurgent economic and political strike movements and insurgencies lowering production are accompanying these demands.

The expectancy of the English and German bourgeoisie that the German workers will be mollified by a lower living standard by always threatening them with a foreign invasion, is utopian. Just like all other societies based on class oppression, capitalism can only exist on the condition that

1. the oppressed classes are guaranteed a rising living standard (albeit very slowly);
2. the oppressed classes are impressed by the solidity of the system of class hegemony.

None of them exists in Germany.

The German bourgeoisie is unable to guarantee its wage slaves a rising living standard. This could only be realised by: a) increasing production of consumer goods for the workers; b) reallocating a larger share of the output at the detrimental of profits. Both conditions are not fulfilled. In the first case the *means of production* should necessarily be ameliorated; obtaining a higher labour productivity from an undernourished, unsatisfied worker would be impossible. Amelioration of the means of production implies a withdrawal of large amounts of goods from actual consumption. Thus real accumulation. In a capitalist society, accumulation is a function of the capitalists. This means at any rate: higher profits, hence an even lower standard of living of the working class. And this during a longer period of time. *To make possible an increase in the living standard of the working class in the future, a further worsening of the actual living conditions of the working class will be required*. This second possibility should thus also be excluded. If the capitalists could agree on transmitting a larger part of their profits to the working class – this is a completely unrealistic, un-Marxist idea – production would stagnate at the actual low level. We do not want to speak about the Entente bourgeoisie, which will react to any improvement in Germany's economic situation by increasing the reparation dues by 5 milliards of gold marks a year because of additional interest payments on another 82 milliard in debt. The capitalist class is therefore unable to render the workers their pre-war living standard and to guarantee a rising living standard.

> For [German] capitalism there was only one way out of this dilemma: by inspiring the proletariat, who is already working at full capacity, to postpone at least their demands, thus by giving the capitalist class the possibility of limiting in this way their personal expenditures in exchange for a faster accumulation, for replacing the destroyed and worn-out means of production producing consumer goods, thus for making later on a higher living standard of the proletariat possible. The *knights of social peace* are preaching the necessity of this solution to the working class. They ask the working class to suspend the class struggle, to work hard, to work even overtime, to demand no '*exaggerated*' wage increases – i.e. which are threatening profits and capitalist accumulation – and, above all, no shorter working time. The Scheidemanns[93] in Germany and the Gompers[94] and Co. in America are operating in this way. But this with little success! The grumbling proletariat is not hoping for a hardly but highly uncertain improvement in its living condition under a capitalist regime in the future, hence, the proletariat is not refraining from attacking capitalism by demanding an immediate improvement in its living conditions.[95]

But this gentle impulse coming from the trade-union leaders will not meet the goals of the capitalists. The proletariat's creed in the firmness and perennity of capitalist society is fundamentally shaken.

> *Material impoverishment was affecting the proletariat in such a particular way that a further reinforcement of its social consciousness was highly favoured*. During the war the ruling classes of all countries had appealed to the patriotism of the proletariat: in the fields, in the factories, in the countryside. One was always calling: the proletarians must save the fatherland, because their readiness for fighting on the battlefields and their labour productivity in the factories will both determine the 'fate of the fatherland'. The proletariat experienced in this manner its overwhelming importance in modern society from the spokesmen of capitalism. In the

---

93 [Philipp Scheidemann (1865–1939) was a German Social Democratic politician].
94 [Samuel Gompers (1850–1924) was president of the American Federation of Labor].
95 Varga 1921e, p. 18.

officially scientific ideology the workers had hitherto only heard talk of their own inferiority in relation to the members of the ruling class. The opposite was now told. In addition, the worker had experienced that he could manipulate weapons as well as the members of the ruling class and their followers – the latter had always served in the past as guardians of class hegemony and they had always been used *against* the workers. This experience had made a profound impression on the proletarians.[96]

A German proletariat acquiescing peacefully to its horrible fate would be contrary to any expectations when taking Russia as an example of a country where an isolated proletariat is holding power under the most harsh circumstances ... And social dissatisfaction is here connected with labour productivity! Again and again, the capitalists are making the reproach that the workers are *consciously* lowering their productivity. That may be exceptionally the case. Insofar as lower labour productivity is not simply the consequence of worn-out means of production and undernourished workers, it is in most cases an unconscious or semi-conscious protest movement of the German working class against the attempt of the German and Entente bourgeoisie to enforce a modern labour system with wages paid a half a century ago upon the German working class! Such an attempt must finally lead either to a physical destruction of the German working class or to a decreasing labour productivity – this is already reflected in today's lowering living standard – and wages descending to the very low pre-war level of the Russian workers! That is why German capitalism – notwithstanding periodical and often only apparent improvements – is entangled in a permanent, hopeless crisis.

The Reparation Plan

The reparation problem appears to most people as a financial problem, because it implies an annual payment in paper money or in gold by the government. This is in reality an economic problem.

Germany has to pay to the Entente a yearly fixed sum of two milliard gold marks and one additional milliard – eventually even more – or a 26 percent *ad valorem* tax based on Germany's total export.[97] When adding to this sum

---

96 Varga 1921e, p. 14.
97 [At the Paris Conference of Ministers of January 1921, a plan was formulated by which Germany was to pay 226,000 million gold marks in 42 fixed annuities (1921–63), and in 42 varying annuities each equal to 12 percent of German exports].

the costs of occupation and different missions, we arrive at a total sum of *3½ milliards of gold marks* or about *50 milliards of paper marks*.[98]

How can Germany pay a yearly sum of 3½ milliards of gold marks?

Obviously not with gold! The gold treasury of the Reichsbank amounts to some one milliard. Even if the German patriots would offer all their hidden gold together with all their jewels – for sure, they do not want to do that – that would hardly suffice to pay an annuity. The German bourgeoisie owns very few foreign assets. What was left is now mainly sold abroad. The national heroes are willingly sacrificing lives of the workers on the altar of the fatherland, but they are not eager to offer their own fortune.

Germany can only pay with goods! And because Germany is impoverished by the war and because the country does not possess large stocks of goods, it must pay these 3½ milliards of gold marks by taking these goods away from the yearly output and by transmitting them to the Entente capitalists.[99]

What do 3½ milliards of gold marks signify to Germany? Before the war, Germany's 'people's income' was estimated at some 25–40 milliards of gold marks.[100] These estimations are only referring to the yearly produced value – i.e. the yearly value of products minus the value of used raw materials, depreciation of the machinery, etc. – which is the equivalent of 40 milliard gold marks of labour time. Many overlaps are included: income from trade, interests, etc. But we do not want to discuss this aspect and we accept this total amount as accurate. Hence, a yearly tribute of 3½ milliards of gold marks equals a tenth of Germany's highest pre-war national income.

---

98 These 3½ milliard gold marks were provisionally placed on the record. Germany had to subscribe, apart from this debt, to a loan of 82 milliards of gold marks carrying a 5 percent interest rate and a 1 percent redemption rate, making together a yearly payment of some 5 milliards. [This arrangement obliging Germany to pay 2 milliards of gold marks plus 26 percent of exports, was drafted in the expectation that this would amount to 3 milliards of gold marks in total. Disputes among historians are ongoing over whether the 82 milliards of gold marks of deferred payments were maybe a sop to inflamed public opinion in France, Belgium and Italy and were not expected to be paid].

99 The solution could be to pay the foreign countries in kind with fixed capital: factories, arable land and real estate. But this would only postpone finding a solution to the problem. The output of this fixed capital would then be exported in the form of goods. If these capital goods were to be expropriated without compensations paid to the German capitalists, the burden on the total German economy would nonetheless remain the same, but this would, however, be to the advantage of the German proletariat insofar as one would not mostly produce for the foreign and not – as is the case now – for the German bourgeoisie.

100 25 milliard, Schmoller; 35 milliard, Ballod; 40 milliard; see *Herr* Karl Helfferich in his propagandistic booklet (1913).

Nobody will assert that the size of today's German gross domestic product [Wertprodukt] is as big as before the war. First of all, Germany's territory has been reduced by ceding large territories. Secondly, the means of production and labour productivity have also been reduced. Germany's production of 1920 is only 50–60 percent of peacetime production if our calculations are right. Hence, 'people's income' – which is nothing but the annual gross domestic product [Wertprodukt] – is also some 50–60 percent of pre-war people's income.

At the Conference of London, the *German government* officially declared that Germany's national income[101] attained 140 milliards of paper marks. *Kuczynski* is contesting the employed account method, but, basing himself on an income estimation similar to that of the Prussian income statistics, he arrived, however, at the same sum of 140 milliards of paper marks. If 1 gold mark equals 14 paper marks, which represents the exchange rate of the dollar's gold value, then 140 milliards of paper marks are worth 10 milliards of gold marks. Kuczynski accepts this estimation. But, in order to prevent disputes, we are inclined to increase this sum by some 50 percent and we estimate Germany's national income to be at 15 milliards of gold marks, thus about a half of its pre-war national income. We are taking into account the fact that the purchasing power of gold has since then declined![102]

Of this amount of 15 milliards of gold marks, the Entente demands 3½ milliards of gold marks, or some *23 percent*.

This means that if the reparation claims are met and its burden is equally spread across the whole population – legislation and a state dominated by the ruling classes will mean that the working classes will pay heavily – real income calculated in consumer goods of the German workers will decline by some *23 percent*, thus their miserable standard of living will be cut by a quarter.[103]

We see that the obligation of paying the reparation burden is seriously sharpening the crisis of capitalism. If its burden will be passed to the proletariat, then the problem already treated in a previous chapter will appear: will the German proletariat, with its increased social self-consciousness, with its

---

101 *Akten der Brüsseler Sachverständigenkonferenz* 1921.
102 During the deliberations on material damages in Northern France, the Entente stated that the actual purchasing power of gold was only half of its pre-war level: this is damaging Germany's interests.
103 Calwer even gives much more pessimistic figures (*Das Wirtschaftsleben*, May 1921, p. 22). Calwer thinks nonetheless that '[t]he living standard of broad masses is nowadays fundamentally better than during the war ... (which seems to be right) ... and on average is not that far beneath peacetime level, as is often generally accepted'. Is this an overture to a further decrease in the proletariat's living standard?

lost belief in the perennity of the capitalist social order, peacefully agree to a further unprecedented reduction in her standard of living? Certainly not!

Then again, we must admit that the problem is not altered so much when the capitalist would be tempted – however improbably – to challenge the reparation burden. Because its amount is so huge that it would swallow more than the whole surplus product reserved for accumulation,[104] a decrease in wealth and a decay of the means of production would be furthered. This means, however, that the country's total production will decline year on year, that the living standard of the proletariat will diminish, and that tensions will grow extremely in the class state. The crisis of capitalism in Germany will grow ever more acute and become ever more inextricably intertwined.

∴

Something different, but beyond our research, is the problem of whether a world market in distress because of an overproduction crisis in America and an underproduction crisis in East and Central Europe[105] would be able to absorb such a large amount of German goods thrown as reparation payments on the world market! One should keep in mind that Germany can only pay in kind, while the Entente countries want Germany to pay interests and amortisations of the reparation bonds worth 50 milliards of gold money in foreign currencies. Hence, it would not be sufficient that Germany makes its own consumer goods worth some 3½ milliards of gold marks available to the Entente. These goods have to be sold on the world market. And rather at least to countries with hard currencies: America, England, France, the colonies. They have to be sold to private capitalists who will only buy these German goods if they are cheaper than any domestic or foreign goods of equal quality. Reparation means therefore a sharpening of German competition. That is already seriously worrying capitalists of all countries against which they want to be protected by higher tariffs and exceptional measures! Reparations are not only sharpening the crisis of capitalism in Germany, but also in the Entente countries. The 5.7 million job-

---

104   The Ministry of Finance estimates (*Deutsche Allgemeine Zeitung*, 13 February 1921) that *income from wages*, civil servants included, amounts to 60 milliards of paper marks. The other incomes – surplus value, interests and earnings of peasants and independent workers – amounts to 80 milliards of paper marks – 5.8 milliards of gold marks. If one were to tax away 3½ milliard of the latter amount, i.e. three-fifths of the reparation burden, nothing would be left for accumulation; moreover, this amount would be taken away from a declining capital stock. Just like during the war, no real accumulation, but impoverishment, disaccumulation, will occur.

105   See Varga 1921d.

less in the United States and the 1.7 million jobless in England will have much patience if Germany will forced to throw goods worth milliards on these markets, because that will prevent them from earning their means of existence.

CHAPTER 5

The Crisis of the Capitalist World Economy

Preface[1]

During the preliminary discussions preparing for the Third Congress of the Third International, the proposal was made for writing an introductory brochure on the topic of the 'economic world crisis' so that the participants of the Congress could have prior knowledge of the subject. That task was assigned to me. The brochure had to be written within a period of four weeks. This is certainly too short a time for having all material collected in Russia, where the after-effects of the 'mental blockade' are still present, and for studying this complex subject. The reader should attribute some minor mistakes in the figures and other imperfections to these circumstances and have me excused! This presentation could also have been much clearer and much more consistent if this work had not been done within this short a period of time.

    E. Varga
    Moscow, 10 May 1921

An economic crisis of an unseen violence has shaken the capitalist world. Millions of workers are unemployed. The means of production are immobilised notwithstanding the population is in distress. In America, grain is burned in large quantities; in Europe millions of people are starving. Although millions of people are wearing rags, the textile mills are not working anymore. The whole folly of the capitalist mode of production, which is not meant to satisfy human needs but to generate profits, is now showing itself from its most abject aspect.

Since the beginning of capitalism periodical crises have existed. It is not our task to describe them, it is a matter of studying them in order to see how far the present crisis differs from a normal crisis; it is a matter of studying whether the actual crisis is, just like all previous ones, only a transient phenomenon as most capitalists and Social Democrats pretend,[2] or whether this crisis is leading to a final decay of capitalism. Answering this question requires that we have to dig deep for our research!

---

[1] [Translation based on *Die Krise der kapitalistische Weltwirtschaft*, Verlag der Kommunistischen International Auslieferungsstelle für Deutschland: Carl Hoym Nachf. Louis Cahnbley, Hamburg 11, 1921].

[2] Not all bourgeois authors believe in a smooth evolution of the actual crisis. W. Federn, editor

Changes in the World Economy because of the War

1. *The basic characteristics of the world economy before the war were:*
The present economic crisis is not a normal crisis of overproduction of the kind capitalism has already survived a dozen times since its very beginning. This crisis of the world economy is caused by changes having resulted from the world war.

The basic situation of world capitalism before the world war was:

Western Europe – roughly defined – the area west of the line Danzig-Trieste, was the *industrial workhouse of the world.* Intensive agriculture did not suffice to feed the population – 300 to 350 million people are living in this small area. Huge quantities of raw materials have to be imported, processed and exported in another form again. As a payment Europe received raw materials and foodstuffs from all other continents. But huge quantities of goods were also received from elsewhere in the form of interest payments and dividends of capital invested in the poorer countries.[3] Revenues obtained from colonial exploitations and profits obtained from shipping should also be added to them.

Western Europe's industrial domination was based on natural and historical location advantages.

Natural advantages: Western Europe has rich coal and iron seams, a deep inland penetration of the sea; navigable rivers, a good climate.

---

of the *Oesterreichischer Volkswirt* (26 February 1921), writes in his paper: 'There is no prospect that the crisis which is hitting the world economy today, will proceed just like in the past ... During the crisis, temporary recoveries may occur and create a hope of recovery, but a real recovery is impossible ... The lingering and aggravating world crisis will urge the workers of the victorious countries to resist. They will not remain passive when wages are cut but industrial prices will remain high. They will not accept that new masses of workers will become unemployed because of a realisation crisis ... *Soon or later at the end of this crisis, a decomposition of the whole social order will happen in accord with the development of the crisis and the temperament of the masses in each country. The social revolution should be everywhere the final stage ...* (our stress)'. Hilferding and Bauer should at least pay attention to these digressions of a downright conservative bourgeois economist.

3 For 1914, [August] Sartorius von Walterhausen estimates English assets abroad at 32 milliard pounds sterling, generating, according to [George] Paish, revenues estimated at 140 million pounds sterling for the year 1906–7; for France he estimates total foreign assets officially at 30 milliard for the year 1900, but Sartorius estimates them at 40 milliard for 1906 and [P.] Arndt at 60 milliard for 1914, Sartorius estimates their yearly revenues at 1.8 milliard and those of Germany at 1.24 milliard marks on an investment worth 26 milliard marks. If adding foreign investments by Holland, Belgium, Switzerland, etc., a total amount of some 150 to 200 milliard gold marks invested abroad is reached.

Historical advantages: Capitalism found its origins here; a skilled industrial working class exists here and, notwithstanding higher labour costs per unit, it is possible to produce at lower costs than in those regions having a cheaper but unskilled labour force (Russia, Japan). Of the non-European regions only the United States have similar natural advantages, but the US had remained until the war an exporting agrarian country.

Western-European capitalism accumulated an incredible amount of richness by exploiting its own proletariat and, indirectly, that of all *colonial countries* – that is how we want to call all countries exporting predominantly foodstuffs and raw materials and importing industrial products. Accumulation of capital is now progressing there very fast. Wealth was acquired by the capitalists. But the crumbs were for the industrial workforce. In Western Europe, the living standard of the industrial working class showed a rising tendency interrupted by crises.[4] Relative social stability in capitalist society was based on this.

The distinct national economies were interrelated by labour time reification [Verdinglichung], i.e. by *ready money*.[5] All countries of European culture used gold money; their paper money was covered by gold; circulating paper money was equivalent to gold. Money was a general equivalent; in general, one could buy everything for money when doing business on the domestic or the international market.

Capitalism seemed to be firmly entrenched. The labouring masses believed in general in the fatality of the existing system of class rule. Some kind of *Bernsteinian* revisionism was the ideological exponent of this belief.

Competition between capitalists from European countries, primarily originating from England and Germany, for the monopoly of exploiting the colonial countries led to the outbreak of the world war. The world war did, however, shake capitalism to its foundations.

2. *The peculiar effects of the world war on some countries:*
The effects of the world war were not the same for all countries. The effects were different for (a) the belligerent countries, (b) the neutral capitalist countries to which the United States and Japan should be added, and for (c) the actual colonial countries.

---

4 I am basing this assessment not really on the very unreliable statistics of wages and costs of living, but more on consumption of some goods of primary necessity, such as grains, meat, sugar, coffee, tea, etc. per inhabitant in those countries where their consumption is increasing.

5 [Ready money: money in the form of cash that is readily available].

a) *The belligerent countries*

We can describe the *consequences of the war on the actual belligerent countries* briefly as follows. Accumulation of real wealth not only stops but can also reverse when a country consumes more than it produces. Stocks not only decrease, but even the means of production become worn out. *Human resources* decline because of productive labour withdrawn from industry, human losses during the war, undernourishment and physical exhaustion. The *physical means of production* are exhausted by wear and tear of machinery and buildings not having been replaced in time, and by indirect war damages. Accumulation only destined to war aims. Impoverishment is hidden by issuing huge quantities of fictitious capital in the form of war loans, bonds, paper money with which the warrior-state pays its citizens for its purchased goods. Hence, the erroneous idea of a general enrichment emanates. Prices increase because of shortages of goods and enrichment. Speculation is keeping goods from the market. The state is invited to control the most important goods and to organise their distribution (war socialism!). But creeping impoverishment is breaking through the false shine of enrichment. The real living standard of workers and civil servants is falling fast. Villages not receiving their necessary industrial products are breaking away from the city. Money is losing its role of a general value equivalent. The peasants are returning to a form of subsistence and barter economy. Food supply of the urban workers is continuously worsening and productivity is declining. We want to outline all these changes by using the concept of 'war-economic deformation'.

This 'war-economic deformation' did not spread equally over all countries. The poorer the country, the more serious this deformation will be; war-economic deformation appears to be stronger in the countries of Central Europe having been cut off from world trade than in the Entente countries; it is stronger in those countries having served as battlefields and differs according to the method of financing war expenditures. Austria suffered most of all, while England was less affected. We shall illustrate this assertion with statistics.

TABLE 5.1 Germany: impoverishment and decline
Stock-breeding (in millions of animals)

		Horses	Horned cattle	Pigs
1914	1 December	3.44	21.8	25.3
1918	4 December	3.42	17.7	10.3

Harvest (in millions of tons)[6]

	Corn	Wheat	Barley	Potatoes	Oats	Processed sugar beets
1913	12.1	4.4	3.6	52.8	9.5	16.9
1914	10.3	3.8	3.0	44.7	8.8	16.0
1915	9.1	3.7	2.4	52.9	5.9	9.6
1916	8.9	3.0	–	24.7	6.9	9.5
1917	7.0	2.2	1.8	34.4	3.6	9.2
1918	8.0	2.5	2.1	29.5	4.7	–

These tables show a growing decline, which is a natural consequence of a shrinking stock caused by shortages of fertilisers.

Production in millions of tons

	Coal	Iron ore	Cast iron	Raw sugar
1913	191.5	35.9	19.3	(1913–14) 2.62
1918	160.5	(1917) 26.9	11.9	1.57

We see a sharp decline in production of the most essential commodities.

War expenditures were practically exclusively financed by printing money. The capitalists did not want to pay for war costs. Public debt of the German Reich increased from 11 milliard at the beginning of the war to 150 milliard mark at the end of the war, paper money in circulation from 2 to 22 milliard mark. The money illusion was nonetheless very strong. Huge price increases followed; the index of wholesale prices rose sharply: from 105 in 1914 to 216 in 1918,[7] but one should, however, keep in mind that price regulation by the German state was far-reaching and that in reality many prices were much higher. The real living standard of the proletariat had already sharply declined. [René] *Kuczynski, one of Germany's best statisticians, estimated this decline to be a third*.[8] During this period a similar decline in labour productivity had occurred. Yearly average productivity per mineworker decreased in Germany

---

6 *Statistisches Jahrbuch für das Deutsche Reich* 1919 and 1920.
7 *Wirtschaft und Statistik* 1921, no. 2.
8 Kuczynski 1921.

from 380 tons in 1913 to 284 tons in 1918. Reports of all capitalist enterprises are filled with complaints about 'deficient work-motivation' and insufficient labour productivity. The same account is given for Germany's allies and also for Poland and Romania.

France. When evaluating the economic consequences of the war, one often makes an erroneous distinction between victors and vanquished countries. This is erroneous. We believe that economic decay was not fundamentally less *at the end of the war* in France, Belgium and Italy than in Germany. France had the advantage of not having been cut off from the world market and having received support from England and America. Foreign assets were mobilised in order to finance the war. However, a large part of the country was destroyed by the war and human losses were comparatively much higher than in Germany. Compared with Germany's cattle stock the French situation is as follows:

TABLE 5.2   French cattle stock (in millions of animals)

	Horned cattle	Horses	Pigs
1913	14.8	7.0	16.8
1920	12.8	4.6	9.4

Wheat harvest was: 81 million of double hundredweights in 1913, 39 million of double hundredweights in 1917, 47.5 million of double hundredweights in 1918.

TABLE 5.3   French industrial output

	Coal in millions of tons	Iron in millions of tons	Shipbuilding in thousands of tons
1913	14.8	7.0	16.8
1918	12.8	4.6	9.4

Total public debt increased from 33 milliard at the beginning of the war to 200 milliard at the end of the war, circulation of paper money grew from 6 to 30 milliard francs. The French wholesale price index was much higher than the German one: 341 compared to 100 in 1913. Inflation was here much higher than wage increases and the purchasing power of the workers had thus diminished. Decline of labour productivity was here not lower than in Germany: daily average production per head of all French coalminers declined from 695 kilos in 1913 to 564 kilos in 1918. Deformation caused by the war economy was not less important in victor-country France than in Germany: France was only able after the war to improve its situation to the detriment of Germany. We will later comment on this issue.

England. Of all countries having been engaged in the war, England's economy is least deformed. The reason is that England had no [standing] army at the beginning of the war and that it only fully mobilised at the war's end. In general, fewer men were utilised for war aims and fewer lives were lost. The richest country on earth was able to cover its war expenditures by selling its foreign assets and opening credit lines without exhausting its means of production. England financed its war expenditures more rationally than other countries: *taxes were immediately raised*, warprofiteering was prevented and a considerable part of war costs was financed out of tax receipts. Thus high inflation was absent. (The wholesale price index [of the *The Statist*] stood at 226 points in November 1918 and according to *The Economist* at 283 points in comparison to 100 in 1913).[9]

TABLE 5.4 Production in millions of tons

	Coal	Pig iron	Steel	Shipbuilding in thousands of tons
1913	292	10.3	7.7	1,932
1918	231	9.1	9.5	1,348

On the other hand, agricultural production *increased*: arable land expanded; the wheat harvest increased from 16.5 millions of double hundredweights in 1914 to 25 millions of double hundredweights in 1918. The economy of England had suffered much, but incomparable less than the continental countries at war!

b) *The neutral capitalist countries*
The influence of the war on the [economies of the] neutral countries – the latter category also includes the United States and Japan – is manifold. As suppliers of the belligerent countries, the small European countries could take advantage of the war. But they could not realise long-lasting war benefits

---

9 See Varga 1921e, pp. 159–82.

because of their smallness and dependency on the world market and their interconnection with the decaying economies of continental Europe; their situation instead even deteriorated.[10] In place of real goods, they hoarded gold and foreign currencies! The purchase of military equipment for defending their neutrality forced them to make sacrifices.

TABLE 5.6   Public debt increased during the war from 1913 to 1919

	Increase in %
Norway	182
Sweden	142
Denmark	156
Holland	138
Switzerland	116

In these countries, inflation was as high as in the belligerent countries.

Two non-European powers, the United States and Japan, were among the war profiteers. England was the leading capitalist country before the war; the United States became that after the war. Hence, we should fully examine the changes having occurred in the United States.

The United States of America possess all location advantages required for developing a flourishing economy on their territory.[11] A mild climate, a fertile soil, rich natural resources, iron, petroleum, copper; an educated and industrious population free from inhibitions that often frustrate in Europe the rationalisation of the production process (ignorance of the peasants, class prejudices,

---

10   TABLE 5.5   Denmark's herd (in millions of animals)

	Horned cattle	Horses	Pigs
15 July 1914	2.5	0.6	2.5
15 July 1918	2.1	0.5	0.6

Because of fodder shortages, Danish pig stock was ruined.

11   See Varga 1921d, pp. 119–46.

etc.). In an overview of the economic development of the United States, we see that during recent years an uninterrupted evolution to a higher stage of capitalist development has occurred. Industrialisation, a rapid rise in the organic composition of capital, and thus also higher labour productivity per worker in agriculture and industry, was realised.[12] At the same time capital was incredibly fast concentrating. The United States did not practice forms of European colonialism because of the country's incredible richness of natural resources. But similar colonisation attempts could nonetheless be noticed during the Spanish-American War. This war resulted in America's first colonies. In our vision, the United States were, however, still themselves a 'colonial country'. In 1905, apart from finished industrial goods worth 460 millions of dollars, the United States exported foodstuffs and raw materials worth 1,000 millions of dollars.

During the war, economic development of the United States was not interrupted, but even speeded up. Freed from competition by England and Germany on the world market, exports expanded tremendously, especially to Central and South America; at the same time, the USA became a supplier of the Entente: war-time materials, foodstuffs, raw materials were supplied in huge quantities. Unprecedented production capacities were fully employed. When in the belligerent countries, England included, production and productivity declined, both would soon expand in the USA. We give here some production figures in millions of tons.

TABLE 5.7   US industrial production (in million tons)

		1913	1918
Coal	tons	517.–	615,–
Pig iron	tons	35.50	39,03 (1917–18)
Copper	tons	5.49	8.56
Petroleum	barrels	284.04	355.09
Wheat (1914)	tons	236.–	310,– (1919)
Cotton	bales	14.09	11,09 (1917–18)
Cotton consumption (1910)	1,000 tons	2,250,–	3,863,– (1918)
Shipbuilding	tons	276,–	3,033,–
Automobiles (1915)	units	892,618	1,974,016 (1919)

---

12   See, extensively, Shadwell 1920. We give here the results of a very interesting survey 'Underproduction in England', published by *The Economist*, 5 March 1921, pp. 505–6.

Of the most important commodities, only cotton production had declined, while coal, iron, copper and petroleum production had increased. The unprecedented growth of the shipbuilding and automobile industry and an important increase of cotton consumption are hinting to growing industrialisation.

TABLE 5.8   Livestock statistics (in millions of animals)[13]

	Horses	Horned cattle	Pig
1910	19.8	61.6	58.2
1920	21.6	68.1	72.9

Contrary to Europe, labour productivity apparently did not decrease during the war in the United States. The evolution of average productivity of a coalminer is exemplary for productivity gains by all workers active in the bitumen and coal-mining sector of the United States:

TABLE 5.9   US bitumen and coal production

	Daily productivity per worker in tons	Number of working days per year	Yearly production per worker in tons
1913	3.61	232	887
1918	3.84	252	968

That under these conditions US inflation had appeared during the war (the Bradstreet's Index gives a yearly average inflation of 125 percent between 1913 and 1918!) is obvious, but in relation to European inflation it is a totally different economic phenomenon.

In Europe, inflation was a consequence of decreased production, shortages, speculation. Higher prices in America were the result of the fact that declining production in the belligerent countries of Europe could not be completely compensated by production growth. The Entente bought any American goods at the highest price.

---

13   *Statesman's Year-Book* 1920. Unfortunately, data of the last counting are not available.

TABLE 5.10 Export surplus of the United States in millions of dollars

1913	1914	1915	1916	1917	1918	1919	1920
69	324	1,776	3,091	3,281	3,117	4,016	2,949

From 1915 to 1920, a surplus for a total amount of 18,230 millions of dollars!

The country's industrial development was in the meantime proved by the fact that already in 1919 finished industrial products worth 2,072 millions of dollars and foodstuffs worth 1,408 millions of dollars – minus imports – were exported. *The United States has become an exporting industrial country!*

What did the United States now receive from Europe in exchange for these 18 milliards?

European-owned American securities returned to America. Their value is estimated at three to five milliard dollars.

More than half of the whole visible gold stock in the world – £1,501 million – is now concentrated in the United States.

The United States have lent several milliards of dollars to the European countries, cities and banks; American capital is holding a big stake in Europe's productive capital through portfolio investment.

We can summarise this development as follows:

America's economy has not been weakened by the war, but fortified. Production and productivity have increased. From an agrarian-colonial country, America became an industrialised exporting country, from an indebted country it became a creditor country, from an 'American' country it became an imperialist world power! An external symptom of America's triumph in Europe is that all European currencies are listing a discount rate of some 10 to 99 percent to the dollar!

The development of Japan. Japan's development is in essence analogous to, though less impressive than, the United States, because the required preconditions, such as the availability of enormous natural resources, accumulated production facilities and the higher productivity of the American workers, are non-existent. Data available for Japan are less complete than those for the US. Hence, we only want to discuss the most striking features.

Official sources[14] inform us that during the four war years, some 14,000 new factories and big workshops employing 270,000 workers had been construc-

---

14   *Der Neue Orient* 1921, 5, 9.

ted for a total investment amount of 440 million yens. According to the same sources, only some 5,000 factories employing 160,000 workers with a total investment worth 360 million yens were operating before the war! Production growth is given in *Table 5.11*.

TABLE 5.11 Japan's industrial production

In millions of double hundredweights						In million pounds sterling		In 1,000 tons	
Coal		Steel		Total steel consumption		Flax		Shipbuilding	
1913	17	1914	2.82	1914	8.15	1910	20	1913	65
1918	210	1917	5.29	1917	17.34	1918	178	1918	490

Bank deposits increased from two to six milliard yens; foreign assets amounted 2.8 milliard yens. Japan's foreign trade expanded especially to the Asian, Indian and East-African markets. But this expansion of the Japanese economy was not favoured by an advantageous natural environment. Hence, as we shall see, the reappearing European competitors were now threatening Japan's success in these markets.

c) *Industrialisation of colonial countries*
A constant shortage of shipping space existed during the war period. The German and Austrian-Hungarian merchant fleet had meanwhile disappeared. Because of the submarine war the Entente's shipping tonnage had temporarily diminished. An important part of the remaining merchant fleet was used for shipping troops and war-materials. Relations with the 'colonial' countries were disconnected. Their commodities could not be shipped. Provision with industrial products from Europe had worsened because of a declining productivity of European industry and cargo shortages. Freight prices were crazily growing. As a consequence *price differences between commodities and industrial goods were formidably growing in the colonial countries.*

Location advantages having made of Western Europe the industrial workshop of the world in a period of regular navigation and normal freight prices had vanished. In all colonial countries local industries had mushroomed and these countries tried to produce their own industrial goods autonomously from the world market.

THE CRISIS OF THE CAPITALIST WORLD ECONOMY

A long period of study and a thick book would be necessary for tracing out and analysing that development in all countries statistically. Thus we have to be satisfied with citing some cases.

In 1910, India's *coal production* was 12 million tons; in 1918 20 million tons.

TABLE 5.12 Total tonnage of ships arriving at British-Indian ports[15]

1913–14	8.6 million tons
1918–19	5.2 million tons

TABLE 5.13 Most important commodities exported from Great Britain to British India (in million £)

	1913	1918
Cotton textiles	35.89	28.61
Cotton fibres	2.27	1.90
Iron and steel products	9.31	2.82
Machinery	5.40	2.53
Wagons and parts	1.36	0.25
Copper products	1.33	0.11
Woollen products	1.39	1.00

One should notice that in England prices did rise by about a half between 1913 and 1918. Hence, it should be clear that the quantity of exported industrial products to India has decreased by a third or a quarter!

This decline must have been compensated partly by Japan, and also partly by the rapidly developing domestic industries.

About industrial development of South Africa during the war, *The Statesman's Year-Book* writes:

---

15 Data taken from *Statesman's Yearbook* 1920.

The conditions brought about by the war gave an impetus to local manufactures. The production of leather, for which this country is most suitable has been more than doubled; a commencement has been made with the manufacture of tanning extract from wattle bark; in dairy products increasing activity is everywhere being shown and the output of cement is rapidly overtaking the demands of the country. The union already produces its own requirements in beer and matches. The manufacture of tobacco satisfactorily maintains its position as one of the most important industries in the country. Amongst other commodities which the union is producing are dynamite, soap, rope, wine, spirits, furniture, vehicles, brooms and brushes, biscuits, earthenware pipes, and firebricks.[16]

The *Manchester Guardian* of 31 March 1921 gives statistics on industrial development in *Australia* (see *Table 5.14*).

TABLE 5.14 Industrial development in Australia

Number of factories		Number of workers		Value of production	
Wool industry					
1913	10	1913	1,790	1913	513,252
1919–20	14	1919–20	2,864	1919–20	1,976,428
Knitting industry					
1913	56	1913	1,221	1913	259,761
1919–20	79	1919–20	2,443	1919–20	1,149,272

On *China*'s industrialisation we read in *Berliner Tageblatt* of 22 October 1920 that industrialisation is progressing there. 'Cotton spinning-mills are mushrooming, most of them are bigger enterprises with 50,000 to 100,000 spools'. Machines are from the Union. Other industrial branches, even shipyards, are developing as well. 'Dormant Chinese capital has waken up and is looking for being employed in modern industrial enterprises'. Mixed Western-Chinese enterprises. Great expectations!

---

16   *The Statesman's Year-Book* 1920, p. 216.

A similar development is going on in all non-European countries.[17] This emerging industry is, for the time being, still weak and may not sustain in peacetime competition by European and American industry.

The Boom after the End of War

After the end of the war, a new economic boom in the world surpassed that of the pre-war period. The reopening of communication lines with the hitherto boycotted Central-European states, tonnage becoming free for shipping peace goods, a delayed consumptive demand by several social groupings of the population, a gradual abolishment of all state regulation of the economy: all this led to a conjunctural economic revival.

We will give here an outline of the actual conjuncture with regard to the following groups of countries: continental Europe, England, the United States, Japan and the colonial countries. We present here their general characteristics:

A highly speculative boom characterised by prices and profits rising faster than production.

Though an apparently excellent conjuncture, continental Europe's decay is mirrored in a deteriorating exchange rate of all European currencies vis-à-vis those of the real victors, i.e. the United States and Japan.

Price fluctuations in countries with stable currencies are given data in *Table 5.15*.

TABLE 5.15 Index of wholesale prices

	England *The Economist*	United States *Bradstreets*	Japan
1918 Jan–Nov on average	225	203	196
1919 " "	235	203	239
1920	293	208	267
1920 (highest score)	310 (March)	227 (January)	321.5 (March)

We see that the world-market prices increased *by more than about 12 percent above the 1918 average exchange level!* Prices are from now on given in Amer-

---

17 See Varga 1921e, pp. 159–82.

ican currency, and no longer in English currency. The latter are no longer set in gold equivalents, but related to the exchange rate of the British currency in New York. In the other countries, where inflation is nonetheless higher and whose economies have suffered mostly, the exchange rate of their currencies versus the gold-backed dollar is continuously worsening and now reaching its lowest level!

We show in *Table 5.15* the exchange rates of the most important currencies in New York at the end of war and in spring 1920 (data from *Archiv für Weltwirtschaft* and *The Economist*).

TABLE 5.16 Currency rates at the end of the war

Conversion method	London $ versus £	Japan $ cents versus yens	Paris francs versus $	Italy lire versus $	Zürich francs versus $	Berlin $ cents versus marks
On par	4.87	49.85	5.18	5.18	5.18	23.83
Exch. rate on 31 Oct 1918	4.75	54.60	5.47	6.36	5.01	3.30[18]
Exch. rates on 25 Mar 1920	3.87	46.25	13.40	19.60	5.84	1.35

The figures shown in *Table 5.16* are not so easy to interpret because of different methods of conversion we will explain here.

The pound sterling depreciated by 2.5 percent at the end of the war, but at the end of the boom the pound depreciated by about 20 percent! In this period, Japan's currency was already *overvalued* by some 10 percent; the exchange rate has now declined by some 15 percent, thus is now depreciated. One paid 5.47 French francs for a dollar in New York at the end of the war. At the end of March 1920 already 13.40 francs were paid for a dollar. The corresponding figures are 6.36 and 19.60 for Italy. The Italian currency has already lost three quarters of its nominal gold value! The German mark lost eighteen times its value!

This fall of the exchange rate led to a corresponding important rise of the price level in the countries concerned and to the well-known phenomenon of currency and commodity speculation putting – with the exception of the United States and some neutral countries – their stamp on this boom period.

---

18   30 October 1919 (first conversion after the war).

Enormous profits were made, but production itself declined, state deficits soared tremendously, the working class became impoverished.

The following data show some parallels between falling exchange rates and inflation:

TABLE 5.17   Declining exchange rates and inflation

Index of wholesale prices	Germany Statistisches Reichsamt	France Statistiques générales	Italy Bacchi
1918 (averages)	216	339.2	409
1920 (March)	1,455	591 (April)	679 (April)
1918 (31 October)	30.30 marks[19]	5.47 francs	6.36 lire
1920 (25 March)	74.90	13.40	19.60

The higher the exchange rate of the dollar, the higher prices will climb! Price rises are ending up with speculation!

Hereafter we will examine some cases belonging to several different groupings of countries.

Germany. That the postwar boom was mainly a speculative boom is best shown by the case of Germany. While prices increased seven times within a period of a year and a half, production, however, decreased after the exchange-rate crisis and prices increased by 100 percent a month if compared to the pre-war price level. Coal production fell from 261 million tons in 1918 to 210 million tons in 1919; production increased again to 252 million tons in 1920 (from 67.8 percent of pre-war production level in 1919 to 75.7 percent in 1920). But because of compulsory coal deliveries to the Entente the economic situation has now become untenable. Half of the factories are standing idle because of coal shortages. Labour productivity rapidly declined. Wages did not keep up with inflation. Workers and civil servants were impoverished. Enormous strike movements and revolts were marking the struggle of the despaired proletariat for improving their living standard: in 1919 more than 5 million workers had gone on strike; 47 million officially registered working days were lost.[20] Paper-money circulation increased during this period with about 20 milliard marks, i.e. twice as much as at the end of the war. Public debt increased with about 40

---

19   30 October 1919.
20   *Statistisches Jahrbuch* 1920.

milliard marks! The market was becoming a *selling-off economy*: old domestic stocks were sold abroad at ridiculously low prices. The 1919 harvest is showing a further sharp decline if compared to 1918 (by about 10 percent).

Apparently, the economic situation of *France* improved in this period, but only because of compulsory deliveries of goods from Germany. There is no strengthening of the domestic economy. Coal production declined from 26 million tons in 1918 to 22 million tons in 1919, rose again to 25 million tons in 1920. Coal shortages lasted until autumn 1920.

France is keeping a standing army of 800,000 troops on war-strength in order to secure German reparation payments. Costs of this army amount to several milliards of francs at the charge of the budget. State revenues do not even cover half of these expenditures. Hence, public debt increased to 220 milliard francs at the end of December 1919, which was much higher than that of defeated Germany (190 milliard marks). During 1919 paper money in circulation increased by an additional 7 milliard of francs. Inflation peaked.

In 1920 production increased erstwhile. Foremost, the wheat harvest increased to 62 millions of double hundredweights, which was nonetheless 25 to 30 percent below the pre-war average level, but that was nonetheless a striking improvement if compared with the war years' production. The same happened to other agricultural outputs. Foreign trade also improved: in 1920 total value of import surpluses decreased to 13 milliards of francs. The situation in Italy and Belgium was similar to that in France, though vehement labour unrest was weakening Italy's economy.

England is the only European belligerent country to have clearly recovered during the boom period. However, production did not increase in all branches. The most important data are given in *Table 5.18*.

TABLE 5.18 Production in million tons

	Wheat	Coal	Iron	Steel	Shipbuilding
	Double hundredweights	In tons	In tons	In tons	In 1,000 tons
1918	25	231	9.2	9.5	1,348
1919	21	233	7.4	7.9	1,620
1920	15.5	229	8.1	9.0	2,056

THE CRISIS OF THE CAPITALIST WORLD ECONOMY 361

Except for shipbuilding, production during the booming years did not surpass output of the last war years and production of raw materials – coal and iron – was considerably lagging behind (in 1913 coal production was 292 millions of tons, output of iron was 10.4 millions of tons). Labour productivity per worker decreased in coalmining; all capitalists of the other production branches were also complaining. Production slowed down because of enormous strikes!

In this period, England could nonetheless consolidate its public finances, increase its tax revenues[21] and clear away its public deficit with funds raised by selling war-materials (about 300 millions of pound sterling). England is furthermore the only belligerent country to have diminished its war debt after the war.[22]

21 TABLE 5.19 Yearly tax burden per inhabitant according to an assessment made by Entente experts

England	Pound sterling 17/0
France	Pound sterling 5/16
Germany	Pound sterling 2/11

One should notice that revenues are much more heavily taxed in England than in its colonies.

TABLE 5.20 Yearly income tax rates

Pound sterling	England	South Africa	Australia	Canada	New Zealand
250	13½	None	4½	10	none
800	14¾	25½	60	32	58¼
800 (unchanged)	165¾	25½	78	32	58¼

22 England's public debt amounted to 8,079 million pounds sterling on 31 December 1919 and to 7,644 pounds sterling on 31 March 1921. *The Economist*, 23 April 1921, p. 811.

TABLE 5.21 Evolution of the currency exchange rates

| | Paris | Italy | Switzerland | New York | Bombay | Berlin | Stockholm |
					12.8.1919	12.8.1919	
31.12.1918	26.6	30.38	23.65	4.765	1,6 1/16	76.50	16.60
31.3.1920	58.45	81.–	22.20	3.88	2.4 3/16	285	18.8

We see that in this period the currencies of all belligerent countries had devalued vis-à-vis the British pound sterling and that England's currency had depreciated by some 20 percent vis-à-vis the dollar.

English industry made enormous profits during this period of rising prices; these profits partly appeared on the balances of 1920.[23] Especially coalmining and shipping companies were robbing entire foreign countries.

The *United States* became in this period the world's first economic power. Not only did the profits of the capitalists increase, but also production. This is shown in *Table 5.21*.

TABLE 5.22 Production in millions

| | Coal | Iron | Cotton | Wheat | Petroleum | Ships | Automobiles |
	Tons	Tons	Bales	Tons	Barrels	1,000 tons	Units
1913	517	31.5	14.9	–	248	276	–
1914	466	23.7	15.1	236	265	200	892,000
1918	615	39.5	11.6	242	356	3,033	1,153,600
1919	494	30.6	12.2	310	378	4,075	1,974,000
1920	600	31.4	13.2	202	442	2,746	2,350,000

---

23   In 1920, the English cotton spinning-mills paid at average a 25.11 percent dividend (*The Manchester Guardian*, 27 January 1921). According to the Central Profiteering Com., the wool industry had generated a net profit of 59.4 percent in 1919, which was still 39.04 percent after war taxes were deduced. The gigantic profits generated by the coalmines are widely known. [Varga is obviously referring to the Central Wool Committee. From 21 November 1916, until 30 June 1920, when the contract with the British Government expired, the Central Wool Committee held complete control of the wool industry of Australia in all its branches. It drew its authority from regulations issued under the War Precautions].

We see that activities increased in shipbuilding, in petroleum production and in the automobile industry; on the other hand, iron production remained strikingly well under its wartime level. The cotton harvest did not yet recover to its peacetime level. Cattle stock is also minimally growing; the number of horses decreased between 1918 and 1920; wheat production is declining, but maize production is increasing. At any rate, the US economy was progressing in this period.

On the other hand, Europe's decay is in particular proven by the fact that in this period the exchange rates of all European currencies suffered colossal losses on the American exchange market. At the beginning of this period, on 31 October 1918, only the Italian currency showed a considerable depreciation of about 23 percent (the currencies of the enemy countries were not yet quoted), the English and French currencies had heavily depreciated, and the currencies of the neutral countries, like the Japanese yen, were at par or had depreciated!

At the end of this period (31 March 1920), however, the exchange rate of the French francs had dropped to 40 percent of its gold value, the Italian lire to 25 percent and all neutral currencies showed a depreciation of 10 to 20 percent! This proves that the European economy was not healthy during the whole 'booming' period.

We also want to stress that speculation played an important role during the boom period of the United States. According to data provided by the 'Comptroller of the Currency',[24] total credit allowed by all American banks amounted to 25,086 million dollars on 30 June 1919 and 30,892 million dollars on 30 June 1920.

A prominent American capitalist, *G.E. Roberts*,[25] Vice-President of National City Bank of New York, mentions that the enormous sum of 6 milliard dollars was used for speculative movements because of the fact that production did not increase; he said that production could not be raised because all machines and workers were employed. – We already want to see in that the beginning of a crisis: additional money capital is needed when goods in the circulation sphere are not sold.

Statistical material about the countries outside Europe is not sufficiently available in order to typify such a short period of time. We only argue that the

---

24 [The Office of the Controller of the Currency (OCC) was established in 1863 as an independent bureau of the US Department of the Treasury. The OCC's primary mission is to charter, regulate, and supervise all national banks and federal savings associations].

25 [George E. Roberts, formerly Director of the United States Mint, was an assistant to the President of National City Bank of New York].

conjuncture had *a highly speculative character*[26] in these areas and that the first incitement to the crisis had come from the Asian countries where silver prices had collapsed and that this had made selling European and American goods there difficult.

The Actual Economic Crisis

The actual economic crisis can especially be characterised by its violence, but also by substantially falling prices and the incredibly high number of unemployed workers and their geographical spreading. Today, there is no single country – except Russia – in the whole world not sharing the miserable fate of the crisis.

When studying the origins and the geographical development of the slump, we discovered that the crisis had started in the economically strongest countries, like America and Japan. Now that the available means of production remain idle in Central Europe because of coal shortages and insufficient transport facilities, the necessary goods for meeting existing demand cannot be produced, while in America and Japan stocks of unsold goods are already constituted. It is noteworthy that [in 1920] wholesale prices reached their highest level in various countries (see *Table 5.23*).

TABLE 5.23 Highest wholesale prices in various countries in 1920

United States	January
Japan	March
England, France, Italy	April
Canada, India	May
Sweden	June
Holland	July
Australia	August

---

26 An interesting description of speculation in the Japanese cotton industry in this period is given by the *Board of Trade Journal* of 2 December 1920. Huge stocks constituted at high prices, a price fall of 50 percent, spinners, cotton traders, yarn traders, yarn exporters, weavers, textile merchants and textile exporters are mutually interconnected. The government intervenes with a credit of 40 million yens to prevent a general breakdown.

Statistics from Central Europe are worthless because price changes are deformed by violently fluctuating exchange rates.

We already noticed that capitalism fiercely resists when in crisis. In spring 1920, business activities were already slowing down in the English textile industry. Asia was buying practically nothing anymore,[27] but prices remained nonetheless rather high during a half a year; only in October [1920] prices would crash! And meanwhile retail prices kept on rising during some months after wholesale prices had already declined. Since the war, consumers are used to paying any price a merchant demands.

Fierce resistance of capital was also turned into growing competition. Hardly a big bank and a large industrial enterprise collapsed. At the beginning of the war, capital's great strength was already based on a fully organised capitalism. Enterprises set up big trusts and integrated concerns led by big banks were so closely knit together that not a single enterprise would be able to break away in case of a collapse of the whole system.

---

27   See weekly reports in *The Economist*.

TABLE 5.24   Evolution of wholesale prices in the United States and England

	United States		England	
1920	Wholesale prices	Retail prices	Wholesale prices	Retail prices
	Bradstreets	Bureau of Labour	*The Statist*	Cost of Living
January	227.2(!)	248	289	225
February	226	249	306	230
March	225.2	253	308	230
April	225	265	313(!)	232
May	216.4	272(!)	306	241
June	210	269	301	250
July	205	262	299	252
August	195.7	250	298	255
September	184	242	293	261
October	170	225	282	264
November	148	207	263	276(!)
December	138	201	243	269

(!)   Index base = 100 added.

1   The Causes of the Present World Crisis

A capitalist economic crisis always appears in the form of an overproduction crisis meaning that a part of the goods produced for a price containing a corresponding profit will remain unsold. But the phenomenon of overproduction is always engendered by a particular form of income distribution.

If we study the causes of the actual crisis from this vantage point, we find a statistically proven overproduction of ships!

TABLE 5.25   Total stock of sea ships (in 1,000 tons) according to *Lloyd's Register*

1914	1919	30 June 1920	English estimation 31 March 1921
49,100	50,900	57,314	59,100

After 1914 total quantity of shipped goods had certainly not increased. Exclusion of Russia from world trade, decreasing production in the Central and Eastern European countries, growing industrialisation of the colonial countries have certainly led to a declining cargo demand. An increase of one-fifth of tonnage supply means a real overproduction. An absolute overcapacity of tonnage appeared after in wartime postponed shipping of goods and transports of troops back home had been realised one and half years after the war's end.

According to the Hamburg-Amerika Linie,[28] no less than 30 percent of world tonnage had been laid up in March 1921.[29]

---

28   [The Hamburg Amerikanische Packetfahrt Actien Gesellschaft (HAPAG) is often mentioned as the Hamburg America Line (Hamburg-Amerika Linie)].
29   This explains the incredibly declining freight prices.

TABLE 5.26   Indian-English freight prices

1914	March 1918	March 1919	March 1921
17/6 sh.	175 sh.	75 sh.	20 to 22 sh.

Price evolution in 1920 is shown in following *Table 5.27*:

Did absolute overproduction also exist in other industrial branches?

According to world trade standards, hardly! In some neutral countries maybe!

During the war, gigantic production facilities consuming an incredible amount of war materials were developed in America and in the neutral countries. These workshops were reorganised for peacetime production purposes (machine building, furniture, etc.). The amount of production facilities increased enormously, especially in the United States, and a *relative* overproduction of many goods grew there very soon. Because of peacetime reconversion the US *domestic market* could not absorb that output increase. Because of falling agrarian prices the American agrarian population lost an important part of its domestic purchasing power.

Deliveries of wartime goods to the Entente armies had ceased. American goods on the free market were now exposed to competition of products produced by European and colonial industries.

Because American industry produces everything cheaper than the new industries of the colonies or the decaying European factories, the former would have certainly won if labour value had been exchanged for labour value and gold value for gold value. But continental Europe has no gold. Because Europe's means of production are decaying, labour productivity is low; Europe has no goods to exchange with the United States. Continental Europe must import everything from America: foodstuffs, raw materials, machinery and manufactures, but has nothing to exchange. Only paper money. If countries having put that money into circulation cannot sell goods, that paper money will lose its

---

Price rates of *one* fare in shillings (Report of the Chamber of Shipping. *The Economist*, 26 February 1921, p. 461). [See also other shipping statistics mentioned in the same issue of *The Economist*, pp. 393–4].

TABLE 5.27 British shipping prices in 1920

	January	April	September	December
England – La Plata	190	150	102	42
Cardiff – Port Said	65	75	30	15
Monthly Charter	25	20	13	10 (*The Times*)

In addition, some three million tons are still under construction in England and seven million tons more in the whole world.

value.[30] Hence, the special situation is created that industrial goods produced by those countries with bad currencies and by an *objectively* expensive production process will be cheaper than American industrial products.

There exists thus a relative overproduction in America, Japan and England, while continental Europe is facing an underproduction crisis. *This relative world-economic overproduction in the countries of 'healthy' capitalism is caused by underproduction in Central and Eastern Europe and by the disappearance of Russia from world trade.* The crisis spread to all neutral and colonial territories. The available means of production cannot be employed because of coal and raw material shortages, which causes a permanent underproduction crisis in Central Europe; the present overproduction crisis is therefore much less sharply felt there. Price falls and unemployment are relatively much lower in Germany than in America or in England.

2   Economic Crisis and Income Distribution

Let us explain the social roots of the crisis. When studying the crisis from this point of view, we see that *the crisis began in the sector of goods of mass consumption which are, however, not indispensable*, such as clothes, shoes and luxury goods. Price falls were very steep in this branch. If taking English prices – the English currency suffered permanently from a 20 percent depreciation *vis-à-vis* the gold price – we can list two kinds of goods: *indispensable goods* and *a kind of luxury goods* (see *Table 5.28*).

[30]   TABLE 5.28   Depreciation of the most important currencies *vis-à-vis* the US dollar in percentages at the end of 1920

Switzerland	21.2	Norway	41.4	Germany	94.3
Holland	22.1	Greece	61.4	Czechoslovakia	94.4
Sweden	26.3	Belgium	68.0	Yugoslavia	96.5
England	27.5	France	69.6	Austria	98.9
Spain	30.3	Italy	82.1	Hungary	99.1
Denmark	41.4	Romania	93.5	Poland	99.2

The especially high depreciation rate of the moneys of the neutral countries is striking. At the end of the war, they were still at parity or at agio, just like the Spanish and Swiss currencies. *Does this mean that neutral Europe had been dragged away by Central Europe's decay?*

TABLE 5.29 Price index of goods
Group 1: Index of indispensable goods, i.e. basic materials

	1 May 1920	1 March 1921	1 April 1921	Price fluctuations since 1 May 1920 in percentages
Wheat, England	234	239.9	285	+21
Wheat, Manitoba	270.5	253.2	246	−8
Potatoes, England	512	336	352	−31
Beef, England	240	276	272	+13
Sugar, England	473.2	405.6	411	−13
Butter, Denmark	230.7	227	227	−1
Pig iron, Cleveland	400	390	300	−25
Export coal	567.9	281.5	281.5	−51
Petroleum, refined	305.9	323.5	325.3	+8

Group 2: Index of luxury goods, i.e. their basic materials

	1 May 1920	1 March 1921	1 April 1921	Price fall since 1 May 1920 (%)
Rice, no. 2	510.5	147.4	173.7	65
Tea, India	159	134.3	109.6	32
Coffee	239.1	144.9	126.8	48
Cotton, America	379.3	99.9	112.3	70
Wool, Merino	530.2	116.4	111.6	78
Hemp, New Zealand	258.3	191.7	187.5	27
Rubber	94.6	38.4	36.6	61

We see that of all prices paid for indispensable goods only the extremely high price of export coal has sharply fallen, while wheat, petroleum and beef prices have increased. The prices of luxury goods, i.e. their basic materials, decreased even with 78 percent.

TABLE 5.30 Prices of some goods having surpassed peacetime price levels[31]

	31 December 1913	28 February 1921	24 April 1921	Highest price in 1920
American wool	7.14 d.	7.13 d.	–	32.41 d.
Crossbred wool	10¾d.	8½ d.	–	29.– d.
Jute	£35/10	£32/0	£34/-	£70/0
Rubber	2 s. 4 d.	10¾ d.	10¾ d.	10½ d.
Tin (tons)	£169/10	£159/15	£168/17.16	£420/0
Lead (tons)	£18 3/9	£17/10	higher[32]	£53/0

Tables 5.29 and 5.30 are showing a kind of socially influenced overproduction: more luxury goods are produced for mass consumption than workers and civil servants can afford with their diminishing real income. This complex of causes is closely related to Central and Eastern Europe's decay: the purchasing power of broad masses, i.e. workers and white-collar workers, has diminished to the bare minimum in these less-producing territories. Relative overproduction elsewhere is caused by an absolute underproduction in these regions.

3 *The Break-Up of the World Market*

We should once again refer to the breaking up of the world market: politically, Central and Eastern Europe are geographically broken up into a series of small countries which are fighting and blocking each other; economically, the colonial countries created new industries during the war seriously competing the industrial world powers; the crisis in the colonial countries should be explained – apart from price falls of all raw materials – on the basis of these circumstances. The different countries only tried to protect their own industries. A new era of building high tariff walls has begun.[33] Even *export taxes* exist in many countries. Not only have the advantages of a worldwide economic division of labour disappeared, but even the world market itself.

---

31 According to several issues of *The Times*.
32 These listings in these and in the other tables show that the lowest price level could have been transgressed.
33 Free-trading England has an anti-dumping law and levies high import taxes on German paints and instruments. France has increased its import tariffs to 300 percent. Ten new tariff walls were recently erected on the territory of the former Austrian-Hungarian Monarchy. India raised its import taxes on British goods to 11 percent, etc.

In addition, one should also mention the incredible currency depreciations and the enormously fluctuating exchange rates! All capitalist calculations are transformed into exchange speculations![34] Small neutral countries with high exchange rates and exporting industries, like Switzerland and Sweden, are suffering most of all from the crisis! Absolute underproduction and relative overproduction are partly caused by this break-up of the world market.

4   The Spread of the Crisis and Unemployment

The actual world economic crisis is spreading over all territories of the whole capitalist world and is everywhere creating high unemployment rates. It is a matter of fact that the crisis is steeper in the most developed capitalist countries like England, America and Japan where the highest numbers of unemployed workers can be found, while unemployment is lower in Central Europe. Thanks to the overproduction crisis, areas suffering from underproduction could get coal and raw materials for starting up their production. In spring 1921, for instance, the Alpine Montan Gesellschaft in German Austria got enough cokes from Czechoslovakia to start up a new blast furnaces after a period of inactivity at the very moment that in America and England blast furnaces were put out!

The number of unemployed workers in different countries can be considered as known and also the fact that the official statistics do not even register the real mass of jobless workers.[35] We only possess detailed data about *the evolution of unemployment* for England and Germany. In England, the trade unions reported that in the first half of 1920 between 0.9 and 2.9 percent of their members were jobless, which is quite 'normal': high unemployment started in October [1920], at the very moment of the Great Strike of the mineworkers, with

---

[34]   TABLE 5.31   Some cases of fluctuating exchange rates on the London market during recent years

1 £	1 April 1920	1 July 1920	1 October 1920	31 December 1920	31 March 1921
German mark	279.00	149.00	213.00	258.00	245.00
Polish mark	637.50	570.00	900.00	2,200.00	3,275.00
French franc	57.75	47.20	51.88	59.72	56.10
Lire	80.62	65.62	83.60	101.75	95.85

[35]   The *Industrie- und Handelszeitung* of 23 February 1921 writes that, according to recent estimations, only about half of the unemployed received unemployment benefits; the same appreciations are given in *Reichsarbeitsblatt*! The situation should be no better in England.

5.3 percent, and progressed then to: 5.7, 6.1, 6.9, 8.5, 10 percent. We do not yet know the official record for April [1921]; that percentage must be significantly higher because of the miners' general strike. According to official statistics, 11.3 percent of the 12 million workers insured against unemployment in England were unemployed! *Unemployment correlates with the price falls, i.e. with the evolution of the crisis itself*. In *Germany*, unemployment correlates strongly with the fluctuating exchange rates: export will decline and unemployment figures will grow when the exchange rate of the mark improves. In other countries with weak currencies, things are going the same way. The neutral countries with overvalued currencies are showing comparatively high unemployment figures. (Switzerland had officially 43.554 full-time and 88,689 part-time unemployed workers on 25 January 1921). It is also certain, although this was not the result of decreasing sales, that the capitalists decided to limit production and to lay-off in order to accustom the workers to wage cuts.

The number of full-time unemployed workers can be estimated at least at 10 million workers in the capitalist countries (the United States 3,500,000, England 1,500,000, Germany 500,000 officially). The certainly not less numerous unemployed 'short-term' workers have to be added to the former category. Working hours were shortened in the textile industry in the whole world. The *International Federation of Cotton Spinners*[36] adopted an international accord on shorter working during half a year in the cotton industry, a measure ending in January 1921. The regulation about *shortening working hours was changed and recalculated in function of a complete stoppage of all spools*. The spinning-mills had thus come to a standstill for 6 working weeks of 48 hours during the 26 workings weeks of that half a year:

6 hours in England,
2½ in France,
7½ in Germany,
1 hour Italy,
13½ (!) in Czechoslovakia,
4.7 in Spain,
7½ in Belgium,

---

36 [The *International Federation of Master Cotton Spinners and Manufacturers* was established in 1904 to address issues related to chronic cotton shortages that resulted in market destabilisation and manipulation; and to foster cooperation among cotton producers, shippers and downstream manufacturers. It comprised associations from 10 European countries including Austria, Belgium, France, Germany, Italy, the Netherlands, Portugal, Spain, Switzerland and the United Kingdom].

1½ in Switzerland,
10 in Poland,
10½ in Austria,
13 (?) in Japan,
none in India.

In the United States: 6,00,000 out of 36,000,000 spools remained idle at the end of December 1920 and 4,450,000 were still idle at the end of January 1921.

Hence, a relative overproduction had led to an absolute decrease of production!

The Postwar Living Standard of the Working Class

Establishing whether and in which measure the real living standard has improved or worsened since the end of war is one of the most important tasks. The available data only provide an unclear and contradictory picture. One has to measure the purchasing power at different moments. Today, we have sequential calculations of living costs for different countries at our disposal; their exactness is, however, contested by workers as well as by employers. The figures of wage tariffs with their fluctuations are so controversial that one only should use them very cautiously.[37] Those are the precautions we will take when studying the particular groups of countries.

1   *Germany and the Central European Countries*
That the living standard of the working class sharply declined in Germany, Poland, German Austria, Hungary, etc. during the war should not be proven. *It is important to know that this situation did not change during the boom period.*

Let us take *Germany* for example. All its data are published in an explanatory memorandum published by the German trade unions: *Die wirtschaftliche Lage der deutschen Arbeiter und die Beschlüsse der Pariser Konferenz* (see Table 5.32).[38]

---

37   The best but also the roughest method of comparing the living standard of the working class consists of comparing prices of consumption goods – bread, meat, sugar, coffee, tea, etc. – with those of commodities. These data are only very recently published; they are, however, less useful for the war period because of the army's particular demand!

38   *Die wirtschaftliche Lage* 1921.

TABLE 5.32 Average wages increased between 1914 and the end of 1920

Wages of		Costs of living	
		Calculations by the trade unions	Calwer Index
1,44,851 workers	9 times	–	–
817,706	6.5 times	15.5 times	17.7 times
37,496	4.2 times	–	–

'*Wages of German workers must increase twice for nearly reaching the pre-war living standard*', is the conclusion of the trade unions.

Based on the same data, the famous statistician [René] Kuczynski arrives at the same conclusion for 1919 and 1920. He writes:[39] 'When including all not vital expenditures (clothes, underclothing, furniture, fares, taxes) into the official statistics of the Reich, I arrive at an existence minimum of 254 marks for February 1920. On the other hand, official statistics give a weekly average wages of male workers in Great Berlin'.

TABLE 5.33 Averages wages of Great Berlin

Building industry	175 Marks
Glass and ceramic industry	171 Marks
Leather industry	199 Marks
Vegetable oils and fat industry	160 Marks

> The average wage of the male workers in Great Berlin can be set on 170 marks, i.e. about one-third under the actual existence minimum (254 marks) of six persons family. One should keep in mind that during the last pre-war year the same existence minimum of hardly 29 marks was laying more than one-sixth under the then paid average wage of 35 marks. [...] *For November 1920 I estimate the weekly average wage at 240 marks, the minimal costs of living at 316 marks. In August 1919 wages were about a quarter beneath the existence minimum.*

---

39   Kuczynski 1921, p. 30.

THE CRISIS OF THE CAPITALIST WORLD ECONOMY

Of course, there are enough advocates of the bourgeoisie arguing that the living standard of the German worker had improved after the war. But is it really necessary to prove the proletariat's impoverishment by using statistical data? Is that not evident when looking at their rags and their increasing leanness, and by data provided by the sick-funds about the spreading of tuberculosis and other diseases in general? Does not everybody know that clothes, underclothing and other belongings of the German workers were sold to the peasant usurer? But we want here to quote some witnesses:

The English politician Charles Roden Buxton and his wife Dorothy Frances Buxton stayed in the Essen coal district with a family of German mineworkers where they observed in detail a family's living conditions. Citing this report discussed in the *Labour Leader*, the *Rote Fahne* writes:

> Sternstraße 7 is the address, but more smoke than stars can be seen when looking out of the windows. *Herr Duda* is a face man. In the year of 1910 he earned about 30 marks a week at average. Today, he earns 300 marks. Prices have multiplied by about 20. Hence, things he once bought for 30 marks, are costing now 600 marks. In other words, he only can buy about half of the things he bought previously. This is roughly indicative of the changes in the living standard everywhere in Germany. Other people are in a worse situation, because they have a larger family and less savings. One should keep in mind that the *mineworkers are now better paid than the other workers* and that they are suffering less from unemployment. At our request, the Duda family reported on their living standard as well. Breakfast consisted of rye bread with a very little bit of melted-down pork fat smeared on it and with imitation coffee. Bread ration is half a pound a day. Our host took *four thin slices of bread with him to the coal mine*. After having returned from his work at noon, he had his main meal. Apart from Sundays, when he had meat, his daily dinner consisted of cabbage and potatoes or peas and potatoes, occasionally completed with a scanty piece of sausage and with bread and coffee. Supper was usually prepared from what was left from dinner and consisted of fried potatoes or potato pancakes, and a little bit of barley soup or cooked rice was served after one or two days. *Of course, we never saw any butter*.
>
> Underwear shortages were even worse than food shortages. We visited a large number of families in their dwellings; they were not at all selected because of their poverty. On our demand they showed us their wardrobes and drawers and we found them near empty. *Hundreds of miners have now switched on a 'one-shirt-system'*. At Sunday night, they go to bed, but *they cannot get up before that only shirt is washed and dry*. With regard

to the children: many of them cannot go to school, because they have no underwear.

This creeping impoverishment of the German population that the Treaty of Versailles is successfully creating, is occurring without provoking any sensation. People do not starve in the streets: if tired and sick and having their clothes in rags, they'll stay at home during their idle moments or go their own way to their workplace without attracting attention from anybody. The children will be kept at home when weak or wearing no shoes or shirt.[40]

And in December 1920, Dr. Grützer, the President of the Government in Düsseldorf who belongs to the Majority Social-Democratic Party, declared publicly: 'For months, children of my civil servants in Düsseldorf are going to school without wearing a shirt'.[41]

We could quote hundreds of such non-communist utterances! And the situation in Poland, German-Austria, Hungary, Romania, etc. is also bad.

2 The Entente Countries

We do not possess such concise data about wage increases in *France* and *Italy*. *Le Populaire*[42] of 23 October 1920 published figures about wage increases of ten groups of metal workers in France. Increases amounted from 275 to 440 percent. The wholesale index stood at 489 in January, 591 in April, 463 in November. As a result a very serious worsening of the living standard happened.

TABLE 5.34   Data about wage increases of the coalminers (French Ministry of Labour)[43]

	Northern Basin		Canal Basin		Loire Basin		Wholesale index; yearly average
		%		%		%	
1913	6.20	100	4.13	100	4.06	100	100
1914	6.34	103	5.59	135	4.85	120	103
1918	13.17	213	11.77	285	10.27	250	341
1919	16.77	270	15.03	360	14.12	345	358

---

40 [Varga gives no further references].
41 *Frankfurter Zeitung*, 29 December.
42 [*Le Populaire* was a Socialist newspaper, published by the SFIO].
43 *Wirtschaft und Statistik*, Herausgegeben vom Statistischen Reichsamt, Berlin, 1921, vol. 1, no. 1.

These figures of *Table 5.34* show also a *worsening of the living standard*. All observers have also come to the general view that the condition of the working class has worsened in France and Italy.

England

TABLE 5.35 Average wage increases paid by the English shipyards (for a working week of 53 or 54 hours in 1914, and 47 hours in 1920) between 4 August 1919 and 31 December 1920 according to the *Labour Gazette*

	Increases in %
Founder	121
Moulder	122
Machinist	209
Plater	123
Riveter	131
Shipyard worker	204

The cost of living index gives a price increase of 169 percent for December [1920]. This is, in general, a worsening. Moreover, a big boom developed in the shipbuilding industry.

TABLE 5.36 Wage increases in comparison with 1914 according to the *Manchester Guardian*

(In percentages 1914 = 100)	
Railway worker, ordinary level	270
Railway worker, higher level	140
Building worker, daily labourer	225
Building worker, weekly pay	190
Mineworker	160
Machinist	145
Shipyard worker	144
Cost of living index	141

After a sharp price decline in October 1920, the real living standard improved. However, in the meantime the bourgeoisie imposed wage cuts, hence the living conditions of the workers did not improve!

TABLE 5.37 Wage increases of the miners compared to peace-time wages

	Wage increases in percentages	Labour Gazette Index = price increases
15 May 1915	15.5	20
1 December 1915	20.5	35
March 1916	25.5	35 to 40
June 1916	29	45
February 1917	33.5	65 to 70
September 1917	56	80 to 85
June 1918	77.5	100

'Wages increased a little bit faster than inflation, but only for a very short period of time'.[44]

In this period, the living standard of the English worker did not keep up with inflation in general.[45]

Neutral Countries

We do not dispose their data.

Denmark

Official statistics. A rising cost of living by 264 percent until January 1921. An increase of hourly paid wages by 296 percent during the third quarter of 1920, an increase of weekly paid wages by 228 percent during the third quarter of 1920.[46]

---

44   *Daily Herald*, 20 March 1921. (Retranslated from German into English).
45   It is very interesting that during the boom the number of officially registered unemployed workers increased substantially. In September 1918, there were 446,600 unemployed workers in England and Wales; 483,148 in December 1919; 494,300 in July 1920; and 542,000 in November 1920.
46   *Reichsarbeitsblatt – Nichtamtlicher Teil* 1921, p. 465.

Sweden

According to the employers, wages increased between 185 to 190 percent from 1914 until 1 January 1921. According to the trade union of the metalworkers, wages increased by 159 percent between 1914 and 1 January 1921. Total costs of living increased (officially) by 171 percent from July 1914 until 1 January 1921.[47] The living standard seems to have undergone little changes.

Holland

The wages of the Rotterdam city workers increased (officially) by 195 percent between 1912 and 1920; the wages of the city's street cleaners increased by 270 percent and those of the carpenters of the city by 165 percent. According to a collective agreement for the printing industry, the wages of the mechanical composers increased from 206 to 272 percent between 1 February 1914 and 1 January 1921, and book printers from 221 to 336 percent. In the metal industry in Amsterdam: hourly wages increased by 167 percent between 1 January 1910 and June 1920; weekly wages increased by 112 percent.[48] The increase in the wholesale price index (*Central Statistical Office*) since 1913: in January 1920 an increase of 193 percent, in December 1920 an increase of 134 percent. The average living standard would thus have improved.

The United States would have been the only country where the living conditions of the working class undoubtedly improved during the war. This could have been possible with regard to our previous analysis of the economic situation of the United States.

TABLE 5.38   Average wages of the workers of the state of New York[49]

	1913	1920	1920 Oct.	1920 Nov.	1920 Dec.
Wages	100	222	228	226	223
US Bureau of Labour Index, total costs of living	100	–	225	207	201.4

---

47 Ibid.
48 Ibid.
49 *Labour Market Bulletin*, December 1920.

According to the *railway companies* (!) wages of their employees increased by some 134 percent between 1914 and 1920, but the costs of living rose by some 94 percent. Information given by the United Steel Company about their 250,000 workers seems to be more reliable.

TABLE 5.39 Average wages of all categories of workers was[50]

	Yearly averages per worker per day in dollars		US Bureau of Labour Index (retail prices)
1913	2.92	905	100
1914	2.97	905	99
1915	3.01	925	100
1916	3.36	1,042	123
1917	4.16	1,296	175
1918	5.38	1,685	196
1919	6.17	1,902	214

Increases in percentages

1913 to 1919	108	111	114

According to these precise data, the living conditions of the workers of the steel trust did not improve at all!

Trustworthy specialists, thus our comrades, knowing the living conditions of the working class, think that, in general, the American working-class wages were well above the normal wage standard during the war, thus that the workers could have saved: *that meant that they were able to survive during this period of high unemployment.*

We do not want to accumulate here more data. We only want to mention the relation between the crisis and the living conditions of the workers. Underproduction in Central Europe has led to a important worsening of the living standard of the proletariat – and even to a more serious worsening of the living conditions of the civil servants. These large groups of consumers had to reduce consumption of inessential goods, such as footwear, clothes, furniture, kitchen utensils, books, etc., to a strict minimum. Hence, the crisis and the price

---

50   *Weltwirtschafliches Archiv* 1920, July p. 42.

fall started first in these production branches. The *'consumers' strike'* holding Europe under its spell is apparently a mass movement expressing a lack of purchasing power.

Labour Productivity Since the Beginning of the War

We repeatedly find complaints about *absence of work motivation and low labour productivity* when consulting reports on capitalist economies and the boom.[51] How real labour productivity developed during the war and then took shape could be a very interesting experience. Relevant data, especially on coalmining, are available. We must, however, be clear that labour productivity depends not only on labour force and work motivation, but also on the technical situation of the production facilities. In countries with a highly productive capitalism the means of production had been improved and, hence, productivity could increase independently of work motivation. On the contrary, in the decaying countries the means of production were worn out, thus hampering labour productivity. We should look at the data in *Table 5.40* when making that consideration.[52]

TABLE 5.40 Performances of the *American mineworkers* in the bitumen and coal industry

	Number of yearly working days	Yearly production per miner in tons	Production per miner in tons per day
1913	232	837	3.61
1914	195	734	3.71
1915	203	794	3.91
1916	230	896	3.90
1917	243	915	3.77
1918	252	968	3.84

---

51 Some examples will be given later.
52 From *The Economist*, *The Times* and other English sources.

TABLE 5.41 Production per *English* miner in tons per day

	All workers	South Wales
1913		243
1915	270	
1918		184
1919		221
1920	200	174
1920 1st quarter		207
1920 2nd quarter		193
1920 3rd quarter		198
1920 4th quarter		163

TABLE 5.42 Production per *German* miner in kg per day[53]

	Ruhr Basin	Upper Silesia
1913	380	145
1918	284	139
1919	230	86
1920	289	106

TABLE 5.43 Production per *French* miner in kg per day[54]

1913	695
1914	668
1916	610
1917	634
1918	564
1919	448

---

53 *Wirtschaft und Statistik* 1921, 1, 2, p. 35.
54 *Wirtschaft und Statistik* 1921, 1, 1, p. 34.

We see that there is an increase in the United States, but a steep decrease in Europe. Only in Germany was there a weak improvement in 1920. In Europe, there is no question of approaching pre-war productivity. The situation is not that different in industrial branches of which statistics are more difficultly to find. The underproduction crisis in Europe is caused not only by low labour productivity of *workers unwilling to work hard under capitalist social conditions*, but also partly by insufficient nourishment of these workers.

Consolidation or Decay of European Capitalism Since the End of War?

Fascinated by the coming of a speculative boom, the adherents of the Two-and-a-Half International pretend that Europe's capitalism is on its way to a new consolidation. And they urge the proletariat to speed up this recovery by working harder.

Did European capitalism really consolidate? There are symptoms of consolidation, but also of a further decay. We shall try to evaluate both tendencies.

With regard to the most important moments in this consolidation process of capitalism we primarily mentioned that *the Central European ruling classes have already regained their self-consciousness*. At the end of 1918 and in 1919, the bourgeoisie was still benumbed and frightened and emigrated with its capital to neutral foreign countries; but, in its role of commander of the economy, the same bourgeoisie is now reorganising and constituting big trusts, allying with English, French and American capital, planning businesses for the coming decades; hence, in brief, the bourgeoisie is preparing to secure capitalism's long-term survival and is trying to make the workers believe in capitalism's immortality by organising class armies.

It is not that easy to assert that the means of production have improved during the war. After having studied all new investments, we must also admit that some progress was made! But statistics also contain erroneous evidences; firstly, currencies have devalued; secondly, war profits were capitalised and share-capital was diluted. We are in need of data about *the natural form of the means of production*. These data are only partially available. The stock of sea ships has enormously multiplied: this is a matter of real accumulation. However, construction activities were minimal; neither dwellings nor railways were constructed in huge quantities. Housing shortages were horrible in all big cities. The condition of the railways' *rolling-stock* is still very bad in Germany, Poland, Austria, Hungary, Romania, etc. With respect to the *means of production in the narrower sense*, we know that complete factories were moved from Central Europe to the neutral countries and from Europe to the colonies. Factories formerly producing war-materials were reorganised into peace-production units, but no enlarged accumulation as yet took place. That would also have been very difficult, because production of the most important goods did not – or only hardly – increase and reaching the pre-war level of output was still far away, a fact we already mentioned at the hand of statistics! *If one does not produce enough, then extended real accumulation will become impossible!*

The champions of capitalist consolidation prefer pointing to the balance-of-trade recovery of the European countries. In 1920 England's trade balance had become quite normal. The English trade deficit was balanced by earnings from freight and by political gains; the French and Italian trade balances only slightly improved after the end of the war.[55] Until now, Germany does not publish statistical data and the statistical data of the other Central-European countries are quite comparable (because of changing borders, currencies, exchange rates). With respect to this domain no changes are perceptible. As a consequence of the crisis, the figures for the first quarter of 1921 show a very important decline in foreign trade, not only in value, but also quantitatively in practically all countries.

The basic fact, however, is that the whole of Europe, England included, is facing a gigantic trade-balance deficit; hence, there exists no economic equilibrium. That was also already the case before the war in Western Europe. However, profits from capital investments in Russia, freight and money transfers from expatriates, were then balancing the trade deficit. Colonial capital has been consumed, only England is earning an income from shipping, and Europe's debt to the United States amounts to 15–20 milliard dollar.

---

55 TABLE 5.44 Balance-of-trade deficit

	France	Great Britain	Italy
	milliards of francs	millions of £	milliards of lire
1918	17.6	783.8	12.7
1919	21.1	562.8	10.6
1920	13.0	378.8	8.1

SOURCE: DATA TAKEN FROM *WIRTSCHAFT UND STATISTIK* 1921, 1, 3, PP. 119–21, AND FROM *THE ECONOMIST*

An improvement occurred in France and Italy in the structure of their foreign trade: more raw materials were imported and more finished goods were exported.

Public finances of the Entente countries have improved: but only England's budget has no spending deficit. French public finances are completely reliant on Germany's reparation payments and the country is financing a standing army of some 800,000 men! Public finances of the vanquished countries, including Poland, show, year after year, month after month, increasing spending deficits![56]

No improvement is observed in monetary affairs; once again an exception should be made for England. In the vanquished countries, circulation of paper money is uninterruptedly growing. Germany, German-Austria and Poland are issuing milliards of paper money a month. Paper money newly put into circulation during the 'period of consolidation', i.e. from the end of 1918 until the end of 1920, increased by *milliards*.

TABLE 5.46 Paper money circulating from the end of 1918 until the end of 1920

France	From	30.25 to	37.90
Germany	From	22.18 to	68.81
Italy	From	9.22 to	22.26
Austria	From	35.58 to	75.(?)

---

56 We give here an interesting summary published in the 'Annual Review' of *The Times*, 28 January 1921. Of course, real spending deficits must have been much huger.

TABLE 5.45 Future state expenditures in percentages covered by tax revenues for the fiscal year of 1920

England	119.7	South Africa	73.2
Czechoslovakia	108.1	Canada	68.0
British India	98.2	Switzerland	62.1
Norway	90.0	Germany	53.5
United States	89.7	Portugal	49.9
The Netherlands	82.6	Greece	46.9
Sweden	87.2	France	44.6
Japan	78.2	Australia	44.4
Spain	76.6	Poland	44.1
Belgium	42.8	Italy	42.5

No improvement was signalled with regard to the exchange rates. In America, the exchange rate of the British pound sterling stabilised but at 20 percent under the gold price. But all other currencies, also those of the neutral countries, showed worsening exchange rates during the *'consolidation period'*.

We began this outline with the analysis that the ruling classes regained their self-confidence after the consolidation of capitalism with the firm will of maintaining the capitalist social order in life. On the other hand, the revolutionary will of the masses increased by resisting capitalist recovery, while especially the communists continued their revolutionary struggle for a higher living standard of the broader masses. The number and spreading of conflicts with the entrepreneurs was never so huge as during this 'consolidation period'. Hence, talk of a consolidation of capitalism is difficult when two coalminers' strikes occur within two years, when English workers are obstructing the start-up of the water pumps in the collieries, when English workers go on strike against the will of their trade-union leaders.

The creed in the eternal existence of the capitalist world order has disappeared from the souls of the masses. That is the most important fact. Class hegemony can only exist as long as the oppressed believe in its firmness. We may ascertain that when considering all these factors, European capitalism has not only consolidated, but also that its decay is progressing. The deep economic crisis shattering today's whole capitalist world is the outcome of a chronic underproduction crisis, of Central Europe's decay shaking the Entente countries and the small neutral countries as well. The whole capitalist world must get sick of an epidemic ravaging Europe's core countries.

There Is No Alternative

We situated the particular characteristics of the actual crisis in the fact that today's relative overproduction is not only a simple result of capitalist anarchy, but a consequence of the changes caused by the war in the reconstruction of the world economy. The crisis was caused by the decaying economies the Central and Eastern Europe, thus by chronic *underproduction* in these regions. These factors and industrialisation of the colonial areas during the war enabled the United States, Japan and England to find an outlet for their goods on the world market.

Can the causes of the crisis be overcome?

Relative overproduction is an essential crisis factor in capitalism. Because of an existing particular income distribution, a stock of goods cannot find sufficient customers at a profitable price. This creates overproduction.

How did one overcome overproduction until now?

Overproduction was overcome: 1) by *falling prices* of the already produced stock of goods, causing price falls to the level whereby they reflected the 'socially necessary needs' of the total stock of goods being brought to the world market; 2) *by a lowering of production costs of the already produced goods, by technical renewal increasing labour productivity, by enhancing labour intensity, thus by lowering production costs meaning that prices adjusted for a while to the actual level of purchasing power;* 3) by a simple limitation of production set by the big monopolies during the highest stage of capitalism until the market had slowly absorbed superfluous goods.

Are these alternatives still possible today?

The price fall is a fact. But would a lowering of production costs also be possible?

Not for continental Europe!

Reduction of production costs is possible *by improving and renewing the means of production and by increasing labour productivity of the proletarian without changing production conditions.* In the first case a considerable real accumulation rate becomes a precondition, i.e. a larger than normal share of the yearly general domestic product should be subtracted from individual consumption for expanding the technical means of production.

But who wants to abandon a share of his income?

The capitalists would answer: the workers! The workers should work harder, but they should not consume more! But the workers of Europe are not willing to submit. The proletariat of Europe is no longer that passive mass of workers accepting capitalism and all its privations as a fatal reality. Europe's proletariat has discovered its own self-respect. The ruling class of the belligerent countries made daily appeals to the proletariat's readiness to concede sacrifices. For years the proletariat has been under arms. The workers learned risking their life with their arms in their hands. They are not willing to endure hardship anymore.

The workers refuse to endure new privations for enabling capital to renew its means of production; they claim a higher standard of living. Not only an improvement of their actual standard of living, but something well above its peacetime level. Hence, we can see that workers' demands for a rising living standard are antagonising the interests of a capitalist mode of production requiring a renewal of the means of production by imposing a regime of intensified accumulation.

The gentlemen capitalists may reduce their standard of living, and in the latter case they can, instead of consuming luxury goods, finance the reconstruction of the means of production themselves! A capitalist spokesman (Rathenau)⁵⁷ asks this from the bourgeoisie. In several countries, imports of luxury goods were forbidden for a while. But it is a fact that the bourgeoisie does not diminish its share of the necessities of life; on the contrary, luxury goods are more abundantly available in Europe today than ever before: the 'new rich', the swindlers and speculators, are more than ever before carousing and debauching when spending their easily won profits.

The other solution could be that *the proletarians should produce more under the same living conditions*. The proletariat should work harder for the renewal of the means of production, thus for a rising living standard of the working class in the future. *But the proletariat is not willing to accept this!* Labour productivity does not increase and the capitalists of all European countries, *England included*, are complaining about low labour productivity.⁵⁸

The most intelligent spokesmen of capitalism understand very cleverly this uncomfortable situation. They know that a capitalist world economy can only be sound if *the superfluous means of production in the United States are put at the disposal of impoverished Central Europe* and the senseless attempt to reconstruct the economies of France, Belgium and Italy at Germany's expense would be abandoned. But all attempts in that direction have remained unsuccessful. The United Sates should cancel their claims on the Entente countries; England

---

57   [Walther Rathenau (1867–1922) was a German Jewish entrepreneur and liberal politician, owner of the AEG (Allgemeine Elektrizitäts-Gesellschaft)].
58   'When the working day was shortened, one predicted that productivity would remain the same or increase. The contrary occurred: productivity per worker and hour decreased ...', Speech of the president of Vickers Electric Comp. *Manchester Guardian*, 21 March 1921 [retranslated from German]. *The Times* of 21 March 1921 writes: 'Labour productivity has decreased during the last half a year in such a way nobody reasonably had could predicted' [retranslated from German]. Speech of the chairman of Davis and Comp.; 'There is no object in dilating upon the vicious effect of the enormously increased wages, with at the same time a greatly decreased rate of production, in all industrties, coal being one of the chief'. (Howard Houlder, Chairman of the Reliance Fuel Company), *The Economist*, 5 March 1921, p. 532; 'Report on Cotton Manufactures blames the trade union for its deliberate policy of restricting output and thus increasing the number of unemployed'. *The Economist*, 5 March 1921, p. 506. 'It cannot be doubted that British industry suffers seriously from underproduction. It is universal, and it is by no doubt principally due to the extraordinarily belief of the workers that they can benefit themselves by restricting their output, by spreading the work'. *The Economist*, 19 February 1921, p. 324. [The quotes from *The Manchester Guardian* and *The Times* could not be traced back in the issues Varga referred to. In a long speech pronounced by chairman Archibald Mitchelson of D. Davis and Sons Limited, published in *The Times* of 21 April 1921, it is only said that 'the results have fallen far short of what might reasonably have been expected'. Chairman Philip A.M. Nash of Metropolitan-Vickers Electrical Co., Ltd., did not report on labour productivity at a company meeting in *The Manchester Guardian* of 31 March 1921].

could then do the same. France, with its heavy foreign debt, should intelligently relieve Germany's debt burden. And the Entente countries should float the vanquished countries of Central Europe (Norman Angell, Keynes) by conceding an important credit. But the bourgeoisie of the United States bluntly rejected England's suggestion of a mutual abolishment of all war debts. A lot of talks and deliberations on credit proposals were organised, but until now without any result. And France continues to ruin Germany, that relatively healthy country of decaying Central Europe, by occupying new territories, by establishing tariff walls, and by imposing an additional 50 percent tax levy.

The Social Democrats of the Second and the Second-and-a-Half Internationals tried, though still participating in government, to stop capitalist decay by means of socialisation and economic planning and to prepare for a peaceful transition (!) to socialism. As long as the bourgeoisie did not feel sufficiently strong enough to openly fight the proletariat, they were not opposed. But Noske,[59] Scheidemann[60] and Kautsky were ousted when the Orgesh[61] was organised. And the beautiful plans for socialisation and economic planning were both thrown into the waste-paper basket.

Would it be possible to drop Russia and the vanquished countries completely and to give the highly industrialised countries a necessarily broader base by developing the colonial countries? This idea is very popular in some American circles. The everlasting revolutions have discredited Europe in the eyes of the American capitalists! They do not want to get involved with Europe anymore!

Is this solution possible?

The colonial territories inhabited by white settlers are too small to replace Central Europe and Russia.[62] However, there exist two large territories that could be much more intensively integrated into capitalism: *India and China!* They each have 300–400 million inhabitants! But they must be completely subjected to capital before they can be exploited. The means of production should be separated from the labour force and the workers should become proletarians, subjected to the discipline of capital and be habituated to higher labour

---

59   [Gustav Noske (1868–1946) was a German politician of the Social-Democratic Party of Germany (SPD)].

60   [Philipp Scheidemann (1865–1939) was a German politician of the Social-Democratic Party of Germany (SPD)].

61   [Orgesh is one of the strange and obscure deities of the charda. It is arguably the best well-known of these inscrutable beings, and the charda view it as an endlessly hungry being requiring constant sacrifices of food to placate].

62   The white population of these territories is insignificant: Canada 8 million people, Central and South America 30 to 40 million people, Australia 10 million people.

productivity. This will, however, take a *long period of time*, two to three generations. For the time being, the amount of *goods* not produced and consumed in these economies is much too small to replace Central Europe and Russia on the world market.

Without Central Europe, the world market becomes too small for the highly developed countries. Notwithstanding a temporary economic upswing, after a while underproduction in Central Europe will engender a new economic crisis. The booming periods will become ever shorter, the periods of crisis will grow ever longer and more intensive; more and more countries will decay and ever-larger groups will join the revolutionary movement of the proletariat. The social revolution will be victorious after a period of long struggles.

'*At the end of this crisis, the dissolution of the entire social order is waiting. This depends on the evolution of the crisis and the temperament of the masses, in one country earlier than in another. But everywhere the social revolution must be the final outcome ...*'.[63] We think that we can agree on this opinion articulated by the capitalist economist W. Federn.[64] On the condition that the revolutionary mind of the proletarian front fighters will not forsake, there will be no alternative.

On the Coming World War

During the coming years, the European proletariat will have to sustain a long struggle and the three great powers, the United States, England and Japan, will meanwhile fight each other for world hegemony. According to the laws of capitalist society, they cannot avoid this struggle. Because of the elimination of Russia and Central Europe's decay, the world market has become too narrow for the imperialist powers. With their arms in their hands they will decide who will be the ruler!

The struggle has already begun. The United States are the aggressive world power. During the war they developed themselves economically to the most powerful country.[65] With [President Warren] Harding leading the country, America's big bourgeoisie is not inclined to accept England's maritime and political hegemonic role on the world market.

---

63 [Varga gives no reference for this quote].
64 [Walther Federn (1869–1949) was an Austrian liberal economist and journalist].
65 According to Garry at the *Annual Meeting of the Iron and Steel Institute*, the United States' share of the world economy for the year 1920 was: 6 percent of the total world population, 7 percent of the earth's surface. See Nearing 1919, p. 187. [Scott Nearing (1883–1983) was a leading critic of imperialism. He shortly joined the American Communist Party].

Disagreements between England and Japan on the one side and the United States on the other become evermore frequent and acute. The United States protested against England's monopoly of petroleum exploitation in Mesopotamia! Acrimonious speeches in the Senate denounced the fact that England is receiving cheap American petroleum from the United States, while American ships have to purchase expensive British petroleum in Asia.[66] England is accused of establishing, i.e. already possessing, a petroleum monopoly outside the United States. More and more frequently a possible war with England is enunciated in American newspapers. On the other hand, the United States protested against the decision of the 'League of Nations' – which has become an instrument of England's world hegemony because of the absence of the United States, Germany and Russia – for having adjudged the isle of Yap[67] in the Pacific Ocean to Japan. England is embittered because of industrial competition by which the United States have undermined during the past years England's centuries-old coal monopoly on the world market.[68] America's refusal to agree on a mutual remitting of the Entente's war debt has roused serious discontent.

TABLE 5.47 US share of world production

20 percent of gold	60 percent of aluminum
25 percent of weath	60 percent of copper
40 percent of steel and iron	60 percent of cotton
40 percent of lead	66 percent of petroleum
40 percent of silver	75 percent of maize
50 percent of zinc	85 percent of motorcars
52 percent of coal	

[In 1901, Elbert Henry Garry (1846–1922) organised the US Steel Corporation with the help of the banker J.P. Morgan. In 1909 he founded the American Iron and Steel Institute].

66 See my article on America. Varga 1921d, 2, 17, pp. 119–46.
67 [Yap belongs to the Caroline Islands in the Western Pacific Ocean. Today, it is a state of the Federated States of Micronesia].
68 TABLE 5.48 US coal exports (in thousands of tons)

	France	Italy	Holland	Sweden
1914	47	776	–	–
1919	532	1,633	722	253
1920	3,646	2,388	2,147	1,247

Italy has signed a five-years' delivery contract for coal from the United States. Not-

And arming for war is already openly acclaimed! The naval programme of the United States has been extended in such a way that the British fleet will be surpassed by half its size. Cadres for a territorial army of several millions of men were formed. An armament programme for the production of new murderous weapon systems, especially poisonous liquids and gases, is designed. The Panama Canal will receive fortifications provided with the most powerful artillery of the world.[69]

General R. Lee Bullard, Commander of the First Division of the American Expeditionary Army in France in 1918,[70] declared in a speech to the [National] Republican Club that America, because it had not been prepared for war, had been put *under command of the English proletariat*, that British troops had been posted between American troops and the enemy, *until they had finished their training!* That should not happen again anymore: America must create a battle-ready army.[71] Before the war, the same arguments were used in Germany. Competition on a narrowed market and increased influence of the war industry during the war are leading to similar policies.

The next war will put an end to a decaying capitalism if the proletariat is not already victorious. Just as the past world war was at the origins of the dictatorship of the proletariat in Russia and decaying capitalism in Central Europe, so the next world war will completely ruin capitalism throughout the whole world.

<blockquote>withstanding a higher exchange rate of some 20 percent, American coal is everywhere crowding out English coal from the market.</blockquote>

69 *Frankfurter Zeitung*, 31 December 1920.
70 [General Richard Lee Bullard (1861–1947)].
71 *The Times*, 21 February 1921.

CHAPTER 6

The Situation of the World Economy and the Evolution of the World Economic Policy during the Last Three Years

1 **The World Economy Three Years after the End of the War**[1]

Three years have passed since the official ending of the world war. (In reality, the war is not yet over). With regard to the tactics of the communist parties of all countries, exceptionally important questions have arisen: did the capitalist world economy reach a new equilibrium, or is it progressing toward a new equilibrium? This question is intimately related to the expected pace of the revolutionary development. Though production statistics are not yet available for the whole year of 1921, one can try to predict the evolution.

As a consequence of the war, the following basic changes occurred in the structure of the world economy:

1. In those countries with a fully developed capitalism that were only indirectly and superficially disturbed by the war, but which made high profits as war suppliers, the means of production are very strongly developed. That is particularly the case in the United States and in Japan and, to a lesser degree, also in England.
2. In the countries with a not fully developed capitalism situated not so far from the former centre of the world economy – i.e. Western Europe – Australia, India, China, South Africa, and South America are in a process of fast industrialisation. Restricted and expensive navigation hampered the previously existing exchanges between the countries producing raw materials and the 'industrial workshops of the world': Western Europe. Plenty of raw materials and shortages of manufactures occurred. Price differences between raw materials on the one hand and finished products on the other were important enough to foster domestic industries. Global division of labour declined; the centre of the world economy shifted meanwhile from Western Europe to the United States of America.

---

1 [Translation based on E. Varga, *Die Lage der Weltwirtschaft und der Gang der Weltwirtschaftspolitik in den letzten drei Jahren*, Verlag der Kommunistischen Internationale, Auslieferungsstelle für Deutschland: Carl Hoym Nachl. Louis Cahnbley, Hamburg, 1922].

3. The countries of Central and Eastern Europe: Russia, the Balkans, Austria-Hungary, counting all together some 300 million inhabitants, broke down under the costs of the war. An unprecedented impoverishment occurred; the soil became exhausted, the industrial apparatus completely worn out, human labour power was exhausted because of under-nourishment, production diminished. Backed by their allies, France and Italy were less damaged, but these countries had nonetheless suffered.

The world economy presented a rather clear and unified character before the world war. The less-developed capitalist regions were concentrically grouped around the highly developed industrial core – Western Europe. The further a country is from the centre, the less its development. Remoteness should not simply be understood in terms of geographical distance, but of absent communications. Geographically distant coastal regions can be economically more developed than adjacent countries with badly opened inlands. Gravity of the whole world system was concentrated in England now dominating the whole world economy by its fleet, its military fortifications all over the world, its huge capital investments abroad, its currency. Apart from England, Germany emerged as a new centre. All sorts of foodstuffs and raw materials were transported from the whole world – the United States included – to Western Europe as a return on capital investment, as a payment for freight, as an equivalent for purchased industrial goods. Gold – only pro forma divided up into national currencies – as a universal means of payment did not disturb international trade. Only the periodically returning crises and the class struggle unveiled that the whole system was antagonistic and revealed its labile equilibrium.

As we already explained, instead of an equilibrated European economic system, the war split the world into three parts and completely disturbed the economic equilibrium:

1. *The United States, Japan and England with their enlarged production facilities, but without finding any possibilities for selling the output of their enlarged production facilities on the world market: a region of relative overproduction.*
2. *The colonial and peripheral countries of the world economy with their infant industries.*
3. *Because of their decreasing production capacity and their impoverishment as buyers and sellers,* Eastern and Central Europe *retrograded: a region of absolute underproduction.*

At the end of the war, the countries affected by these changes were not immediately aware of this basic disturbance of the world-economic equilibrium. A huge shortage of goods in Europe and the colonial countries and a conversion of wartime into peacetime production led the way for a *'postwar boom'* to completely dominate the world market until February 1921. At the end of 1921, a severe great crisis broke out. *The falling apart of the world economy into two or three regions is their characteristic* but sharply contradictory *feature* because of their interconnections having become looser and because of their not complementary economic conditions.

From a narrow-minded Central-European point of view, Social-Democratic political economists try to prove that the postwar crisis of the world economy has already been overcome, that the recovery process is coming soon, that a new equilibrium of the world economy will be found. First of all we want to argue *that since the beginning of capitalism there has never been an unemployment crisis of such a long duration and swell as in 1921*. These facts are widely known.

TABLE 6.1   Average unemployment in 1921

United States	20–15%	Norway	15%
England	12–15%	Denmark	20%
Sweden	25%	Holland	15%

We want to put this question to any smart person: can one talk about a world economy in equilibrium when the bourgeoisie of those countries having not or only slightly suffered is unable to provide work and bread to a fifth of the workers during a whole year? In addition, one cannot argue that a decisive change in a positive direction has already occurred. Signs of improvement exist: in America, the steel and textile industries recovered, and also in England symptoms of recovery were signalled many times, but until now they were always disappointingly ephemeral.[2]

---

2   *The Economist* of 24 December 1921 gives the following pessimistic overview of the English economy in general: 'In the records of British economic history Christmas, 1921, will probably mark the lowest point in the depression following the Great War. How feebly the viral spark has been glowing during the past year will be shown by the various indices which we shall have occasion to lay before our readers in the next few weeks. It will suffice to mention here that coal output, which amounted to 230 million tons in 1920 and 285 million tons in 1913, will barely exceed 160 million tons in the current year, while pig-iron output, which amounted to 10 million tons in 1921. The record of other industries and economic, though perhaps in some cases less startling, will confirm that national production has this year been at an abnormally low ebb, and had left us in mid-winter faced with the stupendous fact of nearly two millions of our industrial population unemployed, at a moment when we are practically free from any important industrial dispute. Such figures are entirely without precedent since

A second visible symptom of the disrupted equilibrium of the world economy is the absolute, unbridgeable gap between the currencies of the countries of overproduction and those of underproduction. The currencies of Russia, Poland, Germany, Austria, Rumania, etc. are exchanged at only a fraction of their previous rate. And the fractioning of the world economy and the ongoing decline of the countries of underproduction are showing year after year – except for some minor upward fluctuations – a permanent worsening of their exchange rates.

TABLE 6.2   The exchange rate of the British Pound in London[3]

	At par	At the end of 1920	At the end of 1921
German mark	20.43	255	769
Polish mark	20.43	2,200	12,000
Austrian krone	24.02	1,425	11,000
Bulgarian lei	25.22	265	612
Serbian dinar	25.22	130	280

Year after year, all Central and Eastern European currencies are losing much of their value; even the exchange rate of the Czech krone last year lost about 8 percent of its nominal value to the British pound.

In addition to this worsening exchange rates, a continually rising deficit of the state budget is causing a growing volume of paper money in circulation; this phenomenon is common to all countries in this region of underproduction.

---

we became an industrial nation, and are indeed so large that, like all enormous numbers, they tend to be mere digits, unrelated to the facts they represent. But at this season of the year we can at least attempt to conceive their human implications in our industrial towns and mining villages, so aptly described by Lord Derby as *our* devastated regions. Actual hunger and want have hitherto been kept within narrower limits than might have been feared, but as month after month has gone by without appreciable improvement in the outlooks, and the members have grown with the approach of winter, savings have melted away, while morale is threatened by those grim allies, idleness and poverty'. 'The darkest hour', *The Economist*, 24 December 1921, p. 1103.

3   Data in *The Economist*, 24 December 1921, p. 1135.

2 The 'Immanent' Recovery Tendency in the World Economy

The very nature of the disturbance of the global economic equilibrium consists of a relative overproduction in specific regions and insufficient production in other regions. The contradiction must be superseded: *the present crisis is characteristic of capitalism and of the irrational tendency in capitalism to overcome this equilibrium disturbance*. An exaggerated expansion of the means of production has occurred in America, Japan, England, in the new countries of Europe. Products do not find buyers there. Hence, capital tries to remedy this disequilibrium *by simply stopping the means of production that are superfluous*. Hence relative overproduction can be avoided by simply sacking a fifth of the workforce.

Busy activities, however, have been noticed in the countries of underproduction. In Germany and in Austria, all workplaces are producing. The increased production in these countries can compensate for production decline in other regions of the world economy. And [Paul] Levi,[4] [Rudolf] Hilferding[5] and friends are now arguing 'that Germany with its unimpaired production facilities, with ... its feverish increased production',[6] holds a strong position. One could otherwise argue that in Germany unemployment in the trades has reached an *average level of 3.9 percent during the first half of 1921, a level that had not even been attained during the severe crisis-period of 1908–9*. Recovery only occurred in the autumn of 1921. But already now, at the end of 1921, at the very moment we are writing these lines, in general, the opinion prevails in Germany that the good situation on the labour market would be over very soon. Already in November a slight slowdown could be noticed in the production process in Germany.

A similar phenomenon occurred in price evolution. While prices in the countries of overproduction were showing a tendency to fall, they were uninterruptedly increasing in the countries of overproduction. A similar recovery tendency existed for world-market prices. However, this tendency could not hold on.

Could the equilibrium of the world economy possibly be re-established by this expedient of increased production and high prices in the impoverished regions and production limitation combined with low prices in the overproduction regions?

---

4 [Paul Levi (1883–1933) was a German Communist and Social-Democratic politician].
5 [Rudolf Hilferding (1877–1941), Austrian-born Marxist economist; German SPD politician, member of the Reichstag, Finance Minister (1923; 1928–9)].
6 See footnote on page [10].

We think that this would be impossible!

Keeping a fifth of the labour force in the overproduction regions unemployed would be socially unsustainable in the long-run. Even for an apparently stable social structure of capitalism, as exists in America and England, such a burden would become unsustainable in the long-term. And we already saw that Lloyd George,[7] who is well aware of the needs of bourgeois hegemony in England, wants to approach his *foreign policy differently: how to absorb English unemployment?*

Hoping that the regions of absolute underproduction will recover by their own efforts and increase their production is an illusion. Germany is the best-equipped country of all. Because of shortages of raw materials,[8] coal and transport facilities, and low labour productivity caused by insufficient nutrition and low productivity standards, output has not yet recovered. Hence, the burden of the capitalist social order is not lighter than in the overproduction regions. There exists a gigantic unemployment combined with a lower living standard; here, full employment exists combined with sub-level living conditions. Thus the question remains as to which of the two situations will prove to be the most unsustainable.

3   The Reparation Question as a Social Problem

Reparation payments to continental Europe imposed on Germany are particularly disturbing the immanent tendencies of restoring the world-economic equilibrium. Although this question is probably important for Germany, we must nonetheless stress that this is only a *minor cause* among others having led to the huge disturbances now shaking the world's economic equilibrium, and its 'solution' – if there is any – should not be identified with solving the problems of the world economy in general, as some people in Germany are likely to believe.

---

7   [David Lloyd George (1863–1945) was a British liberal politician and Prime Minister].
8   The capitalist proxies are not judging the economic situation in Germany as optimistically as Hilferding and Levi. In his speech to the Economic Council (Reichswirtschaftsrat) (*Deutsche Allgemeine Zeitung* of 16 December 1921), [Hugo] Stinnes emphasises that the stock of scarp has been exhausted, that the cokes ovens have fallen into decay and that the German heavy industry will therefore not be able to take advantage of the next boom. And the annual report of the Chamber of Commerce of Hamburg explains: '*The actual export prices paid in combination with a simultaneously declining exchange rate of the mark permit doing business at an ever lower level of activity; however, gains are not sufficient for purchasing the same stock of imported raw materials*'.

What is the essence of the reparation problems within the framework of our analysis of the global economic situation?

As Germany has to renew its production facilities and to grant a decent living standard to its proletariat, it can hardly cede a quantity of goods worth 3½ gold marks a year. This is about a tenth of the national income of a rich, territorially undamaged Germany of the pre-war years. Carrying out this decision literally would mean:

1. That Germany will plunge into full misery; its means of production will become completely worn out; its currency will become valueless on the world market. Social struggles of the most dreadful kind for the inadequate remnants of production will lead the country to a social revolution or plunge it into barbarity;
2. That a smaller world market, which is already unable to absorb all excess goods produced in the regions of overproduction, will be flooded by huge volumes of German export goods. A full application of the reparation arrangements will foster growing competition on the world market as well.

The best solution could be a cancellation of all reparation payments!

This solution can only be applied if Germany would pay reparations to the countries of the overproduction regions. We see that England is already pretty at ease with the idea that Germany does want to pay its due. English statesmen and political economists understand that rescuing the capitalist social order in England imperatively needs a stable world economy facilitating a reduction of the unprecedented and dangerous high rates of unemployment. Because Germany is forced to practise dumping,[9] this will also lead to growing long-term unemployment in England.

Reparation payments are, however, going only for a small part to 'rich' England. The problem could and might thus be solved by a simple remittance. France, Belgium, Italy and Serbia, which are the countries highly dependent on these payments, would receive the largest part of the reparation payments. Let us take France as an example. During the war, France was – just like Germany – living from hand to mouth under the slogan 'The German will pay!'. In France, fewer taxes were paid during the war than in peacetime. When

---

9 We know that the absolute quantum of Germany's exported goods in the years 1920–1 is relatively small, but much smaller than before the war. Before the war, during the period of a relative equilibrium of the world economy, these exports only slightly disturbed the economies of the other capitalist countries – maybe England is an exception. Now that the absorbing capacity of the world market is strongly limited, all countries are nonetheless erecting tariff walls against German exports.

victory was gained, one had to form a national majority after new elections; again, milliards were wasted on the voters.[10] Real material damages France had endured and which – obviously correctly – Keynes had estimated at 20 billion, had already been overestimated three or four times in attendance of German reparation payments, and the capitalists of the occupied territories who had kept 'good relations' were assigned similar exaggerated sums. Hence, France is facing a yearly deficit of 20 milliard francs! Even if France's share of the reparation payments were to be completely paid, this would not balance the whole French spending deficit. That is why France can simply not accept the proposition of cancelling its reparation claims. Considered from a politico-financial point of view, French interests dictate that Germany will pay the whole sum. But Germany cannot and can only finance these payments out of huge export earnings and by a fierce competition with the countries from the overproduction regions, hence, also with France having already become a steel-exporting country after the annexation of Alsace-Lorraine. Meanwhile France is cunningly trying to circumvent this problem by claiming full payment of all reparation dues. This is not in favour of finding a solution, because France has now found protection against German competition behind very high tariff walls. Because Germany is setting world-market prices, German price competition is also affecting other countries.

Moreover, the obligation to pay reparations in gold-backed currencies causes upward pressures on these currencies at due dates which will widen the gap between the regions of overproduction and underproduction. We see: any attempt to collect the reparation dues will aggravate the world economic crisis. But cancelling them would imply a bankruptcy of France.[11]

The Wiesbaden Agreement[12] tries to sidestep these difficulties. The economic essence of this agreement is that Germany will deliver specific goods to France instead of chaotically throwing goods on a world market which cannot possibly absorb them. And those goods delivered for reconstructing the destroyed French regions *are then kept out of the normal French business cycle*. Obtaining goods from Germany without raising unsustainable competition on the world market would be a good deal; these materials and services for reconstructing houses, roads, etc., and also for *private* use would not directly expand the production process and output of goods.

---

10   See the very interesting book of the bourgeois apologist Georges Lachappelle 1921.
11   Even if the reparation payments were fully met, the French State would have to cover for many years a spending deficit of several billions of francs.
12   [In 1921, the Wiesbaden Agreement on German reparations to France was signed in the city of Wiesbaden].

The Wiesbaden Agreement could be favourable to France. But the agreement is not yet ratified: private interests of influential French capitalist groups are preventing it. Germany would not have gained much by that.

The delivery of goods in huge quantities and of homogenous quality could lower production costs. Reparations paid in kind could release Germany of the obligation of paying its dues in currencies obtained at a high exchange rate. But the basic problem remains: how can an impoverished Germany withdraw a quantity of goods worth 3½ milliard gold marks from its reduced production capacity? Indeed, the problem could even become more pregnant *during the coming years if Germany could deliver more goods to France than France's share of the reparation commitments*. Germany could then pay its due in advance and credit France for its additional deliveries. Because of Germany's impoverishment this would be an impossible experiment. But the German economists are quite right when defining the Wiesbaden Agreement as a harmful arrangement.

The reparation problem can only be solved within a general framework remedying the disturbed economic equilibrium: every other specific attempt will lead to a sharpening of *the general crisis*.[13] We shall later tackle this subject again.

4   Conscious Attempts to Restore Economic Equilibrium

Apart from spontaneous tendencies restoring the disturbed equilibrium of the world economy – a production decrease of a fifth in the regions of underproduction can be combined with a subsequent production increase in the regions of underproduction – *conscious attempts to restore the equilibrium* also exist by initiating:
a)   *A breaking up of the international economic division of labour*.
b)   *An opening up of new markets for capitalism*.
c)   *A recovery of the regions of underproduction in Europe*.
We shall discuss these attempts in turn:

a)   *The breaking up of the international economic division of labour*
The economic crisis in the individual countries is a consequence of a distorted equilibrium of the world market. The simplest reaction is creating a national, autarchic economy disconnected from all dangerous disturbances of the world economy. In line with that are the following measures:

---

13   [Editor's stress. Varga uses here the concept of 'general crisis' already at the end of 1921].

Preventing imports of foreign goods by imposing high tariffs and import contingents. We can observe this kind of attempt in all countries: England, the classic country of free trade, establishes protective tariffs; America, France, Italy, are surrounded by high protective tariff walls. The countries of the regions of underproduction do not need them: their depreciated currencies are protecting them better than any high tariff wall.

Hindering the export of particular goods by means of export prohibitions. We can illustrate the changing importance of foreign trade by statistics in Table 6.3.[14] Except for the United States, gold value of total foreign trade was lower in 1920 than in 1913, although the economic conjuncture was quite better. For 1921 the decline will be even steeper.

TABLE 6.3   Foreign trade of England, Germany, France and the United States in 1913 and 1920 (gold value)

	England	Germany	France	United States
1913	1,403.5	20,867	15,301	4,196
1920	3,494.6	230,000*	57,839	13,508
Price index (1920) 1913 = 100	280	1,250	500	200
Foreign trade index (1920) 1913 = 100	1,288	18,400	11,568	6,754

* Approximate figure, official data are not available

An attempt to return to an agrarian economy in the highly developed industrialised countries. Typical of this tendency is the campaign launched in *The Times* by former Minister of Agriculture Erle [sic][15] for developing domestic agriculture, and Lord Northcliff[16] for agricultural colonisation by promoting emigration to Australia. In France, the call for a 'Retour à la terre' had already become fashionable before the war. Incentives to agrarian reforms are serving the same purpose in different countries.

Obtaining foodstuff autarchy is therefore so urgent because food surpluses are only available in countries with hard currencies: the United States, Canada,

---

14   Data from the *Annuaire Statistique de France* and *Wirtschaft und Statistik*.
15   [No British minister with that name was Minister of Agriculture and Fishery. Maybe Varga is referring to one these former Ministers: William Onslow, the Earl of Onslow; Robert Wynn-Carrington, the Earl of Carrington; William Palmer, the Earl of Selborn; David Lindsay, the Earl of Crawford].
16   [Alfred Harmsworth, 1st Viscount Northcliff (1865–1920), was a British press magnate].

Argentina, Australia. Because of exchange-rate differences they will be inaccessible to countries with weak currencies. On the other hand, farmers in America's West are, however, pleading for the use of maize instead of coal for heating,[17] because maize is comparatively cheaper than coal. In his speech to the Assembly of the League of Nations, [Fridjov] Nansen[18] also asserted that in Argentina houses were nowadays heated by burning maize. A better illustration of the chaotic situation of the world economy cannot be given.[19]

Because of all these strained relations a return to agriculture is also privately an advantageous affair; hence, this is therefore partly due to the spontaneously working equilibrium tendencies, just like what happened in the underproduction regions with the poor coal veins which were not suited for exploitation during the former equilibrium period, etc.

What does this tendency to economic autarchy (self-sufficiency) now mean from a point of view of production? Obviously it is nothing other *than a general decline in labour productivity*: the same amount of labour time of all workers of the capitalist world is now embodied in a much smaller amount of useful goods if compared to a world economy with a full-fledged division of labour.

With regard to the regions of overproduction, one may think of finding a temporary solution, but for the regions of underproduction this tendency will lead to a sharpening of the crisis.

Realising such a self-sufficient national economy is naturally impossible because of climatologic conditions. Of all capitalist great powers, only the *United States* are coming nearest to economic self-sufficiency because they possess important natural resources such as foodstuffs, fuel, all sorts of ores, raw materials, fibres which are all locally produced. The United States only have

---

17 ['Colorado coal output cut. Decrease attributed in part to use of corn for fuel', *The New York Times*, 10 November 1921, p. 10]. In the regions of overproduction, prices of organic raw materials fell generally a lot faster than those of industrial products because the latter prices were kept up by powerful cartels.

18 Fridjof Nansen (1861–1930) was a Norwegian diplomat and explorer].

19 The production of coal decreased considerably during the current year. 'According to assessments of the Washington American Geological Institute, the worldwide production of coal has diminished in much quantities during the current year that they will not reach the level of the year 1909 (a year's production of some 1,100 million ton). The three-months strike of the British mineworkers has caused an important production loss of about 52 million ton. A very important loss is also booked in the North-American coal-mining industry: in comparison to some 136 million ton produced during the first three-quarters of 1920, i.e. until now North America's highest yearly output figure, only 366,5 million ton were produced during the same period in 1921' (*Bergwerkszeitung*, 30 December 1921). In addition, in France, England and the United States coal is so largely in stock that many collieries were shut down.

to import particular tropical goods, such as coffee, tea, rubber, etc. They possess unlimited opportunities to increase their resources: they possess a 'colonial empire' within their own motherland!

Of all European countries, France is in a completely different position. France is holding its huge colonial empire economically and socially firmly under control. It is relatively on good terms with its colonial population and, for the time being, it is not facing important colonial troubles.[20] Its colonies supply France with foodstuffs, iron ore, while the North – after reconstruction of the coal mines – provides its with coal and, after construction of additional hydropower stations, more electrical power will become available. On the other hand, France has no basic materials for its textile industry, no colonial produce in sufficient quantities and no petroleum sources on its own territory.

A self-sufficient economy cannot be developed for *Germany* and *Italy*. Both countries must import foodstuffs, textile materials, colonial products, petroleum; Italy must also import its coal and timber.

England is in the worst situation of all great powers. The motherland has plenty of coal and iron, but all the rest is missing. Foodstuffs are produced for only four months per year; timber, petroleum, all kinds of textile materials, colonial products must be imported. Of all great powers England developed into the 'industrial powerhouse' of the world. Notwithstanding all efforts to intensify agriculture, including the successful attempt to grow sugar beets and the creation of a 'national sugar-beet industry', one cannot ignore the fact that only 12 percent of England's population works in agriculture. England cannot, like France, rely on its colonies. The self-governing territories – Ireland also belongs to them – are practising an economic policy tending to autarchy: *but away from the motherland*. If England wants to return to agriculture, then Canada, South Africa, Australia and New Zealand will try to develop their own industry and thereupon give up their agrarian character. In Egypt an India, which are two big *subjected* colonial countries, upheavals have broken out: in Egypt an armed rebellion and in India an intensive but as yet peaceful resistance movement.[21] The British Empire is falling apart: the flames are burning

---

20   With regard to the surprising fact that the French are much more capable of governing their colonial populations than the English, I am referring to the very interesting study of Dr. Rudolf Asmis 1921, pp. 289–308.
21   We think that we are not wrong when reducing the different behaviour between the French and English colonies above all to the higher economic development of the latter. Apart from all nationalist and religiously inspired anti-English ideologies, one sees that the national bourgeoisie of the concerned countries has strongly developed during the world war. The struggle for national liberation is also a battle for the liberation of local capital from imperialist dominance.

bright everywhere. England is fully hit by the collapsing former equilibrium of the capitalist world economy, because the country is the most complex and the most intricate product of world capitalism. Notwithstanding all contradictory appearances and its undeniable but unusual political splendour, we consider England *as the weakest link in the chain of the capitalist world powers*.

The way back to autarchy is not only closed because of the absolute necessity of importing goods which cannot be produced locally: economic activities in England and the United States – but also in France and Germany – are based on exports of industrial products. In order to prevent millions of workers in England and in America from being *permanently* unemployed, these countries must create markets for their superfluous industrial output. None of the capitalist great powers can survive in isolation, in autarchy.

b) *Opening up new markets: the China problem*
When the productive forces created by capitalism had become too large to find buyers for their produce on the capitalist markets, capitalism could find an outlet by opening up new regions for capitalist exploitation. When looking around, we see that Europe, America and Australia have already been completely integrated into the capitalist [world] economy. Africa has been divided up among the European countries: because Africa is thinly populated and productivity of the primitive population is low, prospects are poor; the developed regions, South Africa and Egypt, are difficult to hold under control. That is why only Asia remains. However, of the latter's vast regions, Asia Minor proved to be politically unsuitable for colonisation; India belongs to England, North and Central Asia belong to Soviet Russia. Thus only China with its northern and western territories, Mongolia and Manchuria, is left.

After all, China is a fat titbit, with many hundreds of millions of educated people, mineral wealth, large fertile regions. If integrated into the capitalist world system, China could absorb for many years all superfluous industrial products from the regions of overproduction. Indeed, it looked like an agreement reached by the capitalist world powers about finding a way of opening up China as the major economic issue of the Conference of Washington. But one was gradually going easier and finally everything remained as before.

When looking closer at the present political circumstances, it appears that China will not easily be disclosed and that this will imply the use of important armed forces and making huge costs which are not proportional to the expected profits. All this is closely related to profound political and social changes having occurred in China during the past decade.

If we judge the situation correctly, China is not in decay but *in a transition from pre-capitalist economic relations characterised by feudal-bureaucratic centralism towards a new form of government reflecting the changes Chinese capitalism has undergone during the world war.*[22] Local governments headed by generals, who are also the richest capitalists of the province, clearly demonstrate what is going on: they are governments representing the interests of the emerging national bourgeoisie. But because of the gigantic distances and the badly developed transport and communication systems, the capitalist development process could not yet make sufficiently progress because it lacked a centralised capitalist government system. We should not forget that if China were to fall apart, each part of it will comprise, on average, some 40 million inhabitants, a number that is in full accord with the territorial size required by capitalism at its early stage.[23]

May this explanation be right or wrong, the next facts are at any rate valid:
1. That the Chinese population is not willing to become a colony of the imperialist powers without resisting them.
2. That not unimportant military forces have already been mobilised to resist them.
3. That because of the enormous size of the country huge costs will be needed for a military occupation.
4. That none of the not-directly neighbouring great powers possesses the indispensable strategic bases for going to war against China: neither the United States, nor England or France. Only Japan is strategically capable for launching an attack on China.

According to us, these are the reasons why planning a 'peaceful penetration' of the Chinese world empire has faded away during the proceedings of the Washington Conference. It seems that China's domestic development has sufficiently evolved that all necessary preconditions have disappeared for extending capitalism by an imperialist intervention. *The disrupted equilibrium of the world economy can only be restored by selling industrial products coming from the regions of overproduction to China.*

c)   *The recovery of the regions of underproduction in Europe*
Economic recovery of the economically destroyed regions of Europe – Germany, Poland, Russia and the successor states of the Austro-Hungarian Monarchy (with the exception of Czechoslovakia) and the Balkans – is a third item of the economic policy of the world powers. A complex of some 300 million

---

22   That capitalism is easily developing in China, notwithstanding the chaotic political situation, is proven by the increasing number of all sorts of machinery installed, a fact that is mentioned in articles published by English specialised magazines.
23   See my article in *Internationale Press-Korrespondenz*. [Obviously Varga refers to his article 'Das Rätsel Chinas' 1921, pp. 356–7].

people having already been integrated into the capitalist world economy of which some parts, like Germany, were already spearheading capitalism before the war. Notwithstanding profound political differences between the capitalist countries of Central Europe and the proletarian Soviet Republic, all these states are economically suffering from the same disease, *i.e. from impoverishment by the war*, from shortages of means of production, from insufficient production, all leading to under-nourishment of the working masses. Causes and consequences are enchained into a vicious circle: an insufficient standard of life is engendering a decreasing labour productivity, a diminishing output ...

Hence, the solution of the world economic crisis can – at least theoretically – easily be found: it would only be a matter of exporting superfluous goods from the regions of overproduction to the impoverished regions. But these superfluous goods are privately owned by capitalists. Their export to the impoverished regions can therefore only occur in accord with capitalist laws: thus property rights should be respected and profits should be made. A solution is thus very hard to find.

Attempts to solve the problem have already a long prehistory. English political ideologues like Norman Angell and [John M.] Keynes have addressed the problem. The bankers followed with concrete proposals: the *Ter Meulen Plan*,[24] the *Vanderlip Plan*[25] for an European international bank, etc. followed an unofficial English initiative for mutual remittance of the war debt in combination with a reduction of German reparation payments, *Parvus's*[26] propaganda for an international consortium for the reconstruction of Germany and Russia, Stinnes's English-German cooperation for Russia. Finally, what is very actual at the moment of writing these lines is the decision of the financiers at the Paris Entente Conference to propose the establishment of an international bank with a capital of 20 million pounds to provide loans to all impoverished countries for the reconstruction of their roads and production capacity, but on the condition that they '*guarantee property rights*'. We can see that the plans become more and more concrete and that they will be extended to Russia. Because of the inapplicability of the Chinese plans, international capital is now interested in the vast territories of Russia, Ukraine, Siberia and Turkestan which much-needed huge markets can guarantee its further survival.

Before discussing these theses and their perspectives in detail, we want to argue that an '*unconscious*' *tendency* – i.e. profit-seeking by private capital-

---

24 [Carel E. Ter Meulen (1867–1937) was a partner of Hope & Co. in Amsterdam and a member of the financial committee of the League of Nations].
25 [Frank A. Vanderlip (1864–1937) was President of the National Bank of New York].
26 [Parvus: alias of Alexander Israel Helphand (1867–1924)].

ists – *to bridge the gap in the world economy by capital transfers*, is a process that has already started after the end of the war. This tendency influenced the capitalists of the rich countries in their striving to invest their capital in the underdeveloped regions. This happens in different ways:

1. Capitalist groups in the overproducing countries, producing until recently in their own region and providing from there the actual regions of underproduction with goods, established in the latter countries new production facilities because wages were much lower and profits were higher there. This process means in many cases breaking-up the worldwide division of labour and decreasing productivity if produced in unfavourable locations.
2. Capitalist groups participate in limited liability companies in the regions of underproduction. Appreciation of the exchange rates of their hard currencies facilitates the establishment of production facilities that can produce cheaper than in the rich regions. This is also the case with acquiring rural estates, urban properties, complete factories there.

Both processes signify: oversupply of goods, especially capital goods, coming from the regions of overproduction to the regions of underproduction; in the first case this happens directly, in the second case indirectly by paying for them with foreign currencies (insofar as these are not speculatively hoarded by their new owners). Hence, they are supporting the immanent tendency of restoring the equilibrium of the world economy. Quantification of this process is difficult. Much is not revealed. One thing is nonetheless certain: the 'spontaneous' equilibrium tendency turned out to be much too feeble to bridge the widening gap in the world economy.[27] Until now this process has been halted at the borders of Soviet Russia.[28] Plans of transmitting the idle means of production from

---

27 Characteristic of capitalist anarchy is the fact that *a parallel countertendency* exists. Because of revolutions, seizure of securities, etc., Stinnes and Siemens are setting up new firms on foreign continents and capitals move from poor to rich countries.
28 The changing role of Europe in the world economy can be studied at the hand of *Table 6.4*.

TABLE 6.4   England's foreign trade with Europe decreased in percentages

	1913	1919	1920	1921 (until October)
Import	40.3	15.3	23.3	27.4
Export	37.5	57.0	52.7	33.8

England gives no political credit anymore; hence, a sharp decline in exports to Europe occurred.

the regions of overproduction to the regions of underproduction, thus possibly re-establishing the equilibrium of the world economy, are nothing more than a draft. Two issues are coming to the fore here:

1. *A mutual annulment of inter-allied war debts combined with a reduction of Germany's reparation burden.* Implementation of this measure has until now failed due to the resistance of its main creditor, i.e. the United States, which does not want to give up a claim of some 10 billion dollars and which has also the most powerful *political weapon*. One should also take into account that America is England's main creditor. Notwithstanding serious economic problems, England remains after all a creditworthy country. In addition, England's debtors are actually insolvent continental countries. Because of America's refusal, a mutually concluded inter-allied debt annulment is likely to be out of question.

   One should, however, admit that a mutual inter-allied debt annulment is *not a positive step* towards a solution of the world-economic crisis. This does, however, not mean that the means of production will be transferred from the rich to the poor countries, but only an annulment of claims whose real counterparts have already disappeared during the war. A reduction in the reparation burden would allow Germany to finance its reconstruction by way of its own resources, but this would also signify that France, whose foreign war debt is only representing a theoretical burden because the country is not paying interest, may expect a worsening of its financial situation. A mutual annulment of debts would therefore be only a partial solution to a partial problem, not a contribution to overcoming the global economic slowdown.

2. *An extraordinary international credit accommodation guaranteed to all countries – Russia included – of the regions of underproduction.*
   This would be the only correct and possible way out of the crisis. If carried out fully, this measure could clear away the cleavages created by the world war in the world economy. Abundance of means of production and goods in general in the regions of overproduction should flow to the regions of underproduction, production in these regions could then rapidly recover, normal worldwide trade could resume, and the exchange rates could then stabilise. This should, of course, not signify a definitive stabilisation of the capitalist social order, because the *old contradictions* of class society will remain, will be sharpened by the existence of Soviet Russia and the strengthening of the independence movements in all colonial and semi-colonial countries. But the acute economic crisis would not be overcome.

Economic changes are quantitatively possible. If the output of six million American, two million English and one million other present-day jobless workers could become available during two or three years to the impoverished regions, an equilibrium could be reached.

What is hindering this solution?

It is Germany's and Russia's *political problem*! Notwithstanding the ongoing international intertwining of capitalist interests, the political contradictions of the 'national' imperialisms have remained in essence unchanged!

Let us first of all consider the *political problem* of Germany. Before the world war, England and Germany were primarily struggling for economic supremacy in the the world. The United States was still mainly an agrarian country, while France and Japan were second-rate industrial powers. The world war promoted America to the category of a first-ranking power. After having annexed Alsace-Lorraine, France became an exporter of heavy industrial products fiercely competing with those of the first two countries. Japan was promoted – at least in Asia and Africa – to the rank of a world power. If Germany's economy were to be floated by means of important foreign credits and have its reparation burden alleviated, it could regain its equilibrium and, propped by low wages, reappear as the most dangerous competitor of the industrialised world powers. This evolution would be very dangerous for France. That is why large amounts of French capital are invested in Poland and in the Danube countries, but only exceptionally in Germany; Polish, Czech and other loans can easily been sold to the rich countries, but until now no important German loan …

The situation is quite different for Russia. Profitable investment could become possible without creating a dangerous competitor in the near future. But the dictatorship of the proletariat is still deterring the capitalists. After having given up their hope of bringing down the Soviet government, the necessity of stimulating the Russian market by allowing credits cannot be denied. But they will allow them so parsimoniously that their impact on the restoration of the equilibrium of the world economy will be marginal.

5 Recovery Attempts at the Cost of the Proletariat

Conforming to capitalism's antagonistic character, capitalists are trying to overcome the crisis at the cost of the proletariat by increasing the degree of exploitation. A lengthening of the working day, wage cuts, increased efficiency: that is the 'medicine' capitalism is trying to prescribe to the regions of overproduction as well as those of underproduction. Pressing for increased productivity and a lengthening of the working day is a Sisyphean task when ten million workers are unemployed and unsold goods are at the very origins of the crisis! But the capitalists in England and America argue as follows: goods are unsaleable because *production costs are too high*; the capitalists in Germany, Poland, etc. argue that everybody should work harder in poor countries in order to ban poverty by increasing production ...

That method will lead to any result in any group of countries. A sharpening of the world economic crisis will be its result if the employed workers in the countries of overproduction will produce more, hence the amount of unsaleable goods or even the rate of unemployment will grow. In the countries of underproduction, however, the proletariat is undernourished to such a degree, its living standard is so degraded, the production facilities are so worn out, the rate of surplus value is so high, that, generally speaking, labour productivity cannot possibly increase. Such an attempt must lead to a catastrophically miserable proletariat. Higher labour productivity can in this case only be attained by improving the production facilities, by a better organised production process (in Germany many times applied) and by a temporarily improved nourishment! The equilibrium cannot be restored at cost to the proletariat!

6   The Armed Struggle for World Hegemony

If it is impossible to restore the equilibrium by returning to self-sufficient national economic regions and by opening up new regions, or by reconstructing economically the regions of underproduction to create markets for the unsaleable goods from the regions of overproduction, then there would be no other possibility left than an *armed struggle of the imperialist powers for the control of all world markets having become too small*.

Speaking of future wars must sound like a blasphemy in the ears of the petty-bourgeois Philistines and Social-Democratic ideologues in these days of the Washington Disarmament Conference. When studying the proceedings of the Washington Conference, the following picture can be drawn without any prejudice. The United States are showing the participants at the Conference their splendid weaponry: their weapon factories are producing noxious gases of an unprecedented perfection, their wharfs are constructing gigantic battleships and new murderous weapons. And they tell their competitors: 'if you do not parry, I'll cancel the loans, I'll lend no more money, thus go ahead!' The other countries confirm their peaceful intentions, but will threaten each other mutually in clear terms.[29] The whole Conference is in reality an art of power play for

---

29   Balfour's declaration in Washington – that the number of submarines France wants to built can also be used against England – sounds like a menace of war. 'For and against submarines. Mr. Balfour's case for Britain', *The Times*, 27 December 1921, p. 7.

obtaining, if need be, what already was decided but this time with the same expedients. Until now there were many peace and disarmament conferences. It requires an overdose of naivety to believe that these conferences will prevent future wars; the cause of the last world war was the struggle of the imperialist powers for world hegemony which is today fought out in a more exacerbated manner.

7   Drawing Up the Balance-Sheet of the Past Three Years

Did capitalism consolidate during the last three years?

The answer is not easily given. We observe contradictory facts. I believe that the following answer comes close to the truth: *Capitalism did not consolidate economically. In the defeated countries it is now socially consolidated, but as a whole and in the long-run it certainly does not!*

We think that there is no reason to think of an economic stabilisation, because of the incredibly high unemployment rate, the chaos on the exchange market and the ever-widening gap existing between the regions of over- and underproduction. But we do not argue that the *actual* crisis will nowadays last uninterruptedly until the breakdown of capitalism occurs. For sure, periods of economic revival will come. But until now nothing has been done to strike at the root of all evil, the absence of an equilibrium. This state of affairs must thus always, after a short period of economic revival, result in an acute economic crisis.

Capitalism consolidated in the defeated countries. After having lost its authority because of its defeat in the world war, *the bourgeoisie regained its strength and self-confidence*. Thus the opportunity of liquidating capitalist hegemony was missed. The bourgeoisie reorganised itself, lined up the White Guards and took the offensive.

On the other hand, there are those masses of workers having been attracted by sentimental reasons to the ranks of the revolutionaries because of embitterment engendered by their sufferings during the war, by the breakdown of all hitherto established authorities, by the example of the victorious struggles in Russia; they consciously joined, but now they have deserted because the struggle had not ended into a quick victory. After the great revolutionary wave, a period of depression followed and is still lasting. Capitalism has thus strengthened. But one should not forget that after the desertion of the emotionally moved revolutionary masses, conscious communist vanguards have nonetheless survived in all European countries and that they transformed into really revolutionary organisations. Our enemies can scoff at our weaknesses and the never-ending turmoil in the different communist parties. However, three years ago there existed at best some small communist groupings. Today there exist strong communist parties with thousands of experienced militants. An important historical progress was thus made. But, apart from some 'normal' contradictions in the capitalist social order, the economic equilibrium will remain fundamentally disturbed. Hence, the present period of a depressed revolutionary movement will sooner or later transform into a revolutionary wave luring back all 'emotional revolutionaries' having deserted during the years of depression.

However, we must say to all wavers: Only in a period of depression can you see who is a real revolutionary!

Moscow,
New Year's Day 1922

CHAPTER 7

The Process of Capitalist Decline (Report to the Fourth Congress of the Communist International)

Preface[1]

Fifteen months have elapsed since the last congress of the Communist International, in the present period of revolutionary developments a considerable span of time. It appears therefore necessary to review the changes in the economic life of the world in the light of experience gathered during this interval.

The present review will not be confined to the year 1921–2. The Communist International is on the point of drafting a programme. This requires a searching analysis, from the Marxist point of view, of the changes of the economic substructure. This essay is intended to be a contribution to the discussion of the programme question. I attempted therefore to deal somewhat more fully with the theoretical aspect of the question, at the risk of rendering my disquisition less easy than I should have desired. On the other hand, for the sake of making it possible for each of the Congress delegates to read it through, I have reduced the statistical matter to a minimum.[2]

In stating beforehand the result of our inquiry, I may observe: The crisis of the economic life of the capitalist world has not been overcome, 'normal' capitalism is not restored, thus giving the lie to the advocates of the capitalist interests in the proletarian camp, Cunow,[3] Hilferding,[4] Levi,[5] etc., who have been prophesying prosperity for the last two years. But no final collapse has as yet taken place, which some 'Left comrades' in our ranks have looked for. The forces of reconstruction and destruction counterbalanced one another during the interval of our two Congresses.

---

1 [Originally published by Communist International, in commission: Carl Hoym Nachf. L. Cahnbley, Hamburg 8. Printed by Vereinsdruckerei G.m.b.H., Potsdam, 1922].
2 Readers who need more statistical data will find them in the second edition of my *Krise der Kapitalistischen Weltwirtschaft* (Volume 25 of the Library of the Communist International), then in our new *Internationales Jahrbuch für Wirtschaft, Politik und Arbeiterbewegung*, also in my *Quarterly Reports* in the *International Press Correspondence*.
3 [Heinrich Cunow (1862–1936) was a German Social-Democratic politician].
4 [Rudolf Hilferding (1877–1941) was an Austrian-born Marxist theoretician and politician].
5 [Paul Levi (1883–1933) was a German Communist and Social-Democratic politician].

The unstable equilibrium of the social forces continues; the crisis is ongoing; but bourgeois power outside Russia still occupies a dominant position. It is our task to inquire theoretically, that is, without prejudice and without illusions, into the condition of world capitalism, and at the same time to consolidate the forces of the international proletariat and to prepare the final struggle for power in those sectors of our line of advance where the adversary is most exposed to attack. The struggle will go on for a considerable space of time. It is therefore necessary for the Communist International to lay down, programmatically, the bases and methods of this contest.

Berlin, 29 September 1922
E. Varga

1   Rise and Decline of Capitalism

While the industrial year 1921–2 has not fulfilled the hopes which capital had cherished, there has been in 1922 some improvement in the economic condition of the principal capitalist countries, viz. USA, Great Britain, Japan, and France, as will be seen later on from the statistical tables. The fundamental question must therefore be raised afresh:

Is the present industrial crisis of the world a transitory and usual one within capitalism, which, having run its course, will be followed by a period of prosperity and social consolidation of class domination, in order to give way, some time later, to a less severe and usual crisis? Or is it part of a permanent crisis, which, while it may be broken by spells of prosperity, can no longer be stopped?

Before dealing with this question, before indicating the economic characteristics of the various types of crises, it must be pointed out that the militant attitude of the proletariat forms one of the most decisive factors in the process of social evolution. We must guard ourselves against the mistake into which Social Democracy has fallen – the mistake of scientific fatalism, of merely theorising, in Marxist terms, on the collapse of capitalism and then passively waiting for its tumbling down. Without a protracted and embittered struggle, without the self-sacrificing spirit of the proletariat, capitalism will not fall to pieces. Capital will strive to surmount all difficulties at the expense of the proletariat; it will pauperise the working class; aye, it will drive down society to the pre-capitalist level rather than relinquish one particle of its class domination.

When we therefore speak in the following of a permanent crisis of capitalism, we mean a period in which the contradiction between the forces of production and the conditions of production has come to a head, a period in which the class relations are such that the class struggle of the proletariat can be successful, can lead to the overthrow of class domination. But the struggle must be fought out, in order that victory might be achieved.

And now let us revert to the economic substructure and let us try to indicate the difference between the former crises and the present period of crisis.

The former crises of capitalism were periodically recurring phases in the ascending line of evolution of capitalism. Leaving the periodic crises out of account and bearing only in mind the broad outline of economic evolution, we find that capitalism in general had, up to the world war, exhibited an upward tendency.[6] This is shown by the following:

The capitalist form of production *expanded geographically*; new countries were increasingly opened up to capitalism.

Capitalism *extended its sphere of operation* in the capitalist countries themselves by drawing the pre-capitalist strata of society into its vortex. The gold standard, which considerably facilitates the exchange of goods on a capitalist basis, found favour to a growing degree. Foreign trade increased in weight and value.

Large accumulations of capital formed the basis of these developments, since the falling rate of profit in the highly developed capitalist countries and the effect of the steadily growing higher organic composition of capital was compensated for by the export of capital to less developed capitalist countries, with higher rates of surplus value and profit. The centralisation of capital into monopolist forms of production, covering the whole economic field of a country, reduced the cost of capitalist management.

The result was that, apart from the periodic crises, the level of production rose steadily in the world at large as well as in each particular country. The proletariat's standard of living rose slowly. The credit system and the small company shares permitted the working men and the lower middle class to participate, with their savings, in the appropriation of surplus value. The number of people who had an interest, or who believed they had an interest, in maintaining the capitalist system was on the increase. The proletariat of the imperialist countries received from capital a small share of the surprofits which it got out of colonial exploitation. The upper stratum of the proletariat, the aristocracy of labour, became separated from the mass of the working people and became subservient to capital. All classes submitted to the leadership of capital. The great landowners turned into capitalists, and the capitalists inves-

---

6 Trotsky, in his paper presented to the Third Congress of the Communist International, drew attention to this point.

ted money in land; the tendency of financial capital was to amalgamate all possessing sections of the nation with one another. The crises were transitory phases within an upward development, the effects of the anarchy of the capitalist form of production, and caused by superficial disturbances in the structure of capitalism. The system as a whole, however, lost nothing of its equilibrium.

The aspect of the down-grade, decaying capitalism exhibits quite different characteristics.[7]

1. The geographic expansion of the capitalist form of production is slackening; in addition to capitalist countries there are countries in growing numbers where the proletariat is preparing for dictatorship.
2. Within various capitalist countries there is a growing tendency towards a reversion to pre-capitalist forms of industry.
3. The international division of labour is narrowing; foreign trade is shrinking, the economic life of the world, which used to arrange itself organically round the highly developed industrial nucleus of Western Europe, loses its diverse economic structures.
4. The gold standard of the various countries, which, while it differed in the number of its gold units, was on the whole a uniform and stable currency, is being replaced by an unstable, violently fluctuating paper currency; and there is even a tendency to revert to barter.
5. The former accumulation of capital is being replaced by a progressive impoverishment, disaccumulation.
6. The volume of production is decreasing.
7. The whole credit system is crumbling.
8. The standard of life of the proletariat is getting lower, either through the normal wage not keeping pace with the rise of prices or through wage cuts, or through unemployment.
9. Among the various strata of the possessing class a severe struggle is blazing for the division of the diminishing social product. This manifests itself, politically, in the disruption of the governing coalition parties, in the failure to form new political bodies or to formulate new programmes, etc., etc.
10. The faith in the unity and solidity of the capitalist order of society is being shaken. The governing class, losing its moral authority, has recourse to force and arms itself for the protection of its dominance.

---

7 Compare also Bucharin 1922.

This condition of capitalism, incompletely and cursorily touched upon in those points, we venture to call the decaying stage of capitalism or the period of permanent crisis, or the crisis-period, for short.

The characteristics are, of course, not to be found in an equal degree in all countries. There are countries in which we meet with all those characteristics, but there are also countries in which the crisis is hardly to be noticed yet, aye, which are but in the initial stages of capitalist development. But their rise takes place within a capitalism which, on the whole, is on the down-grade. We shall deal with this question more extensively later.

This period of permanent crisis, or crisis-period, owing to its world dimensions, must be of a long duration. In its course there will be times of improving trade and of acute crisis, just as in the period of ascending capitalism. We thus clearly distinguish three types of crises:

1. Acute crises in the period of ascending capitalism.
2. The crisis-period, or the period of the decline of capitalism.
3. Acute crises within the crisis-period itself.

These distinctions must be borne in mind when dealing with the economic condition of the world. The latter can be characterised in the following manner:

We are no longer in a phase of crisis, as we were at the time of the Third Congress; we are in a phase of improving trade, but still within the crisis-period of capitalism.

This conception of ours will meet with opposition from two sides: (1) from the Social Democrats and generally from all those who are interested in the continued existence of the capitalist order of society and who assert that we have not entered any crisis-period or the period of decline of capitalism, but that we have gone through a crisis that was caused and aggravated by the world war, and which, after its having been overcome, as it now seems to be the case, capitalism will continue to progress; (2) from certain adherents of the 'Left' of our movement who deny that we have entered any phase of improving trade. Against this we shall try to demonstrate the following:

1. that we have actually entered a period of permanent crisis;
2. that the war which gave rise to this crisis-period was no 'accident', but the necessary consequence of the imperialism which is the present evolutionary stage of capitalism;
3. that an improvement in the economic situation is drawing near.

2   Essence and Meaning of the Decline of Capitalism

Let us try, above all, to arrive at a general theoretical view of the decline of capitalism.

The normal economic life of the capitalist world was an organism of an unstable equilibrium, in which a continually extended reproduction was taking place. Marx drew a diagram of a state of equilibrium (or of a continually renewed state of equilibrium, with an extending reproduction), assuming thereby that the whole world was within the capitalist mode of production, or, in other words, while developing his diagram, Marx looked upon the world as a single capitalist country. The crises which periodically occurred in the process of reproduction were explained by the disturbances of the equilibrium, arising from the want of the proper economic ratio between the production (i) of the means of production, (ii) of the necessaries for the proletariat, and (iii) of comforts and luxuries for the well-to-do classes.[8] (*Capital*, Volume I).

In the actual economic life of the capitalist world the conditions of equilibrium were, of course, incomparably more complicated since there was no uniformly or planfully developed system. The equilibrium of the capitalist system, as periodically restored through the crises, had, besides those indicated by Marx, the following bases:

1. As to the equilibrium of the economic life of the capitalist world from the point of view of the *balance of exchange values*:

a)   The centre of the capitalist economic life, Western and Central Europe, received annually, without equivalent, from the whole world large masses of values as profits from investments abroad and as income from their political exploitation of the colonies.

---

[8]   The tripartition given by Marx, like that of Quesnay's *Tableau économique*, is a rough approximation. For, in order to maintain or continually to restore the equilibrium, it is not sufficient to secure the quantitative ratio between the three spheres of production, since within each of the spheres commodities may be produced which in their total exchange-value might correspond to the social demand, but not in their use-value. For instance if the necessary quantity of goods of any of the spheres is produced, but instead of the necessary machinery, tools, etc. for the iron and steel industry there are produced those for the textile industry or agriculture, such a miscalculation in use-values may be the origin of a disturbed equilibrium or of a crisis, although the ratio of the division of production between the spheres I, II, and III is in conformity with the diagram. The real diagram of the conditions of equilibrium would form an infinitely ramified series. The difficulties of establishing such a series manifests itself with brutal directness in the practical attempts of Soviet Russia to produce a harmonious economic plan.

b) The centre exported other and new accumulated masses of values as new investments to the less developed capitalist countries. That a certain equilibrium established itself is proved by the fact that the rates of the foreign bills fluctuated little.

2. From the point of view of the *balance of exchange of commodities*:

The centre received foodstuffs and raw materials from the countries that were industrially less developed and less involved in the capitalist mode of production; as far as these imports did not contain profits from investments or incomes from other forms of exploitation, the centre paid for them with manufactured goods.

Despite the cycle of crises, a certain equilibrium existed in the production and exchange of commodities, as may be seen from the fact that the proletariat, apart from the reserve army of unemployed which is necessary for maintaining the capitalist system, found employment and gradually, though very slowly, improved its standard of life; that all capital found remunerative employment; that, generally speaking, everybody could obtain, for his income, the commodities he desired.

The possibility of maintaining this equilibrium was, however, threatened by the fact that the new accumulated masses of capital of the great imperialist nations, which formed the centre of the economic life of the world, were no longer able to find new opportunities for investments that would yield adequate profits. This led, as we shall show in *Chapter 4*, to the world war; the imperialist powers thought it more suitable to their purpose to have the matter decided by a trial of force as to whom shall fall the possibility of exploiting the non-imperialist regions.

The war, however, destroyed – at least temporarily – the bases of the former equilibrium of the capitalist world.

1. From the point of view the *exchange values*:
a) During the war the European belligerent powers consumed not only the profits of their foreign investments, but the capital sums themselves;
b) The accumulation of capital stopped, and, partly, even a disaccumulation took place. (We must, of course, leave out of account the fictitious accumulations and illusionary riches which are only the effect of the depreciated currencies). This process, to some extent, still continues.

This destruction of the exchange-value-equilibrium of the economic life of the capitalist world manifests itself by the chaos of the currencies.

2. From the point of view of use-values:

The regions which used to supply foodstuffs and raw materials are establishing their own manufactures. The goods of the manufacturing centre therefore find no markets. Hence the glut of manufactured commodities in the highly developed industrial countries, and a glut of foodstuffs and raw materials in the agricultural countries. And this leads to a deliberate limitation of production (cotton, rubber, coffee, etc.) and even to using foodstuffs as fuel. In both regions there is relative overproduction, a want of economic equilibrium.

As against this complex stand the Central and Eastern European countries in which, as a consequence of the war and the blockade, such an annihilation of goods, such a deterioration of the material and human productive forces took place that a constant underproduction has set in, that is, much less is being produced than is required for the renewal of the material and human productive forces. Instead of reproduction on an extending scale, there is a reproduction on a shrinking scale.

This is, in our view, the theoretical outline of the present grave disturbances of the equilibrium of the capitalist system. And this is the essence and meaning of the present crisis-period. The result is that the whole economic life of the capitalist world no longer moves on the ascending, but rather on the descending line.

As those observations may appear to some to be too abstract, we shall deal more fully with the concrete features of the situation which we sketched out in the first chapter and which characterise the decline of capitalism, and we hope to show that they are realities.

In the preceding chapter, the main features of the decline of capitalism have been roughly drawn and the attempt has been made to establish, theoretically, the essence of this decline. It is now our business to deal with those features in greater detail.

1. *The geographic expansion of capitalism is being checked.* For, while capitalist domination makes some advance through getting a foothold in China and South America, it is being eliminated in Russia and the affiliated Soviet Republics as well as in the Far Eastern Republic. It is true that proletarian Russia, isolated and hounded down, is compelled to make concessions to capitalism, whose assistance she needs in the work of reconstructing its economic life, still there is a fundamental difference between Soviet Russia, whose governmental power is in the hands of the proletariat, and the capitalist countries, where the bourgeoisie is in power.

2. *Within the various capitalist countries there is a tendency to return to pre-capitalist economic forms.* This tendency is most pronounced in the centre of the crisis, in Central and Eastern Europe. Instead of production for the market, there is production for the domestic use of the peasantry. Instead of taxation in money, there is taxation in kind (Hungary). Instead of money credits, corn credits. And capital itself, as far as it is not invested in production,

is returning in an increasing measure to the pre-capitalist form of unproductive commercial capital.

3. *The international division of labour is being restricted; the volume of foreign trade is shrinking; the unity of economic life is crumbling.* The restriction of the international division of labour is going on apace. The highly developed manufacturing countries are more and more raising their custom duties for the protection of their home markets. (New custom tariff in USA). The countries which were hitherto agricultural and have lately taken to manufacturing, are surrounding themselves with obstacles against imports and with high custom duties for the protection of their infant industries. The old manufacturing countries, on the other hand, are striving to revive or develop their agriculture (agitation in Great Britain for a return to the land, artificial creation of beet sugar factories, emigration to settlement colonies, etc.). The result is a dissolution of the international economic co-operation, a shrinking of internal exchanges.[9]

---

9 TABLE 7.1   Movement of foreign trade in the main countries in the last decade

	1913	1918	1919	1920	1921	Index number reduced to 1913	Wholesale trade figures of 1921
Great Britain in million £							
Imports	659	1,285	1,461	1,710	980	202	485
Exports	525	501	799	1,334	703	–	350
Germany in million francs							
Imports	10,770	–	–	98,136	119,132*	1,911	9,250
Exports	10,097	–	–	69,311	99,921	–	7,900
France in million francs							
Imports	8,421	22,301	35,799	49,905	23,548	345	6,800
Exports	6,880	6,596	11,880	26,896	21,553	–	6,200
Italy in million lire							
Imports	3,645	16,039	16,623	15,862	20,058	578	3,500
Exports	2,312	3,345	6,066	7,804	9,224	–	1,600
Switzerland in million francs							
Imports	1,919	2,401	3,533	4,200	2,253	195	1,150
Exports	1,376	1,963	3,298	2,374	1,764	–	900
Belgium in million francs							
Imports	5,050	–	5,223	12,942	10,054	368	2,600
Exports	3,716	–	2,289	8,862	7,147	–	2,000
Denmark in million Krones							
Imports	855	946	2,519	2,943	1,635	250	650
Exports	721	758	909	1,962	1,466	–	590

4. Still more than those various symptoms is the fact which lies at the bottom of it, namely, *the decay of the former unified economic life of the world*. In the period of the ascending line of capitalism, economic life was ranging itself fairly uniformly round the most highly developed Western European nucleus. From the centre, capitalism expanded in all directions, and this expansion, it may be noted, was mainly determined not by graphical contiguity, but by traffic facilities, so that those regions were earliest and most strongly drawn into the capitalist system which were easiest reached by overland and maritime routes. In essence, however, all countries followed the sane line of development, but with this fundamental difference that some were active agents of capitalist development, while others were the passive objects of this development, namely, exploited colonies.[10]

The present period of decline of capitalism is characterised by the decomposition of this unified economic life of the world. The centre of gravity of capitalism is moving to the USA and Japan. Central and Eastern Europe are being eliminated from the rank of leading capitalist regions. While the commodities of the still intact region find no effective demand on the world markets,

TABLE 7.1   Movement of foreign trade (*cont.*)

	1913	1918	1919	1920	1921	Index number reduced to 1913	Wholesale trade figures of 1921
USA in million dollars							
Imports	1,749	3,031	3,904	5,279	2,508	148	1,700
Exports	2,446	6,149	7,920	8,228	4,425	–	3,000
Japan in million Yen							
Imports	729	1,668	2,173	2,335	1,613	200	800
Exports	632	1,962	2,099	1,947	1,252	–	620

*   Eight months.

If we reduce the totals of imports and exports in 1921 to the price level of 1913, we perceive at once the considerable shrinking of the foreign trade. (The reduction is but approximately carried out, as the method is only a rough one). Only the exports of the USA and the imports of Japan in 1921 appear to be larger than in 1913. On the other hand, the falling off in the trade of the European countries is very considerable.

10   The rise of an indigenous capitalist class in the colonies, the inevitable effect of their being drawn into the capitalist system, tends to put an end to that difference, either by peaceful means (as in the British self-governing dominions) or by revolutionary means (as in Egypt, India).

the production in Central and Eastern Europe is far from being equal to the daily consumption. We characterised this state of things as the decomposition of the world into two regions: one of relative overproduction, the other of absolute underproduction. Thus the essential difference is distinctly marked. With regard, however, to our programme question, we shall try to illustrate this classification by two salient types of the present period of decline.

The former gold standard has been replaced by a paper currency which is exposed to violent fluctuations. This is, strictly speaking, a partial symptom of the decomposition of the economic life of the world, but it is particularly important, since in its reaction it accelerates the process of decay. This fact is so well known that it hardly needs any demonstration. Apart from the USA and Switzerland there is no country with a real gold standard. The Federal Reserve Bulletins publish a General Index, which is composed of the movements of the various currency rates of the most important capitalist countries,[11] showing the monthly average rates of these currencies in percentages of the dollar at par.

TABLE 7.2 General Index gives the following figures

1918	November	101
1919	February	100
1919	July	92
1919	December	78
1920	July	70
1920	December	55
1921	July	52
1921	December	57
1922	July	55

From these figures it would appear as if in the last two years a certain stability has set in. But this is only to be ascribed to the fact that some of the European currencies – Holland, Great Britain, France – have improved during that period. On the other hand, the currencies of the Central and Eastern European nations, which – with the exception of Germany – do not enter into the composition of

---

11   Belgium, Denmark, France, Germany, Great Britain, Holland, Italy, Spain, Switzerland, Sweden, Canada, Argentina, Brazil, Chile, India, Japan.

the index, have continued their downward course, and have sunk to such a low level which practically deprives them of the character of money.

TABLE 7.3 Monthly average rates in percentages of the American dollar (at par)[12]

Greece	15.33	Germany	0.86
Finland	11.12	Hungary	0.38
Yugoslavia	6.33	Austria	0.02
Bulgaria	3.78	Czechoslovakia approximately	10.00
Rumania	3.13	Poland	0.09

The result of these developments is that these currencies have all but disappeared from the international money market and are even losing in the respective home markets their function as measures of value and medium of exchange. Many manufacturers in Germany have in their business calculation abandoned the mark and adopted foreign currencies; in many businesses it is made a condition that the whole or part payment due to them shall be made in foreign currency.

A greater obstacle than the low rate of the currencies is the process of depreciation to capitalist enterprise in those regions, since this process does not go on in a steadily downward movement, but in violent fluctuations, which render all anticipations, all calculations, all long-term business impossible. Therefore we see the tendency towards a reversion to barter, to the corn price as the basis of all business.[13]

---

12 *Federal Reserve Bulletin* 1922, 8, 8, p. 1014.
13 From the innumerable cases of this sort we take two, which just met our eye writing these lines. We read in the *Deutsche Allgemeine Zeitung* of September 1921:
    'Our own correspondent wires that the Chambre of Agriculture at Weimar has fixed tuition fees for the Agricultural winter courses at Triptis and Marksuhl in corn currency, – namely 1½ cwts. of rye for students from Thuringia, and 2 cwts. for Non-Turingians. – The Power Works Sachsen-Thüringen, Ltd. at Auma which raised last week the price of light to 45 marks and of gas to 36 marks, announces that it is quite willing to be paid for a kilowatt hour light current at the rate of 10 eggs or 3 lbs. wheaten flour or ¼ cwt. potatoes. The Medical Society at Naumburg announces that in order to make it possible for the agricultural population to pay the doctor's fees, they would require to be paid in kind at piece prices. Also the medical men at Braunschweig are asking the peasantry to pay in kind. – "Newspaper Subscriptions in kind"! The *Tageblatt* at Langensalza informs its readers that the subscription price for the coming months amounts to 60 marks, which could also be paid in kind, – 6 lbs. corn or 10 eggs'.

5. *Accumulation is being replaced by a progressive impoverishment.* It is questionable whether this view is universally correct. It is probable that accumulated wealth of the capitalist world is smaller now than it was before the war. It is, however, questionable whether since the war a further impoverishment of the capitalist world has taken place. The available statistical material does not allow us to be positive on this point. But we believe that a further impoverishment may undoubtedly be assumed to have taken place in the centre of the crisis, Germany, Austria, Hungary, Poland, Italy, etc. We shall later on attempt to prove this in the case of Germany.

6. *Production is diminishing.* The subjoined *Table 7.4* shows the production of the most important commodities in the last decade.[14] Many of the figures are only approximately correct, but they suffice to illustrate the tendency of the development.

TABLE 7.4 World production of agrarian products in million double cwts (Russia not included)

	Average 1903–13	**Average 1914–18**	**Average 1912–22**
Wheat	799.0	790.8	800.3
Barley	264.7	250.8	252.9
Rye	213.6	167.1	191.2
Oats	494.4	486.5	478.9
Maize	971.4	974.3	1,056.7
Potatoes	1,133.6	982.0	993.3
Beet sugar	62.7	45.7	43.1
Cane sugar	95.9	120.1	128.9
Coffee	11.6	12.1	9.7
Cocoa	2.3	3.0	3.9
Tea	280.5	343.8	332.8
Cotton	40.7	38.8	36.8
Jute	15.3	15.3	11.3

(a) *Annuaire Statistique Agricole* 1909–21, p. 216 sqq.

---

14 The data are taken from the *Annuaire International de Statistique Agricole*, and from the *Internationales Jahrbuch für Wirtschaft, Politik und Arbeiterbewegung*, as well as from the *Wirtschaftskurve mit Indexzahlen der Frankfurter Zeitung* [Frankfurt: Frankfurter Societäts-Druckerei], August 1922.

Mining products

	1912	1913	1914	1915	1916	1917	1918
In million tons							
Coal	1,377	1,478	1,346	1,340	1,390	1,346	1,331
Petroleum	47	52	55	56	62	67	67
Pig-Iron	73	78	59	62	71	67	–
Steel	–	75	–	–	–	–	–
In 1,000 tons							
Copper	103	103	96	109	144	147	147
Tin	125	133	121	125	125	130	114
Zinc	974	1,000	888	833	956	990	828
Lead	1,182	1,187	1,176	1,116	1,169	1,190	1,195
In 1,000 kg							
Gold	701	692	661	708	683	637	568
Silver	6,980	6,960	5,000	5,100	5,000	5,100	5,600
In 1,000 tons							
Ships	2,900	3,330	2,850	1,200	1,690	2,960	5,400

TABLE 7.5 World's life stock (including Russia) in million heads (according to the census taken immediately before 1911 and 1921)

	1911	1921
Horses	110.5	99.3
Cattle	482.8	510.9
Sheep	617.8	532.2
Pigs	260.2	209.7

Life stock statistics taken from *Annuaire Statistique Agricole*, 1909–21, p. 234 sqq.

From a cursory glance at this table, one might assume that no decrease in production had taken place, for, while these statistics show for the greater part of the items a decrease in production, there are also products which show increases (wheat, maize, cane, sugar, petroleum, ships). But the following two considerations must be taken into account:

Under normal conditions the world's production showed in a like period large increases. Stagnation or a slight decrease means a cessation of accumulation, thus a decline of capitalism.

On an analysis of the world's production we find that the increases took place in the extra-European regions, with a developing capitalism, while Europe itself showed throughout a very considerable decline.

Take for instance *Table 7.6*:

TABLE 7.6 European wheat and cattle production

Wheat	1909–13	Europe (excl. Russia) 35,20 percent of world production
	1919–21	Europe (excl. Russia) 28,8 percent of world production
Cattle	1909–13	Europe (excl. Russia) 127 million heads of world production
	1919–21	Europe (excl. Russia) 122.1 million heads of the worlds production

The products which show large increases, like maize, cane, sugar, cocoa, tea, petroleum, are all extra-European. The production in those parts of Europe where the decay is most pronounced show throughout a sharp decline.

7. *The credit system is collapsing*. This applies, above all, to those countries in which the depreciation of the currency is going on, while in countries with something like a stable currency, the home credit is still intact. In Germany, Austria, Hungary, Poland, etc., the credit system has broken down to such an extent, in view of the rapid depreciation of the currency, that nobody is willing to grant long-term loans. On the other hand, all saving of money in the respective currencies has lost all meaning, since the saved up money is, so to speak, melting away, within a few months, to a fraction. When dealing later on with Germany, we shall give statistics in this respect.

But the *international credit* has also broken down, because those countries in which the crisis is most advanced are not deemed worthy of credit. (Austria has, for years, begged for credit and is offering all sorts of guarantees, but all in vain).

The international private credit between the nationals of countries with a good and a depreciated currency has likewise broken down. American capitalists, for instance, cannot grant any money credit to Germany, because they do not know to what degree the mark will depreciate during the loan period and how many dollars they would receive back on the day of maturity. The German capitalist cannot contract any dollar-credit, for he is calculating in marks and does not know how many marks he would have to pay when the bill became mature.

8. *The standard of life of the proletariat is falling.* Capital is no longer able to secure to the working class a steady wage, let alone a rising one. The growing misery of the working class assumes various forms. In high currency countries it takes the form of widespread unemployment. This is shown in the subjoined Table 7.7:

TABLE 7.7 The most important dates as to unemployment (in percentages of the organised or insured working people respectively)

		Great Britain	Belgium	Holland	Denmark	Sweden	Norway
1921	January	8.2	19.3	16.5	19.7	20.2	10.5
	July	14.8	21.4	7.6	16.7	27.8	15.9
	August	13.2	21.7	7.3	17.7	26.8	14.7
	September	12.2	17.7	7.1	16.6	26.2	14.7
	October	12.8	13.6	7.0	18.3	27.2	15.1
	November	15.7	13.9	10.0	20.8	28.6	16.9
	December	16.2	11.4	17.0	25.2	–	18.3
1922	January	16.2	11.2	20.3	28.9	35.6	20.4
	February	15.7	10.1	21.3	33.1	32.1	21.3
	March	14.6	9.2	14.2	27.9	30.6	21.9
	April	14.4	8.9	11.4	24.0	28.6	21.3
	May	13.5	7.4	10.5	16.1	23.3	16.3
	June	12.7	–	9.5	13.2	21.5	15.2
	July	12.3	–	9.4	12.5	20.2	–
	August	12.0	–	9.3	11.1	–	–
		Canada	Germany	Switzerland	France	Sweden	USA
1921	January	13.1	4.5	34.652	40.000	20.2	–
	July	9.1	2.6	55.605	37.226	27.8	–
	August	8.7	2.2	63.182	–	26.8	–
	September	8.5	1.4	66.646	20.408	26.2	6.5 Mill.
	October	7.4	1.2	74.238	18.831	27.2	–
	November	11.1	1.4	80.692	16.158	28.6	3.5 Mill.*

TABLE 7.7 The most important dates as to unemployment (*cont.*)

		Canada	Germany	Switzerland	France	Sweden	USA
	December	15.1	1.6	88.957	9.602	–	–
1922	January	13.9	3.3	97.000	9.244	35.6	–
	February	10.6	2.7	99.541	8.474	32.1	–
	March	9.6	1.1	89.099	6.009	30.6	–
	April	10.4	0.9	80.799	5.207	28.6	–
	May	8.7	0.7	71.100	4.968	23.3	–
	June	5.3	0.6	59.456	6.027	21.5	–
	July	–	0.6	52.180	–	–	ca. 1.5 Mill.
	August	–	0.7	51.789	–	–	–

* Data of the Labour Office

In countries with depreciating currencies it is not so much unemployment as the steady rise of prices, with which the wage increases never keep pace. This fact is so well known that it is not necessary to give statistical data in support of it. We refer the readers to the second edition of our *Crisis of the capitalist world economy*[15] and our *International Annual*.[16] But also in wealthy Great Britain, the wages of large numbers of working people have been so considerably cut that their standard of life, even at full working time, has fallen far below that of the pre-war period. The civil service, the clerks, etc. are involved in this growing misery. The intellectual workers, who in their way of living and in their mental outlook used to regard the governing class as their model, are sinking to the level of the proletariat. Among the various strata of the possessing class, a sharp struggle is taking place for their respective share in the distribution of the diminished social product. This we find in nearly all capitalist countries. The peasantry, which in the period of capitalist ascendancy hardly ever appeared on the political scene as an independent class, has now become a factor of the first magnitude not only in Central and Eastern Europe, but also in the USA. They even attempt to create an international class organisation. In Poland, Hungary, Bulgaria, Yugoslavia, etc., they are engaged in struggle with the bourgeoisie for the conquest or preservation of political power. The connection between town and village is dissolving. The peasantry refuse to contribute,

---

15 [Varga 1922c].
16 [*Jahrbuch für Wirtschaft, Politik und Arbeiterbewegung*, Hamburg, 1923].

in the form of taxes, material assistance to the rebuilding of the bourgeois state. It is but the fear of the proletariat that keeps the rich peasant and the bourgeois together, while the middling and the poor peasant are making advances to the fighting proletariat.

The small bourgeoisie in the low-currency regions, the independent craftsman and the shopkeeper, are being rapidly impoverished, for, despite their large profits, in nominal money the value of their stock is getting smaller owing to the constant rise of prices of raw materials and goods. Their takings are never large enough to re-purchase from the manufacturer or wholesale dealer the commodities they had sold, since the new wholesale prices are much higher than the former retail prices.

Within the bourgeoisie itself a struggle is going on between the producers of raw materials (heavy industry) who, aided by high protective duties, strive to control the home market, and the producers of manufactured goods, who are suffering from the enormously high prices of the raw materials. The great landowners are putting themselves at the head of the rich peasants in order to press the government for lower taxation and higher protective duties. The diminishing production is forcing each group of society into the affray for a relatively larger share of it.

This war between the various groups of society is not a direct one, but is fought out on the economic and political field, it centres round price fixing, custom duties, and taxation. The decline of capitalism is reflected in the well-nigh hopeless state of national finance. There is, apart from Great Britain, no European country whose budget does not show a deficit. The measures taken for balancing the budgets, namely increased national loans and increased paper money, are themselves contributing to the decline of capitalism. No class is willing to make financial sacrifices for the preservation of the state.

This decline has as its consequence a chronic *political crisis*. In all bourgeois countries, government changes have become a usual occurrence. There is nowhere a stable government party. The sharp divisions among the possessing class are reflected in the splits among the parliamentary parties, and in their incapacity of formulating and pursuing a consistent and independent policy and the rapidly changing, short-lived coalitions. Only the need to keep down the revolted proletariat temporarily united the warring groups and Parties.

10. *Ideologically, the faith in the stability of capitalist class domination has been shaken.* We would overstep the limits of this paper if we tried to deal more fully with this subject. We should like to point out that the former unquestioned authority of capitalist state has disappeared, at least in those countries

where the decline has advanced farthest. Not only is the proletariat, to whom the rise of the Soviet Russia has been an inspiration, proving by its revolutionary struggles, by establishing organisations which try to acquire a certain part of state power, that it has lost faith in the stability of class domination, not only is the colonial population proving the same by rebellions, but also the bourgeoisie itself has lost confidence. The fact that the bourgeoisie has everywhere been compelled to arm itself, to form white guards, demonstrates the weakness of domination. The bourgeoisie cannot afford to leave the protection of its domination any longer to paid persons belonging to another class; it has no longer the possibility of arming a part of the proletariat and employ it for the purpose of keeping down the masses; the bourgeoisie must arm itself. This is not a sign of power, but of weakness of class domination, for the latter is strongest when but the lowest minimum of armed force is needed for preservation, when the mere threat of using state power is sufficient to quell all opposition. It is one more symptom of decline that the armed struggle of the bourgeoisie with the proletariat is going on without the state (March Action, Fascist fights, Spanish Officers' League, Awakening Hungary, etc.).

On the other hand, we see that the bourgeoisie pushes aside the state also economically and puts itself through its organisation the place of the state. There are great capitalist organisations (Stinnes, Reparation Agreement), which are taking over the function of the state.

It is undeniable that the bourgeoisie, aided by Social Democracy, succeeded after the great revolutionary crisis at the termination of the war to re-consolidate its domination. Capital is now at the point of removing the scenes from the political theatre, to eject the Social Democrats, after having done their duty, and to wrest from the proletariat all the revolutionary conquests. The decline of capitalism is, indeed, no automatic process, but a period of conflict, with alternating success and failures of the militant proletariat.

3   The Role of War under Capitalism

The Social Democrats, who hold that the present crisis of capitalism is only a temporary phase which will be followed by a period of growth, are also asserting that the present crisis is 'merely' the effect of the war. As far as their bare statement of fact goes, they are surely right. However, their error or their deliberate falsehood consists in the fact that they regard the war as something accidental, which has no necessary connection with capitalism, a thing that will not repeat itself. Consequently, they are pacifists, were enthused over Wilson, and pretend to believe in the eternal peace of the League of Nations.

But the war was not an incident brought about by wicked politicians; it was a contest prepared for decades by the bourgeoisie of the highly developed capitalist countries. For decades, millions of men were drilled for slaughter; a considerable portion of the annual produce of the nations was invested in warlike instruments. All pacifists and antimilitarist manifestations went for nothing; in vain did Norman Angell attempt to demonstrate that war was bad business. The bourgeoisie did not allow itself to be disturbed in its war preparations or to stop in its work of setting the war ablaze.

And today, four years after the termination of the war, militarism is stronger than ever. The number of men under arms is greater than before, and a still larger portion of the national product is being spent on war preparations. What ingenuousness to regard all this as an accident, as a misunderstanding!

Militarism and war are, as a matter of fact, necessary effects of capitalist development. The theory of Norman Angell, which forms the basis of the pacifist propaganda of Social Democracy, sprang from an antiquated stage of capitalism, and fitted the interest of British commercial capital. In the highly developed capitalist countries, however, it is not commercial capital that determines government policy, but the heavy industry (iron and steel and coal), in alliance with financial capital, and it is not their interest to measure their strength in free competition with their rivals on the world markets, not to create profitable markets, but to conquer and monopolise whole regions for safe investments of capital export.[17] This policy of capital is likewise impelled by the tendency of the rate of profit to sink.[18]

Owing to technical progress, the organic composition of capital is getting higher, the turnover of industrial capital slower, the rate of profit lower. To this a new factor was added in the last decades of the nineteenth century. The proletariat, by means of its organisations, was able to raise its standard of life. The 'historic moment', which 'co-determines the volume of the so-called elementary needs and the mode of their being satisfied',[19] is making for an increase in

---

17   The opposition between industrial and commercial capital manifested itself on the occasion of the Balfour note. The commercial capital of Great Britain was in favour of cancelling the Inter-Allied debts, in order to facilitate a settlement of the Reparation question and to restore Germany as a market for British trade. The British industry as represented by the FBI [Federation of British Industries] was, however, against cancellation of the debts and, open or tacitly, in favour of making Germany sink to the level of a colonial region of the *Entente*. The new custom tariff of the USA means likewise the complete victory of industrial capital over the commercial.

18   Marx 1959, pp. 49–69.

19   [Marx writes: 'On the other hand, the number and extent of his so-called necessary wants, as also the modes of satisfying them, are themselves the product of historical develop-

the rate of wages. Or, in other words, the necessary labour is extended at the expense of surplus labour. The rate of surplus value is falling.[20] At a given sum of variable capital, it effects an acceleration of the falling tendency of the profit rate.

Capital seeks to overcome the falling tendency of the profit rates by various means. Through organising cartels, trusts, mergers, at which centralised capital reduces the *faux frais* of the sphere of circulation and wrests a part of the profits from commercial capital and increases its own rate of profit through fixing monopoly prices at the expense of the other classes. Above all, however, through *exporting capital* to countries, where the necessary labour time is shorter, the rate of surplus value and profit higher. In order to render the exploitation of those regions possible, they must be made pliable to the demands of capital, that is, they must be subjugated. The capital of every highly developed industrial country, in order to retard the falling of the profit rate, is compelled to subdue large colonial regions, and it does not shrink from a war for the protection or conquest of new investment spheres, which are to be converted into monopoly markets.[21]

We can, of course, also imagine a capitalist 'peace of God'. One can imagine that the international organisation, the trustification of capital of the leading countries, will be so far advanced that all rivalry between the 'national' capitals would cease. Only in such a case would bourgeois pacifism have a prospect of realisation. But even in such a case the necessity would remain to keep down by armed forces the aspirations and movements of the oppressed colonial population for emancipation from the imperialist yoke. In reality, we are far from having reached such a point. The tendencies towards an international organisation are far weaker than the antagonism between the various national capitalist interests. And we cherish the hope that the present period of decline of capitalism would not last long enough to render such an universal trustification of capital possible.

The last war was, in any case, not an untoward accident, but the natural outcome of that antagonism, which had manifested itself in the preceding decade

---

ment, and depend therefore to a great extent on the degree of civilization of a country ...'. Marx 1954, p. 171].

20   [This passage is taken from Varga's report, *The Decline of Capitalism*, to the Fifth Congress of the Comintern of 1924].

21   We are thus in agreement with Rosa Luxemburg as to the fact that highly developed capitalism, in its political form as imperialism, leads necessarily to universal conflicts. But we differ as to its motivation. We do not believe that an accumulation or the continued existence of capital is impossible without an extension of the capitalist mode of production to hitherto non-capitalist strata.

of frenzied armaments. The world war, it is true, occasioned the present crisis-period, but it cannot be regarded as its cause which could have been obviated if a better policy had been pursued. And its result is historically considered this, that a dangerous competitor for world dominion, namely Germany, has been knocked out, and that the whole region to the East of the Rhine has been converted into a colony of the victorious *Entente*-capitalism. The world war was thus a symptom of the crisis of capitalism and resulted in the reproduction of the imperialist antagonism on a higher plain; only four imperialist powers facing each other in shining armour. And it is only the fear of the proletarian and colonial revolution which keeps them from jumping at each other's throat.

Finally, we should like to observe that it is altogether not true that the war is, economically, bad business for the leading capitalist circles, the industrial capital. There are statistical data (see *Table 7.8*) available showing, before all, American profits.[22]

TABLE 7.8 Total sum of the net profits of all joint-stock-companies in million dollars

1909	3,125
1910	3,360
1911	3,214
1912	3,832
1914	3,711
1915	5,187
1916	8,766
1917	10,730
1918	9,500*
1919	8,500*

* Estimates

Concerning mining and manufacturers in particular, there are the following data (see *Table 7.9*) available:

22 See Friday 1921, p. 15 and p. 17.

TABLE 7.9　Total net profit, in million dollars

1909	1,326
1910	1,436
1911	1,310
1916	5,026
1917	6,809*

* We have no more recent data

From this *Table 7.9* it is evident that industrial capital has increased its profits fivefold! No bad business, there! And similarly it must have gone on with British, French and German manufactures. As to their war profits we could not acquire any summary reports.

4　The Economic Types of the Period of Decline of Capitalism

We shall now attempt to bring some order into the chaos of the present period by grouping the various countries according to their position in the economic life of the world and to bring into prominence certain types. We can, of course, give here no more than a rough outline. The want of equilibrium in the economic life of the world, as indicated in *Chapter 2*, makes itself felt as a general insecurity, in the co-existence of various economic types side by side with one another.

First Group of Countries with Not Fully Developed Capitalism

Although capitalism has entered the period of decline, there are many countries where capitalism has not yet reached its full development. These are extra-European regions, in which the natural resources have not yet been fully exploited, and which are rich in agricultural and mining possibilities; regions in which during the war (owing to the dearth of shipping, the freights were very high, and the geographical advantages of European industry could not be taken advantage of), the rate of industrialisation was accelerated. These regions, despite their low level of capitalist development, have suffered heavily from the acute crisis; their infant industries are hardly able to withstand the onslaughts of the old manufacturing centres, aided as they are by the low freights prevailing at present; also their agriculture and the production of raw materials are unfavourably affected by the decrease of the purchasing power of Europe.

This group embraces countries which are on very diverse stages of economic and public development. We attempt therefore to divide them into subgroups. The division cannot, of course, be a clear-cut one; with some countries it is doubtful to which subgroup they may assigned.

a) *The oppressed colonial regions of Great Britain, France, Belgium, Italy, in Africa, inhabited by an uncivilised native population.*

These regions are at present on the lowest stage of economic evolution of all countries in the earth. Capital is still completely foreign colonial capital (plantations, commercial capital); the native population, hardly differentiated, is still on the lowest level of civilisation. Capitalism has here against itself a thin, very small population and very unfavourable natural conditions (absence of rain, tropical heat, sleeping sickness).

b) *The oppressed colonies, with a non-European population, but standing on higher level of civilisation.*

To this subgroup belong:

The Spanish, French, and British colonies of North Africa, the British colonies in Anterior Asia, India (British, French, Dutch), the Japanese and American colonies. These regions have a more or less developed capitalism, indigenous capitalism which is in the course of development a rapidly growing native capitalist class, a population that exhibits the beginnings of class divisions, as we generally find them under capitalism, but which are kept together in a certain unity by their common opposition to the oppressing colonial powers. The universal decline of capitalism, on the one hand, hinders their economic growth by making it difficult for them to find profitable markets for their raw materials; on the other hand, they made, during the war, much progress in industrialisation, and wrested from the colonial powers great economic and political liberties. Their emancipation will destroy one of the foundations of capitalist imperialism.

c) *The nominally independent colonial countries.*

In Asia China, Persia, Afghanistan, Turkey; in America Mexico and the various South-American republics. They are nominally independent, because they are not colonies of one single imperialist power, but bones of contention of the Four Great Powers. Their economic structure and cultural development are very diverse. In China there lives an old civilised people; in Brazil, partly quite civilised Indian tribes. Common to all is the possibility of a rapid capitalist development, having at their disposal large and unexploited natural resources; although there exists already in those regions an indigenous capitalism, foreign capitalists have still large scope for their activities there and for export of capital to those countries. It is these regions that the extra-European Imperialist Powers the USA and Japan have marked out for themselves, as soon European Capitalism has collapsed. That these regions have been little affected by the decline of the economic life of the capitalist world is shown by the favourable condition of their currency.[23]

d) *The group of British Settlement Colonies.*
Canada, South Africa, Australia, New Zealand.

Although nominally colonies, they are practically independent and all but fully developed capitalist countries. They all possess a broad agricultural basis, which renders them, in large measure, independent from the world markets. And this makes it possible for them to continue to develop a capitalism of their own. The decline of capitalism makes itself felt there through the decreasing demand for foodstuffs and raw materials on the world market and through the severe competition of the old industrial countries with the newly developed industries on the home markets. These countries will probably have recourse to protective duties and will move along the direction of establishing a self-sufficient economic life. Their essentially healthy economic condition is testified too by the fact that the last acute crisis affected them little. Their currency, budget, and credit organisation *have* remained unshaken.

---

23   TABLE 7.10   Average rates in July, in percentages of the dollar (at par) according to *Federal Reserve Bulletin* 1922, 8, 8, p. 1016

China: Shanghai tael	118.2
Id.: Hesar-Rania dollar	118.0
Id.: Hongkong dollar	121.3
Argentine (peso, gold)	84.8
Brazil (milreis)	42.3
Chile (peso, paper)	64.7
Mexico	97.3
Cuba	99.8
Uruguay	78.7

Second Group of Countries with Fully Developed and Essentially Intact Capitalism

This group embraces the leading imperialist countries of our time. Some of them are already strongly touched by the decline. On the whole, however, their capitalism is still intact, and as their money and credit system is still healthy and their accumulation of capital continues, their faith in the continued existence of the present system is still strong. As the fate of capitalism is to be decided in these countries, it is necessary to deal with each of them separately.

a) *Japan*

This country has grown within a few decades to a fully developed capitalist, imperialist state with all the features that characterise such a stage – militarism, export of capital, colonial expansion. The social structure has, however, remained behind the revolution of industrial life. The social and legal conditions still exhibit a strongly feudal character, so that the creation of those political conditions which are the proper forms of capitalism, namely, equality before the law, political democracy, popular parliament, etc., are regarded as progress. The country has been strongly affected by the decline and by the acute crisis, but the mechanism of production has remained intact, accumulation continues, the money and credit system has remained in a healthy condition, though some speculating firms have gone bankrupt.[24]

Owing to its geographical contiguity to the still unexploited gigantic territories of China and its outer-countries (Manchuria, Mongolia), owing, further, to its position between the healthiest capitalist parts of the world economy, USA, Canada, Australia, it has a prospect of remaining more or less untouched by the rapid decay of Central Europe.

b) *The United States of America*

The USA grew during the war to a fully developed imperialist power of the first rank. Its productive mechanism strongly increased; it turned from an agricultural country into an industrial country, from a capital-importing country into a capital-exporting country, from a debtor country to a creditor country.

It is differentiated from the European imperialist countries, above all, by the fact that its agricultural basis is much larger; it is able not only to supply from its own soil its necessary foodstuffs, but to be the greatest exporter

---

24 During the whole of the period since the termination of the war, the Japanese Yen stood at par, the fluctuations did not amount to more than 5 percent above or below par.

of wheat, maize and cotton. It finds itself in the peculiar position that it must export larger quantities, both agricultural and industrial, of its productive capacity.[25]

It is exactly for this reason that it has been strongly affected by the decline of capitalism after having had in the last decade surplus export of about 22 billion dollars (approximately 90 billion gold marks), after having cleared its foreign debts by re-purchasing its bonds. After having loaned to the Allies more than 11 billion dollars, after having come into possession of 40 percent of total available gold of the world, the USA is facing the following problem: What equivalent can the world and, above all, impoverished Europe give for the supply of American goods? And as, under capitalism, all irregularities in the international exchanges find their expression in the rates of currencies, the question can be thus formulated: How are American exports possible in the face of the enormous depreciation of the continental European currencies? And this question is closely connected to the question of interest and sinking fund payments of the Allied debts. In which form could Great Britain, France, Italy, etc. pay interest and sinking funds to America, without sending its goods? And this to a country like the USA, where six million workmen were unemployed for months and months, because of the glut of goods, for which she cannot find foreign markets?

Also the severance of the agricultural and industrial production may be noticed in the USA. With the relative overproduction of nearly all commodities in 1920–1, the prices of the agricultural products fell even in a larger measure than those of the industrial products, for owing to the big trusts planfully restricting industrial production, prices could be somehow maintained.[26] The result was that the farmers got poorer and their purchasing power considerably decreased, and this impacted, of course, unfavourably on manufacturers. This was the cause of the severe struggle between farmers and the trustified financial-industrial capital and railway capital. (Farmer Block in the Senate, Non-partisan League).

---

25 TABLE 7.11 US surplus exports in the last decade in million dollars

1913	1914	1915	1916	1917	1918	1919	1920	1921	Total in 9 years
737	323	1,779	3,109	3,281	3,118	4,016	2,949	1,917	21,309

26 This matter is dealt with more fully in my *Krise der kapitalistischen Weltwirtschaft*, second edition.

The United States are now attempting to allay the crisis in two ways: (1) through securing the home markets. The new custom tariff brings very high protective duties to agriculture as also to manufacture. The home markets should be entirely handed over to home capital.[27] (2) Through exports of capital. The surplus is, above all, to be invested in the still underdeveloped regions of South America, in China, and in the British Overseas Dominions (Canada is economically already more closely connected with the USA than with Great Britain).

The new custom tariff is anti-European. It is an attempt to disconnect the States from declining Europe, an attempt that has little prospect of success, but which, at any rate, dooms Europe to progressive paralysis. Only the pro-European policy, the cancelling of the Allied debts, granting of large credits to Continental Europe, that is, the transfer of a part of the American overdeveloped productive mechanism to impoverished Europe, may perhaps be a means of creating, before long, a new economic equilibrium, if the proletarian revolution will give capitalism the necessary time for it.

c) *Great Britain and the neutral European Countries*
A third group is formed by Great Britain and the neutral European states. The productive mechanism and the money and credit system of those countries are, on the whole, intact. As they – and particularly Great Britain, Scandinavia and Switzerland – do not possess such abundant resources of agriculture and raw materials as the USA, they depend much more on the world markets than the latter. A much larger percentage of their industrial production must be exported, in order to avert chronic unemployment and to be able to import large quantities of foodstuffs and raw materials from abroad. While capitalism in these countries is, more or less, intact, the prevailing severe unemployment[28] nevertheless shows that, owing to the disappearance of the former equilibrium, the decline has also set in there. And as these countries do not possess any broad agricultural basis which might enable them even to attempt to establish a self-sufficient economic system of their own, and, moreover, as the colonial possessions of Great Britain are now being threatened by the emancipation movement in India, Anterior Asia and Africa, it may be assumed that this group of countries, despite the momentary improvement of business, will be drawn into the decline in a more rapid and stronger manner than the extra-European countries.

---

27   The new tariff means the full triumph of productive capital (agricultural and manufacturing) over commercial and money capital.
28   Cf. the table of unemployment.

As to social conditions, the decline in Great Britain is less noticeable than in America. The fact that there exists in Great Britain practically no independent peasantry makes the proletariat directly confront a bourgeoisie which is essentially unified, except for a certain opposition of interests between commercial and banking capital on the one hand, and manufacturing capital on the other hand, the former advocating some sacrifices with a view to the reconstruction of Europe, the latter fearing a reassertion of German competition, but this opposition of interests among the two sections of the bourgeoisie can hardly be spoken of as a struggle. The proletariat, however, is still on the way to a revolutionary conception of the situation, and is all but completely in the hands of trade-union leaders who are co-operating with the capitalists.

Third Group of Countries in Which the Decay of Capitalism Is Evident

In this group we put all bourgeois countries of Continental Europe which took part in the war. The common feature of all these countries is a large *decrease in production* as compared with the pre-war period, a decrease or complete stoppage of accumulation, or even a dis-accumulation (reproduction on a shrinking scale); the money and credit system more or less shaken; severe depreciation of the currency, violent fluctuations of exchange, disordered budgets, the connection between agriculture and manufactures loosened. In the majority of these countries the authority of the state is considerably shaken; the bourgeoisie itself takes up arms for the defence of its class domination (Orgesch, Fascists, Awakening Magyars, etc.). The class antagonism grows in intensity; there exist neither stable government parties nor stable governments. The parties are split into innumerable fractions and factions, and there is no end to ministerial crises.

These symptoms of decline are showing themselves in the various countries in different degrees. It is just this diversity from land to land, the rapid change of conditions, the general instability of things, which is characteristic of this group of countries. For this reason it is impossible within the narrow limits of our essay to give more than a general outline.

a) *The 'Victorious Countries', France, Italy and Belgium*
France. The economic conditions of France are far more favourable than those of Great Britain, as they rest on a broader agriculture basis; with the normal harvest, France is able to feed herself. The agricultural character of the country renders it somewhat indifferent to the happenings on the world markets. On the other hand, a part of the mechanism of production has not yet been restored, and the human factors of production have been diminished by

war losses and by the gigantic military apparatus. The national finances are in a wretched condition, the rate of the franc has fallen to 40 percent below its gold par.

On the other hand, through the re-conquest of Alsace-Lorraine, France has been turned into an export country of the heavy industry.

This fact, in conjunction with its extensive colonial possessions, its militarism and nationalism, makes France, despite the disordered national finances and currency, along with the USA, Great Britain and Japan, one of the leading imperialist powers. France has extended its influence over nearly the whole of bourgeois Europe east of the Rhine. She threatens Germany through the reparations demands. She controls Poland, Czechoslovakia, Hungary and the little Entente through its investments of capital and military alliances; she seeks to transform into colonial regions all the lands east of the Rhine, aye, even Angora-Turkey and Anterior Asia, all those regions which in consequence of the war have sunk economically to the level of colonies.

However, the economic substructure of France, the small and diminishing population, the feebly developed and war-damaged mechanism of production, which, despite all appearances of large accumulations of money-capital, the disordered currency and the bad condition of the national finances, is by no means strong enough to bear for any length of time such an immensely ambitious superstructure. The contradiction between the feebly developed economic foundations and the overdeveloped diplomatic and military superstructure will, before long, lead to a great collapse (possibly in consequence of a war) and will finally destroy the false appearances of French prosperity.

In *Italy*, the decline of capitalism is more advanced. Continual rises in most of the manufactures, much unemployment, the lire 20 percent of gold par, the national finances disordered, the authority of the state in decay, the class struggle fought out with armed force outside the sphere of the state. The decline is so far advanced that the country has got hardly anything out of the economic improvement of the last year.

b)   *Fourth Group: The Manufacturing Countries of Central Europe in Which the Decline Is Most Advanced*

To this group we should assign four countries – Germany, Austria, Poland and Czechoslovakia.

The first three exhibit the characteristics of decay in their fullest development. Production has considerably diminished, the material mechanism of production worn out, the proletariat underfed, its standard of life continually sinking. The curve of production completely dependent on the fluctuations of the currency: at falling rates, large foreign orders, and the appearances of brisk trade, but as soon as the rates of their currencies and the prices approach those of the world market, there is a slackening of business. As their cost of production is relatively higher (because of their inferior and less fully exploited productive mechanism) than that of the countries of group II, and as each article of the same quality contains more labour time than that produced by group II, they can only compete on the world markets by driving down the standard of life of the proletariat owing to the rise in money-wages always lagging far behind the rise in prices of the necessaries.

The volume of production is considerably smaller than before the war and is not equal to the daily needs. Accumulation of capital has come to a standstill.[29] Despite the enormously increased paper money sales, and paper profits, it is shown that the small trader is not able to re-stock his shop with the takings of his sales, or the craftsman to buy new materials for the continuation of his work, the big manufacturer, who uses foreign raw materials, to procure the same quantity of new raw materials. The industrial mechanism is starved, production is shrinking.

The currency is being rapidly depreciated (see *Table 7.12*).

TABLE 7.12 For an English pound sterling the following rates were quoted in London

	At par	End of 1920	End of 1921	22 Sept 1922
German mark	20.43	258	778	6,300
Austrian crown	24.02	1,500	11,000	335,000
Polish mark	20.43	2,250	12,000	35,000

Still more disturbing is the effect of the violent fluctuations which, in the case of the German mark in the summer 1922, amounted to 50 percent of the rate of exchange.

The home currency loses for this reason its function as a measure of prices as well as a medium of circulation. The business world makes its calculations in foreign 'precious currencies'. And as the available stock of foreign money is being cornered, the mass of the circulation paper money is mounting up to fantastic proportions. The German issuing bank throws daily more than three billions new paper money into circulation, the Austrian bank perhaps 50 billions.

---

29 Within the last twelve months, the total amount of the German saving bank deposits rose by ten percent, but their value in gold mark fell to a tenth part.

The credit system has broken down, nobody is willing to grant long-term loans in the home currency, since at the time when repayment will be due, the purchasing power of the money may have sunk to a fraction. The rates of interest reach fantastic heights. An increasingly larger part of real value, house and land properties are being alienated, that is, transferred to foreign capitalists. The whole region sinks, economically and politically, to the level of a colony of the Allied powers.

The national finances have collapsed. The continued and rapid rise in prices shatters all attempts to draw up real budgets. The floating debt is soaring upwards; the governments are unable to contract any foreign or home loans.

The village severs its connection with the town. While the town is starving, the agricultural production is being restricted.[30]

In the town, the officials, clerks, intellectuals, annuity holders, pensioners, are sinking to the level of the proletariat. The general decay manifests itself in the internecine struggle of the various sections, in the total instability of the political conditions, in the bitter feeling of the labouring classes.

In *Austria*, the decay is most advanced. In Germany, it is being accelerated by the reparation burdens. The position of *Poland* is relatively best, since she has a broader agricultural basis and is free from war indemnities and reparation payments. But, as in the case of France, Poland is being driven in the direction of complete decomposition by its militarism, its undeveloped and disordered economic substructure being in contradiction with its far-flung diplomatic superstructure.

Czechoslovakia occupies a particular position; its economic condition being much healthier than that of all neighbours. And this is the reason, as paradoxical as it may appear, why the country cannot emerge from the acute crisis. Although its currency has fallen to one-tenth of gold par, it is for all its neighbours an inaccessibly high currency. And as Czechoslovakia is a highly developed manufacturing country which must export a considerable percentage products (the industrial mechanism of Czechoslovakia was established for the needs of the 60 million population of the old Austro-Hungarian Empire), the country is suffering from an acute crisis, from which she cannot emerge, unless she participates in the general decline of its neighbouring countries.

---

30 Despite the great want of foodstuffs, the intensive cultivation of the land is decreasing. The area of fallow ground in 1921 was larger by 19.4 percent than in 1913, in the case of pastures by 15 percent, of arable land by 4.1 percent (760,269 hectare). These developments continued into the year 1922.

c) *The smaller countries and border states in Eastern Europe*
This group contains countries of a very different economic character. All of them are strongly drawn into the decline of capitalism; but their broader agricultural basis gives them greater power of resistance than the Central European countries possess. Their money system is disordered,[31] the national finances are bad, the means of production passing more and more into the hands of foreign capitalists.

It would go beyond the limits of this paper to deal with each of these countries separately. The decay is more advanced in the defeated countries – Hungary and Bulgaria – than in the others. Some of these countries receive economic assistance from the imperialist states by their investing capital there, so, above all, Greece from Great Britain.

While the economic decay of these countries is not as conspicuous as that of the manufacturing countries of Central Europe, their social decay is all the more evident; in Bulgaria, Hungary, Yugoslavia, hard contests between the various sections of the ruling classes; in Greece revolution, everywhere continual government and party crises. It appears that these countries, though in a relatively better economic condition, are nearer a proletarian revolution than those of Central Europe, because the dominant classes are not united in their resistance.

d) *The group of Soviet countries*
The existence of Soviet State is the most striking proof of the decline of capitalism. Looking at the world at large, the capitalist class is still stronger than the proletariat, and this fact compelled isolated proletarian Russia to make serious concessions to capitalism in order to accelerate the economic reconstruction of

---

31 TABLE 7.13 The following rates were quoted in London for £1

	At par	End of 1920	End of 1921	22 Sept 1922
Hungary	24.2	–	2,550	11,00
Romania	25.22	276	550	680
Yugoslavia	25.22	127	272	300
Bulgaria	25.22	277	590	800
Greece	25.22	47.5	99	196
Latvia	25.32	–	1,000	1,160*
Finland	25.22	120	221	202

* August 1922.

Russia. On the other hand, the capitalist world, with all its hatred of Bolshevism, has shown itself incapable of destroying Soviet Russia. The deep-seated antagonism of interests of the four imperialist great powers, which make them continually reel on the brink of war; the fear of the revolutionary power of the proletariat in their respective countries, which, for all the sinister doings of the social-patriotic traitors, is on the side of proletarian Russia (in times of danger even the social traitors acknowledge that the collapse of Soviet Russia would be the signal for the destruction of the proletariat in all capitalist countries), definitely preclude all military intervention.

While the decline of capitalism is proceeding apace, the new governmental type, the Soviet power, so full of promise for the future, is growing in strength. It expands geographically, radiating from Central Russia, it is spreading to the coasts of the Black Sea, the Caspian Sea, and across Asia to the Pacific Ocean, to the borderlands of India and China. Throughout Asia its influence is felt as the victorious champion against imperialism.

Soviet Russia is consolidating herself economically. While the depreciation of the currency in Central Europe is going on without interruption, the Soviet rouble is stabilised. While the disorder of the national finances is assuming there unheard of proportions, Soviet Russia is on the point of balancing its budget. While in Central Europe the estrangement between agriculture and manufacture is still advancing, the relations between the two economic factors in Soviet Russia are being restored.

Soviet Russia is also consolidating socially. The bourgeoisie as a class has disappeared. The relations between the peasantry and the Soviet are improving; all rebellions and guerrillas have ceased. Government power is stronger than anywhere in Europe. And in the same measure as Russia is consolidating its forces and is able to overcome difficulties and to raise the level of the working class, we see in the other countries of Continental Europe a growing resistance of the proletarian masses (a) to the continuation of the capitalist order of society, which, in its decline, dooms them to a continually advancing wretchedness, and (b) to any sacrifices on behalf of a restoration of capitalism. In this way Soviet Russia, from the mere fact of its existence and security, is a mighty factor in the process of the decline of capitalism.

5 The Economic Development in the Last Year

At the time of the Third Congress of the Communist International in July 1921, the first phase of the crisis reached its culmination. It was even then possible to foretell that a certain economic improvement was imminent. As a matter of fact, the industrial conditions have, on the whole, improved, and it appears that this improvement has not yet reached its zenith.

It must be observed, however, that with regard to the disorder of the world economy this improvement could not spread in equal measure to all countries. Most pronounced it is in the countries of group I and II, while some of the countries more affected by the decline, i.e. Italy, Czechoslovakia, Hungary, have been unable to overcome the crisis. The disturbance of the equilibrium of the world economy has, for this reason, by no means diminished. The chasm fixed between the countries of group I and II (that is, between the still growing or the still intact capitalist countries on the one hand, and the countries of group III, that is, those which are strongly involved in the decline on the other) is today perhaps greater than a year ago. This is, at least, the inference which one may draw from the further severe drop of the currencies of group III.

It is of course impossible to include all countries in our inquiry. To find out and fix the economic condition of any country for so short a period depends on the available statistical material, unless we mean to be satisfied with mechanically stringing together various trade reports. This consideration determined the selection of countries. Therefore it is, unfortunately, impossible to give details concerning the countries of group I, since there are no data or only older statistics available. On the whole it may be stated that the trade situation of those countries improved, owing in the first place to the rise of prices of agricultural produce.

Group II

a) USA

Trade in the USA, the leading capitalist great power, has decidedly improved in the last year. This may be safely stated, although the aspect as a whole is somewhat obscured by the gigantic strikes of the miners and railwaymen. As a guide to the movement of trade we take the most important data of the *Business Indicator*, of the official *Survey of Current Business*. The data of 1913 are taken as equal to 100, the index numbers show these changes in percent (see Table 7.14).

TABLE 7.14 US industrial production index

	1920	1921	1921 July	1921 Aug	1921 Sept	1921 Oct	1921 Nov	1921 Dec
Production of pig iron	119	54	34	37	38	49	55	64
Production of steel	135	66	36	52	53	73	75	65
Production of copper	99	39	17	21	21	24	22	18
Production of bituminous coal	116	85	76	87	88	110	90	77
Production of anthracite	97	95	92	94	93	99	90	78
Production of petroleum	181	189	194	198	176	172	183	203
Consumption of wool	118	135	132	145	155	166	163	159
Consumption of cotton	117	85	85	97	101	103	109	106
Foreign trade: Imports	294	140	119	130	120	126	141	159
Foreign trade: Exports	331	181	157	177	157	166	142	143
Wholesale trade index of all goods	226	147	141	142	141	142	141	140
Motor cars, in 1,000(*)	183	139	–	–	–	–	–	–

	1921 Jan	1921 Feb	1921 Mar	1921 April	1921 May	1921 June	1921 July
Production of pig iron	64	64	79	81	90	92	–
Production of steel	72	79	107	111	123	119	–
Production of copper	25	37	61	75	87	92	–
Production of bituminous coal	94	103	126	strike	strike	40	–
Production of anthracite	82	89	115	strike	strike	51	–
Production of petroleum	208	197	225	217	224	219	–
Consumption of wool	153	158	176	130	–	–	–
Consumption of cotton	109	98	108	93	103	105	–
Foreign trade: imports	145	144	171	145	170	172	–
Foreign trade: exports	135	121	156	150	149	156	–
Wholesale trade index of all goods	138	142	141	143	148	150	–
Motor cars, in 1,000(*)	91	173	122	214	225	288	–

(*) Monthly average

These figures are a safer indication of the improvement of trade, particularly if one also takes into account the extraordinarily brisk building activity, the excellent trade in locomotives and agricultural machinery. The improvement advanced in the past months, for which no statistical percentages are available. The bank rate is now equal to that of the pre-war period. The number of unemployed, which at the time of the culmination of the crisis amounted to 5–6 million, has sunk to the 'normal' level. In many industries, it is even complained that there is a shortage of 'hands'. Owing to the influx of working people into the building trades, the Steel Trust voluntarily raised the wages of 200,000 workers by 20 percent from 1 September 1922, a sure sign of improving trade. Also the prices show a rising tendency, as in normal times. The declining exports and the rising prices prove that the home market has thoroughly improved. It is the rise in prices of agricultural produce and the good harvest which have caused the industrial improvement. It demonstrates the inherent power of American capitalism, but by no means the improvement of the general condition of the world.

b)   *Japan*
Our information concerning the economic condition of Japan is not as specified as that of the USA. The general aspect of things Japanese, as described in the reports of English trade journals, is that of a crisis, with a slight tendency to improvement. The price index is stable; for the year 1922 the numbers are 206, 205, 200, 197, 194, 197, 201. The rate of the yen is likewise stable, a few percent below the dollar at par, with a falling tendency, probably the effect of a strongly unfavourable balance of foreign trade.

c)   *Great Britain*
The industrial condition of Great Britain has not yet emerged from the crisis. But a certain improvement is noticeable. The subjoined table gives the most important data:

TABLE 7.15 British industrial production statistics

Monthly data	1913(*)	1920(*)	1921(*)	1921 July	1921 Aug	1921 Sept	1921 Oct	1921 Nov
Coal in million tons	24	19.1	13.7	15.2	16.6	16.5	21.1·	17.9
Pig iron 1,000 tons	855	670	218	strike	strike	158	236	272
Steel 1,000 tons	639	756	302	strike	439	429	405	444
% of unemployed among all insured	–	–	–	14.8	13.2	12.2	12.8	15.7
Wholesale prices index (*Economist*) 1914 = 100	–	–	305 (June)	186	188	192	178	174
Rate of £ in dollars	–	–	–	3.57	–	–	3.87	3.97
Exports in million £	–	–	–	52.5	61.3	63.8	72.6	72.7
Imports in million £	–	–	–	80.8	88.6	87.1	84.7	89.2

	1922 Jan	1922 Feb	1922 March	1922 April	1922 May	1922 June	1922 July	1922 Dec
Coal in million tons	17.7	19.8	19.9	29.9(·)	19.1	15.8	23.2(·)	18.1
Pig iron 1,000 tons	228	300	330	394	408	369	399	412
Steel 1,000 tons	328	415	549	404	462	400	473	521
% of unemployed among all insured	16.2	15.2	14.6	14.4	13.5	12.7	12.3	12.0
Wholesale prices index (*Economist*) 1914 = 100	167	166	167	167	170	171	171	166
Rate of £ in dollars	4.22	4.36	4.38	4.41	4.44	4.45	4.45	4.45
Exports in million £	71.6	68.8	74.7	64.7	67	60.9	68.7	70.0
Imports in million £	76.5	69.4	87.9	80.7	88.8	84.3	81.8	83.0

(*) Annual average
(·) Five weeks

These figures indicate a certain improvement in the production of the heavy industry. Also the considerable decrease in the numbers of unemployed in the course of the year speaks for the improvement of the trade conditions. These figures, however, must not be construed in a too optimistic sense. A decrease in unemployment always take place in the summer months. Another consideration is that the protracted miners' strike in the USA brought temporarily a certain improvement in the coal trade of Great Britain. If we further consider that the textile industry of Lancashire has, from 30 September, reduced the weekly working time by 27 percent, that in the textile industry unemployment has increased, then we must describe the economic condition of Great Britain as being still involved in the crisis. A considerable improvement has taken place in the financial position. The sterling rate, measured by the dollar, has risen from 3.54 to 4.45. The bank rate is 3 percent. The budget is balanced. The income tax has been reduced by 1 sh. in the pound.

Group III

In the group of the continental European countries, where the decline is most advanced, the conditions are extraordinarily variegated and contradictory. While some countries appear to have overcome the crisis (France, Finland), there are others (Italy and notably Czechoslovakia) which have not emerged yet from the crisis. Again while some (Germany and Austria), which during the acute crisis have gone through a fictitious prosperity, will in all probability soon have to face an acute crisis. We shall attempt to illustrate this diversity of conditions by statistical figures. Unfortunately, there is here less statistical material available than in the English speaking countries.

a) *The victorious countries: France*

Although the economic life of France has not yet overcome the crisis, there has been a considerable improvement. This is shown, above all, by the curve of unemployment. The number of the relieved unemployed has very considerably decreased, it is even smaller than in the pre-war period.

Below (see *Table 7.16*) is an attempt to illustrate the condition in France by a statistical table, the most important data of which are taken from the *Federal Reserve Bulletins*.

TABLE 7.16 French industrial production statistics

	1913 (*)	1920 (*)	1921 (*)	1921 July	1921 Aug	1921 Sept	1921 Oct	1921 Nov	1921 Dec
Coal output in 1,000 tons	3,400	2,100	2,400	2,330	2,450	2,490	2,500	2,570	2,703
Coal imports in 1,000 tons	1,558	2,005	1,472	660	1,065	1,874	1,301	3,291	2,895
Iron production in 1,000 tons	439(·)	286	280	267	255	244	256	295	301
Steel production in 1,000 tons	391(·)	254	255	223	232	236	260	277	302
Unemployed 1,000	–	40	–	37	–	20	19	16	10
Exports 1,000 tons	1,840	1,871	1,333	1,194	1,035	1,172	1,252	1,515	2,507
Imports 1,000 tons	3,685	4,211	3,165	2,164	2,543	3,993	2,809	5,161	5,167
Exports in million francs	573	2,241	1,796	1,563	1,725	1,775	1,759	1,748	2,182
Imports in million francs	701	4,159	1,962	1,468	1,737	2,225	2,227	2,333	3,154
Wholesale prices index	100	510	345	330	–	–	331	332	326
Rate of the franc in New York	19.30	7.00	7.50	7.80	7.80	7.30	7.30	7.20	7.89
Banknote circulation in billion	5.6	38	39.4	36.9	36.8	37.1	37.2	36.3	36.5

	1922 Jan	1922 Feb	1922 March	1922 April	1922 May	1922 June	1922 July	1922 Aug
Coal output in 1,000 tons	2,669	2,501	2,764	2,479	–	–	2,525	–
Coal imports in 1,000 tons	1,676	2,153	2,081	1,538	2,058	–	–	–
Iron production in 1,000 tons	312	323	386	383	442	416	428	445
Steel production in 1,000 tons	315	317	367	324	364	–	360	390
Unemployed 1,000	9	8	7	–	5	5	6	–
Exports 1,000 tons	1,554	1,520	1,570	1,794	1,538	1,799	1,936	–
Imports 1,000 tons	3,396	4,126	4,434	3,787	4,396	4,307	4,223	–
Exports in million francs	1,639	1,853	1,877	1,963	1,869	1,963	1,887	–
Imports in million francs	1,488	1,847	1,932	1,744	1,810	1,851	1,996	–
Wholesale prices index	314	306	307	314	317	325	325	–
Rate of the franc in New York	8.16	8.73	9.00	9.20	8.24	9.76	8.24	7.70
Banknote circulation in billion	36.4	36.2	35.5	35.8	36.0	36.0	36.4	–

(*) Monthly average
(·) Without Lorraine

These figures show that trade has undoubtedly improved. The level of prices is stable, with a tendency to rise. The note circulation has somewhat decreased. The fluctuations of the franc are, it is true, still very considerable, but the rate does not show a tendency towards deterioration.

But also here it must be observed that we must guard against overestimating the improvement. The production of iron and steel has hardly surpassed that of the pre-war period, in spite of the incorporation of Lorraine and despite the fact that the American miners' strike has diverted British competition from the French market. The productive capacity has only been exploited to the extent of one third. The causes of this are the want of coke and coke coal, deficient organisation, and the absence of connections with the world markets. The harvest was bad, the necessity for importing foodstuffs will result in an unfavourable balance of trade, and will press upon the rate of the franc. As far as the decrease of unemployment is concerned, we must not forget the enormous decrease in the population in consequence of the war.

The weakest point of French economic life is after all to be found in the condition of the national finances. France enters all expenditure that originated in the war into a separate account which should be balanced by the Reparation payments. In the past financial year, more than 16 billion francs were covered in this way. There was besides that a deficit of several billions in the ordinary budget. For the financial year 1923, the ordinary budget has been balanced by transferring its deficit of four billion to the 'Reparation account' under the pretext that they represent the interest of the national debt of 80 billion which France had contracted and advanced to Germany in the shape of compensation payments to those who have suffered financially from the war. Then there is the debt of France to the USA, amounting at the present rate to 40 billion, to Great Britain about 30 billion francs, with no provision in the budget for payment of interest and sinking fund. And it is only the extraordinary thrift of the French petty bourgeois and peasant and their unflinching willingness to put again their savings[32] at the disposal of their bankrupt state which render it possible for their country to go along without issuing paper money and to avert the collapse of the currency. But this cannot last forever. The new reparation policy of France, setting much store by deliveries in kind, is the effect of this consideration. Only in this way France recovers some of its losses, for until now she has got, except the reparation coal, precious little out of Germany.

---

32   According to the *Federal Reserve Bulletin* of July 1922, the savings of the French people were: in 1919, 27 billion francs; in 1920, 47 billion francs; in 1921, 39 billion francs. [*Federal Reserve Bulletin* 1922, 8, 7, p. 809].

Italy

The economic condition of Italy in the interval between the two Congresses has become worse rather than better. We have, unfortunately, few data in support of this statement, for the Italian statistics are deficient. But some figures may be adduced:

TABLE 7.17 Italian economics statistics

	Number of unemployed	Bachi index of wholesale prices	Rate of the lire in New York, par 19.30	Circulation of notes in billions
1921 July	413,000	520	–	17.9
1921 October	455,000	599	4.12	18.3
1922 January	540,000	577	4.37	18.8
1922 February	600,000	562	4.91	18.2
1922 April	513,000	527	4.96	18.2
1922 May	–	527	5.26	17.7
1922 June	–	–	4.57	17.2
1922 July	–	–	4.96	17.6

Of the manufactures of Italy which saw a great development during the war, like iron and steel, shipbuilding, chemical industries, some are now involved in the crisis. The financial condition of the country by no means improves; the currency has sunk to about one fourth of its gold value. The nation is torn by Party and class struggles.

b) *The industrial countries of Central Europe*

From this group of countries we shall pick out two of them which are unlike one another, Germany and Czechoslovakia.

A severe controversy is raging round the question of the economic condition of Germany. While the Germans themselves have a very unfavourable opinion of their economic condition, the Entente experts are judging it as very favourable. The former are basing their opinion on the symptoms of the impoverishment of Germany, sinking of the standard of life, collapse of the mark, state bankruptcy, while the others are supporting their opinion by the fact of full employment of labour, the absence of unemployment. In this controversy we are on the side of the German opinion. Although the German workmen have been fully employed, we think the economic condition of Germany to be catastrophically bad.

We begin, above all, with the production. The harvest of this year has been very bad. This is no mere accident, but the result of the decreased intensity of agricultural production; fallow-ground and pastures increase, the yield per hectare decreases.

TABLE 7.18 Average production per head in Germany according to official data

Corn (exclusive seed)		Meat in Prussia	
1913–14	256 kg	1913	46.15 kg
1921–22	141 kg	1921	28.52 kg

According to the figures given in *Wirtschaft und Statistik*,[33] the officially supervised killing of cattle for butchers' meat amounted in the first six months of 1922 to only 45 percent of that in the parallel period of the year 1913.

Also in all other spheres of production and consumption we meet with the same condition of things. The coal output does not increase despite all efforts. For the German industry there remains, after deducting the coal for reparation and means of locomotion, only a fraction of that of the pre-war period. As to iron and steel, no statistics are published.

Reducing the figures of the foreign trade capital investments and saving bank deposits,[34] the total sum of money in circulation,[35] the dividends, etc.

---

33 ['Saaten- und Erntestand im Deutsche Reich Anfang September 1922', *Wirtschaft und Statistik*, 1922, 2, 17: 560–2].

34 The Deutsche Bank, in its balance-sheets, converts the paper mark sums into gold marks according to the prevailing dollar rate. This reduction gives the following result:

TABLE 7.19 Exchange rate of the paper mark

	1921	1921 in billions	1913
	Paper	Goldmark	Goldmark
Total turn-over	2,125	85	125
Deposits	38.6	0.88	1.58
Credits	9.7	0.22	0.86
Total dividend, in million	–	1.48	25

to gold marks or foreign currency, there is evidently a continued shrinking of German economic life. The takings from the sales suffice only for carrying on the business on a reduced scale. Every merchant, every tradesman, every big employer who has to buy raw materials becomes familiar with this fact. No accumulation takes place; there is an absolute want of capital, and this has resulted in a rise in the bank rate to 8 percent, in reality, a double or triple rate of interest is being paid. Germany is becoming rapidly impoverished.

The apparent paradox of full employment of labour and rapid impoverishment finds its explanation in the following circumstances:
1. A considerable portion of the German produce leaves the country, without equivalent, as reparation by virtue of the Versailles Treaty.
2. The mechanism of production is larger than the actual production, so that the mere upkeep of the redundant part requires much labour power.
3. The output is relatively inconsiderable, owing to underfeeding as well as to social and political disaffection.

It must also be considered that the Deutsche Bank absorbed a number of great and middling banks and that its share capital in 1913 was only 200 million, at present it amounts to nominally 400 millions.

35 In the *Manchester Guardian Commercial* of 3 August 1922, we find the following interesting statistics concerning Germany:

TABLE 7.20 German monetary statistics

	Note circulation in million marks	Rate of British pound	Total value of circulation notes in million British pound
End of 1918	32.8	40	820
End of 1919	49.8	180	270
End of 1920	81.0	250	320
End of 1921	122.2	775	158
January 1922	128.6	860	134
February 1922	128.2	975	131
March 1922	139.6	1,465	98
April 1922	149.8	1,250	120
May 1922	161.6	1,250	129
June 1922	178.0	1,600	110
July 1922	190.0	2,500	76

This continued in August and September 1922 in increasing degree, until it came to a catastrophic stringency of money-tokens in September.

4. The cost of the factor labour power is, compared with the enormously high cost of materials, very low; capital does not mind exploiting labour to the utmost; the consequence is a stagnation of technical progress.

These facts explain the apparent contradiction between the full employment of labour and the actual decline. The collapse of the German mark is assuming catastrophic dimensions (at the time of the Third Congress, the dollar was about 70 marks, at present 4,000) and is but a symptom of the deterioration of the economic condition of Germany.

Austria, which is not burdened with reparation payments, exhibited in the period under report the same picture as Germany; only there the want of capital, the effect of impoverishment, was more conspicuous.

In *Poland*, agriculture improved last year, but its economic structure is under too strong a pressure from enormous demands of its political apparatus (army, diplomacy, bureaucracy) to allow any definite improvement to take place.

A very different development manifests itself in *Czechoslovakia*. The reasons for it we have given above. The Czech crown, which in October 1921 stood in New York at 1.05 cents, rose in September 1922 to 3.35 cents. While eighteen months ago the German mark and the Czech crown were equal in value, the crown is now about 20 marks. This continued rise of the Czech currency as against the currencies of the surrounding countries has led to a catastrophic trade crisis in Czechoslovakia, which does not show as yet any sign of abatement. Whole industrial branches are at a standstill, the workers are emigrating. A comprehensive process of concentration is going on, which is wiping out all the weaker elements. The Government is as little able to stay the upward swing of the crown as the German Government to stop the downward whirl of the mark. Everybody runs away from the foreign currency, everybody is getting rid of it as soon as they get it. The attempts of the Government to buy foreign money in order to stop the rise of the crown have failed. Very considerable amounts of foreign money have accumulated in the State Bank, without any success. Czechoslovakia must come lower down economically in order to be able to overcome the crisis.

c) *The Balkan countries and the border countries*

The statistics of these countries are not sufficiently developed to enable us to report on them for the period 1921–2. It seems, however, that their economic condition has somewhat improved.

6 Tendencies of Development and Prospects for the Future

Looking back at the developments of last year, we may state as follows:

Capitalism acquired a certain firmness and this through its inherent tendencies towards a restoration of the equilibrium. Such tendencies take rise from the activity of economic bodies to increase their profits.[36] As there is no possibility for the goods of the 'overproduction region' to be sold at profitable prices on the world market, many capitalists prefer to shut their factories. The result is a diminution of production. As in consequence of the depreciation of the money the prices of the foreign goods in the 'underproduction regions' rise sharply, their consumption diminishes, and it is attempted to produce them at home. Total result: tendency towards a restoration of the disturbed equilibrium between the rich and the impoverished countries. A similar effect has the alienation, that is, the redundant capital of the rich countries is being employed by their possessors to buy in the impoverished countries real estate, shares, etc., or invest there in production. The industrialisation of colonial countries, which disturbed the former equilibrium, is fought down by ruthless competition of the old industrial countries; the serious deficiency of foodstuffs in the old industrial countries leads to their resuming and extending agriculture. But all these activities are carried on not on a social, but on an individualist, private capitalist basis, unconsciously, quite in keeping with the antagonistic character of capitalism which operates in ignorance of its own laws. These unconscious tendencies have contributed something to the improvement which has taken place. But they have not the power to restore the equilibrium of the capitalist world economy. All the less so, as even the conscious tendencies for a restoration of the economic equilibrium have not been attended by any success. Conscious tendencies I call those economic and political measures which have not been taken for the purpose of increasing profits, but for overcoming the crisis.

The most important line of those tendencies was the desire to remove the unequal division of the productive forces between the countries of group II and III. This was thought to be possible:

a) through removing one of the causes of the reproduction on a diminishing scale in the countries of Europe, namely through the cancelling of the Interallied debts and the reduction of the reparation burdens. For, although Great Britain, of all the Allies, is now on the point to pay the first instalment of interest

---

36 We have dealt more fully with these tendencies in the second edition of our *Krise der kapitalistischen Weltwirtschaft*. [Varga 1921].

and sinking fund of its debt to the USA, these obligations are a very heavy burden upon the shoulders of the concerned countries and are undermining their international credit.[37] The remarks concerning reparation payments showed how difficult it is for capitalist countries not only to pay away great masses of values without equivalent, but also to receive such payments. Were the debtor-country one of the countries from the group of relative overproduction, the transfer of large masses of values without equivalent would then operate in the direction of restoration of the economic equilibrium of the world. Actually, however, the line of obligations runs in an opposite direction, the USA and Great Britain, that is, the countries which suffer from the inability of the world market to absorb their surplus products, are the creditor-countries, and they should receive billion values without payments! This can only have the meaning that they should be paid in kind, which, if really sent there, would but aggravate their own overproduction.[38] And the debtors are countries of group III, with an insufficient accumulation or disaccumulation. The delivery of values without equivalent would have a catastrophic effect on their economic condition as it has on that of Germany.

The antagonistic, discordant and confused nature of the present-day economic policy is best demonstrated by the fact that USA is persistent in demanding repayment of the Allied debts and at the same time surrounds itself with

---

37   At the international bankers conference this was officially stated to be the case concerning Germany. The sum for which Germany should pay interest and sinking fund amounts, as is known, to 50 billion gold marks. France, whose population is smaller by one-third than that of Germany, owes to Great Britain and America about 70 billions paper francs = 30–35 gold francs, that is more than half of the actual reparation debts of Germany.

38   'Who doubts', declared the National City Bank of New York in December 1920, 'that our market would now be in a healthier condition if Great Britain and France had not repaid their joint loan to New York on 15 October 1920 ... Had they not paid the 400 million dollars they would have had by so much a larger sum of money to buy goods from us. Nobody can at the same moment pay off debts and augment his purchases of commodities'. In June 1921, the same Bank again declared: 'For the time being we are more interested in Europeans buying our goods than in their paying off old debts to us. And this position continues. The paying capacity of Europeans serves their and our interests better if employed in buying American goods which we have got in superfluity, than in clearing debts due to our Government ... The high rate of the dollar in the whole of Europe, forms a great barrier to our exports, and if, in addition to this, some Governments of the debtor-countries are on the point of competing with the business world for our dollar, then the rate of exchange will still more be driven upwards. At a time, when the most important question of our traders is to make Europeans purchase our goods by granting them credits, it would be a strange policy indeed to ask our European debtors to strain their paying capacity in order to clear their debts to our treasury'. [Retranslated from the German, as quoted by Max Schippel 1921, p. 16].

a wall of custom duties which prevents imports; that France demands the full payment of reparation from Germany and at the same time sets its face against German competition on French markets.[39]

b) Credits to the impoverished countries of group III

The equilibrium of the capitalist world economy could but be restored if, with the cancelling of the Inter-allied debts and a thorough reduction in the reparation payments, a comprehensive transfer of means of production from the richer to the poorer countries would take place. Under the capitalist regime this would mean large international credit transactions. But all such plans failed, apart from ideological motives of hatred against the former foe, through the resistance of American and British industrial capital, which will not tolerate the idea of Germany as a great industrial power.

The industrial capital of the English-speaking imperialist powers is determined fully to exploit the victory in such a form that the whole of Central and Eastern Europe, and if possible also of France, should be transformed into its colonial sphere. (It must, for the time being, compromise with the powerful position of France). The means of production should, through participation and put that at absurdly low prices, be transferred to British and American capital; instead of producing manufactured goods, those countries should supply the English-speaking capital with plenty of raw materials; the standard of life of the proletariat should be driven down to the level of colonial labour; the defeated 'capitalists' should enter the service of foreign capital and see to it that their workers should work their hardest, for which those 'capitalists' and taskmasters should get a small share of the profits; finally, to guard them against the social revolution, by using the armed force of those colonial countries. The whole world should be transformed into an English-speaking colonial Empire. A *pax anglo-saxonica* should reign throughout the world.[40]

This is the world-economic perspective of the English speaking powers, which, however, does not prevent either of them from aspiring to a world dominion of its own. But as a preliminary to its realisation the two imperialist powers – Japan and France – must above all be laid by the heels and likewise

---

39   The Stinnes-Lubersac Agreement, as well as other similar agreements entered into lately, appear to be calculated to solve the problem for France: the country gets its payments in kind in such a form which lie outside the 'normal' demand of the French market. But they are no solution for Germany: the delivery of masses of values without equivalent, be they in kind, must have a fatal effect on the anaemic state of German economic life.

40   These intentions manifested themselves most clearly at the credit negotiations with Austria – handing over the issuing bank to the Anglo-Bank and the (French) Länderbank, abrogation of the sliding scale, abolition of the eight hour day.

degraded to third rank powers. A new world war lies this way, at which it is by no means a foregone conclusion that both of them would find themselves in the same camp.

Apart from the rivalry of the four imperialist great powers, there are other obstacles to that plan, the revolutionary struggle of the oppressed colonial population for emancipation and the revolutionary class struggle of the proletariat and Soviet Russia. It is a race of opposing forces. The capitalist great powers desire to overcome the crisis of capitalism at the expense of the proletariat. The means to this is the transformation of the whole world into a colonial region of a few great powers and to create in this manner a new world-economic equilibrium on capitalist lines, even if in this process many millions of proletarians should rapidly or slowly perish from starvation and the whole civilisation of Europe be wrecked.

As against this stands the proletarian conception of the dictatorship of the proletariat! What are the prospects for its realisation? To be sure, the crisis of capitalism has not been overcome. We are, no doubt, in the midst of the decline of capitalism, and this offers the objective possibility of a victorious proletarian revolution. But the objective possibility is still far from being a reality. The proletarian control must be fought for. The material development does not automatically result in the collapse of capitalism. If the proletariat is not determined and prepared for a revolutionary contest, then capitalism will overcome the crisis. It will open up the still undeveloped regions to capitalist exploitation, and will reconvert former capitalist lands into non-capitalist in the meaning of Rosa Luxemburg; it will slaughter in further world wars millions and millions of proletarians and will restore at the terrible cost of the working classes its shaken domination.

Never was there a contest for greater things; the fate of a world is the price of this battle. *We shall fight!*

CHAPTER 8

The Decline of Capitalism

Preface[1]

The time when this brochure was written was a very unfavourable one for determining both the more remote and the immediate perspectives of the world situation. Several factors that are important for gauging developments cannot be determined at this time. They are:

The American boom is at an end. But it is impossible at this time to say whether the sharp decline of the boom during the month of April is only a passing phenomenon or the beginning of a crisis. If the latter were the case, a new proof would thereby be furnished to demonstrate our contention that capitalism is, on the whole, on the decline.

The *Report of the Experts' Commission* (Dawes) has been published; likewise the acceptance in principle both of the Powers of the Entente and of Germany. But will an understanding really be arrived at on the basis of this report? Will not the militaristic imperialistic policy of Poincaré gain the upper hand, which in fact would lead to a new catastrophe of the mark, since the Rentenmark, an artificial creation, would by no means be able to withstand such a blow?

The *outcome of the harvest* is of very great importance for shaping the course of the market during the ensuing business year. For the moment the prospects for the harvest are pretty poor in Middle Europe, especially in Germany. A decidedly poor harvest would put an end to the sparse beginnings of a recovery of business in Middle Europe.

It is also unclear what the *relation of Russia* toward the capitalistic states will be in the immediate future.

These and many other factors cannot be estimated at this moment with reference to the influence they will exert.

But it is doubtful whether a later moment would show less fluid conditions. The only stable thing in this period of crises is the uncertainty, the chaos!

> E. Varga
> Berlin, 5 May 1924

---

1 [Originally published by the Communist Party of Great Britain for the Communist International, London, 1924].

1   The Period of Decline of 'Normal' Capitalism

The Communist International adopted its last theses concerning the economic position of the world on the occasion of the Third Congress.

Three years have passed since then. During these three years the proletariat has suffered big defeats in several countries that are very important from the viewpoint of the revolution, viz. in Italy, Bulgaria, and Germany. The bourgeoisie has succeeded throughout the world – barring, of course, Russia – in establishing its hegemony anew. Under these circumstances the question must be raised as to whether the position taken by the Communist International in its theses has proven to be sound or unsound.

The fundamental idea of the theses was that the crisis which followed the short, speculative postwar 'boom' was no ordinary crisis of 'normal' capitalism, but rather the beginning of a *period of crises* for capitalism. Within this period of crises the course of business progresses in cycles, just as it did under the normal capitalism of pre-war days: *periods of booms alternate with periods of crises*. The principal question is that of placing an estimate upon the whole period, and not upon the phases of which it is made up.[2]

In the brochure[3] written for the Fourth Congress of the Communist International, we made an attempt to sketch the difference between the 'normal' capitalism of pre-war times and the capitalism of the period of decline more sharply. We wrote there (page 6) concerning pre-war capitalism:

> The capitalist form of production *expanded geographically*; new countries were increasingly opened up to capitalism.

---

[2] During the Third Congress there was a rather strong opposition, supported by the German delegation, which at that time was very 'left', and by the Italian and Hungarian delegations, which took exception to Comrade Trotsky's and my prediction, made in the theses, to the effect that there was a possibility that the boom period might enter into a new phase. 'The revolutionary character of the period of crises, in the midst of which we find ourselves ... is not expressed sharply enough ... in the theses', Comrade Thalheimer declared (*Protokoll des III Kongresses*, p. 113). Comrade Pogány's criticism went even farther. 'Within the great economic crisis ... the theses ... give too much emphasis to the phase of prosperity and too little to the period of crises within the crisis which obtains today ... We cannot and must not make prosperity and the future second world war our Leitmotiv, but, quite the reverse, we must talk about the crisis and the new civil wars' (*Protokoll des III. Kongresses*, p. 108 and p. 111). And Comrade Pogány was anxious to have the reference to a coming boom-phase eliminated entirely. Actual economic developments have, however, proven the correctness of the theses. Yes, it has even become evident that we ourselves underestimated the duration and intensity of the boom in the United States, the first signs of which were apparent at the time of the Third Congress.

[3] Varga 1922a.

Capitalism *extended its sphere of operation* in the capitalist countries themselves by drawing the pre-capitalist strata of society into its vortex. The gold standard, which considerably facilitates the exchange of goods on a capitalist basis, found favour in a growing degree. Foreign trade increased in weight and value.

Large accumulations of capital formed the basis of these developments, since the falling rate of profit in the highly developed capitalist countries – the effect of the steadily growing higher organic composition of capital – was compensated for by the export of capital to less developed capitalist countries, with higher rates of surplus value and profit. The centralization of capital into monopolist forms of production, covering the whole economic field of a country, reduced the cost of capitalist management.

The result was that, apart from the periodic crises, the level of production rose steadily in the world at large as well as in each particular country. The standard of life of the proletariat rose slowly. The credit system and the small company shares permitted the working men and the lower middle class to participate, with their savings, in the appropriation of the surplus value. The number of people who had an interest, or who believed to have an interest, in maintaining the capitalist system, was on the increase. The proletariat of the imperialist countries received from Capital a small share of the surprofits which it got out of colonial exploitation. The upper stratum of the proletariat, the aristocracy of Labour, got separated from the mass of the working people and became subservient to Capital. All classes submitted to the leadership of Capital. The great landowners turned into capitalists, and the capitalists invested money in land; the tendency of financial capital was to amalgamate all possessing sections of the nation with one another. The crises were transitory phases within an upward development – the effects of the anarchy of the capitalist form of production, and caused but superficial disturbances in the structure of capitalism. The system as a whole, however, lost nothing of its equilibrium.

The whole system of capitalist world economics formed a dynamic whole! The alternating phases of booms and of crises recurred in all capitalistic countries at about the same time. The waves of booms and crises were rapidly transmitted from one capitalistic state to another. Even the larger tendencies of the capitalistic mode of production – concentration and centralisation of capital, etc. – were noticeable in practically the same manner in all capitalistic states.

On the other hand, capitalistic world business did *not form a component whole geographically*. The individual states had reached very different stages of capitalistic development. (This is true even today, although to a somewhat lesser degree). There was *a highly developed centre in Western Europe: England, Germany, Belgium*, and, less important, France, Holland, Czechoslovakia, Italy, etc. This centre, 'the industrial workshop of the world', was characterised by the following:

(1) It was connected much more closely than other countries with the division of labour obtaining in the world business, i.e. a much greater part of the annual values produced was exported into foreign countries in the form of manufactured goods, and large quantities of foodstuffs and raw materials were imported.
(2) These countries annually sent newly accumulated values in the form of new investments into countries capitalistically less developed.
(3) These countries annually received large values in the form of profits derived from their investments throughout the world and as the gain of the political extension of wide colonial areas, without their having to render any service in return.

Outside of Europe there were two other, fully developed, capitalistic countries: the *United States of America* and *Japan*. Also, there were numerous countries in Europe and other parts of the world that were only just developing along capitalistic lines; furthermore, colonies and semi-colonies that served as sources of food and of raw materials under the dominion of the various highly capitalistic countries.

The equilibrium of this system was always an unstable one; disturbances were overcome by periodically recurring crises. That an equilibrium nevertheless existed, on the whole, is proven by the stability of the exchanges.

In the most highly developed countries, capital assumed more and more the form of financial capital, which was intimately connected with the heavy industries. Internal development and the tendency toward a decreasing rate of profit forced the capital in these countries *to secure for the export of its investments opportunities made secure by monopolies*.

In the course of technical development the organic concentration of capital – especially in the heavy industries – becomes ever higher, the realisation on industrial capital ever slower, the rate of profit ever lower. To this must be added another circumstance of the nineteenth century. Thanks to its stronger organisation, the proletariat is gaining for itself an improvement of its standard of living. 'The historical moment', which helps to determine 'the extent of the so-called essential necessities and the manner of satisfying them'[4] creates

---

4 Marx 1954, p. 134. [Marx writes: 'On the other hand, the number and extent of his so-called

a tendency in the direction of increasing the wages. In other words, necessary labour is extended at the expense of overtime labour. The rate for surplus values decreases. When variable capital has reached a certain size, there results an acceleration of the falling tendency of the rate of profit.

Capital employs different means for combating the falling tendency in the rate of profit. One of these is organic combination, whereby capital combined in a trust reduces the *faux frais* of the sphere of circulation, lays claim to a part of the profit of trade capital, and raises its own rate of profit by fixing monopoly prices at the expense of other strata of society. The principal means, however, is the exportation of capital to countries where the time involved in labour is shorter and the rate of profit and for overtime is a higher one. To make possible the exploitation of these areas, they must be subservient to the condition imposed by capital in general; i.e. they must be subjugated. Capital in every highly developed, capitalistic country is compelled, in order to retard the decrease in the rate of profit, to subjugate larger colonial areas.[5]

Essentially, the world war was a conflict of the imperialistic powers for the control of colonies and spheres of influence, carried on with the most modern instruments and methods of mass murder. It ended by reducing the number of imperialistic world powers to four: England, France, the United States, and Japan; with the transformation of the rest of the world – excepting the Soviet Republics – into dependencies of the imperialistic great powers; with the new dividing up of the world among them.

The direct economic consequences of the war were the separation of the world into spheres of relative overproduction and absolute underproduction. This condition was partly overcome during the last six years by the 'imminent tendency' of capitalistic world economics, by its mechanism for 'automatic steering', although it still manifests itself by the 'dearth of credit' or of capital in these countries.[6]

The general crisis in world business during the years 1920 and 1921 was followed by a phase that is economically difficult to define and that is not at all uniform. There was a great boom in the United States; on the other hand a slow

---

necessary wants, as also the modes of satisfying them, are themselves the product of historical development, and depend therefore to a great extent on the degree of civilization of a country ...'. Marx 1954, p. 171].

5 We therefore find ourselves in agreement with Rosa Luxemburg with reference to the fact that highly developed capitalism in the form of imperialism leads to warlike conflicts on a global scale. The reason for this, however, is not the impossibility of accumulation without the existence of non-capitalistic elements, but the simple desire for higher rates of profit.

6 See Varga 1922b.

crisis in Europe with indications that a betterment of conditions was in sight – a betterment which, however, did not synchronise in the various countries with that of the rest of the countries and that did not lead to a general betterment within the whole capitalistic world.

2 Characteristics of the Period of Decline

The period since the end of the war and especially during the last three years was characterised above all by the *confusion of economic conditions*, through the *absence of uniform course of business* in the whole capitalistic world, through the existence of *tendencies and counter-tendencies* that crossed each others' paths in the world's business. For this very reason it is exceedingly difficult to extricate the chief characteristics of this period from this confusion. In an earlier work[7] of mine I made an attempt to summarise the principal characteristics of the period of decline as follows:

(1) The geographical extension of the capitalistic method of production becomes narrower: besides the capitalistic countries there exist and continue to increase in numbers countries in which the workers are already establishing their dictatorship.
(2) Within the various capitalistic countries there is a tendency toward the return to forms of production in existence in pre-capitalistic times.
(3) The international division of work is restricted, trade with foreign countries decreases: world commerce, which was previously grouped uniformly about the highly industrial centre in western Europe, loses its balance and is dissolved into parts that are built economically upon entirely diverging bases.
(4) Gold exchange, previously uniform and differing only as to the size of the various monetary units, is supplanted by uncertain, wavering paper exchanges: a tendency is discernible in the direction of reverting to trade in kind.
(5) The accumulation of capital gives way to progressive impoverishment-disaccumulation.
(6) Production decreases.
(7) The credit system collapses.

---

7 Varga 1922a, pp. 11–21.

(8) The standard of living of the proletariat declines: either as a result of the fact that wages do not keep pace with the rising cost of living or as a result of tremendous unemployment.

(9) Among the various strata of the possessing classes there is an ever-sharpening conflict for the distribution of the decreasing social production of values. Politically this shows itself in the constant change of governments, the collapse and new formation of parties, the absence of a uniform government party in the parliaments, etc.

(10) Ideologically the faith in the eternal and unshakable character of the capitalistic order of society begins to wane: the ruling class is compelled to arm itself for the protection of its dominion.

This condition of capitalism, which has been incompletely and hastily characterised in the above, may be called the declining stage of capitalism or the period of continuous crises.

Not two years have passed since the above lines were written and although they are still true in the main, the importance of several of the ten points has been greatly reduced, e.g. the tendency toward a reversal to economic forms of pre-capitalistic times (Point 2). Whether the accumulation gave way to decumulation throughout the whole of capitalistic business, I set out as doubtful even then.[8] In the light of the boom in the United States which has taken place since then, this sentence can be set down as incorrect. This does not mean, however, that it is to be regarded as incorrect for the European countries that were hit hardest by the crisis.

On the other hand, several very important characteristics of the present period of world economics are missing in the above.

i. The *lack of uniformity in the development of booms* as a sure sign of the absence of a uniform capitalistic form of production.
ii. The *agrarian crisis*, interwoven with the general phase of crises and extending over the whole world.
iii. The *social crisis in Europe and in the leading industrial countries of Europe* as a result of a decline in the division of world economic labour.
iv. The tendency on the part of European imperialistic countries, instead of extending their markets, to hinder production on the part of a competitor and to turn capitalistic development backward.

---

8 Varga 1922a, p. 21.

∴

The result of the entire three years' development seems to us to be the following:

The acute social crisis of capitalism, the instinctive, unorganised rebellion of the working class against capitalistic society, seems on the whole to have been overcome. On the other hand, the 'normal' conflict of capitalistic society seems to have been made very much more acute by thoroughgoing concentration and centralisation on the one hand, and by the birth of revolutionary, communistic [sic!] mass parties on the other.

The economic crisis of capitalism has been lessened but is not yet overcome. Production has scarcely reached pre-war levels; Europe's production has diminished, that of capitalistic countries outside of Europe has increased! Owing to successful *offensives of capital* against the proletariat, owing to the *expropriation of the middle class* through inflation, and owing to the progressive *impoverishment of the farmers* as a result of the low prices of agricultural products compared with industrial goods ('shears'), the distribution of income has been shifted in favour of capital. In this manner capitalistic accumulation was made possible, in many cases at the same time that industry as a whole declined. Corresponding to the antagonistic character of capitalist society, the tendencies that are favourable toward overcoming the crisis have the imminent faculty of changing over into the very opposite; through the reduction of income the buying power of the classes affected is in a like manner reduced, a fact that becomes a source of new wars.

The crisis of economic policy continues unabated. None of the great economic problems – reparations question, international debts, relation of the capitalistic states toward Russia, protective tariffs versus free trade, inflation or return to a gold basis – could be solved during the last three years. Economic chaos continues unchanged.

We shall justly be reproached with the charge that our presentation of the situation is unclear. But we must repeat that the lack of clearness, the existence of contradictory tendencies is a characteristic of the present period. As far, however, as the prospects for a revolution are concerned, we should like to say the following, anticipating the results of our later observations:

The present position of capitalism, although the general feeling of rebellion on the part of the proletariat, observable immediately after the end of the war, no longer exists, *is one of giving good prospects for a successful revolution in Europe*. Whether this possibility becomes a reality depends upon the attitude of the proletariat and of its revolutionary vanguard, the Communist Party. There is no such thing as an economic situation that ensures a victory of the proletariat without long continued, enduring fights calling for numerous sacrifices. And there is no such thing as a situation that offers no way out for the bourgeoisie.

> [Comrades,] we have now come to the question of the revolutionary crisis as the basis of our revolutionary action. And here we must first of all note two widespread errors. On the one hand, bourgeois economists depict this crisis simply as 'unrest', to use the elegant expression of the British. On the other hand, revolutionaries sometimes try to prove that the crisis is absolutely insoluble. This is a mistake. There is no such thing as an absolutely hopeless situation. The bourgeoisie are behaving like barefaced plunderers who have lost their heads; they are committing folly after folly, thus aggravating the situation and hastening their doom. All that is true. But nobody can 'prove' that it is absolutely impossible for them to pacify a minority of the exploited with some petty concessions, and suppress some movement or uprising of some section of the oppressed and exploited. To try to 'prove' in advance that there is 'absolutely' no way out of the situation would be sheer pedantry, or playing with concepts and catchwords. Practice alone can serve as real 'proof' in this and similar questions. All over the world, the bourgeois system is experiencing a tremendous revolutionary crisis. The revolutionary parties must now 'prove' in practice that they have sufficient understanding and organisation, contact with the exploited masses, and determination and skill to utilize this crisis for a successful, a victorious revolution. It is mainly to prepare this 'proof' that we have gathered at this Congress of the Communist International.[9]

The above was said by Lenin in 1920, at a time when the wave of revolution seemed still to be on the upward trend; when the great masses of the workers were on their way to joining the Communist Party; when the 'notorious' Twenty-one Points were worked out in order to protect the Communist International from a flood of opportunistic elements; when the Red Army was in the midst of a triumphant march upon Warsaw.

But if it is true that there are no situations from which there is no way out for the bourgeoisie, it is also true that there are no situations in which the revolutionary proletariat cannot wage successful fights. The honest, earnest struggle of the proletariat for the improvement of its conditions within the capitalist system is a factor of prime importance for hindering the successful averting of

---

9 Lenin 1964d, pp. 226–7.

the crisis. If it is possible for the Communist Party, as the leader in the fight of the whole proletariat, to lead into the fight also the masses of peasants who are exploited by the big landowners and the bourgeoisie, the struggle can lead to victory, even if the 'normal' capitalistic system were apparently to be re-established.

3 World Production and Accumulation

In the light of the characteristics of the present period of decline of the capitalist system mentioned above, we shall try especially to examine into world production and the accumulation of wealth.

World Production

Table 8.17 in the Appendix affords a picture of the world production of the most important goods, insofar as statistics are available. If we compare the production of 1913 with that of 1923, we gain the impression that pre-war production has almost been reached. But in estimating the importance of this table we must emphasise the following:

(1) The year 1923–4 was a very favourable one for wheat and grain; if we were to contrast the average for 1920–3 with that for 1909–13 (this average has unfortunately not been published as yet by the Institute of Agriculture), it would be clear that the normal pre-war production had by no means been reached as yet.

(2) The increase of production applies to the *non-European countries* (United States, Canada, Argentina). Europe still lags far behind the pre-war period.[10]

(3) *Production in the heavy industries, which is especially important to capitalism, has not yet reached that of pre-war times* (see Table 8.2).

---

10 TABLE 8.1 The development of sugar production is characteristic in millions of double hundredweights

	1913	1923
Beet sugar (European product)	62	747
Cane sugar (non-European product)	95.0	127

TABLE 8.2 Production in heavy industries in millions of tons

	1913	1923
Coal	1,344	1,360 (our estimate)
Iron	73	65
Steel	75	73
Shipbuilding (1,000 tons)	3,330	1,643

In these branches of production, which are so characteristic of the capitalistic system, the production of 1913 has not yet been reached, although the year 1923 includes the apex in the American boom.

(4) Under normal conditions the production of *iron and coal shows a tremendous increase from decade to decade*, see *Table 8.20* in the Appendix. During the decade 1913–23 this increase is wanting. Whether it will take place during the coming decade is doubtful. Considering the fact that the peak of the American boom, which before all others furnished the increase in production during the last few years, has no doubt been passed, and considering the fact that European business passed through no such boom, we deem it unlikely that a similar increase is to take place during the ensuing decade.

Production figures therefore furnish no basis for claiming that the critical period has been passed through. The low production in the heavy industries is all the more significant as the *capacity for production* is much greater than before the war. A large part of the plants is not producing at all. At the other extreme we observe the long continuing unemployment; we shall return to it in another connection.

Accumulation

In dealing with the question of accumulation we shall differentiate between the accumulation of *wealth* and the accumulation of *capital*, to avoid the possibility of mistakes. Under accumulation of wealth we understand the increase of the objects of value in the possession of a people, irrespective of classes; in other words, the difference between a year's production of values and their consumption. By accumulation of capital we understand the increase in that part of the wealth that is used as capital and is in the hands of the capitalist. The accumulation of wealth and of capital under normal capitalism run along parallel lines, inasmuch as it is the capitalist class to whom the newly created wealth chiefly accrues in obedience to the law of capitalist production.

There is, however, also the possibility of the very opposite development in the accumulation of wealth and capital. It is possible for the wealth that is in the hands of all classes to remain the same or to become less, while at the same time an accumulation of capital takes place, in that a part of the wealth of the non-capitalist classes passes over into the hands of the capitalists and increases their capital.[11] Disaccumulation (decrease) of wealth and accumulation of capital are not necessarily exclusive one of the other.

The question now arises whether or not at present there is actually an accumulation of wealth and an accumulation of capital. The answer to this question would be interesting for this reason: the comrades who adhere to Rosa Luxemburg's theory of accumulation consider this question as of vital importance in determining the prospects of a revolution. In general they are of the opinion that the capitalistic order of society cannot be maintained without accumulation; some of them draw from the premise that capitalism is still accumulating the conclusion that there is no crisis whatever of capitalism, and that therefore the prospects for a revolution are very slight.

I do not share any of these views, at least not when expressed so dogmatically.

The want of possibility for accumulation means reduced production and therefore a more bitter struggle of the classes for the division of the annual product; hence also better prospects for a revolutionary movement of the proletariat. The cessation of increase in the means of production means – under capitalist conditions – that new generations, on reaching the age when they can work, are unable to find work even during the height of a boom; this fact tends to aggravate the situation. *But the absence of accumulation or even disaccumulation is by no means a guarantee of the breakdown of capitalism.* Capitalism can move in a retrogressive direction; a partial return to pre-capitalistic forms of economy can take place; untold millions can die of hunger or be seized by plagues; one or several capitalist countries can accumulate at the expense of the capitalistic countries that are 'decapitalising' themselves; but the domination of capitalism can nevertheless remain if the proletariat does not wrest power from it by revolutionary means. It seems to us that speculation upon the impossibility of accumulation as a premise to the revolution represents considerable opportunism.

On the other hand, the existence of accumulation by no means proves that a proletarian revolution is hopeless. The accumulation of capital may have been

---

11   For a classic example, see the series of articles by Comrade [Marcel] Ollivier [Aron Goldenberg] in *La Vie ouvrière*, beginning with issue no. 208 of 1923.

forced by reducing the real wages of the workers and by the successive expropriation of the middle class and the peasantry; it therefore by no means precludes the existence of revolutionary situations; in connection to which it may be admitted that a real accumulation of wealth as the result of the raising of the living standard for all classes creates a situation unfavourable to the revolution. The latter situation would, however, develop only if capitalism throughout the world were to take a new lease of life.

It would certainly be useful to determine by means of figures whether or not an accumulation – in both forms, accumulation of wealth and accumulation of capital – took place during the last years.

The answer to this question is exceedingly difficult. The question of actual accumulation of *wealth* is perhaps most easily determined by certain signs; by building activity in the broadest sense; by the size of visible stocks of wares; by the condition of the means of communication and of the cattle, etc.

The most important sign is certainly the *building activity*, since every extension of the establishments in which production takes place also means the extension of building operations, and since, on the other hand, *building activity signifies the conversion of present productive forces into a natural form, the amortisation of which will probably take place in 30–100 years*, and which therefore is the typical form of accumulation.

Now, we observe that in the United States, during the past two years, and presumably also during the year 1924, there is a tremendous building boom. Several milliards of dollars are set aside annually for building purposes – for factory buildings, houses, warehouses, schools, etc. This means real accumulation; as does the investment activity of the railways, the rapid increase in the number of automobiles, etc. This accumulation of wealth certainly also means the accumulation of capital in most cases!

A different situation obtains in Europe. Building activity everywhere is only a fraction of that of pre-war times. In all the large cities there is an appalling dearth of houses. Railway construction and other large operations likewise take place only in a reduced manner. From this one can draw but one conclusion, namely, that the accumulation of wealth proceeds, if at all, at a much slower pace than before the war.

An exception seems to be furnished by France, which during the last few years has almost completely rebuilt its devastated areas. However, in evaluating this fact one must take account of the further fact that operations in other parts of France were exceedingly limited; that France received payments of considerable size from Germany, and that it was supplied with credits from other countries; also, that a part of these investments was paid for at the expense of the middle classes through inflation.

As concerns the accumulation of *capital*, its progress is much more difficult to judge. The estimates of national wealth usually put forth by bourgeois writers, the inclusion of capital in stock companies, the deposits in banks, etc., cannot serve as an acceptable basis. Under national wealth are included *sham items*, such as land values (capitalistic ground rent); through the system of mutual participation and holding companies the same actual item of wealth appears several times; through the depreciation of gold (the purchasing power of which is at present about one-third less than before the war) all estimates seem exaggerated. In countries with unstable exchange, these estimates are encumbered by the further factor of unreliability.

For this reason we can do nothing with estimates of this kind.[12] We must rely upon the general observation of economic facts. These reveal the following:

An accumulation of capital running parallel with the accumulation of wealth in the United States, in the English colonial settlements, and in general in the capitalistic areas outside of Europe.

An accumulation of capital on the basis, for the most part or entirely, not of the increase of wealth, but above all as a result of the transfer, brought about by concentration and inflation, of wealth formerly in the hands of non-capitalist strata of society into the hands of capitalists in the countries of Europe.

Assuming that the sources of errors are about the same, certain interesting deductions may be made: if we eliminate government loans as not real accumulation, new emissions total 186.8 and 144 millions respectively for 1912 and 1913, and 131.1 and 97.9 millions respectively for 1922 and 1923. When we consider the reduced purchasing power of gold and its depreciation, a marked decrease in actual accumulation results. And as the economic position of England, despite the heavy crisis in the export industry, is by no means less favourable with reference to the possibilities of accumulating than that of the other European countries, we may conjecture from this that only limited accumulation is taking place in all of Europe.

---

12   See the *Appendix* for *Table 8.20a* and *Table 8.20b*, containing data about the emission of capital in the United States and England.

4   The Lack of Uniformity in Capitalistic World Economy

One of the most strikng signs of the period of crisis is the lack of uniformity in capitalistic world economy. World business is constituted of loosely connected areas, in each of which the progress of the turn of the market is a different one, with currencies of unstable value substituted for gold as world money, with entirely different conditions obtaining with reference to credits, etc.

The Contradictory Progress of the Course of Business

While under 'normal' capitalism the progress of the course of business is the same for all capitalistic countries, we note the unusual condition of late that the different capitalistic countries have booms at different times, and that the progress of these booms is contradictory and opposite. This is hard to express in figures, since the economic statistics of most countries are not adequate for this purpose. (In the *Appendix*, Tables 20a, b, c, we give the most important economic figures for the United States, France, and England). On the basis of our observations of the turn of the market we can point out the following development on a quarterly basis:

TABLE 8.3   Economic development in USA, England, France, Germany, Czechoslovakia, Poland

Quarter	USA	England	France	Germany	Czecho-slovakia	Poland
1922						
1st	Improved	Poor	–	Good	Poor	Improved
2nd	Good	Poor, but improving	Improving	Very good	Poor	Improved
3rd	Boom declining	Ditto	Improving	Good, declining	Poor	Improved
4th	Good	Improving	Ditto	Ditto	Poor	Improved
1923						
1st	Boom	Improving	Worse	Poor	Improving	Poor
2nd	Boom	Improving	Worse	Poor	–	Poor
3rd	Boom, declining	Worse	Better	Crisis	Declining	Better
4th	Ditto	Improving	Better	Crisis	Uncertain	Better

TABLE 8.3 Economic development (*cont.*)

Quarter	USA	England	France	Germany	Czecho-slovakia	Poland
1924						
1st	Boom, improving	Improving	Better	Improving	–	Poor
2nd	Boom strongly declining	Improving	Better	Improving	–	Poor

This characterisation of the course of the market is, of course, inadequate and vulnerable as to details, since within the individual countries, too, *there is not uniform trend of business in all branches of production*. (Even during the peak of the boom in the United States there were branches of industry that remained below the standard of 1919). Hence, in estimating the course of the market one can arrive at different results depending upon the importance that one attaches to every branch of production. In any case *Table 8.3* demonstrates that the course of business is not a uniform one.

Also, it may be asserted that the improvement in business in one country is bought at the expense of that in another. Thus the improvement in the English heavy industry was attained at the price of the cessation of production in the Ruhr Valley and in part also in France. It would seem that capitalism is unable to bring about a general boom!

The Isolated American Boom

The most important event of the last three years is the American boom. It reached its peak in April 1923. (See *Table 8.20a* in the Appendix). Of fundamental importance is the following:

(1) That the American boom happened as an isolated fact and remained isolated, and failed to draw in its wake a boom of European capitalism.
(2) That it could take place although the crisis continued in Europe.
(3) The American boom depended entirely upon the purchasing power of the home market and had nothing to do with increasing export. This is manifest from the figures for the foreign trade of the United States.

TABLE 8.4   US foreign trade in millions of dollars

	Imports	Exports	Excess of imports over exports
1921	2,509	4,485	1,976
1922	3,113	3,832	719
1923	3,950	4,025	75

We see: the *export of goods* did not increase during the period of greatest boom. If we take into account the very high price of cotton in 1923, the export of goods of all kinds must have been less than in 1921. More characteristic even is the fact that during the highest peak of the boom, during the months of March, April, and May 1923, the United States *had a passive trade balance* – a very exceptional case. The capacity of the home market to absorb the product was so great that, although production had been increased to the utmost, it was not adequate to the needs: Dutch tiles, French iron, English coal – everything found its way to America and was bought there. As the boom subsided, imports decreased rapidly, while exports increased.

This change means that a boom in the United States no longer had a stimulating effect upon the European course of business. European capitalism was unable to participate in this phase of business improvement; so overwhelming was the effect of the *period* of crisis that the *phase* of individual business improvement was suppressed by it.

Some are of the opinion that a boom will come in Europe only after the reparations problem has been solved on the basis of the Experts' Report. We consider this an erroneous standpoint, as we shall develop later. But even if the point were well made, the deduction would have to be made that the economic life of the United States had been completely severed from that of Europe and that boom and crisis do not coincide.

For, *nobody can doubt today that the American boom has reached its end*. All newspaper reports (the official statistics appear only two or three months later) agree in saying that the decline of business has extended to the entire heavy industry. The price of iron was reduced. Of 15 smelters of the Carnegie Company in Feddell, six were extinguished at one time. Tin works are employed at only 50 percent capacity. Production in the steel trust decreased 6–7 percent in April [1924], that of independent steel companies 8–10 percent during March.[13]

---

13   *Usine*, 19 April [1924], *Berliner Börsen-Courier*, 29 April [1924], etc.

Ford is said to have one million cars on hand.[14] We will not presume to predict with certainty that a sharp crisis will soon ensue. But the capitalists of the United States will try to postpone the crisis by forced exportation of industrial product, and thereby greatly detract from the possibility of a European boom that is expected by optimists.

Let us briefly touch upon the special reason for the boom. In our opinion it was largely due to the circumstance that in the United States also accumulation was insufficient during the war. There was too little building and the railway material was not renewed sufficiently. The gigantic boom in the building industry and the enormous orders of the railways were, aside from the automobile industry, the most important factors of the boom which has just come to an end. This urgent call for orders to replace the gaps of the war period has already been satisfied; agriculture, on account of the 'shear', is less able to absorb orders; Europe cannot buy, because it has no goods with which to pay America. For this reason the boom period, which, by the way, lasted for a very long time – for three years – had to come to an end.

The relation of the United States to Europe is one of the weightiest problems of the crisis. Even before the war the trade balance of the United States with Europe was a decidedly active one – average annual export, 1910–14, 63.3 percent, imports, 49.6 percent (see Appendix, *Table 8.22*). The difference was covered by the money sent by immigrants, expenses of Americans in Europe, and interest on American securities in the hands of Europeans. The trade balance became even more favourable over against Europe during the postwar period: export to Europe, 1923, 54.4 percent, import 31.8 percent. And as American securities had during the war been bought back by Americans, the difference had to be made up by the exportation of gold from Europe to America. In point of fact the gold supply of the United States is growing from month to month. The notes of the central bank of issue are actually covered more than 80 percent by gold. The time is not distant when they will be covered 100 percent, in which case the problem of 'gold inflation' will become, acute. The continued accumulation of gold in the United States is a characteristic sign of the shift in the economic importance of Europe and America. At the same time it demonstrates how divided up the world's economy and business has become.

---

14   *The New York Herald*, 16 April [1924]; *The Times*, 25 April [1924], reports a general movement downwards. [See 'McKenna duties – workers. Plea for retention. Motor trade anxiety', *The Times*, 25 April 1924, p. 7].

Unemployment

Somewhat like the boom, unemployment is of an irregular, zigzag-like character, but the opposite of the boom. In this connection it is important to remember that the number of unemployed in the most important capitalistic countries is at present, at the beginning of 1924, at least as high as three years ago, as the following figures in *Table 8.6* show:

TABLE 8.6 Evolution of the number of unemployed (in thousands)

Beginning	USA*	England	Germany	Italy	Czechoslovakia	Poland	Together
1921	34,000	977	300	112	95	74	4,958
1922	2,000	1,926	120	606	113	221	5,086
1923	–	1,493	300	391	441	120	2,745
1924	1,000	1,371	2,200**	270	220***	200***	5,261

*   Unofficial estimates, which, however, coincide with the estimates of the *Federal Reserve Bulletin*.[15]
**   Estimated.
***   December 1923.

These figures are, of course, only approximately correct. The number of unemployed is surely greater everywhere than has here been given on the basis of

---

[15]   TABLE 8.5   US employment in 1919 = index 100

Monthly average 1921	83
Monthly average 1922	90
April 1923, peak of boom	103
January 1924	98

There were in 1919:

Factory workers	9.1 millions
Railway workers	2.0 millions
Office employees	3.1 millions

Adding the workers in petty industries, in commerce, etc., this means 20 million workers. Accordingly, the number of unemployed must be:

official statistics. The unemployed are estimated differently in the different countries. But we may assume that the sources of errors are on the whole the same, so that the comparison is not upset thereby. The total number remains unchanged, taken by and large. (The figure 300 for Germany, 1923, is actually much too low for Germany, inasmuch as there was great unemployment in the Ruhr as a result of the Occupation, which, however, was not registered as such). While in some countries, as for instance in England and Germany at this moment (end of April 1924), the figures are on the decline, they rise in the United States and Poland. There is variation, but no absorption of unemployment, no reduction to 'normal' status of the industrial reserve army. This is proof of the fact that the period of crisis in the phase of booms has not yet passed (see Appendix, *Table 8.23*).

The Exchange Crisis

Now as before there are no stable exchange conditions. Only in two countries, the United States and Sweden, is the money actually backed by gold. All other states are on a paper basis. During the last three years the exchange of Germany, Poland, and Austria collapsed completely, and stabilisation took place artificially on a new basis. We shall speak of the effects of this process upon income and fortunes later. The attempt of England to place the pound sterling back on a par with the dollar was unsuccessful. Nor can one claim that the exchange chaos may be considered as having been ended by the stabilisation of the German and Polish exchanges. The last few months witnessed the collapse of the French franc: down to 130 to the pound sterling and then a rise to 65 to the pound. Several exchanges that were considered quite stable – those of Japan, Denmark and Spain – have depreciated considerably recently. The Japanese already shows a *disagio* of 20 percent.

It would seem superfluous here to discuss in detail the catastrophic effect of fluctuating exchanges upon capitalistic business. These are generally known: instead of calculation and production – speculation; the advancement of trade-and-speculation capital at the expense of solid industrial capital; general insecurity, of which the big capitalists take advantage for the systematic despoiling

1921	25% = 4 millions
1922	13% = 2.6 millions
1923	–
1924	5% = 1.0 million

Dearth of Credit and Capital

An interesting phenomenon of the period of crisis is the enormous difference in the interest charged in the different countries for money loaned. While in the United States and England money is plentiful and interests rate are low – 3 to 5 percent – the interest charged at this time in Germany for gilt-edged credits is 24 to 96 percent. First class industrial undertakings pay 2 percent per month. A similar situation was signalled in Finland, Poland, and in general in the states formerly designated as the 'territory of underproduction'. The term 'credit crisis' is used. In reality it is a question of the *dearth of capital* as a result of the impoverishment of this territory. Under normal circumstances such a divergence in interest rates could not be maintained for a long time, in fact, could not come to pass at all, since capital available for loans is very mobile and in the briefest possible time flows from one country over into another and evens up the rates of interest. (There is a constant difference within each country, depending upon the security of the investment).

For the present, however, the political situation in continental Europe is so uncertain that English and American capital, despite the high rate of interest, makes its way there in only a limited quantity.

On the contrary, capital fled from impoverished Europe to the United States, where, to be sure, the interest was low, but where it seemed to be invested safely. According to the reports of the Department of Commerce,[16] there were bought in the course of the year 1923:

TABLE 8.7 Capital flows from Europe to the US

Foreign securities by Americans	US$ 410,000,000
American securities by foreigners	US$ 394,000,000
American currency by foreigners	US$ 50,000,000

In other words, more capital was brought by foreigners to America than was exported from the United States.

---

[16] 'U.S. international balance-sheet. Capital investment from abroad', *The Times*, 7 April 1924, p. 20.

Says the official report: 'If it proved impossible for us to maintain our position as the first loaning country in the world which we were last year, this not due to lack of capital on our part, but rather to the unsettled conditions abroad, that made the investment in foreign countries less attractive for the Americans'.

To sum up: there is no uniform world economy, since the course of the business, the position of the labour market, the exchange situation, the interest rates do not move along parallel lines in the various countries, but in contradiction to each other.

5   The Decline in the World Economic Division of Labour and the Crisis of the European Industrial Countries

The crisis in the European industrial countries is set off in sharp relief from the general crisis. During the war the special advantage of western European industry – a skilled working class, trained in specialised work, which produced at very little cost per unit of product – was partly eliminated. The normal process of industrialising the colonial lands received a severe blow through the interrupted emigration of the European industrial masses. A native industrial working class, capable of working, and native industrial capital developed as a result.[17]

Upon the ending of the world war, sharp competition set in on the part of European industry for regaining these markets. But these newly industrialised countries are defending themselves, some by cheap labour power, others by tar-

---

17   A general summary of the results of this development is not yet available. We give a few examples, however:
     Canada's industry has grown 300 percent during the last century. (*M.G. Comm.*, 11 October 1923).

   TABLE 8.8   Economic development of Australia and India

Australia	Number of factories	Number of workers
1911	14,445	312,000
1921	18,018	395,000

   Commerce Reports. A Weekly Survey of Foreign Trade, Washington: Bureau of Foreign and Domestic Commerce, US Department of Commerce, 23 September 1923.

iffs! India demands a tariff not only on twine, but even on iron. Canada declined the idea of a united British world empire and of preferential tariffs for the raw materials of the colonies, because it wants to carry out its own policy of protective tariffs. All this leads to increasing greatly the difficulties of exporting to these countries from Europe.

Paralleling this situation there is the phenomenon of the United States taking up ever closer economic connections with extra-European countries. These countries need capital, which they can obtain more easily from the United States than from Europe. The British colonies, especially Canada, but also Australia, lean heavily upon the United States. In South America, the United States have tried to gain economic and political control.[18]

The result of this development is:

(1) *The decrease in foreign trade in the world in general* (see Appendix, Table 8.22).

(2) *The decrease in foreign trade for European industry in particular.*

Let us try to compare the export of the most typical European industrial countries in 1913 with that of 1923 by reducing the data of 1923 concerning the index figures for wholesale trade to those of 1913. This is a rough method and one that gives only approximate results, all the more so since the foreign trade data of France and Germany very rightly are considered as not very reliable.

India	Number of textile factories	Number of spindles
1910–11	226	6.0 million
1921	284	7.8 million

	Production (million yards)	Import
1913–14	1,164	3,197
1922–3	1,725	1,578

Report of Overseas Trade, Board of Trade, London: HMSO, 1922.

China: Of 109 modern textile factories, 77 belong to Chinese, 5 belong to Englishmen 25 belong to Japanese. *The Statist*, 16 April 1923.

18 Interesting details concerning this are contained in Key 1924, p. 47.

TABLE 8.9 Exports in millions of monetary units

	1913	1923	Wholesale index	Transposed in terms of 1913	Minus	Plus
England	634	886	162 (*Economist*)	547	87	–
France	6,880	30,400	419	7,250	–	370
Germany	10,097	6,079	(In terms of 1913)	6,079	4,018	–
Belgium	3,716	8,993	497	1,810	1,906	–
Switzerland	1,376	1,760	181	908	468	–

Thus we see that the exports from the 'Industrial Workshop', with the exception of France, where there was an accretion of territory and an inflation boom, lag far behind those of pre-war times: Belgium 52 percent, Switzerland 30 percent, Germany 40 percent, England 13 percent (in the case of England the severance of Ireland plays a part).

(3) *The decrease in exports hits particularly those branches of industry that are mainly dependent upon export.* This is shown most clearly in the distribution of unemployment in England among the various branches of industry.

In a special Free Trade Supplement of *The Economist* for 17 November 1923, the following very interesting data is given concerning unemployment in the various industrial branches of England. The various lines of business are divided into three groups; one group in which exports exceed imports; one group in which imports predominate; and one, the so-called home industries, such as building trades, hotels, railways, water works, etc. The groups that in England show a surplus of imports are: fine metals, woodworking, silk goods, oil, leather goods, and paper.

The number of unemployed at the end of September 1923, may be divided as follows among these groups:

TABLE 8.10 Division of the number of unemployed

Export Industry	698,337
Local Industries	395,018
Import Industry	83,762

These figures prove that it is not the importation of industrial goods from abroad that is the cause of unemployment in England, for unemployment is greatest in the export industries. For this reason tariffs upon imports would be senseless, all the more so since the importation of industrial products is less than before the war. Nor does the fault lie in the fact that England's share in the world's trade has grown less. On the contrary: according to [Reginald] McKenna's[19] estimates, England's share of the world's trade was as follows: 13.8 percent in 1912 and 17.3 percent in 1922.

The English Free Traders are quite right in their arguments against protective tariffs. In his programmatic free trade speech of 5 November 1923, [Herbert] Asquith[20] was quite right in asserting: 'The first real cause is the fact that the whole trade of the world has dwindled ... The remedy lies in the re-establishment of the productive capacity and exchange power of the world'.

In other words, this means: the restoration of England and Western Europe in general as the 'industrial workshop' of the world. But this seems to be impossible.

'The old markets, that have disappeared, can for the most part never develop again, and that is one of the reasons why continental Europe cannot be reconstructed within its own borders'.[21] The shifting in the international economic relationships, the decrease in the economic division of work thus calls forth a special crisis in industrialised Western Europe. There is a tendency towards establishing a new equilibrium through the exportation of capital, emigration, return to agriculture, and limitation of offspring. But such a rearrangement needs much time and can only be brought about after severe class struggles. We shall revert to this when dealing with the perspectives.[22]

---

19 [Reginald McKenna (1863–1943) was a British Liberal politician and banker].
20 [Herbert Henry Asquith (1852–1926) was a Liberal politician and Prime Minister].
21 Key 1924, p. 7.
22 In the periodical issued by the Russian Communist Academy ['Obzor literatury po mirovomu khozyaistvo', *Vestnik Kommunistcheskoy Akademii*], April–July 1923, Volume 4, p. 415, Comrade [Mieczysław] Bronskiy [Warszawski-Broński] launches an extended criticism of my interpretation of the crisis. He takes especial exception to a certain article published in 1916 under conditions of severe censorship, in which I demonstrate that the theory of the social patriots, according to which the proletariat has an interest in the exportation of industrial product, and therefore an imperialism and war itself, is unsound. I therein cite Germany to prove that even the complete suppression of exports would be more favourable to the proletariat than militarism and war, since the importance of exports as compared with the entire production is much less than the social patriots claim. Comrade Bronskiy seems to have misunderstood the semi-illegal character of this work of mine. I there speak of the relative unimportance of industrial export *in general*, in other words, on the assumption, concealed or covered up there, of a non-capitalistic order of society.

Under capitalist conditions, of course, things stand quite differently, since production there does not take place for the purpose of supplying the need. The president of the American Steel Trust [US Steel Corporation], [James A.] Farrell,[23] was right in stating to the Department of Commerce: 'In every business there is a part of the production roughly estimated at the least at 20 percent that cannot remain unsold if the first 80 percent of the sales are to prove profitable. Remove this last 20 percent and the whole operation will cease to show a profit'.[24]

If, therefore, the individual branches of industry in the *capitalistic* countries are so organised that they dispose of 80 percent at home, but must export 20 percent, and if for these 20 percent there is no market, then this simply means that there is no profit; in other words, it means crisis, unemployment, which, corresponding to the structure of capitalism, becomes transferred to all branches of production.

In our own opinion there is, therefore, no contradiction in my contention on the one hand that the importance of export trade for business 'in general' is overestimated, and on the other that the limitation of export means a heavy crisis for *capitalism*. One must only read my contention aright.

6   The Agrarian Crisis

Closely connected with the general crisis is the agrarian crisis, which has lasted for several years, but has received scant attention. In my *Crisis*[25] I have already referred to the agrarian crisis as an important phenomenon, but only in connection with the economy of the United States. The reason for this was the

---

In general it is quite true that a *large* modern country, such as Germany, France, Russia, or the United States might support its population without exports (hence also without imports). The standard of life would be lowered, poorer clothes would be worn, people would renounce certain pleasures, and possibly even suffer some hunger; but no catastrophe would result. At least none that would equal the world war as far as the proletariat is concerned. Even the English people could, by intensive cultivation of the soil and by fishing, sustain themselves at about the standard of the Irish fifty years ago, provided they got along without meat. The standard of life of the whole world would be lowered through the renunciation of the advantages of an international exchange of commodities, but in our opinion to a much lesser degree than most people believe.

23   James Augustine Farrell (1863–1943) was President of US Steel from 1911 to 1932. He was an early pioneer of steel exports with the help of the shipping subsidiary he founded, the Isthmian Steamship Company.
24   Quoted in Patterson 1922, p. 12.
25   [Varga 1922b].

fact that the agrarian crisis remained concealed for a long time because of the effect of inflation. The harm that came to the farming business through the low prices for agrarian products – low as compared with the general level of prices for industrial products – was compensated for through the automatic depreciation of mortgages, through the actual exemption of farmers from taxation, and through the circumstances that the farmers were able during the inflation period to purchase their industrial products below reproduction costs.

The agrarian crisis is of special social significance, since it has a tendency to separate the small and middle-sized farmers from the capitalist class, and to loosen their identity of interests. This expresses itself most sharply in the United States in the efforts to organise a third party.

The 'Scissors'

The economic reason for the agrarian crisis is the so-called '*scissors*', i.e. the opposite development of prices for agricultural and industrial products during the postwar period. It is exceedingly difficult to express this in figures. From a purely economic viewpoint it is impossible to establish a normal relationship between the prices of agricultural and industrial products, unless one were to assume that the price for agricultural products must be so high that the cultivation of the unrented ground, the yield of which is still necessary for supplying the world market, nets the average profit on the capital. This is theoretically correct, but it can by no means be estimated in figures, since too many factors, modificatory in nature, are brought into play: land hunger, freight rates, varying productivity, depending upon the climate, weather, etc. There is no other recourse for us save to take the relationship of prices in a normal year, in other words, a price relationship uninfluenced by either agrarian or an industrial crisis, as our starting point. Such a year is 1913, which in most cases was also chosen as the starting point for estimating the various index figures. Since, however, inflation has caused confusion in the price relationship and since there are no index figures for prices fixed uniformly for all capitalistic countries, it is hardly possible to use the index figure for determining the 'scissors'. Depending upon the weight attached to the industrial and agrarian products in estimating the various index figures, contradictory figures are arrived at for the different countries.[26]

---

26 The various German index figures are quite contradictory on this point. The index for wholesale trade of the federal statistical office of Germany, for instance, was fixed at the end of November at 98.9 for grain and potatoes, and 155.8 for industrial products, hence a very strong 'scissors'. During the same period of time the index figure for wholesale trade given by the *Industrie- und Handelszeitung* was fixed at 79 for grain, flour, etc., at the same

Under these circumstances it seems best to us to use the figures for wheat, the most important agricultural product, as our starting point. In Appendix *Table 8.27* are given the market prices of certain grades of wheat in the most important produce exchanges of the world, divided into export and import markets, as well as the notations of such European countries as on the whole produce their own supply. The price quotations of pre-war times show that the prices in the export markets were graded quite evenly, depending upon the distance from or freight charges to Western Europe. With the European countries there is a sharp divergence of prices, depending upon whether there is free trade or protection tariff. Thus the price for inland wheat per quarter was (all prices are expressed in gold francs):

TABLE 8.11   Wheat prices, average 1913

Free trade countries		Protection countries	
London	19.86	Berlin	24.56
Antwerp	19.89	Paris	27.82
Rotterdam	20.60	Milan	28.10

If, now, we follow the prices, figured in gold francs, in all important exchanges of the world, we see that with the exception of France the price of wheat everywhere lags far behind the general rise of prices. If we compare the present moment, in other words, the course of prices at the beginning of April 1924, with 1913, we find the following:

TABLE 8.12   Wheat prices and general prices

	Average 1913	Beginning 1924, April
Chicago	17.19	20.37
Karachi (India)	17.26	19.16
Argentina	19.03	18.60
London-Manitoba I	20.90	23.05

time that the general index figure was 145, hence a divergence of almost 100 percent. On the other hand the wholesale index figure for the *Frankfurter Zeitung* during the same period showed the very opposite tendency: food and articles of consumption, 1,584, total index for 98 classes of goods, 1,565.

TABLE 8.12 Wheat prices and general prices (*cont.*)

	Average 1913	Beginning 1924, April
London-Plata	20.61	21.77
Berlin	24.86	21.24
Antwerp	19.89	22.49
Paris	27.82	24.00 (about)
Milan	28.10	25.07
Rotterdam	20.60	24.83

These figures are all reduced to gold francs. If we take into account that the general purchasing power of gold, as reflected in the wholesale trade index figures for the United States, is about one-third less than in 1913, it is evident that the price of wheat at this moment is far below that of pre-war times in the whole world. And as wheat may be looked upon as characteristic for all agricultural products (except textiles), there can be no doubt but that the position of the farmers in the world's markets has become considerably worse, and that there is a 'scissors' in the world market. The difference is sharpest in the countries where there was a high tariff on grain before the war, which, however, during the postwar period was either removed or greatly reduced: Germany, France, Italy.

The Causes of the 'Scissors'

The reason for this difference in the fixing of prices between agricultural and industrial products is above all the fact that during and after the war monopolies were established in industrial concerns in greatly increasing numbers. We have already referred to this in a previous chapter. Through the formation of trusts and monopolistic companies the prices of industrial products are more and more placed outside of competition, and the profits of organised branches of industry are increased at the expense of those not comprised in such combinations. Owing to the fact that there are untold millions of independent producers, a monopolistic fixing of prices is an impossibility in agriculture. The monopolistic fixing of prices can take place only in exporting countries with the help of the government, as was the coffee valorisation scheme in Brazil. Attempts of that sort were made in the United States and Canada, but thus far without success. Were such an artificial concentration of surplus export for purposes of raising prices to come to pass in the most important countries, the 'scissors' would in all probability disappear rapidly. It would be quite sufficient for Argentina and Canada to create a monopoly for the export of grain, since these two states, together with Russia, which monopolises its whole foreign trade anyway, control the world's grain market.

The creation of such monopolies is prevented, however, by the circumstances that the capacity of the European market, which is decisive in shaping prices, to absorb the product is very small as a result of the decline of European capitalism that is taking place just now. Thus the agrarian crisis and the crisis of European capitalism are closely interconnected.

Different Manifestations of the 'Scissors' in the Various Countries

The reaction of agriculture to the 'scissors' was and is different in the different countries. In this connection the divergent policy governing the fixing of prices in the belligerent countries during the world war is of importance. In the countries of the European continent a maximum price was fixed for the agricultural products, at which the farmers were compelled to yield their produce. Although these maximum prices were constantly circumvented by the farmers, this system, taken by and large, nevertheless led to a decrease in the gold earned from agricultural products and also to a decrease in production itself. In the Anglo-Saxon countries, however – England, the United States, and the British colonies – the very opposite price policy was followed. No maximum prices were fixed and everything was left to free competition. But the governments bound themselves to purchase certain agricultural products, above all wheat, for a number of years at a fixed price which was set rather high. This system tended to the very opposite of the fixing of maximum prices in the continental countries of Europe: it led to the extension of production, as this proved very profitable for the producers. The surplus profit of agricultural producers was, of course, turned into capital and led to a sharp increase in the price of land. Then when this system was abrogated after the close of the war, the effect of the collapse in prices that soon followed was felt in the following manner:

In England and the United States, where all land is in private hands, and where the rents had been increased, corresponding with the higher productivity during the war, the crisis was and is severest. It manifested itself in the United States in this manner: hundreds of thousands of farmers went bankrupt and left their farms, streaming into the cities. Other hundreds of thousands were only held on the farms because their creditors left them unmolested, their calculation being that if these debtors sell their land at auction, the creditors will eventually lose everything, while if they left them on their farms there was at least the hope that under more favourable business conditions they might be able to collect. In 1923 the crisis among the wheat farmers in certain parts of the United States (the Dakotas) became such that hundreds of financial institu-

THE DECLINE OF CAPITALISM 493

tions were driven into bankruptcy. The reason for this is the fact that the leases and rents went up during the war, but the farmers, who during the boom bought land at high prices on credit or leased it, are now, in the face of the low prices, unable to pay their interest or rent. In England, where the farms are in the hands of better situated capitalists, such a catastrophe did not ensue.

But in both countries the result is a *sharp shrinkage of the area devoted to the raising of grain*. The area under cultivation was:

TABLE 8.13 Cultivated grain areas, average (in 1,000 hectares)

	1909–13	1917–21	1922	1923	1924
England					
Wheat	767	854	796	704	–
Rye	23	36	34	30	–
Barley	748	611	552	537	–
Oats	1,634	973	873	800	–
USA					
Wheat	19,065	24,670	24,779	23,574	16,263[27]
Rye	905	2,212	2,513	2,118	1,771
Barley	3,084	3,251	2,991	3,228	
Oats	15,118	17,311	16,468	16,498	
Corn	42,181	41,635	41,152	42,152	

In England the area under cultivation is far less in extent than during the pre-war period. In the United States the cultivation of winter wheat in the fall of 1923 was 13 percent less than in 1922. This means that the United States with an equally good harvest has only half as much wheat to export as in 1922.

In *Canada and Argentina* the area under cultivation has increased still further despite the low prices. This is to be ascribed to the fact that there is still free land to be had[28] and that the extension of grain cultivation includes lands that were thus far not tilled at all. The original fertility of this land is made use of, and with intensive cultivation and very small expenses harvests are achieved

---

27 Without summer wheat.
28 Free land in the economic sense, i.e. at prices that from an economic standpoint cannot be regarded as in lieu of rent; for example the low tax in Canada.

that even during the present time of low prices make the effort put into production worthwhile.

TABLE 8.14 The area under grain cultivation in Canada and Argentina, average (in 1,000 hectares)

	1918–19	1917–21	1922	1923
Canada				
Wheat	4,025	7,505	9,074	9,175
Rye	47	325	852	586
Barley	637	1,096	1,052	1,127
Oats	3,884	6,139	5,885	5,372
Corn	125	108	129	129
Argentina				
Wheat	6,496	6,572	6,451	6,967
Rye	34	97	87	128
Barley	93	253	243	258
Oats	970	1,024	1,059	1,112
Corn	3,525	3,285	3,177	3,425

In *continental Europe*, where agriculture is for the most part conducted by peasants, the 'scissors' began to show their full effects only now. Their detrimental effect upon the position of the peasants, as already intimated above, was prevented by the fact that the farmers during the inflation period for the most part got rid of their mortgages; that until very recent times, also as a result of inflation (in Germany, Poland, Hungary, Austria, in part also in France), they had to pay taxes that were minimal in comparison with pre-war times; that they produce but once per year and by the immediate use of the money realised can escape the losses due to inflation; and that, finally, in purchasing goods they profited by the circumstance that industrial products were being sold under production costs.

The peasants began to feel the full weight of the agrarian crisis the minute stabilisation had taken place. Immediately they are loaded down with taxes in gold. The new mortgages must be made out in gold values and the interest paid in gold. The fixing of prices now turns very much against the farmers, in that they must now pay for the industrial products that are manufactured from raw materials at a much higher advance than before the war.

The classic example for this is furnished by Germany, where at present the agrarian rests upon the peasants with all its weight. The change in the fixing of prices is especially significant.

We here cite several figures from the *Börsen Courier* of Berlin for 9 December 1923:

TABLE 8.15A German agrarian prices

	1913	Middle November 1923 per 50 kg	Increase (1913 = 100) (in gold marks)
Production costs for rye	8.22	9.75	119
Rye Bread			
Retail price of rye			
Rye Flour	15.00	31.50	210
Rye Bread	14.00	22.50	160

In other words, hand in hand with an increase of 19 percent in the cost of producing rye there goes an increase in retail prices of 60 and 110 percent respectively:

TABLE 8.15B German agrarian prices

	1913	Middle November 1923 per 50 kg	Increase (1913 = 100) (in gold marks)
Production costs for oxen (live weight)	52.00	115.00	221
Wholesale price for oxen	73.00	325.00	445
Retail price for beef (meat for cooking)	87.50	400.00	444

At the same time that there is an increase of 221 percent. In the costs of production, there is double the increase in the retail price. The difference between the cost of production and the wholesale price has risen from 41 percent to 188 percent, and that between wholesale and retail prices from 20 to 23 percent.

	1913	Middle November 1923 per 50 kg	Increase (1913 = 100) (in gold marks)
Production costs for hides, Munich (1/2 kg)	0.61	0.60	98%
Wholesale price for sole leather	2.25	3.36	149%
Retail price for box calf shoes	12.50	24.67	197%

A reduction in the cost of raw hides of 2 percent is matched by an increase in the retail prices of 97 percent. Conditions have changed but little during the last quarter of a year. German agriculture is in dire need, and this distress is heightened by the fact that credits can nowhere be obtained, inasmuch as all German business suffers from a lack of capital. The big agrarians are looking for a way out through agricultural protective tariffs. This might help agriculture, but through the consequent raising of prices for the necessaries of life, it would make the lot of the German proletariat worse, and would lead to grave wage conflicts. The raising of wages, on the other hand, would lessen the ability of German industry to compete and would cause a still severer crisis in the whole of Germany's economic life.

7   Aggravation of the Class Conflict

During recent years there has taken place, objectively, an aggravation of the class antagonisms within capitalism. The distribution of incomes has shifted to the advantage of the very narrow layer of big capitalists. We can here differentiate between the following:

(1) *Concentration and, the formation of trusts.*
(2) *The expropriation of the middle classes in the cities through inflation.*
(3) *The impoverishment of the peasantry through the 'scissors'.*
(4) *The reduction in the standard of life of the proletariat*, directly through the reduction of wages and the lengthening of working hours, and indirectly through the continuing period of unemployment, which reduces the income of the proletariat as a class. Thus the big capitalists enriched themselves at the expense of the non-capitalist strata. The circle of people economically interested in the continuance of capitalism thus constantly decreases; the exploitation of all classes through the big bourgeoisie grows constantly worse. This supplies the economic basis for further

revolutionary struggles, even though the working class was driven onto the defensive during the period between the Fourth and Fifth Congresses, and though it had to give up positions it had already captured.

Concentration and the formation of trusts. The tendency toward concentration and the formation of trusts was present even before the war, but it has been increased during recent years. It is impossible to determine this in *exact figures*, since capitalistic economy is so tremendously intertwined and interwoven.[29] But nobody can doubt the correctness of this fact, if he observes objectively the manifestations of modern capitalism.

Still more important than the concentration of production in the various branches of production and the centralisation of fortunes in the hands of a small number of capitalists is the formation of trusts and concerns, which give a very small group of big capitalists the possibility of controlling the economic life of a country. Especially characteristic of the last years is the growth of trusts or combinations that include the whole productive process from the raw material to the finished article, that themselves produce the machinery and equipment for their manufactures, and that arrange for transport and distribution, trade and financing, through their own organs. In this way there arise new phenomena, autarchic up to the finished product, which constitute powerful autonomous units within a modern economic system that is still called 'Volkswirtschaft' (popular economics).

The heads of these mighty organisations are in fact the rulers of the modern capitalistic State. They follow their own domestic policy, their own social policy, their own foreign policy. The trustification process was very much encouraged by the sudden drop of prices and, at the end of the postwar period of apparent boom, by the sudden change from boom to crisis that was accompanied by fluctuations of exchange. The establishments that were less firmly founded were unable to withstand these storms and had to save themselves from destruction by fusing with the big concerns.

The activities of these concerns are not limited to their native countries. They take root everywhere, due to the exportation of capital and through mutual interweaving and interlocking. Thus we see how the two mightiest American concerns, the Morgan[30] and the Rockefeller[31] interests, branch out

---

29   Since the war, no statistics concerning business establishments were gathered by any European countries, so that no data are available for the concentration that has taken place. The first census is to be taken in England in 1924.

30   [J.P. Morgan & Co. was an investment banking company founded by John Pierpont Morgan (1837–1913) in New York].

31   [John D. Rockefeller (1839–1937) was an American industrialist and oil merchant, founder of the Standard Oil Company].

more and more in almost all European countries; how under the mask of French or Austrian capital they gain control of the oil production of Poland and Romania; how the whole electrical industry of the world is under their influence.

On the other hand, the formation of such gigantic concerns is not dependent upon wealthy America. It impoverished Germany, we see, during the inflation period, the growth of the [Hugo] Stinnes[32] concern, which swallows up in an almost planless manner all sorts of useful undertakings: coal and iron mines, smelters for the smelting of iron ore, machinery factories for turning out manufactured products of iron, forests for securing wood for the mines, paper factories for taking care of the waste wood, newspapers for using the paper, shipping undertakings for transporting the goods, and pure business concerns for securing freight trade for the steamers. The Stinnes concern, too, is not limited to Germany, but extends to Austria, Czechoslovakia, Poland, Hungary, South America, South Africa, etc.[33]

Of fundamental importance in this connection is the tendency towards bringing into consonance with each other the various species of capital that previously were often antagonistic to each other: baking capital, industrial capital, trade capital, transportation capital, agricultural capital. These become so closely intertwined by the formation of trusts that one can speak of a unified *'concern capital'* in the most advanced capitalistic countries. The further events develop, *the more capital places the proletariats as a unified whole*, and the less hope is there of inner differences of interests between capitalists.

It is further interesting that, while before the war the initiative for the formation of trusts and cartels was usually taken by banking capital, and while the latter usually played a leading role in these trusts, during the postwar period it is industrial capital, especially *in the countries of inflation*, which became the motive power in forming combinations and which controls the trusts, and to a certain degree also the banks. The reasons for this shift are to be found in the mechanism of inflation, as we shall develop later.

The trusts constitute so great an economic force that they make the 'unorganised' bourgeoisie dependent upon them economically and financially. As

---

32   [Hugo Stinnes (1870–1924) was a German industrialist, owner of an industrial empire based on coal and steel. He owned more than 60 newspapers, and in 1919 he became member of the Reichstag for the German Nationalist Party *Deutschnationale Volkspartei* (DNVP) of Alfred Hugenberg].

33   A concrete description of this development would be interesting, but would demand a whole book. In my consideration of this problem I rely largely upon the collection of materials in the hands of Comrade Rolf [Wilhelm Florin], which he has placed at my disposal.

a matter of fact, trust capital dominates the whole economic life and seeks effectively to enlarge its profits at the expense of the bourgeoisie that is not yet organised in trusts. In this way there is a division within the bourgeoisie which does not, however, separate people as before according to the kinds of capital, but into trustified and unorganised capital.

Two important problems arise in this connection:

(1) Has the formation of trusts advanced so far that the heads of these combinations control a sufficiently large part of the industrial and business life to be able to prevent crises? This possibility can be denied with certainty. Trust-forming has advanced furthest in the United States. An attempt was there made to use the credit policy of the central bank of issue to regulate the course of the market. Nevertheless we see that neither could the big crisis of 1920–1 be prevented, nor the present sharp downward movement averted. In other countries there can be even less talk of this. Trust-forming can merely bring it about that the burdens of a crisis are shifted from the capital organised in trusts to the unorganised capital and to the non-capitalistic classes.[34] Great though the power of the trusts is, it does not extend to agriculture nor to the small or middle-sized industries, the economic weight of which is, after all, greater than that of the trustified capital.

(2) Is the international trust-forming and mutual interlocking of the capitalistic interests of the individual capitalistic countries not liable to overcome the antagonisms of the various national capitalisms and thereby to prevent new armed conflicts in future? This possibility, too, can be denied with certainty. The conflicts of interests between the various national capitalisms of 'State-capitalistic trusts', as Bukharin calls them, are considerably greater than the community of interests brought about by mutual penetration. If one reads the list of concerns in Europe controlled by the Morgan or Rockefeller trusts, this sounds quite imposing; but if one attempts to compare their economic weight with that of the entire capitalism of the respective countries, one finds that, after all, theirs is rather small. The sharp competition in armaments on the water, under the sea,

---

34 The following news item (*Berliner Börsen-Courier* for 1 May) is characteristic: 'From the American Steel Industry. According to a report in the *Iron Age*, the producers of steel are adopting the same policy as last year, namely, they bring their activity into accord with the demand. There is nothing to indicate that attempts are being made to obtain orders by reducing prices greatly'. That is, the crisis is overcome, not at the expense of the capitalists through reduction of prices, but at the expense of the proletariat through restriction of production.

in the air, and in chemical factories, engaged in by the imperialistic World Powers, proves sufficiently that there can be no thought of a world peace based upon the mutual community of interests of the capitalists.

The Expropriation of the City Middle Class through Inflation

The petty bourgeoisie, including the smaller capitalists, has been radically expropriated in the countries that have had big inflation, and has been partly reduced to the level of the 'riff-raff' proletariat. The mechanism is as follows:

The fortunes or incomes that were invested in nominal money units were expropriated in proportion to the depreciation that took place. All rentiers who had invested their savings in state or communal bonds or industrial shares bearing fixed interest, grew poorer in proportion to the depreciation of the money. Similarly all those who had deposited their savings as savings accounts with financial institutions. Likewise those who had taken out life insurance or had turned over their savings to them in return for a fixed annuity. The expropriation amounts in France to two-thirds, in Austria, Germany, Hungary, Poland to more than 99 percent of the former fortunes.

Those who gained from this process were: financial institutions, insurance companies, industrial undertakings, and the state as common organ of the capitalists.

The expropriation of tradesmen, little merchants and lesser productive capitalists took place in a different manner: these strata were unable to fit their business practices and methods of calculation to the shrinking exchange in time. Instead of selling at a figure based upon a re-purchasing price plus profit, they sold at the purchasing price (the price at which they bought it) plus profit. Under normal circumstances, where purchasing and re-purchasing price (production price and re-production price) are equal, yes, where the tendency exists that goods may become cheaper due to technical improvements, this method is correct. During the period of money depreciation, however, this led to the ruin of the petty bourgeoisie. For, figured in nominal money units, they made a good profit under this system. But at every turnover of their capital they became poorer since they were able with the money realised from the sale of their goods to re-purchase only a part of them. Their stock, which constituted their fortune, in this way became smaller and smaller and they themselves became poorer and poorer. Many did not realise their mistake until they had to go out of business because of a dearth of capital. Without going bankrupt (no credits were given during the inflation period) they went to pieces, the victims of the big capitalists.

For a long time, the state itself prevented the little fellows from calculating on a basis corresponding to the rules of capitalist economy, when it determined that, on the basis of the principle, mark equals mark, franc equals franc, everybody must be considered as a profiteer and must be punished who demands a higher price than one based upon the purchasing price plus profit in nominal money units.

In so doing the state protected the interests of the big capitalists, especially of those in the heavy industries. The principle of purchasing price plus profit in paper money units was not applicable to the heavy industries and to the large industries combined in trusts which conduct their own production from the raw material to the finished product. These concerns immediately raised their prices to correspond with and even exceed the depreciation of the money. They profiteered systematically at the expense of the small capitalists, the dealers and tradesmen, in that as a class these capitalists bought all goods that they needed for production from these strata, as well as all objects of private consumption, always far below the price which the big capitalistic purveyors received from these strata for the same goods. They profiteered indirectly at the expense of these strata in that the system of selling below the cost of reproduction made it possible for the capitalists to pay very low wages, since the workers received the goods below cost from the petty bourgeoisie. The capitalists sustained the proletariat in part at the expense of the petty bourgeoisie.[35]

In this way it was possible for the big capitalists to accumulate capital through the expropriation of the fortunes of the middle class, *at a time when the accumulated wealth was not increasing, yes, even decreasing*, and at the expense of the petty bourgeoisie. It is no wonder, therefore, that capital in all countries sabotaged the stabilisation of the exchange until the moment that the expropriation of the petty bourgeoisie had been completed or the change over to a calculation based upon the re-purchasing price could no longer be prevented.

This process at the same time meant a shifting in the position of the various kinds of big capital. During the inflation period the path toward getting rich was an easy one: take up credits, invest the money in goods or in production, sell the goods at reproduction prices, but pay back the credits in nominal monetary units. The heavy industries were best able to do this, while the banks, to be sure, as debtors obtained great profits from the inflation, yet at the same time also sustained losses as creditors, so that, as compared with the heavy industries, they issued forth from the inflation period in a weakened

---

35 The very fluctuations of exchange furnish the big capitalists, who are in a position not only to foresee but even to cause them the possibility to rob the uninitiated. A classical example of this is the support given to the French franc in the spring of 1924, an action which brought tremendous profits to the initiated, but to the uninitiated – the whole financial world of Vienna and Berlin – the greatest possible losses.

condition. The deciding influence therefore passed from the banks over to the heavy industries.

Through the inflation the class antagonism between the petty bourgeoisie and capital was objectively heightened greatly. Unfortunately capital succeeded overwhelmingly in diverting the subjective dissatisfaction from itself to nationalism and anti-semitism. The Fascist Movement; the movement of the expropriated, impoverished petty bourgeoisie is apparently directed against the 'unproductive trade and banking capital', but in reality it is a weapon for dividing the proletariat and for averting the revolutionary movement. This movement is in many respects made unnecessary by the existence of the social democracy as a counter-revolutionary factor.

(3) In a previous chapter we have already spoken of the *impoverishment of the peasantry* by means of the 'scissors'.

(4) *The offensive against the working class for the reduction of its standards of life.*

The most important result of the last three years is the offensive of capitalism, successful on the whole, against those points gained by the working class with which during the war capitalism bought the support of the proletariat and at the end of the war quieted the rebellion of the workers: higher wages, eight-hour day, works councils, etc. All throughout Europe there has taken place a reduction in the standards of life of the proletariat. In America alone the proletariat seems to have succeeded in approximately holding its position.

The methods of the offensive were in part those of peaceful economic conflicts, in part also open military or fascist terror.

In connection with the economic conflict capital profited from the weakened position of the trade unions, besides the subjective treason of the social-democratic and trade-union leaders (e.g. the open treason of the transport workers at the time of the English miners' strike; the blackleg work of the English miners at the time of the American miners' strike, etc.). The British trade unions had spent their funds on unemployment doles. The unions in the countries of inflation lost their fortunes through the inflation; their incomes were so small that they were not even sufficient for keeping up their apparatus. Under these circumstances the traditional methods of the trade-union fight – viz. to stick to peaceful refusal to work until the damage arising to the capitalists from the cessation of production becomes greater than the difference in wages for which the struggle is fought – were utterly inapplicable. The workers were able to hold out in a peaceful fight without support for but a brief time. The capitalists, however, organised in gigantic trusts, and closely-knit employers' federations absolutely held the upper hand in a peaceful economic struggle. Thus the economic conflicts usually ended with the defeat of the proletariat and led to the reduction of the standards of living of the working class. The workers lost faith in the trade unions. With but few exceptions (Hungary), the number of workers organised in unions shows a great decrease during the years 1921–4.

In the countries in which the proletariat attempted to resort to political, armed conflicts, these likewise ended with the defeat of the workers. In Italy it was the Fascisti, an organised, armed force of the capitalist class existing outside the state, which vanquished the proletariat; in Bulgaria and Spain it was a bourgeois dictatorship set up by an officers' revolt; in Germany it was the former 'democratic' government which – as in Bulgaria with the aid of the social democracy – step by step became transformed into a real, undiluted, military dictatorship, which compelled the revolutionary proletariat to retreat.

The result is everywhere a sharp decline in the actual standards of living of the proletariat. It would lead us too far afield to produce figures. It is generally known that the real wages of the German, Austrian, Italian, Hungarian proletariat are today not more than 60 to 70 percent of the pre-war period; that the eight-hour day and the rights of the workers in the industrial concerns have for the most part gone by the board.

In England and the states where the conflict was fought with peaceful weapons, the democratic appearance was kept up. There, too, the standard of life of the workers is much lower than before the war. The special crisis of Western Europe shows itself here in a very interesting manner. The wages of the workers in the export industries (mining, machinery construction, textile industry) were forced down far more than those of workers in local industries (building, tailoring, shoemaking). And even within the same branch of production, as for instance coal mining, there are big differences in wages depending upon the districts. In addition the capitalists everywhere try to separate the wage scales, in that they attempt to force the wages of unskilled workers, of women and of children, down further in proportion to those of male skilled workers, so as to divide the proletariat and weaken its ability to strike a blow.

Summing up, then, we can assert: the class antagonisms have, objectively, become aggravated during the last years: subjectively, however, the onslaught of the proletarian, revolutionary forces has been weakened. The working-class movement has been going through the trough of the revolutionary wave: this is also evident from the successes of the social patriots. Not until 1921 are the first signs of a new revolutionary wave discernible.

8   The Crisis of Economic Policy

When we survey the economic policy of the capitalistic powers during recent years, we find there a reflection of the instability of capitalism during its period of decline. None of the great politico-economic problems could thus far be solved. In most cases bourgeois economic policy was not even able to adopt an attitude, much less offer a solution. We shall try quite briefly to sketch the most important problems.

Autarchy or World-Economic Interlocking

We have repeatedly referred to the fact that the economic development of the war period and in part also of the postwar period tended in the direction of autarchy, i.e of the greatest possible self-supplying with all necessaries on the part of each state. This tendency was especially marked in the development of the colonies, which developed a powerful native industry, while in the capitalistic countries an improvement of agriculture took place (extension of the cultivated areas in England, the raising of beet sugar, the production of hemp in many European countries, etc.).

The bourgeoisie had to face the problem of whether to encourage or hinder this development.

The problem is most intimately connected with a political one – the possibility of new wars coming soon. The experiences of the last war have shown that modern war is not only a conflict between two armies: people fight against people, business against business, technical skill against technical skill. Therefore national economy should be so built up that all the things necessary for a war can be produced at home. This is, of course, an utopia. Only such gigantic countries as the United States or Russia can make their arrangements with the possibility in view of supplying themselves. But the preparation for future wars, the desire to introduce as many of the things necessary for waging war upon the home soil as possible, is an important factor in the striving for autarchy!

Free Trade or Protective Tariff

Closely connected with the problem of self-supply or economic interlocking is the question: protective tariff or free trade? We shall deal with both simultaneously.

Bourgeois economic policy has thus far found no unified answer to this question. But in practice there is a strong tendency toward encouraging the decline of division of work in the world economy by positive measures.

In the *United States* a policy tending in the direction of autarchy has thus far held the upper hand. The protective tariff (McKinley bill) came into force in the autumn of 1922. In the spring of 1924 the President made use of his right to increase the already high tariffs still further at his own discretion, in that he increased the duty on wheat by 40 percent. That importation was not prevented by the high duty is explained by the fact that there was a big boom and that the dollar was estimated abroad at more than its real value. The 'American' tendency has likewise triumphed thus far in the question of taking part in the solution of the reparations question.

Almost all European states try to develop their native industries through protective tariffs, embargoes, subventions, etc., and to aim as far as possible at self-sufficiency. Ditto the English colonies and the independent extra-European states.

The situation of the Western European industrial countries is much more complicated. There can be no question of autarchy on their own soil, although there is continued agitation for a 'back-to-the-farm' movement. They attempt to achieve autarchy by including their colonies in the scheme. In this connection *France* has the advantage that there is no industry developed as yet in her colonies and that there is no native bourgeoisie. France can therefore attempt without hindrance to build up its '100 million country' on the principle of self-sufficiency, and it attempts to do this by creating a tariff area that includes the colonies, and by adopting special politico-economic measures. From a military point of view this 'Greater France' suffers from the dearth of petroleum. It is trying to secure this by political and economic penetration of Poland and Romania.

The problem of *Great Britain* is a more difficult one. The British Imperial Conference of 1923 was an abortive attempt at creating a British world empire that was sufficient unto itself and that constituted a single customs area. The plan came to naught because the bourgeoisie in the colonies was unwilling to renounce customs duties against English industry, and to be relegated to the position of merely supplying foodstuffs and raw materials. The plan further came to naught owing to the circumstances that the creation of a customs union would only then have been worthwhile for the colonies if foreign articles of food, coming from places other than the colonies had been loaded down with tariffs – a thing that nobody dared expect of the English consumers. The defeat of the Conservatives put an end to even the meagre beginnings of a protective tariff policy decided upon by the Imperial Conference. The plan for the creation of a self-sufficient British world empire has failed for the time being: England will stick to free trade, while the colonies are heading more and more in the direction of protective tariffs.

The interests of the bourgeoisie are contradictory in this question. As *purveyor* of industrial products they have an interest in being permitted to import into another country free of duty. As exporters of capital, who desire to *produce* in the colonies or in any foreign country for the market there, they are interested in customs duties. In another respect the interests of the colonial native bourgeoisie are contradictory. As a *native* bourgeoisie they are interested in fighting foreign, exploiting imperialism; as a *bourgeoisie* beset by a native proletariat that is awakening to class consciousness they are dependent upon the aid of the foreign bourgeoisie, who are their natural allies. Hence the contradictions in the 'national' movement in India, and in similar colonial states.

Russian Relations

The bourgeoisie was likewise unable to solve the Russian problem. After the attempts to dethrone proletarian rule by force of arms had failed, the united bourgeoisie attempted at Genoa and the Hague to win out by diplomacy. Likewise without success. The united front of the bourgeoisie broke down in due time; although the European bourgeoisie feared connection with the Bolsheviks for inner-political reasons, the Western European commercial crisis compelled it to come to terms individually with Russia and to make economic arrangements. The aggravation of international antagonism compels the capitalistic countries one after the other to recognise Soviet Russia politically also.

But that is not a solution to the problem. The bourgeoisie cannot attain an honest relationship with the workers' state. While for political reasons it proclaims, especially through the mouths of social democrats, that communism is at an end in Russia, that capitalism has been re-established there, it proves the very opposite by its reserve with reference to the investment of capital and credits. It is utterly unable, either by fair means or foul, to make Russia a part of the capitalist system. Russia remains a thorn in its side. The growing prosperity of the Russian people, the raising of the living standards of the Russian working class has more influence with the oppressed European proletariat than all agitation. Thus the Russian problem remains unsolved despite recognition until it will have been solved by the general extension of the dictatorship of the proletariat. In this connection a new attempt at armed intervention on the part of the capitalistic powers is entirely within the realm of possibilities.

Inflation, Deflation or Stabilisation

The bourgeoisie has not succeeded in solving the problem of exchange. Yes, the views concerning the method of solving it are in sharp contrast to each other.

After the conclusion of the war the opinion prevailed that the exchanges were to be brought back to the gold standard by energetic deflation. England made successful attempts in this direction and had already approached gold parity to within 3 to 4 percent. But the heavy industries of England opposed this policy more and more, and openly or half-furtively defended inflation. (See the celebrated memorandum of the Federation of British Industries, etc.). In point of fact, the British exchange since then evinces a falling tendency. Inflationist tendencies are also conflicting very much with the efforts at securing a good franc.

In the previous chapter we showed the mechanism of inflation – how it expropriates the middle classes in favour of the capitalists, and how it compels certain strata that previously lived on their incomes (interest, profit) to go to work. Inflation automatically forced wages down. It practically means freedom from taxation for the ruling classes, in that direct taxes are reduced to a minimum through the delays in fixing and collecting them. This is of special advantage to the industrial bourgeoisie. The industrial bourgeoisie of the countries having inflation are given a great, albeit temporary, advantage in the struggle for conquering the foreign markets. It is therefore but natural that there are strong inflationistic tendencies in every country; that even in England there is hardly any talk of regaining the nominal gold standard; that in the best case stabilisation is attempted only upon a very low basis (Germany, Poland).

The Reparations Problem

The most difficult politico-economic problem with which the European bourgeoisie is wrestling is the question of reparations. It is impossible within the space of this brochure to trace the history of the complicated reparations negotiations. We must assume that the reader is familiar with them. We shall merely try to show the relation of the reparations question to the general crisis of the European industry and to the contradictory methods of solving it.

The original idea was this: Germany was to restore all damage done to the Allies, without taking into consideration whether German industry can bear such a burden and whether under capitalist circumstances the transfer of such huge sums was possible without something being given or done in exchange.

The result of this system is well-known: Germany, which was to pay the reparations bills in foreign exchange, had to buy foreign money at every price. As long as there were people outside of Germany who believed in the economic future of Germany, and therefore purchased marks with the hope of seeing them rise later, the plan was somehow kept in operation. When, however, with the continued catastrophic depreciation of the mark the sale of it was made impossible abroad, when the marks already sold abroad began to pour back, the impossibility of this method of paying reparations became evident. Germany had to plead for a moratorium, which was partly granted in 1922. The correct conclusion was arrived at that Germany could pay reparations directly in foreign exchange only if the country exported more than during the pre-war period (10 milliards of gold marks per annum). If the attempt were made, however, to compel Germany to conduct such enormous export, this would mean fatal competition upon the world's markets for the industrial countries of Europe – in a market that without this was already unable to absorb the products of Western Europe. In other words, unemployment in England would be aggravated and perpetuated.

The problem became still more complicated through the antagonisms between France and England that were becoming constantly aggravated in their struggle for power. The struggle assumed more and more this form: to the sphere of influence of which of the three imperialistic Great Powers – France, England or the United States – was the country which had become impotent of itself, viz. Germany, to be attached? To put it in slogan form: whose colony was Germany to become?[36] It was out of the question for France with its limited population and its dearth of capital to rule over all of Germany. The French plan, therefore, was: to occupy the Rhine, and Ruhr territories, and to unite these with French industry; to separate southern Germany from northern Germany and then to lord it politically over a Germany thus divided up.

England had no real interest in adding Germany to her sphere, for the reconstruction of Germany would mean the resurrection of the most dangerous rival of Great Britain upon the world's markets, just as before the war. The victory of the war would thus be nullified for England. On the other hand, the solution attempted by France was politically and economically unacceptable for England. Politically, because the military power of France hereby would have become still greater, her position of hegemony upon the European continent still more confirmed. Economically, because the union of the entire continental heavy industry would have meant an unbearable threat to English heavy industry.

The only country that could digest Germany economically is the *United States*. The United States is the only country in which in times of favourable business there is a dearth of industrial workers. Until the world war the United States made up this dearth by extended immigration. At present, however,

---

36 When in this connection, we speak of a colony, we naturally do not think of it in the sense in which Marx used the term: not a country that supplies raw materialism and bought industrial products. Germany could be made into such a country only then if, as Clemenceau desired, it were to lose 20 million of its inhabitants. But one can also speak of a colony in another sense: namely, of a country that is economically controlled and exploited by other countries. This will actually be the case with Germany if the recommendations of the Experts are carried out. [Georges Clemenceau (1841–1929) was a French politician and prime minister, member of the Radical Party].

American public opinion decidedly favours the prevention of further immigration, partly out of fear of the communistically infested immigrants, partly out of nationalism, out of fear that the English character of the country may be lost through intensive immigration; socially, in that capitalism by the embargo upon immigration purchases the support of the aristocracy of labour. The 'colonisation' of Germany by American capital would therefore mean that the workers who were lacking in boom periods would not have to emigrate to America but would be put to work in Germany for America; and that the cheap wages paid to German workers would be used to force down American wages. Meanwhile, however, partly on account of the business boom, the enthusiasm for meddling with European affairs was not yet very great. In fact, in the three countries, France, England and the United States, very different interests are opposed to each other on the reparations issue and make a solution difficult.

The struggle for power between France and England prevented the success of all reparations conferences held until the end of 1922. At the beginning of 1923, there came the occupation of the Ruhr. As one surveys the period historically one can assert that the occupation of the Ruhr was provoked by England in the hope of involving France and Germany in an economic and possibly even in a military conflict, and thereby to tie the hands of France, which was getting more dangerous all the time, and to weaken her militarily and economically. We therefore note that England withdraws after the occupation of the Ruhr has taken place, and that it contents itself with strengthening the backbone of Germany secretly and openly through utterances in which the legality of occupying the Ruhr is challenged. The English plan was crowned with success. To be sure, Germany could not in the long-run withstand a France armed to the teeth. Passive resistance was abandoned and the big industrialists of the Ruhr Valley were compelled to sign the 'Micum' agreements[37] and to undertake enormous deliveries to France. But France was weakened very much economically by the struggle and the catastrophical drop of the franc compelled France to accept the help of English-American capital and – at least seemingly – to agree to a solution of the reparations problem such as is outlined in the Report of the Experts.

Before we deal with the latter, let us point out that there has always been agreement between the French and the English bourgeoisie in one respect: viz. in the belief that German industry, thanks to inflation, by which the state

---

37 [MICUM (Mission Interalliée de Contrôle des Usines et des Mines), Franco-Belgian occupation unit in Ruhr; MICUM agreements were signed in November 1923 between the German industrialists and the French government crediting coal advances by MICUM to the reparations account].

itself and industry were cleared of their debts, is in a much better position than its French and English competitors. Lloyd George said this quite clearly in his speech in parliament on 3 August 1922:

> Germany is suffering from the world crisis. This is not the right time for estimating her full capacity. Let us suppose that it is estimated too low – at £1,000 or £1,500. What will happen? Germany has actually got rid of her internal debts. The collapse of the mark may really have had dire consequences for Germany's economic life. But there is no doubt but that she got rid of her state debts … Germany would then be in this position: She would have no internal debt and only £1,000 to £1,500 foreign debts; not a single factory damaged, some of them newly equipped … Germany has a population of 60 millions, of able and highly qualified workers. A time of recovery will come. When this time comes, we shall have a well equipped Germany with a population of 60 millions, without any state debts, with a foreign debt that was fixed when times were exceedingly bad – and an England loaded down with £7,000 million internal and £1,000 million foreign debts, which would have to enter into competition with two great industrial powers, her industrial rivals.[38]

The same train of thought is found in [Raymond] Poincaré's[39] reply to the English proposal of the Paris Reparations Conference at the close of 1922:

> At present Germany has no foreign debt whatever; as a result of the collapse of the mark she has proportionally reduced her internal debts, so that these would not exceed a few milliards of gold marks and at the next collapse of the German exchange would drop to zero. If Germany were then faced by but a single debt, its reparations obligation, and if this were to be reduced to about 20 milliards through the system of discounts outlined in the British plan – a debt that could be amortized in about fifteen years and that amounts to less than one-third of the French national debt – Germany would after a few years be the only country in Europe that had not a foreign debt; with its increasingly population, its industries intact – which industries would not cease to profit by the exceptional situation – with its untouched reservoirs of coal, wood and nitrates, she would

---

38 [Varga gives as source *The Times*, London, 4 August 1922. However, *The Times* of that date gives a different quote from Poincaré's speech].
39 [Raymond Poincaré (1860–1934), French conservative politician and Prime Minister; in 1923 he ordered the French occupation of the Ruhr].

become the master of Europe as compared with a France the population of which would be half as large and that would continually have to bear the burden of reconstructing the devastated areas. The German hegemony over Europe, which the war was to destroy, would be re-established and strengthened through the Allies.[40]

This thought is repeated again and again by the English capitalists, who point out that they must figure in the high taxes that above all are necessary for paying the interest on state debts, in calculating their production costs, write their German competitors have to pay very low taxes because the state debts have been wiped out through the inflation. The English and French agree that the taxes to be paid by German producers must under no circumstances be lower than their own, so that they may not be at a disadvantage over against their competitors.

The Report of the Commission of Experts

The above are the economic and world-political circumstances under which the unanimous report of the Commission of Experts was framed. We shall now attempt to bring out the most essential parts of it, whereby we assume that the reader is familiar with the report itself. The following seem to us to be the essential points:

Reparations payments to be made only with stable exchange. The Experts' Commission takes the position that Germany can make regular reparations payments only if the German exchange is stable since in the event of a depreciating exchange the income of the state automatically shrinks so much that payments become an impossibility. The stability of the German exchange is therefore to be guaranteed despite the reparations deliveries.

Reparations payments in German exchange. From the above it follows logically that Germany's reparations payments – excepting those in kind – are to be made in German exchange only. The prescribed payments are to be deposited by Germany in German money to the credit of the Reparations Commission in the new bank of issue that is to be erected, the Reparations Bank. After the stipulated sum has been deposited, Germany has fulfilled her obligations; it is up to the Allies to see to it how they will get the reparations deliveries made in German money out of the country. This is to be the business of the Entente Commission that is to be appointed. The old question arises: *in what natural*

---

40 [Varga gives no reference for this quote. Poincaré spoke in the French Assemblée on 16 December 1922 and in the Senate on 20 December 1922].

form can Germany make its reparations deliveries, or, what payments in kind can be accepted as reparations payments by the Allies without heavy damage to the industries of France, England, and the rest of the capitalistic world? The experts' report, of course, does not solve this problem, since this problem is by its very nature unsolvable. Provision has been made that the payments of Germany may be accumulated in money up to two milliards of gold marks. The sums that exceed two milliards are to be invested in German bonds, the maximum being five milliards of gold marks. In case it should develop that no form can be devised by which the reparations payments can be taken over, then Germany's payments are to be reduced until such time as the Allies are able to manage the transfer to foreign countries.

The Experts' Report condemns all plans by which the reparations problem was to be solved at one blow by an international loan of milliards of marks; e.g. the proposal of the Cuno[41] government for a loan of 20 milliard gold marks. The whole idea that by America's broadmindedly placing at Germany's disposal the riches heaped up in America, and in part not put to use the tremendous gold reserves of the Federal Reserve Bank, the reparations problem could be solved and with it at the same time a prime reason for the crisis be removed, has vanished into thin air. The Experts' Report provides for one single, modest loan of 800 million gold marks, to be used for meeting the payments of the first year.

From a *world-political point of view* the proposed solution means the *defeat of France's policy of might*, and a victory for England. The policy of France which aimed at the final separation of the Rhine and Ruhr regions from Germany, separatism in Bavaria and the secession of southern Germany from northern Germany, the division of Germany in this manner into three or four parts, may be looked upon as having failed. The report demands that Germany form a unified economic whole. The solution at the same time prevents the union of continental iron and coal in the hands of France, a thing that is of the greatest importance for France's economic and political position toward England.

Germany becomes an international colony. The Experts' Report provides for a strict and systematic control of Germany by the Allies. In carrying out the measures provided for, German industry is put under Entente control. This control will extend to the railways, to the finances of the country, to the whole monetary policy through the control of the central bank of issue that is to be established, with which all existing banks of issue are to be merged, and to the German taxes, the size of which is to be prescribed by the Allies.

---

41   [Wilhelm Cuno (1876–1933) was a German Catholic politician, Chancellor of Germany (1922–3)].

Payments and Germany's capacity to pay. The Report provides for the following payments (see *Table 8.16*).

TABLE 8.16   German reparation payments

1st year	1,000 million gold marks
2nd	1,220 million gold marks
3rd	1,200 million gold marks
4th	1,750 million gold marks
5th	2,500 million gold marks
Total for the first five years	7,670 million gold marks

Of this sum, as is known, 800 millions are to be realised by a loan, so that for the first five years, payments of less than seven milliard gold marks are provided for. From the fifth year, the payments are to amount annually to 2,500 millions and possibly even more. For, a *prosperity index* has been provided for, made up of different, rather heterogeneous elements (railway traffic, population, export trade, consumption of tobacco, budget expenses, and consumption of coal). If these factors, calculated according to a certain system (the means of percentually changing these six factors), later show a raising beyond the standard of 1926–9, the obligations of Germany are to raised accordingly.

The Report provides *from which sources the reparations are to be secured*: in other words, several forms of income are sequestered for the reparations payments.

(1) *The railways* have ridded themselves through the depreciation of the money of all their debts; they represent a capital account of 26 milliard gold marks. Before the war they had a net income of 600 million gold marks, which sum, figured at today's money values, means about 1,000 gold marks, in which connection it is emphasised, however, that during the pre-war period the German railways were not looked upon as profitable enterprises, but above all as means for the economic development of Germany. If the policy governing rates and fares is directed above all toward the realisation of the highest possible income, it is easily possible annually to gain 600 million gold marks out of the railways in the form of interest on bonds and on the amortisation of these bonds; also, to gain 290 millions annually in the form of railway transportation taxes for reparations purposes.

(2) *German industry* has likewise unburdened itself of its debts through the depreciation of the German money. She can, therefore, take upon her-

self a reparations payment of five millions gold marks, which at 5 percent interest, and 1 percent amortisation is to yield 800 million gold marks annually.

(3) In the Versailles Treaty it is stipulated that *taxes in Germany* shall not be lower than in the Entente countries. On this basis it is estimated that until 1928–9 Germany can progressively deliver 1,250 million gold marks from its ordinary budget for reparations purposes. To secure these deliveries, the income from duties upon tobacco, beer, alcohol and sugar, as well as the customs are to be paid into the reparations account of the new bank of issue (the Reparations Bank).[42] If these taxes and customs duties yield more than has been estimated, the surplus will be placed at the disposal of the Reich.

Two questions present themselves in this connection.

(1) *Can the sums here estimated be taken out of the proceeds of German business and industry, out of the annual production of a Germany diminished in size?*

As far as the first five years are concerned, this question can be answered in the affirmative. In our opinion these sums can be realised because of the disappearance of the state debt and the reduction of military expenses, provided, however, that the political control of the bourgeoisie is a firm one and that the productive processes are not disturbed by heavy social conflicts – a presupposition that will hardly obtain. As far as concerns the full payments after five years, however, we must doubt whether German industry can stand the withdrawal of such sums. However, considering the extremely uncertain condition of capitalism very little that is definite can be said about what will happen five years from now!

(2) *Can a form of delivery in kind be found that will make it possible to export out of Germany the payments provided for?*

For the first five years this question can be answered in the affirmative, for when we substract the deliveries of coal and coke which France is not only glad to accept, but which it absolutely needs for its economic life, there will remain only a relatively small balance that must be exported either as exchange or in the form of goods. This balance can, it seems, be taken care of through the sale of German goods in the world's markets, unless a heavy and acute economic crisis crosses these plans. A different situation will arise when after five years the payments are to be made in their

---

[42] [Reparations Bank. In April 1924, Charles G. Dawes proposed a plan for instituting annual payments on a fixed scale].

full sums. Annual payments of 2½ milliard gold marks can be made only if Germany's export of goods exceeds that of pre-war times by many milliards. We say 'by many milliards' because Germany cannot merely export goods, the raw and auxiliary materials for which are to be found in Germany, but it must naturally also import raw and auxiliary materials from abroad. So extensive an export of German goods would, however, lead to grave disadvantages for French and English industry, considering the present limited capacity of the world market to absorb goods, and considering the continuous inability, in our opinion, of all of Western Europe to produce at full industrial capacity because of the want of markets. We are therefore of the opinion that the full payments demanded can neither be supplied by Germany nor accepted by the Entente.

The Meaning of the Experts' Report: Holding Down German Industry
The Report was unanimously adopted by the experts. As we may assume with certainty that the experts acted in agreement with their governments, this merely means that the Entente governments, i.e. the Entente bourgeoisie, consider the solution of the reparations question as submitted to be correct. The difficulties that Poincaré is causing seem to us to be in part election manoeuvres, in part attempts at holding up the others, so as to compel a solution of the inter-allied debt question that shall be favourable for France.

Then what is the economic meaning of the report? In our opinion it is the following:

The Entente bourgeoisie realises that it is impossible to secure reparations payments from Germany in such sums as were provided for in the various ultimatums. The Entente bourgeoisie must choose: either to secure reparations, but at the price of sharp competition by Germany upon the world market, and as a consequence, depreciation of the mark, social unrest, dictatorship of the right or of the proletariat in Germany, continuation of the crisis and unemployment in England and later, after reconstruction has been completed, also in France; or else to renounce reparations in the sums provided for, *but in return to have decisive influence upon the processes of German industry and to exploit it in such a way that Germany shall be held down as an industrial rival*. In other words: fewer reparations, but no resurrection of Germany as a competitor that is dangerous in the markets of the world. The Experts' Report means that the Entente bourgeoisie has accepted the latter solution. When we take this for granted, the provisions of the report, some of which seem queer, become understandable.

The mortgage upon the railways and the control of the German railways means: freight and passenger rates of German railways must be kept high, so that Germany industry may be prevented from encouraging export, as in peace times, by cheap rates and exceptional export tariffs.

The five-milliard mortgage on German industry means that the costs of production of German industry are increased accordingly. It is significant that the experts have declined to lay claims to German agriculture, as Cuno himself had suggested at one time. For them it was important only to impose burdens upon industry.

The control of the bank of issue means that the discount policy of the central banking institution will be determined by the Entente bourgeoisie and that the size of the credits extended to industry, as well as the rate of interest, will be determined according to the needs of the French and English bourgeoisies, so as to hamper the development of German industry through limitation of credits and through high interest rates.

The investment of five milliards of gold marks in German securities means that the Entente bourgeoisie, which already possesses considerable quantities of shares in German industrial undertakings, gains direct control over the most important branches of German industry. This would especially be the case if the Reparations Commission should later undertake to raise the sum provided for.

Altogether this means that Germany is to be placed economically under the control of the Entente bourgeoisie. This control is, above all, to reduce Germany's industrial ability to compete to a degree that is bearable for France and England; on the other hand industry is not to be so weighted down with overlarge reparations burdens as to bring about a new collapse of the mark and the danger of a nationalistic or proletarian dictatorship.

Germany is to be treated like a valuable draught-horse: it is to be permitted to live, but not to become dangerous. The German proletariat is to be enslaved through long hours of work and low wages, so as to furnish a good excuse for the Entente countries to reduce wages and lengthen the hours of work. The German bourgeoisie is to be given the job of exploiting the workers. It is significant that the Entente bourgeoisie emphasises the necessity of raising the taxes on articles of consumption. But of the sums thus realised only so much is to remain as not to raise a dangerous competitor of the Entente bourgeoisie, the position of which continues to be a difficult one on account of the special crisis of Western European capitalism. Thus we see, instead of an attempt to overcome the crisis through extension of the market, the endeavour to hold down economically the opponent who has been defeated in the war, to lessen competition and to hinder the development of capitalism by political means.

The problem of the inter-allied war debts was only partially solved by the English-American agreement. But there is evidence that even for England, whose state finances are well founded, it is quite difficult to fulfil obligations of this sort, and American economists are of the opinion that the acceptance of these sums is harmful to the United States.[43]

The essence of the question is this: in what form of product are these debts to be paid or accepted by the creditor? In view of the fact that the market for industrial products has become smaller through the war the acceptance is often more disastrous than their delivery. Hence there is a strong tendency, especially in English trade capital circles, which favours the cancellation of inter-allied debts. But the industrialists fear that thereby the taxes of the competitor may be reduced and his ability to compete heightened. Their interests would be best served if the debts or interest thereon were indeed collected, but if the goods with which they are paid were somehow to disappear from the world market – either burned or 'thrown into a hole', as [Walther] Rathenau[44] put it concerning deliveries in kind. Thus the bourgeoisie is breaking its head over this problem without arriving at a solution.

Emigration, Immigration, Malthusianism

Just as in economic policy, so also in the policy regarding population there is real chaos. The French bourgeoisie is complaining of the standstill of population without finding a way out. The English bourgeoisie has already abandoned the hope of supporting the gigantic army of unemployed and the young generation of coming workers on industrial labour within their own country. Hence the continuous agitation for regulated emigration into the colonies and for the limitation of population. Malthusianism, which during the ascendancy of capitalism seemed disposed of, is being resurrected in England.[45]

The question is even more complicated in the United States. Immigration was recently limited for every country to 2 percent of the number from that country living in the United States in 1890. This means that the possibilities for persons from southern and eastern Europe are restricted to a mere fraction, while northern Europeans – Englishmen, Scandinavians, and Germans – are afforded greater possibilities. This policy seems to be in crass contradiction to the interests of the capitalists as employers. As a matter of fact, this policy is

---

43   See Varga 1922a, p. 46.
44   [Walther Rathenau (1867–1922) was a German entrepreneur and owner of the Allgemeine Elektricitäts-Gesellschaft (AEG), liberal politician, minister of Foreign Affairs. On 24 June 1922 he was killed by militants of the extreme right].
45   See, for instance, Harold Cox, editor of the *Edinburgh Review*. The advantages by which England was thus far able to support a dense and growing population have disappeared, he contends, and will never return. See Cox 1922, pp. 38–9. [John M.] Keynes, too, subscribes to this Malthusianism.

the result of conflicting interests. It means above all that the semi-fascist aristocracy of labour under the leadership of [Samuel] Gompers,[46] the still more fascist American Legion, and the wholly fascist-nationalist Ku-Klux-Klan have agreed with the capitalists to keep away from America the cheap foreign labour that is not interested in American nationalism, but is difficult to assimilate and is imbued with revolutionary theories. Through the bar upon immigration the American bourgeoisie purchases the support of the aristocracy of labour in the fight against a revolutionary movement.

But while this policy seems calculated to retard the revolutionary movement in the United States, it works in the very opposite way in Europe. It compels the energetic and dissatisfied elements, which previously solved the problem of their well-being individually by emigration, to remain in Europe and to solve their problem through collective methods, i.e. through taking part in the revolutionary movement. The restriction of immigration stops up a safety-valve that is quite necessary for the European bourgeoisie!

Thus, in the question of population, too, we note the same uncertainty, the same helplessness as in all the other politico-economic problems.

9   The Perspective of Development

From the argument developed thus far the reader will see that we stick to the opinion held thus far: *the period of decline of capitalism continues*. This does not mean that *single sections* of the earth, which were only recently encompassed within capitalism, will not pass through a strong economic ascendancy on a capitalistic basis. Nor does it mean that there can be no more business booms for Europe.

It does mean, however, that capitalism as a whole is proceeding along a downward curve. Considered in big periods, the total of production is decreasing, the crises are long and intensive, the periods of boom are of short duration and not big. Unity of capitalistic world economy is not achieved of late: industrial cycles cross each other's paths, the interlocking of world-economic interests becomes less and less. The position of western Europe, especially, remains shaken, the condition of crisis continues almost permanently because of the tendency toward decreasing the division of world work. The end of the reconstruction period in France and the resumption of production in Germany

---

46   [Samuel Gompers (1850–1924) was an American union leader, founder of the American Federation of Labor (AFL)].

after the stabilisation of the mark and after the solution of the reparations problem will aggravate this crisis. This period is characterised by heavy internal class struggles for the division of what has been produced and wars to hinder the opponent forcibly from competing.

The *immediate future* is characterised by the ending of the American boom, increased competition of America on the world markets, and a crisis in Europe that may be expected soon.

It cannot be decided purely from an economic standpoint whether the end of the period of decline will mean the collapse of capitalism or the construction of a new world-economic equilibrium, a new entrenchment of capitalism. In our *Crisis*[47] three years ago we pointed out that within capitalism there are '*imminent tendencies*' for regaining the equilibrium and that conscious efforts are under way for overcoming the crisis. Unquestionably the last three years have witnessed the social entrenchment of capitalism. We recall the words of Lenin which we cited in the first chapter: 'There is no situation for which there is absolutely no way out for the bourgeoisie'. Whether capitalism will work its way out of the period of decline or whether it will collapse depends decisively upon the attitude and actions of the proletariat.

∴

It goes without saying that the question of the future of capitalist economy is much discussed today. The general opinion is a more optimistic one than we hold. The capitalists are always inclined to look upon the present course of business as a permanent thing. It would lead too far to disprove all opposing theories. We shall cull a few representative opinions.

Hilferding's optimism. That the Social Democrats look optimistically upon the future of capitalism is the logical consequence of their whole political attitude, their treaty with the bourgeoisie and their enmity toward a proletarian revolution. For, they can temporarily keep the workers away from the revolutionary movement only if they promise them a *betterment of their condition for the future within the capitalist system*, that is possible, however, only if they assume that in the near future there will be a new upward trend of capitalism.

As an example we cite the opinion of [Rudolf] Hilferding,[48] the recognised economic theoretician of the Second International:

---

47 [Varga 1922b].
48 [Rudolf Hilferding (1877–1941), Austrian-born Marxist economist; German SPD politician, member of the Reichstag, Finance Minister (1923; 1928–9)].

> Even now it is quite evident that the economic crisis has in the main been overcome. One can also discern that the reestablishment of world production will not, as there was reason to fear for a time, take place on a narrower scale, but on a wider. As soon as the problem of the reconstitution of political security in central Europe, in Russia, and in China is solved, a big boom is to be expected as extremely likely, which boom will fully employ all the productive forces that have meanwhile been developed.[49]

Hilferding furnishes no real proof for his interpretation, unless we take the following sentences as proof:

> During and after the war the productive forces have grown tremendously. This expansion was not uniform – above all those branches of industry were increased that were necessary for the conduct of the war: the raising of raw materials in the widest extent possible, the production and workmanship on metals, the chemical industry, shipping; while the industries having to do with the means of consumption, in so far as they were not necessary for the armies, lagged behind. This disproportion is one of the reasons for the world crisis. But in the last analysis the extension of productive capacity means, after the crisis has been overcome, increased production and a new boom. The agrarian revolution at the same time means the extension of the market for industrial products. Thus capitalist economy seems as a result of the war period to have been materially expanded and qualitatively changed on the way to organised-economy.[50]

This theory, which, by the way, coincides with that of Comrade Ollivier[51] mentioned above, suffers from the error that it takes for granted something that must be proven, namely, that we are concerned in the present period with an 'equilibrium of world production and circulation that has been temporarily disturbed', which is to be followed by an era of democracy, of peace, of *'realistic pacifism'*, during which 'the sovereignty of individual states is to be curtailed in favour of a super-state organisation'. Hilferding himself puts a question mark after this sentence, which has been entirely adapted to the foolish and lying homage paid by the Second International to the Entente League of Nations.

---

49   Hilferding 1924c, p. 118.
50   Hilferding 1924a, p. 9.
51   [Marcel Ollivier (Aron Goldenberg) (1896–1993) was a 'Luxemburgist' French Communist who left the USSR in 1928; he broke with Communism in 1933].

But the whole trend of his thought is: ascending capitalism, agreement with the bourgeoisie, democracy, world peace.

For the present, however, we see a business depression not only in the United States, but also in Germany.[52] Not a trace of the boom prophesied. And instead of 'realistic pacifism' we see armaments on sea and land and under the sea, in the air, in the chemical works, in the bacteriological institutes ...

We see as one of the most important reasons for the present crisis the industrialisation of overseas countries, through which Western Europe, with its overdeveloped apparatus for production and the necessity of exchanging articles of food and raw materials for industrial products, is losing its economic basis as heretofore held. The American statistician, Miller,[53] expresses this idea as follows:

> While the nineteenth century brought the conquest of the world through technical and mechanical inventions, and thereby a division of work between the primitive countries that supply raw materials and the more developed industrial countries, the twentieth century signifies a new and opposite phase of development: the turning aside of the countries with raw materials from the principle of division of work and their striving to get back to economic autarchy. This, he holds, is an economic problem of the most fundamental importance, whereby the industrial countries are themselves advancing this process by supplying machinery and equipment.

The editor of the German financial periodical, *Die Bank*, [Alfred] Lansburgh,[54] offers the following objection to this trend of thought: The present 'agrarian countries' were industrial countries during the period of manual trades, and supplied fine industrial goods for Europe.

> The concentrated production and applied science of the so-called cultured nations forced primitive overseas production out, brought about the gradual limitation to the production of raw materials, and thus

---

52 See 'Die Wirtschaftskonjunktur Anfang Mai', *Berliner Börsen-courier*, 2 May [1924]; 'Einer neuen Inflation Entgegen', *Berliner Börsen-courier*: 3 May [1924]: 'German business and industry during the last six weeks shows all the signs not of recovery but of a relapse into the sickness from which it has barely recovered'.

53 [Varga gives no references of information about this Miller].

54 [German economist and editor of *Die Bank*, Alfred Lansburgh (1872–1937) (ps. Argentarius) warned in 1923 of the danger of printing additional marks].

branded them as agrarian countries. This process is today revised backwards; the industrial countries supply the agrarian countries with technical means again to industrialize themselves, and that, too, in modern form. Not, however, in order to renounce their supplying the world market with manufactured goods and to turn their population, trained industrially, over to starvation, but rather to specialize anew and to transform their works so as to manufacture articles that correspond to the tremendous technical developments. Instead of exporting cotton thread, the manufacture of which is now left to the countries that were formerly agrarian, one now begins to export artificial silk; instead of oil and petroleum lamps, one exports electric bulbs and apparatus; instead of old-fashioned guns, modern machine guns; instead of hardware made of iron, articles made of aluminium; instead of a number of articles that one can now do without, chemicals, especially dyes and medicinal articles. And if the accumulation of capital, which follows this advantageous export for the countries supplying these goods, in due time leads to a new phase of the industrial penetration of countries overwhelmingly agrarian, and trains these to produce electrical equipment, chemical preparations, and perhaps even dirigible airships, then progress will again even up the decrease of export of the industrial countries; and other articles, thus far only dreamed of (radio apparatus? accumulators from the energy of the sea?) will be supplied in exchange for the raw materials that may still be needed. Without envy technical inventions and the experience of yesterday are turned over to the agrarian States, and just as unenvyingly the achievements of today will be turned over to them to-morrow, since one is in possession of data that mean progress to-morrow. Thus the transition from one stage in the division of work to another is accomplished without pain, without a shock, and without any possibility of proclaiming a catastrophe.[55]

This trend of thought has much more content than that of Hilferding. Only we do not believe that this transfer will take place 'without pain and without a shock'. We recall the famous report of the Indian Viceroy[56] at the time when the English textile industry conquered India. 'The bones of weavers cover the

---

[55] *Die Bank. Monatshefte für Finanz- und Bankwesen und Chronik der Wirtschaft*, February 1924, p. 63.
[56] [Lord William Bentinck (1874–1934) was governor-general of India and sympathised with liberal ideas. Bentinck showed great courage and humanity by his decision to abolish suttee (*sati*), the Hindu custom of burning widows alive with the corpses of their husbands].

plains of India'.[57] It is open to question whether the European proletariat will take such a fate upon itself. Of course, if the proletariat is eliminated as a revolutionary force, then every crisis can be overcome by the bourgeoisie.

We shall now briefly quote the opinions of several English economic authorities as reflected in a series of articles in *The Nation*.[58]

In an introductory article Lloyd George[59] points out that the population of England has increased by 2,000,000 since before the war. Hence production ought to be 5 percent higher than then. Actually, however, it was only 87 percent of the pre-war period during 1923 (the best of the last three years) according to the estimates of the celebrated Professor [Arthur Lyon] Bowley,[60] or 98 percent according to the estimates of the *Economist*. In any case there is a discrepancy of 10 to 18 percent! Lloyd George looks to the re-establishment of pre-war conditions in a pretty remote future. He has no better advice to give than to prepare for a later boom by improvising the productive apparatus.

William Beveridge,[61] the celebrated expert on the problem of English unemployment, comments on unemployment on a large scale for ten years.

> The modest state of comfortable riches of the Victorian period will never return. We had great prosperity and became a great people during the reign of Queen Victoria simply because we were the first to be able to exploit our coal and iron fully. But we have lost this passing advantage of a first exploitation of our natural resources. Prosperity can in future be vouchsafed only through harder collective labour that will at least be more effective, more scientific, and more harmonious than that of others ... It will not fall into our laps as of yore.

Professor Bowley estimates that from 1930 on, the decline of the birth-rate during the war will ease the labour market. At present, he says, unemployment is not greater than in 1909. It will gradually diminish.

Lord [William] Weir[62] emphasises the necessity of advancing English industry, etc.

---

57   Cited in Marx 1954, p. 432.
58   *The Nation*, 12 April, 19 April, 26 April 1923.
59   [Lloyd George (1863–1945) was a British liberal politician and Prime Minister].
60   [Arthur Lyon Bowley (1869–1957) was a British statistician and economist who was pioneering in sampling techniques in social surveys].
61   [William Beveridge (1879–1963) was a British economist and liberal politician].
62   [Lord William Weir (1877–1959), 1st Viscount Weir, became in 1918 Secretary of State for Air in Lloyd George's government].

In general we see in the case of the leading English economists that there is helplessness and pessimism. Not a trace of Hilferding's optimism of gladly affirming a better future for capitalism! Only, the Social Democrats must see the future of capitalism in a rosy light, for their whole policy is built upon the continuance of capitalism.

The crisis of capitalism continues. No optimistic theories can deceive us. Whether it will lead to the recovery of capitalism or its collapse depends upon the revolutionary proletariat and its party, the Communist World Party. Capitalism has entrenched itself during the last years. But likewise the Communist Movement. In Russia through the economic reconstruction, through the final winning over of the majority of the working class, which is now accepted, into the party organisation; in the bourgeois countries through the rearing and development of a determined advance guard and great mass parties. The power of capitalism has grown, but we, too, have gained strength. The struggle continues on a higher plane.

Appendix

The table below shows that production has scarcely reached the level of the pre-war period. Coal, iron and steel especially behind pre-war times.

TABLE 8.17 Figures for world production (without Russia)[63]
Plant products in millions of double hundredweights

	Average 1909–13	Average 1914–18	Average 1921–2	1923
Wheat	700	791	800	942
Barley	265	251	253	247
Rye	214	167	191	234
Oats	494	487	479	555
Corn	971	974	1,057	900
Rice	693	764	–	695
Potatoes	1,134	982	993	1,161
Beet sugar	63	46	43	47
Cane sugar	96	120	129	127
Coffee	12	12	10	–

63 Plant products from *Annuaire Statistique Agricole 1909–21*, p. 261f.

TABLE 8.17 Figures for world production (*cont.*)

	Average 1909–13	Average 1914–18	Average 1921–2	1923
Cocoa	2	3	4	–
Tea	3	3	3	–
Cotton	41	39	37	34
Jute	15	15	11	–

Mining products (in million tons)

	1913	1916	1917	1918	1919	1920	1921	1922	1923
Anthracite	1,344	1,390	1,345	1,331	1,158	1,300	1,100	1,207	1,300[64]
Petroleum	52	62	67	67	80	90	109	122	145
Pig iron	78	71	67	–	–	61	40	51	65
Steel	75	–	–	–	–	68	41	62	73

(in 1,000 tons)

	1913	1916	1917	1918	1919	1920	1921
Copper ore	103	144	147	147	96	98	53
Tin	133	125	130	114	124	122	–
Zinc	1,000	965	990	822	645	719	458
Lead	1,187	1,169	1,190	1,196	864	849	888

(in 1,000 kilograms)

	1913	1916	1917	1918	1919	1920	1921	1922
Gold	692	683	637	568	549	542	468	457
Silver	6,960	5,000	5,100	5,600	5,500	5,020	4,850	7,141

---

64 Preliminary estimate.

(in 1,000 tons)

	1913	1916	1917	1918	1919	1920	1921	1922	1923
Shipbuilding	3,330	1,690	2,940	5,440	7,140	5,860	4,340	2,467	1,643

World supply of live stock (including Russia), millions of heads, according to the census of live stock closest to the years 1911 and 1921[65]

	1911	1921
Horses	111	100
Cattle	483	511
Sheep	618	532
Pigs	260	210

The table below shows the shift in mine production in favour of the United States.

TABLE 8.18 Shift in mine production[66]

	Before the war				After the war		
	Year	Million tons	Million tons	USA % of world prod.	Year	Million tons	Million tons	USA % of world prod.
Anthracite	1913	1,344	517	38.4	1922	1,207	418	36.6
Petroleum	1913	52	34	65.3	1923	145	105	72.4
Pig iron	1913	78	31	39.7	1923	65	40	61.6
Steel	1913	78	32	42.1	1923	73	45	61.6

65 Figures concerning live stock from *Annuaire international de Statistique Agricole*, Rome: Institut international d'Agriculture, 1909–21, p. 234f.
66 M.G.C., *Wirtschaft und Statistik*; *The Economist*.

		Europe % of world prod.	North America % of world prod.		Europe % of world prod.	North America % of world prod.
Copper	1912–14[67]	11	67	1919–20[68]	7	64
Lead	" "	46	43	" "	30	57
Zinc	" "	65	34	" "	36	61
Aluminium	1913	58	42	1921	48	52

TABLE 8.19 Development of coal and iron production in the most important countries[69]

	USA		England		Germany		France	
Year	Coal	Cast iron	Coal	Cast iron	Coal	Cast iron	Coal	Cast iron
1870	17.3	1.6	113.0	6.0	33.9	1.4	13.3	1.1
1880	42.8	3.8	146.9	7.7	59.1	2.7	19.3	1.7
1890	111.3	9.2	181.6	7.9	89.2	4.6	26.0	1.9
1900	212.3	13.7	225.1	8.9	149.4	8.5	33.4	2.7
1913	478.4	30.9	287.4	10.2	190.0	9.2[70]	40.8	5.2
1923	591.2	40.6	281.4	7.6	80.0[71]	5.0	47.8	5.3

---

67 Average.
68 Average.
69 Brelet 1923, p. 25.
70 Including Luxembourg.
71 Estimated.

TABLE 8.20A   Economic statistics of the United States (1918 = 100).[72] Monthly averages

	1919	1920	1922	1923	1923 Jan	1923 Apr	1923 July	1923 Oct	1924 Jan	1924
Production of pig iron	100	119	54	87	130	126	139	144	123	118
Steel	111	135	64	114	143	151	156	139	141	143
Copper	105	99	39	81	121	110	116	123	130	130
soft coal	99	116	87	85	114	126	107	113	123	127
Anthracite	96	97	99	58	104	114	106	109	114	104
crude oil[73]	154	178	189	224	202	251	283	315	323	272
Consumption of wool	–	–	–	124	121	144	128	105	117	122
Cotton	108	105	97	109	117	131	124	99	116	124
Foreign trade (according to value) Import	218	294	140	177	201?	220	244	192	206	198
Export	319	331	181	154	201	162	157	146	194	191
Wholesale trade	212	226	147	149	154	156	159	151	153	151
Automobiles in 1,00 per month[74]	164	183	139	214	334	243	382	327	365	316
General Index (F.R.B. 1919 = 100)	–	105	80	98	120	121	124	121	118	120

---

72   *Survey of Current Business; Monthly Supplement to Commerce Reports.* United States Department of Commerce, Washington: Bureau of the Census, Bureau of Foreign and Domestic Commerce, Bureau of Statistics.
73   1921 = 100.
74   1913 monthly average = 40,000.

THE DECLINE OF CAPITALISM

TABLE 8.20B The most important data concerning English business.[75] Monthly averages

	1913	1920	1921	1922	1923	1923 Jan	1923 Apr	1923 July	1923 Oct	1924 Jan
Coal, million tons	24.3	19.4	3.81	21.1	23.4	22.4	22.4	22.1	25.7	23.8
Pig iron, 1,000 tons	869	680	222	415	630	577	663	666	605	642
Steel, 1,000 tons	649	768	314	494	719	644	761	634	713	701
% of unemployed among trade union members	–	–	–	–	–	13.7	11.3	11.1	10.9	8.9
Dito, among all insured	–	–	–	–	–	13.1	11.4	11.5	11.7	11.9
Wholesale trade index, *Economist* £ in dollars	100	283	181	160	162	161	165	155	160	172
Exports in million £	4.87	3.66	3.85	4.43	4.57	4.65	4.66	4.58	4.52	4.26
Imports in million £	43.8	111.3	58.6	60.0	63.9	66.8	62.9	59.5	71.3	77.5

TABLE 8.20C The most important data concerning French business[76]

	1913	1920 (a)	1921 (a)	1922 (a)	1923 (a)	1923 Jan	1923 Apr	1923 July	1923 Oct	1924 Jan
Coal prod., 1,000 tons	3,404	2,890	3,213	3,596	3,986	4,199	3,063	4,312	4,862	3,762(b)
Coal import., 1,000 tons	1,558	2,005	1,472	1,861	–	1,888	1,927	2,473	2,272	2,247
Iron prod., 1,000 tons	434(c)	276	280	427	433	486	350	436	514	586
Steel prod., 1,000 tons	396(c)	246	255	373	415	408	355	400	477	541
Unemployed per 1,000	–	–	64.0(d)	9.7(d)	2.4(d)	2.4	1.4	1.6	0.5	1.2
Exports, 1,000 tons	1,840	1,071	1,333	1,885	–	1,896	1,513	1,921	2,170	1,170

---

75 *The Economist*, Monthly Supplement.
76 *The Economist*, Monthly Supplement; *Federal Reserve Bulletin*.

TABLE 8.20C The most important data concerning French business (cont.)

	1913	1920 (a)	1921 (a)	1922 (a)	1923 (a)	1923 Jan	1923 Apr	1923 July	1923 Oct	1924 Jan
Imports, 1,000 tons	3,685	4,211	3,165	4,281	–	4,111	4,175	4,864	4,360	3,933
Exports, million francs	573	2,241	1,648	1,720	2,536	1,696	2,508	2,424	2,814	2,361
Imports, million francs	702	4,159	1,839	1,992	2,718	2,144	2,560	2,616	3,069	2,644
Whole sale trade index	100	509	345	327	419	387	415	407	421	495
Exchange rate of franc in New York	19.3	7.0	7.5	8.2	6.1	6.7	7.0	5.9	6.0	4.67
Banknote circulation, milliard francs	5.7	37.9	36.4	36.4	39.1	37.1	36.9	37.3	37.3	38.8

(a) Monthly average.
(b) Excluding Saar territory.
(c) Excluding Lorraine.
(d) January.

TABLE 8.20D   The most important data concerning German business

Production 1,000 tons	1913	1920 Jan. (a)	1921 Jan. (a)	1922 Jan. (a)	1923 (a) Jan.	1923 Jan.	1923 April	1923 July	1923 Oct.	1924 Jan.	1924 Feb.	1924 Mar.
Anthracite	11,729	10,945	11,351	10,830	5,200	–	–	–	–	8,785	9,726	–
Soft coal	7,269	9,323	10,250	11,423	9,833	–	–	–	–	9,553	8,327	–
Coke	2,639	2,074	2,394	2,426	–	–	–	–	–	1,474	1,742	–
Iron	909	463	625	730	333	–	–	–	–	–	–	–
Steel	1,412	643	750	762	417	–	–	–	–	–	–	–
% of unemployed trade union members	–				3.9	3.9	6.6	3.1	19.3	29.4	28.6	–
Wholesale trade index (St. R.)	1.0	3.3	4.7	3.8	–	2,785	5,212	74,787	7.1 mllrd.	1.17 billn.	1.16 billn.	–
Wholesale trade index in gold	100	14.9	19.1	341.8	–	–	–	–	117.9	117.3	116.2	120.7
Value of imports in gold marks	934	329	479	526	507	–	–	–	436	568	719	–
Value of exports in gold marks	850	300	351	517	507	–	–	–	565	431	466	–
Exchange rate of mark in dollars	23.8	1.8	–	– (b)	0.02 (c)	0.0073 (c)	0.0035 (b)	0.0035 (d)	0.37 (d)	0.23	0.23	–

(a) Monthly average.
(b) For 1,000 marks.
(c) For 100 marks.
(d) For 1 milliard marks.

The table below shows that the exportation of capital decreased greatly in 1928, especially the capital loaned to Europe.

TABLE 8.21A   Emission of capital in the United States (million dollars)

	1913	1920	1921	1922	1923
United States					
Joint Businesses	408.0	774.0	1,420.8	1,279.2	1,112.4
Corporate undertakings	1,645.2	3,106.8	2,635.2	3,424.8	3,640.8
Total(a)	2,053.2	3,880.8	4,056.0	4,704.0	4,753.2
Foreign Countries –	–	261.7	414.4	495.7	312.8
To Governments of these					
Europe	–	177.3	138.3	131.7	70.0
Far East	–	–	12.0	110.7	50.0
Latin America	–	–	188.2	148.3	67.5
North America	–	84.4	75.9	105.0	26.3
To Undertakings of these	–	170.7	161.6	203.9	89.8
Europe	–	15.7	3.3	97.3	18.5
Far East	–	5.9	–	1.3	19.9
Latin America	–	52.7	53.4	57.3	17.3
North America	–	96.4	104.9	48.0	34.1
Foreign Countries Total(b)	–	432.4	576.0	699.0	303.8
Grand Total	–	4,313.2	4,632.0	5,403.0	5,056.8

(a) *Journal of Commerce*
(b) *Federal Reserve Bulletin; Survey of Current Business*

The table below shows that, if we except the govenrment loans, which signify no real accumulation of capital, accumulation is demonstrated to have been much less than before the war.

TABLE 8.21B Emission of capital in England (in million £) (a)

	1912 £	1913 £	1920 £	1921 £	1922 £	1923 £
Great Britain						
Government	nil	nil	37.5	202.9	369.6	77.5
Other	45.3	35.9	290.5	73.2	73.9	56.4
Total	45.3	35.9	328.0	276.1	443.5	133.9
British Possesions						
Government	14.7	26.3	11.9	73.7	58.6	69.4
Other	57.9	49.8	19.7	16.9	16.3	23.3
Total	72.6	76.1	31.6	90.6	74.9	92.7
Foreign Countries						
Government	9.6	26.1	Nil	5.9	14.3	26.5
Other	83.2	58.3	7.8	16.3	40.9	18.2
Total	92.8	84.4	7.8	22.2	55.2	44.7
Grand Total	210.7	196.4	367.4	388.9	573.6	271.3

(a) 'New capital issues in 1923', *The Economist*, 29 December 1923, pp. 1140–1.

The table below shows how the Foreign Trade of the United States has been diverted from Europe, and how trade with Asia is growing in importance. It also shows the tremendous excess of exports to Europe. This was covered in part through the exportation of gold, in part through credits.

TABLE 8.22 Direction in which the Foreign Trade of the United States moves. (a)
In million dollars

	Export					Import				
	1910–14	1920	1921	1922	1923	1910–14	1920	1921	1922	1923
Europe	1,350	4,466	2,364	2,083	2,276	837	1,228	765	991	1,240
France	139	676	225	267	280	130	166	142	143	172
Germany	304	311	372	316	313	177	89	80	118	166
Italy	66	372	216	151	186	51	75	62	64	103

TABLE 8.22 Direction in which the Foreign Trade of the United States moves (*cont.*)

	Export					Import				
	1910–14	1920	1921	1922	1923	1910–14	1920	1921	1922	1923
England	569	1,825	942	856	1,003	279	514	239	257	403
North America	501	1,929	1,130	916	940	347	1,663	755	822	864
Canada	315	972	594	577	577	117	612	335	364	367
South America	121	624	273	226	255	207	761	296	359	496
Argentina	47	214	111	96	110	33	208	60	86	140
Asia and Oceania	165	1,044	646	541	500	276	1,397	653	875	1,140
Japan	45	381	238	222	161	85	415	251	354	372
China	31	179	132	127	–	39	250	113	152	–
Africa	25	166	73	56	54	22	150	40	65	210
Total	2,166	8,228	4,485	3,832	4,025	1,689	5,278	2,509	3,113	–

Percentages

	Of the total export					Of the total import				
Europe	62.3	54.3	52.7	54.4	–	49.6	23.3	30.5	31.8	–
North America	23.1	23.4	25.2	23.9	–	20.5	31.5	30.1	26.4	–
South America	5.6	7.6	6.1	5.9	–	12.3	14.3	11.8	11.5	–
Asia and Oceania	7.8	12.7	14.4	14.4	–	16.3	28.0	26.0	28.1	–
Africa	1.2	2.0	1.6	1.5	–	1.3	2.8	1.6	2.1	–

(a) *Commerce Year-Book*; for 1923 *Federal Reserve Bulletin*.
(b) Including Korea.

TABLE 8.23 Unemployment in %

	England (all who are insured)	Belgium	Trade-union members					Canada	Germany (a)	Switzerland	France	Italy	USA
			Netherlands	Denmark	Sweden	Norway						
1921												
Jan	8.2	19.3	16.5	19.7	20.1	11.7	13.1	4.5	35	64	112	—
Apr	15.0	31.2	11.9	21.7	24.2	17.7	16.3	3.9	49	85	250	—
July	14.8	21.4	7.6	16.7	27.9	17.9	9.1	2.6	56	34	435	6.5(b)
Oct	12.8	13.6	7.0	18.3	27.1	17.1	7.4	1.2	74	14	492	3.5(d)
1922												
Jan	17.2	11.2	20.3	28.9	34.3	23.9	13.9	3.3	97	10	607	3.0(b)
Apr	15.4	8.9	11.6	24.0	28.3	34.4	10.4	0.9	81	7	432	—
July	12.3	5.3	9.5	12.5	18.2	12.5	4.1	0.6	52	4	304	1.5(b)
Oct	12.3	3.9	9.6	11.3	15.5	11.3	3.9	1.4	18	1	321	—
1923												
Jan	13.1	3.9	19.3	21.5	20.5	16.1	7.8	4.2	56	2	392	—
Apr	11.4	2.4	10.4	11.5	14.9	11.2	4.5	7.0	36	1	270	1.0(b)
Jul	11.5 (11.1)(c)	2.2	10.6	7.4	9.1	6.9	2.2	3.5	23	2	183	—
Oct	11.7 (10.9)(c)	1.9	11.0	7.6	8.2	8.6	6.2	19.1	24	—	200	—

TABLE 8.23 Unemployment in % (*cont.*)

			Trade-union members								
	England (all who are insured)	Belgium	Netherlands	Denmark	Sweden	Norway	Canada	Germany (a)	Switzerland	France	Italy	USA
1924												
Jan	11.9 (8.9)(c)	3.7	22.7	21.0	13.6	–	7.5	26.5	28	1	281	1.5(b)
Feb	10.7 (8.1)(c)	3.6	17.3	21.3	12.8	–	7.8	25.1	27	1	259	–
Mar	9.9 (7.8)(c)	–	15.1	–	–	–	–	16.6	21	1	–	–
Apr	–	–	–	–	–	–	–	–	–	–	–	–

(a) *Reichsarbeitsblatt*. Berlin: Reichsministerium, Verlag von Reimar Hobbing.
(b) Estimated.
(c) Percent of trade-union members.
(d) Figures of the Labour Ministry for November.

The table below shows how many American cents were paid per hundred, thousands, million and milliard respectively, of a given unit of exchange. The countries are grouped approximately according to the order of their depreciation. Note especially the depression of certain exchanges that were then far stable: Japan, Denmark, Brazil, Spain.

TABLE 8.24 Dollar-cents per unit of exchange

		Annual average						1923				1924		
	Par.	1919	1920	1921	1922	1923	Jan.	April	July	Oct.	Jan.	Feb.	14.4	18.4
Sweden	26.8	25.5	20.5	22.5	26.2	26.6	26.9	26.7	26.5	26.3	26.2	26.2	26.3	26.4
Holland	40.2	39.1	34.4	33.6	38.5	39.1	39.5	39.2	39.2	38.0	37.4	37.4	37.1	37.2
Switzerland	19.3	19.0	16.9	17.4	19.1	18.1	18.8	18.2	17.6	17.5	17.3	17.4	17.3	17.6
England	486	43	366	385	443	457	466	466	458	44	426	43	428	436
Japan	49.8	51.2	52.4	48.2	47.8	48.6	48.7	48.7	48.8	—	—	—	—	41.8
Argentina	96.5	99.0	92.7	73.0	81.8	78.6	84.7	83.1	77.7	73.7	—	—	—	—
Spain	19.3	—	—	13.3 (e)	14.5 (e)	12.8	15.7	15.3	14.9	13.1	12.8	12.7	12.9	13.8
Denmark	26.8	—	—	16.2 (e)	19.9 (e)	18.4	19.4	18.9	18.0	17.2	16.9	16.0	15.3	16.6
Norway	26.8	—	—	16.1 (e)	15.5 (e)	16.7	18.7	17.8	16.7	14.7	14.1	13.3	13.5	13.8
Brazil	32.42	26.7	22.5	13.1	—	10.2	11.4	10.5	10.4	9.5	—	—	—	11.3
France	19.3	13.7	7.0	7.5	8.2	6.1	6.7	6.7	5.9	5.5	4.7	4.4	4.5	6.3
Belgium	19.3	12.8	7.4	7.4	7.4	5.2	6.1	5.8	5.4	4.7	4.2	3.82	3.9	5.4
Italy	19.3	11.4	5.0	4.3	4.3	4.6	4.9	5.0	4.3	4.4	4.3	4.3	4.3	4.4

TABLE 8.24 Dollar-cents per unit of exchange (cont.)

		Annual average						1923				1924		
	Par.	1919	1920	1921	1922	1923	Jan.	April	July	Oct.	Jan.	Feb.	14.4	18.4
Czecho-Slovakia	20.26	—	—	1.3 (e)	1.73 (e)	2.96	2.85	2.98	3.0	2.9	2.9	2.9	2.9	2.94
Austria	—	—	—	0.25 (e)	0.003 (e)	0.0014 (d)	0.0014 (d)	0.0014 (d)	0.0014 (d)	0.0014 (d)	0.0014 (d)	0.0014 (d)	0.0014 (d)	0.0014 (d)
Hungary	20.26	—	—	—	—	0.00017	0.0004	0.0002	0.014 (d)	0.0054 (d)	0.0040 (d)	0.0034 (d)	0.0015 (d)	0.0015 (d)
Poland	23.8	—	—	—	—	0.014 (a)	0.0042 (d)	0.0023 (d)	0.007 (a)	0.00053	0.00012 (a)	0.00011 (a)	0.00012 (a)	0.00012
Germany	23.8	3.0	1.8	—	—	0.02 (a)	0.0073 (d)	0.0042 (d)	0.0035 (a)	0.37 (c)	0.23 (c)	0.23 (c)	0.23 (c)	0.23 (c)

(a) For 1,000 marks.
(b) For 1 million marks.
(c) For 1 milliard marks.
(d) For 100 kronen or marks.
(e) January.

THE DECLINE OF CAPITALISM

The table below shows that, if we compare the figures for exports and imports with the index figure for wholesale trade for the respective years, the foreign trade is much less than before the war.

TABLE 8.25 The foreign trade of important countries (a)

		Wholesale b Import					Export					Wholesale trade index (b)				
		1913	1920	1921	1922	1923	1913	1920	1921	1922	1923	1913	1920	1921	1922	1923
Great Britain	Million pounds	768	1,932	1,087	1,004	1,098	634	1,557	810	824	886	100	283	181	160	162
Germany	Gold marks	10,770	3,947	5,751	6,312	6,081	10,097	3,724	—	6,199	6,079	100	—	—	—	—
France	Francs	8,421	49,905	22,068	23,901	32,600	6,880	26,894	19,773	30,642	30,400	100	509	345	327	419
Italy	Lire	3,645	26,821	17,266	15,727	17,225	2,312	11,774	8,275	9,297	11,059	100	624	578	562	575
Switzerland	Francs	1,919	4,200	2,248	1,915	2,245	1,376	3,277	2,140	1,690	1,760	100 (c)	—	191	168	181
Belgium	Francs	5,050	12,942	10,055	9,377	12,538	3,716	8,862	7,147	6,110	8,993	100 (c)	—	366	367	497
Denmark	Crowns	855	2,943	1,635	1,467	1,975	721	1,962	1,505	1,242	1,243	100	341	178	181	204
USA	Dollars	1,749	5,279	2,587	3,116	3,792	2,446	8,228	4,485	3,832	4,168	100	226	147	149	154
Canada	Dollars	670	1,337	800	762	908	377	1,303	803	898	1,002	100	241	170	150	154
Argentina	Gold pesos	496	881	635	686	—	519	1,031	672	673	—	100	—	—	—	—
British India	Pounds	122	336	178	155	—	166	262	164	210	—	100 (c)	204	181	180	176
China	US Dollars	416	—	599	775	—	294	—	457	537	—	100	152	150	146	156
Japan	Yen	729	2,335	1,614	1,859	1,984	632	1,947	1,253	1,595	1,447	100	260	201	196	—

(a) *Statistisches Jahrbuch für das Deutsche Reich; Commerce Year-book for 1923; Business and Statistics.*
(b) *The Economist*, Monthly Supplement, 22 March 1924. p. 20.
(c) 1914.

According to the *Bulletin of the International Institute of Agriculture*, Rome, figures for 1921 are in round numbers and transposed into gold francs. The table below shows the movement of wheat prices during the postwar period in gold francs, and the index figures for wholesale trade of the Federal Reserve Board, brought to a gold basis. The statistics show that prices in gold francs have risen far less than the wholesale trade index for all commodities. Prices in Germany, France, and Italy are absolutely lower than those obtaining before the war, since high protection tariffs obtained then.

TABLE 8.26 Price of wheat per quarter in gold francs (at the beginning of each month or the end of the preceding month)

Wheat prices of the exporting countries(a)

	Average 1913	1919 XI	1919 V	1921 II	1921 VIII	1922 II	1922 VIII	1923 II	1923 VIII	1924 II	1924 IV
Canada: Winnipeg (Manitoba 1)	16.76	15.91	17.44	30	31	22.12	25.00	20.34	19.93	18.30	18.08
United States: Chicago (Winter 2)	17.19	16.85	17.73	32	23	23.21	21.30	22.28	18.66	21.52	20.37
Minneapolis (Northern 1)	16.90	16.39	17.32	31	28	26.85	24.75	23.04	21.33	22.66	21.52
New York (Winter 2)	18.52	23.59	20.02	37	27	26.04	24.66	24.61	21.39	24.47	22.80
India: Karachi (White)	17.26	16.74	—	—	—	—	24.14	22.09	18.19	19.65	19.16
Argentina: Buenos Aires	19.03	20.47	18.47	30	30	21.70	23.37	22.88	19.21	18.51	18.60
Grain imported to London: Manitoba 1	20.90	—	—	—	—	28.28	29.52	24.96	23.24	24.75	23.05
Winter 2	20.71	—	—	—	—	26.88	26.21	25.10	21.48	—	—
Plata	20.61	—	—	—	—	26.88	27.14	24.96	21.88	23.21	21.77
Karachi	20.90	—	—	—	—	—	—	26.62	22.16	—	22.54

TABLE 8.26 Price of wheat per quarter in gold francs (cont.)

Wheat prices of the exporting countries(a)

	Average 1913	1919 XI	1919 V	1921 (b)	1921 II	1921 VIII	1922 II	1922 VIII	1923 II	1923 VIII	1924 II	1924 IV
Homegrown wheat:												
Germany, Berlin (from the mk.)	24.56	21.00	24.00		18	14	21.39	21.13	15.67	22.17	18.33	21.24
Belgium, Antwerp	19.89	18.75	–		31	34	25.26	27.86	21.89	22.19	22.50	22.44
France, Paris	27.82	25.50	27.25		36	40	29.36	31.33	27.46	25.55	23.93	–
England, London	19.86	–	–		–	–	24.68	27.81	22.58	28.55	23.27	22.68
Italy, Milan (Soft)	28.10	25.75	26.12		20	26	30.43	29.08	26.94	20.58	22.76	25.07
Holland, Rotterdam	20.60	–	–		–	–	23.47	28.25	22.97	29.04	23.61	24.83

Wholesale trade index of the Federal Reserve Board figured on a *gold basis*

	1919 (b)	1921 (b)	1922 (b)	1923 (b)
Canada	198	150	147	147
United States	211	149	158	164
England	214	156	150	159
France	–	133	136	124
Germany (Fed. Stat. Office)	–	–	–	139 Nov.

(a) All prices are final quotations for goods that can be disposed of.
(b) Annual average.

TABLE 8.27 The table shows the shift in the production of grain in the various parts of the world during the postwar period

Figures for wheat production (exclusive of Russia). (a)
1909–13 (1909–10(b) – 1913–14(b) = 100)

	Wheat				Rye				Barley				Oats			
	1919	1920	1921	1922	1919	1920	1921	1922	1919	1920	1921	1922	1919	1920	1921	1922
Europe	69.1	69.6	89.2	75.7	61.8	54.0	76.9	71.3	68.8	78.0	79.7	84.5	70.6	76.8	77.4	79.2
North America	128.2	123.6	125.7	141.2	225.7	188.0	217.7	334.8	77.5	109.8	93.3	112.1	97.2	135.8	100.9	114.5
South America	138.6	108.9	129.5	124.9												
Asia	83.9	109.6	76.0	106.5	66.3	75.1	110.4	129.9	101.0 (c)	109.6 (c)	96.5 (c)	106.9 (c)	72.1	90.3	76.8	89.0
Africa	79.3	70.7	114.1	77.9					71.6	60.3	107.1	61.5				
Oceania	51.9	156.8	143.4	118.8												
Total	92.5	95.9	103.4	103.5	67.9	59.1	82.2	81.3	77.3	88.8	87.7	92.3	81.9	102.2	97.3	94.5

Percentage of the various continents in the total production

	Wheat					Rye					Barley					Oats				
	1909–13	1919	1920	1921	1922	1909–13	1919	1920	1921	1922	1909–13	1919	1920	1921	1922	1909–13	1919	1920	1921	1922
Europe	45.1	33.7	32.7	38.9	33.0	96.1	87.4	87.9	89.9	84.3	54.0	48.1	47.4	49.1	49.5	54.2	46.7	40.7	48.0	45.4
North America	29.8	41.3	38.4	36.2	40.6	3.7	12.4	11.8	9.8	15.3	17.6	17.6	21.7	18.7	21.3	42.2	50.1	56.1	48.8	51.2
South America	5.9	8.9	6.7	7.4	7.2						20.9 (c)	27.4 (c)	25.8 (c)	23.1 (c)	24.2 (c)					
Asia	12.7	11.5	14.5	9.3	13.0	0.2	0.2	0.3	0.3	0.4						3.6	3.2	3.2	3.2	3.4
Africa	3.3	2.8	2.4	3.7	2.5						7.5	6.9	5.1	9.1	5.0					
Oceania	3.2	1.8	5.3	4.5	3.7															
Total	100	100	100	100	100	100	100	100	100	100	100	100	100	100	100	100	100	100	100	100

(a) *Annuaire international de Statistique agricole*, Rome: Institut international d'Agriculture, 1922.
(b) For the southern hemisphere.
(c) Oceania included.

CHAPTER 9

Introduction to: Materials on the Situation of the Peasant Movement in the Most Important Countries

Making an alliance between the toiling peasants and the working class against the ruling class is one of the pillars of Leninism.[1]

A struggle on two fronts is required to create this alliance: against the agrarians and against the Social Democrats.

Class antagonism between peasantry and big landowners was obvious and unequivocal before the abolishment of serfdom. In capitalism, the big landowners succeeded in wiping out this class antagonism with the slogan of common interests between all 'independent' agrarian producers. On this basis they could bring large masses of peasants, even parts of the poor peasants, under their ideological and organisational influence. Making possible an alliance between the proletariat and the toiling peasants requires making them especially clear that their class interests are not at all coinciding with those of the big landowners and the rich peasantry and that they are members of organisations and parties serving not their own class interests.

Social Democracy has always prevented in two ways the formation of a class alliance between the toiling masses in the cities and those at the countryside by directing them into a counterrevolutionary direction. *Firstly, by propagating the slogan 'property-owners and propertyless people'*, hence by including the toiling peasants, yes even the poor peasants, into the ranks of the property owners. Instead of making a formal distinction between both categories, Social Democracy had in this way served the objective interests of the exploiters and their camp at the disadvantage of the proletarian cause. For the toiling peasants who are labouring their land with the help of their family, ownership does not signify exploiting wage workers; for them employing their own labour force is a natural precondition. As an 'independent' owner of his means of production, the peasant is nonetheless exploited by the capitalist state, by the big landowners, by the monopolist organisations of the coalesced bourgeoisie.

---

1 [Translation based on *Materialien über den Stand der Bauernbewegung in den wichtigsten Ländern*. Herausgegeben und eingeleitet von Eugen Varga, Hamburg: Verlag Carl Hoym Nachf. Louis Cahnbley, 1925, pp. 5–11].

A *second* erroneous slogan Social Democracy used was making a *distinction between producers and consumers*. The whole peasantry was categorised as producers, although the poor peasants have to buy their foodstuffs; they are therefore forced to wage labour. The erroneously drawn watershed between consumers and producers led to the isolation of the industrial workers in their struggle against the ruling classes and to relegating the broad masses of poor and middle peasants to *the camp of the counterrevolutionary forces*.

Both points of view were typical products of the general attitude of Social Democracy as a party of the industrial working class in the narrower sense of the word striving for a better living standard of the industrial workers by changing income distribution within capitalism. The Communist Party, which is undermining capitalism and striving for the establishment of the dictatorship of the proletariat, considers the peasantry as a possible and very important ally to be won over as an ally.[2]

In general, the communist parties originated from Social Democracy and they inherited many of the latter's attitudes and errors they necessarily must abjure. That is also true for the attitude of the communist parties with regard to the peasantry. It should be necessary to put this question once again on the agenda of the Communist International.

The Communist International paid much attention to this question. During the Second Congress in the summer of 1920 the question was principally treated under Lenin's supervision. The adopted theses elucidated essential questions. They all focused on the common knowledge *that the peasantry does not form a homogeneous social class and that only the upper social layer, the rich peasants, share a common interest with the big landowners, that the middle layers should remain at least neutral in the struggle opposing the ruling class to the proletariat, while the majority of the toiling peasants* (small peasants, dwarf peasants, poor peasants) *belongs to the revolutionary camp*. Politically, emphasis was put on the fact that the social layer of the rich peasantry would lose something if the dictatorship of the proletariat were established, while only the middle layers of the peasantry and, especially, the poor peasantry would win with the dictatorship of the proletariat. This political line was inspired by the analysis that the world revolution would follow after the shock capitalism had to endure because of the war.

In the summer of 1922, the agrarian question was put for the second time on the agenda of the Fourth Congress of the Communist International. The

---

2   In his introduction to *The Peasant War in Germany,* Engels already pointed to the fact that the peasantry can become in most countries the most important ally of the proletariat in the latter's struggle for political power.

question was principally treated in the same way as during the Second Congress. But politically one was expecting a slowing down of the pace of the world revolution. *Hence, the theses treated primarily the relations of the communist parties with the peasantry in the period before assuming power.* These theses formulated the tenet that the communist parties should defend the daily demands of the toiling peasants in their struggle for conquering the broad peasant masses and prove by their actions that they are the only political parties representing the real interests of the toiling peasants against the ruling classes within the capitalist system. Meanwhile the communist parties had to convince the peasants that their demands cannot be met within the capitalist system, because of being contradictory to the interests of the ruling classes. In this way they can guide the peasants on their revolutionary road.

The third time the agrarian question was discussed occurred at the Enlarged Executive in January 1923 when the slogan of a workers and peasant government was formulated for building up a class alliance. Some months later the First International Peasants Conference was congressing in Moscow which led to the founding of the International Peasants' Council.

For the fourth time the Fifth Congress discussed the peasant question thoroughly, especially in relation to the agrarian crisis and the necessity for the Communists of the different countries to support the toiling peasants in their struggle for liberating themselves from the ideological and organisational influence of the big landowners and the rich peasantry.

In March 1925, the Enlarged Executive was once more treating the question of the relation between the communist parties and the individual peasant parties. One of the most important social consequences of the war is the fact that the peasantry had been politicised. During the pre-war period the peasantry had been totally subjugated to the political leadership of the big landowners, but in the postwar period independent peasant parties had emerged in the eastern European countries (Poland, Czechoslovakia, Hungary, Rumania, Yugoslavia, Bulgaria). In many cases a division between rich and poor peasants had become apparent. The attempts of the Bulgarian peasantry to conquer state power ended up into a complete defeat. In many countries the activities of the communist parties among the peasantry were successful: they succeeded in organising peasant organisations and communist propaganda, enrolling sympathising peasants into the party or in helping them organising a revolutionary peasants party. All these questions will be thoroughly discussed at the Enlarged Executive.

The objective of this pamphlet is rather modest. It gives an overview of the state of affairs with regard to the most important countries. The material presented here is based on reports made by different communist parties, the International Peasants' Council, and individual comrades.

Unfortunately, the majority of the communist parties did not, or not in time, answer the questions formulated in the forms of the inquiry. As a consequence, many mistakes may have been committed. We nonetheless believe that, in general, a true picture has been drawn of the peasants' movement in the world. The discussion to be organised at the Enlarged Executive will make it possible to have all mistakes corrected and omissions repaired.

We nonetheless have to stress the fact that the words designating the individual social layers of the peasantry are different in all languages, which creates misunderstandings. The German version of this book uses the currently accepted terminology in Germany. Hence, a *Mittelbauer* is a peasant labouring himself on his farm with the help of his family, but he also employs wage workers; in Russia he would be called a small *kulak*; and in France a *propriétaire*. The Russian *srednak*, who is not always employing wage workers, is called a *Kleinbauer* in German, in French he will be called a rather better-situated *petit propriétaire*. The Russian word *bednak* refers to a German dwarf peasant, a parcel peasant. According to existing social class differences, words can have a different meaning in each language or they do not always refer to the same phenomenon. One should keep this in mind.

 E. Varga
 Berlin, 1 January 1925

CHAPTER 10

The Decline of Capitalism: The Economics of a Period of the Decline of Capitalism after Stabilisation

Foreword[1]

The object of this work is to give, in a very small space, a sketch of the most important facts and tendencies within capitalism in decline, in the last few years, since stabilisation. It does not claim to be exhaustive. Many very important theoretical problems are omitted, such as the question of the *determination of prices in the postwar period*; why, in spite of the increased productivity and intensity of labour, in spite of the decrease in the production of gold, involving no considerable decrease in the cost of production of gold – why is the price level 50 percent higher than before the war? An answer to this question would require a detailed analysis of the prices of different commodities on the one hand, and, on the other, the reopening of the old dispute concerning the influence on prices of the cost of the production of gold, and what, taking into account the varied gold content of ore and the variations in the cost of production, actually determines its value. Such a discussion must be reserved for a later and purely theoretical work; the theoretical analysis of the form of capitalist economy with a monetary unit changing, and not constant, in value (*Theory of the economics of inflation and deflation*). But there are a number of important problems which are *general problems of capitalism, and which, at the present time, show no particular characteristics*, either not dealt with at all or only touched upon lightly, such as the problem of the desultory development of capitalism. In the present work we shall confine ourselves to those problems, politically the most important, which are characteristic of the present period; to the facts which demonstrate that the stabilisation of capitalism does not mean the stability of the capitalist system; that the internal contradictions of stabilised capitalism must necessarily lead to new revolutionary situations, that *the period of the decline of capitalism is not ended* ...

---

1 [Originally published by the Communist Party of Great Britain, London, 1928].

In order to assist the reader I have maintained the following plan: the text itself contains the actual examination of the subject and the most important data; the footnotes contain references and supplementary figures and data; and, finally, the Appendix contains the complete tables which are essential to any reader who wishes to become thoroughly acquainted with the statistical bases of this work. I believe that this arrangement will enable readers, and, above all, the workers, to master this publication. It was not, of course, possible to remove all difficulties; the subject itself is too complicated for that. The reader will have to resign himself to reading a few chapters through twice ...

The Author
Moscow, 1 June 1928

1 The Stabilisation of Capitalism

The elemental revolt of the masses during and immediately after the war resulted in the complete overthrow of the capitalists in Russia; in the temporary loss of their power in Hungary, Finland, Bavaria; in capitalism being seriously endangered in all the belligerent European countries.

In that extremely dangerous situation, the capitalists executed a sham retreat all along the line; submitting to the pressure of the masses, they seemed willing to surrender power to the workers or to share it with them. They made enormous sacrifices in order to maintain the capitalist system. In a few countries they even ceased for a while to exploit in order to save the conditions necessary for exploitation, their class supremacy. They resigned from government in favour of the reformist Labour leaders; all the customary *political* working-class demands were satisfied – abolition of the monarchy and upper chamber; universal, equal and secret franchise for all political institutions, freedom of meeting and association, liberty of the press, etc. Similarly with the old *social* demands – the eight-hour day, general social insurance, work found for all demobilised soldiers, rights of the workers in the factories (factory councils), etc. The capitalists were most accommodating with regard to wages also. They pacified the revolt of the masses by setting up 'Nationalisation Commissions', by sham preparations for agrarian reform. *The capitalists had, at any price, to gain time in order to re-establish their crumbling machinery of power and to give the reformists the opportunity of guiding the elemental revolt of the working masses into 'orthodox channels'.*

We wish to emphasise here – in order to avoid any misunderstanding – that we are describing the historical significance, the meaning of events, and not what actually occurred in the immediate consciousness of individual persons. The capitalists, individually, recoiled from the proletarian revolt, for they had neither the courage nor the power to face it boldly. Only a few leading politicians were clearly conscious of the fact that *the bourgeoisie as a class had effected a sham retreat of historical importance*; but that does not affect the significance of events.

The capitalist retreat manoeuvre was crowned with complete success. The great mass of workers believed the statement of the reformists that a victorious and bloodless revolution had occurred. They did not realise that the outward appearances lacked a class content; that although the reformist leaders were ruling, the workers were not in power. The basis of capitalism, private ownership of the means of production, was not touched. The bourgeois state-machine, shaken by defeat, was not destroyed, but renewed and strengthened by the assimilation of the reformist leaders who placed the working-class organisations, which supported them, at the service of the capitalists. What appeared to the workers as their victory – their leaders becoming Presidents, Ministers, Secretaries of State – was actually a victory for the capitalists. The leaders of the bourgeoisie and their reformist lackeys allied themselves together to prevent the social revolution, to avoid the dictatorship of the proletariat!

This sham retreat gave the capitalists what they most wanted – time! And they exploited it excellently. With the help of the reformists they assembled and reorganised the state machinery of force; where necessary, they created armed class troops on a Fascist basis. Assisted ideologically and organisationally by the reformists, and increasing from time to time the use of violence, they defeated the attempts of the revolutionary vanguard to transform the apparent victory of the workers into a real proletarian revolution. As section by section, the workers were defeated, the concessions that the bourgeoisie had been compelled to grant at the end of the war in order to stem the tide of working-class revolt were withdrawn!

In this way, the possibility of realisation of capital was gradually regained. The capitalists of a few countries had already succeeded before this in realising their capital by means of inflation. *The historical function of inflation was to annul economically those concessions granted by the capitalists to the workers for political reasons, to prevent the social revolution.* Real wages were constantly falling. The material achievements gained by the workers were soon lost on the road of inflation. The capitalists expropriated the property of the rentiers, the petty bourgeoisie and the peasants; and, through inflation, they succeeded to some extent in transferring the burden of maintaining the workers on to the independent producers. With decreasing production the large-scale capitalists, by appropriating the surplus value again being created because of inflation, and by the consequent expropriation of the property of the middle classes, were enabled to enrich themselves. *The realisation of capital was restored by inflation, although upon an 'abnormal', temporary and fluctuating basis.*[2]

But inflation is only a temporary method for the realisation of capital, and one which is not suitable for the capitalists of all countries.[3] After having strengthened their position the bourgeoisie had to take up the direct struggle against the workers. And in this struggle they were victorious. Then followed the political 'stabilisation' of capitalism: the relation of forces between capitalists and workers had shifted so far in the favour of the former that struggles for power could for the moment no longer be taken up with any prospect of success.

In internal policy this was evidenced by the fact that the capitalists ruled without the co-operation of the reformists. This afforded the reformists the opportunity of forming an opposition within the capitalist system, of conducting a struggle for the economic demands of the workers and, in this manner, of regaining to some extent the doubtful confidence of the workers. Such a state of affairs is advantageous to the bourgeoisie, for it enables the reformists to act more successfully as capitalist agents within the working class when any acutely revolutionary situation arises – so long as the bourgeoisie has not resorted to capitalist terror – to Fascism – as a system of government. The capitalist victory was, by the reciprocal action of history, both conditioned by and the condition of the *economic* stabilisation of capitalism. The realisation of capital, the production and appropriation of surplus value, accumulation, is again proceeding normally. Exchanges are stable. National and international credit is again restored. The break-up of the capitalist world into two spheres of overproduction and under-production, peculiarly characteristic of the postwar period, was slowly surmounted, the rich countries 'supporting' the poor countries by means of capital exports.

---

2 We wish to emphasise the fact that, in the given relation of class forces, inflation was economically inevitable. It was not consciously arranged by the capitalists; but historically inflation served to accomplish the expropriation of surplus value indirectly, this being impossible directly.

3 Inflation was of no use to the British bourgeoisie because of the lack of a peasant class, and because of the great importance of international financial concerns. It would, by expropriating the rentier class, have brought the capitalists directly face to face with the workers, there being no peasantry to act as a protective buffer class. It would have meant the end of London as the world-banker.

Technical progress set in at a great rate. The machinery of production was rapidly renewed and extended. Production outstripped the level of the pre-war period.[4] The reformists foretold a new, long-enduring boom of capitalism, a growth, already in process of development, towards socialism by way of state capitalism, economic democracy, the co-operatives, small shareholdings, etc.[5] Postwar capitalism is leading to a peaceful *super-imperialism*, whose economic basis is international monopoly, economic co-operation between banks of issue and the balance of forces; whose form of organisation is the *League of Nations*. Later on we shall deal with this theory in greater detail. At this point we only wish to state the following: It would be blind stupidity to attempt to deny the fact of the economic and political stabilisation of capitalism as compared with the position in the years immediately following the war. But it is equally incorrect to overestimate the economic and political results of stabilisation.

Annual production in the capitalist countries of western Europe increased on average by 3 percent in the half century preceding the war. This is a very rough calculation, but it gives an approximately correct picture. For the period 1913–28 this would correspond to an increase of about 50 percent. *Table 10.22*. in the Appendix shows that the pre-war average has not by any means been reached. The waste of the war has not yet been replaced.[6]

As far as the *actual period of stabilisation* is concerned, the increase in production is significant. It would, however, be quite false to assume that this will be the normal rate of progress from now on; it is an exceptional state of affairs, conditioned by the intensity of the postwar crisis and by the fact

---

4 See *Table 10.22* of Appendix: Figures of World Production. This deals only with raw materials, since there are no statistics dealing with the production of finished goods. But it may be assumed that the production of finished goods increased in accordance with that of raw materials, and perhaps increased even more because of the improvements introduced in the utilisation of raw materials (fuel technique, utilisation of old materials, avoidance of waste). The table shows that the production of the most important raw materials outstripped that of the pre-war period, particularly metals.

   This is evidence of the extension in the machinery of production, and of great accumulation. The increase in the production of food and textiles scarcely keeps pace with the increase in population, which shows that the real standard of life of the people as a whole, and of the workers in particular, has not improved.

5 Hilferding writes: '... [T]he extension of productive capacity means finally, after crises have been overcome, an increase in production and new good markets. At the same time, the agrarian revolution means an extension of the market for industrial products'. Hilferding 1924c, p. 10.

6 Taking the world production of coal and pig/iron as indicative of the general trend, we get the following figures in *Table 10.1*:

that 1927 was for Germany (and, for the first half of the year, for the USA also) a year of good markets.

The following is, however, decisive.

Capitalism in the postwar period is no simple restoration of pre-war capitalism. It is a different capitalism. It is no longer a 'dying' capitalism, but one already in the process of mortification, which has lost a sixth part of the world, an important part of its former sphere of hegemony, to its grave-digger, the proletariat. And within the still existing capitalism those contradictions which are peculiar to it are rapidly growing sharper, and are heading straight for a new catastrophe. *The sharpening of these contradictions forms the actual theme of the rest of this work.*

2 The Instability of the Capitalist System

Stabilisation is not synonymous with stability. Capitalism never was, and never can be, stable. In a society where the means of production and the actual producers are separated from each other, where the social connection of human beings appears as the material relation of commodities, where the destinies of men acting blindly for themselves are not made subject to conscious laws, where the great majority is governed and exploited by a diminishing minority – in such a society stability is impossible. It is essentially part of the capitalist

TABLE 10.1 Coal and pig iron production (a)

	Coal mill. tons	Annual increase %	Pig iron mill. tons		Annual increase %
1865	188	–	9.1		–
1875	283	5.05	14.1		5.60
1885	407	4.38	19.8		4.04
1895	583	4.35	29.4		4.84
1905	914	5.68	54.8		8.64
1913	1,242	4.45	77.2	(78.8)(b)	5.02
1921	1,030	-2.13		(37.8)	-6.50
1925	1,229	4.83		(76.9)	25.80
1927	1,300	2.90	85.0		5.42

(a) Figures up to 1905 taken from Cassel 1923; 1913, 1921 and 1925 are from *International Statistical Yearbook*; 1927 figures are estimated percentages calculated by the author.
(b) According to *International Statistical Yearbook*.

system that its balance is unstable, its instability constant. In times of apparent stability, the elements of contradiction are unfolding uninterruptedly until they reach a violent solution in a crisis, and balance is for a moment restored.

'The crises are always but momentary and forcible solutions of the existing contradictions. They are violent eruptions which for a time restore the disturbed equilibrium'.[7]

A stable capitalism without crises is impossible. Marx protests against the idea that within the capitalist system of production there exists merely the possibility of crises, 'as though it were accidental whether or not they occur',[8] as though there could be any measures to prevent the periodic recurrence of crises. Why can there be no capitalist economy without crises? The answer to that is:

> The conditions of direct exploitation, and those of realising it, are not identical. They diverge not only in place and time, but also logically. The first are only limited by the productive power of society, the latter by the proportional relation of the various branches of production and the consumer power of society. But this last-named is not determined either by the absolute productive power, or by the absolute consumer power, but by the consumer power based on antagonistic conditions of distribution, which reduce the consumption of the bulk of society to a minimum varying within more or less narrow limits. It is furthermore restricted by the tendency to accumulate, the drive to expand capital and produce surplus-value on an extended scale. This is law for capitalist production, imposed by incessant revolutions in the methods of production themselves, by the depreciation of existing capital always bound up with them, by the general competitive struggle and the need to improve production and expand its scale merely as a means of self-preservation and under penalty of ruin.[9]

These remarks apply, with equal validity to present-day capitalism; the formation of national and international monopolies can mitigate the harmful consequences of crises for the capital concerned in those monopolies, as we shall show later, and can burden the workers and the independent producers with the full weight of the crisis. But this automatically leads to an intensification of the next crisis, for: 'The ultimate reason for all real crises always remains the

---

[7] Marx 1959, p. 244.
[8] Varga quotes here from the German edition (Stuttgart: Dietz) of the *Theorien der Mehrwert*, Volume 2, p. 287. '... And consequently their occurrence is merely a matter of chance'. Marx 1970, p. 513.
[9] Marx 1959, p. 239.

poverty and restricted consumption of the masses as opposed to the drive of capitalist production to develop the productive forces as though only the absolute consuming power of society constituted their limit'.[10]

The formation of monopolies and rationalisation means, however, a decrease in the proportion of variable capital to the yearly value of products, i.e. a decrease in the working-class share of the total value of the commodities, i.e. a still sharper operation of the 'last cause'.

Balance in the capitalist system itself was again and again restored for a time by an extension of the capitalist market. This occurred through the separation of industry and agriculture;[11] through the change of independent producers cultivating their won land into either wage-earners or small-scale capitalists; and through the peaceful or violent transportation of the capitalist system of production to foreign countries. In this way capitalist society, in spite of the periodically recurring crises, maintained itself as a system.

Bukharin writes on this point as follows:[12] 'The crisis never goes beyond the limits of unsettling the system. Having concluded our examination we see *the system*, moving, fluctuating; but through all the movements and disturbances the balance is again and again restored'.

The fundamental, world-historical difference between all previous crises of capitalism, and that which came to a head in the world war, consists in this, that previous crises did for a moment restore the balance of the capitalist system, *did succeed in solving the contradictions, although by force and with the most violent convulsion, it is true, yet still within the framework of the capitalist system, while this crisis led to the break up of the system itself, to the overthrow of the bourgeoisie and the attainment of the proletarian dictatorship in one of the greatest states of the world.*

The overthrow of the capitalist system and the establishment of the dictatorship of the proletariat within the Soviet Union signifies the beginning of the period of

---

10   Marx 1959, pp. 472–3.
11   '... [O]nly the destruction of rural domestic industry can give the internal market of a country that extension and consistence which the capitalist mode of production requires'. Marx 1954, p. 748.
12   Bucharin 1922, p. 109. [Varga refers to this German edition of 1922. However, this quote differs considerably from the German edition of Bucharin's book. The Bergman edition gives the following translation: '... [I]f we speak of the progress or retrogression of productive powers of society, we mean the rising or falling of social labor productivity; if we speak of the distribution of productive powers, we mean the distribution and redistribution of means of production and labor powers; if we need a sociological definition of productive powers, we can take the technological system of society, the active, changeable "factor" of social development'. Bukharin 1971].

the decline of capitalism, the first ten years of which have already passed, of the historic period of the transition from capitalism to socialism through a series of successful and unsuccessful proletarian revolutions.

The destruction of the Russian bourgeoisie and the erection of the proletarian dictatorship exercise a powerful influence both on the economic sub-structure and on the political and ideological superstructure of the rest of the world. This influence can be summed up as follows: *the existence of the proletarian dictatorship in the Soviet Union intensifies all the* contradictions in the rest of the world and strengthens all those forces which made possible the defeat of the bourgeoisie in Russia itself.

Economic sub-structure: The possibility of overcoming crises by an extension of the capitalist market is limited by the boundaries of the Soviet Union, embracing as it does one-sixth of the earth. This means an intensification of economic crises; increased difficulty in overcoming them temporarily; sharpening of the internal contradictions of capitalism; lessened stability of the entire system. It means a new impetus towards a new re-division of the world.

Social-political superstructure: The downfall of the Russian bourgeoisie raises the class consciousness of the proletariat, strengthens its readiness for struggle: it demonstrates the possibility of overthrowing capitalist class domination throughout the world; demonstrates that capitalism is not an eternal, but merely a historically-transitory form of society.

In the same way the overthrow of the bourgeoisie in Russia affects the opposition offered by the colonial and semi-colonial peoples to imperialist oppression. The Soviet Union is the rallying point of all anti-capitalist forces within capitalism, and this forms a new element of instability.

These effects are intensified by the demonstration not merely of the possibility of overthrowing the bourgeoisie, but also of the fact that the capitalists are not essential for the management of the productive forces concerned in capitalism. The economy of the Soviet Union is developing at a more rapid rate since the conclusion of the civil war than that of the capitalist world.[13]

The political reaction of the existence of the Soviet Union, which exacerbates the social struggles in the capitalist world, is of a twofold character. In imperialist countries the recreation and strengthening of a labour aristocracy (USA); in second-class capitalist countries where the economic basis for a labour aristocracy is lacking, organised terror of the bourgeoisie – Fascism (Italy). In many cases both tendencies are apparent.

---

13 See *Table 10.26* in Appendix.

It is particularly significant of the present period of decline that *parliamentary democracy*, the form of government for which the rising bourgeoisie struggled against feudalism and which embodies capitalist political ideology, is decaying. Even before the war parliamentary democracy had, because of the concentration of capital and the formation of monopolies, become merely a caricature of itself. But the bourgeoisie held on to it as the most suitable means of awakening in the masses the illusion of their participation in power. Today the parliamentary system is legally abolished in Italy and Spain, and practically abolished in Poland and Portugal; in the Balkan countries it exists only as a sham (there are no legal Communist Parties). But even in those countries where the parliamentary regime still exists, the idea of Fascism, the idea of capitalist terror, gains new adherents daily.[14]

When comes this change?

Parliamentary democracy serves as the state form of the bourgeoisie as long as it is a historically progressing class, as long as it can claim to serve the interests of the people as a whole. The Fascist state, organised terror in the interests of the capitalists, is the form of government adapted to the period of decline, when the rule of the bourgeoisie is seriously threatened. At the present time, since a mere handful of the greatest capitalists at the head of powerful monopoly organisations dominate economic and political life, since the class struggle has torn the democratic mask into shreds, the idea of Parliamentarism has lost its power. Its place is taken by the idea of Fascism, of unbridled nationalism, the final attempt to bind the petty-bourgeois masses to capitalism; the proletariat – apart from the labour aristocracy – will no longer be bound to capitalism by any idea whatever. The white terror is taking the place of ideological domination. In the period of decline the bourgeoisie is losing its ideological leadership of the people.

In the sphere of foreign policy the instability of the system becomes increasingly obvious. There is no end to the palaver about eternal peace, disarmament and courts of arbitration, but military preparations on land, on sea, under the sea and in the air continue to be made uninterruptedly and hastily. There have never been military preparations on such a scale as those taking place today. Alliances and counter-alliances which change from day to day, blocs and counter-blocs, herald the coming war. The capitalists of certain countries (Italy, Germany, Hungary) publicly and brutally propose the question of the re-division of the world.

---

14   It is significant of the decline of Parliamentarianism that, in the last elections in Germany, only 12 million took the trouble to vote, out of an electorate of 42 million.

The following main tendencies can be discerned in the general confusion:
(a) *The capitalist world against the Soviet Union*: As a hostile class, the bourgeoisie of the whole world is pursuing a common fight against the victorious proletariat of the Soviet Union.
(b) *Imperialist powers against the colonial peoples*: The capitalists of all imperialist powers have a common interest in maintaining their rule over the exploited colonial peoples. And since the Soviet Union is the natural leader of all anti-imperialist and anti-capitalist struggles the interests of the capitalist class in maintaining its supremacy against the workers in the home country are bound up with its interests in maintaining its domination of the oppressed peoples in the colonies, both coming to a head in a systematic preparation for war against the Soviet Union.
(c) Capitalism is not, however, a unified whole, but is broken up into separate states each carrying on a struggle for its share of the world. Antagonisms among the imperialist states themselves prevent unified procedure. There is unity of principle in our camp because we have a common object, but the capitalist camp is split again and again by imperialist antagonisms. The bourgeoisie of the United States – which will later become the acknowledged leader of the anti-revolutionary struggle because of its position as the strongest capitalist Power – does not yet feel itself directly threatened by the proletarian revolution. Its own colonial sphere, Central and South America, lies far from the Soviet Union, and is less subject to the influence of the Soviet Union, for economic and cultural reasons, than the Asiatic colonies of England. Hostility towards the two other imperialist world powers – Britain and Japan – is at the present time still stronger than towards the USSR. Britain's attempt to unite the European states into one bloc against the USSR brings to light all the hidden antagonisms in the Balkans, in eastern and central Europe. The capitalists of the countries immediately bordering the Soviet Union hesitate to enter into war, for they realise that defeat would mean the immediate overthrow of their supremacy.

All these factors are indicative of extreme instability in all matters of foreign policy, and therefore in the whole system. Apart from the ever intensifying hostility between the two strongest imperialist powers – the United States and Britain – apart from the 'friendship' between England and France forced on them by the military situation,[15] everything is unstable, everything is continu-

---

15 France, by means of long-distance artillery, submarines and aircraft, holds England in

ally changing. But all the powers, without any exception, are arming themselves for a new war against each other.

This accounts for the irresolution of the bourgeoisie in the fight against the Soviet Union. The capitalists of the world, split by internal dissensions, *hesitate* to make the attack. Meanwhile imperialist antagonisms become more bitter, the anti-capitalist and anti-imperialist forces within the bourgeois world increase and organise themselves, the USSR's capacity for defence grows, with the progress of industrialisation. All this *forces* the world bourgeoisie to begin the attack.

Ideologically, the decline of capitalism is completely manifest. The bourgeoisie *no longer possess a political ideology*. The old catchwords of liberty, equality, fraternity are buried. The free trade ideology ekes out precarious existence, for the bourgeoisie of each country demands protective tariffs for itself and free trade in other countries. The political ideology of the American bourgeoisie has been discredited by the tremendous unemployment and the misery of the independent producers; the nationalist-chauvinist ideology of Fascism by the capitalist terror.[16] The economic theory of capitalism today goes back even further than [David] Ricardo; its most prominent representatives altogether deny the need for a theory of value, and disown the old bourgeois classical economists, because their theories lead directly to Marxism, to the doctrine of the historically transitory character of capitalism. No longer [Werner] Sombart, infected with Marxism, but [Gustav] Cassel, the most superficial vulgar economist, is the 'leading theoretician of today'. Marxism is strictly prohibited.[17]

---

check; while, with her superior naval force, England holds France in check by the threat to deprive her of her colonies.

16 The youth of the colonial bourgeoisie, educated in the universities of Europe and America, is seeking in vain for a revolutionary bourgeois ideology corresponding to their class. Nothing is left for them but to employ Marxism as the basis of their struggle against imperialism (which, were the struggle to change from being merely anti-imperialist to being anti-capitalist, they would certainly betray without any qualms). Thus, for example, we see Chiang Kai-Shek justifying the murder of Chinese Communists in 'Marxist' words.

17 The following extracts are typical: 'It is obvious that with this recognition of the complete and fundamental inadequacy of Ricardo's theory of costs, the caricature of it – the Socialist theory of value – proves useless and *we will not waste any time on the hair-splitting of its defenders*'. (Cassel 1923 Volume 1, p. 294, our emphasis). Another luminary of present-day bourgeois economics, [John Maynard] Keynes, regards Marxism with the helplessness of a child: 'But Marxian socialism must always remain a portent to the historians of opinion – how a doctrine so illogical and so dull can have exercised so powerful and enduring an influence over the minds of men, and through them, the events of history', Keynes 1926, pp. 34–5. The American political economists make no mention of Marx at all.

Now, as before, the reformists call themselves Marxists. But reformist economic thought today contains not the smallest grain of Marxism. It is an extraordinary mixture of bourgeois twaddle (proposals for rationalisation, increase in labour productivity) and Sismondism (capitalists should pay higher wages in order to be able to sell more goods).[18]

Summing up:

Instead of the stability and super-imperialism foretold by the reformists, we see the greatest disintegration, the greatest instability in capitalism today, both in its economic sub-structure and in its political-social and ideological super-structure. The contradictions are becoming sharper and are making straight for a new imperialist war, either of the imperialists against the Soviet Union or of the imperialists among themselves, to determine the re-division of the world (a combination of both is possible).

3   The Sharpening of Internal Contradictions: The Widespread Unemployment

'We have developed a fairly definite idea that an employer's business is to eliminate work'.[19]

The fact of chronic mass unemployment in the postwar period is generally acknowledged. We were inclined to treat it merely as the consequence of the serious disturbances experienced by world economy – industrialisation of the transatlantic countries, impoverishment of Europe, and agrarian crises. These factors certainly are contributory causes. But a thorough examination of recent developments shows that the cause of this chronic mass unemployment does not lie primarily in those disturbances, but is a necessary result of the sharpening of the internal contradictions of capitalism. The nature of this contradiction is as follows:

Surplus value, in which the capitalists share, in accordance with definite laws, in proportion to their respective capital, is produced by the workers exploited by industrial capital. By industrial capital we understand, as Marxists, capital which, in its circulation, passes through the cycle of production, assuming and discarding the forms:[20]

---

18   Fritz Tarnow's new pamphlet, *Warum arm sein?* 1928, is of a typical reformist kind of ideology.
19   Tugwell 1927, p. 37.
20   This is a formula expressing the circulation of capital through the process of production.

$$M - C \genfrac{}{}{0pt}{}{L}{M.\ Prod.} Production - C - M'$$

That is, productive capital invested in agriculture, industry, mining and transport. It is true that trading capital, financial capital, and loan capital exploit their workers, but the workers so employed do not directly create surplus value; their wages are a part of the apparent costs of the capitalist system of production. All profit, all income from sources other than labour, whatever the legal title of its source may be, is a part of the surplus value appropriated by industrial capital. The total amount of profit is equal to the total amount of surplus value. Consequently the more workers who are being exploited at a certain rate of surplus value, the greater the mass of surplus value and the mass of profit.

The internal contradiction of the capitalist system of production consists in this, that although total profit equals total surplus value, each individual capitalist concern is constantly endeavouring to reduce the number of workers it exploits, to replace human labour by machines, to reduce the total of surplus value.

For the capitalists, who have no insight into the nature of capitalist economy and view everything through the spectacles of competition, expenditure on the wages of labour forms an element of cost differing in no way from other elements of cost, fuel, raw materials, machinery, etc. Consequently as soon as the opportunity of reducing the costs of production arises, machines are brought in to supplant the worker, the workers are thrown on to the scrapheap, and the surplus value yielded is decreased. *The interests of all the individual capitalist concern to assure to itself a larger share of total profit by reducing its individual costs of production through decreasing wage costs, are therefore in opposition to the interest of the class in having as high a realisation as possible of total capital.*[21]

This fact is responsible for three main tendencies in capitalism:

Starting as money capital (M), it is turned into commodities (C), these commodities taking the form of labour power (L) and means of production (M. Prod.); the process of manufacture or production then takes place, resulting in the capital having been once more transformed into commodities; these are sold, and by their sale the capital (plus the surplus value created) once more takes the form of [more] money.

21 The cheapening of commodities compensates the capitalists as consumers but does not alter the tendency to a falling rate of profit.

1. The tendency to raise the organic composition in capital;
2. The tendency to a falling rate of profit;[22]
3. The tendency to a diminishing number of workers.

At this juncture we shall only deal with the last named. On this question Marx says:

> The accumulation of capital, though originally appearing as its quantitative extension only, is effected, as we have seen, under a progressive qualitative change in its composition, under a constant increase of its constant, at the expense of its variable constituent ... Since the demand for labour is determined not by the amount of capital as a whole, but by its variable constituent alone, that demand falls progressively with the increase of the total capital, instead of ... rising in proportion to it. It falls relatively to the magnitude of the total capital, and at an accelerated rate as this magnitude increases ... With the growth of the total capital its variable constituent or the labour incorporated in it also does increase, but in a constantly diminishing proportion ... The labouring population therefore produces, along with the accumulation of capital produced by it, the means by which itself is made relatively superfluous, is turned into a relative surplus population, and it does this to an always increasing extent. This is a law of population peculiar to the capitalist mode of production ... The greater the social wealth, the functioning capital, the extent and energy of its growth and, therefore, also the absolute mass of the proletariat and the productiveness of its labour, the greater is the industrial reserve army. The same causes which develop the expansive power of capital, develop also the labour power at its disposal. The relative mass of the industrial reserve army increases therefore with the potential energy of wealth.[23]

Up to the time of the world war it seemed as if this tendency, which theoretically must follow from the working of the capitalist system of production itself, did not apply to the sound capitalism of that time. It is true that the number of workers engaged in agriculture fell. But the number of those engaged productively in industry rose rapidly: when markets were favourable,

---

22 Insofar as the cheapening also affects the factors included in constant capital, it counteracts the tendency to a falling rate of profit.
23 Marx 1954, pp. 628–9, 631–2, 644.

the industrial reserve army was absorbed, and complaints made of the lack of labour forces.[24]

This explains the popular belief – which Ricardo combated so long ago – that the workers thrown on to the streets by the introduction of machines will *necessarily* find new opportunities for employment in production.[25]

In the postwar period, since the stabilisation of capitalism, a definite decrease in the number of workers employed by industrial capital – not only in agriculture – has taken place. The tendency towards making workers supernumerary is being completely worked out. This displacement of workers by machinery is no longer compensated for by an extension of production.[26]

This is such an important fact that we must demonstrate it carefully by figures and argument. First, let us meet a possible objection: we are not here dealing with a phenomenon arising from the industrial cycle. We are not dealing with a decrease in the number of workers employed resulting from a decrease in the volume of production caused by a crisis: we are dealing with *unemployment at a time of global markets, of an increased volume of production, and in the leading capitalist countries!*

---

[24] The average figure of unemployment among trade unionists in Germany in the years 1907–13, that is, in the period which includes the grave crisis of 1907–8, amounted to 2.3 percent. Compare that with [*figures in Table 10.2*]:

TABLE 10.2 Unemployment among unionists in Germany (1923–7)

1923	1924	1925	1926	1927
9.6	13.5	6.7	18	8.8

SOURCE: STATISTISCHES JAHRBUCH 1927, P. 536, CALCULATED BY AUTHOR

[25] One example from a thousand: Professor [Paul] Mombert, writing in the *Bergwerkzeitung* (Miners' Journal) of 23 October 1927, says: 'We must not allow ourselves to be puzzled by the fact that rationalisation as we have seen it has temporarily displaced a large number of workers. That was also the case 100 years ago, when machines entered into competition with human labour power. In the long run, it is true that all technical and economic improvements will indubitably increase the opportunities for labour in any country'.

[26] Formerly such compensation applied only to imperialist countries: mass unemployment was avoided by the export of industrial products to the colonies, where countless millions of Indian, Chinese and other hand-workers were displaced and left to die of hunger.

We shall first consider the United States. The following *Table 10.3* shows the development of labour forces and of the volume of production since 1899:[27]

TABLE 10.3 Development of the workforce and the volume of production

	Workers employed in 1,000s		Index for 1925 1899 = 100		
	1899	1925	Workers	Production	Production per worker
Agriculture[28]	10,500	10,500	100	145	145
Mining	600	1,065	177	480	271
Industry	5,200	9,772	188	188	148
Railways	929	1,846	198	198	148
Totals	17,229	23,183	135		183

This table is typical of development in the *former* capitalist epoch in the principal countries: an unchanging number of workers in agriculture, a great increase in industry transport and mining; but an increase in the volume of production of 147 percent corresponds to an increase in number of workers employed of 35 percent. Production per worker increased by 83 percent. *There is a relative displacement of labour power, for the increase in output per worker is less than the increase in the total volume of production. Hence the necessity for additional labour power!*

Analysing the postwar period, we obtain an entirely different picture.

---

27   *Commerce Yearbook* 1926, p. 16. Figures for building, where there was a great increase in the number of workers employed, are lacking.
28   These figures include the farmers themselves, as well agricultural labourers; but this does not change the direction of development.

TABLE 10.4 Development of labour forces and volume of production since 1919[29]

	Workers employed in 1,000s		Index for 1925 1919 = 100		
	1919	1925	Workers	Production	Production per worker
Agriculture	11,300	10,500	93	108	118
Mining	1,065	1,065	100	133	133
Industry	10,689	9,772	91,5	128,5	140
Railways[30]	1,915	1,774	91	104,4	115
Totals	24,969	23,081	93	120	129

We see that there is a decrease in labour employed of 7 percent, but an increase in the volume of 20 percent, and of production per worker of 29 percent, *numerically a decrease of nearly two million. The increase in production per worker exceeds the extension. So labour power was completely dispensed with!*

The same process was clearly continued in the years 1926 and 1927; the census figures do not go beyond 1925, but the index figures of the Federal Reserve Board and of the Bureau of Labor will serve instead:

TABLE 10.5 Index figures for factory industry

	1919	1920	1921	1922	1923	1924	1925	1926	1927
Production[31]	83	87	67	85	101	95	104	108	106
No. of workers[32]	–	–	85.1	88.4	100	90.3	91.2	91.9	88.2[33]

Finally we wish to show how, in particular industries, technical progress in recent years and rationalisation have caused stupendous unemployment.

29 *Commerce Yearbook* 1926, p. 18.
30 Only first-class railways; hence the difference from the previous table.
31 New index of the Federal Reserve Board, average daily production of the years 1923–4–5 taken as 100.
32 US Bureau of Labor Statistics, index 1923 = 100; *Statistical Abstract of the United States* 1926, p. 337.
33 Calculated by the author.

The following tables give changes in American industry in 1923–7, and also the:
(a) percentage changes in the volume of production;
(b) percentage changes in the number of workers;
(c) percentage changes in the demand for labour in relation to the volume of production (calculated on a and b).

TABLE 10.6 Changes in American industry in 1923–7

	(a)	(b)	(c)
Refined petroleum	+84	−5	89
Tobacco	+53	−13	66
Meat slaughtering and packing	+20	−19	39
Railways (1922–6)	+30	−1	31
Automobiles	+69	+48	21
Motor tyres	+28	+7	21
Soft coal	+4	−15	19
Electricity (1922–7)	+70	+52	18
Steel	+8	−9	17
Agriculture (1920–5)	+10	−5	15
Cotton goods	+3	−13	16
Wood products	−6	−21	15
Men's clothing	+1	−7	5

This table shows the five years in which the production per worker in the most important industries rose by about 20 percent. How great is this progress is demonstrated by the fact that Sombart calculates the increase in the productivity of labour in industry for the entire 'high capitalist' period, that is, for the 100 years preceding the war, to be merely 100 percent. Progress has been made in the last five years which formerly took 20 years.[34]

The result of this development is gigantic unemployment increasing from year to year. This is accentuated by the normal increase in labour force, and by immigration. Graphs illustrating this development are given in the Appendix.

Figures for England show the same development.

---

34 Sombart 1928, p. 243.

TABLE 10.7 The number of workers engaged in industry and transport amounted to, in thousands[35]

	Beginning of 1923	Beginning of 1928	
Insured	9,701	8,992	−709
Unemployed	1,333	1,094	−239
Working	8,368	7,898	−470
Index of production[36]	88,7	96,3	+7.6

We see that the number of workers has decreased by about half a million, that is, 6 percent, while the volume of production increased by 7.6 percent. The tendency towards the creation of mass unemployment is clear, particularly if we take into account that there is an annual access of 200,000 new workers into the labour force, and that some ten thousand are each year displaced in agriculture.[37] The statistics available for other countries do not suffice to demonstrate the origin of this widespread unemployment, but the fact of chronic mass unemployment in most European countries is enough to show that the same causes are also at work there.

Where are the workers thus thrown out of employment?

The figures for America and England show that a part of the workers no longer required by industrial capital, the number being increased by the natural growth in labour forces, does find employment elsewhere, otherwise the number of unemployed would be much greater than it is. The following calculation for the United States was made by [Lewis] Corey.[38] Between 1919 and 1926 there was, according to the figures of the National Bureau of Economic Research, an increase in the number of wage-earners of 4,312,000. Since, as a result of technical progress, there were 2,125,000 fewer workers employed by industrial capital, 6,500,000 persons were compelled to seek a livelihood out-

---

35 Insured workers from *Labour Gazette*: the following are not included in the total: distributive trades, commerce, banking, government, hotels, etc., and also the unemployed.
36 London and Cambridge Economic Service, 1913 = 100.
37 The large number of workers employed in the years immediately following the war was the result of development during the war and of demobilisation; the decline is therefore not only due to technical improvements and rationalisation, but is to some extent a return to the former 'normal' conditions.
38 *The Analyst* [New York], 9 March 1928. [Lewis Corey was the pen name of Communist dissident and well-known economic analyst Louis C. Fraina (1892–1953)].

side agriculture, industry, transport and mining. Taking as his basis the increase between 1910 and 1920 in those branches of employment outside the sphere of industrial capital, and making certain additions thereto, the author calculates that of this 6,500,000, the numbers finding situations were as follows:

TABLE 10.8 Number of workers having found a livelihood in services

In commerce	1,000,000
Managers and officials (not in service of industrial capital)	1,000,000
Liberal professions	650,000
Motor trade and service	700,000
Public service	250,000
Various	350,000
Total	3,950,000

Apart from these, about 650,000 new workers found employment in the building trades, which, in any case, is within the sphere of industrial capital. We are then faced with the following results.

A decrease of about one and a half million in the number of workers directly creating surplus value in the service of industrial capital; an increase of about four million in the number employed in distribution and various other services.[39] The capacity of the distribution services to absorb workers is of course a limited one, the whole course of development is abnormal. The rationalisation of trading and of all forms of office work also tends to decrease the amount of labour employed in this sphere. The contradiction between technical-organisational progress, between the immense increase in social wealth, and the growing army of permanently unemployed, is the most powerful element of instability within the most stable capitalism, and it has tremendous social importance.

---

39 Considered in the abstract, this involves a tremendous waste of labour power. As Marx (1954, p. 530) says: 'From a social point of view, the productiveness increases in the same ratio as the economy of labour, which, in its turn, includes not only economy of the means of production, but also the avoidance of all useless labour. The capitalist mode of production, while on the one hand enforcing economy in each individual business, on the other hand begets by its anarchical system of competition, the most outrageous squandering of labour power and of the social means of production, not to mention the creation of a vast number of employments at present indispensable, but in themselves superfluous'.

4   The Sharpening of Contradictions: Rationalisation

'Rationalisation' is a new word for an old phenomenon. Capitalism has always tried, by improvements in technology, by more refined methods of exploitation, to reduce costs of production and thereby increase profits. But in the last few years this has occurred systematically and at a more rapid rate. To understand these processes we must first of all analyse the various methods of rationalisation according to their economic nature.

In our opinion we must first of all differentiate between three processes:

(*a*) *Raising the profits of an undertaking or of one form of capital at the expense of the profits of other undertakings or forms of capital.* This is a re-division among the capitalists of an unchanged total of surplus value; a process which at the time does not in the least affect the working class. If, for example, a number of undertakings are made into a monopoly, prices raised and profits consequently increased, the effects of this process are confined entirely to the circle of capitalists, if for the time being we make the theoretical assumption that labour power is sold at its proper value; the process does not alter either the rate of exploitation of the workers or the proportions in which the product is divided between the working class and the capitalist class as a whole. Nor does this process affect the amount of labour time embodied in the commodities, or the total sum of products.

This section also includes measures which raise the profits of one form of capital at the expense of other forms. If, for example, industrial capital disposes of its goods directly to the ultimate consumer, thereby eliminating trading capital, then the profits of industrial capital – although the period of turnover is extended – are increased at the expense of trading capital profits. This process also does not affect the value of the product nor the division of the product between capitalists and workers.

(*b*) *The second group of measures of rationalisation includes those processes which involve a decrease in the value of the product.* These are: increasing the productivity of labour; diminishing the labour time embodied in the commodities by standardisation.

An increase in the productivity of labour through technical innovations is the classic form of progress in capitalist production. Each worker sets in motion a more complicated machine, makes with the same expenditure of labour a greater change in the materials of his labour, and produces a greater mass of use value than before. We shall deal with technical progress in the last decade in a separate chapter.

As far as standardisation is concerned, there is a saving in labour time not through improved technique but through the elimination of those variations in form and size which are superfluous from the point of view of the use value of the commodities, by which, in accordance with the law of mass production, labour time is saved. Commodities satisfying the same demand are produced with the expenditure of less labour time.[40]

To this category belong also measures to avoid waste in raw materials, unnecessary transport, etc.[41] There is nothing new in this. Marx himself dealt with this thoroughly in many places, particularly in the chapter 'Economy in the Employment of Constant Capital'. But in America it is now being systematically carried out under the patronage of the Government.

(c) *The third form of rationalisation is the raising of the rate of surplus value, the increased exploitation of labour power.* We shall now deal with this aspect of rationalisation.

An increase in exploitation can occur by the production of relative surplus value. When, as the result of the methods of rationalisation enumerated above,

---

40   The following figures concerning the United States show what great success has in many cases been obtained in reducing variety in the same article of use:

TABLE 10.9   Reduction of types produced in industry

Reduction of types	From	To	Percent
Glazed tiles	66	4	94
Beds	78	4	95
Ordinary tiles	44	1	98
Kettles	130	13	90
Forged tools	665	351	47
Milk bottles	78	10	87
Iron plates	1,819	263	85
Warehouse slips	1,000	15	850

SOURCE: BIRNBAUM 1927

Tugwell gives other interesting examples in his above-mentioned book. Tugwell 1927, p. 136. A felt hat factory produced 3,684 kinds of hats. He remarks that 90 percent of its sales occurred in seven kinds of hats in 10 shades. Production was therefore confined to those varieties. A shoe factory turned out 2,500 kinds of shoes in three qualities. This was reduced to 100 kinds of one quality. By this means costs of production were lowered by 30 percent, general factory costs by 28 percent, and sale price by 27 percent. Sales rose by 50 percent.

41   The struggle against waste is one of the principal objects of American economic policy. See, for example, Chase 1925.

the prices of goods consumed by the workers fall, the value of labour power falls also, the necessary labour decreases, the surplus labour increases.

An increase in exploitation also follows from a rise in absolute surplus value, either by an extension of hours of labour or by an increase in the intensity of labour. At a certain point the two methods become mutually exclusive; with very great intensity of labour, the daily or weekly hours of labour cannot go beyond a certain maximum, or else the worker would break down.

But it is more advantageous to capital to allow a shorter working day with a maximum intensity of labour than it is to have a longer day with a lower intensity, for constant capital (particularly the fixed part of it) is in this way better employed, because a certain section of expenditure, lighting, heating, administration, supervision, etc., remains the same whether more or less is produced per day.

This explains the tendency of capital to employ a greater amount of labour power in the shortest time. To accomplish this capitalism has founded a new science, that of scientific management. Piece wages takes the place of time rates. The premium system takes the place of time rates – that is, an increase in piece rates if a certain height of production is reached. And in place of the premium system, or combined with it, the minimum system, every worker who does not reach a certain minimum of production is dismissed. This is combined with time studies, with the dissection of labour into separate, exactly determined and strictly circumscribed movements of the worker.

All this refers to the pre-war period. The latest development shows a dialectical change: *back to time rates, but in conjunction with the introduction of the conveyor belt.* The conveyor belt in conjunction with 'serial' production[42] makes the Taylor system, with all its tremendous supervising and preparatory apparatus, time and movement studies, time cards for each kind of labour and for each worker, entirely superfluous. The conveyor belt establishes an automatic control of labour productivity, keeps the worker to the speed of the conveyor

---

42   The new organisation of labour '… is concerned with two essential factors of productive labour: machine and human activity in a new manner: with mass production, … the processes of labour are dealt with not, as in most former instances of "serial" production, *next to each other*, but *after each other*. While with "serial" production the piece of work, so to speak, goes in search of the appropriate machine, with "traveling" work the continuous stream of work determines where the required machine is to stand. There is no more turning, cutting, planning, but the lathes, cutting machines and planning machines stand between drilling machines, polishing machines, casting machines, in positions necessitated by the time taken by the traveling labour process'. Ludwig Preller (1927), quoted in *Die Rote Fahne*, 26 April 1928. [Ludwig Preller (1897–1974) was a Social Democrat in the government of Saxony].

belt, enforces a superhuman intensity in the expenditure of labour power. Its employment can be observed in all spheres. Motors and machines move along the travelling belt in just the same way as slaughtered animals in the packing factory, the ingredients in a confectionery works, or the incoming mail at an American sorting station.[43]

The use of conveyor belts leads to a multiplication of labour intensity, without raising the productivity of labour. We give a few examples from many:

> In a Silesian shirt factory the same articles were, in the sewing department, dealt with by different methods of work, resulting in astonishing differences in the length of time required to perform the given task. One method, that formerly used in the department, consisted in the following: each sewer received a certain number of, e.g., men's shirts, and sewed them from the separate parts supplied by the cutter into the finished garment. By the second method, a group of six machines were given a certain amount of work to do, each having to perform a certain part of the work.
>
> This involved no change in the arrangement of seats or in technical apparatus. The third method was to employ the idea of the conveyor belt: the work was further subdivided and the workers sat in a long row at the appropriate distance from each other. The pieces of work were carried along this row by a simple moving belt, not in an unbroken movement, but regulated so that the belt moved the length between two workers at intervals of 18 minutes. Within that 18 minutes each worker had to do the required section of work for five shirts. According to the factory management's statistics, which were confirmed by the workers themselves, the following results were given by the three methods in a uniform period of time:
>
> Individual work   100
> Group work   260
> Conveyor belt   350
>
> This result is all the more remarkable because, with the exception of the conveyor belt itself, no increase or improvement of technical apparatus was necessary. This is a case of an extraordinary improvement in production occasioned by nothing but a better organisation of labour.[44]

---

43   See Hirsch 1926. [Julius Hirsch was a former state secretary in the Berlin Economics Ministry and a professor at the Berlin Economics College].
44   Tarnow 1928, p. 32.

This and similar examples show that the increase in labour output by rationalisation is only partly due to an increase in the productivity of labour brought about by technical changes, *and to a much greater extent is simply the result of increasing the intensity of labour*. If the monotony of work at the machines is soul-destroying – as Engels so powerfully describes it in his *Conditions of the English Working Class* – then work with the conveyor belt unmercifully sucks out the strength of the worker to a much greater extent daily than can be renewed.[45] Workers in such conditions are in a state of permanent over-fatigue:

> With the beginning of this fatigue, the production of the worker remains at the same level – he is not in the least aware of his state of fatigue, nor can it be objectively demonstrated, for the output remains the same ... The gradual increase of the burden of work is not apparent to the worker, because the process works itself out slowly ... Any light illness can then make the state of affairs at once obvious or the worker himself realises in time that 'something has gone wrong' ... The impossibility of recognizing the slow appearance of these indefinite results of fatigue is one of the saddest facts which wrecks any attempt at the scientific limitation of admissible labour intensity.[46]

This murderous rate of work has in some cases in America been still further increased by the workers having each to work at two conveyor belts (e.g. in the Hudson-Essex automobile factory).

This intensity of labour in America, increased to the utmost limit, explains why real wages, in spite of great unemployment, have up to the present shown an upward tendency; why some concerns have introduced the five-day week. The expenditure of labour power enforced by the conveyor belt is possible only with good nourishment and a relatively shorter working day, for otherwise the worker would simply break down at his job. And as cattle are better fed for harder work, capitalism is compelled to give more fodder and grant more rest-

---

45 Sombart has pertinently stated the motto for the modern factory worker: '*The soul must be left in the cloakroom on entry*'. [Varga gives no references for this quote]. 'Though operations have become specialized, skill has become less so, and in large stretches of industry labour has become merely automatic machine-tending. In short, American labour today is, to a degree little realised, unskilled labour – the standardization imposed upon the product has also been stamped upon the man'. 'Unemployment in the u.s. – Machinery and men', *The Times*, 9 March 1928, p. 14. [Tugwell is even more explicit: 'The industrial revolution has robbed the worker ... from his professional skills.' Tugwell 1927, p. 7. [This part of the note is published in the French text, but not kept in the English translation].

46 Durig 1928, pp. 4–5.

ing time than formerly to the human automata working at a pitch of intensity hitherto unknown.[47]

In spite of the rise in real wages, the rate of surplus value in American industry is rising. (There are no statistical data on which to base a calculation for other countries).

TABLE 10.10 Rate of surplus value in American industry

1914	1919	1921	1923	1925
121	122	106	118	128

The low rate of surplus value in 1921 reflects the crisis. (For the method of calculation, see the Appendix. The rates of surplus value calculated here are *lower* than is the actual case, for profits of trading capital had to be left out account).

Thus we can observe the following line of development as a result of rationalisation, which only accentuates the tendencies inherent in capitalism.

Absolute decrease in the number of workers by industrial capital, and, at the same time, an increased growth in the intensity of labour and a rise in the rate of surplus value. This is accompanied by a fall in the average rate of profit as a result of the rapid increase in the organic composition of capital. As a whole there is a strong resemblance to the theoretical picture of pure capitalism painted by Marx – particularly in the United States, the leading capitalist country. There is also a process going on which is establishing two rates of profit. Capital included in monopolies is realising a higher rate of profit at the expense of capital not monopolised and of the independent producers. Because of this, and because of the decrease in the total wages of the working class as a result of rationalisation, there is a narrowing down of the home market and, in spite of monopolies, a more acute struggle for markets which must necessary lead to war and to a further redivision of the world.

---

47 '… [W]here we have labour, not carried on by fits and starts, but repeated day after day with unvarying uniformity, a point must inevitably be reached where extension of the working day and intensity of labour naturally exclude one another in such a way that lengthening of the working day becomes compatible only with a lower degree of intensity, and a higher degree of intensity only with a shortening of the working day'. Marx 1954, p. 409.

5 The New Technique and Its Economic Consequences

... [W]ith the single exception of the era which saw the introduction of steam, probably none has witnessed a greater industrial revolution than that in progress today. Changes are taking place in every direction, and many of the conditions under which the great staple industries were built up no longer exist. Electrical energy, generated in many countries by water power hitherto running to waste, has vastly extended the area in which manufacturing can be successfully conducted; it is no longer anchored to accessible coal. Chemical discoveries ... have altered the relative values of raw materials. The development of many new countries, which has been largely due to modern means of communication, has led to a great change in the relative importance the world's markets. In the midst of this changing world new industries, not only in this country, have come into being to meet new requirements.[48]

In the last few years there has been a rapid increase in the output of labour. This is based upon an increased intensity and productivity of labour.[49] Increased productivity is a result of numerous technical innovations which have recently been introduced in connection with rationalisation.[50] It is not our concern to deal with the purely technical aspect of the question, nor have we the technical

---

48 'Artificial silk', *The Times*, 17 March 1928, p. 13.
49 Since these two ideas are often confused, we shall differentiate exactly between them: By productivity of labour we understand that factor in labour output which is determined by the means of production. With the same expenditure of labour power for the same period of time, the output can be greater or less according to the nature and quality of the means of production employed. The use of better machinery, better technique, raises the productivity of labour. The intensity of labour is determined by the quantity of labour power expended in a given period of time. (In the words of Marx, 'The expenditure of human muscular energy, blood, nerves'). It is the number of appropriate movements, of necessary muscular energy, the degree of nerve strain, etc. A change in the intensity of labour can take place while using the same machinery, according to the rate at which it is worked. Increases in the productivity and intensity of labour generally occur simultaneously, but this is not necessarily so. There can be increased intensity with unchanged productivity, but scarcely the reverse. Increased productivity of labour means the production of a greater quantity of consumable values with the same expenditure of human labour power, that is, decreasing value per unit of product. Increased intensity similarly means the production of a greater quantity of consumable values, but in this case their value is proportionately greater, because more intensive labour in the same time is as creative of value as labour of normal intensity employed for a longer time. See Marx 1959, pp. 140–206.
50 We must differentiate sharply between the discovery and introduction of new machines.

knowledge for such a task. We can only try to infer the economic consequences of technical development.

The Economics of Power

We shall begin with power. The following processes must be distinguished.
(a) The better employment of coal,[51] steam turbines in place of the old steam engines,[52] flexible furnaces, coal dust fuel, the beginning of long-distance gas conducting, and liquefaction of coal.
(b) Replacement of coal by oil, peat, water power.

Economic result, international coal crisis!

In spite of progressing industrialisation and the great increase in the volume of production, there is no increase in the amount of coal being used. This is most clearly shown in the United States. Production, which we may take as indicative of consumption, amounted to:

TABLE 10.12 Production, million tons (5-yearly averages)[53]

	1870	1880	1890	1900	1910	1920	1925	1927
	32	62	138	227	455	626	559	601
% increases	–	94	123	65	200	38	−11	7

Often years and decades pass before a new technical invention is sufficiently widespread to effect a change in production; and only in the latter case does it have economic importance.

51 Considering coal from the beginning in the mine up to its utilisation as fuel in a steam engine, only 4 percent of its power was usefully employed because of waste and faulty technique. See American Geological Survey and the Bureau of Mines. Quoted in Chase 1925, p. 247.

52 The great progress made in the use of coal in recent years is shown by numerous data. According to the management of the Austrian Federal Railways, the following amounts of coal were employed per 1,000 British ton miles:

TABLE 10.11 Amounts of coal used by the Austrian Federal Railways

1923	1924	1925	1926	1927
157	126	113	107	104

SOURCE: *BERLINER BÖRSEN-COURIER*, 20 DECEMBER 1927

53 *Statistical Abstract of the United States* 1926, p. 725. Percentages calculated by author.

Following on a serious decline in the upward trend for the periods 1905–10 and 1915–20, there is an absolute decrease in consumption.

(c) *Steam engines are no longer employed as machines for labour, as in Marx's time, but for the generation of electrical power.* As steam power was important in the age of free capitalist competition, so electrical power is important for the age of imperialism. And instead of small electrical concerns satisfying local requirements we now have gigantic works engaged in generating electricity on the site of the actual source of energy (waterfalls and coal mines) and high-tension transmission across very great distances.[54]

The economic consequences of the change to electrical high-tension power are as follows:

(1) *Greater freedom for industry to choose its site of production: the decentralisation of large-scale industry.* The direct use of steam power compelled many industries to set up works on a site as near as possible to the coal areas or in their immediate vicinity, otherwise the freightage costs of coal would have increased the costs of production.[55] By covering the whole country with a high-tension network, industry can move either to the area of raw materials or to the localities where cheap labour is obtainable. We can observe a great moving of industry in the USA from the north-east to the south, in England from the north to the south-east. Industry, formerly concentrated preponderantly in the neighbourhood of coal, is being distributed: the economic structure of the different industrial countries is being equalised, the division into purely agricultural areas and mainly industrial areas is being eliminated. The industrial proletariat, as a class, is spread over the whole country!

(2) The use of electrical high-tension transmission affords a concrete basis for the rapid development of certain areas whose economic development in the age of steam power was hindered by lack of coal. The rapid development of north Italian industry in the last decade would have been impossible without the transmission of electrical areas from the Alps. Long-distance high-tension transmission makes it possible to exploit industrially those areas which produce raw materials and which are badly developed in the way of communications. (Important for Africa and Asia).[56]

---

54 Electricity generated in the Alps is conducted to towns in Lombardy. Electricity up to a pressure of 100,000 volts is transmitted hundreds of miles in America.
55 See Weber's excellent book (1909).
56 The importance of electrical power will become still greater should Marconi's attempt to transmit power by radio succeed, for cables are very expensive.

(3) *The concentration of power supply.* The technical development of electricity generation enforces the interconnection of electricity power stations in a country, the object being to even out the variations in daily and seasonal consumption. Over large areas in Germany and the United States, generating stations are connected up with each other (small works are mostly closed down and production concentrated in a small number of large stations).[57] The central electrical power stations have become decisive economic rulers.[58] The cessation of electric power supply caused by a general strike with a revolutionary mass movement would have much more decisive effects in the great industrial countries than a strike in any other branch of industry.

(4) *Greater mobility within the factory.* Factories working directly on steam power, as Marx described them, were concerns working in a unified manner.

> An organised system of machines, to which motion is communicated by the transmitting mechanism from a central automation, is the most developed form of production by machinery. Here we have, in the place of the isolated machine, a mechanical monster whose body fills whole factories, and whose demon power, at first veiled under the slow and measure motions of his giant limbs, at length breaks out into the fast and furious whirl of his countless working organs.[59]

The replacement of steam power by electricity has changed the appearance of factories.[60] The 'unified impulse' of the steam engine disappears. 'The transmitting mechanism, composed of flywheels, shafting, toothed wheels, pulleys, straps, ropes, bands, pinions and gearing of the most varied kinds'[61] is almost completely disappearing. The factory as a whole is absolutely dependent upon the supply of electricity, but – that guaranteed – is more mobile and elastic than

---

57 This development in America has been summed up in two phrases, 'super-power' and 'giant power'. The name of super-power is given to the system by which the individual electric supply is given to the system by which the individual electric supply companies retain their independence, their connection with each other only consisting of the distribution of their surplus power among themselves. Giant power means the concentration of the total production of, and the total demand for, electricity in a whole State, and correspondingly systematic distribution. See Pinchot (ed.) 1925.

58 The formation of giant power under private ownership 'would be the most dangerous monopoly that has yet existed.' See ibid.

59 Marx 1954, pp. 381–2.

60 In the USA 75 percent, and in Germany about 50 percent of all factories work with electric power.

61 Marx 1954, p. 373.

the old steam factory. Indeed, the idea of complete decentralisation of the factory, of the re-emergence of rural industry on a modern basis, has arisen.[62]

Progress in Machinery Itself

It is difficult to characterise this generally, because it consists of innumerable details. Although certain special new machines greatly assisting production have been introduced (e.g. the Westlake bottle machine), there has not been, as far as we can see, any fundamental, revolutionary change in any branch of industry which works up its raw materials by machinery. Innovations have proceeded in the old channels: further division of the processes of labour and multiplication of special machines for dealing with detailed jobs,[63] mechanisation of the transport of raw materials to the machine, making the labour processes automatic, etc. This last factor has been of great importance, particularly in the textile industry. Human labour is limited entirely to supervision. In America, one worker and two assistants tend 60 machines. We are of the opinion that the increase in labour output is due less to improvements in machinery than to improvements in the organisation of labour. The great increase has been in the intensity of labour, and only secondarily in productivity.

The development of agricultural machinery's exceptional position. In this case the universal machine and not the specialised machine is the object aimed at; a natural consequence of the fact that a certain process has to be carried out only once a year and then for a short period. Hence the development of all-round agricultural machines, moved by tractors, in which the actual implements are interchangeable at will, e.g. one machine for harvesting and threshing.[64] The economic consequences are: a great increase in the organic compos-

---

62   Fisher 1925, p. 96.
63   The shoe industry is a good example of this. See Jones 1921.
64   Julius Hirsch, in the *Berliner Tageblatt* for 28 February 1928, makes a few interesting observations on the growing importance of machines in American agriculture.

TABLE 10.13   The number of horses in the United States

1915	21,200,000
1920	19,900,000
1925	16,500,000
1927	15,300,000
1932 (estimated)	12,000,000

ition of capital in agriculture; decreased opportunity for work on the land; and change in unemployment from being 'latent' into being acute.

The employment of machinery in offices also occupies a peculiar position. It decreases the overhead costs of the capitalist system of production by systematising the keeping of accounts, and by replacing clerks, statisticians and bookkeepers by machines tended largely by unskilled workers. The machine, which groups thousands of items on cards in the form of punched holes, adds and gives the complete calculation; the 'human machine', a recent American invention which deals with accounts transmitted by telephone, indicates the line of development. A similar change is taking place in the rearrangement of labour, e.g. clocking in on separate cards, instead of in books; the conveyor carrying bookkeeping documents from one employee to the other. The economic consequence is a relative surplus of office workers who – as in agriculture and industry – presently become an absolute surplus.

The Conveyor as the Centre of Organisation

The important changes have not taken place in machinery but in the organisation of labour within the factories. The real centre of the factory is not in the machine, but in the conveyor belt. It is not the materials of labour, or their way through the factory, that are adapted to the machinery; it is not the materials of labour which journey from machine to machine, as formerly, but the other way round. The organisational centre is the conveyor, and the machines are so placed as to serve the requirements of conveyor work. The most varied machines are placed along the conveyor in gay confusion; the necessary tools for the workers, if they have to change their tools at all, are placed ready to hand. The old factory organisation, the co-ordination of similar machines or machine systems, is disappearing.

> The estimate for 1932 is based on the present number of foals. Of the most recent machines adopted in American agriculture the following are worthy of attention: (1) The so-called 'Little Combine', which is a combination of mowing, binding and threshing machine. The employment of these machines is, of course, only possible in dry areas – where the corn can be cut quite dry. Such a machine costs 1,285 dollars. The department calculated that the employment of such a machine effected a saving of about 31s. per ton. Recently they are coming to be used in their tens of thousands. (2) The tractor has also been greatly improved, so that it can now be used both for small plots of ground and for hilly, stony and boggy soil. A main-wheel tractor, strong enough for ploughing, is now being sold at 750 dollars, and also, of course, on the hire-purchase system. There is also the mechanical cotton picker. This is still in an experimental stage, and has the disadvantage of leaving more than a quarter of the crop untouched. But doubtless this will be remedied.

The essential condition for the successful employment of the conveyor belt is mass production, the production of exactly similar commodities in unbroken repetition. With the products of the great staple industries, cotton yarn and fabrics, metals, etc., this has been the case for some time. What is new is the extension of mass production to the means of production or their parts (standardisation), and also to articles of consumption (automobiles, houses, shoes, clothes).

The essential condition for mass production is a large market for the commodities produced. This arises partly from the standardisation of demand[65] – which has proceeded furthest in America – and partly from a general increase in the sale of the particular commodity.[66]

Production with the conveyor requires not only a large market, but a correspondingly great capital; it promotes concentration and centralisation of the formation of monopolies.

The economic nature of production with the conveyor is the attainment of the greatest possible output. The arrangement of labour within the factory also

---

65   While there did exist formerly a conventional similarity in the clothing, houses, etc., of the workers engaged in domestic industry or in handicrafts, serial production today enforces a new uniformity of demand. In America millions own the same Ford car, the same shoes, the same bookcases with the same 50 or 100 'best books', etc.

66   The lack of sufficient markets is the chief danger which confronts German rationalisation. The whole tragedy of German rationalisation was aptly described by a German correspondent of the *The Statist* [*A Journal of Practical Finance and Trade*] in the issue of 10 March 1928 [p. 390] in the following words: 'The world's excessive demand for German products ... gave place to an almost complete lack of orders from abroad after the stabilisation of the mark. German goods seemed to have lost suddenly the ability to compete in external markets, whereas German imports of foreign, chiefly American articles, rose steadily. Their lower price, notwithstanding the far higher earnings of labourers in the United States, led in 1925 to a migration of the captains of trade and industry across the ocean in order to see for themselves how America could succeed in underbidding German industry even in its home market ... Upon the return of these explorers "the rationalisation of production methods" became the catchword in Germany. It was said that merely by imitating the American practice of 'recklessly scrapping out-of-date machinery and of mass production of certain standard types, the growing adversity of the German trade balance could be checked and the foreign demand for German articles could be re-established'. But the goal of rationalisation was not reached and the market for German goods abroad showed no increase. '... The only positive results of the rationalisation process appear to be an over-expansion of the production capacity of German industry and an immense increase of its indebtedness, particularly to foreign countries ... Responsible for this failure is the blind imitation of American methods. No attention has been paid to the fact that the United States industry has a far wider domestic market than Germany, and does not beat itself against insurmountable Customs barriers in the nearest vicinity of its headquarters'.

serves this purpose: the elimination of any superfluous movement from the labour process on the one hand, and the production of the greatest intensity of labour on the other.[67] The speed of work has been so greatly accelerated that in many concerns compulsory rest intervals had to be introduced, for otherwise some of the workers would certainly have broken down during the day.

The Advance of the Chemical Industry

Tremendous progress has been made in the chemical industry. Together with electrification the chemical industry gives the technology of today its peculiar character. The production of nitrogen from the air, liquefaction of coal, artificial silk, regeneration of used rubber, synthetic rubber, etc.

The age of capitalism was distinguished from pre-capitalist epochs, as [Werner] Sombart has correctly remarked, by substituting inorganic for organic materials; substituting the products of mining for those of agriculture and forestry – iron instead of wood for tools and materials of construction, coal instead of wood for fuel, petroleum instead of vegetable matter for lighting, etc. Development today is along the lines of replacing rare by 'ubiquitous' – the word is Weber's – raw materials, that is, by raw materials which are found everywhere. Iron and wood are to be replaced by concrete, salpetre by nitrogen, natural petroleum by liquefied coal, silk by artificial silk, etc.

This development also implies the replacement of mechanical by chemical labour. Instead of coal being transported in its natural condition it will be turned into electrical energy, gas or oil, and conducted great distances by wires or pipes without any mechanical labour.[68] Instead of felling and sawing wood,

---

67   The importance of the organisation of labour as compared with developments in machinery is shown by the following: According to the *Balfour Report* (Part 2, *Further Factors in Industrial Efficiency* 1928, p. 11) the increase in wage-costs per unit of product between 1907 and 1924 was greater than the increase in a full week's wages (with the exception of heavy industry, shipbuilding and machine construction). Also the mechanical power employed in industry rose much more than production per head (from 8,000,000 to 13,500,000 h.p.). The reasons for this were insufficient employment of labour power, widespread short time, high overhead charges. Since 1924 the position has improved as a result of the rationalisation then begun. [The Balfour Committee on Trade and Industry studied between 1924 and 1928 British industrial decline and mass unemployment. The *Final Report* concluded in 1929 that what was needed was the rationalisation of Britain's industry and a development of newer industries].

68   In England and Germany, about half of the transport of goods is done by coal; this explains the opposition of the railways to long-distance conveying of gas. The necessary condition for long-distance gas conveying is the invention of welded steel pines which will stand pressure of 30 atmospheres; a riveted pipe, as used formerly, will not stand such a pressure.

instead of digging for iron ore, smelting and rolling iron, cement will be produced. Electrolysis is gaining a growing importance in metallurgy; quite new metals (e.g. aluminum for aeroplanes) are obtaining economic importance.

Economically, this implies a tendency towards the distribution of industry over the whole country, instead of its former concentration in areas producing either fuel or raw materials, with the results which we mentioned above.

The advance in chemistry at the expense of the mechanical working up of raw materials also implies an advance in apparatus at the expense of machinery in the whole system of capitalist production.

'The machine proper is therefore a mechanism that, after being set in motion, performs with its tools the same operations that were formerly done by the workman with similar tools'.[69]

This definition of the machine is not applicable to the mechanism of production in chemical industry. The means of production in the chemical industry are not machines, but apparatus, appropriately constructed container-and-pipe systems in which the objects of labour are handled, and machine processes, such as mixing, shaking and turning, play only an accessory part.[70] Production is becoming automatic; most businesses are almost entirely devoid of workers!

Apparatus production implies a sharp division of labour power in the works concerned, there are no skilled apparatus workers. In the chemical industry there are chemical engineers, about one-fifth of the total personnel; the rest are unskilled workers who do the work of assistants, understand nothing of the processes of production, and on the whole are very badly paid.[71]

Progress in Traffic

In the nineteenth century, railways were the most important factor in overcoming crises and in the opening of new areas for the capitalist mode of production, as Lenin demonstrated in his *Imperialism*. The war and the postwar period

---

69   Marx 1954, p. 374.
70   There appeared before the war a Marxist book on this problem, to which too little attention has been paid, which is even more topical today: Mataré 1913.
71   The technique of the chemical industry, which has always been kept secret, is rapidly changing. The principal chemists of the International Dyestuffs Corporation when they vacate their positions receive their full salaries for three years, but may not accept positions in any other chemical concern. I once asked a director of that concern, 'And if he should go to England or America after the three years?' receiving the answer: 'In three years our technique has changed so greatly that he may peacefully enter into competition with us; he can't harm us any longer'.

showed a relative slowing down in railway construction.[72] In shipbuilding the former development was continued; in the place of the steam-ship came the motor-ship, in the place of coal firing came oil as fuel. New sailing vessels for long-distance voyages were no longer built; the attempt to utilise wind in shipping in a new form, *Flettner's Rotor Ship*, does not seem to be gaining any economic importance. In recent shipbuilding the greatest importance is attached to speed and comfortable, elegant arrangements for passengers. Automobiles and aeroplanes are gaining the lead. The figures are generally known; we shall only refer to the economic consequences.

The automobile makes it possible to link up to the world transport system those thinly-populated areas where railways, on account of the little traffic, would not pay. There are motor roads from the Mediterranean to Baghdad right through Arabia, there is Trans-Sahara transport.

Automobile and air transport establish a very rapid connection between all quarters of the globe. Development is proceeding rapidly. Ford is beginning to manufacture cheap mass aeroplanes, the flight over the Atlantic Ocean has been accomplished,[73] there are motors without fuel,[74] rocket automobiles and aeroplanes.[75]

Motor and air transport serve chiefly to shorten the time of journeys for travellers. The motor mainly serves shorter distances, for connecting up the main railway lines and also town and country. It enables those employed in the town at fairly well-paid jobs to live in the country. It is also rapidly becoming of great

---

[72] TABLE 10.14 The total length of railways in the world amounted to

End of 1913	End of 1924	Increase
1,101,653 km	1,221,066 km	11 percent

[73] The Dornier works are now turning out giant aeroplanes with 12 motors, totaling 5,000 h.p., for American transport. They are to be equipped with nautical instruments and everything necessary for ocean transport.

[74] Early in 1928 in America, Lindbergh, a representative of the War Ministry, the inventor and the capitalists who were backing the invention, tried out a motor which works without fuel, but utilises the electric currents in the earth by means of a magnetic motor. The motor developed 1,800 revolutions per minute, and may be the herald of a revolution in the sphere of transport technology.

[75] The rocket automobile was first used in Berlin in May 1928, and with success. It is claimed that the rocket aeroplane has the advantage of not needing much air for the lifting planes, and can therefore go far from the earth's surface and attain terrific speed. A thousand, even thousands of kilometers per hour is mentioned (?).

importance in freight traffic for short distances, and is successfully entering into competition with the railways for short distances.[76]

Aeroplanes have up to the present only been used in exceptional circumstances for transporting very expensive commodities, for which long delay in transport would involve great loss of interest, or for articles which spoil quickly. This applies to the transport of gold from England to the Continent, and in South Africa; of fresh flowers and fruit from the South of France to London, etc. Its greater importance is for passenger traffic over long distances, particularly if there is no good overland route. In these cases the saving in time is very great indeed. The pressure towards saving time gave rise to the many attempts to cross the Atlantic Ocean by air; it can scarcely be doubted that within a few years there will be a regular air transport service between America and Europe.

The contradiction between the development of transport technique and the division of the capitalist world into numerous small states is becoming more and more acute. Frontier crossing and tariff formalities will soon occupy more time than the journeys themselves.

Process in the Distribution of Information

The last decade has witnessed great progress in the technique of distributing information. Postal transmission by means of motors and aeroplanes has resulted in great rapidity in spreading information. The most important innovation, however, is that contained in the radio, the wireless transmission of news. Radio connects the most distant areas with the centre, and since it requires no cables, the number of those using it can be illimitably extended. The one-sidedness arising from the fact that one can only receive news, but that only the distributing centre can send out news, will soon be overcome. The radio telephone and radio-vision are about to be put into operation.[77] Trans-oceanic cables, for whose possession the imperialists fought so bitterly ten years ago at the conclusion of peace, will soon be worthless rubbish.

Progress in the technique of transport and news distribution has greatly improved knowledge of the world market. Differences in prices arising from a lack of knowledge of market conditions in distant areas, and the speculation which took place because of this, have disappeared. So has the possibility of carrying on credit swindles, which, even in Marx's time, greatly intensified

---

76 Many complaints about this have been made in England, where the railways are now beginning to organise their own motor transport.

77 Judicial superstructure lags behind economic development here also. Recently in America the courts decided that a cheque transmitted by radio cannot be recognised as valid.

crises.⁷⁸ Connections in world economy are growing closer; and the possibilities of crises arising from ignorance of what is happening, less. Crises are now much more due to inherent causes, and much less to accidents.

Technology and Military Preparations

The reason for employing technical inventions is found in the desire of capitalist undertakings to increase their profits. It would, however, be false to overlook the close connection between technique and war preparations, to ignore the fact that many technical inventions were made in the course of the war, and have been put into operation in the hope of making large profits in the next war, meanwhile being supported by the Government. The production of nitrogen from the air originated in Germany during the war, because the supply of saltpetre was cut off; the same is true of the English and American dyestuffs industry, because of the lack of German dyes. The entire chemical industry is most closely connected with war preparations, and this is also true of transport. Civil aviation in all capitalist countries is subsidised by the Government. The British Empire Lines have never yet covered their expenses by their own income. But governments everywhere subsidise civil aviation, for in case of war every aeroplane will immediately be used for military service; every civil pilot is a potential military pilot. Every technical innovation is immediately tested to see what use could be made of it in a future war.⁷⁹ The great industrial countries are gaining an absolute military predominance over the agricultural and smaller countries which, as a result of their incapacity to equip themselves from a technical and military standpoint out of their own resources, can only take part in war as a part of one of the alliances led by an industrial great power.

---

78   See Marx 1959, pp. 392–404.
79   The American [sic!] Brown Boveri Company, in conjunction with a large shipbuilding firm, early in 1928 requested the assistance of the American Government in constructing six 35,000-ton trans-Atlantic passenger steamers. They are to take four days in crossing the Atlantic from dock to dock, and to be equipped as aeroplane carriers. In the plans it was mentioned that the decisions of the Naval Armament's Conference of 1922 do not refer to these ships, and that no naval Power in the world possesses, or is in process of building, such ships. They are to travel at 33 knots, and can cover more than 7,000 nautical miles without stopping for fuel; and, although their normal equipment would consist of 24 aeroplanes for civil purposes, they can be easily adapted to carry 100 aeroplanes in the event of national need. It is further emphasised that the peculiar advantage of these ships is that they require no naval base, this being of particular importance since the USA has no marine base west of Hawaii. Government assistance was nominally refused. [Brown Boveri, now ABB, is a Swiss multinational company].

Technology and Economics

We shall now try to recapitulate the economic consequences of the new technique, with all the reservations which are unavoidable in a subject with which we are so little familiar.[80] *The most widespread result is that the contradictions in capitalism have been intensified!*

(a) The new technique and organisation of labour has increased output to such an extent that the 'setting free' of workers is no longer compensated for by an extension in the domain of the capitalist system of production. While Marx witnessed an increase in the number of workers despite technical progress, today we are faced with unemployment on a gigantic scale, with an increasing army of permanently unemployed in the most highly developed capitalist countries. A diminished number of productive workers are working with a murderous intensity, while millions are unemployed!

(b) The contradiction between production capacity and the possibilities of realisation is growing sharper. The decrease in variable capital, i.e. in the share of total product falling to the working class, means the narrowing down of the home market and gives rise to the necessity for a more bitter conflict for markets outside the 'national' market. Simultaneously, a considerable part of the machinery of production is lying idle!

(c) The rapid technical development increases the danger of 'moral waste', of machinery becoming prematurely out-of-date. This explains the tendency towards the greatest possible utilisation of stock, although this is hindered by the narrowness of the market.

(d) The organic composition of capital is increasing rapidly. This enforces the concentration of capital, for it requires a huge amount of capital to start a new concern capable of competing. Hence the tendency towards the formation of monopolies.

(e) The contradiction between social production and private ownership in the means of production is growing stronger; technical development makes the concentration of capital a necessity. This tendency can be seen partly expressed in state capitalism.

(f) The latest technique liberates industry from being bound to particular areas, enables previously backward areas to develop rapidly, diminishes the contrast between town and country, increases the connections of all quarters of the globe with world economy.

---

80 Some of what is written here has already been commented upon by comrade [Henryk] Brand [Henryk Gustav Lauer] at the Seventh Plenum of the Comintern.

(g) As against this, the latest technique adds to the economic, military and political predominance of the great imperialist industrial countries. The resistance of the smaller countries, expressed in high protective tariffs, gives rise to the break-up of the world market, without affecting the superiority of the great industrial countries.

In the following chapters we shall deal with some of these factors more fully.

Appendix to Chapter 5: Calculation of the Rate of Surplus Value in American Industry

The statistics collected by the Census, which is taken periodically, afford the possibility of making an approximate estimate of the rate of surplus value in American industry. The factors entering into such a calculation are (see *Commerce Yearbook* 1926):

> Total wages = Variable capital.
> Cast of raw materials = Circulating capital.
> Cost of wear and tear of machinery = Fixed capital.
> The value of the product.

For an exact calculation we should also have:

1. The value of the wear and tear of that part of the fixed capital present in buildings; but this is relatively so small that it can be overlooked in any merely approximate calculation.
2. There is also lacking a very important factor, namely, the total of commercial profits, which is a part of the surplus value produced in industry, for in the Marxian theory of value, industrial capital disposes of its goods to commercial capital not at the full production price, but lower than that, at a price which will enable commercial capital, when selling the commodities at their production price, to realise the average rate of profit. Profit on commercial capital is therefore surplus value shown in industry. The necessary data are not, however, at our disposal. Consequently the rate of surplus value in the next table is considerably lower than corresponds to reality.

With these reservations let us turn to the tables:

TABLE 10.15 Rate of surplus value in American industry in million dollars

	Total wages = V.	Cost of materials	Wear and tear of machinery = fixed C	Value produced	Surplus value S = V	Rate of surplus value %
	I	II	III	IV	IV − (I + II + III)	V/I = S/V
1899	2,008	6,576	250	11,407	2,569	123
1904	2,610	8,500	330	14,794	3,354	128
1909	3,427	12,143	500	20,672	4,602	134
1914	4,068	14,278	600	23,988	5,042	121
1919	10,453	36,989	1,600	61,737	12,695	121
1921	8,193	25,155	1,400	43,427	8,679	105
1923	10,999	34,381	1,800	60,258	12,978	117
1925	10,729	35,931	2,300	62,706	13,746	128

For calculating the wear and tear of machines, the figures giving the total value of machines employed in industry are at our disposal.[81]

TABLE 10.16 Value of machines in industry (in million dollars)

1900	1904	1912	1922
2,541	3,298	6,091	15,783

If we consider this table, the most important thing we learn from it is that the 100 percent rate of surplus value assumed by Marx and everywhere described as grossly exaggerated has actually been outstripped in American industry. And we must again emphasise the fact that this rate of surplus value is lower than the actual rate, for it does not include that share of the profits produced in industry, but going to commercial capital.

---

81   Taken from the Official Publication, *Wealth, Public Debt and Taxation: 1922 1924*, p. 18.

We wish to emphasise, moreover, very strongly that we are *dealing here only with a very rough attempt at estimating the approximate rate of surplus value, based on inadequate data and with many deviations from the actual facts*, but at least these deviations tend to make the result lower than the actual rate of surplus value.

6   The Limitation of the Home Market and the Struggle for the World Market

The capitalist system of production has the tendency to decrease the workers' share in the social product, for, with an increase in productivity, those goods which are consumed by the workers fall in value, and necessary labour time becomes shorter, and surplus labour longer. The share of the worker grows less in a corresponding degree. Formerly the share of the working class as a whole, that is, variable capital, only decreased relatively in the great industrial countries. But in the most recent development there has been an absolute decrease.

We have already referred to the decrease in the number of productive workers in the United States. A smaller number of workers are being exploited at a much greater intensity. More intensive labour requires better nourishment. Hence a slight increase in the real wages of full-time workers. The American Bureau of Labor statistics publishes the following index numbers, based upon returns from more than 10,000 concerns employing more than 3,000,000 workers.[82]

TABLE 10.17   Evolution of American wages and the number of workers

	1923	1924	1925	1926
Number of workers	100.0	90.3	91.2	91.9
Total wages bill	100.0	90.6	93.6	95.8
Cost of living index (1913 = 100)	173.2	172.5	177.9	175.6

The number of workers has decreased by 8 percent, the wages bill by 4 percent. Wages have therefore risen relatively by 4 percent. But this increase is practically cancelled out by an increase in the cost of living of 2.5 percent. These figures may be taken as typical. For 1926 was a year of good markets.

---

82   *Handbook of Labor Statistics 1924–1926* 1927, p. 112 and pp. 132–3.

As for the absolute amounts paid out in wages, we have only the figures for industry as they appear in the census returns.

TABLE 10.18 Wages and value added in million dollars[83]

	Wages bill	Salaries	Value added
1923	10,999	3,001	34,481
1925	10,730	3,147	35,936

Wages down by 270,000,000 dollars, surplus value increased by 1,455,000,000 dollars.

In 1925 industrial workers could buy 270,000,000 dollars worth less of their own products than in 1923, although they had increased the values produced by then by 1,455,000,000 dollars. The same is true of most other branches of production in America (particularly agriculture) as well as of other industrial countries for which there are no figures. This explains the diminishing purchasing capacity of the working class.

The prices of goods produced by monopoly organisations are not lowered in a corresponding degree to the decrease in their cost of production. Monopolist capital gets extra profits beyond the average rate of profit. This is at the expense of the profits of independent producers and unorganised capitalists, farmers, handicraftsmen, petty-capitalists, whose purchasing power is proportionately diminished. This involves a further narrowing of the home market. A particular kind of limitation of the home market occurred in the inflation countries, where the income of the rentier classes was expropriated. The consequences of inflation as they affected the home market could not be wiped out for many years.

It may be argued, as has been done by the bourgeois apostles of harmony, that the less the workers, independent producers and unorganised capitalists produce, the more falls in the share of the monopolists; the total purchasing power of society remains the same, the total annual product. Hence the sale of commodities is guaranteed.

This would be so in the case of a regulated economically-planned capitalism, in which production was systematically adapted to the distribution of income. But capitalism today is – in spite of state capitalism and monopolies – an antag-

---

83 *Statistical Abstract for United States*, 1926, p. 745.

onistic and anarchic mode of production, in which each undertaking is anxious to reduce costs of production, for which purpose methods must be employed which must necessarily result in an increase in the volume of production beyond the limits imposed by the antagonistic distribution of income.

This means, first of all, periodically recurring crises, and, secondly, a bitter struggle for foreign markets. This explains one policy, represented chiefly by the reformists: the capitalists should, in their own interests, pay higher wages.[84] The second looks forward to increased consumption on the part of the capitalists themselves. It is true that at the present time the capitalist class is displaying unprecedented luxury, particularly in America. But the Europeans are not behind in this, as is shown by the following description of the journey of Loewenstein,[85] the Belgian capitalist, to America.[86]

> Mr. Loewenstein is traveling rather in the manner of a ruler than as a private citizen. He is accompanied by his wife and five guests: the Count and Countess de Grunne,[87] Count and Countess Montalembert,[88] Commander Daufresne[89] and a personal staff of 15 persons, consisting of four secretaries, two typists, a private detective, a chauffeur, a private pilot, a masseur and a valet. He brought with him on the boat two wonderful automobiles … He will buy a Fokker plane here, which he will use during his stay. The company occupied eight suites and cabins on board … The banker and his wife occupied the most luxurious suite, consisting of three bedrooms with baths, a private consulting-room and a private

---

84 To restore balance between production and sale, the reformists are persuading the capitalists to pay higher wages in order to extend the buying capacity of the home market. Lenin has already answered this; it would be to regard the capitalists as blockheads if one were to serious expect them unnecessarily to surrender a part of their surplus value to the workers merely in order to be able afterwards to sell the workers more commodities.

85 [Alfred Loewenstein (1877–1928) built an international industrial empire in Canada, the United States and Europe, monopolising the production of artificial fibres. In 1927 he tried to acquire the Banque de Bruxelles, which met the opposition of a group of financiers led by Dannie Heineman of the Sofina. On 4 July 1928, Loewenstein disappeared during a flight in his private aeroplane over the Channel].

86 *The New York Times*, 26 March 1928.

87 [Xavier de Hemricourt de Grunne (1894–1944) was a personal friend of King Albert I of Belgium. In 1936 he became senator of the Rexist Party of Fascist Léon Degrelle. He died in a concentration camp in Germany in 1944. He married Anne de Meaux in 1919].

88 [The French family de Montalembert is related to the family de Grunne. Madeleine de Montalembert (1849–1920) was Xavier de Grunne's mother].

89 [Raoul Daufresne de la Chevallerie (1881–1967) would become commander of the Belgian Brigade in Great Britain during the Second World War].

dining-room ... The cost of the journey alone amounted to about 20,000 dollars, and a sum of about 3,000 dollars was spent on wireless telegrams sent by Mr. Loewenstein during the journey.

But so long as there is no economically planned and regulated capitalism – and such there can never be – it is impossible for the capitalists to spend the whole surplus value and give up accumulation.

The struggle for markets is conducted by many methods, such as (1) industrial high protective tariffs, (2) dumping, (3) capital export, (4) colonial policy.

All countries have *industrial protective tariffs*, Spain and the United States the highest.[90] In England only a few industries are protected by tariffs, but their number is increasing from year to year. In spite of the famous *Bankers' Manifesto*, in spite of the fine decisions of the World Economic Conference,[91] new commodities are continually being protected with tariffs, and the already existing tariffs raised. The competition between the different national bourgeoisies for markets prevents any reduction in tariffs. The formula corresponding to the interests of the bourgeoisie would be: prohibitively high protective tariffs for ourselves, free trade for all other countries. Since they cannot compel the bourgeoisie of other countries to adopt free trade, they all raise tariff barriers and engage in dumping.

By dumping we mean selling on the foreign market at lower prices than on the home market, in many cases lower even than the actual cost of production. The foreign market is of great importance for national monopolies, for high prices can be maintained at home only so long as no more goods are placed on the market than can be disposed of at such high prices. That is why it is the strongest monopolies which carry on dumping.[92]

Protective tariffs and dumping are contradictory processes: they mutually neutralise each other's effects. Dumping leads to the establishment of still higher protective tariffs or to international alliances of the national monopoly organisations for the purpose of reserving the home market (the European Steel Cartel).

The export of capital is the principal method employed in the struggle for sales on the world market. The importance of capital export to monopolistic capital was thoroughly analysed by Lenin in *Imperialism*. There is little new to be added to his remarks: 'Typical of the old capitalism, when free competition

---

90 See *Table 10.43* in Appendix.
91 [World Economic Conference, Geneva, May 1927].
92 See *Table 10.43* in Appendix.

held undivided sway, was the export of goods. Typical of the latest stage of capitalism, when monopolies rule, is the export of capital'.[93]

Two factors can be distinguished in capital export, the export of capital for the purpose of exporting goods. This is accomplished in the form of long-term credits, by which the disposition of the goods exported is transferred to the buyer (e.g. the sale of military equipment to foreign states by means of long-term credits).

Capital export proper: capital which, because of the lack of markets and the low rate of profit, cannot be invested at a sufficiently profitable rate at home, is invested abroad, in which case the exporters of capital retain control of it (e.g. railway construction and concerns in foreign countries).[94]

These two kinds of capital export are contradictory to each other. Capital export proper creates a market for goods once, but as soon as production is begun abroad, the export of the country of those goods which are produced abroad as a result of capital investment, decreases to a corresponding extent. In spite of this capital export proper continues to a great degree, urged on by the high rate of profit in the backward countries.

> In these backward countries profits are usually high, for capital is scarce, the price of land is relatively low, wages are low, raw materials are cheap. The export of capital is made possible by a number of backward countries having already been drawn into world capitalist intercourse; main railways have either been or are being built in those countries, elementary conditions for industrial development have been created, etc.[95]

Before the war, Western Europe was the only capital-exporting area. But since then the position has changed. The United States has become the greatest capital-exporting country; France is no longer in the ranks of capital-exporting countries, while Germany has become one of the greatest importers of capital.[96] This is a result of the reparation obligations, and will cease when these have been again regulated and the temporary demand for making up the deficiencies caused by inflation and for carrying out rationalisation have been covered.

---

93   Lenin 1964e, p. 240.
94   'The need to export capital arises from the fact that in a few countries capitalism has become "overripe" and (owing to the backward state of agriculture and the poverty of the masses) capital cannot find a field for "profitable" investment'. Lenin 1964d, p. 241.
95   Lenin 1964d, p. 242.
96   See *Table 10.39* in Appendix.

The best means of ensuring a proportionate share in the world market for the sale of commodities and for capital export is the acquisition of areas controlled by monopoly, the acquisition of colonies. Hence the urge of the capitalist powers towards gaining the greatest number of colonies even in the period of free competition. Today this way is no longer open. The earth is already distributed among the imperialist powers. There still remain South America, but that is under requisition by the United States, Turkey, Persia, Afghanistan, which have, however, freed themselves from the imperialist powers or are in the process of so doing. One large area remains, and it is around this that the struggle is now being waged: China.

But, influenced by the existence of the Soviet Union, and by that of the successful opposition offered to the imperialists by Turkey and Afghanistan with its assistance, it requires increasingly great efforts and expenditure to maintain the suppression of the colonial peoples. Moreover, super-profits have been cut down by the working-class movement in the colonies. A larger area has to be controlled in order to obtain the same amount of profit. This explains the sharpening struggle for colonies, for a re-division of the world.

This re-division is openly demanded by the capitalists of those countries whose internal economic development is in contrast to their lack or insufficient ownership of colonies. Germany and Italy are openly demanding a re-division; Japan is actually carrying it out in China, and the United States in Latin America.

To sum up: the possibility of extending the home capitalist market is strictly limited in the great capitalist countries. Voluntary increases in the share going to wages for the purpose of extending the home market are not to be considered by the capitalists. The growing luxury of the capitalist class is limited by the pressure towards accumulation. The transformation of farmers into agricultural capitalists on the one hand, and into proletarians on the other, has, in essence, taken place. The workers' share of the product has begun to show an absolute decrease. Export to independent countries comes up against tariff barriers; to the colonies against their monopolist rule by individual imperialist powers; to the Soviet Union against the barriers of the foreign trade monopoly. The contradiction between production and the possibilities of realising goods on the market is growing greater. It will come to a head in a grave crisis, which will necessarily be but the prelude to a new war for the re-division of the world.

7   The Formation of Monopolies and the Struggle for the World Market

'Free competition becomes transformed into monopoly'.[97] This is one of Lenin's principal theses. Free competition, at a certain stage of development, must necessarily change into monopoly, because of concentration and centralisation. But 'at the same time monopoly, which has sprung from free competition, does not drive the latter out of existence, but co-exists over it and with it, thus giving rise to a number of very acute and very great contradictions, antagonisms and conflicts. Monopoly is the transition from capitalism to a more highly level developed order'.[98]

And it is true that in recent years we have witnessed an even greater concentration of concerns into monopolistic undertakings, both on a national and international scale.

It is unfortunately impossible to estimate at all reliably the extent of monopoly formation, the proportion of monopoly to total economy, and this for two reasons:

(1)   The most complete form of monopoly-fusion, when the concerns which are being amalgamated completely surrender their independence and form an entirely new undertaking, is not fully dealt with in any statistics. The Steel Trust, or the International Dye-Stuffs Corporation, is today one concern, one monopoly, not a monopolist organisation. It is a matter of economic history that it arose out of fusion of many firms.

(2)   On the other hand, there are very effective monopolies that are not based on any formal, legal organisation. This is particularly the case in countries where there are legal obstacles to the formation of monopolies. Then, there are 'gentlemen's agreements', unwritten associations, of which a breach is punished by boycott and other measures; for example, the famous 'Gary dinners',[99] the amalgamation of apparently independent concerns into one banking firm, where the uninitiated are not in the least aware that Mr. X. represents the interests of a large bank, etc.[100]

---

97   Lenin 1964d, pp. 196–210.
98   Lenin 1964d, p. 266.
99   [Elbert Harry] Gary, the recently deceased president of the American Steel Trust [US Steel], before the formation of the trust, used to invite the leaders of the iron industry to dinner each month, and there agreements as to prices and production were reached.
100   Attempts to understand the formation of monopolies, such as the well-known memorandum of the German Economic Ministry, are of little value, because they are based on external characteristics.

For these reasons it is not possible to compute the extent of monopoly statistically. But it is indisputable that in the great industrial countries, with the exception of England,[101] practically all important industries are already concentrated into monopolies, and that this process in recent years has been developing energetically.

A monopoly implies control of the market.[102] How does this come about? We may distinguish the following causes:

(1) Monopoly of capital. To start a new concern requires so much capital that it can only be managed with the assistance of the banks. Since, however, bank capital has grown up with the existing monopolies as finance capital, co-operation for the purpose of obtaining the capital is refused. If, in spite of that, a concern – usually not very strong financially – is started, it is not difficult for the monopoly, which has strong capital forces, to ruin it by a price war (e.g. the disappearance of independent cement firms because of the cartel in Germany).

---

101   It would be erroneous to believe that there are no powerful monopolies in England. In his valuable book Fitzgerald (1927) gives the following examples of monopolies:

TABLE 10.19 Capital of some British monopolies

	Capital in £
Coats' Cotton Trust	28,000,000
Cotton Dye Trust	10,000,000
Lever Bros.	64,500,000
Mond Chemicals	57,000,000
Royal Dutch Oil	70,000,000
Courtauld's Artificial Silk	32,000,000

This suffices to show that certain organisations are not far behind the largest German concerns, such as the International Dye Trust and United Steel Works, in capital strength. The formation of monopolies is rendered difficult by the absence of any *general* protective tariff, but has recently been making great progress (e.g. the Armstrong-Vickers fusion in heavy Industry, district cartels in coal mining, formation of trusts in the cotton industry, etc.).

102   Control of the market does not mean that all firms which produce a certain commodity must be included in the monopoly. According to the kind of commodity and the situation of the market, 50 percent to 80 percent of total production is enough to give control of the market, and with agricultural products, the supply of which can only be increased on the market after at least one or two years, even less than 50 percent is often sufficient.

(2) Monopoly in the sources of raw materials. Apart from, or in conjunction with, capital monopoly, a monopoly of raw materials is very important. This is particularly the case with regard to mines.

(3) Technical monopoly. With the progress in the chemical industry, a monopoly in technical knowledge is a very important foundation for monopoly. Nowadays inventive work is rationalised, systematised and pressed into the service of large-scale capital. The International Dye Trust employs in its laboratories more than half of all the chemists in Germany. The same applies to many branches of the electrical industry and to the match industry, where the Swedish-American trust possesses all the patents; the position is similar in the machine-made shoe industry, where the American Trust has a monopoly based on the sole possession of a number of complicated machines.[103]

The best basis for a monopoly is the union of a monopoly in capital and technique, and this is the case with all the great monopolist organisations.

The object and purpose of forming a monopoly is to raise the profits of the concerns participating in it. This can be achieved:

(1) By raising the sale price above production price, selling at monopoly prices, i.e. appropriation of a larger share of total profits at the expense of unorganised capitalist and independent producers.[104]

(2) By reducing the cost of production through rationalisation; concentrating production on those works which produce most cheaply. Specialisation of firms in certain commodities, cutting down overhead expenses arising from competition, common employment of all patents and utilisation of technical experience, etc.

(3) By reducing the price of labour power below its value. The strength of trade unions, so long as they merely employ the peaceful strike as the method of struggle, is not great enough to defend the workers against powerful monopolies; the conditions of labour are automatically determined by monopoly capital.[105]

---

[103] See Jones 1921, p. 165.

[104] The agrarian crisis, insofar as it is affected by the 'scissors' and not by the rents fixed in the time of former high prices, is the most obvious expression of the appropriation of a part of the average profits of independent producers by monopoly capital.

[105] Hilferding maintains that progress in the chemical industry is at the expense of heavy industry, and diminishes the antagonism between capital and labour. 'It [the chemical industry] is not in such direct and immediate opposition to the working class as is heavy industry', because the share of wages is less, and such huge profits are made that, in comparison wages seem to decrease. 'Actually, however, the chemical industry pays shamefully low wages, and is carrying out a policy of cutting down wages'. Hilferding 1926a, p. 291.

The form which the monopoly takes corresponds to the purposes enumerated above. We can differentiate between:

Horizontal monopoly. Amalgamation of concerns which produce the same commodities. The purpose here is to raise prices. There are various forms of such monopoly: simple price agreements, cartels to regulate all conditions of sale, quota cartels, trusts (financial co-operation by the mutual interchange of shares), etc., and complete fusion.

Vertical monopoly. Amalgamation of concerns, of which the product of one serves as the raw material for another: coal, coke, iron, smelting works, machine factories, sawmills, cellulose, paper, artificial silk, etc. The object here is to adjust profits to compensate for the fall in the prices of various raw materials and semi-manufactured articles, and to reduce costs of production by systematic organisation of production from the raw material to the finished article.[106]

The economic difference is that horizontal monopoly wipes out rivalry in the commodities which it produces, while vertical monopolies exist side by side and may be in competition with each other at every stage of production, as was formerly the case with the vertical trusts in heavy industry.

The most recent form, the highest stage, is the super-monopoly, the horizontal amalgamation of vertical trusts, as exemplified in the German Steel Works and International Dye Trust, and in the Brunner Mond concern in England. The result is either a complete monopoly or a monopoly within the monopoly of the horizontal cartels controlled at every stage of production by the super-monopoly. For example, the German Steel Works trust possesses concerns in the various monopolies existing in the different processes of heavy industry – iron, steel, wires, pipes – as much as approximately half of the total concerns, and is therefore in a position to influence the policy of the cartels to a proportionate extent. The power of such a super-monopoly is consequently extraordinarily great. They are very closely connected with the banks, and are the most completely developed form of finance capital. The huge profits raked in by the great monopolies are more or less hidden from the public eye. Firstly, a great part of the profits is reinvested in the concerns themselves. The American Steel Trust employed 115,000,000 dollars for purposes of extension in the last four years (this is the so-called 'self-financing'). Du Pont, chief shareholder in General Motors, Ltd., refers to a clear profit of 45,947,832 dollars for 1927 (after payment of preference interest). The share value of General Motors stands at

---

[106] A degenerate form of such organisation was seen in the inflation concerns, when groups of capitalists bought up the stocks of bankrupt firms, e.g. the notorious [Hugo] Stinnes concern. Since they had no basis in technical production, they crumpled up with the stabilisation of the exchanges.

119,774,640 dollars, but on the Exchange it is valued at 538,985,880 dollars.[107] When profits are so great, capital is correspondingly increased. Courtauld's pays a 25 percent dividend, and the capital is increased from £24,000,000 to £48,000,000 by the issue of bonus shares, and only 12 percent is therefore paid in dividends. It is obvious therefore that nothing would be more incorrect than to determine actual profits by the dividend payments of monopolies.

The power of monopolies is so great that they exercise a decisive influence on the state and completely control economic policy. A new form of state capitalism is being evolved, which consists in serving the great monopolies. The state which they control serves their special interests; economic policy is placed at the service of monopolist price policy; foreign competition is excluded by means of protective tariffs, etc. We shall discuss this in the next chapter.

With regard to monopolies, the internal contradictions in the capitalist system of production show themselves in the following ways:

The further monopoly progresses, the more goods are sold at monopoly prices, the higher those monopoly prices become. In other words, since total profits cannot be greater than total surplus value; monopoly profits can only be won at the expense of the profits of capital not organised in the monopolies. The further monopoly progresses, the smaller the proportion of unorganised capital in the total capital of a society grows, the smaller becomes the possibility of appropriating monopoly profits. If total capital were divided among equally strong monopolies, there would be no more monopoly profits, but each form of capital would make the average rate of profit.[108]

Another contradiction: the immediate extent of a monopoly's power is the national state area; as far as the state power of the bourgeoisie extends, so far stretches the power of the national monopolies. Outside the state area there is competition among monopolies, expressed most sharply in the form of dumping. If the opposing monopolies are of equal strength, then dumping by both destroys the monopoly on the home market in spite of protective tariffs (if these latter are not absolutely prohibitive). Dumping and protective tariffs cancel each other out in their effects!

---

107 'Du Pont Co. earned $41,113,968 in year', *The New York Times*, 28 January 1928, p. 21. [Figures Varga gave for Du Pont and General Motors needed corrections].

108 In general there is no price-cutting competition among horizontal monopolies; but there is a struggle between cartels producing different commodities which serve the same purpose, e.g. iron, tiles, cement, wood as building materials, coal, oil, wood, peat, water power as sources of energy. An excessive rise in the price of one of these tends to concentrate consumption on its substitutes. Modern technical development makes it much easier to replace one object by another. This places a limit on increase of monopoly prices.

Limitation to the home demand, if there are protective tariffs, is possible only in the early stages of the development of an industry. As soon as the industry meets all the demands of the home market, monopolist capital is forced to dispose of a part of its production outside in order to avoid surplus supplies on the home market whose capacity for absorbing the goods fluctuates according to the position of the industrial cycle. Sharp competition begins, leading eventually to the formation of super-national monopolies.

Super-national monopolies, embracing many countries, are already numerous, and the number is increasing. They are a super-organisation of the national monopolies, including a few or all countries. Sometimes there are two rival international organisations, such as Standard Oil and Royal Dutch; sometimes national monopolies in a few countries are amalgamated, while the same industry in other countries is still unorganised: the European Steel Cartel includes the Continental steel works, the American Steel Trust controls the American market, while the English steel industry is unorganised. In other instances a monopoly is directly controlled by the industry of other countries. (This is the case with the Swedish-American match trust). There is a great variety in the forms of organisation, and conditions are constantly changing. Finance capital employs the most diverse methods of mutual conflict between firms in order, with a relatively small amount of capital, to gain decisive influence over a whole branch of industry.[109]

In general the basis of organisation consists in guaranteeing the home market for the national monopoly. In many cases foreign markets are also divided among the national monopolies (e.g. the International Incandescent Lamp Cartel). Sometimes the association is valid only for a part of the world – 'undisputed areas' – while competition proceeds in full force in the other parts of the world – 'disputed areas'.

There are also other forms. In those branches of industry where production is divided up among so many firms that the amalgamation of all the producers in the country into a monopoly organisation appears to be impossible, a situation occurring chiefly in agricultural production where there is a very numerous peasantry, a monopoly organisation can only be established by making a detour to cover trading capital. Only a part of the products destined for sale, and particularly that part which is to be exported, is appropriate as a basis for the formation of an international monopoly. So, for example, the wheat export

---

109   See e.g. 'Investment in artificial silk', *The Economist*, 12 May 1928, pp. 968–9, which describes the control exercised by Courtaulds over practically the whole artificial silk industry of the world.

of Canada, Australia and Argentina is concentrated in monopolist organisations, for the purpose of raising wheat prices on the world market. In contrast to industry, a monopoly is in this case desired only for that portion of the product which is to be sold outside the national frontiers; prices on the home market rise only as a part of a general rise in the level of prices on the world market.

International monopolies are not very strong organisations. The struggle of the national monopoly for a larger share of the world market is carried on as a struggle for quotas or market spheres, or by secret underbidding, and destroys many of these organisations. Complete fusion into one concern, which could alone prevent such destruction, it rendered impossible because of the opposing interests of the national capitalist classes as a whole.[110] International cartels imply only a temporary armistice in the struggle for the world market.

For this reason all theories which accept international monopolies as the material foundation of a peaceful super-imperialism are essentially false. Lenin explained this in *Imperialism*:

> Many bourgeois authors express the opinion that international cartels, as one of the most flexible manifestations of the internationalization of capital, offer a hope of the maintenance of peace between the nations within capitalism. This view is theoretically completely unsound, and, in practice, a sophism, a dishonest way of defending the worst sort of opportunism.[111]

At the present time it is the social democrats, above all [Rudolf] Hilferding, who have adopted the theory, utterly destroyed by the world war, held by Norman Angell[112] and the free trade pacifists generally, the theory which is expressed in the catchword 'realistic pacificism'. This, however, does not by any means pre-

---

110   The International Holding Companies are an example of the highest stage of development; the shares of the concerns organised with a monopoly are transferred to another organisation, which issues its own shares in exchange. The profits of all the companies concerned are then pooled and distributed equally as a dividend on the shares of the holding company.

111   [Varga quotes Lenin, but he omits a reference to Kautsky. A later translation (1964) is slightly different: 'Certain bourgeois writers (now joined by Karl Kautsky, who has completely abandoned the Marxist position he had held, for example, in 1909) have expressed the opinion that international cartels, being one of the most striking expressions of the internationalization of capital, give the hope of peace among nations under capitalism. Theoretically, this opinion is absolutely absurd, while in practice it is sophistry and a dishonest defence of the worst opportunism'. Lenin 1964d, p. 252].

112   Angell 1909, one of the most popular pacifist books of the pre-war period.

vent them from most strongly supporting the claims of 'their' bourgeoisie for a re-division of the world.[113]

The bourgeoisie itself is not at all so optimistic with regard to the effects of international monopoly as a means of ensuring peace. De Wendel recently showed, quite calmly, that even before the war a Franco-German iron cartel was in existence, but that did not prevent the outbreak of the war.[114]

Just so little can international monopolies help to prevent Economic crises, as Hilferding believes, or seems to believe:

> A change in capitalism from free competition to organised capitalism is taking place. This is naturally accompanied by greater conscious order in and direction of economic life, which is trying to overcome the anarchy inherent in capitalism of the free competition type by capitalist methods ... If this tendency could be carried into practice without obstacles ... the instability arising from capitalist relations of production would be diminished, crises, or at least their reactions on the workers, would be ameliorated ... Conditions of labour would assume a more constant character, unemployment would be less threatening, its consequences softened by insurance.[115]

Experience shows that monopolies do not prevent crises; such could only be the case with a capitalist planned economy. The formation of monopolies frees the monopolists from the consequences of crises. In free competition capitalism, crises made themselves acutely felt by reducing the value of commodities which were produced in excess of the consumption capacity of society, by a sharp fall in prices to their socially necessary value. In these cases the capitalists bore the chief part of the cost in the form of property losses, bankruptcies, etc. Monopoly capitalism cannot do away with crises, i.e. with the contradiction between the productive forces of society and its consumption power determined by antagonistic relations of distribution. But monopolies are certainly capable of transferring the burden of crisis from themselves, because they can maintain high prices even during a crisis, and bring about stability not

---

113 In one of [Arturo] Labriola's articles in *Die Gesellschaft* [1928, pp. 359–74] there is an utterly chauvinist representation of the interests of the Italian bourgeoisie.

114 The De Wendels are typical representatives of international capital. Before the war one brother was a member of the German Reichstag, the other of the French Chamber. Now, when Alsace-Lorraine is French, both brothers are members of the French Chamber. The one has become a French, instead of a German, patriot.

115 Hilferding 1924c, p. 2.

by depreciating the value of surplus commodities, but by *limiting output*, that is, at the expense of the workers, at the same time being able to reduce wages to a level convenient for them. It is not credit crises, not bankruptcies, not bank failures which characterise the crises of monopoly capitalism, but permanent mass unemployment.[116] The reaction of the crises in the working class is not ameliorated under monopoly capitalism, as Hilferding maintains, but accentuated.[117]

The existence of international monopolies strengthens the position of capital as against the workers in the economic struggle. A labour dispute spread over a whole branch of industry in a country formerly threatened the capitalists concerned with heavy losses in the world market. If, however, strong international monopolies exist, with quotas or capital shares, the capitalists can carry on the struggle without regard to the world market. International monopolies therefore must be met by the internationalisation of trade-union organisations and of the economic struggle.

Recapitulating we can say that the formation of monopolies on an international scale is a method of increasing the exploitation of the proletariat, of the unorganised capitalists and independent producers by finance capital. International monopolies mean a temporary and partial armistice among the national monopolies in their struggle for markets. Monopolies do not prevent either war or crises; they merely transfer the burden of crises from capital to the proletariat.

8   State Capitalism

Capitalism in its imperialist stage leads directly to the most comprehensive socialization of production; it, so to speak, drags the capitalists, against

---

116   I referred to this change in the character of crises in the *Neue Zeit* before the war. [However, Varga only reported on social and political development and on inflation caused by gold production in Hungary].

117   [Werner] Sombart, even better than Hilferding, has recognised the uses of the market cycle for capitalism: 'If capitalism succeeded, during the whole period of its ascendancy, in keeping wages within moderate limits in spite of the rapid increases in capital accumulations, thus safeguarding its own vital capacity and development, this was due ... in no inconsiderable degree, to the actual market cycle. This ensures that, in times of boom, wages do not increase equally with surplus value, because of the rapid rise in prices; but it is also this market cycle which floods the labour market as desired, thereby creating the industrial reserve army, by a regular movement of contraction, by making some labour power unnecessary. This reserve army is an obstacle to rising wages'. Sombart 1927, p. 586.

their will and consciousness, into some sort of a new social order, a transitional one from complete free competition to complete socialization. Production becomes social, but appropriation remains private. The social means of production remain the private property of a few.[118]

State capitalism, in its nature, is an attempt on a capitalist basis to wipe out the contradiction, between productive forces and production relations: an inadequate compromise, which cannot solve the contradictions!

If one reviews the economic activity of capitalist states historically, it can be asserted that such activity is greatest when the bourgeoisie are least able to overcome the contradictions of capitalism with their own forces. In the expanding period of European capitalism, the ideas of laissez-faire prevailed; during the world war, when the existence of the ruling classes was at stake, the economic activity of the state became all-embracing. After the conclusion of the war the destruction of state capitalism began; in recent years, when technical development gives a still stronger impulse to the socialisation of production and the contradictions of stabilisation become apparent, this tendency towards state capitalism is given additional strength.

We can express the contradiction between the forces of production and the relations of production in the following way: the interest of the bourgeoisie as a whole is in contradiction to the special interests of individual capitalist groups. In the interests of the bourgeoisie the necessity arises of socialising certain economic functions. This can occur by these functions being taken over by the organisation of the capitalist class, by the capitalist state and eventually by the municipal organisations. This was the case with certain economic functions which even before the war were exercised by the state, such as the regulation of weights and measures, the organisation of currency (central banks of issue were everywhere, with but few exceptions, either state institutions or under state supervision), and important parts of the traffic system, post, harbours, canals and in many countries railways also.

The twofold character of the capitalist state was shown in this, that not only these economic functions were socialised which, if left in the hands of private capitalists, would be a monopoly dangerous to the capitalist class as a whole; but the state also took over those functions which would not be profitable if exercised by private capitalists – road construction, canals and railways, which, if managed privately, would not pay (strategic railway lines, etc.).

---

118 Lenin 1964d, p. 205.

Social politics is a particular form of state interference. Its class significance lies in this: firstly, to protect the working class, whose exploitation forms the basis of the entire system of capitalist production, from physically deteriorating as a result of immediate exploitation by individual capitalists; secondly, to protect the capitalist class rule as a whole, by concessions to the working class as a whole or to privileged sections of it.

The economy of war-time, the highest stage reached by state capitalism, was similarly built up on this principle. With the existing shortage of commodities state regulation of the distribution of raw materials, of production and of labour forces was so organised as to prevent the special interests of individual capitalists putting any obstacles in the way of concentrating all forces for the purpose of carrying on the war in the interests of the bourgeoisie as a whole.

In the present period, when the struggle for markets is of decisive importance to the bourgeoisie, the chief function of state economic activity is to support the national bourgeoisie in this struggle. The entire foreign economic policy, and to some extent the home economic policy, it subordinated to this object; external economic policy in the form of protective tariffs, trading agreements and the struggle for colonies; internal economic policy in the form of supporting all measures which help to reduce costs of production. According to the strength of the capitalist system in the individual countries, according to whether capitalism in the country concerned is still progressing or has already entered a period of decline, important modifications occur in the direction and extent of state capitalist activity. In the United States, for example, state capitalist participation is directed mainly towards reducing costs of production, chiefly by the avoidance of waste, in the widest sense of the term. It is also aimed at protecting the home market against foreign competition by means of high protective tariff and support and regulation of the imperialist expansion policy of capitalism. In Germany, on the other hand, state participation in economic life extends much further and embraces all aspects of economic and social life.

State activity in the economic life of a country can be divided into two kinds: mere regulative activity and economic activity proper, state capitalism in the narrower sense.[119] In the first case of regulative activity by the state, the means of production remain the private property of the capitalists. The state merely regulates the production and distribution of goods, influencing the distribution of income by regulating prices and conditions of labour without actually appearing itself as a capitalist employer or itself owning the means of produc-

---

119   See Bukharin's report at the 15th Congress of the CPSU 1928, and Lapinski 1928.

tion. The influence which the state exercises, by taxation and the use of the state finances, on the distribution of income belongs to this category; 10 to 20 percent of the national income passes through the hands of the state in this manner.

In state capitalism proper the state owns productive concerns and produces goods which are brought on to the market either in competition with private capitalists or together with them in a monopolist organisation, or else the state acts as a single monopolist. Two forms of state capitalism may be distinguished in this respect:

(1) State undertakings which serve the interests of the bourgeoisie as a whole by withdrawing them from private monopoly (post, harbours, canals, etc.).
(2) Ordinary business undertakings which are also being carried on by private capitalists, such as mines, factories, etc.

The extent to which the state directly participates in economic activity varies in different countries. It is greatest in Japan and Germany, least in the United States. A few figures will illustrate the importance of state economy in the total complex of national economic life. In Germany, 2,501,000 persons are employed in the State service nationally and municipally, or on railways or postal services. This is 8 percent of all wage earners in Germany, but actually the figure should be at least 10 percent, for it does not include those 'working members of families' whose numbers greatly swell the figure of agricultural workers in Germany; and further because it consists to a great extent of better qualified and higher-paid workers. It can be safely asserted therefore that 10 percent of all wage earners in Germany are employed in socialised concerns.[120]

The same book from which the above figures are taken gives the following estimate of property owned by the State, the federal States, municipalities and public corporations:

TABLE 10.20 State property in Germany

Railways	28 milliard marks
Communal works	5 milliard marks
Post	1 milliard marks
Other public property	20 milliard marks
Total	52 milliard marks

---

120   These figures are taken from Hirsch 1926.

Property held publicly amounts therefore to one-fifth or one-sixth of the total national property.

A calculation has also been made for England, which estimates the value of property held publicly at £2,754 milliards.[121] But the property of co-operatives is included in this estimate, and that cannot really be considered as the property of public corporations. In any case, this estimate shows that the total of non-private property is much greater in England than one is accustomed to believe.

Some problems arise with regard to these facts.

Firstly, is the present tendency towards an extension or a decrease in state capitalism? This question cannot be answered satisfactorily for all countries. In some, for example, France and the United States, the reaction against the war-time regulation of the national economic life still continues; former state undertakings are being transferred to private capital, and the regulative activity of the state limited in many respects. On the other hand, there can be observed an increase in state activity in the economic life of England, Germany and particularly of Italy, where the Fascist state is, in its regulative functions, encroaching more and more upon all spheres of economic life.

Taking world capitalism as a whole there is without doubt a tendency towards strengthening State capitalism. This is brought about by the power needed for socialising certain economic functions, such as power supply, a necessity which grows more urgent with increasing technical development; it is also brought about by the accentuation of class antagonisms in the different capitalist countries, which makes it essential for the bourgeoisie to concentrate their forces more strongly in their struggle against the workers; by the increasingly bitter struggle for the world market, which necessitates State support of the bourgeoisie in this struggle; by the necessity to concentrate all capitalist forces for the coming fight for the re-division of the world.

The second problem concerns the attitude of the different classes to this state capitalist development. It is clear that as long as capitalist domination exists, the state is and remains an organ of the capitalist class; in its economic activity, therefore, the state may indeed act in opposition to the interests of individual groups, but never against the interests of the entire capitalist class as a whole or of dominating monopolist capital. If we come across attacks directed against state interference by various capitalist groups we may be sure that the special interests of that group were not sufficiently considered in some concrete instance. It is a part of the anarchic character of capitalism that there is no

---

121   Keynes (ed.) 1928, p. 74.

general economic-political regulation which will satisfy all sections and groups of capitalists equally. That is why there are always some groups which for a time make a stand against state capitalist interference.[122]

In this connection the position of the capitalists in the different countries is of great importance. If the capitalist class feels itself to be strong socially, it is against state interference; if danger threatens its supremacy, it immediately turns to state capitalism. If a particular group of capitalists in a given economic situation can make high profits at the expense of other sections it is against state interference, while the other sections are for it: When markets are good, the feeling of the capitalists is opposed to state interference; when markets are bad they seek the assistance of the state and go so far as to demand state monopolies. '... [S]tate monopoly in capitalist society is merely a means of increasing and guaranteeing the income of millionaires in some branch of industry who are on the verge of bankruptcy'.[123]

But most important of all is the internal change in the character of state capitalism itself which has occurred in the last few years. This change reflects the fact that capital is being very definitely split up into two sections: finance capital organised in monopolies and unorganised small-scale capital. Accordingly the state today is no longer the state of the whole capitalist class, but the state of a small clique of monopoly capitalists. The state no longer represents the interests of the entire bourgeoisie, but the interests of a few monopolists.

This change in the economic basis is expressed in the disappearance of the formerly existing independence of the state machine as against individual capitalists. Powerful monopoly organisations have made the state subordinate to themselves and themselves direct state capitalist activity. The change is particularly clear in the sphere of politics and economic policy. In France, for example, it was the large banks which consistently put obstacles in the way

---

122 For this reason the utterances of leading capitalists against state capitalism must not be taken too seriously. Such speeches were often heard in Germany in the recent period of good markets. Capitalist associations took an unequivocal stand against the system of arbitration and the 'exaggeration of social policy'. The speech of J. Goldschmidt of the Darmstädter und Nationalbank, is very characteristic: 'In our time politics and economics have been drawn closer together than at any other period. But the natural limits of the state and of economics must not be done away with by a complete fusion; still less should the too great interference of one in the sphere of the other endanger the natural course of development ... The state must return to its proper tasks, and must refrain from transforming a free economy into one manipulated by the state ...'. He then quotes approvingly Hallnach's observation: 'The state and economics are at their best when they mutually preserve some distance between themselves'. *Berliner Börsen-Courier*, 12 February 1928.

123 Lenin 1964d, p. 218.

of the execution of the economic programme of the left bloc in the last parliament, and brought about the downfall of the left cabinet by deliberate acceleration of the depreciation of the French exchanges. This was kept up until a finance-capitalist government, under Poincaré, was brought into power, a change which suited them.

In Germany the great monopoly organisations openly control the economic policy of the State. The negotiations for the Franco-German trading agreement had no result until the French and German iron industrialists had concluded their private arrangements. In this private agreement it was laid down how much iron should be exported from France to Germany and under what tariff; also under what tariffs the products of the German iron manufacturing industry should be imported into France. Nominally this private treaty was concluded independently of the trading agreement; it was to enter into operation when the Governments succeeded in concluding a corresponding tariff agreement. But actually the position of dependence was the reverse; the arrangements of the monopoly capitalists were submitted to the respective governments and then issued publicly in legal form.

The same position was even more glaringly apparent in the case of the German-Japanese commercial treaty. A settlement of the treaty was constantly delayed by the Japanese prohibition on the import of German dyes. So a director of the International Dye Trust went to Japan, made a private treaty concerning dye supplies with the Japanese Government, assisted by the German embassy there; and this agreement was quite simply incorporated in the German-Japanese commercial treaty.

The influence of monopoly organisations and capitalist groups on the economic policy of the United States is equally clear. It is quite easy to follow the work of the trusts in the fixing of tariffs. Foreign policy in the USA is in many cases directly determined by the interested capitalists. [Thomas W.] Lamonte, Morgan's business partner, travelled to Japan, discussed loans there, and decided American-Japanese relations. Morrow, a director of Morgan's, was sent as Ambassador to Mexico, and in a short time he succeeded in having the Mexican laws directed against American oil interests annulled, etc.

Summing up, we can say that state capitalism, state participation in the economic life of a capitalist state tends to grow as the contradictions between the forces of production and the relations of production grow, giving an impulse towards socialisation, as the general instability of the capitalist system increases, giving an impulse towards state concentration of forces. But the development does not follow a single course. According to the stage of development of the forces enumerated above, according to the growing strength or weakness of the bourgeoisie, development either progresses, rapidly or temporarily retrogresses. State capitalism cannot of course solve the internal contradictions of capitalism. Reformist speeches concerning the overthrow of capitalism by means of state capitalism and economic democracy only serve the purpose of weakening working-class resistance and the workers' will to fight.

9 The Struggle for the World Market: Agrarianisation and Industrialisation

Capitalism dissolved the pre-capitalist union of agriculture and industry by superseding the elements of industry formerly contained in peasant economy and the peasant household, by breaking up the peasant class and changing the peasants either into small agricultural capitalists or landless agricultural workers. (In so doing the small agricultural capitalists were subjected to the domination of large-scale capital through marketing and credit relations). The division into 'town' and 'country' took a parallel course; the word 'town' being used in the sense of centres of industry. The differentiation took place in all countries; Western Europe became 'the industrial workshop of the world', other parts of the world became sources of raw materials and food supplies.

> On the other hand, the cheapness of the articles produced by machinery, and the improved means of transport and communication furnish the weapons for conquering foreign markets. By ruining handicraft production in other countries, machinery forcibly converts them into fields for the supply of its raw material. In this way East India was compelled to produce cotton, wool, hemp, jute and indigo for Great Britain. By constantly making a part of the hands 'supernumerary' modern industry, in all countries where it has taken root, gives a spur to emigration and to the colonization of foreign lands, which are thereby converted into settlements for growing the raw material of the mother country; just as Australia, for example, was converted into a colony for growing wool. A new and international division of labour, a division suited to the requirements of the chief centres of modern industry springs up, and converts one part of the globe into a chiefly agricultural field of production, for supplying the other part which remains a chiefly industrial field.[124]

---

124 Marx 1954, p. 451.

But along with the antagonistic character of the capitalist mode of production, other counter tendencies are to be observed. The drawing in of a country into the capitalist world market facilitated the change of pre-capitalist forms of capital – commercial capital and loan capital – into industrial capital. Certain industries arose in agricultural countries because of advantages in situation: raw materials, partly worked up, cost less to transport. Concerns grew up for collection and conserving raw materials, for organising transport, etc.

Because of these advantages of situations, contradictions sprang up between the interests of the industrial bourgeoisie as a class and the private interests of individual capitalists. It is to the advantage of industrial capital that no new industries should grow up in these countries which have hitherto bought finished goods. But it is often more profitable for the individual capitalist to establish his works in the country where the raw materials are found and the market is available, than to transport the raw materials to the home country and send the finished goods back again; that is, to have double transport expenses. And individual interests take precedence of wider interests: so the period of the export of capital began, which worked in a contrary direction to that of the division of the world into industrial and agricultural spheres. There came the period of the industrialisation of agrarian countries.[125]

The process of industrialisation was accelerated by the world war. The shortage of ships, high shipping costs and the shortage of industrial commodities in the belligerent countries themselves gave a great impetus to the development of industry in colonial agrarian countries. The lack of sufficient machinery and of skilled workers alone hindered this development.

Military requirements were an added factor in this process. With the shortage of ships it was impossible to meet the military demands of the colonies as formerly from the resources of the home country. British imperialism renounced its policy of putting obstacles in the way of the industrial development of India, and demanded its industrialisation in order to be able to equip the troops fighting in Asia.

After the end of the postwar boom, as soon as the machinery of production was again working in peace conditions, and the products of the European industrial countries again appeared on the markets of the agricultural coun-

---

125 This tendency was, as far as I know, first described by the well-known German socialist-patriot Gerhard Hildebrand (1912) in his book on industrial supremacy and industrial socialism published before the war. He takes up a stand against this development and for capitalist colonial policy. He was at that time excluded from the German Social-Democratic Party, but, after socialist-patriotism had become the official policy of that party, was again admitted into its ranks.

tries, a grave crisis arose in the young industry of these countries. Many concerns which blossomed suddenly in the war as though in hothouses, appeared incapable of life and broke down.

But as industry developed in these countries there arose also a capitalist group, composed of home and foreign capitalists whose main interest lay in maintaining these new industries and making them profitable, and who were ready to defend them. The defence consisted in introducing protective tariffs for the industries.

The efforts to keep national industry going were supported by the interests of national defence. The experience of the war had shown – and the development in armaments since the war confirmed this – that without an industry of its own a country is powerless in time of war. Every country therefore tried to develop at home at least some industries among these necessary for war, by means of high protective tariffs.

At this stage the policy of power entered upon its rights. Subject colonies like Egypt, Korea, French Africa, etc., have no possibility of carrying out an independent customs policy. China's autonomy with regard to tariffs was greatly limited by the imperialists and the lowest customs duties in the world were imposed on her. But all other States, however weak by comparison with the imperialist great powers, tried their utmost to utilise the right of having an independent customs policy in order to create home industries. This is true of the British dominions.

The attempt of *small* States to create home industry was in many cases frustrated by the small capacity of the home market which was unable to absorb the full production of a really modern concern. Small and inferior factories were constructed. A protectionist policy in small States meant consequently an obstacle to the free development of productive forces. On the other hand, the existence of industrial tariffs intensified the contradiction between the class interests of the bourgeoisie in preventing industrialisation – where the capacity of the home market was great enough – and the particular interests of individual capitalists in establishing production in countries protected by tariffs.

After stabilisation, when a market for industrial commodities became the great problem of the European industrial countries, a new politico-economic campaign against the protective tariff system of the agricultural countries was begun.[126] We may call to mind the famous Bankers' Manifesto which con-

---

126 United States industry still produces mainly for the home market. The following percentages of total production were exported:

tained a warning against 'artificial industrialisation' and demanded the abolition of protective tariffs, and of the sharp refusal with which it was met in Poland, Italy and even America.

In the same way the free trade decisions of the World Economic Conference remained ineffective in practice. Protective tariffs were nowhere reduced, while artificial promotion of the growth of industry continued everywhere. We cannot speak of a tendency towards agrarianisation in the sense of a positive decline of industry in agricultural countries. The process can be demonstrated by the relevant figures (see tables in the Appendix).

The textile industry has made absolute progress in most colonial countries and in the less highly industrialised European countries. The employment of machinery has attained more or less the same level in colonial countries. In some countries it is higher, in a few lower than it was before the war.

If we consider the production of iron and steel, the development is less uniform. There is a marked increase in production in Japan, British India and Australia, and an absolute decrease in Canada. Still, it would be quite false to infer from that a decline in the industrialisation of Canada. Special factors must be considered: the local advantages of highly developed American heavy industry are so great that it does not pay to create a domestic heavy industry by artificial means, still less as there is no question of war between Canada and the USA.

The machine industry still remains a monopoly of European and North American industry, so that the 'new' countries are still dependent upon the 'old' industrial countries for their equipment with means of production.[127] In general, development has proceeded in such a manner that it is chiefly the more primitive staple industries, dealing directly with raw materials, which are

TABLE 10.21 Percentages of US total production exported

1899	1904	1909	1914	1918	1921	1923	1925
6.5	5.9	4.9	6.2	8.8	6.2	7.3	7.9

(For 1925 a new method of calculation was used, excluding the double reckoning of raw materials. The figure, therefore, is actually higher for that year. See *Commerce Yearbook* 1926, p. 92).

127 World machine production was divided as follows in 1925: USA 57.6 percent; Great Britain 13.6 percent; Germany 13.1 percent; all other countries 15.7 percent. The share of these three countries in world production *rose* by 3.4 percent since 1913. See 'The Machine Industry of the World', issued by the Association of German Machine Manufacturers for the World Economic Conference [at Geneva in 1926]. Verein deutscher Machinenbauanstalten, 1926.

developing, e.g. the coarse cotton industry among textiles. The finer branches of industry require more skilled workers, technique and a larger market than those possessed by agricultural countries; the latest technical achievements, the most skilful methods of production, ate employed in the old industrial countries.[128]

The statistics available do not afford a basis on which to decide which of the two tendencies is stronger, that towards agrarianisation, or that towards industrialisation. It is, moreover, extremely difficult to find an exact and scientific method for deciding such a question. Statistics of employment are not applicable. In some cases there are none, in others they do not go beyond 1920, while some actually obscure the real process.

India is typical of this. The statistics of employment in India show that for 50 years there has been a decrease in the number of those engaged in industry and an increase in the number of those engaged in agriculture; as far as we know, this is the only country which issues such statistics. Does this mean the agrarianisation of India? By no means! For although the number of workers engaged in the old primitive handicrafts is *decreasing*, large-scale industry of a modern capitalist type is developing.[129] There is no doubt that India today, in spite of the relative decrease in the number of industrial workers, is a more industrialised country than it was 50 years ago.

We might also employ the method of 'weighing' agriculture and industry as wholes. But apart from the difficulties of measurement – only the USA statistics are suitable for this – the following must also be taken into account. In many countries – Canada, Argentina, Australia – there is a twofold development in progress at the same time, a great expansion of agriculture by the development of hitherto unused areas, and the development of capitalist industry. It is possible that in these cases agricultural production grows more rapidly than industrial. Nevertheless, there would not be any sense, economically, in describing the results of these two parallel processes simply as 'agrarianisation'.

Summing up: the tendency in free competition capitalism to transform colonies into areas producing raw materials and foodstuffs for Western Europe, the industrial workshop of the world, came up against a strong counter tendency in the period of imperialism, that of capital export, protective tariffs, war

---

128   This fact has led to the optimistic theory being put forward according to which the industrialisation of agrarian countries involves no injury to the economy of the old industrial countries, for the loss of staple industries is compensated for by an increasing demand for machines and other goods essential for a highly developed technique. The difficulties of British industry prove the falseness of this theory.

129   See economic review for the first quarter of the year 1928. [Varga 1928c].

considerations. The difficulty of disposing of industrial commodities in the postwar period gave rise to the attempt on the part of industrial capitalism among the imperialist powers, to force a policy of agrarianisation on the smaller states. This attempt was brought to grief by the contradiction between the class interest of the industrial bourgeoisie and the private desire of individual capitalists for profits, and by the opposition of the capitalists of the small independent countries, of the dominions and semi-colonies; it could only be fully thrust upon the colonies. Although there is no scientific method for deciding the question, we believe that it is not true to speak simply of agrarianisation; that, on the contrary, the tendency towards industrialisation is stronger than that towards agrarianisation.

10   Preparations for a Re-devision of the World

> The capitalists divide the world, not out of any particular malice, but because the degree of concentration which has been reached forces them to adopt this method in order to obtain profits. And they divide it 'in proportion to capital', 'in proportion to strength', because there cannot be any other method of division under commodity production and capitalism.[130]

The contradiction between the sham ideological struggle against war and the actual preparations for war is one of the basic facts of recent years. The pacifists of all shades of opinion, and above all the Social Democrats, wish to make the world believe that the world war was an 'historical accident', brought about by the militarist policy of monarchs and by a false conception on the part of the bourgeoisie of their own class interests. Now, however, the age of superimperialism, of 'realistic pacifism' is approaching. Its economic bases are international cartels, international trustification, capital export, the closely interwoven interests of the bourgeoisie of the whole world. The League of Nations is its organisation; its instruments the treaties of peace, the non-aggression pacts, and, latest of all, the all-embracing treaty of the 'Outlawry of War'.

But as against all these paper treaties and pretty speeches we can see the actual, iron reality of war preparations. The United States, which sponsors the idea of outlawing war, is at the same time building warships to the value of hundreds of million dollars; all states, without exception, are ceaselessly piling up armaments for the next war.

---

130   Lenin 1964d, p. 253.

We must not be deceived by the Washington naval agreement. It deals with limitations on the construction of battleships, whose value as against the most modern fighting units – small cruisers, submarines and aircraft, has been called into question; with a very costly weapon (a modern battleship costs more than a hundred million dollars); America's threat to compete in the construction of warships forced the financially weaker competitors to give way on this question. The attempt to place a limit on the construction of cheaper types of ships was utterly defeated by the three greatest powers at the Geneva Conference, after which France and Italy refused to take any part whatever in the Conference.

The fact that standing armies today are smaller than before the war is of just as little importance. As against that, technical equipment is incomparably better. Armies have become mechanised. Tank regiments have taken the place of cavalry, machine-guns the place of single weapons, etc. The League of Nations Disarmament Conference was very busy finding new excuses for preventing any genuine tackling of the disarmament problem. All pacifist ideas, disarmament conferences and talk of the outlawry of war, are nothing but manoeuvres intended to obscure the facts and to deceive the workers who detest war, and to produce the illusion of everything possible having been done to prevent war.

The reasons which Lenin adduced for the inevitability of war in the imperialist stage of capitalism apply with equal validity to the present period of capitalist decline. It is unnecessary to restate them. *But it is necessary to give a short sketch of the position and policy of the powers at the present time.*

This picture is in part simpler, in part more complicated, than that of the pre-war period. After the war, Germany, Austria-Hungary and Tsarist Russia were no longer included in the ranks of the imperialist powers. Only four independent imperialist world powers remained: the USA, the British Empire, Japan and France.[131] To that extent the picture is simpler. It is more complicated for the following reasons.

(1) Germany, because of its population and economic importance one of the leading countries of the world, was disarmed after the war, and was deprived of the possibility of imperialist activity. Nowadays Germany combines the characteristics of an imperialist power with those of a colonial country. The economic substructure is imperialist – except for the import of capital, which was forced on Germany by reparation obligations; her disarmament carried out (at least officially), her obligation to pay reparations, foreign control and imports of capital are the character-

---

131   See *Table 10.50* in Appendix: 'The great powers of the world'.

istics of a colony.[132] The German bourgeoisie were driven by economic conditions to take up imperialist activities. They are openly propounding the question of the return of the German colonies. They are trying to find a place for themselves in the industry of French colonies.[133] They are again building railways in Turkey and Persia. Nevertheless Germany is not an imperialist country in the full sense of the word, but a peculiar and contradictory structure: half an imperialist power, half a colony under the control of imperialist powers.

(2) Because of progress in military technique and because of the super-power of the four world powers, it has become impossible for the smaller countries to conduct an independent foreign policy, although they are nominally independent. Their foreign policy consists merely in steering between the imperialist great powers and exploiting their antagonisms. The peculiar aspect of this is that these countries include those with extensive colonial possessions! Holland, which cannot itself defend its own colonies, and relies upon England's protection; Portugal, which, although possessing colonies, has itself sunk into being a semi-colonial possession of Great Britain; and finally Belgium, which is internationally protected and is adjacent to the domain of French power.

(3) The distinctions between independent States, colonies and semi-colonies are fast disappearing. Greece, for example, nominally independent, is actually more dependent upon England than are the British Dominions. The allegiance of Canada or Australia to the British Empire is purely a question of convenience for the capitalists of those countries. Were they to decide on secession, it is scarcely possible that the British bourgeoisie could make any attempt to compel them to remain within the Empire by force of arms.

---

132   In spite of official disarmament, Germany is by no means defenceless. There exist technically well-equipped and well-formed divisions of officers and subalterns which, in the event of war can be immediately changed into a great army if supplemented by trained man power. Germany has extensive civil aviation which can also be used for military purpose in a very short time; it has the best developed chemical industry of the world. Potentially, there is the possibility of constructing tanks in a very short time out of finished motors and armour plates, with the assistance of the engineering industry. What is lacking, and what cannot be improvised, is heavy artillery and ships.

133   Early in February 1921, the French senator Lémery negotiated in Berlin for the establishment of Franco-German trading companies to exploit the French colonies. [Henry Lémery was senator of Martinique. During the Second World War he would become Minister of the French Colonies under Pétain].

(4) A twofold process is going on with regard to the relations between colonies and semi-colonies and the imperialist powers. The formerly independent states of southern and central America are rapidly becoming dependent upon the United States, which is in this case playing a progressive role, insofar as the USA furthers capitalist development and supports the bourgeoisie against the feudal owners of land (on which England relies in these areas); at the same time the USA is bringing these capitalists and the countries themselves under its own sway.

The centrifugal development of the British Dominions within the Empire and the growing opposition of the old colonies and semi-colonies to imperialist oppression is in sharp contradiction to the trend of affairs in America. This opposition has in a few cases (Turkey and Afghanistan) resulted in complete success. In the case of China it has led to a temporary strengthening of imperialist domination (the open penetration of Japan into north China).

(5) The picture is still further complicated by inter-Allied debts and reparations; and finally by the existence of the Soviet Union as the magnetic centre of all anti-imperialist forces; a subject which we have already discussed.

We shall now deal with the characteristics of the principal imperialist world powers.

The United States has in the last decade grown into a fully developed imperialist state; but some features of the former period still remain. America still exports a great quantity of foodstuffs. The home market is still of overwhelming importance; only six percent of the industrial products are exported. American finance capital has not yet developed banking organisations abroad. Certain legal and ideological remains of the earlier period still hinder the free development of imperialist activity. But all such vestiges of the earlier period are being rapidly discarded. Technical development is out-distancing the extension of the home market, mass unemployment is in existence, the export of commodities and capital, and monopolised areas to which to export have become an economic necessity.

The sphere of imperialist activity for the USA is primarily the American continent. The lands bordering the Caribbean Sea have openly been proclaimed as a sphere where the USA has 'special interests'. The protection of the Panama Canal serves as the justification of this proclamation. The rest of South America comes under the Monroe doctrine which is similarly interpreted to meet the requirements of American imperialism. The South American states are daily growing more dependent upon the USA economically, financially and politically (e.g. the Pan-American Conference). Canada, nominally a part of the

British Empire, is being more and more drawn into the sphere of American economic life.

The superiority of the USA in the American continent is economically and militarily unassailable. The USA is, and remains, before all, an American power.

The British Empire, apart from Canada, surrounds the Indian Ocean. England is principally an Indian Ocean power. Around India there is Outer India (Singapore), Australia, New Zealand and Africa. Egypt, Mesopotamia, Palestine, Gibraltar and Malta guard the road to India. England's gains in the war, in near Asia and East Africa, served to round off and complete her rule over the Indian Ocean. (Motor communication direct from the Mediterranean to Baghdad and India; uninterrupted land routes from Cape Town to Cairo). But while imperialism in the USA is on the upgrade, that of England – in spite of the new possessions gained by the war – is going downhill. The great settlement colonies of Canada and Australia are turning towards the United States. The revolt of the workers in the downtrodden colonial and semi-colonial areas is growing stronger, in spite of the fact that the leading capitalists have for the most part aligned themselves with the imperialists in those countries where the national revolutionary movement is developing into an anti-capitalist movement.

Japan is a Far Eastern power. It is much weaker than the Anglo-Saxon world powers. It is partly dependent economically on the USA, which buys the greater part of the silk exports which are so important to Japan and exports capital to that country. Its existence as a capitalist power depends mainly on China. Being itself weak in raw materials, it can only carry on its industry with the help of its colonies – Korea, Manchuria, Shantung, Formosa, and of China itself.

France is predominantly a Mediterranean-African power (although it possesses a valuable colonial area in Indo-China also). The African colonies lie near to the motherland, and are most closely bound to her economically and strategically, France's weakness is in her small and stagnant population; her strength in her military superiority on the continent. Politically and militarily she is closely connected with Poland, Yugoslavia, and Czechoslovakia (the economic connection is not very important), but taken as a whole France is also much weaker than the two Anglo-Saxon world powers.[134]

Between these four world powers, which independently conduct an imperialist world policy, the other States vacillate here and there in changing alliances and blocs insofar as they are not already appendages of one of the world powers. The decisive factor in this connection is the growing rivalry of the

---

134 In particular France's communications with her African colonies are constantly threatened by the sea-power of Britain which possesses powerful naval bases at Gibraltar and Malta.

world powers called into existence by their struggle for markets, raw materials and the possession of monopolised areas. This rivalry is also present at its sharpest between the two greatest world powers, England and the USA. It extends over the whole world; in South America, Canada, Australia, China; everywhere American capital is pressing hard upon English capital, demanding the 'open door' for all areas which it controls, demanding, that is, equal rights. The struggle is also directed against the monopoly in raw materials which British finance capital has achieved: rubber, tin, etc. The struggle over oil – Royal Dutch against Standard Oil – is a vital factor in this antagonism. American armaments are directed principally against Britain's sea supremacy which still exists in spite of the Washington Agreement, since England possesses naval bases everywhere and owns an overwhelming number of merchant vessels which in the event of war could be used as auxiliary cruisers.[135]

There is also continuous antagonism between the USA and Japan. The USA is demanding the 'open door' in China, which it considers to be the best future market. Apart from that there is rivalry over the hegemony of the Pacific Ocean. The USA, at the Washington Conference, thrust Japan out of China and compelled England to sever her alliance with Japan.

France and England are permanent rivals for superiority on the European continent. By the changes in war technique, England has ceased to be an island in the strategic sense of the term. French guns, with long distance ranges, can reach the English coast from the mainland. Aircraft can reach and bombard London in an hour. Submarines – as a result of the greater nearness of the bases and their greatly superior construction – can endanger England's shipping to an incomparably greater extent than did the German submarines during the war, submarines which were both less numerous and more primitive than those of today. In the same way there is a deep antagonism between France and Germany – in spite of the many international monopolies. Germany will, within a short time, have a population twice as great as that of France, and is developing more rapidly than France both technically and economically. The fear of a war

---

135 Tire disputes at the Geneva Naval Disarmament Conference, which were difficult for the lay mind to understand, revolved around the maritime rights of England in the event of a war, around the question of the 'freedom of the seas'. America, being short of naval bases and merchant ships, wanted to fix the type of 'small cruisers' and their equipment in such a manner as to make them superior to England's merchant vessels used as auxiliary cruisers. England was determined on a smaller type with fewer armaments in order to be able, in the event of war, to wage battle against small foreign cruisers with her auxiliary cruisers. For Japan, which is interested only in China, the point was one of indifference; she could therefore play the part of mediator.

of revenge is one of the chief factors governing French foreign policy, in spite of Locarno, Thoiry, and all peace guarantees.

The military supremacy of France forces England to seek allies on the continent. This explains her good relations with Italy which is herself strongly opposed to France. The basis of Franco-Italian antagonism is the fact that in the re-division of the world at the close of the war Italy came out worse than any other of the victorious states, because she had shown herself to be the weakest. The spoils intended for Italy in Asia Minor were lost because of the national rebirth of Turkey. That is why the North Italian industry, which developed so rapidly, is urgently in need of a good position on the world market and of colonies, the Italian home market being particularly small. But the world is divided up. Italy has only received worthless crumbs. The obvious sphere of Italian imperialist expansion would be around the Mediterranean. But wherever Italy turns, she comes up against France.[136] Almost in sight of Sicily lies Tunis, a French possession, where there are more Italians than French. Towards the East, Italy, in its drive towards expansion, comes up against Yugoslavia, which is supported by France. Italy is, therefore, a willing tool in the hands of England for her struggle against France. Apart from Italy, England seeks to strengthen Germany as a counterpoise to France – with whom, by the way, the Entente Cordiale still exists. But Germany is England's greatest rival in the industrial sphere, political interests are therefore in conflict with immediate economic interests.

It would take us to eternity even to enumerate all the antagonisms which divide the Balkans and Eastern Europe; Germany against Poland; Hungary against Romania, Yugoslavia and Czechoslovakia; Poland against Lithuania; Bulgaria against Yugoslavia, etc. These antagonisms are expressed in the most diverse alliances. Such blocs are, however, shortlived; the internal opposition of interests is continuously demolishing them, or they neutralise each other. The foundations of alliances are, for example, the following:

(a) The universal hostility of all capitalist states to the Soviet Union. This bloc is always latently in existence. But the opposition of interests is so strong that up to the present it has not materialised. England's efforts to unite all the central and east European States into a bloc for an attack on the USSR have not yet succeeded, because these attempts themselves bring to light all the latent hostilities in Eastern Europe.

(b) The common hostility of all colonial powers to the colonies and semi-colonies oppressed by them – a subject we have already discussed.

---

136 The Mediterranean is important for England not as a colonial area, but as the road to India. England holds the most important strategic points, Gibraltar, Malta, etc., but apart from Egypt and Palestine it has no colonies there.

(c) The common hostility of all European debtor States to their master creditor, the USA.
(d) The common hostility of all the victorious countries, interested in maintaining the status quo, to the defeated countries which were destroyed or despoiled in the war.
(e) The common interest of all reparations creditors in the operation of the Dawes Plan.[137]
(f) There is a bloc of the States surrounding Hungary – the Little Entente – to protect their possessions.

There is another bloc arising, cutting right across it, composed of Fascist states: Italy, Hungary, Poland, Bulgaria, Romania.

But all this is unstable, changing, brittle. The hostile interests of the world powers disintegrate all these changing alliances, force their policies on the small states, which, exploiting the hostile interests of the powers, are trying to attain a relative independence.

To sum up: the present political relations of power are determined by the opposition of the capitalist world to the Soviet Union, by the hostility of the imperialist powers to the colonies, and by the clash of interests among the imperialist powers themselves (USA-England; USA-Japan; England-France). The smaller states, nominally independent, have either become mere appendages of the world powers or are at any rate incapable of carrying out an independent policy. Finance capital among the Great Powers is uninterruptedly preparing for a war to re-divide the world, and the small states, willy-nilly, will have to take part. There will be fewer neutral states in the next war than there were in the last! League of Nations, disarmament conferences, pacts of non-aggression, outlawry of war, etc., are partly deliberately deceptive manoeuvres, partly expressions of the capitalists' fear of the consequences of a new world

---

137 As on all other points, the interests of the separate national capitalist classes, and the sections within these classes, are in opposition. For England, reparations are not a very important financial affair; the chief desire is to exchange the reparation payments against her debts to America. But for France reparation imports are very important. Finance capital in the USA is mainly concerned with guaranteeing its capital investments in Germany, and is therefore in favour of a revision of the Dawes Plan, but refuses to cancel inter-allied debts for this purpose, although they are not of great financial importance to America. Since, moreover, reparation payments can, in the long-run, only be made via greatly increased export of German industrial products, which would seriously injure the industrial interests of the receiving countries, there is a sharp division among the capitalists of those countries. That is why reparations cannot serve as a lasting foundation for the formation of alliances.

war, which would certainly end with the overthrow of the capitalist regime in a number of countries. That is why the bourgeoisie are anxious to defeat the dictatorship of the proletariat in the USSR before the fight begins among themselves, in order to deprive the revolutionary workers of the world of their organised centre of power.

11 Present-Day Capitalism as Viewed by the Reformists

The world situation, which we outlined in the preceding chapter, shows the instability of the capitalist system, its inherent and fundamental contradictions. It is true that the great revolt of the working class, the attempt to destroy the system in Europe after the war ended with the defeat of the proletariat and the stabilisation of capitalism, because of the cunning manoeuvres of the bourgeoisie, the treachery of the social democrats and the absence of Communist Parties. But the decay of capitalism has nevertheless begun. Capitalism could not regain its mastery over the whole world – one-sixth of the globe is lost to it; the proletariat rules in the USSR! The contradictions within the capitalist world are more marked. In the central capitalist areas the transformation of independent producers into petty capitalists or workers is almost completed. Those workers who become unemployed as a result of technical progress no longer find work, as hitherto, in the expansion of the capitalist market. The result is permanent mass unemployment, accompanied by the idleness of a great part of the machinery of production and the increased exploitation of a small number of workers.

Concentration and centralisation are continuing. The growth of monopolies is increasing by leaps and bounds. A small group of the most important capitalists who are at the head of the monopolies and banks, direct economics and politics. From time to time they continue to form international monopolies and divide the world market between them.

The contradiction between social production and private appropriation becomes ever keener and more intolerable. The state is becoming a tool of the monopolies; bourgeois democracy can no longer conceal the contradictions; in its place there is growing up, to an ever greater extent, the system of capitalist terror as a permanent institution – Fascism.

The rivalry of the world powers, the competition for markets and for the possession of monopoly spheres – in spite of international monopolies – the hostility to the USSR, all these factors lead to the maddest competition in armaments, to violent new world wars, the extent of which it is impossible to foresee.

Only the overthrow of capitalist supremacy, which can only occur by means of an armed struggle, by the destruction of the bourgeois state – and not by any peaceful evolution – can save humanity.

What do the reformists say to this? What picture of the world do they present to the workers?

It is not easy to answer these questions. The theories of the reformists appear in many hues, contain versions of all bourgeois theories veiled in sham Marxist phraseology, and often deliberately shelve the problem. Besides, the same contradictions that exist between the capitalist classes of different countries are also to be found among the various social-democratic parties since they form the extreme left wing of the capitalist parties as a whole. In the following we shall deal principally with Hilferding, for in spite of his degeneracy, he has the clearest head of all the reformists.

The reformist world picture is approximately as follows:

(a) *The present period is not one of capitalist decline.*
The separation of the USSR from the capitalist world does not indicate the beginning of the end of the capitalist system. There has not been a *proletarian*, but a *bourgeois-peasant* revolution. The Bolsheviks, as the ruling party, are obliged to consider the interests of the peasantry as the strongest 'social force' (Otto Bauer). The social and economic system of the Soviet Union is not a socialist one, but a primitive capitalist one. Not the proletariat, but a small clique *above* the proletariat rules in the Soviet Union. The liberation of the proletariat necessitates the fall of the Bolshevik government (Kautsky).

(b) *Capitalism is approaching a new period of expansion.*
'Does this crisis in capitalism', asks Hilferding, 'really mean, as so many say, the end of normal capitalist development, or does it indicate, as Professor [Bernhard] Harms thinks, a new boom in capitalism? Actually, Professor Harms has already demonstrated this new expansion to us, for if one does not limit oneself to any particular national considerations, all the facts which he enumerates are nothing but the foundations of the revival of a vastly-extended world capitalism'.[138]

---

138   Boese (ed.) 1926, p. 112.

(c) *Capitalism today differs from earlier forms of capitalism because it is organised and planned.*

'The era of free competition, in which capitalism was governed solely by blind laws, is being superseded by the capitalist organisation of economy, that is, we are faced with organised economy instead of with a blind play of forces ... *Organised capitalism means ... the replacement of the capitalist principle of free competition by the socialist principle of regulated production*'.[139]

(d) *The action of the state is, in the period of organised capitalism, of decisive importance to the fate of the working class.*

> The better the organisation ... the more intolerable for the mass of producers grows the usurpation of economic power and of social products by the owners of amalgamated and concentrated means of production ... The contradiction disappears through the change in economy from being hierarchically to being democratically organised. Conscious social regulation of national economy by the few for their own purposes becomes regulation by the mass of producers. Capitalism is setting itself the problem of economic democracy ... its establishment is a long historical process in which concentrated capital becomes increasingly subject to democratic control.[140]

(e) *The state today is not an instrument of capitalist domination.*

> Marx certainly gave the state a distinguishing characteristic by saying that the state should not only be considered as a political body, but also according to its social function, which consists in maintaining the supremacy of the ruling classes by means of the state power. But this definition of the state by Marx is not by any means a theory of the state, for it applies to all State forms since the beginning of class societies, and we must therefore elucidate the distinguishing characteristics of state development ... The state is nothing but the government, the machinery of administration and the citizens who compose the State ... [I]n other words, this means that the essential elements of any modern state are the parties, because the individual can only realise his will through the medium of the party. Consequently all parties are necessary

---

139 Hilferding [1927], p. 168.
140 Hilferding 1924c, p. 3.

component parts of the state, in the same way as the government and the administration.[141]

The necessity of a coalition government is an evident consequence of this, in order to be able to influence the state and to overcome, with the help of the state, the contradiction between political freedom and economic slavery.

(f) *The transition from capitalist rule to socialism will not be brought about by the collapse of capitalism, but by the gradual attainment of economic democracy.*

The idea that the collapse of capitalism will automatically take place because there will no longer be any pre-capitalist markets, can be rejected as erroneous. I believe that in this I am in complete agreement with the teachings of Karl Marx, to whom a theory of collapse is always falsely attributed. The second volume of *Capital* shows that production within the capitalist system is possible on an ever-expanding scale. I have often thought that it is not altogether regrettable that the second volume should be so little read, for, in certain circumstances, a panegyric of capitalism might be extracted from it. (Loud laughter and cries of 'Quite right!')[142]

---

141 Hilferding [1927], p. 175.
142 Boese (ed.) 1926, pp. 113–14. In the form of an attack on the theory of passively awaiting the collapse of capitalism, supposed to be propagated by the Communists, the theory emphasised by us, of the necessity for the violent overthrow of capitalism by the proletarian revolution, is ignored, and the purest revisionism is announced as Marxism. For example, Otto [sic] Braunthal writes as follows in his booklet 'Tendencies in the development of Capitalist Economy' destined for the socialist youth: 'Diametrically opposed to the theory of collapse, the theory of concentration is a soundly optimistic theory of development. It believes that the development of capitalist economy – apart from temporary retrogressions – will continue until its transformation into socialism. It also believes that it is possible for the workers to gain a share in the continually increasing production by means of rises in real wages, in spite of the falling value of labour power. And, in conclusion, it considerably lightens the tasks of the socialist transformation by assuming that the organisation of economic life is possible and sensible, step by step. Two advantages of socialist society can be inferred from this conception. Firstly, all tendencies in organisation, which nowadays are penetrating all the nooks and corners of capitalist economy, will become preparations for fulfilling the tasks of socialist organisation. Secondly, the socialist society is not faced with the insoluble problem of changing an anarchic economy into an organised economy by one stroke; but it is faced with the much easier task of gradually changing a semi-organised economic life into a fully organised one'. Braunthal 1927, pp. 44–5.

In order to accomplish the change from an economy organised and directed by capitalists into an economy directed by the democratic State, democracy, and the political power of the working class, to be gained by democratic means and aiming at economic democracy, is necessary.

(g) *Democracy today is not 'bourgeois' democracy.*

> It is historically false and misleading to speak of bourgeois democracy ... Considered historically, the proletariat has always championed the cause of democracy ... We had to wrest it from the rulers in a stiff fight ... [T]he rulers must now turn to the citizens and have their rule continually ratified by a majority in lively conflict with us. Should the bourgeoisie attempt to ignore the democracy, this would lead to the use of violence in the class struggle, to a long-drawn-out, most embittered and extremely costly civil war. If the foundations of democracy are destroyed, the working class is put on the defensive and has no choice but to use whatever means are at its disposal. But social democracy will not turn to civil war as long as democracy is assured, for it realises that ... there is no graver obstacle to the realisation of socialism than civil war, and because we, as socialists, would find ourselves in an extremely difficult position if the proletarian state power were to arise out of civil war. That is why we, as the proletariat, have so strong an interest in the maintenance of democracy.[143]

The catchword of formal democracy is incorrect. Democracy implies a changed distribution of political power. It implies other social effects, and implies also that the will of the state is likewise differently fashioned. It is, therefore, quite false to say that democracy is formal; it is of the greatest real importance in the fate of all the working classes. If there are illusions to be destroyed today they are not those which Marx destroyed in 1848. Today it is not the democratic, but the anti-democratic illusions which are dangerous.

(h) *The immediate object of the workers is the struggle for economic and factory democracy.*

'Economic democracy means the subordination of private economic interests to social interests; factory democracy is the possibility for each individual to rise to the leadership of the concern, according to his capabilities'.[144]

---

143   Hilferding [1927], pp. 172–3.
144   Hilferding [1927], p. 171.

What is actually meant by 'economic democracy' is impossible, with the best will in the world, to determine, although so much has been written on the subject. The various reformists understand quite different things, but all are somewhat vague; participation in the management of monopoly concerns by means of the introduction of state councils, composed of capitalists, workers, and consumers (Otto Bauer), influencing economic policy by the socialist parties participating in the government; economic democracy by means of trade unions and factory committees; workers sharing in the profits of the capitalists by means of workers' shares, profit-sharing, etc.; the supersession of capitalism by the concentration of workers' savings in co-operatives, workers' concerns, etc. – all these are parts of the entirely vague idea of economic democracy.

By factory democracy is obviously meant the equal rights of the workers to decide on the appointment and dismissal of workers, the determination of conditions of labour, etc.

(i) *Since capitalism still has a long lease of life, since it should not be destroyed but is to evolve into socialism, rationalisation must be supported.*

'We need a powerful and not a decadent, impoverished capitalism, for it is to the advantage of the inheritors if their inheritance is as great as possible'.[145]

It is only necessary that the workers should receive a proportionate share of the greater production which results from rationalisation; that, at least, their share of total production should not decrease.[146]

'This is even more necessary in order to prevent capitalism from experiencing great difficulties because of the narrowness of the market'.[147] A larger share of the total must reach such persons as will presumably use it for purposes of consumption. A greater part of the product must fall to the workers. Higher wages are advantageous to capitalism itself.

(j) *The increase in the number of international monopolies is the foundation of realist pacifism, of super-imperialism.*

International monopolies bring order into the capitalist system. The organised distribution of markets makes war superfluous and stupid for economic reasons. The League of Nations is the political expression of this combination of the interests of the national capitalists. Its power should be supported by the

---

145   Hilferding 1926b, p. 115.
146   This is the demand of all trade unionists from [William] Green (USA) to [Léon] Jouhaux (France).
147   Tarnow 1928, pp. 48–9.

Social-Democratic Parties participating in its deliberations, in order to support a policy of peace in their 'own' countries.

The demand for general disarmament and free trade should follow logically from such an attitude. But on these questions the ideas of the various social-democratic parties are sharply divided, reflecting the hostile interests of the national bourgeoisie.

On the military question: the German social democracy is opposed to the militia and supports the Reichswehr (the German Army).

> Our attitude to the Reichswehr cannot be one of opposition in principle; the Reichswehr is in its very nature a system of defence with which we can agree in the circumstances, provided that disarmament, which is nowadays one-sided, does not become international ... We do not therefore struggle against the Reichswehr, but for it, so as to make it a still more reliable instrument in the hands of the republic.[148]

On the other hand, the French social democracy whose member, Paul-Boncour,[149] is well-known as the protagonist of the new French military system, announces the necessity of a general obligation to serve – extended even to women – and the subordination of all the economic forces of the country to the purposes of 'national defence'.

The social democrats of the small countries whose capitalists cannot conduct any independent policy, such as the Swiss, Norwegian, Dutch, Swedish and Danish Social-Democratic Parties, are all in favour of complete or very extensive disarmament.

The attitude of the various Social-Democratic Parties to the question of tariffs is equally contradictory.

We wish to emphasise again that this outline portrayal of the reformists of today is not applicable everywhere, for there is no definite international theory, just as there is no international discipline, among the reformists. But our statement represents the kernel of social-democratic ideas. The central point of their theory is the theory of the state set up in opposition to that of Marx. If the state today is considered not as a tool of the capitalist class, but as an instrument which can be employed, according to the election results, as the tool of one class or another, including the working class, then everything else follows logically from that: the importance of parliamentary democracy, the Utopia of

---

148 Hilferding [1927], p. 182.
149 [Joseph Paul-Boncour (1873–1972) was a French Socialist].

achieving economic democracy by means of the ballot box, the possibility of a peaceful transition from capitalism to socialism – if only the ruling class will respect democracy. The theory that there is no room for Communism also follows from this.[150]

It is unnecessary to refute these social-democratic theories in these pages. Experience refutes them from first to last. Capitalist terror is ruling instead of democracy over an ever larger area. The capitalists prove at every moment that the state today is a bourgeois state, and they only put up with democracy as long as it does not endanger their class supremacy.

But the reformists are not particularly concerned as to whether their theories are true or false. For them, as capitalist agents in the working class, it is enough if large sections of workers believe in the correctness of their theories. They themselves surrender these theories as soon as they involve any danger to their 'own' bourgeoisie. They support the maintenance of imperialist power where the capitalists possess such power (MacDonald);[151] they are in favour of the re-division of the world if their 'own' bourgeoisie feels itself wronged (Labriola);[152] in the victorious countries they support the maintenance of the status quo arrived at after the war; in the defeated countries they favour a revision of the peace treaty; they compromise with the Fascists (Polish Socialist Party) and continuously incite hatred against the USSR. Sometimes they are in opposition, sometimes in office, but even when in opposition they are always the future government party, the party for the defence of the capitalist system. If they are in opposition, they carry on trade-union struggles which, viewed historically, only serve the purpose of retaining the confidence of the working class in order to be able to proceed more strongly and more effectively against revolution when any new and acutely revolutionary situation arises.

The problem is: how can the reformists, with such contradictory theories, hostile to the interests of the working class, daily refuted by practical experi-

---

150   Hilferding said at Kiel: 'The Communists are disappearing, although it may take a longer or shorter time. I can understand that the unemployed, the many desperate persons who lost their money during inflation, that all those who, during the war, lost every but their belief in force, still perhaps, from some blind instinct, vote for the Communists. But the Communist Party is of no importance in the socialist movement. It is lost'. Hilferding [1927], p. 184.
151   [Ramsay MacDonald (1866–1937) was a leader of the Labour Party and British Prime Minister].
152   [Arturo Labriola (1873–1959) was an Italian Socialist ideologue and politician. As an opponent of Mussolini he was exiled to France, but in 1935 he returned to Italy].

ence, how can they keep such great masses of workers under their banner? It would overstep the limits of our work if we were to give a full answer to this question: we should merely like to mention a few points. The labour aristocracy, that section of the working class corrupted by the capitalists, by their very nature and class position, belong to the reformists. The reformists also attract those sections of the proletariat which do not possess the necessary resolution and fighting spirit to join the Communists, but for whom activity in the social-democratic party gives the illusion of struggle against capitalism. The reformists also include those wide sections of the working class which not so very long ago were part of the peasantry and of the middle classes, and who still drag with them the idea of an expansion within capitalism, etc. The more acutely the inherent contradictions of capitalism develop, the more the supremacy of monopoly capital comes to be felt, the quicker will social democracy lose its influence over the workers, as the recent successes of the German, French and English Communist Parties show. Hilferding's contention that the Communist Party is lost, is actually applicable to the Social-Democratic Party as a party of the working class. Its character of a bourgeois party is being more extensively recognised by the proletariat, and all those who are courageous, youthful and eager for the fight are leaving the ranks of social democracy.

Conclusion

The work of Communists is more difficult and complicated now than it was a few years ago. Stabilisation of capitalism means that there is no acutely revolutionary situation in the great capitalist countries. Communists must accomplish the task of working between two waves of revolution as a revolutionary class party, or of creating such a party. They must be the vanguard, steadfastly working towards the revolutionary goal, but not, in so doing, allowing themselves to be separated from the workers, not becoming an isolated sect. They must be mass parties; this means that the daily interests of the working masses, of all the exploited, must be defended; and the bourgeoisie fought consistently and logically even within the framework of capitalism.

In this sphere, the Communists and the reformists are in keen competition for the masses. With stabilisation, the position of the reformists has to a certain extent improved. Wide sections of the working class, temporarily discouraged by many defeats in the revolutionary struggle, believe their promises, that capitalism has entered a new period of expansion, in which the workers will also have their share. The rise in real wages in a few countries in recent years gave some foundation for these hopes. The fact that the reformist trade unions are again conducting separate industrial struggles – at the moment there is no danger of every working-class struggle changing into a revolutionary struggle for power – assists the reformists to gain adherents among the masses. All these factors intensify the difficulties of our task in capitalist countries.

In recent years, the Communist International has gained much ground in colonial countries. At the Fifth Congress the Chinese delegation was the object of amazed curiosity. Today the Chinese Communist Party, beaten, persecuted, outside the pale of the law as it is, is a strong part of the Communist World Party, with great revolutionary experience. All over Asia, in America and Africa, everywhere, in areas which the reformists have always avoided, the Communist movement is rapidly growing.

The European Communist Parties, suppressed by capitalist terror, have learnt to maintain contact with the masses in spite of illegality, and are extending their influence although in some of these countries (Poland and Hungary), there is direct co-operation between the reformists and the Fascists.

Although our task is difficult, although the period of stabilisation is not adapted to revolutionary struggles for power; although we have not attained any great success such as the overthrow of the bourgeoisie in further countries, yet the cause of revolution has without doubt made great progress even in this period of stabilisation. Future capitalist crises will give the Communist World Party, better equipped, ideologically more developed and organisationally stronger than ever before, the opportunity of successfully undertaking the struggle for power in further countries.

But the change is already in progress. The working class is beginning to realise that capitalist rationalisation is not a universal panacea. Mass unemployment is increasing. The last results in Germany and France show a further growth in the influence of the Communist Party, although the social democrats also succeeded in increasing the number of their voters. In England, the Communist Party is on the road to becoming a mass party.

Appendix: Tables

This includes only the most important raw materials, for there are no international statistics for manufactured goods. We may, however, assume that the production of finished goods runs in general parallel to that of raw materials, that, in fact, it oversteps raw materials a little, for one of the most important methods of reducing costs of production is the better utilisation of raw materials and the avoidance of waste.

The table shows that the production of all raw materials is greater than before the war, but that the increase in those raw materials which are included in Division I of Marx's scheme – particularly metals – is much greater than in foodstuffs and textiles. This indicates the great expansion in the machinery of production, and consequently the strong tendency towards accumulation and concentration. Increases in the production of foodstuffs and textile materials just keep pace with the growth of population, which shows that the population's standard of life has not improved, that of the workers certainly not.

The figures are not very reliable (particularly those referring to agriculture), but are adequate for general inference.

TABLE 10.22 The most important figures of production of world economy (in million units)

			Yearly average 1909–13	Yearly average 1920–4	1925	1926	1927
Food							
Wheat(1)	Area	ha. (*)	79.8	83.3	89.6	91.8	–
	Produce	tons	82.2	88.7	90.2	91.8	94.7
Rye(1)	Area	ha.	19.6	18.3	18.7	18.2	–
	Produce	tons	26.1	21.1	25.6	20.4	23.1
Barley(1)	Area	ha.	23.6	24.5	25.5	25.5	–
	Produce	tons	28.7	27.6	30.19	29.5	30.9
Oats(1)	Area	ha.	41.1	44.2	45.6	44.1	–
	Produce	tons	52.1	52.0	58.2	53.8	53.6
Maize(1)	Area	ha.	69.9	70.2	71.7	70.0	–
	Produce	tons	102.9	108.0	113.6	107.0	–
Rice	Area	ha.	48.2	53.6(3)	54.7	54.3	–
	Produce	tons	77.5	83.2(3)	85.3	84.6	–
Potatoes(1)	Area	ha.	12.4	12.5	12.4	12.7	–
	Produce	tons	128.6	128.8	143.6	120.9	145.5
Beet sugar(1)	Produce	doz.	69.7	57.0	73.2	69.1	73.6
Cane sugar(1)	Produce	doz.	96.0	139.0	166.0	159.2	157.3
Textiles							
Cotton	Production	tons	4.84	4.33	6.0	5.99	4.40(8)
	Consumption	bales	23.3 (3)	21.6	23.2(5)	24.7(4)	25.9(8)
Wool	Production	kg.	1.463.0	1,249.0(6)	1,329.0	1,405.0	–
Silk	Production	kg.	29.2	38.2	45.8	47.2	–
Artificial silk	Production	kg.	14.1(2)	49.4(6)	87.0	99.5	130.0
Rubber	Production	kg.	114.0(2)	303.0	504.0	618.0	604.0
Fuel							
Coal	Production	tons	1,098.0	1,126.0	1,187.0	1,217.0	1,283,0
Petroleum	Production	barrels	385.0	869.0	1,067,0	1,095.0	1,234.0

TABLE 10.22 The most important figures of production of world economy (*cont.*)

			Yearly average 1909–13	Yearly average 1920–4	1925	1926	1927
Metals							
Iron	Production	tons	68.3	58.9	76.9	77.5	85.0
Steel	Production	tons	65.2	68.4	90.8	91.6	99.1
Copper	Production	kg.	1,030.0(2)	1,015.0	1,443.0	1,491.0	1,510.0
Lead	Production	kg.	1,194.0(2)	1,084.0	1,524.0	1,587.0	1,643.0
Zinc	Production	kg.	976.0(2)	760.0	1,132.0	1,249.0	1,300.0
Tin	Production	kg.	133.0(2)	128.0	150.0	147.0	–
Aluminium	Production	kg.	63.0(2)	122.0	179.0	211.0	213.0
Gold	Production	1,000 kg.	768.0(2)	525.0	593.0	600.0	600.0
Silver	Production	1,000 kg.	6,964.0(2)	6,467.0	7,514.0	7,454.0	7,454.0
Shipbuilding							
	Launched from docks	1,000 British tons	3,333.0(2)	3,312.0	2,193.0	1,675.0	2,236.0

(*) 1 hectare = 2½ acres.
(1) Excluding the Soviet Union.
(2) 1913.
(3) 1912–13.
(4) 1925–6.
(5) 1924–5.
(6) 1924.
(7) Current figures.
(8) 1926–7.

SOURCES OF FIGURES: *INTERNATIONAL STATISTICAL YEARBOOK 1926*; *INTERNATIONAL YEARBOOK OF AGRICULTURAL STATISTICS 1926–27*. FOR 1927 (AND PARTLY 1926) NEWSPAPERS AND OTHER PUBLICATIONS

TABLE 10.23 World population (in millions) (i)

	1913	1926	Percentage increase over 1913
Europe	467.9	477.6	2.1
North and Central America	133.5	157.5	17.9
South America	56.5	69.7	23.5
Asia	986.7	1,037.9	5.2
Africa	134.2	143.3	6.8
Oceania	7.7	9.0	17.8
Totals	1,786.5	1,895.0	6.1

(i) *International Yearbook of Agricultural Statistics 1926–27*

The table below shows the development in production and consumption of the most important raw materials in Europe. It can be seen that the production of foodstuffs in Europe (excluding the Soviet Union), as well as the consumption of cotton and wool, was, even in 1927, below the pre-war average, although population has increased since then.

TABLE 10.24 European figures of production (in million units)

			Yearly average 1909–13	Yearly average 1920–4	1925	1926	1927(7)
Foodstuffs							
Wheat(1)	Area	ha.	29.3	26.7	27.8	27.9	28.4
	Produce	tons	37.1	30.5	37.8	33.0	34.6
Rye(1)	Area	ha.	18.2	15.4	16.4	16.2	16.3
	Produce	tons	25.1	18.6	23.8	19.0	21.1
Barley(1)	Area	ha.	11.5	10.8	11.1	11.0	11.2
	Produce	tons	15.4	13.5	15.1	15.0	14.6
Oats(1)	Area	ha.	20.0	18.4	18.7	18.7	18.5
	Produce	tons	28.2	23.5	26.0	27.8	27.1
Maize(1)	Area	ha.	10.9	9.9	10.9	10.8	11.4
	Produce	tons	16.0	11.6	15.9	16.9	12.2
Rice	Area	ha.	0.2	0.18	0.2	0.2	–
	Produce	tons	0.7	0.8	1.0	1.0	–
Potatoes(1)	Area	ha.	10.5	10.1	10.4	10.3	10.6
	Produce	tons	114.0	111.0	129.4	104.4	127.0
Beet sugar(1)	Produce	doz.	52.9	46.0	64.2	59.2	64.1

THE DECLINE OF CAPITALISM 637

TABLE 10.24 European figures of production (in million units) (cont.)

			Yearly average 1909–13	Yearly average 1920–4	1925	1926	1927(7)
Textiles							
Cotton	Consumption	bales	12.2(3)	8.3	9.8(5)	10.2(4)	10.3(8)
Wool	Production	kg.	431.0	326.0(6)	331.0	340.0	–
Silk	Production	kg.	4.7	3.8	4.7	4.2	–
Artificial silk	Production	kg.	143.4(2)	34.6(6)	56.9	63.3	93.0
Fuel							
Coal	Production	tons	552.0	491.0	545.0	463.0	610.0
Petroleum	Production	barrels	85.0	51.0	76.0	93.0	104.0
Metals							
Iron	Production	tons	39.2	25.5	37.0	35.1	44.9
Steel	Production	tons	36.0	29.5	40.8	40.5	51.5
Copper	Production	kg.	192.0(2)	86.0	106.0	125.0	–
Lead	Production	kg.	559.0(2)	263.0	371.0	345.0	–
Zinc	Production	kg.	647.0(2)	326.0	514.0	528.0	618.0
Tin	Production	kg.	37.0(2)	30.0	42.0	–	–
Aluminium	Production	kg.	37.0(2)	63.0	104.0	103.0	–
Gold	Production	1,000 kg.	474.0(2)	266.0	327.0	338.0	–
Silver	Production	1,000 kg.	2,914.0(2)	2,427.0	2,030.0	1,428.0	–
Shipbuilding							
	Launched from docks	1,000 British tons	3,333.0(2)	3,312.0	2,193.0	1,675.0	2,236.0

(1) Excluding the Soviet Union.
(2) 1913.
(3) 1912–13.
(4) 1925–6.
(5) 1924–5.
(6) 1924–4.
(7) Current figures.
(8) 1926–7.

SOURCE OF FIGURES: *INTERNATIONAL STATISTICAL YEARBOOK* 1926; *INTERNATIONAL YEARBOOK OF AGRICULTURAL STATISTICS* 1926–27. FOR 1927 (AND PARTLY 1926) NEWSPAPERS AND OTHER PUBLICATIONS

This table below shows that Europe's share in heavy industry production has increased in recent years, while that of America has fallen relatively; development is approaching the conditions of the pre-war period. In the textile industry the development is similar, but much more slow. In considering the figures, the bad markets for the United States in 1927, and the good markets for Germany in that year must not be left out of account.

TABLE 10.25 Europe-America
Percentage comparison of European and American shares in world production

	Europe			United States		
	1909–13	1920–4	1927	190--13	192--4	1927
Coal	50.4	43.6	50.2	42.5	55.7	42.4
Iron	57.3	43.3	53.0	39.8	52.6	43.6
Steel	55.2	43.1	52.1	42.5	53.6	47.2
Cotton consumption	52.5	38.4	40.0	24.0	27.9	27.4

TABLE 10.26 Index figures of the economy of the Soviet Union (taken from the Russian Control Figures for 1927–8)

	1924–5	1925–6	1926–7	1927–8
Industry				
Coal	55.3	84.1	107.2	124.1
Petroleum	76.1	89.8	109.7	120.7
Pig iron	30.6	52.4	70.5	82.3
Metals	39.6	64.1	76.3	85.2
Cotton yarn	67.0	90.6	105.4	112.0
Rubber shoes	56.4	90.7	109.6	132.6
Salt	68.2	80.3	102.0	114.2
Agriculture				
Cultivated area	84.4	89.4	95.1	97.6
Cattle	–	–	96.9	102.8
Wheat	81.0	94.0	108.0	104.0
Rye	108.0	109.0	120.0	127.0
Barley	41.0	65.0	63.0	57.0

TABLE 10.26 Index figures of the economy of the Soviet Union (*cont.*)

	1924–5	1925–6	1926–7	1927–8
Oats	51.0	76.0	105.0	94.0
Maize	149.0	376.0	277.0	278.0
Potatoes	–	219.0	245.0	–
Flax	91.0	110.0	97.0	121.0
Cotton	–	56.0	56.0	–
Hemp	83.0	150.0	134.0	148.0
Sugar	30.0	67.0	60.0	–
Transport freightage (Railways)	–	–	99.1	114.2

The League of Nations has issued the following *index figures of production*, based on the production of 63 raw products (foods, fibrous materials, metals, fuel, chemicals) calculated on 1926 prices.

Tables 9.27 and *9.28* show the great increase in German production in the last few years in every sphere. Although it does not reach the rate of development of industrial production in the Soviet Union, it is still the only example in economic history. It must, however, be taken into account that structural and market factors coincided favourably. It is possible that after the end of the rationalisation market a decrease in the volume of production will set in.

TABLE 10.27 Development of production in the USSR and the rest of Europe

	1913	1923	1924	1925	1926
Europe, excluding USSR	100	87	93	102	93
Europe, including USSR	100	84	89	102	98

The figures show that in 1926 the production of the USSR outstripped that of the rest of Europe.

TABLE 10.28 Production in Germany (1)

		1913	1920	1924	1925	1926	1927
Coal	Million tons	141.0	108.0	119.0	132.0	145.0	154.0
Brown coal	Id.	87.0	112.0	125.0	140.0	139.0	151.0
Coke	Id.	35.0	26.0	25.0	28.0	26.0	32.0
Pig iron	Id.	10.9	6.4	7.8	10.1	9.6	13.1
Raw steel	Id.	11.7	8.4	9.7	12.1	12.3	16.3
Potash	Id.	11.6	11.4	8.1	12.1	9.4	–
Cotton consumption	1,000 tons	486.0(2)	163.0	271.0	368.0	292.0	475.0
Shipbuilding launched from docks	Id.	465.0(2)	242.0	175.0	406.0	80.0	290.0

(1) *Statistisches Jahrbuch für das Deutsche Reich* 1927.
(2) Old sphere territory.

TABLE 10.29 Index figures of German production (1) (1924–6 = 100)

	Total	Industries handling raw materials	Manufacturing industries
1924			
1. Quarter	77.5	73.0	88.2
2. Quarter	86.1	81.0	98.0
3. Quarter	86.1	88.3	81.0
4. Quarter	101.6	101.4	102.5
1925			
1. Quarter	111.8	112.0	111.6
2. Quarter	107.1	107.3	106.8
3. Quarter	103.3	100.4	110.0
4. Quarter	104.1	100.3	112.8
1926			
1. Quarter	94.4	95.0	93.3
2. Quarter	91.4	95.6	82.1
3. Quarter	100.7	105.0	91.0
4. Quarter	116.7	118.5	112.6

TABLE 10.29 Index figures of German production (1) (1924–6 = 100) (cont.)

	Total	Industries handling raw materials	Manufacturing industries
1927			
1. Quarter	121.9	122.7	120.3
2. Quarter	122.5	122.0	123.8
3. Quarter	123.3	122.2	125.9

(1) 'Deutsche Wirtschaftszahlen', *Vierteljahrshefte zur Konjunkturforschung* 1927, 2, 3, p. 114.

Figures of French production show a much slower increase than those for Germany. The stabilisation crisis is reflected in the stagnation of production for the year 1927.

TABLE 10.30 Production in France

		1913	1920	1924	1925	1926	1927
Coal	Million tons	44.0	25.0	45.0	48.0	52.0	52.0
Pig iron	Id.	9.0	3.3	7.7	8.5	9.4	9.3
Raw steel	Id.	7.0	2.7	6.9	7.4	8.4	8.2
Potash	Id.	–	1.2	1.7	1.9	2.3	–
Cotton consumption	1,000 bales	1,010.0	–	1,063.0	1,122.0	1,179.0	1,182.0
Shipbuilding launched from docks	1,000 tons	176.0	93.0	80.0	76.0	121.0	44.0

TABLE 10.31 Production in England (1)

		1913	1920	1924	1925	1926	1927
Coal	Million tons	287.0	233.0	270.0	247.0	131.0	259.0
Pig iron	Id.	10.3	8.2	7.3	6.2	2.4	7.3
Raw steel	Id.	7.7	9.2	8.2	7.7	3.6	9.1
Cotton consumption	In 1,000 bales	3,825.0	–	2,718.0	3,235.0	3,022.0	3,010.0
Shipbuilding	In 1,000 tons	1,932.0	2,056.0	1,440.0	1,079.0	640.0	1,226.0

TABLE 10.31 Production in England (1) (cont.)

		1913	1920	1924	1925	1926	1927
Electrical	(1920 = 100)	–	100.0	–	76.0	87.0	114.0
Motors	(in 1,000 bales)	22.0(2)	–	132.0	176.0	159.0	200.0

(1) *The Economist*, 18 February 1928, p. 320.
(2) 1912.

American production statistics show a more or less uniform rise up to 1926, and a fairly heavy decline in all important industries in 1927.

TABLE 10.32 Production in the United States (1)

		1913	1920	1924	1925	1926	1927(9)
Coal	Million short tons	478	569	484	520	578	520
Anthracite	Id.	91	90	88	62	85	81
Coke	Id.	46	51	44	51	56	50
Petroleum	Million barrels	248	443	714	764	767	890
Iron	Million long tons	31	37	31	37	39	36
Steel	Id.	31	42	38	45	48	43
Copper	1,000 short tons	807	763	1,130	1,102	1,173	–
Lead	Id.	462	530	690	767	799	–
Zinc	Id.	347	463	517	573	618	–
Automobiles(3)	1,000	462	1,883	3,243	3,839	3,937	2,939
Tractors	1,000	24	322	364	473	491	455
Cotton consumption	1,000 bales	5,786	6,762	5,522	6,433	6,687	7,406
Building (4)	Million dollars	858	2,533	3,880	5,043	5,391	–
Value added in industry	Milliards	9.7(6)	24.7(7)	–	26.8	–	–
Wholesale trade index	Id.	100	226(8)	150	159	151	147

(1) *Statistical Abstract of the United States* 1926, and *Commerce Year-Book* 1926.
(2) Bituminous.
(3) Motors for private use in the USA and Canada.
(4) In 27 states.
(5) Value added by manufacture.
(6) 1914.
(7) 1919.
(8) 1919–26.
(9) *Survey of Current Business*.

The following figures do not give a complete picture of unemployment, but only of those officially registered as unemployed, which is considerably lower. For England, figures relating to young workers who have not yet found employment are lacking; for Germany, those relating to persons on poor law and those run out of benefit. The statistics, therefore, can only give a dynamic picture. As such, they demonstrate the *permanent character of mass unemployment in the period of stabilisation.*

TABLE 10.33 Unemployment
Number of unemployed officially registered (in thousands)

		England	Germany	Italy	Poland	Belgium	Austria	Czecho-slovakia	Holland	Switzer-land
4th q.	1920	526	368	104	–	49	16	20	33	15
July	1921	1,804	314	414	65	147	–	33	30	56
Dec	1921	1,934	149	542	173	86	–	33	66	89
July	1922	1,458	20	372	87	36	38(1)	232(1)	33	52
Dec	1922	1,432	43	382	75	26	117	437	50	53
July	1923	1,325	139(2)	183	65	14	87	215	31	23
Dec	1923	1,227	1,528(2)	259	68	24	98	192	45	27
July	1924	1,135	526	118	152	21	66	63	19	8
Dec	1924	1,260	536	150	159	33	154	81	35	11
July	1925	1,327	197	80	175	31	112	42	23	10
Dec	1925	1,243	1,498	112	314	44	179	48	45	17
July	1926	1,737	1,741	80	263	16	152	46	20	11
Dec	1926	1,432	1,749	192	190	33	205	29	36	18
July	1927	1,114	573	388	148	22	137	12	21	8
Dec	1927	1,194	1,188	414	165	56	207	–	–	14

(1) September.
(2) Unoccupied territory only.

Percentages of trade-union unemployed, or of unemployed insured workers

		Holland	Denmark	Sweden	Norway	Germany	England	Canada	USA
4th q.	1920	8.3	8.3	9.3	3.9	4.1	4.5	9.8	–
July	1921	7.6	16.7	27.8	17.9	2.6	14.8	9.1	–
Dec	1921	16.6	25.2	33.2	18.3	1.6	16.2	15.1	–
July	1922	9.1	13.2	21.5	15.6	0.6	15.7	5.3	–
Dec	1922	15.1	20.3	21.3	15.1	2.8	14.0	6.1	–
July	1923	10.6	7.5	9.1	6.9	3.5	11.5	2.2	–
Dec	1923	15.9	19.6	14.1	14.0	28.2	10.7	7.2	–
July	1924	7.0	5.4	6.2	3.9	12.5	9.9	5.4	–
Dec	1924	12.7	17.1	15.5	12.5	8.1	10.0	11.6	–
July	1925	8.3	8.3	7.6	8.3	3.7	11.2	5.2	–
Dec	1925	16.0	31.1	19.4	19.0	19.4	10.5	7.9	–
July	1926	6.9	17.0	8.6	20.4	17.7	14.0	2.3	–
Dec	1926	12.1	32.2	19.1	29.6	16.7	11.9	5.9	–
July	1927	7.0	17.3	8.2	20.9	5.5	9.3	3.3	–
Dec	1927	9.3	30.5	18.6	28.0	12.9	9.8	6.6	17.8

Exact statistics of output and production are not available for Germany as for the USA. The following data make it reasonable to assume that mass unemployment is also developing in Germany. The number of workers in those concerns employing more than five workers, which come into the scope of industrial statistics, amounted to (in thousands): (1)

TABLE 10.34 Increase in output in Germany

	1922	1924	1925	1926	1927
	8,216	7,386	–	6,920	–
National Statistical Dept. index of production 1924–6 = 100	–	100	101	111	125

The index of production is based on a relatively small number of commodities (2), and has only a roughly approximate value. But the following figures for separate industries confirm this tendency to a great increase in labour output, although one cannot judge from them how much is due to increased productivity, and how much to increased intensity. The figures are taken from the Annual Report of the National Credit Company.

	1925	1927
Ruhr coal mining: Increase in production per shift	114	132
Pig iron production: Daily output per worker increased (3)	100	140
Raw steel production: Daily output per worker increased	100	137
	1st quarter, 1925	3rd quarter, 1927
Machinery industry	100	145
National railways: Km. Per head of personnel	100	118.5

(1) Figures for 1922 and 1924 from 1926 *Statistisches Jahrbuch für das Deutsche Reich*; 1926 from *Jahresberichte der Gewerbeaufsichtsbeamten und Bergbehörden für das Jahr 1926*, Berlin: R. von Decker's Verlag, 1927, Part 4. The report contains no figures for metals, building, etc., which are included in the 1924 figures. Judging from the tendency towards a decrease in all industries, this, if anything, makes the figures higher rather than lower.
(2) See *Vierteljahrshefte für Konjunkturforschung* 1927, Berlin: Institut für Konjunkturforschung, 2, p. 26.
(3) 1913 = 100 per head for coal and hard-rock miners.

The statistics collected by the Census, which is taken periodically, afford the possibility of making an approximate estimate of the rate of surplus value in American industry. The factors entering into such a calculation are (see *Commerce Year Book* 1926):

> Total wages – Variable capital.
> Cost of raw materials – Circulating capital
> Cost of wear and tear machinnery – Fixed capital

The value of the product.
For an exact claculation we should also have:
1. The value of the wear and tear of that part of the fixed capital present in buildings; but this is relatively so small that it can be overlooked in any merely approximate calculation.
2. There is also lacking a very important factor, namely, the total commercial profits, which is a part of the surplus value produced in industry, for

in the Marxian theory of value industrial capital disposes of its goods to commercial capital not at the full production price, but lower than that, at a price which will enable commercial capital, when selling the commodities at their production price, to realise the average rate of profit. Profit on commercial capital os therefore surplus value produced in industry, and if we are to find the actual rate of surplus value, it must be the rate of surplus value in the next table is considerably lower than corresponds to reality.

With these reservations let us turn to the tables:

TABLE 10.35 Calculation of the rate of surplus value in American Industry (in million dollars)

	Total wages = V	Cost of materials = C	Wear and tear of machinery C = fixed	Value produced	Total surplus value = S	Rate of surplus value %
	I	II	III	IV	V IV − (I + II + III)	VI V = S I V
1899	2,008	6,576	250	11,407	2,569	123
1904	2,610	8,500	330	14,794	3,354	128
1909	3,427	12,143	500	20,672	4,602	134
1914	4,068	14,278	600	23,988	5,042	121
1919	10,453	36,989	1,600	61,737	12,695	121
1921	8,193	25,155	1,400	43,427	8,679	105
1923	10,999	34,381	1,800	60,258	12,978	117
1925	10,729	35,931	2,300	62,706	13,746	128

For calculating the wear and tear of machines, the figures giving the total value of machines in industry are at our disposal (taken from the Official Publication, *Wealth, Public Debt and Taxation* 1922, p. 18):

(in million dollars)

1900	1904	1912	1922
2,541	3,298	6,091	15,783

THE DECLINE OF CAPITALISM

If we consider this table, the most important thing we learn from it is that the 100 percent rate of surplus value assumed by Marx and everywhere described as grossly exaggerated, has actually been outstripped in American industry. And we must again emphasise the fact that this rate of surplus value is lower than the actual rate, for it does not include that share of the profits produced in industry, but going to commercial capital. We wish to emphasise, moreover, very strongly that we are *dealing here only with a very rough attempt at estimating the approximate rate of surplus value, based on inadequate data and with many deviations from the actual facts*, but at least these deviations tend to make the result lower than the actual rate of surplus value.

TABLE 10.36 Value added by manufacture amounted in American industry to the following (according to the article published in the *American Federationist*, October 1927–March 1928, and based on census returns): 1904 = 100

	1909	1914	1919	1921	1923	1925
Leather	97	97	82	104	99	96
Wood	104	114	106	119	104	107
Railway Workshops	98	97	101	99	97	97
Motors	92	87	97	91	93	82
Transport	92	88	96	93	103	90
Rubber	114	108	121	128	135	120
Paper and printing	98	100	98	104	99	94
Chemicals	92	106	142	153	139	126
Metals (not iron or steel)	101	101	110	118	109	103
Tobacco	95	90	77	90	75	55
Textiles	96	101	83	100	92	94
Iron and steel	96	104	102	113	100	96
Food	92	94	102	115	104	96
Stone, Glass, etc.	98	98	88	92	83	81

The figures show:
1. That the share of the workers was highest in 1921, when wages had not yet followed the sharply falling price level.
2. That with the exception of a few industries, the share of the workers was, even in 1925, lower than in 1914, i.e. *the rate of surplus value had risen*.

It must be pointed out that we are only dealing with the share of the workers actually working, with the relation of S to V; *it is not a picture of the working class as a whole*, for the increasing unemployment is left out of account.

TABLE 10.37 Average height of tariffs of the value of commodities for a few countries

	Textile goods	Iron an iron goods	Machinery and apparatus	All groups
Belgium	14.1	12.4	13.2	11.4
Denmark	14.3	8.8	7.1	13.2
Germany	24.0	16.9	10.9	20.8
France	70.6	110.0	38.9	58.1
Italy	18.6	60.7	25.4	28.6
Yugoslavia	29.9	41.1	22.8	34.8
Austria	14.6	30.8	25.6	19.2
Poland	49.6	56.3	41.6	43.3
Romania	294.3	39.6	22.9	98.4
Sweden	18.6	22.8	15.5	19.5
Switzerland	10.9	29.7	12.5	17.5
Czechoslovakia	28.6	53.3	46.2	36.4
Hungary	29.8	49.2	33.0	31.1

SOURCE: MEMORANDUM OF THE VIENNA CHAMBER OF COMMERCE FOR THE WORLD ECONOMIC CONFERENCE

At the beginning of May 1928, the official prices of the German Iron Cartel were as follows:

TABLE 10.38 Examples of differences between home and foreign prices

	Home prices from 10 May	Export prices in May	Reckoned in marks	Differences in marks	Export repayment in May	Duty on iron
Raw ingots	104.0	4/2/0	83.0	21	19.0	10.0
Finished ingots	111.5	4/3/0	83.5	28	19.0	10.0
Iron rots	119.0	4/13/6	90.0	29	19.0	15.0
Iron plates	124.0	4/14/0	90.0	34	19.0	15.0
Wrought iron	138.0	4/14/0	90.0	48	35.0	25.0
Bar iron	141.0	5/8/0	107.0	34	28.0	25.0
Iron laths	164.0	6/5/0	149.0	15	35.0	25.0
Rolled wire	159.3	5/15/0	117.3	42	21,5	25.0
Rough sheet iron	158.0	5/10/0	112.0	46	22.0	55.0

THE DECLINE OF CAPITALISM   649

Home prices are, as a rule, higher than the price for export plus export expenses. This means that German users pay more for German iron than their foreign competitors.

The following table shows capital export of the two principal countries, USA and England, in recent years, and German capital import. We must point out: (1) that we are only dealing with public issues; (2) that apart from long-term capital export *from* the USA and England, there is also a stream of short-term investment capital *to* these countries.

TABLE 10.39 Capital issues and movement of capital
New issues and capital export: England (issued in million £ (1))

	1912	1913	1924	1925	1926	1927
England						
Government	–	–	13.8	45.7	4.7	66.1
Other	45.3	36.0	70.8	109.3	124.5	140.8
Total	45.3	36.0	84.6	155.0	129.2	206.9
British possessions						
Government	14.7	26.3	50.1	30.7	31.9	55.7
Other	58.0	49.9	22.2	30.2	21.3	44.1
Total	72.7	76.2	72.3	60.9	53.2	99.8
Foreign						
Government	9.6	26.2	40.6	–	23.8	11.8
Other	83.3	58.3	11.8	16.3	24.6	36.6
Total	92.9	84.5	52.4	16.3	48.4	48.4
General Total	210.9	196.7	209.3	232.2	230.8	355.1

The table does not include any conversion operations, but represents exclusively new money capital.

New issues and capital export: United
States (issued in million dollars (2))

	Total	Abroad
1923	4,304	267
1924	5,593	997
1925	6,223	1,086
1926	6,311	1,145
1927	–	1,567

New issues and capital import: Germany (3) (in million marks)

	Internal loans	Foreign loans	Actual amounts raised	Joint stock capital demand
1924 total	176.30	1,002.00	66.00	113.88
1925 total	144.60	1,241.00	593.76	114.12
1926 total	1,306.00	1,517.00	1,242.66	90.38
1927 total	993.70	1,688.38	1,024.13	139.90

(1) *Information financière*, 1 December 1927.
(2) *Commercial and Financial Chronicle*.
(3) *Frankfurter Zeitung*, 1 January 1928.

The following table gives a very rough sketch of real wages in the period of stabilisation in the most important European capitals. They are comparable with each other only with many reservations, for the *method of calculation* varies greatly from town to town.

TABLE 10.40 Comparative index figures of real wages (1)
Calculated on the basis of food prices, London, 1 July 1924 = 100

	1924, 1 July	1927, 1 October
Amsterdam	89	86
Berlin	55	68
Brussels	59	50
London	100	105

TABLE 10.40 Comparative index figures of real wages (1) (cont.)

	1924, 1 July	1927, 1 October
Madrid	57	57
Rome	46	51
Paris	73	56(3)
Prague	56	52
Vienna	47	45
Warsaw	43(2)	42
Łódź	48(2)	44

(1) *International Labour Review*, 1927, 16, 4. The figures of the ILO can be used to determine the *tendency* in wage development.
(2) 1 January 1925.
(3) 1 July 1927.

The table below is taken or calculated from official statistics. In these statistics wages for full-time workers under agreements are given as for the highest paid section; on the other hand, the official cost of living index is too low; in particular, the deductions for taxation and social purposes, much higher than before the war, are not taken into consideration.

TABLE 10.41 Wage changes in Germany, 1913–27

		Weekly wages in marks		Real wage index	
		Skilled	Unskilled	Skilled	Unskilled
	1913	35.02	24.31	100	100
February	1924	28.61	22.86	72	94
December	1924	38.44	28.61	83	90
February	1925	39.18	29.23	81	89
July	1925	43.90	32.37	87	93
December	1925	45.98	33.92	93	99
February	1926	46.02	33.95	94	100
July	1926	45.93	34.05	92	99
December	1926	46.36	34.44	92	98
February	1927	46.43	34.52	91	98

TABLE 10.41 Wage changes in Germany, 1913–27 (*cont.*)

		Weekly wages in marks		Real wage index	
		Skilled	Unskilled	Skilled	Unskilled
July	1927	49.17	36.70	93	100
December	1927	49.43	37.01	93	101

The following table of wage changes in England does not take into account the cheapening in cost of living following upon deflation. *It cannot*, therefore, be used as a basis for determining real wages:

TABLE 10.42 Wage changes in England

	Increase	Decrease
In total weekly wages bill, £ 1,000		
1915	867	–
1916	885	–
1917	2,986	–
1918	3,435	–
1919	2,547	–
1920	4,793	–
1921	–	6,061
1922	–	4,210
1923	–	317
1924	554	–
1925	–	78
1926	49	–
1927	–	359
	16,116	11,025

TABLE 10.43 Wages in the USA
Real wage index in the USA (1)

Yearly average	
1912	100
1923	103
1924	111
1925	107
1926	110
1927	112 (2)

(1) *American Federationist. Offical Organ of the American Federation of Labor*, 34, December 1927, p. 1496. This index figure is calculated on the basis of the prices of goods consumed by the workers.
(2) Average for first nine months.

Real wages. Index numbers according to official statistics

Year monthly average	Total wage index for industrial workers	Department of labour cost-of-living index	Real wage index
1914	100.0	100	100
1920	235.4	198	119
1921	188.0	167	113
1922	191.9	157	122
1923	211.3	161	131
1924	209.5	164	128
1925	214.8	168	128
1926	216.7	168	129
1927 April	218.4	164	133

In the four years 1924–7, real wages changed on average very little in the USA. *Since the fourth quarter of 1927, wage decreases have set in.*

The table below shows that consumption per head of the population, corresponding to the impoverishment of broad masses, is still lower than before the war.

TABLE 10.44 Consumption per head of articles of general consumption in Germany (1)

		1913(2) (1913–14)	1923 (1922–3)	1924 (1923–4)	1925 (1924–5)	1926 (1925–6)	1937(3) (1926–7)
Rye	kg.	153	90	106	87	115	101
Wheat	kg.	96	46	57	63	74	80
Barley	kg.	108	29	42	45	58	66
Oats	kg.	128	57	87	85	86	106
Potatoes	kg.	700	560	433	495	582	473
Meat	kg.	52	31	43	47	48	–
Beer	litre	102	45	61	75	76	–
Spirits	litre	5.4	2.5	1.88	2.8	3.0	–
Sugar	kg.	19.0	19.5	13.3	20.2	20.5	–
Coffee	kg.	2.4	0.6	0.9	1.4	1.7	1.9
cotton	kg.	7.2	3.0	4.3	5.9	4.7	7.5

(1) *Statistisches Jahrbuch* 1927.
(2) Old extent of territory.
(3) Current figures.

The import of the most important foodstuffs, etc., into England is greater than before the war, which can be attributed to the increased purchasing power of the masses following on deflation.

TABLE 10.45 British imports per head of the most important foodstuffs, etc. (3)

		1913 (1)	1923 (1)	1924 (1)	1925 (2)	1926 (2)	1927 (2)
Wheat	lbs.	247.0	247.0	291.0	239.0	240.0	272.0
Flour	lbs.	29.0	29.0	27.0	22.0	26.0	27.0
Maize	lbs.	118.0	82.0	91.0	65.0	79.0	112.0
Beef	lbs.	22.0	30.6	30.4	30.2	32.7	32.3
Mutton	lbs.	13.0	14.5	12.8	13.4	13.3	13.7
Ham and Bacon	lbs.	13.7	22.6	22.3	21.3	20.5	22.3
Butter	lbs.	9.9	12.2	12.7	13.8	13.9	13.8

TABLE 10.45 British imports per head of the most important foodstuffs, etc. (3) (*cont.*)

		1913 (1)	1923 (1)	1924 (1)	1925 (2)	1926 (2)	1927 (2)
Cheese	lbs.	5.5	6.9	7.1	7.3	7.4	7.2
Sugar	lbs.	82.4	71.7	76.9	106.3	88.3	81.7
Tea	lbs.	6.7	8.5	8.8	9.0	9.2	10.1
Tobacco	lbs.	2.06	2.3	2.85	3.97	4.16	4.70
Eggs	lbs.	56.2	52.89	53.5	–	55.1	60.6
Wine	gallons	0.25	0.30	0.34	–	0.43	0.44

(1) *Statistical Abstract for the United Kingdom.*
(2) Calculated by the author on figures published in *Board of Trade Journal.*
(3) Including Northern Ireland.

Of the foodstuffs included in the table above, there is also produced at home: –

Percentage of total consumption

Meat	Eggs	Wheat	Cheese	Butter	Sugar	Bacon
43	38	28	15	10	10	7

TABLE 10.46 Industrialisation
Coal production (1,000 tons) (1)

	1913	1920	1924	1925	1926	1927
Netherlands	1,873	3,941	5,882	6,848	8,650	9,324
Spain	4,016	5,421	6,128	6,117	6,276	–
British India	16,468	18,250	21,514	21,240	21,258	21,324
China	13,776	20,669	20,524	20,500	–	–
Japan	21,316	29,245	30,111	31,459	29,191	30,460
South Africa	7,984	10,409	11,332	11,793	12,458	12,072
Australia	12,617	13,183	14,108	14,739	–	–

(1) *Statistisches Jahrbuch* 1927.

Petroleum produced (in 1,000 tons) (1)

	1913	1920	1924	1925	1926	1927
Romania	1,848	1,109	1,861	2,317	3,241	3,976
Venezuela	–	70	1,330	2,885	5,329	8,520
Persia	248	1,669	4,316	4,622	4,667	5,538
Outer India	1,526	2,365	2,926	3,066	3,064	2,840

(1)   *Statistisches Jahrbuch* 1927.
Current figures given in *The Economist*.

TABLE 10.47 Industrialisation
Iron and steel production (in 1,000 tons) (1)

	1913	1920	1924	1925	1926
Iron					
Italy	427	88	304	482	529
Spain	425	251	497	528	457
Hungary	190	–	116	93	188
Romania	–	19	46	64	85
Yugoslavia	–	6	15	35	–
Canada	1,031	1,015	629	580	749
British India	207	316	891	894	927
Japan	240	721	820	838	864
Australia	48	350	423	446	457
Steel					
Italy	934	774	1,458	1,892	1,712
Spain	242	306	545	626	578
Hungary	443	62	239	231	325
Romania	10	35	87	101	–
Canada	1,059	1,128	670	765	789
British India	32	159	340	456	457
Japan	305	844	1,098	1,168	1,219
Australia	14	170	311	357	366

(1)   *Statistisches Jahrbuch* 1927.

TABLE 10.48 Industrialisation
Number of cotton spindles (1,000) (1)

	1913	1921	1924	1925	1926
China	–	1,800	3,300	3,350	3,426
India	6,084	6,763	7,928	8,500	8,510
Japan	2,300	4,126	4,825	5,292	5,573
Brazil	1,200	1,521	1,700	1,950	2,493
Canada	855	1,100	1,167	1,319	1,167
Mexico	700	720	802	814	830
Italy	4,600	4,507	4,570	4,771	4,833
Holland	479	630	686	817	921
Portugal	480	400	503	503	503
Finland	222	240	251	253	255
Hungary	–	22	–	–	101

(1) *International Statistical Yearbook* 1926.

TABLE 10.49 Industrialisation
Use of machinery, 1913 and 1925 (1)

	Use in million mark		As a percentage of world use	
	1913	1925	1913	1925
Latin America	358	505	2.6	2.3
Japan	109	324	0.8	1.5
China	20	54	0.2	0.2
British India	139	225	1.0	1.0
Rest of Asia	75	76	0.5	0.4
Australia	152	292	1.1	1.3
Union of South Africa	64	99	0.5	0.4
Rest of Africa	43	68	0.3	0.3

(1) *Verein Deutscher Maschinenbauanstalten* 1926.

The following table gives a roughly accurate idea of the distribution of the world among the great powers and of their economic importance. We must point out that since the time to which these figures refer the share of the USSR has considerably increased. America's leadership and China's backwardness in the sphere of production are very apparent from the figures. The figures themselves are not particularly reliable.

TABLE 10.50 The great powers of the world (1)

	1,000 sq. km.	% of earth's surface	Million	% of world population	Million ha.	% of world res.	% of world prod.	% of world res.	% of world prod.
British Empire	38,240	28.0	464	26.0	203(2)	22.5	26.0	18.2	1.9
USA	10,591	7.7	132	7.1	139(3)	46.0	45.3	17.0	71.3
France & colonies	14,714	10.8	99	5.3	31(4)	1.0	5.2	2.2	–
Soviet Union	21,502	16.0	138	7.4	–	3.0	1.5	13.6	5.2
China	11,080	8.1	449	24.2	–	19.4	1.7	2.9	–
Japan	678	0.5	82	4.4	12.6	0.12	2.6	2.6	0.2
Total	96,805	71.1	1,364	73.4	–	92.02	82.3	56.5	78.6
Other countries	39,195	28.9	489	26.6	–	7.98	17.7	43.5(5)	21.4
World	136,000(6)	100.0	1,853	100.0	–	100.0	100.0	100.0	100.0

THE DECLINE OF CAPITALISM

	Iron % of world prod. (1925)	Steel % of world prod. (1925)	Motor driving power 1,000 HP	Railways 1,000 km.	Railways % world	Merchant marine 1,000 tons	Merchant marine % world	State income $million (1924)	Imports $million (1924)	Exports $mill. (1924)	Strength of army (7) (1,000)
British Empire	11.4	10.4(8)	—	249	21.1	21,504	36.6	5,623	9.9	9.2	1,001(9)
USA	49.2	50.9	29,567	415	35.1	11,605	17.7	4,012	4.0	5.2	347
France & Col.	13.9	10.2	6,600(10)	72	6.1	3,262	5.6	1,468	2.5	2.5	801
Soviet Union	2.0	2.1	—	60	5.1	—	—	—	0.12	0.7	600
China	0.6	0.2	—	12	1.0	—	—	490(11)	0.83	0.62	—
Japan	0.6	0.6	2,932	20	1.7	3,741	6.4	657	1.2	0.9	307
Total	77.7	74.4	—	828	70.1	18,673	31.7	40,112	18.55	18.59	—
Other countries	22.3	25.6	—	352	29.9	—	—	—	8.4	6.7	—
World	100.0	100.0	—	1,180	100.0	58,785	100.0	—	27.0	35.5	—

(1) Taken from the *Jahrbuch für Wirtschaft, Politik und Arbeiterbewegung 1925–26*.
(2) Great Britain, Ireland, Canada, India, Egypt, South Africa, Australia, New Zealand.
(3) Excluding colonies.
(4) France, Algeria, Morocco, Tunis.
(5) Large oilfields lie outside the immediate sphere of domination of the imperialist powers, and are objects of continual friction and disputes (Mexico, South America, USSR, Dutch India, Persia).
(6) Excluding polar regions.
(7) Including marines.
(8) Great Britain, Australia, Canada, India, New Zealand.
(9) Only France.
(10) 1919.

In recent years the theory has been maintained in the United States, particularly by Carver, that by means of small shares and workers' shares, an important part of profits is being acquired by the workers. The complete untenableness of this assertion is demonstrated by the following table:

TABLE 10.51 The workers' share of profits in the USA
The class distribution of income from profits in the USA, 1924 (1)

Income group	Number wage earners	% of wage earners	Amount of income from property, milliard $	% of total wealth
Wage earners	27,100,000	63.0	10.0	4.3
Farmers	6,385,000	14.9	39.5	17.0
Wage earners with income below 3,000 $	6,755,000	15.7	26.1	11.2
From 3,000–10,000 $	2,500,000	5.8	57.9	25.0
Over 10,000 $	260,000	0.6	98.5	42.5
Total	43,000,000	100.0	232.0	100.0

(1) Taken from *The New Republic*, 10 August 1927.

The table is drawn up on the basis of individual profit-making property and excludes property held collectively. This means that dividend and interest paid by Joint Stock Companies is included but not the internal accumulation of those Companies.

CHAPTER 11

Accumulation and Breakdown of Capitalism

It may be the case that no author has showed such an unbridled arrogance as Sir [Herr] H. Grossmann in his first book.[1,2] Already in his introduction he argues that his study has resulted 'that the method on which Marx's *Capital* was based has really been reconstructed for the first time, secondly, that an essentially new light was shed on important domains of the *theoretical system of Marx*. One of these newly acquired insights is the subjoined breakdown theory, the pillar of the economic system of Karl Marx'.[3]

Only scoundrels are modest! Grossmann has no modesty. Stressing once more his future merits of having rescued Marx, he declares some lines further: 'According to me, the unsatisfactorily situation of the actual Marx studies can be reduced to the fact *that one has until now utilized no clear research method, but, though this may be striking, one does not care for it*' (our emphasis).

'Though this may be striking', nobody cared thus until now of the Marxist research method! Hence, Grossmann is also railing at all Marxists when referring to them. *Plekhanov* is not even mentioned! *Lenin* is rejected, albeit in cautious terms, as a theoretician of imperialism! (We will return to this subject later). Yes, even *Engels* is accused of having erroneously interpreted the teachings of Marx.[4] Finally, *Marx himself is accused* of only having 'made an attempt' to explain the collapse of capitalism: 'one believes now that the definitive answer will come. But it does not come. Hence, doubts arise with regard to Marx's breakdown theory ...'.[5] Only Grossmann, and he alone, is the preferred teacher developing Marx's 'first attempts' into a theoretical system ...

We now want to see how our Marxist hero reconstructs the Marxist method.

---

1 [Originally published in *Unter dem Banner des Marxismus*, Vienna: Verlag für Literatur und Marxismus, 1930, 4, 1: 60–95].
2 Grossmann 1929.
3 Section V (if not otherwise indicated) stressed by Grossmann.
4 '*Engels has seriously underestimated this problem* (the liberation of money capital in the circulation process of capital) and even *misinterpreted* ...' (our emphasis). Grossmann 1929, p. 324. On page 195 he accuses Engels and Moore for having misinterpreted when editing the chapter on the relation between the profit rate and the surplus-value rate. 'It is in advance credible that there is here an ample chance of misunderstandings and errors and that these errors then could easily have transmitted ... to the chapter of the tendendially falling rate of profit'.
5 Grossmann 1929, p. 15.

1 Grossmann Did Not Understand the Research Method of Marx

Notwithstanding Grossmann's prepotency adjudging himself as being the first one to have reconstructed Marx's method, we nonetheless argue that he did not understand the Marxist method. In particular we want to prove this assertion by referring to his concealment of the fall of capitalism in Russia.

Grossmann's main argument – I want to develop this first – is as follows:

Contrary to the ideas defended by the 'neo-harmonists',[6] Marx's system of ideas contains a breakdown theory. 'Representing the necessity of a breakdown of the capitalist mode of production ... *by a strictly scientific analysis of the capitalist mode of production* – was the real problem Marx put forward in *Capital*'.[7] By trying to prove that capitalism should break down 'purely economically' *because of overaccumulation caused by an insufficient realisation of surplus value*,[8] Grossmann fulfils his task. Take note: this breakdown does not occur, as Marx says, because of a diminishing rate of profit 'leading to a blunting of the stimulus of accumulation',[9] but more likely by the impossibility of realising an ever rising rate of profit.

We must ask the following question:

Does Grossmann really think that he is applying Marx's research method by publishing in 1929 a book on the breakdown of capitalism without mentioning that already in 1917 capitalism had broken down in one-sixth of the world? Does he really believe that it is Marx's method of finding out *in abstracto* a possible – even if necessary – breaking up of the capitalist system, instead of studying its concrete causes? Marx never agreed on this way of proceeding! Marx has very carefully studied concrete reality. During many years he was reading and making excerpts in order to grasp the dialectical movement of his subject of research concretely. In the preface to the second German edition of *Capital*, Volume I, he writes:

---

6 [Grossmann described Otto Bauer as a 'neo-harmonist' who thinks that both workers and capitalists benefit from capitalist development].
7 Grossmann 1929, p. 5.
8 Grossmann 1929, p. 64.
9 [Varga refers here to Marx without giving any references. Marx writes in *Capital*, Volume I, 1954, p. 619: '... [A]ccumulation slackens in consequence of the rise in the price of labour, because the stimulus of gain is blunted'. In *Capital*, Volume III, 1959, pp. 236–7, one can read: 'The rate of self-expansion of the total capital, or the rate of profit, being the goad of capitalist production (just as self-expansion of capital is its only purpose), its fall checks the formation of new independent capitals and this appears as a threat to the development of the capitalist production process'].

Of course the method of presentation must differ in form from that of inquiry. The latter has to appropriate the material in details, to analyze its different forms of development, to trace out their inner connection. Only after this work is done, can the actual movement be adequately described. If this is done successfully, if the life of the subject-matter is ideally reflected as in a mirror, then it may appear as if we had before us a mere a priori construction.

But somebody who publishes in 1929 a book of some six hundred pages on the 'law of the collapse' of capitalism, without saying something about capitalism having already collapsed in Russia, can accumulate as many quotations of Marx and scholarly digressions on the method of Marxism as he wants – he nonetheless is misunderstanding the Marxist research method![10]

Why does Grossmann so tenaciously remain silent on the Russian Revolution?

It is not because he did not collect facts at all: searching everywhere in the world for evidences to underpin his theory,[11] he discovers already the existence of the *overaccumulation of capital* in the seventeenth century in Holland – already in a period when 'civil society', according to Marx, was merely '*emerging*'.[12] (Curiously, capitalism did not yet 'collapse' in Holland!)

---

10 The provisional fall of the bourgeoisie in Hungary was, when compared to the fall of the bourgeoisie in Russia, a rather minor event. Lenin, however, has repeatedly and personally insisted that the history of the fall of the bourgeoisie in Hungary should be written; he said that my book would be 'translated into all languages of the world'. That is how Lenin estimated the importance of the short-lived Hungarian dictatorship for the better understanding of the fate of capitalism. Sir Grossmann, however, passes under silence the Russian Revolution and he thinks he is a Marxist!

11 Many times he finds evidences in history: but one should not forget Lenin's wise words: 'in view of the extreme complexity of the phenomena of social life it is always possible to select any number of examples or separate data to prove any proposition' (Foreword to the French and German edition of *Imperialism*). Lenin 1964e, p. 190.

12 [Varga refers here to Marx's Preface to *A Contribution to the Critique of Political Economy*. See Marx 1977. Marx is, however, giving a broader meaning to the term of 'civil society'. He writes: 'The first work which I undertook to dispel the doubts assailing me was a critical re-examination of the Hegelian philosophy of law; the introduction to this work being published in the *Deutsch-Französische Jahrbücher* issued in Paris in 1844. My inquiry led me to the conclusion that neither legal relations nor political forms could be comprehended whether by themselves or on the basis of a so-called general development of the human mind, but that on the contrary they originate in the material conditions of life, the totality of which Hegel, following the example of English and French thinkers of the eighteenth century, embraces within the term "civil society"; that the anatomy of this civil society, however, has to be sought in political economy. The study of this, which I began

He stubbornly keeps silent on the fall of capitalism in Russia, because *it is evident that those causes leading according to Grossmann to the breakdown of capitalism were not playing a role in the collapse of capitalism in Russia.* Indeed: arguing that capitalism had broken down in Russia because of overaccumulation of capital would be ridiculous because – as it is widely known – the country was lacking capital and therefore it had to import large amounts of foreign capital! For the same reason one cannot speak of overaccumulation of capital in Hungary. Just like a real Talmudist, Grossmann anxiously avoids confronting his theory with reality. We also want to ask: what is the worth of a causal theory of an 'inevitable breaking up' of capitalism if these causes cannot be applied to two *real* cases of a collapsing capitalist regime? Grossmann should at least recognise that capitalist hegemony may also collapse because of other reasons than his fatal breakdown theory. As ancient logic puts it correctly: *De esse ad posse valet consequentia*, or denying something that really exists will be impossible.

For us, who are the *struggling Communists*, it is a great reassurance that the real breakdown of capitalism cannot be imputed to the causal mechanism widely advertised by Sir Grossmann: as we later shall argue, the infallible breakdown scheme of the pseudo-Marxist Grossmann extends capitalism's lifetime by hundreds of years, while the real Marxists, who are not only writing thick books, but who are also actively working at its downfall, are hoping for capitalism's breakdown in the whole world within a foreseeable historical future, long before 'overaccumulation' of capital will succeed in bringing down capitalism.

But Grossmann has another reason for avoiding any analysis of the concrete breakdown of capitalism in Russia and Hungary. In his vision, which is related to that of [Rosa] Luxemburg, much accumulated capital was destroyed by the war and this had postponed the breakdown of capitalism. He writes: 'Far from being a ... circumstance ... speeding up the decay of capitalism ... the destructions and devaluations caused by the war are much more an expedient weakening than a menacing collapse'.[13]

To everybody who knows about the history of the fall of the bourgeoisie in Russia, it should be really clear that the war was one of the most important causes of the breakdown, that without a lost war and without 'the transformation of the imperialist war into a civil war',[14] this breakdown would not have

---

in Paris, I continued in Brussels, where I moved owing to an expulsion order issued by M. Guizot. The general conclusion at which I arrived and which, once reached, became the guiding principle of my studies can be summarised as follows'].

13 Grossmann 1929, p. 369.
14 [Varga is giving a nod to Lenin's *Imperialism* book].

occurred. Grossmann's theory of the war having postponed the breakdown is belied by the facts. (Of course, we should not fall into the error of the opposite and *only* hold that a victorious proletarian revolution is possible as a consequence of the war). Grossmann anxiously avoids mentioning the Russian Revolution because the latter is absolutely contrary to his war theory.

Grossmann's total incomprehension of the dialectical method is shown by his view on the war as a phenomenon. For him a war is a war missing any dialectical concreteness. Any war postpones the breakdown. But for a dialectical Marxist, things look different. By its breaking out a war can postpone a crisis announced by important inventories of unsold commodities if the war is fought outside its own territory, if the war does not last too long and ends up in a victory, eventually accompanied by an acquisition of new colonial territories: such a war *can* postpone an economic breakdown. If a war is lasting for a long period of time, then it can lead to a 'breakdown' and to acute revolutionary situations. In that case it is not the 'attained degree of overaccumulation of capital' that decides on a breakdown or a survival of the capitalist social order, but the armed struggle in a civil war. Grossman's thesis that 'the war' is postponing the breakdown is a mechanical, an un-Marxist, thus an incorrect one. If the World War would have lasted longer, a final downfall of the hegemony of the bourgeoisie in many parts of Europe would have been possible instead of the rise of a short-lived and isolated dictatorship of the proletariat in Hungary.

Furthermore: Grossmann does not consider the imperialist war as an element in a dialectical development of capitalism, but as something fortuitous, influenced from outside. He writes:

> Postponement (Bucharin) is *not the result of economic causes*, not of an inevitable proper economic law of the capitalist mechanism itself, but caused by the war, by an *extra-economic force*, disturbing from outside the production system ... Such a breakdown would mean 'the revelation of a transcending cause that is nonetheless working in the economy'.[15]

Hence, when Grossmann reduces on the one hand the 'breakdown' to just one cause, i.e. overaccumulation, which is also causing competition of foreign trade, capital export and crises (for obtaining just one *causa movens*, he denies all other contradictions), but on the other hand he mechanically separates the war as an 'extra-economic force' from the total capitalist development process in the economy. This is totally undialectical and un-Marxist.

---

15   Grossmann 1929, pp. 47–8.

This undialectical and thus un-Marxist interpretation permeates the whole book. He separates the economy from the class struggle,[16] hence *his* 'breakdown' does not mean the fall of the capitalist social order. It is a pure economic fantasy: it is a matter of reaching the point of no return where, according to Otto Bauer's scheme that is fully accepted by Grossmann, the capitalists should – even if they are unable to do it – nevertheless accumulate. The breakdown does not mean the end of class hegemony for Grossmann, but the incapacity of the bourgeoisie to accumulate as is foreseen in Otto Bauer's schemes.

It should nonetheless be clear that – although accumulation of capital is important for capitalism – to stop accumulating does not also mean an immediate breakdown of capitalism. Hence, (1) in every industrial cycle there is a moment of no accumulation; (2) it is well conceivable that the bourgeoisie in the era of sluggish monopoly capitalism will maintain its class hegemony for a certain period of time, even without accumulating in the form of a simple reproduction, as long as the proletariat does not overthrow them; or the possibility of accumulating is restored again.[17] But Grossmann is practising Talmudism instead of dialectics, hence he is unable to understand this.

A lack of the faintest notion of dialectics characterises the whole book. All digressions on the 'levels of abstractions' in Marx, on the 'system of abstraction', and his attempt to eliminate all contradictions in order to find a single *causa movens* for all phenomena: all this is not Marx's method. *Without dialectics, no Marxist method!*

One can now shrug one's shoulders and reject Grossmann's theory if he had not have given the impression by stockpiling Marx quotes that he is an orthodox Marxist interpreting Marxist theory. This may create confusion. *Grossmann is not afraid of committing gross falsifications* in order to make Marx responsible of his own undialectical, un-Marxist theory of overaccumulation as the single *causa movens*: he quotes sentences Marx used in a totally different context in order to underpin his theory, he eliminates sentences from the quotes if the latter do not please him, but without mentioning it, and therefore *he forges Marx's theory*. Paying ample attention to this book is thus necessary.

---

16   In the preface to his book he protests against the suspicion of 'pure economism': 'Wasting even a word on the relation between economy and politics would be superfluous, he said'! Wasting words is something, but an economy without class struggle is not Marxism.

17   We remind that the German bourgeoisie neglected for a moment not only to accumulate, but even to appropriate surplus value in order to bring the proletariat not in a revolutionary mood and thus gain enough time for the reconstruction of their repressive apparatus having fallen into decay.

Grossmann is finally forging himself. He poses himself as the only true Marxist towering high above the multitude of epigones and neo-harmonists. *But he is completely hiding his political profile!* Throughout his book he neither pronounces himself in favour of the dictatorship of the proletariat, nor in favour of the necessary armed struggle against the bourgeoisie, he never makes a stand in favour of the Soviet Union. However, these are questions separating true Marxists from traitors defending capitalism by using a Marxist phraseology. Grossmann remains silent. One is not communicating if one is not considering the actual regime in the Soviet Union as the beginning of the construction of socialism or, as Kautsky did, does not see the Soviet Union as a kind of primitive, bad capitalism? Grossmann remains silent. But keeping quiet is not permitted for a Marxist; hiding one's political profile is not done! He must speak out, even at the risk of missing the possibility of becoming a professor at the University of Frankfurt! *Hic Rhodus, hic salta!*

2 Grossmann's Great Discovery: The Incorrectness of Bauer's Reproduction Scheme

The essence of Grossmann's book is made by his discovery that O. Bauer's scheme is erroneous – as far as this may prove the possibility of a crisisless capitalist reproduction scheme. According to Bauer's reproduction scheme, accumulation cannot continuously go on: after a certain period of time a 'breakdown' will occur as a result of 'overaccumulation'; the appropriated surplus value will not suffice to feed capitalists and workers when sustaining the strictly dictated pace of accumulation; hence, m will not be large enough to generate the necessary variable capital v; hence, because of overaccumulation of capital, a huge unemployment will develop until the breakdown is there. However, before the moment of breakdown periodical crises will occur and, because of capital destruction, this will lead to a decrease of overaccumulation, etc. which will postpone the moment of breakdown. The main question is now:[18] 'Can accumulation continue further on without stopping the reproduction process, i.e. will the *realisation process* get stuck if considered from a capitalist point of view?' Because the conditions set by O. Bauer cannot be based on these schemes, this should be answered *negatively*. This base is:[19] 'This equilibrium between accumulation and population growth can, however, only be realised

---

18   Grossmann 1929, pp. 92–3.
19   [Otto Bauer 1912–13, p. 869].

on the condition that the accumulation rates increase so fast that, notwithstanding a growing organic composition of capital, variable capital grows as fast as the population'.

But in the long-run the rate of accumulation cannot grow as fast as shown in O. Bauer's scheme. However, there occurs nonetheless a breakdown!

Before going into details, we only want to argue that Bauer and Grossmann put the problem in an undialectical way. From the point of view of the internal laws of capitalism, Marx considers the cyclical evolution of the reproduction process with its periodical crises in which the immanent contradictions, at least for the capitalist mode of production at this level of its development, will inevitably come suddenly to a violent breakdown. *O. Bauer is a harmonist of the future, while Grossmann is a harmonist of the past.* O. Bauer, however, thinks that he discovered thanks to his scheme that an undisturbed, crisisless development of capitalist accumulation is possible. Grossmann explains the crises exclusively by overaccumulation and he necessarily accepts a period of capitalism in which overaccumulation is still absent, in which there are thus no crises, because he does not want to fall back into the ridiculous assertion that the capitalist mode of production started with overaccumulation of capital. Grossmann may attack the neo-harmonists as much as he wants, but in reality he is himself a harmonist, because he has no idea about dialectics!

We now are going to discuss the Bauer-Grossmann scheme.

TABLE 11.1 Otto Bauer's scheme

Years	C	V	K	a_c	a_v	Yearly production value	Consumption of capitalists in % of surplus value	Accumulation rate $a_c - a_v$ in % of surplus value	Surplus value in %k+a_c c+ a_v k+a_c c+a_v
1st I	120,000	+50,000	+37,500	+10,000	+2,500	=220,000	75	25	
1st II	80,000	+50,000	+37,500	+10,000	+2,500	=180,000	75	25	
Total	200,000	+100,000	+75,000	+20,000	+5,000	=400,000	75	25	33
2nd I	134,666	+53,667	+39,740	+11,244	+2,683	=242,000	74.05	25.95	
2nd II	85,334	+51,333	+38,010	+10,756	+2,567	=188,000	74.05	25.95	
Total	220,000	+105,000	+77,750	+22,000	+5,250	=430,000	74.05	25.95	32.6
3rd I	151,048	+57,576	+42,070	+12,638	+2,868	=266,200	73.0	26.96	
3rd II	90,952	+52,674	+38,469	+11,562	+2,643	=196,300	73.04	26.96	
Total	242,000	+110,250	+80539	+24,200	+5,511	=462,500	73.04	26.96	31.3

TABLE 11.1   Otto Bauer's scheme (cont.)

Years	C	V	K	a_c	a_v	Yearly production value	Consumption of capitalists in % of surplus value	Accumulation rate $a_c - a_v$ in % of surplus value	Surplus value in %k+a_c c+ a_v k+a_c c+a_v
4th I	169,124	+61,738	+44,465	+14,186	+3,087	=292,600	72.02	27.98	
4th II	96,876	+54,024	+38,909	+12,414	+2,701	=204,924	73.02	27.98	
Total	266,000	+115,762	+83,374	+26,600	+5,788	=497,524	72.02	27.98	30.3

c   constant capital.
v   variable capital.
k   surplus value consumed by the capitalists.
a_c accumulation of constant capital (Bauer called it α).
a_v accumulation of variable capital (Bauer called it β). The condition is that the whole stock of constant capital of a society should be converted once a year into money.

Everything seems to pass off in quiet harmony. Grossmann's great discovery is that the usefulness of this scheme is limited. Or mathematically formulated: the *curve* of Bauer's scheme does not show a continuous, but a discontinuous trend.

According to Grossmann, Bauer's scheme can only be applied under condition that[20]

> ... [F]or the time being one considers the reproduction process only from the value side (i.e. Grossmann eliminates disproportionality between sector I and II!), and the analysis is constantly carried out under conditions *favourable* for the existence of capitalism, i.e. under condition of an equilibrium between production and turnover.

---

20   Grossmann 1929, p. 105, n. 58.

TABLE 11.2 The Bauer-Grossmann scheme

Years	c	v	k	a_c	a_v	Yearly production value	Consumption of capitalists in %	Accumulation rate a_c-a_v in % of surplus value	Surplus value in % k+a_c c+a_v K+a^c c+a^v
1st	200,000	+100,000	+75,000	+20,000	+5,000	=400,000	75	25	33.0
5th	292,600	+121,550	+86,213	+29,260	+6,077	=535,700	70.93	29.07	29.3
10th	471,234	+155,130	+100,251	+47,123	+7,756	=781,494	64.63	35.37	24.7
20th	1,222,252	+252,691	+117,832	+122,225	+12,634	=1,727,634	43.63	53.37	17.1
30th	3,170,200	+411,602	+73,822	+317,200	+20,580	=3,993,404	17.97	82.03	11.5
35th	5,105,637	+525,319	+0	+510,563	+14,756	=6,156,275	0	104.61(!)	9.3
36th									
a) capital available: 5,616,200	a) population available: 551,584			required: 26,265 deficit: 11,509					
b) capital in operation: 5,499,015(*)	b) active population: +540,075	+0	+540,075	+0	=6,696,350	0	109.35(!)	8.7
surplus capital: 117.185	reserve army: 11,509		required: 561,620 deficit: 21,545	required: 27,003 deficit: 27,003					
			total deficit: 48,548						

(*) 5,616,200 : 551,584 = 5,499,015 : 540,075

Grossmann is so happy with his discovery that he considers the predicted breakdown in his absurd writings as a concrete fact:

> Already for the coming 35 years the k-part of surplus value, thus the capitalists will obtain no foodstuffs for daily consumption, because all available foodstuffs must (!) be used for accumulation, but, nonetheless, there will arise a food deficit of 11,508 a_v ... The system breaks down, the coming crisis of the system epitomizes the collapse of its realisation. (Which realisation? That of capital!) Under the already mentioned conditions no

accumulation of capital will be possible after 35 years. The task of the entrepreneurs will be to manage a production system whose yield will go exclusively to the working class. Already after 35 years accumulated capital will not generate enough profits to guarantee entrepreneurs the necessary k-part for their consumption.[21]

Crises, capital export and imperialism are the outcome of this overaccumulation. This is Marx's real breakdown theory, for which Marx, indeed, drafted 'preliminary texts', but it is Grossmann's privilege to reconstruct this theory. And then he starts an endless series of Marx quotes to convince the reader that Grossmann's breakdown theory has really been inspired by Marx. In order to prove this, Grossmann is not afraid of forging texts by citing sentences Marx never wrote or by employing them in a totally different context and by presenting them as evidences. (This was eased by the fact that he confuses the tendentially falling rate of profit caused by the growing organic composition of capital, which is essentially – but not in a period of crises – a continuing process, with falling realisation caused by overaccumulation). We will give some crass examples of these forgeries.

On page 79, line 80, Grossmann quotes the following sentence of Marx's *Capital*, Volume 3, 1:[22] 'This process would soon *bring about the collapse of capitalist production* if it were not for counteracting tendencies, which have a continuous decentralising effect alongside the centripetal one'.[23]

Let us have a look at the text of *Capital*. Starting with a minor item, we find first of all that Grossmann's words 'bring about the collapse' are *not stressed in Marx's* text, but Grossmann hides this from his readers. Normally, this is especially inadmissible in the case of Marx, who reputedly stressed his words exceptionally! The paragraph, in which Grossmann quotes this sentence in an attempt of saddling up Marx with his breakdown theory, Marx discusses – in a polemic against 'the [fantastic idea of] priest Chalmers'[24] – the question of the growing volume of profits when profit rates are falling. In his conclusion Marx writes:

---

21 Grossmann 1929, pp. 121–2.
22 [Varga refers to the German edition: Marx 1921, *Das Kapital. Kritik der politischen Oekonomie*, Volume 3, 1 (Chapters 1–28), fifth edition, Hamburg: Otto Meissners Verlag. This quote is not on page 227, but on page 228].
23 Marx 1959, p. 241.
24 [In *Capital* (1959, p. 241) Marx refers to Thomas Chalmers (1832, p. 88). Thomas Chalmers (1788–1847) was a Scottish theologian and economist].

> However, this requires a simultaneous concentration of capital, since the conditions of production then demand employment of capital on a larger scale. It also requires its centralization, i.e., the swallowing up of the small capitalists by the big and their deprivation of capital. It is again but an instance of separating – raised to the second power – the conditions of production from the producers to whose number these small capitalists still belong, since their own labour continues to play a role in their case. The labour of a capitalist stands altogether in inverse proportion to the size of his capital, i.e., to the degree in which he is a capitalist. It is this same severance of the conditions of production, on the one hand, from the producers, on the other, that forms the conception of capital. It begins with primitive accumulation [Buch I, Kap. XXIV; English edition: Part VIII. – *Ed.*], appears as a permanent process in the accumulation and concentration of capital, and expresses itself finally as centralization of existing capitals in a few hands and a deprivation of many of their capital (to which expropriation is now changed). This process would soon bring about the collapse of capitalist production if it were not for counteracting tendencies, which have a continuous decentralizing effect alongside the centripetal one.[25]

Any reader should see that 'this process' is not referring to Grossmann's 'pure theory of economic breakdown' caused by overaccumulation, but to the *economic and social process* of centralisation of capital into the hands of a few owners: because of capital centralisation the periodical crises are deepening while the disproportion between the divisions I and II are periodically sharpening.

Meanwhile, the number of people with a stake in the existence of capitalism is also quickly diminishing, the social basis of capitalism is rapidly narrowing and, *in this way*, '[this] process would soon bring about the collapse of capitalist production if it were not for counteracting tendencies which have a continuous decentralizing effect alongside the centripetal one'.[26] Hence, this out-of-context quote of Marx Grossmann uses here for his theory is a matter of crude forgery. One can find many similar forgeries in Grossmann's book.

Let us return to the Bauer-Grossmann accumulation scheme. It is not necessary to be a great mathematician to find out that the Bauer scheme – and any other scheme of a similar nature – must lead to a final 'moment of breaking down'!

---

25   Marx 1959, p. 241.
26   Marx 1959, p. 246.

Indeed: surplus value m contributing to growth of a_c and a_v, always equals v, because the rate of surplus value always equals 100 percent. Because a_c, which is not contributing to the growth of surplus value m, increases each year by 10 percent of c (always available constant capital), but v depends on an increase of m by about 5 percent of the always available variable capital; hence, the moment must necessarily be near – no matter what the initial amount may be – that surplus value m will no longer suffice to sustain the hitherto fast developing accumulation process.[27] (If one splits m into a_c defined as an independent variable,[28] and in a_v and k defined as dependent variables, then it is very clear that k will disappear earlier – the capitalists will no longer be able to consume if they wish to continue accumulating just like before – hence a 5 percent transfer of a_c to v will not suffice).

In a scheme like Bauer's and Grossmann's in which the accumulation rate is constantly increasing, i.e. the part of k reserved for self-consumption of the capitalists, it is on the contrary very clear that k must disappear when nearing a certain level of accumulation.

The question should now be raised: is the Bauer-Grossmann scheme conceived according to Marx? Because of two main reasons this is not the case:

1. The assumption of *a rapid increase in the organic composition of capital* is contrary to the basic tenets of Marx (the scheme starts with a ratio c/v = 2 to 1; after 10 years it is 5 to 1, after 30 years it is 7 to 1), *on the condition, however, that the rate of surplus remains unchanged at 100 percent*. The increase in the organic composition of capital requires increased labour productivity, thus less socially necessary labour time per unity product will be demanded: or, formulated in money terms, a decrease in production cost per unity. The precondition of the increase in the organic composition of individual capitals – total social capital is the sum of all individual capitals – is that the individual capitalist can produce cheaper after having invested in new production processes which will practically always increase the organic composition of capital. Generalised for total social capital, this means a diminishing of the amount of foodstuffs the worker earns in his working time, thus also a decrease in the necessary

---

27 A compound interest increasing with 10 percent a year must result – if the first member of the comparison is a positive number – in a higher growth after a mathematically predictable but very long period than a compound interest growing with 5 percent, even if the first member of the comparison is as large as possible. Hence, a 10 percent increase in constant capital at a mere 5 percent's increase in variable capital cannot continue infinitely!

28 [Varga uses the word 'variant'].

labour time, an increase in the surplus time, i.e. an increase in the rate of surplus labour time. Hence, the Bauer-Grossmann scheme is contradictory to the basic tenets of Marx.[29] If the rate of surplus value would remain unchanged notwithstanding rising labour productivity, this would imply a rapid increase in the living standard of the proletariat together with productivity growth, but this is absolutely contradictory to Marx's theory of wage formation during accumulation.

2. The Bauer-Grossmann thesis of a *rising accumulation rate* is erroneous, i.e. the assumption that the capitalist class will consume an ever diminishing *part* of the appropriated surplus value. By quoting Marx in his polemic with Boudin,[30] Grossmann tries to prove that this was also Marx's opinion; meanwhile *he commits an unprecedented forgery* by quoting the next sentence from *Capital*, Volume 3: 'A fall in the rate of profit and accelerated accumulation are different expressions of the same process only in so far as both reflect the development of productiveness'.[31] If we consult the original text we see that this does not refer to the accumulation *rate* Grossmann is attributing to Marx, but to the *amount* of newly accumulated capitals. And at the end of the paragraph in which he is underpinning his insights, we read explicitly the contrary of which he is claiming: '[...] Through expropriation of minor capitalists, the few direct producers who still have anything left to be expropriated. This accelerates *accumulation with regard to mass, although the rate of accumulation falls with the rate of profit*'[32] (our emphasis). We remark that Marx clearly says the contrary of what Grossmann tries to prove by using a half a sentence situated at the beginning of the same paragraph! Really, this man is not only pretending that nobody else had ever better understood Marx, but also had ever understood the text of *Capital*!

The construction of the Bauer-Grossmann scheme increasing the accumulation rate from 25 percent to 99.5 percent within 34 years, is incompatible with Marx's theory stating that the rate of accumulation diminishes because of a falling rate of profit! Marx would never have supported the stupid idea that, notwithstanding a huge amount of profits, the whole capitalist class would renounce consumption because of accumulation. Moreover, Grossmann

---

29   Grossmann notices this contradiction, but he passes over it.
30   Grossmann 1929, p. 120, n. 79. [Louis B. Boudin (1872–1952), born Louis Boudianoff, was a Russian-born American Marxist theoretician].
31   Marx 1959, p. 236.
32   Ibid.

should not have adhered to the idea that *competition* which is absent in his capitalism theory, *only exists but from the moment when overaccumulation begins!* It is hardly understandable why individual capitalists should increase accumulation at any price and at their own costs until overaccumulation follows even when the incentive of competition is absent. According to Lenin, imperialism's *idleness* is responsible for a diminishing real accumulation of productive capital, a stagnating technical progress and a parasitical rentier capitalism, i.e. all elements which are entirely contradictory to Grossmann's theory!

When integrating these two moments contradictory to Marx into the Bauer-Grossmann scheme – i.e. an increase in the rate of surplus value corresponding to an increase in the organic composition of capital with a falling rather than increasing rate of accumulation – *the special feature of Grossmann's construction, i.e. the 'breakdown' of realisation, would already* have disappeared *at a profit rate of 10 percent.* In a correct scheme the profit rate will tendentially fall to zero, i.e. as is taught by Marx, to the point where the 'incentive' to further accumulation will disappear: of course, this will not occur in a continuous and harmonious process, but in a succession of crises in which the contradictions of the capitalist mode of production will end in a violent solution. In a correctly constructed Marxist scheme there is no place for a 'purely economic breakdown', but, on the contrary, only for a set of economic, social and political assumptions jointly creating an acute revolutionary situation …

The construction of a 'correct' scheme implies no difficulties: but we think that this effort will be in vain; all these schemes will only contribute to the creation of some kind of approximate illustrations of a much more complex reproduction process. Believing like Bauer, Hilferding, etc. that proportionality between I and II can however generate a crisis-free development is an illusion. An inventory of the preconditions for a crisis-free capitalist reproduction process would necessitate an endless scheme impossibly reflecting *reality*!

3 Grossmann's Breakdown Scheme and Reality

As we already saw, Grossmann does not prove the correctness of his theory of the capitalist breakdown in Russia and Hungary by making a reality test. Nor does he want to test his scheme to real capitalism.[33] We want to help him here a little bit.

---

33   Prospecting the dialectical character of Marx's method, he writes: 'Marx's argumentation

Bauer assumes a rather arbitrary population growth of 5 percent. He could do that by setting up a scheme that merely illustrates his arguments against Luxemburg's theory of the impossibility of realising the surplus value within pure capitalism. Grossmann *cannot make such an assumption, because he draws historical conclusions from the scheme concerning the past and future of capitalism!*

During the last year for which statistics are available, population grew according to *Table 11.3* in percentages as follows:

TABLE 11.3   Population growth in percentages

Germany	Belgium	England	France	Italy	Poland	Japan	USA	British India
0.64	0.57	0.44	0.16	1.09	1.39	1.70	0.96	0.89

A population increase of more than 2 percent only exists in the USSR and in some totally insignificant small countries. In all big capitalist countries, except Poland, Japan and Italy, the rate of population growth is lower than 1 percent. A calculated average for the whole world does not exist: it is, however, obvious that it could be about 1 percent. If a scheme is not used as a mere *illustration* of the laws of movement of capitalism, but used for concrete historical conclusions, one should not assume a population growth of 5 percent, but a real population growth of 1 percent!

The assumption of a yearly increase in constant capital by about 10 percent in capitalist society, as presupposed by the Bauer-Grossmann, is also unrealistic. This would lead to the fantastic outcome that constant capital increases 25-fold within 35 years! One should only refer to the numerous surveys of enterprises conducted in various countries to see that such an increase of constant capital is clearly contradicted by reality![34]

---

has the character of a deduction ... With regard to such deductions, Oppenheimer gives the following excellent comment: "Hence, any reference to experience is illicit. A deduction will not be accepted by the fact that its result sconform to the experience"'. Grossmann 1929, p. 63. And that should be Marx's method! Note: the formal correctness of a deduction is not justified by the fact that the result coincides with the experience. But if the *result of the deduction* does not coincide with the scientific meaning of this word, then the deduction should be obviously incorrect.

34   'Capital' of American industry – in this country and type of production, capital has surely increased faster than in the whole world – shows the following growth statistic:

Grossmann is thus abstractly-theoretically spoken right in the following assertion, but on the condition that his arguments are explained in Marxist terms:

> As long as the whole economy is growing faster than population – and the continuous progression to a higher organic composition of capital is a necessary precondition imposed by capitalism – a point has to be reached during this process where realisation will become insufficient and where absolute overaccumulation will necessarily start. Hence, this can only be avoided in capitalism if c is accumulating at the same pace as population growth. But, in capitalism this would mean renouncing to technical progress.[35]

If Grossmann means with the expression that 'realisation will become insufficient' because the profit rate is tendentially falling, thus – with the overcoming of countertendencies – that the rate of profit is nearing the o bottom line, and that this should lead to a *disappearance of driving forces of accumulation*, his explanations are correct: he is only repeating what Marx already said. But when speaking *in this* sense of overaccumulation, that will also really occur, but only *on the condition* that the capitalist mode about overproduction will exist for a sufficiently long period of time. But he is completely wrong when explaining this in his own way by calculating that a 'breakdown' caused by overaccumulation will already happen at a profit rate of 10 percent. As we already argued, a correct scheme set up with a growing productivity accompanied by an increasing rate of exploitation, with a falling rate of accumulation, with data about

TABLE 11.4 Growth of American capital (in milliards of dollars)

	1879	1889	1899	1909	1914	Growth in 35 years
Capital	2.8	6.5	9.8	18.4	22.7	Eightfold
Wages	0.9	1.9	2.0	3.4	4.1	Four-and-a half-fold

As indicated in the *Biennial Census of Manufactures 1925*, the data of 'capital' are giving 'rough approximations only'. It is safe to assume that the value of buildings includes the price of the building site (capitalised building site rent), thus that the given sum is too high. Hence, here where capital accumulation was highest with only an eightfold increase in 35 years, and not with a 25-fold increase as indicated in Grossmann's scheme! Is this only the case in the American economy or also in the whole capitalist world?

35   Grossmann 1929, p. 147.

population growth and with an increase in constant capital near to reality, including also those countertendencies slowing down the falling profit rate, will signify that, until such a low profit rate can be attained and 'realisation is insufficient', a period of 35 years (counted at the hand of an already very high organic composition of capital from 2 to 1) will be insufficient, but also that this would require a period of time much longer than capitalism ever existed in Russia!

On the one hand, we also see that capitalism's real breakdown has already occurred in Russia well before one could have been talking about overaccumulation. On the other hand, as Grossmann tries to explain the crisis of overaccumulation by exclusively referring to overaccumulation, he must already presume the existence of overproduction during the period of the manufacture. Because overaccumulation can only occur in his scheme in the case of an extraordinarily high organic composition of capital (in the scheme a diminishing k part begins with an organic composition of 5 to 11!), such a composition of capital would be unthinkable in such an early period. Grossmann's conclusions based on Bauer's scheme are thus incorrect.

4   Grossmann's Incorrect Crisis Theory

Grossmann's crisis theory is very simple: if abstracting from the polemical passages in which he is attacking the bourgeois theories as well as those of all Marxists (also Engels) explaining Marx's crisis theory, and leaving out of consideration the *trivial games*[36] *with different schemes*, we obtain the following scheme:

The *crisis occurs* – regardless of any disproportionality – *merely as a result of capital overaccumulation* in the form of an 'insufficient realisation' because – on the condition of a constant rate of surplus value – the exploited population cannot generate sufficient surplus value to finance the amount of newly accumulated capital required by this strict scheme. Once accumulation of capital has reached the point of no return, thus where k (thus where the individual

---

36   We can give a humorous example of these trivial games: because Grossmann never paid any attention at checking his arithmetical examples, yes, he even rejects it *in principle*, he takes (p. 216) an organic composition of 200,000 c and 25,000 v as his starting point. We only need to proceed further and, instead of 25,000 v, we take only 20,000 v, i.e. a composition of 10 to 1: in this case the scheme cannot start functioning, because at a surplus rate of some 10 percent surplus value will already be insufficient for covering a^c during the first year. Capitalists and workers must starve!

capitalists start consuming a part of surplus value) is disappearing, there *'the crisis sets in'*. *'The crisis is thus an interrupted and a not yet completely developed breakdown tendency'*.[37] The turning-point of the crisis depends on:[38]
1. the height of the organic composition of capital;
2. the size of the rate of surplus value;
3. the height of the rate of accumulation a_c;
4. the height of the rate of accumulation a_v.

When these elements of the system are known, then one can calculate the period of accumulation and when the final turning-point will be met.

The crisis is shaping the countertendencies against the tendentially falling rate of profit (destruction of constant capital, wage cuts and, hence, also increasing rates of surplus value, etc.) and recreates the possibility of 'realisation within a predictable period of time'; but this will not automatically lead to a 'breakdown', to a new crisis.

In several hundreds of pages he tries to prove:
a) That this is the real meaning of Marx's view on the 'crisis in pure capitalism'.
b) That the symptoms of the crisis given in bourgeois descriptions of the business cycles can only acquire a sense thanks to Grossmann's explanations.

Now we argue:
a) That Grossman's crisis theory is contradictory to the assertions of Marx and Lenin.
b) That the quotes Grossmann borrowed from Marx are not related to real capitalism, but to an unreal case of overaccumulation of capital deduced from Marx's theory.
c) That Grossmann's crisis theory is inadequate to explain the real crisis.

a) Let us start with the first point:

Marx already situated the *possibility* of crises in the very existence of the commodity economy: because the *money owner* is not forced to spend his money at purchasing goods; thus the circulation process C–M–C can always be interrupted at stage M. Furthermore – at a higher level – because money can be used as a means of payment, the claims of payment can be interrupted which can lead to a credit crunch and, hence, also to a general crisis. Marx nonetheless protested against the idea that in a capitalist mode of production the possibility of the crises is given, 'and consequently their occurrence is itself

---

37 Grossmann 1929, p. 290.
38 Grossmann 1929, p. 225.

merely a *matter of chance*'.[39] Hence, as such there is no contradiction between Marx and Grossmann.

The contradiction begins with the stress on the *necessity* of a crisis. Grossmann only knows the problem he constructed himself about overaccumulation caused by failed realisation: *only the value form exists for him*. He wants to explain the crisis by assuming that it is not caused by a realisation problem, that there is no problem between Departments I and II. That the overaccumulation process is necessarily causing a disproportion between Departments I and II and so laying the basis of the periodical crises, that the limited purchasing power of the masses forms an element of disproportion: all these elements are rejected by Grossmann as erroneous or of secondary importance, as obviously contradictory to the views of Marx and Lenin.

We want to remind the reader of the passages in which Marx summarises his views on the problem of the crises best:

> The conditions of direct exploitation, and those of realising it, are not identical. They diverge not only in place and time, but also logically. The first are only limited by the productive power of society, the latter by the proportional relation of the various branches of production and the consumer power of society. But this last-named is not determined either by the absolute productive power, or by the absolute consumer power, but by the consumer power based on antagonistic conditions of distribution, which reduce the consumption of the bulk of society to a minimum varying within more or less narrow limits. It is furthermore restricted by the tendency to accumulate, the drive to expand capital and produce surplus-value on an extended scale. This is law of capitalist production, imposed by incessant revolutions in the methods of production themselves, by the depreciation of existing capital always bound up with them, by the general competitive struggle and the need to improve production and expand its scale merely as a means of self-preservation and under penalty of ruin. The market must, therefore, be continually extended, so that its interrelations and the conditions regulating them assume more and more the form of a natural law working independently of the producer, and become ever more uncontrollable. This internal contradiction seeks to resolve itself

---

39   Marx 1970, p. 513. A general, abstract possibility of a crisis means nothing – as *the most abstract* form of crisis, without content, without real motif. Sale and purchase can fall apart. They are thus *potential sources* of a crisis [Krisen *potentia*]. 'The factors which turn this possibility of crisis into [an actual] crisis are not contained in this form itself'. Marx 1970, p. 509.

through expansion of the outlying field of production. But the more productiveness develops, the more it finds itself at variance with the narrow basis on which the conditions of consumption rest.[40]

Defending the same point of view Lenin asserts: '... [T]he irregular production of a surplus-product (crises) is inevitable in a capitalist society as a result of the disturbance in proportion between the various branches of industry'.[41]

What would Grossmann have said in response to this remark? Well, he would have declared that this passage is not giving the 'most abstract' version of Marx's explanations,[42] that the texts of *Capital*, Volumes 2 and 3, were not correctly edited by Engels![43] Nevertheless, *we* maintain that Engels understood Marx's theory as well as Grossmann did and that there is no reason for a textual revision of Volumes 2 and 3 as requested by Grossmann. That is why there exists an unmistakable contradiction between Grossmann's crises theory of accumulation which is exclusively based on value, and the crisis theory of Marx, Engels and Lenin based on value and the natural form of commodities (disproportions between I and II caused by accumulation), i.e. social purchasing power is here limited because of an antagonistic income distribution and a boundless expansion of capitalist production!

b) But what about the Marx quotes Grossmann is using in order to prove that his theory is the real crisis theory of Marx?

---

40 Marx 1959, pp. 239–40.
41 Lenin quoted in Bucharin 1926, p. 58. See Lenin 1964f, p. 161.
42 Quoting Marx, Grossmann declares explicitly on p. 291: '"Realisation disappears. *In times of crisis* ... the rate of profit, and with it the demand for industrial capital, has to all intents and purpose disappeared" (Marx 1959, p. 500). Unsaleable goods, i.e. their overproduction, are only the result of insufficient realisation caused by overaccumulation. Not disproportionality between expanding production and insufficient purchasing power, thus a lack of consumers, causes the crisis'. We also see here Grossmann's way of quoting. Marx says: 'In times of crisis' (i.e. a moment, an element of crisis) realisation disappears: in a trice Grossmann makes it the only cause of the crisis as if it would be the view of Marx! A glance at the passage of Marx shows that it is there not a matter of the causes of the crisis, but of a contradiction between the demand of loan capital (for payments) and industrial capital during the crisis. In the same way Grossmann explains: 'The result of our analysis is as follows: there is overproduction at the crisis moment. How was the return to the economic upswing carried out? Perhaps that production had been limited? On the contrary, the crisis deepened even more! And the crisis was nonetheless overcome. This is the best evidence that it was neither caused by an insufficient purchasing power, nor by a lack of consumers or by a disproportionality in the sphere of production'. Grossmann 1929, p. 309.
43 See his chapter: 'Why the Marxist theory of accumulation and breakdown was misunderstood'. Grossmann 1929, p. 190 *passim*.

We already had the opportunity of illustrating Grossmann's way of quoting [Marx]. We should continue on this path. Grossmann takes the Marx quotes mainly from the third part of *Capital*, Volume 3, here Chapter 15: 'The law of the tendency of the rate of profit to fall', section 3 'Excess capital and excess population'.[44] Marx begins here with the problem of the '*plethora of capital*' and remarks that the 'plethora of capital always applies' essentially to a plethora of *small capital* 'for which the fall in the rate of profit is not compensated through the mass of profit – this is always true of newly developing fresh offshoots of capital – or to a plethora which places capitals incapable of action on their own at the disposal of the managers of large enterprises in the form of credit'.[45]

This plethora of capital arises from capital overaccumulation by individual capitals not meeting the required size for starting production with any perspective on success. Now Marx asks: 'When would overproduction of capital be absolute?' And he answers:

> There would be absolute overproduction of capital as soon as additional capital for purposes of capitalist production = 0. The purpose of capitalist production, however, is self-expansion of capital, i.e. appropriation of surplus-labour, production of surplus-value, of profit. As soon as capital would, therefore, have grown in such a ratio to the labouring population that neither the absolute working-time supplied by this population, nor the relative surplus working-time, could be expanded any further (this last would not be feasible at any rate in the case when the demand for labour were so strong that there were a tendency for wages to rise); at a point, therefore, when the increased capital produced just as much, or even less, surplus-value than it did before its increase, there would be absolute overproduction of capital; i.e. the increased capital $C + \Delta C$ would produce no more, or even less, profit than capital C before its expansion by ΔC. In both cases there would be a steep and sudden fall in the general rate of profit, but this time due to a change in the composition of capital not caused by the development of the productive forces, but rather by a rise in the money-value of the variable capital (because of increased wages) and the corresponding reduction in the proportion of surplus-labour to necessary labour.[46]

---

44 Marx 1959, pp. 245–54.
45 Marx 1959, p. 246.
46 Ibid.

As we have seen, Marx understands by overproduction of capital something completely different from what Grossmann pretends here. According to Grossmann, *overaccumulation is a situation in which too much capital is available in the form of constant capital and too little capital in the form of variable capital.* That is why, *although a sufficient quantity of labour force is set free*, realisation of additionally accumulated capital becomes impossible. According to Marx, overaccumulation of capital means *a situation in which the whole available labour force is fully employed* ('neither the absolute working-time ... nor the relative surplus working-time could be expanded any further'), so that any further expansion of capital, thus the amount of surplus value, will be impossible! According to Grossmann, it is a matter of relative overaccumulation: the workers can still be exploited, surplus value can be raised: but because of erroneously constructed schemes there is no variable capital – at least on paper – available though the profit rate is still very high! According to Marx there is a real overproduction of capital with regard to the available workers' reserve and to the extremely increased degree of exploitation given the existing production relations. Grossmann overlooks this fundamental difference, he conceals his basically erroneous construction of Marx's theory of capital overaccumulation. Given these circumstances, and premeditated or not, this is nonetheless a case of falsification because Grossmann quotes Marx in this chapter proving *his* conception of capital overaccumulation.

Then Marx describes the *consequences* of the absolute overproduction of capital he presumes: underutilisation of capital, falling profit rates, a fierce competitive struggle of a new kind between capitals deciding which capitals should remain unutilised, restoring economic equilibrium not only by not utilising, but also by destroying capital[47] in its natural form of means of production or in its value form (price fall of commodities), disruption of the circulation and production processes – crises.

> The stagnation of production would have laid off a part of the working-class and would thereby have placed the employed part in a situation, where it would have to submit to a reduction of wages even below the average. This has the very same effect on capital as an increase of the relative or absolute surplus-value at average wages would have had.[48]

---

47   Marx 1959, p. 248.
48   Marx 1959, p. 249.

In addition: new labour-saving machinery, better working methods, devaluation of elements of constant capital will announce a possible production expansion later. Hence, Marx's way of reasoning is:

> ... [A] fall in the intensity of exploitation below a certain point, however, call forth disturbances, and stoppages in the capitalist production process, crises, and destruction of capital. It is no contradiction that this overproduction of capital is accompanied by more or less considerable relative overpopulation ... an overpopulation of labourers not employed by the surplus-capital owing to ... *the low rate of profit which they would yield at the given degree of exploitation.*[49]

As we have seen: *the falling rate of profit is of primordial importance* as a consequence of a presumed absolute overaccumulation (no possibility anymore of increasing the rate of surplus value by utilising more capital). *A surplus of workers is the result.* But according to Grossmann, this surplus of workers is, however, not caused by falling profit rates and decreasing amounts of profit, but by the fact that the appropriation of surplus value cannot be realised because of a lack of workers and an uneven capital distribution between c and v. There is no absolute overproduction of capital, a free labour force is still available to be exploited, *thus the amount of surplus value can grow*; but a crises arises (at a profit rate of 17 percent) because of a disproportion between c and v in an incorrectly set up scheme.

As we saw: the quote Grossmann used in his chapter when proving that his crisis theory gives a correct interpretation of Marx's theory, is fallacious. Moreover, the text of Marx only mentions (grammatically, the conditional is always used) the *possibility* of an absolute overaccumulation, but this does not affirm that the crisis is caused by an absolute overaccumulation of capital, nor is it assured that the law of motion of the capitalist mode of production should necessarily lead to this claimed 'absolute overproduction of capital': further commentaries on the real forms of the motion law of capitalism are based on the *falling rate of profit*.

> The rate of profit, i.e. the relative increment of capital, is above all important to all new offshoots of capital seeking to find an independent place for themselves. And as soon as formation of capital were to fall into the hands of a few established big capitals, for which the mass of profit compensates

---

49 Marx 1959, pp. 250–1, our emphasis.

for the falling rate of profit, the vital flame of production would be altogether extinguished. It would die out. The rate of profit is the motive power of capitalist production. Things are produced only so long as they can be produced with a profit. Hence the concern of the English economists over the decline of the rate of profit.[50]

The limitations of the capitalist mode of production come to the surface: In that the development of the productivity of labour creates out of the falling rate of profit a law which at a certain point comes into antagonistic conflict with this development and must be overcome constantly through crises.[51]

According to Grossmann, 'the point of no return to the crisis' is reached at a profit rate of 17 percent and an unemployment rate of 5 percent. There exist two different concepts of overproduction, respectively overaccumulation of capital; but according to the quotes Grossmann borrowed from Marx (almost all crucial quotes are taken from this chapter), the crisis would be the result of a capital overaccumulation *in the sense he argues*. This is thus a unscrupulous falsification of Marx's views.

c) That Grossmann's theory is inappropriate to explain the real crisis is proven by the fact that:

Periodical economic crises have existed since the beginning of the nineteenth century.[52] But talking about capital overaccumulation in 1815? The assumption that in those days such a high organic composition of capital had already existed that, because of shortages of variable capital, a further enlarged reproduction process could be prevented and thus causing a crisis, makes no sense.

We want to add some concrete examples: The organic composition of capital is certainly highest in American big enterprises. If we try to calculate the organic composition of capital in American industry by using data of the 1925 census, we obtain the following results:

---

50 Marx 1959, p. 254.
51 Marx 1959, p. 253.
52 Engels writes in a footnote added to a sentence of Marx: 'The industrial cycle is of such a nature that the same circuit must periodically reproduce itself, once the first impulse has been given'. Marx 1959, p. 477. And also: 'In the early years of the world commerce, 1815–47, it can be shown that crises occurred about every five years; from 1847 to 1867 the cycle is clearly ten years ...'. Marx 1959, p. 478. According to [Wesley Clair] Mitchell in the *Business Annals* (New York 1926), the [industrial] production cycle starts in the United States in the year 1790!

TABLE 11.5 Organic composition of American capital (1925)

	Milliards of dollars	
	Consant capital = c	Variable capital = v
Wage sum = v		10.7
Costs of raw materials = circulating capital = c	35.9	
Value of machines (1922) = fixed capital = c	15.8	
Buildings (our estimation) = c	10.0	
Total c	61.7	

c : v = about 6:1

With profit rate of 14 percent and this organic composition of capital there exists not yet a crisis in Grossmann's scheme of the year 1925. How to explain a crisis having occurred in England in 1815 as a result of overaccumulation when the organic composition of capital was incomparably lower then? (According to official surveys the organic composition of capital was between 3 and 4 to 1 in America's big industry).

Grossmann is also inconsistent and he staggers between crises as a result of overaccumulation in his meaning of the word – too much c and too little v: insufficient realisation = a low profit rate – and unprincipled ups and downs. He argues:

> The circumstances weakening the breakdown tendency, i.e. overcoming the crisis, are of a manifold nature, but with regard to their impact they can be reduced to the fact that either the value expression of capital has diminished or that surplus value has increased, by which the profit rate, thus realisation of advanced capital, increases and improves.[53]

But, according to his scheme, the crisis is not the result of a low profit rate: the profit rate is, when the 'turn to the crisis' sets in, thus as the sinking of k begins at 17.1 percent, and in the year of the announced 'breakdown', when the accumulation rate should attain 104.6 percent of the surplus value, it is still 9.3 percent! How can such a low a profit rate be at the very origins of the crisis?

---

53   Grossmann 1929, p. 295.

Furthermore: the height of the organic composition of capital, i.e. the approximation of the 'breakdown' moment in the distinct capitalist countries is very different because of their [uneven] economic development. How could economic crises touching all countries of the world have been generally possible? Grossmann refers to 'the medium of imports of commodities', 'transmitting the boom from one country to another'.[54] But how can a crisis arise when there is no overaccumulation in the country concerned? When tackling Grossman's crisis theory one is everywhere confronted with nonsense!

If *overaccumulation of capital had caused crises in England after 1815, then there clearly exists no relation between Grossmann's 'purely economic breakdown' and the capitalist system's real breakdown!* According to Grossmann, the crisis is *'an interrupted and not completely developed breakdown tendency'*,[55] but England was not subjected to a purely economic breakdown during the past 115 years and no *real* breakdown of capitalist domination happened here. It is not at all clear why according to Grossmann's 'purely economic' theory capitalist domination could exist in England for some more centuries. Hence, Grossmann's proud construction of an economically necessary breakdown of capitalism is here destroyed. Who the hell needs today, in a world in which the breakdown of capitalism has already begun, an economic theory about an inevitable collapse of capitalism over probably several centuries?

3   Grossmann's Erroneous Theory of Capital Export

We neglect here Grossmann's treatise on the countertendencies thwarting the breakdown tendency (they are a bad version of Marx's treatise on the causes hindering the profit rate to fall). He begins with the following sentence: 'Capital export is as old as today's capitalism itself'.[56] He argues that the idea 'that *higher profit rates* in the less developed countries are causing capital export' is 'banal'. Thus, 'not the profit rate, but the *amount of surplus value* realised on a pro rata capital base is higher in these countries'.[57] He bitterly polemicises against Otto Bauer, Hilferding, Bukharin, Varga – we will later discuss this issue – and then he begins[58] a new chapter entitled: '*Overaccumulation and*

---

54   Grossmann 1929, p. 448.
55   Grossmann 1929, p. 290.
56   Grossmann 1929, p. 490.
57   Grossmann 1929, p. 505.
58   Grossmann 1929, p. 316.

capital export according to Marx's vision', and here he commits the most flagrant and the most shameless of all his forgeries.

Beginning with citations from Marx on the possibility of absolute overproduction of capital (we already dealt with this), Grossmann concludes that capital export occurs when capital becomes 'superfluous from a capitalist point of view'[59] and in the following footnote he argues: 'One should interpret the other passage in the same sense where is said: "If capital is sent abroad, this is not because it could absolutely not be applied at home".'[60]

In this footnote he tries to make the reader believe that Marx had used the word '*absolutely*' here in a sense that capital cannot be applied *in a non-capitalist social order* and that it would therefore be overaccumulated in capitalism.[61]

Let us have a look at what Marx wrote: 'If capital is sent abroad, this is not done because it absolutely could not be applied at home, *but because it can be employed at a higher rate of profit in a foreign country*'.[62]

This sentence we emphasised absolutely excludes this possibility, but Grossmann conceals this and he only quotes the first part of the sentence: a cruder form of falsification can hardly be imagined.[63] When preparing in his way a completely erroneous theory of capital export for the reader, Grossmann attacks everybody, Bauer, Hilferding, Varga, Bukharin, Lenin,[64] who formulated the

---

59 Grossmann 1929, p. 526.
60 Marx 1959, p. 251.
61 This is demanding very much of Marx, because Marx writes somewhere else: 'However, even under the extreme conditions assumed by us this absolute overproduction of capital is not absolute overproduction, *not absolute overproduction of means of production*'. Marx 1959, p. 250. We see that Marx identifies capital with *means of production*. Means of production is a general category of any economy: capital is a historical category of a particular mode of production. Demanding that Marx should speak of capital in a non-capitalist society would be really too much!
62 Marx 1959, p. 251.
63 A premeditated falsification is here undoubtedly open to suspicion. Grossmann indicates *Kapital*, III, 1, page 218, as the page of this mutilated Marx quote. But this quote is found in *Kapital*, III, 1, sixth edition, at page 238. Moreover, in his preface Grossmann mentions the editions of Volume 1 and Volume 2 he is citing, but he does not indicate the edition of Volume 3. The reader who is not finding this quote on p. 218 may therefore think that Grossmann has used a different edition. All this is thus open to suspicion.
64 Grossmann does not only falsify the works of Marx, but also Lenin's! Lenin writes on capital export in his usual concreteness: 'As long as capitalism remains what it is, surplus capital will be utilised ... *for the purpose of increasing profits by exporting capital abroad* to the backward countries. **In these backward countries profits are usually high**, for capital is scarce, the price of land is relatively low, wages are low, raw materials are cheap' (**my emphasis**). Lenin 1930, p. 57. [Lenin's quote is not on page 57, but on page 71]. [Lenin 1964e,

clear thesis that capital is only exported in case there is any perspective on obtaining higher profits abroad than at home!

He cites the following sentence of mine (which is almost literally of Marx, as we already showed above): 'Not because it would be absolutely impossible to accumulate capital domestically without penetrating non-capitalist markets, but only because there is a perspective on making *higher* profits if capital is exported'.[65] And then he attacks me very sharply. He passes to my account for having defended in principle the possibility of 'an unlimited domestic investment', and he edifies me that my assertion 'contains an insoluble contradiction with regard to any labour theory incompatible with the latter. However, surplus value is labour! But in any country labour is a given quantity and from a given population one can only extract a maximum quantity of surplus value, although this is a little bit extensible. The assumption that capital can infinitely grow implies that surplus value can also increase, which means nothing else than that surplus value can infinitely increase, thus that the growth of surplus value is not dependent on labour'.

He also tars Bukharin, Bauer, Hilferding and – indecently – Lenin, who, as we already have seen, shares this opinion. Therefore we want to study his arguments more closely.

Indeed, there exists an '*unrestricted investment possibility*' for 'capital' on the domestic market, but there is no unrestricted possibility of investing capital in the form of *industrial capital* able to indirectly create surplus value in the production process. If at a given moment *all* workers of a country without any exception would be *fully* employed (extensively and intensively) to their utmost capacities in the production process, in that case thinking of new investments in industrial capital would be inconceivable, because the capitalist would not find the commodity named labour force on the market. It is thus not a problem of 'realisation', but of technical impossibility: investing cap-

---

p. 241]. Except for the last sentence, in which Lenin is arguing about the necessity of capital export, Grossmann is smuggling all the time, but, ironically enough, he uses inverted commas when speaking of 'overripe' capitalism in some countries, where the possibility of a 'profitable' investment is lacking. Grossmann, however, uses this quotation in order to underpin *his* views and meanwhile he highlights what he needs but without indicating it! (p. 520). Haughtily he argues: 'Lenin does not explain what that "overripeness" is'. And already earlier: '... Lenin's description does not go beyond the level of empirically detectable relations; in Lenin we find no theoretical analysis proving the necessity of capital export in the highest stage of capitalism' (Ibid.). Condescendingly he apologises for Lenin's omission 'because of the popular character of his writings' (Ibid.). Sir Grossmann is really a sly old dog!

65   Varga 1927, p. 363.

ital in the form of industrial capital would be impossible, even if free labour is available and realisation possible, but no labour force available on the labour market!

Does this now signify that capital cannot be 'created' at all if absolute overaccumulation of capital described by Marx as a possibility when 'additional capital for purpose of capitalist production = o'[66] is a reality? By no means! Capital can also be 'created' by investing loan capital, by using bank depositories, etc. It never happened that loan capital did not earn *any* interest when the interest rate was = o. Of course, in that case neither the amount of surplus value, nor the amount of profits will grow; but a larger amount of capital should then share the same amount of profits.

In practice, however, even industrial capital can be created in a situation of absolute overaccumulation by using technically better-equipped fresh offshoots of individual capitals producing at a lower cost than the older or smaller enterprises, by paying higher wages and by attracting workers from other firms by offering them better working conditions. The total amount of profit will then *diminish*, thus not increase because of these fresh offshoots of capital; but, viewed from this angle of total social capital, formation of new capital could be really a superfluous exercise: the process of capital formation will never come to a standstill.

Nonetheless, we should ask this question: is the problem of absolute overproduction of capital thus a situation in which 'neither the absolute working-time supplied, nor the relative surplus working-time by this population, can be extended any further'[67] – once qualified by Marx as a *potentiality* – but, according to Grossmann, also a reality? No! Except for a period of a few months of economic boom during the 10–20 year cycle, there will always be an industrial reserve army available,[68] there will always be a real possibility of accumulating capital as *industrial* capital and increasing the total amount of surplus value and profits by new investments. If happening abroad, it will be the result of better prospects of making higher profits.

I have some final remarks about Grossmann who argues that: 'In every country the size of the labour force is given, and from a given, but anyhow expanding

---

66 [Marx 1959, p. 246].
67 Ibid.
68 The most recent development of capitalism is engendering 'structural', 'technological', *permanent* mass unemployment in countries with a high degree of capital export – America, England. When the American and English capitalists export capital, they are certainly doing that because of higher profit rates, not because of realising additional surplus value they cannot possibly realise at home!

population, one can barely squeeze a rather limited, but albeit slightly elastic amount of surplus labour'.[69]

Is this right?

Yes, but only for a well-defined period of time; no, if considered dynamically.

Suppose that France would prohibit immigration. Would this mean that the 'maximum amount of surplus labour' would not increase in the future, thus that the amount of surplus value and profit will always remain at the same level? Not at all! The total labour time that a given working population can provide will always remain stable, hence, the total amount of newly produced value (v + m) will remain the same. Hence, necessary labour time proportionally diminishes within total labour time, but surplus labour and surplus value increase. Why?

Because of labour shortages capital will be incited to make technical progress: labour-saving machines and processes are introduced on a larger scale and, hence, notwithstanding a stagnating number of workers, an industrial reserve army will be created, labour productivity will rapidly increase; labour time per unit product of foodstuffs consumed by workers will significantly drop; necessary labour will become less, surplus labour produced by every individual worker will grow and, hence, total surplus value produced by a 'given population' as well. The profit rate will nevertheless rapidly fall, but, nonetheless, there will not occur a dynamic, absolute overaccumulation of capital in the sense that new investment of capital will hamper the growth of the total amount of surplus value. – We also believe that Grossmann's reproval at our (and Hilferding's, Bauer's, Bukharin's and Lenin's) address – is completely superfluous. We may quietly assume that higher profit rates, and not the *impossibility* of investing at home, are at the very origins of capital export, because investing at home – even at a lower profit or interest rate – remains possible for individual capitals, even in case of 'absolute overaccumulation'.

We do not want to pay attention to Grossmann's historical elucidations on capital export. We only argue that omitting the *location problem* means that an intelligent discussion on the history of capital export cannot possibly be conducted. Hence, we ask Grossmann how to apply his overaccumulation schemes to France, a country already exporting capital for several decades before the war, but that after the war, when capital was invested at home, workers were immigrating massively? How can one explain by referring to the 'realisation need' of capital that before the war workers and capital were emigrating for many decades? Why did English capitalists not employ their workers at home

---

69 Grossmann 1929, p. 499.

in order to valorise capital [Verwertung des Kapitals]? Why did English capital emigrate with English workers to America, Canada, South Africa? This only occurred because better location conditions were offered for many of their production branches, i.e. manufacturing costs per single unit of product were lower here, i.e. the profit rate was, *ceteris paribus*, higher there than in England in case the same English capitalists wanted to employ the same number of English workers in the same production branch. This is the grist of the matter; Grossmann's arguments are thus meaningless. Paying no attention to the location problem means that one is also neglecting *uneven development*! That is what Grossmann is doing. If one would ask him why development was proceeding during the last decade by leaps and bounds in the industry of Northern Italy, he would have certainly been unable to give a correct answer. Due to the distribution system of high-tension electricity, Northern Italy could obtain cheap energy from the Alps. This modified the country's location situation in its advantage; instead Grossmann would have divulged some generalities about the accumulation process ...

4   Grossmann's Erroneous Theory of the Reserve Army

Grossmann's theory of the reserve army in capitalism has an erroneous starting point. Somewhere in his scheme he has to integrate unemployment caused by overaccumullation. Hence, he had to disrupt that something can only be separated violently.

> Liberation of the worker, the growing reserve army of which Marx is referring to in his chapter on accumulation, – which has been until now completely neglected in literature – is not technically brought about by introducing machines, but by a lack of valorization appearing at a higher level of accumulation; hence, this can only be brought about by the specificity of the capitalist mode of production. Workers are set free, not because they are replaced by machines, but because at a certain level of capital accumulation profits are too small for financing the necessary machines, etc.[70]

---

70   See p. 130; ibid., p. 167, p. 380, etc., where he is always referring to Marx! Note that the vague relation between the insufficient valorisation caused by the falling rate of profit and Grossmann's specific impossibility of valorisation due to overaccumulation are here, however, directly juxtaposed as 'accumulation *is not worth the trouble* (because of a too low a profit rate) and therefore an insufficient amount of profit'!! (p. 130).

Hence, machines are not crowding out workers and making them jobless, but the low profit rate at a certain level of accumulation. But why did the profit rate sink so low? Because workers were replaced by machines! *A high organic composition of capital, a low profit rate and a crowding out of the workers by machines are different aspects of the same process*, that is already included in Marx's definition of the concept of organic composition [of capital]. The dialectical process in which each individual capitalist is replacing workers by machines for *increasing* temporarily the share of his individual profit, must lead to a tendentially falling rate of profit for total capital, but this does not exist for Grossmann. Workers replaced by machines is for him not a fact.[71] Progressing capital accumulation and falling profit rates are two *different things*. That they are two aspects of a single process does not bother him! And this man wants to reconstruct Marx's method!

His theory is only a corollary to his scheme of capital accumulation: he argues that a huge shortage of labour power existed in the beginning of capitalist development. 'Only the technical revolution in the last third of the 18th century created a fundamental change'.[72] Then followed a period of overpopulation, of Malthusianism.

> Fear of overpopulation was obvious in a period when human labour was replaced by machines, but capital accumulation was still in its initial phase and no additional employment was available for redundant workers. Constant plus variable capital, c plus v, were too insignificant compared to population. But, Malthusianism could and should only be a transitory current of ideas in a mode of production based on exploitation of human labour. Then, growing capital accumulation and its impact meant that capitalism in the developed countries of Western Europe acceded to a new level of development. Because of the enormous volume

---

[71] That is why he declares, short and snappy: 'This liberation of labour will occur *in any* mode of production, even in a socialist plan economy in so far as this will bring technical progress into practice'. (p. 129). But it is not a matter of liberating 'labour' – as Grossmann formulates it here – a formulation we cannot find in Marx (as far as I can remember!), but of *liberating the workers*. In capitalism the liberated worker is starving; in a socialist planned economy no worker will remain jobless, but due to technical progress, instead of the eight-hour day, the seven- or six-hour work day will become the rule and instead of having a holiday each seventh day, each fifth day will become a holiday, etc. What is the political sense of talking about the 'liberalization of labour' in capitalism and socialism instead of digressing about the *different fate of the workers?* It is obviously a matter of hiding the difference between capitalism and socialism!

[72] Grossmann 1929, p. 398.

accumulated capital of the leading capitalist countries, accumulated capital c plus v becomes too big in relation to population, i.e. population growth by a given percentage will be insufficient for providing the required amount of surplus value required for a normal valorization of the already accumulated and in percentages faster growing stock of capital. But an ever growing population needs additional capital a_c plus a_v for its employment, that can only be taken away from the stock of surplus value m. However, as this amount will not be sufficient in order to valorize the actually accumulated capital stock, the amount of surplus value will not be sufficient for additional accumulation. Hence, notwithstanding overaccumulation, a reserve army of unemployed workers must therefore be formed. In general, growing unemployment in capitalist countries is in essence quite different from Malthus's time. In those days c + v was too small in relation to the population; today c + v is too large. On the other hand, $a_c + a_v$ is nowadays too small. Unemployment is thus the consequence of an insufficiently large population.[73]

Hence, it is up to the reader to judge whether this theory of the reserve army – a small c + v in the beginning and, later on, a bigger c + v engendering a growing reserve army (until now we thought that only v played a role in this development) – is compatible with Marxist theory. Hence, we only want to ask here two questions:

a) If unemployment was a result of insufficient accumulation ('c + v was too small in relation to the population') in the period of Malthusianism – which lasted until 1850–60 – how can one defend the thesis that during the first half of the nineteenth century any crisis was announcing a breakdown caused by overaccumulation?

b) Grossmann argues that there exists such a huge unemployment because 'c + v is too large, but $a_c + a_v$ is nowadays too small'. But this means that the c to v ratio is too high, thus making it not profitable for the capitalists to employ more workers. This makes sense. However, there exists no difference between Marx's theory of the tendentially falling rate of profit and Grossmann's overaccumulation theory stating that the overaccumulation process is already beginning long before the profit rate is threatening to sink to a dangerously low level. However, if 'c + v is nowadays too large' signifies something different, then this would make no sense! Enormous production units are today only operating at 50–80 percent of their

---

73 Grossmann 1929, p. 415.

production capacity. At the same time millions are unemployed! If these workers were employed in production, then the amount of surplus value would increase; hence, profits and, *ceteris paribus*, accumulation ($a_c + a_v$) would also grow. Obviously, not $a_c + a_v$ smallness must be the cause of unemployment, but, on the contrary, huge unemployment is the reason that – in spite of the fact that all means of production are available – the sum of surplus value, profits and accumulation are too small. By only paying attention to his accumulation scheme, by haughtily abhorring Marx's sentence that the purchasing power of capitalist society is always lower than its production capacity, Grossmann cannot have a clear view on the relation between unemployment, crisis and insufficient demand.

5 Grossmann's Erroneous Theory of Competition and Monopoly

Grossmann's theory is necessarily a result of his erroneous theory of competition. He writes:[74] 'Marx ... accepts the equilibrium situation as a starting point of his analysis ... The *struggle for turnover* and capital investment markets must *begin* when at a certain level of capital accumulation valorization falters. Competition is thus the result of *insufficient realisation*, not its cause!' (my emphasis).

Once more one can see Grossmann's complete incomprehension of Marx's method. Marx analyses price fixing according to the predicament that supply always meets demand and that competition is eliminated, in order to reveal the '*essence*': price fixing by value. But Grossmann hypostatises this precondition by pretending that there would have been a competition-free capitalism in the beginning and that competition has found its origins in overaccumulation and insufficient valorisation. This is a completely incorrect idea: there has always been competition; without competition there would have been no tendentially balanced profit rate. Even if we assume that supply and demand could be by chance perfectly balanced for a *certain* period of time, a perfect equilibrium of the capitalist system (i.e. a wholly unrealistic condition), unequal development would lead in the shortest time to competition between individual enterprises in the same branch – and to competition between the industrial branches for a larger share of the market. In other words: disproportion between the limited purchasing power of capitalist society and the struggle for an unlimited expansion of the productive forces are for Marx typical for this mode of pro-

---

74 Grossmann 1929, p. 285.

duction, hence competition has always existed in capitalism, but Grossmann thinks that competition only appears when overaccumulation begins and its consequences become concrete.

Grossmann's monopoly theory is also incorrect. His central idea is:[75] 'The breakdown tendency is weakened by monopolistic price increases pumping additional amounts of surplus value from abroad into the economy of a country having a monopoly position'.

The second part of the sentence is correct: monopoly profits from abroad are pumping additional profits, *surplus profits*, into a country, representing of course additional surplus value: but so what? But does this also mean that 'the breakdown tendency is halted'? Not at all. Monopoly profits are by definition profits *not* included in the profit rate balance; this is typical for their monopolistic character. Monopoly profits, 'the additional amount of surplus value', devolve to the monopolists and improve the valorisation of *their* capital, but this does not signify that non-monopolistic capital is also relieved (on the contrary); the average profit rate is not rising, the breakdown tendency is not weakened. This is one of the many 'silly blunders' made by Grossmann.

Hence, Grossmann's polemic against Lenin's monopoly theory is also erroneous.[76] He does not understand Lenin's basic thoughts – they are already contained in Marx's *The Poverty of Philosophy* – that monopolies are a necessary outcome of free competition leading to concentration. Therefore he puts artificially created privileges by governments in the beginning of the capitalist mode of production simply on a par with monopolies having arisen in the age of imperialism! Thus his monopoly theory is not worth a penny!

6   Marx's Method and Grossmann's Method

Grossmann pretends that he is the first one to have revised Marx's method 'nobody had ... yet grasped'. In reality, however, he does not understand Marx's method of which he has no idea although he quotes – if I am not mistaken –

---

75   Grossmann 1929, p. 466.
76   In spite of occasional bans, one can spot an open or anonymous polemic with Lenin. Already in his preface he writes: '... [C]ompletely empirically detectable tendencies of the world economy, which are characteristic of the *newest* stage of capitalism development (and which are cited in many publications on imperialism: monopoly organisations, capital export, struggles for the partitioning of territories with raw materials, etc.), are *superficial phenomena* of minor importance primarily rooted in the *essence* of capital accumulation'. Grossmann 1929, p. x. This means: *'Lenin only saw the superficial phenomena, but I, H. Grossmann, explain the essential features Lenin could not grasp'*.

the well-known phrase of Marx: 'But all science would be superfluous if the outward appearance and the essence of things directly coincided'.[77] *But he did not grasp that appearance and reality are one and the same to Marx.*[78]

Marx looks through the outward appearances, thus going from reality to essence and to 'the intrinsic connection between the economic categories or the obscure structure of the bourgeois economic system'.[79] He gives an explanation for the appearances, i.e. reality through its basic essence. The price exists in reality: its essence is its value. There exists in reality various appearance forms of profit: interests on loan capital, profits of commercial capital, entrepreneurial profits, etc.; their essence is nonetheless based on surplus value. Hence, reality, i.e. the appearance form, is explained by functionally linking the latter to 'the obscure structure of the bourgeois economic system',[80] thus to the essential categories: the price is in the first instance value, the amount of values is the sum of all prices; the sum of surplus value is the sum of profits, etc.

This distinction between the 'intrinsic connection' and the world of the phenomena, i.e. reality, has, of course, nothing in common with [Immanuel] Kant's 'thing-in-itself' [Ding an sich] and the world of the phenomena.[81] Kant claimed that the thing-in-itself cannot be known, none of its properties is accessible to mankind's speculative reason. The essence, Marx's intrinsic connection, cannot be known, but its appearance is also the only method to acquire knowledge of reality, i.e. the world of the phenomena and the essence are connected to the same object: the bourgeois economic system. The degree of knowledge of both of them is only different. Vulgar economic science is exclusively operating within the world of phenomena, is transforming the motives influencing the capitalists' behaviour into vulgar categories and remains enticed by the 'appearance of competition'. Marxism, however, recognises the essence of social connections, the intrinsic connection of the bourgeois economic system. The reality known in its deepest connections is the 'essence'.

Grossmann has completely misunderstood this basic thought of the Marxist method. He believes that events occurring in reality can *indirectly* be explained by an analysis of their essence. He believes that the specific moments of the essence, which can only be known by Marxist theoreticians, are indirectly caus-

---

77 Marx 1959, p. 797.
78 For instance, he writes: 'But in *reality* (*i.e. in the world of phenomena*) the matter is reversed'. Marx 1959, p. 46, my emphasis.
79 Marx 1970, p. 165.
80 [Ibid.].
81 [The things as they appear to an observer].

ing effects on the appearances, i.e. on the reality of people. He concentrates his attention on his accumulation scheme – a scheme belonging to the domain of the essence, i.e. the 'intrinsic relations' – and then he believes that the capitalists are, just like he, anxious about the diminishing amount of surplus value: that they are not exporting capital abroad because of higher profit gains there, but because of their rising stock of surplus value! Marx is speaking about the 'appearance of competition', but he thinks that competition did not really exist before overaccumulation appeared, etc. He completely forgets Marx's brilliant analysis in Volume 3 [of *Capital*] that because of the development of *particular* forms, in which profit is splitting, not only surplus value but also profit as such is disappearing from the capitalists' perception; the working capitalist is hence confronted with interest-bearing capital and his 'entrepreneurial profit' will appear to him as a wage paid in exchange for his highly qualified labour force. In Grossmann's view, the capitalists are *indirectly* acting on the basis of the essence.[82] Thus Grossmann completely misinterprets the unity of appearance and essence and, hence, he is not only hampering the ambitioned reconstruction of Marx's method, but also how to understand Marxism and acquire a clear insight into capitalism. That is why all problems Grossmann is dealing with, though his presentation is partially based on Marx quotes, can only lead to incorrect interpretations contradictory to Marxism and Leninism. Our analysis of his mistakes is by no means exhaustive.

∴

The following question should be asked: why pay so much attention to such an uninteresting book?

The answer is: there exists the danger that Grossmann's book, just like Luxemburg's book in the past, may create confusion and damage. The book is based on phenomena of present capitalism which are explained by referring to a unique cause, i.e. overaccumulation, assuring the reader that a 'breakdown' will be inevitable and that even the moment of collapse can be theoretically predicted, which is opening the door to widespread fatalism and passivity. Because of basing his assertion on countless Marx citations – many of them are also forged – he gives the impression that a real revolutionary is here revealing the final breakdown theory of Marx which had been until now concealed by

---

82   Marx writes nonetheless: 'The existing market-price is for the capitalist what the presupposed value of the product is for the theory and the inner relationship of production'. Marx 1970, p. 333. Grossmann did not notice this.

the neo-harmonists. The reader, especially here someone of the younger generation, may be confused by all these contingencies and withhold him from actively struggling against the bourgeoisie. Revealing Grossmann's forged theory was therefore necessary.

CHAPTER 12

The Great Crisis and Its Political Consequences: Economics and Politics 1928–34

Foreword[1]

This book is an endeavour to give a brief review of the period between the Sixth and Seventh Congresses of the Communist International. It is *not a history* but an analysis looking towards the future.

Such an effort is beset with particular difficulties. The crisis of the capitalist mode of production, the clash of the two systems, the imperialist antagonisms, the struggle between the bourgeoisie and the proletariat, and so on – all the factors that determine world events at present, act *simultaneously, and in every respect are interlinked* on all sides. Language, however, allows us to describe matters only in time sequence! Hence the alternative of either making constant repetitions or making an analysis, which, though incomplete at first, would be completed in the later chapters. We have chosen the second path. The book should be read and judged *as a whole*. Each separate chapter is not complete in itself.

Although we endeavoured to write *popularly, without vulgarisation of course*, the first chapter will present certain difficulties to a reader not well-versed in Marxism. *A clear understanding of the peculiarities of the great economic crisis and of the special nature of the present depression is possible only on the basis of Marx's theory of crisis and cycles*. Since this question is of the utmost importance to the outlook for the development of the revolution, we deemed it necessary to give this theoretical chapter at the beginning. The difficulties of this chapter should not deter the reader from reading further. Even without the first chapter the book represents a complete whole.

The analysis is made not according to countries, but by problems. Consequently, the unevenness of development in various countries has not been reflected sufficiently. However, an exposition according to countries would require too much space and would involve too much repetition.

---

1 By E. Varga, Formerly Professor of Political Economy in University of Budapest, Director of Institute of World Economy and Politics in Moscow; report published in London: Modern Books Limited, Printed by The Marston Printing Co., Nelson Place, Cayton St., London, England.

The book does not pretend to be complete. The problems of the economic struggle of the working class, and the strategic and tactical problems of the Communist Parties have not been dealt with. It would be overweening on our part to venture to express an opinion on this point before the convening of the Congress, which will embrace the collective experience of all Parties.

E. Varga
Moscow, 4 September 1934

Introduction

Six years have elapsed since the Sixth Congress of the Communist International. Six short years sufficed to change radically the world aspect of capitalism. At that time, stabilisation; now, the eve of the second round of revolutions and wars; then, prosperity; now – after four years of an unprecedentedly deep economic crisis – a depression of a special kind, without any prospect of a new prosperity phase. Then, as a result of stabilisation, fresh illusions arose among the working class as to the possibility of peaceful advance within the limits of capitalism on the basis of 'industrial democracy'; now, the rapidly growing recognition that there is only one way out for the proletariat: the revolutionary overthrow of the rule of the bourgeoisie. Never before has the contradiction between productive forces and production relationships stood out in such stark relief. Never before has there been such a glut of commodities alongside the misery and starvation of the working-class masses. Never before has it been so clear that the capitalist system of society must be overthrown, if mankind is to live as men!

The change that has set in during the last six years is tremendous. How presumptuous and haughty were the spokesmen of capitalism at that time! Dazzled by prosperity, they proclaimed a new and lasting advance of capitalism; they proclaimed that the capitalist system of society remained unshaken. President Calvin Coolidge,[2] the steward of American finance capital, in his last message to Congress, 1 December 1928, at the end of his term of office, declared:

> No Congress, of the United States ever assembled, on surveying the state of the Union, has met with a more pleasing prospect than that which

---

2 [Calvin Coolidge (1872–1933) was a Republican politician, President of the USA (1923–9)].

appears at the present time. In the domestic field there is tranquility and contentment, harmonious relations between management and wage-earner, freedom from industrial strife, and the highest record of years of prosperity ... The great wealth created by our enterprise and industry, and saved by our economy, has had the widest distribution among our own people ... The requirements of existence have passed beyond the standard of necessity into the region of luxury. Enlarging production is consumed by an increasing demand at home and an expanding commerce abroad. The country can regard the present with satisfaction and anticipate the future with optimism.

The captains of American industry were no less optimistic. Charles Schwab, president of the Bethlehem Steel Corporation, stated: 'I say with confidence that there has been established a foundation upon which there may be built a structure of prosperity far transcending anything we have yet enjoyed'.[3]

Alfred Sloan, president of General Motors, declared: 'My standpoint regarding 1929 is based on the conviction that our general economic and industrial situation is thoroughly sound; therefore I do not see why the general progress should not continue and ensure us an excellent flow of business and still increased prosperity'.[4]

At the bankers' conference in Cologne in the autumn of 1928, Jacob Goldschmidt, leader of the German finance oligarchy at the time and director-general of the Darmstädter- und Nationalbank (which finally collapsed in 1931), proclaimed the new revival of capitalism in the same proud manner:

> While the end of the capitalist age and the replacement of individualist profit economy by that of state socialism engages the attention of prophetic minds, and the idea that the present economic system of society is doomed and is to be replaced by new economic forms often haunts mankind like a hallucination, the practical management of industry, with its capitalist methods, energetically continues its advance. In spite of capitalist the adverse atmosphere of a revolutionary period, it was erected an economic machinery upon the ruins of a lost World War, which, though, far from ideal, operates for the present quite satisfactorily. Starting with an obsolete technology, it did this within the brief space of less than five years ...

---

3   *The Iron Age*, 1 November 1928.
4   *The New York Times*, 29 October 1928. [This quote could not be traced].

The leaders of Social Democracy, the lackeys of the bourgeoisie, followed their masters in proclaiming the new rise of capitalism. [Rudolf] Hilferding,[5] in his articles and speeches, has supplied a 'Marxist' theoretical foundation for this stand ever since 1924.

> Productive forces grew to an extraordinary degree during and after the War. This growth was not uniform: the branches of industry necessary in waging war were most highly developed ... while industries manufacturing consumers' goods fell behind. This disproportion is one of the causes of the world crisis. But in the long run, after the overcoming of the crisis, *extension of productive capacity signifies an increase in production and a new boom*. Materially widened and qualitatively changed as a result of the war period, capitalist economy appears to be *on the way to organic economy*.[6]

This glorification of the future of capitalism was linked with the counter-revolutionary theory that the *state*, ruled by coalition governments composed of Social Democracy and the bourgeois parties, was *above all classes* and was effecting the peaceful transition from 'organised capitalism' to socialism through 'industrial democracy'. In a book of a programmatic nature published by the German General Trade Union Federation in 1928, this theory was expounded as follows.

The development of the capitalist mode of production proceeds from the individual to the collective enterprise, from free trade capitalism to organised capitalism (the expression 'monopoly' is carefully avoided). Consequently, the contradiction between the power of the owners of the means of production and the masses of the population becomes ever greater. Hence a change in the social order must be had. In the period when capitalism was completely unfettered, it seemed that there was no other conceivable alternative for unorganised capitalism than the socialist organisation of economy as a whole; it therefore seemed hopeless and purposeless to try to make any change in the despotism of the capitalist system.

'But gradually it became apparent that the structure of capitalism is changeable and that capitalism can be *bent* before it is *broken*'.

The force which is to bend capitalism in the direction of industrial democracy is the state. Industrial democracy can be achieved only through political democracy.

---

5   [Rudolf Hilferding (1877–1941) was an Austrian and German Social-Democratic politician].
6   See, for example, Hilferding 1924d, p. 119.

> Hence industrial democracy signifies the extension of political democracy through the democratization of economic relations ... Complete industrial democracy is identical with collective economy ... The state is a commonwealth, i.e. it is a public body transcending all individuals and expressing a definite will. The essence of industrial democracy is therefore only achieved when production is no longer controlled by private individuals as private property used for private ends, but is in the hands of an economic commonwealth embodying a collective economic will, where the decisive factor is not the private use of individuals, but the collective use of the whole.[7]

How unutterably out-of-date, how foolish and ridiculous does the chatter of the Coolidges and the Goldschmidts, the Hilferdings and the Naphtalis[8] sound today! And on the other hand, how true have the Marxist-Leninist analysis and prognosis made by the Communist International shown themselves to be. The Communist International was not deceived by the temporary improvement in the situation of capitalism; it fully exposed the empty chatter of capitalism's apologists. It revealed the temporary nature and the inner contradictions of capitalist stabilisation, and proclaimed that these contradictions would inevitably lead to the end of stabilisation in the near future, that stabilisation would be followed by a new revolutionary wave!

In the middle of 1928, the Theses of the Sixth Congress of the Communist International stated that a new, third period of postwar capitalism had set in, whose essence was formulated in the Theses as follows:

> For the capitalist world the third period is a period of the rapid development of technique, of increased development of cartels and trusts, and of tendencies towards state capitalism. At the same time it is a period of the most intense development of the contradictions of world capitalism, operating in forms determined by the entire course of the general crisis of capitalism up to now (shrinkage of markets, the Soviet Union, colonial movements, growth of the inherent contradictions of imperialism). This third period, in which the contradiction between the growth of the productive forces and the shrinkage of markets has become particularly accentuated, is inevitably leading to a new phase of wars between the imperialist states, of wars against the Soviet Union, wars of national lib-

---

7   Naphtali 1928, pp. 14–15.
8   [Fritz Naphtali (1888–1961) was a German journalist and trade-unionist, Israeli politician].

eration against imperialism, imperialist interventions, and gigantic class struggles. This period, in which all international antagonisms are growing more acute (antagonisms between the capitalist countries and the Soviet Union, the military occupation of North China – the beginning of the partition of China – and the mutual struggles between the imperialists, etc.), in which the inherent antagonisms in the capitalist countries are coming to head (the swing to the Left of the working-class masses, intensification of the class struggle), and in which movements develop in the colonial countries (China, India, Egypt and Syria), inevitably leads, through a further development of the contradictions of capitalist stabilisation, to a renewed disturbance of capitalist stabilisation and to the extreme aggravation of the general crisis of capitalism.[9]

The historically brief interval between the Sixth Congress and the Seventh has furnished *practical* confirmation of the absolute truth of the Comintern's conception and of the utter emptiness of the Social Democrats' apologetics. The economic crisis broke out like a devastating hurricane in the middle of 1929; it brought unheard-of misery to the working masses all over the world and abruptly ended all talk about the strength and durability of capitalist stabilisation.

The cyclic crisis of 1922–33 plays a special role in the history of capitalism.

Ever since the full development of the capitalist mode of production, its movement has proceeded in cyclic fashion. Each upward swing ended with a violent explosion of all the contradictions of the capitalist system in the cyclic crisis of overproduction, which, however, provided a violent solution for these contradictions to a considerable extent. Thus cycle followed cycle, crisis followed crisis.

Yet this repetition of cycles and crises does not denote a mechanical addition of qualitatively equal units. Each cycle and each crisis has its own concrete historical peculiarities; each cycle and each crisis has its specific historical place in the history of capitalism. The change in the nature of the capitalist system itself: the transition from industrial capitalism to imperialism and to the era of the general crisis of capitalism as a particular stage of imperialism, likewise proceeds cyclically.

---

9 [This passage differs in its formulation from the 'Theses and Resolutions of the VI. World Congress of the Communist International', in *International Press Correspondence*, 23 November 1928, p. 1568].

What is, then, the historical place of the crisis which broke out in 1929?

As Comrade Stalin pointed out at the Sixteenth Congress of the Communist Party of the Soviet Union, it is the first world crisis after the War, in the period of the general crisis of capitalism. The place of this crisis in history also determines its concrete peculiarities. It is undoubtedly a cyclic crisis of overproduction, but by no means is it a 'normal' crisis, a 'mere repetition of previous crises'. Its course was greatly influenced by the general crisis of capitalism (on the basis of which it is running its course), by the increasingly monopolist character of postwar capitalism, by its intertwining with the agrarian crisis (which is a part of the general crisis of capital) and by the extraordinarily sharp fall in prices, which represents in part the liquidation of the excessively high price level dating back to the World War. Other factors were the measures taken by monopoly capital and its state for the artificial solution of the crisis, which led to considerable delay in the outbreak of the credit crisis and – in the long-run – to the prolongation and deepening of the crisis as a whole.

The final result is that the first world crisis in the era of the general crisis of capitalism has proved to be much deeper, of longer duration and in every respect more devastating than any of the previous cyclic crises. This crisis also reveals qualitatively new aspects: currency depreciation in almost all the capitalist countries, almost universal non-payment of foreign debts, and practically complete cessation of capital export. These are qualitatively new aspects, which were not present in any of the previous crises.

While the crisis reduced capitalist production to below the pre-war level, the development of productive forces in the Soviet Union proceeded at a tremendous pace under the Five-Year Plan. The economic crisis has strikingly demonstrated the superiority of the Soviet system to the capitalist system for all the toilers of the world. The struggle between the two systems has been decided in favour of the Soviet system in the economic, social and cultural fields. This impels the world bourgeoisie still more to seek the use of armed force, to turn the scales of battle between the two systems in its favour.

The crisis has led to a very marked change for the worse in the conditions of the working class and of the toiling peasantry throughout the world, and hence to an extraordinary accentuation of class contradictions. This has had far-reaching political consequences. The influence of Social Democracy on the working-class masses is rapidly diminishing. Under the pressure of the radicalisation of the masses, almost all the Social-Democratic parties are experiencing a crisis, manifested in the formation of Left and Right factions, in resignations and splits. While some of the leaders openly desert to the camp of the bourgeoisie and even to fascism ([Ramsay] MacDonald[10] and [Philip] Snowden[11] in England, the neo-fascists [Adrien] Marquet[12] and [Marcel] Déat[13] in France, [Paul] Löbe[14] and [Carl] Severing[15] in Germany), the revolutionary Social-Democratic workers in ever greater number seek affiliation to the Communist International, in order to close the split in the ranks of the working class and to wage a united struggle against the bourgeoisie. The crisis in the Second International is plain to all. The weakening in the influence of its main social bulwark and the growth in the influence of the Communist Parties more and more compel the bourgeoisie to brush aside parliamentary democracy, which has become a hindrance, and to take refuge in fascism – in open, violent dictatorship.

At the same time the crisis has led to a general economic war of all countries with one another, representing a kind of prelude to war itself. It has resulted in the beginning of the struggle for the violent repartition of the world in the Far East, to 'small' wars in South America and Asia, and to a deliberate orientation of economic policy to the coming imperialist war and to a counter-revolutionary war against the Soviet Union. The conquest of Manchuria by Japan and the wars between Paraguay and Bolivia, between Peru and Colombia, between Ibn-Saud [Arabia] and Yemen, and between China and Tibet, are the forerunners of the new world war.

Thus the cyclic crisis has brought about and hastened the end of capitalism's temporary stabilisation. It has caused a profound disturbance of the entire capitalist system, initiated a new and higher stage of the general crisis of capitalism, and resulted in the maturing of the objective prerequisites for the revolutionary crisis. 'The tremendous strain of the internal class antagonisms in the capitalist countries, as well as of the international antagonisms, testifies to the fact that the objective prerequisites for a revolutionary crisis have matured to such an extent that at the present time the world is closely approaching a new round of revolution and wars'.[16]

However great the suffering inflicted by the crisis on toiling mankind in the capitalist countries, and however great the role it has played in accelerating the

---

10 [Ramsay MacDonald (1866–1937) was a British Labour politician].
11 [Philip Snowden (1864–1937) was a British Labour politician].
12 [Albert Marquet (1875–1947) was a French right-wing socialist politician].
13 [Marcel Déat (1894–1955) was a French right-wing socialist politician].
14 [Paul Löbe (1875–1967) was a German Social-Democratic politician].
15 [Carl Severing (1875–1952) was German Social-Democratic politician].
16 *Theses and Decisions. Thirteenth Plenum of the* E.C.C.I. 1933, p. 5.

process of the collapse of stabilisation, *it would yet be theoretically and politically incorrect to regard the cyclic crisis as the cause of the end of stabilisation.*

Theoretically: The Communist International never considered stabilisation as anything but a transient phenomenon within the enduring general crisis of capitalism, as a trough in the waves of the revolutionary movement. The same inherent causes which – together with the World War – necessarily produced the general crisis of capitalism, also led to the end of stabilisation; to the maturing of a new revolutionary crisis.

The cyclic economic crisis, like all cyclic crises, was the necessary result of the most fundamental laws of capitalism. 'As long as capitalism exists, cyclic fluctuations are inevitable. – They will accompany it in its death-throes, just as they accompanied it in its youth and maturity', state the Theses of the Third Congress of the Communist International. Therefore, we can consider the cyclic crisis only as a trigger force, as the immediate cause terminating the process of shattering stabilisation.

Politically: If the cyclic crisis were the cause of the end of stabilisation, it would follow that, should capitalism succeed in overcoming the cyclic crisis, stabilisation would be restored and a new trough in the wave of revolution would follow.

This conception would inevitably lead to opportunism, to denying the further maturing of the revolutionary crisis in the not impossible event of some delay in the outbreak of the next world war.

1   The Economic Bases of Business Crises

The major feature of the six years that have elapsed between the Sixth and the Seventh Congresses of the Communist International is the economic crisis, which occupies almost the whole interval. Three periods may be *roughly* distinguished; we shall fix the dividing lines between them somewhat arbitrarily.

(a) From the middle of 1928 to the middle of 1929, when the industrial production of the world was still on the upgrade, but the commodities produced could not be marketed completely, when stocks were accumulating and the crisis was already beginning in some countries.

(b) From the middle of 1929 until approximately the end of 1933 – the actual crisis phase in the strict sense of the term, which reached its nadir approximately in the middle of 1932.

(c) From 1934 on – the phase of the 'depression of a special kind', which, though differing from the crisis in the dynamics of industrial production, of price formation, etc., nevertheless represents a continuation of the crisis in its social and political effects, and – for the present at least – offers no basis for a further prosperity phase.

We shall deal only with the crisis and the depression; the period between the middle of 1928 and the middle of 1929 not requiring any special analysis. Before proceeding to a *concrete* analysis of the crisis, however, we shall make one or two theoretical observations by way of a preface.

The Apologists of Capitalism Deny the Inevitability of Crises

For a hundred years bourgeois political economists have tried in vain to solve this question: Why does every prosperity phase end in a crisis? Just when profit-making seems to be in full swing, why does overproduction, with no market for commodities, suddenly occur?

Bourgeois political economy always poses the problem as follows: the production of every commodity also creates a corresponding purchasing power for the purchase of this commodity. The value of the raw and auxiliary materials is paid to their respective producers. The increase in value arising in the process of manufacture is divided into wages paid the workers and the capitalists' profit. Therefore no new value can be produced without at the same time creating the purchasing power for the sale. Putting it differently: the total purchasing power of society equals the total value of the commodities produced. The anarchy of capitalist production, its lack of planning, may lead to disproportions; too much may be produced of *one* or of *several* kinds of commodities. But in this case, no little must have been produced of other commodities, in relation to the purchasing power of society. A simultaneous overproduction of all commodities is therefore impossible. The causes of crises are disproportions, which arise *accidentally* but do not follow from the nature of the capitalist system of society. This, in essence, is also the opinion of [Karl] Kautsky, [Rudolf] Hilferding, etc.[17] Hence, it follows that a capitalist 'planned economy', 'organised' state capitalism is required to prevent the outbreak of crises.

In other words progressively increasing capitalist production would be possible without any crises, provided disproportions were avoided.

More than half a century ago Marx disclosed with perfect clarity the reasons why the periodic recurrence of crises is inevitable under capitalism. The ideologists of capitalism rejected this explanation, however. The bourgeois economists and the revisionist wing of the Social Democrats did so openly.

---

17 In *Das Finanzkapital*, Hilferding wrote: '... [A]t the same time these formulæ [of Marx] show that in capitalist production, both simple and progressively increasing reproduction may proceed undisturbed, provided these proportions are maintained'. Hilferding 1910, blz. 318.

The centrists: Kautsky, Hilferding, [Otto] Bauer, etc. – whom Rosa Luxemburg mordantly called the 'Apostles of Harmony' – paid lip-service to Marx, called themselves Marxists, and still do so to the present day, but they distorted and falsified the theory of Marx to such an extent that nothing was left of its revolutionary content.

> I believe I am ... in full agreement with the theory of Karl Marx, *to whom a theory of collapse is always wrongly ascribed*. Precisely the second volume of *Capital* shows how *progressively increasing production* is possible within the capitalist system. I have often thought that *it is not such a bad thing that this second volume is so little read, since under certain circumstances a pæan to capitalism might be construed out of it*.

This is how Hilferding expressed himself before an intimate, purely bourgeois circle at the Vienna Conference of the Union for Social Policy.[18] No wonder that the minutes at this point read: 'Laughter and applause; cries of "Hear, hear"'. However, he who denies Marx's theory of revolutionary collapse must needs either deny his theory of crisis or falsify it in an opportunist fashion.

The Theory of Crises and the Revolutionary Collapse of Capitalism

Marx was the first to make clear the course of the process of capitalist reproduction and circulation. The value of all capitalistically produced commodities consists of three factors: *constant capital*: c (machinery, raw and auxiliary materials), which *does not increase in value* during the process of production, but transfers its value to the newly produced commodities (machinery, buildings, the 'fixed' part of constant capital, transfer only part of their value, corresponding to their depreciation, to the commodities produced with their aid); *variable capital*, expended for wages: v, which increases in value through the exploitation of the workers; and surplus value: m.

All commodities fall into two main divisions, according to their use value:

> Division I: *means of production*, which serve for further production.
> Division II: *means of consumption*, which are directly consumed by capitalists and workers.[19]

---

18 Hilferding 1926c, pp. 113–14, my emphasis.
19 At this stage of his analysis, Marx, for the sake of simplicity, presupposes a 'pure' capitalist society, composed of capitalists and workers only; he temporarily leaves out of account the existence of all pre-capitalist classes, such as toiling peasants and artisans, in order not to complicate the analysis.

All the commodities produced in capitalist society during a certain period of time, say, one year, may therefore be represented according to value and use by the following formula (omitting the portion of fixed capital which is not consumed during the given year and is to serve in production during the following year).

$$\text{I } 4{,}000\, c_1 + 1{,}000\, v_1 + 1{,}000\, m_1$$
$$\text{II } 2{,}000\, c_2 + 500\, v_2 + 500\, m_2$$

The figures taken by Marx (they may signify millions or milliards in money units) are chosen arbitrarily as far as absolute magnitude is concerned. If production is to begin again or be continued on the same basis ('simple reproduction') in the following interval of time, however, *the proportion between them is strictly determined by the use to which the commodities are put*. This is proved by the following argument:

v_1 and m_1, variable capital and surplus value in Division I, are produced in their *natural form* of means of production; they cannot serve for individual consumption, for which they are destined *socially* as wages and surplus value. They must be exchanged for goods of Division II. c_2, the value of constant capital in Division II, is produced in the natural form of means of consumption, and therefore cannot be used further in Division II as means of production. $v_1 + m_1$ of Division I must therefore exchange places with c_2 of Division II.

If, therefore, production is to be continued on the same scale, the sum of v_1 + m, viz. *variable capital plus surplus value of Division I*, must equal c_2, *the constant capital of Division II*. Only in this case of an 'ideal, normal production', as Marx says, would simple reproduction, without any crises, be abstractly *theoretically* possible.

But this is *only* an abstract theoretical possibility. In actuality, even simple reproduction would also inevitably entail crises for the following reasons:

(a) Fixed capital (machinery, buildings) cannot be renewed in every enterprise, parallel with its depreciations. It must be renewed step by step, after value has been accumulated parallel with wear over a considerable period of time, which must almost inevitably lead to the disturbance of the 'ideal, normal production'. This particular movement of fixed capital, as Marx says, forms the 'material basis' for the cyclic course of capitalist production. 'This illustration of fixed capital', he writes,[20] 'on the basis of an unchanged scale of reproduction, is striking. A disproportion of the

---

20   Marx 1957, p. 469, my emphasis.

production of fixed and circulating capital is one of the favourite arguments of the economists in explaining crises. That such a disproportion can and must arise even when the fixed capital is merely preserved, that *it can and must do so on the assumption of ideal normal production* on the basis of simple reproduction of the already functioning social capital is something new to them'.

(b) The above formula covers only the most general movement of commodities. Even if the general proportion ($v_1 + m_1 = c_2$) is maintained, tremendous disproportions may occur. For instance, too many ships may be produced in Division I or too much cotton goods in Division II. Overproduction in one or several *important* branches of industry leads to unsaleability of goods, to a drop in prices and wholesale bankruptcies, which, in view of the mutual intertwining of credit under capitalism, draw the other branches of industry into the crisis as well.

However, these statements of Marx as to the possibility and the necessity of crises in simple production merely serve to facilitate an understanding of the process of capitalist reproduction by means of an assumption made for the sake of greater simplicity. In reality, capitalist production increases progressively.[21] '*Essentially, the capitalist process of production is simultaneously a process of accumulation*', says Marx.[22] That means that the bourgeoisie, as a class, never consumes all of the surplus value appropriated by it, but accumulates a part of it, which it uses for the further extension of production. Under pain of ruin, every individual capitalist is compelled by competition to convert part of his profits into capital, and to improve his means of production, in order to be able to reduce production costs. This means that:

The total value of social capital increases from year to year.

The organic composition of capital is enhanced: the distribution of capital between constant and variable capital (capital invested in means of production and that paid out in the form of wages) changes in favour of the former.

Within constant capital, there is a shift in favour of fixed capital: that part of capital invested in buildings, machinery, tools and means of transport increases at a more rapid rate than that invested in raw material.

There is a relative diminution of the total profit (tendency of the rate of profit to decline) *as well as of the wage fund*, as compared with the total value of the annual production of goods.

---

[21] During crises and depressions there are short periods of *simple reproduction*, but for longer periods of time increasing reproduction is the rule.

[22] Marx 1959, p. 213.

The 'consuming power' of capitalist society, viz. the sum available for the purchase of commodities for *individual consumption*: v + (m − a) (wages plus that part of surplus value which is not accumulated but used by the capitalist class for the purpose of satisfying its personal needs), is thus constantly diminishing *in relation* to the development of capitalist production.

The distinction between the *'purchasing power'* and the *'consuming power'* of capitalist society is of the greatest importance for an understanding of crises. *The purchasing power of society is c + v + m; it tends to equal the sum of the value of the products* (without that fixed part of c, which is not used up in one year, but which, although partially depreciated and therefore diminished in value, continues to serve in the production process). Bourgeois economists always refer to this equation when they deny the possibility of *general* overproduction. The consuming power of capitalist society, v + (m − a), is only a small part of purchasing power, and with the progress of accumulation a relatively diminishing one.

This relative diminution of the consuming power of society, which is necessarily connected with the development of capitalism and which is based on the contradiction between social production and private appropriation, *poses the problem of markets in an ever acuter form, making it ever more difficult to dispose of commodities*. For in the final analysis, as Lenin says, *all means of production serve for the production of means of consumption*. The extent to which the available industrial plant can be utilised, and hence in the long-run the sale of means of production as well – the course of business in Division I – depends, at bottom, upon the sales volume of means of consumption. Productive consumption, according to Marx: '... is at first independent of individual consumption because it never enters the latter. But this consumption definitely limits it nevertheless, since constant capital is never produced for its own sake but solely because more of it is needed in spheres of production whose products go into individual consumption'.[23]

References of bourgeois political economists to the fact that the corresponding purchasing power is produced together with the production of a commodity, that the total value of the products is equal to the purchasing power of society, prove to be meaningless. The limitation of the *consuming power*, its continual and inevitable relative diminution, is what decides the fate of capitalism.

The contradiction between the limited consuming power of society, and the boundless expansion drive of capital, due chiefly to the proletarian condition

---

23   Marx 1959, pp. 299–300.

of the masses, must necessarily *lead to periodically recurring crises of overproduction.* 'The ultimate reason for all real crises always remains the poverty and restricted consumption of the masses as opposed to the drive of capitalist production to develop the productive forces as though only the absolute consuming power of society constituted their limit'.[24]

The constant relative diminution of consuming power (disregarding the cyclic course of production) compared to the development of the productive forces leads to a chronic accentuation of the contradiction between the productive power and the consuming power of capitalist society, since the individual capitalists, driven by the necessity of winning in the competitive struggle, develop the productive forces without taking the relative diminution of consuming power into consideration. This is *the economic basis for the general crisis of capitalism,* for the chronic idleness of a large part of the productive apparatus, for chronic mass unemployment.

The relative diminution of the consuming power of society does not affect capitalists and workers alike. At first the working class grows *relatively* impoverished. The value of labour power sinks in conformity with the reduction in the value of the necessities of life required to maintain the working class – a reduction due to the increase in the productivity of labour. The 'necessary labour time' – the labour time during which the worker is working for himself – grows shorter and shorter, while the time during which he is working for capital grows longer and longer. The rate of exploitation rises with the rise in the productivity of labour. The proletariat receives a diminishing portion of the *value of the product,* capital getting an increasing portion. This means that v represents a relatively diminishing portion of the consuming power of capitalist society, and $(m - a)$ a relatively increasing one. Put in popular form: even if the proletariat were to receive the value of its labour power in the form of wages, it could only purchase a continuously diminishing part of the value produced by it with these wages.

Alongside this relative impoverishment of the working class, which goes on continually under capitalism, the *absolute impoverishment of the working class* comes to the fore more and more strikingly in the period of the general crisis of capitalism. In the first place, a large proportion of the workers is chronically unemployed. Secondly, this permanent glut of the labour market enables capital, concentrated in monopolist organisations and dominating the state, to increase the intensity of labour and force down the wages of the employed workers below the value of their labour power. The relative and absolute impov-

---

24   Marx 1959, pp. 472–3.

erishment of the masses of the working class, with capital less able to maintain a privileged, corrupt labour aristocracy, together with the wholesale ruin of the toiling peasantry (the causes for which we shall discuss later), reinforce the subjective forces necessary for the overthrow of the rule of the bourgeoisie, for the revolutionary collapse of capitalism.

The Marxist-Leninist theories of periodic crises, of the general crisis of capitalism and of its revolutionary collapse, are thus indissolubly connected. Although Marx's theory of crises is patently correct, the defenders of capitalism – both bourgeois and Social-Democratic – must either reject or distort this theory because acknowledging it entails recognition of the inevitability of capitalism's revolutionary collapse.

Accumulation as the Cause of the Cycle Course of Capitalist Production

Anarchy of production, 'lack of plan', is the constant *prerequisite* for economic crises. The contradiction between social production and private appropriation is the *ultimate cause* of crises. This contradiction manifests itself in the constant conflict between the limited dimensions of consumption on a capitalist basis, its continual relative shrinkage, and a production that is always exceeding these limits.

The question now arises: why is there permanent overproduction in capitalism under these circumstances? Why, until now, have crises, depressions, revivals and prosperity phases followed each other in regular sequence?

The answer to this question is not only of economic but also of revolutionary and political importance. The exceptional depth and acuteness, the unusually long duration of the economic crisis of 1929–33 has caused many comrades to believe – to an even greater extent than during the first postwar crisis – that there is absolutely no way out of this cyclic crisis. At that time Lenin,[25] and now Stalin,[26] resolutely opposed this conception, which must inevitably lead to the theory of the *automatic collapse* of capitalism and to opportunist passivity on the part of the proletariat.

The cause of the cyclic course of capitalist production is the accumulation of capital. The accumulation of capital in its *real*[27] form signifies an extension

---

25 Lenin 1964c, pp. 17–118.
26 Stalin 1955a, pp. 288–388.
27 We distinguish between '*real*' accumulation, i.e. an increase in the value of social capital in its productive form (buildings, machinery, raw materials, finished products), and *accumulation in the form of loan capital* (deposits in banks and savings banks) which represents only formal, potential accumulation of capital.

of the purchasing power of capitalist society, an enlargement of the capacity of capitalist markets to absorb commodities. *It is the immediate motive force behind revival and prosperity, but on a higher plane it is also the immediate cause of crises.* Once the process of real accumulation in the prosperity phase has reached a certain stage, *a change of quantity into quality occurs*. The role of accumulation changes abruptly. Hitherto the basis for the boom, it now becomes the immediate cause of the crisis.

Let us explain this in greater detail:

Competition, as we have already explained, compels every capitalist enterprise, 'under pain of ruin', to reduce its cost of production. One of the chief means to this end is *increasing the productivity of labour*: enlarging and improving the machinery operated by one worker, 'technical progress'. In other words, the *real accumulation* of fixed capital, of that part of constant capital (buildings, machinery, apparatus, tools) which successively transfers value to the product in the repeated turnovers of circulating constant capital, while it continues to function in its natural form in the production process until its natural or *moral* depreciation.

> The cycle of interconnected turnovers embracing a number of years, in which capital is held fast by its fixed constituent part, furnishes a material basis for the periodic crises. During this cycle business undergoes successive periods of depression, medium activity, precipitancy, crisis. True, periods in which capital is invested differ greatly and far from coincide in time. *But a crisis always forms the starting-point of large new investments.* Therefore, from the point of view of society as a whole, more or less, a new material basis for the next turnover cycle.[28]

Only on rare occasions do these elements of fixed capital serve in the production process up to the point of their *natural* wear. The capitalists' efforts to reduce the cost of production, which are dictated by competition, force them to renew their fixed capital, to install new, more efficient machines in place of the old ones, although the latter are still capable of functioning. The renewal of fixed capital is usually begun in the phase of depression ('a crisis is always the starting point of a large amount of new investments'), is *expanded* in the revival phase, reaches its *climax* in the prosperity phase, and stops almost completely with the outbreak of the crisis.

---

28   Marx 1957, p. 186, my emphasis.

This peculiar movement of fixed capital forms the material basis for the cyclic course of capitalist production, but it is not its cause. It is not actual wear nor technological progress that determines when fixed capital is to be renewed on a large scale. The cause of the cyclic movement is accumulation, one form of which is the expansion of fixed capital.

As long as accumulation is in full swing, in the phases of revival and prosperity, it enlarges the *purchasing power* of capitalist society together with the production of commodities in Division I. In these phases, sales present no difficulties, since the capitalists themselves are the principal purchasers of one another's commodities.

> The development of production (and, consequently, of the home market) chiefly on account of means of production seems paradoxical and undoubtedly constitutes a contradiction. It is real 'production as an end in itself' – the expansion of production without corresponding expansion of consumption. But it is a contradiction not of doctrine, but of actual life; it is the sort of contradiction that corresponds to the very nature of capitalism and to the other contradictions of this system of social economy.[29]

Accumulation, the expansion of production by increasing the means of production, denotes not only an expansion of purchasing power, but also entails a certain temporary expansion of the consuming power of society. The expansion of production in Division I is accompanied by an increase in the number of workers employed and in the variable capital of this division; the consuming power of the proletariat is raised. The increase in the number of employed workers – provided the rate of exploitation remains the same – is accompanied by a growth in the total surplus value, and consequently in the demand for consumers' goods on the part of the capitalists of Division I. Hence, larger sales and increased production in Division II, an increase in its variable capital, in its surplus value and in consumption by workers and capitalists in that division. At the same time, Division II renews its fixed capital to an increased degree, and gives orders to Division I, thus raising the latter's production still further. Revival mounts to the stage of prosperity. The capitalists can see no reason why this should end in a crisis.

But accumulation is a two-sided dialectical process. As long as the process is going on, its effect is to expand the purchasing power of capitalist society and, within the limits of this society, its consuming power as well. But at the

---

29   Lenin 1964e, p. 56.

same time the ultimate effect of accumulation is to accentuate the contradiction between the productive and consuming power of capitalist society, since of necessity it reduces the consuming power of capitalist society still further, relatively speaking. This follows from the nature of accumulation. It signifies a higher organic composition of capital, a rise in the productivity of labour through the application of improved and larger machinery, a decrease in v compared to c, the tendency of the rate of profit to sink, and the reduction of the consuming power of society: $v + (m - a)$, relative to the productive power of capitalist society, which grows rapidly just because of real accumulation.

Accumulation thus gives rise to two contradictory processes; on the one hand, expansion of the purchasing power of society and (as a part of the same) of consuming power, as far as the latter's absolute magnitude is concerned; on the other hand, a relative decrease in the consuming power of society compared to its productive power.

Thus, as Marx says, accumulation means continual relative overproduction. '... [A] *continuous relative over-production, in itself identical with accumulation, even at those average prices whose level has neither a retarding nor exceptionally stimulating effect on production*'.[30]

Or elsewhere: 'But the whole process of accumulation in the first place resolves itself into *production on an expanding scale,* which on the one hand corresponds to the natural growth of the population, and on the other hand, forms an inherent basis for the phenomena which appear during crises'.[31]

This is why the revival and prosperity caused by real accumulation cannot last forever. In the process of social reproduction, the means of production serve to produce consumers' goods. As *means of production,* they can serve this purpose alone. (For the capital which produces means of production, the object is of course the appropriation of profit.) Therefore, *in the final analysis,* the production of means of production is limited by the consuming power of capitalist society. The relative decrease in consuming power caused by accumulation must therefore sooner or later put an end to the expansion of production. *The phase of prosperity must lead to a crisis,* which temporarily puts an end to the process of real accumulation.

It is this function of accumulation to diminish consuming power comparatively which caused Marx to identify it expressly as 'relative overproduction'.

To put it more simply: prosperity continues as long as the process of real accumulation is in full swing, as long as new factories, harbours, railways are

---

30 Marx 1959, p. 656.
31 Marx 1969, p. 492.

built, and old machines are replaced by new ones. But as soon as this process reaches a certain conclusion, after a considerable number of new production plants have been completed, the demand for the commodities of Division I (building materials, machinery, etc.) diminishes, entailing a drop in the demand for consumers' goods as well, since the workers in Division I are becoming unemployed. At the same time, the supply of commodities increases, since the new and the reconstructed factories begin to pour goods into the market. Overproduction already exists, but the open outbreak of the crisis is delayed, since the capitalists (who never believe that a prosperity phase will come to an end) are producing for inventory. But production exceeds consumption to an ever greater extent, until the crisis bursts into the open.[32]

⁂

Glancing back in the light of the foregoing over the course of the industrial cycle in the postwar period, we find the following:

(a) The first postwar crisis of 1920–1 was not a 'normal' crisis of overproduction. During the World War, as a result of the tremendous unproductive consumption of the armies and the devastation of large territories, consumption in Europe exceeded production. The tremendous accumulation of fictitious capital (war loans) was accompanied in reality by a 'dis-accumulation' of capital; at the end of the war, machines were worn out (with the exception of munition plants newly built during the war), stocks of commodities and raw materials were far below normal, the soil was exhausted, houses were out of repair, etc. This devastation of the productive forces led to a general impoverishment and underproduction. 'The present crisis in Europe is a crisis of underproduction', the Theses of the Third Congress declare. There was underproduction in the belligerent countries of Europe combined with overproduction in the neutral and overseas countries.

(b) This great demand for means of production in Europe, brought about by the war, made it possible to overcome the first postwar crisis *quickly*. Rapid reconstruction of production plants was begun, largely financed by American loans, and this formed the economic basis for the revival and the period of prosperity. *But it was precisely this wholesale renewal of fixed*

---

32 In this chapter we deliberately treat the problem of crises in a greatly simplified and incomplete manner. The crisis involves the outbreak and the temporary solution of *all* the contradictions of capitalism. We have only emphasised those which are of particular importance for the *present* situation.

capital, coupled with a great increase in the intensity of labour ('rationalisation') which led to an exceptional accentuation of the contradiction between productive power, expanding by leaps, and consuming power, extremely restricted as a result of rationalisation. In other words, this led to a particular accentuation of the problem of markets. The general crisis of capitalism grows deeper. The bourgeoisie is incapable of utilising the productive forces it has created. Hence, growing chronic, wholesale unemployment, growing idleness of production plant and the exceptional depth, acuteness, and long duration of the industrial crisis.

(c) The surplus of production plant (together with the chronic agrarian crisis) is the principal economic basis for the special character of the present depression. The inner forces of capitalism were sufficient to overcome the lowest point of the crisis and to effect a transition to the phase of depression; but a revival and a prosperity period are impossible without real accumulation on a large scale, i.e. without the renewal and expansion of fixed capital. The surplus of unutilised production plant, which existed even before the crisis, represents a serious hindrance to the investment of capital in new means of production.[33]

Thus the contradiction between the development of productive power and consuming power in capitalist society, which necessarily grows more acute, determines to an ever increasing extent the course of the industrial cycle and forms the economic basis for the accelerated maturing of the revolutionary crisis.

2 The Great Crisis of 1929–33

Each cyclic crisis occupies a particular place in the history of capitalism. Each crisis possesses its own features which differ from those of all previous crises.[34] Therefore the outline of the *general foundations* of the cyclic course of the process of capitalist production given in the previous chapter is by no means sufficient for an understanding of the great crisis of 1929–33 in its manifold concrete aspects. *In making a concrete analysis, it is necessary to omit some of the*

---

33 In a later chapter we shall deal in greater detail with the special character of the depression.

34 Marx based his theory of crises on a concrete analysis of all the details of the crises of 1848 and 1858. This is proved by his footnotes in *Capital* and in *Theories of Surplus Value*, his correspondence with Engels and the enormous collection of quotations and figures to be found in the Marx-Engels Institute.

methodological simplifications which Marx made in order to render the general causes of the crisis more understandable, and on the other hand to introduce the new circumstances created by the development of capitalism.

(a) In his general analysis Marx starts with the assumption of a 'pure' capitalism – a society composed of only two classes – the bourgeoisie and the proletariat. In reality, however, the majority of the world's population, down to the present day, consists of *'independent producers'* – peasants and artisans. The peasantry is one of the most important purchasers of the commodities of capitalist industry. The produce of peasant agriculture becomes a component part of constant capital in the form of raw material, and serves to feed the workers. Peasant agriculture and capitalist industry are interwoven. And although capital penetrates into agriculture more and more, subjugating the peasantry and exploiting it in the most varied ways, the state of peasant agriculture is, nevertheless, an important factor affecting the course of individual cyclic industrial crises. Good conditions in agriculture mitigate crises; an agrarian crisis like the present one intensifies and accentuates them.

(b) *Marx regards all of capitalist society as 'one nation', and the capitalist market as an integral 'world market'*. At this stage of his analysis he disregards the fact that capitalist society is organised in separate territories divided by state frontiers, as well as the differences between 'home' and 'foreign' markets. In analysing individual crises, and especially the last crisis, we must pay particular attention to the subdivision of capitalist society into separate states which isolate themselves from each other more and more. This has led to an unprecedented shrinkage of international trade, to the collapse of the 'world market' in the old sense of the word, to an exceptionally intense struggle for every sales opening it the world market, to the disintegration of the international system of credit, etc.

(c) The economic theory of Marx in general, and his theory of crises in particular, are based upon industrial capitalism, *upon the capitalism of free competition*. Present-day capitalism, however, is *monopoly* capitalism – imperialism. The monopolist character of capitalism, which necessarily evolves out of free competition through concentration of capital as a result of accumulation and centralisation, limits the consuming power of capitalist society and hence the absorbing capacity of the market general still further. Monopoly denotes the sale of commodities *above* their price of production (cost price plus average profit). The continuous 'normal' shifts in the division between capital and labour, between the bourgeoisie and the proletariat of the *new* value created annually, the increase in m at the expense of v – shifts which are occasioned by the rise in the productivity of labour – are supplemented by a new element in the development of capitalism: monopoly profit, the *artificial* rise of the share of monopoly capital in the total profit at the expense of the income of the smaller capitalists and the 'independent producers' still operating. At the same time, within the bourgeoisie there is a shift in favour of the narrow inner circle of the finance oligarchy. The consuming power of capitalist society and hence, in the final analysis, the absorbing capacity of the entire capitalist market are still further limited by the rise of monopolies.

The reasoning of bourgeois economists – that solely the absolute magnitude of the newly produced value determines consuming power (with distribution between the bourgeoisie and the proletariat and, within the bourgeoisie, between the finance oligarchy, the middle and petty bourgeoisie, of no significance) – is incorrect, as we have explained above. All of v, the total income of the proletariat, is consumed individually, expended for the commodities of Division II. Only a part of the total m, the income of the bourgeoisie, is consumed individually, while another portion is accumulated. An increasingly large part of m, of the total income of the bourgeoisie, is taken by the narrow circle of the finance oligarchy, and a relatively smaller part – notwithstanding the insane luxury indulged in by these topmost monopolist exploiters – is spent on commodities of Division II.

Monopoly capital, as an employer, is in a particularly strong position against the working class. This enables it to force wages down below the value of labour power, directly by wage cuts and indirectly by means of increases in the monopoly prices of those commodities which are consumed by the workers.

Monopoly profit does not arise exclusively from the sale of commodities controlled by the monopolies at prices higher than their cost of production, but also from the *purchase of raw materials and other goods at monopoly prices which are lower than the cost of production*. In purchasing agricultural products from the peasants and industrial goods from the artisans, home workers and small capitalists, monopoly capital appropriates part of the value by purchasing at prices which in many cases do not leave the independent producers even a wage worker's income. This reduces the consuming power of these groups still further.

With the development of the monopolist character of capitalist society, the latter's consuming power diminishes more and more, relatively speaking, and since *in the final analysis* the magnitude of consuming power also determines the magnitude of purchasing power, the contradiction between the production and marketing possibilities grows greater and greater and the problem of markets more and more insoluble.

Monopoly capital, however, restricts the *purchasing power* of capitalist society, not only indirectly through the restriction of consuming power, but directly as well. Sales at monopoly prices are possible only when the supply of monopolist commodities to the market is restricted. To ensure this, the development of production must be retarded and the construction of new production plant in the monopolist branches of industry must be adapted to the sales artificially limited by high prices.

Hence a new contradiction arises in monopoly capital. The endeavour to restrict the supply of commodities in order to maintain high prices tends to prevent the expansion of production. On the other hand, the drive to *lower the cost of production prompts the erection of new, technically more perfect plants, necessarily entailing expansion of production capacity.* (We must never forget that monopoly does not eliminate competition, that sharp competition exists with the outsiders in a given branch of industry, as well as competition among monopolies whose goods may serve as a substitute for each other, and among the various monopolies for the 'consumer's dollar', i.e. for their commodity's share as use value in the total consumption of society).

The net result is that cyclic crises *under monopoly capitalism are much deeper and more acute than under free competition capitalism*. The thesis advanced by Hilferding in his *Finance Capital*, viz. that crises grow milder in the period of imperialism, is absolutely untrue. *This thesis* is based on Hilferding's false fundamental concept: that crises are caused solely by the involved nature of the market and the resulting disproportions. He fails to see that the fundamental cause of crisis lies in the contradiction between social production and private appropriation, as expressed in the contradiction between productive power and consuming power, which must lead to *periodic overproduction of all commodities*. He mechanically differentiates between the consuming power of society and the proportionality of the various branches of industry.

'"The consumer power of society" and the "proportional relation of the various branches of production" – these are isolated, independent of, and unconnected with each other', according to Lenin. 'On the contrary, a definite condition of consumption is one of the elements of proportionality'.[35]

Since Hilferding assumes that competition dies out and the market becomes 'easier to survey' with the development of the monopolist nature of capitalism, he concludes that crises grow weaker[36] whereas they must grow more and more

---

35 Lenin 1964f, pp. 58–9.
36 In his programmatic article, 'Probleme der Zeit', in the first number of *Gesellschaft* (1924b, p. 2), Hilferding wrote: 'A transition takes place from free competition capitalism to organised capitalism. Parallel with it there develops conscious order and management of industry which endeavours, on a capitalist basis, to overcome the inherent anarchy of free competition capitalism. If this tendency could assert itself without hindrance ... crises, or it least their effects upon the workers would be mitigated employment becomes more steady, unemployment grows less menacing and its consequences are mitigated by insurance'.

acute under monopoly capitalism according to the correct Marxist-Leninist theory. The concrete analysis of individual crises in the era of imperialism fully confirms this.

(d) Marx developed his theory of crises on the basis of a rising capitalism which was expanding at a rapid pace, intensively and extensively. *The great crisis of 1929–33 developed on the basis of the general crisis of capitalism, and this accounted for its special nature.*[37]

Ten years sufficed to prove conclusively the absolute baselessness of this allegedly 'Marxist' analysis.

We cannot make an exhaustive analysis of the general crisis at this point.[38] We must limit ourselves to those aspects that are of greatest importance in their effects upon the industrial crisis.

(a) The blocus to the capitalist system of society, manifested in the existence and flourishing progress of the Soviet Union on a socialist basis, in the existence of Soviet China, in the expansion and intensification of the colonial revolutionary, anti-imperialist movement, and in the maturing of the revolutionary crisis in the capitalist countries, which are bringing closer the beginning of a second round of revolutions, are generating a feeling of general insecurity and are making new capital investments and long-term enterprises rather difficult all over the world.

(b) *The contradiction between productive forces and production relationships in the capitalist world is always of an acute nature*. This manifests itself in the chronic narrowness of the market under capitalism, leading to a sharp fight for every sales opportunity and to such an accentuation of imperialist antagonisms as to bring us close to the second run of wars. Capital's manoeuvring possibilities are thus considerably restricted. The chronic narrowness of the market manifests itself economically in the following way:

   (1) *The chronic agrarian crisis* permanently reducing the agricultural population's purchasing power for industrial commodities.

   (2) *The chronic surplus of capital*, particularly of industrial capital (permanent idleness of large portions of the production apparatus),[39]

---

37 The crisis of 1920–1 also occurred in the period of the general crisis of capitalism, but, as already mentioned, its specific nature was determined principally by the effects of the war.

38 See *Programme of the Communist International* 1929; Stalin 1954c, pp. 242–349; the symposium *Obshchiy krizis kapitalizma* 1933–4.

39 The production capacity 41.4 of German industry, taking 48 hours a week as a basis, was utilised only 67.4 percent in 1929, and only 35.7 percent in 1933.

as well as of trading capital ('congested trade') and of loan capital (except during the acute phase of the credit crisis).

(3) *Chronic mass unemployment*, which differs from the industrial reserve army of the industrial capitalism era in that it does not disappear even in the prosperity phase, growing bigger and bigger (if we disregard the cyclic movement).

These are the major aspects of the general crisis of capitalism which determine the exceptional depth, intensity and duration of the great crisis of 1929–33.

The Depth of the Crisis

Let us take the decline of industrial production as a measure. A comprehensive index is available for Germany only.

TABLE 12.1 Changes in the industrial outlook of Germany according to cycles[40]

Boom year	Year of lowest point of crisis	General index			Means of production			Consumer goods		
		Boom year	Crisis year	% change	Boom year	Crisis year	% change	Boom year	Crisis year	% change
1865	1866	15.9	16.0	+0.6	12.4	12.4	0.0	26.0	26.3	+1.2
1872	1874	22.9	21.5	−6.1	17.6	16.9	−4.0	38.0	34.3	−9.7
1885	1886	32.2	32.7	+1.6	27.7	28.3	+2.2	45.0	45.1	+0.2
1891	1892	41.4	40.0	−3.4	35.5	33.8	−4.8	58.0	57.7	−0.5
(1898)	(1900)									
1900	1901	64.7	64.9	+0.3	62.1	61.1	−1.6	75.0	72.2	−3.7[41]
1906	1908	34.3	78.8	−6.5	83.0	76.0	−8.4	89.2	87.0	−2.5
1922	1923	46.9	71.4	−34.4	70.7	43.4	−38.6	76.3	58.8	−22.9
1929	1932	103.1	61.2	−40.6	103.0	48.4	−53.0	106.2	79.4	−25.3

This table illustrates our foregoing statements most clearly:

(a) *In the era of industrial capitalism*, when German capitalism was developing rapidly, the crises in the decisive sphere of production was very mild. During three crises there was no decline in industrial production at all, merely a slackening in the rate of growth.

---

40 Calculated by the Institut für Konjunkturforschung of Berlin.
41 The figures refer to the years 1898 and 1900. The crisis began earlier and ended earlier in Division II, hence, the general index shows a rise whereas the two partial indexes, each separately, show a drop.

(b) *In the era of industrial capitalism,* when the development of productive forces was not yet limited by monopolies, the decline in the production of means of production was not greater than that in the production of consumers' goods, but less.

(c) *In the era of imperialism,* and particularly in the period of the general crisis, the rate of decline in industrial production during the crisis suddenly increases. At the same time the centre of gravity of the crisis shifts to Division I, as a result of the effect of monopoly and of the surplus of means of production that characterises the general crisis.

(d) *In depth the last crisis by far surpasses all its predecessors*; the production of means of production, in particular, has dropped more than half, whereas the production of consumers' goods has declined only 25 percent.

No general indexes calculated on this basis are available for other countries. We use as substitutes the data available for long periods of time for the older industries. The following table shows the percentage declines[42] from the year of prosperity to the lowest crisis year.

TABLE 12.2 United States of America: decline in production in %

	Coal	Iron	Steel	Cotton consumption
1857–8	1.7	20.2	–	27.4
1865	+0.5 (rise)	17.9	–	–
1874–5	9.1	27.0	+8.5 (rise)	9.6
1884–5	7.5	12.5	10.7	15.4
1893–4	6.4	27.3	18.4	19.8
1907–8	13.4	38.2	40.0	8.9
1920–1	27.5	54.8	53.0	20.0
1929–33	41.7	79.4	76.3	31.0

In essence this table reveals the same dynamics as those prevailing in Germany. The enormous decline in the output of steel and iron, the typical, raw materials in the production of means of production, is particularly striking in the last crisis. The picture presented by England and France is somewhat different. In England, the percentage decline in production was less in the present crisis

---

42 The figures have been compiled by the Economic Research Section of the Institute of World Economy and World Politics, Moscow.

than in the first postwar crisis. This is due to the fact that the general crisis is particularly acute in England; therefore, there was no ideal upswing there in the years 1928–9. In France, on the other hand, the crisis of 1920–1 was relatively mild (the decline in the general index of industrial output was only 11 percent, as compared with 31 percent in the recent crisis), because the reconstruction of the devastated areas created a big special market for industry. But this unevenness in the case of individual countries does not alter the fact that the world crisis of 1929–33 was by far the deepest crisis in the history of capitalism!

Decisive for the exceptional depth of the last crisis was the chronic surplus of means of production, which has hit Division I particularly hard on a world scale, as the following *Table 12.3*[43] shows:

TABLE 12.3   Index of world industrial production (1928 = 100)

	1913	1929	1930	1931	1932	1933
Means of production	69	110	96	82	62	75
Consumers' goods	81	105	98	91	89	96

In 1932, the lowest crisis year, *the output in Division I dropped some 10 percent below the 1913 level*, whereas the output in Division II *was still about 10 percent above the level of 1913*.

The decline in production according to divisions in the most important countries in 1932 is given in the following *Table 12.4*.

[43] Includes the Soviet Union. No statistics for the capitalist world, without the Soviet Union, are available for 1932–3. The figures are as follows for the previous years:

TABLE 12.4   Index of world production without the Soviet Union

	1913	1929	1930	1931
Means of production	69	109	94	78
Consumer goods	81	104	93	92

As we may see by a comparison of the figures for 1931, *the inclusion of the USSR affects the world index considerably in favour of Division I*. Figures from Wagenführ 1933, p. 67; for 1932–3, see *Wochenbericht des Instituts für Konjunkturforschung*, 7, 17, 11 July 1934, pp. 129–32.

TABLE 12.4 Index of world production without the Soviet Union (repeated)

	1913	1929	1930	1931
Means of production	69	109	94	78
Consumer goods	81	104	93	92

These figures reveal great inequalities among the different countries. The decline in the output of means of production was greatest in the USA and *Germany*, the two countries where the industrial production apparatus, as a result of rationalisation, was the most modern and the most strongly developed prior to the crisis (in Poland the lack of capital and the complete cessation of capital imports played a great role). *France* occupies an exceptional position throughout the entire crisis: its decline in Division I was always less than in Division II. The most important reasons for this were: the late beginning and the lesser extent of rationalisation before the crisis; large-scale construction of fortifications, harbours and canals during the crisis; and the importance of its luxury industries in Division II, which were particularly hit by the crisis. In *England* the decline in production was generally less because production was already at a very low level in 1928, which is taken as a basis. In *Japan* the lowest point of the crisis was reached as early as 1931.

Of the various branches of industry, the building, shipbuilding and machine industries suffered most under the crisis, in addition to the iron and steel industry, i.e. those branches of industry chiefly producing commodities used as fixed capital. The following passage indicates the methods adopted to avoid any increase in fixed capital:

> During the last six months very few orders for machine tools were placed in Germany. They came mostly from small and medium-sized firms. The big plants and concerns have stopped all buying of production equipment. *They cover their urgent needs from the machinery inventory of the plant departments that are operating at less than capacity.*[44]

Influenced by the chronic surplus of production capacity, *the production of means of production in some countries during the crisis has dropped to such an extent that output did not even cover current natural wear and tear*. Bourgeois

---

44   Schoening 1933.

authorities have already admitted that this holds true for 1931. Thus, the Institut für Konjunkturforschung writes in its weekly report of 9 March 1932:

> In 1931 the reduction of total existing plant in Germany's national economy due to current wear and tear and obsolescence of old plants was much greater than the total replacement investments and the isolated cases of new investments. In other words, German national economy has been living on its capital in 1931.

The annual report of the American steel trust (United States Steel Corporation) for 1931 reads: 'The average annual production during the ten years, 1922 to 1931, inclusive, was 43,000,000 tons, compared with a production of 26,000,000 tons in 1931'.

It seems reasonable to suppose that on the basis of average demands in the United States for steel products during the past ten years, the requirements of this country for maintenance and current uses alone, exclusive of development and expansion, should call for steel products in considerably greater tonnage than was consumed in 1931.[45]

But in 1932 steel output in the USA dropped to half that in 1931. It is therefore obvious that production was far from sufficient to cover current wear and tear.

In some cases the decline of fixed capital during the crisis may be ascertained directly. Let us cite two examples: *the American railways and the cotton industry*.

While American railways used over two million tons of new rails annually for replacement in the five years preceding the crisis, only 500,000 tons of rails were relaid in 1932.

The same holds true for US railway rolling stock, as may be seen from the following table:

TABLE 12.6 Rolling stock orders

	1929	1931	1932	(Until Sept 1931)
Locomotives	1,212	235	0	–
Passenger cars	2,303	11	0	–
Freight cars	111,000	11,000	2,000	–

---

45 [Varga gives as source *Iron Age*].

Repairs of locomotives and cars were neglected to such an extent that the number of locomotives at present in operation is many thousands less than in the pre-crisis period. (Data obtained from various numbers of the *Railway Age*).

TABLE 12.7 Number of installed spindles (in millions)[46]

	1 August 1929	1 February 1933	Decrease	Percent decline
Total capitalist world	156.7	148.4	8.3	5
England	55.9	48.0	7.9	14
USA	34.8	31.0	3.8	11
Germany	11.3	9.9	1.4	13

The textile industry declined in the leading capitalist countries, but in the colonial countries there was a certain expansion of the textile industry even during the crisis; the decline for the world as a whole therefore is less than in the three leading capitalist countries together.

Tonnage of sea-going vessels reveals a similar state of affairs:

TABLE 12.8 World sea-going tonnage – millions of gross tons[47]

	Total	Steamships	Motorships
June, 1929	68.07	59.78	6.63
June, 1934	65.58	53.75	10.60
	−2.49	−6.03	+3.97

These figures, however, conceal the antagonistic and uneven nature of development. Almost 9,000,000 tons of *new* ships were completed from 1929–33, so that scrapped vessels represented approximately 12,000,000 tons. No less than 11,600,000 tons were laid up and withdrawn from service in the middle of 1933. But international competition and preparations for war forced the building of

---

46 *International Cotton Statistics*, Manchester: International Federation of Cotton and Allied Textile Industries, March 1934.

47 *Monthly Bulletin of Statistics*, Geneva: League of Nations, July 1934, p. 292.

new and faster motorships. New ships totaling 1,200,000 tons were being built in the middle of 1934.

Taken by countries, the figures reveal the same uneven state of affairs as in the cotton industry.

TABLE 12.9   Loss of tonnage between the middle of 1929 and 1934 (millions of tons)

England	USA	Germany
2.43	1.48	0.4

Various small nations, on the other hand, increased their tonnage. The tendency to abandon worldwide division of labour is in evidence here just as in the cotton industry.

These facts and figures – which could be repeated ad lib – disclose the exceptional depth of this great economic crisis surpassing all previous crises. Production would have dropped still lower *if not for the tremendous war preparations*, which provided certain sections of industry with orders. The decay of capitalism is clearly manifested by these facts.

The All-Embracing Nature of the Crisis

The last crisis differs from all previous crises in its all-embracing character, as Comrade Stalin pointed out in his report at the Seventeenth Party Congress. In studying the history of previous crises, we find that there always were particular countries and certain branches of industry that were unaffected by them.[48] This crisis, through its link with the chronic agrarian crisis, has affected all countries: industrial as well as agrarian countries; imperialist nations and colonies; the means of production as well as consumers' goods; the production of food and raw materials; domestic and foreign trade; stock exchange and credit; all without exception!

Only those branches of industry *directly* involved in preparation for war: airplane construction, the artificial silk industry, etc., constitute an exception. Production rose in these branches of industry even during the crisis and their production capacity has been augmented by the construction of new plants, although the available plants are fare from working at full capacity.

---

48   Thorp 1926.

TABLE 12.10 World production of artificial silk in thousands of metric tons[49]

1928	1929	1930	1931	1932	1933
17.4	20.8	20.0	23.4	24.0	30.2

Development was very uneven. In Japan the output of artificial silk went from 750 tons in 1929 to 4,400 tons in 1933, according to estimates given by the League of Nations.

The Long Duration of the Crisis

The recent crisis is undoubtedly the longest in the history of capitalism. It is difficult to obtain exact comparative figures for the following reasons:

(a) The time of the open outbreak of the crisis can be fixed precisely (although the crisis matured for a long time in the form of an accumulation of unsold goods). On the other hand, the transition from the crisis to the depression phase is a process which is not clearly delimited and is interrupted by relapses. The time when the crisis – after reaching its lowest point – passes into the depression can be determined only more or less arbitrarily. Only the interval of time between the *highest point of production and the lowest point of the crisis* can be stated accurately, but this low point does not signify the end of the crisis.

(b) For technical reasons: *no monthly* data of production, are available for the older cycles, only annual data. We will therefore confine ourselves to a few examples from the USA.

TABLE 12.11 USA – duration of the decline in production (in months)

Crisis	Iron	Coal	Building contracts
1907–8	3	6	9
1920–1	16	4	9
1929–32	39	41	57

---

49   *Statistical Yearbook of the League of Nations* 1933–4.

The long duration of the decline in production down to the lowest crisis point, which also determines the unusually long duration of the crisis as a whole, follows from the general crisis of capitalism, from the effect of monopolies, which endeavoured to prevent the drop in prices of their goods, and partly from the endeavours of the bourgeoisie to overcome the crisis rapidly by means of state measures which only resulted in a prolongation of the crisis.

The Price Decline during the Crisis

With the exception of the postwar crisis the *price decline during the recent crisis was incomparably greater than* during any of the previous crises.[50] This tremendous price decline is the basis for a number of important qualitatively new factors in the crisis: depreciation of currencies, non-payment of foreign debts and cessation of capital export.[51] We must therefore deal at greater length with its causes.

During the crisis, prices moved as follows in the major countries:

TABLE 12.12 Index of wholesale prices[52] (1913 = 100)

Annual average	Germany	France (gold francs)	England (*Economist*)	USA	Japan
1929	137	127	127	137	166
1930	125	113	107	124	137
1931	111	102	89[53]	105	116
1932	97	87	86	93	122[54]
1933	93	81	87	94[55]	136

---

50 The fall in prices in previous crises amounted to approximately 10 percent. *The great period of falling prices in the nineteenth century, from 1873 to 1896, was not of a cyclic character.* The price decline was the result of the great agrarian crisis and of the decrease in the value of capitalistically produced commodities due to technical progress, the rise in the productivity of labour, which was very great during this boom period of capitalism.
51 The unevenness in the drop of prices (the decline in monopoly prices was much slighter than the drop in prices of non-monopoly commodities; the drop in price of manufactured goods was slighter than that of agricultural commodities, etc.) is a special factor in accentuating antagonisms during the crisis. We shall discuss this later on.
52 *Monthly Bulletin of Statistics*, League of Nations, 1934, 17, 7.
53 Inflation since September, 1931.
54 Inflation since the end of 1931.
55 Inflation since March 1933.

These series *cannot be compared* with each other since various commodities or the same commodities weighted differently serve as a basis. But the *movement* of the price level is the same (allowing for the effect of inflation).

TABLE 12.13 Price decline in percent from 1929 to 1933 (annual average)

Germany	France	England	USA
32	36	31	31

Prices have dropped approximately by an equal percentage in all countries *where there was no great depreciation of the currency*. The causes of this big price decline are to be found not only in the acuteness of the crisis, but also in the following factors:

During the war the demand for commodities exceeded supply to such an extent that the prices of almost all commodities rose considerably above their value. This assertion seems to contradict one of the main theses of Marxism, according to which the price of commodities is determined by their value. However, this is not so. Under *extraordinary* circumstances, when demand exceeds supply for a long time, prices can and must rise above value. Only in general, only under 'normal' conditions, are prices determined by their value.

> In so far as crises arise from *changes in prices and revolutions in prices*, which do not coincide with *changes in the values* of commodities, they naturally cannot be investigated during the examination of capital in general, in which the prices of commodities are assumed to be *identical* with the *values* of commodities.[56]

Thus Marx considers that 'price revolutions' are possible without changes in value. Moreover, in each cycle the actual market prices rise *above* value during the boom and fall *below* value during crises. The equality of total price and total value of commodities holds good only when averaged over the entire cycle. Marx says:

---

56   Marx 1969, p. 515.

... [I]n periods of prosperity, particularly during the times of bogus prosperity, in which the relative value of money, expressed in commodities, decreases also for other reasons (without any actual revolution in values), so that the prices of commodities rise independently of their own values.[57]

Hence the detachment of price from value during the World War as a result of demand constantly exceeding supply in no way contradicts the theory of Marx. On the contrary, that is what had to happen. (Artificial price recovery effected by state measures – guaranteed minimum prices in the USA and in England – also played a role). By the end of the World War, prices *in gold* had risen to more than twice the 1913 level. This excessive price rise was only half liquidated in the crisis of 1920–1; prices were then stabilised on this level, which was still much too high. The gold price index hovered around 150 in 1922–9, taking 1913 as 100. The reason why prices did not drop to about the pre-war level was not a decline in the value of gold compared with the pre-war period, since no technical innovations were introduced such as might have reduced considerably the labour time contained in the gold unit of weight. In our opinion, the reason for this lay in the fact that the level of very important elements in production costs; leases, rent, freight, officials' salaries, overhead expenses, taxes, etc. were fixed in long-term contracts, or by government decree. These excessively high factors in production costs kept prices high, although supply and demand tallied more or less. A second major crisis was required to destroy all these bonds and to adjust prices to the value of commodities, which had undoubtedly declined compared with the pre-war period (due to the increase in the productivity of labour). But this adjustment was a violent process which accentuated the crisis even more, and hence, overcoming the crisis was rendered more difficult. It undermined the entire international gold and credit system and it is one of the factors accounting for the exceptional character of the present depression.

Reduction of Profits

Every crisis involves a decrease in the appropriated *surplus value*, since *the number of exploited workers drops sharply* and wage reductions cannot keep up with the fall in prices. The reduction in the total appropriated surplus value is tantamount to a reduction in total profits.

---

57 Marx 1957, p. 410.

Furthermore, the heavy price decline results in *profits dropping even faster than surplus value*. The market price of commodities is not determined by the actual price of production, but by the price of reproduction! When the elements of constant capital – raw materials, auxiliary materials, etc. – drop in price during the process of production, the market price of the finished goods will not be governed by the actual expenditure, but by the outlay necessary at the time of sale for purchasing raw and auxiliary materials, etc. Hence every turnover of capital ends in a loss when prices are falling rapidly. The workers are exploited, surplus value is appropriated, but there is no profit. The longer the production period, the greater the loss.[58] Naturally, idleness of production plant, which tangibly raises the cost of production, is also an important factor.

TABLE 12.14 Company balances of the most important industrial countries[59]

	USA	England	Germany
	Net profit of 4333 industrial corporations (Standard statistics) (1928 = 100)	Profits (1924 = 100)	Total profits in million of marks
1929	113.5	120.1	315
1930	67.6	119.4	207
1931	28.0	92.5	116 (loss)
1932	7.0	75.8	73

We emphasise that these figures do not refer to profits in our sense of the term, but only to *employers' profit* (i.e. after deducting interest, amortisation and taxes). But this gives a roughly approximate picture nonetheless. It is probable that many corporations, whose credit was already jeopardised, 'trimmed' their balances, i.e. show a profit instead of the actual losses.

These summary figures conceal major inequalities. The deeper the crisis in particular branches of industry, the longer the process of production, the

---

58 The price decline, by cheapening the elements of constant capital, lowers the organic composition of capital, and therefore raises the rate of profit at the expense of a great loss of capital. But this effect is evident only after the drop in prices is over.

59 *Vierteljahreshefte zur Konjunkturforschung*, 1933, 8, 2, part A, p. 98.

greater the loss. Let us take the USA[60] as an example. In 1932 employers' profits (profit after deducting interest on borrowed capital, taxes and amortisation) were as follows in the most important branches of industry in the USA:

TABLE 12.15 Monopolies as against customers and producers

	Number of enterprises	Capital (in millions of dollars)	Employers' profit	Percent
Food industry	41	785	44.1	5.6
Dairy produce	10	321	19.8	6.2
Bakeries	21	366	27.9	7.6
Tobacco	28	894	110.3	13.5

These two-edged monopolies, purchasing their raw materials from the unorganised farmers at very low prices and selling their commodities directly to the ultimate consumers, can therefore maintain prices at a high level. With a very short production period (in bakeries practically only one day), and with sales not declining very much, relatively speaking, they piled up respectable profits even during the crisis.

This does not hold true for all enterprises of Division II, however, as may be seen from the following figures in *Table 12.16*:

TABLE 12.16 Losses made in the textile industry

	Losses in millions of dollars
Cotton industry	13.7
Wool industry	11.0
Other textile industries	11.6

On the other hand, the heavy industry enterprises, with a longer production period and a greater decline in production, which produce their own raw materials or buy them at high monopoly prices from other monopolies, have sustained great losses in spite of their strong monopolist position.

---

60   Data taken from the *National City Bank Bulletin*, April 1934.

TABLE 12.17 Losses of heavy industry

	Number of enterprises	Capital (in million of dollars)	Loss
Iron and Steel	51	4,030	160.9
Machinery plants	73	527	39.0
Automobile factories	20	1,382	40.5
Building materials	44	601	19.5
Capper production	14	450	10.7

We shall deal later with the effect of the decline in prices of agricultural produce.

The Credit Crisis and Its Peculiarities

Every crisis in the sphere of production is not without its effect in the sphere of credit. But the beginning of the credit crisis need not coincide with the outbreak of the crisis in the sphere of production. The distinguishing feature of the present crisis is that the open outbreak of the credit crisis occurred after a day of two to three years. In Germany it broke out in the summer of 1931, while in the USA it assumed the dimensions of a catastrophe only in March 1933. The far-reaching fusion of bank capital and industrial capital into finance capital *caused the big banks to mobilise all their resources to prevent the open outbreak of the credit crisis, which might have become very dangerous for them,*[61] as the bankruptcy of all the big German banks has shown. But the longer this outbreak was delayed in any one country, the more catastrophic were the forms assumed by the credit crisis. It was most acute in the USA, where all the gold institutions had to close down in March 1933.

The violent outbreak of the credit crisis could not be prevented mainly because of the tremendous fall in prices which increased the real burden of indebtedness by 30 or 40 percent during the crisis.

The price decline meant a vast shift in the distribution of real income in favour of creditors (those living on income) at the expense of debtors (industrialists, peasants, house owners, artisans). Putting it otherwise: loan capital in

---

61 In the crises of the period of industrial capitalism, when the banks advanced credit chiefly on bills of exchange and their stake in a given debtor was relatively small, they drove their debtors into bankruptcy with less hesitation in order to save their claims.

all its forms was to receive the same amount as before in interest and amortisation out of total profits, which were greatly reduced by the crisis. This could not go on forever. There were three ways out:
(1) *Elementary cancellation of debts through bankruptcy.*
(2) *Depreciation of currency, thus adjusting the real debt burden to the lowered price level.*
(3) *Non-payment of debts*, both internal and foreign, *sanctioned by the state.*
The anarchic method of cancelling the intolerable portion of the debt burden through bankruptcy, which is the normal method under capitalism, could not be allowed to run its course during this crisis. The bankruptcies affected such commanding institutions of finance capital as the Darmstädter Bank, the Dresdner Bank, the Vienna Kreditanstalt, the Kreuger Match Trust in Sweden, the Insull Trust in the USA, etc. Owing to the depth of the crisis and the tremendous price declining the number of bankruptcies threatened to reach such enormous proportions as to involve the complete collapse of the credit system, and politically to endanger the hegemony of the bourgeoisie over the peasantry and the urban petty bourgeoisie. *The wave of bankruptcies had to be stopped.* This was done either through depreciating the currency or through governmental decrees reducing the interest rate and prohibiting sales at auction, etc. at home, and by moratoria on debts owed abroad. Thus the credit crisis grew into a bank crisis and a crisis of currencies.

The Depreciation of Currencies
Depreciation of the currencies of most countries is a *qualitatively new factor*, not found in any previous crisis.[62]

The general economic basis for the wave of inflation is the fact that the burden of domestic and foreign debts had become intolerable owing to the heavy price decline. The *immediate* cause was different in various countries. In agrarian countries with foreign indebtedness, the balance of payments is negative *as a result of the heavy decline in the prices of agricultural produce, so that*

---

62 Previous cases of the depreciation of gold currencies, including depreciation during the postwar crisis, were almost exclusively the result of wars which had led to genuine inflation, to the issue of paper money to cover the cost of war. Present currency depreciation is *nowhere the result of 'inflation' in this classical sense of the word*, which is an increase in the circulation of paper money to cover the State deficit. In some countries the banknote circulation has increased during the crisis, true enough, though it should have decreased in view of the drop in prices and reduced production. But this increase was not undertaken with the direct object of covering the budget deficit, but because cash reserves in banks and other enterprises were greatly augmented on account of the credit crisis, as is always the case in such times.

the net export surplus no longer meets interest and sinking funds payments on the foreign indebtedness. In England the balance of payments was negative for the moment and there was a large outflow of gold owing to the sudden withdrawal of a considerable part of the foreign short-term capital invested in London. In the USA, despite a favourable balance of trade, the currency was depreciated by governmental measures deliberately instituted to lighten the burden of debt, which had brought the entire credit and banking system to the verge of destruction.

Roughly speaking, inflation proceeded in three waves. The *first wave* caused inflation in a number of overseas agrarian countries. The *second*, in the autumn of 1931, was marked by England's leaving the gold standard and the adjustment of the respective currencies to the depreciated pound sterling in ail the British dominions, India and the Scandinavian countries. The *third wave* began in the early part of 1933 with the departure of the USA from the gold standard. The process of inflation is by no means concluded and continues in the phase of depression as well. The situation in the middle of 1934 is as follows:

(a) *There are still four countries on a real gold standard,* that is, where banknotes may be exchanged for gold at par whenever desired, and gold may freely be exported: France, Switzerland, Holland and Belgium.

(b) *There is a group of countries with a formal gold standard.* In relations with other countries, the currency is exchanged on the basis of gold parity. But this is attained nor through the free movement of gold, as is the case in countries on a real gold standard, but through the strictest regulation of foreign trade and currency transfer, and prohibition of the export of banknotes. In some countries, this is supplemented by the *non-payment* of foreign debts, which we shall discuss later. This group includes Germany (after devaluation), Italy, Poland, Hungary, Rumania, Czechoslovakia, Bulgaria, Latvia and Lithuania. In some of these countries, as in Germany, there are actually *two rates of foreign exchange*: the official one, corresponding to the gold parity, for foreign exchange allocated by the government; and another rate at a discount of between 20 and 50 percent for marks in possession of foreigners usable only in Germany (registered marks, etc.). Mark notes are dealt with abroad at a discount of 20 to 50 percent.

(c) *All other countries have an openly depreciated currency.* These countries comprise three groups:

(1) *The sterling bloc.* This is a group of countries closely linked economically with Great Britain, which have 'tied' their currencies to the pound, i.e. the rate of exchange of their currencies in terms of gold is regulated according to the quotation for the pound. To put it in other words, in their case the British

pound, as it were, plays the role of a world money. This group includes all the British dominions and colonies, the Scandinavian countries, Portugal, Argentina and Brazil.

The British bourgeoisie was doubtless forced to *abandon the gold standard* because of the temporarily unfavourable balance of payments, which led to a large outflow of gold. It did so very reluctantly in view of the big profits it reaps from its position as banker to the world. This is proved by its endeavours to procure the foreign exchange needed to maintain the gold standard by floating big loans in the USA and in France. Conditions on the world stock exchanges did not permit the foreign securities in Britain's possession to be thrown on the market to obtain foreign exchange, since this would have led to a catastrophic stock exchange collapse. But when depreciation proved to be unavoidable, the British bourgeoisie derived the greatest possible benefit out of it by utilising the depreciation of the pound in its struggle for world markets, and by re-establishing the pound's position as a world currency in spite of its depreciation (which it quickly checked by re-establishing free gold dealings). The Bank of England's gold reserves are now greater than ever.[63]

(2) *The second group constitutes the dollar bloc*; the USA and a few Central and South American states, whose currency is regulated according to the depreciation of the dollar.

Abandonment of the gold standard by the USA was not due to *monetary* compulsion, an outflow of gold which began to eat into the gold reserves, as in the case of England or Japan. (The outflow of gold at the beginning of 1933 was bound to come to a stop as soon as the relatively insignificant short-term balances of foreign banks had been withdrawn). In general, no attempt was made to use the tremendous gold reserves – more than four milliard pre-inflation dollars – to protect the currency. Departure from the gold standard was deliberately undertaken with the object of easing the untenable position of the debtors, who were collapsing under the debt burden – shifting the division of profits between industrial capital and loan capital in favour of the former.

But abandoning the gold standard alone was not sufficient to produce depreciation of the dollar. The trade balance of the USA in contrast to that of England is a very favourable one. The same is true of the balance of payments. Therefore, exceptional methods had to be applied. The USA's favourable balance of payments was enough to maintain the new gold value of dollar notes without their being exchangeable for gold.

---

63   Over £100,000,000 of gold was pumped out of India.

The issue of unbacked paper money to cover the budget deficit would have been the proper method of forcing depreciation still further. (Roosevelt had obtained the power to issue three milliard dollars of additional paper money from Congress). But Roosevelt was still afraid of this 'open' inflation, and struck a path that was quite new in the history of capitalism; purchasing gold at prices higher than the current dollar rate in gold francs – artificially lowering the dollar rate of exchange. By the end of 1933 he had succeeded, through this procedure, in reducing the dollar rate of exchange by about 40 percent, at which level the dollar was actually stabilised at the insistence of dominant sections of the big bourgeoisie, without re-establishing the gold standard.

(3) The third group consists of those countries that have not 'tied' their currencies either to the pound or to the dollar. Most of them are agrarian debtor nations, which could no longer pay interest and amortisation on their foreign debts out of their export receipts in consequence of the sharp fall in prices of agrarian produce. After their gold reserves were exhausted, they were compelled to resort to inflation and to stop payments on their foreign debts. The following instance may serve as an illustration:

TABLE 12.18 Argentina's balance of payment during the crisis (millions of dollars)[64]

	Net favourable trade balance	Interest and dividend payment abroad	For other services[65]	Total	Gold export	Increase in indebtedness to foreign countries
1927–8	+199	–182	–52	–35	–146 (import)	131
1928–9	+114	–188	–49	–123	+119	38
1929–30	–103	–158	–38	–299	+56	167
1930–1	+43	–117	–22	–96	+123	10

These figures show that net income from exports dropped from US$ 199,000,000 to US$ 43,000,000, whereas payments of interest and other obligations to foreign countries dropped only from US$ 234,000,000 to US$ 39,000,000. During the crisis, Argentina paid out US$ 218,000,000 in gold. As long as it was able to, it contracted new foreign debts to pay the interest on

---

64   *Statistical Yearbook of the League of Nations*, 1932–3, p. 173.
65   Ocean freight and the like.

the old loans; but in 1930–1 it could no longer obtain any new loans. Inflation and cessation of interest payment to foreign countries became inevitable.

Thus we see that although the sharp drop in prices was the *general economic basis* for the depreciation of currencies, the concrete economic mechanism that led to inflation differed in various countries (or types of country).

A Few Words on Gold Standard Countries

It is striking that all the countries formally or in fact remaining on the gold standard *are countries that already went through the experience of very severe inflation in the postwar period* (except the typical *rentier* states, Holland and Switzerland). The tenacity with which the German, Polish, Hungarian bourgeoisie, and the like, hold on to the gold standard naturally does not imply that capitalist economy in these countries is on a sounder economic basis and less undermined by the crisis than in the USA or England. It merely means that they fear they will be unable to set any limits to currency depreciation once it sets in, because of their economic weakness. Depreciation resembling that of the postwar period would dangerously accelerate the maturing of the revolutionary crisis, since it would alienate the petty-bourgeois bank depositors and intensify the proletariat's discontent tremendously.

In our publications, currency depreciation is often treated much too simply as merely a means of struggle for foreign markets, as a means for supplementary exploitation of the working class, as a phenomenon which has only favourable aspects for the bourgeoisie. This is naturally incorrect and undialectical. *The depreciation of currency is not a remedy voluntarily employed against the crisis, but a symptom of the disease as well as an elementary factor intensifying the crisis still more.* To the first countries compelled to inflate, depreciation of the currency offers a transient advantage in the struggle for world markets, an advantage which disappears as soon as most currencies are depreciated. The low gold prices at which inflation countries sell their goods abroad mean that they are *selling them under their value*; it signifies the impoverishment of these countries, while a few inflation profiteers grow rich. Certain sections of the bourgeoisie, principally the heavily indebted agrarians, rich peasants and industrialists, derive an advantage from inflation at the expense of loan capital; but they must run the risk of exchange fluctuations which will make all long-term calculation impossible. Inflation increases the exploitation of the workers and means expropriation of the property of the savings bank depositors (i.e. chiefly the petty bourgeoisie) in favour of the big bourgeoisie. But it also involves the rapid accentuation of class antagonisms, with the threat of the petty bourgeoisie going over to the side of the revolutionary proletariat.

In contrast to the view that inflation is a remedy voluntarily employed by the bourgeoisie to overcome the crisis, we should like to emphasise the following:

The healthy, normal functioning of capitalism requires a stable gold standard currency. The fact that inflation has been introduced in an overwhelming majority of countries, that even in the phase of the present depression the process of currency depreciation has not come to a standstill, proves the far-reaching devastation of world capitalism which the crisis has entailed. Currency chaos is an element in the special character of the present depression. The almost general abandonment of the gold standard has now restricted the big shifts in the distribution of gold that took place during the crisis. The result of the struggle for gold is shown by the following table:

TABLE 12.19 Gold reserves of central banks and governments in millions of gold dollars[66]

	USA	England	France	Germany	Total Europe	Asia	Latin America
July 1929	3,974	688	1,462	512	4,511	728	801
1933	4,009	925	3,213	58	6,922	481	367

The table reveals quite clearly the following interesting facts:
(a) During the crisis all newly-mined gold was absorbed by Europe.
(b) The debtor countries (Latin America, Asia, Germany, etc.) were obliged to part with a large proportion of their gold reserves.
(c) Within Europe, France appropriated an enormous part of the gold reserves of the world.

The Decay of the Credit System and of Capital Export

Together with inflation, the debt burden, which the crisis and steep price decline had made intolerable, resulted in a disintegration of the credit system. This took on various forms:

In many countries, particularly in those which remain on the gold standard either formally or in fact – the debt burden was reduced by state intervention: prohibition of sales by court order (sheriff sales) and reduction of the interest rate. Moreover, government credit has taken the place of private capitalist credit to an ever greater extent – guarantee of savings bank deposits and reorganisation of bankrupt banks, which are transformed into semi-governmental

---

66   *Federal Reserve Bulletin.*

institutions. The net result is a tremendous shrinkage in the total volume of credit. Short-term indebtedness throughout the capitalist world shrank from 57 milliard marks in 1931 to 25 milliard marks at the end of 1933 (Reichskreditgesellschaft estimate).

Payment of *international* debts became impossible owing to lack of gold or of an adequate export surplus, and to a large extent had to be abandoned. Reparations and inter-allied debts are no longer being paid. A large number of nations have declared a complete or partial moratorium on government loans.[67] Several nations have declared a moratorium even on private debts, e.g. Germany (standstill agreement in regard to short-term debts and loans), Austria, Hungary and a number of South American countries.

The natural consequence of this general non-payment of foreign debts is an almost complete *cessation of capital export*, even after the acute credit crisis had been passed and capital became available in the imperialist countries for export purposes.

TABLE 12.20 New issues of capital for foreign countries[68]

	1928	1929	1930	1931	1932	1933
USA (millions of US$)	1,325	763	1,020	255	27.0	1.6
Great Britain (millions of £): Colonies	219	159	127	37	29.0	30.0
Foreign countries		86	54	70	9	0.3	8.0

Capital is now exported abroad only when foreign policy and preparations for war demand it. (England's loans to the dominions and to Argentina, the French loans to Rumania for equipping the latter's army, and the loans of the USA to the government of Chiang Kai-shek). The cessation of the 'normal' export of capital, which is one of the cornerstones of imperialism, shows how deeply capitalism has been shaken by the crisis. *The cessation of capital export is an important factor in the exceptional nature of the present depression*. This does not imply the cessation of the struggle for capital investment, however, the best proof of which was Japan's protest in April 1934 against the investment of capital in China by other nations.

---

67 Almost all the countries of Central and South America, the Balkan States and the countries of Central Europe (Germany, Austria and Hungary).
68 *Statistical Yearbook of the League of Nations* for 1932–3 and 1933–4.

The collapse of the credit system also manifests itself in the peculiar fact that a tremendous abundance of *short-term funds* is paralleled by a lack of long-term credit, with the issue of stock and bonds at an extremely low level.[69]

The decline is general, continuing in 1933, except in Great Britain. The trend is highly uneven: the USA declined over 90 percent, while France and England lost only one-half. In Japan the issue of capital increased threefold in consequence of the war boom.[70]

The Bank of France has 25 milliard francs of *non-interest bearing deposits*. The American government was able to dispose of short-term treasury notes at an interest rate of 0.12 percent per annum. Worry over the safety of capital and fear of tying up capital in long-term investments under the generally prevailing conditions of political and economic insecurity outweigh the desire to invest at greater advantage. The property of money to become potential capital, the characteristic feature of capitalism, asserts itself with ever greater difficulty.

The Shrinkage of Foreign Trade

Every cyclic crisis entails a drop in foreign trade. In this crisis, however, the shrinkage is extraordinarily great. The reasons for this are as follows:

(a) *The fight for markets* has brought about a situation in which every commodity that can be produced at home at all is produced within the country under tariff protection, or with imports prohibited. This holds true both in industry and in agriculture.[71]
(b) Preparations for war have the same effect.
(c) In many countries *the lack of foreign exchange* necessitates the reduction of imports.
(d) *The almost complete cessation of capital export.*

---

69   TABLE 12.21 Issue of capital – except for refunding (in millions)

	USA dollars	Great Britain pounds	France francs	Germany marks	Italy lire	Japan yen
1929	10,183	254	19,245	2,664	7,280	2,662
1932	1,862	113	14,432	972	3,647	3,818
1933	936	133	10,429	–	3,344	6,617

70   Data from *Statistical Yearbook* of the League of Nations for 1933–4, p. 226.
71   This led to the most insane state of affairs: England subsidises sugar-beet cultivation, although enormous quantities of sugar are stored all over the world; Germany subsidises the cultivation of vegetable oil plants, and so forth.

TABLE 12.22 World foreign trade in milliards of pre-inflation gold dollars[72]

	1928	1929	1930	1931	1932	1933
Imports	34.7	35.6	29.8	20.8	14.0	12.5
Exports	32.8	33.0	26.5	18.9	12.9	11.7

World foreign trade has shrunk one-third, approximately half of the loss being due to the drop in prices, and the other half to the reduced volume of trade. The drop in total continued in the years 1933–4 as well.

The shrinkage of foreign trade proceeded unevenly, of course. Some countries, such as Japan, were able to increase their share of world trade during the crisis, while the shares of Germany and the USA diminished.

In many cases the shrinkage of foreign trade was the cause of inflation, as we have shown above. Conversely, protection of the currency in countries on an actual or nominal gold standard led to further shrinkage of foreign trade. The whole mechanism of international trade is out of gear. Commodities are no longer exported from countries where they can be produced most cheaply to countries where their production is most costly. Foreign trade is more and more regulated on the principle of a *'net balance'* between any two countries, i.e. every country buys from every other only as much as the other takes in exchange, so that no net balance need be paid in gold or foreign exchange. A kind of international 'barter in kind' develops: the USA exchanges wheat for coffee with Brazil; Hungary exchanges wheat for timber with Austria; Japan exchanges cotton goods for raw cotton with India, etc. Not a trace is left of the free trade that was typical of the period of rising industrial capitalism.

This gives rise to the *ideology of 'autarchy'*. The shrinkage of foreign trade, the tendency to abandon the worldwide economic division of labour, involves reduced productivity of labour and is a sign of the progressing decay of capitalism.

---

[72] The difference between import and export consists of freight charges, interest losses and difference in price between exporting and importing countries. The figures are taken from the statistics of the League of Nations.

3   The World Agrarian Crisis

The industrial crisis ran its course interwoven with the chronic agrarian crisis persisting since the end of the War. This deepened and prolonged the industrial crisis, and accentuated the agrarian crisis, making it more general. All the countries of the world and all branches of agriculture: cereals, stock-raising, dairy farming, industrial crops, were affected most acutely by the agrarian crisis. Its social and political consequences are stupendous; the peasantry of the entire bourgeois world is in motion. The tradition, formerly so natural, hegemony of the bourgeoisie over the masses of the peasantry – with whose help it was usually able to crush the revolutionary movement of the proletariat – is endangered. The bourgeoisie is compelled to resort to complicated and perilous manoeuvres to divert the peasant masses temporarily from the revolutionary road. For the Communist Parties the agrarian crisis has opened the road to the exploited rural masses.

In this chapter we shall analyse the agrarian crisis principally from the economic standpoint. Its social and political effects will be dealt with later.

The basic cause of the agrarian crisis is the same as that of cyclic industrial crises: the contradiction between social production and private appropriation, with its contingent poverty and restricted consumption for the masses. In this sense, agrarian crises are 'capitalist crises', as Lenin said. The outward form is also the same: *both are overproduction crises*, which involve a drop in prices and the wholesale bankruptcy of producers.[73]

---

[73]   TABLE 12.23 Agricultural sales income

	USA (millions of dollars)	Germany (millions of marks)
1929	11,918	10.2
1933	5,143	6.5 (1932–3)

TABLE 12.24 Number of sheriff sales of peasant farms in Germany

1930	1931	1932
4,318	5,798	6,961

YEARBOOK OF AGRICULTURE
1933, VOLUME 9, NO. 1, P. 25

There are, however, very important differences. Whereas industrial crises under capitalism recur periodically at intervals of eight or twelve years, *there is no such periodicity in agrarian crises*. The history of capitalism records only two general agrarian crises of long duration: the European agrarian crisis of 1873–95 and the present *world agrarian crisis*. (Former agrarian crises, such as the English crisis after the Napoleonic wars, were of a local character. Before railways were built there was no world market for agrarian produce, merely isolated markets limited by the undeveloped state of transportation). The following problems must therefore be cleared up:

(a) Why are there no periodically recurring crises in agriculture as in industry?
(b) Why do agrarian crises outlast several industrial cycles?
(c) What connection is there between agrarian crises and industrial crises?
(d) What is the difference between the present agrarian crisis and that of the nineteenth century?

We shall endeavour to answer these questions as briefly as possible:

(a) There are no periodically recurring agrarian crises because *the simple production of goods and production for the producer's own use predominates in agriculture*. Although the capitalist mode of production has been predominant for over a hundred years, although the peasant producers were subjugated by capital and exploited by it in a thousand different ways, and although agriculture has been long carried on largely by capitalist leaseholders in the advanced capitalist countries (England), nevertheless even today the bulk of the agricultural produce on the market is not produced by capitalists, but by peasants. Peasant agriculture today still outweighs capitalist agriculture.

Another factor is the backwardness of agriculture in general: its low organic composition of capital and the relatively minor role played by fixed capital (the 'material basis' of crises, as Marx says) even in capitalist agriculture. If the organisation of agriculture were as capitalist as industry with the role of fixed capital just as large, and if the retarding effect of ground rent did not operate, agricultural production would exhibit the same cyclic movement as industry.

(b) The duration of the agrarian crisis, persisting through several industrial cycles, is also due mainly to the slight development of capitalism in agriculture. The specific conditions of agricultural production account for the fact that production is not reduced at the outbreak of the crisis as it is in industry. The crisis does not take on the form of a sudden decline in production, but of the accumulation of large, unsold stocks, with production unrestricted.[74]

The reasons for this are as follows: Since the production costs in large-scale capitalist agriculture are much lower than on peasant farms operating under the same natural conditions, the former can continue production at a profit for a long time, even during the crisis. The peasants, however, are compelled to continue production on the old scale until production involuntarily declines owing to the degradation of agriculture. The peculiarities of agricultural production lie in the circumstance that the percentage of the fixed costs that do not vary with the scale of production is much higher than in industry.[75] Ground rent in the form of leasehold payment and mortgage interest, amortisation interest on buildings and machinery, fodder and replacement of draft animals, taxes and finally wages of the full-time labourers, which total at least 70 percent of the individual costs of production, remain almost unchanged when the area under cultivation is reduced. Therefore, restriction or total cessation of operations in agriculture involves far greater losses than in industry. In addition, it is very difficult for the peasant to find employment for his own labour power and that of his family off his farm, without abandoning it altogether. The peasant, therefore, continues production even when he can make only a minimum living wage. All endeavours made hitherto to induce agricultural producers to restrict their production voluntarily have failed because of this circumstance. Moreover, the prices of agricultural produce fluctuate according to the results of the harvest, temporary price rises awakening hopes for improvement and inducing the producers to stay on their farms. These are the most important causes accounting for the long duration of agrarian crises.

(c) Although the dynamics of agrarian and industrial crises differ, industry and agriculture constantly react on each other. *Every industrial crisis makes the situation in agriculture worse*, since the demand for industrial raw materials

---

[74] TABLE 12.25 The League of Nations index of world foodstuffs production (cereals, meat, wine, coffee, tea, cocoa, etc.) reveals the following picture (1925–9, taken as 100)

1925	1926	1927	1928	1929	1930	1931	1932	1933
98	97	99	103	103	104	102	104	103

We see that the tremendous drop in prices during the last four years has not brought about a reduction in output. Nor was there a reduction in the output of textile fibres or rubber. Some countries (mainly the European importing countries) have increased their agricultural output, while the exporting countries (USA and Canada) have reduced their output considerably. The size of the annual crop is another important factor, of course.

[75] Kondratiev's wrong theory of 'long cycles', which was largely accepted also by Trotsky, is based on the effect of the great nineteenth-century agrarian crisis upon industry.

declines, while the demand for foodstuffs, particularly those of better quality (meat, milk, butter, eggs) drops as a result of the declining income of the working class. Prices, therefore, sink. But this does not yet mean an agrarian crisis. Conversely, the course of industrial cycles changes under the influence of the agrarian crisis, which greatly restricts the capacity of the agricultural population to purchase manufactured goods. The agrarian crisis tends to accentuate and prolong industrial crises, while the boom phases grow shorter and less pronounced.[76]

(d) The most important economic and political question is the difference in character between the present agrarian crisis and the great agrarian crisis of the nineteenth century. Before we answer this question, however, we must dwell in brief on the important *role that ground rent plays in agrarian crises*. We presume that the reader is acquainted with the Marxian theory of ground rent and we shall therefore deal only with the role of ground rent in the agrarian crisis.

Ground rent is that portion of the surplus value appropriated in agriculture which does not enter into the establishment of the average rate of profit, owing to private ownership of land, but is taken by the landowner as rent. This is made possible by the fact that the organic composition of capital in agriculture is lower than the average of the total capital of society. If not for this there would be no absolute rent, merely differential rent. Theoretically, it is assumed that the capital invested in agriculture (the capital of the capitalist lessee) yields the average rate of profit, and that the landowner takes only that part of the surplus value gained by the lessee which represents the latter's profit over and above the average rate of profit on his invested capital.

But the landowner does not get the economic rent, which varies according to the yield of the harvest, and the course of prices. *The amount of rent is not fixed annually after accounts are settled, but is fixed in the lease or in the purchase price*,[77] *on the basis of the results of previous years*. As soon as the lease is signed,

---

[76] TABLE 12.26 Proportion of fixed-charges increases with decreasing income following official data for the USA (in millions of dollars)

	Gross income	Interest	Percent	Taxes	Percent
1929	11,913	554	4.7	777	6.5
1932	5,143	510	10.0	620	12.0

[77] The *price of land* (apart from the sum expended on clearing and improving the soil) *is nothing but ground rent capitalised at the current rate of interest.*

or the land bought on credit, subject to a corresponding mortgage, the rent signifies a definite fixed charge for the future, as far as the lessee or landowner is concerned, representing an element in his individual production outlay but not of the social cost of production. If the price of agricultural produce falls while the cost of production remains unchanged, the lessee or the indebted landowner is unable to pay the excessive lease rent or mortgage interest. He is ruined, although his own costs of production would allow him to make an average profit if he had no rent or not a too high rent to pay (in the form of lease rent or mortgage interest).

This is the special role that rent plays in an agrarian crisis. *Not the existence of rent in general* (which is a *constant* burden on agriculture), *but the fact that it is fixed at too high a level*, hits agricultural producers most severely during crises.

This accounts for the long duration of the agrarian crisis, since reducing *ground rent*, fixed on the basis of former high prices, to a level that corresponds to the fallen prices is a long drawn-out process, involving the wholesale ruin of the agricultural producers. (We will deal with the usury rent that poor farmers have to pay in the chapter devoted to the social effects of the crisis).

We return once more to the difference between the two great agrarian crises.

Engels characterises the agrarian crisis of the nineteenth century as follows:

> But everything is transitory. The trans-oceanic steamboats and the railroads of North and South America and India enabled very peculiar stretches of land to enter into competition upon the European grain markets. There were on the one hand the North American prairies, the Argentine pampas, steppes, made fertile for the plough by nature itself, virgin soil, which yielded rich harvests for years to come even with primitive cultivation and without any fertilization. Then there were the lands of the Russian and Indian Communist communities, that had to sell a portion of their product, and an increasing one at that, to obtain money for the taxes wrung from them by the pitiless despotism of the state, very often by means of torture. These products were sold without regard to their cost of production, sold at the price offered by the dealer, because the peasant absolutely had to have money when tax day came around. And against this competition – of the virgin prairie soils and of the Russian and Indian peasants ground down by taxation – the European tenant, farmer and peasant could not maintain themselves at the old rents. Part of the soil of Europe fell definitely out of competition for grain growing, the rents fell everywhere ... Hence the woes of the agrarians from Scotland to Italy,

and from Southern France to East Prussia. Fortunately, far from all prairie land has been placed under cultivation. There is enough left to ruin all the great landed estates of Europe and the small ones into the bargain.[78]

We see that the agrarian crisis of the nineteenth century was *not a world crisis* like the present one, but a *European* crisis. There was no agrarian crisis in North and South America nor in Australia. It was not an all-embracing crisis like the present one, but a crisis of grain production.[79] Stock-raising and industrial crops were not affected by the crisis. *It was a crisis within the capitalist system, whereas the present crisis is part of the general crisis of capitalism itself.*

Engels's hope that there was enough prairie to 'ruin all of European landed property including the small proprietors', did nor materialise. The agrarian crisis was surmounted within the framework of capitalism. But what is of decisive importance is that the manner in which the agrarian crisis was overcome in Europe in the nineteenth century does not apply to the present agrarian crisis.

How was the previous agrarian crisis in Europe overcome?

We can distinguish the following ways:

(a) The agricultural centre of gravity was shifted from cereals to stock-raising, together with the importation of cheap fodder (Scandinavia, Holland, Belgium, Western Germany), while ploughed land was turned into pasture and meadow (England).

---

[78] Footnote to p. 842, Volume 3, chap. 43 of *Capital*, evidently written at the beginning of the nineties. The preface to Volume 3 is dated October 1894.

[79] This is best shown by the price movements in the *British* markets, which at that time could rightly be considered as the world market, during the agrarian crisis of the nineteenth century.

TABLE 12.27 Wholesale prices in London

Annual average	Cereals			Livestock products	
	Wheat (112 lbs.)	Oats (112 lbs.)	American corn (480 lbs.)	Prime beef (8 lbs.)	Pork (av. 8 lbs.)
	s. d.	s. d.	s.	s. d.	s. d.
1851–75	12 5	8 8	33	4 3	4 2
1876–82	10 1	8 5	26	4 11	4 5
1883–1900	7 1	6 6	23	4 8	3 6

SOURCE: DATA TAKEN FROM SERING 1929

(b) Considerable reduction in the cost of production was effected by rationalisation. The substitution of green fallow land for bare fallow land, the introduction of better crop rotation, deeper ploughing (the iron plough), improved machinery artificial fertilisers and seed improvement were the chief means employed. While large sections of the middle peasantry, who lacked the necessary funds for such rationalisation, were ruined, the big capitalist agricultural enterprises and the rich peasants succeeded in *reducing the cost of production through higher yields per acre*, in this way managing to get through the period of low grain prices.

(c) Production costs were reduced through reductions in the cost of the means of production supplied by industry. This was still in the epoch of free competition, when advances in labour productivity benefited the consumers.[80]

(d) Grain prices were raised artificially through the introduction of protective tariffs, in grain importing countries of continental Europe, such as France, Italy and Germany.

(e) Finally, in the course of a long drawn-out process – against the bitter resistance of the landowners – the level of ground rent adapted itself to the new price level, and the agrarian crisis was overcome.

The ways and means of overcoming the agrarian crisis of the nineteenth century (with the exception of the last method) *are not applicable in the present agrarian crisis since they can be effective only under the conditions of advancing capitalism.* This necessary prerequisite was a great increase in the consumption of animal husbandry, products due to the rapid increase in the industrial (urban) population of Europe and to the swift expansion of colonial exploitation, which gave rise to a broad stratum *of people living* on unearned income and which enabled the European bourgeoisie to maintain a numerically grow-

---

[80] TABLE 12.28 The movement of the English Sauerbeck Index during the agrarian crisis

	1871–5	1891–5
Mineral raw materials	115	68
Textiles	100	56

The price 'scissors' operated only in the case of agricultural products, but not for animal husbandry products.

ing labour aristocracy. Therefore the crisis in European grain production could be overcome on an *ascending curve*: through a rise in commodity production and through specialisation in agricultural crops; through expanding reproduction; technological progress (improved means of production), agricultural advances (better utilisation of the soil), etc. The level of European agriculture at the end of the great nineteenth-century agrarian crisis was undoubtedly higher than at the beginning of the crisis. Under capitalism this process was achieved, of course, at the cost of proletarianising millions of formerly independent peasants. But these proletarianised peasants were able to earn a living partly in the rapidly developing industries of Europe which at that time give employment to millions of new workers, and partly in the overseas immigration areas.

At the present time it is impossible to overcome the agrarian crisis on an ascending curve.

(a) There are no opportunities for extending the consumption of animal husbandry products in the period of the general crisis of capitalism. Chronic mass unemployment, the decline of the labour aristocracy in number and position, the tendency to reduce the number of workers employed by industrial capital in the advanced capitalist countries, the rapid impoverishment of the urban petty bourgeoisie under monopoly capitalism, the expropriation of pensioners and savings bank depositors through inflation – in short, the tendency to reduce the consuming power of the urban masses makes this impossible.

The rapid expansion of industry in the nineteenth century gave rise to a greatly increased demand for raw materials, and to wider cultivation of industrial crops. At present, we see a reverse process: the catastrophically low prices[81] of raw materials have led to a rapid restriction of the area under cultivation.

---

81   TABLE 12.30 Prices of important industrial raw materials in gold francs (per hundred pounds)

July	Cotton New Orleans	Jute London	Rubber New York	Raw silk Yokohama	Hemp London	Copra London	Soya London
1929	97	36	110	23	82	27	13
1932	30	12	15	6	34	12	5
1933	39	13	29	7	41	10	5

Coffee, tea and cocoa suffered a similar price decline.

TABLE 12.29 Area under industrial crops in the capitalist world (in millions of acres)[82]

	1929–30	1930–1	1932–3
Sugar beet	5.48	4.84	4.37
Tobacco	5.98	5.98	5.12
Cotton	83.10	76.35	72.00
Jute	3.44	1.86	2.15
Hemp	1.16	0.86	0.67

(b) Technically, the lowering of production cost through *rationalisation*, through the employment of improved means of production, etc., is possible now as well. But the unbelievably low wages paid to agricultural labourers render such rationalisation unprofitable from the standpoint of private business. The overwhelming majority of agricultural producers lack the necessary capital. The collapse of the credit system makes the partial acquisition of the necessary working capital impossible, at least for the present. The capital that does enter agriculture expands the area under cultivation in the overseas countries through improved technique (tractors, combines), thus accentuating the crisis for the peasantry, since it leads to an increase in production and makes liquidation of the enormous stocks in hand,[83] which keep prices down, still more difficult.

---

82 *International Yearbook of Agricultural Statistics*, 1932–3.
83 Up to 1933 stocks of agricultural produce increased or remained almost undiminished in magnitude. Only the catastrophic crop failure in the northern hemisphere in 1934 will lead to a reduction in carry-over, but if the bad harvest does not recur, this will exert only a passing effect.

TABLE 12.31 World stocks of agricultural produce (in April of each year)

	1929	1930	1931	1932	1933	1934
American cotton (thousands of bales)	2,879	3,870	7,000	9,930	11,174	9,236
Wheat (millions of bushels)	497	518	600	584	526	483
Sugar (thousands of tons)	6,190	6,125	8,453	9,091	8,903	8,046
Tea (millions of pounds)	260	210	242	213	276	251
Coffee (millions of bags)	15.4	37.5	31.1	36.9	26.9	–
Rubber (thousands of tons)	245	426	547	646	646	673

SOURCE: DATA FROM THE LONDON AND CAMBRIDGE ECONOMIC SERVICE, QUARTERLY SUPPLEMENTS

(c) Reductions in the price of the means of production used in agriculture are impeded by production and distribution monopolies which maintain high prices. The 'scissors' between the prices received by the agriculturists for their commodities and the prices they have to pay for their means of production is wide open.[84]

(d) The maintenance of high agricultural prices in the importing countries by means of tariffs, etc., meets with the obstacle of the limited consuming power of the urban population. Under the influence of higher prices, production expands so rapidly (as is clearly proved by the example of Germany and France in 1933) that domestic production meets domestic requirements, so that tariffs and quota measures become ineffective.

(e) The adjustment of rent to the changed price situation also proceeds in an anarchic fashion in this crisis, involving the ruin of millions of agricultural producers and a *degradation of agriculture*, which was not a general phenomenon in the previous agrarian crisis.

The degradation process in agriculture is manifested in various forms in the several countries: reduced use of artificial fertilisers, inadequate replacement of agricultural machinery and implements, reduction in livestock inventory and deterioration in its quality, poorer land cultivation and smaller crop yields, the decay and neglect of the peasant farm in general.

[84] TABLE 12.32 Data of prices of agrarian and industrial products

	USA (1909–14 = 100)a			Germany (1913 = 100)b		
	Price of farm produce	Prices of goods bought by farmer	Ratio	Agricultural produce	Manufactured goods	Ratio
1929	138	152	91	–	–	–
1930	117	144	81	–	–	–
1931	80	124	65	111	136	82
1932	57	107	53	97	118	82
1933	63	109	58	93	113	82

(a) *Monthly Summary*, US Department of Agriculture, April 1934.
(b) *Vierteljahrshefte zur Konjunkturforschung*, 1934, 9, 2, B.

A few European countries (France, Switzerland, Sweden) were able to prevent the growth of a 'price scissors' by means of high tariffs, import prohibitions and the establishment of governmental minimum prices. This holds true on paper at least, since the poor peasants receive much lower prices in the countryside than those quoted on the commodity exchanges.

The process of degradation in agriculture comprises two phenomena differing economically and socially.

A more or less voluntary extensive *development of capitalist agriculture* – adjusting methods of production to the changed price situation, such as the substitution of horse-drawn ploughs for tractors, since gasoline is expensive while oats are cheaper and unsaleable; reduced use of artificial fertilisers, since it does not pay to use them at prevailing low crop prices; the return to manual labour in place of complicated machinery,[85] since wages have dropped very steeply.

Furthermore, forced general deterioration of the peasant farm, since the peasant's net income is not enough to maintain simple reproduction in spite of the greatest personal privations suffered by his family; the dying cattle cannot be replaced, worn-out implements cannot be renewed, etc. Decrease in labour

---

[85] TABLE 12.33 Decline in use of agricultural machinery

	1928	1929	1930	1931	1932	1933
USA. Domestic sales of agricultural machinery (millions of dollars)	–	458	381	192	65	–
Germany. Domestic sales of agricultural machinery (million of marks)	245	215	155	100	25	– (first six months)
Poland. Domestic orders for agricultural machinery (1928 = 100)	100	77	25	10	2.2	2.9
Imports of agricultural machinery (1928 = 100)	100	70	36	17	4.9	5.2

The major portion of the decline is, of course, accounted for by the fall in prices. The decline in actual sales, however, is also tremendous.

TABLE 12.34 Sales of agricultural machinery in the USA (units)*

Highest annual figure in the period	Tractors	Combines	Harvesters	Threshers
1921–9	160,637	19,666	53,219	14,662
1931	93,632	8,172	22,675	5,280

No later figures are available, but the decline in the operations index number of the agricultural machinery industry from 93 in 1931 to 37 in 1932 and 42 in 1933, shows that sales declined still further.

The drop in sales of machinery in the western agricultural districts of Canada is still more acute. Sales of units were as follows:†

output in agriculture, limitation of production for the market and the trend to confine production to the needs of the peasant household proper.

We see that the methods successfully adopted in the nineteenth century to overcome the agrarian crisis cannot be applied today. *The present agrarian crisis is part of the general crisis of capitalism and cannot be solved within the framework of the capitalist system of society.* (Naturally enough, temporary improvement, in 1924–8, is possible and even probable). The agrarian crisis has led to an unprecedented wholesale ruin of the toiling peasantry, to the pauperisation of the poor peasants and agricultural labourers, and to a revolutionary mass movement of the toiling agricultural population.[86]

That is why the only solution (temporary though it may be) of the agrarian crisis at all conceivable within the framework of capitalism – ruining all the 'inefficient' (i.e. the poor and middle) peasants, and driving them off the land; transferring their land to the elements possessing more capital; letting the 'superfluous' land lie fallow and restricting production to fit the restricted, 'able to pay' demand, on the pattern of the industrial trusts – is impracticable for the bourgeoisie.[87]

In the epoch of the maturing revolutionary crisis, the bourgeoisie, confronted by a proletariat which is rising to storm the ramparts of capitalism, cannot force the solution of the agrarian crisis by deliberately hastening the wholesale ruin of the toiling peasantry. Hence the search (vain though it be) for another solution of the agrarian crisis; hence the experiments and manoeuvres of the bourgeoisie!

TABLE 12.35 Sales of agricultural machinery

	Tractors	Threshers	Combines
1928	17,143	6,247	3,657
1933	777	182	77

* *Farm Independent News*, 22 June 1933.
† *Canadian Farm Implements*, December 1933.

86 In subsequent chapters we shall deal with endeavours to overcome the agrarian crisis artificially, as well as with its social and political consequences.
87 Such a solution was proposed by some of the ideologists of the American bourgeoisie. See, for instance, Mead and Ostrolenk 1928; or Ostrolenk 1932. Roosevelt, afraid of the farmers' revolts, struck out along the opposite road.

4 The Crisis in the Colonies

The colonies are most acutely affected by the crisis. This follows from their *position* as colonies, as subjugated areas. The Theses of the Second Congress of the Communist International 'On the Colonial Question' state that 'in the main, European capitalism draws its power not so much from the European industrial countries, as from its colonial dominions'. Capital in the imperialist countries shifts a considerable part of the crisis burdens to the colonies and hence the crisis is especially deep and devastating there. The most important factors in this situation are the following:

(a) The overwhelming majority of the colonies and semi-colonies are *agrarian countries*. They therefore suffer the full force of the chronic agrarian crisis and its accentuation as a result of the industrial crisis.

(b) Imperialism has largely turned the colonies into raw material appendages of the home countries. A number of colonies and semi-colonies are *one-crop countries*, whose economic life depends on the sale of one (or a few) commodities in the capitalist world. Egypt, for instance, produces cotton, Australia – wool and wheat, India – rubber, Cuba – sugar, Brazil – coffee, etc. These countries are extraordinarily limited in their opportunities for economic manoeuvring. Overproduction has led to an enormous drop in prices,[88] which is ruining them. They now have to sell two to six times the quantity of their major export commodity to industrial countries for the same amount of money they received before the crisis. In consequence their export surplus no longer sufficed to meet the interest on their foreign debts; their balance of payments became unfavourable, and they were therefore compelled to turn over their

---

88 Some examples of the drop in prices of typical colonial commodities (in gold francs per 100 lbs.).

TABLE 12.36 Prices of colonial products

	Rice (Saigon 1st) London	Cane sugar (Cuba) New York	Tea (Ceylon) London (per lb.)	Coffee New York	Copra London	Soya London	Cotton (bales) Alexandria	Rubber New York	Jute London New York	Raw silk New York (per lb.)
Dec 1928	14.8	11.1	1.45	93.5	29.7	14.1	196	93.5	40.8	26.7
Dec 1932	5.6	4.3	0.45	43.0	12.5	5.6	45	16.8	11.5	7.5

THE GREAT CRISIS AND ITS POLITICAL CONSEQUENCES

gold reserves, small as they were, to the imperialist usurers.[89] In this way they fall into still greater dependence on the latter, succumbing to inflation,[90] which makes the burden of their debts (contracted in foreign currency) even heavier.

Let us take India as an example.[91]

TABLE 12.38 Foreign trade of India, year ending March 31 (millions of rupees)

	1929	1930	1931	1932	1933
Net export surplus	860	790	620	348	34
Net gold imports	212	143	125	–	–
Net gold exports	–	–	–	580	683

(c) The price 'scissors', which accentuates the crisis in agrarian countries in general, strikes the colonies with particular force:

---

89   TABLE 12.37 Gold reserves of some of the colonial and semi-colonial countries (in millions of their respective currency units)

	Brazil (milreis)	Argentine (pesos)	Mexico (pesos)	Dutch East Indies (gulden)
End of 1928	1,242	641	39	170
End of 1932	129 (1930)	215	10	104

90   The colonial and semi-colonial countries occupy first place in relation to the extent of currency depreciation. By the middle of 1934 currency depreciation (percent of gold) was as follows: Mexico, 67; Argentina, 66; Columbia, 65; Uruguay, 54; Brazil, 58; Bolivia, 58; China, 52 (percent of 1929 rate of exchange), etc.

91   Official figures: *The Statist*, 11 November 1933, p. 670.

TABLE 12.39 Price indices (1913 = 100)

	USA	Germany	England		Colonial commodities			
	Manufactures	Pig-iron	Coal	Indian cotton (London)	Jute (London)	Tea (London)	Cane sugar (New York)
1929	136	157	132	122	114	102	138	71
1930	127	150	126	120	74	69	112	53
1931	111	186	110	114	59	54	74	48
1932	101	110	100	112	65	52	65	33

These figures, however, are far from giving a correct picture of the increase in non-equivalent exchange between the colonies and the imperialist countries during the crisis, since they give the prices received imperialist countries during the crisis, since they give the prices received by the European dealers in colonial products, i.e. the prices ruling on the exchanges. The prices the peasant receives in the colonies dropped even lower. With the prevailing oversupply the big international monopolies, such as Unilever, themselves fix the prices that their buyers are to pay for the commodities in the colonies. 'Capitalism has succeeded in somewhat alleviating the position of industry *at the expense ... of the peasants in the colonies and economically weak countries* by still further forcing down prices for the products of their labour, principally for raw materials, and also for foodstuffs'.[92]

(d) Most of the colonial and semi-colonial countries either have a silver currency, or silver (sometimes, as in China, copper as well) forms the legal circulating and paying medium at home while a formal gold standard exists in commerce with foreign countries. The tremendous fall in the price of silver during the crisis enabled the imperialist countries to obtain raw materials from these countries at exceptionally low prices.

These factors resulted in the rapid impoverishment of the colonial peasantry: accelerated transfer of the land to the hands of the landlords;[93] a growing hun-

---

[92] Stalin 1955a, p. 296.
[93] Korea may be taken as an example: The proportion of the area cultivated by landlords rose from 54.1 percent to 56.4 percent between 1928 and 1932. The number of landless tenant farmers rose from 1,191,000 in 1926 to 1,393,424 in 1931. (Figures are taken from Pavel A. Mif, *Gegemoniya proletariata v kolonialnoy osvoboditelnoy borbe*).

ger for land; growing 'over-population' in the countryside, which is enhanced by the accelerated return to the land of urban artisans ruined by the development of domestic capitalist industry and by foreign competition, as well as of workers thrown out of employment by the industrial crisis.[94]

Impoverishment is further intensified by the manifold exploitation of the peasantry. The feudal landowners, village usurers, the native and the imperialist bourgeoisie exploit the colonial peasantry in various ways: 'The disadvantages of the capitalist mode of production, with its dependence of the producer upon the money-price of his product, coincide here therefore with the disadvantages occasioned by the imperfect development of the capitalist mode of production'.[95]

This general characterisation of colonial economy by Marx is even more true of the era of crisis. Chronic starvation and periodically recurring famine are now the lot of hundreds of millions of colonial peasants. Slavery is on the increase; it is an everyday occurrence for parents to sell their daughters into slavery.[96]

The degradation of agriculture is especially pronounced in the colonies. The manifold exploitation of the peasants deprives them of so much of their hard-earned income that they are not even able to continue the process of simple reproduction. The peasants are unable to buy the necessary quantities of urban fertilisers needed for the intensive cultivation so indispensable in the thickly populated areas of China. Livestock is diminishing, while its quality grows worse. In many regions of China the irrigation system, the basis of Chinese agriculture, is falling into decay. Imports of rice and wheat are increasing, while the area under poppy cultivation for opium production is expanding in Kuomintang China. In the one-crop countries specialisation is being reduced and production for one's own needs is returning.

This general impoverishment of the population in the colonies during the crisis in many ways modifies the process of the development of the consumers' goods industries in the colonies and semi-colonies. The process of expansion

---

94   In India, where periodic censuses have been taken for decades, the proportion of the agricultural population – in contrast to imperialist countries – is constantly higher. The same is obviously true of China, where no census is taken.
95   Marx 1959, p. 791.
96   'In the suburbs of Kiangfu and on the shores of the Sienyang Ho (Shensi Province) a "human market" has been established, where girls under ten are sold for two to three dollars per head. The price for girls above ten years is five dollars'. *South China Morning Post*, 2 November 1932.

of light industry undoubtedly continues during the crisis. The shrinkage in the capacity of the market to absorb local manufactures is compensated for by the fact that the impoverishment of the population increases the demand for the *cheapest kinds of commodities* of inferior quality, which are produced by the colonial (and Japanese) industries.

Moreover, the great currency depreciation in colonial and semi-colonial countries, particularly the drop in the price of silver, served as protection against the competition of foreign goods. As early as 1931, the yearly report of the Bank of China stated: 'In the last three years Chinese industry has manifested signs of improvement, owing to the cheaper price of the goods of domestic industries as compared with that of imported goods, which is a result of the fall in the price of silver'.[97]

These factors operated to produce an increase in domestic production and a sharp decline in the import of manufactures in many of the colonies and semi-colonies (the rise in tariffs also plays a certain role). The following figures[98] show this is true in the case of China:

---

[97] TABLE 12.40 Index of imported manufactured goods in Shanghai, in silver (1926 = 100)

1929	1931	1933
110	160	153

[98] Figures taken from an article by Gamberg, 'Polozhenie kitayskoy promyshlennosti vo vremya krizisa', *Problemy Kitaya*, 1933, no. 12.

TABLE 12.41 Import of manufactures in the colonies

	Textiles			Cigarettes		Matches	
	No. of cloth looms	Output (1,000 pieces)	Import of cotton goods (million yds.)	Output (1,000 packages)	Imports (millions)	Output (1,000 cases)	Imports (1,000 cases)
1929	25,818	14,658	868	750	9,547 (including Manchuria)	600	8,424 (including Manchuria)
1933	39,564	20,122	372	1,123	250 (excluding Manchuria)	800	73 (excluding Manchuria)

Numerous new plants for knitted goods, rubber goods, soap, caps, enamelware, paper, ink, pencils, as well as electric bulbs, radio sets, cement, bricks, and the simplest kinds of machinery, etc., have been established during the crisis especially in the Shanghai and Hong Kong areas. (On the other hand, the depreciation of silver reduced the imports of foreign machinery, hampering the development of industry, particularly those industries owned by Chinese).

Similar phenomena are observed in the other colonial and semi-colonial countries. (Many new textile factories erected in the interior of India; the growth of the textile, boot and shoe, and other industries in Brazil and Chile during the crisis). But the following factors must be emphasised in our estimate of this course of development:

(1) The crisis is extremely severe in the branches of industry that produce semi-finished goods for export: raw silk, tea, oil-seed mills, etc.

(2) The erection of factories by *foreign* capital, is the principal factor in increased production in light industry and the growth in the number of enterprises, thus increasing dependence upon imperialism.

(3) The growth of light industry (though limited in extent) is attained through a big rise in the rate of exploitation of the colonial proletariat – wage reductions, lengthening of hours of work, increased labour intensity – which capital was able to force through despite the worker's resistance.

The ruin of the artisan trades and the uninterrupted impoverishment of the toiling peasants under the hammer-blows of the crisis and of manifold exploitation by the landowners, imperialists, domestic bourgeoisie and usurers, continued to throw new hinds into the industrial labour market, making more difficult the often heroic struggle against capital of the colonial proletariat – largely consisting of women and children, and drawn directly from the village.

5 Unsuccessful Endeavours to Overcome the Crisis Artificially

During the last five years the bourgeoisie has made innumerable efforts to overcome the crisis artificially. They all proved to be failures, as was to be expected. Both the *general crisis* of capitalism and the cyclic overproduction crises are consequences of the 'natural laws' of capitalism, as Marx often puts it. The general crisis of capitalism only expresses the fact that the capitalist system of society, as a historically transient form of society, is now passing through the period of its unevenly proceeding revolutionary collapse. No artificial measures can alter this.

The cyclic overproduction crises represent the violent outbreak of capitalism's contradictions but at the same time they also involve their temporary solution. The endeavours to mitigate the crisis, or to hasten its end, lead in the final analysis to a prolongation of the crisis.

How is a cyclic overproduction crisis overcome? The most important factors are the following:

Production is so greatly restricted that consumption exceeds production.[99]

Part of the surplus products is physically destroyed.

The drop in prices reduces the price total of commodities to the social requirements. Surplus stocks of commodities are absorbed. Prices do not decline further. Cheapening of the elements of constant capital increases the utilisation of total capital.

During the crisis wages are cut, the intensity of labour increased, labour conditions grow worse, causing a temporary decrease in consuming power. At the same time, however, better utilisation of capital (as the prerequisite condition for the resumption of investment) and an expansion of the market for Division I are made possible.

The credit crisis reduces social capital through bankruptcies and company reorganisations, thus increasing the profit rate on the capital remaining. The prerequisites are present for new capital investments in the sphere of pro-

---

[99] The question might arise as to where this consuming power comes from if production is so restricted. This question is not hard to answer. The bourgeoisie and those living on unearned income, government officials and a large part of the salaried employees continue consumption during the crisis on almost the same level as before. The unemployed live on their savings plus unemployment insurance.

duction. At the same time the credit crisis eliminates the insolvent debtors; the credit chain, broken during the crisis, and mutual 'confidence' are reestablished. Large amounts of loan capital are once more available for the resumption of real accumulation. Crisis passes into depression.

The bourgeoisie is just as unable to comprehend the overproduction crisis as it was a hundred years ago. Hundreds of books, hundreds of thousands of articles on the crisis have been published by bourgeois writers within the last five years, without having advanced the understanding of the latter in the slightest degree. Sometimes this is acknowledged by the ideologists of the bourgeoisie themselves.

Ernst Wagemann, director of the German Institut für Konjonkturforschung, wrote as follows in the *Wochenbericht* of 26 August 1931:

> In many places the outbreak of the acute credit crisis has affected the foundations of economic development and thus interrupted the organic course of the depression. Such events affecting national economy from the outside cannot be foreseen by research methods any more than earthquakes, fires, etc. Nor are their consequences ... subject to any quantitative predictions.[100]

Under the heading 'The Failure of the Economists', the *Manchester Guardian* of 9 January 1931 wrote:

> We know more of the velocity of an electron than we do about the velocity of money. We know far more about the cycle of the earth about the sun and the sun about the universe than we do about the cycle of trade. We can predict the movements of unseen and inconceivably remote heavenly bodies with vastly greater accuracy, than we can predict the end of the trade slump.[101]

In contrast to this total confusion in the heads of economists, each section of the ruling class deliberately pursued the aim of making economic policy serve its own interests. Victory in the struggle among these conflicting interests was finally gained by the financial oligarchy, monopoly capital, concealed though it was behind all sorts of manoeuvres.

---

100   Wagemann 1931, p. 89.
101   *Manchester Guardian*, 9 January 1931, p. 8.

The bourgeoisie sees in the crisis *chiefly the unsaleability of its commodities at profitable prices*. All the measures suggested for overcoming the crisis moved within this circle.

'*Our goods do not sell because of overwhelming foreign competition*', declares the capital producing for the home market. Hence, tariff rises, quotas and import prohibitions to surmount the crisis.

'*We cannot sell our goods abroad*', the exporters cry. Hence, government subsidies, freight rebates and state-organised dumping.

'*The value of our currency is too high*', shout the exporters of all countries, demanding inflation (or more inflation wherever it exists already).

'*The value of our currency is too low*', cry the importers of foreign raw materials, the creditors and the coupon-clippers. 'Only maintenance of the gold standard ensures economic stability, credit and a way out of the crisis'.

'*Our production costs are too high*', industrial capital cries. Hence, wage cuts, a longer working day, labour speed-up – the effort to overcome the crisis at the expense of the workers, which restricts the capacity of the domestic market to absorb manufactures still further.

'*Our selling prices are too low because of unrestricted competition*', the monopolists say. Hence, government aid in the formation of monopolies (England), compulsory cartels, prohibiting the establishment of new enterprises (Germany), government sanction of cartel prices, minimum prices fixed by the government. This artificial maintenance of high monopoly prices[102] increases

---

102 In some countries the 'free' prices and those that are fixed, i.e. the cartel prices, are combined in the indices of the government institutes of business research. The maintenance of high monopoly prices is clearly shown in the following table:

TABLE 12.42 Price index in Germany, Austria and Poland

	Germany		Austria		Poland	
	(1928 = 100)		(1923–31 = 100)		(1928 = 100)	
	Cartel prices	Free prices	Cartel prices	Free prices	Cartel prices	Free prices
1928	102	107	–	–	–	–
1929	105	97	99	100	108	94
1932	84	48	93	73	105	53
1933(a)	84	48	94	73	93	49

(a) Ten months.

the profit of monopoly capital, but it slows up the liquidation of surplus stocks, and prolongs the crisis.

'*Consuming power must be increased*', demand the leaders of the trade unions and Social-Democratic economists. '*The crisis is a result of under-consumption*'. The capitalists should increase wages, the state should put more money in circulation, and should put through public works. Then the capacity of the domestic market will increase and the crisis will be over.

This agitation foundered on the resistance of capital, which is not disposed to accept the nonsensical plan of paying higher wages out of its own pocket to be able to sell more goods. (Roosevelt manoeuvres with this catchphrase for demagogic reasoning).

'*This crisis is due to insufficient credit*'. The state should provide for credit expansion. Efforts in this direction have failed (Hoover's Reconstruction Finance Corporation). The 'credit-worthy' capitalists do not require any additional loan capital in view of the diminished business during the crisis. Those who do require money to pay old debts are not 'credit-worthy'.

'*The burden of debts is ruining us*', cry the debtors. Hence, reorganisation (of course only of the biggest enterprises) through state subsidies, governmental purchase of shares, reduction in the interest rate and relief of the debt burden through inflation.

'*The crisis can be overcome only by re-establishing free circulation of commodities in the world market*'. Tariffs should be reduced, quotas, import and export prohibitions should be abolished and international credit and capital export should be restored.[103] This policy was advocated by the British bourgeoisie at the beginning of the crisis. It failed because the bourgeoisie of every country (and the British bourgeoisie with increasing determination) endeavoured to monopolise its domestic market. They succeeded in destroying the world market in the old sense. There are no longer world market prices in the old sense, the international division of labour is being more and more restricted and foreign trade is shrinking. The ideological expression for all this is the senseless catchword 'autarchy'.

The difference in prices is tremendous. In reality, the difference is probably less, since the official cartel prices are secretly evaded and underbid by the individual cartel members in various ways.

103 The re-establishment of 'free trade' as it existed before the crisis would benefit the strongest imperialist industrial countries, but would place the weaker countries at a disadvantage. It would not solve the crisis, since the purchasing power of the capitalist world as a whole would not be raised in the least.

We do not wish to tire the reader by prolonging this list. The conflicting interests of the various strata of the ruling classes led to a constant struggle around the state's economic policy, to uninterrupted parliamentary 'log-rolling' to increasingly frequent cabinet crises, and to an uncharted zig-zag policy, which is one of the bases for the fascisisation of the state.

Roosevelt's 'New Deal' represents the most grandiose effort to overcome the crisis by governmental measures. The essence of this policy is:

(a) Saving the credit system from utter collapse by a government guarantee of deposits;
(b) Reducing the burden of debts by 40 percent through the depreciation of the dollar;
(c) Artificially raising the prices of agricultural produce through a reduction of output prescribed and subsidised by the government;
(d) Furthering the organisation of monopolies by means of the Codes, which in many cases amount to compulsory cartels;
(e) Combating unemployment by undertaking big public works and by reducing the working hours per week;
(f) Regulation of wages: fixing minimum wages in the Codes, which in practice became maximum wages.

As we know, the effort led to a very sharp rise in industrial output in the summer of 1933 (accumulation of stocks and increased purchases by the rich in anticipation of the inflationist rise in prices), and to a sharp relapse in the autumn of 1933. This was followed by a gradual renewed improvement in the first half of 1934 and by a new decline beginning with July. Since housing construction as well as the renewal and increase of fixed capital are very slight up to the present and the purchasing power of the working class has not increased, the artificial increase in production clashed with the limited capacity of the market and collapsed after a few months had elapsed. In the final analysis the increase in production remains within the bounds that the inner forces of capitalism would lave reached; its progress, however, was no longer more or less even, but followed an unsteady zig-zag.

All the efforts to overcome the crisis artificially failed in the long run. The fact that the acute phase of the crisis came to an end and passed into the depression of a special kind, is not due to the manoeuvres of the bourgeoisie. It was effected by the inner forces of capitalism tending to overcome the cyclic crisis, which were reinforced by the increased preparations for war and (in some countries) temporarily by inflation.

A few words on the efforts to overcome the agrarian crisis artificially. Their main object was *a rise in prices*. The methods attempted in the importing countries differed from those in the exporting countries.

In the *importing countries* an effort was made to make domestic prices independent of the movement of world market prices, through quotas, increased tariffs, import prohibitions, and so forth. This policy was pursued chiefly by the West European countries: Germany, France, Italy, etc. By 1933 this policy had succeeded in making domestic prices two to three times higher than world market prices.[104]

This development of prices led to an expansion of the farmed area; the increased harvest, however, soon covered the domestic demand[105] (reduced by the crisis), and protectionism became ineffective. The new drop in prices could be halted only by the introduction of government-fixed prices (France, Germany. Czechoslovakia) and the organisation of state control of the grain trade.

In the exporting countries, the endeavour was made to raise the world market price through purchasing the surplus quantity and keeping it off the world market: Canadian Wheat Pool, Federal Farm Board in the USA, coffee valorisation in Brazil, etc. All these efforts ended in failure, since production continued to increase, stocks accumulated still further, and the organisations could not stand the burden. Either they went bankrupt (Canadian Wheat Pool), or the bourgeoisie no longer desired to bear the losses (Farm Board in the USA); prices again fell steeply.

---

104 TABLE 12.43 Prices in gold francs, July 1932

	Berlin	Paris	London	Chicago	Buenos Aires
Wheat per 100 lbs.	13.4	14.8	5.4	4.7	4.0
Pork per 100 lbs. (on the foot)	47.7	66.2	–	23.6	–

SOURCE: *INTERNATIONAL YEARBOOK OF AGRICULTURAL STATISTICS* 1932–3

105 Germany may serve as an example. The area under wheat cultivation increased from 4,000,000 acres in 1929 to 5,700,000 acres in 1933.

Domestic production met the country's need as follows (in percent):

TABLE 12.44 German domestic production

	1926	1929	1932
Wheat	48	72	97
Meat	91	94	99
Butter	70	72	85

This experience shows that *prices cannot be maintained at a high level unless production is restricted*. A campaign was begun for voluntary restriction of the area under cultivation (particularly in the USA); bonuses were paid for reduction in cultivated area and efforts were made to conclude international agreements for restricting the production or export of various agricultural commodities. These efforts also failed by and large, although the prices of certain commodities produced chiefly on capitalist plantations (rubber, sugar, tea) rose considerably in consequence of restricted production. The enormous weight of fixed costs (*Chapter 3*) renders restriction of production difficult in agriculture. Effective control is scarcely possible in view of subdivision into millions of small farms. It proved impossible to restrict production according to plan as was indicated in the chapter on the agrarian crisis.

Hence, as early as two years ego, a bad harvest was awaited as a blessing. *The Minneapolis Tribune* (USA) wrote: 'We, who learned to pray for our daily bread, are now praying that it be taken away from us; a heresy as peculiar in the field of theology as in the field of economics'.

A similar contradiction exists between the entire ideology of agricultural education, whose aim is to teach how to get the biggest crops, between the traditional system of state awards to farmers with the biggest crops, and the agitation and legislation for reducing the cultivated area and the crops by prohibiting the use of larger quantities of fertiliser (American cotton regions), and the like.

Finally, the only recourse left was the systematic, wholesale *destruction of agricultural produce of every kind*. In 1933, 24,700,000 acres of ripe cotton (approximately one-quarter of the total area) was ploughed under in the USA. In Brazil ten million bags of coffee (almost the total annual world requirements) are burned, dumped into the sea or used as road construction material every year.

Tea is not gathered; rubber trees are not tapped. Whole shiploads of oranges were dumped into the sea in London. Five million hogs were bought by the US government and destroyed in the autumn of 1933. In Denmark, 1,500 cows were slaughtered weekly and converted into fertilisers. In Argentina, hundreds of thousands of older sheep were killed and abandoned to make room for the young; the cost of transportation to the slaughter houses would have exceeded the money received for them. And so on and so forth! All this is happening at a time when millions upon millions of unemployed and their families are starving and are clad in rags. *Never before in the history of mankind has anything like this ever occurred*. The decay of capitalism – the contradiction between the productive forces and the production relationships – is tangibly obvious to every peasant and worker!

The long and tedious process of the degradation of agriculture and the crop failure of 1934 will finally bring about the reduction of stocks so ardently desired and will raise prices somewhat.[106] This will only be a short interlude, however. In a year or two, overproduction stimulated by the higher prices will be still greater than at present. A solution to the agrarian crisis within the framework of the capitalist system of society is nowhere in sight; at most, only a temporary mitigation of the crisis may occur.

∵

The principal result of the efforts to overcome the crisis artificially (and of all capitalist economic policy during the crisis) is the intervention of the state in every detail of economic life in favour of the ruling classes in general, and of monopoly capital and the big agrarians in particular. Monopoly capital makes use of its control of the state machinery to effect a systematic shift of national income in its favour and to rob the state treasury in various ways and under all sorts of pretexts. 'State capitalism' tendencies have grown considerably. A transition from monopoly capitalism to a 'state war-monopoly capitalism', as Lenin called capitalism in the period of the World War, is taking place to a certain extent.

In fact the present situation of capitalism very much resembles that during the World War. First, *because the preparations for the next world war dominate the economic policy of all nations more and more.* The economy of most capitalist countries, especially of Japan and Germany, already manifests pronounced features of war economy, which inevitably involves increasing the role of the state in economy.

Second, *the rapid maturing of the revolutionary crisis,* the threat to the bourgeoisie's domination compels the latter to consolidate its state power for the purpose of better defence. The resulting fascisisation of the state apparatus is connected with the strengthening of state-capitalism tendencies.

We shall endeavour to indicate the chief outlines of the strengthening of state-capitalism tendencies.

(a) *The suddenly increased role played by the government budget.* While the value of the products of society (according to bourgeois terminology: the national income) had dropped very heavily as a result of production restrictions and the fall in prices, a large part of it, unchanging

---

106 The effects of the crop failure upon the condition of the toiling peasants will be dealt with later.

in magnitude was appropriated by the state and redistributed.[107] This means that the proportion of the national income taken by the state has increased.

(b) *Foreign trade has in essence become a concern of the state.* The innumerable restrictions of foreign trade (tariffs, quotas, prohibitions, allocations of foreign currency, barter between nations, etc.) have created a situation in many countries (Germany, the Baltic states, and Japan) which very much resembles a state trade monopoly.

(c) *Credit has actually become state credit*; in most nations (chiefly Germany and the USA) the banks are governmental or semi-governmental banks and in every respect depend on the state.

(d) The state has acquired increasing control over the distribution of labour power ('voluntary' labour service in the USA, Germany, etc.; state measures for creating work).

(e) *The prices of many commodities are determined by the state*: directly through price fixing by the state (all the prices of agricultural commodities in Germany); indirectly through the organisation of obligatory cartels and through foreign trade and currency policy.

The effect of this and other kinds of state interference is that the profits of each enterprise (and even of some commercial transactions) depend on the rapidly growing number of governmental measures. In general, all government measures tend to benefit monopoly capital, but in individual cases, they very much

---

[107] TABLE 12.45 Budgets of the most important countries during the crisis (in millions of the respective currency units)

	USA		Japan		England		Germany		France	
	1929	1934	1929	1934	1929	1934	1929	1934	1929	1934
Expenditures	3,848	7,105	1,815	2,309	818	830	8,002	6,647	455,000	505,000
National Income (a)	80,500	39,800	–	–	3,849	3,381	75,400	46,500	245,000	206,000
Governmental expenditures in % of National Income	4.8	17.8	–	–	21.3	24.6	10.5	14.3	18.4	24.5

(a) In every case the figures for the national income of the previous year are taken for comparison.

depend on the bureaucrats, rapidly growing in number, who 'interpret' and enforce the laws and the decrees. The importance of these bureaucrats (and their corruption) has grown immensely. Although this basis is general, the differences between the various countries are often far-reaching. We shall return to the same question in later chapters.

6   The Special Nature of the Present Depression

In his report the Seventeenth Party Congress, Comrade Stalin stated that 'industry in the principal capitalist countries had already passed the lowest point of decline and did not return to it in the course of 1933'.

The following *Table 12.46* shows this in figures:

TABLE 12.46 Index of industrial output (1928 = 100)[108]

	Capitalist world (June)	USA	England	Germany	France	Japan	Poland
Month of highest output in 1929 (average)	109.8	114.4	107.9	107.2	113.4	–	105.8
1929 (average)	106.0	107.2	106.0	100.4	109.4	111.4	99.7
1930 (average)	90.5	86.5	97.9	90.1	110.2	105.6	81.8
1931 (average)	77.9	73.0	88.8	73.6	97.6	100.7	69.3
1932 1st quarter	69.5	62.5	80.1	62.0	79.5	101.0	52.2
1932 2nd quarter	64.2	54.7	89.4	61.3	74.0	104.8	54.5
1932 3rd quarter	63.3	55.3	82.7	59.6	73.2	107.2	54.0
1934 4th quarter	67.4	59.5	90.0	61.8	76.1	118.7	54.0
1933 1st quarter	66.6	56.5	89.9	64.1	80.8	120.9	48.2
1933 2nd quarter	75.7	70.9	91.7	67.6	85.8	125.7	55.2
1933 3rd quarter	82.6	82.6	91.8	70.8	87.4	129.0	58.0
1933 4th quarter	75.3	67.3	99.5	73.4	84.3	138.1	60.1
1934 1st quarter	80.5	73.0	103.3	81.8	82.7	132.6	60.2
1934 2nd quarter	–	76.5	104.1	87.7	79.5	–	63.8
Lowest point in 1932	61.5 (July)	52.3 (July)	82.7 (2nd quarter)	58.5 (August)	72.4 (July)	91.4 (May 1931)	46.5 (March 1933)

---

108   The figures are taken from the League of Nations statistics. Figures of world output have been taken from the data of the Berlin Institut für Konjunkturforschung.

Industrial output in most countries reached its lowest point in the middle of 1932. Some countries, such as Japan (war and inflation boom), reached it as early as 1931, while others, like Poland, passed it only at the beginning of 1933.

The lowest point in the price decline was reached somewhat later, in 1933; the fall in prices is still continuing in some countries possessing a stable currency.

Price formation is greatly distorted owing to currency depreciation. Recalculation on a gold basis at the rate of exchange is impracticable since the rise in prices during inflation always lags considerably behind the depreciation of the currency.

The accumulation of stocks of agricultural products (see table in *Chapter 3*) came to a standstill at the same time. *The stocks of industrial raw materials* began to diminish. *The stocks of industrial finished products diminished considerably*, falling below the normal level by the end of 1932.[109]

TABLE 12.48 World stocks of industrial raw materials

April	1929	1930	1931	1932	1933	1934
Tin (1,000 tons)	27	41	60	62	52	22
Lead (1,000 tons USA)	–	41	116	151	173	198
Zinc (1,000 tons USA)	35	90	140	138	137	105
Petroleum (million of barrels)	599	639	591	560	504	502
Copper (1,000 tons)	324	–	586	701	647	506

The figures are taken from the London and Cambridge Economic Service; figures for copper from the *Berliner Börsenzeitung* of 2 August 1934 (1929–30 = annual average).

No statistics are available for the stocks of manufactures in other countries; the trend, however, is undoubtedly similar. The continuing drop in prices prompted all enterprises, particularly the wholesale and retail trade, to reduce invent-

---

109 TABLE 12.47 Index of stocks of manufactures in the USA (1923–5 = 100)

	1929	1930	1931	1932
December	119	120	108	96

ory minimum. During 1933, the world economic crisis had thus reached a stage which is ordinarily described as a transition to the depression.

Marx and Depression

In Marx's analysis of cycles, the focus of interest is always the crisis, as that phase of the cycle in which all the contradictions of capitalism break out openly and violently, the capitalist system of society is shaken to its very foundations, the proletariat is freed of the illusions arising during the prosperity phases, and the historically transient nature of capitalism is strikingly demonstrated. The other phases of the cycle interested Marx principally as phases preliminary to the next crisis. That is why only scattered remarks on the depression are found in Marx's works. Parenthetically the *term* 'depression', characterising a certain phase of the cycle, is not found in Marx's works at all. (When the term is used it is used in the *English* sense of 'crisis'). Marx uses the expression 'stagnation', 'state of rest', 'the phase of the industrial cycle immediately following a crash',[110] and 'the melancholic period'. However, Marx's meaning is clear, and it is useless to quibble about words.

Marx characterises the phase of depression in greatest detail in the following passage:

> ... [I]n the phase of the industrial cycle immediately following a crisis, when loan capital lies around idle in great quantities. At such times, when the production process is curtailed (production in the English industrial districts was reduced by one-third after the crisis of 1847), when the prices of commodities are at their lowest level, when the spirit of enterprise is paralysed, the rate of interest is low, which in this case indicates nothing more than an increase in loanable capital precisely as a result of contraction and paralysation of industrial capital. It is quite obvious that a smaller quantity of a circulation medium is required when the prices of commodities have fallen, the number of transactions decreased, and the capital laid out for wages reduced; that, on the other hand, no additional money is required to function as world-money after foreign debts have been liquidated either by the export of gold or as a result of bankruptcies; that, finally, the volume of business connected with discounting bills of exchange diminishes in proportion with the reduced number and magnitudes of the bills of exchange themselves. Hence the demand for loanable money-capital, either to act as a medium of circulation or as a

---

110 Marx 1959, p. 473.

means of payment (the investment of new capital is still out of the question), decreases and this capital, therefore, becomes relatively abundant. Under such circumstances, however, the supply of loanable money-capital also increases, as we shall later see.[111]

Let us enumerate the most important features of this quotation:
- *Production is restricted;*
- *The spirit of enterprise is crippled;*
- *Prices of commodities are at their lowest level;*
- *Loan capital lies idle in vast amount;*
- *The rate of interest is extremely low.*

All these features were undoubtedly present in 1933. The crisis passed into depression, not an ordinary depression, but one of a 'special kind'.

Stalin on the Present Depression

Does this mean that we are witnessing a transition from a crisis to an ordinary depression, to be followed by a new upswing and flourishing of industry? No, it does not. At any rate, at the present time there is no evidence, direct or indirect, to indicate the approach of an upswing of industry in the capitalist countries. More than that, judging by all things, there can be no such evidence, at least in the near future. There can be no such evidence, because all the unfavourable conditions which prevent industry in the capitalist countries from making any considerable advance continue to operate. I have in mind the continuing *general* crisis of capitalism, in the circumstances of which the *economic* crisis is proceeding; the chronic under-capacity operation of the enterprises; chronic mass unemployment; the interweaving of the industrial crisis with an agricultural crisis; the absence of tendencies towards a more or less serious renewal of fixed capital, which usually heralds the approach of a boom, etc., etc.

Evidently, what we are witnessing is a transition from the lowest point of decline of industry, from the lowest point of the industrial crisis, to a depression – not an ordinary depression, but a depression of a special kind, which does not lead to a new upswing and flourishing of industry, but which, on the other hand, does not force industry back to the lowest point of decline.[112]

---

111   Marx 1959, p. 474.
112   Stalin 1955a, pp. 296–7.

What is of decisive importance is the following: considered mechanically, the present depression is hardly to be distinguished from all preceding phases of depression, as characterised by Marx;[113] considered dynamically, there is a fundamental difference: *the present depression* (in contrast to 'normal' depressions) *does not furnish a sufficient basis for a boom in capitalist economy. The special nature of the depression consists in the deformation of the industrial cycle under the influence of the general crisis of capitalism.*[114]

This deformation is clearly evident in the entire development of capitalist economy since the lowest point of the crisis, in the middle of 1932. In the cycles of rising capitalism a few months sufficed to raise production and business from the bottom of the crisis to the peak of the preceding boom phase. In some cases (see *Chapter 3*) there was no drop in production at all during the crisis, but merely a retardation of the rate of growth. Up to now in the period of imperialism it usually took one or two years for the previous peak to be reached again after the bottom point of the crisis.

What do we see today?

More than two years have elapsed since the crisis touched bottom, but the volume of the capitalist world's industrial output is still 20 per cent below what it was in 1928; after two years of recovery, production is still way below the preceding peak than at the lowest point of the crisis in former cycles.

It is also obvious that *the ascending line of economy again snapped in the summer of 1934*. There is a pronounced relapse in the USA, as in 1933; the German economy is heading for a catastrophe; in France the slow decline continues; in England improvement has come to a standstill, etc. There is no doubt that in the third quarter of 1934 the volume of industrial production is lower, and the condition of capitalist world economy as a whole is worse, than a year ago.[115]

---

113   The principal difference is the completely disrupted state of the monetary and credit system at the present time.

114   This deformation was manifested as early as the cycle of 1921–9; the boom was *not general*. Some countries (England, for instance) and whole industries (coal, shipbuilding, cotton) participated in the boom only to a very slight extent. The boom would have been even slighter if not for the necessity to make good the devastations of the war.

115   It should be emphasised that the transition from the crisis phase to the depression phase of the industrial cycle does not mean an improvement in the economic position of the agricultural countries in general. In countries (such as the Balkans, South America and China) where industry represents no more than 10–20 percent economically, an increase of even 25 percent in industrial output involves an improvement of no more than 2.5–5 percent in the total economy of the country. *Should the condition of agriculture grow worse at the same time* (crop failure), then in spite of the transition to the depression in the field of industry, *the whole economic condition of the country will grow still worse*. The depression involves an improvement in every case only for the industrial countries. For

It is obvious that *the contradiction between the productive forces and the production relationships is so acute in the present period of the end of capitalist stabilisation that increased production prematurely hits a snag in the market's limited absorption capacity before the boom phase is reached.*

The inner mechanism of capitalism was effective enough to overcome the lowest point of the crisis, to bring about the transition to a depression, and in some countries to create a limited revival; but it does not prove to be effective enough to produce a real boom, a prosperity phase.

We must now determine why the rise in production once begun is now prematurely blocked by the market's absorption capacity at the present time. The decisive factors are as follows:

(a) The 'material basis' of the boom is the expansion of the market for goods of Division I, especially the expansion and renewal of fixed capital in the process of real accumulation (see *Chapter 1*). The chronic failure to utilise in full the available production apparatus and the chronic surplus of industrial capital characterise the period of the general crisis of capitalism. Germany serves as an example:

TABLE 12.49 Utilisation of capacity of German industry (in percent)[116]

1929	1930	1931	1932
67.4	52.2	44.5	35.7

Thus, even in the year of maximum production, 1929, the production apparatus of German industry worked at only two-thirds of capacity. The other capitalist countries present a similar picture. Needless to say, the bourgeoisie is reluctant under such circumstances to renew or increase fixed capital except in the armament industries, because the existence of unutilised plants reduces the rate of profit, the surplus value being divided among an unnecessarily large capital. But without it a boom is impossible.

---

the agrarian countries it may be accompanied by further deterioration depending upon the actual conditions.

116 *Vierteljahrshefte zur Konjunkturforschung*, 1934, 9, 2B, p. 119. As a rule, 48 working hours a week are taken as complete utilisation of capacity.

(b) The great crisis led to a tremendous process of centralisation. The establishment of monopolies,[117] the monopolist nature of capitalism, has developed enormously. In some countries (Germany, England, USA) the formation of monopolies was aided by governmental measures. But the stronger the monopolies, the stronger also the brakes on technical progress and the slighter the incentive to renew fixed capital.

Naturally, this does not mean that technical progress has come to a stop altogether; under capitalism, this is impossible. (Even the feverish improvement in *armament technique* would be impossible without certain technical progress in other spheres of industry). The following seems to us to be the qualitatively new element: owing to low wages and the great surplus of fixed capital *only such technical improvements are introduced as secure a very great reduction in production costs*, i.e. a particularly great reduction in the labour power required. A slight reduction in the lost of production is not enough to induce new investment of capital.

(c) The increased formation of monopolies lessened the fall in prices of monopoly goods (see above). Trade monopolies and the rise in turnover and consumption taxes resulted in *retail prices dropping much less than wholesale prices*.[118] This restricted sales to the ultimate consumer, which in the final analysis also determine the level of production in Division I.

(d) In previous cycles, the capitalist market expanded through drawing the independent peasant producers, working largely for their own needs, into the capitalist exchange of commodities. In this connection Lenin says:

> The basic process of the formation of a home market (i.e. of the development of commodity production and of capitalism) is the social division

---

117 Some of the international cartels and trusts collapsed during the crisis; in the period of depression a revival of the tendency to establish (or re-establish) international monopolies may be noticed. During the crisis, the organisation of monopolies within individual countries proceeded at an accelerated rate with the aid of State measures.

118 TABLE 12.50 Comparative wholesale and retail prices, annual average (1913 = 100)

	USA		Germany		Poland	
	Wholesale	Retail	Wholesale	Retail	Wholesale	Retail
1929	137	171	137	154	127	113
1933	95	132	93	119	81	87
Reduction in percent	31	23	30	23	37	23

SOURCE: LEAGUE OF NATIONS STATISTICS

of labour. This consists of various forms of processing raw materials (and various operations in this processing) separating from agriculture one after another and becoming independent branches of industry, which exchange their products (now *commodities*) for the products of agriculture. Thus, agriculture itself becomes industry (i.e. produces commodities), and the same process of specialization takes place in it.[119]

The differentiation and disintegration of the peasantry proceeds along with the spread of commodity production; an agricultural bourgeoisie is formed on the one hand, and an agricultural proletariat on the other, whereby the capitalist market continues to expand notwithstanding the impoverishment of wide sections of the peasant population.

> The formation and development of a peasant bourgeoisie creates a market in twofold fashion: firstly and mainly on account of means of production (the market of productive consumption), since the well-to-do peasant strives to convert into capital those means of production which he 'gathers' from both landlords 'in straitened circumstances' and peasants in the grip of ruin. Secondly, a market is also created here on account of personal consumption, due to the expansion of the requirements of the more affluent peasants.[120]

In the present depression the following change has taken place: the process of 'depeasantizing', as Lenin calls it, i.e. drawing the agricultural producers into the capitalist market, is essentially completed in the most highly developed capitalist countries: the USA, England and Germany. In the present agrarian crisis the process of differentiation develops into the wholesale ruin of the small and middle peasants. At the present time, however, this process is interlinked with the degradation of agriculture as already indicated in *Chapter 3* – and hence there is *no* expansion but a decrease in the capitalist market. Sales of the means of production are reduced because horses and human labour replace machinery, the use of artificial fertilisers is declining, and so forth. The transformation of the peasantry into an agricultural proletariat does not create a market for consumers' goods since the proletarianised peasant chiefly increases the army of the unemployed! The chronic agrarian crisis is one of the main obstacles in the path of a boom! (The crop failure of 1934 will increase the

---

119   Lenin 1964e, p. 67.
120   Lenin 1964e, p. 181.

misery of the toiling people in the countryside enormously; the rise in prices – relatively insignificant due to the pressure of large stocks – will not compensate for the loss in the size of the harvest even for most of the landowners and rich peasants).

(e) In former cycles the capitalist market was enlarged extensively by drawing new regions into the capitalist mode of production: by the conquest and opening up of colonies. Today the world is already partitioned; there are no more rulerless regions to conquer. Intensive exploitation of the colonies as markets is hampered by the development of consumers' goods industries in the colonial and semi-colonial countries themselves, a process which has not stopped even during the crisis.

(f) During the period of imperialism the export of capital was one of the most powerful levers for expanding the boundaries of the capitalist market. All export of capital means supplementary *sales of goods*,[121] which would be impossible if the respective countries had to pay the equivalent of the delivered goods at once. *At present the export of capital has almost completely ceased.*[122]

The main reasons for this are as follows:

1. *Economically*: the crisis has shown that with the present tendency to abandon the world economic division of labour, with the chronic agrarian crisis and with tariff walls, it is very difficult for the capital-importing debtor countries to transfer the interest or the profit on the foreign capital invested there, since the creditor countries do not want to buy the debtor countries' goods.
2. *Politically*: the world is close to the second round of wars, but the coalitions of countries for the next world war are not yet definite. Each country faces the menace of *strengthening its future enemy* through the export of capital, and losing its capital in the war.

The prospect of an impending war hampers replacement of the 'morally obsolete' fixed capital; the capitalists expect that war with its enormous demand and high prices will render even obsolete plants, now fit to be scrapped, profitable.

But the world is also close to the second round of revolutions. The menace of the proletarian revolution impedes capital investments in general, and capital export in particular. The bourgeoisie tries to keep its capital in liquid form; it sacrifices higher profits for greater security.

(g) *The huge decline in the income of the working class* as a result of mass unemployment, reduced earnings, increased taxes, and so on, is one of the most

---

121 Only in very rare cases is capital exported in the form of gold; as a rule it assumes the form of commodity export.
122 See *Chapter 2* for data.

important factors limiting the market for consumers' goods. The transition to depression has done very little to change this.

Production has increased, the number of exploited workers has increased, but the total purchasing power of wages his scarcely risen.[123]

The *changed character of rationalisation* during the crisis plays a great role in this regard.

Before the crisis the task that capital set its scientists, technicians, organisers and speed-up men, was approximately as follows: 'Reduce my production cost per unit. If that can't be done without increasing the quantity of goods produced, don't worry about it. Sales are my affair. There is always a market for a good commodity at a low price'.

The crisis has taught capital that in the period of the general crisis of capitalism there are very narrow limits to the expansion of the capitalist market. The crisis has taught capital that in many cases the cost of production in the 'thoroughly rationalised' plants equipped for mass production, where the entire process is mechanised and runs on the conveyor system, has risen to a far greater extent owing to the reduced output, than in the less modern plants.

In the crisis, capital therefore set its scientists, technicians, organisers and speed-up men the following task: *'Reduce the cost of production per unit provided that this does not lead to an increase in the quantity of commodities produced,* since there is no prospect of increased sales'. Or still more concretely: 'Attain lower production costs with the plant running at far below capacity, as at present'.

Scientists, technicians, engineers and speed-up men have carried out capital's orders. Although plants were running at far below production capacity, the cost of production has dropped considerably.

Of the methods employed for this purpose, the following seem to us to be most important:

(1) Concentrating production in the best plants of the monopolist organisations and closing down the inferior plants. *Within the plant* only the latest machinery is used, while the others are shut down, or vice versa, the conveyor is abandoned for more primitive methods of production better suited to the limited sales.
(2) Choosing the workers who are 'best': from the standpoint of capital, workers who accept speed-up and increased intensity of labour with as little resistance as possible.

---

123 For details see next chapter.

(3) *Increased intensity of labour accompanied by severe reductions in wages.* Part-time work[124] in various forms enables capital to increase the intensity of labour to the maximum during the actual working day. And if the workers are rapidly and prematurely worn-out by this murderous speed-up, capital need not worry; the millions of unemployed always provide plenty of fresh material for exploitation.

(4) The division of the labour process into separate, absolutely simple movements and the extensive mechanisation of the labour process reduces the number of skilled workers who are more difficult to replace, and converts the great mass of workers into easily replaceable unskilled and semiskilled workers.

Thus, new forms of rationalisation enabled monopoly capital to increase the workers' output during the crisis considerably and to make the proletariat bear the burden of the crisis to a large degree.

This peculiarity of crisis rationalisation is an important element in the special nature of the present depression. The reduction in production costs at the expense of the workers lessens the incentive to renew fixed capital, thus limiting the expansion of the market for the means of production, while lowering wages narrows the market for consumers' goods.

∴

To sum up, the transition to the stage of depression has increased the return on capital. Capital succeeded, as Stalin says, in improving its position somewhat at the expense of the workers, at the expense of the peasantry, and at the expense of the colonies. This was also the case in previous depressions. But formerly the better return on capital led to large new investments, to the expansion of the market for Division I, and hence for Division II as well, and thus to a new boom. This is not the case now. New investments of capital are reduced to a minimum; the 'material basis' for a boom is lacking. That is why increased production strikes the snag of the limited market after a few months, commodities do not find an adequate sale, the stocks of manufactured goods again pile

---

124 In America, the workers work only two or three days a week in the coal, iron and steel, automobile and other industries, although the factory runs full-time. The factory's labour time does not coincide with the labour time of the employed workers. The factory 'employs' double the number of workers it can accommodate, but most of them work only every other day. This was the case in many branches of industry in the USA, even during the boom period.

up[125] and a new setback occurs. These setbacks would have been still greater and industrial production still lower if the rapidly growing preparations for war did not provide a supplementary market even though it be of an unproductive character.[126]

The Outlook

In recent years the economic prerequisites for the revolutionary collapse of capitalism have developed by leaps and bounds. The contradiction between productive forces and production relationships has become palpable. The bourgeoisie is incapable of utilising the productive forces created by it; there is a chronic surplus of capital together with a surplus of population, closed down plants and starving armies of unemployed. The large-scale 'methodical' destruction of capital and of every kind of commodities shows how far the decay of capitalism has proceeded. The finance oligarchy, in trying to improve its position at the cost of all the remaining sections of the population is expropriating the weaker capitalists and the petty bourgeoisie through concentration of capital and, in using the state apparatus dominated by it to plunder the entire population, accentuates the contradictions between productive forces and the production relationships still further. It restricts ever more the consuming power of society and intensifies the general crisis of capitalism.

The same causes that entail the particular nature of the present depression also determine the further course of capitalist economy. The general crisis of capitalism, the end of temporary stabilisation and the ensuing aggravation of imperialist and class contradictions, as well as the general instability of all relations, will produce another and still greater deformation of the industrial cycle. Except for a few countries, perhaps, the present depression will drag on for many years, with brief booms and sharp relapses, without passing into a period of prosperity, *and finally, it will be succeeded by a new, deeper and more devastating economic crisis.*

Such would be the outlook if the outbreak of world war and *the outbreak of a proletarian revolution were delayed for many years to come*. This, however, is highly improbable. Dissatisfied with the slight improvement in the return on capital in the present depression of a special kind, the bourgeoisie will look to

---

125   This is most clearly shown in the USA. The index of stocks of finished goods, which had dropped to 96 by December 1932, rose to 110 in December 1933 (192 for textiles).

126   The quantitative extent of the increased preparations for war may be determined approximately, but only through very complicated calculations. We estimate that from 10 to 40 percent (depending on the individual countries) of the increase in industrial production of 1933 was due to war preparations.

war as a way out. The proletariat, whose situation in the depression is hardly any better than it was in the crisis, will – with the help of the toiling peasantry and the oppressed colonial peoples – seek its way out in the offensive against the rule of the bourgeoisie.

7. The Social Consequences of the Economic Crisis

Accentuated Struggles within the Ruling Class

Crisis and depression have seriously deranged the capitalist system of society. The inner conflicts among all the sections of capitalist society have become very acute.

The economic basis for this is the decrease in total profits during the crisis. As outlined above, the total appropriated *surplus value* has diminished during the crisis because the increased rate of exploitation did not compensate for the reduction in the number of workers were exploited. The effect of the prolonged and heavy drop in prices during the crisis was that goods were very often sold at a loss. The workers were exploited, but capital realised no profit. Under these circumstances the struggle for the division of the profits (or losses) necessarily became extremely sharp. This struggle is proceeding along various contradictory lines. All sections of the bourgeoisie in countries of agricultural imports combat the artificial maintenance of high ground rents, which raise the price of foodstuffs, make wage-cutting difficult, and hamper the reduction of production costs, thus hampering their ability to compete in the world market.

Agrarians and peasants, the industrial bourgeoisie and the petty bourgeoisie fight jointly for the reduction in interest charges against loan capital, against the coupon-clipping class. The finished goods industries combat the raw material monopolies, the peasants fight against the big trading monopolies, and so on.

The struggle revolves around tariff policies, price policies, the incidence or shifting of taxes, government orders, subsidies, credits, etc. – *in short, control of the state*. In some countries, such as Germany, Japan and Austria, this struggle is already taking the form of political murders and armed struggles. The 'crisis in the ruling class' is unmistakable.

Impairment of the Condition of the Urban Bourgeoisie

The situation of all sections of the urban petty bourgeoisie has grown considerably worse. The *'independent' strata* – artisans, café owners, small shopkeepers, doctors, and the like – have suffered a catastrophic diminution of income, largely because of the impoverishment of the proletariat, which furnishes most of their clientèle. The growing competition of the co-operative societies, of department and chain stores, direct sales to consumers by capitalist bakeries, milk companies, canning plants, and so on, account for an ever-increasing share of the shrunken market. Most of the independent petty bourgeoisie fall more and more into debt to capital; they grow poorer and go bankrupt. Hence, the popularity of the fascist demagogy, 'Break the chains of interest slavery', 'Abolish department stores', among these groups.[127]

The Social Effects of the Crisis upon the Non-independent Petty-Bourgeois Strata

The condition of the non-independent petty-bourgeois sections, the so-called 'new middle classes', is still more disastrous. The crisis threw engineers, chemists and technicians out of industry *en masse*. The rationalisation of office work threw millions of clerical employees out of work. Armament expenditures increase rapidly, but the bourgeoisie can find no money for cultural purposes. Wholesale unemployment exists among teachers and scientific workers. Those who still hold positions have had to accept salary reductions. Since there is a shortage of funds, teachers receive no salaries, sometimes for years on end; this occurs not only in such countries as China and Rumania, but in Chicago and other big cities of rich America as well. Tens of thousands of college graduates are glad to earn some sort of living as street sweepers, waiters or odd-job workers.

The Social Effects of the Crisis upon the Various Sections of the Peasantry

In *Chapter 3* we dealt with the agrarian crisis as a whole. Now let us examine its effects upon the toiling peasantry.

Although all agricultural producers are affected by the fall in prices, by the growing burden of too high rents, intolerable debts and high taxes, it is a matter of course that (except for the agricultural labourers) the crisis hits the middle and small peasants worst of all. The reasons for this are as follows:

(a) The production costs of the small farm are higher than those of the capitalist large-scale farm. With the present state of prices the peasant produces at a loss at a price level of agricultural commodities, allowing big farms to yield a profit.

(b) The rent paid by the peasant as tenant of a landlord's acreage is always 'usury rent' in the sense that it not only swallows the excess of appropri-

---

[127] The number of artisans has diminished during the crisis, as far as one can judge, but the number of 'independent' small shopkeepers *has not* decreased, since more and more of the unemployed are resorting to street hawking to eke out a miserable existence.

ated surplus value over and above the average profit, but the entire profit and even part of the wages as well.

(c) The rate of interest that the toiling peasants must pay the small provincial savings bank and village money-lenders is usurer's interest; it is considerably higher than the interest the big landowner pays on his mortgage, obtained at the original source.

(d) The 'price scissors' hits the middle or small peasant much harder than it does the big producer, since the former is obliged to sell his commodities to the provincial trader (whose debtor he very often is) below the prevailing market price, or else his selling price is dictated by the big monopolies (dairy companies, flour mills and slaughter houses). At the same time he buys his manufactured articles from middlemen at higher prices. For the toiling peasants, therefore, the gap in the 'price scissors' is much wider than that in the official indices based on wholesale prices. When minimum prices for agricultural produce are fixed by the state, they are gotten only by the big landowners and the rich peasants, whereas the middle and the small peasants have to sell their produce cheaper.[128]

(e) The taxes the toiling peasants have to pay are considerably higher per acre or in proportion to their income than those paid by the landowners and rich peasants, who are able, through their dominating position in the governmental and communal machinery, and through their 'connections' to shift the tax burden largely to the shoulders of the toiling peasantry.

(f) Ninety-nine percent of the *aid* which the capitalist state offers 'agriculture' in the form of cheap credit, remission of debts, subsidies, and so on, is obtained by the big landlords and rich peasants; the toiling peasant are left empty-handed.

Thus the agrarian crisis hits the middle and poor peasants most heavily all along the line.

The effects of the agricultural crisis can therefore be formulated from the class point of view as follows:

The process of continued differentiation characteristic of all capitalism – the sinking of part of the middle and poor peasants into the ranks of the village poor and the proletariat, and the rise of a very tiny section into the ranks of the

---

[128] A minimum price of 127 francs per quintal of wheat was established in France in 1933; but the peasants received only 80 to 90 francs (see *The Statist. A Journal of Practical Finance and Trade*, 21 April 1934).

rich peasantry – is intensified in the agrarian crisis to the point of *mass ruin of the poor and middle peasants*. The toiling peasants are expropriated at a rapid rate. More and more of the land passes into the hands of the banks, usurers and speculators; the former owner becomes an exploited tenant on what was formerly his own land.[129]

The degradation of agriculture, which is discussed in *Chapter 3*, strikes the middle and small peasants most of all. Their income – after deducting taxes, rent and interest – is not enough to maintain simple reproduction even in spite of the greatest personal privations and the strenuous labour of the entire family. Worn-out machinery cannot be renewed, livestock that dies cannot be replaced. The peasants incessantly sink lower and lower into hopeless misery.

This holds true for the 'independent' middle and small peasants. The situation of the village poor, who cannot live without extra earnings from wage labour, is desperate. The almost complete standstill of building construction, mass unemployment in industry, and the compulsory enrolment of the unemployed is 'auxiliary labour' on the firms of well-to-do peasants (Germany), all make it impossible for the village poor to find the extra employment as wage labourers that is absolutely necessary for them to make a living. Their position is hopeless and starvation is daily at their door.

Marx already pointed out that in agriculture the replacement of workers by the machine is irrevocable. Before the general crisis of capitalism, the labour power released in agriculture could find employment in industry. Today this is no longer the case. During the industrial crisis, the tide of unemployed workers, of industrial workers deprived of unemployment insurance, began to flow back from the cities to the countryside, to their relatives, in order to escape

---

129   TABLE 12.51 The percentage of farmers in the USA working leased land exclusively according to census data

1900	1920	1925	1930
35.3	38.1	38.9	42.4

In 1930–4, this process of dispossessing the farmers from their land continued at an even faster pace. At the present time probably as many as 50 percent of the farmers in the USA are working leased land. (The farmers who lease other land in addition to their own are not included in these figures).

death from starvation. Opportunities for the village poor to get employment become still rarer. *The more difficult it is to find employment, the stronger the drive of the poor rural population to cultivate land themselves, so as to utilise their idle labour power* and keep from starving. While millions of former peasant proprietors were deprived of their land during the crisis, millions of others strove to lease small plots of land at usurer's rentals, thus retarding the adjustment of land rent to the changed price level still further.

A few concrete examples suffice to show the impoverishment of the toiling peasantry in various countries. We cite bourgeois sources exclusively:

USA (Arkansas)

> The last remnants of their meager harvests are now used up. The livestock is taken off to the woods – to end there. The children cannot go to school, for they have no clothes. The Red Cross is the last hope.[130]

USA (Oklahoma)

> Debts which they will never be able to pay and the mortgage foreclosures are rapidly reducing the number of independent farmers. They have become tenants. Large areas of Oklahoma are now in the hands of the insurance societies, whose wage-workers the farmers now are.[131]

Canada (Saskatchewan)

> In South Saskatchewan the farmer received in the middle of January 35 cents for a bushel of wheat no. 1, the best quality, and 15 cents for poor quality. Few of them have much to sell. There are some who do not receive sufficient from the sale of their wheat to pay the threshing costs. In those parts in which such conditions exist, the poorer classes of farmers are reduced to a ration of rough house-baked bread with syrup, alternated by a few potatoes, for their sustenance. Cases have been cited in which fried field-mice and other earth-inhabiting creatures and soup of Russian thistles have been the only means of preventing death by starvation.[132]

---

130   *The Chicago Tribune*, quoted in *Literary Digest*, 28 February 1931.
131   *The Times*, 17 November 1930.
132   *The Times*, 19 February 1930.

Italy

'Polenta must take the place of honour as of old, and there must be little bread and hardly any more in the peasant diet. I see no other way out of our present troubles'.[133]

'Fortunately, the Italian people is not used to several meals a day, and since its standard of living is modest, it feels shortage and privation much less'.[134]

Hungary

Two years ago a Hungarian illustrated paper printed a picture of a horse found on a country road with a rag tied to it; wrapped in the rag there was a horse's passport together with a letter which read:

> 'I have completed my autumn work with this horse. I have no fodder to keep it through the winter. I cannot sell it because there are no buyers. I haven't the heart to kill it. I'm letting it go free; perhaps somebody will take it in and feed it'.

Conditions in a large German village in Hungary, with 2,000 inhabitants, are described as follows in an article by L. Leopold in the *Pester Lloyd*, 19 November 1933:

> Only one paper is received in the whole village. The total annual consumption of pencils is ten dozen, including the school. The barber relates: 'There isn't any money at all left in the village. The peasants haven't a red cent and get a shave only for big holidays ... The people here have no money. Hardly a few pengő in the whole village. They gradually stopped counting in money terms. Since the village shop-keeper himself has no cash and cannot buy either wheat or rye, nobody even talks of money prices'.

---

133   The fascist professor, [G.] Bizzorero, in *Corriere Paduano* of 14 June 1931, quoted in *The Economist*, 29 August 1931, p. 396. [Varga does not mention that the author of this article in *The Economist* was Gaetano Salvemini, a former Italian prime minister].

134   Mussolini, speech in the Senate, 18 December 1930.

Japan

> The agrarian crisis, which has ensued since the end of the war, has never been paid so little attention as now. Its results have been a decisive reduction of the number of peasant landlords, the growth of conflicts between tenants and landlords, the desertion of the farmers by the progressive youths and girls, the continued deficit in the peasants' budget and the continuous accumulation of unpayable debts ... The farmer is disillusioned by the repeated relief campaigns, which in the long run are undertaken at his expense, and had no other effect but to perpetuate the conditions of his suffering.[135]

These quotations could be continued indefinitely. Everywhere we have the same picture – the consistent impoverishment of the exploited rural population under the blows of the crisis. Discontent is widespread and finds expression in numerous peasant revolts, to which we shall return later.

It is self-evident that the 1934 crop failure – hailed with delight by some of the landowners – has turned the miserable condition of the village poor and of the small peasants, who always must buy additional foodstuffs, into a disaster. The situation of the middle peasants, whose harvest *this* year was not enough to meet their own requirements, has grown still worse. The rise in prices that followed the crop failure benefits only a small upper crust of landowners and rich peasants, but entails still greater misery for the exploited sections of the rural population.

The Impoverishment of the Proletariat

The absolute and relative impoverishment of the proletariat proceeded at an accelerated rate during the interval between the Sixth Congress and the Seventh. In spite of the growing resistance of the proletariat, in spite of great, stubborn, often bloody strikes (particularly in 1933 and 1934), the capitalist offensive *proved successful on the whole*. Capital has largely succeeded – to an uneven degree, in different countries, and by varying methods – in making the proletariat bear the burden of the crisis.

The impairment of the workers' conditions proceeded along the following main lines in all countries:
(a) Increase in the number of unemployed (and part-time workers);
(b) Reduction in the *real wage* of the employed workers;

---

135   S. Washio in *The Trans-Pacific* [Tokio], 7 December 1933.

(c) Increased intensity of labour;
(d) Curtailment of social insurance.

We must definitely emphasise the fact that the official figures used by us below, as the only ones available for investigating the condition of the working class, *have been falsified in many crises*. The bourgeoisie endeavours to have the conditions of the working class appear in a better light. In many cases this falsification can be proved from the official figures themselves. In most cases, however, exposure of the frauds requires more space than we have at our disposal. But the impairment of the conditions of the working class is clearly evident even from bourgeois statistics.

(a) Mass unemployment and increased labour output during the crisis

There are no reliable statistics of unemployment throughout the world. Unemployment among agricultural labourers and semi-proletarians is nowhere recorded. We can only reproduce the official statistics and prove by a few examples how they are falsified.

TABLE 12.52 Percentage of unemployed industrial workers

	1929	1930	1931	1932	1933	1934 (first six months)
Germany (trade unions)	13.2	22.2	34.3	43.8	44.7[136]	17.5[137]
Austria (receiving dole)	12.8	16.2	20.2	27.2	31.1	29.4
Belgium (receiving dole)	1.3	3.6	10.9	19.0	17.0	19.0
Canada (receiving dole)	5.7	11.1	16.8	22.0	22.3	19.4
Denmark	15.5	13.7	17.9	31.7	28.8	24.7
USA (trade unions)	12.0	21.0	26.0	32.0	31.0	23.0
Norway (trade unions)	15.4	16.6	22.3	30.8	33.4	37.3
Holland (insured)	7.5	9.7	18.7	29.9	31.4	30.7
England (prolonged unemployment)	8.2	11.8	16.7	17.6	16.4	14.8
England (together with the 'temporary stopped')	11.8	16.8	23.1	25.5	23.2	17.4

---

136 Last figures of the Allgemeiner Deutscher Gewerkschaftsbund (General Federation of Trade Unions in Germany), May [1934].
137 Statistics of Kraft durch Freude (German Labour Front).

These figures do not give a complete picture of the prevalence of unemployment. Unemployment among agricultural labourers and poor peasants, and part-time *work* (although the latter is very widespread) are not listed. Nonetheless they show that the officially listed percentage of unemployed rose everywhere up to and including 1932 and that the percentage of unemployed is much higher than in any of the preceding crises.

Of particular importance, however, is the fact that the transition to the *period of depression and the increase in industrial production in 1933 was accompanied by a disproportionately slight reduction in the percentage of unemployed.*

The explanation for this peculiar fact is that the *trend towards the reduction in the number of workers employed by industrial capital,* as Marx uses the term – agriculture, industry, building, transport – a tendency pointed out by us before the crisis, at the Sixth Congress of the Comintern,[138] *has been increased considerably by crisis rationalisation in the highly developed capitalist countries.*[139]

---

138   Varga 1928c, ch. 3.
139   *The trend of the number of workers* employed in industry to diminish, even before the crisis, is evidenced by the following figures in *Table 12.53*:

TABLE 12.53   Number of workers employed in industry and in craft trades in Germany (*in millions*) (In enterprises more than five workers)

1925	1926	1927	1928	1929	1930
9.5	7.6	8.9	9.1	8.3	7.5

We see that the number of workers employed was far behind that of 1925. (All the figures are *official*). The tendency towards reduction of the number of productive workers, producing value and surplus value, is most clearly shown in the United States. The following official census figures illustrate this particularly well:

Workers (in thousands)

	1919	1925	1929	1931
Agricultural workers(a)	2,336	–	2,733	–
Railwaymen	1,960	1,786	1,694	1,283
Miners	888	–	788	–
Industrial workers	9,041	8,384	8,839	6,523
	14,225		14,054	

(a)   Figures for 1920 and 1930.

In other words, in the period of the general crisis of capitalism, the process of displacing workers as a result of increased productivity and intensity of labour (a process which is inherent to capitalism) can no longer be compensated by an increase of production. At increasingly short intervals the expansion of production clashes, as we have pointed out above, more and more sharply with the limits of the capitalist market which grows increasingly narrow with the continued development of the general crisis of capitalism and with the chronic aggravation of the contradiction between the production and sales possibilities. Today the correctness of Engels's thesis, written 40 years ago, is proved with special clarity: 'The daily growing speed with which production may be enlarged in all fields of large-scale industry today, is offset by the ever-greater slowness with which the market for these increased products expands. What the former turns out in months, can scarcely be absorbed by the latter in years'.[140]

Hence, because of lack of a market, it is impossible to have such an expansion of production as could – except for cyclic fluctuations – prevent a reduction in the number of employed workers in the most advanced capitalist countries.

The following table compiled by the National Industrial Conference Board, a bourgeois institution, may serve as an illustration of this development in the USA:[141]

Even during the peak of the boom in 1929 the number of workers exploited by industrial capital did not equal the total for 1919, although the index of industrial production (mining + industry) was 83 in 1919, 119 in 1929 (1923–5 = 100). An increase of more than 40 percent in the volume of industrial production was achieved with a reduction in the absolute number of workers employed.

140   Marx 1959, pp. 428–9.
141   *The Conference Board Bulletin*, National Industrial Conference Board, 8, 20 February 1934, p. 10.

TABLE 12.54 US employment and production (1923–33) (1923–5 = 100)

	Production	Employment	Labour hours	Wages paid	Output per worker	Output per working hour	Labour cost per unit of output
1923	101	104.2	106.5	103.4	97.3	95.0	102.3
1924	94	96.2	93.9	95.7	97.7	100.1	102.1
1925	105	99.6	99.9	100.9	105.1	104.8	96.5
1926	108	101.4	101.6	104.3	106.5	106.3	96.6
1927	106	98.8	98.0	102.0	107.1	107.9	96.6
1928	112	97.2	97.0	101.8	114.8	115.0	91.3
1929	119	101.1	101.8	107.7	117.8	117.0	90.7
1930	95	87.8	80.7	87.4	108.4	117.9	91.9
1931	80	74.4	64.4	66.0	107.7	124.4	82.2
1932	63	62.0	48.3	45.3	101.2	130.3	72.1
1933	76	66.2	52.0	47.5	114.8	145.0	63.4

This *Table 12.54* indicates quite clearly the roots of the growing chronic mass unemployment and the economic basis for the declining trend in the number of workers employed in the industries of highly developed capitalist countries (and in production as a whole).

In the course of ten years the output per worker has increased by 17.5 percent and the output per worker-hour by 50 percent. (The smaller increase in the output per worker is due to the *shorter working day* during the crisis; *up to 1929 the rise in the output per worker and per hour run parallel*). The increase in output was particularly steep during the crisis owing to crisis rationalisation. The output per hour increased from 118 to 145 during the interval 1931–3. As a result, an increase in the production index from 63 in 1932 to 76 in 1933 (i.e. by 20 percent) was accompanied by a rise in the index of employment by 4.2 or only six percent. If as many workers had full-time employment as in 1923, with the present output per worker in American industry, production would be fully 50 percent greater. And *if as many workers were now employed as in the last prosperity year, 1929, the volume of production would exceed that of 1929 by 25 percent and be almost double that of 1933*. In fact, *it would be much more than double*, since the increase in the output per worker would undoubtedly continue still further. But even the most optimistic ideologists of American capitalism would not have the courage to prophesy such an increase in production. This means that

American industry will never again employ as many workers as it did in 1919 or even in 1929. This means that the process of discharging workers from American industry as well as from agriculture and mining, which began in 1919, will continue. This means that chronic mass unemployment will tend to increase, aside from cyclic fluctuations.

The increase in output per worker in the USA as a result of crisis rationalisation was most strikingly shown in the period preceding the general introduction of part-time work through the NIRA.[142]

TABLE 12.55 Official statistics of American industry (1923–5 = 100)

	Volume of industrial production	Employment	Wages
May 1932	61	61	46
May 1933	80	60	42

In the course of one year production was increased 31 percent, while the number of workers employed dropped, and wages fell by ten percent.

This great increase in output per worker during the crisis is not peculiar to American industry alone.

The German Institute of Business Research gives the following figures for the increase in output per worker per hour for the whole of German industry.[143]

TABLE 12.56 Increase in output per worker in German industry

1925	1928	1929	1930	1931	1932
87.3	100	106.6	115.6	121	124.4

---

142   NIRA (National Industrial Recovery Act): the law empowering the president of the United States to regulate industry by means of decrees ('codes').
143   *Wochenbericht des Instituts für Konjunkturforschung*, 5 July 1933, 6, 14, pp. 63; Germany's Economic Situation at the Turn of 1933–4, 1934.

TABLE 12.57 Output per pit-worker in German coal mines (1913 = 100)[144]

1925	1928	1929	1930	1931	1932	1933
103.6	126	134	144	163	180	187

It is clear that such an increase in output must eventually lead to a further reduction in the number of employed workers in Germany as well.

A similar trend is seen in England. Industrial production in 1933 was 98.5 (1924 = 100) according to the official Board of Trade Index, whereas the index of employment was only 86.3.

A rapid increase in the output per worker also took place in the coalmining industry in France.[145]

TABLE 12.58 Average output per shift in pounds

1930	1931	1932	1933
1,350	1,588	1,725	1,875

Finally, let us take the increase in output per worker during the crisis in the Japanese textile industry, which is the country's major industry.[146]

TABLE 12.59 Increase in output in the Japanese textile industry

	Cotton yarn output of bales per worker per month	Number employed workers per 1,000 spindles
1927	1.23	35.3
1929	1.46	27.5
1930	1.51	23.5
1931	1.75	20.6
1932	1.85	20.1

---

144 Germany's Economic Situation at the Turn of 1933–4, 1934; *Glückauf*, 3 June 1934.
145 Data of the Coal Committee.
146 Data of the Japanese textile cartel, *The Japan Advertiser* [daily], Special Supplement, January 1933.

TABLE 12.60 Number of Japanese workers per 100 looms

	Men	Women	Total
1927	132	660	792
1929	122	494	616
1930	113	430	543
1931	90	357	447
1932	79	368	447

Parallel with the trend towards reduction in the number of workers employed by industrial capital, who directly create value and surplus value, the number of workers employed in trade, banking, etc., who do not create value, tends to increase. This is best seen in Great Britain:

TABLE 12.61 Shift in number of productive and non-productive workers employed in Great Britain[147] (in thousands)

	Industry, mining, building and transport	Percent	Trade, banking, etc.	Percent
1928	7,940	77.2	2,344	22.8
1929	7,926	73.4	2,875	26.6
1930	7,507	71.9	2,933	28.1
1931	7,024	69.9	3,021	30.1
1932	6,890	69.1	3,077	30.9
1933	7,111	69.2	3,165	30.8

As we see, the number of non-productive workers *increased* by 300,000 during the crisis, whereas the number of productive workers creating value and surplus value diminished by 800,000. The decay of capitalism is manifested here most strikingly.

∴

---

147 Taken from the *Labour Gazette*. From the total number on a certain day in the various branches of industry, the average number of unemployed deducted.

Owing to the lack of reliable data it is impossible to ascertain definitely the absolute number of unemployed. The official figures record only the number of 'registered' unemployed. Since the cuts in unemployment insurance have eliminated the incentive for the workers to register, statistics give a completely false (or deliberately falsified) picture of unemployment. The following figures are interesting (but not reliable), therefore, as showing *the trend of world employment, but they must not be taken as absolute figures.*

TABLE 12.62 World unemployment

	Index[148]		Number in millions[149]
1929	100	March 1931	21
1930	168	December 1932	28
1931	241	March 1933	30
1932	297	March 1934	32.5
1933	279		

That the number of unemployed is falsified, as in Germany for example, is proved by comparing the following figures (all of them official).

TABLE 12.63 Unemployment in Germany

	August 192 (in millions)	August 1933[150] (in millions)
Number of employed according to sickness insurance fund statistics	18.77	12.72
Unemployed	1.27	4.12
Total	20.04	17.84

---

148 'Statistics', *International Labour Review*, 29, April 1934, p. 571.
149 'Die Arbeitslosigkeit im Ausland', *Wirtschaft und Statistik*, Herausgegeben vom Statistischen Reichsamt, Berlin, 14, 10, May 1934, p. 316.
150 In order to 'trim' the statistics, the fascist government included various categories of forced labourers (who receive no wages) in the sickness insurance statistics, so that the 'corrected' number of employed was announced as 13,725,000 in August 1933.

2,200,000 *workers have simply disappeared from German statistics in the course of four years*; they are neither employed nor officially unemployed. To this there must be added some hundreds of thousands representing the difference between the number of workers who have reached the working age and the old workers who have dropped out of the labour market either through death or disability.[151] Finally, there are the hundreds of thousands of small peasants, artisans, petty shopkeepers, who were robbed of their 'independent' existence in the crisis and thrown into the ranks of the unemployed. To sum up: chronic mass unemployment, this terrible scourge of the proletariat in the capitalist countries of today, is not a transient cyclic phenomenon. The transition to depression has mitigated it to only a small extent. *It is impossible to place the army of unemployed in production again*, as was the case with the industrial reserve armies in boom period before the crisis of capitalism. This would require a production level far exceeding that of 1929 of which, however, there is no likelihood.

Thus the situation has arisen which Marx foresaw as a hypothesis: 'A development of productive forces which would diminish the absolute number of labourers (the number of workers employed is under discussion – E.V.), i.e. enable the entire nation to accomplish its total production in a shorter time span, *would cause a revolution*, because it would put the bulk of the population out of the running'.[152]

The development of productive forces has reached this stage; the period of the general crisis of capitalism is the period of the social revolution.

(b) The reduction in real wages

Bourgeois wage statistics are so falsified and so unreliable that they give no picture of the lowering of real earnings even of workers who are fully employed. All the calculations given below must therefore be used with the greatest reserve. In order to avoid any charge of exaggeration, we have taken, in all doubtful cases, the figures that are more favourable to the workers.

---

[151] TABLE 12.64 According to German official estimates, the number of persons reaching the working age was (in thousands)

1930	1931	1932	1933	Total
664	575	594	745	2,538

[152] Marx 1959, p. 251.

The wages of the full-time workers were reduced in three different ways:
(1) Elimination of 'wages above agreement schedules'.[153]
(2) Lowering of *collective agreement wages*.
(3) Increase in *taxes and wage deductions*.

Germany

TABLE 12.65 Decline of average earnings in the building trades from August 1929 to August 1932 (in percent) (for all cities with more than 100,000 inhabitants)[154]

	Bricklayers	Carpenters	Semi-skilled building workers	Excavation workers
Reduction in percent of gross earnings	41.8	34.9	33.5	33.9

Between August 1932 and August 1933 (i.e. already under the fascist regime) the collective agreement wages in the building trades were further reduced some five percent.

Reductions in the collective agreement wages of other trades were somewhat smaller. Between October 1929 and February 1933 typical wage cuts were as follows: skilled workers in the metal industry 18.1 percent; chemical industry 18.7–18.9 percent; textile workers 13.9–15.5 percent. In addition, earnings above the collective agreement rates were cut by 5–8 percent.

The wages paid the workers are further reduced, moreover, during the crisis by numerous new taxes and imposts,[155] which together comprise about five percent of wages.

---

153 'Wages above agreement rates' are used in these statistics to mean additional wages which piece-workers receive over and above the hourly wage fixed by the collective agreement.
154 *Wirtschaft und Statistik*, Statistischen Reichsamt, Berlin, 1933, 12, 17, p. 544.
155 (a) Increase in social insurance deductions: rise of 1.5 percent of wages in unemployment insurance contribution;
    (b) *'Crisis tax'* (newly introduced): one percent on wages exceeding 100 marks per month;
    (c) *'Aid to married people'*: all unmarried workers have to pay 2 percent on monthly earnings of 75 to 150 marks, and 3 percent on monthly earnings of 150 to 300 (more than half the industrial workers are unmarried);
    (d) *'Donations to work creation'*: 'voluntary'(!) contribution of 1 to 2 percent of wages (now abolished);

The reduction in money wages of the fully employed worker totals between 25 and 52 percent, depending on the branches of industry. Wage cuts for the higher-paid trades were greater than for the lower-paid ones.

TABLE 12.66 Compared with this the official cost of living index (1913–14 = 100)

	1921	August 1934	Rate of fall
Total	158.8	123.3	22
Rent	126.2	121.3	4.5
Food	154.5	118.5	23

The official figures *doubtless* list the drop in the cost of living too high rather than too low.[156] But even if we accept the official figures, we get a drop in real wages of between 5 and 32 percent in the case of the full-time workers.

The full-time workers represent a minority of the German class, however. According to trade-union statistics, average employment was as follows in 1932 (in percent):

TABLE 12.67 German average employment

Full-time workers	Part-time workers	Totally unemployed
33.6	22.6	43.8

The total income of the German working class as a whole, including the unemployed, has diminished enormously during the crisis, especially since unemployed insurance benefits have been cut at a rapid rate and the burden of maintaining the unemployed has been shifted to an increasing extent to the shoulders of the employed workers.

(e) *Winter aid donation*: approximately one hour's wages per month;
(f) Numerous 'collections', compulsory subscriptions to the fascist press, etc.;
(g) *Citizen tax*: six marks per annum.
156 Particularly rent, which remained relatively stable, has been inadequately weighted. Moreover, the prices of those foods that the worker now buys, because of his diminished money income, sank less than the average while some, such as margarine, have risen sharply.

The total income of workers, office employees and civil servants was as follows, according to the estimate of the Institut für Konjunkturforschung (milliards of marks):[157]

TABLE 12.68 Total income of German workers

1929	1930	1931	1932	1933
44.5	41.0	32.5	25.7	26.1

The decline from 1929 to 1933 is 41 percent. To this we must add an increase of at least 5 percent in taxes and deductions, hence a total *decline in money income of 46.6 percent.*

The decline would be still greater for the *workers alone* since there is less unemployment among the higher employees and civil servants, and the latter's wages are cut much less. Even assuming that all the official figures and the official calculations of a drop of 21 percent in the cost of living are correct, we find a *net reduction of 26 percent in real wages for all workers, office employees and civil servants.* The actual reduction in the real wages of workers alone is undoubtedly a few percent higher. According to our estimate, the real income of the German working class has declined about one-third during the crisis.

United States

Real wages of the full-time workers as well as the income of the working class as a whole declined considerably in the United States during the crisis.

---

157   For 1933 see *Konjunkturstatistisches Handbuch* 1933, p. 80; *Wochenbericht des Instituts für Konjunkturforschung,* 6, 23, 6 September 1933, p. 96.

TABLE 12.69 Average weekly earnings of all industrial workers[158]

	1928	1929	March 1933 (minimum)	March 1934	Decline in % since 1929
	27.88	29.17	14.56	20.49	29.8
Cost of living[159] (1923 = 100)	100.8	100	71.8	78.5	21.5

It must be emphasised that this cost of living index, like the German one, is based on a standard of living that is much too high, and inapplicable to the period of crisis. For instance, only 33 percent of total expenditure is allocated for food. Hence the rise of 20 percent in the food index between March 1933 and March 1934 is quite independently reflected in the total index.

The American census of manufactures enables one to calculate the *rate of surplus value* in industry with some degree of accuracy on the basis of wages paid and the increase in value due to production. The result is as follows:

TABLE 12.70 Trend of the rate of surplus value in US industry[160]

1899	1909	1919	1921	1923	1925	1927	1929	1931
128	130	122	106	118	128	133	152	147

We can see that the rate of exploitation shows a decidedly rising trend. The drop in the crisis year 1921 – and to a slighter extent in the present crisis – *does not denote a diminution in the exploitation of the productive* workers, who create surplus value, but indicates a relatively higher proportion of wages paid to the unproductive, supervising, guard and office personnel, due to plants being operated at far below capacity during the crisis.

The impairment of the condition of the working class in the USA was largely due, however, to the *tremendous unemployment*. According to various estimates (there are no official statistics) the number of totally unemployed has exceeded

---

[158] Data from *The Conference Board Bulletin*, National Industrial Conference Board.
[159] Index of *The Conference Board Bulletin*, National Industrial Conference Board.
[160] See Appendix for the method of calculation.

THE GREAT CRISIS AND ITS POLITICAL CONSEQUENCES

ten million for many years. Part-time work is likewise widespread. This enormous unemployment is manifested in the huge decline of wages paid.

TABLE 12.71 Index of wages paid in big American industries[161] (Federal Reserve Board, 1923–5 = 100)

1929	1930	1931	1932	1933	1934 (first 4 months)
109	89	68	46	49	61

Thus, the total wages paid in 1933 was only 45 percent of the 1929 level. This enormous drop is not mitigated by any sort of unemployment insurance. The workers ate up their savings,[162] they sold their automobiles, furniture, houses and fell into the hands of their creditors. In 'rich' America, millions are homeless and starving; they become tramps and sink to the level of the *lumpen*proletariat.

In conclusion some data on the impairment of the condition of the workers in Japan:

---

161 These figures are based on data supplied monthly by the big plants which together employ approximately three million workers. We have reason to believe that wages in small enterprises, in agriculture and trade, have dropped at least as much.

162 TABLE 12.72 Savings bank deposits and depositors in the USA

	Deposits (millions of dollars)	Number of depositors (thousands)
June 1929	62,764	28,218
June 1933	39,268	21,421

Thus, almost seven million depositors consumed all their savings between 1929 and 1933. The total sum of the deposits dropped 23,500,000,000 dollars in four years. There is no doubt that it is largely the workers who ate up their savings. Inflation further reduced what remained by 40 percent!

TABLE 12.73 Trend of real wages in Japan[163] (1926 = 100)

	1929	1930	1931	1932	1933	March 1934
Hourly wages	98.6	96.2	91.3	88.1	85.1	83.5
Actual earnings	103.9	98.7	90.7	88.1	89.2	91.6
Cost of living (1914 = 100)	–	–	135.5	136.8	145.6	149.0 (May)

The increase in the actual amount of earnings while wages per hour decline is due to the overtime and night work prevalent in the armament industries. In recent years *real wages* fell by 20–25 percent even according to these figures taken from capitalist sources.

We can dispense with figures for other countries, as they present the same picture.[164]

The wages of agricultural labourers have declined to a greater extent than those of industrial workers. Here are a few instances.[165]

TABLE 12.74 Wages of agricultural workers

	Canada	USA (wage per day)	New Zealand (weekly wage)
	(1914 = 100)	(1927 = 100)	(1914 = 100)
1929	194	99	179
1932	106	49	125
1933	100	48	115

We can easily form an idea of the frightful poverty of the agricultural labourers in the capitalist world when we take into consideration the enormous unem-

---

163 Data from the Economic Bureau of the Mitsubishi concern.
164 According to official data the real wages of full-time workers have declined least of all in England and Sweden.
165 Data from the *Statistical Yearbook of the League of Nations*, 1933–4.

ployment in agriculture, the absence of any sickness, accident or unemployment insurance in most countries on the conditions of the peasantry quoted above.

(c) Cutting down social insurance

In the last four years social insurance has been cut all along the line in every country. Unemployment insurance exists only in England, practically speaking (and there it is reduced by the Means Test). In all other countries where unemployment insurance existed, nothing but miserable shreds of it are left.

Germany may serve as an example. By forced labour, by discharging workers in whose families there is a wage earner, by hiring workers who draw an unemployment dole, by stopping unemployment relief to Communists and Social Democrats, and by imprisoning the unemployed in concentration camps, unemployment insurance has been practically abolished by the fascists.

TABLE 12.75 Registered unemployed in various categories (in percent)

	Receiving unemployment insurance	Receiving crisis relief	Public welfare relief	Receiving no relief
January 1929	78.8	5.1		
June 1934	10.5	33.0	32.0	24.5

But the number of those receiving no relief in fact exceeds 50 percent since, as we have shown above, at least 2,200,000 and probably 3,000,000 unemployed do not register at all, having given up all hope of ever getting work or unemployment relief.

Paralleling the withdrawal of relief, the amount of relief itself was cut for all categories. As the cities have no funds, public welfare relief has been reduced to the most pitiful alms. Similar cuts have been made in all other forms of social insurance.

(d) Working Hours

A few words about working hours. Motivated by fear of the millions of unemployed, the bourgeois governments and the reformist trade unions in many countries have advocated a compulsory reduction in working hours, the 'planned distribution of work' (naturally with a corresponding reduction in earnings). This was carried out on a large scale only in Roosevelt's 'Codes', which *on the whole*, however, only sanctioned the existing state of affairs. In 1932, the working hours per week in the factories of the USA averaged 34.8.[166] But this average covered the most glaring disproportions. In 1932, nine factories in the woollen industry worked 60 hours a week in the night shift, two factories 65 hours, and one 67.5 hours (likewise in the night shift). In the cotton industry, 39 factories worked 11 hours daily in the night shift and ten factories 12 hours.[167]

Capital's complete indifference to the fate of the workers (and the uneven employment index in different factories) is shown by the fact that *in Britain, with hundreds of thousands unemployed in the very same branch of industry*, not only part-time but also overtime is worked. The following *Table 12.76* gives British data for September 1933.[168]

TABLE 12.76 Unemployment and overtime hours in Great Britain

	Percent of workers	Overtime hours per week	Percent of workers	Number of hours less per week
Worsted industry	26.5	6	12	11
Woollen industry	23.0	7	16	10
Shoe industry	16.0	7.25	37	9.5

There are similar phenomena in France. Although part-time work is quite general, there are plants where the hours of work are inhumanly long. The laundries and millineries of Paris work up to 18 hours a day, confectioneries 12 hours, and so on. Overtime is worked regularly in the armament plants. No doubt this is also the case in other countries that do not publish such detailed statistics.

(e) Increasing the intensity of labour

We have furnished exhaustive data above on the increased labour output during the crisis. This increase was due almost exclusively to the increased intens-

---

166 *Survey of Current Business*, Washington: Department of Commerce, Bureau of Foreign and Domestic Commerce, 1933, 13, 1, p. 28.
167 According to the official figures of the US Labour Department, cited in *The American Federationist*, Washington, D.C.: American Federation of Labor, 1933, 40, 2, p. 184.
168 *The Ministry of Labour Gazette*, 1933, 40, 10.

ity of labour. Productivity of labour probably increased only in exceptional cases, since on the whole no improved machinery was introduced during the crisis. The most important methods employed to increase the intensity of labour were as follows: speeding up machinery; increasing the number of looms operated by one worker in the textile industry; introducing the conveyor and running it at a faster rate; 'scientific' management (Bedaux): increasing the supervising staff, introducing the espionage system, fines, etc.

(f) Forced labour

Finally, we should like to point out a *new* phenomenon: the ever-wider growth of various forms of 'voluntary' forced labour, to which youth is subjected in an increasing number of countries. It is furthest developed in Germany and in the USA. The youths are quartered in camps and employed as unskilled labourers (road building, drainage, canals, military fortifications, and so on), at the same time undergoing military training. Another form of forced labour is the allocation of unemployed workers to rich peasants on whose farms they have to work through the summer for food, lodging and a little pocket money. In case they refuse to undertake this work, they are deprived of unemployment or welfare relief. The forced labour system, which has existed in the colonies for a long time, is now being more and more extended in various forms to the most advanced capitalist countries.

(g) The frightful conditions of the workers in the colonies

The conditions of the colonial workers have doubtless grown worse more rapidly than those of the workers in the imperialist countries. Colonial capital has cut wages and impaired labour conditions by using the most brutal force. There is no statistical data that is at all usable. We must confine ourselves to a few concrete instances taken at random from bourgeois sources.

Cuba

> Labourers are working for 10 cents a day throughout Cuba, and large numbers are unable to get jobs even at that wage ... Families carrying children in their arms are seen asleep in vacant doorways others prowl about garbage pails for something to eat.[169]

---

169   *The New York Herald Tribune*, 25 January 1934.

Puerto Rico

> 'It is estimated that there were about 200,000 unemployed family heads on the island; since the average family has 5.6 persons, about 1,120,000 persons are affected, two-thirds of the total population of 1,600,000'.[170]

India

> 'Taking the City and Island of Bombay, it is seen that 5 out of 84 mills have been scrapped ... Twenty-nine mills have been closed down ... The total number of unemployed workers is thus easily more than 61,000 ...'.

> 'In other words, for every 100 persons employed, there are 70 workers who are thrown out of employment ... In the midst of the closure of 29 mills no less than 14 mills are working night shift ...'.

> 'Forty-eight out of the remaining 50 mills which are working have made cuts varying from 7 percent, to 44.5 pet cent ...'.

> 'There are only two mills in Bombay which have so far made no direct cut in wages. But these have been put on the rationalisation basis by giving more looms and spindles to the workers ...'.[171]

> 'Unemployed coolies from the tin mines and the rubber estates drift through the streets like ghosts ... Thousands of Chinese and Indian labourers are beggars repatriated every month ... Every Mohammedan store has its crowd of beggars ... Chinese women hide behind the pillars of the shops watching their children invade the parked cars with their hands to their mouths as a sign of hunger, mumbling broken petitions between their spread fingers ...'.[172]

The quotations could be continued endlessly.

---

170   *The New York Times*, 8 April 1934.
171   *The Bombay Chronicle*, 8 February 1934.
172   *The Manchester Guardian*, 17 February 1933.

8   The Rise of the Soviet Union

The six years since the Sixth Congress have shown the workers of the whole world, through the example of the Soviet Union, what it really means to have the productive forces freed from the shackles of the capitalist mode of production. For in these six years the Dictatorship of the Proletariat – which Kautsky and Co., the lackeys of the bourgeoisie, claimed had 'stabilised hunger and suffering' – has rendered possible rapid progress in the technical, economic, social and cultural fields such as the world has never known. The gigantic First Five-Year Plan, which the bourgeoisie and the Social Democrats called a fraud or at best a utopia, was completed in four and a quarter years. In order to measure the tremendous extent of the progress which has been made in these six years, let us sketch the principal features of the Soviet Union's situation in the fiscal year 1927–8.

Compared with the leading capitalist countries, the Soviet Union was a decidedly *backward country in the field of technology*. Only the simplest machines could be made within the country itself. The decisively important means of production – lathes, tractors, combines, automobiles, airplanes, chemicals, etc. – were not made in the country. Agricultural technique was completely backward, very little different from that of the pre-war period; even the wooden plough was still widely used.

In the economic field the Soviet Union was still an agrarian country in 1927–8. Agriculture accounted for 51.3 percent of the gross value of production, industry for only 48.7 percent. (The situation had scarcely changed compared to the pre-war period; at that time agriculture accounted for 57.9 percent and industry for 42.1 percent).[173]

At that time the Soviet Union was largely dependent on the capitalist countries economically, because it had to import the principal means of production. Industry still produced articles of consumption primarily; *only 27.2 percent of the gross value of industrial production represented means of production, while 72.8 percent were articles of consumption.*[174]

A boycott by the capitalist countries could therefore have cut off technico-economic progress. Development of the country's defences was also dependent on the outside capitalist world. Equipping agriculture with modern instruments of production, without which the transition to socialist agriculture is impossible, was out of the question.

---

173   Stalin 1954c.
174   Ibid.

The problem that Lenin had posed still faced the Bolsheviks in all its magnitude: *Either catch up with the capitalist countries economically and surpass them, or perish.*

At that time capitalism still possessed strong roots in the Soviet Union. Some 12 percent of industrial production was still in private hands, while some 17 percent of the industrial workers were employed by exploiters.[175] Still more important: private ownership dominated agriculture. There were about 24,000,000 peasant farms, with a tendency to further division. They comprised roughly: 7,000,000 poor peasants, 16,000,000 middle peasants, 1,000,000 kulaks.

The kulaks owned about 10 percent of the land, and they exploited at least one-quarter of the agricultural population, either directly as workers, or indirectly through renting out draught animals and machines, through usurious loans, etc. In the middle of 1928, Stalin said: '... [R]aising the level of individual small and middle peasant production ... is still the chief aim of our work in the sphere of agriculture'.[176]

The transition from this policy of improving the small and middle *individual* peasant farms, of combating and limiting the capitalist elements,[177] to the policy of liquidating the kulaks as a class, on the basis of thorough collectivisation, was only contemplated as yet.

This means that the great question which had been posed by Lenin – 'Who will defeat whom?' – had not yet been finally settled in the Soviet Union, *that possibilities still existed for the restoration of capitalism!* Even after the Sixth Congress of the Comintern, Stalin said in this connection:[178]

---

175   Larin 1927.
176   Stalin 1934a, p. 48. [In this quote, Varga deliberately truncated Stalin's text. In Stalin's *Works* a slightly different version is published: 'The specific feature of the present moment is that fulfillment of the first task, that improving individual small- and middle-peasant farming, while it is still our chief task in the sphere of agriculture, is already insufficient for the solution of the problem as a whole'. Stalin 1955, p. 218].
177   'The proletarian state power has succeeded in restricting within narrow limits the upstarts of capitalism that unavoidably spring up in town and country as a result of N.E.P. ...'. 'Resolution on the Situation in the Soviet Union and in the C.P.S.U.' 1928, p. 1578.
178   [Varga quotes here Stalin's speech on the *Right danger in the Soviet Union* in Stalin 1934b, p. 60. However, this text differs sensibly from the text in Stalin's *Works*, Volume 11. Stalin: '*Under the conditions of Soviet development*, when capitalism has already been overthrown, but its roots have not yet been torn out, the Right deviation in communism signifies a tendency, an inclination that has not yet taken shape, it is true, and is perhaps not yet consciously realised, but nevertheless a tendency of a section of the Communists to depart from the general line of our Party in the direction of bourgeois ideology. When certain circles of our Communists strive to drag the Party back from the decisions of the Fifteenth

Do the conditions exist in our Soviet country that make the restoration of capitalism *possible*? Yes, they do exist. That, comrades, may appear strange, but is a fact. We have overthrown capitalism, we have established the dictatorship of the proletariat, we are intensely developing our socialist industry and are closely linking it up with peasant economy;

Congress, by denying the need for an offensive against the capitalist elements in the countryside; or demand a contraction of our industry, in the belief that its present rapid rate of development is fatal for the country; or deny the expediency of subsidies to the collective farms and state farms, in the belief that such subsidies are money thrown to the winds; or deny the expediency of fighting against bureaucracy by methods of self-criticism, in the belief that self-criticism undermines our apparatus; or demand that the monopoly of foreign trade be relaxed, etc., etc., it means that there are people in the ranks of our Party who are striving, perhaps without themselves realising it, to adapt our socialist construction to the tastes and requirements of the "Soviet" bourgeoisie. A victory of the Right deviation in our Party would mean an enormous strengthening of the capitalist elements in our country. And what does the strengthening of the capitalist elements in our country mean? It means weakening the proletarian dictatorship and increasing the chances of the restoration of capitalism. Consequently, a victory of the Right deviation in our Party would mean a development of the conditions necessary *for the restoration* of capitalism in our country. Have we in our Soviet country any of the conditions that would make the restoration of capitalism *possible*? Yes, we have. That, comrades, may appear strange, but it is a fact. We have overthrown capitalism, we have established the dictatorship of the proletariat, we are developing our socialist industry at a rapid pace and are linking peasant economy with it. But we have not yet torn out the roots of capitalism. Where are these roots imbedded? They are imbedded in commodity production, in small production in the towns and, especially, the countryside.

As Lenin says, the strength of capitalism lies "in the strength of *small production*. For, unfortunately, small production is still very, very widespread in the world, and small production *engenders* capitalism and the bourgeoisie continuously, daily, hourly, spontaneously, and on a mass scale" (see Vol. XXV, p. 173) ... "As long as we live in a small-peasant country, there is a surer economic basis for capitalism in Russia than for communism. This must be borne in mind. Anyone who has carefully observed life in the countryside, as compared with life in the towns, knows that we have not torn out the roots of capitalism and have not undermined the foundation, the basis of the internal enemy. The latter depends on small-scale production, and there is only one way of undermining it, namely, to place the economy of the country, including agriculture, on a new technical basis, the technical basis of modern large-scale production. And it is only electricity that is such a basis. Communism is Soviet power plus the electrification of the whole country. Otherwise, the country will remain a small-peasant country, and we have got to understand that clearly. We are weaker than capitalism, not only on a world scale, but also within the country. Everybody knows this. We are conscious of it, and we shall see to it that our economic base is transformed from a small-peasant base into a large-scale industrial base. Only when the country has been electrified, only when our industry, our agriculture, our transport system have been placed upon the technical basis of modern large-scale industry shall we achieve final victory" (Vol. XXVI, pp. 46–47)'. Stalin 1954d [1928], pp. 236–7].

but we have not yet torn out the roots of capitalism. Where are these roots implanted? They are implanted in the system of commodity production, in small production in the towns, and particularly in the villages. As Lenin said, the strength of capitalism lies 'in the strength of small production, for unfortunately, small production still survives in a very, very large degree, and small production *gives birth* to capitalism and to bourgeoisie, constantly, daily, hourly, spontaneously and on a mass scale'.[179] Hence, since small production is a mass phenomenon, and even a predominant feature of our country, and since it gives birth to capitalism and to a bourgeoisie constantly and on a mass scale, particularly under the conditions of NEP, it is obvious that the conditions do exist which make the restoration of capitalism *possible*.[180]

In this regard Lenin said:

> As long as we live in a small-peasant country there will be a firmer economic basis for capitalism in Russia than for communism. That must always be kept in mind. Everyone who has carefully observed village life as compared with the life in the city, knows that we have not eradicated the roots of capitalism and that we have not undermined the basis, the foundation of our internal enemy ... Only when the country is electrified, only when industry, agriculture and transport are placed on the technical basis of modern, large-scale industry – only then will our victory be complete.[181]

Viewed dynamically, the Soviet power still rested essentially on two contradictory foundations at that time: '[O]n the basis of large-scale socialist industry, which *destroys* the capitalist elements, and on small, individual peasant firming, which *engenders* elements'.[182]

In the social sphere: the condition of the industrial working class had already improved considerably, but average yearly earnings were still only 843 rubles; there still was considerable unemployment, housing conditions were still very

---

179 Quoted from Lenin, *Doklad o rabote v derevne na VIII partsezde VKP(b)*, in *Lenin Sochineniya*, Volume 25, Moscow, p. 173. [See Lenin 1966b, p. 24].
180 Stalin 1954b [1928], p. 60.
181 Quoted from Lenin, *VIII Vserossiyskiy sezd sovetov. Doklad o deyatelnosti Soveta narodnykh komissarov 22 dekabrya*, in *Lenin Sochineniya*, Volume 26, Moscow, pp. 46–7. [Lenin 1966c, p. 516].
182 Stalin 1955b, p. 176; Stalin, *From the First to the Second Five-Year Plan* 1934, p. 115.

bad, and the large-scale construction of workers' dwellings had only begun. *The condition of the agricultural workers and of the village poor* was far from uniform; their dependence on the kulaks and their exploitation were very great in many districts, where the local Soviet machinery was under the latter's influence. The kulaks conducted an active struggle against the Soviet Union by refusing to deliver grain, and there were moments in 1928 when the alliance of the working class and the middle peasantry was imperiled.

The technical specialist personnel of all kinds, with the exception of the army, still consisted predominantly of old, bourgeois elements, very many of whom were hostile to the Soviet Union. In many cases, as the Shakhty trial proved, this went as far as active counter-revolutionary sabotage, under instructions from *émigré* white-guards or the general staffs of foreign countries.

Progress in the cultural field was already very great; yet only 58 percent of the population could read and write. The workers and sons of workers studying at the universities were still very slight in number; the bourgeoisie's monopoly of education was still unbroken. Development of the various national cultures had only begun.

This, in the roughest outlines, is the picture of the Soviet Union at the time of the Sixth Congress. *The six years that have elapsed since then have involved an unprecedented change, giant progress, in all fields*, the results of which were summarised as follows by comrade Stalin at the Seventeenth Congress of the CPSU:

> During this period, the USSR has become radically transformed and has cast off the aspect of backwardness and medievalism. From an agrarian country it has become an industrial country. From a country of small individual agriculture it has become a country of collective, large-scale mechanised agriculture. From an ignorant, illiterate and uncultured country it has become – or rather it is becoming – a literate and cultured country covered by a vast network of higher, secondary and elementary schools functioning in the languages of the nationalities of the USSR.[183]

Let us illustrate this for the entire period from 1928 to 1934.

In the field of technology: construction of the most complicated machines and tractors has been commenced (motors, tractors, combines, giant turbines, blooming mills, rotary printing presses, airplanes, etc., etc.). The chemical industry has been newly created; this is the only country in the world where

---

183   Stalin 1934f, p. 24 [See also Stalin 1954e, p. 313].

synthetic rubber is produced on a factory basis. Production of the most complex metal alloys has been undertaken, etc.

In the field of economics: industrial production has increased by leaps and bounds, and thousands of new industrial plants have been established, which in size and modernity exceed those in European countries, and are equalled only in the USA.

TABLE 12.77 Growth of industrial production (1929 = 100)[184]

	1928	1929	1930	1931	1932	1933	1934 (Plan)
Soviet Union	79.4	100	129.7	161.9	184.7	201.6	243.9
Capitalist world[185]	93.7	100	87.1	73.1	62.6	71.1	70.0

The volume of industrial production has tripled during six years. During the same period, production in the capitalist world has decreased 30 percent. It is now approximately on the 1913 level, whereas production in the Soviet Union has more than quadrupled since then. This one contrast is enough to demonstrate the absolute superiority of the Soviet system over the capitalist system! Trotsky's counter-revolutionary chatter to the effect that the economy of the Soviet Union is 'regulated' by the economy of the capitalist world has been proved completely false. The rise of industrial production in the Soviet Union has proceeded untouched by the severest industrial crisis in the capitalist world.[186]

The reason why there is no over-production crisis in the Soviet Union, and why there cannot be any, is as follows:

Under capitalism, the extent of production run by the consuming power of society, 'by the poverty and restriction of consumption of the masses'. In the Soviet Union the reverse is true: *the expansion of consumption is governed by the extent of production* (and by the requirements of socialist accumulation).

---

184   We supplement the figures given by Stalin, with data for the year 1928, and for the 1934 plan, according to the State Planning Commission data.

185   From the figures of the German Institut für Konjunkturforschung, Sonderheft 31 [see Wagenführ 1933], and *Vierteljahrshefte zur Konjunkturforschung* 1934, 9, 2, B, recalculated from a 1928 to a 1929 basis. For 1934, my estimate is used.

186   The agrarian crisis made it more difficult to export agricultural products; the industrial crisis hampered the export of raw materials, but likewise reduced the purchase price of industrial goods. On the whole the influence of the crisis in the capitalist countries on the economy of the Soviet Union was very slight.

There is no *social* obstacle to limitless increase in the consumption of the working population of the Soviet Union, until the latter is many times greater than at present. The sole limitation is the magnitude of production itself. In other words, there is *no market problem in the Soviet Union* in the capitalist sense of the term; when production increases, the consuming power of the population increases parallel with it.[187]

The following figures [see *Table 12.78*] show the conversion of *the Soviet Union from an agrarian country into an industrial country*.

TABLE 12.78 Ratio of industry and agriculture in the total production of the Soviet Union (at 1926–7 price level)

	1928	1929	1930	1931	1932	1933	1934 (Plan)
Industry	53.1	54.5	61.6	66.7	70.7	70.4	79.2
Agriculture	46.9	45.5	38.4	33.3	29.3	29.6	20.8

The transformation of the Soviet Union from an agrarian country to an industrial country is shown not only in this rapid increase in the proportion of industrial production, but in *the changed relationship between Divisions I and II as well*. There is a very rapid proportional increase in the production of the means of production. Although, as we have shown above, the exceptional severity of the crisis in capitalist countries is determined precisely by the extremely large decline in the production of the means of production, although the bourgeoisie issues the slogan of stopping the expansion of production capacity and, finally, although it is precisely in the leading capitalist countries that an anarchic (and in many cases organised) destruction of the means of production has taken place during the crisis, in the Soviet Union every effort is exerted to develop the production of the means of production. These efforts are meeting with complete success, as the following figures show:

---

187 Because of the necessity for rapid expansion of the productive apparatus, i.e. for using a very large part of the value produced for socialist accumulation, consuming power, that is, the demand for consumers' goods, actually exceeds the supply. Hence the temporary 'goods famine' at times.

TABLE 12.79 Ratio of divisions I and II in large-scale industrial production of the Soviet Union (at 1926–7 price level)

	1928	1929	1930	1931	1932	1933
Division I	46.7	48.5	52.6	55.4	57.0	58.0
Division II	53.3	51.5	47.4	44.6	43.0	42.0

Between 1928 and 1933 the proportion of machinery production in the total value of industrial production has risen from 13.3 percent to 26.1 percent. *More than one-quarter of total industrial production is the production of machinery*, something which has probably never been the case in any capitalist country.

And this fundamental reconstruction of Soviet industry, the new construction of thousands of factories, of powerful central power stations, canals, railroads, and great new cities in former waste areas, *has all been created by the workers of the Soviet Union themselves*. In the years 1929–33 alone, sixty milliard rubles were invested in industry in the Soviet Union, at a time when new capital investments in the capitalist world had fallen almost to zero. The means for industrialising the country were obtained not with the help of foreign loans,[188] not by plundering colonies, as in most capitalist countries, but through the enthusiastic work of the toilers of the Soviet Union.

What made it possible for the Soviet Union to carry through this tremendous task with its own forces? It is the *dictatorship of the proletariat*, the superiority of the Soviet system to capitalism, that performed this miracle. The most important factors in this respect are the following:

(a) *There are no parasites in the Soviet Union*. The wide class of landowners, bourgeoisie, coupon-clippers, priests, etc., and the enormous train of servants and hangers-on they maintain, does not exist. There are no English lords with their town palaces and country manors, with their hundreds of stewards and servants, cooks, chamber-maids, stable-boys, masters of the hounds, hunters, governesses, chauffeurs, pilots, etc. The whole insane, stupid luxury – the ruling classes, the daily new costumes of the bourgeois ladies, the display of wealth in jewellery and the like – the dictatorship of the proletariat has swept all these idle trappings of bourgeois society beyond the borders of the Soviet Union. There is no equality of income,

---

188 The slight commodity credit that the Soviet Union gets abroad is quite insignificant compared to the investments made.

indeed; high output gets higher pay. The stage of communism, when everyone will consume according to his needs, and work according to his abilities, has not yet been reached. A few outstanding writers, architects, physicians, have relatively high incomes. These are exceptional cases; in general the standard of living of a factory director, who has millions of rubles at his disposal, or that of a People's Commissar, is no higher than that of an intermediate official under capitalism. This is not asceticism, but the *conscious temporary limitation of the entire population's needs*, to make possible a speedier tempo of socialist construction!

(b) *In the Soviet Union there are no unemployed.* While half of those seeking employment in capitalist countries are unable to find work because the rotting system of capitalism, undermined by the fever of the crisis, is unable to give the workers jobs, every healthy person in the Soviet Union, without exception, is at work. Although in capitalist countries it is considered distinguished to lead an idle life, in the Soviet Union it is considered a disgrace not to work if one is able to.[189]

(c) *In the Soviet Union every worker feels responsible for production.* The mechanical class discipline of capitalism, the speed-up system, is replaced by a voluntary socialist discipline of work, which the workers impose upon themselves, as the ruling class. Socialist competition, the system of shock brigades, and the moral pressure of the majority of workers, who are consciously striving to make their factory progress, sweep along with them the minority of workers, only recently recruited from the villages, who are still less advanced. The workers, especially the Party members, feel that they share responsibility for the factory's success; in many meetings the collective experience of the workers is gathered and used for the benefit of the factory. The relationship between the workers and the factory is totally different from that under capitalism.

(d) *The economy of the Soviet Union is directed methodically.* The 'overhead waste' of the capitalist mode of production: the cost of competition, of advertising, of bad investments, the periodically recurring destruction of values in crises, etc., do not exist in the USSR. The entire output of the population is usefully employed.

---

189 According to the laws of the Soviet Union social pensioners (invalids, the aged, etc.) may work as workers or employees without any reduction in their pensions, and without receiving a lower wage or salary for the same work than that paid to 'ordinary' workers.

(e) *To these must be added the intensive utilisation of the already available means of production.* The superiority of Soviet economy to capitalist economy is demonstrated particularly clearly in the *degree of utilisation* of the means of production. Under capitalism, in general, the utilisation of production equipment 48 hours a week is regarded as full employment; but in the Soviet Union, where work is done in three shifts of seven hours each, 147 hours a week is so regarded. We can illustrate the significance of this by taking the British cotton industry as an example. The British cotton industry has 52,000,000 spindles, of which only 39,900,000 were in use in 1932, for 35 hours a week, i.e. 1,400,000,000 hours a week. In the Soviet Union, with the customary full utilisation of all spindles 147 hours a week, they would work 7,620,000,000 hours a week, or more than five times as much! *With the full utilisation customary in the Soviet Union, the English textile industry could produce one and a half times the total world demand for cotton goods.*

The methodical complete utilisation of all productive forces by the proletariat as the ruling class made it possible to *double the national income in five years.* The latter rose from 25,000,000,000 rubles in 1928 to 50,000,000,000 in 1933. And since there are no parasite classes in the Soviet Union to squander a large part of the national income on meaningless luxury, since there is no wholesale destruction of values such as takes place under capitalism, a very large part of the national income can be used for socialist accumulation while raising the living standards of the entire population. In this way the Soviet Union was able, with its own forces, to convert the country from a backward agrarian land into a leading industrial country. *Only the dictatorship of the proletariat could accomplish this!*

New industrial construction covers *all parts of the territory of the Soviet Union*, from the polar regions to the deserts of Central Asia. Industrial centres have risen everywhere in the midst of the peasant population, which is of great importance in solving the problem of agriculture.

During these years real revolution has taken place in agriculture! The voluntary union of the toiling peasants into collective farms has turned a country of backward peasant agriculture into a country of the most modern large-scale farms.

TABLE 12.80 Development of collectivisation

	1928	1929	1930	1931	1932	1933	1934 (June)
Number of collective farms (in thousands)	33.3	57.0	85.9	211.1	211.05	224.5	233.5
Number of collectivised farmsteads (in millions)	0.4	1.0	6.0	13.0	14.9	15.2	15.7
Collectivization of peasant farms in percent	1.7	3.9	23.6	52.7	61.5	65.0	70.8

Some 230,000 large-scale collectivised enterprises have taken the place of 16,000,000 peasant farms. This was paralleled by the establishment of big Soviet farms on hitherto uncultivated land. This transformation would have been impossible without the tremendous progress in the production of the most modern agricultural machinery.[190] Only because the advantages of machine farming could be demonstrated to them in practice through experience did the poor and middle peasants voluntarily decide to give up their private farms and to unite in collectives.

As a result of these changes the 'private sector' is rapidly disappearing from Soviet economy. In industry the proportion of the private sector is now no more than one percent. (The concessions of foreign capitalists have outplayed their part and almost all of them have been taken over by Soviet industry). In agriculture the proportion of individual peasant farms is about 15 percent, and is constantly decreasing.[191]

---

190   TABLE 12.81 Mechanical equipment in the Soviet farms and collective farms in 1933

Tractors	Combines	Motor trucks
204,100	25,000	24,400

In 1928 there was scarcely any such machinery employed in agriculture!

191   Collectivisation has progressed furthest in regions where grain cultivation predominates, because there the advantages of collective farming are greatest. At the opposite pole are

The collectivisation of agriculture signifies a fundamental turn of the village towards socialism. Before collectivisation there were approximately 1,000,000 kulaks in the agricultural population, exploiting 7,000,000 poor peasants. (Large differences in income also existed among the middle peasantry, depending upon the possessions of the individual peasants). *The basis for exploitation disappeared with the pooling of the land and means of production*[192] *in collective farms*, and the acceptance of poor peasants as members enjoying full rights. There is no longer any necessity for the poor peasant to let himself be misused by private exploiters; the kulaks, whose land and means of production have been pooled in the collective farms, are no longer able to exploit the labour of others. *The kulaks are thus liquidated as a class*. The size of the agricultural population's income now depends primarily on the *number of days of work done on the collective farm* and on the quality of work of the whole collective!

As a result, at the present time, *the middle peasant* – who, as Lenin said, felt attracted as a working man toward socialism, but as a *small producer* felt attracted to the old, familiar capitalism – is no longer the *central figure in the Soviet village. Now, the central figure is the collective farmer*, whose working conditions approach those of the industrial worker more and more closely (work in large enterprises, in brigades, in socialist competition, and with modern machinery), and whose whole attitude toward life is undergoing a corresponding change. Lenin said the following in this regard:

> The middle peasant in a communist society will come over to our side only when we improve his standard of living. If tomorrow we could procure 1,000,000 first-class tractors, supply them with gasoline and mechanics (and, as you all know, that at present is a sheer fantasy), the middle peasant would cry, 'I am for the *communia!*'[193] (i.e. for communism).[194]

---

the nomad peoples, still numerous in the territory of the Soviet Union, where one cannot even speak of collectivisation as yet.

192 Collectivisation, as is generally known, was temporarily overdone, in that the milk-cows and smaller livestock serving the needs of the family itself were collectivised together with the means of production and the draught animals. In many cases communes were formed with complete community of property, income and consumption, instead of working associations ('artels'). The Party opposed these excesses, which were historically premature. (See Stalin's famous article, 'Dizzy with Success', March 1930). [Stalin 1954f.]. Instead it issued, and is also putting into practice, the slogan that every collective farmer should have at least one cow of his own.

193 *Communia* is the term used by the peasants and repeated by Lenin. *Ed.*

194 Stalin, 'A year of great change', *Leninism*, Volume 2, p. 177. [This text differs sensibly from the one published in Stalin's *Works*: 'The past year has shown that the Party is successfully coping with this task too. We know that by the spring of the coming year, 1930, we shall

With the change of the basic masses of peasants from small commodity producers to collective farmers, and the step-by-step transformation in their psychology, there also disappears the former intellectual influence of the petty bourgeoisie on the industrial working class, which Lenin considered so important a factor.

It is obvious that this tremendous change in class relationships could not be brought about without the bitterest resistance by the kulaks, without 'revolutionary overhead costs'.[195] The establishment of political sections in the tractor stations, to which tens of thousands of the best Party members were sent for day-by-day contact with the collective farmers, serves to facilitate the transition from individual to collective economy, as well as to liquidate the remainders of the kulak's ideological influence upon the collective farmers.

The present situation of the Soviet Union is summarised as follows in the Theses and Resolutions of the Seventeenth Party Congress:

> Already during the first Five-Year Plan period, thanks to the heroic struggle of the working class, the foundation of socialist economy was laid, the last capitalist class – the kulaks – was defeated and the basic masses of the peasantry – the collective farmers – became a firm support of the Soviet government in the countryside. The USSR finally established itself on the socialist road.[196]

The position of the working class in the Soviet union has improved very much in every respect during the years since the Sixth Congress. While chronic mass unemployment is constantly on the increase in the capitalist countries (aside from cyclic fluctuations), unemployment has been completely liquidated in the Soviet Union, and there is a permanent shortage of workers, although the number of workers and employees increased from 11,600,000 in 1928 to

---

have over 60,000 tractors in the fields, a year later we shall have over 100,000 tractors, and two years after that, over 250,000 tractors. We are now able to accomplish and even to exceed what was considered "fantasy" several years ago. And that is why the middle peasant has turned towards the "kommunia"'. Stalin 1954g, p. 141].

195 The major overhead cost was the great decline in the number of cattle, partly because the kulaks and the elements influenced by them slaughtered *a lot of* cattle during the collectivisation campaigns, and in part because the transition from the individual keeping of livestock to big collective livestock ranches required a change in working methods which could not take place without some friction. At the present time the number of cattle is again increasing rapidly.

196 *Resolution on The Second Five-Year Plan of Development of the National Economy of the USSR*, 1934, p. 639; *Socialism Victorious* 1934.

23,400,00 in 1934, or more than 100 percent. While wages were cut in the capitalist world, *the average earnings of an industrial worker in the USSR have risen from 843 rubles in 1928 to 1,610 rubles in 1934*, although the working day has been reduced to seven hours (six hours for workers underground and in occupation injurious to health). Social expenditures are being reduced everywhere else, but in the Soviet Union they rose from 1,063,000,000 rubles in 1928 to 1928 to 5,871,000,000 in 1934.[197]

However, it is not at all necessary to cite figures to demonstrate the tremendous improvement of the position of the working class during these years. One can see it with one's own eyes. *Torn shoes and patched clothes no longer prevail in the streets of the cities*. Hundreds of thousands of new dwellings and large, wholly new cities shelter the workers. Millions of workers engage in sports or occupy themselves with music. Hundreds of thousands who used to be manual workers have become technicians, factory directors and inventors.

The enormous achievements in the cultural sphere are known to our readers, and are acknowledged even by the bourgeoisie of the whole world. Illiteracy has been almost completely liquidated in the Soviet Union; seven years of compulsory school attendance now prevails.

TABLE 12.82 Number of students

	Elementary schools (millions)	Intermediate schools (thousands)	Universities, etc. (thousands)
1928	11.9	2,415	180
1934	19.7	6,991	471

The number of pupils attending intermediate schools has increased tenfold in six years, and of those in the schools of higher learning has almost tripled!

Although under capitalism a worker who got as far as university study was looked upon as a rarity, 51.4 percent of the university students in the Soviet Union in 1933 were workers. The result of this gigantic cultural progress is the *final abolition of the education monopoly of the specialists of bourgeois origin*. The Soviet Union already has its new intelligentsia, stemming from the working class and working for socialist construction with all its might.

---

197   In 1934 approximately every fifth worker spent his vacation in a sanatorium or rest-home.

Under capitalism the selection of those capable of the highest mental achievements is made only from the narrow circle of the ruling classes. The son of a poor peasant or of an ordinary worker – although he may possess the genius of a Newton, a Hegel, or a Marx – finds the road to the development of his talent closed by the bourgeoisie's monopoly of the means of education. The sons of the ruling classes, on the other hand, no matter how unfit they may be for menial work, are helped by private tutors, by bribes, and by connections, in getting their university degrees. *In the Soviet Union, the selection of those fitted for the highest mental achievements takes place from among the entire people.* Every worker and every peasant is offered the opportunity of developing his abilities and, what is more, each is assisted in his efforts to educate himself. Every talent is discovered, whether in man or woman, young or old, a Russian or a member of any other nationality in the Soviet Union. *This systematic selection of all the talented from the entire population* (not merely from the narrow circle of the ruling classes) *ensures the future mental superiority of the Soviet Union to the capitalist world in all fields: technique, science and art.*

The cultural advance embraces *all the nationalities in the Soviet Union*. The uncultured state forced upon the peoples of Russia by the Great Russian chauvinism of the tsarist era making it impossible for them to develop a national culture, has been done away with. Dozens of nations have been awakened to a new cultural life. Newspapers, magazines and books are being printed in the languages of the formerly oppressed nations, and schools of all grades are established in these languages. An entirely new cultural world is being created.[198]

The gigantic advances of the Soviet Union in all fields – the undeniable fact of the superiority of the country of the dictatorship of the proletariat to the capitalist world – has enormously increased the Soviet Union's revolutionary influence upon the proletariat and the exploited strata of the agricultural population in the capitalist countries, as well as the oppressed colonial peoples. The apologists of capitalism have the greatest difficulty in discovering any arguments to counteract the growing drive of the proletariat to follow the Russian example. Even the mere recording of all the slanders, lies and distortions that the bourgeoisie uses to combat the revolutionary influence of the Soviet Union would lead us too far afield. We propose only to characterise the methods briefly.

---

198 The sale of books is fantastically high, compared with that in capitalist countries. 19 million copies of Gorky's books were sold during the past few years. Single novels by other writers attain editions of over one million copies. Scientific works appear in editions of as high as 50,000 copies. Total daily newspaper circulation has risen from 8,800,000 in 1928 to 38,500,000 in 1934.

1. *The method of gross lies and slander* (Kautsky, the Archbishop of Canterbury, etc.): There is no material or cultural progress in the Soviet Union. The Five-Year Plan is a swindle; the statistics of the Soviet Union are forged. Suffering is widespread, and millions are dying of hunger.
2. *Denial of the socialist character of the Soviet Union*: The material advances are recognised as a fact, but the social advances are not. Kautsky says: Not the dictatorship of the proletariat, but '*dictatorship of a minority over the proletariat*'. Trotsky's characterisation: 'Degeneration and Thermidorianism'. The following line of argument, by Dan,[199] is characteristic of this 'finer' falsification, intended to mislead the workers of the capitalist world.

   The elimination of the private economic sector by no means signifies that the capitalist trends in Soviet economy have been successfully destroyed. Capitalism, as a system of social relations in the productive process, is characterized by certain very definite traits. The immediate producers are no longer owners of the means of production, which, on the contrary, as 'capital' stand in opposition to them and rule them. It is not the immediate producers who determine the tasks and conditions of their own work, but the owners of 'capital', who appropriate a part of their work as surplus value and who occupy the position of a 'ruling class' with respect to them. However much the cloak of 'proletarian dictatorship' may disguise, it still cannot hide the fact that all these traits of a 'capitalist' economy are also characteristic of Soviet economy.[200]

This refined demagogy deserves a few words by way of exposure. *Dan consciously concludes the technical category of large-scale production with the social category of capitalism.* A railway or a chemical *combinat*[201] cannot under any conditions be the private property of the immediate producer; only in a small-scale artisan production can the producers be the individual owners of their tools. In the Soviet Union the means of production are the *collective property of the people*, not the property of the bourgeoisie! In large-scale production it is impossible that the 'tasks and conditions' of work be individually decided by each worker, as in craft manufacture. Under capitalism the bourgeoisie decides this, but in the Soviet Union the decisions are made by the organs of planned economy, the leaders of Soviet economy or of the individual enterprises, to whom this task has been entrusted by the entire working class. But these social

---

199 [Teodor Dan (1871–1947) was a leading Menshevik politician].
200 Dan 1932.
201 An industrial aggregate of several component plants.

functions, entrusted to them by the working class, in no way makes them a 'ruling class'. There is no possibility for them to 'appropriate surplus value';[202] their salaries are at most twice the earnings of skilled workers.

The bourgeoisie, the fascists, and the social-fascists[203] combat the revolutionising influence of the Soviet Union with all sorts of lies, libels and slanders: the religious crusade, the dumping campaign, the indictment of 'Red imperialism', etc., etc.

But the truth slowly prevails nonetheless. Bourgeois individuals of all kinds, such as [Édouard] Herriot[204] and the American, Cooper,[205] world-famous writers like [George] Bernard Shaw and [Henri] Barbusse,[206] and many, many others speak up for the truth. The working class of the capitalist world does not allow itself to be fooled by the Trotskys, Kautskys, Dans and Bauers.[207] Its pressure even forces the Social-Democratic leaders to recognise the truth. Not long ago, for example, the French Social Democrat [Jean] Ziromski[208] said at a united-front mass meeting in Paris: 'It is undeniable that the Soviet Union represents an element of social Progress, where a new civilization is being built on the basis of love for work. The overthrow of the Soviet Union would be a historical catastrophe'.[209]

Truth does prevail!

---

202 Even in the Soviet Union the individual worker does not receive the 'full product of his labour'; one part of it goes towards socialist accumulation, another towards the maintenance of the sick, the aged and those unable to work. But the entire product of the labour of all the working population does go either directly to its own benefit or to that of its children; no exploiter, no parasite has any share of it.
203 [This qualification of the Social Democrats as social-fascists had survived in the English and American editions of Varga's report. The Spanish, German and Russian versions of the report contained the same qualification, but the French report spoke about 'les social-démocrates'. Though Varga finished the report on 4 September 1934, the first Russian edition (50,000 copies) was only printed on 8 March 1935].
204 [Édouard Herriot (1872–1957) French Radical politician].
205 [John Gordon Cooper (1872–1955) was a former railway worker and Republican member of the House of Representatives for Ohio].
206 [Henri Barbusse (1873–1935) was a French pacifist novelist].
207 [Otto Bauer (1881–1938) Austrian Marxist and Social-Democratic politician].
208 [Jean Ziromski (1890–1975) belonged to the Socialist Left, but after the war he joined the PCF].
209 L'Humanité, 25 August 1934.

9   The Second Breach – Soviet China

The most important social phenomenon of the last few years, besides the rise of the Soviet Union, is the occurrence of a second breach in the structure of bourgeois society, the emergence and consolidation of Soviet China. Although Soviet China has not been recognised as yet by any capitalist country, although the heroically fighting Chinese Red Army is called a 'robber band' by its enemies, and although the frontiers of Soviet China still shift and the individual Soviet regions do not yet form a single connected whole, the significance of Soviet China as a factor in colonial revolution and foreign policy cannot be overestimated.

The struggle and the success of Soviet China by its deeds concretely point out to the suppressed colonial peoples the road to their liberation. It shows the milliard colonial peasants that under the guidance of the bourgeoisie they will never be able to sweep away the landlords and usurers who suck their lifeblood, and take possession of the land they cultivate. It shows them that this can be done only through armed struggle under the hegemony of the proletariat. It shows them the betrayal of the 'national' bourgeoisie – its alliance with the imperialists against the working people. It shows them the possibility of a material and cultural advance through establishing the democratic dictatorship of the workers and peasants in the form of the Soviet system. It shows them that the capitalist stage of development can be skipped. The revolutionising example of the Soviet Union is now reinforced by the revolutionising example of Soviet China which is much closer to the colonial peoples. From the standpoint of foreign policy: the continued existence of Soviet China is the main obstacle to the final dismemberment of China among the imperialists, and thus constitutes an important factor in the struggle for the Pacific Ocean!

After the bourgeoisie betrayed the movement for the liberation of the Chinese people, Soviet China became the centre of the struggle against imperialist oppression. The proletariat possesses the hegemony in this struggle.

The rise of Soviet China occurred in a very short time. Six years ago, at the time of the Sixth Congress, the Chinese revolution had just experienced a severe defeat.

> The first wave of the broad revolutionary movement of workers and peasants, largely marching under the slogans and (to a considerable extent), under the leadership of the Communist Party is over. In a number of centres of the revolutionary movement, it ended in extremely grave defeats of the workers and peasants, in the physical extermination of a part of the Communist cadres of the workers' and peasants' movement, and

of the revolutionary cadres as well, in a sharply expressed development of the extreme camps of the social forces, in the formulation of precise political slogans of the contending classes, in the complete exposure of the Kuomintang leadership, in the acquisition of tremendously great revolutionary experience by the toiling masses, and, finally, in the transition of the entire mass revolutionary movement of China to its new phase: the Soviet phase. In connection with the regrouping of classes it is beyond doubt that a certain consolidation of the reactionary forces is taking place. The bourgeoisie has not only made a definite alliance with the counter-revolutionary feudal lords and militarists, but actually came to terms with foreign imperialism ...[210]

This was at the time when Trotsky wanted to bury the Chinese revolution and issued the slogan of a 'constituent assembly'. That was when several leading Chinese comrades lost courage and became renegades (Tan Pin-shan, Chen Tu-hsiu), and when others tried to speed up the revolutionary movement by force, by putsch attempts and terror against the workers. In the resolution mentioned above, the Comintern characterised these events in the following manner: '... [C]*ertain symptoms show that the workers' and peasants' revolution is on the way to a renewed mighty upsurge*'.[211]

It demanded that the mass work of the Party among the workers and peasants be strengthened, that Soviet regions be created, that the guerrilla troops be consolidated and transformed into Red Armies led by Communists.

'The ECCI holds that the main task of the Party in the Sovietised peasant districts is to carry out the agrarian revolution and organise Red Army detachments, having in view that these detachments gradually unite into one common national Red Army'.[212]

The six years since then have fully confirmed the correctness of the Comintern's line. Soviet power was established in one area after another. The Chinese workers and peasants in the Red Army, the Red Guards, etc., organised under the leadership of the Communist Party of China, have defended Soviet China in heroic battles. Although the Red Army possesses no arsenal in the central Soviet area[213] and although it is largely compelled to obtain its arms by capture

---

[210] 'Resolution on the Chinese Question' 1928, p. 321.
[211] Ibid.
[212] 'Resolution on the Chinese Question' 1928, p. 322.
[213] Only in the Soviet region in Szechwan are there two arsenals; the Central Soviet Area merely possesses shops for the production and repair of small arms.

from the enemy,[214] it succeeded in victoriously repulsing five major campaigns by Chiang Kai-shek (the sixth is still under way), and in annihilating armies up to five times its size, organised by trained European officers (General von Seeckt, etc.), and equipped by the imperialists with the latest arms.

How was this miraculous success possible? The heroism of the Chinese Red Army is unquestionable. But this alone was not enough. The decisive factor is that the Red Army is supported by the entire working population, young and old, men and women, and that most of the soldiers in the Kuomintang armies did not want to fight against the Red Army, but took advantage of the first opportunity to surrender their arms and desert to the Reds. The superiority of the Soviet system to the reactionary Kuomintang regime and the mortal hatred for their oppressors felt by the workers and peasants conscripted into the Kuomintang armies are the underlying reasons for the Red Army's victories.

What Lenin said about the Soviet Union at the Third Congress of the Comintern holds true in even greater measure for the Chinese Soviet Republic: 'Only because the revolution is developing throughout the world is the international bourgeoisie unable to strangle us, although it is a hundred times stronger than we are economically and from a military standpoint'.[215]

Only when we compare the conditions of the working population in Kuomintang China and in Soviet China are we able to understand the successes of the Red Army.[216]

During the six years since the victory of the counter-revolution in China the conditions of the working masses rapidly grew worse all along the line. The Kuomintang regime proved itself unable to solve a single problem of the bourgeois revolution. The *dismemberment of the country* still persists. The power of the Nanking government is felt only in the provinces around Shanghai and Nanking, while a hostile government rules in Southern China. The rival government in Fukien was wiped out only with the utmost effort; the North is ruled by a clique in Japan's pay; all sorts of generals rule in Szechwan, etc.

---

214   According to Wellington Koo's estimate in the *Memoranda presented to the Lytton Commission* 1933, p. 764, 25 percent of the arms were bought in the foreign concessions, 10 percent manufactured in the Soviet areas; the balance, in one from or another, came from the enemy.

215   See the minutes of the Third Congress: *Protokoll des III. Kongresses der Kommunistischen Internationale* 1921, p. 748.

216   The following sections are based largely upon the preliminary work of our Chinese Institute, especially of Comrades Kara-Mursa, Grinevitz and Potopalov, as well as the very valuable collection of documents in *Räte-China* 1934. [Varga's institute was developing studies on the Far East after having absorbed the China Institute].

The Kuomintang regime was unable to liberate the land from the Imperialists' yoke. On the contrary, it capitulated to the latter completely in order to obtain their support in its struggle against Soviet China. The Japanese imperialists have seized Manchuria; they are pressing onward to Mongolia, are the rulers of Northern China, and are preparing to sever it from Kuomintang China and establish a new puppet government there. Chiang Kai-shek capitulated to the Japanese long ago. He betrayed the battle of the 19th Army and of the Shanghai proletariat against the Japanese; he has *de facto* recognised Manchukuo; and he retreats before the Japanese invasion without offering battle. England and France are pressing forward in the south-west.

The Kuomintang regime has not solved the agrarian problem. On the contrary, conditions have grown appallingly worse. Irrigation works are falling into ruin, while the rivers flood the country year after year. Famine has become a constant phenomenon. The degradation of agriculture is apparent; it is no longer able to feed the population! Importation of food for the cities is assuming ever greater proportions! Although suffering chronic starvation, the great mass of working peasants is no longer able to continue simple reproduction because it has been and still is fleeced on all sides by the landowners, the usurers, the state and the militarists. In many districts the price of land has fallen 50 percent. Let us cite some data from bourgeois sources.

The burden of ground rent. In Hupei province rent formerly ate up 20 percent of the crop, in 1928 the figure was 40 percent, and now 50 percent. In Kiangsi the tenant must give the landowner 11 *piculs*[217] of the rice crop out of every 17.[218] The landlords, who control the provincial administration, have the tenant farmers who cannot pay rent thrown into jail. 'In the district prison of Chansa (Kiangsi) 380 tenant farmers were under arrest in May 1933'. To keep too many peasants from feeling a desire to get their bread in jail 'they are compelled to pay for everything: water, bread, and even for using the toilet'.

The burden of usury. The peasant must pay at least 12 percent interest monthly on money borrowed, 24–36 percent on the average, and in many cases *100* percent, as in Kwantung.[219] The Nanking government has officially sanctioned this usury, issuing a decree early in 1933 with the following provision: 'In view of the fact that usury interest has risen of late to 20–30 percent a month, *it is hereby forbidden to charge more than 10 percent interest monthly*'.[220]

---

217 One picul = 133.5 pounds.
218 See report of the [Ludwik] Rajchman Commissioner of the League of Nations. [Rajchman 1934].
219 *The China Weekly Review* [Shanghai], 23 December 1933.
220 *Chuanbao*, 17 January 1933.

From now on, of course, nobody lends money at less than 120 percent per annum. The usurer dispossesses the peasants of their land; in making a loan a contract is often signed whereby the land becomes the usurer's property if the debt is not paid on time.

The burden of taxation. The taxes weighing down upon the peasants have been raised repeatedly since 1928 – not only the land tax, but the various other taxes – to an even greater extent. If the Chinese peasant wants to sell anything in the market, he must pay all sorts of tolls on the way: upon entering the city, for use of the market place, when leaving the city, etc. In some instances, the tax burden is greater than the value of the entire rice crop.

Plundered by the militarists. Looting by the militarists, which knows no limits, has the most devastating effect upon the condition of the peasantry. Preparation for any war, either among the individual generals or against Soviet China, begins with a plunder campaign against the peasants. Here are some instances: in 1929, more than US$1,956,690 were extorted as war taxes from nine districts in Northern Honan and Southern Hupei, more than four times the 'normal' taxes. In the spring of 1928, US$29,631,070 were extorted as war taxes in Northern Shansi, *or 26 times the normal taxes.*[221] In many areas the militarists have already extorted taxes from the peasants for *decades in advance.*

Exploitation of the peasantry proceeds in a hundred different ways. Merchants of entire districts set very low purchase prices for silk cocoons, tobacco, cotton, rice, etc., with the connivance of the corrupt administration. Administrative heads 'visit' the districts, accompanied by a huge suite; the peasants must feed them and supply them with everything they require, etc., etc. All the various forms of feudal and capitalist exploitation grind down the unfortunate peasants of Kuomintang China. They are often compelled to sell their children, forsake their village, and become bandits.

The condition of the Chinese peasantry is described as follows in an article in the *North China Herald* of 24 January 1934:

> They [the Chinese peasants] cry for help, but their feeble voices are drowned completely in the deafening clamour of factional disputes and resultant civil wars. The return from their yearly toil, pouring into the Government treasury and the warlord's purse, only brings back more torture instead of relief. Forlorn and desperate, they desert their farms, turn into bandits or Communists. This makes the situation worse and affords the militarists additional excuses for their gladiatorial adventures ...

---

221 [*Nankai*] *Weekly Statistical Service* 9 [Nankai University, Tientsin], 27 March 1933.

The figures given by the International Famine Relief Commission indicate that the annual income of 76.6 percent of the farm families is below US$ 201 but their average expenditures amount to US$ 228.32. That means that only 23.4 percent of them is able to live without going into debt, and this only in a normal year.

High rent, low wage, exorbitant taxes, usurious interest on credit and unfair exploitation of cereal merchants are responsible for reducing the peasant income to such a deep-sunken level ...

Rural China is now bankrupt. Millions of farmers have perished. Millions are deprived of their homes, land and all means of subsistence. Millions are struggling between life and death. Even the luckiest ones are suffering terribly under their ever-growing burden ...

Facing calamities on all sides, the farmers seem to be compelled to take one of two desperate steps, to desert their farms for other places or to join the ranks of bandits, or Communists. Everywhere the villages have been witnessing a silent but continuous exodus. Everywhere honest and peaceful peasants go 'bad' or Red.[222]

Under such circumstances it is natural that the secret peasant organisations, such as the 'Red Lances', the 'Big Knives', the 'Black Flag', etc., etc., should grow constantly, that peasant revolts should never cease, that civil war is a chronic phenomenon in China, and that every landowner is compelled to turn his estate into an armed fortress! All this explains why Kuomintang armies, recruited predominantly from the peasantry, disintegrate in battle against the Red Army.

In contrast with this, the revolutionary solution of the agrarian question has improved the conditions of the peasantry in the Soviet territories tremendously. The most important factors in the agrarian revolution are as follows:

1. The land of the landowners (gentry), officials and monasteries was confiscated without compensation and distributed among the poor and middle peasants, agricultural labourers, Red Army men and the workers of the village. The land which the kulaks formerly leased to others, as well as all of their land in excess of the general norm, was taken from them.
2. The landowners' means of production, their cattle and the kulaks' surplus cattle were confiscated and distributed among the poor and middle peasantry. The Soviets publicly fix the price at which the kulaks are obliged to

---

[222] Yao Hsin-Nung, 'Rural China's collapse', *The North China Herald* [Shanghai], 24 January 1934.

hire out their cattle to the village poor for farming the soil. Committees of the Village Poor supervise the enforcement of the agrarian laws.
3. Usury has been eliminated. All usury contracts were declared null and void. All the peasants' debts have been annulled. All property held in pawn was returned to its owners. Interest on new loans was reduced to one percent per month.
4. All rivers and ponds important in irrigation were nationalised (as well as forests and pasture land).
5. All former taxes and military imposts were declared null and void, with a uniform progressive income tax instituted in their place. The village poor owning 3 to 5 mu[223] of land were freed of all taxation. The rest of the peasantry pays 5–20 percent of the crop as taxes (in addition to various minor levies for Cultural purposes, for the purchase of airplanes and for the Red Army).

The agrarian revolution has made the middle peasant the central figure of the village in Soviet China. The condition of the entire working peasantry, especially of the former village poor and the agricultural labourers, has considerably improved, representing an unattainable ideal under the Kuomintang regime, for the peasantry in Kuomintang China. It is understandable that the peasants fighting in the ranks of the Chinese Red Army will make every effort to defend their new land and their new life against the landowner armies of Chiang Kai-shek.

Influenced by the agrarian reforms, the cultivated area has already been extended in the Soviet districts, the crop yield has increased, and agricultural productive forces are growing. The Soviets see to it that seed grain is improved, that the fields are regularly fertilised, etc. While millions of peasants in Kuomintang China are starving, there is an abundance of food in Soviet China.[224]

The Chinese bourgeoisie together with the imperialist bourgeoisie made use of the victory of the counter-revolution to make an unprecedentedly violent attack upon the working class. The revolutionary class trade unions were dissolved; the Communist Party was forced underground, and innumerable courageous comrades have been murdered. The Chinese working class offered heroic resistance in large-scale, stubborn, big strikes and numerous clashes, but the bourgeoisie succeeded in forcing working conditions down considerably,

---

223 One mu = one-sixth of an acre.
224 This is self-evident: all the food that formerly was appropriated by the parasite classes as taxes, rent and interest, etc., in kind (part of which was consumed on the land itself, another part being sold in the cities) is now left with the working population of Soviet China.

aided as they were by the imperialists, by the influx of millions of peasants driven from their homes, and by the entrance of artisans ruined by the advance of native and foreign manufactured goods into the labour market.

As opposed to this, the living conditions of the rural industrial workers in Soviet China have been basically improved. (There are no big industrial enterprises in the Soviet China districts). Wages have been greatly increased – doubled and tripled. The ten to 17-hour working day has been shortened to from eight to ten hours. The usual system in China of the labour agency concluding a contract with the employer and taking part of the worker's wages for itself has been forbidden and employment agencies were made a Soviet monopoly. Obligatory social insurance was instituted, and a considerable number of workers were organised into trade unions, which supervise compliance with working conditions. Women's work was placed on the same level as the work of men, provided their output is the same.

Despite the comparatively small number of industrial workers in Soviet Chinese territory, the hegemony of the proletariat is assured. Industrial workers – some of them from Kuomintang China – are at the head of the Party organisations, the Red Army and the Soviet organs. The Communist Party of China is increasingly successful in solving the complicated task of simultaneously governing the Soviet areas as the ruling party and leading the revolutionary movement in Kuomintang China as an illegal, persecuted party.

The cultural revolution now in process in Soviet China is of special importance. In 2,932 villages of the Central Soviet District alone there are 3,052 schools for children and 32,388 schools for eliminating illiteracy among adults. Primitive schools have been established in the vacant rooms of the expropriated landowners' houses. In some areas 92 percent of the children go to school, as against 20 percent in Kuomintang China. Schools have been politically organised to a considerable extent. Pioneer and youth organisations now exist. Adults are first of all taught the ideographs for the most indispensable concepts; new simple ideographs have been introduced for the new political terms. Classes are held in the afternoon and evening. Several technical schools have been founded in the Central District, as well as its first university. Towards the end of 1933 the Soviet government made an appeal to all the professors of Kuomintang China to support the cultural progress of Soviet China. Clubs, libraries, dramatic circles, sport circles are springing up everywhere. There are 34 newspapers, the official newspaper having 50,000 circulation, and the youth paper 28,000. Pamphlets and schoolbooks are being printed.

Women participate in the cultural revolution with especial zeal. They are in the majority among those taking evening courses. This cultural upsurge forms a trenchant contrast to the cultural decay in Kuomintang China.

The things that Chinese reaction can offer by way of offsetting the achievements of Soviet China in the sphere of improving the material and cultural conditions of the working masses are slander and violence.[225] The slanders are of little use, for the Chinese workers and peasants know quite well that the conditions of the working masses in Soviet China are much better than their own. That is why all attempts at the annihilation of Soviet China by force end in failure.

A White Russian *émigré*, G. Sokolsky,[226] writes as follows in the American magazine *Asia* (December 1932):

> Each spring the Nanking government appeals to the Shanghai bankers to lend hundreds of millions of dollars to save the nation from Communism. Each summer hundreds of millions of dollars are squandered and tens of thousands of lives are destroyed in an effort to wipe out Communism. Then the autumn rains come; the canals are again swollen; rivers are impassable; the roads grow muddy ... The anti-Communist campaign is over. Five mighty anti-Communist campaigns has Chiang Kai-shek marshalled against them [the Red Armies]. Five times have the best units of the national, German-trained, modernly equipped army, sometimes mounting to as high as half a million men, hurled themselves against the Red Armies. Each campaign has been a failure. Last summer ended with another failure. It is practically impossible to suppress the Communists by military prowess; for where does the Red Army end and the peasant population begin in these southern provinces? The national troops find only hungry peasants, ground almost out of existence between the high taxes collected far in advance and the usurious rates of moneylenders and landlords. Chiang's army advances: the peasants are an armed body of troops in his rear. His men surrender: the Communists have arms and munitions.

The story is always and everywhere the same. Communist propaganda demoralises the armies of Chiang Kai-shek because, as Sokolsky says, 'Chiang's officers and men ... too are peasants or sons of peasants'. The Red Army grows in

---

225 Neither 'Left' manoeuvres and phrases, nor the founding of the 'Reorganisation' Party, was of any avail. At present the Kuomintang resorts more and more to a reactionary, religious, fascist ideology. Chiang-Kai-shek's 'new life' propaganda aims at the rehabilitation of the feudal ideology of passive submission to fate.
226 [George E. Sokolsky (1893–1962) was a radio broadcaster, columnist and writer].

size[227] and becomes better armed as deserters come over from the enemy and volunteers enter its ranks (parents themselves put their sons in the army).[228] Although it is comparatively poorly armed, yet wherever it goes it is aided by the entire population, which supplies it with information, furnishes it food, diverts the enemy through false reports, attacks the enemy's rear at night, and so forth. The *Red Army and Soviet China have three hundred million workers and peasants as its adherents in China, in the enemy's territory; that is why they are invincible.*

Chiang Kai-shek can depend only on this small group: the feudal nobility, the big bourgeoisie and the rich peasants, as well as on the aid afforded by the foreign imperialists.[229]

But this support makes the people hate him all the more. The masses realise that the Kuomintang government is a tool of the imperialists, a government of perpetual terror and civil war against the working masses.

Chiang Kai-shek may succeed in defeating certain sections of the Red Army, again subjecting individual Soviet districts to the landowners' rule. But new Soviet districts are in other sections of China; new red Armies are formed. *He cannot prevent the final victory of the revolution in China!*

---

227 In China, with its traditional ideology of peace, soldiery is considered a very inferior occupation.

228 TABLE 12.83 Approximate size of the Red Army

1928	1929	1930	1931	1932	1933	1934
10,000	22,000	62,000	145,000	170,000	200,000	350,00

Czan-Shi 1934, p. 273.

229 Every time the Red Army menaces or captures a city on the coast or on the Yangtze River, the united imperialist fleets appear and decide a battle in favour of reaction. The American *Foreign Policy Reports*, issue of 26 April 1933, on the Communist movement in China complacently records the gratitude of *The China Weekly Review*, which stated on 30 September 1932, that the foreign gunboats 'in this particular case performed a good service for the Chinese Government by helping to drive the Communists out of Changsha ... hence there has been no outcry on the part of the Chinese authorities at this most recent activity of foreign gunboats in China' [Bisson 1933].

10 The Effects of the Crisis on Foreign Affairs

With the general instability of relations, the existence of a large number of inner-European antagonisms led to a constant regrouping of states. But one main trend plainly appeared out of all these multifarious and constantly changing groupings, the trend of struggle against the Soviet Union.[230]

The instability of foreign relations, which the Sixth Congress indicated in the case of *Europe*, spread during the subsequent years, *and today applies to the whole world*. The crisis has destroyed the foreign policy bases of stabilisation and has accentuated the antagonisms between *all* countries. Lenin's phrase of 1915 that: 'The old national states have become too cramped for capitalism', is today truer than ever. All countries are constantly conflicting with one another in the struggle for markets. The conflicts criss-cross one another in the most complex manner. All bourgeois states are manoeuvring uninterruptedly on all sides. All bourgeois states are feverishly arming for a new war, in the hope of solving their own market problem by force at the expense of their competitors. but just this multitude of antagonisms has until now prevented the formation of firm war *blocs* such as existed among the great powers before the first World War. In addition to their fear (increased by the maturing of the revolutionary crisis) that the imperialist war will be turned into a civil war, their fear of the rapidly increasing military strength of the Soviet Union, their fear of entering a war inadequately prepared from the military standpoint (in view of the unusually swift development of the military technique) this is another reason why the outbreak of the second round of the World War has been delayed. This is why the wars still in progress or those that occurred in the last few years (Japan's attack on China, Paraguay-Bolivia, Peru-Chile, Arabia-Yemen, Tibet-China) have not yet ignited the World War. But, with the universal aggravation of all antagonisms and the prevalent armament competition, the world war may break out any day despite these inhibiting factors.

'Again as in 1914 the parties ... of war and revenge are coming into the foreground. Quite clearly things are moving towards a new war'.[231]

The multitude of foreign events and regroupings that have taken place between the Sixth Congress and the Seventh, and the extraordinary complex-

---

[230] 'Theses and Resolutions of the VI. World Congress of the Communist International' 1928.
[231] Stalin 1934, p. 10. [However, the text here is slightly different: 'Again as in 1914 the parties of bellicose imperialism, the parties of war and *revanche* are coming into the foreground'. In Stalin's *Works*: 'Once again, as in 1914, the parties of bellicose imperialism, the parties of war and revanchism are coming to the foreground'. 1955a, p. 298].

ity of the present situation make it impossible to give a thorough and complete analysis briefly. Our presentation must necessarily be incomplete and schematic.

The Sharpening of the Struggle between the Two Systems and the Success of the Peace Policy of the Soviet Union

In 1925, Comrade Stalin summarised the international situation as follows: 'Then we have two stabilisations: the temporary stabilisation of capitalism and the stabilisation of the Soviet system. The setting in of a certain temporary equilibrium between these two stabilisations – such is the characteristic feature of the present international situation'.[232]

A certain mitigation of the forms of struggle between the two systems took place in the period of relative stabilisation. The bourgeoisie considered the 'new economic policy' (NEP) the beginning of a return to capitalism. They were strengthened in this illusion by the counter-revolutionary chatter of the Trotskyite opposition regarding the 'degeneration' of the Soviet power. In this period of 'democratic pacifism' there took place the *de jure* recognition of the Soviet Union by England (the first [Ramsay] MacDonald Cabinet), France ([Édouard] Herriot) and Italy.

But the situation had already changed considerably at the time of the Sixth Congress. The 'democratic pacifist' episode had reached its inglorious end. The illusion that the NEP meant a return to capitalism had evaporated. The period of 'peaceful intercourse of the two systems' was broken by a period of brutal provocation under the leadership of England: the Arcos raid, the Zinoviev letter, the break of diplomatic relations with England; the withdrawal of [Christian] Rakovsky from Paris; the murder of [Pyotr L.] Voykov in Warsaw, the attack on the Soviet Embassy in Peking, etc. Parallel with this went the efforts to draw Germany into the anti-Soviet front, efforts which met with a friendly reception among a part of the German bourgeoisie. The 'western orientation' began to outweigh the so-called 'eastern orientation'. The Theses of the Sixth Congress [of the Comintern] state that:

> The growth of monopolist capitalism in Germany leads on one hand to an increasing disintegration of the Versailles system, and on the other to

---

232   Stalin 1934d, p. 152. [In Stalin's *Works*, Volume 13, this text has been remastered: 'Thus, we have two stabilisations. At one pole capitalism is becoming stabilised, consolidating the position it has achieved and developing further. At the other pole the Soviet system is becoming stabilised, consolidating the positions it has won and advancing further along the road to victory'. See Stalin 1954a, p. 95].

Germany's adopting a more definitely 'Western' (i.e. imperialist and anti-Soviet) orientation. While in the days of her economic decline and her political and national humiliation Germany sought an agreement with the proletarian state, the only state that opposed her imperialist enslavement, the matured tendencies of German neo-imperialism are forcing the German bourgeoisie more and more towards an anti-soviet position.[233]

The crisis has brought a new accentuation of the tension between the capitalist world and the Soviet Union, after a certain temporary abatement during the phase of prosperity.

Therefore, every time that capitalist contradictions begin to grow acute the bourgeoisie turns its gaze towards the USSR as if to say:

> Cannot we settle this or that contradiction of capitalism, or all the contradictions taken together, at the expense of the USSR, the land of the Soviets, the citadel of the revolution, which, by its very existence is revolutionizing the working class and the colonies, preventing us from arranging for a new war, preventing us from dividing the world anew, preventing us from being masters of its extensive internal market, so necessary for capitalists, particularly today owing to the economic crisis? Hence the tendency to adventurist assaults on the USSR and to intervention, a tendency which is bound to be strengthened as a result of the developing economic crisis.[234]

The danger of a counter-revolutionary war of aggression against the Soviet Union has been threatening without interruption ever since the outbreak of the economic crisis.

What has prevented this attack until now? The following important factors can be distinguished:

(1) *The increase of the military strength of the Soviet Union by leaps and bounds*. Its basis is the growth of the Soviet Union's economic forces at an

---

233 ['Theses and resolutions' 1928, p. 1569].
234 Stalin 1934e, pp. 260–1. [In Stalin's *Works*, the text is slightly different: 'That is why, every time the contradictions of capitalism become acute, the bourgeoisie turns its gaze towards the U.S.S.R., wondering whether it would not be possible to solve this or that contradiction of capitalism, or all the contradictions together, at the expense of the U.S.S.R., of that Land of Soviets, that citadel of revolution which, by its very existence, is revolutionising the working class and the colonies, which is hindering the organisation of a new war, hindering a new redivision of the world, hindering the capitalists from lording it in its extensive home market which they need so much, especially now, in view of the economic crisis'. Stalin 1954e, pp. 262–3].

unprecedented rate during the successful completion of the First Five-Year Plan and the first year of the second plan. The development of heavy industry and the machinery industry have made it possible to equip the Red Army as well as any capitalist army, independently of the capitalist world. The liquidation of the kulaks as a class on the basis of collectivisation, and the coming to the fore of the new type of collective farmer, closely bound up with the working class, as the central figure in the village hive made for an even greater social superiority of the Red Army over the bourgeois armies, which are growing more and more demoralised even in peacetime, owing to the intensification of class antagonisms.[235] Another factor is the thorough replacement of the old bourgeois military specialists by Party comrades, or by new leading military personnel, predominantly of working-class origin, and devoted to the Soviet Union through life and death.

This rapid reinforcement of the Soviet Union's military strength and the growing disintegration of the bourgeois armies make any attack against the Soviet Union an extremely dangerous undertaking from the purely military standpoint. This is an important reason why the Japanese war-mongers, for example, have for three years delayed their attack on the Soviet Union time and again, in order to make better preparation for it.

(2) *The thoroughgoing peace policy of the Soviet Union*. This rapid reinforcement of the Soviet Union's military strength makes the thoroughgoing peace policy of the Soviet Union more impressive and more successful, because it cannot be regarded as the consequence of military weakness. The Soviet Union makes use of every opportunity to document its readiness for peace; in every country it supports every movement, no matter how weak, working for the preservation of peace. The government of the Soviet Union adhered to the Kellogg Pact; at the Disarmament Conference it was the only power which fought (though of course without success) for real disarmament.

This thoroughgoing policy of peace has resulted in a tremendous strengthening of the Soviet Union's international position. Today the Soviet Union is the magnetic pole for all the small countries that have nothing to gain in a war, for all countries that are threatened by the danger of dropping to the status of colonies of some imperialist world power during the next world war, and for all countries at present in favour of peace. The external expression of the success of the Soviet Union's peace policy is the creation of a whole network of non-

---

235 The mutinies in the British, Dutch, Chilean, and Greek fleets, and in the Japanese army at Shanghai, the mass desertion of Kuomintang troops to the Chinese Red Army in every battle, the desertion of Manchukuo troops to the guerrilla bands, etc., are evidence of this process of disintegration.

aggression pacts. In evaluating this success, one must avoid two diametrically opposed errors. The significance of the pacts and treaties *must not be overestimated*. By no means would the bourgeoisie of the capitalist countries be afraid to break these treaties at a moment favourable to them. The pre-war Triple Alliance was not concluded with the social enemies of the bourgeoisie, but among capitalist countries on an equal social basis, and it was formally signed by their kings. But this, as we know, did not prevent Italy from entering the war opposed to its allies.

On the other hand, it would be altogether incorrect to underestimate the value of the non-aggression pacts because of this. They form an important obstacle to the ideological preparation for war against the Soviet Union. When the bourgeoisie of the neighbouring countries concludes non-aggression pacts with the Soviet Union, and solemnly declares that it will work together with the Soviet Union for the preservation of peace, it cannot begin a war against the Soviet Union *immediately*. It needs a certain amount of time to prepare public opinion for the change in policy, for war against the Soviet Union. And even if this reorientation would not require a long time, in view of the bourgeoisie's monopoly of the legal press, the pacts do guarantee some gain in time in any case. At the same time they strengthen the movements and forces in every country which are working for the preservation of peace.

This thoroughgoing peace policy makes it more difficult for the enemies of the Soviet Union to stir up the peoples with the lying tales of 'Red Imperialism'. Japan's refusal to sign the non-aggression pact repeatedly proposed by the Soviet Union shows the workers of the whole world who is for war and who is for peace.

An important step in the peace policy of the Soviet Union is its entrance into the League of Nations. The exit of Japan and Germany – the two powers whose leading statesmen are not only preparing for a counter-revolution war against the Soviet Union at present, but openly advocating it – has placed the League of Nations under the domination of those great powers (France above all) whose bourgeoisie champions the maintenance of the Versailles system. They are therefore in favour of the maintenance of peace in general (even if only for a short time), and hence for peace with the Soviet Union. This makes the entrance of the Soviet Union into the League of Nations possible and advisable for the maintenance of peace. Wide circles of the petty bourgeoisie and working class in many countries, who are convinced of the pacifist mission of the League of Nations, will consider the entrance of the Soviet Union as the most striking evidence disproving the slanderous charge of 'Red Imperialism'.

(3) *The effect of imperialist antagonisms*. The economic crisis produced a pronounced intensification of imperialist conflicts (cf. next section for details) and

this has made the relations of some imperialist states with the Soviet Union more friendly of late, at least temporarily. Japan's attack on Manchuria led to the recognition of the Soviet Union by the USA, plus a certain degree of *rapprochement*. The establishment of the Hitler government produced a sharp turn in France's attitude towards the Soviet Union. The politicians who only four years ago demanded that France lead the anti-Soviet front have passed into the background, and a more friendly policy toward the Soviet Union has won the upper hand. For the same reason a more peaceable attitude toward the Soviet Union seems to be arising for the time being among some of the bourgeoisie in England.

(4) *The accentuation of class antagonisms*. One of the most important factors hindering counter-revolutionary war against the Soviet Union is the accentuation of class antagonisms in all capitalist countries and the accelerated maturing of the revolutionary crisis in some countries that now stand in the forefront of the anti-Soviet front: Germany and Japan. A war against the Soviet Union would make acute the threat of overthrowing the power of the ruling classes. As much as nine years ago, Stalin said: 'Our country no longer stands alone, for it has the workers of the West and the oppressed peoples of the East for its allies ... A war against the Soviet Union would also be a war waged by imperialism against its own workers and colonies'.[236]

The great increase in the military strength of the Soviet Union, its thoroughgoing peace policy and the aggravation of imperialist antagonisms and class antagonisms in the capitalist world are the main causes that have delayed the daily threatening attack on the Soviet Union.

The Liquidation of the Foreign Policy Foundations of Stabilisation

The unsettling of temporary stabilisation, which was already under way at the time of the Sixth Congress, was completed by the crisis in foreign affairs.

According to Stalin, the stabilisation of capitalism was manifested concretely in the following:

> First, in that America, England and France have temporarily succeeded in coming to an understanding as to how and to what extent will despoil Germany ... Secondly, the stabilisation of capitalism has found expression in the fact that British, American and Japanese capital has temporarily managed to come to an understanding as to the allotment of spheres of influence in China ... as to the ways of plundering it ... Thirdly, the stabilisation of capitalism has found expression in the fact that the imper-

---

[236] Stalin 1934d; p. 156. [See Stalin 1954a, p. 101].

ialist groups of the advanced countries have managed for the time being to come to an understanding mutually to refrain from interfering in the plunder and oppression of 'their' respective colonies ...[237]

Uneven development rapidly unsettled temporary stabilisation, as Stalin predicted in the same speech. The crisis brought it to an end. 'The world has come close to the second round of revolutions and wars'. Only the multiple crisscrossing of imperialist antagonisms, the extraordinarily complex and swiftly changing foreign political situation – still further complicated by the increased international significance of the Soviet Union, the fear of the united strength of the Soviet Union plus the workers fighting to turn the imperialist war into a civil war, as well as of the colonial peoples fighting for their independence, have thus far prevented the 'little wars' now in progress from growing into a world war.

(1) *The collapse of the Versailles system is nearing its end.*

Of Versailles's three main pillars – reparations, disarmament, and territorial provisions – only the last is still in force, and its revision also is imminent. It was only in 1929 in the Young Plan, that the victorious powers 'finally' fixed Germany's reparations as lasting 59 years(!), but under the blows of the economic crisis [Herbert] Hoover hastened to declare a moratorium on reparations and inter-allied debts as soon as 1931, by which they were *de facto* ended forever.

The disarmament of Germany was brought to an end by the German bourgeoisie itself, after fascism came to power. (Hungary and Bulgaria are secretly arming). In this, Germany correctly depended upon the multitudinous antagonisms among the victorious powers, which prevented a war to stop Germany's rearmament. At this point we can but incompletely sketch these complexities in the roughest outlines.

The Anglo-French antagonism exists on the European continent, as well as outside Europe: in the Near East, South China, Africa, etc. It is the traditional policy of the British bourgeoisie to prevent any one country from gaining hegemony on the European continent if possible.

Therefore it supported Germany against France (up to a certain point) throughout the entire postwar period. It manoeuvred in Poland and Belgium to weaken French influence, and tried to use Italy against France (most recently in the unsuccessful 'Four-Power Agreement' on armaments).

But these anti-French manoeuvres of British policy were always kept within very narrow limits by the basic, Anglo-American antagonism. The overseas

---

[237] Stalin 1934d, pp. 154–5. [See Stalin 1954a, pp. 98–9].

'interests' of the British bourgeoisie which exploits 500,000,000 people in colonial countries, outweigh its European continental interests. Britain's position as a world power must be constantly defended against the USA. War between these two biggest world powers is unavoidable if the proletarian revolution does not forestall it. The centre of the British world empire, however, the British Isles themselves, have strategically lost their island character, because of the development of military technique after the war: long-range guns, submarines and airplanes, with which France is particularly well equipped. Britain cannot wage war against any third power if it is not sure of France's benevolent neutrality. Therefore the English bourgeoisie always abandoned its manoeuvres in German's favour whenever France demanded this as an ultimatum, uniting with the French bourgeoisie at Germany's expense.

Recently the rearmament of Germany, which is proceeding at a rapid pace, in particular the very rapid growth of its air fleet, has helped the anti-German, pro-French tendency in British politics to gain supremacy, at least temporarily. At this moment England does not appear to be sufficiently well prepared for war; it is especially backward in air armament.[238] The British bourgeoisie is afraid that German fascism will seek an escape from the threatening economic catastrophe through a 'premature' precipitation of the world war. Baldwin's statement that the Rhine, and not the Dover cliffs, is England's defence frontier, undoubtedly signifies a warning to Germany not to attempt adventure in the West.

Still more contradictory is the Franco-Italian-German relationship! The French system of alliances in Southeast Europe not only serves to guarantee the traditional provisions of the Versailles system against the vanquished countries (Germany, Austria, Hungary and Bulgaria), but is also an obstacle to the Italian policy of expansion in the Balkans. The interests of French and Italian imperialism clash in North Africa, in the Near East, and in the question of controlling the Mediterranean. Hence one line of Italian policy: co-operation with the 'vanquished' – Germany, Hungary and Austria – against France, for revising all the provisions of the peace treaties (including the territorial provisions) and support of England's anti-French tendencies, within the framework of a general friendly relationship with England.

But the aggressiveness of Hitler fascism, which has sought to gain one victory in international politics, at least in the Austrian *Anschluss*, has brought

---

238 Although the English navy is today the strongest in the world (the USA has not built its navy up to parity), the English air fleet stands in fifth place. That is why England and the British Empire are now building planes very rapidly so as 'to have the strongest air fleet in the world'.

Italy into the sharpest conflict with Germany (the demonstrative massing of Italian troops at the Austrian border to prevent *Anschluss* by force if necessary), and has brought it into a common front with France, on *this one* question. On this basis France now endeavours to reach a further *rapprochement* with Italy through certain concessions in North Africa and in naval armaments, in order to isolate fascist Germany on the South.

The position of *Poland*, which wavers and manoeuvres between Germany France, England and the Soviet Union, but has veered sharply towards Germany (evidently counting upon Britain's approval), under the influence of traditionally anti-Soviet circles of the bourgeoisie, as a reaction to the *rapprochement* between France and the Soviet Union, is equally contradictory. So is that of Hungary, which maintains 'connections' with Germany and France, in order not to fall into wholly one-sided dependence on Italy. Likewise, that of Yugoslavia – which in general is one of France's vassal states, but which is opposed to the Franco-Italian policy on *Anschluss*, because it considers this a factor strengthening its arch-enemy, Italy, etc., etc.

Universal instability has taken the place of the stabilisation founded on the suppression and exploitation of the vanquished states. The *Deutsche Führerbriefe* (*German Letters to Leaders*) correctly stated on 17 April 1934: 'What characterises the latent tension in Europe is that no one is able to say "Yes" in order to satisfy one side without all the other partners in the game thinking it is a "No" aimed at them'.

(2) *The struggle for domination in the Pacific.*

Japan's attack on Manchuria, and its penetration of North China and Mongolia, constitute a forcible violation of the Washington Nine-Power Treaty on the common exploitation of China, which was an important factor in temporary stabilisation.

The centre of gravity of world politics was thereby moved from Europe to the Pacific Ocean, where the redivision of the world by force had already begun, where the four biggest imperialist powers – the USA, England, Japan and France – are competing for their share in the exploitation of China, and thus for the mastery of the Pacific Ocean. This struggle is complicated by the intertwining of imperialist antagonisms with the struggle of the two systems, and by the existence of Soviet China, the second revolutionary breach in the system of bourgeois society!

Why was Japanese imperialism the first to resort to arms for the redivision of the world?

It would be altogether mistaken to explain this as a consequence of Japanese imperialism's strength. On the contrary, in a certain sense it was the economic weakness of Japan that impelled the Japanese ruling classes to this policy of force. Japan is a poor country; the *per capita* income of the population is equal to that of the poorest European countries: Latvia, Lithuania or Rumania. Moreover, inequalities in distribution of income are greater than in all other capitalist countries. In cross-section, Japan has 30 milliardaires, 3,000 who are rich, and 30,000 well-to-do. Most of those in the next stratum, the peasants and the urban petty bourgeoisie, are poor, while the workers' living standard approaches that of colonial workers. This inordinate income distribution *limits the population's power of consumption to a minimum, and forces Japanese industry to seek foreign markets for a large part of its production*. But with international competition as bitter as it is at present, sales are certain only in markets under monopoly control. To this must be added the fact that Japan has no raw materials (except silk and copper) in sufficient quantity on its own territory. Iron and steel, cotton and wool, wood and oil, etc. – all must be imported. That is why Japanese imperialism is constrained to try to seize colonial areas rich in raw materials, in order to be able to monopolise the exploitation of raw materials,[239] as well as the sale of industrial goods.

Japan's campaign of conquest has been successful thus far. There were plenty of *paper* protests. The League of Nations condemned the conquest of Manchuria in careful terms. The Japanese puppet-state of Manchukuo was not recognised by a single country, except El Salvador (demonstration against the USA). America formally declared that it would not recognise the validity of any changes brought about by force. But up to now there has been nothing beyond these paper protests!

The reasons for this are as follows:

By its occupation of Manchuria and its penetration of Mongolia, Japan is erecting a military barrier between the Soviet Union and Soviet China, at the same time preparing a base area for war against the Soviet Union. In this sense it is acting as the vanguard of the world bourgeoisie in the struggle between the two systems. That is why France and England actually supported Japan in the first stages of its plundering campaign (though under the guise of pacific gestures). While fascist Germany placed itself openly on Japan's side.

The motive also played a certain role in the passive behaviour of the USA.[240] But the following factors were the decisive ones:

---

239 Japanese capital has forced its competitors out of Korea completely; more than 90 percent of Korea's foreign trade is monopolised by Japan.
240 It must be emphasised that there is no conflict of interests between the USA and Japan in the sphere of foreign trade. The USA is Japan's best customer: it holds first place in Japanese exports, with about 40 percent of the total, and first place in Japanese import, with

The fundamental Anglo-American antagonism does not allow the USA to enter into an open conflict with Japan at the present time without an agreement with England; but all the efforts of the American diplomats to induce England to common action against Japan have remained unsuccessful.

The strategic position of the USA with regard to Japan is very unfavourable. The USA's great naval base, Pearl Harbour, in Hawaii, is far too distant from the Asiatic coast, while the naval bases of Guam and in the Philippines have not been modernised, in accordance with the Washington Naval Treaty. The American navy is supposed to be superior to the Japanese in the ratio of five to three, but Japan has actually built its navy up to the limits permitted by the Washington Treaty, while the USA is only endeavouring this year to make up for lost time by forcing the expansion of its fleet. *Because of the Anglo-American antagonism, the USA can never use its entire fleet against Japan* (even if England declared its neutrality), while Japan's whole navy can await the attack of the American fleet in its home waters, supported by its numerous naval bases. Under these circumstances, Japan's strategic superiority in Asiatic waters is apparent. In order to gain time for further armament (particularly for the development of a powerful aviation base in the Aleutian Islands), the USA must, under these conditions, limit itself for the present to peaceful methods of struggle: recognition of the Soviet Union and support of the Nanking Government through loans and through furnishing war material and military instructors, in the hope of creating an army in China capable of fighting Japan, thus gaining a closer base of operations against Japan.

But this hope of the American bourgeoisie has not been realised. The Chinese ruling classes, its generals, and the rotten Chiang Kai-shek government, which also sabotaged the heroic struggle of the Chinese masses against Japan's attack on Shanghai, have surrendered to Japanese imperialism *de facto* in order to be able to concentrate all their energy on the fight against the Red Army of Soviet China. In this fight they enjoy the support of all imperialist powers! But the Chinese Kuomintang army cannot be had for a fight against Japan. This gave the Japanese imperialists the courage to claim a

---

about 28 percent (Japan occupies second place in the USA imports, and fourth place in the export trade). Until very recently there was scarcely any competition in the world market between the two; the USA exported raw materials and means of production, while Japan exported the products of light industry. American capital is invested in Japanese industry in not insignificant amounts (principally in electric power). Under these circumstances, it is natural that a pro-Japanese tendency also exists within the bourgeoisie of the USA.

protectorate over all China in the notorious declaration of 17 April 1934, by the Foreign Office.[241]

While the American-Japanese antagonism is thus objectively becoming increasingly acute (though not breaking out into war for the present), *a certain change has taken place during recent years in the relationship of England and France toward Japan.*

The Anglo-Japanese relationship is highly complicated and contradictory. Although the British bourgeoisie had no objection to the conquest of Manchuria and Mongolia or to the development of a basis for attack against the Soviet Union, and though it regards Japan as a potential ally in the (sooner or later) inevitable war against the USA; despite the dissolution of the alliance which existed until 1922, it is nonetheless disturbed by Japan's penetration of North China, which is aimed directly at Britain's interests. Japan's claim to a protectorate over all China cannot be tolerated by England. Japan's propaganda, using such slogans as 'China for the yellow race!', 'Against all white conquerors!' and 'Asia for the Asiatics', in itself constitutes an attack upon the British bourgeoisie's positions throughout Asia. It threatens the heart of English colonial power: India. (This is supplemented by the growing competition of Japanese goods in the world market, particularly the increasing displacement of English cotton goods from all colonial markets).

That is why Britain is penetrating further in the direction of Western Szechwan, Tibet and Sinkiang, forcing the establishment of a chain of naval bases from Singapore to Australia (including the Dutch East Indies) to prevent future penetration of the Indian Ocean by Japan, and endeavouring to develop united air defence for the whole empire. Despite all its 'friendship', the British bourgeoisie is undoubtedly preparing for a war against Japan in the distant future. At the same time Britain has taken severe measures against Japanese imports into its colonies[242] (reduction of Japanese imports to the pre-war level by means of the quota system). This has led to a certain estrangement of the two powers which were formerly so friendly. The fighting between English and Japanese troops in North China during the summer of 1934 is symptomatic of this. There are many indications that at the naval disarmament conference in

---

241 This statement was a trial balloon to ascertain the reaction of the USA, and particularly England.
242 In the recent period the relationship of the British dominions to Japan has somewhat changed in that Japan has become an important buyer of Australian wool and wheat. It is also a large buyer of Indian cotton, which enabled it to compel the recent agreement with India regarding the import of textiles. Relationships in the Pacific Ocean are becoming more complex day by day.

1935 an Anglo-American front will be directed against Japan – especially on the naval parity problem – rather than an Anglo-Japanese front against the USA.[243] (Although the Anglo-American antagonism is the basic one, it by no means excludes a temporary co-operation between the two powers in individual questions). It is a matter of course that there are several trends within the British bourgeoisie, with influential circles advocating collaboration with Japan.

The comparative estrangement between France and Japan is founded primarily on Hitler's seizure of power. As we stated above, the French bourgeoisie seeks a guarantee against Hitler in Eastern Europe through a more friendly attitude toward the Soviet Union, while German fascism, with its far-reaching international isolation, looks to Japan as an ally in war against the Soviet Union. Under these conditions, the traditional friendship between France and Japan must cool off to some extent.[244]

Thus, the European antagonisms fit into the more worldwide antagonisms in the Pacific.

The successes of Japanese imperialism in Manchuria have been dearly bought, however. The resistance of the Chinese population engages large Japanese forces in Manchuria. The newly-formed Manchurian army is unreliable: mutinies and desertions to the partisans are regular occurrences. Preparations for war require enormous expenditures. Japan's weak economic foundation is not able to bear these demands forever. Today, though the 'great war' has not yet begun, unproductive military expenditures are already greater than the excess of production over consumption. The country, which seems to be prospering economically, is in fact becoming poorer and poorer. In order to defray the cost of armaments, the Japanese ruling classes are exploiting the workers and peasants, as well as the oppressed colonial peoples, even more intensely, thus creating the objective conditions for the overthrow of their rule. And while the imperialist robbers are contending for the division of their Chinese booty, the power of Soviet China is growing, its territory is expanding, and in constant struggles there is being formed that power of the workers and peasants which alone is destined to overthrow the rule of the foreign and native exploiters, to chase the imperialists out of China, and to solve 'the problem of the Pacific Ocean' in proletarian fashion!

---

243 Naturally, this by no means excludes the possibility or joint deals. In the summer or 1934 a delegation of the English financial oligarchy, including Lord Barnby, President of the Federation of British Industries, visited Japan and Manchuria to investigate the opportunities for British capital investment in Manchuria. (Japan urgently needs foreign capital to continue arming).
244 Japan's intrigues in Siam are also a source of anxiety for the French bourgeoisie.

(3) *On the Eve of a New World War.*

The Sixth Congress had already determined that the course of events 'is inevitably giving rise ... to a new phase of wars among the imperialist states themselves; wars of the imperialist states against the Soviet Union; wars of national liberation against imperialism'.[245]

The economic crisis and the depression greatly intensified the bourgeoisie's urge to solve the market problem by crushing their enemies by force, by the forcible redivision of the world, and by seizing new monopoly-controlled areas. The economics and politics of the capitalist world are being governed more and more by the preparations for war.

(a) Economic preparation for war is in progress all along the line. Rapidly growing sums, constituting an ever greater portion of government expenditures, are devoted to war preparations.

TABLE 12.84 Open war expenditures in the budget of major countries (a) (percent of total budget)

	Germany		Japan		France	
	Million marks	%	Million yen	%	Million francs	%
Expenditures, 1928	755	10	492	28	9.6	23
Expenditures, 1933	674	10	697	35	11.6	23
Estimates, 1934	750	–	852	37	11.4	20
Estimates, 1935	1,354(b)	21	937	44	11.2	19

(a) Official figures.
(b) Of this total, 250,000,000 marks for the Storm Troops and police.

---

245 See the thesis on the international tasks of the CI. 'Theses and Resolutions of the VI. World Congress of the Communist International' 1928.

	USA		England		Poland	
	Million dollars	%	Million pounds	%	Million złoty	%
Expenditures, 1928	732	20	117	14	824	32
Expenditures, 1933	801	15	103	13	761	35
Estimates, 1934	716	10(a)	108	14	762	35
Estimates, 1935	839	19	114	15	762	35

(a) The great fall in percent is a result of the increase of civil expenditures under Roosevelt.

It must be emphasised, however, that the open war expenditures, admitted in the budgets as such, are *only a part of the actual war expenditures*! These figures are useful, if only indicative. The trend of expenditures, not as absolute sums. They show the exceptionally rapid growth of war expenditures in Germany and in Japan; the latter's open war expenditures are officially placed at 44 percent of the total estimated budget for 1935.

Besides the open expenditures, entered in the budget of the war ministry, war expenditures are concealed in the budgets of *all* ministries. The ministry of the interior covers the outlays for the police, the frontier guards and the militia; the ministry of transport meets the expenses for civil aviation and for the railway rolling stock intended for military purposes; the ministry of public works finances the construction of largely strategic roads, frontier fortifications, etc.; the ministry of education handles the military education of youngsters in school; the ministry of labour pays for the 'voluntary' labour camps, which are disguised military formations, etc., etc. It is therefore quite impossible to determine the actual war expenditures of the capitalist states. As a rough estimate, the actual expenditures for military purposes are at least 50 percent higher than the amounts indicated in the budgets.

In judging the significance of the above sums it must also be borne in mind that feeding and clothing soldiers now costs much less than in 1928, owing to the sharp drop in the price of food and agricultural raw materials. Hence expenditures for armament, for the actual instruments of murder, have increased much more than military expenditures in general.

The organisational rearrangement of national economy for war is being carried out systematically. Every nation has 'militarised' its industry. The 'mobilisation plan' for shifting industry to war production is ready everywhere. Most factories already have in hand their orders in the event of mobilisation, so that they can put the shift into effect without delay. In the USA there are regularly recurring trial mobilisations of industry.

Every nation tries its utmost to produce on its own territory the foodstuffs, raw materials and arms most necessary for war. Hence governmental aid for sugar-beet growing in England and for oil-seed planting in Germany; hence the 'battle of grain' in Italy. This is the reason behind government subsidies for shipping, for the construction of speedy commercial vessels that can be used as auxiliary cruisers in time of war, for civil aviation, for copper production (in Germany), etc., etc., *ad infinitum*. Every little state endeavours to establish on its own territory a minimum of heavy industry, of armament manufacture and of artificial silk manufacture to avoid being wholly dependent on imports in case of war.

This striving for self-sufficiency, originating in military considerations, coincides with the bourgeoisie's effort to monopolise the domestic market in every country as thoroughly as possible and to exclude foreign goods. The result is a tendency to *destroy the division of labour in world economy*: a certain 'agrarianisation' of the industrial countries and an artificial industrialisation of the agrarian countries have taken place during the crisis and the depression of a special kind. The *ideological expression of this trend is the theory of autarchy*[246] which has been enunciated most emphatically by the German fascists. (Moreover, 'autarchy' is always taken to mean *the limitation of import alone, never a voluntary limitation of exports*).

The mobilisation and militarisation of all labour power in the event of war is also provided for (compulsory 'labour-service' for the youth in Germany, etc.).

The enlistment of national economy for war has made the greatest advances in Germany and Japan. In Germany the various branches of industry are united in compulsory artels, while raw materials are centrally distributed to the factories under state control. Reserve stocks are being stored for war, and production of all kinds of 'substitute goods' has already begun. The transition to an 'organised starvation' can take place at a moment's notice. As for Japan, its economy largely bears the character of war economy already: absolute precedence of war production, inflation, higher prices, starvation.

---

246 Real 'autarchy', i.e. a complete isolation from the world market, is out of the question under capitalism. German industry uses 45 to 50 percent of foreign raw materials, and its textile industry as much as 90 percent The restriction of raw material imports in the summer of 1934, due to the shortage of foreign exchange, has taught the German people a painful lesson in the senselessness of the fascists' autarchy demagogy.

(b) *Technical preparation for war* has been carried on at a feverishly accelerated pace ever since the Sixth Congress. Although capitalism is introducing technical innovations only in the rarest instances during the crisis and the present depression, one 'improvement' follows on the heels of another in the field of armament. Capitalism's degeneracy is manifested with particular crassness at the present time, in that armaments – the preparations for new mass slaughter – form the principal basis for technological progress.

It goes beyond the confines of our task to describe in detail the perfection of murder instruments since the Sixth Congress. Moreover, the data would rapidly grow obsolete. We shall confine ourselves to a few examples.

Artillery: The range of light guns has been raised from 7.5 to 11 miles, that of 4.1-inch guns from 9 to 16 miles, and that of the giant railway guns (14-inch) from 22 to 40 miles. The longest-range guns have a range as high as 93 miles. The total weight of the shells that an artillery division can fire at the enemy during a given time has risen some 50 to 100 percent.

Infantry: Ordinary rifles are being replaced more and more by automatic repeating rifles, while the number and effectiveness of machine-guns have been greatly increased. An American infantry division, which formerly could fire 107,000 shots a minute from its machine-guns, can now fire more than 200,000.

The new types of weapons, tanks and airplanes have undergone enormous development. The speed and the radius of action of all types of tanks have been doubled since the Sixth Congress! Heavy tanks travel on wheels at a speed of 60 miles per hour, and cross-country at 30 miles per hour on *caterpillar tread*. Tanks have become enormous moving fortresses as well as irresistible battering rams that 'jump' trenches, swim rivers, and know no obstacles. The horsepower of pursuit plane motors increased from 500 to 1,000 h.p. between 1929 and 1933, their speed rose from 175 miles per hour to over 250, and their maximum flying altitude from 27,000 to over 40,000 feet. The number of military airplanes possessed by the major powers is as follows:

TABLE 12.85 Number of military airplanes

	England	USA	Japan	France	Germany
1929	1,824	3,129	1,260	5,000	–
1934	3,000	5,000	2,200	6,000	1,000

The importance of the aerial weapon in the whole system of armaments has increased by giant strides, as is best shown in the war budgets. The radius of action of bombing planes increased from 300 to 750 miles. Thus, almost all the territory of West European countries is exposed to air attacks by neighbouring countries.

Many military specialists consider the airplane the decisive weapon of the future world war.

New discoveries and improvements of every sort are being made daily in all types of weapons: Germany's 'pocket battleships', electrical gun – aiming at the target, remote control of ships and airplanes, Tesla's[247] 'death-rays', cutting out a motor's magneto ignition by means of special rays, rockets flying hundreds of miles, giant flame-throwers mounted on tanks and airplanes, and so forth – not to mention the advances in preparation for 'prohibited' chemical and bacteriological warfare, regarding which the greatest secrecy is maintained.

The horrors of the coming war will many times exceed those of the past war. The 'front' will no longer be a 'line' several miles broad, but an area dozens of miles deep. The new frontier fortifications erected at tremendous cost, into which hundreds of thousands of tons of steel have been sunk, will hardly be able to prevent this. On both sides tanks will penetrate far into the enemy's territory; with their bombs airplanes and airships will destroy cities hundreds of miles behind the front; and the entire civilian population of the enemy-country will be decimated by gas attacks as a potential army. Every factory, and even agricultural land, will be regarded as part of the military, and will be laid waste. The 'devastated areas' will embrace entire countries.

(3) *The ideological preparation for war* is what is most difficult for the bourgeoisie. The masses of the people, especially the older generation that experienced the horrors of the first World War, want to have nothing to do with a new war. The masses are undoubtedly filled with a profound desire for peace. Only the big bourgeoisie, which makes enormous profit in war,[248] and the regular army officers (for whom war means promotion) are interested in war. Under these conditions no government had the courage openly to advocate an ideology of aggressive warfare. Therefore the pacifist phrases mounted on all sides.

---

247 [Nikola Tesla (1856–1943) was a Serbian-American electro-technician. His work fell into relative obscurity after his death].
248 It is typical of the bourgeoisie's 'patriotism' that the munitions industrialists sell their weapons to any country, friend or foe, for cold cash. They did this even during the World War! They are connected with one another in the most complex fashion. See Fenner Brockway's *The Bloody Traffic*, London [Gollancz], 1933, for many interesting facts and especially the testimony before the US Senate Committee in the summer of 1934.

The feverish preparations for war continue to be masked in pacifist guise as essential for 'defence' of the fatherland. In the question of national defence there is a united front of all the bourgeois parties, from the fascist wing on the extreme Right to the Social Democrats.[249] But whoever approves of national defence, *whoever is in favour of a 'defensive war' is in favour of war in general*, for every war is represented as a defensive war by those who start it.[250] Whoever is for national defence is for maintenance of the rule of the bourgeoisie.

The *disarmament conference* that collapsed so ingloriously also served as a pacifist disguise. Its final collapse was due to the aggravation of imperialist antagonisms in general, and to the aggressive policies of Japan and of fascist Germany in particular. Limitations of armaments was conceivable (and was even effected for naval armaments at the Washington and London conferences to a limited extent)[251] as long as the main task seemed to be the joint suppression by the victors of the disarmed countries vanquished in the World War, as long as the redivision of the world was not a pressing problem during the period of relative stabilisation of capitalism. Any thought of armament limitation became impossible when fascist Germany, demonstratively leaving the disarmament conference, threw off the armament restrictions imposed on it at Versailles, and when Japan started its war for the redivision of the world. Deceiving the toiling masses with talk about 'disarmament' could no longer be continued along this line.

The chauvinistic ideology of conquest and revenge now came to the fore more and more strongly (especially in Germany and Japan), disguised and interwoven with agitation against the 'inferior' races and against the Soviet Union, but without relinquishing pacifist phrases, with continued emphasis upon the defensive character of armaments. Every effort was made to reawaken the nationalist, chauvinist and militarist spirit, especially among the youth. Youngsters are systematically inoculated with the spirit of chauvinism from the kindergarten to the university. The daily press, the moving-pictures, the radio, the theatre, literature, art and science, are all used for this purpose. Brilliant military parades are supposed to make one forget the horror of war.

---

249 During recent years the congresses of the legal socialist parties one after another have adopted resolutions for national defence, e.g. the congress of the French party at Tours [1920], the Social-Democratic Parties of Denmark, Holland, Switzerland, etc.
250 Since all imperialists want war, all aggressors are also on the defensive.
251 Agreement on limiting the construction of battleships was made easier by the gigantic sums that such ships cost, and by the doubt which has been raised in naval circles, after the experience of the World War, regarding the value of super-dreadnoughts against submarines and comparatively cheap airplanes.

The ideological mobilisation of the population for the coming war meets an obstacle in the impoverishment of the workers, the toiling peasants and the petty bourgeoisie during the crisis; in the resultant intensification of the class struggle; in the anti-militaristic work of the Communist Parties (insufficient this still is in many countries); and in the maturing of the revolutionary crisis. Hence, the greatest anxiety of the bourgeoisie is the army's reliability in case of war. That is why special detachments have been established to maintain discipline in the next war. That is the basis of Fuller's[252] proposal to create small armies of reliable class composition, equipped with the latest achievements of military technique. But this concept has turned out to be impossible to execute. The army of the next war will undoubtedly be a mass army. The entire male population will be armed, except for those indispensable for the production of war materials. This means that the more the revolutionary crisis matures in the different countries, the more unreliable will the mass army be for the ruling classes. Moreover, the more complex the whole modern army mechanism becomes, the more complex present-day weapons are as machines, the greater must be the effectiveness of the proletariat's anti-war, class struggle, activity in determining the outcome of the war.

The new world war is unavoidable if the proletarian revolution does not forestall it. *History places these alternatives before the proletariat: Either to be sacrificed once again in the slaughterhouse in the service of the bourgeoisie, or to turn its weapons against its own bourgeoisie under the leadership of the Communist Party, turning the imperialist war into a civil war for the overthrow of the rule of the bourgeoisie!*

11   The Changes in Method of the Dictatorship of the Bourgeoisie

The entire period of the general crisis of capitalism is characterised by an uneven, zigzag process of exposing the democratic-parliamentary disguise of the bourgeoisie's[253] dictatorship. Bourgeois democracy was the given form of the bourgeoisie's rule during the ascending period of capitalism, while the latter was still fulfilling its historical mission of developing the forces of pro-

---

252   [John Frederick Charles Fuller (1878–1966) was a British General pioneering in mechanised warfare].

253   As early as 1920 the Theses of the Second Congress of the Comintern declared: 'The centre of gravity of political life at present has been completely and finally transferred beyond the limits of parliament'. 'The Communist Party and Parliamentarism', *Theses and Statutes*, 1920, p. 43.

duction, while the bourgeoisie could still lay claim to being a progressive class. During the period of the general crisis of capitalism, bourgeois democracy had to be undermined and abolished since the capitalist mode of production has become an obstacle to the further development of social productive forces; since the contradiction between the forces of production and the production relationships are becoming more and more acute; since the number of people interested (or imagining themselves to be interested) in the maintenance of the capitalist system of society is growing less and less as the result of the centralisation of capital, the mass ruin of the toiling peasants and the impoverishment of the working class; and since the struggle of the oppressed classes against bourgeois rule grows more and more intense.

Moreover, the struggle among the various groups of the ruling classes for a share in the social profit, which tends to decrease, also grew more acute. This found political expression in splits of the bourgeois parties, in the system of coalition governments, in parliamentary 'log-rolling' and in the rapid succession of cabinets. All this undermined the confidence of the masses in bourgeois democracy and parliamentarism, and lessened the prestige of the ruling classes. The bourgeoisie was less and less able to maintain its rule by peaceful, ideological methods. Instead it had to set its machinery of force in motion more and more often, and more and more systematically, in order to protect its rule. This trend was characterised as follows in the Theses of the Sixth Congress:

> ... [T]he imperialist states develop more and more severe methods and weapons for suppressing the revolutionary detachments of the proletariat, particularly the Communist Parties ... These measures ... reflect the general aggravation of class antagonisms, and the intensification of all forms and methods of the class struggle, as expressed in the increasing application of fascist methods of oppression by the bourgeoisie.[254]

The great crisis, which sped up the process of the centralisation of capital tremendously, which ruined millions of hitherto 'independent' petty bourgeois and peasants, and rendered half of the working class unemployed, abandoning them to the most frightful misery, accelerated this trend. The fascisisation of the government machinery is becoming a common phenomenon. Governments are becoming more and more independent of parliaments; government

---

254   Resolution of the Sixth Congress on 'The International Situation and the Tasks of the Communist International'. 'Theses and Resolutions of the VI. World Congress of the Communist International' 1928, pp. 1567–77.

by decree based on 'extraordinary powers' is becoming more and more the rule. (Even such traditionally democratic states as the USA and France are no exception). In the course of the crisis and depression the bourgeoisie did away with bourgeois democracy even in form in Germany and in several smaller countries, defending its imperiled rule against the revolutionary proletariat by establishing the fascist form of its dictatorship.

The growth of fascism and its coming into power in Germany and in a number of other capitalist countries means:
(a) That the revolutionary crisis and the indignation of the broad masses against the rule of capital is growing;
(b) That the capitalists are no longer able to maintain their dictatorship by the old methods of parliamentarism and of bourgeois democracy in general;
(c) That, moreover, the methods of parliamentarism and bourgeois democracy in general are becoming a hindrance to the capitalists ...
(d) That in view of this, capital is compelled to pass to open terrorist dictatorship.[255]

The Crisis of Social Democracy

The great crisis, which led to rapid acceleration of the process of fascisisation, made the crisis in Social Democracy apparent. The crisis has seized both the Second International and the Amsterdam Trade Union International, as international organisations as well as the individual Social-Democratic parties. It is manifested in the increasing transfer of the best, most revolutionary Social-Democratic workers to Communism; in the severe internal struggles which lead to splits and defections in practically all the Social-Democratic parties; in the ideological confusion prevailing in the biggest of these parties; in the decline of the influence exercised by Social Democracy over the working class; and finally in the fact that the bourgeoisie in a number of countries no longer looks upon and treats Social Democracy as its main social support, but on the contrary abandons it to fascist terror.

This change in the bourgeoisie's attitude toward Social Democracy takes place very unevenly in the various countries, depending upon the extent of economic disintegration and the menace to bourgeois rule occasioned by the maturing of the revolutionary crisis.

---

255 *Theses and Decisions* 1934, p. 6.

From this standpoint the following groups of countries may be differentiated:
(a) Countries where Social Democracy either participates in the government, or is considered as the future government party: Sweden, Denmark, England, Czechoslovakia;
(b) Countries where the Social-Democratic parties constitute legal opposition parties, as in the United States, France, Spain, etc.;
(c) Countries where legal and semi-legal Social-Democratic parties exist under a fascist regime, e.g. Hungary and Poland. (Beginnings of collaboration in Italy and Austria as well);
(d) Countries in which Social Democracy is suppressed and persecuted as a party, as in Germany and Austria.

This very different situation of the various Social-Democratic parties is the chief cause of the crisis in the Second and Amsterdam Internationals as central organisations.

The differing positions of the individual Social-Democratic parties which participate in the government in some countries, while they are illegal and persecuted in others, do not allow of even formally unanimous decisions on any problems.

Moreover, the accentuation of imperialist contradictions more and more sharply divides the various Social-Democratic parties, which side with their respective bourgeoisies. Although the Second International in its decisions before the World War threatened to declare a general strike if war broke out, and although Kautsky's theory that 'the International is an instrument of peace' was originated only during the course of the War, today we see more and more Social-Democratic parties, even before the outbreak of war, openly advocating national defence.[256]

However, the crisis in the international reformist organisations (which had never exercised much influence on the individual parties) is not important for our struggle, but rather the crises in the individual Social-Democratic parties.

(1) *The social basis of the crisis in Social Democracy is the impairment of the conditions of the working class in general and of the labour aristocracy in partic-*

---

[256] It is particularly interesting that not only do the Social-Democratic Parties participating in government or in the legal opposition advocate national defence, but that Otto Bauer (who has since been driven out of Austria) offered the already illegal Social-Democratic Party of Germany the following advice: 'In case of war, German Social Democracy will have to fight so that a democratic-socialist revolution *tears down those obstacles to the development of the full defensive strength of the German people* ... Not defence in the sense of 1914, or even of May, 1933 ... *but neither the defeatist refusal of any and all national defence*'. Bauer 1933, pp. 320–1.

ular during the period of general crisis and especially during the course of the great crisis and of the depression of a special kind. '... The labour aristocracy ... is constantly being weakened by the abolition of the privileges of separate groups of the proletariat through the general decay of capitalism, the levelling out of the condition of the working class, and the generalized extent of its need and insecurity'.[257]

After the victory of reformism and the transformation of the *ultimate goal* into an empty holiday phrase, the basis of Social Democracy's influence was the belief of a large section of the working class (a belief consistently nurtured by the Social-Democratic leaders in the interests of bourgeois rule) that it is possible to better its conditions within the framework of capitalism by utilising bourgeois democracy, the peaceable trade-union movement and the parliamentary influence of the Social-Democratic parties. This faith was fostered by the fact that certain more or less narrow sections of the working class – *the corrupted labour aristocracy in the imperialist countries and the labour bureaucracy* (members of parliament, officials of the trade unions, the party, and the cooperatives, employees of sick benefit organisations, etc.) actually could better their conditions within the framework of capitalism. The opportunist leadership of the Social-Democratic parties would have been unable to retain control for so long a time if not for this objective basis.

The illusions of the working class regarding bourgeois democracy and the possibility of improving its conditions under capitalism grew considerably immediately after the war, especially in the defeated countries. During the first round of revolutions, the bourgeoisie's rule was acutely threatened in these countries by the revolt of the masses, embittered by their sufferings during the War, and by the collapse of the bourgeois machinery of force as a result of defeat in the War. *Hence the bourgeoisie made far-reaching concessions to the revolutionary masses within the framework of the capitalist social order*. In the defeated countries all the traditional demands of the Social-Democratic workers were met; overthrow of the monarchy; universal, equal and secret suffrage; freedom of assembly and of organisation; the eight-hour day; unemployment insurance, etc. At the same time the bourgeoisie handed over the government to the Social-Democratic leaders.

In view of the breakdown of its machinery of force, it was impossible for the bourgeoisie to meet the revolts of the masses with violence at that moment. The bourgeoisie had to mollify the revolt of the masses by offering them con-

---

[257] Theses on the Trade Union Movement, Factory Committees and the Third International. *Theses and Statutes of the Third International* 1920.

cessions, in order to gain time for the restoration of its machinery of force. The fact that the Social-Democratic leaders were in the cabinet created the illusion in the working masses of having already defeated the bourgeoisie. The Social-Democratic leaders nurtured these illusions with such slogans as 'Socialism marches on', by instituting commissions for socialisation, etc. Under these circumstances, there was a strong influx of workers, officials and petty bourgeois into the Social-Democratic parties immediately after the War. Participation in the government enabled the German and Austrian Social-Democratic parties to extend their base within the bureaucracy by making hundreds of thousands of their followers state and municipal officials.

But with the recovery and strengthening of bourgeois rule and with capital's offensive against working conditions, the illusions of the masses of workers were disappointed more and more. The great crisis, which impaired the condition of the masses of workers to an unprecedented degree, also undermined the privileged position of the labour aristocracy by *reducing its numbers and its privileged position in comparison to the masses of the workers and by fully extending unemployment to it as well.*

Presenting the impairment of the labour aristocracy's condition concretely, in figures, meets with the difficulty of determining what categories and groups of the working class are to be considered as belonging to the labour aristocracy. We cite the following figures from the book by [Jürgen] Kuczynski (with all necessary reservations).[258]

TABLE 12.86 Index of real wages of the labour aristocracy (1900 = 100)

	Germany	USA	England
1929	93	143	93
1933	49	115	95

These figures, which are not very accurate owing to the complexity of the calculations, indicate a very severe impairment of the position of the labour aristocracy in Germany and the USA, with slight improvement in England.[259]

---

258 Kuczynski 1934.
259 The impairment of the situation of large sections of the labour aristocracy can be demonstrated in England as well, the classical country of corruption of the topmost stratum of

(This includes losses sustained through unemployment, as well as income from unemployment relief).

In general we note that the major tendency in the condition of the working class during the crisis is a levelling out on a lower plane. This downward levelling tendency during the crisis is clearly manifested, for instance, in the official statistics of German workers' wages.

TABLE 12.88 Invalid insurance classification of German workers according to weekly wage (in percent)

	Up to 6 marks	6–12 marks	12–18 marks	18–24 marks	24–30 marks	30–36 marks	Over 36 marks
1929	3.5	12.3	16.5	13.0	8.8	8.1	37.8
1934 (first quarter)	4.0	25.1	19.4	14.4	10.7	9.5	16.9

the working class. The weekly wage collectively agreed upon for skilled workers is as follows in *Table 12.87*:

TABLE 12.87 Weekly wages of skilled workers

	4 Aug 1914		31 Dec 1933		Percent increase	Percent increase in cost of living
	s.	d.	s.	d.		
Metal trades	41	8	62	4	50	–
Shipbuilding	41	7	60	0	43	43
Building	39	0	65	5	67	–

These figures indicate that the real wages of the labour aristocracy (when fully employed) improved as compared to the pre-war period. But unemployment his hit just these layers extremely hard in the course of the crisis. As late as May 1933, unemployment among shipbuilding workers totalled 47.6 percent, with up to 33 percent among metal workers of various categories. Wages above the collective contract level were greatly reduced. The official cost of living index is falsified to a considerable extent. Although certain new sections of better-paid workers develop (motor, radio) the position of the labour aristocracy in England has undoubtedly also been impaired on the whole by the crisis.

Before the crisis, 42 percent of the workers earned from 6 to 24 marks; at present this group totals 59 percent. Before the crisis 37.8 percent earned more than 36 marks; now 16.9 percent, or less than half, earn that much. The number of workers with an income of more than 48 marks has been reduced to a minimum. If we take into consideration the tremendous unemployment, the increase in taxes and wage deductions, and the cuts in unemployment relief (which had already commenced while the Social Democrats were in the cabinet), we can understand why the illusions of the German working class regarding the possibility of advance within the framework of capitalism, through the peaceful methods advocated by Social Democracy, evaporated during the crisis. The principal basis for the political crisis in the Social-Democratic parties is: disillusionment caused by the failure of democracy and by the futility of the 'positions of power' plus the workers' dissatisfaction with the anti-Soviet and war policy of the Social-Democratic leaders.

The Political Crisis of Social Democracy

Social Democracy was transformed from an originally revolutionary party into the main social support of the bourgeoisie, by having in practice substituted reformism for revolutionary international Marxism even in the pre-war period; by having openly gone over to the side of its bourgeoisie during the World War, urging the proletarians to murder each other; by splitting the working class and causing the collapse of the revolution in its first round through the use of subtle manoeuvres plus armed violence together with the bourgeoisie; by slandering the Soviet Union in every way and seeking to discredit it among the workers.

> The petty bourgeois democracy of the capitalist countries represented as its advanced section by the Second and the Two and a Half Internationals is at the present moment the chief support of capitalism in so far as the majority or at least a considerable part of the industrial and commercial workers and employers remain under its influence. The latter are in fear of the advent of the revolution; they fear the loss of their petty bourgeois prosperity created by imperialist privileges. But the growing economic crisis is aggravating the conditions of the wide masses everywhere. This together with the inevitability of imperialist wars (which is becoming more manifest every day) is shattering this mainstay of capitalism.[260]

---

260 'Thesis on the tactics of the Russian Communist Party', 1921, pp. 121–2.

The political essence of the crisis of Social Democracy is the conflict between its function as the main social support of the bourgeoisie and its proletarian (and petty-bourgeois) *mass base, a conflict that grows more and more irreconcilable in, the crisis and depression.* The bourgeoisie demands that the reformist leaders get the workers to accept the impairment of their working conditions peacefully. The Social-Democratic workers demand that they organise and lead the resistance against the attack of capital. The bourgeoisie demands that the Social-Democratic bureaucracy in government office, such as Severing, Grzesinski,[261] MacDonald and others, defend bourgeois rule against the workers by armed force. The Social-Democratic workers demand that the Social-Democratic leaders take advantage of the government 'positions of power' held by them to conduct the struggle against the bourgeoisie.

The bourgeoisie demands of the leadership of Social Democracy that it perpetuate the split of the working class, isolating the Social-Democratic workers from the influence of the Communists, and assuring the hegemony of the bourgeoisie over the workers. The Social-Democratic workers want to conduct a united struggle with the Communists against the hegemony of the bourgeoisie over the workers; they demand the united front, negotiations and reconciliation with the Communist International.

The bourgeoisie demands of the Social-Democratic leaders active participation in preparations for the new imperialist war; the Social-Democratic workers want to have nothing to do with a new imperialist war.

The bourgeoisie demands of the reformist leaders active participation in the ideological and organisational preparation of the counter-revolutionary war against the Soviet Union. The Social-Democratic workers understand that the Soviet Union is realising the ultimate socialist goal for which the labour movement has been fighting since its beginning; not only do they reject any war against the Soviet Union, but they demand that the latter be defended, in struggle against their own bourgeoisie if necessary.[262]

This conflict, existing on every front, between the function of Social Democracy as the main social support of the bourgeoisie and its proletarian mass base, and the resultant political crisis of Social Democracy do not develop evenly in all countries. The crisis of Social Democracy is less acute in those countries where the conditions of the workers during the crisis have grown worse to a lesser extent, relatively speaking, where the traditions of the revolutionary workers' movement are less and the influence of the Communist Parties

---

261 [Albert Grzesinski (1879–1948) was a German Social-Democratic politician].
262 This is naturally not a complete summary; the conflict develops in every field without exception.

weaker, as in England, Sweden, Norway or Denmark. Therefore the Social-Democratic parties in these countries can still participate in their governments or aspire to be the future government parties, and yet retain their mass influence, or in many cases, as in Sweden for instance, even extend their influence during the crisis.

Likewise, the crisis in Social Democracy is somewhat less acute for the present in those countries where the Social-Democratic parties are in constant 'opposition', where they support 'Left' governments, it is true (as in France), but their leaders do not participate directly in the cabinet, and where the party officialdom is not fused with the state machinery.[263] In such countries the function of the party as the main social support of the bourgeoisie is more easily concealed from the working masses by employing manoeuvres and revolutionary phrases.

On the other hand the war question plays a very big role in the crisis of the French party (as well as in several other Social-Democratic parties). While the 'Left' and Centrist leaders continue to manoeuvre with pacifism, under the pressure of the masses who want to have nothing to do with a new war, the leaders of the Right, under pressure from the bourgeoisie, take an open stand for a new war. This, as we know, has led to the split of the Socialist deputies' group and to the emergence of the neo-fascist Marquet-Déat group.

The crisis of Social Democracy has gone as far as the complete disintegration of the party in Germany, which was very hard hit by the crisis, where the condition of the proletariat in the postwar period, and especially during the great economic crisis, had grown worse to an exceptional degree, where the leaders of Social Democracy constantly participated in government,[264] and where the party officialdom had been most extensively interwoven with the bourgeoisie's machinery of force. Hence, Social Democracy's responsibility for the reduction of wages, for the cuts in social insurance, and for the murder of demonstrating workers could not be hushed up. Hence, a strong Communist Party, rapidly gaining in influence, made it more and more difficult for the Social-Democratic leaders to carry out their anti-working-class policies. The inner dialectics of development of the crisis in Social Democracy is therefore best illustrated in Germany.

---

263 However, the fact that the Social-Democratic Party of France controls numerous municipalities has led to a pronounced interlinking of the Party apparatus with the municipal bureaucracy. This constitutes a strong pillar of opportunism.
264 Social Democracy 'ruled' uninterruptedly in Prussia from the end of the war until the Braun government was driven out by [Franz] von Papen in 1932.

The leaders of German Social Democracy 'honesty' endeavoured to meet the demands of the bourgeoisie all along the line. [Fritz] Tarnow[265] frankly declared: 'The crisis must be solved within the framework of the capitalist social order, with the sacrifices by the working class necessary to that end'.[266]

The Social-Democratic arbitrators reduced the workers' wages.[267] The Social-Democratic trade-union leaders prevented strikes, and expelled the Communists from the trade unions.

The Social-Democratic chiefs of police allowed policemen, members of Social-Democratic organisations, to shoot down demonstrating workers.[268] And so forth.

But this anti-working-class policy led to the undermining of Social Democracy's influence among the working masses, and the rapid growth in influence of the Communist Party of Germany (Kommunistische Partei Deutschlands, KPD). Election votes showed that the KPD had won the majority of the working class in such important centres as Berlin and the Ruhr area, and was definitely on the road towards winning the majority of the working class in the entire Reich. (Yet, since the majority of the working class continued to follow the leadership of the Social-Democratic SPD – Sozialdemokratische Partei Deutschlands – and it controlled the mass organisations, especially the trade unions and the workers in the big factories, its weakened influence was still sufficiently powerful to hinder a united struggle of the working class in general,

---

265 [Fritz Tarnow (1880–1951) was a German Social-Democrat politician and trade-union leader].
266 *Die Rote Fahne*, 10 December 1930.
267 The first wage reduction enforced by the government was based, as we know, on Severing's Oeynhausen arbitration decision.
268 How very conscious the Social-Democratically organised police officials were of their counter-revolutionary role is shown by the following letter sent by the Brotherhood of Social-Democratic Police Officials to the Leipzig Convention of the Social-Democratic Party of Germany (SPD) in 1931: 'The forthcoming emergency decree provides for another reduction in the salaries of officials. We do not want to repeat the arguments generally valid against such a proviso. But in the justifiable defence of the interests of police officials, to which we are certainly entitled as members of the trade union of government officials, we merely want to protect our members against heavy and unbearable sacrifices and to inform the Party Convention of our political apprehensions, arising from such a reduction. We should like to put the question frankly: *Where in the world has any state, in times of stress and danger, ever reduced and cut the means of livelihood of the protectors of governmental order? When has a state ever alienated the armed forces that protect it in the hours of extreme danger?* It is the duty of the German republic to forestall an agitation among police officials that is counter to the public interest, by assuring them their means of livelihood. Will it really be the fate of the German republic to treat its police officials to a reduction in salary exactly at the moment when it needs them urgently?'

and in particular to prevent the general strike proclaimed by the KPD against the fascists' seizure of power).

The decisive sections of the bourgeoisie reacted to the decrease in influence of the SPD by supporting and extensively financing the fascist movement, in order to subject the workers to intensified pressure and terror and, in view of the probable failure of the Social Democrats in their role of the bourgeoisie's main social support to have a ready substitute in the fascists. (Although Hitler's agitation was much more 'anti-capitalist' than that of the Social-Democratic leaders, the captains of industry: [Fritz] Thyssen,[269] [Martin] Mutschmann,[270] and the rest, knew quite well that it was no more earnest than the phrases of the Social-Democratic leaders regarding the class struggle and the ultimate revolutionary goal).

Thus the Social-Democratic leadership was subjected to many-sided pressure. The bourgeoisie demanded that it stifle the economic and political struggles of the proletariat, and threatened to replace it by the fascists; in endeavouring to meet the demands of the bourgeoisie, the leaders of the SPD drove the workers towards the Communists, and the petty bourgeoisie (plus certain tiny sections of the working class) to the fascists. The leadership of the SPD supported every reactionary government, and tried to justify its betrayal to the working class by its 'theory of the lesser evil'.

'There was only this alternative: the Brüning Cabinet or open fascist dictatorship', according to [Wilhelm] Sollmann's[271] political report at the Leipzig Party Convention in 1931.

'If we overthrow the Brüning cabinet the scorpions of Hitler and Hugenberg will succeed the whip of Brüning', [Wilhelm] Dittmann[272] said at the same convention.

They also avoided any serious clash with fascism, for they feared that such a struggle would develop into a revolutionary movement against the bourgeoisie. They prepared the way for Hitler's advent to power by suppressing the Red Front Fighters' League, by disarming the workers, by tolerating the organisation of the Storm Troops and the Special Guards, by giving the fascists police protection against the workers while the former were still weak, and so forth. They opposed [Ernst] Thälmann's[273] candidacy for the presidency, supporting

---

269 [Fritz Thyssen (1873–1951) was steel magnate from the Ruhr and Hitler's fundraiser].
270 [Martin Mutschmann (1879–1947) was a leading Nazi and businessman from Saxony; in 1947 he was executed in Moscow].
271 [Wilhelm Sollmann (1881–1951) was a German SPD politician and journalist].
272 [Wilhelm Dittmann (1874–1954) was a German Social-Democratic politician].
273 [Ernst Thälmann (1886–1944), German Communist leader].

[Paul von] Hindenburg (who later took Hitler into the cabinet) with the slogan: 'A vote for Thälmann is a vote for Hitler'. Their struggle against Hitler consisted in trying to convince the bourgeoisie that the latter could find no better support than they themselves were. 'We are playing the role of capitalism's physician'. But all their manoeuvres could not abolish the crisis. *The more they laboured to serve the bourgeoisie, the more their ideological influence upon the working class declined*, the less was their usefulness to the bourgeoisie. The leaders of German Social Democracy could not break through this vicious circle by any sort of manoeuvre. Until Hitler's seizure of power they continued their policy of splitting the working class. They refused the KPD's offer for common struggle, even when von Papen simply expelled them from the Prussian government. They remained unshakably faithful to their masters until they were driven out. The German proletariat, however, is paying, under Hitler's whip, for the fact that their traitorous leaders prevented the Social-Democratic workers from carrying on a united struggle together with the Communists against the bourgeoisie.

∴

The 'Left' Austro-Marxists could not bridge the conflict between their role as the main social support of the bourgeoisie and their proletarian mass base any more than could the Right leaders of the SPD. Essentially, they pursued the same policy of the lesser evil, although they could easily see whither it led by the fate of the SPD. After having played their part they were driven off the scene practically without a struggle, by the weak Austrian bourgeoisie, divided by its own inner conflicts.[274] This is the best proof that the fate of the SPD is no exception due to exceptional circumstances, but *represents the typical fate awaiting all Social-Democratic parties* if the Social-Democratic workers do not realise the united front with the Communists against the menace of fascism, if they do not shatter that baneful influence of their leaders, who serve the bourgeoisie, and do not follow the only practicable revolutionary path, blazed for them by the Russian Bolsheviks.

The crisis in the Amsterdam International is less advanced than that in Social Democracy. In many countries (especially where each trade-union member is automatically a member of the Social-Democratic party, as in Norway,

---

274   The heroic struggle of the Schutzbund, unwanted and unsupported by the leaders, had to collapse because it had no political, revolutionary goal. The purely defensive slogan of defending freedom's rights – not struggle for the overthrow of the bourgeoisie – had to result in defeat: the strategic and tactical errors inevitably followed from this false political approach.

Hungary and Great Britain), Social Democracy finds support in the free trade unions. In the USA the AFL is undoubtedly growing considerably at the present time; hundreds of thousands of workers went on strike in 1934 for the right to organise in unions within the framework of the AFL.

The reasons for the greater stability of the Social-Democratic trade unions compared to the Social-Democratic parties are many and various. The most important are as follows: the individual union-organised workers are directly and materially interested in the existence of the trade unions. The trade unions can adapt themselves to a regime that is going fascist much more easily than the Social-Democratic parties can. Moreover, practically all the Communist Parties have done insufficient work in the trade unions. But the same causes that account for the crisis in the Second International must also aggravate the crisis in the Amsterdam International.

The Ideological Crisis of Social Democracy

The ideological (and organisational) crisis of Social Democracy is interlinked with its political crisis.

The period of relative stabilisation enabled Social Democracy to renew and extend its pre-war revisionist policy, which it had masked with 'Left' phrases, during the first revolutionary crisis.

In the field of economics, Hilferding, Kautsky and Tarnow announced that there was no general crisis of capitalism;[275] that capitalism still had a long period of advance before it; that the October Revolution had been a bourgeois revolution, and did not signify the beginning of the overthrow of the capitalist social order (Otto Bauer); that capitalism was developing into a planned state capitalism, free of crisis; and that the transition to socialism had already begun.

As to the theory of the state, their position was as follows: *The state is above classes; parliamentary democracy is the only road to the conquest of state power*, which can only proceed step by step. Until Social Democracy obtains an absolute majority at the polls it participates in coalition governments and occupies 'positions of power' in the governmental machinery, but it cannot fully carry out its programme of 'industrial democracy', socialism (as they understand it), even when governing alone. 'The Labour Party is in office, but not in power'. Democracy involves the rejection of all use of force, of all dictatorship, even the dictatorship of the proletariat.

---

[275] Even as late as 11 November 1930, in the midst of the great economic crisis, Hilferding declared at the Landgemeinde Convention: 'The present economic crisis is much more severe than previous ones, but as a crisis of capitalist economy it is only a cyclic phenomenon that will be overcome. The basic drive of our economy points upwards'.

This ideology, which temporarily satisfied the bourgeoisie and also kept the majority of Social-Democratic workers from coming over to the revolution, could not withstand the hammer-blows of the crisis. The drop in production to below the pre-war level, the rapid impoverishment of the proletariat, and the ejection of half the workers from the process of production, gave the lie to the theory of the advance of capitalism, and destroyed the illusions that had arisen during the period of stabilisation among some of the Social-Democratic workers regarding the possibility of an existence worthy of a human being within the framework of the capitalist social order. But the fact that in all countries (including those where Social Democrats were in the cabinet) the offensive of capital was made with the support of the state, and that the workers' resistance was smashed, when necessary, by the most brutal application of the state machinery of force, undermined faith in the state standing above classes. Under the blows of the crisis, the Social-Democratic workers again became receptive to revolutionary Marxism, championed by the Communists. The walls that the Social-Democratic leaders had erected between the Social-Democratic workers and the Communists began to give way.

With unconcealed revisionist ideology the leaders of Social Democracy could no longer keep the workers firmly under their influence. The political crisis was reflected in the ideological crisis. Some of the leaders again began to develop 'Left' theories: Löbe stated that the crisis of capitalism was general; Otto Bauer demanded that democracy be defended against Fascism with armed force; Seydewitz[276] and Co. even demanded the dictatorship of the proletariat.

The ideological crisis grew even greater after the victory of fascism in Germany and Austria. The leaders faced the task of finding a new ideology that would quiet the Social-Democratic workers, embittered over the complete failure of the policy of the lesser evil, but at the same time would not block the way for further collaboration with the bourgeoisie later on.

The ideology of peaceful parliamentary democracy had to be sacrificed for the time being.

'Against *despotism* no parliamentary or constitutional opposition is possible, but only the weapon of revolution', is the phrasing of the first programmatic pamphlet of the SPD leadership from exile.

'In the struggle against the National Socialist dictatorship no compromise is possible, there is no place for reformism or legality', declares the January programme of the SPD.

---

276   [Max Seydewitz (1892–1987) was a German Social-Democratic politician].

But the 'revolution' is to be directed only against the fascist form of the bourgeois dictatorship, and not against the rule of the bourgeoisie itself. The revolutionary phrases are intended for the workers, while the bourgeoisie is set at ease by the decisive rejection of Bolshevism.

'The new socialist battlefront ... must reject the Bolshevik goal programmatically. Replacing the National-Socialist prison by the Bolshevik penitentiary cannot be the goal of the great struggle for freedom against the fascist state' (January Programme).

'Back to democracy', is Kautsky's slogan. 'Through dictatorship to democracy', is the slogan of the exiled Austro-Marxists.

As we see, this clique of leaders, though driven out or locked up in concentration camps, still serves the bourgeoisie, by employing the vestiges of its remaining influence among the working masses against the united front of the proletariat, against the proletarian revolution, and for the re-establishment of a legal dictatorship of the bourgeoisie. But the German and Austrian workers have learned a lesson from the events of the last few years, and see through this double-dealing of their leaders more and more clearly.

The crisis in ideology is a problem for the whole Second International, and not only for the German and Austrian Social-Democratic leaders already driven out by the bourgeoisie. The problem is to create a new ideology, *a new programme, that on the one hand would satisfy the workers temporarily and keep them with the Party, and on the other would keep the bourgeoisie from (following the example of the German bourgeoisie) driving out the reformists and making the fascists their main social support*. Or putting it otherwise, to create a programme that would enable Social Democracy to continue successfully playing its role as the main social support of the bourgeoisie, despite the crisis.

The 'most successful' attempt in this connection was made by de Man,[277] whose 'Programme of Labour', which was formally adopted by the Belgian Social-Democratic Party, united 'Left' phraseology with a semi-fascist content that is acceptable to the bourgeoisie. The workers are given to understand that the plan constitutes 'an attack on the structure of capitalism itself', and that its fulfilment would constitute a step towards realisation of the ultimate goal, since the banks, railroads, power production and mining would be 'nationalised'. The bourgeoisie is reassured that confiscation of its property is out of the question, and that the fulfilment of the plan will take place only by peaceful means, by winning a majority among the people or in parliament. The side of the plan shown the workers is the revolutionary phrases; the side shown the

---

277   [Hendrik de Man (1885–1953) was a Belgian Socialist politician and ideologue].

bourgeoisie is an offer of government by coalition on the basis of systematising state aid to the enterprises of monopoly capital facing bankruptcy.[278]

The crisis programmes of the British Labour Party, the Swiss Socialist Party, the French Neo-Socialists, etc., run essentially along the same lines.

That this endeavour, to keep the Social-Democratic workers from the united front and revolutionary struggle by means of 'Left' phrases,[279] did not have the anticipated success is demonstrated by the organisational crisis of the Socialist parties.

The Organisational Crisis of Social Democracy

The organisational crisis of Social Democracy is the result of the political crisis, which the leaders attempt to overcome, without success, by changing its ideology and by 'Left' manoeuvres. This organisational crisis is manifested in defections and splits to the 'Right' and to the 'Left', and in transfer to the Communists, not only by individual workers, but whole Social-Democratic organisations.

These defections and splits take place along two main lines. Some of the Social-Democratic leaders want under no circumstances to share the fate of [Otto] Wels,[280] [Ernst] Heilmann[281] and Otto Bauer. *They want to remain in the favour of the bourgeoisie under all circumstances*. Such are the MacDonald-Snowden group in England, the neo-fascist Marquet-Déat group in France, and [Gustav] Noske,[282] [Carl] Ulrich,[283] Löbe and Severing in Germany.[284] But through their open desertion to the bourgeoisie they lose their influence over the workers, and with it their value for the bourgeoisie.

---

278   See my detailed criticism in the *Communist International*, nos. 12–13, 1934, 'The De Man Plan is a Fraud on the Workers'.
279   The use of 'Left' phrases assumes various forms. De Man speaks of an 'attack on the structure of capitalism itself'. Otto Bauer, for the time being, proclaims the necessity of armed uprising to overthrow the fascist regime in Austria, etc. All this is for the purpose of keeping the Social-Democratic workers from coming over to the Communist Parties. Only the former extreme Right-wing leader of Spanish Social Democracy, [Largo] Caballero, has advanced, under the pressure of the revolting masses, from 'Left' slogans to participation in the revolutionary struggles.
280   [Otto Wels (1873–1939) was a German Social-Democratic politician].
281   [Ernst Heilmann (1881–1940) was a German Social-Democratic politician].
282   [Gustav Noske (1868–1946) was a German Social-Democratic politician].
283   [Carl Ulrich (1853–1933) was a German Social-Democratic politician].
284   In Germany the entire Social-Democratic leadership was ready to go over to Hitler had Hitler been willing, as was proved by Wels's speech in the Reichstag on 17 May 1934; the whole technical-bureaucratic staff of the Free Trade Unions has been taken over by the 'Labour Front' and is continuing its work under fascist leadership.

Other Social-Democratic leaders attempt to serve the bourgeoisie by placing themselves at the head of the leftward movement of the working class in order to prevent the workers from going over to the Communist Party: the ILP[285] in England, the Socialist Labour Party [Sozialistische Arbeiterpartei, SAP] in Germany, etc. They cannot fulfil their role since the workers are beginning more and more to recognise the difference between the revolutionary struggle of the Communists and the 'Left' phrases of these most dangerous representatives. The aggravation of the whole situation prevents the formation of any extensive Centrist groups.

The organisational crisis is also manifested in the fact that the 'founder parties' themselves are split into 'Right' and 'Left' fractions in the most varied fashion, as was shown most clearly at the last congress of the French Social-Democratic Party.[286]

The organisational crisis is most severe in Germany and Austria, where there is no longer any central Social-Democratic Party at all, *but merely loose groups, most of which refuse to have anything to do with the émigré party leaderships.* The case of Germany proves most strikingly how unstable a basis were the labour aristocracy and the Social-Democratic bureaucracy. The huge Social-Democratic bureaucracy in the Reich, in Prussia, in the cities and towns, in the trade unions and co-operatives, have as a body entered the service of the fascists (except for those who were kicked out). For years, many had carried the fascist party card in their pocket alongside the Social-Democratic one. As for the highly skilled Social-Democratic workers, most of them, as indispensable to capital, have remained in the factories. But the great majority have become politically 'neutral' and are not inclined to jeopardise personal freedom and jobs by engaging in Social-Democratic Party work.[287] The functionary staff of the Party, which had been recruited from these privileged strata, no longer exists as an organisational entity.

The political, ideological and organisational crisis of Social Democracy, the complete bankruptcy of the policy of the mighty German and Austrian Social-Democratic parties, the blows struck the workers by fascism, and the courage and resoluteness of the German and Austrian Communists in their illegal work,

---

285   [Independent Labour Party].
286   This organisational chaos is most strikingly evidenced in Switzerland where the Right Social-Democratic chief of police of Zurich had the 'Left' Social-Democratic party secretary arrested.
287   A certain change has taken place in this respect since 30 June, which revealed the internal weaknesses of the Hitler regime as by the lightning flash. The old Social-Democratic functionaries are again beginning to try to do some Party work.

are making more and more Social-Democratic workers begin to lose faith in Social Democracy. They begin earnestly comparing the policy of the Social Democrats with that of the Communists, and groups of really sincere, Left Social-Democratic, revolutionary workers are being formed. The road to the united front in struggle against fascism and the bourgeoisie is opening before us.

The Growth of Fascism

The growth of fascism – both the fascisisation of the state machinery and the fascist movement itself – had already begun, prior to the Sixth World Congress, on the basis of the general crisis of capitalism. The great economic crisis and the present depression of a special kind have forced the bourgeoisie to speed up the process of fascisisation, though unequally in different countries, depending on the degree to which the rule of the bourgeoisie has been weakened and the revolutionary crisis has ripened.

We use the word forced advisedly. It is not merely for pleasure that the bourgeoisie replaces the democratic-parliamentary disguise of its rule by the method of fascist terror. The establishment of the fascist regime, although it does represent a heavy blow to the proletariat, is not the result of the strength but rather the weakness of the bourgeoisie's position, the loss of its ideological-political hegemony over the majority of the people, which forces it to take refuge in the systematic use of terror.

If the impairment of the position of the proletariat in general, and of the labour aristocracy in particular, is the major basis of the crisis in Social Democracy, the impoverishment of the peasant and petty-bourgeois masses constitutes the social base for the growth of the fascist movement.[288]

Intense discontent and a widespread revolt against existing conditions were the political consequences of the mass ruin of the peasantry during the economic crisis. (Demonstrations, boycotting the supply of foodstuffs to the cit-

---

288   This is shown most clearly in the votes received by the fascists in Germany. Their vote was as follows (in percent of all votes cast in the Reich):

TABLE 12.89 The Fascist vote in Germany

Stabilisation period			Crisis-period		
1924 May	1924 Dec	1928 May	1930 Sept	1932 July	1932 Nov
0.2	2.5	2.6	18.3	37.4	33.1

ies, mass refusals to pay taxes, interference by force with sheriff sales, etc.). Throughout the world, the toiling peasantry – hitherto the reserve of the bourgeoisie, but at the same time the great potential reserve of the proletarian revolution – has been stirred to activity. Although this activity, like all petty-bourgeois activity, lacks any clear political goal, it represents a menace to the rule of the bourgeoisie, the danger of which grows with the intensity of the latter's struggle with the proletariat, with the maturing of the revolutionary crisis in a given country. In all capitalist countries the bourgeoisie has always looked to the sections of the peasantry that it led and misled for support in its struggle against the revolutionary proletariat. What they have in common is private property, with the working peasants usually unable to distinguish between peasant property and exploiters' property. As fanatical defenders of peasant property, which to them seems indispensable as the natural basis for the employment of their labour power, they readily permit themselves to be misused for the defence of exploiters' property. Hence, the general revolt of the peasantry against existing conditions, caused by the agrarian crisis, represents a serious threat to bourgeois rule.

The toiling 'peasantry' (which in this context we take to include tenant farmers, small farmers and middle farmers, i.e. all the agricultural toilers living wholly or in part by cultivating their own or leased land by their own labour) constitutes the absolute majority of the earth's population and the most numerous single section of the population in most capitalist countries (with the exception of England and Belgium).[289]

The importance of the peasantry for the bourgeoisie is increased by the *special role it plays in the bourgeois state's machinery of force*. It is largely the sons of peasants who form the human material for the bourgeois state's machinery of force: the gendarmes, the militia, the police, the prison guards, are recruited

---

289 According to the latest available census figures, the percentage of persons gainfully employed in agriculture is as follows:

TABLE 12.90 Persons employed in agriculture

USA	Germany	France	Czechoslovakia	Italy	Spain	Poland
26.7	30.5	38.4	40.5	55.7	57	76.2

Rich farmers, as well as landless agricultural wage labourers, must be deducted from these totals.

Data from *Statistisches Jahrbuch für das Deutsche Reich* 1932, pp. 24–5.

for the most part from the sons of the peasantry. The army, especially the professional cadres of non-commissioned officers, consists very largely of sons of the peasantry, to an extent even higher than the percentage of peasants in the total population. (For class reasons, workers are not readily promoted to positions as non-commissioned officers). Therefore the general dissatisfaction of the peasantry imperils the reliability of the machinery of force, which is now of such decisive importance in the struggle with the working class.

It follows from all this that the attitude of the toiling peasantry is of decisive importance for the success of the proletarian revolution. This was already emphasised at the Second Congress of the Communist International, which pointed to the necessity of winning the village poor, of neutralising the middle peasantry, and of decisive struggle against the rich peasants.

Victory of the proletarian revolution is extremely difficult in most countries (and in many countries impossible) so long as the ruling classes succeed in keeping the 'peasantry' (in the wider sense of the word) under their moral and political influence, with the help of the rich peasants, 'who are the most numerous of the bourgeois strata, the direct and determined enemies of the revolutionary proletariat'. That is why the Theses of the Second Congress state: *'In the work of the Communist Party in the rural districts chief attention must be given to the struggle against this element, to the liberation of the labouring and exploited majority of the rural population from the moral and political influence of these exploiters'.*[290]

Unfortunately, it must be stated that only in a few such countries, such as Bulgaria, Greece, China and some other colonial countries, and to some extent in Poland, have the Communist Parties succeeded in using the favourable situation arising from the peasants' revolt to accomplish this task.[291] In most capitalist countries, especially in Germany, the fascist movement has suc-

---

290   'Theses on the Agrarian Question', *Theses and Statutes* 1920, p. 78.
291   The task of the Communists was made more difficult by the traditional agrarian policy of Social Democracy, which systematically established a barrier between the urban working class and the poor and middle farmers. It pictured the peasants (without class differentiation) merely as producers of foodstuffs in contrast to the industrial workers as *consumers*, as buyers of foodstuffs. Instead of the class distinction between exploiters and exploited in town and country, *the contrast of 'urban consumers' and 'rural producers' was stressed.* Instead of showing that industrial and agricultural workers, as well as poor and small farmers, are all exploited by the same ruling classes in town and country, Social Democracy drew a line between the urban and rural districts. Thus there arose a peculiar 'united front' between Social Democracy and the agrarians. Social Democracy objectively supported the policies of the agrarians who proclaimed the community of interests of all 'farmers'. This basic line was not changed by the agrarian reformism of [Eduard] David and [Paul] Hertz, and by occasional manoeuvres intended to catch peasant votes.

ceeded, with the help of an unscrupulous hypocritical demagogy ('Breaking interest slavery', 'Subdivision of large estates', etc.), in absorbing the revolt of the peasantry and temporarily turning it into a force hostile to the working class. The National-Socialist movement did not confine its demagogy to economic questions. Slogans such as 'Blood and Soil', 'A People Without Space', and so on, paved the way for demagogy in the race question, and for chauvinism. A huge 'scientific' literature was supposed to prove that the peasants represent the pure *Nordic blood* in the German people, that the (free) peasants and the nobility were of common descent; they spoke of the 'peasant nobility', etc.[292]

In this way the peasantry became a mass base for fascism; as a result the shaky hegemony of the bourgeoisie over them was (with a changed ideology) temporarily restored. The inability of Social Democracy to influence the peasant movement, and the success of the fascists in demagogically deceiving the peasantry were important factors in the turn of the German ruling classes, from Social Democracy to fascism.

With similar demagogic, chauvinistic, reactionary, 'anti-capitalist' slogans, such as 'Against greedy capital', 'Abolish department stores', etc., the fascist movement succeeded in attracting the urban petty bourgeoisie, which the crisis had abandoned to ruin: artisans, small shopkeepers, intellectuals, as well as the very numerous 'new middle classes': government officials, clerks, office workers, technicians, etc., who comprise almost half the total of actual wage earners in the highly developed capitalist countries.

We cannot give a thorough analysis of fascist demagogy here. Its characteristic features are the unscrupulousness with which absolutely contradictory demands are set up for different groups at the same time, its great flexibility, and its appeals, not so much to the reason, as to the lower instincts of the petty-bourgeois masses.

A constituent of fascist demagogy common to all countries is the cult of nationalism, of jingoism, the presentation of one's own people as the finest, the bravest, the noblest in the world, and of all other peoples as inferior, second-rate. That is why fascism is almost always a movement of the ruling nation in countries with mixed national groups. This demagogy is intended chiefly for the petty bourgeoisie. The peasant, who never leaves his native village as long as he lives and falls victim to the 'idiocy of rural life', the small-town artisan and small shopkeeper, with their narrow outlook, fixed by the limited extent of their economic relationships, and the government official who knows only the

---

292 See, for example, [Walther] Darré's book, *Das Bauerntum als Lebensquell der Nordischen Rasse*, Munich 1933, third edition.

room where he works, are especially susceptible to this narrow-minded patriotism and nationalism! (The big bourgeoisie pretends to be patriotic, but is always ready to change its 'fatherland', if business so requires; it is always ready to deliver munitions to any enemy of the fatherland, if only he pays a good price!)

Nationalism and patriotism lead to chauvinism, which is indispensable in the ideological preparation for war and as a counterweight to the revolutionary internationalism proclaimed by the proletariat. In many cases (Germany, Japan) nationalism and chauvinism are bound up with a special race demagogy[293] or with anti-semitism. However, anti-semitism is not a universal method of fascist demagogy. In Italy, for example, Fascism does not use it. In Poland, only one wing of fascism is anti-Semitic, while [Józef] Piłsudski[294] and his inner circle are friendly to the Jews. In Palestine there is a big Jewish fascist movement, which is directed against the Arabs and the revolutionary Jewish workers.

Everywhere, fascist demagogy makes use of the existing, historically determined ideology of the petty-bourgeois masses. In Japan, fascist demagogy ties itself to the traditional veneration of the monarch and the military virtues: in Austria, to Catholic fanaticism on the one hand, and to German nationalism on the other, etc.

Despite the elasticity of its demagogy, the *fascist movement has nowhere succeeded in penetrating the proletariat of the major industries*; at most it has been able to win over agricultural workers, domestic workers, youths and unemployed (partly because of the material advantages of membership in the Storm Troops). The National Socialists even tried to call a few strikes, taking part in the Berlin transport strike, but they could make no headway in the industrial working class.

This petty-bourgeois mass basis is fascism's principal weakness. Irresolute vacillations are characteristic of the petty bourgeoisie. Lenin said in this regard:

---

293   The concept of the 'race' is handled according to political circumstances. At one time it is the entire 'Aryan' race, which is set aside from all others, especially the 'Semites'; at another time it is the 'Teutons' who are superior to the Slavs. But since the French are largely descended from the Germanic race of Franks, the Germans are 'racially' sub-divided in turn, and the 'Nordic race' is placed above all the other peoples in the world. For the German fascists the Japanese are a '*noble race*' in contrast to the Chinese, while the Japanese themselves contrast the 'yellow race' with the white, the Asiatics with the Europeans, etc.

294   [Józef Klemens Piłsudski (1867–1935) was a Polish Chief State (1918–22) and leader of the Second Republic (1926–35)].

> ... [T]he small proprietor, the small master (a social type that is very widely represented in many European countries), who, under capitalism, suffers constant oppression and, very often an incredibly sharp and rapid worsening of conditions of life and even impoverishment, easily becomes extremely revolutionary, but is incapable of displaying perseverance, ability to organise, discipline and firmness. The petty bourgeois, in a 'frenzy' over the horrors of capitalism, is a social phenomenon which, like anarchism, is characteristic of all capitalist countries. The instability of such revolutionariness, its barrenness, its liability to become swiftly transformed into submission, apathy, fantasy, and even into a 'mad' infatuation with one or another bourgeois 'fad' – all this is a matter of common knowledge.[295]

And, in fact, the petty-bourgeois following of the National Socialists in Germany began to waver in the fall of 1932, even before the seizure of power, as the drop in the National Socialist vote showed. This, and the lack of any influence among the industrial proletariat proper, is the reason why the German big bourgeoisie hesitated so long before handing the government over to Hitler; and why in England, for example, only a few big capitalists support the fascist movement up to the present time. For the very reason that fascism everywhere has its mass basis in the constantly vacillating petty bourgeoisie, and not in the industrial proletariat, *it can never completely replace Social Democracy as the main social support of the bourgeoisie*. The greater the relative importance of the proletariat of the major industries in a given country, the more is this true.

This explains the efforts of the bourgeoisie, even after it has placed the fascists in the government, to call upon the collaboration of the Social Democrats at difficult moments, above all upon the reformist leaders of the trade unions. (The PPS[296] in Poland, D'Aragona[297] and Co. in Italy, the negotiations between the [Kurt] Schuschnigg government in Austria and the Social-Democratic leaders, and between the Hitler agents and Wels after the great fascist slaughter of 30 June 1934).

The fact that the rural and urban petty bourgeoisie serves as the mass basis for fascism, and that fascism makes use of anti-capitalist demagogy in its fight to win the masses, has in some cases led even Communists, as we know, to

---

295 Lenin 1964e.
296 [Polish Socialist Party: in Polish: Polska Partia Socjalistyczna, PPS].
297 [Ludovico D'Aragona (1876–1961) was a right-wing Italian trade-union leader. After the establishment of the fascist dictatorship (1922), he advocated the self-dissolution of the General Confederation of Labour].

fail to recognise its character as a tool of finance capital against the proletariat! Fascism was mistaken for an independent class movement of the petty bourgeoisie (the Right wing of the Communist Party of Poland), and even as a movement of the declassed intellectual *lumpen*-proletariat (Remmele).[298] Inadequate insight into the nature of fascism led to such serious errors as active support of Piłsudski's seizure of power by sections of the Communist Party of Poland (CPP). Such facts show how successful fascist demagogy is, and how essential it is to have a correct understanding of the class character of fascism in order to fight it successfully. Failure to recognise the real nature of fascism necessarily results in weakening the struggle against it. On the other hand, since the fascisisation of the bourgeois regime and of the bourgeois parties is a general phenomenon, and the rule of the bourgeoisie often takes on fascist characteristics step by step, the Communist Parties also made the error in many cases (KPD) of stating that a fascist dictatorship already existed, when only an increased fascisisation of the bourgeois regime was taking place. This, too, necessarily led to a weakening of the struggle against fascism, because the workers said to themselves that this fascism was not so very terrible, so that the struggle was diverted from the real fascist danger.[299]

To sum up: the mass ruin of the petty bourgeoisie in town and country, and the mass unemployment of the intellectuals, employees and the youth, provide the base for the fascist *mass movement*. An unscrupulous and elastic nationalist, chauvinist, and anti-capitalist demagogy, adapted to the separate strata of the population, serves to win the masses. Financial support by a few groups of the ruling classes makes it possible to organise a huge paid machine for propaganda, agitation and terror. Open or disguised co-operation with the state machinery of force[300] facilitates the terror campaign against the proletariat in general, and against the Communists in particular, even before the seizure of power. The split of the working class by Social Democracy, the latter's policy of step-by-step surrender, of avoiding every revolutionary class struggle (the

---

298 [Hermann Remmele (1880–1939) was a German Communist leader].
299 The renegades Trotsky and Thalheimer did everything they could to confuse the workers, by calling fascism 'Bonapartism': the rule of a clique which, based on the petty bourgeoisie and the *lumpen*-proletariat, governs against the bourgeoisie!
300 The kind of co-operation with the state machinery of force differs depending on the country. Japanese fascism is very closely connected and interlocked with military circles; we therefore speak of 'military fascism' in Japan. In other countries, such as Latvia, it is the conservative, governing parties which are fascisising the governmental machinery and themselves. This took a special turn in Austria, where the struggle between the two fascist camps – the pro-German, fighting for *Anschluss*, and the pro-Italian, fighting for an 'independent' Austria – to some extent undermined the state machinery of force itself!

theory of the 'lesser evil'), the terror employed against the Communists by Social-Democratic cabinets and government officials, in short, the fascisisation of Social Democracy (which is most glaringly manifested in defections and desertions to fascism), all pave the way for fascism. The mistakes of the Communist Parties, especially the inadequate or incorrect use of the united front tactic for mobilisation of the working masses against the danger of fascism, makes the victory of fascism easier.

But it would be the most fatal error if the counter-revolutionary theory that the victory of fascism is inevitable were to spread through all countries: the theory of a whole 'epoch of fascism'. This theory is equivalent to denying the general crisis of capitalism and the ripening of the revolutionary crisis. It declares that the struggle against fascism is hopeless, and it demoralises the masses. Therefore it must be combated most resolutely.

Fascism in Power

'In periods of acute crisis for the bourgeoisie', the *Programme of the Communist International* states, 'fascism resorts to anti-capitalist phraseology, but after it has established itself at the helm of state, it casts aside its anti-capitalist rattle and discloses itself as a terrorist dictatorship of big capital'.[301]

The reader is already familiar with this process of discarding the anti-capitalist trappings, from the history of Italian and German fascism. With Hitler, the toning down of his anti-capitalist phrases began to some extent even *before* the seizure of power. (Hitler's 1928 interpretation of Par. 17 of the National-Socialist party programme, according to which only 'land *that had been acquired unlawfully*' could (not must!) be subject to confiscation). On the other hand, it would be quite incorrect to interpret this point in the programme of the Comintern as meaning that fascism would discard the 'anti-capitalist rattle' *immediately after the seizure of power*. The seizure of power does not yet mean the 'consolidation of power'. Therefore fascism continues its anti-capitalist demagogy to some extent, even after the seizure of power.

Two opposed processes begin with the fascist seizure of power. On the one hand, the swift elaboration and ideological-organisational consolidation of the state machinery of force, which is cleansed of all 'unreliable' elements and fused with the fascist party machinery. At the same time, the regime's ability to manoeuvre increases as a result of the abolition of the parliamentary system (which had become a fetter) and it becomes more suitable for the thoroughgoing execution of finance capital's policies. On the other hand, with the

---

301 *Programme of the Communist International* 1929, p. 13.

seizure of power there begins the disillusionment of the urban and rural petty-bourgeois masses who had been deceived by fascist demagogy, and wait in vain, after fascism's seizure of power, for the fulfilment of its demagogic promises. Fascism's mass base begins to weaken. The big bourgeoisie therefore faces the danger that the disillusioned petty bourgeoisie may swing toward the side of the revolutionary proletariat and take part under the latter's leadership in the revolutionary struggle for the overthrow of the bourgeoisie.

The weakening of fascism's mass base after its seizure of power makes it more difficult to carry out its principal aim, 'the destruction of the revolutionary labour vanguard, i.e. the Communist sections and leading units of the proletariat'.[302] Fascism is therefore forced to do considerable manoeuvring, even after seizure of power, in order to retard the process of its followers' disillusionment, and if possible to isolate the Communist vanguard from the great mass of workers. Here we can mention only the most important forms of these manoeuvres:

- Providing jobs for their 'old' supporters in the state machinery, especially in the machinery of force; favouring their followers in the free professions by displacing the Jews (the *numerus clausus* in Hungary and Germany); preferential employment of unemployed fascist workers and clerks in the factories, and guaranteeing their jobs;[303]
- Expanding its mass base by favouring the rich peasants and the richer middle peasants at the expense of the great masses of middle and small peasants and the agricultural workers: the hereditary farmstead law, Mussolini's 'battle of grain', assigning unpaid farm hands, tax concessions, etc.;
- Certain concessions to its urban petty-bourgeois followers, at the expense of Jewish shopkeepers and artisans.

As for the proletariat, fascism, once in power, must limit itself, except for high-sounding phrases like 'restoration of the honour of labour' and the like, to minor manoeuvres (the demonstrative arrest of a few unpopular directors) and petty gifts: lengthening vacations and the period of giving notice for a few categories of workers, cheaper margarine for the unemployed, 'winter relief' and 'Hitler relief', cheaper moving-picture tickets, etc. – petty gifts, which of course

---

302   Ibid.
303   In this way a new type of 'labour aristocracy' develops, on the basis of chronic mass unemployment. This consists of workers who in general do not get any higher wages – like the real labour aristocracy – but who have the assurance that they will be the last to lose their jobs, and who therefore betray the working class to the bourgeoisie, serve as strike-breakers, denounce Communists, etc. In contrast to the real labour aristocracy, however, they are very largely isolated from the working masses in the shops, because their role as betrayers of the working class is rather obvious.

can effect no change in the enormously worsened position of the working class, and which for this very reason can have only a very transitory influence at most on those receiving them.

Once in power, fascism immediately sets up a *monopoly of legal ideological influencing of the population*. Schools, the press, radio, moving-pictures, the theatre and literature are placed completely in the service of fascist ideology, i.e. in the service of finance capital. All anti-fascist activity, and much more so, all Communist activity, is forbidden; all non-fascist organisations and parties are dissolved. Undoubtedly this monopoly of ideological influence must have a certain effect, especially upon the youth, when it lasts for a long time as in Italy, and is not counteracted by sufficiently strong illegal Communist work among the masses.

This process of setting up the fascist party's monopoly of the government machinery and of all legal political, organisational and ideological activity develops very unequally in different countries, according to the concrete historical conditions. In Italy, where fascism's mass base at the time of the seizure of power was very narrow, this process lasted a very long time. In Poland and Hungary, only the Communist Party is illegal; the bourgeois parties and Social Democracy adapted themselves to the fascist regime,[304] and are legal even though often persecuted. In Bulgaria, after various modifications in the regime, the other bourgeois parties were prohibited only this year! The National Socialist Party's monopoly in Germany of all legal activity was carried out at a very rapid rate by the liquidation of all bourgeois and Social-Democratic organisations.

Needless to say, the prohibition of parties does not destroy the classes they represent nor the latter's struggles, however much the fascists may shriek about the abolition of the class struggle and of 'Marxism'. The working class continues its class struggle illegally, as well as by using all legal possibilities, predominantly under the leadership of the Communist Parties. The conflict within the ruling classes and the disillusionment of the petty-bourgeois masses – who have been deprived of the opportunity for open expression – appear as the struggles of tendencies and cliques within the fascist party, in many cases – as in Germany on 30 June 1934 – turning into a mass murder of their own supporters.[305]

---

304 The SP of Hungary co-operates with fascism by supporting the foreign policies of the fascists, by not organising the agricultural workers and poor peasants, by leading the trade unions in a strictly reformist spirit, and by combating the Communists and delivering them into the hands of the police.

305 Hitler's mass murders of his own followers, as well as of prominent bourgeois persons such

The race between the disillusionment and revolutionising of the masses, and the elaboration on a party basis of a secure fascist state machinery of force for the suppression by the revolution, is characteristic of fascist dictatorship. The more severe the crisis of capitalism, the less are the possibilities for manoeuvring against the working class in general and against fascism's own supporters in particular, and the less willing is the big bourgeoisie to tolerate 'Left' manoeuvres. So much more clearly does the character of fascism appear as an unveiled terrorist dictatorship of finance capital, the more does the fascist party take on the character of a 'party of order', chiefly supported by the armed forces, and the greater does the role of the Communist Parties become (provided their policies are correct) as the leader of the masses in struggle for the overthrow not only of the fascist form of bourgeois dictatorship, but of bourgeois rule in general.

The fascist form of bourgeois dictatorship is historically the last form of bourgeois rule. A lasting return to the democratic form is made impossible by the increasingly monopolist character of capitalism, by the accentuation of class antagonisms during the period of general crisis (especially conditioned by the end of capitalist stabilisation), and by the nearness of war. This does not at all exclude the possibility that in some countries the open fascist dictatorship may be temporarily replaced by somewhat 'more democratic' form of monopoly capital's dictatorship. This is primarily what the Social-Democratic leaders in exile are aiming at. Even after their exile from the country they still try to serve the bourgeoisie as a reserve by nourishing democratic illusions in the working class, and offering it the prospect of automatic *'ruin'* of fascism as a result of the inner contradictions in the camp of the bourgeoisie. They thus endeavour to hold the working class back from revolutionary struggle against fascism, against bourgeois rule. The émigré Social-Democratic leaders tell the bourgeoisie rather frankly: 'We are always ready to resume our role as a bulwark against the proletarian revolution within the country itself, whenever you offer us the opportunity of doing so'.

The Communist Parties in the countries of open fascist dictatorship must therefore continue to wage a struggle on two fronts: against the fascists and against those Social-Democratic leaders who sabotage the revolutionary struggle against the bourgeoisie. With good Bolshevik organisation and leadership, this struggle must be victorious, and finance capital's fascist rule of force

---

as Schleicher, [Erich] Klausener [leader of the Catholic Action], etc., on 30 June 1934, has thrown a severe scare into the petty-bourgeois masses abroad and temporarily deterred sections of the bourgeoisie in other countries (as in England, for instance) from further support of the fascist movement.

must be replaced by the dictatorship of the proletariat. The victorious proletarian revolution, under the leadership of the only revolutionary world party, the Comintern, will overthrow the rule of the bourgeoisie, and will free the proletariat simultaneously from the yoke of capital and from the terror of the fascists.

12   The Fight for the United Front and Victory

Since 1921, in numerous resolutions, the Communist International has stressed the necessity for creating a united front of the proletariat in struggle against the bourgeoisie, instructing the Communist Parties to conduct the struggle for its realisation. (The earliest detailed document in this regard is the resolution of the Executive Committee of the Communist International adopted 18 December 1921).[306] The bases for this were the strivings of the working masses themselves towards unity for struggle, because they correctly ascribed their defeat in the first cycle of revolutions chiefly to the division of the working class, and they wanted to fight unitedly against the new attack by capital.

The resolution referred to above states: 'under the influence of the increasing attacks of capital there has awakened among the workers a spontaneous, literally irresistible striving for unity, which goes hand in hand with the gradual growth of confidence in the Communists among the masses of workers'.

It is not our task to give a history of the Communists' struggle for realisation of the unity of the working class, and of the tactical errors committed therein. We shall confine ourselves to the most important factors that make the struggle for unity more favourable at present, and are of importance for the prospects of revolutionary victory in the coming second round of revolutions.

The primary difficulty encountered by the struggle for unity of the working class in the first period was that most of the Communist Parties had just been founded, and therefore faced the necessity of demarcating themselves sharply from the reformists, primarily in order to make the workers understand why a new revolutionary party of the proletariat was absolutely essential. This sharp demarcation from the Social Democrats – the precise formulation of the fundamental conflict between the Communists, as the party of the revolution, and

---

306   'Theses on the united front of the proletariat and on relations to the worker adhering to the Second, 2½ and Amsterdam Internationals and to the workers supporting the Anarcho-Syndicalist organisations (Unanimuously adopted by the Executive Committee of the Communist International on December 28th, 1921)' 1922, *International Press Correspondence*, pp. 17–20.

the Social Democrats, as the party of reform, between the party of struggle for the overthrow of capitalism and the party for the defence of capitalism – was all the more necessary, since remnants of Social-Democratic ideology were still very strong within the Communist Parties themselves, and many former leaders of Social Democracy had come over to Communism only under the masses' pressure, against their inner conviction.

The Social-Democratic leaders fought the Communist Parties by painting them as splitters, demanding organisational unity as opposed to unity for struggle. They used the correct principle of unity and proletarian discipline as a pretext for demanding that the Communists reunite with the Social Democrats or at least refrain from all criticism before the broad working-class public, as a prerequisite for fighting unity – conditions which the Communists could not possibly accept and can never accept.

In the countries where a small Communist Party confronted a large Social-Democratic party (e.g. England, Austria and the Scandinavian countries), the argument was repeatedly advanced that the unity of the working class was already realised in the Social-Democratic party and that the necessary premises for a united front did not exist.[307]

In the period of relative stabilisation, the pressure of the workers for unity relaxed somewhat. Exploiting the tactical errors of the Communists, the Social-Democratic leaders had succeeded in strengthening their own ranks and building a wall between the Communist Party and the Social-Democratic workers, by excluding the active Communist workers from the trade unions and expelling many revolutionary workers from their party. The Social-Democratic leaders were aided in their fight against the Communists and against the united front by the Communist Parties' tactical errors: putting the Social-Democratic leaders on a plane with the Social-Democratic workers; calling all the Social Democrats social-fascists; and slogans such as those issued by Comrade [Fritz] Neumann[308] – 'Smash the trade unions', 'Smash the ADGB (German General Trade Union Federation)'.

Such tactical errors by the Communist Parties originated in a sectarian attitude toward the masses of workers. In many cases the difficulties of work in the

---

307 As recently as the 1932 convention of the Social-Democratic Party of Austria, Otto Bauer declared (*Arbeiter Zeitung*, 15 November 1932): 'As far as the united front of the proletariat is realisable at all, it is in Austria already realised in Austrian Social-Democracy. Those who have set about destroying the actually existing unity of the Austrian proletarian in order to negotiate regarding the united front later on ... are simply swindlers'. Bauer held that only international negotiations, between Moscow and Zürich, were of any use!

308 [Fritz Neumann (1902–37) belonged with Ruth Fischer to the KPD leftists].

trade unions led in practice to the organisation in some cases – as a substitute for this work rather than an extension of it – of special revolutionary trade unions, which for the most part did not attain a mass character and made struggle for trade-union unity more difficult.

The third period, the great economic crisis, the end of the relative stabilisation of capitalism, and more particularly the victory of fascism in Germany and Austria, brought a new sudden intensification of the working masses drive for unity in the struggle against fascism, and against the rule of the bourgeoisie in general. In 1933, the Social-Democratic leaders already had to initiate new manoeuvres because of the mass pressure, although in July 1932, when the Braun-Severing government of Prussia was expelled by von Papen,[309] and this much-touted 'commanding height' of German Social Democracy was razed by the bourgeoisie without song or ceremony, the SPD refused the KPD proposal for a general strike.

Even now the essence of its manoeuvres is the same: *organisational unity instead of unity for struggle*,[310] with renunciation of criticism by the Communists as a preliminary condition for common struggle. [Friedrich] Stampfer[311] (as well as Léon Blum)[312] demanded a 'non-aggression pact' between the Communists and the Social Democrats.[313] At the beginning of February 1933, the Centrist Parties (ILP, the Norwegian Workers' Party, the Dutch Independent Labour Party, the German Socialist Labour Party the French Proletarian Unity Party and the Polish Independent Labour Party) submitted a proposal to the Second International and the Communist International that negotiations be undertaken between the international organisations.

The Communist International, as is known, answered in a manifesto calling on all our parties to make proposals to the Central Committees of the parties affiliated to the Second International for joint, definite actions against fascism and against the offensive of capitalism.[314]

---

309   [Franz von Papen (1879–1969) was a German Conservative politician].
310   Some members of our parties, such as [Jacques] Doriot, [Josef] Guttmann (both expelled since then) and [Paul] Merker, acting on this basis, committed Right opportunist mistakes.
311   [Friedrich Stampfer (1874–1957) was a Czech Socialist journalist having become in 1931 editor of the German *Vorwärts*].
312   [Léon Blum (1872–1950) was leader of the French socialist party SFIO].
313   This was connected with a veiled attack on the Soviet Union, in that the statement was made that the Social Democrats were no worse than the governments of capitalist countries with which the Soviet Union concludes 'non-aggression pacts'.
314   The ECCI proposed the following points as a basis:
    '(a) The Communists and Social-Democrats are to commence at once to organise and carry out defensive action against the attacks of fascism and reaction on the political,

The Second International, in its answer (31 March 1933), on the contrary, 'urgently recommended' its affiliated parties to refrain from all separate negotiations with the Communist Parties in their countries, 'because only negotiations between the two Internationals as such can lead to an understanding'. In accordance with these instructions, the Central Committees of all the Social-Democratic parties rejected the offer of joint struggle, some politely, some rudely.

The meaning of this attitude is clear. The leaders of the Second International are afraid of negotiations in the several countries on concrete issues of struggle, because the Social-Democratic workers, with their intense urge towards unity and struggle, would exercise pressure on their leaders to this end. The gentlemen of the Second International would prefer to negotiate far away from the masses of workers, in genteel bureaucratic seclusion, in order to make an agreement impossible.

In 1934, the crisis of Social Democracy (which we discussed in the foregoing chapter) led to a break in the Second International's anti-unity front; the French Social-Democratic party was forced, much against the wishes of the Second International's leadership, to conclude the well-known united front agreement with the PCF. This was soon followed by the Italian SP (which is of little importance in view of the very slight following it possesses in Italy), and by the united front of the Communist Party of Poland with the 'Bund'. All the other parties, however, stubbornly persist in their refusal, and those participating in bourgeois governments or on the verge of such participation do so with special emphasis.

---

trade union, co-operative and other workers' organisations, on the workers' press, on the freedom of meetings, demonstrations and strikes. They are to organise common defence against the armed attacks of the fascist bands by carrying out mass protests, street demonstrations and political mass strikes; they are to proceed to organise committees of action in the factories, the labour exchanges and the workers' quarters, as well as to organise self-defence groups. (b) The Communists and Social-Democrats are to commence at once to organise the protest of the workers, with the aid of meetings, demonstrations and strikes, against any wage reductions, against attacks on the working conditions, against reduction of social insurance, against the cutting down of unemployment benefit, against dismissals from the factories. (c) In the adoption and practical carrying out of these two conditions the ECCI considers it possible to recommend the Communist Parties during the time of common fight against capital and fascism to refrain from making attacks on Social-Democratic organisations. The most ruthless struggle must be conducted against all those who violate the conditions of the agreement in carrying out the united front, as strike-breakers who disrupt the united front of the workers' ('For the United Front Against Fascism', *International Press Correspondence*, 9 March 1933, p. 262).

The most important reasons for the acceptance of the offer of common struggle in France were as follows: the ominous charge of the French fascists on 6 February 1934, which led to the fall of the [Édouard] Daladier[315] cabinet; the French Social Democrats' fear of sharing the fate of the German and Austrian Social-Democratic parties; the strength of the Paris organisation of the PCF, and the energy with which our French Party immediately mobilised the workers for a counter-attack against the fascist bands, thus drawing along with them a considerable section of the Social-Democratic workers. *Actually the united front from below had already been established to a considerable extent before the leadership of the French Social-Democratic Party finally decided to accept the offer of our Party for a united front*,[316] placing the leaders of the Second International in an extremely uncomfortable position.[317]

The French example clearly shows that in the present severe political, ideological and organisational crisis of Social Democracy, the Communist Parties – by placing themselves boldly and decisively at the head of the struggle, and by setting up demands and slogans whose correctness is apparent to the working masses – can establish a united front of the working masses from below in the struggle against fascism, in order to realise the slogan of 'Class Against Class' *and to compel the Social-Democratic leaders either to join in this united front or under the Communists' criticism to lose the remainder of their authority among the Social-Democratic workers*. It is obvious that unity of the proletariat

---

315 [Édouard Daladier (1884–1970) was leader of the French Radical Party].
316 The difficult position in which the leadership of French Social Democracy had been placed is apparent from the report of the *Populaire* on the meeting of the National Party Council on 15 July 1934.
317 On 22 July, the Brussels *Le Peuple* published an article by [Émile] Vandervelde (reprinted verbatim by the *Information Bulletin* of the Second International) which clearly reflects the difficult position in which the leaders of the Second International found themselves. Vandervelde writes: 'Let it be understood at the start that I am in complete agreement with Léon Blum, Paul Faure and [Jean-Baptiste] Lebas that it would have been morally impossible to decline this proposal flatly ... because the initiative for joint action, which was started in Paris after the February days, obviously satisfies the strongest feelings of the masses of workers, at least in the capital but not only must the decision or recommendation of the National Party Council in favour of the united front – which stands "at the edge of the International" – be immediately justified before the International, but the Socialist and Labour International [SLI] must at once concern itself with the entire problem. And here one must not be deceived – the matter will doubtless not run so smoothly in the Executive of the SLI as in the National Party Council of the French Socialists'. The remainder of the article is an effort to present the action of our French Party for unity as if it were action, not in the interest of the French proletariat, but of the foreign policy of the Soviet Union. Parenthetically, at the request of the French, discussion of the French question was tabled at the meeting of the Executive of the Second International.

in struggle can and must be established not merely on a political basis but also in trade-union struggles which under present-day conditions always tend to turn into political struggles.

The formation of the united front is taking place in a different way in Austria. The defeat suffered by the Austrian proletariat, despite the heroic struggle of the Schutzbündlers and the Communists, finally showed the Social-Democratic workers how incorrect and traitorous was the policy of the 'lesser evil' which Renner,[318] Seitz[319] and [Otto] Bauer continued even after Hitler's victory. The leadership has lost all authority. The Austrian Social-Democratic Party no longer exists as an organisational unit! Its very name is scorned by the workers. The best and most active Social-Democratic workers have joined together in a new illegal party, under the name 'Revolutionary Socialists'. The disillusionment of these revolutionary workers with their former leaders and their readiness to fight together with the Communists is evidenced in their well-known letter to the leadership of the Second International:

> The fascist dictatorship has smashed all the democratic and reformist illusions of the proletarian masses here. Today the workers know that the fascists' might can be broken only by the might of the proletariat ... The goal of the revolution (for the overthrow of fascism) cannot be other than the conquest of state power, the dictatorship of the proletariat. In the struggle against the fascist dictatorship there is no difference between the socialist workers and their Communist-organised class comrades. They have to endure the same persecutions and sufferings, and, as they have always aimed at the same goal, now, under the fascist dictatorship, there are no longer any antagonisms in the tactics of struggle.

This is the voice of *genuine Left Social-Democratic workers*, who, organised together with their functionaries, are on the road to Communism, who have lost faith in their own leaders but still have illusions with respect to the Second International – illusions that will also disappear rapidly.[320]

---

318 [Karl Renner (1870–1950) was an Austrian Social Democrat].
319 [Karl Seitz (1869–1950) was an Austrian Social Democrat].
320 The answer that Friedrich Adler 'as a private individual' gave the Revolutionary Socialists is in essence a defence of the 'policy of the lesser evil'.
  'One must understand that the labour movement uses two methods side by side, that of revolution and that of reform. One method or the other stands in the foreground, depending on the historic-economic conditions of a country. In fascist countries it is revolution, in democratic countries it is reform. If we undertake a rational division of labour, it will

After the armed uprising in Spain had been crushed, the Comintern addressed the Second International with a proposal to organise international united front activity against Spanish fascism in defence of the Spanish workers. The Second International rejected the proposal.

The movement among the workers to form the united front was, however, so strong that the *Executive Committee of the Second International, at its session in November in Paris, was unable to maintain its prohibition of the formation of the united front in various countries*. On this question – the most important of all for the fighting proletariat of the whole world – the Second International split. The social-democratic parties which are participating in bourgeois government or are preparing to do so (Great Britain, Denmark, Sweden, Belgium, Holland, etc.) still reject the united front, so as not to compromise themselves in the eyes of the bourgeoisie, nor to lose their 'eligibility' for participation in the government. On the other hand, a number of social-democratic parties (France, Spain, Italy, Austria, etc.) found it necessary to issue a declaration of their special standpoint, emphasising the necessity for negotiations between the Second International and the Comintern for the formation of the united front.

It would, of course, be a dangerous illusion to imagine that the social-democratic leaders, in those countries where unity for struggle has been formed at the present moment, will not try again to disrupt the united front when circumstances permit.

Favoured by the severe crisis in Social Democracy, the united front of the proletariat against fascism and against the rule of the bourgeoisie is being

---

be found that the two methods do not conflict, but complement each other. And thus the unity of action will be realised for each of the two methods'.

Instead of calling for the unity of all proletarian forces in struggle against fascism, Adler incites against the Communists libeling us in the most shameless manner, by accusing us of sabotaging the fight against fascism.

'It is not at all surprising that today, just as in 1919, many readily wavering elements, stunned by the events, go over to the Communists. If they were then motivated by the fantastic hope of the impending world revolution, now it is the boundless despair over the defeat we have suffered which is driving them into the arms of the Bolshevik belief in miracles. I can only say that, just as in 1919, I considered the Bolshevik perspective false, today I am convinced that it is a dreadful misfortune for the international labour movement *that the Bolsheviks still do not understand the conditions of struggle in the democratic countries*, and that, trapped by the delusion that fascism must be victorious everywhere, they themselves contribute to its advance by making the defensive struggle of the workers' parties more difficult – yes, and by sabotaging it'.

The revolutionary Austrian Social-Democratic workers did not succumb to the blandishments of this slanderer.

achieved in unrelenting struggle against those leaders of the Second International who are indissolubly linked with the bourgeoisie, and in the interests of capital *either strive to perpetuate the split of the working class or to realise unity in the form of organisational liquidation of the Communist Parties.* (Otto Bauer's article for another Hainfeld!).[321] Initial successes have been obtained but the struggle for a united front must be continued for a long time to come, with great patience, persistence and elasticity. With the Communist vanguard alone, without the united front of the proletariat, *without mobilising the great masses of Social-Democratic and non-party workers for the struggle to overthrow bourgeois rule, victory in the second round of revolutions now beginning is impossible*! The unity of the working class in struggle is not merely the premise for successful defence against fascism, but also for the victory of the proletarian revolution as a whole!

If the fight against the bourgeoisie is to be successful, the unity of the working class in struggle must be established not only in the political sphere, but in the trade-union field as well. It was never the aim of the Communists to establish special revolutionary trade unions. This was forced upon them by the trade-union bureaucracy which had formed a united front with the bourgeoisie and was systematically expelling the revolutionary workers from the trade unions with utter disregard for trade-union democracy. In this field, therefore, it would be possible to overcome the split at once through organisational reunion, provided the class struggle character of the trade unions is insured! Although the Communist Parties' relinquishing of their independence is out of the question of course, we have no objection in principle to an organisational merger of the trade unions, because the trade unions are fighting organisations of the whole working class, irrespective of the political views of the individual workers.

∴

The bourgeoisie and the proletariat are both preparing for the second round of revolutions on the basis of their experiences in the first. The factor of surprise (in the historical meaning of the word), which played a part in the first round, is now excluded. The seventeen-year history of the Soviet Union has eliminated faith in the invincibility of bourgeois rule, the belief that the capitalist order of

---

321　The 1892 [sic!] unity convention of the Austrian workers' parties. [On their congress held on 30 December 1888–1 January 1889 in Hainfeld, the Austrian Social Democrats adopted their programme].

society is the only possible one, the belief that the proletariat is not able to govern a country. Today the bourgeoisie in all countries knows that in the second round of revolutions, it must fight for its life.

The first round of revolutions developed out of the World War. (The Russian Revolution, which was rapidly maturing even before the outbreak of the World War, is perhaps an exception). Without the World War, the crisis in the ruling classes and the loss of their authority, especially in the defeated countries, would not have occurred at that time. Without the terrible suffering of the War, the mass revolt in Europe would not have taken place at that time – and both of these are necessary conditions for a revolution.

'The revolution', Lenin writes, 'was imminent in 1914–16, concealed in the womb of war, growing out of the war'.[322]

The main and decisive historic difference between the first round of revolutions and the maturing second round is that now the revolutionary crisis is maturing before the second rounds of war. It is possible, of course, that the second round of revolutions will coincide with the new world war and be interwoven with it. This is even probable. If the beginning of the world war or of a counter-revolutionary war against the Soviet Union precedes the revolution, undoubtedly the outbreak of the latter will be greatly accelerated. *But war is by no means an essential condition for the beginning of the second round of revolutions*, as it was in the first round. The circumstance that the revolutionary crisis is now maturing before the war, without war, is a consequence of the accentuation of antagonisms in the period of the general crisis of capitalism, a consequence of the extraordinarily severe economic crisis of the last five years. Viewed historically, the conditions for a victory of the proletarian revolution in the coming second round are therefore much more favourable than they were in the first round, even though there are a few unfavourable factors. Let us first consider the latter.

The factor of surprise (as stated above) is eliminated! The bourgeoisie is very consciously preparing for defence against the danger threatening it.

The bourgeois machinery of force, which at the beginning of the first round of revolutions had completely collapsed in the defeated countries and was considerably demoralised in the victor countries as well, is now considerably stronger. Fascisisation makes it possible to concentrate the power of govern-

---

322 Lenin, *On the Junius Pamphlet*, in *Collected Works*, Volume 29, Russian edition, p. 188. [In the fourth edition of Lenin's works: 'Revolution was on the order of the day in the 1914–16 period, it was hidden in the depths of the war, was emerging out of the war'. Lenin 1964d, p. 317].

ment in a few hands. Special reliable civil-war formations (secret police, armed fascist bands, etc.) serve in the struggle against the proletariat. This is not true of the armies as a whole (although there are also special civil-war detachments within the armies), which have already lost much of their reliability for the bourgeoisie because of the intensification of class antagonisms, and which in the event of general mobilisation would be largely permeated by revolutionary elements. The proletariat itself is disarmed to a great extent, whereas in the first round it still possessed many weapons from the imperialist war.

Finally, the influence that fascism temporarily exercises over large sections of the rural and urban petty bourgeoisie, instilling a counter-revolutionary spirit in them and mobilising them on the side of the bourgeoisie against the proletariat, is also an unfavourable factor.

But these unfavourable factors are outweighed by much more favourable factors.

The Revolutionary Role of the Soviet Union

The decisive factor among the favourable prerequisites for the victory of the proletarian revolution in the second round is the greatly increased revolutionising role of the Soviet Union.

During the first round of revolutions the Soviet Union had to cope with the greatest economic difficulties, partly because of the War and the Civil War and partly because of the inevitable 'overhead costs of the revolution'. That was the time when the world proletariat was called on for famine relief for the Soviet Union. Although the world proletariat energetically supported the Soviet Union in its struggle against intervention, the bourgeoisie and the Social Democrats were able, nonetheless, to take advantage of the Soviet Union's serious economic situation. The slogans of the bourgeoisie – 'It is impossible to keep production going without the bourgeoisie!' 'The dictatorship of the proletariat means hunger and suffering!' – did not remain without effect on the less class-conscious workers, checking the development of the prerequisite subjective conditions for a revolutionary crisis.

Now the situation has fundamentally changed. *The Soviet system has proved its superiority in the struggle of the two systems.* In the capitalist world, crisis and serious depression, the decline of production below the pre-war level; in the Soviet Union, the increase in production at the most rapid rate. In the capitalist world, chronic mass unemployment; in the Soviet Union, shortages of workers. In the capitalist world, mass ruin of the peasantry and degradation of agriculture; in the Soviet Union, the rise of the working peasantry on the basis of collectivisation and the rapid development of agriculture. Under capitalism, cultural decay everywhere; in the Soviet Union, mighty cultural progress. Under capitalism, the inescapable impoverishment of the masses; in the Soviet Union, joyous work on the clearly outlined road towards a classless society!

Under these conditions, the example of the Soviet Union has an incomparably greater revolutionising influence than during the first round of revolutions, on the industrial workers, as well as on the exploited sections of the peasantry throughout the entire world.

The Crisis in Social Democracy

The second decisive factor is the crisis in Social Democracy. Without the latter's aid it would have been impossible for the bourgeoisie (outside of Russia) to overcome the revolt of the masses during the first round. By soothing the masses of workers with fine phrases about socialisation, and by taking over the government, promising (and in part carrying out) various social reforms, it gave the bourgeoisie the respite it needed to reorganise its machinery of force. By splitting the working class and isolating the revolutionary Communist vanguard from the great masses of the workers, it enabled the bourgeoisie to repress the revolution by force.

Owing to the severe crisis in Social Democracy (see the preceding chapter) its influence is today much less than it was, with the exception of a few North European countries, and it is generally on the downgrade. In the next round it will by no means be able to play its counter-revolutionary role as the support of the bourgeoisie with the same success as in the first round. The more successful the Communist Parties are in their struggle for the united front, the less successfully will it be able to play this role.

The Change in the Nature of the Revolutionary Movement in the Colonies

During the first round of revolutions, the colonial revolutions developed almost exclusively under the hegemony of the bourgeoisie (Kemalism, Gandhi-ism, the Kuomintang under the leadership of Sun Yat-sen).[323] In the colonial revolutions during the first round, on the whole the proletariat played the role of a force subordinated to the bourgeoisie. Now the situation has fundamentally changed. The revolutionary struggles of the colonial peoples for emancipation are developing on the widest front, in South and Central America, as well as in Asia, taking on more and more the character of class struggles not only against the imperialists, but also against the national exploiters – the feudal landlords

---

323 [Sun Yat-sen (1866–1925) was a Chinese nationalist and founding father of the Republic of China].

and the bourgeoisie – who for their part turn more and more to the imperialists for protection against the revolting peasant masses.

Hegemony in the struggle for national liberation is shifting to the proletariat more and more. Communist Parties, trying to assure the hegemony of the proletariat in the movement, have arisen in almost all the colonies. Although the development of the subjective factor still lags far behind that of the objective factors of revolution, this change in the nature of the colonial liberation movement is nevertheless one of the most important factors making the outlook for a victory of the proletarian revolution in the coming second round more favourable than it was in the first.

This change in the character of the colonial liberation movement is reinforced by the successes of Soviet China in repulsing all the attacks of the better-armed Kuomintang troops, supported by the imperialists, and in improving the condition of the working masses (see *Chapter 9*).

The Revolt of the Peasantry in the Capitalist Countries

The agrarian crisis, which was scarcely mitigated by the transition to the depression of a special kind, led to a widespread revolt of the peasant masses. With the help of the fascist movement, the bourgeoisie has succeeded for the time being in diverting this revolt, which is really directed against capitalism, into a counter-revolutionary channel. But since the bourgeoisie and its fascist tools can in no way prevent the mass ruin of the toiling peasantry, it is primarily up to the correct work of the Communist Parties to turn these peasant masses, now in motion, into a revolutionary force, as the Russian Bolsheviks did. That the peasantry has entered into such tremendous activity is a favourable circumstance to the revolution.

The Progress of the Subjective Factor of the Revolution

The main reason for the defeat of the proletariat outside of the Soviet Union during the first round of revolutions was the weakness of the Communist Parties, which in part were sects without any mass influence, or (in some countries) mass parties with strong Social-Democratic vestiges. In many cases they were headed by persons who had come over to Communism temporarily, under the proletariat's pressure, and who returned to the camp of the proletarian revolution's enemies when the first wave of the revolution subsided. The Communist Parties did gain in experience during the first round itself, making advances towards Bolshevisation. But the progress in the development of the subjective factor during the revolution itself could not catch up with the impairment of the objective conditions for revolution. This was the principal reason for the defeat of the proletarian revolution in the first round.

One of the decisive factors for the better prospects of victory in the impending second round of revolutions is the process of Bolshevisation that has taken place in the Communist Parties during the last ten years. Although in many countries the Communist Parties are still very weak, and although there are still many inadequacies in several fields, particularly in work in the trade unions, in winning over the middle sections and in carrying out the struggle for unity, *it nevertheless cannot be doubted that the Communist Parties of today are somewhat different qualitatively from the Communist Parties in the first round.*

But even today, despite this progress of the Communist Parties in Bolshevisation, the development of the subjective factor still lags behind the development of the objective prerequisites. This is the reason why the proletariat has not succeeded in fighting through to the revolutionary way out of the economic crisis.

The revolutionary crisis is continuing to mature. But victory, the prerequisite conditions for which are much more favourable objectively than in the first round, depends primarily on the Communist Parties. *Victory must be fought for!* That is why we want to call Stalin's words to mind:

> Some comrades think that as soon as a revolutionary crisis occurs the bourgeoisie must drop into a hopeless position, that its end is predetermined, the victory of the revolution is assured, that all they have to do is to wait for the bourgeoisie to fall and to draw up victorious resolutions. This is a profound mistake! The victory of revolution never comes by itself. It has to be prepared for and won. And only a strong proletarian revolutionary party can prepare for and win victory. Moments occur when the situation is revolutionary, when the rule of the bourgeoisie is shaken to its very foundations and yet the victory of the revolution does not come, because there is no revolutionary party of the proletariat sufficiently strong and authoritative to lead the masses and take power. It would be unwise to believe that such 'cases' cannot occur.[324]

It is probable that in many countries the struggle for power during the next imperialist war will be very closely interwoven with it, in the form of changing the imperialist war into a civil war. The tasks of the Communist Parties will be tremendous and complicated. But the most important task is *to overcome the split in the working class, to establish the united font against the bourgeoisie. If this succeeds, the victory of the proletariat during the coming second round of revolutions and wars seems assured in s number of countries!*

---

324   Stalin 1955a, pp. 304–5.

Supplement: Computation of Surplus Value in American Industry

The data of the periodic census afford the opportunity of approximately computing the rate of surplus value in American industry. The following are available as elements in this computation:
- Total wages paid = v
- Cost of raw material = circulating c
- Cost of wear and tear of machinery = fixed c
- Value of products = w

For exact computation the following are lacking:
1. The value of wear and tear of that part of fixed capital invested in buildings; but this part is so comparatively slight that it can be neglected in this necessarily rough computation.
2. One very important element is missing, however, i.e. the total commercial profit, which constitutes a split-off part of the surplus value produced in industry. For according to the Marxian theory of value, industrial capital does not turn commodities over to commercial capital at the full production price, but below it, at a price enabling commercial capital to realise the average rate of profit on its own capital by selling the commodities at their production price. Hence, the profit of commercial capital is therefore contained in the surplus value produced in industry, and, therefore, if one is to find the actual rate of surplus value, it must be added to the surplus value produced in industry. But the data necessary for that purpose are not available.

The rate of surplus value computed in the table below is therefore considerably lower than it actually is in reality.

With these reservations in mind the following table can be computed:

TABLE 12.91 Rate of surplus value

	I Total wages (= v)	II Cost of raw material (= circulating c)	III Wear and tear of machinery (= fixed c)	IV (= I+II+III+V) Value of products (= w)	V Total surplus value (= m)	VI (= V) I
1899	2,008	6,576	250	11,407	2,573	128
1904	2,610	8,439	330	14,618	3,239	124
1909	3,427	12,065	500	20,450	4,458	130
1914	4,068	14,278	600	23,988	5,042	124
1919	10,462	37,233	1,600	62,042	12,747	122
1921	8,202	25,321	1,400	43,653	8,730	106
1923	11,009	34,706	1,800	60,556	13,041	118
1925	10,750	35,936	2,300	62,714	13,748	128
1927	10,849	35,133	2,300	62,718	14,436	133
1929	11,621	38,550	2,600	70,435	17,664	158
1931	7,226	21,420	2,100[325]	41,333	10,587	147

Data expressing the total value of the machinery utilised in industry were available for computing the depreciation of machinery:[326]

TABLE 12.92 Depreciation of machinery (millions of dollars)

1900	1904	1912	1922
2,541	3,298	6,091	15,783

In accordance with commercial usage we have assumed a yearly depreciation of 10 percent of the value, extending the data by interpolation to the years

---

325   The decrease in the amounts set aside for amortisation of machinery reflects (as in 1921) the decrease in prices of machinery as well as reduced actual amortisation as a result of the standstill of large parts of the production apparatus.

326   Taken from the government publication, *Wealth, Public Debt, and Taxation* 1924, p. 18.

not given, under the basic assumption that the value of machinery rises more rapidly than the value of production, corresponding to the rise in the organic composition of capital.

In studying this table, the major fact deduced is that the 100 percent rate of surplus value accepted by Marx (which was generally declared to be quite exaggerated) is exceeded in American industry. At the same time it must be emphasised again and again that this rate of surplus value is lower than it actually is, since commercial capital's share in profits, which is also produced in industry, is not expressed here.

We expressly emphasise that *this is merely a very rough attempt at an approximate determination of the rate of surplus value on the basis of inadequate data, doubtless deviating considerably from actual reality*. We can only say that this deviation tends towards too low a figure for the actual rate of surplus value.

Addendum

On page 167 after the words '... illusions that will also disappear rapidly'.

The formation of the united front between the Communists and social democrats in Spain took place in a different way in the joint heroic armed struggle (while the anarcho-syndicalists, as we know, betrayed the Spanish revolution).

After the armed uprising in Spain had been crushed, the Comintern addressed the Second International with a proposal to organise international united front activity against Spanish fascism in defence of the Spanish workers. The Second International rejected the proposal.

The movement among the workers to form the united front was, however, so strong that the Executive Committee of the Second International, at its session in November in Paris, was unable to maintain its prohibition of the formation of the united front in various countries. On this question – the most important of all for the fighting proletariat of the whole world – the Second International split. The social-democratic parties which are participating in bourgeois government or are preparing to do so (Great Britain, Denmark, Sweden, Belgium, Holland, etc.) still reject the united front, so as not to compromise themselves in the eyes of the bourgeoisie, nor to lose their 'eligibility' for participation in the government. On the other hand, a number of social-democratic parties (France, Spain, Italy, Austria, etc.) found it necessary to issue a declaration of their special standpoint, emphasising the necessity for negotiations between the Second International and the Comintern for the formation of the united front.

It would, of course, be a dangerous illusion to imagine that the social-democratic leaders in those countries where unity for the struggle has been formed at the present moment, will not try again to disrupt the united front when circumstances permit.

Erratum

P. 17 et seq. The sign 'm' is used to denote surplus value. In English 's' is more usually used, as is done in the authorised translation of *Capital*.

PART 3

The General Crisis of Capitalism (1939–64)

CHAPTER 13

The Imperialist Struggle for a New Redivision of the World

Never has human history been so rich in events, nor the succession of social formations so rapid as in the last century.[1] This will be clear if we picture the world as it was a hundred years ego.

In 1840, the capitalist mode of production was already in the main the dominant one in the majority of the countries of the world. But the capitalist system had reached its highest development in several of the countries of Western Europe and in the United States of America; only in these countries had the bourgeoisie won political power and established a political regime answering to the interests of the capitalist mode of production.

Germany was still split up into 36 States, each with strong survivals of feudalism, its own currency and customs duties and its own laws. In the 1867 Preface to *Capital*, Marx said of continental Europe, contrasting it to England, as follows:

> ... We, like all the rest of Continental Western Europe, suffer not only from the development of capitalist production, but also from the incompleteness of that development. Alongside of modern evils, a whole series of inherited evils oppress us, arising from the passive survival of antiquated modes of production, with their inevitable train of social and political anachronisms. We suffer not only from the living; but from the dead. *Le mort saisit le vif!*[2]

The Habsburg monarchy on the Danube was a feudal absolutism in every respect. Italy was partly split up into a multiplicity of tiny States, and was partly under the foreign yoke of the Habsburgs. In Russia, serfdom and the tsarist autocracy continued in full sway. In Turkey, which at that time embraced all

---

1 [Originally published in *Bolshevik* (Moscow), 1940, 9: 9–18. English translation in *The Labour Monthly* (London), 1940, 22, 11 (November): 578–88, and in the *Daily Worker* (New York), 27, 28, 29 and 30 August 1940. German translation in *Die Kommunistische Internationale* (Stockholm), 1940, 21: 377–88].
2 [Marx 1954, p. 9].

Asia Minor, Northern Africa and the Balkans, a feudal system prevailed, headed by a military-clerical chief in the person of the Sultan. Japan, which was still completely cut off from the outer world, was partly under the sway of a pre-feudal system. As to Asia, with the exception of India and Africa, only its outskirts had been opened up by the capitalist powers of Europe.

Capitalist technique was still very primitive seen through the eyes of today. Textiles were the predominant branch of capitalist industry. In all Europe there were only 3,000 kilometres of railways, while in Asia and Africa there were no railways at all. Electricity, gas, automobiles and the chemical industry were still unknown.

But those were times of unhampered technical development of technology, of free competition and falling prices. Marx and Engels wrote in 1848, in the *Communist Manifesto*, that '[t]he cheap prices of its [the bourgeoisie's – E.V.] commodities are the heavy artillery with which it batters down all Chinese walls, with which it forces the barbarians' intensely obstinate hatred of foreigners to capitulate'.[3]

The cyclical movement of capitalist reproduction and the periodical crises of overproduction had already begun in Western Europe. But the rapid expansion of the capitalist market as the result of the conversion of the peasants, who had hitherto maintained a self-sufficient economy, into purchasers and producers of commodities facilitated and expedited the passing of the crises.

It was a time when capitalism still signified progress and the rapid development of productive forces. It may still have seemed to the bourgeoisie that its special class interests coincided with the interests of society in general. Hymns of praise were sung to capitalism.

But amidst the chorus of eulogisers of capitalism, discordant notes, the warning voices of accusers and doubters, like Sismondi[4] and the utopians, could already be detected. In England the mass movement of the Chartists had already arisen and was criticising the capitalist evil. But the man who was destined to discover the inherent laws of the capitalist mode of production and its historical transitional character – Karl Marx – was then, in 1840, still a student at the Berlin University.

It was a time when England was indisputably the leading capitalist country, the 'workshop of the world', the mistress of the seas, a country which fought for its interests by the hand of foreign mercenaries, by the hand of other nations. England's hegemony had already lasted for about half a century.

---

3 [Marx 1976, p. 488].
4 [Jean Charles Léonard Sismonde de Sismondi (1723–90)].

This was the 'comparatively peaceful' era of capitalism, as Lenin called it. Since the struggle for markets was chiefly waged by means of cheap prices, it was enough for British capital to open new trading ports in other countries. There was no need for it to conquer these countries outright. Even as late as 1852, Disraeli,[5] the British Conservative Prime Minister, declared: 'The colonies are millstones around our necks'.[6]

∴

But 60 years later, in 1900, the world presented an entirely different picture. The capitalist mode of production had brought the whole world under its sway. At the same time, the character of capitalism itself had changed. By virtue of its inherent laws of development, capitalism of the period of free competition had been converted into monopoly capitalism, imperialism. The transition to imperialism had been attended by profound changes, with which the reader will be familiar from Lenin's brilliant work, *Imperialism, the Highest Stage of Capitalism*. We shall only dwell on the factors which have a direct bearing on the wars for the redivision of the world.

Combined in monopolies, finance capital seeks to secure maximum profits not so much by increasing the sale of commodities at low prices, as was the case in the period of free competition, as by high monopoly prices. This is attainable only by the artificial restriction of supply, by the elimination of free competition. For this purpose, associations of employers are first of all formed in the various branches of production in each country; after this, foreign competition is eliminated, or at least weakened, by the introduction of protective tariffs; the 'home market' is protected so as to allow only home monopoly capital access to it. In some cases the monopolistic combines of the stronger imperialist power share up the world's markets and form international cartels.

But owing to high monopoly prices, the capacity of the home market is insufficient for capital, which accordingly experiences a need for foreign markets. And as the finance capital of all imperialist countries is striving for the same end, competition, ousted from the home market, is resumed in the foreign market and in an even more acute form, the form of dumping, that is, the sale of commodities abroad at below the cost of production, and sometimes even below self-cost. Only a monopoly of foreign markets makes it possible to sell

---

5 [Benjamin Disraeli (1804–81)].
6 Lenin 1964e, p. 256.

goods abroad, too, at high monopoly prices. Consequently, monopoly capital, unlike the capital of the time of free competition, strives to bring foreign countries *under its political sway*, to transform them into colonies, to redivide the world among the imperialist powers in order to safeguard their monopoly in the markets.

There is one other reason that induces monopoly capital to subjugate other countries.

The high superprofits accumulate in the hands of the monopolistic combines in the form of money. This newly accumulated capital cannot find a fruitful field of investment in one or another branch of production in the home country, for if it did the production and supply of goods would exceed the capacity of the market (in view of the high prices imposed by the monopolies), which would lead to a fall in prices. Hence the tendency to export capital to countries capitalistically still undeveloped, where 'profits are usually high, for capital is scarce, the price of land is relatively low, wages are low, raw materials arc cheap'.[7]

But in order to invest its capital profitably in a foreign, backward country and to compel the native population to work as wage labourers, the financial oligarchy needs a guarantee of the security of its property and the right to dispose of the labour power of the natives. That is achieved best of all by conquering and enslaving the backward country, by converting it into a colony. And so, the export of capital is a stimulus to the imperialist policy of conquest.

An industrial monopoly is best guaranteed against the appearance of new competitors when the sources of raw material required for the production of its goods are its own exclusive property. Hence the hunt for sources of raw material all over the world, often enough not so much for the exploitation of these source as to prevent them falling into the hands of competitors, present or future.

How is the monopoly of sources of raw material to be secured? The best way is for the imperialist power concerned to seize the country in which these sources lie and convert it into its own colony or semi-colony. The hunt for sources of raw material is therefore another stimulus to the imperialist policy of conquest.

But as the financial oligarchies in all imperialist countries pursue a similar policy of conquest, wars among the imperialist marauders for periodical redivisions of the world are inevitable.

---

7 Lenin 1964e, ch. 6.

During the last quarter of the nineteenth century, parallel with the transition to monopoly capitalism, another highly important change was in progress among the imperialist countries: as a result of the law of unevenness of capitalist development, Great Britain was overtaken by two of her competitors – Germany and the United States of America – who ousted her from her monopoly position as the 'workshop of the world'. Here are a few figures in illustration:

TABLE 13.1 Production of coal, iron, steel and cotton in Great Britain, the USA and Germany

	Production			
	Coal (millions of tons)	Iron (1,000 tons)	Steel (1,000 tons)	Cotton (1,000 tons)
1850				
Great Britain	49.0	3,200	–	640
USA	6.3	564	–	–
Germany	5.2	208	6	18
1870				
Great Britain	110.0	6,000	200	1,100
USA	29.5	1,665	69	263[†]
Germany	26.4	1,391	170	81
1900				
Great Britain	225	9,000	4,900	1,540
USA	241	13,789	10,188	875
Germany	109	8,521	6,646	307
1913				
Great Britain	287	10,300	7,700	1,920
USA	509	31,900	31,301	1,307
Germany	190*	19,300	18,329	487

* Plus 87,000,000 tons of brown coal.
[†] Figures for 1871.
SOURCE: VARGA 1937

As we see, Great Britain which, in 1870 still far surpassed her competitors in all the more important branches of production, by the end or the nineteenth century had been overtaken and outstripped by her competitors – Germany and the United States – in all branches except the textile industry, whose importance had relatively diminished compared with heavy industry. This particularly applies to the highly important 'new' branches of industry, of which figures are not available for purposes of comparison. But it may be safely said that Germany had surpassed Great Britain in every branch of the chemical industry, and that the United States as well as Germany had surpassed her in the machine-building industry. There can be no doubt that on the eve of the first world imperialist war, both German and American capitalism, if we take only their power at home, were much stronger than British capitalism.

But the possession of colonies did not keep pace with the development of the internal strength of the leading capitalist powers. Significant in this respect are the figures cited by Lenin in *Imperialism, the Highest Stage of Capitalism*.[8]

TABLE 13.2 Colonial possessions of the imperialist powers on the eve of the World War of 1914

	Great Britain	France	Germany	Russia	USA	Japan
Territory (millions of sq. km)	33.5	10.6	2.9	17.4	0.3	0.3
Population (millions)	393.5	55.5	12.3	33.2	9.7	19.2

The size of the population of the colonies is, of course, economically more important than their territory, which may, as was the case with Germany's African colonies, consist chiefly of sterile deserts. We find that the population of the colonies exploited by British imperialism was three times as large as the population of all the colonies of the other five Great Powers together!

In particular, the colonial possessions of Germany and the USA, which had economically outstripped Great Britain in the last quarter of the nineteenth century, did not at all correspond to the economic, military and political might of these two powers.

---

8 Lenin 1964e, Chap. 6.

Actually, British capital occupied an even more privileged position. In addition to its own colonies, it intensively exploited those belonging to the small states, especially the Portuguese colonies in Africa and the Dutch colonies in Asia. In the 'semi-colonies' (China, Turkey, Persia) whose population Lenin estimates at 361,200,000, as well as in a number of the South American 'dependant' countries like Argentina and Uruguay, Great Britain had vast capital investments and powerful economic and political interests. According to the laws of imperialism, such a state of affairs was bound to raise the problem of a forcible redivision of the world.

At that period American finance capital was by no means as interested in a redivision of the world as German finance capital. The vast territory of the USA abounded in sources of raw material of all kinds: coal, oil, ore, cotton, etc. Part of the arable area was still uncultivated. Neither was there any particular urge to export capital, as it could be quite profitably invested at home. Consequently, there was no 'superfluous' capital in the United States; on the contrary, right up to the First World War, America imported capital, and at the time of the outbreak of the war owed some US$ 7,000 million to other countries, including US$ 4,000 million to Great Britain.[9]

What American monopoly capital needed most of all was additional sources of cheap labour power. These it acquired not in the way the imperialist states of Europe did – by exporting capital to colonial countries where labour was cheap – but by importing millions of immigrant workers from all parts of the world. This influx of immigrants, or new consumers of goods, made possible the constant and extensive enlargement of the home market. Hence the export of goods was not as important for the USA as for the European countries. The United States exported less than 10 percent of its output, whereas Great Britain, France and Germany exported approximately 23 or 25 percent.

Quite different was the position of German monopoly capital. Germans had no sources of the highly important raw materials, such as oil, non-ferrous metals, textile staples and fats, on her own territory; she also lacked foodstuffs. In order to import all these Germany had to export large quantities of her industrial manufactures, and this brought her into conflict with the colonial monopoly of the imperialist powers, especially that of Great Britain.

The apologists of British imperialism, of course, never tired of asserting that in accordance with the 'most favoured nation' principle the British colonies were opened to the trade and the capital of all countries on an equal footing with those of Great Britain. Formally speaking, this was correct, but actually

---

9 Lewis 1938.

it was far from the case. The building of railways and ports, electrification, the supply of rolling stock and the exploitation of sources of raw material in the British world empire were virtually a monopoly of British capital. Unless he has the 'protection' of the authorities, no capitalist can secure in the colonies the labour power he needs. British capital likewise controlled the shipping, the banks and the credit system of the colonies. It was very hard for 'foreign' capital to find any profitable field of investment in the British or French colonies.

Quite different was the case in the colonial possessions of states which were poor in capital. While Tsarist Russia was engaged in colonial conquest in Manchuria and Central Asia, the raw material resources of the Ukraine and of Baku were being intensively exploited by British, French and Belgian capital. Russia had become entangled in debt to the Western Powers and was dependent on them.

The English have always been fond of asserting that the Germans may acquire in the market the raw materials secured in the British Colonies on the same terms as British merchants. The British imperialists pretend to be oblivious of the fact that even so the colonial superprofits derived from the production of raw materials remain in the pockets of the British colonial capitalists.

The contradictions between the economic might of German monopoly capitalism (which in 1913 had undoubtedly far outstripped Great Britain), and the fact that the colonial population under its sway amounted to only 3 percent of the population of the British colonies must be borne in mind when elucidating the causes that gave rise to the first World Imperialist War, Great Britain's reply to Germany's attempt to create her own colonial empire in Asia Minor (nominally under the rule of Turkey)[10] by building a railway from Berlin to Baghdad was to encircle Germany. Great Britain concluded military treaties with France, Japan and, in 1907, Russia, with which she had never found herself in the same camp ever since the Napoleonic wars. (Tsarist Russia felt that Germany's advance was a menace to her colonies in Central Asia and to her claims to Constantinople).

British diplomatic intrigues had prepared the way for Italy's desertion of Germany and for the adhesion of the United States to the British bloc. The First

---

10   That German finance capital chose this particular territory for the foundation of a colonial empire was not fortuitous. Whereas Germany possessed a more powerful army, England enjoyed superiority on the high seas. Colonial seizures in overseas countries would have met with the resistance of the British Navy, whereas Asia Minor could be reached by internal waterways led through Austria-Hungary and the Balkans.

World Imperialist War was essentially a war between Germany and Great Britain for colonial possessions. As Lenin said, the problem of colonial possession was decided on the battlefields of Europe.

The issue of the war was not in Germany's favour. Under the Versailles Peace she lost even those not very valuable colonies which she had possessed before the war; large pieces were cut off from her European territory, and a huge burden of reparations was imposed on her. All this was done with the object of preventing German capitalism from ever recovering and becoming a competitor of equal strength to Britain. Turkey was deprived of all her regions that had a non-Turkish population. Great Britain rounded out her colonial empire in Africa, obtained a straight road from Cape Town to Cairo, and established new lines of communication with India through Arabia and Iraq. Such a division of the world was even more advantageous to Britain and France than the one that had existed before the World War. Italy was left out in the cold.

The nations under the colonial yoke of Tsardom were liberated by the Great October Socialist Revolution. Turkey, Persia and Afghanistan, with the aid of the Soviet Union, largely or entirely shook off their dependence on imperialism.

As a result of the first imperialist world war and the changes that had directly sprung from it, the relation of forces by the time of the outbreak of the second imperialist war was as follows:

TABLE 13.3 Colonial possessions of the Great Powers (millions of km² and millions of inhabitants, 1932)

	Colonies		Home countries		Total	
	Area	Pop.	Area	Pop.	Area	Pop.
Great Britain	34.9	466.5	0.25	46.2	35.1	512.7
France	11.9	65.1	0.55	42.0	12.45	107.1
Germany	–	–	0.47	64.8	0.47	64.8
USA	0.3	14.6	9.4	124.6	9.8	139.2
Japan (without newly conquered provinces of China)	0.3	28.0	0.4	65.5	0.7	93.5
Total – five Great Powers	47.4	574.2	11.07	343.1	58.42	917.3
Colonies of other Powers (Belgium, Holland, Denmark, Italy, Spain, Norway and Portugal)	9.6	87.6	–	–	9.6	87.6

TABLE 13.3 Colonial possessions of the Great Powers (*cont.*)

	Colonies		Home countries		Total	
	Area	Pop.	Area	Pop.	Area	Pop.
Semi-colonies and dependent countries (Arabia, Bhutan, Nepal, Siam, Central and South American countries, Abyssinia and Liberia)	–	–	–	–	34.9	150.0
Countries fully or mainly liberated from imperialist dependence (China, Turkey, Persia and Afghanistan)	–	–	–	–	3.0	480.7
Other countries (capitalist)	–	–	–	–	3.98	224.1
USSR	–	–	–	–	21.2	163.2
Mongolia and Tuva People's Republic	–	–	–	–	1.4	1.6
The World	–	–	–	–	132.5	2,924.5

Table 13.3 shows that Great Britain's superiority in the colonial world had become even greater than before the First World War. Great Britain had over 466 million colonial people under her sway (a small part of this number – the inhabitants of Canada, Australia, New Zealand and part of South Africa, a total of about 20 million – are English; they are not colonial people in the true sense of the word, but they are in a state of economic and financial dependence on England), while France, the USA and Japan together had only 108 million until she conquered Abyssinia, Italy's colonies – were only of slight value; Germany had no colonies at all.

∴

Since the First World War, the importance of colonies to the monopoly capital of the imperialist powers has increased. The general crisis of capitalism, which was still in an embryonic state before the World War, has now developed to the full. In all capitalist countries, the contradiction between the tendency of capital to extend production, on the one hand, and the relative restriction of the markets, on the other, has grown more acute. Hence the chronic idleness of a large share of production capital, chronic mass unemployment and a chronic redundancy of loan capital.

The finance capital of the imperialist powers is seeking a way out of the situation by strengthening its monopoly in its colonial markets, which is clearly shown by the following figures, borrowed from G. Clark's *The Balance Sheets of Imperialism*.[11] This tendency has markedly developed in the past six years.

TABLE 13.4   Great Britain's trade with her colonial empire (percentage of total trade)

	1904–13	1919–28	1929–34
Import	25.7	33.0	32.9
Export	34.8	40.5	44.6

TABLE 13.5   France's trade with her colonial empire (percentage of total trade)

	1904–13	1919–28	1929–34
Import	10.6	10.8	16.4
Export	12.4	14.9	24.1

These figures quite clearly reveal the rapidly increasing importance to these countries of their own colonies as markets, and show why wars for colonies, for a new redivision of the world, are inevitable in the era of imperialism in general, and in the period of the general crisis of capitalism in particular.

This increase in trade with the colonies was achieved by the abandonment of the 'most favoured nation' principle and the introduction of tariffs for the protection of English goods in the colonies and of colonial goods in England. Trade between the component parts of the British Empire had likewise increased.

The most complete monopoly is that of Japan in the Korean market. In 1936, of Korea's total imports amounting to 762 million yen, 717 million yen came from Japan and Manchuria, and of total exports amounting to 593 million yen,

---

11   Clark 1936.

goods to the value of 518 million yen were exported to Japan and of 56 million yen to Manchuria.[12] An almost one hundred percent monopoly.

We find the contradiction between the economic might of the monopoly capital of Germany and of Great Britain, on the one hand, and their colonial possessions, on the other – which was one of the chief causes of the First World War – reproduced in a far more acute degree two decades later.

The plan of the British and French finance oligarchy to hold their dangerous competitor – German finance capital – in a state of permanent economic suppression suffered a fiasco. It did so owing to the inherent laws of the capitalist mode of production, owing to the rivalry between Great Britain and France and the rivalry between Great Britain and the United States.

Notwithstanding the predatory Versailles peace imposed on Germany, notwithstanding the heavy burden of reparations, German capitalism entered a new phase of progress, partly with the help of American and British loan capital. By 1938, German capitalism had again taken first place among the capitalist countries of Europe, which is incontrovertibly proved by the following figures quoted in the *League of Nations Year Book* for 1938–9:

TABLE 13.6 Output of coal. Brown coal, iron, steel aluminium and electricity in 1938

	Germany	Great Britain	France
Coal (millions of tons)	186	232	47
Brown coal (millions of tons)	195	–	–
Iron (millions of tons)	18.6	6.9	6.0
Steel (millions of tons)	23.2	10.6	6.2
Aluminium (thousands of tons)	160	23	45
Electricity (billions of kilowatts)	55	25	19

These figures show that Germany has again considerably outstripped her European rivals economically. As is inevitable under capitalism, economic development was accompanied by growing military power. The measures that had been taken to limit German armaments ceased to be effective and by 1939 Germany again possessed a powerful army and a stronger air force than any capitalist country in the world. Between the economic and military might of German capitalism, on the one hand, and its total lack of colonial possessions on the

---

12   Rösner (ed.) 1939, p. 291.

other, there was a similar if not more acute contradiction than in 1914. German monopoly capital began to demand an appropriate share in the exploitation of colonies. As in 1914, the reply of the British bourgeoisie was a new attempt to encircle Germany.

The importance of colonies as sources of raw material has grown considerably since the First World War. The British Empire's monopoly of certain raw materials, such as nickel, tin and rubber (the monopoly of rubber is shared by Great Britain and Holland), has become the source of vast superprofits. With the progress of technology, such rare metals as manganese, chromium and molybdenum have become indispensable to modern metallurgy.

How true today is what Lenin wrote 24 years ago!

> ... [M]onopolies are most firmly established when *all* the sources of raw materials are captured by one group, and we have seen with what zeal the international capitalist associations exert every effort to deprive their rivals of all opportunity of competing, to buy up, for example, ironfields, oilfields, etc. Colonial possession alone gives the monopolies complete guarantee against all contingencies in the struggle against competitors, including the case of the adversary wanting to be protected by a law establishing a state monopoly. The more capitalism is developed, the more strongly the shortage of raw materials is felt, the more intense the competition and the hunt for sources of raw materials throughout the whole world, the more desperate the struggle for the acquisition of colonies.[13]

Alongside the economic importance of the colonial sources of raw material, their strategic importance is now greater than ever before. Oil, iron ore, nonferrous metals, rare metals, rubber and many other kinds of raw material are indispensable for the conduct of modern warfare.

The bourgeoisie of the imperialist countries which lacked colonies suffered politically as well as economically. With the development of the general crisis of capitalism, the growing acuteness of the class struggle between the bourgeoisie and the proletariat, the formation of strong Communist parties in the capitalist countries, and the stimulus furnished to the revolutionary working-class movement all over the world by the progress of socialist construction in the USSR, it has become more important than ever to the bourgeoisie to have a buttress within the working class in the shape of a bribed labour aristocracy. Only when

---

13   Lenin 1964e, p. 260.

this social basis of opportunism in the working-class movement existed could Social Democracy play its traditional role as the main social buttress of the bourgeoisie. But to maintain a labour aristocracy, colonial superprofits, foreign capital investments and the brutal exploitation of defenceless colonial peoples were required.

The possession or lack of colonies explains the difference in the position of the Social-Democratic parties in the various capitalist countries today. Two sharply defined groups of countries have arisen in the past ten years. The first group consists of the 'rich' countries, the countries with extensive colonial possessions and huge capital investments abroad and with a corrupt labour aristocracy at home: Great Britain, France, Holland, Belgium and the Scandinavian countries (the latter do not possess large colonies and, with the exception of Sweden, have no foreign capital investments, but they are to a large extent appendages and satellites of the British Empire). In all the countries of this group, the Social Democrats are a legal mass party, are represented in the bourgeois coalition governments, and continue to be the main social buttress of the bourgeoisie. But Social Democracy is encountering the growing resistance of the working class, a result of the activities of the Communist parties.

The second group consists of the 'poor' countries, countries with no foreign investments and with no, or only very small, colonial possessions: Germany, Italy, Spain, etc. The bourgeoisie of these countries is not in a position to maintain a labour aristocracy large enough to guarantee success to the activities of Social-Democratic parties in the interests of the bourgeoisie. Accordingly, the bourgeoisie of these countries has entirely dispensed with the services of the Social-Democratic parties, has driven them underground, and has attempted to transfer to other parties the function of main social buttress of the bourgeoisie hitherto performed by the Social-Democratic parties.

Colonies are not only of economic and political but also strategical value. Today more than ever before, every newly conquered region serves as a strategical base for further conquest. Any rocky island, however sterile and deserted, is of the utmost value if it helps to strengthen the strategical position of some imperialist country; territory is important in itself, irrespective of its economic value. Hence the increased tendency on the part of the imperialists to seize any area they can, if only to prevent it becoming a military base for others. Economic, political and strategical factors in conjunction render a struggle for a new redivision of the world inevitable in the period of the general crisis of capitalism.

The present war is an imperialist war for the redivision of the world. And what Lenin said of the World War of 1914 likewise applies to the present war.

The way for this war was similarly paved by *all* the imperialist countries. The financial oligarchies of all the imperialist countries bear an equal responsibility for it.

Lenin wrote in 1916, and repeated the idea several times before the October Revolution, that the proletarian revolution would break out 'in connection with war'.[14] At that time it never occurred to the ruling classes that their rule was in any way endangered. But they know it today, and are afraid of it. The example of the Soviet Union is a warning to them. Nevertheless, the inherent laws of capitalism drive them to launch again into a struggle for a redivision of the world. The power of the Soviet Union, the strength of the Red Army, their fear of the working masses in their own country, and Stalin's wise peace policy all helped to frustrate the Munich policy of a united front of the imperialist powers against the Soviet Union. The antagonisms among the imperialist powers over the division of the world have temporarily proved to be stronger than the fundamental antagonism between capitalism and socialism.

The war between the imperialist states is undoubtedly weakening the entire capitalist system. The superiority of socialism stands out all the more clearly and distinctly. The conditions for successful proletarian revolutions are ripening in a number of other countries, and so are the conditions for successful anti-imperialist revolutions in the oppressed colonial and semi-colonial countries.

---

14   Lenin 1964e, p. 110.

CHAPTER 14

Changes in Capitalism during the War

For the second time in a quarter of a century, the imperialist bourgeoisie is driving millions of proletarians to mutual slaughter, driving the population of whole continents into starvation and untold suffering.[1] The big bourgeoisie has inflicted this disaster upon mankind not by their own 'free will', not because of whim, but in obedience to the inexorable laws of imperialism, which make wars for the redivision of the world inevitable.

Remembering what occurred during and after the first imperialist war, the big bourgeoisie, or at all events the wisest of its representatives, is well aware of the dangers for capitalist society involved in the second imperialist war, particularly in the vanquished countries. It is mobilising all its forces and is waging a struggle on two fronts: against the external enemy – its imperialist rivals – and against 'the enemy at home' – the revolutionary working class, the masses of the peasantry and the progressive intelligentsia. This double task entails changes in the economics and politics of present-day capitalism, which to a far larger extent than in the First World War is being, as Lenin said, *transformed from monopoly capitalism into monopoly war-state capitalism*.

Lenin described this state monopoly capitalism as follows: '... [S]tate-monopoly capitalism is a complete *material* preparation for socialism, the *threshold* of socialism, a rung on the ladder of history between which and the rung called socialism *there are no intermediate rungs*'.[2]

Let us examine the main trends of the changes in capitalist economy in this second imperialist war.

---

1 [This article was originally published in *Bolshevik* 1940, 9: 9–18, and must have been a policy paper destined to Stalin's Politburo. This version is taken from *International Review* (New York) June 1941: 3–11. The same text was also published in four issues of the *Daily Worker* (New York) on 17, 18, 29, 30 August 1940. A shorter version was also published in *The Labour Monthly* (London), July 1941, pp. 312–18. A German version was published as 'Der Kampf der Imperialisten um die Neuaufteilung der Welt', in *Die Kommunistische Internationale*, 1940, 6: 377–88. This text would serve as an outline for a series of articles Varga started writing during the war which were fused in his later book on the changes of the capitalist economies during the war. The ideas about 'total war' inspired Varga to analyse the economic role of the state organising the war and its transformation into 'state monopoly war state capitalism'. In this article Varga does not mention the role of Fascism or the person of Hitler, and reflects the position of the Soviet government *vis-à-vis* Germany's war policy].
2 Lenin 1964e, p. 359.

The present war is causing a general diminution in real wealth in the belligerent countries far more rapidly than the World War did. This is due to the following reasons:

The present war is a 'total war' to a far larger extent than the World War was. The war is being waged not only against the enemy's army and navy, but also against his economic resources, and against the whole people. The devastation caused by aerial warfare, which is assuming ever greater importance in modern war, is greatly accelerating this process of impoverishment. On the other hand, the war is being waged not only by armies, navies and air forces, but literally by the whole people. The activities of the workers in the factories, the peasants in the field, the scientists in their laboratories and the housewives in their kitchens are all subordinated to the war. All of them, in their way, are contributing either to success or failure in the war.

The present war is much more costly than the first World War. It costs ever so much more in the present war to equip an army which now needs tanks, trucks and aircraft, anti-tank and anti-aircraft guns, and vast quantities of machine-guns and automatic rifles. Not only are armies more heavily armed, but the weapons themselves cost more than they did in the World War, not only in money,[3] but also in labour time. The cost of producing a battleship, a gun, a tank or an airplane[4] is many times higher than it was in the first imperialist war. This means that a much larger part of the labour product in the belligerent countries assumes the form of war materials of every kind and, consequently, a much smaller amount is left available to replace used up capital and to supply the individual needs of the civilian population. This gives rise in the belligerent countries to the necessity of constantly increasing state control of capitalist economy.

If the bourgeois state, which represents the class interests of the big bourgeoisie as a whole, allowed the capitalist system to run its own way during the war, if it did not deeply penetrate into the process of capitalist production with a view to controlling it, the following would result. The prices of all commodities would rapidly rise. The limited supplies of consumer goods would be largely bought up and hoarded by the well-to-do classes. The labour power of the industrial workers, the regular reproduction of which is essential for the continuous production of all war materials, could not be maintained owing

---

3 At the end of 1940, England's expenditure amounted to £12,000,000 per day. Germany's expenditure – if we take the increase in the national debt and two-thirds of the revenues from taxation as war expenditure – amounts to between 5 to 5.5 billion marks per month.
4 Information from various sources clearly indicates that the average cost of the airplanes that Great Britain buys in the United States is no less than $100,000 each.

to the malnutrition of the workers. Output would rapidly sink, and this would mean defeat in the war and the acceleration of the revolutionary crisis at home.

It is therefore in the interests of the big bourgeoisie to ration, at prices fixed by the state, the limited available quantities of consumer goods among the working people commensurate with the importance of the work they are doing for the conduct of the war. Workers engaged in heavy work get more meat and fats than other workers, and those engaged in the heaviest work get more than those engaged in heavy work.

This 'fair' distribution of consumer goods also serves to combat the 'enemy at home', since it is drilled into the workers' minds that 'all citizens equally bear the burdens of the war' and that as far as the distribution of food is concerned, the workers even have priority over the well-to-do classes. But the bourgeoisie can satisfy its requirements by purchasing the available supplies of the more costly articles of food, such as game, poultry, fruit, choice vegetables, etc., the sale of which is not controlled, and which the workers cannot afford to buy. As for clothes, underclothing, footwear, etc., the bourgeoisie always have supplies to last them for many years.

If the capitalist state did not intervene in the distribution of raw materials in the interests of the bourgeoisie as a whole, these raw materials, in consequence of the anarchy of the capitalist market, would be bought up by those capitalist firms that could pay the highest price for them. Enterprises that are directly or indirectly of the highest importance for the conduct of the war might be left without raw materials. That is why the state in all belligerent countries controls raw materials[5] and distributes them among the capitalist enterprises commensurate with their importance for the conduct of the war.[6]

This state control of raw materials is at the same time an important method of increasing the power of capitalist monopoly at the expense of the medium and small enterprises, and particularly of the small artisans, who as a consequence of the shortage of raw materials brought about by the war are compelled to give up their – often fictitious – independence and become wage-workers.

---

5 The control and distribution of raw materials extends not only to newly produced materials, but also to old materials that can be temporarily or permanently diverted from their hitherto peaceful use. The iron gates and fences of parks and gardens, copper and aluminum domestic utensils, church bells, etc., are mobilised for war purposes no less than wastepaper, waste textile fabrics, etc.
6 The only exception is the United States, where, owing to the abundance of raw materials in the country, state control has not been established. The state confines itself to importing and storing large quantities of materials that are essential for war purposes and are totally lacking, or scarce, in the country. Among these are tin, manganese, copper, antimony, etc.

If the capitalist state allowed the economy of the country to run its own way during the war the available means of production in the country would be used to manufacture goods that were useless, or of minor use, for war purposes. The present total war, however, demands that the whole productive capacity of the country be adapted to war purposes, the more so that, if the war lasts a long time, the normal replacement of used up fixed capital will become impossible. That is why the state in the belligerent countries controls the utilisation of the means of production in the interests of the big bourgeoisie as a whole, and decides which articles, and in which quantities, shall be produced in the different enterprises.

The present total war is causing a shortage of labour, particularly of skilled metalworkers. If the state in the belligerent countries allowed the customary anarchy to prevail on the labour market, the capitalist employers would entice workers away from each other by the offer of higher wages. This would not be in the interests of the bourgeoisie as a whole, nor would it guarantee continuity in the production of war materials. That is why workers are prohibited from changing their jobs, and why the state is distributing labour power.

For the same reason the state is controlling the transport system: allocating the available shipping for transporting cargoes that are most important for the conduct of the war, controlling railways and motor transport, controlling exports and imports, etc.

The machinery of state control in wartime – once it is set in motion in one sphere of economic life – must necessarily extend to other spheres until the whole capitalist economy is brought under state control, and monopoly capitalism is transformed into monopoly war state capitalism.

∴

The need for state capitalism in the belligerent countries is increased by the break-up of capitalist world economy into a few large and more or less isolated parts. The continent of Europe is cut off from the overseas countries. Japan and her colonies and occupied territories are becoming more and more isolated from the rest of the capitalist world. This breakdown of international commercial intercourse, which is making itself felt in Europe too (Great Britain is cut off from the Scandinavian countries, which used to supply her with timber, cellulose, paper, butter, bacon and iron ore; hence the shortage of these articles in Great Britain and the superfluous stocks of timber, cellulose and paper in the Scandinavian countries), increases the necessity of state control of the short, or overabundant, supplies of goods.

Consequently, the development of state monopoly in wartime is not confined to the belligerent countries, but extends also to the neutral countries. Cut off from their usual export and import markets, restricted by the economic war regulations in the big capitalist countries, and their economy dislocated by extensive armaments and partial mobilisation, the neutral capitalist countries are also compelled to introduce state control and to ration the consumer goods of which there is a shortage.

For other reasons state intervention takes place in the overseas agrarian countries. In Argentina the state buys maize at 45 pesos per ton and sells it to the railways at 20 pesos per ton to be used as fuel instead of coal, because it is now difficult to obtain coal from Europe. In that country there are superfluous stocks of flax seed, in Brazil there are superfluous stocks of coffee, etc.

The war monopoly state capitalism of the big imperialist countries is not confined to its own countries, but extends to other countries in various ways. For example, the British government has bought the whole of the wool clip in Australia, New Zealand and South Africa, the whole of the cotton crop in Egypt, the whole of the cocoa crop in the French colonies that are controlled by de Gaulle, etc. The economy of the United States is being largely adjusted to meet Great Britain's war requirements. Germany not only controls the economy of the occupied territories, but exercises far-reaching influence on the economy of countries like Hungary, Yugoslavia and Rumania. She enters into contracts with those countries for the cultivation and delivery of oilseeds at prices fixed beforehand by the respective governments, for the delivery of ores, hogs, etc. The governments also make mutual arrangements as to the kinds and price of manufactured goods Germany is to deliver in payment, and also the rates of exchange of their currency.

The organisation of war monopoly state capitalism calls for an immense increase in the state apparatus. Millions of people are withdrawn from the sphere of production to arrange for and control the purchase and distribution of foodstuffs, raw materials, manufactured consumer goods, machinery, transport facilities and labour power. Thus the state control of capitalist economy, which necessarily arises in order rationally to direct the inadequate supplies of the elements of capitalist production into the channels necessary for conducting the war, dialectically becomes a factor in the further impoverishment of the country.

Under war monopoly state capitalism the power of the state apparatus over the individual worker is almost unlimited. The state apparatus decides where the worker shall work, how long he shall work, how much he shall be paid, how much and what he shall eat, what he should or should not read, what he should or should not hear over the radio, what he may talk about, and what he must remain silent about. This power also extends over the peasants, the artisans, the small shopkeeper, and over all working people. The big bourgeoisie uses this apparatus to strengthen its power over the working people and to safeguard its profits.

In order to counteract the growing discontent of the masses, the cry has been raised in many countries that this time the bourgeoisie must not make any war profits; war profits must be taxed 100 percent; dividends must be kept within pre-war limits, etc. Needless to say, the big bourgeoisie, which controls the state apparatus, has numerous ways and means of circumventing these laws that are passed to pacify the working people.

The state capitalist organisation has been built up much faster in this war than it was in the First World War. In the last war the statesmen in the belligerent countries banked on a short war; they had not yet gained experience and slowly groped their way in the dark. In the present war, they are being guided by the experience of the First World War and are making the changes much more systematically, quickly and determinedly.

The leadership and personnel of the controlling apparatus are not quite the same in all countries. In the United States and Great Britain, big capitalist magnates are openly at the head of all the most important war economic state capitalist organisations: Knudsen,[7] former director of General Motors in the United States, Lord Beaverbrook,[8] and others, in Great Britain. To weaken the resistance of the workers to the oppression of the state capitalist apparatus, reformist trade-union leaders and labour politicians were extensively brought into this apparatus: Bevin,[9] Attlee,[10] Greenwood[11] and Morrison[12] in Great Bri-

---

7   [William Signius Knudsen (1879–1948) was a leading manager of Ford Motor Company and later of General Motors. He joined the Franklin Roosevelt administration as a Lieutenant General in the US Army to help head the US war material production effort during Seond World War].

8   [William Maxwell ('Max') Aitken, 1st Baron Beaverbrook (1879–1964) was a Canadian-British media tycoon and politician].

9   [Ernest Bevin (1881–1951) was a British trade-union leader (Transport and General Workers' Union) and Labour politician. He was Minister of Labour in the war-time coalition government].

10 [Clement Attlee, 1st Earl Attlee (1883–1967) was the Leader of the Labour Party (1935–55). He held the office of Deputy Prime Minister under Churchill's wartime coalition government before leading the Labour Party to a landslide election victory in 1945].

11 [Arthur Greenwood (1880–1954) was a Labour politician. He rose to prominence within the party as secretary of its research department from 1920. Churchill appointed him to the War Cabinet in 1940].

12 [Herbert Morrison, Baron Morrison of Lambeth (1888–1965) was a Labour politician who held a number of senior governmental positions].

tain, and Hillman[13] in America. The 'theory', familiar to us from the World War, that war-state capitalism is a step in the transition to socialism, is 'war socialism', has been revived and put into circulation. Taught by their experience of the last World War, however, the masses of the workers in the capitalist countries will have nothing to do with this 'theory'.

In some countries the apparatus of state capitalism differs somewhat from that in the Anglo-Saxon countries. The capitalists themselves remain more in the background and push the military and professional politicians, the majority of whom have risen to the position of the big bourgeoisie, into the foreground. Instead of reformist leaders it is these representatives of the ruling party known to the workers who are performing the function of adjusting the working class and all working people to the requirements of the war and to the interests of the imperialist bourgeoisie.

Thus, all along the line we see the twofold function of war monopoly state capitalism: to organise and centralise all the economic resources of the country for war against the external enemy; and to organise all the forces of the bourgeoisie and of its state against the 'enemy at home', against the revolutionary working class and the masses of the working people.

Important though the role of the present war may be in the development of state capitalism, it would be quite wrong to attribute this development entirely to the war. Its roots lie far deeper. The war is merely accelerating and extending the trends that have been operating throughout the period of the general crisis of capitalism.

The methods by which the bourgeoisie utilises the state have undergone considerable change since the bourgeoisie has been in power.

At the time when, with the assistance of the masses of the working people, the bourgeoisie overthrew the feudal state and released the productive forces of society from the fetters of feudalism, it restricted the functions of the state mainly to the protection of private property. This was the period of the predominance of the 'Manchester School' of free trade, when the theory that predominated among the bourgeoisie was that the state must not interfere in capitalist economy. This was the period of the rapid expansion of capitalist markets, when the contradiction between the unlimited tendency of capital to expand and the relatively limited consuming capacity of capitalist society

---

13   [Sidney Hillman (1887–1946) was the founder of the Amalgamated Clothing Workers of America and its President from 1914 to 1946. He sought 'constructive cooperation' between the union and garment firms to ensure the economic health of the industry and raise the standards of workers within it. He was a close advisor to President Franklin D. Roosevelt].

found expression in periodical crises of overproduction. On the whole, in this period capital could find extensive investment without the direct assistance of the state.

With the development of monopoly capitalism, the contradiction between the tendency of capital to expand and the limited consuming capacity of society has asserted itself more sharply and permanently. The bourgeoisie cannot eliminate this contradiction on a general world scale; but the bourgeoisie in each capitalist country has tried to utilise the state as a means of eliminating it within its own territories. The theories of the 'Manchester School' gave way to the 'theory' that the state must protect the economy of the country. This explains the efforts of the state to protect the home market by means of high tariff, by monopolising colonial markets for home industries, state-subsidised dumping, etc.

In the period of the general crisis of capitalism, the contradiction between the tendency of capital to expand and the limited consuming capacity has become still more acute and chronic. The cyclical process of capitalist reproduction has been disturbed. The crises of overproduction have become very deep and acute; they are followed by long periods of depression; the economic revival is tardy and periods of boom hardly occur.

The bourgeoisie is no longer capable of utilising the available means of production to their full capacity; a very large part of fixed capital remains permanently idle. The bourgeoisie is no longer able to make use of the fertility of the soil; with the assistance of the state, the crop area is reduced and large quantities of foodstuffs are withdrawn from the market and destroyed. The bourgeoisie is no longer able to employ its wage slaves; a large section of the proletariat remains permanently unemployed. The bourgeoisie is no longer able to transform its profits realised in money form into productive capital; an increasing share of these profits is accumulating as idle capital. Capitalist society is obsolete; it has become an obstacle not only to the further development of the productive forces but even to their mere utilisation.

This historical obsolescence of capitalist society serves as the basis of state capitalist development in the period of the general crisis of capitalism, also irrespective of the war. In this period there is a constant increase in armaments. The economic difference between peacetime capitalism and wartime capitalism steadily disappears.

> When capitalists work for the defense, i.e., for the state, it is obviously no longer 'pure' capitalism but a special form of national economy. Pure capitalism means commodity production. And commodity production means work for an *unknown* and free market. But the capitalist 'working'

for defence does not 'work' for the market at all – he works on government orders, very often with money loaned by the state.[14]

The old methods of high tariffs and dumping are no longer adequate. The bourgeoisie seeks other methods of using the state to help it to utilise its capital. These methods are very diverse in their character. We will enumerate only a few of the most important of them.

The monopoly undertakings that collapse during a crisis are saved by huge state credits and subsidies, or by the state purchasing large blocks of their shares. In many large undertakings, private capital is replaced by state capital. In many cases these 'nationalised' enterprises are restored to 'private ownership' after a crisis by the government selling its holdings. In other cases, as in Italy, for example, the state becomes the permanent principal shareholder of the most important enterprises in the country.

Undertakings that make no profit, but which are essential for armament purposes, or for certain capitalists, are initiated and carried out by the state, as, for example, the building of canals, motor roads, airways, enterprises for the exploitation of poor iron mines, various chemical works, etc.

State-organised social insurance appropriates a part of the wages of the proletariat that is working and distributes it in the form of unemployed, sick, disablement benefits, or old-age pensions, among the non-working section, thus relieving capital and laying the foundation for the legend of the 'social state'.

In the interests of the bourgeoisie the state regulates foreign trade, restricts or completely prohibits imports of goods that might compete with the home product at the request of groups manufactured of capitalists it enters into barter treaties with other countries, etc. Thus, we see that even before the outbreak of the new imperialist war there was a marked development of state capitalism in all countries, including old, free-trade England.

Naturally, in no country have these state capitalist measures overcome the restricted capacity of the home market. Consequently, their purpose was changed. They were no longer directed toward the attempt to expand the home market – which was shattered by the inherent laws of capitalism – but to the end of systematically adjusting production to the limits of consumption, of securing the organised reduction of production by means of compulsory cartels, the prohibition of the erection of new enterprises, etc. But this merely served to bring out more strikingly than ever the contradiction that is characteristic of present-day capitalism, namely, the vast concentration of production

---

14   Lenin 1964r, pp. 68–9.

in vast enterprises and the very limited capacity of the home market of the small countries.

In the present war the imperialist great powers are making an effort to eliminate the chronic contradiction between the limits of the home market and the high concentration of capital, which demands enormous markets, by expanding the economic field, by absorbing the small countries in their own economic area.

∵

We think that the further progress of capitalist economy will be on the following lines:

The longer the war lasts, the more the belligerent countries will become impoverished in real wealth: the stocks of raw materials and finished goods will become exhausted, machinery, buildings and railways will become worn out,[15] the fertility of the soil will diminish. The production will diminish correspondingly.

To continue the war the belligerent countries will be compelled to control their economy still more strictly, to reduce consumption on the part of the working people still further, and compel the proletariat to make still greater exertions for the victory of their bourgeoisie. That means that war monopoly state capitalism will develop still further. But this will all the more intensify the

---

15   Prof. K.M. Hettlage, in an article in *Der Deutsche Volkswirt*, of 20 December 1940, entitled 'Who Is Paying for the War?' ['Wer bezahlt den Krieg?'], writes as follows: 'No data are available for estimating the shrinkage of production of articles for private consumption. In foodstuffs it must range between 4.5 to 5 billion Reichsmark [RM] ... The production of manufactured goods must have shrunk by about 9 million RM ... Consequently, in 1940 alone, as a result of non-consumption, the Reich had placed at its disposal for war purpose goods and services to the value of about 14 billion RM more than before. This discrepancy between deterioration and replacement, expressed in money, is by no means small. In private enterprises it must amount to at least 6 billion RM per annum: and in residential building alone it must range between 1.5 and 2 billion RM. In war time such replacements can only be made in enterprises essential for the war ... From the economic aspect, the real wealth which should have been used for replacements, but was consumed for war purposes in 1940 must be estimated between 3 and 4 billion RM. To this must be added the further shrinkage of real wealth as the result of the exhaustion of stocks of raw materials and goods. In the World War this mounted to about 20 billion marks. In 1940, this sum must have ranged between 5 and 6 billion RM'. [Hettlage 1940, p. 476]. [Karl Maria Hettlage (1902–95) was SS-Hauptsturmführer and advisor to Albert Speer; after the war he was appointed professor and higher civil servant; 1962–7 High Commissioner to the European Community for Coal and Steel; 1967–9 Secretary of State of Finance Minister Franz-Josef Strauß].

contradiction between the two objects of modern war capitalism, between victory over the external enemy and the suppression of the revolutionary forces. The first object, victory over the external enemy, can be achieved only by subjecting the working population to ever increasing burdens and privations. In the effort to achieve this object, namely, the victory over the external enemy, the bourgeoisie is compelled to pave the way for its own defeat by the 'enemy at home'.

As Lenin wrote: 'The dialectics of history is such that the war, by extraordinarily expediting the transformation of monopoly capitalism into state-monopoly capitalism, has *thereby* extraordinarily advanced mankind towards socialism'.[16]

In order to allay the discontent of the workers with their conditions during the war, the bourgeoisie is promising them a paradise – after the war: freedom, democracy, socialism, large apartments and private automobiles. But, remembering what happened after the First World War, the masses of the people are very sceptical about the promises. Such promises cannot dam the rising tide of resistance of the masses of the people and of the revolutionary working-class movement.

---

16   Lenin 1964q, p. 359.

CHAPTER 15

Plans for Currency Stabilisation

Of special interest among postwar economic problems is the question of currency stabilisation.[1] Undoubtedly, there is a danger of general devaluation of currencies as was the case after the First World War. At the present time it is quite clear that when the war is over, European countries will be threatened by a new currency devaluation.

A situation of this kind is bound to arise after the war unless timely measures are taken to prevent the threatened devaluation of money. This problem is the subject of lively discussion in the foreign press, and a number of schemes have been advanced, the most important of which are, first, the British scheme drafted by the well-known economist Keynes, providing for the setting up of an international clearing union; and secondly, the American plan, elaborated by White,[2] which calls for the creation of a huge stabilisation fund, and international bank.

The Keynes plan takes into account the special position of Britain.

Implementing the Keynes Plan would undoubtedly help Britain to recover the role of international banker in the postwar period, although stabilising currencies on an international scale could never be secured by means of the creation of an international clearing union.

The existence of an international clearing union could, to a certain extent, modify or postpone foreign devaluation but could not eliminate it. The Keynes plan alone cannot secure currency stability after the war. Only with the continuation of government restriction or individual consumption and investment, with strict control of foreign trade, and also with extensive capital export from rich countries to countries ruined by war, could the aim of the Keynes plan of currency stabilisation be achieved. But the employment of all these means – which incidentally are hardly possible of realisation in peacetime under the existing social system, inasmuch as they run contrary to the selfish interests of influential circles – could secure a stable currency without an international clearing system.

---

1 [Originally published in *Voyna i rabochiy klass*, 1944, 13: 3–10. English translation in *Commercial and Financial Chronicle* (New York), 4230, 2 March 1944, and *The Communist*, March 1944: 282–3].

2 [Harry Dexter White (1892–1948) was an American economist appointed at the Treasury. He was a major architect of the IMF and the World Bank].

The White Plan was submitted to the Senate in April 1943, by Morgenthau,[3] Secretary of the *Treasury*. The central idea of this plan consists in the mobilisation of international finance, the turnover of the huge gold stock in the USA which finds no use at the present time. It proposes, in the first place, a 5,000 million dollar currency fund as a basis for stabilisation. This fund is to be formed from shares payable by all member states.

There is no doubt that the currency fund planned by White could become a substantial factor in world economy and secure currency stabilisation more effectively than the clearing union proposed by Keynes.

The leading position envisaged for the USA by the White Plan not only rests on the anticipation of the USA being the dominant partner in the currency fund, the British press stresses, but also on the anticipated participation of the countries of Central and South America, which are under the strong economic and political influence of the USA. In addition to the stabilisation fund, the White Plan also provides for the organisation of a bank for reconstruction and development by the United Nations and nations joining them. Undoubtedly the planned bank, together with the currency fund, would represent a tremendous economic power.

But precisely because of this there is considerable opposition to this plan, not only outside, but also inside the USA. For fully understandable reasons, even stronger objections to the White Plan are raised in Britain.

Compromise between the two plans is hardly possibly, since Keynes is trying to solve the problem of stabilisation of currency by eliminating gold, and White on the basis of gold; moreover, both these plans correspond to the special economic interests of their respective countries.

Naturally, Soviet public opinion cannot but be interested in economic plans of postwar reconstruction discussed in the countries of our allies. The special character of the economic system of the Soviet Union determines its attitude to the question of the stabilisation of currencies. As a state engaged in foreign trade, the Soviet Union, just as Britain or the USA, is interested in the stability of the currencies of the countries it is trading with, in preventing currency speculation in other countries from interfering with the normal course of foreign trade.

---

3   [Henry Morgenthau Jr. (1891–1967) was during the period 1934–45 Secretary of Treasury of the Roosevelt Administration. He devised a plan, known as the Morgenthau Plan, advocating harsh measures against Germany: the country was to be partitioned into two states and its heavy industry dismantled. Although Roosevelt and Winston Churchill signed a modified version of the plan in September 1944 at the Second Quebec Conference, the plan was never fully implemented].

If all the Soviet Union's trade with the rest of the world could be conducted on the basis of gold currency with an unchanging value, this would undoubtedly render trading operations easier.

As regards the Soviet Union's currency, it is known that here prices – and consequently also the purchasing power of the rouble – in the state trade turnover, are fixed by plan. This means that the stability of Soviet currency is secured by methods entirely different from those in other countries. This also obviates the possibility of any kind of proposals in the field of economic policy as far as the Soviet Union is concerned by any future organisation, be it international bank or currency fund.

On the other hand, the Soviet Union is undoubtedly interested in the beginnings of measures capable of accelerating the restoration of her economy, as well as of the economies of other countries devastated by the fascist brigands.

This question is of the greatest importance in estimating the financial plans on the part of the Soviet Union.

CHAPTER 16

World Currency Headache

Of special interest among postwar economic problems is the question of currency stabilisation.[1] Undoubtedly there is the danger of a general devaluation of currencies as was the case after the First World War. And at the present time it is quite clear that when the war is over, European countries, first and foremost, are threatened with new currency devaluation. Huge sums consisting of bank and savings bank deposits have accumulated in all countries in the course of the conflict. Apart from internal sources of inflation – accumulated purchasing power – there are also external sources of inflation having their origin in foreign trade. The export capacity of European countries will be extremely insignificant because of economic destruction and the necessity of satisfying home needs. Consequently the countries of Europe will have an adverse trade balance. A situation of this kind is bound to arise when peace comes unless timely measures are taken to prevent or allay the threatened devaluation of money.

This problem has been the subject of lively discussion and a number of schemes have been advanced, the most important of which is the one drafted by the well-known British economist, John Maynard Keynes. He proposes the establishment of an international clearing union. Another plan is the one formulated by Harry White,[2] of the United States Treasury Department. He calls for the creation of a huge currency stabilisation fund and international bank. Both projects are directed towards one and the same aim. Nevertheless they call for quite different methods and means of implementation. One of them would obviate the other. There are also some schemes representing compromises.

The Keynes plan takes into account the special position of Britain. Before the war the City occupied the role of international banker – the prerequisites of this role being the stability of the British pound and the free circulation of gold which in turn necessitated a favourable balance of payments and the presence of adequate gold reserves to cover temporary adverse balances.

The war and its consequences have destroyed these conditions. Britain's balance of payments is in danger of becoming an adverse one in the postwar period. And apart from this almost the whole of Britain's gold reserve has been

---

1 [Originally published in *New Masses*, 4 January 1944, pp. 11–12, also published as 'Plans for postwar currency stabilisation', *Commercial and Finance Chronicle*, New York, 4230, 2 March 1944].
2 [Harry Dexter White (1892–1948) was an American economist and civil servant].

transferred to the United States while in the course of the war the British colonies have accumulated considerable sums in sterling in London. From this it follows that Britain cannot count on preserving her role of international banker during the postwar period by the means she used before the war. Implementing the Keynes plan would undoubtedly help Britain recover this role in the postwar period, although stabilising currencies on an international scale could never be secured by means of the creation of an international clearing union. Such a union could to a certain extent soften or postpone foreign devaluation but could not eliminate it.

The Keynes plan alone cannot secure currency stability. Only on condition of continued government restriction of individual consumption and investments, with strict control of foreign trade and also with extensive export of capital from the rich countries to countries ruined by the war, could the aims of the Keynes plan for currency stabilisation be achieved. But the employment of all these means – which incidentally are hardly possible to realise in peacetime under the existing social system inasmuch as it runs contrary to the selfish interests of influential circles – could secure a stable currency in each country also without an international clearing system.

The White plan was submitted to the Senate in April 1943, by Henry Morgenthau,[3] the Secretary of the Treasury. The idea of this plan consists in the mobilisation for international financial turnover of the huge gold stocks in the United States which find no use at the present time. The idea of the White plan is the creation in the first place of a five billion dollar currency fund as the basis for stabilisation. This fund is to be formed of shares payable by all member states. There is no doubt that the currency fund planned by White could become a substantial factor in world economy and secure currency stabilisation more effectively than the clearing union proposed by Keynes. The leading position envisioned for the United States by the White plan rests not only on the anticipation of the United States being the dominant partner in the currency fund, as the British press stresses, but also on the anticipated participation of the countries in Central and South America which are under the strong economic and political influence of the United States.

In addition, the White stabilisation plan also provides for the organisation of a bank for reconstruction and development of the United Nations and nations joining them. The bank's capital of ten billion dollars can be formed by member states in the same way as the capital of the currency fund. Undoubtedly the planned bank with its colossal capital of ten billion dollars, together with

---

3   [Henry Morgenthau (1856–1946) was an American businessman and diplomat].

the currency fund which pursues an identical aim, would represent tremendous economic power. But because of this there is considerable opposition to this plan outside as well as inside the United States. It is as yet far from clear whether the White plan in its present form can count on success even in the United States. For fully understandable reasons even stronger objections to the White plan have been raised in Britain. Efforts to draw up something in the nature of a compromise between the Keynes and White plans have hitherto brought no results. And indeed a compromise between the two plans is hardly possible since Keynes is trying to solve the problem of stabilising currency by eliminating gold, and White on the basis of gold. Moreover, both these plans correspond to the special economic interests of their respective countries.

Naturally, Soviet public opinion cannot but be interested in the economic plans for postwar reconstruction discussed in the countries of its allies. The special character of the Soviet economic system determines its attitude toward the question of the stabilisation of currencies. As a state engaged in foreign trade, just as Britain or the United States, it is interested in the stability of currencies of the countries with whom it is trading and in preventing currency speculations in other countries from interfering with the normal course of foreign trade.

If all the Soviet Union's trade with the rest of the world could be conducted on a basis of gold currency with unchanging value, this would undoubtedly render trading operations easier. As regards the Soviet Union's currency it is known that here prices – and consequently also the purchasing power of the ruble – in state-trade turnover are fixed by plan. This means that the stability of Soviet currency is secured by methods entirely different from those in other countries. So far as the USSR is concerned this also motivates the possibility of any kind of proposals in the field of economic policy by any future organisation, be it an international bank or a currency fund. On the other hand, the Soviet Union is undoubtedly interested in beginnings and measures capable of accelerating the restoration of her economy as well as of the economy of other countries devastated by the fascist brigands. This question is of the greatest importance in estimating the various financial plans on the part of the Soviet Union.

CHAPTER 17

Toward a New Crash?

The end of the war in Europe makes the question of the course of economic life in the capitalist world a very actual one.[1] What is the prospect for the immediate future, or to speak more exactly, what will be the movement of the first industrial cycle after the war?

It would be too risky to attempt to forecast already the course of this cycle, all the more because the lack of statistical material prevents any accurate judgement even on the present economic situation. Nevertheless, the Marxist method and understanding of the economic situation which existed after the end of the First World War, and also such statistics as are available about the economy of the United States – that decisive factor in world capitalist economy – make possible a scientific analysis of the problem and an indication of the general lines of the industrial cycle following on the war. Obviously it would be wrong to believe that after this war what happened following on the last war will be quite simply repeated. There are quite important differences between the situation in that period and now.

We shall deal with these differences in detail.

By way of a starting point, we can use the fact that every world war breaks the course of the industrial cycle, suspends the cyclical features of the productive process during the period of the war and brings about a phase of 'boom of a special kind'. This results from the distortion of the economy under the influence of the war. In peacetime the most difficult problem for capital is the question of the realisation of the value of commodities, how to pass over from the commodity form to the money form of capital. The problems of realisation, or to put it in another way, the problems of the market, do not exist in wartime. The military needs far exceed the productive possibilities which have remained unused in peacetime as the result of the lack of markets.

In war, the government appears on the market as a buyer with unlimited purchasing power. Under war conditions the capitalist has to worry, not about the sale of his products, but about how to transform the capital which he has in money form into productive capital. He has to strive to replace the elements of productive capital: labour power, raw materials, means of production and

---

1 [Originally published in *Mirovoe khozyaystvo i mirovaya politika*, 1945, 9: 23–34. English translation in *New Masses*, 29 January 1946, 57, 5: 3–5].

transport. It is not the consumers' demand that sets limits to capitalist production, as is the case in time of peace, but on the contrary, the insufficient production sets limits both to the productive and to the unproductive demand of the civilian population.

The longer the war continues, the greater the extent to which the consumers' demands of society exceed its productive capacity. The values used up, that is, the productive capital which is not renewed in this form, sits idle in the bank in the form of money capital, since the productive capital is unable to renew its form as a result of the shortage of raw materials, machinery, buildings and labour power. The same takes place with that portion of the profit which is destined for accumulation. The income of workers, employees, officials and officers cannot be spent fully owing to the shortage of consumers' goods and the balance, therefore, for the most part sits idle in various savings funds.

All these immense sums of accumulated consumers' demands await the end of the war, and after the removal of government restrictions will rush with full force into the commodity markets.

Thus all the prerequisites are present, after the ending of the war and a short period of difficulties in passing over from war to peace, for the beginning of the ascending phase in a new industrial cycle. This was the case after the First World War, but the period of rising production was extremely short. Indices of industrial production show that the highest point was reached in the United States in March 1920, in Britain in the first quarter of 1920 and in France in November 1920. Thus in the two most decisive capitalist countries, the United States and Britain, the rise of production after the end of the war lasted only about fifteen months.

As for the countries of Continental Europe, with the exception of the neutral countries, all of them were so impoverished (in real terms) as a result of the war, that the effect of accumulated consumers' demands in the form of banking deposits and savings and partly also in cash, did not lead to a rise in production, but to inflation. There was an effective demand for goods, but production could increase only very slowly because in these countries the material elements of production were lacking – the raw materials, machinery and transport. At that time we characterised the economic situation of those countries as a crisis of underproduction, having in view the fact that the low level of production was not the result of overproduction and insufficient demand for goods, as is the case with the 'normal' crises of overproduction. It was due to a shortage of means of production, that is, to the impoverishment of those countries.

Statistics also show that in the course of the brief rise of the productive cycle after the war, nowhere in Europe, as distinct from the United States, did production reach the pre-war level. This level was only reached some years after the

1920 crisis – in France in 1924, in Germany 1927, England only in 1929, that is, immediately before the new world crisis of 1929–33. This means that after the end of the last war, the chief European countries needed six, nine and eleven years before their industrial production reached the pre-war level.

The index of wholesale prices after the last war shows that the highest level was reached in the United States in January 1920, and in Britain in March 1920. But what is of even greater significance is the fact that during the 1920–1 crisis, although prices fell sharply they did not drop to the 1913 level; and this in spite of the fact that there can be no doubt that the rising productivity of labour lowered the value of products of the same quality (that is, the social labour time embodied in them). The level of prices should have fallen below the level of 1913, but the strength of monopoly and the fact that the war resulted in a piling up of overheads on production (taxes, rents, transport costs, and so on) maintained market prices at a far higher level than before the war. And it was only in the crisis of 1929–33 that prices fell in accordance with the fall in value, that is, to such an extent that they fell even below the level of 1913. The artificial maintenance of a high level of prices through the 1920–1 crisis undoubtedly contributed towards the depth and sharpness of the crisis of 1929–33.

If we compare the economic consequences of the Second World War, so far as the capitalist world is concerned, with the consequences of the First World War, we can say with full assurance that at the end of the present war the distortion of economy in the capitalist world will be much greater than in 1918.

Although the 1914–18 war was also a world war, it was in great measure a European war so far as its direct effects were concerned. In the case of this war, the impoverishment of the capitalist world as a whole will be much greater than it was then.

Moreover, the difference in the economic situation of those countries which did not become a theatre of war operations, as compared with those which did, will be much greater. The economic situation in those countries not directly involved – in the first place the United States and the British Dominions, and to some extent also Britain, South American countries and the European neutrals – will be in sharp contrast with the economic situation of the capitalist countries overrun by Germany in Europe, which will be absolutely impoverished, short of everything and involved in a complete collapse of their economy.

On the other hand, the United States, also Canada, South Africa, etc., will come out of the war with their productive apparatus much increased and improved, while in the countries of continental Europe ravaged by the war, the means of production will, for the most part, have been worn out or destroyed and their towns and transport systems greatly damaged. For this reason, shortly after the end of the war, the countries of the first group will be 'countries of overproduction', while in the ravaged countries, as after the First World War, there will be 'a crisis of underproduction'. But the territory covered by this second group will be much greater than it was after the First World War. In the countries of Eastern Europe allied with the Soviet Union, this crisis of underproduction will not be so sharp thanks to their closer economic relations with the Soviet Union.

Britain will occupy a kind of intermediate position. Although it was not a theatre of war operations, there was considerable material loss as a result of air attacks. During the war it spent or lost a considerable part of its overseas investments and will come out of the war with a far higher indebtedness to its Dominions and Colonies. According to the practically unanimous estimates of British economists, it will be necessary for Britain after the war to increase its exports by fifty percent as compared with pre-war, in order to import the food and raw materials it needs to restore the pre-war standard of living. In order to guarantee this, Britain will have to carry out a very flexible economic policy.

The existence in the United States of a greater and more efficient productive apparatus and of a 'deferred' demand of some fifty billion dollars, will undoubtedly produce in the United States a short-lived prosperity, just as after the First World War. This demand will in the first place be directed towards consumers' goods of secondary necessity, such as automobiles, refrigerators, television sets, furniture, houses, etc., the production of which during the war was either prohibited or very much restricted. The demand for goods of prime necessity, such as food, clothing and shoes, will be only slightly in excess of normal, as production of these during the war was very little affected. On the other hand, the demand for means of production will in all probability be *lower* than before the war owing to the great extension of the productive apparatus during the war.

For a correct judgement about the future course of the industrial cycle, we must also take into account the rise in the productivity of labour as a result of the technical improvements carried out during the war. The fact that industries no longer had to worry about markets and were being pressed to satisfy the needs of the war led to a great number of technical innovations, some of which were already known, but had not been used because of market difficulties. The increase in labour productivity in the United States during the war is estimated at about four percent per annum as compared with two percent in peacetime. This is one of the most powerful factors which will influence the course of the trade cycle after the war.

Thus we see that the conclusion of the war and the changeover of enterprises from war production to peace products will threaten many departments of American economy with overproduction, in spite of the fact that there will be a considerable deferred demand for consumers' goods and housing. The effect on the market of this deferred demand will be counteracted by considerable unemployment, shorter working hours and the return of workers from the armed forces. This mass unemployment will result in a reduction in the current income of the working class and, therefore, of its purchasing power.

Certain factors, therefore, will act in the direction of curtailing the length of the ascending phase of the industrial cycle in the United States, which we have assumed will follow the close of the European war. But on the other hand, a number of important factors will act in the direction of lengthening the ascending phase. We refer to the most important of these factors below.[2]

As for the question of prices, the increase during the war in the belligerent countries has been much smaller than in the First World War. There are two reasons for this:

First, in the larger capitalist countries there was considerable unused productive capacity before the war.

Second, government regulation of prices became effective earlier in this war and was more systematic.

The index of wholesale prices shows that up to 1943, the rise compared with 1939 had been only 35 percent in the United States and 67 percent in Britain. In the neutral countries, the rise was much greater – Sweden 79 percent, Switzerland 106 percent, Turkey 478 percent.

The fact that prices have risen less sharply in the United States and Britain might lead to the assumption, by analogy with the First World War, that at the conclusion of the war there will be a very great increase in prices. We do not, however, believe that this will take place. The gradual transition of economy to peace production, the maintenance of state control on prices and their regulation during the transition period, and particularly in the United States the surplus productive capacity in agriculture and in the raw materials industries, partly also in the manufacturing industries, will work against the rise in prices in countries with stable money and will in any case weaken the tendency to rise.

It must here be emphasised that although even in the United States there is not a great rise in prices as compared with 1939, all the same prices, just as in the First World War, are on the average above value. Insofar as the increased productivity of labour has resulted in a reduction of the social labour time embodied in each unit, as compared with pre-war, prices expressed in gold or

---

2 [Varga here refers to the probability of the Japanese War continuing for some time and thus easing the transition both in the United States and in Britain. This paragraph is omitted].

in dollars should have been lower than pre-war. For this reason, in the United States in the postwar period, we should not anticipate any significant rise in prices, while further in the crisis phase which will follow this rise, a very important fall of prices is to be expected. It will be much the same in those countries whose exchange maintains a firm relation to the dollar as, for example, Britain and the British Dominions.

The course of the postwar industrial cycle will be quite different in the countries of continental Europe. In their case, we cannot speak of any ascending phase of production in the postwar period, such as would bring their production to the pre-war level. It is true that the effective demand for goods will exist, but there will be no possibility of producing the goods to satisfy this demand. In these countries a crisis of underproduction will be inevitable, just as after the First World War. The shortage of all kinds of means of production and transport will considerably restrict the possibility of productive enterprise. The danger of inflation will be extremely great. In order to avoid sharp inflation or at least to modify it, it is possible for the countries of continental Europe to maintain for many years after the war government regulation of production of consumers' goods, of prices, and so on.

The degree that this inflationary crisis of underproduction will reach in Europe, the period it will last, and the extent to which it will result in open inflation, will depend in considerable measure on *how* soon and to what extent the countries with an undamaged or stronger economy – United States, Canada and perhaps Britain – are prepared to help in the process of restoration in Europe by advancing credits for the means of production. France has already received credits from the United States for the purchase of locomotives and rolling-stock, raw materials and food. The countries of Eastern Europe will receive aid in the first place from the Soviet Union.

The projected organisation of an International Exchange Fund and an International Bank for Reconstruction should help these aims.

The immense resources of the United States not only allow it to export considerable amounts of capital to Europe, but because of the danger of overproduction and the threat of mass unemployment, such export becomes in the highest degree desirable.

Certainly the export of capital in considerable sums raises the problem of transfers, that is the question of how the profit or interest on the capital exported by the United States can be paid in some natural form. This question aroused a good deal of discussion after the First World War. It is characteristic that the National State Bank in its monthly bulletins in 1920–1 repeatedly expressed strong views against the European governments being asked to pay the United States their war debts.

The possibility of payment in raw materials has been reduced as a result of the war. After the war, imports of many important types of raw material will fall to a greater or less extent. So far as America is concerned, this refers particularly to rubber, vegetable oils and silk. These together amount to about one-sixth of American imports and in the postwar period they will fall to insignificant amounts as the result of the development of synthetic rubber, soya bean production and improvements in the quality of artificial silk (nylon). Hence after the war it will be necessary for the United States to import new types of commodities. It is clear that the old tariff policy of the United States does not correspond to the new position of the United States in the world market. This was a point which Roosevelt had already called attention to during the war.

Summing up, we may say that after the conclusion of the war, countries whose productive apparatus has not been damaged, or has been improved, will pass through the ascending phase of a productive cycle in the course of two to four years. This phase will end with a crisis of overproduction, which in all probability will be more prolonged than the crisis of 1920–1. This crisis of overproduction will in turn worsen the situation of the countries of continental Europe, which by that period will have raised their production as compared with the extremely low level at the end of the war, but all the same will still be struggling to overcome the crisis of underproduction and the danger of inflation.

After this postwar crisis has been overcome, and the stabilisation of at least some European currencies has been achieved, a new full industrial cycle will begin. But this cycle will not be like the cycle of 1921–9 with its relatively strong ascending phase (especially in the United States and in Germany) but will resemble rather the cycle of 1929–37 with its 'depression of a special kind' and will not reach the full phase of prosperity. The factors which then prevented the full ascending phase from developing – the sharp contradiction between the unlimited drive of capital for its extension and the restricted limits of the purchasing power of society, and the consequent chronic underemployment of the productive apparatus, together with chronic unemployment – will act with even greater force in the first 'normal' postwar cycle.

Certainly it is necessary to emphasise that the Soviet Union, whose economy excludes the possibility of a crisis of overproduction, will be a stabilising factor for the economy of the countries of Eastern Europe. The cyclical crisis of overproduction in the United States and Britain will find its reflection in the economy of all other countries in the capitalist world, while the absence of crisis in the USSR will be a beneficent influence on countries which are linked.

CHAPTER 18

The General Crisis of Capitalism (Features of the Home and Foreign Policy of the Capitalist Countries during the Epoch of the General Crisis of Capitalism)

The home and foreign policy of the capitalist countries during the period of the general crisis of capitalism exhibits certain specific features which distinguish it from the policy of capitalism prior to this period.[1] Stalin, in his speech of 9 February 1946, pointed out: 'Marxists have more than once declared that the capitalist system of world economy conceals within itself elements of general crisis and war conflicts'. In point of fact, during the periods when capitalism was still developing along an ascending line, Marx founded the theory of the inevitable collapse of capitalism, showing that capitalism is a social order that is historically transitory and far from the final form of the organisation of human society, as all bourgeois economists and politicians at that time maintained.

Historical experience demonstrates that the transition from one social order to another everywhere in the world demands a fairly prolonged period of time. This period can be called that of the general crisis of the particular social order in question. Lenin, as is well known, called imperialism – capitalism in decay; it is quite obvious that to say that a social order is in decay is the same thing as saying that it is in a state of crisis.

In order to characterise the foreign and home policy of the capitalist countries during the epoch of the general crisis of capitalism, it is necessary, first of all, to make clear when this crisis began. It would, of course, be incorrect to designate any particular year, month or day as that when the general crisis of capitalism began. But on the basis of what Lenin has said of imperialism as capitalism in decay, the conclusion can be drawn that the general crisis of capitalism began when the transition from free capitalism to monopolistic capitalism was completed in the most important countries of the capitalist world, i.e. approximately at the beginning of the twentieth century.

---

1 [Originally published in *Mirovoe khzyaystvo i mirovaya politika*, 1946, 6: 8–17. English translation in *The Labour Monthly*, 1947, 29, 1: 23–8, 2: 56–61].

As has been pointed out in the *Short History of the* CPSU(b),[2] the First World War was already a reflection of the general crisis of capitalism. Although, however, the general crisis of capitalism existed already before the First World War, the existence of this crisis was not then a political factor such as could exercise a decisive influence on the foreign and home policy of the capitalist countries. Marxism teaches that with an alteration of the economic basis there is an alteration also of the political superstructure of society, of ideology, of the consciousness of the masses. But this process of change of the economic basis and of the political superstructure does not proceed simultaneously. The general phenomenon to which Marx, Lenin and Stalin pointed is the lag in the change of the political superstructure in relation to the change of economy. This, indeed, is understandable. Persons who experience the changes taking place in the economic base do not immediately draw the corresponding political conclusions. The bourgeois revolutions constitute a forcible explosion, an adaptation of the political superstructure to an economic base that has already long before undergone alteration.

As a matter of fact, prior to the First World War, apart from Lenin and the Bolsheviks in Russia, no one in the capitalist world saw the existence of the crisis of capitalism, or that the replacement of the capitalist system by a socialist system was a task that had become historically mature.

Besides the general tendency for political consciousness to lag behind the change in the economic base, there also existed concrete historical reasons why the fact of the existence of the general crisis of capitalism had still not penetrated into the consciousness of people. The half century which preceded the First World War was a period of the greatest progress of capitalism. In this half century capitalist production increased approximately four-fold; it was a period of great technical progress, a period when the capitalist countries took possession of numerous colonies and thereby extended the capitalist market. The bourgeoisie utilised colonial super-profits to buy the labour aristocracy. During this period, reformism struck deep roots in the labour movement. It should also be remembered that during this half century there were no wars between the great powers. The last war between great powers was the Franco-Prussian War; after it only a number of local and colonial wars took place.

The participants in the First World War were bourgeois countries of the same kind. There was, of course, a difference between Great Britain, France and America – countries in which the bourgeois revolution had been completed – and Germany, which still possessed strong relics of feudalism, and Tsarist Rus-

---

2 [*History of the Communist Party* 1939].

sia; but basically these were bourgeois countries of the same kind, the peoples of which were convinced that whatever the outcome of the war, all the countries participating in it would nevertheless remain bourgeois countries.

This 'conception' was shattered by the October Revolution in Russia. It came with great unexpectedness for the bourgeoisie throughout the world (including the Russian bourgeoisie) and for the working class outside Russia. The victory of the October Revolution at one stroke demonstrated to the whole world the existence of the general crisis of the capitalist system, which found its political reflection in the fact that the socialist country made its appearance alongside the capitalist countries. From that moment concern for the preservation of the capitalist system became the chief content of both the home and foreign policy of the bourgeoisie. The danger for capitalism was most real in the conquered countries, where the bourgeoisie that had lost the war was discredited and the governmental authority shattered, while the defeated army did not form a reliable bulwark of bourgeois rule; the bourgeois capitalist world was faced with a problem: how to preserve the capitalist system.

The bourgeoisie attempted to solve this problem, first and foremost by making an alliance with the reformist labour leaders. The chief method used by the bourgeoisie was the isolation of the still young Communist parties from the basic masses of the workers. With this aim in view the bourgeoisie made a number of political concessions to the working class: the bourgeoisie agreed to satisfy those demands of the working class which were compatible with the preservation of bourgeois power. At the same time the basic factors of bourgeois power – private ownership of the means of production and governmental power – remained untouched. The bourgeoisie succeeded in isolating the Communist parties. Simultaneously it combined its political manoeuvres with the employment of the most savage terror, destroying part of the most revolutionary-inclined workers and left leaders of the working class.

This policy can be most vividly traced in the history of Germany after the First World War. Parallel with it a struggle was conducted against the Soviet Union. This fight was waged by various means ranging from various forms of ideological struggle to direct intervention, which, as is well known, proved unsuccessful.

Of course the struggle against the Soviet Union does not exhaust the content of the foreign policy during that period; there continued to exist very acute internal imperialist contradictions. The chief of these in Europe were the contradictions between Great Britain and France. Britain did not want France to become the strongest power on the Continent and therefore supported Germany against France. The chief contradictions on a world scale were those between Britain and the USA.

In the period between the two world wars, the general crisis of capitalism was considerably deepened. This was reflected in the very profound and prolonged economic crisis of 1929-33. This crisis was succeeded by a depression of a special type, characterised by mass unemployment on a huge scale. The economic features of the general crisis became very clear and tangible for the working masses in the capitalist countries. A political consequence of this was that reformism found it more and more difficult to fulfil its role as the chief bulwark of the bourgeoisie. In some countries, reformism already proved to be incapable of fulfilling this role. In Germany, for example, the Communist party won a minority of the workers in the decisive industrial centres – in Berlin and the Ruhr area. Under such conditions the German, Italian and Hungarian bourgeoisie was compelled to look for a new party, a new lever, for holding the working class under its influence. Such a means was found in fascism, the fascist movement and the fascist party. Fascism is a political product of the general crisis of capitalism, and, as Stalin has pointed but, the passing to fascism indicates not only the strength, but the weakness of the bourgeoisie. Especially characteristic of the fascist movement in connection with the general crisis of capitalism is the fact that, as a rule, the fascists did not come forward as open defenders of capitalism, they did not say that they were backing capitalism, and that the capitalist order was the most perfect social order. On the contrary, they came forward everywhere with anti-capitalist demagogy, because, to come out with an open defence of capitalism in the conquered countries of Europe would have prevented them from acquiring influence among the toilers.

This circumstance confused, for a time, even some of the leading elements of the working class. The theory that fascism is the power of the petty bourgeoisie, the power of declassed elements, that it is Bonapartism, a power above classes, etc., acquired a certain popularity. All these views, of course, were completely devoid of reality. We know now that Italian, German and Hungarian fascism was financed by monopoly capitalists in these countries.

Fascism, of course, has its specific features in the different countries, for it is everywhere connected with the old reactionary forces of the given country, but basically fascism is the political expression of the deepening of the general crisis of capitalism. Fascism was victorious and came to power first and foremost in those countries which were conquered in the First World War or which were virtually in the position of conquered countries as, for example, Italy, despite the fact that she belonged to the camp of the victors. In those countries where the bourgeoisie achieved a new, forcible re-division of the world, the bourgeoisie helped the fascist forces because the fascists were not only anti-Marxists, but also chauvinists who undertake the task of defending the capitalist social order and preparing the people for a new war. It should not be forgotten that after the First World War, the majority of the people in all the conquered countries did not want a new war; social democracy was pacifically inclined, which also lowered its value for the aggressive bourgeoisie of these countries.

This article does not aim to give an analysis of the causes of the Second World War. We shall limit ourselves merely to pointing out that the Second World War, unlike the first, did not begin between countries of the same kind. On one side were the fascist aggressors, on the other the democratic countries; moreover, in the camp of the latter were both the highly developed capitalist countries and the Soviet Union. It is obvious that this circumstance was bound to exert a strong influence on the entire home and foreign policy of the capitalist countries.

The fact that the Soviet Union and the highly-developed capitalist countries were in the same camp of powers fighting against the fascist aggressors meant that the struggle between the two systems in the democratic camp was temporarily mitigated, suspended; but this, of course, did not signify the end of the struggle. At the same time, the struggle between the two systems assumed its most acute form when the fascist aggressors attacked the Soviet Union. The Allies assisted the Soviet Union, but it cannot be said that, in so doing, they forgot about the difference in social systems. The secrecy about the atom bomb is sufficient as an example of this. In the sphere of domestic policies, the Communist parties of the countries of the democratic camp – Great Britain, America, etc. – on the basis of the just nature of the war, helped their governments in the war. Against the fascists, urged them towards the opening of the Second Front despite the efforts of reactionary circles in the Allied countries. They defended their people from the danger of German fascism.

It goes without saying that the Anglo-American contradictions – the decisive inter-imperialist contradictions – were also relegated to the background during the war, while the contradictions between the democratic countries and the fascist aggressors came into the foreground; but the Anglo-American contradictions did not disappear and the struggle between America and Britain continued even during the war years. Thus, during the war the Americans took good care that the commodities exported from England should not include more than 10 percent of the materials which England received by lease-lend. During the war American capital endeavoured, not without success, to squeeze out British capital from its positions in Latin America, and to obtain markets in India and the British Dominions. The Americans put on the black list of firms with which trade was forbidden, not only purely Argentine enterprises, but also those which had British capital. In the Near East, the struggle for oil continued also during the war.

THE GENERAL CRISIS OF CAPITALISM

When the Second World War came to an end, the struggle for the preservation of the capitalist system once more became the chief problem in the domestic policy of the capitalist countries, just as it had been after the First World War. The bourgeoisie is scared by the general swing to the left in the working-class movement throughout the world after the end of the war. The forms taken by this swing to the left, and its degree, differ in the different countries. If we take such first-ranking capitalist countries as the USA and Great Britain, it will be found that the swing to the left there was expressed above all in a strengthening of the reformist labour movement. As is known, the Labour Party in Britain won a victory in the parliamentary elections. In the USA mass strikes are taking place and the trade-union movement has grown stronger. In these countries, although a strengthening of the Communist parties has taken place, they are not yet an important factor in the domestic policy of these countries. The capitalist system in these countries has not been shaken in consequence of the war. This is understandable. In the countries which were victorious in the war, the bourgeoisie was not discredited, the state apparatus remained as before, while the army was even strengthened as compared with the pre-war period. One of the characteristic features of postwar policy is the strengthening of militarism in the Anglo-Saxon countries and especially in the USA, which has become the most powerful military state of the capitalist world.

The situation is quite different in the countries of continental Europe. In these countries the bourgeoisie is discredited. In the life of one single generation the population of the European countries has experienced two big wars. Now it is forced to starve and, moreover, it is, of course, the industrial workers, the intelligentsia and the urban population who are starving first and foremost, and not the bourgeoisie or the well-to-do peasantry. Under such circumstances, radicalisation, a swing leftward of the working masses and toilers in general, is inevitable. To this must be added, also, another factor, namely, the strong polarisation of capitalist society during the war. Millions of people from the middle strata – artisans, traders, middle bourgeoisie – lost their independence during the war and became workers. Inflation during and after the war reduces to nothing the savings of the middle strata. The tendency towards the polarisation of modern society, to the formation of two camps – the big bourgeoisie and its immediate environment on the one hand, and workers, office employees, intelligentsia, who do not own property, on the other – is extremely strong. This tendency found expression in the defeat of the typical parties of the middle bourgeoisie of town and village as, for example, the Radical-Socialist Party in France or the Liberal Party in Britain.

The bourgeoisie of the countries which were subjected to German occupation became particularly discredited, because, in the main, the big bourgeoisie of France, Belgium, Holland, Czechoslovakia and Hungary collaborated with the fascist invaders. True, there were isolated exceptions: there were some capitalists in each country who took part in the resistance movement. In the main, however, the bourgeoisie collaborated with the occupationists and this, alongside the military defeat, was the chief factor in its discrediting.

In addition, however, a number of new, important political factors distinguish the present situation from that after the First World War. *One of these new factors is the changed role of the Communist parties of Europe.*

As is known, the Communist parties of Europe won great popularity as a result of the leading role they played in organising the resistance movements in all the European countries.

'The growth of the influence of the Communists', declared Stalin in his interview with a *Pravda* correspondent on Churchill's speech, 'cannot be regarded as an accident'.[3]

It is sufficient merely to recall the figures of the latest postwar elections in the European countries to be convinced of the tremendous growth of influence of the Communist parties in Europe. In France, the Communist Party is practically the largest political party in the country: at the elections on 21 October 1945, and 2 June 1946, it obtained more than five million votes. In Italy, the Communist Party has a membership of two million and is one of the leading political parties in the country. The influence of the Communists has grown considerably also in such countries as Holland, Belgium, Norway, Luxembourg, in Czechoslovakia the Communists obtained about 2.7 million votes and have become the strongest party in the country. In Hungary about 800,000 people voted for the Communist Party. In almost all the countries of the European continent Communists are taking part in the government and are playing a leading role in restoring the economy of their countries. Finally, Communist parties have achieved outstanding successes in Poland, Yugoslavia, Czechoslovakia and Bulgaria, where they are the leading force in the Popular and Fatherland fronts.

In all the countries which were subjected to Hitlerite occupation and where the big bourgeoisie collaborated with the invaders, the resistance movement against the invaders was inevitably also a movement against the big bourgeoisie of the country concerned. The Communists gained their successes as a result of the policy which their parties are now pursuing in all countries on the basis of the experience of the First World War. The Communist parties defend the interests of all the working people – workers, office employees, peasants and

---

3 [*Pravda*, 11 March 1946].

intelligentsia. This policy makes impossible the old tactics of reaction – the isolation of the Communists from the working people.

The second new factor distinguishing the present situation from that created after the First World War is the radical change in the position and role of the Soviet Union in world politics. The growth of the influence and prestige of the USSR as a world power has had to be recognised even by the enemies of the Soviet Union.

After the end of the Second World War the main line in the home and foreign policy of the capitalist countries is once more, as after the First World War, the defence of the capitalist system.

It should be mentioned that Great Britain followed this line during the war itself. Thus, for example, reactionary emigrant bourgeois governments found asylum in Britain. Preparations were carried on to ensure that after the liberation of the countries in question they would be able to return to their countries as the lawful bourgeois rulers.

After the liberation of a number of Western European countries, the question was raised of disarming the guerrillas and of excluding, as far as possible, the leaders of the resistance movement from the newly-formed governments. Of course, it is far more difficult now than it was after the First World War to come forward in open defence of the capitalist system in the form in which it existed before the war. In America, it is true, there are influential persons and groups, like [Lyndon B.] Johnson,[4] Senator [Arthur H.] Vandenberg[5] and the circles supporting them, who call for the return to pre-war capitalism. But they are exceptions. In the main, it is everywhere admitted that a profound reform of the capitalist system is necessary; everywhere ideological trends are to be found, such as the striving for a planned economy under capitalism, the introduction of social insurance, the strengthening of state capitalism, etc.

In Britain, as is known, certain important branches of industry are being nationalised. The fact that the bourgeoisie itself is compelled to begin nationalisation of the means of production is, in itself, an admission that the system of private ownership of the means of production is obsolete. There is, of course, a vast difference, between nationalisation in Great Britain and nationalisation in those countries of Eastern Europe which may be called countries with a democracy of a new type. In these countries, feudal survivals in the form of

---

4 [Lyndon B. Johnson (1908–73) was a Democratic politician, member of Congress, later President (1963–9)].

5 [Arthur H. Vandenberg (1884–1951) was a Republican Senator from Michigan].

large-scale land ownership have been abolished, a considerable part of the means of production has become state property and the state itself is not an apparatus of the rich for suppressing the working people, but operates in the interests of the latter.

In the countries of the old type of democracy, for example, in Great Britain, nationalisation does not alter the distribution of the national wealth and national income, because the owners receive compensation approximately equivalent to their former incomes. In the countries with a new type of democracy, on the other hand, nationalisation means a profound change in the distribution of the national income at the expense of the former owners of the nationalised means of production.

By what methods is the struggle being waged now to preserve the capitalist system, in the first place in Europe?

Firstly, attempts are being made to strengthen reformism in the labour movement to convert once again the Social-Democratic Party and the reformist labour movement in Germany, Hungary, Italy and France into the main social bulwark of the bourgeoisie. In the European countries, an intense struggle to win the Social-Democratic movement is developing between the progressive and reactionary forces. This constitutes the chief content of the domestic policy of the capitalist countries. At the same time, of course, this struggle goes on inside every social-democratic party, between the right and left wings, between the social-democratic working masses, who are much more inclined to march together with the Communists, and the reformist leaders of the Social-Democratic parties, who are endeavouring to revive Social Democracy in its former, pre-war form.

This struggle can best be followed from the example of Germany. A considerable part of social democracy has broken with the former policy of its party and called for unity with the Communists. On 21–22 April 1946, a unity congress of the Social-Democratic and Communist Parties of Germany took place, at which a united party of the working class was formed – the Socialist Unity Party – of Germany. A large majority of the Social Democrats in the Soviet-occupied zone were in favour of the amalgamation of the two workers' parties. Despite the counter efforts of the British and American occupation authorities, the union of the Social Democrats and Communists in the Soviet-occupied zone met with a warm response also in Western Germany.

The emergence of a united party of the working class in Germany is a serious blow to the reformist movement. It is natural, therefore, that all the reactionary elements are up in arms against the new party. Ruling circles in Britain and the US immediately came out against the unification of Communists and Social Democrats and are now giving decisive support to the group of reactionary social-democratic leaders headed by Schumacher,[6] who are trying to revive the old reformist Social Democracy in the Western zones of Germany for defence of the capitalist system of society.

It is characteristic that the Schumacher group has been joined by the majority of the old compromised leaders of Social Democracy, such as [Kurt] Severing,[7] [Gustav] Noske,[8] Paul Loebe,[9] etc., who are tried and tested defenders of the bourgeoisie. The British press openly calls for reliance on this wing of Social Democracy.

Undoubtedly, the further internal political development of the capitalist countries to a considerable degree depends on the outcome of his struggle to win over Social Democracy and on the struggle within Social Democracy.

The second line of defence of capitalism lies in increasing the influence of religion, of the church. The Catholic Church, headed by the Pope, is creating something in the nature of a 'Catholic International'. The Vatican recently appointed as cardinals 32 prominent Catholics of various countries in order to increase its influence in those countries. The same effort is also characteristic of the Protestant Church. Definite attempts are made to use the Moslem Church as a means of political struggle. The clearest expression of this is seen in India.

Most peculiar tactics are adhered to by the bourgeoisie.

In those European countries where the extreme Right-wing reactionary parties are prohibited, the bourgeoisie employs very special tactics. In those countries the bourgeoisie tries to influence the most Right-wing of the permitted Left parties and to get into its hands the leadership of these parties and to obtain a majority for them in the country. A classic example of these tactics is the behaviour of reaction during the recent elections in Hungary. The closest to the Right of the Left parties in Hungary is the Smallholders Party. It was found, after the elections, that this party had obtained the majority of the votes in Budapest, in districts where there is not a single bit of land suitable for cultivation. The whole bourgeoisie and those elements which still follow the bourgeoisie voted for it.

Capitalism's third line of defence, which so far is manifested still in a very veiled form, is encouragement of the fascist movement. If it is true that fascism is the political expression of the deepening of the general crisis of capitalism, it is

---

6 [Kurt Schumacher (1895–1952) was a politican of the SPD].
7 [Paul Severing (1875–1952) was a politican of the SPD].
8 [Gustav Noske (1868–1946) was a politican of the SPD official].
9 [Paul Loebe (1875–1967) was a politician of SPD].

to be expected that fascism will be revived. Lenin pointed out that the domination of monopoly capitalism inevitably engenders reaction. In his article entitled 'A caricature of Marxism and its imperialist economism', he wrote: 'The political superstructure of this new economy, of monopoly capitalism (imperialism is monopoly capitalism), is the change *from* democracy *to* reaction. Free competition is accompanied by democracy. Democracy corresponds to free competition. Monopoly is accompanied by political reaction'.[10]

In the capitalist countries at the present time a certain revival of political reaction and fascism is undoubtedly taking place. There are also fascist countries, such as Spain and Portugal. In addition, there is an illegal fascist movement in countries where fascism formerly ruled: Germany, Italy, Hungary, etc.

But there are undoubtedly signs of the revival of the fascist movement in the democratic countries also. Evidence of this is due activity of the fascist party in Britain, the Ku Klux Klan and other fascist groups in America, etc. In Greece, where the British virtually control policy, after dozens of changes of government Royalist reactionaries have finally been established in power; objectively and subjectively they differ little from fascists.

Of course, in the countries with a new type of democracy the revival of fascism is made very difficult because agrarian reform has done away with the landowning class and because nationalisation of the basic means of production has undermined the economic power of the big bourgeoisie. If we add to this the fact that state power in these countries is in the hands of progressive forces, it becomes clear that the revival of fascism there is made extremely difficult.

As always, the domestic policy of the capitalist countries at the present stage is closely interwoven with the foreign policy.

The methods of struggle against the Soviet Union at the present time differ, of course, from those employed after the First World War. 'Intervention' in the old sense is impossible. But the reactionary forces of the different countries are conducting an intensified campaign against the Soviet Union, and are endeavouring to isolate her and build up an anti-Soviet bloc.

In his statement on 27 May 1946, Molotov pointed to certain extremely characteristic tendencies in British and American postwar policy which had been shown during the preparation of the peace treaties. Molotov repulsed the attempts of the reactionary forces to belittle the importance of the Soviet Union and to minimise its role in the postwar world.

---

10   Lenin 1964s, p. 43.

Very typical of the policy of the bourgeoisie is the way British reaction uses the Right wing of Social Democracy in Europe for the struggle against the USSR. Naturally, the Labour Party and the Labour Government are the most suitable for using this wing of Social Democracy to achieve the foreign-political aims of the British bourgeoisie. In this respect, the existence of a Labour Government is more advantageous to the British bourgeoisie than a Conservative Government would be. To this must be added that, whereas supporters of the Labour Party sometimes came out against the foreign policy of the Conservative Government, and thus there existed a potential opposition to this policy, the Conservative Party has no grounds for opposing Bevin's[11] foreign policy. Of course, the British workers do not approve of this reactionary policy of Bevin and the Labour Government. This dissatisfaction finds expression in the opposition to Bevin's policy within the Parliamentary Labour Party.

Today also, the struggle between two systems is not the sole expression of the foreign policy of the capitalist countries. Imperialist contradictions between the big capitalist countries, in the first place between Britain and America, are reviving, despite the fact that on a number of international issues these powers form a common diplomatic bloc. The British-American contradictions, which were the basic contradictions of the capitalist world before the Second World War, or, rather, before German fascist aggression became a menace to both Britain and America, have since the defeat of Germany once again become the decisive contradictions within the capitalist world. American policy strives now first and foremost to smash the British colonial empire and to win equal conditions for American capital in the competitive struggle throughout the world. This is its chief aim.

The striving to put an end to the British, French and Dutch Empires shows itself in a great variety of forms. During the war one manifestation of this was the draft British-American Alliance, the proposal for joint tutelage over colonies, etc. Sometimes this striving even assumes ludicrous forms. For example, an American publicist recently wrote a book[12] in which he sharply criticised British, French and Dutch colonial policy. After such a criticism one might have thought that he would propose that the colonial peoples should be given their independence. Instead, however, the author declares that the colonial peoples are not yet ripe for independence and proposed that all of them should themselves select their guardians, but should not have the right to select as their guardian the imperialist power which rules them at the present time, i.e. the

---

11 [Ernest Bevin (1881–1951) was British Labour politician].
12 [Viton 1943].

British colonies may not select Britain as their guardian. The author assumes that they will all most certainly choose the Americans, because the latter, he thinks, behave so well towards colonies and can ensure their prosperity.

The movement against the colonial regime has become stronger. An important factor in this is that the British, French and Dutch have lost their prestige in the colonial countries; the colonial peoples no longer feel their former fear of them. The colonial peoples took part in armed struggle side by side with the troops of some imperialist countries against other countries; they witnessed the defeat and capture of American, British and Dutch soldiers.

Economic causes also exert an influence in strengthening the anti-imperialist movement. During the war some of the colonies grew very strong economically; some colonial countries became financially independent of Britain and themselves became creditors of her. It goes without saying that public opinion in the Soviet Union is in favour of satisfying the just demands of the colonial peoples. The plan for a Western bloc is also connected with the colonial problem. A Western bloc which would unite Britain, France, Belgium, Holland, Portugal and perhaps some of the Scandinavian countries in one political alliance is directed first and foremost against the Soviet Union and represents an attempt to revive the notorious *cordon sanitaire*, only not now on the frontiers of the Soviet Union, where it is politically impossible, owing to the existence of friendly neighbouring countries, but in Western Europe.

But another aspect of this Western bloc should be borne in mind. A Western bloc comprising Britain, France, Belgium, Holland and Portugal would unite 95 percent of the colonies of the world. This creation would be an attempt to defend the colonies against the endeavour of the USA to smash the old colonial regime and assimilate these territories economically, and also an attempt to strengthen resistance to the national liberation movement in the colonies.

Naturally, within the limits of this article it is only possible to state the most fundamental lines of domestic and foreign policy during the epoch of the general crisis of capitalism. A full elaboration of this theme, and especially of the political consequences of the Second World War, is a task requiring a series of special studies.

CHAPTER 19

Democracy of a New Type

One of the most important political results of the Second World War is the emergence of democratic states of a new type: Yugoslavia, Bulgaria, Poland, Czechoslovakia and also Albania.[1] We understand by a 'democracy of a new type' a state of affairs in a country where feudal remnants – large-scale landownership – have been eliminated, where the system of private ownership of the means of production still exists but large enterprises in the spheres of industry, transport and credit are in state hands, while the State itself and its apparatus of coercion serve not the interests of a monopolistic bourgeoisie but the interests of the working people in town and countryside.

The social structure of the states differs from all those hitherto known to us; it is something totally new in the history of mankind. It is neither a bourgeois dictatorship nor a proletarian dictatorship. The old State apparatus has not been smashed, as in the Soviet Union, but reorganised by means of a continuous inclusion in it of the supporters of the new regime. They are not capitalist States in the ordinary sense of the word. Neither, however, are they socialist states. The basis for their transition to Socialism is given by the nationalisation of the most important means of production and by the essential character of the State. They may, with the maintenance of the present State apparatus, gradually pass over to Socialism, developing to an ever increasing extent the socialist sector which already exists side by side with the simple commodity sector (peasant and artisan) and the capitalist sector, which has lost its dominant position.

The general historical prerequisite, applying in all cases, for the emergence of these states of democracy of a new type is the general crisis of capitalism, which has very considerably intensified in consequence of the Second World War.

The historical conditions specific to these countries are:

---

1 [Published in *Labour Monthly*, 1947, 29, 8: 235–42; 29, 9: 276–9 and in *The New Masses* of 28 October 1947, pp. 3–5, and 4 November 1947, pp. 14–15. A complete version of this article was published in German: *Demokratie neuer Art*, Berlin: Verlag 'Tägliche Rundschau', s.d. [1947], 23 pages. This paper was announced as a part of Varga's forthcoming book *Wandlungen in der Politik des Kapitalismus im Ergebnis des Zweiten Weltkrieges* (original: *Izmeneniya ekonomike kapitalizma v itoge vtoroy mirovoy voyny*, Moscow: Gospolitizdat, 1946)].

1. The discrediting of the ruling classes and their political parties in the eyes of the broad masses of the people, as a result of their policy of collaboration with Hitler fascism before and during the war, which led to the occupation of these countries by German troops and the fierce suppression and impoverishment of the working masses.
2. The leading role of the Communist parties in the resistance movement, as a result of which unity of the working class was achieved and a people's front formed for struggle against fascism, large-scale landownership and big capital – the economic basis of fascism.
3. The moral, diplomatic and economic support which these countries find in the Soviet Union. Without this support the states of democracy of a new type would be hard pressed to withstand the attacks of reaction, both external and internal. Very edifying in this respect is the fate of Greece.

The following features are characteristic of the *economy* of the states of a democracy of a new type:

Private ownership of the means of production continues to exist: the peasant is the owner of his land, the artisan of his workshop, the trader of his shop, the small capitalist of his factory. Big enterprises, however, in mining, industry, transport and banking are nationalised and are under state management. There still exists the appropriation of surplus value, but it is restricted to a relatively narrow sphere[2] – not only because there is considerably less privately-owned capital but also because the trade unions and the state successfully protect the workers against the capitalists.

We would like, here, to stress the decisive significance of the special character of the state for the development of the economies of these countries. Where the state is controlled by monopoly capital and serves its interests it can own a very considerable part of the means of production without in the slightest degree altering the character of the social system. In Hitler Germany the railways, Imperial Bank, Discount Bank, Prussian State Bank, large industrial enterprises (e.g. Hermann-Göring-Werke), power stations, agricultural and forest areas, etc., were the property of the Reich, individual lands or municipalities. The existence of such considerable public property, however, did not at all alter the fact that the economy of Hitler Germany remained a monopolistic economy and the social order a bourgeois one. The change in the character of the state – its transformation from a weapon of domination in the hands of the

---

2 The bourgeoisie, nevertheless, which still almost entirely dominates in the sphere of trade, receives large profits, thanks to the sale of the commodities of the socialised enterprises; withal it frequently enjoys the support of former officials who have remained in the State apparatus.

propertied classes into the state of the working people – this is what determines the real significance of the transfer of a decisive part of the means of production into the hands of the state in the countries of a democracy of a new type.

The change in the character of the state explains also why the influence of nationalisation on the distribution of the national revenue is totally different in the democratic States of a new type from that in the bourgeois-democratic countries such as Great Britain.

Nationalisation in the new democratic states signifies a special sort of economic revolution. The property of traitors to the country, of fascist capitalists, was confiscated without compensation. Other big capitalists received compensation, but their income after compensation was only a small part of the surplus value they previously appropriated.[3]

The contradictions between the social character of production and the private character of appropriation have sharpened to such a degree as the result of the deepening of the general crisis of capitalism that in the postwar period the wave of nationalisation has embraced almost all countries with fully developed capitalist relations, with the exception of the USA. Nationalisation in these countries *is an attempt to solve the contradictions between the social character of production and the private character of appropriation within the framework of the bourgeois social system*. It is precisely this which explains the introduction of nationalisation *with full compensation for the capitalists*. Thus in Britain, for example, the shareholders of electricity companies were given compensation to the amount of £450,000,000 sterling. This sum was calculated on the basis of the Stock Exchange value of the shares before nationalisation. Similarly, compensation amounting to £1,035,000,000 was fixed for owners of transport enterprises due to be nationalised. This means that the shareholders were not harmed. The distribution of the national income remains almost unchanged.[4]

These various methods of carrying out nationalisation show the difference between a bourgeois democracy and a democracy of the new type.

The economic importance of the nationalisation of big industrial enterprises naturally differs very greatly in various countries of democracy of a new type. In countries where agriculture predominates and where industrial

---

3 Difficulties arose in connection with the fact that British and American capitalists were partners in numerous enterprises taken over by the state. Many capitalists, who have fled abroad, are rapidly becoming American citizens and demanding, with the support of the authorities of their new 'motherland', full compensation or the return of their enterprises.

4 Nevertheless, bourgeois nationalisation also signifies progress in the direction of the new type of democracy.

development is inconsiderable – Bulgaria and Yugoslavia – its importance is relatively less. In Poland, which has a big coal mining and heavy industry, the importance of nationalisation is far greater, the more so as it extends also to industrial enterprises of medium size. In Czechoslovakia, which is much more highly developed industrially, and where industry was expanded by Germany during the war, nationalisation plays the greatest role, despite the fact that in this country it embraces a smaller number of medium enterprises than in Poland. While industry in Yugoslavia and pre-war Poland was almost completely destroyed during the war, the industry of Czechoslovakia suffered extremely little from military operations. The fact that in Bulgaria and Yugoslavia it was not necessary to nationalise so many individual plants does not detract from the importance of this measure for the future economic development of these countries, which are being transformed from agrarian appendages of Germany, as they were before the war, into independent agrarian-industrial countries.

The second important feature of the economies of the countries of democracy of a new type is the complete and final elimination of large-scale landlordism, of this feudal survival inside the capitalist system of economy. The social and political power of the big landowners, dating back a thousand years, has been destroyed. The big landed properties were confiscated by the state and distributed among peasants having little land and landless agricultural labourers. The number of peasant households (i.e. private owners of land) increased very considerably in these countries.

The division of the lands among many hundreds of thousands of peasants who had little or no land has converted the overwhelming majority of these peasants into loyal supporters of the new regime. The mistake made by the Hungarian Communists in 1919, when they wanted to leap over an essential historical stage by converting the confiscated large landed properties into state farms, instead of dividing them up among the peasants and so satisfying the land hunger, has nowhere been repeated.

The cultivation of land by the peasants using their own resources and giving them the opportunity of selling their produce on the market (in some countries only after fulfilling tax payments and deliveries to the State) make possible the preservation or re-emergence of commodity capitalist relations in the economy of the country. As Lenin pointed out, 'small-scale production engenders capitalism and the bourgeoisie continuously, daily, hourly, spontaneously and on a mass scale'.[5]

---

5 Lenin 1964i, p. 24.

Thus, the social order in the States of democracy of a new type is not a socialist order, but a peculiar, new, transitional form. The contradiction between the productive forces and relations of production becomes mitigated in proportion as the relative weight of the socialist sector increases.

The nationalisation of the land of big landowners and its distribution among the peasants had a different significance in different countries. In peasant countries like Bulgaria and old Serbia there existed no large-scale land ownership in the proper sense of the word. Only a relatively small amount of land could be distributed among the peasants there. In other parts of Yugoslavia, previously belonging to Hungary, e.g. in Croatia and the Banat, considerably more land could be distributed. In Czechoslovakia an agrarian reform was carried out already after the First World War: here the estates, first and foremost of expelled Germans, were distributed among the peasants.

In Poland the agrarian reform is of decisive importance for the political development of the country. Here the position of the peasantry was at its worst. *'Polonia infernum rusticorum'* ('Poland is the peasant's hell') was said of it already some hundreds of years ago. Here landownership of the feudal type was retained in its entirety, both on the territory of pre-war Poland and in the Western districts which were previously under German domination. The elimination of landlordism opens up a new era in the economic and political life of Poland.

It is quite clear that the class of big landowners by no means intends to accept these changes peacefully but is resisting the new regime in every way. Nationalisation of the land does not mean that the big landowners immediately lose their political influence. True, some of them fled abroad, but many remained inside the country. A considerable part of their property was in the form of valuables, works of art, furniture, houses, which remained in their hands. In many cases the former big landowners, e.g. in Poland, succeeded in penetrating into the State apparatus, above all into the agricultural administration, and in sabotaging the carrying out of the agrarian reform. More important still is the fact that there remained in the country a stratum of people enjoying some influence, whose existence wholly or partially depended on the big landowners. Among these are the rural clergy, notaries, judges and teachers, who regularly received money, food, firewood, etc., from the landowners; various estate employees, agronomists and other persons who were in service of the landlord; state officials, judges, officers, who obtained their posts through the influence of the landlord; deputies elected by the population at his behest. In short, the elimination of the economic basis of the power of the agrarians does not signify simultaneous destruction of their political influence inside the country.

The same can be said of the big bourgeoisie. Although their enterprises were nationalised, in the majority of cases considerable personal property still remained in their hands. A large part of the former managers, leading engineers and other persons in the service of this bourgeoisie remained in the nationalised enterprises. To this day, persons sponsored by the big bourgeoisie are to be found in the state apparatus and the various economic organisations – Chambers of Commerce and so forth – which continue to exist. The representatives of the big bourgeoisie have close contacts with the middle bourgeoisie whose enterprises have not been expropriated. Since the nationalisation of their enterprises they have not yet completely lost their influence.

Here too the general rule that changes in the economic base do not immediately evoke corresponding changes in politics, continued to operate. Deprived of their economic power, the landlords together with the expropriated and unexpropriated capitalists and the adherents fight with every means at their disposal against the new democratic regime, organise oppositional political parties and through priests, teachers and notaries already debauched by them conduct agitation among the new peasants (who often lack the necessary means of production) for giving back land to the landlords. They frighten the peasants by telling them they will be hanged in the event of the old system being restored, because they 'stole' the land. They organise plots against the government, arm bandits, etc. They seek and find active support in reactionary circles abroad.

The big bourgeoisie, still to a degree playing a dominant part in home and foreign trade,[6] struggles against the new regime in the economic sphere as well, attempting to plunder the state and discredit the social system. With the help of accomplices bribed by them in the state enterprises and the state apparatus they often obtain commodities at less than cost price, hide them, send them to foreign countries or sell them inside the country exclusively in exchange for gold or foreign currency. The representatives of the big bourgeoisie try to cause inflation or increase the existing inflation, thereby to provoke dissatisfaction among the working people and turn them against the new regime.

In a word, it is by no means a peaceful idyll that reigns in the countries of new democracy but, on the contrary, a sharp, extremely fierce class struggle that is in progress, just as in the old capitalist countries.

As regards the class struggle, however, there exists a difference in principle between the states of democracy of a new type and the old bourgeois coun-

---

6   The co-operative bodies are still not sufficiently strong to squeeze out private capital in the circulation of commodities, and in many cases they are tied still to the capitalists.

tries. In the old bourgeois countries the state is a weapon of domination in the hands of the propertied classes. The entire state apparatus – officials, judges, police and as a last resort, the standing army – *is on the side of the propertied classes.*[7]

The opposite is to be seen in the countries of new democracy. Here the state protects the interests of the working people against those who live by appropriating surplus value. When conflicts arise the armed forces of the state are to be found, not on the side of the capitalists, but on the side of the workers. It is wholly inconceivable that the armies of these states should be used against the working people. State officials and judges serve the interests of the working people.

This distinction vividly demonstrates the fact that power is in the hands of the people – the new character of the states in the countries indicated. The state influences the economic life of the country far more and in a different direction than in the old bourgeois countries, though there too the economic functions of the State have greatly extended as compared with the pre-war period. In the countries of democracy of a new type, however, the trend of economic policy is different in principle. In the capitalist countries the economic policy of the state serves the interests of maintaining the existing social order in general and the interests of monopoly capital in particular.

In the states of democracy of a new type, economic policy is directed to strengthening and developing the socialised sector of economy, accelerating economic development, improving the position of the working people, establishing a fair distribution of income in accordance with services rendered to society. To raise the standard of life of the whole people requires an increased output of production. The economic policy, therefore, aims at the utmost development of the productive forces and the elimination of restrictions on their development caused under capitalism by the scramble for profits.

To realise these aims, the states of democracy of a new type seek to influence the development of economy in a planned way. Economic plans calculated over several years have been drawn up.

It is obvious that there can be no planned economy, as understood in the USSR, in these countries. It is impossible owing to the presence of private

---

7 This does not, of course, prevent the organs of the bourgeois state in certain cases settling wage disputes between capitalists and workers in favour of the latter. This, however, never happens should it threaten the foundations of the bourgeois social system – private ownership of the means of production. The passage of social legislation – the shorter working day, health insurance, unemployment benefits – can be explained by the well-understood interests of the bourgeoisie.

ownership of the means of production. Genuine planned economy is possible only under Socialism, when all the means of production are nationalised.

However, nationalisation of the decisive enterprises in mining, industry, transport and credit gives the states of new democracy far greater possibility, than in the case of the states of monopoly capital, to influence by means of planning the economic activity of individual small private producers, the more so because the planned influence of the state is in the interests of the overwhelming majority of these small private producers, primarily the peasantry, and is not against their interests. Undoubtedly, this influence will increase as the countries of new democracy become more industrialised. All these facts show that the planned influence of the state on the economy of the countries of new democracy is sufficiently effective not only to be an obstacle to their reconversion into capitalist social systems of the old type, but also to encourage the development of these countries in the direction of Socialism. Not only does the general line of historical development push them along this road, but also concrete practical needs.

Thus, for example, many former agricultural workers have been given land but do not possess the means of production, traction power and implements, with which to cultivate it. The means of production of the big estates – tractors, steam-ploughs, etc. – distributed among the peasants are unsuitable for cultivating small peasant plots. The new rural proprietors, lacking the means of production, are threatened by the danger of becoming economically dependent on the prosperous peasants who, for money, or part of the harvest or labour, will cultivate their lands.

The practical needs of the peasants who possess land but not the means of production, urge them, therefore, towards joint cultivation of the land, in order to make use of the existing means of production which can only be used to advantage on a big farm. Various forms of artels[8] have arisen. In a number of artels the peasants jointly plough and cultivate the land. After this the boundaries of the individual plots are re-established and each peasant gathers the harvest on his own field.

In Bulgaria, where old traditions of cultivating the land on a co-operative basis exist, co-operatives for joint cultivation of the land have been formed on a voluntary basis. All the land of the members of the co-operative (which often includes all the peasants of a village) is cultivated jointly and the harvesting

---

8 [Artel (Russian: артéль) is a general term for various co-operative associations that existed in the Tsarist Russia and the Soviet Union].

is also done jointly. But the harvest is distributed not according to the purely Socialist principle of the number of days worked: besides the number of days worked, account is also taken of the size of the land which the peasant put at the disposal of the co-operative and also the amount of the means of production put in. It is a solution of the problem which corresponds to the transitional character of the social system.

By giving support to this new type of agricultural co-operative in the form of credits, tractors and seed, etc., the government encourages its development and extension and influences the development of economy in a progressive direction.

Although the same social order exists in all the countries of democracy of a new type, there are differences of no little importance, conditioned historically in both economy and policy. This applies particularly to the national policy of the States under review. It might seem that in this sphere a sharp contradiction exists between the policy of Yugoslavia on the one hand, and that of Czechoslovakia and Poland on the other (Bulgaria is almost united as regards its national composition). Czechoslovakia and Poland expelled to Germany almost all the Germans who previously lived on the present territory of their countries. In Yugoslavia all nations have equal rights and it is a federation of various nationalities. This contradiction, however, is only a seeming contradiction. In Yugoslavia it is a question of nations which (torn from their common Slav nationality) were oppressed by the Germans and fought against the invaders. During the war they belonged to one camp.

At the same time the Germans in the Sudeten region and Poland were a tool of Hitler fascism even before the war. They openly betrayed the country of which they were citizens. During the world war they fought on the side of Hitler against their motherland. It is comprehensible that, with this experience in mind, the Czechoslovak and Polish peoples have no desire to expose themselves to a possible danger by keeping these treacherous elements in their countries. The complete equality of rights of Slovaks and Czechs in Czechoslovakia clearly demonstrates the nature of its national policy, based on historical experience.

On the completion of the expulsion of Germans and the voluntary migration of Ukrainians from Poland to the Soviet Union (and Poles from the Soviet Union to Poland) the national composition of the States of the new democracy will be as follows: Bulgaria and Poland will be almost completely homogeneous as regards national composition, Czechoslovakia will consist of two nations with equal rights (probably with a Hungarian minority, which the population unwillingly accepts). Yugoslavia, on the other hand, is a federation of equal nations. This national policy of the new Yugoslavia is particularly important for the prosperity of the country and friendship among the peoples living on its territory, because its pre-war regime left behind an extremely unfavourable heritage in this respect. Although the country was called Yugoslavia, i.e. the land of southern Slavs, it was the Serbian bourgeoisie which exercised actual domination and oppressed the other peoples. Precisely for this reason everything which in the slightest degree could be interpreted to mean a continuation of the pre-war Serbian policy of oppression was deleted from the Constitution and practice of the new Yugoslavia.

There remains in Yugoslavia a small German (and Magyar) minority. Since Yugoslavia, however, has no common frontier with Germany, and its regime is politically extremely stable, it can, unlike Czechoslovakia and Poland, safely leave this minority in its country.

All the states of democracy of a new type are People's Republics: the working people determine the policy of the government. The form which the political rule of the workers takes is not, however, the same in each case. Czechoslovakia, Poland and Bulgaria are parliamentary republics with universal, equal and secret electoral rights. The governments in these countries are made up of coalition parties forming a majority and are responsible to parliament. Their electoral rights differ from the suffrage in the old bourgeois democracies, in that fascist parties are not allowed to operate and fascist traitors have no electoral rights. At the same time Yugoslavia is a federative republic, its constitution being similar in many ways to that of the Soviet Union.

In this connection an important theoretical question arises: the idea was widely held in the Communist parties that the political domination of the working people, as is the case in the Soviet Union, could only be realised in the form of Soviet power. This is not correct, nor is it an expression of Lenin's opinion.

In my book on the Hungarian Soviet republic, *Politico-economic Problems of Proletarian Dictatorship*, published in 1920, I wrote the following phrase:

> The hostility of the prosperous peasants and all strata of the ruling classes towards the proletarian state does not depend on the form the latter takes: whether this system is Soviet, a government of trade unions or a parliament with a Labour majority – this is all the same to the ruling classes. They will offer equally strong resistance to whatever form is assumed, once serious steps are taken to build up socialist economy.

This phrase which allows of the possibility of other forms of political rule by the working people was regarded by a number of comrades as incorrect. Lenin, however, who made sharp notes of criticism in the margins of some pages of my book, made no remarks at all concerning the phrase quoted above, but merely underlined part of it.[9]

The rise of the states of new democracy shows clearly that it is possible to have political rule by the working people even while the outward forms of parliamentary democracy are still maintained.

The foreign policy of the States of new democracy is determined by the transitional character of their social order. It is owing to their social order that the capitalist States, primarily the United States of America and Britain, do everything in their power not only to hinder the progressive social development of these countries but to throw them back and once more convert them into ordinary capitalist states. This effort becomes all the stronger on account of the fact that the present state system of these countries excludes the possibility of their once more becoming economically dependent countries as they were before the war in relation to Germany. It is this which explains facts in the daily press which are all too well known to the reader: the repeated attempts at interference in the internal affairs of these countries, the hullabaloo about the absence of democracy because reactionary plotting is severely dealt with, attempts to discredit the elections, support of every display of opposition, i.e. of all reactionary (in the present historical situation) and objectively counter-revolutionary parties and politicians, etc. The intensity of these attempts at interference differs in relation to the different countries. It is relatively weak in relation to Czechoslovakia, because the bourgeoisie there are so discredited by their collaboration with the German fascists that they cannot, at least for the present, act openly as a political force and foreign reaction is deprived, therefore, of internal support. The democratic character of Czechoslovakia, therefore, cannot be disputed. In Poland, where Mikołajczyks's[10] Peasant Party[11] serves as the chief legal centre of reactionary forces inside the country and a bulwark for foreign reaction, attempts at interference assume the most intense character. One of the chief tasks of the foreign policy of these countries, therefore, is to protect their political conquests at home and their new social system from all these attacks.

It can be understood from these circumstances why the states mentioned maintain the closest friendly relations among themselves and render each other economic and political aid. Of the States mentioned, Yugoslavia and Bulgaria on the one hand, and Czechoslovakia and Poland on the other, have common frontiers which facilitate their economic ties. (There are two countries –

---

9   See *Lenin Symposium*, Vol. VII, p. 371, Russian Ed.
10   [Stanisław Mikołajczyk (1901–66)].
11   [Polish Peasant Party, 'Piast', Polskie Stromictwo Ludowe (PSL)].

Hungary and Rumania – between these two groups of states, which, although at the present time not belonging to the countries of democracy of a new type, are clearly developing in this direction).

It is equally understandable that these countries maintain close, friendly relations with the Soviet Union. This is so not only because it was precisely the victorious troops of the Soviet Union that liberated their countries (Yugoslavia being, in part, an exception) from German occupation, and not only because they are all Slav states, but primarily because the present social order brings them close to the Soviet Union, because of all the great powers the Soviet Union alone is interested in the maintenance and further progressive development and can afford them diplomatic support against the reactionary offensive from outside.

The Soviet Union is at the same time interested in the maintenance by these countries of the existing regime and their further development in a progressive direction. The present regime in these countries provides the guarantee that they will not, in the future, again voluntarily serve as a *place d'armes* for any power which tries to attack the Soviet Union. For this reason the Soviet Union is interested in these States being as strong as possible in the economic, political and military sense, in order that they may defend themselves against foreign attack at least until such time as the Soviet armies can come to their aid and so avert their forcible conversion into a military *place d'armes* against the Soviet Union, as happened during the Second World War.

This situation signifies that the states of democracy of the new type are the junction of the postwar struggle of two systems. It was not for nothing that during the war Churchill frequently called for the opening of a Second Front in the Balkans instead of a genuine Second Front in the West, in order that, by the end of the war, British armed forces would be on the spot to safeguard the old order. But these proposals were rejected by Roosevelt and Stalin as being incorrect from the military viewpoint.

All this points to the extremely close interweaving of home and foreign policy at the present stage of the general crisis of capitalism.

CHAPTER 20

Anglo-American Rivalry and Partnership: A Marxist View

It may perhaps seem presumptuous for one living in faraway Moscow to venture into an American periodical with his opinion concerning relations between the United States and Great Britain.[1] But the outlines of a mountain range are better seen when viewed from a distance. And so perhaps also the essential features of Anglo-American relations can be better discerned from afar – and with the aid of the Marxist outlook – than close at hand.

Since the Second World War the United States and Britain are – apart from the Soviet Union – the two remaining Great Powers. Their relations, viewed in perspective, appear a peculiar combination of antagonism and cooperation, as result of which the United States is constantly gaining ascendancy over Britain, reducing her more and more to the status of a second-rate power in both economic and political respects. This process began nearly half a century ago, but owing to the different effect of the war upon the economies of the two countries it has been immensely speeded up.

The decisive role which England played in world economy and world politics in the nineteenth century came to an end at about the century's close. That role had been based on the following factors: England's earlier industrial development, as the result of which she became 'the workshop of the world'; her richness in coal; a climate particularly favourable for the development of the textile industry then of overwhelming importance; her vast empire, created in 300 years of wars of conquest, which towards the end of the nineteenth century had a population of about 400,000,000, or one-fourth of the total population of the globe; her merchant marine; and her banking system with its worldwide ramifications. She was the banker of the world, including the United States of America.

In those days England was herself a free-trade country and a champion of free trade, in theory and practice, throughout the world. Thanks to her headstart in industrial development and the consequent lower production of her industries, she was in a position to outbid any competitor in the world market. For this reason she could also afford to permit the free import of goods

---

1 [Published in *Foreign Affairs* (New York), 1947, 25, July: 583–94].

from other countries into her colonies. (It goes without saying, of course, that English firms were given priority in capital investments, railway construction, mining concessions, government contracts, banking, etc.). The United States and the industrial countries of continental Europe, on the other hand, put up high tariff walls to protect their relatively weaker industries against the strong English competition which they could not meet in a free market.

Politically, that was the epoch of England's 'splendid isolation'. She needed no allies and looked for none. It was the time, in naval terms, of the two-power standard – 'Britannia rules the waves'. It was the epoch of 'Pax Britannica'. Britain's mastery of the seas was also a guarantee of peace for the American continent and made the Monroe Doctrine possible, thus extending immunity to foreign invasion to all Latin America.

But towards the end of the nineteenth century Britain lost her position as the world's leading industrial power. She fell behind the United States and Germany, which had meantime developed industrially at a swift pace. Here, however, I shall disregard Germany's development and confine myself to a comparison between the United States and Britain. In the second half of the century industrial production in the former developed at a much more rapid rate than in the latter, as the following index figures show:

TABLE 20.1 Industrial production of Britain and the United States

	Britain	United States
1860	34	8
1880	53	17
1900	79	54
1913	100	100[2]

In other words, in the 50 years before the First World War, Britain's industrial output trebled, while that of the United States increased twelvefold.

Since the totals are not comparable, I shall cite figures which are comparable (in thousands of tons) for the output of three leading industries:

---

2   Wagenführ 1933, p. 69.

TABLE 20.2 Production of coal, iron and steel in Britain and the United States

	Coal		Iron		Steel	
	Britain	USA	Britain	USA	Britain	USA
1871	117,000	42,000	6,6000	1,700	200	2,000
1900	225,000	241,000	9,000	13,400	4,900	10,200
1930	244,000	48,000	6,200	31,800	7,300	40,600
1946	192,000	520,000	7,800	41,000	12,700	60,000

Table 20.2 shows that, whereas in 1871 the United States was far behind Britain in respect to the output of coal, iron and steel, by 1900 she had left Britain far behind. In 1930 the United States produced twice as much coal as Britain (apart from 123,000,000 tons of oil), and five times as much iron and steel. It also far outstripped Britain in most branches of the engineering industry – in the production of machine tools, agricultural machinery, office machines, automobiles, etc.

The underlying reasons for the swift industrial development of the United States are well known: its vast natural resources, good climate and large areas of fertile land per head of population, and the fact that its rich deposits of coal, oil and ores could be developed unimpeded by feudal survivals (with the exception of the cotton-growing sections in the South). Farming developed in what Lenin referred to as the 'American way', i.e. it developed from the very beginning on the lines of capitalist commodity production untrammelled by landlords. All this created a big internal market. As is generally known, the United States exports, on the average, less than 10 percent of the commodities produced in the country,[3] with agricultural produce still representing a relatively larger share than manufactured goods.

The policy of isolationism was a reflection of the fact that there existed a large internal market. Compared with the industrial countries of Europe and with Japan, the United States was less interested in colonies. Not that it waged no wars of conquest. But its aim was expansion on the American Continent, into areas that could actually be made part of the home market, and in the Caribbean. The conquest of the Philippines was an exception. The availability of a large internal market was the economic reason for the withdrawal of the

---

3 *Statistical Abstract of the United States 1946*, p. 888.

United States from European affairs and her refusal to become a member of the League of Nations after World War I.

Two factors limited the American economic advance in the nineteenth century: capital and manpower. Both of these the United States was receiving from Europe – capital primarily from England and manpower from the whole of Europe. The shortage of labour had a definite effect upon the development of American industries in the nineteenth century. Many of the immigrants, after some years of work in the industries of the east, proceeded westward to settle as farmers on the still free land. Wages in industry were relatively high. It was therefore more profitable to introduce expensive machinery than it was in England and in continental Europe, with their lower wages. The result was that the United States left England far behind in regard to productivity of labour, to output per man-hour. British capital equipment became antiquated in comparison. More industries in the United States became able to produce more cheaply than the same industries in Britain. The high American tariffs further impeded the import of British manufactures,[4] while some American manufactures were conquering the world markets. In certain commodities, American exports in 1914 reached the following percentages of the total American output: sewing machines, 40.5 percent; typewriters, 30.9 percent; cash registers, 20.1 percent; bicycles, 13.3 percent.[5] 'Manufactures were gaining in relative importance in American exports before the war and losing ground relatively in the import trade'.[6] English economists watched these developments with anxiety. I might recall Arthur Shadwell's book, *Industrial Efficiency*, published in London at the beginning of the present century, which drew attention to the danger threatening England.[7]

American competition became still keener after the First World War. At that time, as pointed out in the Balfour Report, about half the exports from Britain were already going to countries within the Empire.[8] An important contributing factor was the preferential tariffs established by the Dominions for British goods, with margins amounting on an average to 9 percent of the *ad valorem* duties.

---

4 American tariffs on 'staple British exports' averaged 19.5 percent in 1914 (the *ad valorem* level of American duties on British goods) and 32 percent in 1924. Committee on Industry and Trade 1927.
5 Committee on Industry and Trade 1927, p. 459.
6 Committee on Industry and Trade 1927, p. 452.
7 [Shadwell 1906].
8 '... [B]etween 40 and 50 percent of our total exports are directed to Empire markets', *Final Report of the Committee on Industry and Trade* 1929, p. 22.

By way of reciprocating, Britain had by then introduced tariffs on various commodities (tobacco, sugar, coffee, cocoa, etc.) and granted preferences to the Dominions. During the great economic crisis of 1919–34 this development took the shape of the system of imperial preferences established at the Ottawa Conference in 1931. The system of imperial preferences has enabled Britain all this time to direct about a half of her exports to Empire markets. For example, she sold the following percentage of her exports in Empire markets: in 1913, 36; in 1929, 45; in 1937, 49; in 1945, 54; and in 1946, 50.[9]

These figures make obvious how vital it is for Britain to maintain the system of imperial preferences. This is especially the case today, in view of the difference in the economic effects of the Second World War upon the United States, Britain's main rival, from the war's effects upon Britain herself.

The United States took part in the war during a much shorter period and – in relation to population – with smaller forces than Britain. Her casualties were relatively slight – 262,000 killed, or one per 500 of the population. The number of men killed in action was much smaller than the number of Americans killed during the same period in accidents (355,000).[10] There were no hostilities on United States territory, nor did it suffer from air raids.

The war, which created a practically unlimited demand for goods of every sort, resolved – for the time being – the hardest problem that had confronted United States economy after World War I, namely the contradiction between the output capacity of industry and agriculture and the capacity of the home and foreign markets. American industries, during the period between the two World Wars, worked at only 50–60 percent of their capacity (calculated on the basis of 300 shifts per annum),[11] and millions of workers in the United States were chronically unemployed during those 20 years. Another result was the wholesale destruction of farm produce in the thirties.

The war provided the opportunity to make full use of the productive forces that remained unutilised in the years of peace, and led to a further expansion of the output capacities of American industries.[12] Plants were renovated and improved and the process of production further automatised. The result was

---

9   Calculated on the basis of figures cited in the *Statistical Abstract for the United Kingdom*, Volumes 1913–37, and *The Board of Trade Journal*, London.
10 See 'Front toll 1,070,524: Home front, 36,355,000', *The New York Times*, 13 October 1945, p. 4.
11 Even in the boom period, 1915–29, American industry worked at only 79 percent of capacity, according to the calculation of Nourse (1934). But even these calculations contain serious methodological errors. See my book, Varga 1939b, Ch. IV.
12 The Government alone built new factories valued at US$16 billion, or about one-quarter of the value of all categories in the United States before the war. See *Additional Report of the Special Committee*, 1944.

that productivity of labour – output per man-hour – increased during the war by approximately 20 percent. The gap between the United States and Britain was thus vastly widened.

While the United States grew richer during the war, Britain – despite lend-lease aid from the United States and contributions from the Dominions – lost nearly a quarter of her national wealth (at home and abroad). According to official English figures,[13] the decline by the middle of 1945 amounted to £5,083 million: £4,198 million abroad (£2,879 million representing the increase in foreign debts and £1,118 million the reduction of investments in foreign countries), and £885 million in Britain. This sum does not include damage caused by the war, deterioration of buildings due to lack of repair, or the depreciation and loss of household articles and various stocks. Britain's total loss of national wealth may be put, in round figures, at £7,500 million, or approximately a quarter of the total. And, what is worse, it is not apparent in what way Britain can make good this loss.

Britain's output is now undoubtedly below prewar. True enough, in December 1946 there were approximately 19,500,000 men and women 'employed', against approximately 18,500,000 in June 1939. But these included an additional 1,000,000 in the armed forces and 700,000 in 'public services'.[14] Hence the number of men and women employed in production was smaller than before the war.[15] Obviously, also – in view of the wear and tear of machinery – the productivity of labour is not higher, and in many cases it is even lower.

In the United States, the volume of industrial output in 1947 was 60 percent above the figure for 1939. No postwar index figures have so far been published for Britain. But in the *White Paper* we read: 'By the end of the year [1946] the rate of national output was probably not significantly below prewar over the economy as a whole'.[16] British economy is in fact in a vicious circle. If the national wealth is to reach the pre-war level again, larger amounts of capital must be accumulated yearly than before the war. If consumption is to reach the pre-war level, it is necessary to produce considerably more than before the war. Since fewer persons are employed in production, the productivity of labour must be

---

13   *Statistical Material Presented During the Washington Negotiations* 1945, pp. 12–13.
14   *Economic Survey for 1947* 1948, p. 36.
15   The most serious setback for Britain is the continuing decline of productivity in the coal-mining industry. Here is the output per wage-earner of saleable coal in tons per annum: 1938, 301.9; 1940, 299.4; 1942, 274.8; 1944, 259.2; 1945, 246.2. 'The coal crisis', *The Times*, 20 February 1947, p. 5. The output is barely enough to meet Britain's domestic requirements.
16   *Economic Survey for 1947* 1948, p. 14.

higher than before the war. This could be achieved only by a thorough renovation of antiquated plants, as well as by the replacement of plants used up in the war or destroyed by bombing. But this would involve heavy capital investments. In other words, in order to accumulate capital, more capital has to be invested first.[17]

So far, British economy, as admitted in the *White Paper*, has not been able to break out of the vicious circle: '... [C]apital equipment and maintenance work ... done in 1946 ... was probably much the same as in a normal prewar year. But this does not go far towards making up arrears from six years deferred maintenance'. Even this accomplishment was possible only by keeping the standard of living of the large masses of the British people at about 10 percent below pre-war by means of rationing nearly all consumer goods. This is something no Conservative Government could have achieved without provoking big mass strikes.[18]

Closely connected with this question is the problem of increasing exports and balancing Britain's payments. In order to make up for the lost income from overseas investments, Britain would have to increase exports sufficiently above the pre-war level to attain a favourable balance of payments. In 1946, receipts from exports and re-exports amounted to £900 million, against £533 million in 1938.[19] Still, there was an adverse balance of payments, the deficit amounting to £450 million (compared with £70 million in 1938).[20] To balance the payments,

---

17   American and Canadian credits are of some help, but far from enough – the less so since nearly half of the American loan so far used has been spent to purchase, not capital equipment, but foodstuffs.
18   [*Economic Survey for 1947* 1948, p. 18].
19   [It is unclear on which sources Varga is basing himself here. *The Economist* of 25 January 1946 gives in the 'business notes' slightly different figures for Britain's overseas trade by value:

TABLE 20.3 Britain's overseas trade by value

	1938	1945	1946
Total imports	919,508,933	1,103,693,217	1,297,682,580
UK exports	470,755,320	399,275,982	911,686,238
Re-exports	61,524,646	50,988,697	50,348,445
Total deficit	387,228,967	653,428,538	335,647,897

The Economist, 25 January 1946, p. 158.

20   Receipts from 'oil, shipping, insurance' are not included in the balance of payments.

exports would have to be increased by £450 million.[21] Since, however, British export goods contain foreign raw materials, such as copper, nickel, manganese ore, chromium, cotton, wool, etc., to a value of about 20 percent, exports would have to be increased by a further £90 million. They would have to be raised still more if lost overseas investments were to be built up again. So far this is out of the question. As *The Economist* wrote in its issue of 25 January 1947: 'The country is still running into debt abroad. Each month our balance of overseas payments is still unfavourable'.[22]

To add to the difficulties in the way of balancing overseas payments, Britain is buying heavily from the dollar area, while her sales in that area are much smaller. As *The Statist* reported on 8 March 1947: 'In 1946 we took 35.1 percent of our imports, against only 22.3 percent before the war, from the dollar area, while exporting to that area only 7.6 percent (against 10.1 percent before the war) of our total exports ... That is why the dollar loans are running down so fast'.[23]

The balancing of overseas payments seems to be a virtually unattainable task, the more so since the imminent crisis of overproduction in the United States will reduce the chances for the export of British goods.

In order to make up for the adverse balance of payments for a few years to come, Britain asked the United States for a loan on non-commercial terms, pleading that her sacrifices in the war had been bigger than those of the United States. After protracted negotiations the loan was granted. But the United States categorically demanded that Britain should give up or at least mitigate the imperial preferences system. This demand is quite in line with the interests of big business in the United States. For the United States today holds a position in the capitalist economy similar to that of England in the nineteenth century. Given equal opportunities, she could best all competitors in the world markets. Hence the demand for the Open Door all over the world. But, unlike England of the nineteenth century, the United States is opposed to free imports. Even though American industry can hold its own against any capitalist competitor, big business still insists on maintaining high tariffs.[24]

---

21 [*Economic Survey for 1947* 1948, pp. 16–17].
22 [This is a quote from *The White Paper* by *The Economist*, not a comment of the latter. See 'Let us face the present', *The Economist*, 25 January 1947, pp. 129–30].
23 ['Export crisis', *The Statist. An Independent Journal of Finance and Trade*, 8 March 1947, p. 199].
24 In the past 50 years protective tariffs have undergone a functional change. Whereas in the nineteenth century they served as a means of protecting new and still-feeble industries against the competition of older industrial countries, in the twentieth century they serve

It is true that in the loan agreement a reduction of American tariffs was promised in return for the abolition of imperial preferences. But the prospects of such a reduction are very slight. Business representatives are, indeed, in favour of reducing tariffs on raw materials which they have to import, but they object to a reduction of tariffs on goods which they manufacture. That is the stand taken by the Iron and Steel Institute, the National Association of Wool Manufacturers, the American Tariff League, and the like. Many of the unions belonging to the [American] Federation of Labor are also opposed to a reduction of tariffs. The victory of the Republican Party in the recent elections has further diminished the chances of any material reduction of tariffs. Any changes may be rendered worthless by the application of the 'escape clause', which stipulates that the contracting countries may revoke the tariff reductions if they lead to an increase in imports which may prove seriously harmful for an industry.

On the other hand, the experience of the twentieth century, and especially of the 1930s, has not been lost on American capitalists and economists. They are aware of the weaknesses of the American economy. They understand that American industry, with an output capacity which has increased by one-third during the war, cannot dispose of its entire production in the home market, that it is essential to push exports to the utmost in order to prevent a situation where more than a half of the industrial plant is constantly idle and there is a permanent army of unemployed, ten million strong. With Germany, Italy and Japan for the time being out of the running in the rivalry for world markets, and since for some time to come the European Continent can buy American goods only on credit, American competition is directed primarily against Britain, against the institutions which give her a position of advantage in her own Empire – preferential tariffs, sterling bloc, colonies. The ultimate aim of American policy is to break up the British Empire.

Naturally, British statesmen as long as possible took a sharply negative attitude to the demand for the abandonment of preferential tariffs and the sterling bloc, and strongly resented American criticism of British colonial policy.

---

in older industrial countries like the United States as a means of protecting the superprofits of the big trusts. These latter, protected by high tariffs against foreign competition, are enabled to maintain high prices within the country and to dump goods (which are sold at high monopoly prices inside the country) at low prices on the world markets. The Aluminum Company of the Mellon family furnishes a graphic example of what high tariffs mean to a trust. For decades prices of aluminum in the United States could be maintained above world prices with the aid of protective tariffs. This netted the Alcoa additional millions in profits every year.

Everyone remembers Churchill's statement: 'I have not become the King's First Minister in order to preside over the liquidation of the British Empire'. During the framing of the Atlantic Charter and the negotiations for the lend-lease agreement, he insisted on the insertion of clauses protecting the imperial preferences system.

Since circumstances made it imperative for Britain to obtain an American loan, the British eventually had to yield. But the American policy evoked a great deal of bitterness among British Conservative leaders. This is clearly discernible in a book by Mr. L.S. Amery,[25] in which the blunt charge is made that America's foreign economic policy endangers the prosperity of other countries and the peace: 'The American system means a free field for irresponsible American surplus production and financial power to create chaos and instability in a world of small economic units forbidden to cooperate for their mutual benefit and tied down by the restrictive effects of a rigid international monetary system'.[26]

Another prominent Conservative leader, Lord Woolton,[27] was reported by *The Times*, 24 January 1947, to have stated:

> It was also stipulated that there should be conversations regarding preference within the Empire. There was no harm in that so long as they ended in the right direction. There was no price in gold or in dollars which should induce us to give up Empire trade. There might have to be changes, but he was certain it would be a very bad day for this country if it abandoned its right to trade within its own Empire or to trade among its own people under conditions which it determined. It would be a bad day if it allowed any other country, however friendly, to dictate the terms of its economic policy.[28]

I have pointed out above that the United States is now assuming the position in capitalist world economy which England held in the nineteenth century. As has always been the case in history, the change in economic position has led to a change in foreign policy. Gone are the days when American foreign policy was based on the Monroe Doctrine, on interests confined to the American Continent, on 'isolation' from European affairs, on aloofness from the League of Nations.

---

25 [Leo Amery (1873–1955) was a British Conservative politician].
26 Amery 1946, p. 153.
27 [Lord Woolton (1883–1964) was a British Conservative politician].
28 'Empire preference', *The Times*, 24 January 1946, p. 2.

'The epoch of isolation ... is ended. It is being replaced by an epoch of American responsibility', wrote *The New York Times* on 12 March 1947.[29] Today the United States is pursuing a world policy of imperialism in the fullest sense of the term. She has a bigger navy than all other countries of the world combined. She has the strongest air force. She has naval and air bases all over the world. She has the secret of the atom bomb. She has the biggest war budget of all countries of the world.

Today the United States is the land in which militarism is most in vogue. Big business is bent on using the country's military power for the economic subjugation of the world. Dazzled by this military power, many Americans insist that the twentieth century must become 'the American century'. The present foreign policy of the United States – the conversion of China and Japan into semi-colonies; expansion in the Middle East (oil concessions and pipelines); the far-reaching penetration of American capital into Italian industries and aviation; the position taken by the United States in Africa; the 20 percent share of the United States in the foreign trade of British India, despite preferential tariffs; the entire foreign economic policy of the United States – entails squeezing Britain out of her positions in every part of the world.

Historical development is unquestionably driving towards the disintegration of the British colonial empire. Even the most astute manoeuvring of British colonial politicians cannot delay India's liberation much longer. And, as [George] Curzon[30] once said, without India there is no British Empire. The need to balance overseas payments makes it impossible for Britain to continue overseas government expenditure at the rate of £300 million (the sum spent in 1946) per annum. That is why she had to yield her positions in Greece and Turkey to the United States. Should American policy succeed in breaking down the system of imperial preferences and the sterling bloc, and, consequently, severing the special economic ties binding the Dominions to Great Britain, the latter will be reduced to a second-rate power with a population of 48,000,000. The United States will then remain the only capitalist great power.

As reported in *The Times* on 7 March 1947, Churchill said in the course of the debate on India in the House of Commons that 'it was with deep grief that he watched the battering down of the British Empire with all its glories and all the services it had rendered to mankind'.[31] (To be sure, the peoples of India, China and Africa have a different opinion regarding the 'services rendered' by the British Empire).

---

29   'Mr. Truman goes to Congress', *The New York Times*, 12 March 1947, p. 24.
30   [George Curzon (1859–1925) was a British Conservative politician, Viceroy of India].
31   'Mr. Churchill opposes India time limit', *The Times*, 7 March 1947, p. 4.

The change in the economic basis had led to a change also in the domestic policy of the United States. Roosevelt, as a great statesman, understood that it was in the interests of the American bourgeoisie itself to blunt the edge of the class struggle between the bourgeoisie and the proletariat by timely concessions which did not imperil the existing system. After his death, the forces of social reaction have been gaining the upper hand in the United States. The Republican victory in the latest elections further strengthened these forces. The numerous plans designed to circumscribe the rights of the working class, President Truman's order to remove from the civil service all persons suspected of Communist sympathies, the suggestions that the Communist Party should be outlawed, are all signs of the times.

The internal policies of Britain and the United States are moving in opposite directions. The Labour Government has a programme of nationalisation and peaceful transition to Socialism, and the British bourgeoisie displays flexibility in avoiding a showdown fight with the working class. In the United States, there is growing reaction harbouring the danger of Fascism. As George Catlin aptly remarked in *The Fortnightly* for January 1947, 'The British Tory shows himself these days, by comparison with his American brother, as already half a Socialist'.[32]

How does it happen that, in spite of all these contradictions, as Foreign Minister Molotov has pointed out, the United States and Britain form a bloc in the sphere of foreign policy?

The basis for this bloc is the joint fight waged by the United States and Britain to maintain the system of society existing outside the USSR and to counter the influence of the Soviet Union in world affairs. The Truman doctrine, a turning point in American foreign policy, is a clear departure from Roosevelt's policies; whereas Bevin's[33] policy is a direct continuation of Churchill's. Churchill, as is now generally known, was opposed to a second front in the west and favoured an invasion of the Balkans in order that a British army might be in existence there as a counterpoise to the Soviet Army at the end of the war. Roosevelt's and Stalin's objections thwarted this scheme.

The Truman-Bevin policy is finding increasing opposition in the ranks of the Labour Party, while the British Liberals are finding justification for Bevin's policy in Britain's economic dependence on the United States. W[illiam] Rydal[34] wrote in *The Fortnightly* in March 1947: 'The Socialist rebels who berate Mr. Bevin for a foreign policy which, to all intents and purposes, makes Britain

---

32   Catlin 1947, p. 27.
33   [Ernest Bevin (1881–1951) was a British Labour politician].
34   Rydal 1947, p. 163.

into a satellite of the mighty USA might reasonably be asked to face up to the unpalatable economic and financial facts'.[35]

The United States and Britain are pursuing policies which have many aspects in common. Truman's recent proposal to finance the arming of Greece and Turkey was described by *The New York Daily Mirror* as the most determined anti-Communist step taken by the United States since 1917. And Henry Wallace[36] has pointed out that Truman's policy aims at having American troops patrol the frontiers of the Soviet Union.

Britain, on the other hand, and more specifically the Labour Party leadership, is conducting an ideological struggle against the rising Communist influence in continental Europe. The American ideology of unrestricted capitalism and free enterprise is hardly likely to find a congenial soil in present-day Europe. As Attorney General Sir Hartley Shawcross stated in a speech early this year: 'The political conflict in Europe today is not that between Conservatism and Socialism; it is between Social-Democracy and totalitarian Communism'.[37]

So we see that, in spite of the serious differences dividing the United States and Britain, the two nations are united in the chief aims of their foreign policy. They are waging a common diplomatic policy, as was shown, for example, at the Conference of Foreign Ministers in Moscow. The money and armaments to prop up the far-from-democratic governments of China, Greece, Turkey, etc., are supplied by the United States. In its struggle against Communism, the new democracy and the Soviet Union, American reaction has taken the British Labour Government in tow, despite the increasing opposition which the latter is encountering from its own left wing.

Such are the main features of American and British policy, as seen from a distance.

---

35 Naturally, England is trying to pursue a foreign policy of her own, too. The schemes to create a Western bloc are directed not only against the Soviet Union; they also represent an attempt to bring together the European countries possessing colonies into a bloc capable of standing up against the United States.

36 [Henry A. Wallace (1888–1946) was Vice-President of the United States (1941–6), Secretary of Agriculture (1933–40), Secretary of Commerce (1945–6). He opposed Truman's cold war policy].

37 Quoted in a letter from Zilliacus to *The Times*, 25 January 1947, p. 5. [Konni Zilliacus (1894–1967) was a left-wing member of the Labour Party and an opponent of Great Britain joining NATO].

CHAPTER 21

The Increased Role of the State in the Economy of the Capitalist Countries

One of the most striking features of the Second World War is the fact that in *all bourgeois countries* – the belligerent as well as the neutrals – *the state acquired a decisive role in the war-time economy*.[1]

During the last centuries the relation of the state with the economy underwent many changes.

In the period of full development of industrial capitalism after the fall of feudalism and the liberation of the productive forces from their feudal chains, the role of the state was limited to protection of private property. That was the period of 'Manchesterian' free trade and of the creed that if all individuals pursue their particular interests society could maximise its wealth and that therefore the state should not interfere in capitalist economy. The economic rationality of this theory was based on the fact that in those days the capitalist market was quickly expanding in connection with capitalist development and the inclusion of non-capitalist elements (peasants, home workers, hand workers, etc.) into the circulation process of commodities. Hence, the contradiction between capitalism's strive for unlimited expansion and a limited social purchasing power was not very clear; that only happened during a relatively short period of crisis in the industrial cycle. The doctrine of free trade reflected in the first place the interests of England being in those days the 'workshop of the world'.

The role of the state in the economy increased because of the already present development of the monopolistic character of capitalism and the growing contradictions between the expansionary tendencies of capital and the limited consumption capabilities. Everywhere (except in England) the doctrine of free trade was now replaced by the doctrine of protectionism practised by the state. This inspired protectionist policies of the domestic market by means of tariffs,

---

1 [Originally published in E. Varga, *Izmeneniya v ekonomike kapitalizma v itoge vtoroy mirovoy voyny*, Moscow: Ogiz Gosudarstvennoe izdatelstvo politicheskoy literatury, 1946, Chap. 1, pp. 15–33; translated from Eugen Varga, 'Die gewachsene Rolle des Staates in der ökonomie der kapitalistischen Lander', *Veränderungen in der ökonomie des Kapitalismus im Ergebnis des zweiten Weltkrieges*. Als Manuskript für Funktionäre gedruckt, Zonenleitung der K.P.D., britische Zone, Spezialdruckerei Pittroff & Co. AAM 40 Wuppertal, Klasse B – 8127 9. 47 1500].

colonial markets monopolised by industries of the motherland, state subsidies, dumping practises, etc.

During the First World War, economic activities of the state had enormously increased. War-time state interference differed, however, fundamentally from that of peacetime. In peacetime the capitalist state is helping enterprises in finding profitable *outlets* for their commodities. During the war, when demand of commodities (with only a few exceptions) exceeds supply and 'marketing problems'[2] are inexistent, and when war demands are beating all records, the state will influence production and consumption in such a way that war demands will always be met first.

The one-sided interference of the state in the economy during the First World War caused thoroughgoing changes in a country's economy.

On this phenomenon Lenin comments:

> When capitalists work for defence. i.e., for the state, it is obviously no longer 'pure' capitalism but a special form of national economy. Pure capitalism means commodity production. And commodity production means work for an *unknown* and free market. But the capitalist 'working' for defence does not 'work' for the market at all – he works on government *orders*, very often with money loaned by the state.[3]

Well known is that Lenin therefore characterised the war-time economy of the First World War as a '*war-time state-monopoly capitalism*'.[4] This characteristic is completely appropriate to the Second World War as well. This means that the war-time economy of the bourgeois countries is not some kind of war-time socialism, but a *capitalist* economy. It appears as an economy of monopoly capitalism, while the interests of the big monopolies are predominantly represented; it is a *war-time* economy because production and consumption remain subordinated to war preoccupations; it emerges as *state capitalism*, because the adaptation of the economy is realised in function of the warfare preoccupations of state power representing the coalesced interests of the bourgeoisie.

After the end of the First World War the regulating activities of the state were rapidly curtailed. The role played by the state in the capitalist economy during the interwar years remained, however, by far more important than before the First World War. The state also penetrated deeper into the economy, but this

---

2 We will treat this problem more thoroughly elsewhere in this book.
3 Lenin 1964r, pp. 68–9.
4 [Varga is probably referring to Lenin 1964p, p. 357].

time not by means of protective tariffs, but by using quota systems and import-prohibiting measures, exchange controls, compulsory cartelisation, state subsidies and reorganisations, etc.

The state gained, however, an unprecedented influence on the economy during the Second World War. This mirrored the nature of the Second World War and the necessity of using all available resources of the country as much as possible for warfare. This would have been absolutely impossible if full anarchy of production existing before the war would have remained in war-time; in war-time it would have been impossible to decide on the use of raw materials, allocating workers, distributing insufficient consumer goods to the population and setting their price by trusting exclusively on the point of view of the private entrepreneurs.

If the state had not mostly decided on *the kind of goods to be produced*, many enterprises would have preferred manufacturing goods generating higher profits instead of producing war materials. Instead of producing weapons, they would have mostly manufactured luxury cars; instead of building factories for armament production, they would have built mansions for the rich, etc. If the state had not regulated *the allocation of raw materials*, they would have been purchased by those enterprises able to pay for them the highest price. Hence, the war industry would not always have acquired all necessary raw materials.

If the state had not *allocated* the insufficiently available *labour force*, then not those enterprises entrusted with the production of war materials would have been firstly supplied, but those enterprises able to pay the highest wages. The urban workers' physical forces, whose recovery was however indispensable for securing normal production in the war industry, would have certainly not restored because of insufficient nourishment.

In short one can say that *the bourgeois state as an organisation of the coalesced bourgeoisie was compelled to subjugate the private interests of particular enterprises and persons to the conduct of war*. Of course, this would only have been met with partial success. The stronger the different monopoly enterprises are, the more difficult it will be for the state to subjugate the private interests to the war economy, especially if the representatives of the monopolies and the special interest organisations are exercising a determining influence on the regulation departments of the state.

The role of the state, the degree of its influence on the economy of the developed capitalist countries, depends in the first place on the relation between available resources and war demands. The more this relation becomes unfavourable, the stronger the role of the state will become; the more this relation is favourable, the weaker the role of the state will be. The influence of the state was strongest in Germany, where any economic activity, even that of collecting and delivering fragments of glass, was 'regulated'. In the other belligerent countries, the role of the state was weakest in the USA where enormous natural resources were available and where particular sectors of economic life had also remained in war-time beyond state control.

The regulating activities of the state – in order to subdue the economy to war demands – are somehow contradictory. The more the state controls and regulates, the more the workers will disappear from the productive sector. State bureaucracy is growing enormously. In the USA, the number of civil servants and office workers grew during the war with 1.5 million people. People employed by state enterprises and civil servants working for the different states and municipalities are not included in this number. We do not possess data about the number of German civil servants during the war. Information published in the press[5] about the Berlin district Kreuzberg give us an impression. According to this newspaper some 7,000 families, having obtained a food-card from the registry office, were living in this district. In addition, the registry office also distributed raw materials to handicraft workers living in the same district. About 600 civil servants were employed in this registry office.

One had registered some 20 million families in Germany. If one includes the countryside, where the peasants are supplying themselves with foodstuffs and where the registry offices have a smaller staff, one can nonetheless estimate the total number of people working at the registry offices at 1.5 million (in Germany there are some tens of million copies of 62 different sorts of food-cards numbering printed monthly). To this number of office workers one should add also those of the *Reichsnährstand* – which is collecting all agricultural products, i.e. the produce of each individual farm – and also those office workers controlling prices, foreign trade, foreign currencies, registration of raw materials and their distribution, the transport system, etc. One may assume that the state bureaucracy is employing – apart from the enormous repressive institutions, such as Gestapo, SS, etc. – some 4 million people. The workers of the state enterprises, the municipalities and the railways are not included in this number.[6]

We will now try to illustrate at the hand of statistical data the role the state is playing in the war-time economy.

---

5   *Berliner Börsen-Zeitung*, 3 May 1942.
6   Compared with the data of the USA: the number of state and municipal workers was 5.9 million at the beginning of 1945. *Monthly Labor Review* 1945, 60, 3, p. 5.

a) The state was the most important buyer of commodities on the market. In the belligerent countries the state bought much more than a half of all goods produced during the war. One may take England as an example.

During the war England's National Income was spent as follows:[7]

TABLE 21.1   England's National Income (in percentages)

	1938	1941	1944
War expenditures	8	53	53
Civil consumption	87	62	57
Savings	5	–	–
Decrease of national wealth	–	15	10

One can see that more than a half of the National Income was working for the war effort. The following data are available for 1943 (in millions of pounds sterling):

National Income (*)	8,075
State expenditures (*)	5,782

SOURCE: *STATISTICS RELATING TO THE WAR EFFORT OF THE UNITED KINGDOM* 1944, PP. 33–4

We may assume that 60 percent of all state expenditures have a material character, i.e. payments for goods, and that 40 percent of the expenditures have a personal character: salaries of civil servants, army officers and soldiers, debt service (it is possible that the percentage of material expenditures is much higher because of enormous military spending). In 1943 the English state purchased goods worth about 3,500 millions of pounds sterling; this amount represents about 45 percent of England's National Income. Because the latter includes large sums which do not represent values newly created during the past year, but in reality only a redistribution of income (salaries of civil servants, fees of physicians, lawyers, artists, debt service, etc.), it is possible that the state has purchased more than half of all values incorporated into the commodities produced in the country.

---

7   Official data in 'The statistical background', *The Economist*, 15 December 1945, p. 875.

In the USA the situation is rather similar. The relative share of state expenditures is the following:[8]

TABLE 21.2   Relative share of US state expenditures (in milliards of dollars)

Year	Production value	Public spending (during the fiscal year)(*)		Civil consumption	Accumulation
		Military	Civil		
1941	120.5	13.3	13.2	74.6	19.4
1942	151.5	49.5	12.4	81.9	7.7
1943	187.8	82.5	12.3	90.9	2.2
1944	198.7	86.3	13.0	97.6	1.8

(*)   Fiscal year ends in June.

As the American army was still numerically small and large sums were invested in developing weapon factories, public spending for buying *commodities* was then higher than in England. One may assume that the share of government spending for commodities reached here 75 percent. This means some 59 milliards of dollars for the fiscal year of 1942–3.

US National Income is estimated at some 110 milliards of dollars and for 1943 at some 148 milliards of dollars.[9] For the budget year 1942/3 one can thus presume an average expenditure of 128 milliards of dollars. When deducing (as we already did for England) the regrouped figures, commodities purchased by the US government only represent a half of all new values yearly created in the country. (The amount mentioned above with regard to the US National Income includes salaries of all personnel of the armed forces).[10]

The following quote of the London-based journal *The Economist* of 25 December 1943 reveals the particular importance of the US state as a commodity purchaser.

'If the war should end today there would be outstanding *more than $75 milliards* worth of war contracts on which deliveries had not yet been made'.[11]

---

8   *Federal Reserve Bulletin*, 1944, 30, 3, p. 479.
9   *Federal Reserve Bulletin*, May 1944, p. 418.
10 Ibid.
11 'American survey', *The Economist*, 25 December 1943, p. 846.

This amount roughly equals total output of US industry before the Second World War.

No data are available for Germany; it is however obvious that compared to the Anglo-Saxon countries the state purchased an even larger part of all produced commodities.

b) State property increased very sharply during the war period.
In England, the state constructed an import part (and in the USA even a predominant part) of the new armament factories, because the capitalists were unwilling to take the risk of this investment. In the USA, the state built factories worth 16 millions of dollars, while total value of privately-owned factories amounted in the USA to an estimated 50 to 60 milliards of dollars;[12] in addition, the state built a new commercial fleet measuring 15 to 20 millions of tons of water displacement, etc. In Germany an important part of the industrial enterprises of the occupied countries was acquired by the state; this property transfer occurred either directly or indirectly (i.e. via the Hermann-Göring-Werke). In Italy – maybe more than in any other country – state participation in industry and banks was of a particular importance.

c) In war-time a significant bigger part of National Income was withdrawn by the state from its citizens in the form of taxes than in peacetime.
In England, evolution of National Income and tax receipts were as follows:[13]

TABLE 21.3 England's National Income and tax receipts (in millions of pounds sterling)

Year	1938	1940	1941	1942	1943	1944
National Income	4,804	5,744	6,436	7,088	7,684	8,043
Tax receipts	1,016	1,254	1,831	2,343	2,881	3,154
Tax receipts (%)	21	22	29	33	37	39

In all other belligerent countries the situation was similar.

---

12 *Additional Report of the Special Committee Investigating the National Defense Program* 1944.
13 *An analysis of the sources of war finance and estimates of the national income and expenditure in the years 1938 to 1944* 1945, p. 15 and p. 21.

In the USA tax receipts (without tolls) amounted to:[14]

TABLE 21.4 US tax receipts (in milliards of dollars)

Year	1941–2	1942–3	1943–4	1944–5
Fiscal year (ends on 30 June)	13.7	23.4	45.4	47.7

In the fiscal year of 1943–4, tax receipts amounted to some 25 percent of total nominal National Income and to some 35 percent of real National Income, i.e. the newly created value.

Only semi-official data are available on *Germany*'s tax receipts. According to these data yearly receipts amounted to 40 milliards of marks, i.e. also about 35 percent of total nominal National Income.

d) Apart from tax receipts the state withdrew in the form of war loans a part of its citizens' income and fortune for its own consumption.

In 1943 loans covered 30.5 percent of England's expenditures. In 1943 total public expenditures amounted to 5,782 millions of pounds sterling. Public expenditures had risen to 71 percent of total nominal National Income. Of course, this does not mean that the population of England only disposed of 29 percent of total produced values for its consumption: the amount of values withdrawn from the population in the form of taxes and loans returned to the population in the form of pays to soldiers, army officers, civil servants, or as interest payments on bonds and payments for purchased goods. Consequently one cannot speak of a definitive withdrawal as is often argued in bourgeois economic science, but of a redistribution of income and wealth.

Public debt of all countries participating in the war increased sharply during the war years. After the war the state had to pay interests on the phenomenally increased public debt. Today the state is also intervening more than ever before in income redistribution and expenditures of its citizens. In most countries inflation brutally eliminates the contradiction between real impoverishment of the country and high interest incomes generated by interest payments on public debt.

---

14   'Financial, Industrial, Commercial Statistics United States' 1945, 1946.

e)   In general, the state disposed of the labour force of all citizens employed by the army or being at the latter's service behind the front.

Until the middle of 1943 about 8 million workers had been brought under military discipline. They were tied to their present jobs by Essential Work Orders; they were only authorised to leave their workplace after official military decision. The majority of other workers could not change of employer without official permission.[15]

In spring 1943, 'total mobilisation' concerned all men between 16 and 45 years old and universal labour conscription was decreed for all other men in Germany. When 'super-total mobilisation' was decreed (in the middle of 1944), all inhabitants of the country, pupils, old and sick men, without any distinction of sex, were mobilised for the army.

In the USA, where labour shortages were practically unknown, control of the use of the labour force was rather weak.

f)   The state decided on the use of the major part of the material means of production.

The state distributed raw materials in case of shortages, but in Europe a shortage of practically all raw materials existed. The state determined which means of production should be used (for instance, machines of the textile industry), the construction of factories for the production of consumer goods, etc. The state had all kinds of means of transport at its disposal. By standardisation the state could determine the quantity and quality of produced manufactures.

g)   The state limited consumption of its population.

The state determined the quantity and price of the distributed foodstuffs under its control.

The extent of these state activities regulating consumption was determined by the degree to which the economy had been put under constraint in war-time; this happened to be most extended in Germany and in its occupied countries, but much less in the USA. In Germany, all foodstuffs and also all bilberries (at least in theory) were brought under state regulation. In the USA rationing by assignment was only temporary and applied to some particular foodstuffs like meat, coffee, sugar.

The state also limited consumption of industrial products by civilians. In the USA, production of durables, like cars, refrigerators, etc., was mainly limited. In Germany, the civil population got practically any industrial consumer

---

15   'The last lap', *The Economist*, 25 September 1943, p. 420.

goods at the beginning of the fifth war year; only children and victims of bombings received sometimes clothes and footwear. The situation of the countries occupied by the Germans was even worse. In other countries the degree of consumption restraints varied with regard to the already mentioned two countries.

Consumption restraint of civilians aimed at assigning a possibly bigger share of output to the military. During the war, military demand was strongest in Germany and relatively lowest in the USA.

During the Second World War, when all natural resources of a country were destined to war aims, figuring out which part of production was destined to military consumption and which part to civil consumption was difficult. The pattern of labour force distribution confirms the already sketched changes in the tables in the beginning of this chapter.

TABLE 21.5 Distribution of the labour force in the USA (in millions of people at the end of the year)

	1941	1942	1943
Employment in the war sector of the economy	7.3	17.5	20.0
Employment in the civil sector of the economy	29.4	20.8	19.0
Employment in agriculture	8.9	8.5	7.5
Total	45.6	46.8	46.5

SOURCE: OFFICIAL DATA

As labour employed in the agricultural sector, i.e. farmers, was also mostly producing for military purposes by delivering foodstuffs to the army and to workers employed in the armament industry, it is clear that at the height of war production some half of the US labour force was working for the military or, in other words, that a half of total output was covering military demands.

In July 1944, the number of workers employed in the British armament industry amounted to 4,034,000 individuals. In 1943 allocation of workers working for the government was as follows:

TABLE 21.6 Workers working for the British government (1943)

Industrial branches	Percentage
Textiles	49
Garment	39
Footwear	20
Others	79

SOURCE: *STATISTICS RELATING TO THE WAR EFFORT OF THE UNITED KINGDOM* 1944, PP. 6–7

The following official data of total public and war expenditures are available for England:

TABLE 21.7 British public and war expenditures (in millions of pounds sterling)

Fiscal year	National income	Total public expenditures	Military expenditures
1938–9	4,490	1,055	400
1941–2	6,619	4,776	4,085
1942–3	7,384	5,637	4,840

It is well known that any estimation of the National Income must be very imprecise. Growth of England's National Income during the war can primarily be demonstrated by price increases but also slightly by increased output. As public expenditures also follow inflation, rising prices had no influence on the interrelation between war expenditures and National Income. Hence, war expenditures amounted to some two-thirds of nominal National Income.[16]

In Germany, a significant part of newly created value was already used for war aims. In 1938 this share already amounted to 42 percent, in 1939 to 46 percent. This percentage would grow during the war and in 1943 some two-thirds, and maybe much more, of the newly created value had been used for war aims.

---

16 However, this does not mean that two-thirds of National Income are really spent on war expenditures, because a part of them is covered by foreign and domestic capital and further financed by the Dominions and other payments.

In the countries occupied by Germany and in Germany's allied countries, the situation was quite the same. Even in the *neutral* countries of Europe a very large part of National Income was spent on armaments and on creating military stocks.

h) The state curbed the general tendency of rising commodity prices.
This tendency was caused by the war-time economy because demand of goods remained always stronger than their offer.[17] One should notice that official price indexes of consumer goods are giving much lower inflation percentages for the costs of living than they really are – a discrepancy that was many times remarked by the representatives of the trade unions.

In the USA, and also in England, inflation was less significant between 1939 and 1943 than in the period of 1914–18. The following *Table 21.8* shows this:

TABLE 21.8 Growing costs of living during the Second World War (in percentages)

Countries	Years	General index	Nourishment %	Clothes	Heating, etc.
USA	1914–18	63	78	111	45
	1939–43	26	47	32	10
England	1914–18	103	115	211	74
	1939–43	28	22	64	30

SOURCE: *MONTHLY LABOR REVIEW* 1944, 58, 2

'This is due partly to the greater volume of excess capacity and unutilised resources at the beginning of the Second World War, but more to the greater degree of control'.[18]

Important governmental aid contributed to regulating prices of foodstuffs in England. The state paid yearly nearly 300 millions of pounds sterling of subsidies to support foodstuff prices.

Immediately after the declaration of war, prices were frozen in Germany at the price level of that time. Officially, prices were only rising slowly.

---

17   In all countries a 'black market' exists where commodities are circulating outside the regulated state system. On this market goods are traded at much higher prices than the official stores.
18   'Diary. Changes in the cost of living index: USA and UK' 1944, p. 116.

TABLE 21.9   Official price index in Germany (first semester of 1939 = 100)

Year	1940	1941	1942	1943	1944
Wholesale prices	103	105	107	109	110

Prices of goods regulated by the state did not increase as uncommonly fast as 'black market' prices.

The method of fighting inflation differed fundamentally in England and Germany. In England the government tried to stimulate production by paying lucrative prices to the producers for the foodstuffs they provided and in the meantime food prices were kept constantly low.

In Germany, however, all agrarian producers had to deliver their produce to the state at fixed prices. On the one hand this stimulated production limitation and on the other hand selling the produce on the 'black market'.

It is clear that all these measures taken by the bourgeois state – as we shall see in another chapter – are not featuring a planned economy. Many of these state measures were not implemented or were adapted to the interests of the big monopolies exercising a decisive influence through their representatives on the regulation boards of the state.

i) The belligerent big powers did not only limit their activities to the national territory.

For their warfare activities they tried to use as large a part as possible of the resources of other countries, or they tried to at least prevent these resources from being used by an enemy country.

The US war-time economy was largely implied in the countries of South and Central America. The USA provided capital for the development of blast furnaces and rubber production in Brazil and the development of copper mining in various other countries. The USA bought copper produced in the Latin American countries at a price that was higher than domestic market prices.

The English state regulated the economy of the colonies and sometimes also that of the French, Belgian and Portuguese colonies as well. The English government bought the integral wool production of Australia, New Zealand and South America, the entire cotton harvest of Egypt, the entire cacao production of West Africa at fixed prices. In the middle of 1944 the English government signed a treaty with New Zealand for the delivery of all butter, cheese, beef, veal and mutton exported during a period of four years. The public Commercial Corporation coordinated all England's foreign trade during the war.

The governments of the USA and England, the USA and Canada, England and France coordinated in some particular domains their economic activities by setting up a series of common state boards. Hence, a common Anglo-Saxon Combined Food Board[19] was purchasing all oil and fat offered on the market; England and the USA established a trade monopoly purchasing goods in various countries. Through the already mentioned board, England purchased the whole tea harvest of India and Ceylon, etc.[20]

The Joint War Production Committee was involved in the production of war materials in the USA and Canada; the Combined Raw Materials Board supervised the development and exploitation of raw materials; the Munitions Assignment Board distributed arms and ammunition to the USA, England and the other countries of the United Nations.

The Combined Shipping Board coordinated the activities of the British Ministry of War Transport, the American Shipping Board and other agencies. In the beginning of the war the Anglo-French-Purchasing Board was purchasing foreign goods for both countries.

In the beginning of the occupation of foreign countries, Germany simply robbed other countries. When it later appeared that this was an inefficient method now that one had to face a prolonged war, Germany chose to use the productive resources of the occupied countries for its war-time economy as well. The peasants were forced to grow those crops Germany urgently needed (oil seeds, hemp, flax). Fuels, raw materials and means of transport were only assigned to those factories working for the German army, etc.

In the same way, Japan also tried to exploit the resources of its conquered countries, but finally without any special result.

It must be clear that there exists a difference between the methods applied by the democratic countries and those of the fascist countries with regard to the use of resources of foreign countries for strengthening their war potentials.

England and the USA succeeded in this without transgressing on the property rights of the owners in the countries concerned. The USA paid much higher prices for copper in South America than offered to the producers in their own country, etc.

The difference in this is that the inclusion of the occupied countries and satellite states into Germany's war-time economy was accompanied by *plunder*. In the occupied countries of Western Europe, Germany formally recog-

---

19 The Combined Food Board was established in 1942 by Great Britain and the United States to allocate food to the Allies during the Second World War. (*Editor's note*).

20 'Industry and trade', *The Economist*, 26 September 1942, p. 398.

nised the property rights of the owners, but, in reality, only the rights of those capitalists willing to collaborate with the conqueror; then Germany forced them to cede the majority of their shares to German monopolies at a ridiculously low price. In order to obtain this collaboration, the Germans withdrew from those enterprises raw materials, means of transport and workers. In the east – in Poland, in the temporarily occupied Soviet territories, in Yugoslavia – the Germans did not respect property rights. They simply took the soil, the buildings, the industrial enterprises, etc., and they plundered stocks and private houses.

∴

The economic role of the state was growing not only in the belligerent counties, but also in the few neutral countries. Because of a fragmentation of the world economy caused by the war, the neutral countries' connection with those countries that they had previously provided with goods, and to which they served as export markets, had become impossible or their trade with the neutral countries (Switzerland, Sweden) had become considerably limited. Hence, in these countries the state was forced to ration consumption of foodstuffs, organise production and distribution of raw materials and exercise strict control on exports which had then become of military, and thus also of political, importance.

The role of the state in the war-time economy is, according to this explanation, far from exhaustively treated. There is no domain of economic life having not been more or less regulated by the state during the war.

The fast growing economic activities of the state necessitates a *corresponding enlargement of the state bureaucracy*, thus the creation of new agencies. Discussing all these new economic agencies in the different countries would require too much space here, because all frequently underwent numerous organisational changes during the war.

The governmental agencies exercising economic activities of the capitalist state are, as far as we are talking about leading positions, not occupied by professional officials, but by entrepreneurs recruited as specialists from the economic sectors created by state regulations and who were defending the interests of these sectors in general and those of the big monopolies in particular. Often they only received a 'symbolic' financial compensation (in the USA a dollar a year). Apart from them, the highest military officers in rank of the armed forces were invited to participate in these war-time economic agencies; in the democratic countries the representatives of the trade-union movement and the consumers' organisation were represented as well. However, in many cases the most important functions were nonetheless occupied by entrepreneurs.

A typical example of this is maybe the composition of the *National Defense Advisory Commission* formed in May 1940. Members were: E.R. Stettinius,[21] President of a steel trust (US Steel Corporation); W.S. Knudson,[22] President of an automobile trust (General Motors); Chester C. Davis,[23] governor of the Federal Reserve Board; E. Budd,[24] President of the rail car manufacturing firm Edward G. Budd Mfg. Co.; L. Henderson,[25] economist and civil servant; S. Hillman,[26] trade-union leader; H. Elliott,[27] consumer commissioner.

A similar situation can be observed in England. Appointments at the Ministry of Supply can be mentioned as a good example.

John Rogers, who was appointed director of the division of explosives, is director of Imperial Chemical Industries Ltd. [ICI], African Explosives and Industries Ltd. [AE&I], Cape Explosive Works Ltd. in Cape Town.

Arthur Rose, director of Webley and Scott Ltd., a well-known producer of shotguns, and director of two metal works, was appointed at the department of 'machine tools'. Gavin Smelly Mackley, an advisor to the director of the department ammunition provision, was director of eight firms mainly active in the steel industry.

---

[21] [Edward Reilly Stettinius Jr. (1900–49) worked with General Motors and later with the US Steel Corporation, which he left in 1939. In 1940 he became President of the War Resources Board and in 1944 he was appointed Secretary of State].

[22] [William Signius Knudson (1879–1948) was an expert of mass production. He worked first for the Ford Motor Company and later for General Motors. In 1942 he was commissioned a Lieutenant General in the US Army as well].

[23] [Chester C. Davis (1887–1975) was a farmers' leader and journalist born in Iowa. In 1933, he became director of the production division of the US Agricultural Adjustment Administration, member of the board of governors, Federal Reserve System, 1936–41; president of the Federal Reserve Bank of St. Louis, 1941–5; associate director, Ford Foundation, 1951–4; and study on rural credit in India for the Indian government, 1953–4].

[24] [Edward G. Budd (1870–1946) was a stamped-steel engineer who started producing all-steel car bodies for the Detroit automotive industry and streamlined stainless steel cars and locomotives for the Burlington & Quincy Railroad (Chicago)].

[25] [Leon Henderson was head of the Research and Planning Division (National Recovery Act); in December 1942 he resigned as price administrator].

[26] [Sidney Hillman (1887–1946) was a labour leader and a founder of the Congress of Industrial Organizations (CIO). He served on Roosevelt's first Labor Advisory Board (1933–6)].

[27] [Harriet Wiseman Elliott (1884–1947) resigned in 1941 and became Chairman of the Woman's Division of the War Finance Committee (1942–6), Deputy Director of the Office of Price Administration, and US delegate to the UN Conference on Education, Science and Cultural Organization (UNESCO) in London in 1945].

Percy Herbert Mills,[28] representing the building industry at the directory board of eight firms, was appointed deputy-director at the supervisory board of the artillery works.[29]

The representatives of the big monopolies who are regulating the war-time economy on behalf of the government, are doing that in their own interests.

In Germany, the war-economy agencies were already completely developed under Göring's leadership before the war began.

That happened under the cloak of a Four Year Plan. Unlike in the USA and England, workers and consumers were not represented at the boards of the agencies, but, on the other hand, the influence of the general staff was great. But agriculture, which was led by the National Food Agency [Reichsnährstand], i.e. the big landowners and the capitalists of the food industry, formed here an exception. In individual provinces the general staff was sometimes represented by a plenipotentiary for war production. During the war a thoroughgoing reorganisation was carried out. After the defeat at Stalingrad, the German economy was put under increased economic constraints and 'control' of industry was taken over by industry agencies representing the industrial sectors. Zangen[30] of the all-German industry association [Reichsgruppe Industrie] who was representing the interests of all industrialists, would however become in reality the leader [Führer] of the war industry.

Unlike the state apparatus in peacetime with its usual rigid structure and well-defined functions of each department, the various newly created war-time agencies were often combating each other and each agency was occasionally defending some particular interests of specific economic sectors. In the past the struggles between the monopolies, and also between the different monopolies and the non-monopolistic circles, were not seldom fought out within the different agencies. In the past, these conflicts between the different interest groups were fought publicly and during the war secretly.

Unlike the 'normal' state apparatuses functioning permanently, the war-time economic agencies were created from the very beginning for a short period of time, i.e. for the war-time period; after the war they would mostly disappear.

∴

28 [Percy Herbert Mills (1890–1968), later 1st Baron Mills, was Controller-General of Machine Tools at the Ministry of Supplies].
29 *The Daily Worker*, 20 October 1930.
30 [Wilhelm Zangen (1891–1988) was a director of the Mannesmann-Werke. He became leader of the Wirtschaftsgruppe Metall and later leader of the Reichsgruppe Industrie].

At the end of the war the economic role of the state diminished, but remained nonetheless more influential than before the war.

This is in particular the case with countries having been occupied by the Germans and which were impoverished as a consequence of the war. Food shortages, the threat or existence of inflation, forced the state to carry on their regulating activities. England as the traditional country of 'free enterprise' belonged to this category of countries. It was already made public that the rationing system would be prolonged until 1949 and that after the end of the war control on foreign trade and exchange would also be maintained.

Assets of states formerly controlled by Germany increased after expropriation of local capitalists having collaborated during the war.

Nationalisation of important industrial sectors were decreed in several countries. After the victory of the Labour Party in England, nationalisation of the coal-mining industry, the railways, etc. was put of on the agenda. In France, large segments of the coal industry, the energy sector, the railways and the banks are already nationalised.

In the bourgeois-democratic countries nationalisation was realised by taking over enterprises at market prices. This kind of nationalisation does not alter distribution of national income and the capitalist characteristics of the economy as a whole. In Hitler's Germany the railways, the *Reichsbank* (Central Bank) and various industries were state owned. The specific weight of state assets was not less important in fascist Germany than it will be in England if the programme of the Labour Party is realised. But fascist Germany remained a capitalist and imperialist country.

Nationalisations in the democracies of a new type have a different character. In Czechoslovakia, Poland, Rumania, Yugoslavia, etc., where nationalisations brought about an essential change in the distribution of national wealth and income to the advantage of the state, although private property of the means of production has also remained unaltered in these countries.[31]

As we already argued above, the economic role of the state declined after the end of the war, but remained significantly more important than before the war.

---

31 A systematic nationalisation of the important means of production was carried out in Czechoslovakia. By a decree of 24 October 1945 entire sectors of the basic industry and the banks were nationalised. (In reality, however, the factories were already administered by workers' committees after liberalisation). In Bohemia and Moravia, 227 banks and industrial concerns owning 85.7 percent of all share capital were nationalised. All mines, blast furnaces, big glass works, all sugar mills and gin-distilleries (though with some minor exceptions), chemical works, were nationalised. In total, more than 10,000 enterprises are now nationalised. They are employing more than 60 percent of the workforce (on a total of 3 million people).

The countries of a democracy of a new type are here an exception, because the economic role of the state has increased faster after the end of the war.

After the end of the war, the international war-economic organisations were progressively disbanded. But a series of new and very important economic organisations were then created. They were designed for a long-term policy and countries are their members. These organisations are: the International Monetary Fund, the International Bank [for Reconstruction and Development], the International Wheat Pool, the European Commission for Coal Distribution,[32] etc. Other international organisations, such as the United Nations Relief and Rehabilitation Administration, were created for a period of several years.

These powerful international economic organisations constitute an important new momentum and framework in postwar capitalist economy.

---

32   [The deficit of coal in Europe, led in 1946 to the establishment of the European Coal Organization, bringing together producers and consumers of coal from Western and Central Europe. This organisation evolved into the Coal Committee of the UN European Economic Commission].

CHAPTER 22

The Impoverishment Tendencies in the War Economy of the Capitalist Countries

The war economy is a part of the *impoverishment* tendency of the belligerent countries.[1]

The concept of 'impoverishment' must be clearly distinguished from the generally well-known concept of 'Verelendung of the proletariat'.

Impoverishment of the country means that a country's national wealth in its real sense of the word, i.e. the sum of values created by human labour, is worth less at the end of the year than at its beginning. How wealth is distributed and later redistributed among the social classes will not be examined within this context. Impoverishment is a specific feature of capitalism created by the war and is caused by the sum of civil and war-determined consumption and war destructions. In wartime real wealth does not increase as it is normally the case in peacetime, but diminishes. In Marxist terminology: the country consumes more than v + m, consumes even a part of c, i.e. a part of constant capital.

According to the teachings of Marx, *the impoverishment of the proletariat* is a *constant* phenomenon in capitalist society and determined by the basic laws of its development. Theoretically speaking, it is always working, even in peacetime and also in wartime. Income distribution between the social classes is of crucial importance, *not* the amount of this income or national wealth.

A country's impoverishment does not precondition the proletariat's impoverishment; on the contrary, Marx underlines that the more wealth is accumulated at the top of capitalist society, the more misery will augment at its bottom.

It is clear that in a country with a full-fledged war economy the impoverishment process of the proletariat will go hand in hand with social polarisation within capitalist society and that the misery of the toiling masses will reach a

---

1 [Originally published in E. Varga, *Izmeneniya v ekonomike kapitalizma v itoge vtoroy mirovoy voyny*, Moscow: Ogiz Gosudarstvennoe izdatelstvo politicheskoy literatury, 1946, Chap. 2, pp. 67–84; translated from Eugen Varga, 'Verarmungstendenzen in der Kriegsökonomie der kapitalistischen Länder', *Veränderungen in der ökonomie des Kapitalismus im Ergebnis des zweiten Weltkrieges*. Als Manuskript für Funktionäre gedruckt, Zonenleitung der K.P.D., britische Zone, Spezialdruckerei Pittroff & Co. AAM 40 Wuppertal, Klasse B – 8127 9. 47 1500].

high level never seen before. It is also obvious that, as we already argued in our third chapter,[2] centralisation of capital also progresses during the impoverishment process of the country: an increasing part of decreasing national wealth is concentrated in the hands of big capitalists. Meanwhile capital of the big monopolies may grow in absolute terms during a country's impoverishment process.

Impoverishment of capitalist society is engendered by the characteristics of a war economy. Because of *general mobilisation* an ever increasing part of the working population is usually withdrawn from productive labour. Under the same circumstances this will lead to a concomitant decrease in produced value.

Another important portion of the working population and the means of production is now used for weapon and ammunition production, etc. and for the production of their indispensable means of production. *Weapons and ammunition differ fundamentally from all other goods*, because the means of production producing them cannot be used for the production of consumerables; these goods do not belong to Marx's sector I. *But they are also not consumer goods in the common sense of the word*; they are not variable capital, they are not used for the restoration of the labour force consumed during the production process. Because they are neither means of production nor consumer goods, *they appear as means of destruction. Using them also implies, at the very end, destroying them*. With the exception of scrap collected on the battlefields, they will not reappear in the circulation process of capital.

All goods, with the exception of weapons and ammunition, possibly used in the army differ from the latter because they replace a particular part of civil consumption. People will wear clothes and shoes, even when staying civilians. But clothes, shoes, etc. worn by soldiers are, of course, much more important for the army than for civilians. Civil life also permits a much more careful use of these goods. The situation is not that different with regard to all other army goods in the broadest sense of the word (cars, horses, rolling stock of the railways, etc.). In the poor countries, the amount of foodstuffs consumed by the army is higher than average civilian consumption before the war.

There are also the destructions caused by acts of war: sinking ships, air bombardments, systematic destruction of factories, buildings, railways and stocks of goods by retreating armies, and destruction of besieged cities by artillery fire, etc.

These factors – withdrawal of labour from production, unprecedented consumption of weapons and ammunition and increased depletion of many other

---

2 See Part 3, Chap. 11.

goods by the army, and, finally, destructions caused by the war itself – are the driving basic tendencies leading to impoverishment during the war.

Hence, we stress that *it is not a law, but a tendency weakened by countertendencies that can be overcome under particular conditions.*

In the first place, we want to stress that there exist different degrees and sorts of 'war economies'. Well before the outbreak of war a country's economy can be largely transformed into a war economy, as was the case in Hitler's Germany. On the other hand, individual countries can formally make war, but without transforming their economy into a war economy. That was, for instance, the case in Japan during the First World War. At that time Japan was formally in the war with Germany, but Japan did not put its economy on a war footing, because the acts of war were rather insignificant and these operations did not last for a long period of time, and also because Japan had not become a battlefield. In the Second World War, Brazil was a belligerent country which even sent troops to Italy; but pretending that Brazil's economy was a war economy in the real sense of the word would be incorrect. In many cases the neutral countries surrounded by belligerent countries had to transform their economies much more thoroughly than countries formally at war, but deploying very little real warfare activities.

The impoverishment tendency only develops – we are making here a exception for countries having only put their economy partly on a war footing – if the economy of a belligerent country has a *completely developed war economy*:

a) *a complete mobilisation* of the possibly largest part of the population by the army;
b) *warfare participation proportionally to the army's numerical strength*; proportional consumption of ammunition, weapons, war materials, etc.
c) *a more or less long-lasting participation in war operations*;
d) *war operations on the country's territory.*

If all these conditions are met, a country's total 'consumption' – consumption by both the army and the civil population, and war destructions taken as a whole – will exceed actual production. As a consequence of the war its costs are covered at an important degree by a decrease of real wealth created before the war, i.e. by an impoverishment of the country.

A similar impoverishment of the belligerent countries of Europe occurred during the First World War. The decrease in German national wealth during the First World War was estimated at some 20 milliard marks.[3] It is widely known

---

3 Hettlage 1940, p. 476. [Hettlage mentions only 20 milliard marks]. [Karl-Maria Hettlage (1902–

that the First World War caused an economic crippling and an impoverishment of Tsarist Russia.

'The war was undermining the economic life of Russia. Some fourteen million able-bodied men had been torn from economic pursuits and drafted into the army. Mills and factories were coming to a standstill ... *The war was eating up the resources of the country*'.[4]

It is clear that the impoverishment tendency had become much more apparent during the Second World War than during the First World War because armaments (tanks, mechanised divisions, air forces) are not only more expensive, but they also cost much more if measured in real labour time. Unfortunately, at this moment we do not possess sufficient data about this problem.

Almost all European economists confirm these impoverishment tendencies in the war economies of the capitalist countries. In 1940, at the moment when British war expenditures were still rather insignificant, Keynes wrote:

> There can be little doubt that during the first months of war our rate of private consumption has exceeded our surplus of production on a scale which cannot be continued indefinitely. Government demand has been greatly increased. There is no reason to suppose that private consumption has been sufficiently diminished. It is by drawing on our stocks of commodities and foreign resources and on our working capital that the deficiency has been met.[5]

And on another page:

> Indeed it is certain ... that the existing rate of government expenditure leaves no margin for increased private consumption; and that the maintenance of consumption is already leading to a reduction in stocks of commodities and of foreign reserves at a higher rate of depletion than ... is safe.[6]

---

95) left the Catholic Zentrum Party in 1933; he became SS-Hauptsturmführer and Albert Speer's advisor as well. After the war he was appointed at the Board of Commerzbank, professor at the University of Mainz, Secretary of State at the Ministry of Finance in Bonn, member of the High Authority of the European Community of Coal and Steel (1962–7)].

4   *History of the Communist Party of the Soviet Union (Bolsheviks)* [1939], p. 173. (My stress – E.V.).
5   Keynes 1940, p. 19.
6   Keynes 1940, p. 16.

The British Employers' Confederation wrote: 'What does seem clear is that the world as a whole emerge from the present war even more impoverished than it was by the last war ...'.[7]

The German fascist economists also recognised Germany's impoverishment during the war.

> The labour force, machines and raw materials used during the war and for arms production are irrevocably lost. This fact cannot be denied, nothing can change this, notwithstanding the amounts written off on the balance sheets. According to the balance sheets capital is available, but its only nominally and does not exist really.[8]

> Another difficulty consists of enterprises being unable to afford in many cases renewals and rationalisations. During the war they are obliged to postpone technical improvements because of shortages of materials, machines, raw materials and labour.

The thesis of an impoverishment tendency in a war economy during the Second World War is at first sight contradicted by the fact that some belligerent countries, in the first place the USA and Canada, did not impoverish during this war; on the contrary, their national wealth really increased if compared with the beginning of the war, although they sent important quantities of all sorts of war materials to the allied countries without receiving equivalents for these goods. (Deliveries through Lend-Lease; Canada's contribution to England's war costs amounting to one milliard dollars).

Though the USA did not impoverish much during the war, compared to the pre-war period less new private capital was invested. This is shown in the official statistics (see in *Table 22.1*).

TABLE 22.1 New capital investments (in milliard dollars)

Year	1941	1942	1943	1944	1945
Amount	19.4	7.7	2.1	1.8	6.0

SOURCE: DEPARTMENT OF COMMERCE, BUREAU OF FOREIGN AND DOMESTIC COMMERCE, *SURVEY OF CURRENT BUSINESS*, WASHINGTON D.C., FEBRUARY AND JULY 1945, VOLUME 25

---

7 *Social Insurance and Allied Services* 1942, p. 7.
8 *Der Wirtschaftsring*, 7 November 1941.

During the war state investment became very important. At first glance these well-known figures contradict the well-known fact that the whole US war industry had been built up during the war period. Capital investment in war industries was apparently fostered by lower writing-offs in other industrial branches, by shrinking stocks, etc. This means a redistribution of national wealth at the advantage of the war industry.

The reason why no impoverishment occurred in the USA and Canada was the following:

As we already mentioned, a 'well-developed war economy' in the proper sense of the word did not exist at the end of 1944. At the end of 1944, only 8 to 9 percent of the population had been called up – this is much less than the average percentage. Until the landing in France, acts of war by American forces were comparatively insignificant. One may assume that until that time not more than 1 to 1.5 million American soldiers of all arms – by land, sea and air – were participating in armed actions. Hence, consumption of weapons, ammunition, etc. was relatively insignificant. Finally, the country was not disturbed by acts of war (if one excludes sinking of merchant ships); practically no destructions were signalled on US territory. The same should be said of Canada and the English Dominions.

One should also mention countertendencies especially very strongly softening the impoverishment tendencies in the USA, while resources like labour, capital, raw materials and arable land were only partly used. We only want to give here an account of the most important countertendencies to be described in other chapters. These countertendencies are:

a) integration into the productive process of persons having remained until then unemployed or not working at all;
b) a lengthening of the working day;
c) an increase in labour productivity by means of rationalisation, fragmentation of the production process and its automation;
d) restriction of civil consumption by interdicting production of industrial goods for individual consumption, by prohibiting construction of houses, by rationing foodstuffs, clothes, etc.;
e) resources of other countries were used to satisfy the needs of one's own war economy.

In the USA – where some 10 million people were jobless before the war, where a comparatively small proportion of women had a paid job, where the average working week of the industrial worker (because of reduction of working hours) was only 35 hours a week, where only 67.5 percent of capital was employed, where the state was already subsidising during a long period before the war and even during the war output restriction of wheat, cotton, tobacco, etc., where all countries on the American continent could be mobilised in case of danger – these countertendencies were clearly superseding the impoverishment tendencies. But nonetheless it cannot be denied that the vast majority of the belligerent countries, especially the countries of continental Europe, were impoverished.

Impoverishment is touching all forms of national wealth. Stocks of goods and raw material of enterprises and traders were continually depleting. Buildings, railways, machines were worn out. Arable land was exhausted because of a shortage of fertilisers. Livestock was decreasing and lost weight. Forests were cut down, etc. Family stocks of foodstuffs diminished; supply and quality of durables (furniture, clothes, footwear, household equipment) diminished. Depending on concrete conditions in individual countries, impoverishment could evolve faster or slower.[9]

It must, however, be clear that the engendered impoverishment process will furthermore accelerate this tendency. Worn out machines will hamper the production process. Reduction of livestock and its changing composition of cattle will imply a deterioration of the soil and hence lead to poorer harvests. This will signify diminishing food supplies to the working people and engender a further decrease of labour productivity, etc. A chain reaction will be set in motion until the country is completely exhausted.

Impoverishment during the war went hand in hand with increased investment of fresh capital into enlarged industrial production facilities being of crucial importance for warfare activities. All main belligerent countries were building during the war new aircraft and tank factories, ovens for the production of electrical steel, works producing liquid fuels, synthetic rubber, etc. More than 90 percent of the US war industry was built up during the war. In many countries, new railway tracks, oil pipelines and strategic highways were constructed, new ports were developed for opening new shipping lines, etc.

∴

Although the impoverishment of the belligerent countries is very clear and undisputable, reliable data sufficiently underpinning this process in the differ-

---

9 Emaciation of the continental-European population, primarily of the urban population, took a particular form of impoverishment. The average loss of population's weight was about 5 kg per person, which represents a loss of 1.5 million tons on a total population of 300 million people. In this case about 15 million tons of additional foodstuffs were needed to recover the body mass and its subsequent loss of labour force. One may assume that in China and in India people lost even more weight.

ent countries are still difficult to find. Forthcoming postwar statistics will reveal the degree of impoverishment in these countries. The next considerations can only illustrate our general assumptions.

Obviously, notwithstanding the plundering of the whole of Europe, *fascist Germany impoverished nonetheless most countries during the war*. It is noteworthy that Germany, when bringing its economy on a war footing before the war, had practically utilised all its means of production as well, but, unlike the USA and England, it did not dispose of important natural resources.

Official data concerning Germany's impoverishment were not published. Being on their guard, the Hitlerians did not communicate on the disaster they had caused. Germany's impoverishment had already been very far-reaching during the First World War. According to calculations made by the Dresdner Bank, Germany's national wealth could be estimated at 250 to 255 milliard marks in 1913, and at 211 milliard marks in 1922.[10]

Hence, after having endured four war years, impoverishment had by then amounted to one-sixth of total pre-war national wealth.

With regard to the Second World War we can agree with the estimations made by the fascist professor [Karl-Maria] Hettlage. By the end of 1940 he wrote:

> ... [O]nce converted into money, this balance-sheet depreciation and its coverage are not that unimportant. For the private economy, it accounts at least for some 6 milliard marks a year; depreciation of housing stock amounts at 1.5 and 2 milliard marks on a year base. In a war period, the demand of replacing worn-out means of production can only really be met in those sectors of the economy having become of crucial importance for the military ... Seen from the point of view of fluctuating commodity stocks *postponing production of substitutes for worn-out means of production implies that the country's real capital stock will be used for war aims. In Germany, this kind of consumption could be estimated at 3 to 4 milliard marks in 1940*.
>
> One should also add to this material losses and even consumption of stocks of hoarded raw materials and finished goods. Consumption of stocks which had not been replenished during the World War, amounted to some 20 milliard marks. *One may thus assume that in 1940 stocks valued at some 5 to 6 milliard marks had been consumed*.[11]

---

10   *Die Wirtschaftliche Kräfte der Welt* 1930.
11   Hettlage 1940, p. 476.

This Fascist author calculated that the devaluation of basic capital and raw materials and commodity stocks amounted to 8 to 10 milliard marks during the first war year. Assuming that during the following war years impoverishment had remained at the same level, total losses should then amount at some 50 milliard marks by the end of 1944.

But, as is well known, 1940 was a very 'quiet' year. After the very fast German attack on the neighbouring countries in the west, practically no new military operations would follow. Hence, consumption of war materials remained very insignificant. Many troops were sent on leave and working in the hinterland. It is clear that after the surprise attack on the Soviet Union requiring an enormous consumption of war materials and leading to 'total' and even 'super-total' mobilisation, national wealth diminished.

One should also notice that Hettlage did not discuss the decrease in national wealth with regard to agriculture. Impoverishment was fast growing in this sector during the war period. Horses were confiscated, machines were not replaced, an important part of the livestock was slaughtered and the remaining herd was emaciating; because of shortages of fertilisers the soil was losing its former fertility. Delivery of agricultural machines replacing the worn-out old ones had drastically diminished.

The following official data (see *Table 22.2*) illustrate how important livestock diminished in Germany.[12]

TABLE 22.2   Decrease of livestock in Germany

Years	Horned cattle (millions of animals)	Hogs (millions of animals)
1939	23.5	29.0
1942	22.8	17.3
1943	22.9	15.4

Data of 1943 are referring to the month of June; more recent data are not available.[13] Once imports of livestock and – that is even more important – also imports of fodder from the temporarily occupied countries had stopped,

---

12   *Deutsche Allgemeine Zeitung*, 9 March 1944.
13   After Germany's capitulation a secret edition of the *Statistisches Jahrbuch für das Deutsche Reich* was discovered. Unfortunately, these data refer to a territory with boundaries changing year after year, thus making the figures incomparable.

slaughtering of cattle was obviously increasing. A short report published in the middle of March [1944] in all German newspapers confirmed:[14]

> Horned cattle has become the most important source of meat provision for our nourishment. When during the first year of the war economy beef and veal provided only 46 percent of total deliveries to the butchers and the sausage makers, this share had risen to 75 percent in the fourth year of the war economy. In the near future this proportion of beef and veal consumption will further rise.

This short report also refers to the fact that the number of milk cows has grown, but 'that livestock made fat for slaughtering was decreasing after the beginning of the war and continuously diminished during the whole war period'.

Air bombings played an important role in the impoverishment process of Germany, but not in such a way as English propaganda pretended.[15] After Germany's occupation it became obvious that until the fourth quarter of 1944 Germany had succeeded in repairing the armament factories. A secret report of Armament Minister Albert Speer from early 1945 mentioned that the Germans had repaired six to ten times their destroyed works and that output of arms and ammunition was only seriously decreasing during the fourth quarter of 1944: about 30 to 40 percent less than the *Wehrmacht* demanded. Having observed the results of the bombing raids in occupied Germany, one can only say that the factory buildings works were seriously damaged, but also that the works themselves, especially the mechanical industry, had only suffered superficial damages. Before and especially during the war, many German weapon factories were manufacturing in underground facilities or were relocated somewhere in the forests.

That is why the air bombings during the first years of the war did not seriously damage Germany's war potential.

Because of the air attacks Germany's private wealth had decreased in real terms. Many houses had been destroyed. One should also add all personal belongings, such as furniture, plates and dishes, foodstuffs, clothes, etc., to

---

14   We are reproducing the text of this short report as it was published in the *Völkischer Beobachter*, 11 March 1944.

15   Having based ourselves on these sources, we had overestimated in our publications 'the exhausting of natural resources of Germany' caused by air bombings and the pace of their exhausting. [In 1941 and 1942 Varga had published a pamphlet on the exhaustion of the German economy; this publication was translated into different Soviet languages and in the Comintern's *Kommunisticheskiy Internatsional* of 1941, 8: 15–29, and 1942, 2: 14–20].

the losses caused by these destructions. A fascist author, a certain [Heinrich] Hunke,[16] writes: 'Let's assume that 100,000 people have become homeless. This means that 30,000 families have lost all their belongings and that national wealth has diminished with at least a half a million marks'.[17] In the autumn of 1944 the war activities of the Allies on German territory – East-Prussia and West Germany – caused important destructions. When retreating, the furious Hitlerians destroyed even their own country, though by then Germany had already clearly lost the war.

It is obvious that at the end of the war a significant part of Germany's real capital was lost.[18]

Germany's impoverishment would have been much more important during the Second World War if a larger part – about a quarter to a third according to our calculations – of the war expenditures had not been covered by plundering the occupied countries.

The countries having suffered from German occupation are especially impoverished. Germany plundered them, forced their entire economy to produce for the German war effort and the occupied territories were mercilessly destroyed when evacuation time came.

The situation of the countries mentioned above can be illustrated by the case of France, although one should notice that, due to the fast retreat of the Germans and the successful operations of the Resistance, France had been comparatively less destroyed than, for example, Italy, Yugoslavia, Poland and Hungary.

During the occupation the Hitlerians forced France to pay 620 milliard francs for 'occupation costs', i.e. about 12.4 milliard dollars at the exchange rate of 50 francs for one dollar fixed by the Allies. We do not speak here of individual plunder committed by German soldiers. Other serious factors of impoverishment of France were: deportation of two or three million workers over a period of several years – prisoners of war and 'recruited' workers, i.e. in majority people deported by force to Germany; means of production working for Germany's war aims; devastations caused by war activities on French territ-

---

16 [Professor Dr. Heinrich Hunke (1902–2000) was a NSDAP official and economic ideologue; member of the Reichstag; official of the Ministry of Economic Affairs, president of the German Economic Council; he became director of the *Deutsche Bank* in 1943. After the war he joined the Bund der Heimatvertriebenen und Entrechteten (BHE)].
17 Hunke 1943, p. 833.
18 England's decrease in national wealth (see further) was officially estimated at a quarter; as Germany had been a battlefield, it goes without saying that the decline in national wealth should be much larger.

ory; destruction of the Atlantic ports and railways[19] and damages caused by air attacks of the Allied and German air forces.

France's national wealth clearly suffered very huge losses during the war. The cowardly and treacherous policies of the traitors of the fatherland, of the French reactionaries aiming at establishing their own dominance over the French workers by their collaboration with and submission to the Hitlerian regime would cause very heavy material damages to France.[20]

An official American source gives a general overview of German plundering of Belgium.[21] The Germans took 45 percent of the country's output in the period 1943–4. Belgium's national income – in prices of 1939 – diminished from 64 milliard francs before the war to 27.5 milliard in 1944. A substantial impoverishment of the country was obviously its result.

An even more important impoverishment occurred in all economies of the countries of Eastern Europe having been occupied by Germany and its allies. *Szabad Nép* (of 2 June 1945), the newspaper of the Central Committee of the Hungarian Communist Party, writes about the damages Germany had caused with the help of 'allied' Hungary. The paper publishes abstracts of a speech delivered by Minister of Reconstruction Ferenc Nagy:[22]

> About 30 to 40 percent of our transforming industry is destroyed and its production is not as high as half of its pre-war total output. Because of damages many of our mines are flooded. Dismantling of factories by the Germans had bad consequences, especially for the heavy industry and the building materials industry. Our agriculture will only be recovered after several decades of its damages caused by the war and the rapacity of the Germans. Not more than 25 percent of the horses and 30 per-

---

19   At the end of 1944 the French railway workers described the situation of the railways: in August, about 4,200 km of the railway network was damaged, among them were 800 km of main railway tracks. During the liberation 100 central stations and 24 junctions (of a total of 40) were out of order. Before the war the SNCF possessed 15,000 locomotives. After deliveries to the Germans 11,000 locomotives were left. An important number of them had been destroyed or damaged by the Germans during the advance of the Allies. Hence, only 2,500 locomotives were left to France. Thanks to the efforts of the railway workers, 5,600 locomotives are now operational. Before the war, the SNCF owned 450,000 wagons; but today, after reparation of some 20,000 wagons, there are 140,000 wagons available.
20   Because an important part of the young male population of France was abroad for several years, demographic problems will soon arise.
21   Szymczak 1945, p. 10.
22   Ferenc Nagy (1903–79) was a member of the Hungarian Small-Holders Peasants Party.

cent of the horned cattle stock have survived the war. Transportation has mostly suffered from war destructions. Only 12 percent of the locomotives and some 8 percent of the rolling stock of the railways are available. The Germans destroyed especially the railway-embankments. They blew up points, railway stations and power lines. Not a single one of the bridges on the large rivers has remained intact.

An American author reported (see *Table 22.3*) on the depletion of cattle stock on the European continent by the end of 1942.[23]

TABLE 22.3 Depletion of cattle stock by the end of 1942

Year	Sheep* 14 Countries	Cattle† 21 Countries	Hogs‡ 17 Countries
1939	78,414,000	95,933,000	66,303,000
1942	72,759,000	80,150,000	48,114,000
Percentage decrease	7%	16%	27%

* Norway, Denmark, France, Spain, Portugal, Italy, Switzerland, Czechoslovakia, Poland, Greece, Bulgaria, Rumania, Estonia, Finland.
† Norway, Sweden, Denmark, Netherlands, Belgium, France, Spain, Portugal, Italy, Switzerland, Germany, Austria, Czechoslovakia, Poland, Yugoslavia, Greece, Bulgaria, Rumania, Latvia, Estonia, Finland.
‡ Norway, Denmark, Netherlands, Belgium, France, Spain, Portugal, Italy, Switzerland, Germany, Czechoslovakia, Poland, Yugoslavia, Greece, Bulgaria, Rumania, Finland.

In the period of 1943–5, decay was even more important than during the first 3 and a half war years. One may assume that only a half of the livestock of the European continent is left.

Information about *England's* impoverishment during the war is available.

The English White Paper published in 1945 gives the following figures (see *Table 22.4*) about changes in 'capital wealth'.[24]

---

23 Brandt 1945, p. 141.
24 *The White Paper on the National Income and Expenditure* 1945, p. 19.

TABLE 22.4 Changes in 'capital wealth' (in million pounds)

Year	1940	1941	1942	1943	1944	In 5 years
At home	+76	−81	−78	−123	−88	
Abroad	−796	−795	−666	−684	−655	
Total	720	876	744	807	843	3,990

Real increase in domestic capital was even larger, because the *White Paper* does not give the real stock of commodities in current prices per year. If one looks at inflation during the war years[25] and at the shrinking national income during the first semester of 1945, the sum of real capital decrease should be estimated at almost one milliard pounds.[26]

This decrease in the *amount of private wealth goes hand in hand with an increase in state assets* formed during the war by the establishment of state-owned factories at costs we ignore. These war industries would become mostly obsolete after the war and they are nowadays of little value.

Official statistical data provided by the English delegation during the negotiations on a US loan contained the following figures for the period between September 1939 and June 1945 (see *Table 22.5*).[27]

TABLE 22.5 Decrease in British national wealth between September 1939 and June 1945 (in million pounds sterling)

Selling of foreign investments	1,118
Increase of foreign debt	2,879
Decrease of gold reserves, foreign currencies, etc.	152
Losses due to bombings	1,480
Replacement of basic capital]	885
Losses of merchant ships and cargo	700

---

25 Kalecki 1944, pp. 131–5.
26 According to the *White Paper*, a net increase in private wealth amounted to 275 million pounds during the year of 1938.
27 *The White Paper*, p. 6708, p. 875; 'The Trade Proposals', 'The Washington Documents', in *The Economist*, 15 December 1945, pp. 853–4, pp. 867–73.

Together with diminished commodity stocks, total decrease in national wealth was estimated at 7,300 million pounds, i.e. about a quarter of England's national wealth, predominantly formed by foreign assets.[28]

It must be nonetheless clear that England has not only lost a big part of its foreign assets, but also owes huge sums to other countries. During the war, accumulated debts to India, Egypt and other countries amounted to more than 2 milliard pounds. Debts of the Land-Lease are not included. It is also obvious that without exploiting the resources of other countries – by importing commodities or by paying with English foreign assets and with the help of foreign credit – real impoverishment of England would have been much more important.

Hence, the British Employers' Confederation stated: 'It also seems clear that this country will emerge from the war as a debtor country, and that our foreign investments – which before the present war played such a vital part in helping to bridge the gap between the cost of our Imports and the value of our Exports – will have largely ceased to exist.'[29]

As we already mentioned, the United States is an exceptional case among the belligerent countries. Colossal reserves accumulated before the war made production growth possible during the war. US consumption of weapons and ammunition remained until the middle of 1944 relatively insignificant. As a consequence, the USA could expand in wartime their production facilities by establishing new factories worth more than 20 milliard dollars. Agricultural output increased and livestock augmented.

Apart from this, utilisation of the enormous natural resources not previously explored helped to keep national wealth unimpaired, although an important part of the country's output was used for war production. *The Survey of Current Business*, i.e. the official voice of the US Trade Department, provides the following data (see *Table 22.6*) about war expenditures in percentages of the National Product.[30]

---

28   In addition, many valuable objects and personal fortunes of rich people, especially objects of art, rare books, were sold to foreign countries, in the first place to the USA.
29   *Social Insurance and Allied Services* 1942, pp. 7–8.
30   The 'Gross National Product' is at any rate much bigger than National Income, because it also includes the written-off part of constant capital.

TABLE 22.6 US war expenditures in percentages of the National Product

Year		In %
1941	First semester	8
	Second semester	13
1942	First semester	26
	Second semester	39
1943	First semester	44
	Second semester	43
1944	First semester	44

A decline in that basic capital used for civil production was a reality during the war in the USA. In a report of Truman it is stated: 'Practically no steel has gone into the civilian economy in the last 2 years, except small quantities for uses essential to maintaining war production, such as transportation and farm machinery'.[31]

It must be clear that the USA has become, unlike the European countries, really wealthier. But the future will show if this is also true. Much will also depend on the way the USA can adapt the facilities exclusively built for wartime production to peacetime production and which part will be considered obsolete and thus will be worthless.

How the enlarged investment of capital for war purposes can contribute to a real increase in national wealth after the war will depend on technical and economic factors.

Technically speaking, this will really depend on the way machines, apparels, mechanical works, etc. can be utilised for peacetime production. Unfortunately, we do not find any authentic information on these questions in American literature. Truman's report gives some information about the span of time necessary for a transition to peacetime production, about required new capital investments, but he did not touch on the problem of how the means of production can be technically adapted to peacetime production. Some indications allow us to assert that about 20 to 25 percent of the means of production cannot possibly be used for peacetime output.

---

31   *Investigation of the National Defense Program* 1944, p. 91.

In the 1943 annual report of General Motors it is said that before the war the firm owned 69,000 machine tools, about 17,000 of which could not be utilised for war production and were stored, while 3,000 others had been sold for peace production.[32] It appears thus that a quarter of the machine tools could not be adapted to wartime production. One may thus assume that readapting machines for wartime to peacetime production will possibly cause the same problem.

About the possibilities of utilising basic capital accumulated during the war *economically*, one can resolutely predict that the same reasons having caused that only about 65 percent of the production facilities had been utilised during the 20 years before the Second World War, will also be at work after the war; hence, capacity utilisation of actually invested basic capital will be even lower. Hence, pretending that the enlargement of US basic capital during the war will also imply a growth of national wealth in the postwar years, is obviously wrong.

As we already argued, the impoverishment tendency is now meeting a serious countertendency we will have to study in another chapter.

32   *The Commercial and Financial Chronicle*, 27 March 1944, p. 1251.

CHAPTER 23

Concentration and Centralisation of Production and Capital during the War

Concentration of production and capital is a characteristic of the capitalist mode of production.[1] The war has reinforced this process. Concentration and centralisation of capital developed exceptionally fast during the Second World War. For a long period of time the results of these changes will be recognisable after the end of the war.

During the war, *concentration of industrial production* was fostered by the state. Actual war demands of the belligerent countries stimulated the mobilisation of all economic means in the interest of war production. As the war intensified and went on, shortages of important means of production, i.e. labour, means of production and raw materials became more and more scarce. Hence, governmental policies consisted of concentrating labour as much as possible in the most modern industrial enterprises employing the best machinery and using raw materials in the most rational way, i.e. those enterprises which had best of all organised labour productivity and production under equal conditions. Normally this will be in the biggest enterprises. Hence, numerous small and middle-sized enterprises were shut down by governmental decree.

In fascist Germany, all these phenomena can be observed on a large scale. Well before Hitler declared war to the whole world, this concentration process had already been speeded up now that military preoccupations were completely determining Germany's economic policy.

During the war, and especially during the period of 'total mobilisation', small and middle-sized enterprises were shut down by the cruel methods of Hitler's fascists. Hundreds of thousands of enterprises were standing idle, entire industrial sectors producing consumer goods for the civil population stopped production. The Hitlerites spared only those small industrial enterprises as well as

---

1 [Originally published in E. Varga, *Izmeneniya v ekonomike kapitalizma v itoge vtoroy mirivoy voyny*, Moscow: Ogiz Gosudarstvennoe izdatelstvo politicheskoy literatury, 1946, Chap. 3, pp. 51–66; 'Die Konzentration und Zentralisation der Produktion und des Kapitals während des Krieges', Als Manuskript für Funktionäre gedruckt, Zonenleitung der K.P.D., britische Zone, Spezialdruckerei Pittroff & Co. AAM 40 Wuppertal, Klasse B – 8. 47 1500].

those important artisan firms having completely specialised in producing parts for the war industry.[2]

These figures (see *Table 23.1*) are showing centralisation of capital in Germany.[3]

TABLE 23.1 Capital centralisation in Germany

Total liabilities of firms (in 1,000 RM)	Number of limited liability companies				Capital (in million RM)
	End 1927	End 1931	End 1942	Until 1 November 1943	Until December 1943
Until 5	604	342	19	19	0.1
5–50	1,635	1,126	127	117	3.8
50–100	1,367	1,252	182	173	10.0
100–500	3,802	3,340	1,515	1,463	344.0
500–1,000	1,482	1,352	841	859	556.0
1,000–5,000	2,378	2,255	1,843	1,840	3,970.0
5,000–20,000	540	578	617	632	5,736.0
20,000–50,000	98	121	153	156	4,477.0
+ 50,000	60	71	107	108	14,639.0
Totals	11,966	10,437	5,404	5,367	29,735.9

The figures show that about a half of the liabilities belong to the 108 biggest firms, each with a capital worth more than 50 millions of marks. Some small firms were transformed into limited liabilities companies during the fascist regime. During the war many small limited liabilities companies and several privately owned firms were closed down. In the region of Łódź, the Germans already closed down some 40,000 of the 43,000 commercial firms.[4]

---

2 Since 1943 German policy changed *vis-à-vis* small and middle-sized and important artisan enterprises located outside the urban areas. Bombing of the big German cities and the industrial centres meant that one preferred establishing small enterprises in villages and small towns which were less vulnerable to air attacks.
3 *Deutsche Allgemeine Zeitung*, 28 November 1944, based on official data.
4 *Deutsche Allgemeine Zeitung*, 11 November 1944.

We do not have exact figures about the number of small firms having been shut down, about the number of entrepreneurs having been previously 'independent' but now having been transformed into wage workers in the big factories of the war industry. Their number should undoubtedly exceed some hundreds of thousands.

In England, concentration of production was usually realised by agreements reached in the same industrial sector.[5]

Until the end of 1942, 2,700 industrial enterprises of different sectors were shut down, setting about 250,000 workers free for the war industry. About 5,000 enterprises of the same sectors were permitted to continue production. In contrast to Germany stopping production did not necessarily mean a final shut down of the enterprise. Enterprises stopping production continued their activities as commercial organisations not trading their own output, but the produce of other factories in their sector.

In the USA compulsory concentration was less sizeable than in Germany or in England. Because of their gigantic reserves of all means of production – labour force, means of production, raw materials – the USA were able to double production during the war without taking that kind of decision. Until March 1944, US consumption of war materials was not that huge in comparison with the strength of its armed forces. Hence, the necessity of mobilising all economic resources by shutting down a large number of enterprises was not that urgently felt. However, a number of US enterprises in the sectors of the agricultural machinery works, typewriters, bicycles[6] and others were shut down and their production was concentrated in the remaining enterprises.

In the USA governmental orders were used as a basic method for concentrating production into big monopolies.

From June 1940 until the end of November 1942, state orders amounted to about 60 milliard US\$.[7] 70.1 percent of these orders went to 100 enterprises; one-third of the orders (almost 20 milliard US\$) went to five enterprises[8] (see Table 23.2).

---

5 At the beginning of the war, concentration of war production was less important than in the USA and in Germany; there existed for instance about 9,000 coal-mines and 82,000 companies employing fewer than 20 workers.
6 Hence, 10 out of 12 factories producing bicycles were shut down.
7 Not included are small orders worth less than 50,000 US\$.
8 'From concentration to monopoly', *The Economist*, 25 September 1943, p. 427.

TABLE 23.2 State orders going to five US enterprises (in milliard US$)

Enterprises	Milliard US$
General Motors	7.25
Curtiss-Wright Aircraft Corp.	4.61
Bethlehem Steel Company	2.95
Douglas Aircraft	2.37
United Aircraft	2.34

It is obvious that only a part of the orders was executed by these five enterprises in their own factories; a larger part of it was subcontracted by tens of thousands of smaller firms. More details will follow.

The enormous importance of big orders worth 20 milliard US$ obtained by the already mentioned five firms in two years time should be situated in this context: according to official statistics, gross value of total production of the American manufacturing industry had declined between 1929 and 1933 from 70 milliard US$ to 31.4 milliard US$.[9]

On the other hand, the already mentioned sum of 20 milliard US$ equals England's yearly total pre-war income.[10]

In *England* a substantial sum of the budget also went to a small number of factories. According to official sources, the Ministry of Air distributed 80 percent of all its orders to 50 enterprises. In addition, some 15,000 subcontracting enterprises were producing parts for these orders.

Information about Germany is missing, but a small number of big monopolistic enterprises must have undoubtedly obtained the biggest share of all war orders. A particular form of production concentration was accompanying this phenomenon; many artisan enterprises were reduced to the status of *suppliers of parts producing for some big enterprises*.[11] This particular method

---

9   *Statistical Abstracts of the United States* 1938, p. 749.
10 Clark 1937, p. 89.
11 The well-known automobile producer Chrysler, producing tanks and airplanes instead of cars during the war, was outsourcing 58.2 percent of its production; 3,000 out of 4,500 parts for tanks were produced by subcontractors; subcontracting firms produced 5,881 out of 11,542 parts of the wings of the bomber Martin B-26. In comparison to the peacetime period the number of suppliers of parts working for Chrysler had quintupled. If any

of concentrating production was widely used in all belligerent countries. All these enterprises remained formally independent and autonomous; economically they became, however, dependent on one gigantic firm; they provided, year after year, the big companies with parts. This kind of relation could be rather profitable to these small firms as long as the war lasted. However, it became very difficult or even totally impossible for these firms having been transformed into subcontractors to break with this kind of dependency after the war by producing and selling their goods independently on the market in order to regain their former status.

Another serious factor contributing to increased concentration of production during the war was that the *newly created enterprises during the war were in general gigantic*. This assertion refers not only to the newly established American airplane, engine, shipbuilding and aluminium plants but also to English and German works in these branches.

As a consequence of all these already mentioned changes, an important part of industrial production had now become more concentrated into big enterprises than before the war. However, statistical data of the whole industry in the belligerent countries are not yet available.

The kind of giants created during the war in the USA is best illustrated by the case of General Motors. The report on the year of 1943 mentions:

> In the USA, the General Motors Corporation manages 99 factories owned by the company and 16 factories which are owned by the government. In these factories about 130,000 machines are utilised for the production of war materials and similar goods; 69,000 of them are owned by the General Motors Corporation. Among them, 17,000 machines, which are not used during the wartime, were stored. About 3,100 machines were sold. The total amount of wages amounted to 1,321,999,829 US$, the number of workers employed amounted to 448,848 people. The total number of workers employed attains approximately 500,000.[12]

---

supplier, however, did not deliver just in time, this would contribute to a disorganisation of the production process in this gigantic enterprise. See *Iron Age* of 11 March 1943. This journal obtained the figures for this report from the firm's general manager [Herman L.] Weckler.

12   *The Commercial and Financial Chronicle*, 27 March 1944, p. 1251. [Retranslated from Russian and German].

According to these figures, one can argue that the number of workers employed here approximately equals the number of workers of an industrialised country like Belgium. General Motors employed itself about 500,000 workers and clerks. But subcontractors producing different parts for General Motors employed about the same number of workers.

Apart from General Motors, there existed nine large trusts in the USA employing (according to reports) each more than 100,000 workers in 1943 (see Table 23.3).

TABLE 23.3 Large US trusts employing more than 100,000 workers

	Number of employed workers (in thousands)
US Steel Corporation	340
Bethlehem Steel Company	289
Ford	193
General Electric	175
Curtiss-Wright Aircraft Corp.	140
Dupont	115
Westinghouse Electric	115
Chrysler	109
Goodyear	102

SOURCE: *ECONOMIC OUTLOOK*, SEPTEMBER 1944

Reports for 1943 illustrate the unprecedented degree of concentration of capital in the USA; eight firms are owning liabilities worth more than 1 milliard US$ (see Table 23.4).

TABLE 23.4 US firms owning liabilities worth more than 1 milliard US$

	Liabilities in 1943 (in million US$)
Standard Oil of New Jersey	2,328
General Motors	2,265
US Steel Corporation	2,106
Curtiss-Wright Aircraft Corp.	1,295

TABLE 23.4 US firms owning liabilities (cont.)

	Liabilities in 1943 (in million US$)
Dupont	1,115
Bethlehem Steel	1,045
Socony-Vacuum Oil Co.	1,030
Ford	1,009

SOURCE: *INVESTIGATION OF CONCENTRATION OF ECONOMIC POWER*, NO. 29, P. 328; *BUSINESS WEEK*, 22 JULY 1944

Though they were not that large and numerous, comparable giants developed in other belligerent capitalist countries as well.

A report for the year of 1944 published by Bethlehem Steel Company shows that the company's turnover amounted to 42 million pounds sterling and that the firm employed then about 50,000 workers.[13] In Germany one could notice a similar development. The *IG Farbenindustrie* represents a gigantic concentration of economic power in Germany. According to a report issued by *General Eisenhower*, the firm dominated several sectors (see *Table 23.5*)

TABLE 23.5 IG Farbenindustrie dominating different industrial sectors

	Percentages of total production in Germany
Artificial rubber	100
Lubricating oil	100
Vaccines	100
Poisons	95
Nickel	95
Plastics (bakelites, etc.)	90
Magnesite	88
Explosives	84
Nitrogene	75

---

13   *The Times*, 25 March 1945. [This reference could not be traced in *The Times*].

During the war, the IG Farbenindustrie employed more than 400,000 workers. Total worth of its assets was estimated at 6 milliard US$.[14]

Parallel with increasing concentration of production *an ever-faster concentration of capital occurred*. This happened both by means of accumulation and centralisation.[15]

Concentration of capital by accumulation is playing a leading role; the preconditions for centralisation of capital by stronger companies taking over weaker ones can only be created if some enterprises are making larger profits than others and thus accumulating faster.

Because profits are higher during the war, concentration of capital by accumulation proceeds faster than in peacetime. No marketing problems exist in a full-fledged war economy; on the contrary, managing the indispensable elements of the production process, i.e. raw materials, machines and workers, remains the main problem. An unlimited purchasing power and effective demand of war materials exist in a war economy. Mass demand of similar goods is boosting a further product specialisation and engendering cost reductions while real wages are declining as well.[16] The state is also supporting the monopolies by providing them with plants, machines, credit, etc. Hence, profits of industry are higher during the war than in peacetime. One should furthermore notice that profits are very unevenly obtained: profits are very huge

---

14   *Metal Bulletin*, 26 October 1945.
15   In general, concentration of production on the one hand and concentration of capital on the other hand are wrongly distinguished. Marx distinguished two kinds of concentration of capital: *concentration by accumulation and concentration by centralisation*. In the first case capital of the enterprises grows because a part of the appropriated surplus value is not consumed, but added to the enterprise's capital. In the second case, already existing capital of another enterprise is appropriated. Marx distinguishes 'the [first – E.V.] kind of concentration which grows directly out of, or rather is identical with, accumulation'. Marx 1954, p. 625. On centralisation of capital, however, Marx writes: 'It is concentration of capitals already formed, destruction of their individual independence, expropriation of capitalist by capitalist, transformation of many small into few large capitals. This process differs from the former in this, that it only pre-supposes a change in the distribution of capital already to hand, and functioning; its field of action is therefore not limited by the absolute growth of social wealth, by the absolute limits of accumulation'. Ibid.
16   In the belligerent capitalist countries *hourly* real wages have fallen and the surplus rate has increased. According to official statistics, *yearly* real wages of workers have apparently increased notwithstanding full employment and longer working days in most countries. Because of shortages of consumer goods, workers could not spend all their money wages. Hence, despite their hard work, their living conditions were constantly worsening during the war economy if compared to the period of peace. The degree of worsening, however, differed from country to country; the US is an exception.

in the war industries; but they are strikingly lower in industries producing for peace demand.

Official data provided by the American Securities and Exchange Commission show these higher profits (see *Table 23.6*).

TABLE 23.6 Return on invested capital in 1942

Company	Before taxes	After taxes
Jacobs Aircraft Engine Company	679.2	175.2
Beech Aircraft Corporation	563.1	153.0
Bellanca Aircraft Corporation	200.8	143.7
Parker Alliance Company	255.5	121.8
Consolidated Aircraft Corporation[17]	578.3	117.0
Elastic Stop Nut Corporation of America	515.6	133.3

SOURCE: ALLEN 1944, P. 6

One should also notice that the big corporations 'perfected' the art of drawing up their balance sheets in such a manner that they only reveal a part of all accumulated profits. An important part of them disappeared under the heading of 'hidden reserves' for 'bad times'. The state taxes away a large part of the profits inscribed on the balance sheet. We can illustrate this with data of profits made by American corporations (see *Table 23.7*).

TABLE 23.7 Profits made by American corporations (in milliard US$)

	1939	1940	1941	1942	1943	1944
Before taxes	5.4	7.4	14.4	19.0	22.8	–
After taxes	4.1	4.8	7.3	7.4	8.2	9.9

SOURCE: *SURVEY OF CURRENT BUSINESS*, JANUARY 1944 AND JULY 1945

---

[17] [In March 1943, Consolidated Aircraft and Vultee Aircraft Corporation merged and formed Consolidated Vultee Aircraft Corporation (Convair). In 1954, Convair merged with Electric Boat and formed General Dynamics].

Net profits on the balance sheet increased much more slowly than did total profits before taxes. As we already said, an important part of profits remained as 'hidden' revenues in the enterprises. In this way a large concentration of capital is occurring by the process of accumulation.[18]

Public subsidies are an influential source of capital concentration. In individual countries they can take different forms. As we already pointed out, in the United States, where before the war plenty of fixed capital had reputedly remained idle,[19] the entrepreneurs could not decide to invest in new factories for war production. They feared that the war would not last a sufficiently long period of time for possibly writing off their investments. On the other hand, a reconversion of them for peace production after the war would not only increase the already existing overcapacity, but also cause additional marketing problems.[20] As we already have mentioned in our first chapter [of this book], many factories were established at governmental costs in the USA.

The American journal *Steel*[21] gives an interesting overview of the activities deployed by the state with regard to the build up of the war industry. The Reconstruction Finance Corporation *will own half of the production capacity of all engineering works of the country*. This corporation built 521 aircraft factories and will also own them. *These aircraft factories are 2.7 milliard US$ worth or more than a tenfold of total worth of all privately owned aircraft industries together*.

The Defence Plant Corporation spent about 1 milliard US$ on building blast furnaces. Plants producing 92 percent of total production capacity of manganese were built for this corporation. Total worth of these works: 430 mil-

---

18 One should notice that accumulation is fostered by accumulation of fictive and not real capital. With exception of the war industries in the narrowest sense, the share of real values (buildings, machines, raw materials, manufactures) in the composition of capital declined year after year; the part of war loans, bank deposits and cash money, increased constantly. This shift mirrors the fact that a country's war expenditures are partly covered by current production. The biggest part, however, will be covered by the country's public wealth.

19 According to our calculations, fixed capital was utilised in America at 67.5 percent in the period between 1925 and 1934. Full capacity utilisation was here based on working in one shift during 300 days a year. (See Varga 1939b, pp. 46–57).

20 These fears still existed during the war. At the end of August 1943, the United States Chamber of Commerce announced the formation of a committee on utilisation of war plants and surplus property, in order to tackle the postwar problems. The Chamber declared: 'As the war goes on and comes to a close, the problem of the disposition of surplus property will become increasingly important. There will be the problem, at the end of the war, of the proper and efficient utilisation of the great special-purpose manufacturing plants'. 'Chamber to study war-plant puzzle', *The New York Times*, 29 August 1943, p. 29.

21 *Steel*, 11 October 1943, p. 141.

lion US$. Nine works producing aluminium having a yearly capacity of some 600,000 tons were built; this is more than a trice of total production capacity in this sector. Works producing yearly 800,000 tons of artificial rubber but exceeding about a third of peacetime demand were built at the costs of the state. In addition, the government invested large sums in works producing high-octane petrol, in pipelines as well as in research, development and production of raw materials. After the end of the war, it became publicly known that the government had invested two milliard US$ in facilities for the production of the atomic bomb.

The government was, however, not itself operating these newly built factories, but had given them to capitalist monopolies managing them during the war period. Either the government leased these newly built plants to the capitalists, or the whole production process was directly managed by capitalists receiving a management fee from the government. Even the plants producing atomic bombs were directed by Dupont Corporation. The capitalists had the right – but not the plight – to acquire the factory from the government at the end of the war by reimbursing the building costs minus depreciation.

Though to a lesser extent than in the USA, the English and German state also built factories and acquired machines for the weapon industry and all these were then rented or used by big capitalist enterprises.[22] The Japanese big corporations were subsidised by the state.

A larger concentration of capital was the consequence for the implied enterprises.

∴

Centralisation of capital is progressing faster in a war economy than in a peacetime economy. Many thousands of small and medium-sized enterprises were shut down. When continuing production, the owners are either hindered by acquiring raw materials and hiring workers, or, as we already argued, the state will oblige them to shut down their factories. Capital of the privately owned companies will sooner or later, freely or not, come under the aegis of big companies continuing production. In the democratic countries this will lead in most cases to signing a voluntary agreement, but in the fascist countries this will only happen after coarse coercion by the state.

---

22   In 1943 a decree was published in Germany that the capitalists were obliged to buy and to pay for the machines provided by the government. They could easily afford this because they had already drained large sums of money to their bank accounts. Transforming that money into productive capital was not possible.

CONCENTRATION AND CENTRALISATION OF PRODUCTION AND CAPITAL

The process of compulsory centralisation of capital revealed the rapacious nature of German imperialism and the greedy endeavour of German financial capitalists enriching themselves at any price. The latter process was carried out by using three basic procedures.

Capital of German Jews, estimated at a total amount of 6–8 milliard of marks, had been taken away (already before the war) from the owners and, with a few exceptions, handed over to 'Aryan' big capitalists. The higher ranks of the Fascist party took a share of that Jewish capital.

Industries and banks of the conquered countries were violently annexed and confiscated or, at least, brought under control of German finance capital. Methods used were different in the West and in the East. In Upper Silesia and in Poland the industrial enterprises were simply robbed from their owners and handed over to German monopolies – the Hermann-Göring-Werke, the heavy industry, the big banks – and distributed to them. *No indemnity was paid for these works*. Some formalities were nonetheless respected in Austria, in Czechoslovakia and in the Western countries. In the first place, German big banks 'took over' all shares owned by English, American and French capitalists in the banks of the occupied countries. If this was insufficient for controlling these banks, the Germans purchased shares of the banks on the free stock market or forced the banks to emit new shares and they could then buy the complete emission. Big *industrial concerns* 'took over' important enterprises in the occupied or vassal countries or they became their 'stakeholders'. The Hermann-Göring-Werke acquired the weapon industry of Austria and in Czechoslovakia.

The following technique was applied in the occupied countries of Western Europe. The owners of the enterprises that were really important to the German monopolies were strongly 'persuaded' to double their share-capital and then to sell the newly emitted shares to related German monopolists at a relatively low price. If the directors of an enterprise refused to place their firm into German hands, the German occupation authorities could withdraw their access to raw materials and transport facilities; they could withdraw their orders and exercise enough pressure to have them change their mind. Payment for these shares was financed out of the paid 'occupation costs'. The latter were fixed at such a high amount that the Germans had no possibility of spending them on the purchase of goods in the occupied countries. Acquiring shares was thus nothing but a form of investment by German capital. In reality, however, German capital did not invest a penny in these countries. All 'capital investments' were financed at the account of the occupation costs squeezed out of the population.

The highest reward for having rapaciously acquired foreign property went to the Hermann-Göring-Werke. The latter company increased its capital to 4 milliard mark and became Europe's biggest enterprise.[23] The Hermann-Göring-Werke acquired some works in Austria; in Czechoslovakia they robbed the *Škoda Works*, the *Brünner A.G. Rüstungsproduktion*, and a number of coal mines and blast furnaces. In Poland, they acquired the lion's share of the *Oberschlesischen Bergwerksgesellschaft*. In Rumania, they controlled four-fifths of the mining and steel industry. In Norway, Sweden, France, and Belgium, a whole network of enterprises was formed, mainly put together by iron-ore mines, blast furnaces and other enterprises having some importance for the German war economy. The Hermann-Göring-Werke also wanted to lay hands on the heavy industry of Ukraine. During the occupation the German Hermann-Göring-Werke 'administered' the iron mines and blast furnaces of Krivoy Rog and the manganese mines of Nikopol too.

The heavy industry of Alsace-Lorraine was handed over to the German heavy industry. Röchling, Otto Wolf, Göring (having inherited the expropriated works of Thyssen), etc. got the booty.

IG Farben was the most active of all enterprises by 'acquiring' related industries in occupied and 'allied' countries and by taking over big chemical enterprises like *Ugine Kuhlmann* in France.

It is clear that after the defeat of Hitlerite Germany all properties robbed by German finance capital in the occupied countries were returned to these countries.

Well before the war a third form of compulsory centralisation of capital was introduced in Germany by means of *compulsory cartelisation* of entire industrial branches under the aegis of the monopolies.

Centralisation was even more speeded up during the war by closing down hundreds of thousands of small enterprises (liquidation of small enterprises reached a climax during the period of 'total mobilisation'). The possessions of the closed-down enterprises, i.e. raw materials, machines, office furniture, business offices, etc., were acquired by the big enterprises continuing production.

In England, concentration of capital was already very strong before the war. According to calculations made by [Harry] Campion in his book *Public and Private Property in Great Britain*,[24] 6.7–7.4 percent of the adult population owning in 1936 in England more than 1,000 pounds sterling, possessed 83.3–85.8 percent of total private capital.

---

23 Documentation on German enterprises is taken from the booklet *Occupied Europe* 1944, p. 41.
24 Campion 1939.

According to calculations made by Beveridge, 84.5 percent of England's private wealth was owned by 7.1 percent of the adult population of the country.[25]

It is well known that in the USA a large concentration of capital had already occurred before the war. During the war centralisation of capital was speeded up in the other democratic capitalist countries, but exact information about its importance is still unavailable.

In agriculture, concentration and centralisation did not go beyond the already mentioned normal tendencies. An acute labour shortage in agriculture gave the middle and small farms relying on the labour force of the family the possibility of preserving, more or less, their survival.

∴

Finally, increased concentration of production, reinforced concentration and centralisation of capital are partially a result of the world war; they are not a temporary phenomenon, but have a lasting character (with the exception of the compulsory acquisition of enterprises in continental Europe by German robbery capital). The exact size of this process of accelerated concentration and centralisation shown by the figures will only be known some years after the end of the war when relevant statistical data and calculations will be available.

The social consequences of this process are nonetheless clear without these data: an important decline of the urban middle class; an even sharper polarisation within society between the two main social classes, with on the one hand the class of workers and clerks, and on the other hand the big bourgeoisie; a stormy growth of the giant firms.

We will illustrate this with some data taken from the annual report of the American firm *Douglas Aircraft*.

> When the war began, the company employed 8,500 workers; at the beginning of 1945, the firm employed 187,000 workers. In 1935, turnover amounted to 11 millions US$. In 1943, the company delivered combat planes worth 1 milliard US$ to the American armed forces. The company reduced direct man-hours a plane unit more than 50 percent, but lowered per-unit costs to the military a 22 percent. The company paid out more than 50 million US$ of taxes. The company produced more than 16 percent by

---

25   'Beveridge-As-You-Go', *The Economist*, 25 December 1943, pp. 836–7.

weight of the national plane output purchased by the American armed forces. *At the beginning of 1943, the company had a current backlog of war orders totalling 3 milliard US$*, i.e., largest in the company's history. With its current backlog *Douglas Aircraft* ranked fourth in the nation. Three of the major plants were working throughout the year of 1943 at maximum production capacity, by peak output at the two new plants in Oklahoma and the 33 millions US$ Chicago factory would not be reached until mid-1944.[26]

These sparse data nonetheless give us a picture of this giant firm which one could have hardly imagined a few decades ago.[27]

A huge concentration of production and capital by a relatively small number of exceptionally large enterprises will lead after the war – but unimaginable before it – to an ever-closer collaboration within powerful cartels. But once the demands unsatisfied during the war are met, an even stronger contraction of the markets can be predicted. This will then lead to a unprecedented sharp competition between the giant firms having been formed during the war.

26 'Douglas Aircraft had record output', *The New York Times*, 5 January 1944, p. 27; 'Douglas Aircraft has record year: Issues annual report', *The New York Times*, 27 March 1945, p. 34.
27 The question of what kind of goods *Douglas Aircraft* should produce after ending the war stands on its own. According to optimistic prognoses, not more than 5 percent of the actual production capacity of the American aircraft industry can be used in order to cover total demand of the civil aviation.

CHAPTER 24

Economic Regulation and Absence of Planning in the Capitalist Countries during the War

During the First World War, the German reformists praised the war economy of that time because of its 'equal' distribution of all sorts of foodstuffs; they discovered in this war economy an important 'social progress' and called it 'war socialism'.[1] During the Second World War, the concept of 'war socialism' was rarely used. The great success of the economy of the Soviet Union during the pre-war period created a widespread popularity of the idea of 'economic planning'. When simply denying the successes of the Soviet Union had become impossible, reactionary circles ardently proclaimed that they were simply admiring the results of a planned economy independently of its socialist character. Almost in all countries 'Four Years' Plans', 'Five Years' Plans', 'Ten Years' Plans' were drafted, that were either not realised, or exclusively destined – as was the case with the German 'Four Years' Plans' – to put the economy on a war footing.[2]

In this war the superiority of the Soviet economy became apparent: '... [T]he economic foundation of the Soviet State has proved to possess infinitely greater vitality than the economy of the enemy states'.[3]

As a consequence of all this, the idea of a planned economy got an even greater popularity among the toiling masses. This explains why some foreign economists called the regulations of the war economy 'economic planning', which is completely wrong.

In the capitalist war economy, planning more or less the needs of the army a long time in advance was necessary. As the war was consuming much more than half of the actual production, regulating in advance a significant part of the forthcoming production was necessary to meet in the first place all

---

1 [Translation based on E. Varga, *Izmeneniya v ekonomike kapitalizma v itoge vtoroy mirivoy voyny*, Moscow: Ogiz Gosudarstvennoe izdatelstvo politicheskoy literatury, 1946, Chap. 4, pp. 67–84; translated from Eugen Varga, 'Wirtschaftsregulierung und Planlosigkeit in den kapitalistische Laändern während des Krieges', *Veränderungen in der ökonomie des Kapitalismus im Ergebnis des zweiten Weltkrieges*. Als Manuskript für Funktionäre gedruckt, Zonenleitung der K.P.D., britische Zone, Spezialdruckerei Pittroff & Co. AAM 40 Wuppertal, Klasse B – 8046 10. 47 1500].
2 See extensively, Varga 1935.
3 Stalin 1944.

demands of the army. *If all means of production* – any kind of machinery, raw materials, transport facilities and workers – would have been fully available, the activities of the capitalist state could have been confined to placing war orders to private enterprises. However, this did not happen. The state was therefore obliged to reserve a significant part of the means of production for war production. The state was forced to increase production of insufficiently available goods and to limit in particular their consumption by civilians. But when talking about the means of production, one should keep in mind that industrial enterprises producing goods for civil consumption should limit their output. A redistribution of workers and transport facilities by the state was imposed by the same necessity.

The importance of a 'planned' interference of the capitalist state into the economy depends in the first place on the interaction between the resources of a belligerent country and its war demands;[4] but historical conditions also exercise their influence. Having the most 'regulated war economy', Germany combined the dimension of the country's military needs and the shortcomings of its war potentials with the historical tradition of an unconditional submission of its economy to the political authority.

The enormous war needs and the limited availability of resources led in the belligerent countries to the creation of a system of regulations and planning during a certain period of time.

This system, however, *differs fundamentally from our planned economy*. The difference consists of the following elements:

a) A 'planned economy' cannot be created in a capitalist economy, because it cannot be reconciled with production relations based on a system of private property of the means of productions. In these countries planning is nothing other than the outcome of external coercion enforced by the war. Our planned economy is in complete harmony with production relations based on collective ownership of the means of production. There is no question of external coercion here, only of an autonomous principle of an economy regulating the functioning of our economy in periods of war or peace.

b) In the capitalist countries, 'regulation' is an *exceptional measure* dictated by the necessities of the war and only envisaged for a war period. *For us, the planned economy is a permanent and important part of our social system*. Our planned economy remains the same during war- and peacetime,

---

4 This does not, of course, apply to countries like China, i.e. countries having not yet completely chosen for the road to capitalist development and not yet having a centralised state exercising full control over the whole country.

and the kind of goods produced, their distribution, etc., are in complete harmony with the war needs.
c) War regulations in capitalism *only regard those elements of the economy satisfying the needs of the army*; no economic planning concerns the other sectors of the economy or the economy as a whole. Our planning system regards *the whole sphere of Soviet life* – not only the economy as a whole, but also all sorts of professional training, the functioning of cultural institutions, etc.
d) In the capitalist countries (except for Germany that had put its economy on a war footing long before the beginning of the war) regulating organisations were set up during the war by the state; however, these institutions were of a provisional kind. For nearly 30 years we have a functioning central planning system covering the whole economy of our gigantic country. During the war its organisation was functioning without any failure.

In the capitalist countries – this happened in accord with the existing social order – state officials could meet the representatives of the different social classes in committees being in charge of the planning of the war economy: entrepreneurs, in the first place representatives of the big monopolies, 'consumers' and workers. (In Germany, no real representatives of the workers and the consumers were represented in these organisations). This meant that all contradictions existing between the several social classes and social layers, between the monopolies and the outsiders, between entrepreneurs and consumers, reappeared in these 'planning' organisations making their functioning very difficult and their advisory work contradictory.

Only in the Soviet Union, however, the existence of barely two befriended social classes creates the possibility of a harmonious functioning of the planning offices of our economy, even during a period of war.

All shortcomings of 'planning' in the war economy of the capitalist countries are revealed by all these arguments.

· During the war the means of production also remained in private hands. During the war, the capitalist enterprises also produce goods for making profits; in the USA and England the new works established by the state during the war were even handed over to private entrepreneurs for making profits.

The interests of the entrepreneurs in making huge profits and in organising production also persisting during the war are in a permanent contradiction with the state aiming to, as much as possible, bring production and consumption in accord with the war aims. The big monopolies exercise, also during the war period, a determining influence on the economic policy of the state, i.e. particularly on the activities of the economic institutions in which they are occupying a determining key position and which they were concretely leading. Their country's victory in the war was in the *general* interest of the monopolies; but their *private* interests forced them to get possibly highest war profits for their own enterprises. Directing an economy is in such condition really impossible.

Unlike the fascist countries, the contradictions between on the one hand the aims of the state, i.e. mobilisation of all war resources, and on the other hand the strivings of the individual big monopolies for possibly making a huge profit, were clearly perceptible in the USA where they were openly discussed in the press during the war.

Notwithstanding high profits realised on war deliveries, American capitalists refused to invest capital in new enterprises and production facilities having a considerable military importance, such as factories producing airplanes, tanks, ships, aluminium. Notwithstanding their high war profits, they feared that they could not write them properly off in case the war would not last for a sufficiently long a period of time. They foresaw that after the end of the war these works would not be needed for peace production and that they would thus become obsolete. It is well known that before the war the means of production of American industry were only partly in operation. During the war the entrepreneurs forced the state to invest US$16 milliards in production facilities. Most of these works were built by capitalists but paid by the state and they were later handed over to them in order to keep them operating.

How chaotically production capacity was used during the war in the USA is demonstrated by the fact that new factories were built by the state for the big automobile firms while the state shut down the old automobile plants.

Contradictions between the private interests of the big enterprises and the interests of the state are clearly coming to the fore in the case of the Ford [Motor Company]:

> Though the government shelled out $66,000,000 for the Willow Run plant and its highly specialized machinery, the Ford company was allowed to do things its won way. Its own way included locating the plant thirty miles from the chief source of manpower, Detroit; the hiring of workers who were overwhelmingly male, white, and draftable; complete neglect of the elementary problem of housing and active opposition to the government's attempt to solve this problem, and the use of over-elaborate and inflexible tooling methods that delayed production and now make it difficult to introduce the frequent minor changes of design which modern warfare requires. The Ford company built an ideal plant – for civilian cargo planes after the war. 'When the war is over', Henry Ford told a group

of reporters back in September 1941, 'we are going to retain the building we are erecting and construct airplanes on a mass production scale'.[5]

The same can be said of Chrysler:

> And to a greater extent than most other auto companies Chrysler has sought to restrict its war activities to new plants built by the government and to such items as require little change from peacetime production (it is, for example, the nation's largest producer of military vehicles).
>
> At the same time that acres of Chrysler plant space lie unused, the government is building in Chicago for the Dodge division of Chrysler one of the largest industrial units in the world which will manufacture Wright aircraft engines ... 'What will happen to this huge plant after the war?' I asked a representative of the Chrysler company. He shrugged his shoulders. 'It won't be any good to the auto industry', he said ... Economic considerations seem to be back of the Chrysler Corp.'s relatively greater resistance to conversion. Chrysler is more concerned about its competitive position after the war than is General Motors or Ford. Lacking the huge financial surplus of its two principal rivals and holding second place in car production by a very narrow margin over Ford, Chrysler has sought to organise its war activities in a way that would enable it to shift to the postwar manufacture of cars more rapidly and more cheaply than either of its competitors.[6]

Similar examples can be cited for any other industrial sector. A social order based on private property of the means of production makes the creation of a really planned economy impossible.

Particularly difficult is the integration of agriculture into a regulated system, because in all countries some millions of 'independent' farms exist. The problem becomes even more complex because of the parcelling out of the peasant's land.[7]

---

5 Magil 1943.
6 Magil 1943, p. 16.
7 A German fascist journal wrote: If a farm of four acres is parcelled into 72 dwarf parcels or if a bigger farm of 30 ha is parcelled into 162 tiny plots and one has to cover at least 206 km in order to reach all plots, it will be impossible to strive successfully for getting a higher yield. If such a multitude of small plots is also a serious obstacle in peacetime, this must create during the wartime period to an intenable situation. The scattered fields are incompatible with the demands of a rational use of labour, draught animals, fertilisers and agricultureal implements. How can foreign agricultural workers orient themselves on a plot which boundaries

Integration of small businesses into a 'planning' organisation of the war economy was also very difficult. This was realised by transforming small enterprises into suppliers of parts for the big enterprises or by destroying them (especially in Germany).

Because a planned regulation of the capitalist countries was exceptional and only foreseen for the war period, these countries *did not possess a functioning planning organisation for the war economy.* (Only Germany had already established the foundations of its war economy before the war broke out). The indispensable institutions were built during the war and only in case shortages were threatening the demands of the army. The foundations of these institutions became mutually intertwined: new overall organisations coordinating their activities and dealing with competence conflicts were constantly established. Also in these overall organisations functions became interlocked and, instead of a harmoniously functioning planning system, a very chaotic situation as created.

The highly praised country because 'exemplary organised' – Germany – can be cited as an illustration of this.

'Regulation' of the German economy in function of the war economy started soon after Hitler's take-over. In 1934, regulation was delegated to the Ministry of Economy headed by [Walther] Funk.[8] In 1936, [Hermann] Göring was assigned to head the office charged with directing the Four-Years' Plan; the Ministry of Economic Affairs was subordinated to the latter organisation. In practice both organisations were not closely working together, as is proved by their contradictory directives. In early 1940 a third organisation, the Ministry of Armaments and Munitions, was founded in order to regulate the country's entire economy. Because of the stressed military and economic situation this organisation became of an ever increasing importance: in the beginning of the autumn of 1943, coordination of the activities of the war-economic organisations was delegated to the Ministry of Armaments and Munitions, which was then headed by [Albert] Speer.[9] The task of the Ministry of Economic Affairs was limited to providing the civil population with industrial products. Because this Ministry was only responsible for goods the army did not need, its role was limited to providing the civil population with industrial products. Speer was formally subordinated to Göring. The fourth war organisation was in charge of plundering the occupied countries.

---

    can hardly be determined by the village constable, and how can one organise the required supervision?

8 [Walther Funk (1890–1960) was a leading German official and Nazi].

9 [Albert Speer (1905–81) was a leading German official and Nazi minister].

Apart from these organisations there existed organisations grouping individual industrial branches; they constituted in fact cartels disposing of means of coercion. The National Coal Board ('Reichsvereinigung Kohle'), the National Iron and Steel Board ('Reichsvereinigung Eisen und Stahl'), etc., were among them. They had the right to close down individual enterprises and to distribute raw materials. In this way, the biggest monopolies were exercising their authority on industry and especially on the industry of their own branch.

Everything was conceived, organised and streamlined with German precision. Individual enterprises were usually submerged by an avalanche of thousands of contradictory regulations. Even the fascist press was forced to react against this kind of 'excessive organisation'; these interventions had in reality no effect.

On 2 July 1944, an article signed by Muthesius[10] was published in the *Deutsche Allgemeine Zeitung*, in which the author argued:

> Today, one can hardly find a thing that is not regulated. The workforce and raw materials are regulated; capital and tourism are regulated, consumption and all human activities are regulated. Leading people have already argued that the amount of forms and the avalanche of papers, i.e., a tower of Babel of decrees, contingents, concessions, prohibitions and the like, are representing neither our economic world view, nor our ideal, that we have today to deal with measures caused by the war and that one should suppress them as soon as possible, even the sooner the better.

The journal *Das Reich* of 6 August 1944 published an essay authored by Hans Schwarz van Berk[11] in which was argued:

> Here in Germany, priority given to organisation is really a national disease. We have two expressions articulating this perfectly. The first one is about 'complete registration', the second one is about 'uniform execution'. In both cases, they are hiding a strive for power fed by the generals of the card systems and the princes of the fiches, as well as by the narrow-mindedness of people imagining that they will succeed in directing life by including in their indexing system every angler and by prescribing how long the worms for angling should be. But behind this something more serious is hiding: it is the idea that one can realise something exceptional

---

10 [Karl Volkmar Muthesius (1900–79) was a journalist specializing in economic issues].
11 [Hans Schwarz van Berk (1902–73) was a journalist and Nazi propagandist close to Joseph Goebbels].

in economic affairs when sitting at one's office desk or even by making telephone calls. This riskless and easy way of doing business means also delaying and hindering the execution of orders, which is during the war very dangerous. Between each slab of steel leaving the factory and the firing of a gun in Normandy a huge mountain of rustling paper is erected ... *In the same way, the state apparatus and the self/governing bodies are also overloaded and they will find themselves in a situation of double or triple submission.*

An exceeding amount of regulating organisations and private interest groups of monopolists are contradicting themselves and their representatives, who are administering these organisations, are hampering the provision of the army, even in a rich country like the USA.

The subcommittee [on Military Affairs] headed by Senator [Harley M.] Kilgore[12] stated in its considerations of 1943:

> Our various war programs, all essential, are out of balance with one another and in most cases are short of the goals set ... We find inadequate steel capacity, with the result that one program must be sacrificed to another. We find that facilities have been over-expanded in certain industries, while small plants able to do the job have gone unused.[13]

∴

It is true that the regulations in the belligerent capitalist countries provided, more or less, the army systematically with all necessary goods, but this also made that the previous disproportions of the capitalist economy were even growing during the war. Most important is that share capital [Grundkapital] and production capacity of sector I (the war industry included) kept on growing very fast, while production capacity of sector II was growing slower or not at all. During a long period of time after the war this disproportion would overburden the enterprises of sector I, except for those countries having suffered from destructions. In the USA, for instance, the state built aluminium works with a projected production capacity of some 500,000 tons; but already in 1943 it became obvious that an overproduction of aluminium could be foreseen and seventeen aluminium works were later shut down.

---

12   [Senator Harley M. Kilgore (1893–1956) was a Democrat from West Virginia].
13   'New Super Board for War Output is urged by Senate Military Group', *The New York Times*, 13 May 1943, p. 13.

In the USA, the establishment of engineering works was strongly promoted during the war. During the war about a million of new machine tools were built. Overproduction followed already in 1943 and about one-third of the production capacity of the enterprises was shut down. [Paul V.] McNutt,[14] Chairman of the War Power Commission, pointed to the fact that supplying the industry with too many machine tools is a wasteful expenditure because the overwhelming majority of the enterprises of the war industry was *producing in only one shift*. If work had been organised in two or three shifts or – in other words – if the already available machine tools had been more intensively used, a larger part of the newly produced machine tools would have been superfluous.

Shipping tonnage had undoubtedly become insufficiently available of all means of production in 1940–2, in the belligerent democratic countries. Hence, one could imagine that the available shipping tonnage was fully planned and assigned to war needs. However, as some individual cases reveal, reality was obviously quite different.

In 1940, in a period of acute shortages of tonnage, a British Member of Parliament informed the House of Commons that an English cargo vessel going to Suez had been sailing half-loaded while rounding Africa; on its way back to England it had thousand tons of sand as ballast on board; this sand had thus made a trip around the world.

In the issue of 10 September 1944, *The New York Times* published the following tale about six American vessels having been forgotten in Murmansk:

> Washington, Sept. 9 (AP) – The story of a 'forgotten convoy' which spent eight months in Arctic north Russia was told today by the War Shipping Administration.
>
> In January, 1943, six ships, loaded with food and war materials, sailed from New York to join eighteen other Allied freighters, bound for Murmansk. After weathering storms and Nazi air attacks off Norway, the convoy made its destination in two months, and the crews settled down to await the formation of a new convoy for the return trip. It was *eight months* before their ships were put into a return convoy.[15]

---

14 [Professor Paul V. McNutt (1891–1955) was a Democrat, Governor of Indiana. In 1942, Roosevelt made him chairman of the War Manpower Commission, which had to balance the labour needs of agriculture, industry and the armed forces, but the position carried little real power].

15 'Forgotten convoy kept an icy vigil. Six American ships were held in Russian port 8 months, awaiting orders', *The New York Times*, 10 September 1944, p. 16.

Labour supply was one of the weakest links in the regulation project during the war. In this domain, there were not only important mistakes made, but they were, strange enough, made during the First World War as well.

In Germany, as well as in England, mobilisation of all vital labour forces in the coal-mining industry was insufficiently carried out. Soon a shortage of mineworkers, especially of qualified hewers, caused a decline in coal production. Just like in Germany, England had also demobilised a number of mineworkers. Not enough attention was further paid to the recruitment problem, i.e. the problem of replacing mineworkers having fallen out because of illness or death. Not enough applicants could be found among the school-leavers choosing the dangerous job of a coal cutter in a period of a general acute shortage of workers. Hence, even in England, the government was forced to use means of coercion to supply the coal-mining industry with a sufficient number of young workers. In Germany, the Hitlerites tried to drag workers away from Ukraine and other temporarily occupied countries for working in the coal pits of Western Germany, Belgium and Luxemburg.[16] It is obvious, however, that productivity of this forced labour was very low.

Regarding one of the hurdles hampering an efficient use of workers in the USA, McNutt, Chairman of the War Power Commission, said the following in 1942:

> It is estimated that there are 6,000,000 Negroes in the workforce of the country, but not all are employed in the use of their best skills ... When, for example, a Mobile shipyard fails to put Negro workers on the job but imports labour from a thousand or more miles away ... The employment rolls of nine defence plants in a Eastern city leaped from 52,494 in January, 1941, to 71,169 in September. In that period more than 10,000 local Negro workers remained unemployed. Meanwhile, rents skyrocketed. Transportation facilities were intensified. Migrant workers, homeless and exploited [by the landlords, E.V.], quit their jobs, left town.[17]

[Paul V.] McNutt enumerates other similar obstacles hindering a total use of the available workforce: resistance of the entrepreneurs to employing women, handicapped people or workers of a certain age.

---

16   [Luxembourg did not possess coalmines].
17   Paul V. McNutt, 'Our greatest waste: while we mobilize workers for war industries millions of manpower hours are lost daily. Chairman McNutt tells how to plug the leaks', *The New York Times Sunday Magazine*, 13 September 1942, p. sm 9.

Because of labour-market anarchy, many goods were wasted. In California, stocks of sugar-beets weighting 4 million English pounds were wasted. In Arizona, about a half of the melon crop was not harvested, etc.

Anarchy in the labour market was reinforced by big differences in wage standards in individual production branches. In 1944, weekly wages of workers paid in the aircraft industry amounted to US$ 46, in shipbuilding to US$ 53, but only amounted to US$ 37 in the mining industry. Hence, workers in metal mining left for sectors paying higher wages. But metal production was vitally important to the war industry. During the first five months of the war the Butter copper mines of the Anaconda corporation lost 1,000 men the mines only could replace by contracting 400 new workers. In June [1942], production of some pits had fallen by 50 percent because of manpower shortages.[18] In the meantime the state had to purchase copper at a high price in South America.

The contradiction between the general interests of the state and the private interests of the entrepreneurs was particularly sharp in matters of price regulation.

In the big belligerent countries price increases were lower in the state sector than during the First World War. One should nonetheless notice that prices fixed by the government were often officially transgressed. The more acute the shortages, the huger the price differences were between the state-regulated and distributed goods and the prices paid for the same goods on the free or black market.

The state could not fix a price for a series of non-standardised goods. Landed property, houses, art objects, antiques, collections, etc. belonged to that category. Superfluous money capital which was not necessary for the war economy, was used to acquire such goods, especially when a currency devaluation was threatening.[19] That is why prices rose so high.

Now that fixed prices for *new goods* were introduced, prices of used goods rose much faster than those of new ones. 'Automobiles that sold, new, for $1,000 in 1941 are being sold to dealers, after two years of depreciation, for a price of from $1,200 to $1,400, the dealer in turn disposing of them for a $200 markup'.[20] In the USA an old refrigerator costs nowadays more than a new one.

The 'egg war' is a good example of the absence of planned prices in the USA. The State of New York had introduced a price ceiling for eggs during the winter

---

18 'American notes', *The Economist*, 5 September 1942, p. 14.
19 In Germany, people were eager to buy shares of industrial firms. Prices of shares were rising so fast that the state was forced to fix their prices, which, in practice, meant suspending the activities of the stock exchange.
20 *The Economist*, 22 April 1944, p. 533.

of 1944. In that year, the market was, however, oversupplied with eggs and huge stocks of eggs were piling up in New York City. Notwithstanding this situation the merchants kept up their prices. Being confronted with this problem, Mayor [Fiorello] La Guardia[21] of New York City advised the population not to buy eggs as long as the merchants would not lower their prices.[22]

These and other similar cases illustrate that, notwithstanding state interference, anarchy in matters of price regulation still existed during the war.

Anyway, the best evidence for the impossibility of price regulation and money circulation is the fact that inflation sprang up everywhere, except in the USA, England and countries having formed a monetary bloc with them during or after the war.

State regulation of prices and high taxes were introduced in order to prevent soaring war profits. A report issued by Chairman [Harry S.] Truman of the Special Committee of the Senate stated that this target had not been attained. Furthermore, the state tried to recuperate milliards of excessive war profits when bargaining with the big suppliers of war goods in the so-called Commission of Renegotiation.[23] Only one enterprise – the United Aircraft Corporation [of East Hartford, Conn.] – 'voluntarily' reimbursed US$ 286 millions of its super-profits of the [war] years 1941–5!

The executives of these enterprises tried to hide a part of their profits for taxation by applying the most sophisticated techniques and by using them for their own private expenditures. *Harper's Magazine*, an American journal that can be hardly qualified as a radical publication, comments:

> One hears of huge banquets given at our leading hotels at staggering expense for food, drink, decorations, and entertainment. In one case every feminine guest was presented with a $10 purple orchid or a $25 white orchid; in another, the bill *for entertainers alone* was $700. A leading hotel man in one of our largest cities tells me that the amount of money spent for liquor on his premises is beyond his wildest imaginings of a few years ago. 'The sky is the limit,' he says. Where the money comes from is obvious: 'It's on the company' – 'The government's paying for it.' One hears of corporations purchasing hotel and Pullman accommodations which are used by the executives if needed and otherwise simply

---

21 [Fiorello La Guardia (1885–1947) was a Republican Mayor of New York City (1934–5)].
22 'La Guardia urges boycott of eggs; live poultry "strike" on', *The New York Times*, 4 January 1944, p. 19.
23 *Additional Report of the Special Committee Investigating the National Defense Program* 1944, p. 45.

remain unoccupied – 'With the tax situation what it is, the government's paying for them.' One hears of a corporation – not in the liquor business – keeping on hand several hundred cases of liquor for entertainment purposes. Just how much of the cash that flows nowadays in our hotels and night clubs, in Florida resorts, and in fees to ticket scalpers comes out of corporate entertainment funds (however disguised on the books) it is impossible to say, but the proportion is probably large.[24]

The fact that the means of production are in private hands always favours an illegal use of state regulations.

In fascist Germany, where the state tried to control all economic activities, regulations were continually broken during the war. German newspapers reported day after day on sentences pronounced for having hidden goods belonging to the state. Although since 1940 death penal sentences were pronounced with regard to illegal slaughtering of cattle and illicit meat trade, steeling butter from canteens, etc., lawsuits were filed until the war's end against people having broken the management regulations of the economy.

But offences against economic regulations were also regularly committed in the democratic countries. We only give here some examples of this:

> [In England] there is hardly a person in the country who does not see or hear of flagrantly unnecessary motoring: cars with CD or 'Doctor' on them drawn up at Hurlingham or in functions in London; petrol allowances for visiting foxhounds; uniformed officers on war savings business driving leisurely about the Home Counties, when a perfectly adequate train service is available; and so on.[25]

In the USA, Secretary of Agriculture [Claude R.] Wickard,[26] estimated the amount of meat illicitly brought to the market at more than 20 percent of the total meat provision fixed by the government.[27] At the market of Chicago alone, illicit purchases of meat amounted to about one million dollars a week. After the introduction of ration-books, cattle arriving at the legally operating slaughter houses decreased: pigs –28 percent, calves –26 percent, horned cattle –12 percent.[28]

---

24   Allen 1944, p. 9.
25   'Industry and trade', *The Economist*, 31 October 1942, p. 552.
26   [Claude R. Wickard (1893–1967) was Secretary of Agriculture (1940–5)].
27   Kent 1943, pp. 721–7.
28   Kent 1943, p. 722.

The situation did not improve during the war. Senator Elmer Thomas,[29] Chairman of the Senate Committee [of Food Investigation], stated on 10 April 1945 that he did not know what to do against the black market of meat 'because you cannot prosecute the whole United States ... We are making a nation of outlaws ... New York City is just one big black market'. He had heard that there, and in most major cities, 90 percent of the meat was sold in the black market.

Senator [Kenneth S.] Wherry[30] asserted that 60 tons of meat was being sold every week in Washington on the black market at wholesale prices twice the official price.[31]

And here is an example of the exchange market.

> Charles Leonard, of Heathview, Crompton Avenue, Hampstead, was fined £40,000 and ordered to pay £50 costs by Mr. McKenna at Bow Street Police Court yesterday for failing to cause $112,387 (£27,818) to be offered $112,387 (£27,818) to be offered for sale to the Treasury. He pleaded 'guilty'. It was said that he was liable to a maximum penalty of £83,454.[32]

Under the existing conditions, state intervention in the economy in the interests of individuals led inevitably to more corruption within the 'planned economy'. This occurred especially in fascist Germany. Here an example for the year of 1944.

> Director Kapp, forty years old, member of a board of armaments and munitions participated in deliberations about closing enterprises which are not important for war production. This Kapp disseminated secret information he officially got and he contacted an enterprise that was on the closure list. He offered to prevent this. In return he demanded a certain amount of shares in the enterprise.[33]

Some similar cases were made public; many others were kept secret.

All this proves that, notwithstanding state regulations, anarchy of production and a lack of planning remained characteristic of capitalism, even during the war.

---

29 [Elmer Thomas (1876–1965) was a Democrat representing Oklahoma in the Senate (1926–51)].
30 [Kenneth S. Wherry (1892–1951) was a Republican Senator of Nebraska].
31 'New York "One big black market"', *The Times*, 11 April 1945, p. 3.
32 'Dollars not offered to the Treasury', *The Times*, 20 December 1941, p. 4.
33 *Preußische Zeitung*, 12 October 1944.

During the war scientific societies for capitalist 'planning' were formed in the USA and England; a number of books and pamphlets were published on this subject.[34]

Now, after the war, the 'planning' problem comes to the fore together with a decreasing of the regulatory role of the state. The latter's role will resurface within two or three years when the next crisis breaks out.

---

34 Among the membership of the American National Planning Association are well-known people like professor Alvin H. Hansen, Beardsley Ruml, Isador Lubin and others. At the end of the war they had published some 40 pamphlets. Accurate plans were elaborated after the war and published in a booklet entitled *National Budgets for Full Employment* [1945]. Any reference as to how to achieve these plans is lacking!

CHAPTER 25

Towards an Economic Crisis in the USA

At the beginning of January [1953], President Eisenhower presented his first message to Congress on the State of the Union.[1] However hard his economic advisers tried to embellish the situation, it looked far worse than a year ago. The facts testify that the promises that Eisenhower made before the elections have remained unfulfilled. He promised prosperity, but his ministers could not prevent the beginning of a crisis of overproduction; they have only secured huge profits for the big monopolies.

'There Is No Crisis'

The 'scientific' economists of the USA, the big capitalists and the right-wing trade-union leaders can no longer deny the facts of a fall in production, a rise in unemployment, a fall in prices, etc. However, afraid of revealing the very deep contradictions of the capitalist mode of production, they avoid the word 'crisis' in every way possible, and use instead a host of more agreeable expressions: 'a slowing up of tempos of growth', 'normal adjustment to a new situation', 'lull', 'readjustment', 'falling tendency', etc. 'There is no crisis', American economists declare. Use of the words 'depression' and 'crisis' is considered dangerous.

Marx gave the only true, the only scientific theory of economic crises. He showed the inevitability of the periodic recurrence of crises of overproduction under capitalism. During the last hundred years there have been no fewer than ten world crises alone which have gripped the main or all capitalist countries. Nonetheless bourgeois economists try to picture the crisis of overproduction as arising not from objective causes, but from every kind of subjective reason. It turns out, for example, that talk of 'crisis' shakes confidence and brings on a crisis! [Benjamin Franklin] Fairless,[2] president of the steel trust United States Steel Corporation, announced this at the Economic Club in Detroit: 'We ourselves can bring on a crisis by our talk about crises'. Capitalists and their economists – consciously or unconsciously – confuse cause and effect.

---

1 [Originally published in 'K ekonomicheskiy krizis v SShA', *Pravda*, 28 January 1954].
2 [Benjamin Franklin Fairless (1890–1962) served as President from 1938–52 and Chairman and CEO (1952–5) of US Steel Corporation. During that time he served on President Dwight Eisenhower's committee of Citizen Advisers on Foreign Aid].

It stands to reason that after the beginning of a crisis, arising as a consequence of objective causes, people adjust their behaviour in the economic field to the new situation and thus deepen the crisis. But this is not 'subjective' action; it is also objective necessity. Each capitalist, anticipating a fall in prices, tries to buy less in order to protect his profits, to clear old stocks more quickly, and to put off the replacement of his fixed capital. Such activity brings about an acceleration of the fall in production and prices. Workers and employees, seeing the increasing frequency of mass dismissals, fear the future for quite objective reasons. They reduce all their purchases, as far as possible, especially of durable consumer goods: furniture, clothing, footwear, radios, etc., in order to have at least some resources for the period of impending unemployment. Their actions reduce the size of the home market, increase overproduction and deepen the crisis. Farmers, suffering heavily from the fall in prices, reduce purchases of agricultural machinery, fertilisers, and consumer goods. This deepens the crisis. But all this happens, not as a result of 'talk of crisis', not from subjective causes but because of the existence of a crisis of overproduction.

Fall in Production in the USA

An increase in production in the USA continued for a fairly long time after overproduction had already set in. In their scramble for maximum profit the capitalists increased production even more, produced for stockpiling, sold goods on credit, at the expense of the future consumer power of the population, hoping that the difficulties of realisation would be transient. It has been just the same in the past before every economic crisis. Huge stocks of goods have been created in the USA. In September 1953, stocks of private entrepreneurs in industry, wholesale and retail trade, amounted to US$80,000 million. Stocks of farm produce held by the state, and stocks in farmers' barns, on security of which they had received state credit, are valued at US$6,000 million. The value of state stocks of strategic raw materials has reached US$5,000–6,000 million. The value of the huge stockpile of arms and munitions of all types (atom bombs, tanks, guns, etc.) amounts to not less than US$100,000 million. The total of consumer credit amounted to US$28,200 million in October 1953, according to official data. Stocks continued to increase until November 1953; and the total of consumer credit continues to increase at the present time.

But neither production for stockpiling nor sales on account of the future purchasing power of society can ward off the crisis overproduction. The following facts are evidence of this:

TABLE 25.1 Index of physical volume of US industrial production (1934–5 = 100)

December 1952	235
March 1953 (maximum)	243
September 1953	234
November 1953	228
December 1953 (our estimate)	226

Thus the fall in production amounts to seven percent, even according to official figures.

Marx and Lenin taught that deterioration of the position of the working masses and their low purchasing power inevitably puts a periodic limit to the striving of the capitalists to extend production without limit and the proletarian condition of the masses makes overproduction inevitable.

Analysing American official statistics, we find concrete confirmation of this proposition of Marxism-Leninism. In those branches of industry which are chiefly engaged in satisfying the demand of the working people, the fall in production began several months earlier than the general fall in production. Thus, production of cotton textiles and knitwear had already begun to contract at the beginning of 1953. Production of footwear had already contracted 20 percent between March and July.

The influence of the different rates of development of purchasing power of various strata of the population is particularly evident in the US motorcar market. A year ago a surplus of second-hand motorcars, which are bought by working people, was already being felt. Market difficulties for the ordinary new motorcars which are bought by the prosperous section of farmers, small and medium businessmen, salaried employees, and officials, began in the middle of the year; but in the market for expensive, luxury cars, which are bought by big businessmen, no sales difficulties have been noted up to the present.

Lenin pointed out that the final aim of production is always production of means of consumption. Means of production are produced only in order to produce means of consumption with their help. The overproduction of consumer goods, which was already evident at the beginning of 1953, inevitably leads also to overproduction of means of production, and to a fall in their production. And this is what has actually happened in the last two months of 1953. Production of steel, the chief material from which industrial equipment is made, fell by 22 percent in December, compared with the maximum (March). The number of active blast furnaces is decreasing daily. In the centre of the iron and steel industry – around Pittsburgh – only 19 out of 25 blast furnaces were working in the middle of December 1953, and 11 out of 14 open-hearth furnaces. Engineering works are reducing the number of workers. Thus the present crisis is developing along '*classical*' lines: the filling up of warehouses with goods, then a decrease in production of means of consumption, and finally, growth of crisis in the field of means of production.

All the facts point to the inevitability of a further fall in production in the USA (That, however, does not exclude an increase of production in particular months, as took place in August 1953. The fall in production in times of crisis never proceeds uninterrupted). This can be anticipated on the basis of the following concrete facts:

(a) the total of unfulfilled orders of US enterprises at the end of October 1953 was US$ 13,000 million lower than at the end of October 1952. This means a decrease of 18 percent. The total of new orders in October was US$ 2,000 million lower than a year earlier. In November and December the position worsened still further.

(b) the sharp fall in production of steel means that a reduction is taking place in production of means of production. This is testified also by numerous reports in American newspapers of a reduction in production and by dismissal of workers in individual enterprises.

(c) in October 1953, new housing begun was 10 percent lower than in October 1952.

(d) commodity stocks of private entrepreneurs amounted to nearly US$ 80,000 million at the end of October.

Stock piles can be reduced only as a result of a decrease in production, of a fall in prices, and also partially, by means of their deterioration and destruction. Only thus – by means of a crisis – are normal relations between production and stocks of goods restored under capitalism.

Fall of Prices as a Sign of Crisis and a Factor in Its Intensification

The big US monopolies, in spite of overproduction, had maintained the prices of their goods up to the autumn of last year at a higher level than in 1952. But the prices of the goods of unmonopolised enterprises experienced a marked fall.

TABLE 25.2 Prices of typical monopoly commodities

	Sept 1952	Sept 1953	Percentage increase
Steel (dollars per ton)	66	81	23
Aluminium (cents per lb.)	20	21.5	7.5
Copper (cents per lb.)	24.2	29.6	21
Petrol (cents per gal.)	12.9	14.2	10
Sulphuric acid (dollars per ton)	20	22.35	11

There was no fall in the factory prices of new motorcars; and, of course, prices of armaments remained at a high level. This high price level in a number of basic branches of heavy industry is, of course, linked with the carrying out of the arms race policy. Quite a different situation exists for these commodities the prices of which the monopolists are trying to reduce. Since September 1952, the buying price of cotton has fallen 16 percent, wheat 9 percent, beef 20 percent, scrap iron 24 percent. These facts, by the way, once again confirm how little average figures mean: the general index of US wholesale prices was 107 in September 1952, and 106 in September 1953 (1948 = 100). As if nothing had changed. Actually the monopolies had raised prices of their goods in this period up to 20 percent, in this way obtaining huge super-profits; but wholesale prices of farm produce fell 10–20 percent, and hundreds of thousands of farmers were ruined.

However, since October–November 1953, the big monopolies have had to take note of the existence of overproduction and to reduce their prices. The steel monopolies have, since October, been paying the cost of railway transport for delivery of goods, which buyers have had to pay before. The prices of several special sorts of high-grade steels have been reduced US$ 2–13 per ton. At the beginning of December the General Electric Company reduced the price of air-conditioning equipment by 25 percent. The oil trusts have two or three times cut the prices of petrol. The big speculative builders have reduced the price of newly-built one-family houses from US$ 24,500 to US$ 22,500, but even then there are no buyers. All these facts confirm that militarisation of the national economy does not remove the inevitability of economic crisis. On the contrary, it leads to the growth of a new, profound economic crisis, and creates the conditions for its onset.

Increase of Unemployment and Poverty

The newspapers daily announce the mass dismissal of workers from enterprises in the motorcar, aircraft, iron and steel and other industries. Only in the middle of November did official US statistics for the first time admit a decrease during the month in the number of jobs, and an increase in the number of unemployed of 300,000. In December it was admitted that the number of unemployed rose by 422,000 persons. This is all the more significant, because in December the number of unemployed always decreases, since department stores, shops, clothing factories, etc. take on additional workers and shop assistants temporarily for the Christmas and New Year sales. In January of the present year, unemployment increased at no less a rate.

The number of unemployed officially amounts to only 1,850,000 persons. Actually it is several times greater. It is well known that American statistics do not count as unemployed those who have worked even one hour a week, and also those who are actually unemployed, but for whom a 'workplace' has been kept or to whom work is promised in the course of the succeeding month. The information on dismissals does not square in any way with the official number of unemployed. It must also be taken into account that every year in the USA 700,000 youth begin work; but the number of employed workers, even by official figures, is less than last year. Short time is widespread. The average employment of workers in industry fell significantly between December 1952 and December 1953. Enterprises are closed several days a week, etc. As a result average weekly earnings of employed workers had already fallen by two dollars a week between March and September 1953. At the same time retail prices, especially of foodstuffs, have not been reduced, although wholesale prices are falling.

To sum up: the number of wholly unemployed has risen by at least a million persons; weekly earnings of employed workers have decreased by two dollars, while the cost of living has risen by two percent in half a year. Even these figures are evidence that the US working class is *already* experiencing a further fall in its standard of living as a result of the development of crisis phenomena. Of course, the worsening of the workers' position will lead to a fall in their purchasing power and above all to a fall in demand for manufactured goods which is a factor in intensifying the crisis.

∴

At the end of December 1953 a conference of 300 leading American economists recognised at last, under pressure of the facts, that a period of 'recession' had begun. The economists declared that in 1954 the national income will be five percent less than in 1953, that the value of industrial production will decline by US$ 20,000–25,000 million, and that the index of industrial production will fall 10–15 percent. Of the 300 economists, including 100 working in state institutions, only half-a-dozen expressed the view that 1954 production would begin to increase. The overwhelming majority had to admit the inevitability of the fall continuing even into 1955.

Of course, it is difficult to paint an exact picture of the further development of crisis phenomena in the complex present-day circumstances of the ever greater intensification of the general crisis of capitalism. But one thing is clear – the crisis of overproduction in the United States is becoming to an even greater extent an actually operative factor.

CHAPTER 26

Crisis Hits the USA

Professor Eugen Varga, the well-known Marxist economist and member of the Academy of Sciences of the USSR, recently gave an interview to a correspondent of *Neues Deutschland*, daily newspaper of the Socialist Unity Party of the German Democratic Republic, and discussed with him questions concerning the present economic situation in the USA.[1] We print below the questions put by the correspondent and Professor Varga's replies.

Question: What is your opinion about present economic developments in the USA?

Answer: There is no doubt that a cyclical crisis of overproduction has begun in the USA, which has deepened in the last few months. The high point of US industrial production was achieved in December 1956. At that time the index stood at 146 (1947–9 equals 100). But for nine whole months afterwards, industrial production remained more or less static at about this level. The fact of overproduction, which already existed, was covered up. As a consequence, the crisis which has now begun was sharpened and deepened. Despite the existing overproduction, the level of industrial production was maintained throughout the first nine months of 1957 by the following means:

By Increase of Stocks

Between September 1956 and September 1957, stocks (inventories) in manufacturing industry were increased from US$ 50.8 milliard to US$ 54.1 milliard, i.e. by 6.5 percent. Stocks in wholesale and retail trade, however, remained the same – i.e. the traders had already begun to reduce their stocks, if the price increases which took place during the course of the year are taken into account, in expectation of the crisis.

---

1 [Originally published in *Marxist Review* (Toronto), August–September 1958, 17, no. 162, pp. 13–15; also published in *World News* (London), 1958, 5, no. 9, pp. 135–6; Hungarian version in *Uj szó* (Budapest), 11 February 1958].

By the Sale of Consumer Goods on Credit

That is, by anticipating future purchasing power and by dipping into the future income of society. The sums outstanding for consumer credit were:

September 1956, US$ 40 milliard.
September 1957, US$ 43 milliard.

By Driving on Exports

Between January and September 1957, the USA exported goods to the value of round about US$ 16 milliard as against imports of roughly US$ 10 milliard. The gigantic export surplus which it accumulated has, once again, resulted in an acute 'dollar shortage' in all the other capitalist countries.

Through Speeding Up Delivery of Old Orders

Deliveries excluded new orders and the position worsened month by month. In January 1957, American industry had orders to the tune of US$ 64 milliard. By September orders had declined to US$ 56 milliard.

From October 1957 onwards, the onset of the crisis could no longer be restrained by these methods. In December 1957, the index of industrial production fell to 136, i.e. by 10 points, or by 7 percent compared with December 1956. The papers published reports every day of shutdowns in the most varied places. Unemployment grew and at this moment it is probably around the 5 million mark. Official statistics systematically conceal the real extent of unemployment. This is clear from the fact that the numbers given as employed decline more rapidly than the numbers given as unemployed increase. Sections of workers who have lost their jobs are not officially registered as 'unemployed' but as 'not included in those at work'.

Along with those fully unemployed, the numbers on short time increase rapidly. In September 1957, the total wage index in manufacturing industry had declined from 171 in December 1956, to 162 (1947–9 equals 100). At the present time it has probably declined to about 150.

The measures which contributed to the artificial maintenance of production are now resulting in a deepening of the crisis. The workers who are now unemployed can no longer pay the instalments due on the durable consumer goods they bought – e.g. on motor cars. These are taken from them and go to the dealers. The market for cars is being ruined. The same applies to TV and radio sets.

The retail traders, now feeling the pinch, are reducing their stocks. They are selling – but are not buying – which reduces sales by industry even more. Workers and employees, now uncertain of the future, are reluctant to buy the things they need on credit. The capitalists, whose profits in 1957 showed a not inconsiderable reduction compared with 1956, are limiting investment. All this leads to a further reduction in production and an increase in unemployment. So one thing leads to another in deepening the crisis.

Question: Will American budget spending act as a cure?

Answer: The American capitalists are pinning their hopes on an increase in military expenditure to help them to bring the crisis to a speedy end. These hopes have no real foundation.

According to the *Survey of Current Business Business*, November 1957, US military expenditure (in the narrow sense of the term, i.e. without including foreign aid) was (see *Table 26.1*):

TABLE 26.1 US military expenditure (calculated on the basis of expenditure in the first nine months)

In milliards of dollars		
1955	1956	1957
39.1	40.4	44.0(*)

(*) (Calculated on the basis of expenditure in the first nine months)

Thus we can see that the crisis began although military expenditure in 1957 was US$ 4 milliard, or 10 percent higher than in the previous years.

How can a further increase of a few milliard dollars bring the crisis to an end? The reduction of the incomes of the workers and employees by 1 percent means reduction in the purchasing power of the American people by two milliard dollars. There is thirdly to be a reduction in the income of the above groups of the order of 10 percent in a few months time. What can an increase in the military budget by a few milliards signify in the face of a situation like this (apart entirely from the fact that an increase in military expenditure means a further, corresponding decrease in the purchasing power of the people)?

Question: What are some of the likely effects of crisis developments in the USA on those countries which have military and economic ties with the USA?

Answer: It is obvious that the crisis in the USA will involve all other capitalist countries in a world economic crisis. The United States is responsible for half the total industrial production in the capitalist world. A crisis of overproduction in the USA must extend itself to all other capitalist countries through its repercussions on foreign trade, the Stock Exchanges, international credit, and the undermining of confidence, especially when in each of these countries conditions for a crisis have been maturing.

This is true in all the most important capitalist countries of Europe – England, France and Western Germany – where there is stagnation of production, declining investment, a currency crisis in England, the end of the investment boom and export difficulties in Western Germany, currency crisis in France, etc. The sharp fall in raw material prices – copper, zinc, tin, rubber – reduces the purchasing power of the underdeveloped countries, makes it difficult for them to buy the industrial products of Western Europe and thereby intensifies export problems. The sharpening of the agrarian crisis has the same effects.

All the preconditions for the extension of the crisis of overproduction in the USA to Western Europe seem to be present.

(August–September 1958)

CHAPTER 27

Problems of the Postwar Industrial Cycle and the New Crisis of Overproduction

If we look at the course of events from the standpoint of the surface of phenomena it may appear that the cycle which ended in 1957 by letting loose a world economic crisis lasted for 20 years.[1] The cause of this, the apologists of capitalism again began to proclaim, just as they did before the crisis of 1929, is that capitalism has found a means of avoiding crises. At times a weak echo of this nonsense can be discerned in the reasoning of individual Communists.

But a 20-year cycle is only the appearance and not the essence of the phenomenon. World War II, like every great war,[2] interrupted the normal progress of the cycle; it created enormous, extraordinary demand for war materials, accompanied by cuts in the production of civilian goods, giving rise to an excess of effective demand over supply which continued for several years.

The essence of a cycle, its basic function, is the creation, in the course of all its phases, of premises for a crisis of overproduction. In war years conditions conducive to the overproduction of commodities do not exist. In view of this one should not include the years of a great war in the cycle. Some comrades object to this. They say that the cyclical character of reproduction is a result of the action of the general laws of capitalism. And capitalism remains capitalism even during a war. Therefore the cyclical process of reproduction continues even during a world war.

We consider such an approach a dogmatic one. It lacks what Lenin called the living soul of Marxism: a concrete analysis of a concrete situation. True,

---

1 A chapter from the forthcoming book of Varga's *Problems of the Political Economy of Capitalism*. [This chapter was first published in Moscow in *Kommunist* 1958, 8: 140–57, and in *Mirovaya ekonomika i mezhdunardnye otnosheniya* 1958, 6: 18–35; many translations can be traced back in many communist journals: *Rinascita* (Rome, 1958, 8: 1–6); *Mondo economico* (Milan 1958, 40: 24–8); *Estudios sociaes* (Rio de Janeiro, 1958, 2: 154); *Sowjetwissenschaften/Gesellschaftswissenschaftliche Beiträge* (Berlin, 1958, 10: 1173–94); MSZP KB, *Külügyi Osztály Tájékoztatója* (Budapest, 1958, 12). This translation follows the American edition of Varga's *Problems of the postwar industrial cycle and the new crisis of overproduction*, published by International Arts and Sciences Press in New York in 1958].
2 Even such a relatively small war as the war in Korea exercised significant influence on the progress of the postwar cycle, as in the stockpiling of strategic materials, a sharp increase in military expenditures and a price rise.

Marx established the laws of capitalist world economy. However, though there were wars in his time, they influenced the economic life of capitalism relatively little. In Marx's lifetime there was no 'military economy'.

Some of our economists have expressed the opinion that, in view of the extraordinary development of the branches of industry producing armaments and of those connected with them (ferrous and non-ferrous metallurgy, metal manufacturing, chemicals and others) and the serious lag of branches producing consumer goods, war itself creates the premises for crises of overproduction, that is, war creates great disproportions within the capitalist economy. This is an echo of the bourgeois and revisionist theory that the cause of crises of overproduction is not capitalism itself, not the contradiction between the social character of production and the private character of appropriation, and the poverty and proletarian status of the masses born of this contradiction, but a disproportion in the growth of individual branches of production.[3]

This is not so. If at the end of a war the productive capacity of some branches of industry is too large, while that of others is insufficient, this may cause a *partial crisis* in some branches of industry which served the needs of the war, but it cannot bring about a general crisis of overproduction because in many important branches of industry, especially in Department II, demand continues to be in excess of supply.[4]

In fact, after the end of the war in the second half of 1945, in 1946, and partially in 1947, the level of industrial production in all countries was lower than in the war years. This was not a cyclical phenomenon, but rather a natural

---

[3] The starting point of this theory is the teaching of English classical political economy that the production of every commodity generates wages, profits and rent, that is, that the production of a commodity in itself creates the purchasing power ensuring its sale, and that therefore a general crisis of overproduction is impossible. This theory is false. It was refuted by Marx himself. But it has currency even now. In the January issue of the organ of one of the largest American banks, The Guarantee Trust Company, we read: ... '[E]very portion of the money value of every commodity and service produced is income, or purchasing power, to someone ... When goods remain unsold, it is not because there is a deficiency of purchasing power but because people do not use the purchasing power they have'. (*The Guarantee Survey*, January 1958, p. 3).

[4] The share of Department II, even in the United States where the organic composition of capital is higher than in other capitalist countries, is not smaller than that of Department I. During 1957 the total sales of nondurable goods and of durable goods were the same – about US$170 milliard each (*Survey of Current Business*, February 1958). Under durable goods are included some consumption goods: cars, furniture, etc. On the other hand, coal and petroleum, which serve mainly as means of production, are included by American statisticians under nondurable goods. Yet, on the whole, the division of goods into nondurable and durable goods more or less corresponds in Department I and Department II.

PROBLEMS OF THE POSTWAR INDUSTRIAL CYCLE   1063

consequence of the transition from a wartime economy to a peacetime economy. Some of the plants employed in the war effort were put into mothballs and some were re-equipped and transferred to the production of consumption goods (while some continued to produce armaments). Industry had to readjust itself to the production of a new assortment of goods. Such a readjustment required time and it was accompanied by a decrease in the volume of production. Thus *we should take the year 1947 as the beginning of the postwar cycle and the length of that cycle as from 10 to 11 years.*

In respect to length, the first cycle after the end of World War II differed sharply from the cycle which followed World War I, when the crisis of overproduction was of short duration and was not deep, and began only two to three years after the end of the war. The reasons for this difference are that World War I was considerably shorter, required a much smaller quantity of war materials, a smaller number of countries participated in it, and the productive capacity destroyed by it was considerably less. That is why the economy of world capitalism underwent fewer changes then than occurred as a result of World War II.

Here a theoretical question arises: what causes the differing lengths of individual cycles?

The material basis of the cyclical course of reproduction is fixed capital. If we exclude from our calculations such extraordinary occurrences as war, crop failure, etc., the length of the cycle depends upon the volume and character of the renovation and expansion of fixed capital: the larger the new capital investments, the longer the ascending phases of the cycle – revival and boom (and overextension).

In studying cycles, we usually consider only the total of new capital investment and pay little attention to the character of this new capital investment. Such an approach is faulty: the same total of new capital investment may exercise different influences on the length of the cycle.

The most important questions are as follows:

1. Are the capital investments made mainly undertakings (such as plants and factories) which, immediately after their completion, increase the supply of goods on the market, or (as was the case, say, in the middle of the nineteenth century) mainly for undertakings (such as railroads, ports, ships, highways, bank buildings and department store buildings) which increase the supply of goods on the market only indirectly? It is clear that in the first case conditions of an overproduction crisis would mature more rapidly than in the second case.
2. What is the relationship between the new capital investment and the value of goods thrown on the market after the completion of a given

undertaking? For example, the construction of a hydroelectric station requires a sizeable capital investment, but it produces relatively little of the new commodity (depreciation proceeds very slowly). On the other hand, the factories and plants with a lower organic composition of capital send to the market more goods in proportion to the capital invested in them, thus causing overproduction of commodities more quickly.

3. How long are the new undertakings under construction? On the one hand, with the progress of technique and the concentration of capital, larger and larger plants and combinates are built, requiring more time for their designing and construction than the small plants built a hundred years ago. On the other hand, the tempo of construction is considerably higher now than a hundred years ago.

Special Features of the Postwar Cycle

Though for more than a hundred years industrial cycles have regularly followed one another; and though the causes and intrinsic character of all cycles are identical, nevertheless each cycle has its own features, depending upon the concrete historical conditions in which it develops. The main features of the present postwar cycle are as follows: (a) the postwar cycle developed while two economic systems were in existence, under continuous conditions of a 'cold war'; (b) it developed in a situation in which the colonial system of imperialism was breaking down; (c) it began after a world war that lasted for six years, a war that caused great destruction and brought changes into the world capitalist economy; (d) the progress of the cycle in the countries affected was extremely different because the various capitalist countries – neutral countries, the United States, victorious countries, defeated countries – found themselves after the end of World War II in quite different economic (and political) conditions; (e) with the exception of some neutral countries, the cycle developed in the presence of general inflation, when a strong and constant rise of prices was observed; this price rise was to a small degree a result of an artificial raising of prices by monopolies, as well as the usual result of the boom phase of the cycle; (f) the majority of capitalist countries in the course of the cycle experienced a dollar shortage; (g) the cycle developed within a setting of a new intensification of the agrarian crisis.

Let us now analyse the influence of these concrete historical features on the progress of the cycle.

The chief consequence of the 'cold war' was that very soon after the end of the war the capitalist countries, and first of all the United States, resumed large-scale production of armaments, which continued at an accelerating tempo during the whole course of the cycle. Military expenditures, according to our calculations,[5] represented the following percentages of the national incomes:

TABLE 27.1 The course of the economic cycle in the US, UK and France

	1937–8	1948–9	1953–4
United States			
percent of the official estimate of the national income	1.5	6.5	15.8
percent of the national income if double counting is eliminated			about 22
Great Britain			
percent of the official estimate of the national income	4.1	7.7	9.5
percent of the national income if double counting is eliminated			about 12
France			
percent of the official estimate of the national income	5.9	6.1	13.3
percent of the national income if double counting is eliminated			about 16

In 1957–8 the share of military production in the national income will increase even further.

A predominant part of the military expenditures was made for the production of weapons. These weapons, in the course of the cycle, became more complex and expensive. Military technique was developing so rapidly that frequently by the time new weapons reached the stage of mass production they were obsolete. This means that the monopolies – the suppliers of armaments – even in peacetime were obtaining renewed and exceedingly profitable armament orders. For this reason, the strained international situation and the continuation of the policy of 'cold war' were extremely advantageous to the monopolies: the part of armament orders in industrial production was considerably higher than in the national income, while in total profits the share of profits from armament orders was even higher.

Armament production carried out in peacetime exercises a different influence on the process of reproduction, depending upon concrete conditions. If there is in a country – because of insufficient effective demand – an unutil-

---

5 See Varga 1957, p. 42.

ised surplus of productive capacity, raw materials and labour power (and in the epoch of the general crisis of capitalism, as a rule, such is the case), armament orders would result in an increase of production and in an expansion of the volume of the market, and would tend to lengthen the phase of revival and boom (and overextension), that is, would tend to lengthen the cycle, at the same time bringing about or intensifying inflation. If there is in a country no unused productive capacity, armament production would not result in an expansion of the volume of production as a whole, but would be achieved only at the expense of civilian consumption. If the volume of armament production is larger than the economic resources of the country can permit, the result will be the overextension and deformation of the economy such as takes place under wartime conditions.

The influence of armament orders on the course of the cycle may be clearly seen in the case of the crisis of 1948–9 in the United States. It is not important in this connection whether that crisis was an intermediary one, or whether the Korean War prevented its development into a genuine crisis of overproduction. This question will be touched upon later. There is no doubt, however, that the Korean War stimulated an increase in production. For example, the index of industrial production in the united states rose from 95, the lowest point, reached in July 1949, to an average of 112 in 1950 (average of 1947–9 = 100), that is, by 18 percent.[6]

The state of the British economy in the last three years of the postwar cycle may serve as an example of the case in which armament production cannot bring about a general expansion in the volume of production and the size of the market. Though the volume of British armament production was large, the total volume of British production remained on the same level in 1955, 1956 and 1957. In spite of the fact that productive capacity was utilised almost in full, too large a part of armament production brought about inflation and a foreign exchange crisis. On the other hand, relatively small military expenditures in Western Germany and Japan were undoubtedly one of the factors which made possible the rebuilding in these countries of destroyed productive capacity and the great expansion of fixed capital, resulting in a considerable growth of production in the boom phase of the cycle.

The foregoing data show that armament production exercises a great influence on the course of the postwar cycle. Taking the system of capitalist economy as a whole, we may say that armament production may tend to lengthen

---

6 These figures are taken from various issues of the *Federal Reserve Bulletin*.

the phase of boom and overextension and, at the same time, the cycle itself. However, armament production is not a means of eliminating crises of overproduction, as is clearly shown by the crisis of overproduction in the United States which began in the autumn of 1957 and spread rapidly in 1958 to other capitalist countries.

The statements of the press, which serves as a mouthpiece of monopolies, enriching themselves on armament orders, are wrong about the stabilising influence of armament orders on the process of reproduction. The feverish development of military technique intensifies the anarchy of production.

The expenditures of the United States on various types of armaments changed as follows:

TABLE 27.2 US expenditures on armaments (US$ milliard)

	1957	1958
Artillery, ammunition, means of transportation for the land forces	3.6	0.7
Rocket weapons	0.2	2.5
Airplanes	4.9	7.2

SOURCE: 'BUSINESS AND ECONOMIC CONDITIONS', *FIRST NATIONAL CITY BANK MONTHLY LETTER*, NOVEMBER 1957, P. 125

Such large increases exercise not a stabilising, but a disorganising influence on the economy. Changes in the type of planes produced for the Department of Defence resulted frequently in mass unemployment in various cities of the United States.

The breakdown of the colonial system exercised an influence on the course of the cycle first of all through changes in the export of capital. The export of capital ceased to former colonial or semi-colonial countries which had entered the road of socialism (China, Vietminh, North Korea). The decisive factor in the selection of countries for the export of capital became the political factor – the existence of 'safety' and 'order' in the country and the absence of the threat of nationalisation. The breakdown of the colonial system changed the volume and geographic distribution of export of capital. During the years of the postwar cycle the total export of private capital was considerably lower than during the cycle of 1921–9. The geographic distribution of the export of capital has changed; private capital has been going chiefly to those countries which, from the point of view of the capitalists, are the most reliable, that is, to Canada, South America and Africa (with the exception of the Arab countries).

A new feature is the existence on a large scale of the export of state capital, especially from the United States, in the form of economic and military subsidies to various countries. From the point of view of the course of the cycle, there is no difference between the export of private capital and the export of state capital or subventions.[7] What happens is that a country exports goods without simultaneously importing other goods, as is the case with ordinary foreign trade, and this results in a temporary expansion of the volume of the market and, other conditions being equal, in lengthening the industrial cycle.

The loss of resources, because of the formation of two economic systems, and the breakdown of the colonial system did not result in a shortage of raw materials in the capitalist world. During the postwar cycle a shortage of some raw materials on the capitalist market and a rapid rise of prices were observed only in 1950, when the United States was feverishly buying up various strategic materials for military stockpiling. With the help of new techniques the capitalists were able to discover many new sources of raw materials in Canada, South America, central and southern Africa and even on the territory of the imperialist countries themselves (petroleum in the state of Texas in the United States, and in Germany and France), and to substitute new kinds of raw materials for the raw materials in short supply.

That the statements concerning shortages of raw materials in the capitalist world are groundless may be proved by the fact that overproduction occurred and prices fell in the field of industrial raw materials before the crisis in industry arose.

As may be seen from *Table 27.3*, the prices of some raw materials – copper, tin, rubber, leather – first began to fall in 1957. A fall, of approximately the same or even greater magnitude, in the prices of raw materials had been observed in the whole capitalist world, though in January 1958 clear signs of the crisis of overproduction appeared only in the United States.

---

7 Of course, there is no difference between the export of capital and subventions only insofar as the course of the cycle is concerned. In essence subventions, in spite of the statements of some Soviet economists to the contrary, are not identical with the export of capital, because subventions do not have that characteristic which, according to Marx's definition, is the essence of capital – self-increasing value.

TABLE 27.3 Prices of the most important kinds of industrial raw materials in the United States

	1956 the highest level	1957 January	1958 January
Copper (cents per pound)	45.9	35.8	24.8
Scrap iron (dollars per ton)	67.0	63.0	33.0
Zinc (cents per pound)	13.5	13.5	10.0
Tin (cents per pound)	106.5	102.2	92.2
Rubber (cents per pound)	37.2	33.5	27.2
Leather (cents per pound)	13.5	10.0	9.2

SOURCE: *THE GUARANTEE SURVEY*, JANUARY 1958, FEBRUARY 1958, PP. 12–13

World War II, in which all industrial countries of the world participated, except Sweden and Switzerland, was of decisive importance for the course of the postwar industrial cycle.

During the war the level of consumption – civilian and military, also considering the destruction wrought by the war – was substantially above the level of production. The national wealth decreased.[8] Stocks of goods were greatly reduced. Fixed capital, with the exception of the armament industries, suffered great wear and tear, both physical and moral. The demand of the population for goods, especially for durable goods – housing, furniture, cars, household appliances – was not satisfied for years, because their production was prohibited in order to free productive forces – labour, raw materials and machines – for the production of means of war. The consumption of foodstuffs by the urban population – except for the consumption of the rich who used the black market – was restricted by rationing. At the end of the war a large unsatisfied demand had accumulated both for means of production and means of consumption.

This extraordinary demand was an effective demand. The state was paying capitalists high prices for military supplies. Profits, accumulated appropriations to offset depreciation of assets, and accumulations formed because of reduction of stocks, remained in the form of bank deposits, state bonds (which

---

[8] Even in the United States, which did not suffer from war destruction and which took part in the war for a shorter period than the European countries, the national wealth, excluding that part of it which belonged to the state, was, according to the calculations of American economists, not larger in 1945 (in prices of 1929) than in 1929. See Kuznets and Goldsmith 1952, pp. 327–8.

could at anytime be turned into cash), and cash in the hands of capitalists. The wealthier part of the population and even some categories of industrial workers were compelled, because of the shortage of consumer goods, to keep part of their income in the form of savings. Thus in countries of the most different types – industrial and underdeveloped (Brazil), belligerent and neutral – the amount of money in circulation increased from three to five times, while in the vanquished countries (Italy and Japan) it increased almost twenty times.

TABLE 27.4 Amount of money in circulation (in milliards, at the end of the corresponding year)

	USA USD	Canada CND	Brazil cruz.	UK pounds	Sweden Kronas	France francs	Italy liras	Japan Yen
1938	5.8	0.24	3.6	0.46	1.04	112	19	2.9
1945	26.5	1.06	14.3	1.34	2.79	577	368	54.8

SOURCE: *UNITED NATIONS STATISTICAL YEARBOOK* 1956, P. 484 *PASSIM*

To money in circulation should be added bank deposits.

TABLE 27.5 Bank deposits (in milliards, at the end of the corresponding year)

	USA(a) USD	Canada CND	Brazil Cruz.	UK pounds	Sweden Kronas	France francs	Italy liras	Japan Yen
1938	26	0.9	8.5	1.2	76	2.5	27	3.1
1945	76	2.5	27	3.1	3.8	436	290	36

(a) The *Federal Reserve Bulletin* gives even higher figures. Presumably the difference is due to the inclusion in the total of interbank deposits and state deposits.

SOURCE: *UNITED NATIONS STATISTICAL YEARBOOK* 1956, P. 484 *PASSIM*

The tempo of the growth of deposits approximately coincides with the tempo of the rise in monetary circulation.[9] Taken together they show an enormous growth of purchasing power in the respective societies as a result of the war. To

---

9   In Italy and Japan a strong inflation was taking place during these years; so the growth of deposits was smaller than the rise in monetary circulation.

this should be added the growth of deposits in savings banks and the amount of outstanding state bonds – war loans in the hands of private persons and corporations. Of course, purchasing power would not have grown if commodity prices had risen at the same tempo as the amount of money in circulation and the deposits in banks and savings institutions. However, this was not the case.

TABLE 27.6 General index of wholesale prices, annual averages (1953 = 100)

	USA	Canada	Brazil	UK	Sweden	France	Italy	Japan
1938	46	46	13	31	37	4	2	0.4
1945	62	60	40	52	65	14	39	1.0

In those countries which are of decisive importance for the study of the cycle – the United States, Great Britain and Canada – prices during the war rose considerably more slowly than the rise of money in circulation and deposits in banks and savings institutions. In other words, the deferred demand by the end of the war was a fully effective demand.

Thus, at the end of the war the size of the capitalist market in Department I and Department II was considerably above 'normal', a primary factor in determining the course of the postwar cycle. The capitalists began to replace worn-out fixed capital at extremely high tempos as well as to expand it rapidly – in the victorious countries immediately after the war and in the vanquished countries[10] some years later. This was the main reason why the postwar cycle had such a long phase of revival and boom. As an example, we may give data for the United States, Great Britain and Western Germany.

Expansion of fixed capital continued at an increasing tempo even during the first half of 1957. If the fall in the purchasing power of the dollar during the whole postwar cycle is taken into account, then it may be stated that the scale of expansion of fixed capital was several times greater than in the pre-war cycle.

---

10   Neutral countries, especially underdeveloped countries, which had not taken an active part in the war, also experienced a shortage of fixed capital at the end of the war because the industrial countries, which had participated in the war, could not supply them with means of production.

TABLE 27.7 Expenditures on new equipment in the United States (annual average in US$ milliards)

1929–38	1945–9	1950–4	1955	1956	1957
3.5	14.4	25.5	28.7	35.1	37.0

SOURCE: *HISTORICAL STATISTICS OF THE UNITED STATES* 1949; *FEDERAL RESERVE BULLETIN*, JANUARY 1958, P. 60. (DATA FOR 1957, ESTIMATES. ACTUAL EXPENDITURES WERE SMALLER)

A similar situation was observed in England and Western Germany.

TABLE 27.8 Expenditures for fixed capital in Great Britain (in millions of £)

	1938	1950	1955	1956
In current prices	656	1,702	2,955	3,139
In prices of 1948	1,559	1,647	2,124	2,234

SOURCE: *ANNUAL ABSTRACT OF STATISTICS*, 1956 AND 1957, TABLES 285 AND 287, GROSS FIXED CAPITAL FORMATION

In Western Germany capital investments in means of production and construction were as follows:

TABLE 27.9 Expenditures for fixed capital (in milliards marks)

1938	1950–4 (average annual)	1955
7.1	27.8	39.8

SOURCE: *STATISTISCHES JAHRBUCH FÜR DIE BUNDESREPUBLIK DEUTSCHLAND* 1957, P. 561

The purchasing power accumulated as a result of the war was utilised to expand fixed capital as well as to increase inventories, which by the end of the war had reached a very low level. For example, in the United States the stock of goods in industry and wholesale and retail trade had by the end of war reached the low level of US$ 25 milliard, but during the course of the cycle inventories continued to grow, amounting to US$ 91.3 milliard in August 1957. A similar development took place in other industrial countries. Production to replenish depleted inventories played an important part in lengthening the phase of revival and boom in the postwar cycle. In the United States inventories began to decrease only in the fourth quarter of 1952. But the rapid growth of inventories, in comparison with the amount of sales, signalled even before that time the sluggish rate at which they moved to consumers, an indication of an overproduction of goods.

The third factor which contributed to the lengthening of the boom phase – one not caused by the war in this instance, but, on the contrary, by the absence of additional demand and the rack of effective demand – was an artificial expansion of the market volume for consumption goods by means of a great increase in consumer or instalment credit, that is, through utilising the future purchasing power of capitalist society. This development occurred mainly in the United States, where consumer credit increased from US$ 5.7 milliar at the end of 1945 to US$ 43.5 milliard in November 1957. To a smaller degree, the growth of consumer credit was also observed in England as well as in a number of other industrial capitalist countries.

These three factors – an exceptionally great volume of renewal and expansion of fixed capital, the creation of a large stock of goods for manufacturing, and trade and sales by mortgaging the future income of society – determined the length of the postwar cycle and are of great importance for the course of the crisis which ended the postwar cycle.

The history of world industrial cycles shows that in each cycle considerable differences appear in the course of the cycle in various countries, depending upon the concrete historical situation in a given country. These differences were especially great in the postwar cycle, though, if we look only at the results of the cycle, they may appear not to be so great; all countries, victors and vanquished, industrial and underdeveloped, raised the level of their industrial production considerably after the war.

TABLE 27.10 Index of physical volume of industrial production (1953 = 100)

	The whole capitalist world	USA	Canada	Sweden	UK	France	Italy	W. Germ.	Japan	India
1937(a)	56	46	43	60	76	78	63	78	80	74
1947	68	75	76	84	76	71	62(c)	41(c)	29	78
1955	110	104	107	111	113	119	118	129	117	115
1956	116	107	114	114	112	133	128	139	142	126
1957	118(b)	107	114	118	114	145	138	147	161	139

(a) The year 1937 was chosen for comparison because 1938 was a year of crisis, and 1939 was in part a year of war.
(b) An average for the first three quarters of the year.
(c) 1948.
SOURCE: UNITED NATIONS DATA

Although these data are not precise and should be used only to compare the dynamics of developments inside each country, they nevertheless show the basic cause of the differences in the course of the cycle in the individual countries. This cause lies in the different position that each country occupied after the end of the war, at the beginning of the cycle in 1947, that is, when the transition from a war economy to a peacetime economy was completed. The different positions at the starting point explain the differences in the course of the cycle in each of these countries. Here three groups of countries may be roughly distinguished.

1. *Countries which did not suffer from the war*: United States, Canada, Sweden and other neutral countries. In these countries the cycle began at a level of industrial production which was considerably higher than that of 1937. Consequently the growth of production in these countries during the course of the cycle was smaller; in the United States two intermediary crises occurred in the course of the cycle.

2. *European industrial countries, participants in the war, which suffered considerably from it*: Great Britain, France, Italy and others. The cycle in these countries began under conditions in which their industrial production was on the level of 1937 or even lower. In other words, the war put these countries ten years back. In addition to satisfying the deferred demand for peacetime needs, these countries had to make up for wartime destruction. Production in these countries therefore increased more rapidly than in the United States and in the neutral countries, and the intermediary crises of the United States found practically no reflection in the course of their cycles.

In this connection we should like to touch upon this question: by what means does a crisis beginning in one or several countries spread to other industrial countries? The main routes are as follows:

Countries in which a crisis takes place try to ameliorate its effects at the expense of other countries[11] by expansion of their exports and reduction of their imports.

The existence of a crisis in one country or another undermines the confidence of the capitalists and tends to reduce new capital investments. The fall of stock exchange quotations brought about by the crisis is reflected on the stock exchanges of all capitalist countries.

If a monetary-credit crisis occurs, withdrawal of capital lent on a short-term basis may produce a monetary-credit crisis in those capitalist countries.[12]

Indirectly a crisis may spread as follows: in a number of countries a crisis may bring about a sharp fall in the prices of raw materials, thus greatly reducing the ability of countries which depend upon the export of only one product to import industrial goods.

The influence of these factors differs, depending upon concrete conditions in individual countries. The influence of foreign trade upon the development of a crisis of overproduction is greater in countries in which exports and imports provide an important part of the total production, as in Great Britain and Belgium. But, as a rule, a crisis of overproduction spreads to other countries only when domestic conditions in these countries are more or less ripe for this development. If, for example, exports make up 25 percent of production, as is the case in Great Britain, the fall of exports by 10 percent would amount only to 2.5 percent of the total production. In the majority of countries the share of exports is even smaller.

3. *Principal vanquished countries*: Germany and Japan. These countries suffered greatly from war, occupation, destruction of their former world connections, etc. For these reasons industrial production in these countries amounted in 1947 to about one-third of their production in 1937, and several years were needed for them to reach the pre-war level. At the same time the boom in the last three years of the cycle was more intensified in these than in other countries. Thus, though the level of industrial production in the capitalist

---

[11] Serving as an example is the sharp increase of the favourable trade balance of the United States in 1957: from US$ 2.9 milliard in 1955 to US$ 4.7 milliard in 1956 and US$ 6.5 milliard in 1957 (these figures do not include export of armaments).

[12] For example, the crash of Germany's large banks in 1931 was caused by withdrawal of short-term American credits.

world as a whole at the end of the cycle was approximately double that of 1937, the differences among individual countries in respect to the level of production reached and the tempo of development were very large.

Let us now return to the postwar cycle in the United States.

The author of this article and a number of other economists considered the crisis of 1949 as the beginning of a genuine crisis of overproduction in the United States, the development of which was interrupted by war in Korea. Other Soviet economists considered that crisis as an intermediary one. Of course, it is possible to discuss endlessly what form that cycle in the United States would have taken if there had been no war in Korea, but such a discussion would be pointless and scholastic. From the point of view of the world industrial cycle, the crises of 1948–9 and 1953–4 in the United States were intermediary crises and the year 1947 should be considered as the starting point of the postwar cycle. Such an approach would make it possible to understand better the postwar cycle and the cycles that will follow it.

Of course, the basis of both intermediary and genuine crises is the contradiction between the social character of production and the private character of appropriation; the cause is the proletarian position of the masses. Both types of crisis are crises of overproduction. The difference between them is that in a 'genuine' crisis the overproduction embraces all or almost all spheres and branches of the capitalist economy, while in a partial or intermediary crisis it embraces only some branches, while others continue their upward movement. If the branches in which boom conditions continue have great relative importance in the economy of the country, the branches which suffer from the crisis of overproduction will overcome it in a relatively short time. As a result no depression follows an intermediary crisis, which itself is followed by a boom phase. Such was the case in the United States after the crises of 1948–9 and 1953–4, which might better be considered as intermediary crises. The difference between genuine and intermediary crises is that the latter are not observed in each cycle.

An important feature of the postwar cycle is a constant inflationary depreciation of the money of all capitalist countries, something that did not occur in any other cycle of the twentieth century. The depreciation was manifested by the selling of gold for industrial purposes everywhere, including the United States at prices higher than the Treasury rate for gold, set by the United States at US$ 35 per ounce; this depreciation, in turn, was reflected in the depreciation of other currencies in terms of dollars, and chiefly in the rise of prices which continued in part after the beginning of the crisis in the United States. As the value of commodities, that is, the labour time embodied in a commodity unit, was undoubtedly reduced because of the rapid technical progress in the course of the cycle, the price rise signifies an inflationary break of prices with the value of goods.

The basis of the inflation is first of all World War II, which produced an enormous increase in the amount of money in circulation and of deposits in the banks and savings institutions, while the production of goods for civilian consumption was reduced; secondly, the excessive military expenditures of the principal capitalist countries soon after the end of the war and the deficits of the state budgets; and finally, the destructive influence which the United States exercises on the economies of other capitalist countries.

However, we should not ascribe the price increases during the course of the cycle solely to inflation, as the bourgeois economists do. The bourgeoisie uses inflation as a pretext for an offensive against the working class, asserting that the cause of inflation is that wages are too high (!). Undoubtedly, some of the price rise is the result of the cycle, because in the boom phase market prices, when supply lags in comparison to demand, begin as a rule to exceed the prices of production. To a certain degree, also, the price rise is undoubtedly the result of the policies of monopolies which artificially increase prices above the prices of production; this is the main source of the excess profits of monopolistic capital.[13]

While it is impossible, of course, to determine what part of the rise in prices is due to this or that particular factor, the decisive factor is inflation.

The rise in prices, if it continues for many years, tends to lengthen the boom (and overextension) phase and the cycle itself. Businessmen, expecting further price rises, increase their inventories and try to transform their money-loan capital into 'real values'. Consumers, expecting prices to rise further, try to buy, frequently on credit, goods which they may need in the future. The boom phase is prolonged. These tendencies are characteristic only of a 'slow' inflation. If the tempo of the inflation becomes too rapid, the result is a breakdown of normal economic relationships. That is why the bourgeoisie again resorts to stabilisation of exchange rates or at least tries to stabilise them. The fight against inflation may accelerate the explosion of a crisis of overproduction.

---

13   The influence of monopolies on the rise in prices may be seen from comparison of prices of non-monopolised raw materials with prices of goods produced by monopolies from the same materials in the United States, for example, the price of wheat and of white bread, of pigs and of pork products. Between January 1957 and January 1958 the price per ton of scrap iron fell from US$63 to US$33, but the price of steel, despite the crisis, increased during the same period from US$73 to US$77.5.

During the course of the cycle almost all capitalist countries experienced a 'dollar shortage', that is, a continued shortage of dollar foreign exchange.[14] The cause of the dollar shortage is well known: the excess of exports over imports in United States foreign trade,[15] brought about by various measures limiting the import of goods into the country and carried out in the interests of the monopolies, and federal dumping on the world market of goods produced by the monopolies. As a result, the United States' balance of payments is highly active in character and the gold stock of the United States grew almost uninterruptedly at the expense of other capitalist countries. The shortage of dollars was an important additional cause of inflation in many capitalist countries, for example, in Great Britain.

During almost the whole course of the cycle an acute agrarian crisis existed. This is not a special feature of this cycle; it was observed during the preceding cycles of the period of general crises. Overproduction of foodstuffs took place only in 'rich countries' with a large area of land per capita: Canada, the United States, Australia and Argentina. Hundreds of millions of human beings in the underdeveloped countries ate less in quality and quantity at the end than at the beginning of the cycle, while huge amounts of 'surplus' foodstuffs were being accumulated in the United States and Canada. The government of the United States spent about US$ 5 milliard annually to pay farmers to reduce the sown area, while the Soviet Union during the same years expanded its cultivated area by 35 million hectares.

The existence of an agrarian crisis tended to shorten the length of the industrial cycle. However, one should not overestimate this influence. In the highly developed industrial countries, such as the United States or Great Britain, the share of agriculture in the total economy, and the incomes and purchasing power of the agricultural population are too small to exercise a significant influence on the course of the cycle (the share of agriculture in the gross national product in 1956, according to the United Nations, amounted to 5 percent in the United States, to 4 percent in England, to 8 percent in Western Germany, and to 10 percent in Canada). The agrarian crisis reduces the

---

14 The exceptions here are countries with a large output of gold, also countries which are large exporters to the United States of strategic raw materials; and Switzerland, which became a haven for capital of doubtful origin (German fascists and all types of speculators place their wealth in Swiss banks which strictly observe the 'inviolability of banking secrets').

15 The favourable trade balance of the United States during the cycle of 1947–57, according to United Nations data, amounted to US$ 49.3 milliard.

ability of underdeveloped countries to purchase means of production from industrial countries.

In the course of the cycle the capitalist press gave much space to the question of the industrialisation of underdeveloped countries. Every day news items could be read about the construction in such countries of a new factory or some enterprise. Undoubtedly, the industry of underdeveloped countries expanded considerably percentage-wise during the course of this cycle. Nevertheless the ratio of the industry of underdeveloped countries to world capitalist industry probably became smaller than it had been at the beginning of the cycle.

Problems of the New Crisis of Overproduction

The main problems of capitalist economics are now (beginning of May 1958) as follows:

1. What will be the characteristics of the crisis of overproduction in the United States? Short-lived and not deep, as is asserted by a number of bourgeois economists, or deep and prolonged, as we believe?
2. What will be the influence of the anti-crisis measures which the government of the United States will attempt to carry out?
3. Is the American crisis the beginning of a world crisis of overproduction?

Let us consider each of these problems separately.

President Dwight D. Eisenhower, like President Herbert Hoover in 1929, predicted in his economic report to Congress[16] that 'the dip in economic activity' will not be long, though in his appearance on television in February 1958 he boldly predicted that beginning with March 'the crisis will begin to abate'.[17] Several days later, however, the chief economic adviser to the President, Gabriel Hauge,[18] considered it necessary to announce that the statement had been misunderstood, and that President Eisenhower wished only to say that the situation on the labour market would improve in March.[19]

---

16 [*Economic Report of the President Transmitted to the Congress, January 20, 1958*].
17 [Eisenhower said on 26 February 1958: '... [T]here certainly are some indications that there will be more job opportunities in March – some increased job opportunities, probably not great, but some; and if that occurs, we believe it can mark the beginning of the end of this recession'. Available at: http://www.presidency.ucsb.edu/ws/index.php?pid=11309 (accessed on 20 January 2013)].
18 [Gabriel Hauge (1914–81) was a prominent American bank executive and Harvard and Princeton economist. Hauge served as assistant to the President for Economic Affairs during the administration of Dwight D. Eisenhower].
19 [According to Richard E. Mooney, Gabriel Hauge said in a speech 'that he expected to see

Dwight D. Eisenhower is a soldier; he is not strong in economic questions and in his position such a statement is forgivable. But a luminary of modern economic science, in the United States, Professor Sumner Slichter[20] of Harvard University, insisted as early as on 3 March 1958 that the crisis in the United States would not be deep or prolonged. The arguments of Professor Slichter show once more how little the bourgeois economists understand of the laws of capitalist economics.

Professor Slichter reasons as follows: the crisis affected only industry and primarily the production of durable goods; 64 percent of the drop in employment occurred in that branch of production, which employs one-fifth of all employed persons (excluding agriculture). 'In the fields of wholesale and retail trade, government, services, and miscellaneous employments, which provide three-fifths of the wage and salary employment outside of agriculture, the number of jobs in January was less than one-tenth of one percent below August – too small a difference to be statistically significant'[21] (that is, before the beginning of the dip).

The respected professor forgets that the backbone of the long boom was the great expansion of fixed capital, that is, the working at full capacity of the plants in Department I. He fails to notice that the main part of the newly created value, that is, the primary national income, is created, under American conditions, in industry. The income of persons employed in trade, the state apparatus and services is mainly secondary, and a crisis in industry will therefore with a certain delay bring unemployment to these fields of economic activity, too. Thus the whole reasoning of Professor Slichter is faulty.

Before examining the essence of the question we should like to make the following comments.

The history of cycles and crises shows that the longer the phase of the boom, the deeper and longer, as a rule, the crisis of overproduction which ends the cycle. This is understandable: the longer the boom, the deeper the contradiction between the tendency of capital to expand production without limit and the narrow limits of the purchasing power of society. Judging by historical analogy, the crisis in the United States should be deep and not short in duration.

---

the downturn "slow to a stop" during the April–June quarter of this year. He said some people had misread the President's economic statement last week as a prediction of an upturn in March'. Richard E. Mooney, 'Federal Reserve frees 500 million to combat slump', *The New York Times*, 20 February 1958].

20   [Sumner Hubert Slichter (1892–1959) was an American labour economist and the first Lamont University Professor at Harvard University].

21   *The New Republic*, 3 March 1958, p. 8.

The depth of the crises in the United States in the twentieth century may be measured by the fall of the general index of production from the highest point reached in the boom phase to the lowest point in the crisis phase.

TABLE 27.11 The fall of index (in %) of US production

1903	1907	1913	1920	1929	1937	1948	1953
2.2	16	10	23	47	40	10	11

SOURCES: VARGA (ED.) AND TRAKHTENBERG [1937]; ALSO OFFICIAL STATISTICS OF THE UNITED STATES

As may be seen from the above table, in the periods of world crises the fall of the production index varied from 16 percent to 47 percent. The crisis of 1918, 1948 and 1958 were not world crises, but crisis in the United States alone.

Let us now consider the more important factors which make inevitable a further deepening of the crisis in the United States.

1. Fixed capital in United States industry expanded to such an extent during the postwar cycle that already in the boom phase it was used far below full capacity.[22] Here an important role was played by technical progress: automation, cybernetics, atomic energy, etc. Competition compels entrepreneurs to renovate and expand their fixed capital in order to utilise new techniques. It is clear that when a crisis begins, the capitalists start reducing their investments. The 10 percent reduction in investments,[23] which competent circles anticipated for 1958, will amount to US$5 milliard.[24] According to a survey published at the beginning of March 1958, by the US Department of Commerce, expenditures for fixed capital in 1958 would be reduced by 13 percent from the level of 1957. According to the data of the US Department of Labor, the construction of new houses in February 1958 (on an annual basis) went down to 890,000 apartment units as compared with 1,080,000 units in January 1958.

---

22   The *Federal Reserve Bulletin*, 40, 1, January 1958, pp. 1–7, points out that in the boom phase in 1955–6 the production of the most important kinds of industrial raw materials – pig iron, steel, aluminum, copper, cement, artificial fibres, wood pulp, coke, paper, petroleum products and the more important chemical goods – only used from 80 to 85 percent of their capacity. President George Meany of the AFL-CIO in his speech of 11 March 1958, declared that 'more than 25 percent of our productive capacity is idle'.
23   'Investments' is a broader concept than 'expenses for the construction of plants and equipment'.
24   *Monthly Economic Letter*, First National City Bank, New York, February 1958, p. 14.

2. A very important factor in the further deepening of the crisis in the United States is the persistent reduction of the monthly totals of new orders. During 1956 and the first half of 1957 industry received new orders amounting to a monthly average of US$ 28 milliard. Nevertheless the crisis broke out. Now the amount of new orders is falling from month to month at an accelerating tempo. A reduction in new orders must be followed by a fall in production. For a year industry has already been partly occupied with filling the backlog of old orders. This backlog was reduced from US$ 64 milliard in January 1957 to US$ 51.8 milliard in December 1957.

TABLE 27.12 New orders received by industry in the United States (in US$ milliards)

January 1957	August 1957	September 1957	October 1957	November 1957	December 1957	January 1958	February 1958
28.9	27.3	26.6	26.3	26.0	25.2	24.2	25.2

SOURCE: *SURVEY OF CURRENT BUSINESS*, VARIOUS ISSUES

3. The crisis brought about a rapid growth in unemployment. According to official data the number of unemployed increased from 3.2 million at the beginning of 1957 to 5.1 million in February 1958. Moreover, many persons are partially unemployed. According to an estimate of George Meany, president of the AFL-CIO,[25] the partially unemployed equalled 1.8 million persons in terms of the fully unemployed. In fact, the number of unemployed should be considerably higher than the official figures. This may be seen from the following: in July 1957 the highest number of employed (not including armed forces) was 67.2 million persons. In January 1958 this number fell to 62.2 million persons, or by five million. But in July 1957 three million unemployed. Thus the number of unemployed should be eight million. The difference is explained by the fact that American statisticians include many millions under the heading 'not part of the labour force'. This group increased from 47.5 million persons in July 1957 to 50.8 million in December 1957. The average length of the work week was reduced from 41 hours in December 1956 to 38.7 hours in January 1957.

---

25 [William George Meany (1894–1980) was President of the American Federation of Labor (AFL) from 1952 to 1955. As President of the AFL, he proposed in 1952 and managed in 1955 its merger with the Congress of Industrial Organizations (CIO). He served as President of the combined AFL-CIO from 1955 to 1979].

Additional earnings of workers from overtime also fell. All this means that the total wages received by workers have fallen considerably.

Total wages were reduced during the year, to judge by the most conservative estimates,[26] by about US$15 milliard.[27] Only a very small part of this amount, as will be shown below, is offset by unemployment benefits received by workers. Such a reduction in total wages should inevitably bring about a considerable slackening in demand for industrial goods of Department II. This factor also will contribute to a further deepening of the crisis in 1958.

'Optimists' among the American economists point out that the American people (up to January 1958) continued to buy the same volume of goods in spite of the crisis. But this is a temporary phenomenon. During the twenty-year period when there was a shortage of goods during the war and prices rose in the years of the postwar cycle, Americans have become accustomed to spending their money quickly and to falling into debt. Now they are spending their savings, buying goods on credit, etc. But soon this will come to an end. In February 1958, according to the Department of Commerce, the volume of retail sales fell by US$1.4 milliard as compared with January 1958, or by almost 11 percent. As to the ruling classes, the amount of their profits was lower in the fourth quarter of 1957 than in the corresponding period of 1956.[28] In 1958 profits will be even lower. As a result, the production of luxury goods will also be reduced.

Considering all these factors, there is no scientific basis whatsoever for a belief that the crisis of overproduction in the United States will end soon. On the contrary, the fall of the production index in March 1958 to 128, that is, 13 percent below the highest point reached in the course of this cycle (in December 1956) does not mean that the crisis has reached its lowest point. According to the March 1968 survey of one of the largest banks, 'businessmen do not base their plans on a hope of a quick change; they are wary and watchful'.[29]

---

26 The wages of the additional four million fully unemployed would amount, at US$70 per week, to US$14 milliard per year. The weekly pay of the workers employed in manufacturing industries fell between December 1986 and December 1957 by US$1.13, or by a total of US$18 million per week and US$1 milliard per year. The wages of other, less well-organised categories of workers fell off even more.

27 According to the estimates of Mr. Leon Keyserling, former Chairman of the President's Council of Economic Advisers, wages fell by about US$20 milliard per year.

28 Total profits received by the largest industrial monopolies in the fourth quarter of 1952 were 16 percent less than during the corresponding period of 1956 (*Bank Monthly Economic Letter*, First National City, New York, March 1958, p. 27). The profits of smaller corporations undoubtedly reduced even more.

29 *Monthly Economic Letter*, First National City, New York, March 1958, p. 25.

What can anti-crisis measures of the United States government contribute toward overcoming the crisis?

It would be incorrect to say that government measures cannot exercise any influence on the crisis. But it would be even less correct to say that such measures can stop the deepening of the crisis. The fact is, the influence of these measures, directed at softening the impact of the crisis, is considerably smaller than the influence of those factors which tend to deepen the crisis. Among all the arguments adduced for the effectiveness of the government's anti-crisis measures, the principal ones are as follows:

1. In a letter of Secretary of Defence Neil H. McElroy[30] to President Eisenhower, he states that in the first half of 1958 he will give industry new orders to the amount of US$ 10 milliard, that is US$ 4 milliard more than in the first half of 1957. This is a large sum, of course, and the big monopolist suppliers will again obtain high excess profits. In terms of the further development of the crisis, however, the influence of this sum is not great if we remember that in January 1958 the total of new orders was US$ 4.7 milliard lower than the total in January 1957.

2. Congress appropriated US$ 1.8 milliard for public works, construction of roads, hospitals, etc. This sum is relatively small and its influence on the crisis will not become apparent for many months.[31] Moreover, it will be spent for wages of low-paid workers who buy few industrial goods.

3. Payment of unemployment benefits will be extended by 13 weeks. This measure cannot be important for industry, however, because additional expenditures connected with the extension of payment of unemployment benefits are estimated at a total of US$ 0.6 milliard. Statements that unemployment benefits are a means of solving crises have no sense whatsoever. Less than half of the unemployed receive such benefits. In size they are small, varying in different states from US$ 19.70 per week in North Carolina to US$ 38.70 in Nevada, with an average of US$ 25 to US$ 30 per week, or less than half of the average wage.[32] Unemployment benefits are paid at present for a period of 18 to 26 weeks depending upon the state. Extension of the payment of benefits for 13 additional weeks is of no importance so far as the sale of industrial goods is concerned. Since

---

30 [Neil Hosler McElroy (1904–72) was Secretary of Defence (1957–9). Formerly, he had been president of Procter & Gamble].

31 Director of the Bureau of the Budget [Percival F.] Brundage stated in February 1958 that public works may increase purchasing power 'maybe in one year'.

32 *U.S. News and World Report*, 28 February 1958, p. 42.

the benefits are hardly sufficient to pay for rent, utilities and scanty food, nothing will be left for the purchase of industrial goods.

4. Credit measures, such as lowering the interest rate and making it easier to obtain credit, have insignificant influence. Reduced production and trade turnover make money available from the circulation channels. At this stage solid corporations do not need credits, and those which need them do not enjoy confidence (an exception may be credit for the construction of small apartment houses).

All these government anti-crisis measures, taken together, will have a much smaller effect than the influence of the inner process by which the crisis is deepened, and they cannot change its course. Moreover, they inevitably will contribute to the intensification of inflation.

Of course, as it develops, the crisis solves 'for a moment' the contradictions which brought it to life. There are no perpetual crises of overproduction. And in this crisis the reduction of overproduced goods has already begun. Inventories were reduced by US$1.3 milliard in December 1957.

A special feature of the current crisis is the fact that the most important means for overcoming the crisis – a fall in prices – has not yet begun to exercise its influence. Monopolies continue to maintain their high prices. Inflation also acts against any lowering of prices. As a result retail prices do not fall.[33] This, of course, delays the liquidation and prolongs the crisis.[34]

Balancing these arguments we may say that though the crisis in the United States will probably not be as deep and as long as the crisis of 1929–33, *it will be deeper and more prolonged than the preceding crises of overproduction and it is the starting point of a world crisis of overproduction.*

---

33 Index of prices in the United States (1947–9 = 100).
34 It is interesting to note that in spite of the decline in production and profits, the quotations of industrial stocks are falling relatively little. An index of stocks of 170 enterprises (1930 = 100) fell from the highest point of 468 in July 1957 to 370 in December 1957. See the *Federal Reserve Bulletin*, 44, 1, January 1958, p. 50. The causes are: there is, as yet, no credit crisis in the United States; a large number of shares is in the hands of investment trusts, insurance companies and pension funds; if their stocks were thrown on the market this would cause even larger losses for their owners than if they continue to hold them.

The Crisis in the United States as the Starting Point of the World Crisis of Overproduction

The United States is responsible for approximately half of the industrial production of the capitalist world. For this reason a crisis in the United States cannot fail to influence the economies of other capitalist countries. Intermediary crises in the United States did not bring crises to other countries, because in those countries domestic conditions for crises were absent, and they are of decisive importance. Now the situation is different.[35] In the majority of capitalist countries the conditions for a crisis have ripened. In fact, the world crisis of overproduction has begun. This may be seen from the following factors:

1. Overproduction and a considerable fall in prices of raw materials throughout the world: of non-ferrous metals, coal (Great Britain, United States and Western Germany), steel (the steel industry is using only half of its capacity), petroleum, wood pulp (Scandinavian countries), etc.
2. A world crisis in shipbuilding and the steamship market. Three million tons of shipping were idle in February 1958.[36] Newly-built ships from the shipbuilding yards go straight to ship reserves. Orders for new ships are being rescinded. Freight rates are 70 percent lower than a year ago.
3. Cutting of investments not only in the United States, but also in other industrial countries. In the course of the cycle in these countries new capacity was created which is superfluous under new market conditions.

It is impossible at present to give an analysis of the development of the world crisis of overproduction. We will limit ourselves to brief remarks.

The crisis manifested itself with the greatest force in Canada because of her close relationship with the United States. In February 1958 about 600,000 in Canada were already unemployed. The index of industrial production (1953 = 100) fell from 119 in June 1957 to 105 in December 1957, and it continues to fall.

Industrial production has been marking time in Great Britain for three consecutive years. There is a crisis of overproduction in shipbuilding and in the steamship charter market. A crisis is starting in coal production and in the field of investments. According to a questionnaire of the Union of British Industrialists the volume of new orders received by members of that union during the last six months fell by 45 percent. Anti-inflationary measures of the govern-

---

35 British professor Thomas T. Balogh writes: 'The weakness of the rest of the non-Soviet world is too great to be able to tolerate even a minor American depression if protracted'. Balogh 1957, p. 60.
36 'More idle ships', *The Economist*, 8 February 1958, p. 514.

ment further complicated the situation. For the first time in twenty years prices for coal and steel were reduced.

The 'economic miracle' of Western Germany ceased to be a miracle. The index of industrial production (1953 = 100) fell from the highest point of 162, reached in November 1956, to 144 in January 1957. Expansion of fixed capital is being reduced. The volume of construction is falling. In the Ruhr three million tons of coal are piled up, while the working time has been shortened by one shift a week. Production in various branches of heavy industry is falling.

The crisis of overproduction also spread to Japan: it can be observed in shipbuilding, the steamship charter market and the textile industry. The index of industrial production fell from the highest point of 169 (1953 = 100), reached in July 1957, to 151 in January 1958.

Thus in the decisive industrial countries, as well as in a number of small countries such as Belgium, Norway, etc., a crisis of overproduction is already in existence.

It is hardly possible to doubt that the crisis in the United States is the beginning of a world crisis of overproduction.

CHAPTER 28

The Problem of Inter-imperialist Contradictions and War

In[1] the autumn of 1951, when the draft of the textbook on political economy[2] was being discussed, the following question was raised: does Lenin's theory on *the inevitability of wars between imperialist counties* apply in modern conditions, when the world is split into two camps – the socialist and the capitalist – when the cold war is at its height and there is an ever present threat of thermonuclear extinction?

The participants were almost unanimous in the opinion that Lenin's theory was also correct in modern conditions.

Like all other controversial issues, this question was referred to Stalin, the chief arbiter of the conference, whose answer was categorically affirmative. Stalin said that those who were denying the inevitability of wars between imperialist countries saw only the external phenomena and failed to see the abysmal forces which, operating almost unnoticeably, would decide the course of future events.

Twelve years have passed – a long time if we consider how rapidly events develop nowadays – and there is less likelihood of a war between the imperialist powers today than there was in 1951.

There are dogmatists who reiterate that inter-imperialist wars are unavoidable even today. But they are wrong because they disregard the profound changes that have taken place in the world since the time when this theory was formulated.

The 20th Congress of the CPSU has put an end to this misguided view on the fatal inevitability of wars. The resolution of the Congress reads: '... The Leninist precept that so long as imperialism exists, *the economic basis giving rise to wars will also be preserved*, remains in force. That is why it is necessary to display the greatest vigilance ... But war is not fatalistically inevitable'.[3]

The problem could be considered solved. And yet there are those who think that the denial of the inevitability of wars refers only to wars between the

---

1 [Originally published in E. Varga, *Politico-Economic Problems of Capitalism*, Moscow: Progress Publishers, 1968 [1964], pp. 75–84].
2 [See Ostrovityanov 1954].
3 *Resolutions of the 20th Congress of the C.P.S.U.* 1956, p. 11, my italics.

imperialist and socialist camps and that it does not apply to inter-imperialist wars, even under modern conditions. Some dogmatists therefore continue to reiterate the erroneous arguments advanced by Stalin. For this reason we consider it necessary to take a closer look at Stalin's reasoning.

Stalin admitted that the theoretical contradictions between capitalism and socialism are stronger than those between the capitalist countries. He pointed out that this had been true even before the Second World War, and that, in spite of it, when Hitler attacked the Soviet Union, the Anglo-Franco-American bloc not only failed to join forces with Nazi Germany, but, on the contrary, had to enter into a coalition with the USSR against Nazi Germany.

This argument lacks what according to Lenin *'constitutes the very gist, the living soul, of Marxism – concrete analysis of a concrete situation'*.[4]

Both before and during the Second World War, the Soviet Union was the only socialist country. A large proportion of the bourgeois world was convinced that the victory of socialism in Russia had been an 'accidental' result of the absence of democracy under Tsarism. They considered socialism in the Soviet Union a transient historical phenomenon which would crumble under the impact of an external blow or domestic difficulties.

Today there exists a powerful socialist world system. The capitalists are now particularly afraid that some of the countries which have thrown off the imperialist yoke are embarking on the socialist road of development and that *socialism is spreading even without war*. Today *nobody* in the capitalist world considers socialism in the Soviet Union transient, and those who declare that it can spread only through violence are few and far between. Capitalist diehards now admit that socialism can emerge in underdeveloped countries but not in the rich advanced capitalist countries.

It goes without saying that the prevailing historical situation today differs radically from that which obtained on the eve of the Second World War. Socialism has become the decisive factor in world historical development. This does not imply that the socialist world is able to dictate to the capitalist world, but it does mean that prior to taking important foreign or even domestic policy measures every imperialist country must carefully balance the effects of these measures on the relations between socialism and capitalism. This makes the present historical situation different from that before and during the Second World War.

Under modern historical conditions the argument that despite the contradictions between socialism and capitalism the Anglo-Franco-American bloc

---

4 Lenin 1964l, p. 166, my italics.

had to enter into a coalition with the Soviet Union against Nazi Germany, becomes invalid. The coalition with the Soviet Union was formed *not before but after* the outbreak of the inter-imperialist war. The behaviour of the British and French military missions in Moscow in 1939 proved beyond doubt that before its outbreak, British imperialism had no serious intention to conclude a military alliance with the USSR. The Western imperialists entered into an alliance with the USSR only after Hitler had attacked them, had smashed the French Army and occupied nearly the whole of Western Europe, was threatening to carry the war into British territory and to become the dictator of the whole of Europe. They formed this coalition with the Soviet Union not to defend the latter, but in the hope that they would succeed in weakening both Hitler and the USSR.[5] It was also for this reason that they delayed the opening of the second front. The memoirs of Churchill and of other Western political leaders relate how they tried to prevent the entry of Soviet troops into Central Europe. In any case it would be wrong to use the events that unfolded in the concrete conditions of the Second World War to assess an entirely different historical situation.

The present historical situation also differs from all other stages of the imperialist epoch in the following respect: *formerly there have always been opposing coalitions of imperialist powers*. Before the First World War there was the Triple Alliance and the Franco-Russian Entente. Before the Second World War there was the Rome-Berlin-Tokyo Axis and the British-French-American group. Now under the impact of socialism's rapid advance *all Western imperialist powers*, in spite of the sharp differences between them, *form a single military bloc* – the North Atlantic Treaty Organization [NATO]. This is a radical change as compared with the situation prevailing before the Second World War. Now American, British and French troops are stationed on West German territory; West German troops are holding manoeuvres; there are joint manoeuvres on land, sea and in the air; and all weapons, except thermonuclear ones, are being gradually standardised.

NATO is not a stable military alliance. For all we know it may collapse when faced by a serious military test, as did the Triple Alliance before the First World War. NATO is shaken by one crisis after the other. But these crises are resolved by negotiations and compromises. The Common Market and the plan for an 'integration' of Western Europe are aimed at creating an organisation that will smooth out and eventually solve the economic and political contradictions

---

5 Harry Truman openly demanded that a policy aimed at weakening both Germany and the USSR be conducted.

between the continental imperialist powers, and will enable them to resist the USA's attempts at world domination. Stalin's assertion that the contradictions between the large NATO member-countries will inevitably lead to military conflict is unscientific.

To avoid ambiguity, let us repeat – the existence of NATO, the Common Market and other imperialist alliances, does not result in a political stabilisation of capitalism. Let us remember the events that shook the capitalist world in 1962: the war in Algeria; the terrorist actions of the OAS[6] in Algeria and France; the political crisis in France; the crisis of the Adenauer[7] regime in West Germany; the war between the Yemen and the United Arab Republic (UAR) on the one hand, and Saudi Arabia and Jordan on the other; the war in the Congo, which in reality was a war against the people of the Congo, and at the same time a war under the UN flag against Britain and Belgium, who supported [Moïse] Tshomhe[8] and defended the interests of the Union Minière du Haut Katanga; the crisis in Rhodesia; the war between Portugal and its African colony of Angola; the smouldering civil war in South Africa; the semi-war between India and Pakistan; the uprisings and military coups in the Latin American countries; the 'war' on Cyprus in the beginning of 1964; the 'confrontation' between Malaysia and Indonesia; the conflict between Panama and the USA and that between Somalia and Ethiopia. Let us also remember that for many years now the South Vietnamese have fought the aggression of the USA and its puppets.

There is no political stabilisation of capitalism. But this does not mean that inter-imperialist wars are inevitable.

The historic events of the past 12 years have refuted the concept on which Stalin built his theory on the inevitability of inter-imperialist wars. His conception was based on the view that economically the USA will always have the edge over Britain, France, West Germany and Japan and that 'to think that these countries will not try to set on their feet again, will not try to smash the US "regime", and force their way to independent development, is to believe in miracles'.[9]

But Stalin completely forgot Lenin's law of uneven development under imperialism. The defeated imperialist powers needed no war to free themselves from US economic domination. The uneven development removed this dom-

---

6 [Organisation de l'Armée Secrète. Right-wing terrorist organisation set up in 1961 combating President de Gaulle's Algerian policy].
7 [Konrad Adenauer (1876–1967) was a German politician, Chancellor of the German Federal Republic (1949–63)].
8 [Moïse Tshombe (1919–69) was a Congolese politician from Katanga].
9 Stalin 1953, p. 39.

ination by peaceful means. The economy of West Germany, France, Italy and Japan developed rapidly, that of the USA lagged behind; the share of the US in world industrial output dropped to 40 percent, its share in foreign trade turnover fell even more substantially; it lost about a third of its gold reserves, which by the end of 1962 were smaller than they had been before the Second World War. The chronic deficit in US balance of payments due to far too extensive foreign expenditure on the defence of the capitalist world created a constant danger to the stability of the dollar. The USA had to ask West Germany, France and Italy to help it maintain the stability of the dollar, not to exchange their dollar reserves for gold, to pay their debts ahead of time, to buy more armaments in the USA and to assume a larger share in the war expenditure of the capitalist world, etc.

The USA can no longer dictate in the economic field, as it did in the initial postwar period. It is compelled to ask its Western allies for financial help to maintain the stability of the dollar. And all this has come about without a war. With the creation of the Common Market the position of the continental imperialist powers has grown even stronger.

The other imperialist powers have no need to war with the USA to further their economic development; in fact, they *are as yet unable to wage such a war*.

The supremacy in this field enjoyed by the USA in the capitalist camp will be difficult to overcome, not only because of its strategic superiority but also for purely economic reasons. In the 1962/3 fiscal year the USA earmarked some US$ 60,000 million for military requirements (we are including in this sum also expenditure on atomic energy, or military aid to various countries, etc.). In 1960 the aggregate national income of the principal West European countries was US$ 179,000 million, of which West Germany accounted for US$ 54,000, France for US$ 44,000, Italy for US$ 25,000 and Britain for US$ 56,000 million.[10]

These figures are not accurate. But they do show that neither West Germany nor France could *on their own* compete with the USA in the field of armaments. Even if all four powers united their forces against the USA, they would have to spend about one-third of their national incomes on armaments even during times of peace, and for internal political reasons this is hardly possible.

∴

---

10   *Statistical Yearbook of the United Nations* 1961, p. 486 (recalculated into dollars according to the official rate of exchange by the author).

When the problem was discussed in 1951 our main argument against the inevitability of a new inter-imperialist war was that the statesmen of the imperialist powers had learnt a lesson from history. The First World War resulted in the destruction of the bourgeois and landowner rule in Russia; the Second overthrew capitalism in Central and South-Eastern Europe, China and North Korea. The statesmen of the imperialist powers must realise that a third world war would have fatal consequences for the capitalist system as a whole.

Stalin refuted this argument too. He wrote that 'war with the USSR, as a socialist land, is more dangerous to capitalism than war between capitalist countries; for whereas war between capitalist countries puts in question only the supremacy of certain capitalist countries over others, war with the USSR must certainly put in question the existence of capitalism itself'.[11]

We consider Stalin's theory on inter-imperialist war incorrect. It does not take into account the fact that defeat in a large-scale modern war (even if it is waged between the capitalist countries) will also endanger the further existence of capitalism, especially in the defeated countries. Any defeat in war discredits the ruling class, its government and social system, destroys discipline in the army, which in the imperialist countries, in addition to professional officers, consists in the main of factory and office workers, i.e. of people who are not objectively interested in the existence of the capitalist system,[12] and unleashes class forces both within and without the army that result in the overthrow of bourgeois rule. The events of the twentieth century show that the overthrow of the capitalist system in developed countries – in Russia, Hungary, etc. – followed in the wake of a military defeat of the bourgeoisie of those countries.

One must not overlook the possibility that the armies of the victorious imperialist countries might completely occupy the vanquished countries in order to defend the capitalist system there. The US and British armies disarmed the partisans in France and Italy in 1944 purely to defend capitalism. But in the unlikely event of a large inter-imperialist war not involving the socialist world, the historical situation would be different from that in 1944. As a result of such a war the imperialist world as a whole would be considerably weakened, while the socialist world would gain strength. This would enable the socialist world easily to fulfil its internationalist duty and to defend those nations endeavouring to throw off the capitalist yoke.

---

11   Stalin 1953, pp. 39–41.
12   In Italy and France the Communist Parties regularly poll 25 percent of all votes. The share of Communists in the army is probably even higher, since the anti-communist parties gain many votes from among women, old people, and the ruling classes, who do not serve in the army.

It is equally obvious that a third world war between the imperialist countries – the socialist world remaining neutral – would be no less dangerous for the capitalist system than a war between capitalism and socialism.

We therefore consider that even though there are economic reasons for inter-imperialist wars, and even though the struggle for raw material sources and markets, and for the export of capital is no less acute between the imperialists today than it was before the Second World War, bourgeois statesmen have learnt a lesson from the First and Second World Wars, which robbed capitalism of its power over one-third of the world's population, and that they therefore see the dangers entailed to their class in a new inter-imperialist war. This alone will stop them from allowing a new war to come to a head.

The likelihood of a large inter-imperialist war is also lessened by the fact that not only have the class and economic risks resulting from such a war become much greater, but the *chances of monopoly capital winning have become much smaller*. The only advantage it stands to gain is an increase in war orders.

Inter-imperialist wars were waged in the past either to gain colonies or recarve them. Speaking about the First World War, Lenin said that 'the fate of the colonies outside of Europe is being decided on the battlefields of Europe'.[13] In spite of all the talk about a 'new order in Europe' and 'Asia for the Asians', Germany and Japan waged the Second World War to subjugate the European and Asian countries, and to exploit them as colonies.

In modern conditions it is extremely unlikely that an imperialist country will unleash a war against another country to seize colonies. We saw the disintegration of the colonial system of imperialism after the Second World War. Only few remnants remain of the former large colonial empires, and their future is in no doubt. Monopoly capital has learned to exploit the ex-colonies, which have remained bourgeois, by neo-colonialist methods, without dominating them politically.

Technological progress in general, and that of weapons and equipment in particular, is very important in our time. Military equipment now becomes obsolete in a year or two. Sometimes a new weapon becomes obsolete even before it is produced. This happened to the British thermonuclear weapon *Blue Streak*,[14] for the development of which Britain spent several hundred million

---

13   [Varga gives no reference here. He is probably quoting Lenin by heart. Lenin wrote in *Socialism and War*: 'The peculiarity of the situation lies in that in this war the fate of the colonies is being decided by war on the Continent'. Lenin 1964o, p. 303].

14   [*Blue Streak* was a medium range ballistic missile (MRBM), and later the first stage of the *Europa* satellite launch vehicle].

pounds, but which had to be scrapped because it had become obsolete even before it could be produced.

This means that the big monopoly capitalists are obtaining steadily increasing war orders without a war. It is common knowledge that from 1950 on the war budgets of all imperialist countries increased with every passing year. From this point of view too, monopoly capital, which determines the foreign policy of the imperialist countries, does not want war.

At the same time the ruling classes in the imperialist countries realise all too well that the Second World War brought *a substantial decrease in the national wealth of the warring countries*. Even in the USA, whose territory was untouched by war, the aggregate volume of private property decreased as a result of the Second World War;[15] the total sum of state property increased but very little. Some big monopolies, the principal suppliers of war materials, and some speculators did get rich on the war, but the ruling classes of Britain, France, West Germany, Italy and Japan undoubtedly incurred considerable losses. Wars for the purpose of enrichment have become senseless.

We shall not attempt to guess what weapons would be used in an inter-imperialist war, if it were to break out. With the crazy tempo at which war equipment is developing these days, this cannot be foreseen. Much depends also on whether it will involve the USA with its powerful thermonuclear arsenal. But there is no doubt that even if the USA did not participate, it would be more destructive than the Second World War. Weapons have changed. Many countries have a certain stock of tactical thermonuclear weapons, bombers are more powerful, incendiary bombs more effective, tanks are larger, rifles better, etc. The losses of the warring countries and the destruction wrought would undoubtedly be much larger than during the last war.

Scientists throughout the world, broad circles of the intelligentsia and people in general, irrespective of what class they belong to, are becoming more and more aware of the fatal consequences of a thermonuclear war. Even the very rich will be unable to avoid its consequences, for war, like cancer, does not distinguish the rich from the poor. This awareness of a common danger is a powerful deterrent against war.

Let us now summarise what has been said above: imperialist contradictions exist and therefore the danger of inter-imperialist wars cannot be dismissed. However, it is extremely unlikely that a third world war will be sparked off. No single country has anything to gain from such a war. The havoc wrought would undoubtedly be even greater than it was during the Second World War; the

---

15   Kuznets 1961.

downfall of capitalism in the defeated countries is almost inevitable and the consequences of a thermonuclear war would be fatal to humanity. The possibility of a new inter-imperialist war is not excluded. But as long as the decision of war or peace is not left to the discretion of a madman like Hitler, but to bourgeois *statesmen aware of the threat such a war involves for the capitalist system, it will not come to pass.*

CHAPTER 29

Changes in the Reproduction Cycle Following the Second World War

In investigating this problem Marxist economic science has to answer the following questions:[1]
1. Why does the reproduction cycle of the 20 years following the end of the Second World War differ substantially from that of the inter-war period? Is this difference due only to the far-reaching changes in capitalism during and after the Second World War or are other reasons responsible for it?
2. Why are there such striking differences in the development of that cycle, on the one hand in the USA, Canada and to a certain extent in Britain, where slight improvements rapidly alternated with shallow crises, and on the other hand in the continental European countries (France, West Germany, Italy), where no crisis of overproduction (the drop of industrial output below the level for the preceding year) have as yet set in?

   Admittedly, never in the history of capitalism have cycles fully complied with Marx's scheme. The laws of the reproduction cycle, like all laws, are no more than scientific abstractions, and are determined by the different tendencies and counter-tendencies at work in capitalist economy. But the history of capitalism has never before known so great and enduring a divergence between the two main parts of the capitalist world – North America and continental Europe.
3. Finally the most important question – will capitalist reproduction, so long as capitalism continues to exist, follow the pattern of development of the USA or that of the West European capitalist countries?

∴

Let us remind the reader that during the inter-war period the production cycle was running relatively normally. There were three world crises of overproduction: 1920–1, 1929–33 and 1937–8. Of them the 1920–1 crisis was not long lived

---

[1] [Originally published in E. Varga, *Politico-Economic Problems of Capitalism*, Moscow: Progress Publishers, 1968 [1964], pp. 207–39].

and not deep; the 1929–33 crisis the longest and most prostrating in the history of capitalism, and the 1937–8 crisis of average intensity.

Below, in *Table 29.1*, are the indices of world industrial output during that period.

TABLE 29.1 General index of the capitalist world's industrial output[2] (1929 = 100)

1913	68.2
1920	66.9
1929	100.0 (pre-crisis peak)
1932	63.8 (minimum)
1933	71.9
1934	77.7
1935	86.0
1936	96.4
1937	103.7
1938	93.0

Though these data do not claim absolute accuracy, they are accurate enough to show the cyclic course of reproduction. If we had monthly figures, the amplitude of oscillation would be even greater. The figures show that between 1920 and 1938 production grew by about 50 percent, or by an average of 3.5 percent a year. But growth was confined to the period between 1920 and 1929. From 1929 to 1938 there was practically no growth; nor was there any real upswing after the 1929–33 crisis.[3] The 1937 peak exceeded the 1929 level by only 4 percent.

The 20 years since the end of the Second World War differ considerably from the two decades following the end of the First World War. World industrial output grew at a more rapid pace, the cyclical movement was expressed much less clearly and the oscillations were less pronounced.

---

2 Varga (ed.) 1939, p. 362.
3 The exception was Germany where war preparations altered the reproduction cycle.

TABLE 29.2 Index of the capitalist world's industrial production[4] (1953=100)

1937	1938	1946	1947	1948	1950	1952	1955	1956	1957	1958	1959	1960	1961	1962[5]
56	51	61	68	73	84	93	112	117	121	118	130	139	144	153

During the postwar period industrial output more than doubled. The average yearly growth was 5.5 percent, i.e. higher than during the inter-war period.

As mentioned above, production growth was not the result of industrial development in the less developed countries, but was due almost exclusively to an expansion of output in the highly developed capitalist countries.

The UN gives the following percentages for the shares of groups of countries in the world industrial output between 1938 and 1958:[6]

TABLE 29.3 Industrial output in percentages in the world economy (1953 = 100)

	USA and Canada	Western Europe	Japan	Enumerated countries *in corpore*	Rest of capitalist world
1953	55.0	32.6	2.1	89.7	10.3
1958	49.5	36.3	3.5	89.3	10.7

During the five years in which the imperialist countries were beating the drum about the development of productive forces in the less developed countries, the share of the latter in the capitalist world's industrial output increased by only 0.4 percent – a figure well within the limits of statistical error. The highly developed countries continue to account for the bulk of the world's industrial output.

During that same period the cyclic movement of *world* capitalist production was expressed only feebly. In the crisis year of 1958 the industrial output of the capitalist world dropped by only 3 percent below the 1957 level. There was no

---

4   UN data. *Statistical Yearbook of the United Nations* 1955, p. 115; 1961, p. 60; *Monthly Bulletin of Statistics*, May 1962, p. vi; June 1963, p. vi.
5   Recalculated by the author from 1958 = 100.
6   *Statistical Yearbook of the United Nations* 1961, p. 62 *passim*; *Monthly Bulletin of Statistics*, February 1963, pp. xii–xiv.

depression phase – indeed the 1959 output level was considerably above the preceding peak.[7]

And yet development remained *extremely uneven* in the highly developed capitalist countries. It depended on the degree to which their economies had been dislocated during the war and, in particular, on the state of their productive apparatus (fixed capital, raw materials, etc.). The countries which were not exhausted by the war and had not been devastated, began to increase their output as soon as they had overcome the difficulty of shifting from war to peacetime production; but the countries which had been devastated by war and whose productive apparatus had been seriously damaged, needed several years before they were able to expand their output.

Below we give figures on industrial output in the important capitalist countries, grouped according to the 1947 production level (see *Table 29.4*).

The table shows that:

a) the vanquished countries, whose postwar output was extremely low, managed to raise their output without an interim critical drop; the 1958 crisis affected their production growth rate only to a very slight degree;

b) in 1962 the industrial production level in these countries was about 200 percent higher than it had been in 1937 – i.e. they had developed quicker than the USA and Britain. The causes for this rapid development will be explained below;

c) as distinct from the vanquished countries, a number of comparatively slight crises hit the USA. During the past eight years production has grown very slowly both in the USA and Britain.

TABLE 29.4   Index numbers of industrial production (1953 = 100)[8]

	Japan	West Germany	Italy	France	USA	Britain	Canada
1937[9]	80	78	63	78	46	76	43
1947	29	–	–	71	75	76	76
1948	38	40	62	81	78	83	79
1949	48	57	68	88	72	88	80

---

7   A consideration of monthly data would furnish a slightly greater difference.
8   UN data. *Statistical Yearbook of the United Nations* 1955, p. 117 *et passim*; 1961, p. 71 *et passim*. *Monthly Bulletin of Statistics*, May 1962, p. 16 *passim*; June 1963, p. 16 *passim* (1962 recalculated by the author from 1958, p. 100).
9   We are comparing with 1937 and not 1938 because the latter was a crisis year, and 1939 marked the outbreak of the war.

TABLE 29.4 Index numbers of industrial production (1953 = 100) (cont.)

	Japan	West Germany	Italy	France	USA	Britain	Canada
1950	55	72	79	88	84	94	85
1951	74	85	90	99	90	97	91
1952	82	92	91	103	93	94	94
1953	100	100	100	100	100	100	100
1954	108	112	109	109	93	107	98
1955	116	129	120	120	106	111	110
1956	144	139	128	133	109	112	120
1957	167	147	137	144	110	114	120
1958	168	151	142	150	102	112	120
1959	208	162	158	156	116	118	129
1960	261	180	180	174	119	126	130
1961	317	191	200	184	120	128	133
1962	345	200	206	196	122	129	141

Marxist economists are divided on the interpretation of these facts, some declaring that the cycle following the 1937–8 crisis continued right through the war and ended with the regular crisis of overproduction in 1946.

We disagree. The Second World War, like every other great war,[10] interrupted the normal course of the cycle and created an enormous demand for war materials and a corresponding reduction in civilian production, with the result that, for a number of years, the effective demand outweighed supply. In conditions when nearly half the gross national product of a capitalist society goes to satisfy war needs, when enormous wealth is destroyed by the war, when the main problem of capitalist enterprises becomes not how to sell their goods, but where to get the necessary raw materials, machines and labour force to produce them, there can be no overproduction of commodities and no crises of overproduction, and hence no cyclic movement of reproduction. Thus world war interrupts the cyclic movement of reproduction; indeed cyclic reproduction and crises of overproduction are simply inconceivable.

The main function of the cycle, of both its course as a whole and its separate phases, is to create the conditions for a crisis of overproduction. During the war

---

10 Even the comparatively small war in Korea exerted a considerable influence on the post-war cycle-reserves of strategic raw materials were created, military spending increased steeply and prices soared.

years no such conditions are created. For this reason periods of prolonged war must not be included in the cycle.

There are those who object to this argument. They say that the cyclical nature of reproduction stems from the operation of the general laws of capitalism and that capitalism remains capitalism even in times of war. For this reason, they say, the cyclic course of reproduction continues even during the world wars.

We consider this approach too dogmatic. It lacks what Lenin called 'the living soul of Marxism' – a concrete analysis of a concrete situation. After all, Marx established the laws of the capitalist economy *in peacetime*. Even though there were wars in his time, they did not exert a great influence on the economy and 'military economy' simply did not exist.

Some of our economists expressed the opinion that the war itself creates the conditions for a crisis of overproduction because of the excessive development of the war industry and its associated branches (ferrous and non-ferrous metallurgy, the metalworking, chemical and other industries) and the lagging behind of industries producing consumer goods, i.e. creates a major disproportion within the economy. This theory echoes the bourgeois and revisionist view that it is not capitalism itself that is responsible for the crises of overproduction, nor is it the contradiction between the social character of production and the private capitalist form of appropriation with the ensuing poverty and proletarianisation of the masses, but a disproportion between the various branches of production.[11]

This is incorrect. The fact that after a period of war the productive capacity of some industries is too high, and that of others too low, may cause a *partial* crisis in some war industries, but cannot bring about a general crisis of overproduction. In many important industries, especially those producing consumer goods, demand continued to exceed supply even after the war.[12]

---

11 This theory is based on the tenet of English classical political economy stating that every commodity includes wages, profit and rent, i.e. that the production of a commodity in itself creates the purchasing power ensuring its sale, and that a general crisis of overproduction is therefore impossible.

   This tenet is wrong – indeed it was refuted by Marx. Even so it continues to circulate to this day. In the mouthpiece of the Guaranty Trust, the largest American bank, we read that every bit of the cash value of any article produced or any service rendered represents somebody's income or purchasing power ... If goods are unsold this is not an indication of low purchasing power but of the fact that this power is not utilised to the full.

12 Even in the USA, where the organic composition of capital is much higher than in the other

The only fact which could be interpreted as an indication of overproduction during the war was the drop in the general index of industrial output in the USA in 1944 from a peak 244 (1935–9 = 100) in February to 230 in July.[13] However, this drop was due primarily to an overestimation of the requirements for means of transport and heavy armaments; the drop in production therefore affected mainly engineering (including the production of tanks, guns, etc.) and transport machinery building.

The facts show that this drop in production was not of a cyclical nature: a) in 1946 there was still a general shortage of peacetime goods in all capitalist countries; overproduction was observed only in war materials; b) there was a drop in production in the second half of 1945 and in 1946 not only in the capitalist countries, but also in the Soviet Union, in spite of the Soviet economy's planned and crisis-free development.

There was little difference in the manner in which the transition from war to peacetime economy was made in the capitalist countries and in the Soviet Union: war production stopped; millions of people had to be moved over enormous distances (soldiers, the evacuated population, POWs); people who normally did not work in industry quitted their jobs; production had to be adjusted in all industries which had ceased operating during the war, etc. Thus, even though this adjustment proceeded according to plan, the level of Soviet industrial output (1913 = 100) dropped from 782 in 1945 to 652 in 1946 in spite of the growth of the production of consumer goods from 295 in 1945 to 335 in 1946.[14]

In all countries, the industrial output level was lower in the second half of 1945 and in 1946, and partly in 1947 than it had been during the war. This is not a cyclic phenomenon but the natural result of the switchover from wartime to peacetime economy. Part of the military plants was temporarily put out of use, part was re-equipped and transferred to the production of peacetime goods, while a part continued to produce weapons. Industry had to adjust itself to the production of a new range of goods. This transition took time and was attended

---

capitalist countries, the share of Department II is not smaller than that of Department I. During 1957 an equal amount of durables and non-durables was sold – about US$170,000 million worth of each (*Survey of Current Business*, February 1958, p. S-3). The durables included consumer goods such as cars, furniture, etc. On the other hand, American statistics include coal and petrol, which are used predominantly as means of production, in the non-durables group. But on the whole, the division of goods into durables and non-durables more or less corresponds to the division into Departments I and II.

13   *Statistical Abstract of the United States* 1944–5, p. 796.
14   See *Narodnoe khzyaystvo SSSR v 1960*, p. 219.

by a drop in output. Thus, *1947 should be regarded as the beginning of a postwar cycle lasting from 10 to 11 years.*

In this respect the first cycle following the Second World War differed greatly from that following the First. Then the crisis set in two to three years after the end of the First World War. True, the 1920–1 crisis was not long-lived and not very deep. The difference is explained by the fact that the First World War was comparatively short, fewer war materials were needed, fewer countries were involved and the damage wrought to productive capacities was smaller. The changes world capitalist economy underwent as a result of the First World War were therefore much smaller than those wrought by the Second.

This poses a theoretical question: what determines the difference in the length of individual cycles?

The expansion and renewal of fixed capital is the material basis of the reproduction cycle. If we disregard extraordinary events – wars, crop failures, etc. – the length of the cycle depends on the size of the fixed capital being renewed or expanded and the use to which it is put. The larger the amount of new capital investments, the longer the upward phases of the cycle – revival, boom (and overstrain).

In studying the cycles we generally consider only the sum total of new capital investments and pay little attention to their nature. This is wrong: equal amounts of new capital investments can exert different influences on the cycle's duration depending on:

1. Whether capital investments are made predominantly into factories, etc., i.e. projects which immediately upon completion directly increase the supply of commodities on the market, or (as was the case in the middle of the nineteenth century) into projects which increase the supply of goods on the market only indirectly, such as railways, ports, vessels, highways, bank buildings, department stores, etc. In the former case, the conditions for a crisis mature much quicker.

2. The ratio between the new capital investments and the value of commodities being put on the market after the new projects are commissioned. Thus, for example, the building of a hydropower station requires large capital investments, but it supplies only a comparatively small amount of new commodities and investments are recouped very slowly. At the same time factories with a lower organic composition of capital supply the market with more commodities (in relation to the amount of invested capital) and overproduction sets in much sooner.

3. The length of time during which projects are under construction. On the one hand, technical progress and the concentration of capital make for the building of large factories and groups of factories, the designing and

building of which takes much longer than the small factories of a century ago. On the other hand, the rate of construction is now much higher than ever before.

The factors which have caused this speeding up in the cycle are described below.

Distinguishing Features of the First Postwar Cycle

Even though for the past one hundred years, trade cycles have assumed a definite regularity, and are all identical in their causes and nature, each has its own particular features, dependent on the concrete historical conditions in which it unfolds.

The principal features of the cycle following the Second World War were:
a) the existence of two world systems, the continuous influence on world economy exerted by the Cold War;
b) the disintegration of the colonial system of imperialism;
c) the changes in the world capitalist economy wrought by the six-year long world war;
d) the different economic (and political) circumstances in which various capitalist countries – neutral countries, the USA, the West European countries, the victorious countries and the vanquished countries – found themselves after the war and consequent difference in the length of the cycle in the various countries;
e) the general inflation and steady and rapid price advance in all but a few neutral countries resulting partly from an artificial boosting of prices by the monopolies, and partly from the usual increase accompanying such economic upswings;
f) the dollar deficit experienced by most capitalist countries;
g) the marked intensification in the agrarian crisis.

Let us try to analyse briefly the influence exerted on the cycle by concrete historical conditions.

The principal result of the Cold War was that the capitalist countries, and notably the USA, took up large-scale production of arms soon after the end of the war. This continued throughout the cycle at a steadily increasing rate. According to our computations, military spending as a percentage of the national income comprised:[15]

---

15 See Varga 1957, p. 42.

TABLE 29.5 Military spending as a percentage of the National Income

	1937–8	1948–9	1953–4
USA			
Percentage of national income	1.5	6.5	15.8
Percentage of national income after exclusion of double entries	–	–	ab. 22
Britain			
Percentage of national income	4.1	7.7	9.5
Percentage of national income after exclusion of double entries	–	–	ab. 12
France			
Percentage of national income	5.9	6.1	13.3
Percentage of national income after exclusion of double entries	–	–	ab. 15

The share of war production in the national income continued to grow in later years.

The bulk of the military spending was channelled to the production of arms, which themselves were becoming steadily more intricate and expensive. Military technology developed so rapidly that weapons were often obsolete even before their serial production was taken up (this happened to the British atomic weapons *Blue Streak*[16] and *Skybolt*[17]). This means that even in peacetime the monopolies producing armaments are getting new and higher profitable orders. Continued international tension and the Cold War policy thus become extremely profitable for the monopolies. The share of military deliveries is much higher in the aggregate industrial output than it is in the national income, and it is even higher in the sum total of profits.

The influence war production exerts on reproduction in peacetime depends on the concrete historical conditions. If, owing to a lack in effective demand, there are surplus productive capacities, raw materials and labour force in the

---

16 [*Blue Streak* was a medium range ballistic missile (MRBM), and later the first stage of the Europa satellite launch vehicle].

17 [The Douglas GAM-87 Skybolt was an air-launched missile (ALBM), equipped with a nuclear warhead, developed in the US. The UK joined the programme in 1960. A series of test failures and the development of submarine-launched ballistic missiles (SLBMs) eventually led to its cancellation in December 1962].

country (during the general crisis of capitalism this is the normal state),[18] military orders promote production and economic growth, extend the market, lengthen the revival and boom (and overstraining) phases of the cycle, and hence the whole cycle. However, at the same time they produce or strengthen inflation. If, on the other hand, there are no idle production reserves, military production does not increase the aggregate industrial output but is effected at the expense of the output of the civilian branches and, finally, if the scale of war production is greater than that warranted by the country's economic resources, the result will be an overstrained and unbalanced economy similar to that in times of war.

The influence exerted by war orders on the cycle can be clearly seen from the example of the 1948–9 crisis in the USA. (In this connection it is not particularly important whether it was an interim crisis or whether the war in Korea stopped it from developing into a real crisis of overproduction). The war in Korea gave an impetus to production growth. The index of industrial output rose from its lowest point of 95 in July 1949 to an average 112 in 1950 (1947–9: 100), i.e. by 18 percent.[19] This shows that under certain conditions a steep increase in war orders can produce a revival and upswing in the economy.

However, Britain's economy in the last three years of the postwar cycle indicates that not all war orders produce a general expansion in production and market capacity. Even though the volume of war production was considerable, the volume of aggregate production did not change throughout 1955, 1956 and 1957. Production capacities were used almost to the full and the high share of war production became responsible for an inflation and currency crisis. On the other hand, the comparatively low war expenditures of West Germany and Japan greatly contributed to the rapid rehabilitation in these countries of destroyed productive capacities and to an expansion of the fixed capital, resulting in substantial production growth during the upward phase.

18 TABLE 29.6 Idle capacities in the USA (%)

1954	1955	1956	1957	1958
16	8	14	22	20

Data from 12th *MacGraw Hill Survey*. In practice even more of the fixed capital stood idle, for the above figures are based on only 300 shifts a year.

19 *Federal Reserve Bulletin*, various issues.

All these facts show that war production exerted a major influence on the course of the first postwar cycle. As regards the system of capitalist economy as a whole, we find that war production is able to lengthen the upward and overstrain phases, and hence the whole cycle, but cannot avert a crisis of overproduction, as has been conclusively proved by the 1957–8 crisis.

In their newspapers, the monopolies, which are thriving on war orders, propound the theory that such orders have a stabilising influence on the course of reproduction. This is pure fantasy. The feverish development of military equipment intensifies anarchy of production.

The data in *Table 29.7* show how quickly the expenditure on the main kinds of war materials changes in the USA:[20]

TABLE 29.7 Percentage expenditure on the main kind of war materials in the US

Year	Vessels	Tanks, ammunition	Aircraft	Electronics	Missiles
1953	6.8	50.0	31.5	11.2	0.5
1961	7.8	12.4	28.2	18.0	33.6

Such leaps do not stabilise the economy but disorganise it and often bring mass unemployment to US towns.

The disintegration of the colonial system also had a telling influence on the course of the cycle. The export of all capital to the former colonial and semi-colonial countries which embarked on the socialist road of development – China, North Vietnam and North Korea – ceased. Politics became all-important in deciding to which country capital should be ported. This meant that capital could be exported only to countries in which there was 'law and order', in which there was no threat of nationalisation, i.e. in which there existed conditions favourable to a profitable investment of new capital. The disintegration of the colonial system also changed the volume and geographic destination of the capital exports. During the postwar cycle the sum of private capital exported (especially if we consider the drop in the purchasing power of all currencies) was much smaller than it had been during the 1921–9 cycle. Geographically, too, there were changes: capital was exported primarily to countries which from a capitalist point of view were safest – to Canada, the Latin American countries, and, in some cases, Africa.

---

20   'Regions at war', *The Economist*, 13 October 1962, p. 144.

A recent development is the large-scale export of capital in the form of economic and military subsidies by various governments, especially the USA. As regards the course of the cycle there is no difference between the export of private and state capital or subventions.[21] All it means is that commodities are exported from a country while no commodities are imported, as distinct from normal foreign trade. This brings a temporary expansion of the market and, all other conditions being equal, a lengthening of the trade cycle.

The loss of resources brought about by the formation of the world socialist system and the disintegration of the colonial system did not produce a shortage of raw materials in the capitalist world. During the postwar cycle a shortage in some raw materials and a steep increase in their price was observed only in 1950 when the United States was feverishly buying up various strategic raw materials to create military reserves. Modern technology helped the capitalists to open up many new deposits in Canada, South America, Central Africa and even in the imperialist countries themselves (oil in Texas, West Germany and France), which provided a new source of raw materials for those in short supply.

The false assertion that the capitalist world is short of raw materials can be seen from the fact that the overproduction and a drop in prices of industrial raw materials began before the industrial crisis.

TABLE 29.8 Prices on industrial raw materials in the US[22]

	1956 peak	1957 January	1958 January
Copper (cents per pound)	45.9	35.8	24.8
Steel scrap (dollar per ton)	67.0	63.0	33.0
Zinc (cents per pound)	13.5	13.5	10.0
Lead (cents per pound)	106.5	102.2	92.2
Rubber (cents per pound)	37.2	33.5	27.2
Hides (cents per pound)	13.5	10.0	9.2

---

21 The effects of capital export and subventions are identical only as regards the course of the cycle. Actually subventions, in spite of the contentions of some Soviet economists. are not an export of capital, since they do not possess what Marx described as the essence of capital-self-increasing value.
22 *The Morgan Guaranty Trust Survey*, January 1958, pp. 12–13; February 1958, pp. 12–13.

This shows that the prices for some types of raw materials (copper, lead, rubber, hides) began to drop in 1957.

The Second World War in which all industrial countries in the world, except Sweden and Switzerland, participated, *exerted a decisive influence on the course of the first postwar cycle*.[23]

During the war the consumption level – military and civilian with due account being taken also of the devastation wrought by the war – was considerably higher than the production level. The volume of national wealth decreased.[24] Commodity stocks diminished. Fixed capital, excluding that in the military branches, wore out and became obsolete. Consumer demand, especially for durables (housing, furniture, cars, household appliances), was not satisfied for years, since the production of these articles had been prohibited in order to free the productive forces (workers, raw materials and machines) for war production. The food consumption of the urban population (excluding the rich, who bought what they needed on the black market), was limited by the rationing system. By the end of the war there was a tremendous unsatisfied demand for means of production for the 'peaceful' branches and for consumer goods.

This extraordinarily high demand was effective. The government paid the capitalists high prices for military supplies. Profits, accumulated depreciation funds and accumulations resulting from the decrease in stocks took the form of bank deposits, bonds (which could be readily converted into money) and cash. The well-to-do part of the population and even some categories of industrial workers could not spend the whole of their income because of the shortage of consumer goods and whether they liked it or not, were forced to save part of it.

The following US data (see *Table 29.9*) show clearly that owing to the consumer goods shortage during the war, the population was unable to spend all of its income.

---

23 Even the economy of the neutral European countries was upset by the war: the warring countries, and notably Germany, were buying from them all types of goods at high prices.

24 According to American economists, even in the USA, which suffered no devastation in the war and which participated in it for a far shorter time than the European countries, the national wealth (excluding that part which was government-owned) was no larger in 1945 than it had been in 1929 (in 1929 prices). Kuznets and Goldsmith 1952, pp. 327–8.

TABLE 29.9 Personal savings in the USA[25] (thousand million US$)

1939	1942	1943	1944	1945	1947
2.9	27.8	33	36.9	28.7	4.7

The picture is so clear that no further comment is needed. At the same time money circulation and deposits were growing, due partly to the wartime inflation.

TABLE 29.10 Money in circulation[26] (thousand millions at the end of the year)

Year	USA dollars	Canada Canadian dollars	Brazil cruzeiros	Britain Pounds sterling	Sweden kronor	France francs	Italy lira	Japan yen
1938	5.8	0.24	3.6	0.46	1.04	112	19	2.9
1945	26.5	1.06	14.3	1.34	2.79	577	368	54.8

Both in industrial and less developed countries (Brazil), those which participated in the war or remained neutral, the supply of money in circulation grew by 200 to 400 percent, in the vanquished countries (Italy and Japan) it grew nearly 20 times over.

Bank deposits should be added to the above.

---

25 *Economic Report of the President* 1961, p. 145.
26 *Statistical Yearbook of the United Nations* 1956, p. 484 *passim*.

TABLE 29.11 Deposits[27] (thousand millions at the end of the war)

Year	USA[28] dollars	Canada Canadian dollars	Brazil cruzeiros	Britain Pounds sterling	Sweden kronor	France francs	Italy lira	Japan yen
1938	26	0.9	8.5	1.2	1.9	80	21	4.7
1945	76	2.5	27	3.1	3.8	436	290	36

The deposit growth rate coincided roughly with the money circulation growth rate.[29] Taken together they show that, as result of the war, the purchasing power of society increased enormously. To this we should also add the deposits in savings accounts and the war bonds held by private persons and companies. Naturally there could have been no growing effective demand if prices had risen in proportion to the supply of money in circulation, long- and short-term deposits in savings banks. However, they did not.

TABLE 29.12 Average yearly general wholesale price index (1953 = 100)

Year	USA	Canada	Brazil	Britain	Sweden	France	Italy	Japan
1938	46	46	13	31	37	4	2	0.4
1945	62	60	40	52	65	14	39	1.0

In the countries which were of overriding importance to the industrial cycle (USA, Britain, Canada) at that time, prices advanced during the war far less than the supply of money in circulation, long- and short-term deposits in savings banks. In other words, *by the end of the war the postponed demand in these countries were fully effective*, even though black market prices were higher than official ones. The situation differed in France and Italy, which had already been stricken by a deep inflation during the war.

---

27   Ibid.
28   *Federal Reserve Bulletin* gives even higher figures. The difference is probably due to the fact that the sum of deposits includes inter-bank and state deposits.
29   In Italy and Japan there was a strong inflation at that time and the growth of deposits was therefore smaller than the growth in the supply of money in circulation.

Following the end of the war the capacity of the capitalist market was above 'normal' both as regards the output of Department I and Department II, and this above all determined the course of the postwar cycle. The capitalists began to renew the worn fixed capital at an extremely rapid rate and also began to expand it: in the victor countries this took place immediately after the war, in the vanquished countries[30] a few years later. This was the main reason for the length of the revival and boom phases in the postwar cycle. This can be seen from the figures for the USA, Britain and West Germany given below.

TABLE 29.13 Expenditure on new equipment in the USA[31]
(thousand million US$, average per year)

1929–38	1945–9	1950–4	1955	1956	1957
3.5	14.4	25.5	28.7	35.1	37.0

The expansion of fixed capital continued steadily until the first half of 1957. Even taking into account the falling purchasing power of the US$ throughout the postwar cycle, the scale of the expansion was several tim6s larger than it had been in the pre-war cycle.

The same state of affairs obtained in Britain and West Germany.

TABLE 29.14 Gross fixed capital formation in Britain[32]
(million pounds sterling)

	1938	1950	1955	1956
Current prices	656	1,702	2,855	3,139
1948 prices	1,559	1,641	2,124	2,234

---

30   The neutral countries, and especially those that did not participate in the war directly, also renewed fixed capital towards the end of the war. Warring industrial countries were unable to supply them with means of production.
31   *Statistical Abstract of the United States* 1951, p. 444; 1956, p. 498; 1961, p. 492.
32   *Annual Abstract of Statistics* 1956, p. 249; 1957, p. 252.

TABLE 29.15 West Germany capital investments in means of production and construction comprised (thousand million marks)[33]

1938	1950–5 average yearly	1955
7.1	27.8	39.8

Funds which had accumulated during the war were used to expand the fixed capital and to replenish commodity stocks, which by the end of the war had fallen to a very low level. In the USA, for example, commodity stocks in industry, wholesale and retail trade had by the end of the war fallen to US$ 25,000 million; during the subsequent cycle they grew to US$ 91,800 million (August 1957). Similar conditions obtained in the other industrial countries. Production for the replenishment of stocks played a major role in lengthening the revival and boom phases of the postwar cycle. In the USA stocks began to decrease only in the fourth quarter of 1957. But the enormous growth in commodity stocks as compared with the sum of sales indicated even earlier that stocks were too high and that there was an overproduction of commodities.

The third factor which made for a lengthening of the upward phase had nothing to do with the war, but was due to an artificial expansion of the consumer goods market by considerably extending consumer credits. This step was taken when the additional demand of the first postwar years was satisfied and the effective demand ceased to correspond with the volume of production. It was then that the future income, the future purchasing power of capitalist society, was used to save the present situation. This was practised particularly widely in the USA, where consumer credit grew from US$ 5,700 million at the end of 1945 to US$ 45,300 million in November 1957. On a smaller scale, consumer credit also grew in Britain and other capitalist countries.

These three factors – the extraordinary large volume of the renewal and expansion of fixed capital (in the war-devastated countries also the reconstruction of destroyed factories, houses, etc.), the creation of large commodity stocks in production and trade, and sales on account of future incomes – were responsible for the length of the postwar cycle.

---

33   *Statistisches Jahrbuch für die Bundesrepublik Deutschland* 1957, p. 561.

In this connection we should also explain why the 1957–8 crisis of overproduction which completed the first postwar cycle did not spread to such highly developed countries as France, West Germany, Italy and Japan.

In the light of the present discussion it is interesting to look into the mechanism by which a crisis emerging in one or several countries spreads to other industrial countries. Countries afflicted by a crisis attempt to ease their position at the expense of other countries by expanding exports[34] and restricting imports. The development of a crisis stops new capital investments.

The fall in share quotations caused by a crisis is registered on the stock exchanges of all capitalist countries.

In the event of a credit-monetary crisis the withdrawal of short-term loan capital from other countries may even cause a monetary-credit crisis there.[35]

Other factors can also lead indirectly to the same result. A crisis may become responsible for a sharp drop in raw material prices in some countries, and force countries with a mono-cultural economy to cut down on the import of manufactured goods.

Prevailing conditions in the various countries decide which of these factors becomes the most active. The influence exerted by foreign trade in bringing about a crisis is felt most strongly in countries having high export and import quotas, for example in Britain and Belgium. But, as a rule, *a crisis of overproduction spreads to new countries only if the conditions for a crisis have to a greater or larger extent already matured in their domestic economy.* This becomes clearer if we consider that, even with an export quota of about 25 percent (as in the case of Britain), a 10 percent drop in exports comprises only 2.5 percent of total production. In most countries this percentage is smaller.

Even the sharp increase in industrial output between 1948 and 1958, to a level exceeding the pre-war by about 100 percent, did not fully abolish the economic consequences of the Second World War, nor did it create the conditions for a crisis of overproduction.

Thus, although by the end of the cycle the industrial output level of the capitalist world as a whole nearly doubled the 1937 level, there were considerable differences between individual countries as regards their level of production

---

34 Indicative in this respect is the steep increase in the active side of the US trade balance in 1957. It rose from US$ 2,900 million in 1955 to US$ 4,700 million in 1956 and to US$ 6,500 million in 1957 (excluding the export of arms). *Statistical Abstract of the United States* 1961, p. 865.

35 The crash of the German *Grossbanken* (big banks) in 1931 following the withdrawal of American short-term loans serves as an example.

and the rate at which the production cycle developed. If the war in Korea had not given an impetus to US industry (and that of a few other countries) the differences in the development of the cycle, between the victorious and the vanquished countries would have been even greater.

An important feature of the first postwar cycle was the constant devaluation of the currencies of all capitalist countries as a result of inflation – a feature that was absent in all the nineteenth-century cycles. This devaluation could be seen from the fact that in all countries, including the USA, industrial gold was sold above its official dollar rate of US$ 35 an ounce. This in turn depreciated all other currencies and resulted in an increase in prices, which to some extent continued even after the crisis in the USA had set in. Owing to rapid technological progress the value of commodities, i.e. the labour time embodied in a commodity unit, decreased during the course of the cycle, and the price advance therefore indicated an inflationary break-away of commodity prices from true value.

A price advance stretching over many years lengthens the boom (and overstrain) phase and, with it, the whole cycle. Entrepreneurs, expecting a further growth in prices, increase their stocks and strive to invest their money-loan capital into material values. The consumer, expecting a further growth in prices, hurriedly lays in goods (often on credit) for the future. The boom phase extends. There can be no doubt that inflation was one of the factors responsible for the longer duration of the first postwar cycle.

Nearly all capitalist countries experienced a dollar deficit during the cycle.[36] This was the result of various governmental measures taken in the interests of the monopolies to restrict imports, state dumping of monopoly-produced goods on the world market, and the extremely favourable US balance of payments resulting from it, and finally the steady increase in US gold reserves at the expense of the other capitalist countries. The dollar shortage was an important contributory factor to the inflation in many capitalist countries, for example, Britain.

The cycle was attended almost throughout by a sharp agrarian crisis. This was characteristic not only of the present cycle but of all cycles in the era of the general crisis of capitalism (as we hope to prove in the next essay[37]).

---

36 The exceptions were: 1) large gold producers; 2) large-scale exporters of strategic raw materials to the USA; and 3) Switzerland, which became a haven for all capital of doubtful origin (Nazis and speculators from all over the world deposit their money in Swiss banks, which take care not to divulge 'bank secrets').

37 'The problem of agrarian crisis', pp. 240–85.

Distinguishing Features of the Second Postwar Cycle

Typical of the second postwar cycle is the continued struggle of the two systems; the completion, in the main, of the political liberation of the colonies, and a deepening of the agrarian crisis.

The most important features distinguishing the second postwar cycle from the first are the following:

a) the vanquished countries are no longer lagging behind in industrial output; all highly developed countries entered the new cycle at an approximately equal level, as compared with 1937;

b) the economic supremacy of the USA over all other capitalist countries has decreased considerably. Instead of the dollar deficit typical of the first cycle, the USA now has a considerable balance of payments deficit and a steady drain on its gold reserves. It has even been compelled to seek financial aid from the West European countries. The long-term settlements by France and West Germany of their state debts to the USA; the agreement obliging the West European banks to back the dollar; the sale of US government bonds on the West European money market; the US$ 500 million loan given to the USA by the International Monetary Fund, etc., were some of the measures taken to stop this gold drain and to stabilise the dollar. The unusually high share of the USA in world industrial output, exports, and the volume of gold reserves, and also its political weight in world affairs proved to be only temporary conditions brought about by the Second World War. It turned out that in spite of the natural riches of the USA and high labour productivity based on up-to-date equipment, its economic might is insufficient to enable it permanently to play the role of the defender of capitalism on a world scale;

TABLE 29.16 Index of consumer prices[38] (1958 = 100)

	France	West Germany	Italy	Britain	USA	Japan
End of 1964	114	105	104	105	103	110
End of 1962	119	109	109	110	105	118

---

38 *Monthly Bulletin of Statistics*, April 1963, p. 146 *passim*.

c) the inflation in the highly developed countries characteristic of the first postwar cycle has lifted; the currency rates expressed in dollars relative to gold have stabilised; but this stabilisation does not mean that prices have stopped advancing, especially the retail prices being paid by consumers. The price increase was due to the activities of the monopolies and their state, which raises indirect taxes and duties and thus shifts an ever increasing share of the state expenditure on to the shoulders of factory and office workers;
d) there were great changes on the world market. During the first postwar cycle, and especially immediately after the war, American goods dominated the world market. The vanquished countries produced goods predominantly for home consumption, and exported very little. This is no longer true in the second, postwar cycle. Sharp competition reigns on the world market, and the USA and the Common Market are introducing penalty duties. Japanese electronic products are infiltrating into the American market. Cotton cloth and other products of the less developed countries are in demand on the British market. Complaints about dumping are heard everywhere. All this shows that the world market is once again becoming too narrow for the steadily expanding productive capacities;
e) increasing structural unemployment is becoming the scourge of the working class, and a persistent worry, to the big bourgeoisie in the USA, Britain, etc. By resorting to stubborn class struggle, the working class is able to fight the high cost of living more or less effectively, but cannot combat the structural unemployment resulting from technological progress, and, in particular, automation. The only measure that could, albeit temporarily, solve this problem, would be to reduce the working time of the whole working class to about 30 hours a week. Naturally the capitalists are unwilling to agree to such a radical decrease in surplus value.

The statement made by William McChesney Martin,[39] Chairman of the Board of Governors of the Federal Reserve System, to the Joint Economic Committee of the US Congress, shows extent to which monopoly capital is concerned

---

39 [William McChesney Martin (1906–98) was a former president of the New York Stock Exchange and during World War II he supervised the disposal of raw materials on the Munitions Allocation Board. President Harry S. Truman appointed him as head of the Export-Import Bank. In 1951 Truman appointed him Chairman of the Board of Governors of the Fed].

with the rapid and incessantly growing structural unemployment. 'The number of people having jobs rose 1.2 million in 1962 ... Yet the average rate of unemployment declined only to 5.6 percent in 1962 from 6.7 percent in 1961'. Furthermore, despite an increase in industrial production to a level 8 percent above the previous high in the first quarter of early 1960, the number of workers on the production lines of the nation's factories declined 500,000, or 4 percent, in the same period.[40]

The honourable banker is less worried about the fate of the millions of unemployed than about the consequences mass unemployment would have for US economy and the domestic market. He says: 'We also face the inescapable challenge of a faster growing population of working age. Many more jobs will have to be found each year. About a million and a quarter persons are expected to be added to the labour force in each of the next 5 years compared with only about 800,000 in the past 5 years. By 1965, the burgeoning population of 18–24 years of age will account for more than half of the annual growth in the labour force. Unemployment rates are now very high among these young people, especially those with insufficient education. The long anticipated expansion in demand for homes, cars, and all sorts of goods and services will hardly materialize if we fait to find job opportunities for our growing population'.[41]

This is one of the most important problems for the future course of reproduction in the USA, Britain, and the other highly developed countries. Even though the second postwar cycle develops in conditions differing considerably from those of the first, there still are distinctions between the way it unfolds in the victorious and in the vanquished countries. In the victorious countries (the USA, Britain, Canada) the growth rates are slower and there have already been crises – in the USA in 1960–1, in Britain in 1962–3 – but no upward phase worth mentioning.

---

40 'Statements to the Congress: Monetary policy and the economy', *Federal Reserve Bulletin* 1963, 49, 2, p. 123.
41 'Statements to the Congress: Monetary policy and the economy', *Federal Reserve Bulletin* 1963, 49, 2, p. 128.

TABLE 29.17 Index of Industrial Production[42] (1958 = 100)

Year	Japan	West Germany	France	Italy	USA	Britain
1959	124	107	101	111	113	105
1960	156	119	110	128	116	112
1961	186	126	116	142	117	114
1962	201	132	123	156	126	115

The table shows that in the second postwar cycle, too, there are differences in the type of cyclical movement in the USA and Britain, on the one hand, and the large industrial capitalist countries of continental Europe, on the other.

∵

How then will the reproduction cycle under capitalism develop in the future?

At present the cycles differ in the two decisive parts of the capitalist world. We think it illogical for this state of affairs to continue within the single framework of monopoly capitalism. Sooner or later a cycle of a single type[43] will be established throughout the capitalist world. In our opinion *this cycle will resemble the postwar development of the USA*.

The tendency for the cycle to shorten is based on the general laws of capitalist reproduction. The contradiction between the social character of production and the private capitalist form of appropriation, which forms the basis of the cyclical movement, or to be more exact, the contradiction between the striving of the capitalists for an unlimited expansion of production and the limited consumption capacity of capitalist society becomes steadily deeper.[44] For this reason crises of overproduction will become more frequent.

---

42   United Nations data. *Monthly Bulletin of Statistics*, June 1963, p. 18 *passim*.
43   This should not be understood dogmatically; there are and will be deviations from this rule in individual countries.
44   The social consumption capacity is the sum spent on consumer articles, i.e. $v + m - a$ (where a is accumulation). This is less than the social effective demand, which is $c + v + m$ (c in this case being the share of the worn-out fixed capital). But since all production in the final analysis serves to produce consumer articles, the social consumption capacity is the decisive factor in the contradiction between the striving of capital for a boundless expansion of production and the narrow limits of consumption.
      Lenin proved that Tugan-Baranovskiy's theory was wrong because it ignored the difference between consumption capacity and effective demand.

CHANGES IN THE REPRODUCTION CYCLE

A hundred years ago Marx discovered this tendency of the cycle to shorten. He wrote: 'Up to now the cycle usually lasted ten to eleven years. But we have no reason to believe that this is a constant figure. On the contrary, the laws of capitalism we have described give us reason to believe that this is a changing figure and that it will gradually decrease'.[45]

Right through the history of capitalism, cycles tended to shorten. Between 1825 and 1857 when regular crises of overproduction could be observed only in Britain, then the most highly developed capitalist country, the cycle lasted 11 years. In the second half of the nineteenth century, when crises had already assumed a worldwide scale, the following sequence was observed – 1857, 1866, 1873, 1882, 1890, 1900.

According to Marx's theory of crises and cycles, the crisis is the final (and initial) phase of the cycle.

Between 1857 and 1900 there were five cycles with an average duration of 8.5 years each.

In the early twentieth century there were crises in 1907, 1914, 1920, 1929. This shows that over 29 years there were four cycles of an average length of 7 years each. It should also be remembered that in 1914 there was no noticeable crisis because of the outbreak of the First World War. Thus even though there actually were four crises during these 29 years, only three were noticeable.

We may well ask whether in future, too, the cycle will tend to shorten.

We think that this tendency will persist and that the cyclical movement in the whole capitalist world will acquire an ever closer resemblance to that of postwar USA, i.e. there will be *shorter intervals between less serious crises, and real boom phases will be less pronounced.*

Some of our colleagues tried to bypass this question, styling all postwar crises in the USA and Britain (except the 1958 crisis) 'interim', 'partial', 'preliminary' or 'post-crisis'. All these expressions have been used by Marx, especially in his letters. But in *Capital* Marx developed only the theory of genuine crises and cycles.

In our opinion there are no real grounds for regarding all postwar crises in the USA (except the 1958 crisis) as interim. Marx says that 'false' crises occur within the normal cycle, but are not part of it, for they may occur in one cycle, and fail to appear in another. However, what we observe in the USA and Britain

---

45   Marx 1977, p. 1150. These lines are an addition by Marx to the French translation of *Capital*. Engels (for reasons unknown to us) did not include them in the complete German edition; for this reason they do not appear in the second Russian edition of K. Marx's and F. Engels's *Works*, published by the Institute of Marxism-Leninism.

is a constant, regular and relatively rapid succession of minor crises. We therefore should not call them interim, although whatever we style them does not affect their nature.

We therefore maintain that the regular cycle for the capitalist system as a whole will come to resemble the postwar cycles in the USA and Great Britain, i.e. will be shorter than it was before the Second World War.

We think that in addition to a general aggravation of the contradictions of capitalism, *in the postwar period some new factors have tended to shorten the duration of the cycle.*

It is commonly known that the reproduction cycle is determined by the fixed capital, or to be more exact, every crisis is the starting point for a mass renewal and expansion of the fixed capital undertaken for the purpose of lowering production costs. This is because every capitalist thinks that the difficulty of selling his commodities is due to their high cost of production. Similarly, the laws of competition operating under monopoly capitalism force capitalists to renew and expand their fixed capital. This means that they buy equipment (machines, devices), commodities for the building of new factories, for the accumulation of new stocks of raw materials, etc., and this in itself effects an extension of the market.

But the position changes as the renewal and expansion of the fixed capital draws to a close. Capitalists stop buying the commodities and equipment they previously needed to build and equip new factories, just as the new capacities begin to supply the market with an additional mass of commodities.

During the postwar period the renewal and expansion of capital is characterised by the following important new factors:

1. Owing to speedy methods of construction, factories are built and put into operation much quicker than before the war.
2. Owing to rapid technological progress, equipment becomes obsolete sooner than it did before.
3. The rapid replacement of equipment and of the whole fixed capital is encouraged under state-monopoly capitalism. The governments of the highly developed capitalist countries allow the monopolies to deduct from profits depreciation sums which are often two to three times larger than the actual wear. In the USA, for example, any equipment at enterprises, which are considered important from a defence point of view, is written off in five years and less. This provides capitalists with an ideal opportunity of renewing their fixed capital frequently at the expense of the taxpayer and tends to shorten the cycle.
4. Capital investments in the developed capitalist countries are used mainly for the modernisation of equipment in operating factories and not

for the building of new factories. In the USA spending was distributed as follows in *Table 29.18*:

TABLE 29.18 Distribution of capital investments in the USA (percent)[46]

	Expansion	Replacement and modernisation
1959	37	63
1960	35	65

The reason is that capacities are underemployed and result in the following: a) the same amount of new capital investments enables capacities to be enlarged to a far greater extent than if these funds were spent on the building of new factories;[47] b) the time between the investments into capacities and the time when the capacities start producing is reduced. Both these factors accelerate the maturing of the prerequisites for a crisis of overproduction and shorten the cycle.

Since these factors operate not only in the USA but in all highly developed capitalist countries, a further reduction in the length of the cycle can be expected throughout the capitalist world.

It is also interesting to establish which of the cycle phases is becoming shorter. If we look at postwar development in the USA it becomes obvious that, first and foremost, it is the depression phase. This is only logical if capitalists are able to renew and expand their fixed capital out of their depreciation funds, the phase of depression, i.e. the period when production stagnates, must become less enduring.

But *the upward phase is also reduced and sometimes does not even set in at all*. Under conditions when a large portion of available equipment is constantly underemployed, even the introduction of small new capacities results in overproduction. For this reason the upward phase is shorter and the rise a very small one. The curve describing the cycle flattens out.

---

46   *Business Week*, 30 April 1960, p. 28.
47   A thorough study of German pre-war industry (made in connection with the reparation problem) showed that machines and equipment account for an average of 45 percent of the total value of industrial enterprises.

We may expect subsequent crises to deepen in comparison with the first postwar period – indeed the postwar crises in the USA exhibited a definite tendency to deepen. The economists of the American National City Bank determined the depth of the crises of overproduction in the USA according to monthly indices. The figures in *Table 29.19* clearly express this tendency of crises to deepen.[48]

TABLE 29.19 Crisis of overproduction in the USA

Year	Depth of crises (percentage drop of production)
1948–9	8
1953–4	10
1957–8	14
1960[49]	10

It is to be expected that in future the large monopolies will be even more determined to shift the burden of these crises onto the shoulders of small capitalists, farmers, the working class and especially the populations of the less developed countries, by capitalising on the further deterioration of the terms of trade between them and the highly developed countries – the drop in raw material prices and unchanged high prices on the commodities produced by the industrial monopolies.

A substantial growth in unemployment is also likely to ensue for two reasons: 1) the number of people coming of age and qualifying for work is increasing since the population movement of the war and early postwar years has stopped; 2) the rapid development of automation constantly decreases the number of people needed to produce the same amount of commodities. Especially important in this respect is the mechanisation of office work – copying machines, computers, accounting machines, etc., etc. All this means that unemployment is also coming to the 'white-collar workers'. This is very important from a political point of view since this layer of the proletariat, which has grown steeply during the past century and at present comprises 30 to 40 per-

---

48 *First National City Bank Monthly Letter*, March 1960.
49 Based on data from the *Federal Reserve Bulletin*.

cent of all employed, formerly considered itself nearer to the bourgeoisie than to the manual workers. We may therefore expect this huge army of office workers and civil servants to become far more revolutionary than it is at present. Such indications can already be observed in Britain and France.

A general intensification of the class struggle is to be expected, for the big bourgeoisie will attempt to counteract the drop in commodity sales by lowering production costs through wage cuts.

Nor should we forget the contradiction between the direct economic interests of the capitalists and their political interests. Their direct economic interests demand that they advance on the working class and cut down the wages and living standard of the workers. But because of the struggle between the two world systems, the bourgeoisie is unable to devote all its attention to direct economic interests alone. Struggling tooth and nail against the socialist world system, the bourgeoisie must take full account of the political consequences that any offensive against the working class would have, especially in those countries where the proletariat comprises a large slice of the population, such as the USA, Britain and West Germany.

Last but not least, researchers into this cycle should pay particular attention to the peculiar change in the crisis phase over recent years. Formerly the crisis generally took the form of an explosion where there was a sudden transition from the boom to the crisis phase. In America and Britain we now see that the outburst is delayed, that instead of an outburst there is often *a marking of time on the achieved high level of production*, which lasts for months, sometimes up to half a year, until a drop in production finally sets in.

The capitalists now have a far deeper knowledge of the overproduction following a boom and also of world market conditions than they had in Marx's time or even 30 years ago. At that time, much less relevant information was available and it was published only after great delay. Most important of all, it was *retrospective* and recorded only past events.

Now we have efficient *projected* statistics.

In the highly developed industrial countries, information on new orders, unfulfilled orders, contracts on new building work, proposed capital investments by joint-stock companies, questionnaires on projected car sales, records of commodity stocks at factories, in wholesale and retail trade, etc., are now being published regularly (and expeditiously). Many large enterprises and monopoly cartels have special organisations engaged in full-time market research for their commodities. This information enables capitalists to pregauge consumer demand and thus avoid an overproduction of commodities.

The monopoly capitalist state also takes steps to this end. It publishes forecasts on the national income, on total wages, oil future state expenditure, etc., for several years in advance. These predictions, though inaccurate, afford a certain guidance to the capitalists.

Besides, when a recession is in the offing, the state can accelerate the placing of orders, increase their volume, lower taxes to increase effective social demand, etc. But it is easy to overestimate the importance of state 'anti-crisis measures', for their potential value is extremely limited. Under capitalism there can be no state planning, no crisis-free capitalist reproduction. State measures are, however, able to slightly reinforce some of the factors which lower the intensity and duration of the upward phase and the depth and duration of crises in future cycles.

In any case, the long and powerful growth in output observed up to the present in the vanquished industrial countries is unlikely to continue in the future. This is recognised also by many bourgeois economists. Per Jacobsson, Director of the International Monetary Fund,[50] addressing young economists in New York said: 'A new situation has arisen which shows certain similarities with what happened in the early 1930s ... I do not intend to convey the idea that we must repeat the sad experiences of those years, but I do think we will have to take definite measures to see that they are not repeated'.[51]

The deepening of the general crisis of the capitalist system is expressed by the growth in the number of industries which are in a state of perpetual crisis, such as the coal, textile and shipbuilding industries, and those being gradually drawn into this state – the iron and steel and motor industries.

---

50   [Per Jacobsson (1894–1963) was managing director of the IMF from 1954 until his death in 1963].
51   'Postwar expansion is over', *The Times*, 20 February 1963, p. 10.

CHAPTER 30

Problems of State-Monopoly Capitalism

Lately considerable progress has been made in the study of state-monopoly capitalism.[1] The new Programme of the Communist Party of the Soviet Union (CPSU) based on Lenin's teachings gives a clear picture of state-monopoly capitalism. The development of state-monopoly capitalism in the most important countries has been recently described in a number of writings of the Marxist trend.[2] Although there have been profitable discussions on this problem, we still think that some problems remain unsolved.

Internal Contradictions of State-Monopoly Capitalism

In conformity with Marxist theory, a general theoretical analysis of state-monopoly capitalism should regard monopoly capital as a *single force*, and the whole monopoly bourgeoisie as a class or as the leading layer of the capitalist class with common class interests. In his *War and Revolution* Lenin said: 'The old capitalism, the capitalism of the free-competition age [was growing – E.V.] into the capitalism of giant trusts, syndicates, and cartels. This group introduced the beginnings of state-controlled capitalist production, combining the colossal power of capitalism with the colossal power of the state into a single mechanism and bringing tens of millions of people within the single organisation of state capitalism. Here is economic history, here is diplomatic history, covering several decades, from which no one can get away'.[3]

The coalescence of *two forces* – the monopolies and the state – forms the basis of state-monopoly capitalism. This view is further developed in the Programme of the CPSU which states: 'State-monopoly capitalism combines the strength of the monopolies and that of the state into a single mechanism whose purpose is to enrich the monopolies, suppress the working-class movement and the national liberation struggle, save the capitalist system, and launch aggressive wars'.[4]

---

1 [Originally published in *Politico-Economic Problems of Capitalism*, Moscow: Progress Publishers, 1968 [1964], pp. 51–75].
2 Dalin 1961; Pevzner 1961; Khmelnitskaya 1959.
3 Lenin 1964e, p. 403.
4 *The Road to Communism* 1961, p. 471.

We want to emphasise that both Lenin and the Programme of the CPSU speak of a fusion of *two forces*. This means that *monopoly capital and the state are independent forces*, which in the epoch of monopoly capitalism unite to achieve definite aims. This is not a simple unilateral 'subordination' of the state to monopoly capital, as asserted by Stalin, and as some of our economists dogmatically continue to assert to this day.

We have made an attempt to define the essence of state-monopoly capitalism somewhat more concretely: 'State-monopoly capitalism is the alliance of the forces of the monopolies and the bourgeois state for the achievement of two aims: 1) the preservation of the capitalist system in the struggle against the revolutionary movement inside the country and in the struggle against the socialist world system, and 2) the redistribution by the state of the national income in favour of monopoly capital'.[5]

In this general formula monopoly capital is defined as a single power. But if we analyse monopoly capital more deeply we shall discover that the monopoly bourgeoisie fully agrees on some questions, but sharply disagrees on others. And this is only natural. Marx pointed out that the bourgeoisie is united in its attempts to squeeze out of the working class as much surplus value as possible, but that this unanimity disappears completely when it comes to the distribution of the surplus value which has now become profit. Lenin emphasised that competition remains under monopoly capitalism, and therefore also under state-monopoly capitalism, and that this excludes a complete community of interests among the bourgeoisie.

Thus, in Soviet writings one could encounter the erroneous tenet declaring that in every monopoly capitalist country there exists a centre which represents the interests of the monopoly bourgeoisie and gives directives to the state apparatus (such as the Federation of British Industries or the National Association of Manufacturers in the USA). But even though the monopoly bourgeoisie has certain common interests, its individual layers controlling the various economic branches have their own specific interests which contradict those of the monopoly bourgeoisie as a whole. There are even constant contradictions among the various monopolies in a single branch. The monopoly bourgeoisie have the following interests in common:

a) *to safeguard the capitalist social system*. This is an aim shared by the whole monopoly bourgeoisie without exception;
b) *to keep wages at the lowest possible level*. This too is a common interest of the whole monopoly bourgeoisie;[6]

---

5 Varga 1961b, p. 112.
6 The monopolies in the different branches have their own specific interests. They all want the

c) *to reduce the taxes paid by the bourgeoisie* and to shift the tax burden to the other classes and social strata.

In other respects the interests of the various strata of monopoly bourgeoisie differ and contradict each other. Even though the whole monopoly bourgeoisie is interested in establishing high monopoly prices, their interests diverge when it comes to fixing them. The monopolies in the metal industries strive to establish the highest possible prices for their commodities, while the monopolies buying these commodities (the motor, engineering and other industries) are interested in acquiring them at the lowest possible price. *All* monopolies are interested in high protective customs tariffs on industrial goods. But the monopolies of every branch try to establish the highest protective tariffs for the goods *they* are producing; and they certainly are not interested in protective tariffs which boost the prices of the goods they use for production.

Many similar examples could be given, but we think that those enumerated above show that there are only a few spheres in which the interests of the *whole* monopoly bourgeoisie coincide, namely, the safeguarding of the capitalist social system, the high degree of exploitation of workers, and the shifting of the tax burden to the other classes. In all other spheres the monopolies in the different branches have some common interests but also a great *many individual* interests.[7]

The monopolies of any single branch have many interests in common but there are also sharp contradictions between them. Competition leads to the ruination of the weaker. All the monopolies in the same branch are interested in receiving government orders which bring in high profits, and therefore fight each other tooth and nail to obtain these orders for themselves.

A constant struggle goes on between the monopolies of different branches and frequently between those of a single branch for the share of goods to be placed by each on a limited market or, in other words, for their share in total profits. This struggle (disregarding cyclical fluctuations) tends to aggravate constantly, since the gap between the productive capacities and the capacity of the market widens all the time.

The struggle between the monopolies of a single branch is particularly accentuated when war orders become the bone of contention. In March 1968,

---

wages of their workers to be as low as possible. But the monopolies producing non-essential consumer goods (small cars, radios, TVs, etc.) are interested in an increase in the effective demand of the workers of other monopolies.

7 The contradictions are smoothed over through the formation of monopolies which combine enterprises of different branches, by the intertwining of finance capital, etc., but they are not removed.

US Defence Secretary [Robert] McNamara wanted to place an order for US$ 6,500 million (the largest order in US history) with the Dynamics Corporation for TFX military aircraft, but after bitter discussion the Senate was forced to hand it over to their rival, the Boeing Corp.[8]

Many of the contradictions between the monopolies of a single branch, or between separate monopoly enterprises and the interests of monopoly capital as a whole, give rise to conflicts between the state and the monopoly capitalists of a particular branch, or between the state and separate monopoly enterprises. Let us remind the reader of the battle between the American steel smelting industry and President Kennedy in 1961, when state pressure forced the monopolies to abandon their plan of raising prices on steel; and of the conflict between [Ludwig] Erhard,[9] West German Minister for the Economy and the Volkswagen AG, which refused to comply with Erhard's demand that the firm desist from raising the prices of its cars. In retaliation the government considerably lowered import duties on cars.

Such conflicts are explained by the fact that *under state-monopoly capitalism the state represents the common interests of monopoly capital*, interests which may well contradict those of separate monopolies or monopoly groupings. This shows that the definition of state-monopoly capitalism based on Stalin's conception ('state-monopoly capitalism implies the subordination of the state apparatus to the capitalist monopolies'[10]) is wrong.

There is no one-sided 'subordination' but a joining of forces, which, in spite of this merger, still maintain a certain autonomy. There is certainly no subjection of the state apparatus to separate monopolies or the monopolies of a certain branch, for this would exclude conflicts between the state and separate monopolies. The dogmatists once again forget the basic precept of Marxist philosophy, declaring that *all* capitalist laws are no more than tendencies which are *always* opposed by counter-tendencies.

The relations between monopoly capital and the state are complicated by the parliamentary form of government in the monopoly capitalist countries (under a bourgeois dictatorship of the fascist type this complication is removed). The state apparatus, in the narrow sense of the word, i.e. the aggregate

---

8   'U.S. storm over £2,300M. arms contract. Congress hostile to Mr. McNamara', *The Times*, 15 March 1963, p. 12.

9   [Ludwig Erhard (1897–1977), German politician and professor, successively Minister of Economic Affairs (1949–63) and Chancellor (1963–6) of the German Federal Republic].

10 *Politicheskaya ekonomiya. Uchebnik* 1955, p. 266. The 3rd revised and supplemented edition of the textbook appeared in 1960. The definition on page 250 has been improved. But Stalin's formula about the 'subordination of the state apparatus to the monopolies' has not been altered.

of civil servants, the coercion machinery, etc., is a permanent body,[11] while the top layer of the state apparatus, the government and the legislative bodies, change periodically[12] in conformity with parliamentary election results. A change in the parliamentary majority and a change of government do not necessarily entail a substantial change in the relations between monopoly capital and the state, even when the government is formed by the Labour Party or, as in Sweden, by Social Democrats.[13]

But this does not mean that the parliamentary system, the campaigning of the various parties to win the elections, is *irrelevant*. If the monopolies had their way there would always be a Conservative government in Britain. But the monopolies cannot always do as they please. What is the reason for this?

The reason is that in the state-monopoly capitalist countries, factory and office workers and civil servants constitute the majority of the population, and hence of the electors. The bourgeois parties and the government must take this into account, and they, therefore, camouflage and deny the existence of monopoly capitalist domination. In some cases, this results in a certain change of government policy. John F. Kennedy, the son of a millionaire, and worth hundreds of millions of dollars, was naturally no enemy of monopoly capital. But since the electors of the Democratic Party are composed primarily of factory and office workers, he declined the unanimous demand of the monopoly bourgeoisie of all parties in the summer of 1962 for an immediate cut in taxes on monopoly capital. The tax cut was postponed to 1963 in order not to jeopardise the chances of the Democratic Party in the 1982 elections. This shows that in spite of the fact that the monopoly bourgeoisie and the state join forces, the relations between them are more complicated and contradictory than would seem at first glance.

State-monopoly capitalism embraces a single country (we shall discuss the emergence of supra-national state-monopoly capitalist organisations later in

---

11   When an opposition party gains victory over the ruling party in the US a large number of civil servants belonging to the old party are dismissed and replaced by adherents of the new ruling party. This is not done in Western Europe.

12   The permanent state apparatus is often more important than the constantly changing government. The British Prime Minister Lloyd George once said that although people speak all the time about government decisions, 95 percent of these decisions are taken by the apparatus, the remaining five percent by the government according to recommendations of that apparatus.

13   In the USA the monopolies secure their interests by financing the election campaigns of both parties: one part of the monopoly bourgeoisie belongs to one party, the other to the second. In [Lyndon B.] Johnson's Government the two key posts, that of War Secretary and Finance Secretary, are held by Republicans.

the book). This means that the contradictions between the interests of monopolies of different countries breed contradictions and clashes between the relevant countries. This has always been the case under imperialism. The development of state-monopoly capitalism has changed nothing in this respect.

∵

We should like to remind the reader of the *radical contradiction* between two principal aims of the monopoly bourgeoisie: that of safeguarding the capitalist social system, and that of utilising the state to redistribute the national income in favour of monopoly capital. In the struggle for the first and principal aim – the safeguarding of the capitalist social system – the monopolies have the support of all those capitalists whose incomes are fully or partly derived from the exploitation of labour – the non-monopoly bourgeoisie, landowners, rich farmers, and petty bourgeoisie and also highly paid employees, civil servants, the corrupt workers' bureaucracy and workers' aristocracy, in short, of all those elements who do not want a socialist transformation of society. In implementing its second major aim – that of redistributing the national income in favour of monopoly capital with state assistance – the monopolies are treading on the toes of those layers of capitalist society which support the monopoly bourgeoisie in the achievement of the first aim. They alienate them and thereby create conditions for the formation of a broad anti-monopoly-capital front embracing the working people and those layers of the bourgeoisie whose interests have been harmed by the monopoly bourgeoisie.

We shall give only one example to demonstrate how the monopoly bourgeoisie resorts to state assistance to infringe upon the interests of the non-monopoly exploiting classes. On 17 May 1962, [Cyril] Osborne, a Conservative MP,[14] submitted to the British Minister of Trade [Sir Keith Joseph] an interpellation on the high price of ammonium sulphate that the Imperial Chemical Industries (ICI) were charging farmers. ICI have the monopoly on the production of chemical fertilisers in Britain. He quoted the following facts. For the past 20 years importers of ammonium sulphate paid an import duty of four pounds a ton. On 3 May 1962, the duty was raised to seven pounds a ton. This enabled ICI to sell farmers ammonium sulphate at £20 a ton. At the same time ICI exports large amounts of that chemical at £12 a ton and foreign firms are willing to supply Britain at the same price. Osborne asked the Minister to abol-

---

14   [Cyril Osborne (1898–1969) was a MP for the Louth constituency in Linconshire from 1945 until his death].

ish the protective duty on ammonium sulphate. The Minister of Trade did not deny the facts but refused to abolish the tax on the grounds that the export at lower prices makes for a better use of productive capacities and thus lowers production costs. This argument has been used time and again to justify the superprofits of monopoly capital.

But it did not stop at that. In the course of the debates it was pointed out that the British Government is paying the farmers a subsidy of £8/15 per ton of superphosphate with the alleged aim of expanding agricultural output through wider use of artificial fertilisers, but that this money is almost fully appropriated by ICI in the form of high monopoly prices. The Minister of Trade defended this state of affairs, to which Labour MP Douglas Jay remarked: 'Is there anything ICI could do of which the Government would disapprove?'[15]

Obviously, even if British landowners and farmers do support monopoly capital in defending the capitalist social system, they oppose it when it comes to the distribution of the national income. The contradictions between them are mitigated by the fact that the richest landowners are closely linked with monopoly capital.

This example also illustrates the devious means by which the national income is redistributed in favour of monopoly capital. The British Government uses the taxpayers' money, including that collected from the workers, to pay the farmers' subsidies, which are then appropriated from the farmers by ICI which sells them superphosphate at a price exceeding that quoted on the world market by £7 a ton. Thus, a part of the money earned by British workers (being subjected to direct capitalist exploitation) is siphoned into the money bags of the monopolies. We see that the fusion of state power and monopoly capital proceeds dialectically and contains innumerable contradictions which come to light during a concrete analysis.

Stalin's formula on the 'subordination' of the state to the monopolies stops us from seeing things in a true light through a concrete analysis.

The Uneven Development of State-Monopoly Capitalism

Like all processes under imperialism, the development of state-monopoly capitalism is irregular both in time and in various countries. Some manifestations

---

15 Taken from the Parliamentary Records published by *The Times* on 18 April 1962 on p. 6. It is noteworthy that several months after this debate Hugh Gaitskell, the late leader of the Labour Party, announced that in the event of a Labour victory, the Imperial Chemical Industries would not be nationalised.

of state-monopoly capitalism could be observed even before the First World War. For example, the trade agreement signed between Germany and Japan contained a special clause regulating the supply of dyes to Japanese textile firms by the German chemical industrialists' association. However, the final transition to state-monopoly capitalism began only during the First World War.

Lenin said: 'World capitalism, which in the sixties and seventies of the last century as an advanced and progressive force of free competition and which at the beginning of the twentieth century grew into *monopoly* capitalism, i.e., imperialism, took a big step *forward* during the war, not only towards greater concentration of finance capital, but also towards transformation into *state capitalism*'.[16]

Since that time state-monopoly capitalism has developed unevenly. It weakened after the end of the First World War, became stronger during the 1929–33 economic crisis, ebbed after the crisis, intensified during the Second World War, weakened slightly after it, and now experiences a *qualitatively new* upswing, expressed in the setting up of supra-national state-monopoly organisations and in the attempts to create a supra-national state-monopoly capitalism.

This undulating development is due to the fact that the tendency towards the strengthening of state-monopoly capitalism is opposed by strong counter-tendencies, which at times gain the upper hand. But their victory is short-lived because the tendency towards the strengthening of state-monopoly capitalism is victorious in the end. If we compare historically similar periods, for example, the first decades after the First and the Second World Wars, we discover that after the Second World War, following the end of the inevitable period of weakening, state-monopoly capitalism rose to a considerably higher level than it had occupied during the corresponding period following the First World War.

This undulating line of development is easily explained. Obviously, the monopoly bourgeoisie as a whole strives for the main aim of state-monopoly capitalism, which is the safeguarding of the capitalist social system, and the redistribution of the national income in its favour. But, on the other hand, it objects to state 'interference' in the economy and to social legislation on principle. To this day its ideal is 'to be master in its own house'. This contradictory attitude of the monopoly bourgeoisie to state-monopoly capitalism explains why it grows unevenly – makes a leap forward when there is a genuine threat to the existence of the capitalist system and recedes a bit when that danger disappears. Lenin said: 'War and economic ruin have forced all countries to advance

---

16   Lenin 1964m, p. 267.

from monopoly capitalism to state-monopoly capitalism. This is the objective state of affairs'.[17] The Programme of the CPSU gives an identical definition: 'World wars, economic crises, militarism, and political upheavals have accelerated the development of monopoly capitalism into state-monopoly capitalism'.[18]

It is also clear that state-monopoly capitalism must grow stronger *in the historical aspect*. The internal contradictions of capitalism are constantly worsening: socialism is winning the battle, the system of colonial rule is rapidly approaching its final collapse, the former colonial peoples are enemies of imperialism and more and more of them strive to embark on the road to socialism. Socialism is to an ever greater extent becoming the decisive factor in historical development. This signifies that the very existence of the capitalist social system is being subjected to an ever-increasing danger. The monopoly bourgeoisie has but one way out, that of strengthening the capitalist system through state-monopoly capitalism. In our opinion the best definition of the development of state-monopoly capitalism has been given by O.V. Kuusinen,[19] who said:

> Initially it was regarded as a sort of 'emergency measure', resorted to only during wartime or during a grave economic or political crisis and abandoned the moment the 'emergency' had passed. At present, the imperialist bourgeoisie can no longer maintain its domination without state-monopoly capitalism even during relatively normal periods. This is due to the aggravation of the general crisis of the capitalist system, to the growing disintegration of capitalism and weakening of its internal forces – economic, political and ideological.[20]

The monopoly bourgeoisie (finance oligarchy) has taken this historically unavoidable road and to this day continues to travel along it by fits and starts, stopping on the way to limit the state-monopoly capitalist superstructure when it feels that its supremacy has somewhat consolidated. Both in Britain and in West Germany a substantial part of formerly nationalised enterprises have been denationalised and handed over to private capital on favourable conditions. In West Germany not only state enterprises built under Hitler (such as

---

17   Lenin 1964c, p. 170.
18   *The Road to Communism* 1961, p. 471.
19   [Otto V. Kuusinen (1881–1964) was a Finnish-born Bolshevik, member of the Politburo of the CPSU].
20   Kuusinen 1960, p. 7.

the Volkswagenwerk which was financed by workers' money, collected on the false promise that the workers would be provided with cheap cars) but also state property, which belonged to the Prussian state even in the nineteenth century, have been handed over to private capital. In Italy, on the other hand, the power industry is being nationalised, although naturally, the former owners are paid a lavish compensation. All this is a perfect example of the unevenness of capitalist development. Yet, in spite of the denationalisation of some state enterprises in West Germany, in 1962, 74 industrial companies with a subscribed share capital of 100 million marks each were state property; their total share capital amounted to 20,200 million marks, *22 of them accounting for a total capital of 5,800 million marks were state-monopoly enterprises.*[21] If we add state incomes to that figure we can see that even denationalisation has not wrought substantial changes in the state property's share.

In the United States, where the bourgeoisie considers its rule relatively secure, it constantly fights against state 'interference'. The demands of the extreme Right-wing of the Republican Party, supporting the fascist Birch Society,[22] are typical in that respect. They supported the candidacy of reactionary Senator Barry Goldwater[23] for the Presidency.

Below are some of the demands advanced by this movement:
– the repudiation of all social and economic legislation promulgated after 1932;
– curtailment of trade-union rights;
– promulgation of laws on the right to work;[24]
– abolition of state housing construction;
– abolition of income tax;
– the refusal to enter into disarmament agreements with or without guarantees.[25]

This fascist gang openly demands what the American monopoly bourgeoisie only dares to dream about, namely, that all taxes be paid by the mass of consumers, that all legislative or trade-union restrictions on the exploitation of labour be abolished and that nothing be allowed to hamper the arms race.

---

21   *Berichte*, Berlin (GDR): Deutsches Wirtschaftsinstitut, 1962/3, 13–14, pp. 290–1.
22   [The John Birch Society is an American anti-communist organisation founded in 1958].
23   [Barry Goldwater (1909–98) was a businessman and five-term United States Senator from Arizona and the Republican Party's nominee for President in the 1964 election].
24   This includes laws legalising strike-breaking, which give entrepreneurs the right to offer workers worse conditions than are fixed in the collective agreement, etc. In short, it boils down to 'being master in one's own house'.
25   Brant 1962, p. 16.

Obviously, the monopoly bourgeoisie will not reject the chance of getting war orders, no matter how much it talks about disarmament. War orders yield much higher profits than any other investment. Only occasionally is some data on this subject published. An investigation conducted by a committee under Senator [John Little] McClellan[26] on the deliveries of Nike missiles, for which the Government paid US$ 2,500 million, revealed the following facts. The order was given to the Western Electric Company which handed 40 percent of the order over to subcontractors. Profits were divided as follows: Consolidated Steel supplied the Douglas Aircraft Company with commodities amounting to US$ 140 million, making on them a profit of US$ 9 million. In order to make a profit, the Douglas Aircraft Company added a further US$ 10 million to the price and sold the output to the Western Electric Company. The latter added another US$ 9.8 million. The cost of production for the government order was US$ 146 million, but it netted the three participants a total of US$ 28.8 million profit, or almost 19 percent of the total.[27]

No matter how much some monopolies may be against state 'interference', against state-monopoly capitalism, no matter how much they may deride state functionaries among themselves, they never reject government orders, which are an important cog in the mechanism of state-monopoly capitalism.

What the big capitalists think of the people holding key government posts can be seen from the following statements:

> In the quiet, high-ceilinged dining rooms of the Detroit Athletic Club, where the movers and shakers of the automotive industry gather, they added a new tooth to an old saw: 'FDR showed that the Presidency can be a lifetime job, *Truman showed that anyone can be President, Ike that we really don't need a President, and Kennedy that it can be dangerous to have a President*'.[28]

But the top-brass of the finance oligarchy who call the tune, or at least some of them, are political realists and cherish no illusions on the situation. They are compelled to reckon with the socialist countries and also with the power of the trade unions. For political reasons they therefore attempt to create the illusion that the state opposes the monopolies. For propaganda reasons the state

---

26 John Little McClellan (1896–1977) was a Democrat representing Arkansas in the Senate (1942–77).
27 'Locking the defence door', *The Economist*, 21 April 1962, p. 250.
28 *Newsweek*, 16 July 1962, p. 11, my emphasis – E.V.

'struggles' against cartels, which are 'prohibited' by law in the USA. In 1961–2 the US Government accused the General Electric Co. (GEC) and 28 other firms in the electrotechnical industry of having, by mutual agreement, sold the government heavy electrotechnical equipment at excessive prices. Various organs of state power and private firms lodged 1,600 similar complaints.

The clash of the government with GEC was settled out of court: the company had to pay the government US$ 7,470,000 compensation. The government expects all other claims to be settled in the same way, and according to the London *Economist* this will yield the government a further US$ 50 million. This may seem a considerable amount but actually it comprises only 20 percent of company profits for 1961. However, the swindle becomes obvious when we realise that 'if the Internal Revenue Service decides that the damages qualify as deductions from taxable income, the Treasury ... may actually be worse off'.[29]

The government gives the company with its left hand what it takes back with the right.

The development of state-monopoly capitalism is both complex and contradictory. In the final analysis all the profits are always reaped by the largest monopolies, although the manner in which this is done is by no means simple.

State-Monopoly Capitalism and the Proletariat

The constant development of state-monopoly capitalism is an objective process. Historically it is the final phase of imperialism, the preparatory stage for socialism. In his famous definition Lenin says: 'state-monopoly capitalism is a complete material preparation for socialism, the *threshold* of socialism, a rung on the ladder of history between which and the rung called socialism *there are no intermediate rungs*'.[30]

On the surface this would warrant the conclusion that the Social Democrats are right in declaring that the proletariat should *indiscriminately* support *all* measures which tend to strengthen state-monopoly capitalism. They even allege that state capitalism already is socialism, which is pure demagogy since the domination of the bourgeoisie continues. As stated above, the relation of the bourgeoisie to state-monopoly capitalism is both contradictory and inconsistent, and changes depending on how stable or unstable their domination is at any given moment.

---

29   'GE makes good damage', *The Economist*, 4 August 1962, p. 444.
30   Lenin 1964d, p. 359.

Should the proletariat adopt a positive attitude to all state-monopoly measures irrespective of their nature?

Of course not! State-monopoly capitalism contains a dialectical contradiction: on the one hand, it creates the material and organisational preconditions for socialism; on the other, it becomes responsible for a temporary strengthening of the capitalist system and the more intense exploitation of the proletariat with the assistance of the state. For this reason the proletariat should support or oppose state-monopoly measures, depending on their concrete historical content.

We shall give two examples relating to the same historical period. While the laws adopted in connection with president Roosevelt's 'New Deal' were aimed at saving American imperialism from the economic breakdown threatening it as a result of the crippling 1929–33 crisis, the social *legislation* of the 'New Deal' – freedom and recognition of trade unions, limitation of the working day, etc. – was undoubtedly in the interests of the American working class, and since the prerequisites for the overthrow of bourgeois rule had not yet matured in the USA it would have been stupid to oppose Roosevelt's 'New Deal', and particularly the socio-political measures.

Quite a different situation developed in connection with the state-monopoly measures taken by Hitler. Any support of his measures would have been a betrayal of the proletariat, and the support given them by the Right-wing Social Democrats and trade-union leaders cannot be regarded in any other light.

In every concrete historical situation the attitude of the proletariat to the state-monopoly measures of any government depends first and foremost on the maturity that the preconditions for the socialist revolution have attained. If there is a struggle for power, it would be senseless to support any measures of the government tending to strengthen the capitalist system. But while there is no revolutionary situation in a country and bourgeois rule is still stable, the struggle to curb the arbitrary rule of monopoly capital, and for a democratic nationalisation of the key branches, may be a good method of mobilising the masses.

Depending on concrete conditions, nationalisation has a different significance for the bourgeoisie and for the proletariat. On principle, the bourgeoisie is against nationalisation. As Lenin once said, the bourgeoisie favours the nationalisation of economic branches running at a loss, only, of course, if they receive ample compensation for their nationalised assets. Under adverse political conditions, they may even consent to the nationalisation of profitable branches, but attempt to regain them as soon as political conditions make this possible.

This can be seen from the nationalisation carried out in Britain when the Labour Party won the election immediately after the Second World War, and the subsequent denationalisation in 1951 when the Conservatives returned to office.

After the Second World War, as after the First, the deep dissatisfaction of the British working class with the capitalist system brought victory to the British Labour Party. Right-wing leaders of the Labour Party recommended extensive nationalisation as a means of pacifying the workers. With the consent of the bourgeoisie the government nationalised many industries, paying the ex-owners ample compensation.

The further fate of the nationalised industries is a case in point. The coal industry, which is in a state of permanent crisis (and not in Britain alone),[31] is state property to this day. The British bourgeoisie never demanded its denationalisation, not even under the Conservative government. The reason for this is not hard to see. The government pays the former mine owners compensation, and supplies capitalist industry with coal at a loss which is covered by the taxpayer.[32] The surplus value being created by the miners is thus indirectly appropriated by the industrial bourgeoisie as a whole. An identical state of affairs can be observed in the railways.

Conversely, the profitable enterprises which were nationalised by the Labour government – the steel-smelting industry and motor transport – were denationalised by the Tory government on conditions favourable to the monopolies. By the middle of 1962 only a small part remained state property.

---

[31] TABLE 30.1 Data showing the development of the British coal industry

	1938	1951	1960
Coal output (million tons)	227	223	194
Number of miners (thousands)	782	699	602
Coal output per miner/shift (tons)	3.0	3.2	4.0

SOURCE: *ANNUAL ABSTRACT OF STATISTICS* 1961, PP. 135 AND 138. THE NUMBER OF MINERS DECREASED BY 100,000 IN TEN YEARS, THE LABOUR PRODUCTIVITY ROSE BY 25 PERCENT!

[32] According to the United Kingdom *Annual Abstract of Statistics* (1961, pp. 256–7), state expenditure on the coal-mining industry from 1951 to 1961 exceeded income by £531,000,000. This sum probably does not include all losses.

Fundamentally, the proletariat favours the nationalisation of monopoly-dominated branches. This is true both of the Communists, who see in nationalisation an important material and organisational step on the road to socialism, and also of non-Party workers whose economic aims it advances.

Even though the monopoly capitalist state defends primarily the interests of monopoly capital, there is a great difference in the conditions under which the workers struggle for wage increases in private monopoly-owned enterprises, and in state-owned enterprises. The struggle for wage increases threatens to cut the monopoly bourgeoisie's profits. The management of every enterprise is directly and materially concerned with the outcome of the struggle. In state-owned enterprises, the workers are opposed by directors, Ministers, etc., who have no direct material interest in the outcome of the struggle. Therefore their resistance to the workers' demands is usually less stiff than that of the monopoly bourgeoisie. Fascist countries, however, are an exception to this rule. In the advanced state-monopoly capitalist countries with a parliamentary form of government, where factory and office workers constitute the bulk of the electors, political motives also play a major role. For tactical reasons the ruling party does not want to alienate electors by an outright refusal to increase the wages of factory and office workers. Important are also the Cold War policy and the existence of the world socialist system, and, as mentioned above, the desire not to alienate the workers by provocations which would induce them to lend a more willing ear to communist ideas.

The revolutionary proletariat *fights for nationalisation* because this helps to enlist into the struggle against the monopolies not only factory and office workers, but also broad layers of the peasantry and the petty urban bourgeoisie, who are similarly oppressed by the monopolies.

Moreover, they realise that a democratic management of the nationalised enterprises can alleviate the conditions of the working people.

Supra-national State-Monopoly Organisations

An important new phenomenon in the development of state-monopoly capitalism after the Second World War is the rapid growth of state-monopoly organisations embracing several countries. Hundreds of such organisations are now in existence.

Like all other social phenomena, supra-national organisations also had their predecessors before the Second World War. A good example is the Bank for International Settlements in Basel, which was originally set up to deal with Germany's reparations after the First World War. Later it began to conduct transactions on an international scale between central emission banks, all of which are state or semi-state institutions. The Bank also functioned during the Second World War, and, through its board meetings enabled the monopolies of the warring countries to arrange their common business (on international cartels, trusts, payments, etc.) on neutral ground.

With the assistance and participation of the relevant governments international cartels were formed and functioned even before the Second World War. There was a series of inter-state agreements on railway transit traffic, postal and telegraph communications, etc. But before the Second World War they were the *exception*, now they have become the *rule*.

In general, the causes and aims of state-monopoly capitalism on a supra-national scale differ but little from those of state-monopoly capitalism on a national scale. The ever increasing concentration of production in giant enterprises makes the domestic market of a single country too narrow for the requirements of monopoly capital, a state of affairs that has been aggravated by the disintegration of the world market following the Second World War, the creation of arbitrary currency zones, the restriction of imports, state control over the import and export of capital, high duties, etc. Supra-national state capitalist measures were intended to alleviate this situation.

The aims of supra-national organisations are identical to those of state-monopoly capitalism on a national scale the defence of the capitalist social system and the securing of high monopoly profits.

Both economic and military-political organisations serve to defend the capitalist social system. The difference between them is negligible, for all supra-national economic organisations have a political character. The International Monetary Fund, for example, an economic supra-national organisation commanding many thousands of millions of dollars, is first and foremost concerned with maintaining the stability of the imperialist countries' currencies when their balance of payments shows a deficit. The International Bank for Reconstruction and Development (and the financial institutions associated with it) is expected to direct the development of the emerging countries in a way favourable to the monopoly capital of the imperialist powers, i.e. to perpetuate their dependence on these powers. To this day the United States has the final word in both organisations since it owns the bulk of their capital.

A number of agreements between countries and organisations (international agreements on wheat, coffee, etc.) are aimed at preventing a drop in prices arising from the agrarian crisis of overproduction affecting almost all branches of agriculture. Their other aim is to render economic support to well-to-do farmers who are staunch defenders of private property.

So far only the first shoots of supra-national state-monopoly organisations have sprung up in the sphere of production. These are the powerful coal and steel community of six West European countries (ECSC),[33] and Euratom. But their number will undoubtedly increase. The closer coalescence of the monopolies of different capitalist countries that is being achieved through mutual capital investments paves the road for this development.

No full picture can be gained of the intertwining of capital since statistical methods in the separate countries vary considerably. The picture is also distorted by the constant migration of short-term capital-bank deposits, funds used for gambling on the stock exchange, etc.

The following example illustrates this interlinking of capital. According to the Department of Trade, US long-term private capital investments abroad in 1961 amounted to US$ 49,000 million, foreign long-term private capital investments in the United States to US$ 21,000 million.

According to data issued by the Federal Statistics Board at the end of 1960, 261 foreign shareholders owned 53 percent of the share capital in 2,537 West German joint-stock companies, accounting for 17 percent of the total share capital in the country. British shareholders held 932 million, Dutch – 422 million, French – 215 million marks' worth of stock. This does not include the capital of the branches of American, British, Belgian and other firms in West Germany whose capital is unknown.

At the beginning of 1961 the private foreign capital investments of West German companies accounted for 2,758 million marks, of which 963 million were invested in Western Europe.

According to data issued by the industrial association IRI,[34] at the close of 1960 long-term foreign capital investments in Italy exceeded US$ 3,000 million; Italian capital investments abroad – US$ 2,000 million.

Other links include participation in international institutions (the International Monetary Fund, the World Bank), the exchange of patents and licences, etc.

But no matter how important this mutual coalescence of capital, *its significance should not be exaggerated*, for now, as before, *national* monopoly capital continues to be the decisive factor in the economy and policy of every highly developed country.

---

33   According to the ECSC new capital investments in the coalmining and steel-smelting industries comprised US$ 1,500 million in 1961.

34   [IRI: Instituto per la Recostruzione Industriale. Italian public holding company established in 1933].

Supra-national organisations, such as North Atlantic Treaty Organization (NATO), CENTO,[35] etc., serve to defend the capitalist system both militarily and politically. They differ from military-political unions, typical of the former period, by a more rigid organisation, including the joint command over a part of the armed forces, the deployment of NATO forces in foreign countries, especially in those bordering on the socialist countries, joint manoeuvres, standardisation of part of the armaments, etc. They are also more long-lived than those of former periods. In spite of constant internal crises,[36] NATO and the other military-political unions of the highly developed capitalist countries will probably continue to function in one form or another as a means of struggling against the socialist countries right up to the final collapse of capitalism.

The Common Market is a new and important phenomenon in the development of supranational state-monopoly capitalism. However, since it has been widely discussed by the Soviet press and literature, a detailed study of this question is unnecessary.

Although the Common Market *is something new*, in many respects it is a return to the conditions that existed before the First World War. It is an attempt to overcome the dividedness of the world market by uniting the markets of six countries; to re-establish equal conditions for competition through the universal application of the most favoured nation principle in trade agreements, to ensure the free flow of capital and the stability of the gold content of the currencies of most capitalist countries, etc. Equal conditions for competition are to be promoted through the mutual abolition of duties. These measures serve primarily the interests of the big monopolies.[37] At the same time the Common Market is an attempt on the part of the West European imperialist powers to consolidate their position following the political liberation of the colonial countries, to enable them to conduct a vigorous political neo-colonialism and to compete with the United States.

Politically, the Common Market is a desperate attempt to resolve imperialism's inevitable internal contradictions and to oppose the socialist world system by a single imperialist front, or at least by an apparent unity. All imperial-

---

35 [CENTO: Central Treaty Organization or Pact of Baghdad concluded in 1955 by Iran, Iraq, Pakistan, Turkey and the United Kingdom. It was dissolved in 1979].

36 The main reason for the discord within NATO is the US nuclear monopoly, giving America the decisive say in problems of war and peace. In spite of the pressure exerted on the USA by its NATO partners it refuses to relinquish this monopoly.

37 This is clearly illustrated by the internal struggle in Britain over the question of her entry into the Common Market. Monopoly capital favours this entry; landowners, farmers and the bulk of the workers frown upon it.

ist statesmen – [Charles] de Gaulle, [Walter] Hallstein,[38] [Winston] Churchill, etc. – admit that in the creation of the Common Market political aims outweigh the economic.[39]

For these political reasons the United States supported the union of the West European countries in the Common Market and exerted pressure on Britain to join the EEC, even though this union would accelerate the waning of US economic and political influence.

The Common Market member-countries are trying to conduct an independent economic policy vis-à-vis the United States. The following episode is a case in point. Under pressure from interested monopolies, President Kennedy declared in May 1962 that duties on glass and carpets would be raised. Belgian glass exports to the USA were the hardest hit. In reply, the Common Market countries raised the duty on a number of synthetic fibres and materials made from them from 20 to 40 percent[40] as from 17 July 1962.

The Common Market is a house divided against itself. West Germany and France have still been unable to fix common prices on agricultural products. The Italian industrialists are selling France refrigerators at a price that is 25 percent lower than their price on the French domestic market – in the first half of 1963 alone they sold France 140,000 refrigerators. In reply the French Government issued orders stating that refrigerators imported from Italy could be sold only with special permission from the Minister for Industry.

At the Congress of the West German Pig Iron and Steel Union held in Düsseldorf in June 1963, complaints were voiced about the loss inflicted by the Common Market on the West German iron and steel industry. [Hans-Günther] Sohl,[41] the Chairman of the Union, said in his report that '... while other large steel producing countries enjoy stable prices on the domestic market, protected by duties and taxes, the West German steel market has become an export field for all countries. Owing to the devaluation of the French franc by almost 30

---

38   [Walter Hallstein (1901–82) was a German professor and politician, former member of the Nazi Party, first President of the European Commission (1958–67)].

39   During his visit to Western Europe in the summer of 1962 Dwight D. Eisenhower said at a press conference in London that the Common Market was an important question that should be regarded as a union of the free world against 'aggressive communist imperialism', i.e. against the socialist community.

40   'Six relation measures', *The Times*, 7 June 1962, p. 18. The squabble between the USA and the Common Market broke out in 1963.

41   [Hans-Günther Sohl (1906–89) was a former director of the Vereinigte Stahlwerken; after the Second World War he became director of Thyssen AG. Between 1956 and 1969 he was President of the Wirtschaftsvereinigung Eisen- und Stahlindustrie and President of the Bundesverband der Deutschen Industrie (BDI)].

percent, French steel became in 1957–8 cheaper than domestic steel. Besides, the blocking of steel prices by the French Government has widened the price gap to the detriment of West Germany. Belgian and Luxemburg iron and steel works are exerting a strong pressure on the West German market price'.[42] The Congress noted that the reserves created by high domestic prices had made the Belgians particularly successful in expanding their position in the Common Market.

Political contradictions are no less acute. De Gaulle blocked Britain's entry into the Common Market on political grounds, because he considered Britain the instrument of American influence in Western Europe; while Belgium and the Netherlands were for Britain's entry on political grounds, believing that it would offset the threat of West Germany's political domination in Western Europe.

Even politicians in the same country hold contradictory views on the lines along which the Common Market should develop. [Walter] Hallstein is trying to steer a course of close economic union between the Six and advocates a common economic policy. De Gaulle and Erhard on the other hand were strictly against this course. At a meeting of the Ministers and Ambassadors of the Six, Erhard said that he strove not for a centralised European state but for European federation in which different countries and peoples could live their own lives according to their ideals, although the economic integration of the Six was achieved through political decisions, he continued, the striving for centralisation in economic policies should not predetermine Europe's future political structure. Erhard specifically warned against accepting the recommendation of the Common Market Commission advocating a fusion of the national economic policies of the member-countries.

Inter-imperialist contradictions cannot be resolved. US monopoly capital is rapidly setting up branches of industrial enterprises in Western Europe so as not to be excluded from the domestic market of the united countries. The more countries join the Common Market, the more diverse will become its internal contradictions.

The Programme of the CPSU says: 'The dialectics of state-monopoly capitalism is such that instead of shoring up the capitalist system, as the bourgeoisie expects, it aggravates the contradictions of capitalism and undermines its foundations'.[43]

---

42   *Neue Zürcher Zeitung*, 7 July 1963. [Reference was not found in this issue of the Swiss paper].
43   *The Road to Communism* 1961, p. 472.

Bibliography

Works Cited in Introduction, by André Mommen

'A. Sultan-Zade' 1986, in *Biographical Dictionary of the Comintern: New, Revised, and Expanded Edition*, edited by Branko Lazitch with Milorad M. Drachkovich, Stanford, CA: Hoover Institution Press.

Adibekov, Grant M. 2002, *Das Kominform und Stalins Neuordnung Europas*, Frankfurt: Peter Lang.

Ahmed, Mesbahuddin 1986, *The British Labour Party and the Indian Independence Movement, 1917–1947*, New York: Envoy Press.

Altvater, Elmar (ed.) 1969, *Die Krise des Kapitalismus und ihre politischen Folgen*, Frankfurt and Vienna: Europäische Verlagsanstalt/Europa Verlag.

Amo, A. [Amatuni] 1932, 'Borba za shistotu marksistko-leninistkoy teorii krizisov', *Bolshevik*, 9, 10: 80–94.

Andreu, Maurice 2000, *Sur la théorie de la crise 'générale du capitalisme'. La genèse du concept de 'CGC'. Contribution à une histoire des idées économiques dans l'Internationale Communiste de 1919 à 1929*, PhD Université Paris XIII – Paris Nord, Faculté de Sciences Économiques et de Gestion.

Andreu, Maurice 2001, 'Que faire des Théories sur la plus-value? L'exemple des économistes de la Troisième Internationale', Congrès Marx International III, Section Économie, Atelier 15, 29 September, Unpublished Congress Paper.

Andreu, Maurice 2003, *L'Internationale communiste contre le Capital 1919–1924, ou comment empoigner l'adversaire capitaliste?*, Paris: Presses Universitaires de France.

Babitschenko, Leonid G. 1993, 'Die Kaderschulung der Komintern', *Jahrbuch für historische Kommunismusforschung*, Berlin: Akademie-Verlag, 1: 37–59.

Barnett, Vincent 1998, *Kondratiev and the Dynamics of Economic Development: Long Cycles and Industrial Growth in Historical Context*, New York: St. Martin's Press.

Barnett, Vincent 2004, *The Revolutionary Russian Economy 1890–1940: Ideas, Debates and Alternatives*, London and New York: Routledge.

Barnett, Vincent 2005, *A History of Russian Economic Thought*, New York and London: Routledge.

Bauer, Otto 1912–13, 'Die Akkumulation des Kapitals', *Die Neue Zeit*, 31, 1: 831–75, 861–87.

Benedikt, Ottó 1929, 'Die Akkumulation des Kapitals bei wachsender organischen Zusammensetzung', *Unter dem Banner des Marxismus*, 3, 6: 869–911.

Boccara, Paul 1967, 'On State Monopoly Capitalism', *Political Affairs*, 46, 4: 25–34.

Borsányi, György 1993, *The Life of a Communist Revolutionary, Béla Kun*, Boulder, CO and High Lakes, NJ: Social Science Monographs and Atlantic Research and Publications.

Brailsford, H.N. 1945, 'Introduction', in *In Search of the Millenium*, by Julius Braunthal, London: Victor Gollancz Ltd.

Braunthal, Alfred 1927, 'Die Konjunkturpolitik der Reichsbank', *Die Gesellschaft. Internationale Revue für Sozialismus und Politik*, 4, 12: 520–33.

Braunthal, Alfred 1929, 'Der Zusammenbruch der Zusammenbruchstheorie', *Die Gesellschaft*, 6, 2: 289–304.

Broué, Pierre 1977, *Le parti bolchevique. Histoire du PC de l'URSS*, Paris: Les Éditions de Minuit.

Broué, Pierre 2006 [1971], *The German Revolution 1917–1923*, Chicago, IL: Haymarket Books.

Der Brüsseler Kongreß gegen Imperialismus und für nationale Unabhängigkeit vom 10.–15. Februar 1927 in Brüssel [1927], Berlin: Liga gegen Imperialismus und für nationale Unabhängigkeit.

Bucharin, Nikolai 1925a, *Der Imperialismus und die Akkumulation des Kapitals*, Vienna and Berlin (Marxistische Bibliothek, Volume IX).

Bucharin, Nikolai 1925b, 'Der Imperialismus und die Akkumulation des Kapitals', *Unter dem Banner des Marxismus*, 1, 1: 21–63; 2: 231–90.

Bucharin, Nikolai 1925c, 'Das wirtschaftliche Wachstum und das Problem des Arbeiter- und Bauernblocks', *Internationale. Zeitschrift für Theorie des Marxismus*, 8, 3–4: 3–17.

Bukharin, Nikolai 1928a, 'Draft Programme of the Communist International. Adopted by the Programme Commission of the E.C.C.I. on May 25, 1928', *International Press Correspondence*, 8, 30: 549–64.

Bukharin, Nikolai 1928b, 'The International Situation and the Tasks of the Comintern', *International Press Correspondence*, 8, 41: 727–40.

Burns, Arthur F. and Wesley C. Mitchell 1946, *Measuring Business Cycles*, New York: National Bureau of Economic Research.

Carr, Edward H. 1982, *Twilight of the Comintern, 1930–1935*, New York: Pantheon Books.

Chandler, Alfred D. 1977, *The Managerial Revolution in American Business*, Cambridge, MA: Harvard Belknap.

Cherkasov, Piotr 2002, *IMEMO: Institut Mirovoi Ekonomiki i Mezhdunarodnykh portret na fonde epoki*, Moscow: Ves Mir.

Churchill, Winston S. 1939, *Step by Step 1936–1939*, London: Macmillan.

The Colonies and Oppressed Nations in the Struggle for Freedom. Resolutions Adopted by the Executive Committee of the League against Imperialism and for National Independence, Berlin, June 2, 1931, Berlin: International Secretariat of the League against Imperialism.

Cot, Pierre 1974, 'Compte rendu de mission en URSS (mars-juillet 1944)', *Cahiers d'Histoire de l'Institut Maurice Thorez*, 8, 6/7/8: 52–74, 162–76, 262–77.

Dalin, Sergey A. 1936, *Ekonomicheskaya politika ruzvelta*, Moscow: Ekonomicheskoe Izd-vo.

Day, Richard B. 1981, *The 'Crisis' and the 'Crash'. Soviet Studies of the West (1917–1939)*, London: NLB.

De Man, Henry 1919, *The Remaking of a Mind. A Soldier's Thought on War and Reconstruction*, New York: Charles Scribner's Sons.

Der koloniale und nationale Befreiungskampf 1931, Berlin: Internationales Sekretariat der Liga gegen Imperialismus und für nationale Unabhängigkeit.

Deutscher, Isaac 1949, *Stalin: A Political Biography*, New York: Oxford University Press.

Dimitrov, Georgi 1951, *Selected Speeches and Articles. With an Introduction by Harry Pollitt*, London: Lawrence & Wishart.

Dobb, Maurice 1957, 'Some Economic Revaluations', *The Marxist Quarterly*, 4, 1: 2–7.

Dobbs, Michael 2013, *Six Months in 1945. FDR, Stalin, Churchill and Truman – From World War to Cold War*, London: Arrow Books.

Dubrovskiy, Sergey M. 1963 [1925], *Stolipinskaya zemelnaya reforma*, Moscow: Nauka.

Duda, Gerhard 1994, *Jenö Varga und die Geschichte des Instituts für Weltwirtschaft und Weltpolitik in Moskau 1921–1970. Zu den Möglichkeiten und Grenzen wissenschaftlicher Auslandsanalyse in der Sowjetunion*, Berlin: Akademie-Verlag.

Dunlap, John R. 1927, 'Why Panics Now End Quickly. How the Federal Reserve Banking System has Abolished Prolonged Industrial Depressions', *Industrial Management*, 73, 1: 5–8.

Dupeux, Louis 1979, *National bolchevisme: stratégie communiste et dynamique conservatrice*, Paris: H. Campion, 2 vols.

Engerman, David C. 2009, *Know Your Enemy: The Rise and Fall of America's Soviet Experts*, Oxford: Oxford University Press.

Fischer, Georg 1979, *Vom aufrechten Gang eines Sozialisten. Ein Parteiarbeiter erzählt*, Berlin and Bonn: Verlag J.M.W. Dietz.

Gaddis, John Lewis 1997, *We Now Know: Rethinking Cold War History*, Oxford: Clarendon Press.

Gansauge, Petra 1989, *Eugen Vargas Beitrag zur Gestaltung der marxistisch-leninistischen Monopoltheorie innerhalb der Kommunistischen Internationale*, PhD, Karl-Marx-Universität, Sektion Wirtschaftswissenschaften, Leipzig.

Gilbert, Martin 2006, *Churchill and America*, London: Pocket Books.

Goitsch, Heinrich 1944, *Niemals!*, Munich: Zentralverlag der NSDAP.

Göncöl, G. 1969, 'Some Aspects of the Theoretical Work of Eugen Varga', *Acta Oeconomica*, 4, 1: 89–98.

Grossmann, Henryk 1929, *Das Akkumulations- und Zusammenbruchsgesetz des kapitalistischen Systems. (Zugleich eine Krisentheorie)*. Schriften des Instituts für Sozialforschung an der Universität Frankfurt am Main, Leipzig: C.L. Hirschfeld Verlag.

Grossmann, Henryk 1992 [1929], *The Law of Accumulation and Breakdown of the Capitalist System. Being also a Theory of Crisis*, London: Pluto Press.

Grossmann, Henryk 2000, 'The Theory of Economic Crisis', in *Value, Capitalist Dynam-*

ics, and Money: Research in Political Economy, edited by Paul Zarembka and Susanne Soederberg, 16: 171–80.

Gurland, Arkadij 1930, 'Absatz und Verwertung im Kapitalismus: zur neuesten Diskussion des Zusammenbruchsproblem', *Der Klassenkampf. Marxistische Blätter*, 4, 3: 75–83.

Gurvich, Esfir I. 1937, *Poslevoennaya Amerika. Zagnivanie amerikanskogo kapitalizma*, Moscow: Gos. Ekonomicheskoe Izd-vo.

Haithcox, John Patrick 1971, *Communism and Nationalism in India: M.N. Roy and Comintern Policy 1920–1939*, Princeton, NJ: Princeton University Press.

Harrison, James P. 1970, *The Communists and Chinese Peasant Rebellions: A Study in the Rewriting of Chinese History*, London: Victor Gollanz Ltd.

Hedeler, Wladislaw s.d., 'Nicolai Bucharins Studie über die Akkumulation des Kapitals (1914/1925)', unpublished paper, available at: http://www.internationale-rosa-luxem burg-gesellschaft.de

Hevesi, Gyula 1959, *Ergy mérnök a forradalomban. Negy évtized történelmi időkben*, Budapest: Európa Könyvkiadó.

History of the C.P.S.U.(b): Short Course 1954, Moscow: Foreign Languages Publishing House, 1954.

Hochman, Jiří 1984, *The Soviet Union and the Failure of Collective Security, 1934–1938*, Ithaca, NY: Cornell University Press.

Horn, Gerd-Rainer 1996, *European Socialists Respond to Fascism: Ideology, Activism and Contingency in the 1930s*, Oxford: Oxford University Press.

Howard, M.C. and J.E. King 1989, *A History of Marxian Economics: Volume 1, 1883–1929*, Princeton, NJ: Princeton University Press.

Hutchinson, Lester 1935, *Conspiracy at Meerut*, London: Allen & Unwin.

James, Harold 1996, *International Monetary Cooperation Since Bretton Woods*, Washington DC/Oxford: International Monetary Fund/Oxford University Press.

Jones, Mike [s.d.], 'Germany', available at: http://www.marxists.org/history/etol/rev hist/backiss/vol5/no2/jones.html#n19

Kahan, Vilém 1976, 'The Communist International, 1919–1943: The Personnel of its Highest Bodies', *International Review of Social History*, 21, 2: 151–85.

Kaldor, N. and M.F.W. Joseph 1943, *Economic Reconstruction After the War*, London: English University Press.

Kautsky, Károly [Karl] 1907 [1906], *Marx gazdasági tanai*, Budapest: Grill Károly.

Kautsky, Karl 1918, *Die Diktatur des Proletariats*, Vienna: Wiener Volksbuchhandlung.

Keins, Dzh. M. [John Maynard Keynes] 1922, *Ekonomyckeskie posledstviya mira*, Moscow: Goz. Izd-vo, translated by D.P. Konchalovskiy and Zh.M. Dvolaitskiy.

Kennan, George F. 1947, 'The Source of Soviet Conduct', *Foreign Affairs*, 25, 4: 566–82.

Kennan, George F. 1967, *Memoirs 1925–1950*, Boston: Little, Brown and Company.

Kershaw, Ian 2002, *Hitler 1936–1945: Nemesis*, London: Penguin Books.
Keynes, John M. 1940, *How to Pay for the War*, London: Thornton Butterworth.
Kohn, Hans 1960, *The Mind of Germany: The Education of a Nation*, New York: Harper Torchbooks.
Komját, Irén 1982, *Die Geschichte der Inprekorr. Zeitung der Kommunistischen Internationale (1921–1939)*, Frankfurt: Verlag Marxistische Blätter.
Kondratieff, N.D. 1927, 'Das Problem der Prognose in Sonderheit der socialwirtschaftlichen', *Annalen der Betriebswirtschaft*, 1, 1: 41–62; 2: 221–52.
Kondratieff, N.D. 1944 [1926], 'The Long Waves in Economic Life', in *Readings in Business Cycle Theory, Selected by a Committee of The American Economic Association*, Philadelphia, PA: The Blakiston Company.
Korsch, Karl 1996, 'Krise des Marxismus. Schriften 1928–1935', in *Karl Korsch Gesamtausgabe*, Volume 5, edited and introduced by Michael Buckmiller, Amsterdam: Stichting Beheer IISG.
Kozlov, Nicholas N. and Eric D. Weitz 1989, 'Reflections on the Origin of the "Third Period": Bukharin, the Comintern, and the Political Economy of Weimar Germany', *Journal of Contemporary History*, 24, 3: 387–410.
Krausz, Tamás 2011, 'Lenin's Legacy Today', *The Platypus Review*, September, available at: http://platypus1917.org/2011/08/31/lenin%E2%80%99s-legacy-today/
Kriegel, Annie and Stéphane Courtois 1997, *Eugen Fried. Le grand secret du PCF*, Paris: Éditions du Seuil.
Kuhn, Rick 2004, 'Economic Crisis and Socialist Revolution: Henryk Grossman's Law of Accumulation, its First Critics and his Responses', in *Neoliberalism in Crisis, Accumulation, and Rosa Luxemburg's Legacy (Research in Political Economy*, Volume 21), edited by Paul Zarembka and Susanne Soederberg, Amsterdam: Elsevier Jai.
Kuhn, Rick 2006, 'Henryk Grossmann on Imperialism', Paper for 'New Directions in Marxist Theory', Historical Materialism Conference, School of Oriental and African Studies, London 8–10 December.
Kuhn, Rick 2007, *Henryk Grossman and the Recovery of Marxism*, Urbana, IL: University of Illinois Press.
Kuhn, Rick 2013, 'Introduction to "The Change in the Original for Marx's Capital and Its Causes"', *Historical Materialism*, 31, 3: 117–37.
Kun, Béla 1921, *Von Revolution zu Revolution*, Vienna: Neue Erde.
Kuo, Thomas C. 1975, *Ch'en Tu-hsiu (1879–1942) and the Chinese Communist Movement*, South Orange: Seton Hall University Press.
Lange, Peer Helmar 1969, *Stalinismus versus 'Sozialfascismus' und 'Nationalfaschismus'; Revolutionspolitische Ideologie und Praxis unter Stalin 1927–1935*, Göppingen: A. Kümmerle.
Le Blanc, Paul 2013, 'Spider and Fly: The Leninist Philosophy of George Lukács', *Historical Materialism*, 21, 2: 47–75.

Lederer, Emil 1920, *Deutschlands Wiederaufbau und weltwirtschaftliche Neueingliederung durch Sozialisierung*, Tübingen: Verlag von J.C.B. Mohr (Paul Siebeck).

Lederer, Emil 1927, 'Monopole und Konjunktur', *Vierteljahrshefte zur Konjunkturforschung, Ergänzungsheft*, 2, 2: 13–22.

Lederer, E. [Emma] 1975, *Die Geschichtsauffassung der bürgerlichen Radikalen; die historischen Schriften von Pál Szende*, Budapest: Académiai Kiadó.

Lejbzon, Boris M. and Kirill K. Sirinja 1975, *Povorot v politike Kominterna*, Moscow: Mysl.

Lenin, V.I. 1965a [1920], *Kommunismus* in *Lenin Collected Works*, Volume 31, Moscow: Progress Publishers.

Lenin, V.I. 1965b [1920], *The Second Congress of the Communist International. July 19–August 7, 1920*, in *Collected Works*, Volume 31, Moscow: Progress Publishers.

Lenin, V.I. 1972 [1918], *The Immediate Task of the Soviet Government*, in *Collected Works*, Volume 27, Moscow: Progress Publishers.

Lewerenz, Elfriede 1975, *VII. Kongress der Kommunistischen Internationale. Referate und Resolutionen*, Frankfurt am Main: Verlag Marxistische Blätter.

Maiski, Ivan M. 1967, *Memoiren eines Sowjetischen Botschafters*, Berlin: Das Europäische Buch.

Manchester, William 1989, *The Last Lion. Winston Spencer Churchill: Alone 1932–1940*, New York: Bantam Double Day.

Manchester, William and Paul Reid 2013, *The Last Lion. Winston Spencer Churchill: Defender of the Realm, 1940–1965*, New York: Bantam Books Trade Paperbacks.

Marx, Karl 1954, *Capital: A Critique of Political Economy*, Volume I, Moscow: Foreign Languages Publishing House.

Marx, Karl 1959, *Capital, A Critique of Political Economy*, Volume III, Moscow: Foreign Languages Publishing House.

Materialien über den Stand der Bauernbewegung in den wichtigsten Ländern 1925, edited and introduced by Eugen Varga, Hamburg: Verlag Carl Hoym Nachf. Louis Cahnbley.

McDermott, Kevin 1995, 'Stalin and the Comintern During the "Third Period", 1928–33', *European History Quarterly*, 25, 3: 409–29.

Mekhlis, L., Y. Varga and V. Karpinsky 1938, *The USSR and the Capitalist Countries*, Moscow: Foreign Languages Publishing House.

Mendelson, L. [Lev A.] 1931, 'O nekotorykh problemakh mirovogo krizisa', *Bolshevik*, 12, 6: 21–37.

Mitchell, Wesley C. 1927 [1913], *Business Cycles: The Problem and Its Setting*, with a Foreword by Edwin F. Gay, New York: National Bureau of Economic Research.

Molotov, V.M. 1930, *The Developing Crisis of World Capitalism. The Revolutionary Crisis and the Tasks of the Comintern. Report of the Delegation of the Communist Party of the Soviet Union in the Executive Committee of the Communist International. Report and Concluding Speech Delivered at the XVI Congress of the C.P.S.U., Moscow, July 5–7, 1930*, London: Modern Books Ltd.

Mommen, André 2002, *Eens komt de grote crisis van het kapitalisme. Leven en werk van Jenő Varga*, Brussels: IMAVO.
Mommen, André 2010, 'Jenő Varga and the Economic Policy of the Hungarian Soviet Republic', in *A Magyarországi tanácsköztársaság és a kelet-európai forradalmak*, edited by Tamás Krausz and Judit Vertés, Budapest: L'Harmattan-ELTE.
Mommen, André 2011, *Stalin's Economist: The Economic Contributions of Jenő Varga*, London and New York: Routledge.
Motylev, Wolf 1931, 'Osnovye problemy sovremennogo myrovogo krizisa', *Bolshevik*, 12, 4: 56–70.
Motylev, Wolf 1935, 'Critical Introduction to Rosa Luxemburg's Economic Works', available at: http://libcom.org/library/critical-introduction-rosa-luxemburgs-economic-works-wolf-motylev [Russian text available at: http://trst.narod.ru/rl/00.htm].
Muhs, K[arl] 1931, 'Das Gesetz der Fallenden Profitrate und die Zusammenbruchstendenz des Kapitalismus', *Jahrbücher für Nationalökonomie und Statistik*, 135: 16–18.
Neisser, Hans 1927, 'Zur Theorie des wirtschaftlichen Gliechgewichts', *Kölner Sozialpolitische Vierteljahresschrift. Zeitschrift des Forschungsinstituts für Sozialwissenschaften in Köln*, 6, 2: 123–37.
Neisser, Hans 1931, 'Das Gesetz der fallenden Profitrate als Krisen- und Zusammenbruchsgesetz', *Die Gesellschaft. Internationale Revue für Sozialismus und Politik*, 8, 1: 72–85.
Neisser, Hans 1944, *The Problem of Reparations, Studies in Postwar Reconstruction*, 4, The American Labor Conference on International Affairs, New York, July.
Neisser, Hans 1936, *Some International Aspects of the Business Cycle*, Philadelphia, PA: University of Pennsylvania Press.
[Pannekoek, Anton] 1934, 'Die Zusammenbruchstheorie des Kapitalismus', *Rätekorrespondenz. Theoretisches und Diskussionsorgan für die Rätebewegung*, 1, 1(June): 1–20.
Pawlowski, Dr. Eugen [Eugen Varga] 1921, *Der Bankrott Deutschlands*, Hamburg: Verlag der Kommunistischen Internationale, Auslieferungsstelle für Deutschland: Carl Hoym Nachf. Louis Cahnbley, Druck von Konrad Hauf, Hamburg 8.
Pawlowski, Dr. Eugen [Eugen Varga] 1923, *Deutschland eine Kolonie?*, Berlin: Vereinigung Internationaler Verlagsanstalten.
Péteri, György 1984 [1979], *Effects of World War I: War Communism in Hungary*, New York: Brooklyn College Press.
Protokoll. Erweiterte Exekutive der Kommunistischen Internationale. Moskau, 22. November–16. Dezember 1926 1927, Hamburg: Verlag der Kommunistischen Internationale.
Protokoll des III. Kongresses der Kommunistischen Internationale (Moskau, 22. Juni bis 12. Juli 1921) 1921, Hamburg: Verlag der Kommunistischen Internationale.

Protokoll Fünfter Kongresses der Kommunistischen Internationale 1924, Hamburg: Verlag Carl Hoym.

Radek, Karl 1923, 'Leo Schlageter: The Wanderer into the Void, Speech at a Plenum of the Executive Committee of the Communist International, June 1923', *The Labour Monthly*, 5, 3: 152–8.

Report of the National Conference of the League against Imperialism (British Section) 1931, London: League against Imperialism.

Resolutions Passed at the Session of the General Council Held in Brussels on the 9th, 10th and 11th December 1927 [1928], Berlin: League against Imperialism.

Robrieux, Philippe 1975, *Maurice Thorez. Vie secrète et vie publique*, Paris: Fayard.

Roh, Kyung Deok 2010, *Stalin's Think Tank: The Varga Institute and the Making of the Stalinist Idea of World Economy and Politics, 1927–1953*, PhD of Philosophy, Chicago, IL: University of Chicago.

Rue, John R. 1966, *Mao Tse-tung in Opposition 1927–1945*, Stanford, CA: Hoover Institution on War, Revolution and Peace, Stanford University Press.

Sakmyster, Thomas 2012, *A Communist Odyssey: The Life of József Pogány*, Budapest and New York: Central European University Press.

Schmitt, Carl 1932, *Der Begriff des Politischen*, Berlin: Duncker & Humblot.

Schorske, Carl E. 1998, *Thinking with History: Explorations in the Passage to Modernism*, Princeton, NJ: Princeton University Press.

Sharma, G.K. 1963, *Labour Movement in India (Its Past and Present)*, Jullundur, Delhi and Ambala: University Press.

'Sixth World Congress of the Communist International (Full Report)' 1928, *International Press Correspondence*, 8, 39–70: 705–1277.

Smyser, William T. 1999, *From Yalta to Berlin: The Cold War Struggle over Germany*, London: Macmillan.

Soviet Views on the Post-War World Economy: An Official Critique of Varga's 'Changes in the Economy of Capitalism Resulting from the Second World War' 1948, translated by Leo Gruliow, Washington, DC: Public Affairs Press.

Sovremennyi kreditnyi krizis – Diskussiya v Institute Mirovogo, Khozyaystvo i Mirovoi Politiki Komakademii 1932, Moscow: Partizdat, 1932.

Stalin, Joseph V. 1947, *Report on the Work of the Central Committee to the Seventeenth Congress of the C.P.S.U.b*, in *Problems of Leninism*, Moscow: Foreign Languages Publishing House.

Stalin, Joseph V. 1954, *The Fourteenth Congress of the C.P.S.U.(B.). Political report of the Central Committee*, in *Works*, Volume 11, Moscow: Foreign Languages Publishing House.

Stalin, Joseph V. 1955a, *Report to the Seventeenth Party Congress on the work of the Central Committee of the C.P.S.U.(B.), January 26, 1934*, in *Works*, Volume 12, Moscow: Foreign Languages Publishing House.

Stalin, Joseph V. 1955b, *Political report of the Central Committee to the Sixteenth Party Congress of the C.P.S.U.(B.), June 27, 1930*, in *Works*, Volume 12, Moscow: Foreign Languages Publishing House.

Stalin, Joseph V. 1975, *The Seventh Enlarged Plenum of the E.C.C.I., November 22–December 16*, in *On the Opposition*, Peking: Foreign Languages Press.

Sternberg, Fritz 1929, *Der Imperialismus und seine Kritiker*, Berlin: Soziologische Verlagsanstalt.

Sternberg, Fritz 1947, *The Coming Crisis*, New York: The John Day Company.

Tarnow, Fritz 1928, *Warum arm sein?*, Berlin: Verlagsgesellschaft des Allgemeinen Deutschen Gewerkschaftsbundes.

'Tenth Plenum of the E.C.C.I.' 1929, *International Press Correspondence*, 9, 40–53: 834–1144.

Theses and Resolutions. XII Plenum E.C.C.I. [1932], London: Modern Books.

Thomas, Albert, Emil Lederer and Otto Suhr 1928, *Angestellte und Arbeiter. Wandlungen in Wirtschaft und Gesellschaft. Drei Vorträge gehalten auf dem 3. AfA-Gewerkschaftskongreß in Hamburg 1928*, Berlin: Freier Volksverlag GmbH.

Tikos, Laszlo 1965a, *E. Vargas Tätigkeit als Wirtschaftsanalytiker und Publizist in der ungarischen Sozialdemokratie, in der Komintern, in der Akademie der Wissenschaften der UdSSR*, Tübingen and Cologne: Böhlau-Verlag.

Tikos, Laszlo 1965b, 'Eugen Varga: A Reluctant Conformist', *Problems of Communism*, 14, 1: 71–4.

Tooze, J. Adam 1999, 'Weimar's Statistical Economics: Ernst Wagemann, the Reich's Statistical Office, and the Institute of Business Cycle Research, 1925–33', *Economic History Review*, 52, 3: 523–43.

Toward the United Front. Proceedings of the Fourth Congress of the Communist International, 1922, 2012 [1923], edited and translated by John Riddell, Chicago, IL: Haymarket Books.

Trachtenberg, Marc 2005, 'The Marshall Plan as tragedy', *Journal of Cold War Studies*, 7, 1: 135–40.

Trotsky, Leon and E. Varga 1921, *The International Situation: A Study of Capitalism in Collapse (Presented to the Moscow Congress, 1921)*, London: Communist Party of Great Britain.

Tugwell, Rexford Guy 1927, *Industry's Coming of Age*, New York: Harcourt, Brace and Company.

Tugwell, Rexford Guy 1977, *Roosevelt's Revolution. The First Year – A Personal Perspective*, New York: Macmillan.

Turner, Carl B. 1969, *An Analysis of Soviet Views on John Maynard Keynes*, Durham, NC: Duke University Press.

Van Slyke, Lyman P. 1967, *Enemies and Friends: The United Front in Chinese History*, Stanford, CA: Stanford University Press.

Varga, Eugen 1921a [1920], *Die wirtschaftspolitischen Probleme der proletarischen Diktatur*, Vienna: Verlag der Arbeiter-Buchhandlung; Hamburg: C. Hoym Verlag.

Varga, Eugen 1921b, 'Die Krise der kapitalistischen Weltwirtschaft', Hamburg: C. Hoym Verlag Nachf.

Varga, Eugen 1921c, 'Economic Basis of Imperialism in the US of North America', *The Communist International*, 2, 16–17: 58–67.

Varga, Eugen 1922a, *Die Krise der kapitalistischen Weltwirtschaft. Zweite, vermehrte und umgearbeitete Auflage*, Hamburg: Verlag der Kommunistischen Internationale, Carl Hoym Verlag Nachf. Louis Cahnbley.

Varga, Eugen 1922b, *Die Lage der Weltwirstschaft und der Gang der Weltwirtschaftspolitik in den letzten drei Jahren*, Verlag der Kommunistischen Internationale, Auslieferungsstelle für Deutschland: Carl Hoym Nachf. Louis Cahnbley, Hamburg.

Varga, Eugen 1922c, *The Process of Capitalist Decline. Report to the IV. Congress of the Communist International*, Communist International, in Commission: Carl Hoym Nachf. L. Cahnbley, Hamburg 8.

Varga, Eugen 1924, *The Decline of Capitalism*, London: Communist Party of Great Britain.

Varga, Eugen 1927a, 'Kapitalexport in der Weltwirtschaft', *Die Internationale*, 10, 12: 363–9.

Varga, Eugen 1927b, 'Issledonavie konyunkturi i teoriya krizisov', *Mirovoe khozyaystvo i mirovaya politika*, 2, 12: 1–15.

Varga, Eugen 1927c, 'Die ersten zehn Jahre der Niederangsperiode des Kapitalismus', *Die Kommunistische Internationale*, 7, 45–6: 2206–15.

Varga, Eugen 1928a, *The Decline of Capitalism: The Economics of the Decline of Capitalism after Stabilisation*, London: Communist Party of Great Britain.

Varga, Eugen 1928b, 'Problemy kapitalisticheskoy ratsionalisatsii', *Mirovoe khozyaystvo i mirovaya politika*, 3, 5: 12–18.

Varga, Eugen 1929, 'Amerikanskiy birzhevoy krakh i obshchiy krizis', *Problemy ekonomiki*, 1, 12: 142–51.

Varga, Eugen 1930a, 'Akkumulation und Zusammenbruch des Kapitalismus', *Unter dem Banner des Marxismus*, 4, 1: 65–95.

Varga, Eugen 1930b, 'Nakoplenie i krakh kapitalizma', *Problemy ekonomiki*, 2, 3: 31–62.

Varga, Eugen 1930c, 'Krizis v SShA-Obshchiy ekonomicheskii krizis', *Mirovoye khozyaystvo i mirovaya politika*, 5, 2: 5–8.

Varga, Eugen 1930d, 'Mirovoy krizis ego problemy. Ispravlennaya stenogramma dokladat. Vargi v Institute Ekonomiki LOKA 10 maya 1930 g.', *Problemy marksizma* [Leningrad], 3, 4–6: 89–110.

Varga, Eugen 1930e, 'Razvitie i perspektivy mirovogo ekonomicheskogo krizisa', *Bolshevik*, 11, 23–4, 36–59.

Varga, Eugen 1931, 'Wirtschaft und Wirstschaftspolitik im 3. Vierteljahr 1931', *Internationale Pressekorrespondenz*, 11, 18: 2381–408.
Varga, Eugen 1932a, 'Diskussiya po voprosu o problemakh mirovogo krizisa. Zaklyuchitelnoe slovo. Institut mirovogo khozyaystva i mirovoy politiki, 29-XII-1931 g., 14-I-1932 g.', *Problemy mirovogo krizisa*, Moscow: Partizdat.
Varga, Eugen 1932b, 'Sotsial-fasisty za interventsiyu', in *Sotsial-fashism – organizator interventsiyu*, Moscow: Partizdat.
Varga, Eugen 1933, 'Wirtschaft und Wirtschaftspolitik im 2. Vierteljahr 1933', *Rundschau über Politik, Wirtschaft und Arbeiterbewegung*, 2, 30 (25 August): 1109–32.
Varga, Eugen 1934a, 'Wirtschaft und Wirtschaftspolitik im 4. Vierteljahr 1933', *Rundschau über Politik, Wirtschaft und Arbeiterbewegung*, 3, 18 (27 February): 2633–58.
Varga, Eugen 1934b, *Novoye yavleniya v mirivom ekonomicheskom krizise*, Moscow: Partizdat.
Varga, Eugen 1934c, 'De Man's Plan is a Fraud on the Working Class', *The Communist International*, 11, 7: 514–24.
Varga, Eugen 1935a [1934], *The Great Crisis and Its Political Consequences*, London: Modern Books Limited.
Varga, Eugen 1935b, 'Dva goda fashizma v Germanii', *Bolshevik*, 12, 1: 57–75.
Varga, Eugen 1935c, 'Wachsende Schwierigkeiten des deutschen Faschismus', *Die Kommunistische Internationale*, 16, 1: 63–84.
Varga, Eugen 1938, *Kapitalizm i sotsializm za 20 let*, Moscow: Partizdat, 1938.
Varga, Eugen 1939a [1937], *Two Systems – Socialist Economy and Capitalist Economy*, London: Lawrence & Wishart; American edition: New York: International Publishers (translation by R. Page Arnot).
Varga, Eugen 1939b, review article, 'Winston S. Churchill, *Step by Step*', *Mirovoye khozyaystvo i mirovaya politika*, 14, 9: 249–50.
Varga, Eugen 1940, review article, 'John M. Keynes, *How to Pay for the War*', *Mirovoye khozyaystvo i mirovaya politika*, 15, 6: 200–2.
Varga, Eugen 1946, *Izmenenniya v ekonomike kapitalizma v itoge vtoroi mirovoi voiny*, Moscow: Gosudarstvennoe izdatelstvo politicheskoi literatury.
Varga, Eugen 1947a, 'Democracy of a New Type', *The Labour Monthly*, 27, 8: 235–42; 9: 276–9.
Varga, Eugen 1947b, 'The General Crisis of Capitalism (Features of the Home and Foreign Policy of the Capitalist Countries During the Epoch of the General Crisis of Capitalism)', *The Labour Monthly*, 29, 1: 23–8; 29, 2: 56–61.
Varga, Eugen 1947c, 'Anglo-American Rivalry and Partnership. A Marxist View', *Foreign Affairs*, 25 (March): 583–94.
Varga, Eugen 1947d, 'The Marhall Plan and the Approaching Economic Crisis in America', *New Times*, 5, 39: 5–7.
Varga, Eugen s.d. [1947], *Demokratie neuer Art*, Berlin: Verlag 'Tägliche Rundschau'.

Varga, Eugen 1949, 'Protiv reformitskogo napravleniya v rabotakh po imperializmu', *Voprosy ekonomiki*, 2, 3: 79–88.
Varga, Eugen 1955 [1953], *Grundfragen der Ökonomik und Politik des Imperialismus (nach dem Zweiten Weltkrieg)*, Berlin: Dietz Verlag.
Varga, Eugen 1968, *Politico-Economic Problems of Capitalism*, Moscow: Progress Publishers.
Varga, Eugen 1974, *Izbrannye proizvedeniya*, Moscow: Nauka, 3 Vols.
Varga, Eugen 1976, *A proletárdiktatura gazdaságpolitikája. Válogatott írások 1912–1922*, Budapest: Kossuth Könyvkiádo.
Varga, Eugen 1978, *A nagy válság. Válogatott írások, 1924–1943*, Budapest: Kossuth Könyvkiádo.
Varga, Eugen 1979a, *Neue Erscheinungen während der Weltwirtschaftskrise*, in *E.S. Varga. Ausgewählte Schriften 1918–1964*, Volume 2, *Die Wirtschaftskrisen*, Berlin: Akademie-Verlag.
Varga, Eugen 1979b, *Ausgewählte Schriften 1918–1964*, Volume 2, *Die Wirtschaftskrisen*, Berlin: Akademie-Verlag.
Varga, Eugen 1981, *A tőkés gazdaság a II. Világháború után. Válogatott írások (1945–1954)*, Budapest: Kossuth Könyvkiadó.
Varga, E. and A. Lozovskiy 1921, *Mirovoi krizis. Zadachi i taktika Profsoyuzov*, Moscow: Profsoyuz.
Volodin, Viktor S. 1950, 'Izheteoriya Keinsa', *Voprosy ekonomiki*, 3, 1: 108–14.
Volodin, Viktor S. 1953, *Keins – ideology monopolisticheskogo kapitala*, Moscow: Izd-vo Akademii Nauk SSR.
Wagemann, Ernst 1927, 'Einführung in die Probleme der Konjunkturforschung', in *Arbeitsrecht, Arbeitsmarkt und Arbeitsschutz. Ausgewählte Vorträge aus einem Ausbildungskursus der Reichsarbeitsverwaltung*, Berlin: Verlag des Reichsarbeitsblattes (Reimar Hobbing), Sonderheft zum *Reicharbeitsblatt*, 38: 27–32.
Wagemann, Ernst, Hans Vogel and Henry Bruere 1931, *Economic Crises: Unemployment*, Paris: Erné.
Wahl, Manfred P. 1953, *Varga und die neuere kommunistische Kritik am modernen Kapitalismus*, PhD, Eberhard-Karls-Universität zu Tübingen.
Watson, Derek 2005, *Molotov: A Biography*, Basingstoke: Palgrave.
White, Dan S. 1992, *Lost Comrades: Socialists of the Front Generation 1918–1945*, Cambridge, MA: Harvard University Press.
'Das Wirtschaftsabkommen mit der Sowjet-Union. Von unterrichteter Seite', *Der Deutsche Volkswirt*, 14, 21: 658–9.
Woodcock, George 1974, *Who Killed the British Empire? An Inquest*, London: Jonathan Cape.
Woytinski, Wladimir 1927, 'Unterkonsumtion als Krisenursache', *Magazin der Wirtschaft*, 3, 21: 822–6.

Wurm, Cristoph 1929, 'Die Reservearmee. Die Arbeitslosigkeit in der Nachkriegsperiode', *Die Kommunistische Internationale*, 10, 2: 395–416.
X 1947, 'Communism in Eastern Europe', *The Economist*, 7 June: 893–4; 14 June: 942–3.
XI Plenum IKKI 1931. Stenograficheskiy otchet 1932, Moscow: Partiynoe Izdatelstvo.
XIII Plenum IKKI. Stenograficheskiy Otchet 1933, Moscow: Partizdat.
'Zur Marxschen Akkumulations- und Zusammenbruchstheorie' 1934, *Rätekorrespondenz. Theoretisches und Diskussionsorgan für die Rätebewegung*, 1, 4 (September): 1–18.

Works Cited by Eugen Varga

Additional Report of the Special Committee Investigating the National Defense Program, Harry S. Truman, Chairman, 3 March 1944, Washington: Government Printing Office.
Additional Report of the Special Committee Investigating the National Defense Program 1944 Washington: US Government Printing Office.
Additional Report of the Special Committee Investigating the National Defense Program pursuant to S[enate] Res[olution] 71, Harry S. Truman, Chairman, 1944, Washington.
Allen, Frederick Lewis 1944, 'Who's Getting the Money?', *The Harper's Magazine*, 189, 1129 (June): 1–10.
Annual Abstract of Statistics 1956–, Published by Office for National Statistics: London: HMSO.
Annual Abstract of Statistics 1961, London: HMSO, Central Statistical Office.
An analysis of the sources of war finance and estimates of the national income and expenditure in the years 1938 to 1944. Presented to Parliament by the financial secretary to the Treasury by command of His Majesty, April 1945, London: HMSO, Cmd. 6623.
Akten der Brüsseler Sachverständigenkonferenz vom 16. bis 22. Dezember 1920, 1921, in *Sammlung von Aktenstücken über die Verhandlungen auf der Sachverständigenkonferenz zu Brüssel vom 16. bis 22. Dezember 1920*, Berlin: Auswärtigen Amt.
Allen, Frederick Lewis 1944, 'Who's getting the money?', *Harper's Magazine*, 189, 1129: 1–10.
Amery, Leopold Stennett 1946, *The Washington Loan Agreements. A Critical Study of American Foreign Policy*, London: MacDonald and Company.
Angell, Norman 1909, *The Great Illusion*, London: Peace Committee of the Society of Friends.
Angell, Norman 1919, *The Peace Treaty and the Economic Chaos of Europe*, London: Swarthmore Press.

Asmis, Rudolf 1921, 'Afrikanische Weltprobleme', *Preußische Jahrbücher*, Berlin: Verlag von George Stilte, 128, December: 289–308.
Ballod, Karl 1919, *Der Zukunftstaat. Produktion und Konsum im Sozialstaat*, Stuttgart: J.H.W. Dietz.
Balogh, Thomas T. 1957, *The Political Economy of the Cold War*, London: The Hogarth Press, Fabian International Essays.
Barker, J. Ellis 1920, 'The World's Oil Resources and the United States', *The Contemporary Review*, 118, 659: 671–80.
Bauer, Otto 1912–13, 'Die Akkumulation des Kapitals', *Die Neue Zeit*, 31, I: 831–8 and 862–74.
Bauer, Otto 1919, *Der Weg zum Sozialismus*, Vienna: Ignaz Brand.
Bauer, Otto 1933, 'Der deutsche Faschismus und die Internationale', *Der Kampf. Sozialdemokratisches Monatschrift*, 26, 8–9: 320–1.
Berliner, Hans 1919, *Der bolschewistische Staat. Die Gestaltung der Russischen Sowjetrepublik durch die Kommunisten (Bolschwiki) dargestellt*, with an introduction by J. Borchardt, Berlin-Lichterfeld: Verlag der Lichtstrahlen.
Biennial Census of Manufactures 1925 1928, Washington: US Department of Commerce, Bureau of the Census, US Government Printing Office.
Birnbaum, Bruno 1927, *Organisation der Rationalisierung Amerika-Deutschland*, Berlin: Reimar Hobbing.
Bisson, T.A. 1933 *The Communist Movement in China*, New York: Foreign Policy Association, *Foreign Policy Reports*, 9, 4.
The Board of Trade Journal, London: HMSO.
Boese, Franz (ed.) 1926, *Krisis der Weltwirtschaft. Übervölkerung Westeuropas. Steuerüberwälzung, Verhandlungen des Vereins für Sozialpolitik in Wien*, Munich and Leipzig: Duncker & Humblot.
Brandt, Karl 1945, *The Reconstruction of World Agriculture*, New York: W.W. Norton & Company Inc.
Brant, Irving 1962, 'The Anti-Communist Hoax. I. Who are the right-wing's real enemies?', *The New Republic*, 28 May: 15–18.
Braunthal, Alfred 1927, *Die Entwicklungstendenzen der kapitalistischen Wirtschaft*, Berlin: Laubsche Verlagsbuchhandlung, Reichsleitung der Jungsozialisten mit Unterstützung von Dr. Max Adler, Wien/Engelbert Graf, Dr. Anna Siemsen.
Brelet, M. 1923, *La crise de la métallurgie. La politique économique et sociale du Comité des Forges*, Paris: Sagot.
Brockway, Fenner 1933, *The Bloody Traffic*, London: Gollancz.
Bucharin, N.I. 1922, *Oekonomik der Transformations-periode*, Hamburg: Verlag der Kommunistischen Internationale, Carl Hoym Nachf. Louis Cahnbley.
Bucharin, Nikolai 1926, *Der Imperialismus und die Akkumulation des Kapitals*, Vienna and Berlin: Verlag für Literatur und Politik.

Bucharin, Nikolai 1928, *Die internationale Lage und die Aufgaben der Kommunistischen Internationale. Bericht der Delegation der KPSU(B) beim EKKI an den 15. Parteitag*, Hamburg: Verlag Hoym Nachf.

Bukharin, Nicolai I. 1971 [1922], *Economics of the Transformation Period, with Lenin's critical remarks*, New York: Bergman Publishers.

Campion, Harry 1939, *Public and Private Property in Great Britain*, London: Oxford University Press.

Clark, Colin 1937, *National Income and Outlay*, London: Macmillan.

Cassel, Gustav 1923, *The Theory of Social Economy*, 2 Volumes, translated by Joseph McCabe, London: T. Fisher Unwin, Ltd.

Catlin, George 1947, 'Britain and the American elections', *The Fortnightly*, 167, 1: 27–34.

Chalmers, Thomas 1832, *On Political Economy in Connexion with the Moral State and Moral Prospects of Society*, Glasgow.

Chase, Stuart 1925, *The Tragedy of Waste*, New York: The Macmillan Co.

Clark, Grover 1936, *The Balance Sheets of Imperialism*, New York: Carnegie Endowment for International Peace, Division of Economics and History, Columbia University Press.

Commerce Yearbook 1926, United States Bureau of Foreign Commerce, Washington: US Government Printing Office.

Committee on Industry and Trade 1927, *Survey of Overseas Markets: Based on Material, Mainly Derived from Official Sources, with Regard to the Conditions Prevailing in Various Overseas Markets which Affect British Export Trade, Together with Statistical and Other Information*. London: HMSO.

Cox, Harold 1922, *The Problem of Population*, London: Jonathan Cape.

Czan-Shi 1934, 'The Chinese Red Army', *The Communist International*, 11, 7: 272–83.

'Der einheitliche Konsumverein in Sowjetrußland' 1920, *Russische Korrespondenz*, 1, 2: 6–8.

'Diary. Changes in the cost of living index: USA and UK' 1944, *Bulletin of the Oxford University Institute of Statistics*, 6, 7: 114–16.

Dade, H. 1921, 'Der Friedensvertrag und Deutschlands Versorgung mit landwirtschaftlichen Erzeugnissen', in M. Julius, H. Bredow, H. Dade et al. (eds.), *Der Friedensvertrag und Deutschlands Stellung in der Weltwirtschaft* (Herausgegeben von der Deutschen weltwirtschaftlichen Gesellschaft), Berlin: Springer.

Dalin, S.A. 1961, *Voenno-gosudartsvennyi monopolisticheskiy kapitalizm*, Moscow: Izd. Akademii Nauk.

Dan, Theodor 1932, 'Kriegsgefahr in Sicht!', *Der Kampf. Sozialdemokratisches Monatschrift*, 25, 4: 149–57.

Darré, Walther 1933, *Das Bauerntum als Lebensquell der Nordischen Rasse*, Munich: J.F. Lehmann.

Degras, Jane (ed.) 1956, *The Communist International 1919–1943 Documents*, Volume 1 1919–1922, Oxford: Oxford University Press.

Degras, Jane (ed.) 1957, *The Communist International 1919–1943 Documents*, Volume 2 1923–1928, Oxford: Oxford University Press.

Durig, Arnold 1928, 'Fließarbeit und Arbeitschutz', *Reichsarbeitsblatt*, 8, III, *Arbeitsschutz*, 2: 1–7.

The Economic Report of the President Transmitted to the Congress. January 18, 1961 1961, Washington: United States Government Printing Office.

Economic Survey for 1947 – The Battle for Output 1948, London: Popular Edition Prepared by the Central Office of Information, HMSO, Cmd. 7046.

Economic Report of the President Transmitted to the Congress, 20 January 1958, Washington: United States Government Printing Office.

Engels, Frederick 1977 [1844], *The Conditions of the Working-Class in England. From Personal Observation and Authentic Services*, in *Karl Marx and Frederick Engels Collected Works*, Volume 4, London: Lawrence & Wishart.

Erhebungen von Wirtschaftsrechnungen minderbemittelter Familien im Deutschen Reich; 320 Haushaltsrechnungen von Metallarbeitern 1909, Sonderheft zum Reichsarbeitsblatt: Berlin: Deutsches Kaiserlichen Statistischen Amt.

Final Report of the Committee on Industry and Trade 1928, Committee on Industry and Trade, London: His Majesty Statutory Office.

Final Report of the Committee on Industry and Trade 1929, London: HMSO.

'Financial, Industrial, Commercial Statistics United States' 1945/6, *Federal Reserve Bulletin*, Washington: Board of Governors of the Federal Reserve System, 31, 5; 32, 1.

Fisher, Irving 1925, 'The Decentralization and Suburbanization of Population', *Giant Power. Large Scale Electrical Development as a Social Factor. Annals of the American Academy of Political and Social Sciences*, 118: 96.

Fitzgerald, Patrick 1927, *Industrial Combination in England*, London: Pitman.

Friday, David 1921, *Profits, Wages and Prices*, New York: Harcourt, Brace and Howe.

From the first to the second five-year plan. A symposium by J. Stalin, V. Molotov, L. Kaganovich, K. Voroshilov, G. Orjonikidze, V. Kuibyshev, Y. Yakovlev [and] G. Grinko 1934, New York: International Publishers.

Further Factors in Industrial and Commercial Efficiency Being Part II of Survey of Industries, with an Introduction by the Committee [on Industry and Trade] 1929, London: His Majesty Stationary Office.

Germany's Economic Situation at the Turn of 1933–34 [Deutschlands wirtschaftliche Lage an der Jahreswende 1933–34] 1934, Berlin: Reichs-Kredit-Gesellschaft.

Grossmann, Henryk 1929, *Das Akkumulations- und Zusammenbruchsgezetz des kapitalistische Systems (Zugleich eine Krisentheorie)*, Leipzig: C.L. Hirschfeld.

Handwörterbuch der Staatswissenschaften 1909–11, 8 Volumes, Jena: G. Fischer Verlag.

Handbook of Labor Statistics 1924-1926 1927, United States Department of Labor, Bureau of Labor Statistics, Washington: United States Government Printing Office.

Helfferich, Karl 1913, *Der deutsche Volkswohlstand, 1888 bis 1913*, Berlin: G. Stilke.

Hettlage, Karl Maria 1940, 'Wer bezahlt den Krieg?', *Der Deutsche Volkswirt; Tägliche Rundschau*, 15, 12–13 (20 December): 475–80.

Herz, Friedrich Otto [1918], *Die Produktionsgrundlagen der österreichischen Industrie vor und nach dem Kriege: insbesonders im Vergleich mit Deutschland*, Vienna: Verlag für Fachliteratur.

Hildebrand, Gerhard 1912, *Die Erschutterung der Industrieherrschaft und des Industrie Sozialismus*, Jena: G. Fischer.

Hilferding, Rudolf 1910, *Das Finanzkapital. Eine Studie über die jüngste Entwicklung des Kapitalismus*, in *Marx-Studien. Blätter zur Theorie und Politik des Wissenschaftlichen Sozialismus*, Vienna: Verlag der Wiener Volksbuchhandlung Ignaz Brand & Co., VI. Gumpendorferstraße 18.

Hilferding, Rudolf 1924a, 'Probleme der Zeit', *Die Gesellschaft*, 1, 1: 1–29.

Hilferding, Rudolf 1924b, 'Handelspolitik und Agrarkrise', *Die Gesellschaft*, 1, 2: 113–29.

Hilferding, Rudolf 1924c, 'Probleme der Zeit', *Die Gesellschaft*, 1, 1/1: 1–29.

Hilferding, Rudolf 1924d, 'Handelspolitik und Agrarkrise', *Die Gesellschaft*, 1, 2: 113–29.

Hilferding, Rudolf 1926a, 'Politische Probleme. Zum Aufruf Wirths und zur Rede Silverbergs', *Die Gesellschaft*, 3, 4: 289–302.

Hilferding, Rudolf 1926b, intervention in *Krisis der Weltwirtschaft. Übervölkerung Westeuropas. Steuerüberwälzung, Verhandlungen des Vereins für Sozialpolitik in Wien*, edited by Franz Boese, Munich and Leipzig: Duncker & Humblot.

Hilferding, Rudolf [1927], 'Die Aufgaben der Sozialdemokratie in der Republik. Rede gehalten auf dem Parteitag zu Kiel, Mai 1927', in *Sozialdemokratischer Parteitag Kiel 1927*, Kiel: Chr. Haase Druck.

Hilferding, Rudolf [1927], 'Die Aufgaben der Sozialdemokratie in der Republik. Rede gehalten auf dem Parteitag zu Kiel, Mai 1926c, [lecture in] *Krisis der Weltwirtschaft. Übervölkerung Westeuropas. Steuerüberwälzung, Verhandlungen des Vereins für Sozialpolitik in Wien*, edited by Franz Boese, Munich and Leipzig: Duncker & Humblot.

Hirsch, Julius 1926, *Der amerikanische Wirtschaftswunder*, Berlin: S. Fischer.

Hirschberg, Dr. Max 1919, *Bolschewismus. Eine kritische Untersuchung über die amtlichen Veröffentlichungen der russischen Sowjet-Republik*, Leipzig: Duncker & Humblot.

Historical Statistics of the United States 1789–1945, A Supplement to the Statistical Abstract of the United States, prepared with the cooperation of the Social Science Research Council 1949, Washington: Bureau of the Census, United States Government Printing Office.

History of the Communist Party of the Soviet Union (Bolsheviks). Short Course [1939], New York: International Publishers Co. Inc.

Hunke, Heinrich 1943, 'Die Kernfragen des wirtschaftspolitischen Kampfes in der Gegenwart', *Die Deutsche Volkswirtschaft. Nationalsozialistischer Wirtschaftsdienst*, Berlin, 12, 27: 833.
International Yearbook of Agricultural Statistics 1926–7, Rome: International Institute of Agriculture.
International Yearbook of Agricultural Statistics 1932–3, Rome: International Institute of Agriculture.
International Statiscal Yearbook 1926, Geneva: League of Nations.
Investigation of the National Defense Program. Additional Report of the Special Committee Investigating the National Defense Program, Harry S. Truman, Chairman, 3 March 1944 1944, Washington: United States Printing Office.
Jahrbuch für Wirtschaft, Politik und Arbeiterbewegung 1925–26, Hamburg: Carl Hoym Verlag.
Jones, Eliot Logan 1921, *The Trust Problem in the USA*, New York: The Macmillan Co.
Kalecki, M. 1944, 'The White Paper on Employment Policy', *Bulletin of Oxford Institute of Statistics*, 6, 8: 131–5.
Kautsky, Karl 1907, *Die soziale Revolution*, 2nd edition, Berlin: Buchhandlung Vorwärts.
Kautsky, Karl 1909, *Der Weg zur Macht*, Berlin: Vorwärts.
Kautsky, Karl 1910, *Der Weg zur Macht. Politische Betrachtungen über das Hineinwachsen in die Revolution*, Berlin: Buchhandlung Vorwärts.
Kautsky, Karl 1919, *Terrorism and Communism. A Contribution to the Natural History of Revolution*, translated by W.H. Kerridge, London and Manchester: The National Labour Press.
Key, Helmer 1924, *Der Bankrott der Rekonstruktionspolitik und die Kolonialpolitik*, Berlin: W. De Gruyter.
Keynes, John Maynard 1920, *Economic Consequences of the Peace*, London: Macmillan and Co.
Keynes, John Maynard 1926, *The End of Laissez-Faire*, London: The Hogarth Press.
Keynes, John Maynard (ed.) 1928, *Britain's Industrial Future Being the Report of the Liberal Industrial Inquiry*, London: E. Benn.
Keynes, John Maynard 1940, *How to Pay for the War. A Radical Plan for the Chancellor of the Exchequer*, New York: Harcourt, Brace and Company.
Khmelnitskaya, E.L. 1959, *Monopolisticheskiy kapitalizm v Zanadnoy Germanii*, Moscow: IMO.
Koch, Waldemar 1910, *Die Industrialisierung Chinas*, Berlin: J. Springer.
Konjunkturstatistisches Handbuch 1933, Berlin: Institut für Konjunkturforschung.
Kuczynski, Jürgen 1934, *Die Entwicklung der Lage der Arbeiterschaft in Europa und Amerika 1870–1933. Statistische Studien zur Entwicklung der Reallöhne und Relativlöhne in England, Deutschland, USA, Frankreich und Belgien*, Basle: Philographischer Verlag.

Kuznets, Simon 1961, *Capital in the American Economy: Its Formation and Financing*, Princeton, NJ: Princeton University Press.

Kuusinen, Otto 1960, 'Modern Monopoly Capital and its Perspectives', *World Marxist Review*, 3, 4: 6–12.

Kuusinen, Otto 1964b, *War and Revolution*, in *Collected Works*, Volume 24, Moscow: Progress Publishers.

Kuusinen, Otto 1964c, *Revision of the Party Programme*, in *Collected Works*, Volume 26, Moscow: Progress Publishers.

Kuusinen, Otto 1964d, *One of the Fundamental Questions of the Revolution*, in *Collected Works*, Volume 25, Moscow: Progress Publishers.

Lachapelle, George 1921, *La vérité sur notre situation financière, la gestion des finances publiques, les moyens de trésorerie et l'accroissement de la dette, le problème des réparations, les dangers de l'inflation, remèdes et réformes*, Paris: G. Roustan.

Larin, Yuri 1927, *Chastnyi kapital v SSSR*, Moscow: Goz. Izd-vo.

Kent, George 1943, 'Black Market Meat', *American Mercury*, 20, 6: 721–7.

Kuczynski, René 1920, *Das Existenzmiminum und verwandte Fragen*, Berlin: Verlag Hans Robert Engelmann.

Kuznets, S. and L. Goldsmith 1952, *Income and Wealth of the United States: Trends and Structure*, International Association for Research in Income and Wealth: Income & Wealth Series, Cambridge: Bowes & Bowes.

Lederer, [Emil] 1921, 'Die Liquidation der Krise in den Vereinigten Staaten und ihre Lehren', *Weltwirtschaftliche Korrespondenz*, 2, 1 (7 February): 1–2.

Lenin, V.I. 1930 [1917], *Der Imperialismus als höchstes Stadium des Kapitalismus*, Vienna-Berlin: Verlag für Literatur und Politik.

Lenin, V.I. 1964a [1918], *The Immediate Tasks of the Soviet Government*, in *Lenin Collected Works*, Volume 27, Moscow: Progress Publishers.

Lenin, V.I. 1964b [1918], *The International Position of the Russian Soviet Republic and the Fundamental Tasks of the Socialist Revolution*, in *Lenin Collected Works*, Volume 27, Moscow: Progress Publishers.

Lenin, V.I. 1964c [1918], *Extraordinary Fourth Allrussian Congress of Soviets, March 14–18, 1918*, in *Lenin Collected Works*, Volume 27, Moscow: Progress Publishers.

Lenin, V.I. 1964d [1920], *Report on the International Situation and the Fundamental Tasks of the Communist International, July*, in *Collected Works*, Volume 31, Moscow: Progress Publishers.

Lenin, V.I. 1964e [1917], *Imperialism, the Highest Stage of Capitalism*, in *Collected Works*, Volume 22, Moscow: Progress Publishers.

Lenin, V.I. 1964f [1899], *Reply to Mr. P. Nezhdanov*, in *Collected Works*, Volume 4, Moscow: Progress Publishers.

Lenin, V.I. 1964g [1898], *A Note on the Question of the Market Theory*, in *Collected Works*, Volume 4, Moscow: Progress Publishers.

Lenin, V.I. 1964h [1899], *The Development of Capitalism in Russia*, in *Collected Works*, Volume 3, Moscow: Progress Publishers.

Lenin, V.I. 1964i [1920], *Left-Wing Communism: An Infantile Disorder*, in *Collected Works*, Volume 31, Moscow: Progress Publishers.

Lenin, V.I. 1964j [1916], *The Junius Pamphlet*, in *Collected Works*, Volume 31, Moscow: Progress Publishers.

Lenin, V.I. 1964k [1920], *The Eight All-Russian Congress of Soviets. December 22–29, 1920*, in *Collected Works*, Volume 31, Moscow: Progress Publishers.

Lenin, V.I. 1964l [1920], *Kommunismus: Journal of the Communist International*, in *Collected Works*, Volume 31, Moscow: Progress Publishers.

Lenin, V.I. 1964m, *A Turn in World Politics*, in *Collected Works*, Volume 23, Moscow: Progress Publishers.

Lenin, V.I. 1964n [1916], *Opportunism and the Collapse of the Second International*, in *Collected Works*, Volume 22, Moscow: Progress Publishers.

Lenin, V.I. 1964o [1915], *Socialism and War*, in *Collected Works*, Volume 21, Moscow: Progress Publishers.

Lenin, V.I. 1964p [1917], *The impending catastrophe and how to combat it*, in *Collected Works*, Volume 25, Moscow: Progress Publishers.

Lenin, V.I. 1964q [1917], *Can we go forward if we fear to advance towards socialism?*, in *Collected Works*, Volume 25, Moscow: Progress Publishers.

Lenin, V.I. 1964r [1917], *Introduction of socialism or exposure of plunder of the state*, in *Collected Works*, Volume 25, Moscow: Progress Publishers.

Lenin, V.I. 1964s [1916], *A caricature of Marxism and its imperialist economism*, in *Collected Works*, Volume 23, Moscow: Progress Publishers.

Labriola, Arturo 1928, 'Das Adriatische Problem', *Die Gesellschaft*, 5/1, 5: 359–74.

Lapinski, Pavel 1928, 'Der monopolistische Staatskapitalismus und die Politik des Imperialismus', *Die Kommunistische Internationale. Organ des Exekutivkomitees der Kommunistischen Internationale*, 9, 21: 1144–57, and 22: 1214–31.

Lewis, Cleona 1938, *America's Stake in International Investments*, Washington: Brookings Institution.

Magil, A.B. 1943, 'Detroit's Big Three', *New Masses*, 48, 25 May: 15–16.

Marx, Karl 1954, *Capital*, Volume I, Moscow: Foreign Languages Publishing House.

Marx, Karl 1957, *Capital*, Volume II, Moscow: Foreign Languages Publishing House.

Marx, Karl 1959, *Capital*, Volume III, Moscow: Foreign Languages Publishing House.

Marx, Karl 1969, *Theories of Surplus-Value*, Volume 2, London: Lawrence & Wishart.

Marx, Karl 1970, *Theories of Surplus Value*, Volume 2, London: Lawrence & Wishart.

Marx, Karl 1972, *Theories of Surplus-Value*, Volume 3, London: Lawrence & Wishart.

Marx, Karl 1977 [1859], 'Preface', *A Contribution to the Critique of Political Economy*, Moscow: Progress Publishers.

Marx, Karl 1979 [1852], *The 18th Brumaire of Louis Bonaparte*, in *Karl Marx and Frederick Engels Collected Works*, Volume 11, London: Lawrence & Wishart.

Marx, Karl and Frederick Engels 1976, *The Communist Manifesto*, in *Karl Marx and Frederick Engels Collected Works*, Volume 6, London: Lawrence & Wishart.
Marx, Karl 1977, *Le Capital. Livre premier (1867)*, in *Œuvres. Économie*, Volume 1, Préface par François Perroux et édition annotée par Maximilien Rubel, Paris: Gallimard.
Mataré, Franz 1913, *Die Arbeitsmittel Maschine, Apparat, Werkzeug*, Munich and Leipzig: Duncker & Humblot.
Mead, Edward Sherwood and Bernhard Ostrolenk 1928, *Harvey Baum: A Study of the Agricultural Revolution*, Philadelphia, PA: University of Pennsylvania Press.
Memoranda Presented to the Lytton Commission by V.K. Wellington Koo, Assessor 1933, Volume 2, New York: The Chinese Cultural Society.
Mitchell, Wesley C. 1926, 'Business Cycles as Revealed by Business Annals', in *Business Annals, United States, England, France, Germany, Austria, Russia, Sweden, Netherlands, Italy, Argentina, Brazil, Canada, South Africa, Australia, India, Japan, China*, by Willard Long Thorp, New York: National Bureau of Economic Research.
Monthly Bulletin of Statistics 1946–, New York: United Nations, Statistical Office.
Naphtali, Fritz 1928, *Wirtschaftsdemokratie, ihr Wesen, Wege und Ziel*, Berlin: Verlagsgesellschaft des Allgemeinen Deutschen Gewerkschaftsbundes GmbH.
Narodnoe khzyaystvo SSSR v 1960 godu. Statisticheskiy ezhgodnik 1961, Moscow: Tsentralnoe Statisticheskoe Upravlenie.
National Budgets for Full Employment 1945, Washington: National Planning Association, Planning Pamphlets 43–44.
Nearing, Scott 1919, *The American Empire*, New York: Rand School of Social Science.
Nourse, Edward Griswold 1934, *America's Capacity to Produce*, Washington: The Brookings Institution.
Obshchiy krizis kapitalizma 1933–4, 2 Volumes, Moscow: Partizdat.
Occupied Europe; German Exploitation and its Postwar Consequences 1944, London: Royal Institute of International Affairs.
Ostrolenk, Bernhard 1932, *The Surplus Farmer*, New York: Harper.
Ostrovityanov, K.V., D.T. Shepilov, L.A. Leontiev, I.D. Laptev, I.I. Kuzminov, L.M. Gatovskiy and A.I. Pashkov 1954, *Politicheskaya ekonomiya. Uchebnik*, Moscow: Politizdat.
Patterson, Ernest Minor 1922, 'Western Europe and the United States', *Annals of the American Academy of Political and Social Science*, 104: 1–131.
Pevzner, Y.A. 1961, *Gosudartsvenno-monopolisticheskiy kapitalizm v Yaponii posle vtoroy mirovoy voyny*, Moscow: Akademii Nauk.
Pinchot, Gifford 1925, 'Introduction', in *Giant Power. Large Scale Electrical Development as a Social Factor*, edited by Gifford Pinchot, *Annals of the American Academy of Political and Social Sciences*, 118: vii–xii.
Philippovich, Eugen von 1908, *Grundriß der politischen Ökonomie*, Volume 1, Tübingen: J.C.B. Mohr.

Politicheskaya ekonomiya. Uchebnik 1955, 2nd edition, Gospolitizdat.
Preller, Ludwig 1927, 'Der Betriebsschutz bei Fließarbeit', *Reichsarbeitsblatt, Nichtamtlicher Teil*, 10 February, 7, 5: 21–7.
Programme of the Communist International. Together with the Statutes of the Communist International 1929, London: Modern Books.
Protokoll des III. Kongresses der Kommunistischen Internationale (Moskau, 22. Juni bis 12. Juli 1921) 1921, Hamburg: Verlag der Kommunistischen Internationnale, C. Hoym.
Protokoll des III Kongresses der Kommunistischen Internationale (Moskau, 22. Juni bis 12. Juli 1921) 1921, Hamburg: Verlag der Kommunistischen Internationale, Auslieferungstelle für Deutschland: Carl Hoym Nachf. Louis Cahnbley.
Rajchman, Ludwik 1934, *Report of the Technical Agent of the Council on His Mission in China from the Date of His Appointment until April 1st 1934*, [Geneva]: League of Nations.
Räte-China 1934, Moscow: Verlagsgenossenschaft ausländischer Arbeiter in der UdSSR.
Reichsarbeitsblatt – Nichtamtlicher Teil 1921, Ambtsblatt des Reichsarbeitsministeriums und des Reichsamts für Arbeitsvermittlung, Verlag des Reichs-Arbetisblattes (Reimar Hobbing), Berlin sw61, Volume 1 (new series), 31 March.
'Resolution on the Situation in the Soviet Union and in the c.p.s.u.' 1928, *International Press Correspondence*, 8, 83: 578.
'Resolution on the Chinese Question presented on behalf of the c.p.s.u. delegation and the C.P.Ch. by Comrades Bukharin, Stalin, Sian and Lee. Ninth Plenum of the e.c.c.i. (Full report)' 1928, *International Press Correspondence*, 8, 16: 321–2.
Renner, Karl 1906, *Grundlagen und Entwicklungsziele der österreichisch-ungarischen Monarchie. Politische Studie über den Zusammenbruch der Privilegenparlamente und die Wahlreform bei den Staaten, über die Reichsidee und ihre Zukunft von Rudolf Springer*, Vienna and Leipzig: F. Deuticke.
Renner, Karl 1918, *Marxismus, Krieg, Internationale. Kritische Studien über offene Probleme des wissenschaftlichen und des praktischen Sozialismus in und nach dem Weltkrieg*, Stuttgart: J.H.W. Dietz.
Resolutions of the 20th Congress of the cpsu 1956, Moscow: Foreign Languages Publishing House.
Ritter, Kurt 1921, *Die Einwirkung des weltwirtschaftlichen Verkehrs auf die Entwicklung un den Betrieb der Landwirtschaft, insbesondere in Deutschland*, Berlin: Paray.
The Road to Communism. Documents of the 22nd Congress of the Communist Party of the Soviet Union, October 17–31 1961, Moscow: Foreign Languages Publishing House.
Roberts, George E. 1920, 'The Present Price and Credit Situation as Preliminary to a Return to Normal Times', *The Economic World*, 20, 27 November: 760–3.
Rösner, Ernst (ed.) 1939, *Otto Hübner's Weltstatistik, Tabellen aller Länder der Erde*, 73rd edition, Vienna: Verlag L.W. Seidel & Sohn.

Rydal, William 1947, 'The Exposure of England', *The Fortnightly*, 167, 3: 161–5.

Sartorius von Waltershausen, August Freiherr 1970, *Das volkswirtschaftliche System der Kapitalanlage im Ausland*, Berlin: Georg Reimer.

Schippel, Max 1921, *Amerikas Wirtschafts- und Finanzlage und die Wiederaufrichtung Europas*, Stuttgart: Verlag von Ferdinand Enke.

Schoening, H. 1933, 'Die deutsche Werkzeugmaschinenindustrie in Gegenwart und Zukunft', *VDI Zeitschrift*, 77, 9: 209–10.

The Second Five-Year Plan of Development of the National Economy of the U.S.S.R. (1933–37) 1934, in *Socialism Victorious*.

Sering, Max 1929, *Internationale Preisbewegung und die Lage der Landwirtschaft in den aussertropischen Ländern*, Berlin: Parey.

Shadwell, Arthur 1906, *Industrial Efficiency: A Comparative Study of Industrial Life in England, Germany and America*, 2 Volumes, London, New York and Bombay: Longmans, Green.

Shadwell, Arthur 1920, *Industrial Efficiency: A Comparative Study of Industrial Life in England, Germany, and America*, 2 Vols, New York, Bombay, Calcutta and Madras: Longmans, Green.

Shaw, George Bernard 1919 [1910], *Der Sozialismus und die geistig Begabten. Eine Erwiderung an Herrn Mallock*, translation by Hedda Korsch, with a foreword by Karl Korsch, Hannover: 'Freies Deutschland'. [George Bernard Shaw 1910, *Socialism and Superior Brains. A Reply to Mr. Mallock*, published and sold by the Fabian Society, London: Fifield].

Social Insurance and Allied Services. Memoranda from Organizations. Appendix G to Report by Sir William Beveridge. Presented to Parliament by Command of His Majesty 1942, London: HMSO, November, Cmd. 6405.

Sombart, Werner 1928, *Das Wirtschaftsleben im Zeitalter des Hochkapitalismus*, Munich and Leipzig: Duncker & Humblot.

Stalin, Joseph 1934a [1928], *The Results of the July Plenum of the Central Committee*, in *Leninism*, Volume 2, edited by J. Fineberg, Moscow: Co-operative Publishing Society of Foreign Workers in the USSR.

Stalin, Joseph 1934b [1928], *Right danger in the Soviet Union*, in *Leninism*, Volume 2, edited by J. Fineberg, Moscow: Co-operative Publishing Society of Foreign Workers in the USSR.

Stalin, Joseph 1934c [1929], *A Year of Great Change*, in *Leninism*, Volume 2, edited by J. Fineberg, Moscow: Co-operative Publishing Society of Foreign Workers in the USSR.

Stalin, Joseph 1934d [1925], *The Results of the Work of the Fourteenth Conference of the Russian Communist Party*, in *Leninism*, Volume 1, edited by J. Fineberg, Moscow and Leningrad: Co-operative Publishing Society of Foreign Workers in the USSR.

Stalin, Joseph 1934e [1934], *Political Report of the Central Committee to the Seventeenth*

Congres of the C.P.S.U., in *Leninism*, Volume 1, edited by J. Fineberg, Moscow and Leningrad: Co-operative Publishing Society of Foreign Workers in the USSR.

Stalin, Joseph 1934f [1934], *Report of the Central Committee of the Communist Party of the Soviet Union*, in *Socialism Victorious*, New York: International Publishers.

Stalin, J.V. 1944, 'Speech at Celebration Meeting of the Moscow Soviet of Working People's Deputies and Moscow Party and Public Organizations November 6, 1944', available at: http://www.marxists.org/reference/archive/stalin/works/1944/11/06.htm

Stalin, J.V. 1953, *Economic Problems of Socialism in the* USSR, Moscow: Foreign Languages Publishing House.

Stalin, J.V. 1954a [1925], *The Results of the Work of the Fourteenth Conference of the* R.C.P.(B.). *Report Delivered at a Meeting of the Active of the Moscow Organisation of the* R.C.P.(B.), in *Works*, Volume 7, Moscow: Foreign Languages Publishing House.

Stalin, J.V. 1954b [1928], *The Right Danger in the* C.P.S.U. (B.). *Speech Delivered at the Plenum of the Moscow Committee and Moscow Control Commission of the* C.P.S.U.(B.) *October 19, 1928*, in *Works*, Volume 11, Moscow: Foreign Languages Publishing House.

Stalin, J.V. 1954c [1928], *Results of the Plenum of the* C.C., C.P.S.U.(B.). *Report to a Meeting of Activists of the Leningrad Organisation of the* C.P.S.U.(B.) in *Works*, Volume 11, Moscow: Foreign Languages Publishing House.

Stalin, J.V. 1954d [1928], *Results of the July Plenum of the* C.C., C.P.S.U. (B.), in *Works*, Volume 11, Moscow: Foreign Languages Publishing House.

Stalin, J.V. 1954e [1930], *Political Report of the Central Committee to the Sixteenth Congress of the* C.P.S.U.(B), *27 June 1930*, in *Works*, Volume 12, Moscow: Foreign Languages Publishing House.

Stalin, J.V. 1954f [1930], *Dizzy with Success. Concerning Questions of the Collective-Farm Movement*, in *Works*, Volume 12, Moscow: Foreign Languages Publishing House.

Stalin, J.V. 1954g [1929], *A Year of Great Change. On the Occasion of the Twelfth Anniversary of the October Revolution*, in *Works*, Volume 12, Moscow: Foreign Languages Publishing House.

Stalin, J.V. 1955a [1934], *Report to the Seventeenth Party Congress on the Work of the Central Committee of the* C.P.S.U.(B.), in *Works*, Volume 13, Moscow: Foreign Languages Publishing House.

Stalin, J.V. 1955b [1933], *The Results of the First Five-Year Plan. Report Delivered on January 7, 1933*, in *Works*, Volume 13, Moscow: Foreign Languages Publishing House.

Starling, Ernest H. 1919, *Report on Food Conditions in Germany*, [London]: His Majesty's Stationary Office, Cmd. 280.

'Statements to the Congress: Monetary Policy and the Economy' 1963, *Federal Reserve Bulletin*, 49, 2: 122–44.

Statesman's Year-Book 1920, London: Macmillan.

Statistics Relating to the War Effort of the United Kingdom 1944, London: HM Stationary Office, Cmd. 6584, November.
Statistical Abstract for the United Kingdom Volumes 1913-37, London: United Kingdom, HMSO.
Statistical Abstract of the United States 1946 1947, Washington: US Department of Commerce.
Statistical Abstract of the United States, US Department of Commerce, Bureau of the Census 1951-, Washington: US Government Printing Office.
Statistical Abstracts of the United States 1938, Washington: United States Government Printing Office, 59.
Statistical Yearbook of the United Nations 1946-, New York: United Nations, Statistical Office.
Statistical Material Presented During the Washington Negotiations 1945, London: HMSO, Cmd. 6707, December.
Statistical Yearbook of the League of Nations 1932-3, 1933-4, Geneva: League of Nations.
Statistisches Jahrbuch für das Deutsche Reich 1932, 51, Herausgegeben vom Statistischen Reichsamt, Berlin: Verlag von Reimar Hobbing.
Statistisches Jahbuch für das Deutsche Reich, 1919/20, Berlin.
Statistisches Jahrbuch für das Deutsche Reich 1919, 40; 1920, 41, Berlin: Verlag von Puttkammer & Mühlbrecht, Buchhandlung für Staats- und Rechtswissenschaft.
Statistisches Jahrbuch für die Bundesrepublik Deutschland 1957, Wiesbaden: Statistisches Bundesambt.
Statistical Yearbook of the United Nations 1961, New York: United Nations, Statistical Office.
Statistical Abstract of the United States 1926, Washington: US Government Printing Office.
Statistisches Jahrbuch für das Deutsche Reich 1927, Berlin: Statistische Reichsamt.
Szymczak, M.S. 1945, 'Economic Problems of Belgium', *Federal Reserve Bulletin*, Washington: Board of Governors of the Federal Reserve System, 30, 1: 10–15.
Tarnow, Fritz 1928, *Warum arm sein?*, Berlin: Verlagsgesellschaft des Allgemeinen Deutschen Gewerkschaftsbundes.
Theses and Decisions. Thirteenth Plenum of the ECCI 1934, London: Modern Books.
'Theses and Resolutions of the VI. World Congress of the Communist International' 1928, *International Press Correspondence*, 8, 83: 1568–77.
Theses and Statutes of the Third International (Communist) International. Adopted by the Second Congress, July 17th–August 7th 1920, Moscow: Publishing Office of the Communist International.
'Theses on the united front of the proletariat and on relations to the worker adhering to the Second, 2½ and Amsterdam Internationals and to the workers supporting the Anarcho-Syndicalist organisations (Unanimuously adopted by the Executive Com-

mittee of the Communist International on December 28th, 1921)' 1922, *International Press Correspondence*, 2, 3: 17–20.

'Thesis on the tactics of the Russian Communist Party. (Adopted at the 17th Session, July 5th, 1921)', in *Theses and Resolutions Adopted at the Third World Congress of the Communist International (June 22nd–July 12th, 1921)*, New York City: The Contemporary Publishing Association.

Thorp, William Long 1926, *Business Annals. United States, England, France, Germany, Austria, Russia, Sweden, Netherlands, Italy, Argentina, Brazil, Canada, South Africa, Australia, India, Japan, China*, New York: National Bureau of Economic Research.

Trotzky, L. 1919, *Arbeit, Disziplin und Ordnung*, Berlin: Verlag Gesellschaft und Erziehung. [Trotsky, Leon 1919, 'Work, discipline, and order to save the Socialist Soviet Republic', *The Class Struggle*, 3, 3: 366–82].

Tugwell, Rexford G. 1927, *Industry's Coming of Age*, New York: Harcourt, Brace and Company.

Varga, Eugen 1916, 'Geld und Kapital in der Kriegswirtschaft', *Die Neue Zeit*, 34, I, 26: 815–24.

Varga, Eugen 1921a, *Die wirtschaftspolitischen Probleme der proletarischen Diktatur*, (2nd edition), Hamburg: C. Hoym Nachf.

Varga, Eugen 1921b, *Die Krise der kapitalistischen Weltwirtschaft*, Hamburg: Verlag der Kommunistischen Internationale.

Varga, Eugen 1921c, 'Die Wirtschaftslage des englischen Weltreiches', *Die Kommunistische Internationale*, 2, 15: 159–82.

Varga, Eugen 1921d, 'Die wirtschaftliche Grundlagen des Imperialismus der Vereinigten Staaten von Nordamerika', *Kommunistische Internationale*, 2, 17: 119–46.

Varga, Eugen 1921e, 'Die politische und sociale Lage des englischen Weltreich', *Kommunistische Internationale*, 2, 15: 159–82.

Varga, Eugen 1921f, 'Das Rätsel Chinas', *Internationale Pressekorrespondenz*, 1921, 1, 40–1: 356–7.

Varga, Eugen 1922a, *The Process of Capitalist Decline. Report to the IV. Congress of the Communist International*, Hamburg: Communist International in Commission: Carl Hoym Nachf, L. Cahnbley.

Varga, Eugen 1922b, *Die Krise der kapitalistischen Weltwirtschaft, zweite vermehrte und umgearbeite Auflage*, Hamburg: Verlag der Kommunistischen Internationale, ausgeliefert für Deutschland: Carl Hoym Nachf. Louis Cahnblei.

Varga, Eugen 1922c [1921], *Die Krise der kapitalistischen Weltwirtschaft*, Zweite, vermehrte und umgearbeitete Auflage, Hamburg: Verlag der Kommunistischen Internationale, Carl Hoym Nachf. Louis Cahnbley (Bibliothek der Kommunistische Internationale, 25).

Varga, Eugen 1927, 'Kapitalexport in der Weltwirtschaft', *Die Internationale. Zeitschrift für Theorie des Marxismus*, 10, 12: 363–9.

Varga, Eugen 1928a, 'Wirtschaft und Wirtschjaftspolitik im I. Vierteljahr 1928', *Internationale Presse-Korrespondenz*, 8, 28: 847–84.

Varga, Eugen 1928c, *Die Wirtschaft der Niedergangsperiode des Kapitalismus nach der Stabilisierung*, Hamburg: C. Hoym Nachf.

Varga, Eugen 1934, 'The De Man Plan is a fraud on the workers', *Communist International*, 11, 7: 514–23.

Varga, Eugen 1935, *Proizvoditelnye sily buntyut protiv kapitalizma. Planovoe khozyaystvo u nash, 'planovy obman' u vikh*, Moscow: Partizdat.

Varga, Eugen (ed.) 1937, *Mirovoe ekonomicheskie krizisy 1848–1935 gg.*, Volume 1, Moscow: Ogiz.

Varga, Eugen 1939a [1937], *Two Systems: Socialist Economy and Capitalist Economy*, New York: International Publishers.

Varga, Eugen (ed.) 1939b, *Mirovoye khozyaystvo. Ezhegodnik. 1938/1939*, Moscow: Sotsekgiz.

Varga, Eugen 1957, *Osnovnye voprosy ekonomiki i politiki imperializma (posle Vtoroi Mirovoy Voyny)*, Moscow: Gos. Izdvo Polit. Lit.

Varga, Eugen 1961, *Twentieth Century Capitalism*, Moscow: Foreign Languages Publishing House.

Varga, E. (ed.) and I.A. Trakhtenberg [1937], *Mirovoye ekonomicheskie krizisy 1848–1935*, Volume 1, Moscow: Ogiz.

Vialatte, Achille 1907, *L'avenir économique du Japon*, Paris: Marcel Rivière (*Annales de l'École libre des Sciences Politiques*).

Verein deutscher Maschinenbauanstalten 1926, *Denkschrift über die Maschinenindustrie der Welt*, Berlin-Charlottenburg: Karl Lange.

Viton, Albert 1943, *American Empire in Asia?*, New York: The John Day Company.

Wagemann, Ernst 1931, 'Prognose der Arbeitslosigkeit', *Wochenbericht des Instituts für Konjunturforschung*, 4, 22: 89.

Wagenführ, Rolf 1933, *Die Industriewirtschaft: Entwicklungstendenzen der deutschen und internationalen Industrieproduktion 1860 bis 1932*, *Vierteljahrshefte zur Konjunkturforschung*, Sonderheft 31, Berlin: Hobbing.

Wealth, Public Debt, and Taxation: 1922. Estimated National Wealth 1924, Department of Commerce. Bureau of the Census, Washington: Government Printing Office.

Wealth, Public Debt, and Taxation: 1922. Estimated National Wealth. Compiled as Part of the Decennial Report on Wealth, Public Debt, and Taxation 1924, Department of Commerce, Bureau of the Census, Washington: Government Printing Office.

Weber, Alfred 1909, *Reine Theorie des Standorts*, Tübingen: JCB Mohr.

Weltwirtschaftliches Archiv 1920, Jena: Fischer Verlag.

The White Paper on the National Income and Expenditure in the Years 1938–1944 1945, London: HMSO, Cmd. 6623.

Die Wirtschaftliche Kräfte der Welt 1930, third edition, Herausgegeben von der Dresdner Bank, Berlin: Denter & Nicolas.

Wirtschaft und Statistik 1921, Berlin: Statistisches Reichsamt.

Die wirtschaftliche Lage der deutschen Arbeiter und die Beschlüsse der Pariser Konferenz: Der Allgemeine Deutsche Gewerkschaftsbund an die Regierungen und Völker der Ententeländer 1921, Berlin.

Woldt, Richard 1911, *Das großindustrielle Beamtentum: eine gewerkschaftliche Studie*, Stuttgart: J.H.W. Dietz Nachf.

Woldt, Richard 1921, *Wiedergutmachung und deutsche Wirtschaft*, Berlin: Verlag Hans Robert Engelmann (Jahrbuch der Finanzpolitischen Korrespondenz 1).

Wirtschaft und Statistik 1921, 1, Berlin: Statistisches Reichsamt, Verlag von Reimar Hobbing.

Zahn, Friedrich 1909, 'Beruf und Berufstatistik', in *Handwörterbuch der Staatswissenschaften*, Jena: Fischer.

Zahn, Friedrich 1924, *The Decline of Capitalism*, London: The Communist Party of Great Britain for the Communist International.

Index

abolition   218, 461, 549, 614, 863, 884, 886, 979, 1136
accumulation   58–60, 128–29, 132, 228, 472–75, 666–68, 674–75, 677, 681, 692, 694–95, 715, 717–19, 1027, 1029
accumulation process   58–59, 79, 692, 718, 1029
advanced capitalist countries   749, 755, 796, 811
AFL-CIO   1081–82
Africa   33, 40, 242, 405, 410, 437, 441, 534, 577, 633, 636, 908, 913, 915, 981
agrarian countries   51, 191, 410, 521–22, 612, 615, 731, 739, 760–61, 780, 813, 817, 819, 855
agrarian crisis   65, 67, 71–72, 74, 488–89, 492, 494, 748–54, 757, 759, 770, 772–73, 788–90, 793, 1078
agricultural production   72, 149, 191, 199, 349, 445, 456, 601, 615, 749–50
Algeria   660, 1091
Alsace-Lorraine   293, 299, 326, 400, 443, 603
Argentina   3, 403, 424, 472, 490, 492–94, 534, 540, 602, 615, 741–42, 745, 761, 1169, 1174
armaments   613, 616, 621, 624, 850, 852, 854, 856–58, 926, 929, 1040, 1063, 1065, 1067, 1092
artisans   97, 152, 710, 722, 738, 787–88, 802, 837, 880, 885, 927, 951, 959–60
Australia   248, 251, 356, 362, 364, 385, 402–5, 438–39, 484–85, 611, 614–15, 618, 620–21, 656–58, 660
Austria   3–4, 84, 86, 372–73, 396–97, 425–26, 428, 745, 847, 862, 875–76, 881–83, 889–90, 893–94, 1031–32

bank deposits   192, 354, 1029, 1069–70, 1110–11
banknotes   150, 201–2, 204, 216–17, 219, 221–23, 228–29, 740
bankruptcies   25, 42, 66, 75, 260, 273, 275, 400, 493, 603–4, 609, 712, 738–39, 748, 766
Bauer, Otto   14, 16, 58–61, 63, 157, 667–69, 673, 675–76, 687–89, 829, 862, 872–73, 875, 889

Belgium   330–31, 334, 344, 348, 368, 372, 385, 388, 422, 424, 486, 952, 958, 1014–15, 1087
Bolsheviks   66–68, 92, 111, 130, 158, 179, 192, 506, 625, 814, 894, 1149, 1154–55, 1158–59
bourgeois   13, 16, 107, 109, 251, 255, 697, 709, 713, 715, 882, 886, 960–61, 965, 1093–94
bourgeois democracy   83–84, 89–90, 119, 126, 179, 624, 628, 859–61, 863, 961
Brazil   424, 437–38, 491, 537, 658, 741, 747, 760–61, 765, 771–72, 926, 996, 1005
breakdown of capitalism   60, 412, 474, 662, 664, 666, 687
British Empire   19, 25, 99, 404, 617–18, 620, 659, 847, 917, 920, 979–81, 1160
British imperialism   22, 25, 40, 92–93, 99, 612, 912–13, 1090
British India   25, 41, 355, 385, 614, 656–58, 676, 981

capital export   59–61, 78–79, 81, 438–39, 441, 593–95, 612, 615–16, 650–51, 687–91, 744–46, 783, 933, 1067–68
capital investments   384, 394, 443, 483, 506, 594, 623, 720, 745, 783, 913, 972, 1031, 1122–23, 1125
capitalists   121–22, 186–87, 230–32, 336–38, 407–11, 497–503, 549–51, 556–61, 592–93, 616–19, 628–32, 665–70, 697–98, 716–17, 1132–35
capitalist system   6, 46–47, 61–62, 109–10, 419–21, 423, 553–55, 561–62, 705–7, 946–48, 953–55, 1093–94, 1126–28, 1134–35, 1139–40
capitalist world   419–21, 426, 556, 623–25, 818, 826–29, 842–43, 897, 941, 945–47, 1068, 1089, 1091–92, 1097–99, 1120–21
China   131, 405–6, 437–39, 619–21, 658–60, 705, 761–64, 830–32, 837, 839–40, 848, 850–52, 915–16, 981, 1169–70
Churchill, Winston   100, 927, 981–82, 1090, 1147
circulation   150–51, 216–20, 222–24, 227, 229, 347–48, 360, 367, 385, 444, 454–57, 560, 1070–71, 1077, 1111–12

civil servants   162, 165–66, 168–69, 173, 175, 180–83, 186, 190, 224, 228, 322–23, 805, 987–88, 991, 1131–32
class antagonisms   112, 192, 442, 496, 502–3, 544, 608, 743, 843, 845, 860, 887, 897
class consciousness   4, 24, 215, 276, 278, 506, 556
class domination   31, 89, 173, 415–16, 432, 442
classes   44, 108, 110, 119, 182, 205–6, 256–57, 278, 416–17, 430–32, 473–75, 496, 872–73, 1094–95, 1129
class hegemony   125, 154, 336, 338, 386, 666
class struggle   42, 52, 129–30, 198, 203–6, 214, 250–51, 278, 286, 666, 859–60, 886, 964, 1118, 1125
coal industry   246, 248, 381, 1001, 1140
cocoa   426, 428, 525, 750, 755, 975
colonial exploitation   344, 416, 465, 754
colonies   27–28, 31, 101, 504–6, 508, 595, 618, 622–23, 760–63, 842–43, 909–10, 912–17, 919–20, 957–58, 1094
Comintern   12–14, 18–20, 22–23, 25–27, 35–37, 39–41, 44–45, 50–51, 53, 57, 62–63, 77–78, 86–88, 831–32
commercial capital   207, 218, 433–34, 437, 588–89, 612, 646–47, 697, 901
Communists   4–5, 39–41, 89–90, 96–98, 631–32, 834–35, 867, 869–71, 873, 875–77, 882–83, 885–86, 888–91, 893–95, 952–54
consumers   133, 135, 160, 207, 209–12, 545, 681, 717–19, 726, 782–85, 940, 942–44, 998, 1037, 1073
cooperatives   194, 199, 201, 207, 863
copper   106, 161, 230, 263, 274, 350–52, 449, 527–28, 776, 924, 996–97, 1054, 1060, 1068–69, 1109–10
crisis of capitalism   26, 41, 45, 106, 121, 129, 340–41, 435, 462, 524, 802, 873, 887, 947
crisis theory   48, 62, 681, 684, 710, 1151
Cuba   438, 760, 811
currency depreciation   24, 75, 78, 245, 706, 739, 743–44, 761, 776
cycle   16–17, 705, 734, 777, 779, 945, 1061, 1063–68, 1073–80, 1101–2, 1104–5, 1107–9, 1114–17, 1120–23, 1125–26

Czechoslovakia   97–98, 368, 371–72, 443, 445, 448, 458, 620, 622, 952, 962–63, 967–69, 1001, 1015, 1031–32

democracy   76, 179, 520–21, 628, 631, 866, 872–74, 953–54, 956, 959–61, 963, 965, 967, 969, 1001–2

Eastern Europe   33, 96–97, 125, 227, 264, 368, 370, 394, 421, 423–24, 430, 446, 461, 517, 622
economic policy   3–4, 70, 72, 189, 191–92, 225, 404, 406, 504, 606, 609–10, 770, 773, 935, 965
Eisenhower, Dwight D.   1079–80, 1147
elections   73, 156, 284, 292, 952, 955, 969, 979, 982, 1050, 1131, 1136, 1140
Engels, Friedrich   42, 124, 137, 189, 545, 573, 661, 678, 681, 685, 720, 752–53, 908, 1121
engineers   183, 278, 784, 788
Entente   28–29, 210, 262, 266, 269–70, 307, 338, 340–41, 351–52, 359, 433, 443, 463, 515
entrepreneurs   158, 335, 386, 671, 998–99, 1022, 1029, 1037–38, 1044–45, 1081, 1116, 1136
exchange rates   75, 128, 202, 280, 323, 331, 334, 340, 357–59, 363, 372, 384, 386, 396, 408–9
exploitation   191, 196, 569–71, 604, 606, 683–84, 710, 714, 717, 785, 787, 806, 848–49, 910, 914
export markets   28, 40, 106, 490, 998
expropriation   5, 8, 10, 142, 144, 148, 152–54, 157–58, 160–61, 191–93, 216, 226, 500–1, 672, 674

factories   7–9, 125, 173, 175–76, 178, 210–11, 219, 337, 578–81, 810, 820–21, 854–55, 891, 1022–24
farmers   145–46, 250, 274–75, 440, 489, 491–92, 494, 757, 759, 790–91, 793, 835, 1051–52, 1054, 1133
fascism   71, 73, 76, 84, 86, 88–90, 556–57, 707, 870–71, 876–77, 880–87, 890–95, 949, 955–56, 960
fascist dictatorship   882–83, 887, 893
  open   69, 870, 887

fertilisers   196, 250, 293, 296, 347, 772, 1009, 1011, 1039, 1051
First World War   7–8, 96, 916, 918–19, 927, 932–33, 939–44, 947–53, 985, 1005–6, 1044–45, 1090, 1093–94, 1104, 1134
fixed capital   41–42, 65, 339, 588, 646, 711–12, 716–17, 728–29, 749, 780–81, 783, 1029, 1071–73, 1107, 1122–23
foodstuffs   145–48, 195, 199–206, 211–15, 229–30, 268, 274–75, 317–20, 403–4, 634, 636, 879, 992–93, 995–96, 1009
Ford   480, 581, 584, 1025–26, 1038–39
foreign policy   100, 557–58, 610, 618, 830, 886, 892, 946, 948, 950, 953, 956–58, 969–70, 980, 982–83
France   245–47, 251–54, 331–32, 399–406, 442–43, 452, 454, 460–61, 508–9, 511–12, 620–22, 844–49, 913–16, 1013–15, 1091–93
free trade   99, 209, 402, 470, 490, 504–5, 559, 593, 630, 747, 769, 928, 971, 984

General Motors   599–600, 702, 927, 999, 1019, 1023–25, 1039
gold reserves   79, 512, 741–42, 744, 761, 936, 1016, 1092, 1116–17
Gompers, Samuel   129, 277, 337, 518
great powers   403–6, 437, 447–48, 462, 467, 613, 618, 623, 659, 840, 844, 915–16, 947, 970–71, 981
Greece   97, 368, 385, 425, 446, 618, 879, 956, 960, 981, 983, 1015
Grossmann, Henryk   58–63, 67, 661–99, 1151
ground rent   80, 145–47, 749–51, 754, 833
growth   76–77, 221, 497–98, 562, 677, 703–4, 765, 952–53, 1053–54, 1070–71, 1073–74, 1098, 1112, 1116, 1126

hegemony   19, 120, 281, 464, 508, 553, 621, 665, 739, 748, 830, 837, 846, 867, 898–99
Hitler, Adolf   90–93, 852, 870–71, 875, 882, 884, 922, 967, 1020, 1040, 1089–90, 1096, 1135, 1139, 1153
Holland   344, 350, 364, 368, 424, 658, 663, 740, 743, 894, 903, 915, 919–20, 952, 958

Hungary   8–12, 52, 97, 128–30, 160–63, 173–75, 192–94, 197–99, 202–5, 446, 657–58, 663–65, 846–48, 885–86, 954–56

ideology   76, 79, 86, 111, 121, 124, 177, 181–82, 206, 277, 560, 747, 772, 857, 873–75
immigration   275, 509, 517–18, 566, 691
imperialism   19, 32–33, 35, 37–38, 40, 42, 58–59, 252, 704–5, 909, 912–13, 946, 1133–35
imperialist powers   109, 406, 558, 595, 616–18, 623, 848, 850, 910, 912–13, 916–17, 921, 1088, 1090, 1092–93
imperialist war   21, 31, 74, 83, 242, 244, 664–65, 840, 846, 859, 866, 897, 900, 920, 922–23
imports   295, 310–11, 422–23, 449, 451, 453, 479–80, 485–88, 529–30, 533–34, 746–47, 763–65, 945, 978–79, 1075
India   40–41, 101, 103, 251–52, 369–70, 404–5, 423–24, 522–23, 615, 620, 660, 740–41, 760–61, 851, 981
industrial bourgeoisie   41, 507, 612, 616, 787, 1140
industrial capitalism   616, 705, 721, 725–26, 738, 984
industrial countries   505, 508, 521–22, 588, 591, 817, 819, 972–73, 978–79, 1069, 1071, 1073, 1075, 1110, 1113–15
industrialisation   43, 51, 59, 265, 351, 356, 386, 436–37, 459, 559–60, 576, 611–12, 614, 616, 656–58
industrial proletariat   143, 147–48, 150, 174, 197, 206, 214, 577, 882
international trade   23, 26, 95, 128, 147, 208, 210, 231, 233, 394, 721, 747
iron   165, 167, 274, 330–31, 361, 390–91, 454–56, 473, 522–24, 582, 599–600, 648–49, 657, 918, 973

Kautsky, Karl   2, 10, 82, 86, 112, 119, 122, 141, 149, 157, 292, 709–10, 828–29
Keynes, John Maynard   25–26, 94, 109–11, 282, 323, 389, 400, 407, 517, 559, 608, 934, 937–38, 1006
Kondratiev, Nikolai   16, 87, 750
kulaks   51–52, 204, 814, 817, 824–25, 835, 843
Kun, Bela   3–5, 12, 14, 77, 88
Kuusinen, Otto   40, 53, 56, 71, 1135

labour aristocracy 24, 47, 84–85, 235, 278, 416, 465, 509, 518, 556–57, 632, 862–65, 876–77, 885, 920
labour discipline 8–10, 52, 121, 154, 171, 173–75, 177, 180, 195
Labour Party 100, 872, 927, 957, 982–83, 1001, 1131, 1133, 1140
labour productivity 6–8, 127, 130–41, 174–80, 263–64, 324–25, 327–29, 333–34, 336–38, 388, 569, 571–73, 575, 714, 976
landlords 148, 194, 197, 762, 782, 793, 830, 833, 838, 963–64, 973, 1044
Latin America 22, 532, 595, 658, 744, 950, 972
Leninism 37, 41, 544, 698, 824, 1156, 1171–72
loan capital 218, 292, 561, 681, 690, 697, 715, 725, 738, 741, 743, 767, 769, 777–78, 787
Luxemburg, Rosa 19, 34–35, 42, 47–49, 51, 53, 58, 65, 70, 434, 462, 467, 710

machinery 140, 245–46, 263, 301–2, 324, 552, 578–80, 587–89, 611–12, 710–12, 715–16, 863–64, 901–3, 925–26, 940
Malthusianism 517, 693–94
Marshall Plan 100, 109
Marx, Karl 48–49, 65, 131–33, 554–55, 661–63, 671–75, 679–85, 688–90, 695–98, 709–14, 718, 720–21, 777–79, 1121
Marxism 1–2, 5, 57, 64, 68, 112, 559–60, 627, 663, 666, 697–98, 700, 734, 886, 947
mass unemployment 53, 81–82, 110, 112, 563, 567, 582, 633, 643, 645, 783, 790, 794, 944, 949
Mattick, Paul 62–63
Mesopotamia 19, 25, 262, 282–83, 391, 620
Molotov, Vyachevslav 56, 66, 73, 94, 100–1, 103, 956
money capital 42, 218–19, 363, 441, 561, 661, 940
monopolies 108, 554–55, 595–605, 624, 695–96, 721–23, 726, 781, 909–10, 917–19, 1064–65, 1077–78, 1105–6, 1127–33

national bourgeoisie 40, 404, 593, 606, 630, 830

nationalisation 97, 126, 208, 219, 953–54, 956, 959, 961–64, 966, 1001, 1139–41
New Deal 80, 770, 1139

overaccumulation 60–61, 662, 664–68, 671–72, 675, 677–78, 680–81, 683, 687, 692, 694–96, 698
  result of 686
overproduction 17, 19, 136, 366, 386–87, 681, 712, 719, 942, 1042–43, 1050–52, 1057, 1085–86, 1103, 1120–21

parliamentarism 119, 557, 859–61
parliamentary democracy 86, 557, 630, 707, 872, 969
peasants 145–47, 193, 197–98, 200–4, 221–24, 227, 229–30, 494–95, 749–50, 787–90, 830–34, 838–39, 877–80, 962–64, 966–67
petty bourgeoisie 27, 87–88, 179, 500–2, 550, 722, 743, 786, 825, 844, 859, 870, 880–81, 883, 949
planned economy 6, 9, 12, 43, 141, 171, 233, 603, 693, 709, 828, 965–66, 1035–36, 1039, 1048
Poland 97, 373, 385, 410–11, 425–26, 443, 445, 477–78, 482–83, 498, 622–23, 881–83, 962–63, 967–69, 1015
Popular Front 63, 77, 87–88, 90
private property 10, 98, 121–22, 139, 152, 225–26, 605–6, 704, 828, 878, 928, 984, 1032, 1036, 1039
production costs 7, 221, 296, 329, 331, 387, 411, 494–96, 511, 735, 749, 754, 756, 784–85, 787–88
productivity 128–29, 131, 133–34, 136–38, 175–76, 180, 264, 266, 269, 323, 327–28, 351, 353, 388, 390
proletariat 3–6, 118–22, 124–26, 141–44, 146–51, 153–54, 178–84, 234–37, 255–61, 415–17, 429–33, 442–47, 501–3, 892–900, 1138–39

Radek, Karl 28, 37
Renner, Karl 131, 159–60, 893
rents 145–46, 224, 317, 492–93, 598, 735, 751–52, 757, 788, 790, 804, 833, 836, 941, 1044

INDEX

reproduction cycle 1097–99, 1101, 1103–5, 1107, 1109, 1111, 1113, 1115, 1117, 1119–23, 1125
revolution 4, 19–20, 39, 148–50, 158–59, 173, 192–94, 207, 259–60, 474–75, 873–74, 887–88, 893, 895–900
Roosevelt, F.D.R. 80, 94, 99, 742, 759, 770, 810, 854, 934, 945, 970, 982, 999, 1043
Russia 120, 158–59, 161–63, 172–74, 179–81, 192–94, 196–97, 199–201, 209–15, 389–92, 406–7, 409–10, 426–28, 506, 662–64

sabotage 12, 140, 158, 173, 183–85, 187, 209, 887
Second Five-Year Plan 73, 816, 825, 1164, 1171
Second International 113, 259, 519–20, 707, 861–62, 872, 874, 890–95, 903
Second World War 101–2, 108–9, 950–51, 953, 957–59, 970–71, 984–86, 995, 1005–6, 1019–20, 1089–90, 1094–95, 1097–98, 1134
semi-colonies 25, 40, 103, 105, 466, 616, 618–19, 622, 760, 763–64, 910, 913, 981
shipbuilding 262, 266, 351–52, 361, 363, 455, 473, 526, 582, 584, 635, 637, 640–41, 728, 1086–87
Social Democracy 77, 84, 86, 257, 432–33, 502–3, 544–45, 632, 861–62, 866–68, 871–72, 879–80, 882–84, 920, 954–55
socialist revolution 5, 159, 261, 1139
Spain 84, 87, 89, 262, 368, 372, 385, 424, 482, 656–57, 894, 903, 915, 920, 1015
Stalin, Joseph 38, 44–45, 65, 71, 73–79, 90–95, 99–100, 102, 813–18, 824–25, 840–42, 845–46, 1088–89
state apparatus 72, 82, 158, 773, 786, 926–27, 951, 960, 963–65, 1000, 1042, 1080, 1128, 1130–31
state capitalism 12, 45, 552, 587, 591, 600, 604–11, 704, 925, 928, 930, 953, 1127, 1134, 1138
steel 391, 395, 449, 451, 454–56, 498–99, 524–26, 528–29, 531, 596, 599, 648, 973, 1052–55, 1086–87
stock exchanges 107, 273, 731, 1045, 1060, 1075, 1115
sugar 161, 165, 213, 215, 271, 274, 291, 297, 369, 373, 428, 655–56, 756, 760, 762

surplus value 59–60, 186–87, 225–26, 560–61, 588–89, 591–93, 668–70, 673, 678–79, 686, 689–91, 694, 696–98, 710–12, 901
Switzerland 7, 344, 350, 368, 371–73, 422, 424, 486, 740, 743, 1015, 1069, 1078, 1110, 1116

textile industry 301, 332, 334, 372, 395, 404, 419, 452, 503, 579, 614, 638, 730, 737, 811
Thälmann, Ernst 870–71
trade 169, 208, 210, 231–34, 448, 454, 485, 489, 581–82, 800, 917, 974, 980, 1132–33
Trotsky, Leon 20–22, 38, 45, 55, 82, 87, 184–85, 416, 750, 829, 831
Turkey 437, 595, 618–19, 622, 907, 913–16, 943, 981, 983, 1144

underproduction 17, 20, 96, 368, 371, 388, 390, 396, 400, 408, 410, 412, 719, 940, 944–45
unemployment 47–48, 54–56, 275, 371–72, 429–30, 441, 454–55, 481–82, 486–88, 563, 694–95, 794–95, 810–11, 865–66, 1058–59
United States 22–25, 247–48, 253–55, 262–70, 275–85, 349–53, 388–95, 475–80, 491–93, 590–95, 937–45, 971–76, 978–83, 1064–69, 1071–87
urban proletariat 9, 143–44, 190, 195, 198, 203, 205–6, 213, 221

vanguard 39, 143, 205, 235–36, 632, 849
Volodin, Viktor S. 110–11

wages 145–47, 173–78, 186–88, 297, 320–24, 333–35, 376–80, 502–3, 589–91, 652–54, 709–14, 803–4, 806–8, 865, 1083–84
War Communism 51–52
war expenditures 96, 347, 349, 854, 923, 988, 994, 1013, 1017–18, 1092
war industries 42, 165, 392, 986, 1000, 1008–9, 1016, 1021–22, 1028–29, 1042–43, 1045, 1102
war loans 123, 217, 346, 719, 991, 1029, 1071
wheat 145, 274, 294–95, 297, 369, 426, 428, 490–94, 542–43, 634, 636, 638, 655, 771, 791–92

White Terror   12, 118–19, 557
world capitalism   20, 39, 65, 77, 243, 344, 405, 415, 608, 704, 744, 1063, 1134
world crisis   78, 248, 510, 520, 703, 706, 727, 753, 1050, 1081, 1086, 1097

world market   19, 21–22, 247–49, 329, 333–34, 341, 350–51, 370–71, 390–91, 399–401, 441–42, 602, 721, 978–79, 1118

Zhdanov, Andrei   73, 100–1